Anne Norman

7.15
aw 645

The Birds of Derbyshire

Edited by Roy Frost and Steve Shaw
on behalf of the Derbyshire Ornithological Society

Liverpool University Press

First published 2013 by
Liverpool University Press
4 Cambridge Street
Liverpool L69 7ZU

Copyright © 2013 Derbyshire Ornithological Society

The authors' rights have been asserted in accordance with the Copyright, Designs and Patents Act, 1988.

All rights reserved. No part of this book may be reproduced, stored in a retrieval system, or transmitted, in any form or by any means, electronic, mechanical, photocopying, recording, or otherwise, without the prior written permission of the publisher.

British Library Cataloguing-in-Publication data
A British Library CIP record is available

ISBN 978-1-84631-956-3

Designed and typeset by BBR (www.bbr.uk.com)

Cover illustrations by Andrew Shaw
Frontispiece by Paul Leonard

Printed and bound by Gutenberg Press, Malta
Gutenberg Press prints for BirdLife Malta

Contents

vi	Glossary, Abbreviations and Terms
vii	Foreword
viii	Introduction
ix	Acknowledgements
1	A History of Derbyshire Ornithology
5	The Derbyshire Ornithological Society
12	Ringing in Derbyshire
15	A General Description of the County of Derbyshire
20	A Summary of Derbyshire Statistics
21	Changes to the County Boundary
23	Place-names and the History of Birds in Derbyshire
25	The Natural Areas
41	A Chronology of Additions to the Derbyshire List
43	Fossil Species
	Photo Section
45	Derbyshire Habitats and their Typical Species
71	A Selection of Derbyshire Rarities
74	The Breeding Bird Survey
78	The Species Accounts
334	Important Records for 2012
335	Escaped and Released Species
342	Unacceptable Historic Records
343	Table of Breeding Species in Order of Frequency of Occurrence
345	Gazetteer
366	Bibliography
372	Index

Glossary, Abbreviations and Terms

1968–72 Atlas	*The Atlas of Breeding Birds in Britain and Ireland* (Sharrock 1976)
1988–91 Atlas	*The New Atlas of Breeding Birds in Britain and Ireland* (Gibbons *et al.* 1993)
1984–88 Winter Atlas	*The Atlas of Wintering Birds in Britain and Ireland* (Lack 1986)
amsl	above mean sea level
BBRC	British Birds Rarities Committee
BBS	Breeding Bird Survey
BOU	British Ornithologists' Union
BTO	British Trust for Ornithology
BWP	*Birds of the Western Palearctic* (Cramp *et al.* 1977–94; Snow & Perrins 1998)
CBC	Common Birds Census
DAJ	*Journal of the Derbyshire Archaeological and Natural History Society*
Defra	Department for Environment, Food and Rural Affairs
DOS	Derbyshire Ornithological Society
DWT	Derbyshire Wildlife Trust
EMP	Eastern Moors Partnership, a consortium of the National Trust and the Royal Society for the Protection of Birds set up to manage Big, White Edge, Ramsley and Clod Hall Moors and Leash Fen; the EMP moors were surveyed in 2010 (Frost & Taylor 2011)
Frost	*Birds of Derbyshire* (Frost 1978)
GP	(in charts) Gravel Pits
JNCC	Joint Nature Conservation Committee
Jourdain	'Birds' section of *The Victoria County History of Derbyshire* (Jourdain 1905)
Jourdain additions	Annotations by Jourdain in his personal copy of Whitlock
NR	(in charts) Nature Reserve
OS	Ordnance Survey
recent years	(in the Species Accounts) since 1980
Res	(in charts) Reservoir
RSPB	Royal Society for the Protection of Birds
RSPCA	Royal Society for the Prevention of Cruelty to Animals
SBSG	Sheffield Bird Study Group
SF	(in charts) Sewage Farm
SSSI	Site of Special Scientific Interest
tetrad	2km × 2km square of the OS national grid
WeBS	Wetland Bird Survey
Whitlock	*The Birds of Derbyshire* (Whitlock 1893)
10km square	10km × 10km square of the OS national grid

Foreword

This new volume on the birds of Derbyshire is not for me just another book, because I was born in the county and spent the first 18 years of my life in New Whittington, near Chesterfield. This was the area where my early interest in birds was sparked, and where I learnt for myself the rudiments of bird biology. Since I left home for University, I have spent depressingly little time in the county, mainly restricted to occasional short visits. But my early experience there has stayed with me, and much of the northern part of Derbyshire holds many cherished ornithological memories. One of the highlights of my early birding was an excellent view of a Kentish Plover on the newly formed Ogston Reservoir, which many years later I learnt was the first record for the county. In the ensuing 50 years, more than 200 species were recorded at that site, including rarities such as Sabine's Gull and Wilson's Phalarope.

Given this background, I fell upon the text of this book in a mood of anticipation and excitement, and I was not at all disappointed at the breadth and depth of detail found within its pages. It was interesting to see how much the avifauna has changed within my own lifetime, and heart-warming to learn how much our knowledge of the county's birds has improved in this time. This increased knowledge is clearly due, as elsewhere in Britain, to the greater numbers and mobility of birders, and also to the leadership shown by all those dedicated individuals who have kept the records over the years, organized meetings and surveys, and periodically brought the information together for all to share. In the growth of this knowledge for Derbyshire, we owe a great debt to Roy Frost who wrote *Birds of Derbyshire* (1978), some 85 years after the previous compendium on the subject. Another 35 years on, Roy also acted as main editor of this present volume, with the able assistance of Steve Shaw. However, in the pages that follow, it becomes clear just how many other people have been involved in the production of this book, emphasizing the extent to which voluntary bird study has become a collective endeavour.

Where I grew up in the 1950s, I knew of no-one locally with whom I could share my interest (the Derbyshire Ornithological Society was formed in 1954, unknown to me) but now, it seems, there are knowledgeable and well-travelled birders scattered over the whole county. The current volume emerges at a time of unprecedented coverage, when bird distributions in Derbyshire are better known than at any previous time. Taken along with the many other records accumulated over the years, this book documents the changing status and habits of various species within the county, and provides a firm basis against which future changes can be assessed.

Situated in the middle of England, Derbyshire makes up for its lack of a sea coast in other ways, its varied geology supporting a range of habitats from lowland farmland with river valleys and man-made lakes and gravel pits, to upland conifer forests and open moorlands. As in the rest of Britain, most of the variations in bird populations recorded over recent decades result from changes in land use and habitat availability. Since I was a teenager in the 1950s, much of the damp farmland has been drained, leading to declines in the once-common Lapwing, Redshank and Snipe, and other changes on farmland have resulted in big declines of some once very abundant songbirds. The Grey Partridge, Linnet and Yellowhammer are far less plentiful than they were, and the Corn Bunting may have ceased to breed altogether. On the other hand, the construction of various reservoirs and gravel pits, together with the cleaning of once-polluted rivers, has greatly increased the numbers and variety of wetland birds that nest and winter in the county. Other species, heavily persecuted in the past, have also increased and spread, including the Raven which now breeds over many parts of the county, and fish-eaters such as the Grey Heron, Cormorant, Red-breasted Merganser and Goosander, the latter three apparently being new colonists. Sixty years ago, only the Kestrel and Sparrowhawk among raptors nested commonly in the county, but Merlins were still found breeding on the moorlands. Others were no more than rare visitors or very sporadic breeders. But in recent decades Buzzards have become widespread, Peregrines have returned in numbers and are even nesting on buildings, while Goshawks and Hobbies breed in large parts of the county, and Red Kites are frequently seen and will surely be nesting within a few years. This was unthinkable in the 1950s. It is a pity that parts of the Peak District have such an unfortunate record of recent raptor persecution, for without it some of the larger species might be more numerous and widely distributed than they are now, and the Hen Harrier could have again become a regular breeder.

During the twentieth century, the county lost a few breeding species which also declined more widely, including the Black Grouse, Corncrake and Red-backed Shrike. On the other hand, it gained others not previously recorded as nesting, including the three fish-eating species mentioned above, the Little Ringed Plover and Collared Dove. In 2009, a pair of Mediterranean Gulls attempted to breed, and it is probably only a matter of time before the Little Egret is proved to nest. Under the growing influence of climate change, who knows which species will colonize the county in the years to come?

For the time being, however, this impressive book gives unprecedented detail on Derbyshire's birds, together with an accurate snapshot of bird status and distributions as they now are. Whether you live locally or further afield, you will find much of interest in its pages, and I congratulate the editors and many other contributors on a job well done.

Professor Ian Newton OBE FRS

Introduction

Although the idea of updating the 1978 book, *Birds of Derbyshire*, had long been in the minds of some members of the Derbyshire Ornithological Society (DOS), certain restraints, and in particular the acquisition of data from some sites in the county, had caused a start to be postponed. A tetrad atlas was first mentioned in the February 1988 DOS Committee meeting, but it was agreed to await the completion of the first breeding season efforts of the British Trust for Ornithology's second atlas project before embarking on further work. A Breeding Bird Atlas was then proposed by Dave Budworth at a General Committee meeting of the DOS on 7th March 1994, the idea being a project to mark the fortieth anniversary of the formation of the Society. The possibility of a full avifauna covering all birds (not just breeding birds) recorded in Derbyshire was raised during this meeting but was not discussed in detail. A steering group to organize the Breeding Bird Survey was formed, but this was not concerned with an avifauna at that stage.

It was not until 24th November 1996 that a Special Committee Meeting was held to decide if the Breeding Bird Atlas Project, which by then had gathered data for two breeding seasons, should result in a tetrad atlas or a complete avifauna. After a long and detailed discussion of what should be attempted, and some of the problems and pitfalls that would ensue, it was agreed (taking into account the wishes of members who voted by proxy) that the full avifauna project should be embarked upon.

An Avifauna Steering Group was established, with Dave Richardson agreeing to be Project Manager of the operation, while Roy Frost agreed to become Acting Editor-in-Chief, but making it clear that *this* book really would have to be a team effort. Andrew Hattersley, the Chairman of the Society, kept a watching brief initially and later agreed to be Assistant Editor; and Steve Shaw, General Secretary, extended his work into this project. The Society was also incredibly lucky in having as a member Trevor Poyser, a name known throughout ornithological publishing, who readily agreed to share his knowledge and experience. Also, members of the group agreed to look after certain specialist areas; Mike Muddiman agreeing to act as photographic editor, for example.

The group began the awesome task by analysing recently published avifaunas of other societies and gradually building a specification of what the publication should contain and how it would appear. Writers, artists and photographers were approached at an early stage to find out if they would be willing to help. Many did of course, and a skills questionnaire was issued to all Society members to ascertain what other assistance we might be able to call on, such as proofreading.

By mid-1998 the specification for the book had been more or less established, but although some of the introductory sections could be written, it was impossible to make a serious start on the Species Accounts until the Breeding Bird Survey fieldwork was completed, in 1999.

It was agreed that the book would contain an account of the ornithological situation in Derbyshire up to the end of 1999, which was considered a sensible cut-off point, and that the new book would be called *The Birds of Derbyshire* to distinguish it from its 1978 predecessor. It was also decided that any information which came in from 1st January 2000 would as far as possible be incorporated, albeit that no further specific Breeding Bird Survey work would be undertaken. For example, it was thought essential that the remarkable influx of Honey Buzzards in September 2000 should not go without mention.

A set of instructions and all the necessary data was sent out to 27 authors in November 2000 so that they could begin the Species Accounts section, although the accounts of some 80 very rare species had been drafted almost a year before, as it was thought that the information regarding them would be likely to change little. By the deadline for the receipt of Species Accounts of the end of March 2001, some 230 accounts had been received by the Editor-in-Chief, with the rest obtained shortly afterwards. Although much work had been done, it was clear that, by the time of the General Committee meeting in March 2002, it would be impossible to meet an August 2002 publication date and a decision was take to postpone publication by one year.

In May 2003, a meeting with Nick Moyes of the Derbyshire Museum Biological Records Centre helped greatly in the progress of the book's production, in that he demonstrated that small maps could be produced which were perfectly legible if placed in a single column approximately 80mm wide. An almost instant decision was taken to change the previously proposed size of the book to a 'near-A4' size with two columns, which solved many of the very awkward layout problems associated with the previous specification.

During the years when writing and editing were being carried out, periodic meetings were held to discuss progress, discover problems and encourage the participants. These were held at various venues, mainly public houses (such as the Anchor, Oakerthorpe, the Swan & Salmon, Alfreton and the White Swan at Duffield) chosen to even out travelling for those involved, living as they did across a wide area that stretched from Burton upon Trent to Sheffield.

The monumental task of editing the Species Accounts and all of the remaining parts of the book fell on the shoulders of Roy Frost. Bearing in mind all his other interests and commitments, it became clear that this was going to be a long task. All manner of difficulties, setbacks, queries and hold-ups occurred, which involved the exchange of numerous emails and sometimes the holding of specially convened meetings. For example, it was discovered quite late on that the text in the Species Accounts contradicted the distribution dot maps in many cases. Two special brainstorming days were held in Derby with a team of seven who painstakingly worked their way through every one of the 130 or so maps, comparing them to the data which had been used to generate them, until all errors had been eliminated. This alone accounted for scores of man-hours.

In mid-2010 it was decided that the cut-off date for information to be included would be 31st December 2009 (except for additions to the county bird list and other important records), when as much up-to-date information would be incorporated up to the point of going to print. Later it was decided to extend the cut-off to 31st December 2011. While all this was going on other jobs, such as selecting the photographs, were carried out.

Acknowledgements

This book is very much the result of a large collaborative effort by many individuals over a long period of time, both members of the Derbyshire Ornithological Society and others, who willingly gave their time. All who helped are sincerely thanked, and we offer our apologies for any omissions.

Breeding Bird Survey 1995–99

Much of the Species Accounts text is based on the results of this survey.

Organizers

Oliver Biddulph
Dave Budworth

Square stewards

The late David Amedro	The late Chris Falshaw	Rob Lord	Richard Taylor
Mark Beevers	Brian Foster	Dave Mallon	Adrian Tissier
Irene Blagden	Malcolm Hopton	Anthony Messenger	Bill Underwood
The late Tony Botham	Geoff Howe	Mike Muddiman	Eddie Walker
Steve Branch	George Hudson	Martin Roome	Peter Welch
John Cameron	Richard James	Steve Ryan	Andrew Wilkinson
John Clark	Mark Keighley	Tony Sinnott	Michael Williams
The late Gavin Coleman	Mick Lacey	The late Trevor Smith	
Howard Elliot	Ralph Lord	The late Paul Stanley	

In addition to those above, a great number of observers supplied casual records and routine observations, all of which were taken into account in drawing the tetrad maps.

Our thanks are also given to the many landowners, their agents, gamekeepers, farmers etc who allow responsible birdwatchers onto their land.

Preparing the text

The various parts of the text were written by many different individuals, although so much time has elapsed since their first drafts that many changes have had to be made, partly as the result of new information being obtained and partly in an attempt to present a consistent style. Consequently, the authors of some of the Species Accounts may hardly recognize their original work. The original authors, and those carrying out most of the research in the sequence as presented in the Species Accounts, were:

Mute Swan to Egyptian Goose::   Mark Keighley
Ruddy Shelduck to Wigeon: Richard James
American Wigeon: Steve Shaw
Gadwall to Garganey: Richard James
Blue-winged Teal: Steve Shaw
Shoveler: Richard James
Red-crested Pochard and Pochard: Tom Cockburn
Ring-necked Duck and Ferruginous Duck: Steve Shaw
Tufted Duck to Common Scoter: Tom Cockburn
Surf Scoter: Rodney Key
Velvet Scoter: Tom Cockburn
Bufflehead: Rodney Key and Barrie Staley
Goldeneye to Ruddy Duck: Tom Cockburn
Red Grouse and Black Grouse: The late Derek Yalden
Red-legged Partridge to Pheasant: John Clark
Red-throated Diver to Great Northern Diver: Rob Thatcher
Black-browed Albatross to Gannet: Steve Shaw
Cormorant to Bittern: Mark Keighley
Little Bittern to Cattle Egret: Steve Shaw
Little Egret: Barrie Staley
Great White Egret: Steve Shaw
Grey Heron: Mark Keighley
Purple Heron: Steve Shaw
Black Stork: Roy Frost
White Stork to Spoonbill: Steve Shaw

Little Grebe to Black-necked Grebe: Eddie Walker
Honey Buzzard: Roy Frost
Black Kite: Steve Shaw
Red Kite: Mick Taylor
White-tailed Eagle: Rodney Key and Barrie Staley
Marsh Harrier to Montagu's Harrier: Trevor Grimshaw
Goshawk: Mick Taylor
Sparrowhawk: Mick Lacey
Buzzard: Anthony Messenger
Rough-legged Buzzard: Mick Taylor
Golden Eagle: Steve Shaw
Osprey: Mick Lacey
Kestrel to Merlin: Mick Taylor
Hobby: Anthony Messenger
Peregrine: Trevor Grimshaw
Water Rail: John Clark
Spotted Crake and Baillon's Crake: Steve Shaw
Corncrake to Coot: John Clark
Crane and Little Bustard: Steve Shaw
Oystercatcher: Anthony Messenger
Avocet: Mick Taylor
Stone Curlew: Steve Shaw
Little Ringed Plover and Ringed Plover: Martin Roome
Killdeer and Kentish Plover: Steve Shaw
Dotterel: Trevor Grimshaw

American Golden Plover: Steve Shaw
Golden Plover: The late Derek Yalden
Grey Plover: Anthony Garton
Sociable Plover: Steve Shaw
Lapwing: Mick Taylor
Knot to Temminck's Stint: Anthony Garton
Least Sandpiper and Baird's Sandpiper: Steve Shaw
Pectoral Sandpiper and Curlew Sandpiper: Anthony Garton
Purple Sandpiper: Ron Blagden
Dunlin: The late Derek Yalden
Broad-billed Sandpiper: Rodney Key and Barrie Staley
Ruff: Anthony Garton
Jack Snipe and Snipe: Roy Frost
Great Snipe: Steve Shaw
Woodcock: Roy Frost
Black-tailed Godwit to Whimbrel: Anthony Garton
Curlew and Common Sandpiper: The late Derek Yalden
Spotted Sandpiper: Steve Shaw
Green Sandpiper to Greenshank: Ron Blagden
Lesser Yellowlegs: Steve Shaw
Wood Sandpiper: Ron Blagden
Redshank: Mick Taylor
Turnstone: Ron Blagden
Wilson's Phalarope and Red-necked Phalarope: Steve Shaw
Grey Phalarope: Ron Blagden
Pomarine Skua: Steve Shaw
Arctic Skua: Rob Thatcher
Long-tailed Skua: Steve Shaw
Great Skua: Rob Thatcher
Sabine's Gull: Steve Shaw
Kittiwake: Rodney Key
Bonaparte's Gull: Steve Shaw
Black-headed Gull and Little Gull: Rodney Key
Laughing Gull: Steve Shaw
Franklin's Gull: Roy Frost
Mediterranean Gull and Common Gull: Rodney Key
Ring-billed Gull: Steve Shaw
Lesser Black-backed Gull to Great Black-backed Gull: Rodney Key
Sooty Tern: Steve Shaw
Little Tern: Andrew Hattersley
Gull-billed Tern to Whiskered Tern: Steve Shaw
Black Tern: Andrew Hattersley
White-winged Black Tern: Steve Shaw
Sandwich Tern and Common Tern: Andrew Hattersley
Roseate Tern: Steve Shaw
Arctic Tern: Andrew Hattersley
Razorbill: Steve Shaw
Little Auk: Oliver Biddulph
Puffin and Pallas's Sandgrouse: Steve Shaw
Rock Dove: Mick Lacey
Stock Dove and Wood Pigeon: Roy Frost
Collared Dove: Mick Lacey
Turtle Dove: Roy Frost
Ring-necked Parakeet: Steve Shaw
Cuckoo: Mick Taylor
Barn Owl: Anthony Messenger
Little Owl: Martin Roome
Tawny Owl: Anthony Messenger
Long-eared Owl: Martin Roome
Short-eared Owl: Anthony Messenger
Nightjar: Andrew Hattersley
Needle-tailed Swift: Steve Shaw
Swift: Dave Richardson
Pallid Swift and Alpine Swift: Steve Shaw
Kingfisher: Dave Richardson
Bee-eater and Roller: Steve Shaw
Hoopoe to Lesser Spotted Woodpecker: Dave Richardson
Golden Oriole to Lesser Grey Shrike: Steve Shaw
Great Grey Shrike: Mick Taylor
Woodchat Shrike: Steve Shaw
Magpie to Hooded Crow: Dave Richardson
Raven: Mick Lacey
Goldcrest and Firecrest: Roy Frost
Blue Tit to Bearded Tit: Dave Mallon
Woodlark and Skylark: Roy Frost
Shorelark: Steve Shaw
Sand Martin to House Martin: Malcolm Hopton
Red-rumped Swallow and Cetti's Warbler: Steve Shaw
Long-tailed Tit: Dave Mallon
Pallas's Warbler and Yellow-browed Warbler: Steve Shaw
Western Bonelli's Warbler: Rodney Key
Wood Warbler to Whitethroat: Barrie Staley
Dartford Warbler: Steve Shaw
Grasshopper Warbler: Sean Cole
Savi's Warbler and Aquatic Warbler: Steve Shaw
Sedge Warbler: Sean Cole
Marsh Warbler: Steve Shaw
Reed Warbler: Sean Cole
Great Reed Warbler: Roy Frost
Waxwing: Andrew Hattersley
Nuthatch and Treecreeper: Dave Mallon
Wren and Starling: Trevor Grimshaw
Rose-coloured Starling: Steve Shaw
Dipper and Ring Ouzel: The late Derek Yalden
Blackbird: Jon Hornbuckle
Black-throated Thrush: Steve Shaw
Fieldfare: Jon Hornbuckle
Song Thrush: Roy Frost
Redwing and Mistle Thrush: Jon Hornbuckle
Spotted Flycatcher: Dave Mallon
Robin and Nightingale: Jon Hornbuckle
Bluethroat: Steve Shaw
Black Redstart to Wheatear: Jon Hornbuckle
Pied Flycatcher: Dave Mallon
Dunnock: Trevor Grimshaw
House Sparrow and Tree Sparrow: Oliver Biddulph
Yellow Wagtail: Malcolm Hopton
Citrine Wagtail: Rodney Key
Grey Wagtail and Pied Wagtail: Malcolm Hopton
Richard's Pipit and Tawny Pipit: Steve Shaw
Tree Pipit: Malcolm Hopton
Meadow Pipit: Roy Frost
Red-throated Pipit: Steve Shaw
Rock Pipit and Water Pipit: Malcolm Hopton
Chaffinch and Brambling: Roy Frost
Serin: Steve Shaw
Greenfinch: Tony Sinnott
Goldfinch: Mick Taylor
Siskin: Tony Sinnott
Linnet: Mick Lacey
Twite: Roy Frost
Lesser Redpoll: Tony Sinnott
Mealy Redpoll: Dave Mallon
Arctic Redpoll: Roy Frost
Two-barred Crossbill: Steve Shaw
Crossbill: Roy Frost
Parrot Crossbill and Common Rosefinch: Steve Shaw
Bullfinch: Mick Lacey
Hawfinch: Roy Frost
Lapland Bunting and Snow Bunting: Tony Sinnott
Yellowhammer: Oliver Biddulph
Cirl Bunting to Little Bunting: Steve Shaw
Reed Bunting: Oliver Biddulph
Corn Bunting: Steve Mann

Dave Budworth wrote the ringing accounts for almost all of the above species, where relevant. Steve Shaw wrote most of the rarity accounts at an early stage and these were later expanded and updated by Rodney Key and Barrie Staley.

Acknowledgements

The authors of the remainder of the book were:

Introduction and Acknowledgements: Roy Frost and Steve Shaw
Glossary, Abbreviations and Terms: Steve Shaw
A History of Derbyshire Ornithology: Roy Frost and Steve Shaw
The Derbyshire Ornithological Society: Steve Shaw
Ringing in Derbyshire: Dave Budworth
A General Description of the County of Derbyshire: Steve Shaw and Paul Bingham
A Summary of Derbyshire Statistics: Steve Shaw
Changes to the County Boundary: Steve Shaw
Place-names and the History of Birds in Derbyshire: The late Derek Yalden
The Natural Areas Introduction: Steve Shaw and Roy Frost
The Dark Peak and the South West Peak: The late Derek Yalden
The White Peak: Roy Frost
The Peak Fringe: Paul Bingham and Roy Frost
The Coal Measures and Magnesian Limestone: Roy Frost
The South Derbyshire Claylands: Paul Bingham and Roy Frost
The Trent Valley and National Forest: Roy Frost
The City of Derby: Paul Bingham
A Chronology of Additions to the County List: Richard James and Steve Shaw
Fossil Species: The late Derek Yalden
Introduction to the Species Accounts: Roy Frost and Steve Shaw
Important Records for 2012:   Roy Frost
Escaped or Released Species: Malcolm Hopton
Unacceptable Historic Records: Steve Shaw
The Breeding Bird Survey: Oliver Biddulph
Gazetteer: Steve Shaw
Bibliography: Steve Shaw and Roy Frost

Other contributors were Sean Taylor and David Speight (weather) and Gerry Shaw (geology).

Many people assisted the project by reading specific chapters, by answering the editors' queries, or in other ways: Mike Archer, Mark Beevers, Nick Brown, Rod Brown, Roger Carrington, Tom Cockburn, Bill Cove, Paul Glaves, Kevin Gould, Trevor Grimshaw, Andrew and Georgina Hattersley, Stephen Jackson, Steve Mann, Geoff Mawson, Anthony Messenger, Barry Potter, Jamie Rowlston, Tim Sexey, Mick Stoyle, Mick Taylor, Bill Underwood, Margaret White, Mike Williams, David Wilson and the late Derek Yalden.

The British Trust for Ornithology is thanked for supplying details of common bird censuses and ringing recoveries carried out in the county.

The Society also wishes to thank John Clayton and Peter Conole of The Information and Management Directorate of The Western Australian Police Service, Perth, Australia, for their considerable efforts in piecing together the history of Frederick Bulstrode Lawson Whitlock while he was in Australia, and Peter Cascoigne (PC1580), Assistant Staff Officer to The Chief Constable of Nottinghamshire Police, Sherwood Lodge, Arnold, Nottingham who made some useful suggestions regarding Whitlock's history.

The following are thanked for a great deal of help, in a variety of ways: Paul Bingham, Anthony Garton, Malcolm Hopton, Richard James, Rodney Key, Dave Richardson, Barrie and Anita Staley, and Bryan and Kathleen Barnacle.

In addition to producing this book our publisher, Liverpool University Press and in particular Anthony Cond (Director), Jenny Howard (Marketing Director), Katherine Pulman (Marketing Executive) and Janet McDermott (Sales), and Chris Reed and Amanda Thompson of BBR, are thanked not only for the mechanics of producing and marketing the book but also for their friendly advice, encouragement and understanding during the final stage of the project.

Illustrations, photographs, charts and maps

The cover was painted by Andrew Shaw.

The black and white vignettes were drawn by:

Sean Cole: Teal, Quail, Little Egret, Arctic Skua, Kittiwake, Green Woodpecker, Grey Wagtail, Savi's Warbler, Great Grey Shrike and Tree Sparrow

Ashley Fisher: Shelduck, Water Pipit, Stonechat, Sedge Warbler, Firecrest and Snow Bunting

Stephanie Hicking (neé Thorpe):   Red-throated Diver, Leach's Petrel, Killdeer, Grey Phalarope, Little Gull, Iceland Gull, Caspian Tern, Skylark, Lesser Whitethroat and Raven

Felicity Jackson: Mute Swan, Canada Goose, Grey Heron, Coot, House Martin, Dunnock, Robin, Great Tit, Coal Tit, Nuthatch, Rook and Goldfinch

Paul Leonard: Pochard, Golden Pheasant, Cormorant, Little Ringed Plover, Jack Snipe, Common Gull, Stock Dove, Hoopoe, Black Redstart, Magpie, Brambling, Twite, Crossbill, Yellowhammer, Black Tern, Turnstone and Wood Warbler

Norman Richardson: Egyptian Goose, Mandarin, Smew, Ruddy Duck, Black Grouse, Water Rail, Oystercatcher, Redshank, Barn Owl, Meadow Pipit, Dipper, Bearded Tit and Short-eared Owl

Steve Roberts: Honey Buzzard, Red Kite, Sparrowhawk, Buzzard, Osprey, Hobby, Golden Plover, Dunlin, Woodcock and Curlew

Ray Scally: Black-tailed Godwit, Corn Bunting, Dartford Warbler, Fulmar, Little Stint and Pintail

Andrew Shaw: Little Grebe, Bittern, Hen Harrier, Merlin, Turtle Dove, Nightjar, Ring Ouzel, Redwing and Hawfinch

John Wright: Scaup, Common Scoter, Slavonian Grebe, Goshawk, Knot, Pectoral Sandpiper, Green Sandpiper, Bonaparte's Gull, Mediterranean Gull and Common Tern

The photographic editor was formerly Mike Muddiman and latterly Richard Pittam, and photographs, which are credited individually, were supplied by:

Paul Bingham	Iain Leach
The late Tony Botham	Neil Loverock
George Briggs	Jon Lowes
British Birds	Steve Mann
The late Gavin Coleman	Mike Muddiman
Tony Davison	Richard Pittam
The Derbyshire Times	Dave Richardson
Stephen Elliott	Richard Rogers
Roy Frost	Raymond Rowe
Mark Hamblin	Peter Roworth
The late Tony Hamblin	Glyn Sellors
Paul Hobson	Alan Shaw
Malcolm Hopton	Ken Smith
Dave King	

The general mapping was prepared (in draft form) by Steve Shaw, and then produced by Dave Richardson. The solid geology and rainfall maps are reproduced from *The Nature of Derbyshire* (1986) with kind permissions of the author, Trevor Elkington, and copyright holders, Derbyshire Naturalist Trust (now Derbyshire Wildlife Trust).

The distribution maps and comparison maps were prepared by Dave Budworth and Dave Richardson among others.

The distribution maps were based on DMAP, an application by Dr Alan Morton, who is thanked.

All the background bases for the maps in this publication are reproduced with kind permission of Ordnance Survey © Crown Copyright, licence number NC/03/15041.

The charts were prepared by Anthony Garton and Steve Shaw.

Norman Richardson is thanked for the design of the Society logo.

A History of Derbyshire Ornithology

By way of outline, the early history rests largely on publications, written records and renown and it is of little surprise that the earliest to venture into print were from fortunate and educated backgrounds. Of these, five were clergymen or related, one was an aristocrat and two were of the gentry and presumably of private means, with but one each from the military, manufacturing and commerce. The written record starts with Pilkington in 1789 and flourishes in the latter half of the nineteenth century with the two giants of the time, Whitlock and Jourdain, who had been born within six years of each other, in the 1860s. Interestingly, the authors of the previous avifaunas (Whitlock 1893; Frost 1978) were both writing in their 30s, displaying early dedication and talent.

The first book of importance, praised by both Whitlock and Jourdain, was the Reverend James Pilkington's *View of the Present State of Derbyshire* (1789) in which the final chapter, comprising 17 pages, was devoted to birds. Pilkington was a minister of the Unitarian chapel in Derby. The Reverend David Peter Davies held the same post, but for Belper and Milford, and published the *New Historical and Descriptive View of Derbyshire* in 1811, which simply reissued Pilkington's list in the section concerning the birdlife of the county. Indeed, the preface states 'Mr Pilkington's valuable History has been used as a text-book'.

Pilkington was updated in 1829 in Stephen Glover's *The History and Gazetteer of the County of Derby*. Again, a 28-page chapter of this two-volume publication dealt with birds, but was largely based on Pilkington's work, although Mr O. Jewitt of Duffield added some further records. Whitlock noted that several of the rare birds in Glover's list lacked supporting detail and were thus omitted from his avifauna.

Next came John Wolley (1823–59), who was born at Matlock but moved at an early age to Beeston, Nottinghamshire where his father was the vicar. Though he made notes on local birds, recording the Rough-legged Buzzard influx at the end of the 1830s, he is best remembered as an oologist who travelled widely in northern latitudes, particularly Swedish Lapland, where he lived from 1853 to 1857. Of independent means, he gave financial help to the small community of Muonio (just inside Finland) through the severe winter of 1856/57 after the harvest had failed. He also fathered the twin boys of a local girl and left the family a considerable sum in his will, but by then the girl had married a local man and they used the money to buy tickets to America. His memorial stands near the village to this day.

With the help of locals, Wolley had amassed a very extensive collection taking, for example, 27 clutches of Gyr Falcon, and among his particular finds were the first ever nests 'for scientific purposes' of such birds as Jack Snipe and Waxwing. He died at the early age of 36 and was buried in Matlock churchyard in accordance with his final wishes, while there is a memorial plaque that lists some of his oological feats in Southwell Minster in Nottinghamshire. His collection of 20,000 eggs was given to Alfred Newton, later professor of anatomy at Cambridge University, who published details of the collection and all of Wolley's notes in *Ootheca Wolleyana*, two vast tomes, in 1864 and 1906.

Then in 1836, Neville Wood, who lived at Foston Hall, published a book called *British Song Birds*, which gave a useful account of the status of birds of his neighbourhood. He was followed by one of the most active ornithologists of the mid-nineteenth century, John Joseph Briggs (1819–76) of King's Newton, who grew up at Elms Farm which had been the family's ancestral home for three centuries. After leaving school he became apprenticed to a firm of printers but ill-health caused him to return to the farm. A careful observer, he was not only a naturalist but also a topographer, poet and historian. He published the first of his three histories of Melbourne at the age of 20 and contributed valuable notes to the *Zoologist* between 1843 and 1875, including an interesting series of articles entitled 'Birds of Melbourne' in the 1849–50 volumes.

One of Whitlock's correspondents was Henry Seebohm (1832–95), a steel manufacturer in Sheffield. Though he gave local ornithological data to Whitlock, Seebohm is best known for his foreign ornithological expeditions, in particular to Siberia. These resulted in two books, *Siberia in Europe* (1880) and *Siberia in Asia* (1882), combined in 1901 into a single volume entitled *The Birds of Siberia*.

A legendary figure in local ornithology was Sir Vauncey Harpur Crewe (1846–1924), who lived at Calke Abbey, where he succeeded his father in 1886. Owning over 12,000 acres in Derbyshire and an extensive estate in north Staffordshire, he was also lord of 15 manors. He attended neither school nor university and became reclusive early in life, for much of which his only close friend and confidant was Agathos Pegg, the head gamekeeper. Though deriving most of his income from farming, he took little interest in agriculture and forbade his tenants to cut and lay hedges or drain their land. In effect, Sir Vauncey ran the estate as a huge game reserve, with his gamekeepers busy keeping out poachers, and so disturbance of wildlife was minimal. His overwhelming interest lay in adding to his natural history collection at Calke, and by the end of his life over 30 rooms were filled to overflowing. He also bought specimens from a wide variety of sources and his collecting obsession led to a rather uncritical approach to the provenance of some of his acquisitions.

An article on the birds shot by the Reverend Francis Gisborne between 1761 and 1784, and published in the *Journal of the Derbyshire Archaeological and Natural History Society* (*DAJ*) for 1892, by the Reverend Charles Molineux, has proved to be one of the more interesting and valuable historical accounts. Gisborne was a popular, if eccentric, rector of Staveley between 1759 and 1821, when he died, a bachelor, aged 89. He had succeeded his father, James Gisborne in the post and between them they occupied Staveley Rectory for 150 years. A keen observer, he recorded the weights and dimensions of many of the birds he shot.

Natural History of Tutbury and Neighbourhood is the title of a book by Sir Oswald Mosley and Edwin Brown published in 1863, a considerable portion of which deals with birds and contains a bird list compiled by both. Shortly afterwards, in 1866, came a small book, *Wild Flowers of Repton and Neighbourhood*, which contains a bird list complied by A.O. Worthington. The book was revised in 1881 with the bird list undertaken by W. Gurneys. Still concerning the southern regions of the county were notes by

The Reverend Francis Gisborne.

G.W. Pullen entitled 'The Birds of Derby and Neighbourhood', published in *The Young Naturalist* of 1883–84. Two years later Whitlock wrote an article on Peakland birds for *The Naturalist*, based mainly on observations in the Kinder Scout area.

The colourful and energetic Frederick Bulstrode Lawson Whitlock was born in Nottingham on 3rd June 1860, the eldest of seven children, and lived in Beeston, Nottinghamshire. It is unclear why he should have received such an unusual pair of middle names as his mother's maiden name was neither Bulstrode nor Lawson, but Mary Taylor. He attended Loughborough Grammar School.

His *Birds of Derbyshire* was published in 1893. Most of his birdwatching was done in the Trent Valley along the Derbyshire–Nottinghamshire border and his ideas seem generally sound, well over a century later, particularly considering the paucity of ornithologists and the gaps in ornithological knowledge at that time. He was greatly helped by A.S. Hutchinson, who was a Derby-based taxidermist of renown, and the book was headed 'annotated, with numerous additions, by A.S. Hutchinson'. Hutchinson began his trade in the 1870s and died in 1909. He worked for private collectors and for various museums, including those at Derby and at Sheffield, where he set up the Seebohm collection. Though he prepared many specimens of British birds, he is perhaps better known for his cages of exotic birds. Whitlock described him as being 'gifted with excellent powers of observation'. Whitlock also corresponded with several other ornithologists regarding the avifauna, most of them resident in south Derbyshire.

Sadly, Whitlock, who was a bank manager in Nottingham, decided (at least temporarily) that money was more important than ornithology. On 15th November 1897, he emptied the safe of his bank and fled the city 'with a large amount of money' as it said in a Reward Notice (ref 3837/98, dated 28th December 1897) issued by the Nottingham City Police. It offered £100, which was a considerable sum at that time, for information leading to his arrest and contained a photograph, and his description, which included the wording 'he has a shifty expression when talking. He is a clever bicyclist; and a collector of birds and birds' eggs, upon which he is a considerable authority. He usually converses on the subject when in company'. It was almost certainly issued worldwide but he managed to elude the authorities, despite the fact that they were on his trail, and found his way to the port of Fremantle, Western Australia.

Interestingly, a duplicate of the reward notice was found some years ago in a copy of Whitlock's book owned by the late writer, broadcaster and well-known ornithologist, James Fisher, but where it had come from is unclear. However, it is worth noting that James Fisher's father, K. Fisher, and his uncle, A.W. Boyd, were both keen ornithologists in the latter part of the nineteenth century, with large libraries of their own, and it may well be that it had been passed down the generations. The Reward Notice is reproduced below.

Little seems to have been known of Whitlock's fate until recently. After receiving a request for help from the Derbyshire Ornithological Society (DOS), the Western Australian Police Service kindly undertook some considerable research for the Society in the early part of 2000. Their library historian discovered that Whitlock was arrested, in somewhat mysterious circumstances, by Officers Connell (who became one of Western Australia's most prominent police officers and its longest-serving Police Commissioner) and Wilson, at a town called Kanowna. This was a lawless place founded at the start of the 1894 gold-rush and lying about 80km north of Kalgoorlie. It was often referred to as 'the cement workings' due to the impenetrably heavy clay soil, and was originally not so much a settlement as a collection of tents and temporary shacks providing crude shelter from the summer heat (of well over 40°C) and the freezing nights. Many of the prospectors died in these conditions and from disease, such as typhoid.

By the time Whitlock arrived, the settlement had grown to about 12,000 and he must have felt he would escape justice, hiding away in such a place, but he was found and arrested at about 1600hrs on 3rd May 1898. He was charged on a provisional warrant with 'embezzling a large sum of money, the property of

The Reward Notice for F.B. Whitlock.

a bank at Nottingham England, of which said bank, the said Frederick Bulstrode WHITLOCK was manager'. Property seized at the time of his arrest included a silver watch and chain, a magnifying glass, a knife and a portmanteau containing 'clothes and sundries'. However, the money was not found among these few possessions, and indeed has never been recovered. He was taken to Perth and, on 22nd May 1898, remanded in custody and extradited to England. An officer of the Nottingham Police, Sergeant Bryan, was dispatched to escort him back to England.

In about 2000 David Wilson, one of the DOS founder members, discovered that the Reverend Francis C.R. Jourdain had a copy of Whitlock's book, now in the Alexander Library, Oxford, which includes (speculatively), in Jourdain's own handwriting, the annotation 'FBW was convicted of embezzlement & sentenced to [the number of years is, infuriatingly, not stated] years imprisonment.'

Despite all the effort and cost of fetching Whitlock back from Australia, it must be concluded that the authorities did not consider embezzlement a particularly serious crime. Although he was convicted and given a custodial sentence, it could not have been a lengthy one, as he was apparently back in Australia as early as 1901. Note also that in the journal *Emu* (1940), in an account of Whitlock's exploits, Major H.M. Whittell says 'he was compelled for reasons of health to seek a more equitable climate[!]'. He had became known as the 'Birdman of Kanowna'.

Whitlock eventually completed the most extensive range of collecting undertaken by any single ornithologist in Western Australia. He collected for H.L. White from 1908 to 1927, chiefly in Western Australia, but also made a visit to the Hermannsburg Range in central Australia to try and find the Night Parrot *Geopsittacus occidentalis*. His bird-skins are in the Western Australian Museum, Perth, the National Museum, Melbourne (H.L. White Collection), along with most of the eggs he collected, and in the American Museum of Natural History, New York (Mathews Collection). Many Australian species' nests and eggs were obtained by Whitlock, including, in 1909, the Grey Honeyeater *Lacustroica whitei*, the last 'new' Western Australian bird to be discovered.

Honorary life memberships of the Royal Australian Ornithologists Union and Western Australian Naturalists' Club were conferred on him and, between 1909 and 1915, he was honoured by having a genus and a number of bird species named after him, mainly by G.M. Mathews. These include (in the trinomial system) the Shy Heathwren *Hylacola cauta whitlocki* and the Australian Crested Dove *Ocyphaps lophotes whitlocki*.

The J.S. Battye Library of West Australian History in Perth, Western Australia holds Whitlock's diaries and notebooks including records of ornithological expeditions to Lake Way (1909), Shark Bay (1920), Nullabor Plain (1921), Fortescue River (1922), central Australia (1923), Fitzroy River (1924–25) and Bunbury (1948–50). There are also notes on petrels, terns and others, and a copy of R. Hall's *Key to the Birds of Australia and Tasmania* (1899) with copious notes by Whitlock (11 volumes).

He died a widower, on 15th June 1953, aged 93, at Bunbury, Western Australia where he was living in retirement with his daughter, well over half-a-century after his crime. His wife, formerly Clara Ellen Neale, predeceased him by some six months on 22nd December 1952. Following the publication of Whitlock's *Birds of Derbyshire*, several notes relating to Derbyshire birds appeared in such journals as the *DAJ*, the *Zoologist* and *The Field*.

The county's most famous ornithologist, the Reverend Francis C.R. Jourdain, comes next on the scene, writing a 30-page chapter given over to birds based largely on Whitlock's work for Part One of the *Victoria County History of Derbyshire* in 1905. Born in the village of Derwent on 4th March 1865, Frank, as he was usually known, was the second of ten children. His father was vicar of the church, the ruined outline of which is now usually submerged under the waters of Ladybower Reservoir. In 1878 the family moved to the south of the county where he attended Ashbourne Grammar School. His drawings were once shown to Queen Victoria by one of the Ladies of the Royal Household and the monarch was impressed enough to offer him training as an artist. This he declined as he had already made up his mind to study oology and ornithology, graduating from Magdalen College, Oxford with a BA in 1887 and an MA in 1890, in which year he was also ordained.

Following two appointments in Suffolk, he became vicar of Clifton (near Ashbourne) from 1894 to 1914. He was then appointed rector of Appleton in Berkshire, a few miles from Oxford, where he remained for 11 years until retiring in 1925. Following a brief stay in Norfolk, he moved to Bournemouth, where he died just before his seventy-fifth birthday. In 1896 he had married a Clifton woman, Frances Emmeline Smith, by whom he had a daughter and two sons, and he was buried back in Derbyshire in the cemetery remote from the church in Clifton.

It must be remembered that collecting skins and eggs was an accepted form of research in the nineteenth century and those who indulged in these activities were regarded as pioneers, admired both by their colleagues and the public. Gradually,

The Reverend Francis C.R. Jourdain.

however, the need to take huge numbers of specimens came into question and Jourdain recognized this issue. In 1915 he read a paper to the British Ornithologists' Club entitled 'The bearing of oology on classification'. By 1927 he took the opportunity to redefine the role of the oologist when he read a paper on 'Palearctic birds' eggs and egg collecting' to the British Oological Association. But eggs, by then, were a minor facet of Jourdain's studies, which encompassed every aspect of breeding and behaviour. In 1930, he published an important paper in *British Birds* entitled 'Our present knowledge of the breeding biology of birds'. He was indefatigable in his efforts to accumulate accurate data on a wide variety of subjects and in encouraging others to follow his example. He classified and tabulated every fact concerning the breeding biology of Palearctic birds from published sources, correspondents and, not least, from his own fieldwork. He was without peer, leading Desmond Nethersole-Thompson to comment in 1978 that 'Jourdain was by far the greatest scholar of them all: we have no-one with anything like his encyclopaedic knowledge today' (cited in Cole & Trobe 2000).

Jourdain worked tirelessly to support both national and local ornithological societies and publications. He was an assistant editor of both *British Birds* and *Ibis*, and joint editor of the *Oologists' Record*. He served the British Ornithologists' Union as a committee member and vice-president, and was later on the council and the Scientific Advisory Committee of the British Trust for Ornithology. Among his posts with the British Oological Association was that of president, from 1932 to 1939. A measure of the esteem in which he was held nationally was shown by the award of honorary membership of five overseas ornithological societies.

He made a large contribution to the publication of Witherby's *A Practical Handbook of Birds* (1919–24) but most important of all was his joint editorship of *The Handbook of British Birds*, with Witherby, Ticehurst and Tucker. This was published between the years 1938 and 1941 and, by the time of his death in 1940, he had completed notes up to Volume 4 and left careful records for his fellow editors to use in the final volume.

Jourdain's physical ability rivalled that of his intellect. Of wiry build, he was an excellent tree-climber, and his energy in the field was remarkable. It was said that he would stay up, blowing eggs, long after his companions had retired to bed. He made a great number of trips to many parts of Europe and to North Africa, travelling light and being happy to stay in primitive and often remote accommodation and live off the land. Large numbers of eggs were collected on these trips, but only for genuinely scientific purposes and not simply to accrue a vast collection.

He had an amazing memory and felt it his duty to correct any statement that he thought inaccurate. This could be done in a severe and rather caustic style, which led to both friends and enemies referring to him as 'Pastor Pugnax'. In particular, his exchanges at oological meetings with Percy Bunyard were sometimes very unpleasant. The latter's eggs were largely purchased and less scientifically valuable than the self-collected ones exhibited by Jourdain and no doubt led to differences between the two men. This confrontational reputation has tended to overshadow Jourdain's true character, for in his personal relations he was sensitive and kind, and went to great lengths to advise and assist other ornithologists, especially the younger ones. In the words of Harry Witherby, 'It may be truly said of him that ornithology never had a truer or more enthusiastic and devoted servant' (cited in Cole & Trobe 2000). At a local level, he impressed upon contributors to county bird reports the importance of keeping accurate records and it is fair to say that without Jourdain much would have been lost for ever, both in Derbyshire and elsewhere. Derbyshire ornithologists past and present can be grateful that, despite his international renown, Jourdain took such an involved interest in our county and the accuracy of its bird records.

A bird report appeared almost annually in the *DAJ* from 1904 to 1954 of which Jourdain was editor until he moved to Berkshire in 1914. These early reports were compiled from the observations of a small number of contributors (usually fewer than ten) though Jourdain warmly welcomed the records of the Midland Railway Natural History Society from 1911 onwards.

From 1908 the report was renamed 'a zoological record' as it also dealt with mammals and insects, although H.C. Hayward became editor of the entomological sections from 1912. The ornithological editor for 1915 only was Dr William Shipton of Buxton, who wrote his account from the eastern Mediterranean, where he was on active service. Shipton was succeeded by Norman H. Fitzherbert of Somersal from 1916 to 1925. However, the number of correspondents remained very small. From 1918 into the 1920s (and again in the 1940s) one of the contributing observers was Ralph Chislett (1883–1964), who was a chartered accountant at Rotherham. He was active in the Peak District, which features in the first three chapters of his 1933 book, *Northward Ho! for Birds*. The 1919 report includes his photographs of Black-headed Gulls nesting near Baslow. Chislett will, however, be best remembered for his painstaking book, *Yorkshire Birds*, published in 1952.

In the 1923 report, Fitzherbert protested about ornithologists who shot rare birds to add skins to their collection, and also said that a very well-known ornithologist had driven away the Red-backed Shrikes nesting in Dovedale. The following year's report contained a reply from Jourdain, who was correctly presumed to be the target of Fitzherbert's comments on the grounds that few other very well-known ornithologists lived in Derbyshire! Jourdain said that he had taken just one shrike clutch from the Dovedale area, from a nest known to local boys, which he believed to be deserted. He went on to attack overzealous game preservers and also the Royal Society for the Protection of Birds, which he said was run by ladies ignorant of ornithology, with disastrous results. Fitzherbert was very apologetic for his own efforts in 1925, saying lack of time constrained him from devoting due attention to the task. There was no report for 1926–29 though Jourdain, who resumed the editorship from 1930, added a few late records for 1928–29. By then, Jourdain was resident in Bournemouth but often visited Clifton. In the 1934 record he paid tribute to Ernest Grindey of Thorpe, who had died aged 52, and who had been a very active and respected naturalist. Jourdain remained editor until 1939, relinquishing the task shortly before his death in 1940.

Following Jourdain's death, his egg collection was rather neglected for a time and apparently damaged by bombs exploding nearby. The collection was bought by Vivian Hewitt and later passed to the British Museum of Natural History (now the Natural History Museum). Some of the eggs still remain to be matched up with the relevant data (Mearns and Mearns 1998). It is also sad that the British Oological Association changed its name after his death to the Jourdain Society in his memory, as this society was later associated with illegal egg-collecting.

We pass on now to Captain Walter Kinsman Marshall (1888–1982) of Radbourne who became County Recorder from 1940 and whose first task was to pay tribute to his late predecessor. Marshall, who worked as the agent for the Radbourne and Sudbury estates in south Derbyshire, occupied the post until he moved to Monmouthshire in 1957, remaining there until his death in 1982, at the age of 94. As much as anyone, he was responsible for the inauguration of the DOS on 30th October 1954. The last annual bird report to be incorporated in the *DAJ* was that for 1954, to which there were 40 contributors. Marshall had clearly been thinking about the formation of a county bird club for some time as in 1946 he suggested that local birdwatchers might like to meet for a meal, and the 1947 publication records that 25 people did so. After lunch in Derby, they were entertained by Charles Wells' film from Scotland, and slides taken by Stanton Whitaker and A.W. Ward.

The Derbyshire Ornithological Society

Founding, organization and running of the Society

In the early 1950s Captain Walter K. Marshall, ornithological County Recorder from 1940 but always acting under the auspices of the Derbyshire Archaeological and Natural History Society (DANHS), and Stanton Whitaker, who was to become Chairman of the new society, wished to form an organization which would be separate from the existing DANHS. They thought that the practical and financial aspects of such an arrangement would be better, as the nub of the matter was that the DANHS wanted a general subscription from members *plus* an additional subscription from the birdwatchers to finance an ornithological sub-section with a more extended report. This extra payment was considered by the birdwatchers to be unreasonable.

John S. Weston, subsequently a Derbyshire Ornithological Society (DOS) member, was present at a DANHS meeting (although no minutes can be found) on 30th October 1954. He wrote to the Secretary in 1995 (in connection with the fortieth anniversary of the Society) about his recollections: 'What followed was a more "colourful" meeting than the rather prosaic report in DOS *Bulletin* No. 1 would imply. At this open meeting convened by the DANHS on 30th October 1954 to discuss the possibility of forming a sub-section for ornithology ("with tactics more redolent of a boardroom"), by a majority vote of the 35 persons present, it was decided that the interests of ornithology and ornithologists in Derbyshire would best be served by the formation of a separate society devoted entirely to the study of birds. It would seem that at this point the Chairman vacated his seat, whereupon further discussions took place without him.'

The original (hand-corrected) list of interested members, headed 'LIST OF MEMBERS of Derbyshire A&NHS INDICATING INTEREST IN ORNITHOLOGICAL SECTION – UP TO & INCLUDING June 15th 1954' still exists (see below). As can be seen, they were mainly from the south and east of the county, a situation still reflected in the present membership list.

Arrangements were put in place to hold an inaugural meeting of the DOS at The Hayes, Swanwick, on 4th December 1954, the agenda being reproduced overleaf: what the 'informal conversazione [*sic*]' produced is not known. Also shown overleaf are the minutes of this meeting (with the typing errors and hand-correction left in place) and the 'Members Present' sheet that those attending were fortunately asked to sign.

Happily, the Society has always been run on a democratic basis by a Committee, sometimes referred to as the 'Executive Committee' in the early years. It is interesting to note that the Rules in the first *Derbyshire Bird Report* (1955) state that 'The management of the Society shall be vested in the following officers: President, Vice-President(s), Chairman, Secretary, Treasurer, Recording Secretary and Field Meetings Secretary, together with a General Committee of not more than 10 members, who shall be representative of the County'. This would suggest that the President and Vice-Presidents were expected to

```
          of Derbyshire A + NHS.
LIST OF MEMBERS INDICATING INTEREST IN
ORNITHOLOGICAL SECTION – UP TO & INCLUDING
          June 15th 1954.


Mr G.H.Large            302 Nottingham Road, Ripley, Derbys.
Mrs M.H.Mills           Lumsdale House, Matlock, Derbys.
Mr J.F.C.Kent           Lumsdale House, Matlock, Derbys.
Mrs V.Alford            36 Manor Road, Borrowash, Derby
Mr M.W.Alford           36 Manor Road, Borrowash, Derby
Mr G.H.N.Spencer        30 Morley Lane, Stanley, Nr. Derby
Miss P.D.Smith          Buena Vista, Wirksworth
Mrs J.P.Spickernell     Fairfield House, Quarndon, Derby
Dr W.A.Timperley        4 Backmoor Crescent, Sheffield 8
Mrs M.Dalby             Castle Donington, Derby
Mr W.D.White            175 Derby Road, Chellaston, Derby
Mr L.M.Waud             45 Breedon Hill Road, Derby
Mr C.E.Brown            199 Blagreaves Lane, Littleover, Derby
Mr D.L.Jones            "Vivian House", 55 Mapperley Road, Nottingham
Mr D.R.Wilson           33 Whiteley Wood Road, Sheffield 11
Mr Derek C.Hulme        1 Melton Avenue, Littleover, Derby
Mr Edgar Osborne        Morley, Derby
Capt. W.K.Marshall      The Silver Hill, Radburne, Derby
Dr. J.W.C.Holmes        Dunstead, Langley Mill, Nottingham
Mr J.W.Milne            The Hayes, Swanwick, Derby
Rev. C.L.Currey         Wyndesmore, Little Eaton, Derby
```

The original list of interested members on 15 June 1954.

The agenda of the inaugural meeting on 4 December 1954.

The first page of the minutes of the inaugural meeting on 4 December 1954.

The list of members attending the inaugural meeting on 4 December 1954.

take an active part in the running of the Society. This concept was abandoned at some point however, and these positions became purely nominal, as was probably the generally accepted practice for such organizations at that time. Meetings were held in members' homes for many years, but this became impracticable as the Committee grew, so suitable accommodation was hired. Unfortunately, the first Committee Minutes' book was mislaid and has never been found. This covered a period of some three years from the formation of the Society up to a meeting on 21st November 1957, from which point the meetings are all fully documented.

The early to mid-1960s were a very difficult time for the Society, as few members were willing to take on the various tasks required. For example, the Committee did not meet at all between the tenth, eleventh and twelfth Annual General Meetings, and the minutes' book is silent as to an AGM in 1968. This unsatisfactory state of affairs culminated in an Extraordinary General Meeting on 22nd November 1969, with some 55 members present. The appointment of a Steering Committee consisting of six members (later known as the Sub-committee) was suggested and agreed, and first met on 15th January 1970, and thereafter fairly frequently (for example, in October and November 1970 and January 1971). At the beginning, the Rules stated that the officers should be elected annually. Various alternatives, including service for three years, were tried, but it was agreed at the AGM in 1975 that all officers should be elected annually and this has remained the system to date.

The names of principal post holders are shown at the end of this chapter. In more formal times, forenames were not used, of course, and generally did not appear in the various minutes of meetings, *Reports* and *Bulletins*, but where these are known they have been introduced here for the sake of completeness. The Society, being somewhat traditional, and perhaps less than 'politically correct', has never introduced terms such as 'Chairperson'. Decorations and qualifications have been omitted for the sake of space.

Many officers carried out other functions at various times over many years, but their names and those of others holding posts such as Indoor Meetings Organizer, Field Trips Organizer, Ringing Secretary and Conservation Officer, and also those serving on sub-committees, are not listed. A curious phenomenon of the Minutes' books is that names appear indicating presence at Committee meetings, but with no prior mention of election to office! This may be partly explained by the fact that the Committee had the power to co-opt members between Annual General Meetings.

The functioning of the Society seems to have been a little haphazard at times. The 1965 AGM ratified the introduction of area Representatives making a Committee of 15, and also introduced the concept that 'the remaining six general committee members [no longer being referred to as 'Executive' at this point] should serve for no more than three years, with two members falling out each year and being ineligible for re-election until a year had elapsed'. This was surely well intentioned, but it seems that there were never enough willing hands to make this a practicable proposition, and many Committee members served for long periods, particularly from the late 1990s to the present time. It seems that the concept was abandoned from about 1980, by which time the benefits of 'continuity and experience' were more appreciated.

The minutes of the aforementioned Extraordinary General Meeting of 22nd November 1969 contain the comment that 'Mr F.G. Hollands (Secretary) suggested the Committee should make out a proper Constitution', presumably as no formal document was written before this date. By March 1986 the minutes of a Committee meeting show that it was by no means clear, even by then, whether the Society had a formal constitution (as distinct from 'Rules'). However, the problem was addressed in lengthy discussions and by October 1986 a new set of Rules had been thrashed out and the idea of a 'constitution' had been abandoned. The Rules were ratified at the 1987 AGM and although they have been slightly modified several times since, they are still essentially intact.

By 1997, the Committee had grown to 24, with Independents limited to six. But as some members fulfilled more than one task, the maximum number present at any meeting was 21, and usually only about 16 or 17. The size of the Committee was considered by some to be rather large, but the strategy was to have as many members familiar with the running of the Society as possible, so that the inertia which befell the Society in the 1960s would be avoided should any major player have to drop out. A system of Sub-committees (Editorial, Rarities, Publicity, Conservation and Policy Review) was in place by about 1986, and these were intended to do the donkey-work on any problems, find a solution and report back to the General Committee for its recommendations to be rubber-stamped. This proved a reasonably effective strategy for some of the more complex problems in later years, such as those regarding insurance and our charitable status.

The *Derbyshire Bird Report*

It almost goes without saying that the annual *Bird Report* is the most scientifically valuable product of the Society's endeavours. It was the primary source of information, both for Roy Frost's 1978 avifauna, and for the present work. Since 1955 the Society has been responsible for publishing the *Derbyshire Bird Report*, under the supervision of, or (more usually) edited by, the County Recorder. Reporting has been by calendar year since 1959, whereas the two previous editions covered the periods 1st November 1956 to 31st October 1957, and 1st November 1957 to 31st December 1958 respectively. The concept of 'Area Recorders' feeding information to the County Recorder, who would then write the *Report*, was raised in the late 1950s, but seems to have been quietly dropped.

The first annual report published by DOS was for 1955. It was 22 pages long and 49 contributors were acknowledged. By 1980 it had expanded to 72 pages with 238 contributors, while there were 200 pages for 2011, listing no fewer than 500 individuals and 15 organizations as contributors. Not all of these would have been members of DOS; some were members of other ornithological societies which exchange information with DOS. Chief among these is the Sheffield Bird Study Group (SBSG), whose recording area covers parts of north-eastern Derbyshire and the Derbyshire Peak District. Liaison with SBSG has always been good, as it is with the ringing groups in the county and also with the two more recently formed local raptor study groups.

The formation of a Rare Birds Committee to assist in the task of authenticating rare bird records (an issue which is referred to many times in the Minutes over the years) was first mentioned in a meeting of the Executive Committee on 15th September 1960, and was approved at the following AGM. At first it comprised Gordon Hollands, Ray Hawley, Stanton Whitaker, Arthur Whitehouse and the Secretary. Later, the Rare Birds Committee became known as the Records Committee and is now simply referred to as the Rarities Sub-committee, whose important function is, of course, to ensure the accuracy of the records in the *Report*. The great majority of annual reports, especially since 1968, have included articles which have encompassed a range of subjects, including the results of surveys of specific areas or species, ringing, nest-box studies and much more.

Financial difficulties in the 1960s led to calls to economize on the *Report*, for example by omitting the cover picture and publishing fewer records, but thankfully these were on the whole resisted, thus maintaining the value of these editions for posterity. Three years were combined in the single *Report* for 1965–67. Happily, since 1974, the *Report* has been published annually in the year following that which it covered, except in one or two cases. 1978 saw the adoption of Voous (relinquishing Wetmore) for species sequence and nomenclature, and in 2002 a new order introduced by the British Ornithologists' Union was employed (to the dismay of many).

From 1974 to 1983 it was the practice to use the cover illustration for two consecutive years, but from then on each year was unique in this respect. The first *Report* to include vignettes was 1980, under the editorship of Roy Frost, and from then on there were accounts, with descriptions of species new to the county, later broadened to include species not recorded by the DOS. At first, these were written by the finder of the bird concerned but lately mainly by the chairman of the county Rarities Sub-committee. A further improvement was the introduction of a colour cover in 1989, and two further changes took place in the following issue with the introduction of colour plates and a small amount of advertising to help pay for them. The first edition using 'perfect binding' (as opposed to being folded and stapled) was produced in 1996. A General Secretary's Report, to record the annual activities of the Society for posterity, was introduced in 1987, and a Chairman's Report was included in 2010. For 2012 these were combined into a Joint Report.

Because of the large effort involved in producing a modern report, it was decided in 1991 that the Society should appoint an additional Joint Recorder with responsibility for this task. The *Report* was sent to the printer on computer disk for the first time in 1994, with all the text written and assembled on the Society's own computer, saving money and allowing greater control and the ability to make last-minute alterations. Higham Press has printed the *Report* since 1972 but publication was always by the Society itself.

The monthly *Bulletin*

The function of a monthly newsletter is to unify and encourage the membership in its activities by publishing the latest news. From its inception, the Society has published a monthly newsletter, always known as the *Bulletin*, and the five-hundredth edition was published in February 2001. It has been available to members in every month (except July) despite numerous difficulties in the early days, including typing it on to wax stencils with copies run off on a Gestetner machine, a time-consuming process which meant that the publication was usually limited to four sides of foolscap. The *Bulletin* was occasionally sent out late, so the deadline dates for the following edition, and the confirmation of Trip and Indoor Meeting dates, was somewhat haphazard.

Professional production of the *Bulletin* was considered in the 1970s. More prosaically, the purchase of a secondhand typewriter (for the then not-inconsiderable sum of £15), was later agreed. Then, photocopying was introduced in 1988, which enabled the introduction of illustrations and advertisements, and the quality was gradually improved as the first computers became available. For four years in the late 1990s, the Society owned its own secondhand photocopying machine, which kept costs well down, but it was beyond economic repair after producing a quarter of a million copies, and the duplication was then done professionally.

In 1999 the latest computer technology was purchased, including desktop publishing software, which allowed a professional-looking document to be produced. Dispatching the *Bulletin* by e-mail was discussed towards the end of 2000, but this proved more complicated than had been anticipated and few members had the appropriate software to receive it. And the positive response from only 13 members out of 550 killed the project overnight. The possibility of using the Yahoo Groups website was investigated in late 2003.

However, in 2008 Adobe software became freely available allowing the pages to be instantly converted to PDF documents. These were sent to the printer (Stewart Heathcote, Copyit) and the dispatchers (Brian and Jean Hallam) and also, by the end of 2012, over 160 members were receiving the *Bulletin* (in colour) by email. This not only saved printing and mailing costs but relieved the tireless dispatchers (who have done this job for well over 20 years) of some of the 'stuffing and stamping' each month.

A major, perhaps the most important, part of every *Bulletin* has been the comprehensive *Bird Notes*, much more detailed than in the newsletters of many similar groups. Of course, this has only been made possible by the diligent and regular submission of records by the general membership. Its form was reviewed more than once, with occasional pleas for a discursive view of the month's birds and it only settled down in about 1969, when a monthly 'highlights' was followed by a systematic list, remaining the accepted format to this day.

Sadly, only a few complete sets of the *Bulletin* are known to have survived, possibly because of the large amount of space a set takes. Perhaps the changeover to electronic form will solve that problem in the future.

Surveys

These have always been a most important feature of the Society's activities and details may be found in the *Derbyshire Bird Report* for the appropriate year. They have generally been organized by the Field Officers, whose names appear at the end of this chapter.

Field trips

These featured in the Society's activities from the very start, and were an important aspect of the DOS for many years. But all was not well; the minutes of the eighth AGM in 1963, for example, recording 'surprisingly [the] field meetings had been poorly supported'. Over the years this aspect of the Society's activities has fluctuated in its popularity.

Over 70 venues have been visited, however, including most of the major sites within a day's travel of Derbyshire. Several short breaks to Scotland were organized and, in 1961, Barry Potter organized a very ambitious trip by plane to Holland from Burnaston Aerodrome. A sea trip on the *Yorkshire Belle* was made in September 1994. Nor were the local hot spots neglected and the Society has visited many of the most interesting sites in Derbyshire, and those of adjacent counties. But it seemed latterly that birdwatchers preferred to find their information on the various pager systems which became available in the 1990s, and more recently from the Internet, and go in their own transport to where the rarer birds could be found, rather than spending many hours on a coach. So 'away-day' trips were ended from 1996 due to lack of demand and, of course, the ever-mounting cost of coach and minibus hire due to various new regulations. Nevertheless, 2002 saw a short revival under the leadership of Paul Dexter, with an experimental trip to the Brecks, and 2003 saw a repeat of this successful visit. The local trips, with members using their own transport, remain reasonably popular, with understandably variable attendance. Over 300 species have been recorded on well over 400 field meetings.

Computerization of records

This was the subject of a very comprehensive article (Richardson 2001) which is too long to be reproduced here. It must be emphasized that this has been a highly successful project and it is hard to imagine how the Society could now function adequately without it.

The system is known as Derbyshire Ornithological Records and Information Service (DORIS). Well over 600,000 records are presently in place and as well as providing data for the Society's own work, sales of access to the data to various organizations exceeded £13,000 by the end of 2012; an extremely useful addition to the Society's funds.

Website and e-mailing

The website (Derbyshireos.org.uk) has helped immensely in promoting the Society (with over 150 members having joined online) and in providing a service, not least by letting members and other birders know about the birds to be seen in Derbyshire. Credit goes to Dave Richardson who worked almost single-handedly for a considerable time, taking it online on 1st June

2001. The site quickly proved to be very popular and had had over 475,000 'hits' by spring 2013. Dave has continued to improve it and keep it constantly up to date, and has relaunched it several times. Rodney Key and several other members have also made significant contributions. Another benefit, almost overlooked, was that it eliminated overnight the need to set up a 'Bird-line' telephone service!

By the end of 2003, many Committee Members were using e-mail, easing communication, passing along their contributions to the *Bulletin* and the *Report*, and exchanging information about the preparation of this book.

Photographic and other archives

Mike Muddiman has organized the photographic and other archives for many years. He sadly left the Committee in 2003, but kindly agreed to remain the Society's photographic advisor.

Very little exists in the way of documentary archival material apart from the handwritten Minute Books (but, as previously mentioned, the one covering the period up to 1957 is missing). However, a small but interesting piece came to light in 2002, submitted by founder member and ex-Recorder, David Wilson – a receipt for his subscription dated 18th December 1954. David wrote on the reproduction which he kindly sent to the Society: 'I was the original [first] Life Member, but when receipts were sent out mine was No. 2 [the Treasurer having issued No. 1 to himself!!].' David makes no further comment!

The library

Setting up a library was first mooted on 13th October 1962, as the Society owned a number of books, generously donated over many years. From 1975 to 1989 they were housed in two sections in Derby City Library, with one available to the general public and the other only to DOS members. Books were taken to the various indoor meetings for a while, but this arrangement seems to have stopped, presumably due to lack of interest. The books were catalogued in 1989 and have since been held successively at the homes of David Amedro, Martin Roome and, most recently, Andrew Hattersley where they continue to attract little attention. Their sale has been discussed at various times, but potential legal difficulties have discouraged any decision.

Membership

The fluctuation in number of members has at times been difficult to understand. They were at a peak in the mid-1980s ('reportedly over 600' at the 1986 AGM) but fell off most markedly in the early 1990s. However, numbers picked up later, following a strong recruitment campaign mounted by the Publicity Sub-committee together with the strategy of offering a 16-month membership for one year's initial subscription. As the twentieth century drew to a close and early retirement and increased leisure time took hold, numbers remained at around 500, and topped the 550 mark by mid-2002. In terms of circulation, it is known that the *Bulletin* and the *Report* are passed around to others so the actual readership could be as high as 750.

Fortunately, the severe economic climate of 2008–13 did not have a great impact, with numbers holding fairly steady throughout.

Indoor meetings

In the early years there were constant problems in finding suitable venues for meetings. The minutes of meetings endlessly referred to 'why not try here' and 'what about there', the problem being that Derbyshire is a difficult county in which to organize an entirely acceptable set of winter venues, being divided by the Pennines which are always a potential winter travel hazard. Meetings have been held mainly in Derby and at places along the eastern side of the county, including Alfreton and Ripley where the majority of members live, at Bakewell and Buxton, and in the north-east at Chesterfield. And joint meetings with groups such as Carsington Bird Club, Bakewell Bird Study Group and Buxton Field Club have also helped swell attendances and defray costs.

A meeting in each month from October to March has been the norm since 1994, although September and April meetings were held for many years, and September has recently been reinstated. A December meeting was not held from 2010 to 2012. Speakers have included the Society's own members, and national and local celebrities. Although meetings have sometimes been poorly attended, the average over many years has made this a very worthwhile and important aspect of the Society's activities. These presentations were invariably talks, often illustrated by film in the early years or more recently with slides (and occasionally with audio content). Two videos have been shown, and very clear images are now successfully presented using PowerPoint software on a laptop computer.

The Annual Dinner and Members' Evening

Dinners were held for many years and were often long-drawn-out affairs on Saturdays, sometimes beginning as early as 1500hrs and not finishing until 2300hrs. Committee minutes in the mid-1960s once recorded that 'a few small snags were that some people had little tea!' Never mind about the birds, as long as there's enough tea! This aspect of the Society's activities gradually proved less popular, and the last Annual Dinner was held in 1987, when 40 members attended. It was, in effect, replaced by the Members' Evening, introduced in 1986. This proved a popular event, for a time, with members contributing food, slide shows, quizzes, a raffle and prizes, and was usually combined with the DOS Award presentation. But it was discontinued from 2010 onwards because of the very poor attendances in 2008 and 2009.

Other societies, clubs and organizations

The DOS has enjoyed good relations with almost 50 other similar groups both within and without the county, some of which have sent in vital records over many years. While formal representation of these groups on the DOS Committee has been intermittent in some cases, a concerted effort was made from the mid-1990s to form stronger links with the neighbouring counties and three successful meetings were held to this end.

Finances

The financial position of the Society was up and down in the early days but never at crisis point, thanks to a few hard-working individuals. Increased subscriptions were suggested from time to time, sometimes followed by counter-proposals to reduce costs (and standards). The subscription rates during the lifetime of the Society have been as follows:

Year	Price
1954	10/– (50p)
1970	£1
1975	£1.50
1976	£2
1981	£4
1987	£6
1991	£8
1993	£10
2004	£12

It is interesting to note that had the subscription rate been increased in line with (say) the Retail Price Index, they would have stood at about £45 by 2004.

Life membership was proposed on 21st November 1957 at the rate of £10 – excellent value for anyone who took advantage of it – but later abandoned as being too costly for the Society. Donations from Bird Race participants and others were received from time to time, and revenue from advertising in the *Report* and in the *Bulletin* helped to finance these publications, as did the considerable amount earned from sales of the *Report* to non-members through local bookshops.

Fortunately, the financial position of the Society in the mid-1990s was dramatically improved with the first payment for 'professional' survey work. This made the Society so financially stable that it was able to avoid an increase in the annual subscription rates for the ten years up to 2003. However, in June 2003 the Committee voted to increase the subscription to £12, keeping the Junior rate at £5, to encourage the younger members.

In 2006, the financial position of the Society was again improved when it was approached by Dr Stuart Pimm of Duke University, North Carolina, USA, who (conditionally) donated approximately £2,000 to the Society. The money emanated from an international award worth $150,000 for his work on species extinction and conservation. Stuart wanted to recognize the help and support that he received in Derbyshire as a young birder from Barry Potter (Chairman and later President) and the late David Amedro (who was his schoolmaster at Bemrose School). He wanted the money to be used to help young birders get out into the field and learn about birds, so the Society arranged finance from a ring-fenced 'Pimm Fund' for young members to visit places as far afield as Madagascar and Kenya, partly on charity work.

Bird Races

Taking part in the annual 'Bird Races', organized on a national basis, not only generated interest in the Society's activities, but also raised a good deal of money with sponsorship from both individuals and corporate entities. Some of this was earmarked for colour plates for the *Derbyshire Bird Report*, while much found its way into conservation projects, both at home and abroad. Latterly, some of the teams gained national recognition with substantial prizes, and details of their exploits can be found in various *Bulletin* articles.

The Frank Constable/DOS Award

Originally instituted by a former Chairman, Frank Constable, and bearing the title 'The Frank Constable Award', this feature of the Society's year was resurrected in 1988 after a lapse. The intention was to encourage and reward young members of the Society in whatever field they had chosen to help the Society, but it was always understood that it would not be awarded to a serving Committee Member.

Generously funded by Frank until 1991, once by an anonymous donor (when it was retitled 'The DOS Award'), and subsequently by Barry Potter, it has been awarded to 16 members and in every year since 1991, except for 1992, 2003, 2010 and 2011.

The fiftieth anniversary of the Society

The fiftieth anniversary of the Society was celebrated in 2004 and a suitable way of marking this occasion was sought. Barry Potter, the President, suggested planting a small area of woodland, and this was enthusiastically endorsed. A site was found at Darwin Forest Country Park, near Two Dales, thanks to the generosity of the owners and the co-operation of the manager, Ian Grant. The Society was not given ownership of the land, but a promise by the owners to allow it to remain undisturbed in perpetuity. It is a roughly triangular area, approximately 30m long on the north and east sides, with a curved south-west-facing boundary of about 45m. Donations for the purchase of trees were requested from members and well over £1,300 was raised. This was spent mainly on a variety of native English hardwoods of various sizes (sessile oak, English oak, silver birch, rowan and hazel), but also on the necessary requisites: stakes, tubes, fertilizer and delivery to site. The trees were planted by a small band of volunteers in October 2004, following the mechanical excavation of holes by the site owner, and Barry Potter then affixed a small brass plaque to a post to mark the date. Conceived with 'an eye to the future', the woodland was well established by the end of 2011

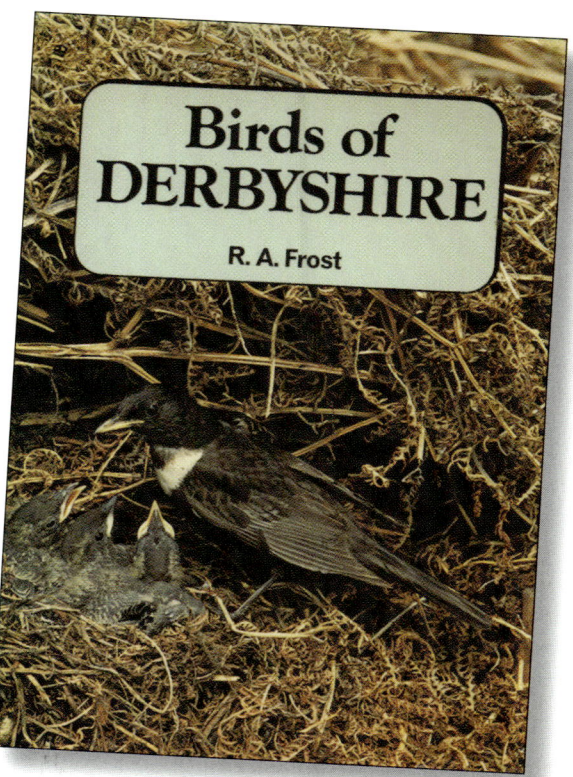

and already generating records for the *Bulletin* and the annual *Derbyshire Bird Report*.

County avifauna

The second ornithologist to write a county avifauna was Roy Frost, who first suggested the idea to the Committee on 6th March 1970. It was published in 1978 to excellent reviews in the ornithological press.

Society helpers

The invaluable contribution made by many individuals to the various aspects of making the DOS function successfully over many years is far too large to catalogue, but the Society would certainly have ceased to operate had it not been for their help: they are all sincerely thanked.

Officers of the Society

President
1954–78   Rt. Hon. Viscount Scarsdale
1978–87   Mrs Marjorie H. Mills
1989–date   Barry C. Potter

Vice-president(s)
1954–70   Capt. Walter K. Marshall
1970–78   Capt. Walter K. Marshall and F. Gordon Hollands
1978–83   Capt. Walter K. Marshall, F. Gordon Hollands and Richard H. Appleby
1983–85   F. Gordon Hollands and Richard H. Appleby
1985–2003   Richard H. Appleby
2004–date   Frank Constable and Andrew P. Hattersley

Chairman
1954–65   Stanton Whitaker (pictured opposite)
1965–70   F. Gordon Hollands
1970–73   Tony B. Wassell
1973–78   Frank Constable
1978–88   Barry C. Potter
1988–95   David V. Haslam
1995–2003   Andrew P. Hattersley
2003–date   Bryan A. Barnacle

Vice-chairman
1985–88 David V. Haslam
1988–2001 Mike J. Cross
2001–03 Bryan A. Barnacle
2003–date Dave A. Richardson

General Secretary
1954–71 F. Gordon Hollands (assisted at times by Richard H. Appleby)
1971–87 Mrs H.E. ('Gin') Roe
1987–date Steve Shaw

Treasurer and Membership Secretary
1954–63 Frank Price
1963–70 Conrad N. Whipple
1970–75 Mrs Pat Kerridge
1975–83 Alan Boiling
1983–86 Alan T. Scahill
1986–2001 Mike Daykin

In 2001 the post of Treasurer and Membership Secretary was split, as the combined workload had become too onerous for one individual to handle.

Treasurer
2001–04 John Clark
2004 Bryan A. Barnacle
2004–date Malcolm Hopton

Membership Secretary
2001–date Barrie Staley

County Recorder(s)
1954–57 Capt. Walter K. Marshall
1957–60 David R. Wilson
1960–63 Derek C. Hulme
1963–65 Norman A. Kerridge
1965–71 Conrad N. Whipple
1971–80 David Amedro
1980–91 Roy A. Frost and Rodney W. Key
1991–date Roy A. Frost, Rodney W. Key and Richard M.R. James. During this period Rodney Key was responsible for the recording of Rare Birds, Roy Frost likewise for Rare Breeding Birds and Richard James the editorship of the *Derbyshire Bird Report*.

Report editors have been as follows:

1955 Capt. Walter K. Marshall, with Wally J. Milne, John F.C. Kent and Mrs Marjorie H. Mills
1956 Capt. Walter K. Marshall
1957–59 David R. Wilson
1960–62 Derek C. Hulme, with Norman A. Kerridge, Anthony B. Wassell and Conrad N. Whipple
1963–64 Norman A. Kerridge, with Anthony B. Wassell and Conrad N. Whipple
1965–67 DOS Rarities Sub-committee
1968 David Amedro, with Roy A. Frost and Conrad N. Whipple
1969 David Amedro
1970 David Amedro, with Rodney W. Key
1971 David Amedro
1972–73 David Amedro, with Roy A. Frost, Rodney W. Key, Philip Shooter and Trevor G. Smith
1974–75 David Amedro, with Roy A. Frost, Rodney W. Key, Philip Shooter, Trevor G. Smith and Mick F. Stoyle
1976–79 David Amedro
1980–88 Roy A. Frost
1989 Roy A. Frost and Richard M.R. James
1990–2012 Richard M.R. James

Overall responsibility for producing the *Bulletin* has been assumed by:

Richard Appleby
Mrs H.E. ('Gin') Roe
Tony Davison
David Haslam
Steve Shaw (1994–date)

Bird Notes Editors
1963–68 Conrad N. Whipple
1968–89 Rodney W. Key
1989–91 Anthony P. Messenger
1991–95 Martin Roome
1995–97 Mick Lacey
1997–99 Mark A. Beevers
1999–date Bryan A. Barnacle

Field Officer
1973–80 Philip Shooter
1981–84 Geoff P. Mawson
1985–89 Richard M.R. James
1990 Anthony P. Messenger
1991–2004 Brian T. Foster
2005–11 Dave Budworth
2012–date Richard Winspear

Stanton Whitaker.

Ringing in Derbyshire

Historical

There are now about 2500 licensed ringers throughout the UK, who provide a huge amount of information about the birds breeding in or passing through these islands. The annual total of birds ringed is now of the order of 800,000, comprising both free-flying birds and nestlings. The technique of scientific bird study by the attaching of a uniquely numbered metal ring to a bird's leg began in Britain in 1909. Two schemes were established: one in Scotland by Sir Landsborough Thompson, then an undergraduate at Aberdeen University, and the other in England by Harry Witherby, after his launch of the journal, *British Birds*, in 1907. The former scheme folded during the First World War but the Witherby scheme continued and annual ringing totals had reached 50,000 by 1935. The foundation of the British Trust for Ornithology (BTO) in 1933 provided a further opportunity for this new study method to develop and the management of the ringing scheme was handed over to this body in 1937.

Early ringing activities in Derbyshire were centred on the areas around Buxton, Derby and Sheffield. The earliest Derbyshire recovery was of a Robin, ringed by A. Broomfield as a fledgling on 27th July 1912 at Chapel-en-le-Frith. This was found dead in the same vicinity in December of that year. The first recovery involving a longer distance was that of a Blackbird, ringed as a nestling at Hope by Miss J. Crookes on 12th May 1912 and recovered at Monard, County Tipperary on 18th January 1913. Interestingly, another nestling Blackbird, ringed also at Hope by Miss Crookes on 28th April 1913, was again recovered in Ireland in Clonmel, County Waterford during the following winter on 22nd December 1913. A Willow Warbler, ringed as a nestling in Buxton in June 1927, was recovered in Warminster, Wiltshire two years later. This was the first recovery of a true migratory species involving Derbyshire.

The activities around Derby were generally at the gravel pits to the south and at Egginton Sewage Farm, but other early locations included Doveridge, Repton and Ticknall. These latter two sites were part of the studies carried out by Wilfred Bullock, a master at Repton School, and included many Sparrowhawk nestlings in woods in the south of the county. He discontinued his ringing in 1962 after leaving the area, but had by then begun training Tony Wassell, who inherited his equipment and rings. Tony's study area was based around Darley Abbey, the Willington area gravel pits and Egginton Sewage Farm. During this period he trained his colleague, Conrad Whipple, and they still continue to ring as a partnership. In the Allestree area, Barry Potter and John Weston were active ringers between 1954 and the 1970s. This was a few years before mist nests came into general use and until then the majority of ringing of small birds still involved nestlings, but some adults were caught by Potter (no connection) and Chardonneret traps, which attract birds into a baited cage.

As the interest in ringing expanded, a need for official training became a requirement and a permit system was introduced by the BTO in 1956. This was well timed since one had to obtain a licence to trap wild birds following the 1958 Wildlife Protection Act. There was also a need for reliable identification skills, especially as more free-flying birds were being caught following the introduction of mist nets. The BTO therefore embraced these new legislative requirements, and the organization was vested with the issuing and control of the licensing system.

Further ringing in the south of the county was centred on the Drakelow Nature Reserve, where Gordon Mortiboy organized a group of people to carry out a number of ringing studies, both on the wildfowl reserve and in the surrounding district. In particular a Swallow breeding study was concentrated on several farms between Burton upon Trent and Swadlincote. This group of people included Tom Cockburn, Malcolm Giles and David Frost, and their efforts were also directed to the annual round-up and ringing of Canada Geese, initially under the leadership of Clive Minton, with help from Bert Coleman. At this same time Dave Budworth moved from the north-east of the county to the Swadlincote area and became the secretary of the newly formed (1970) Drakelow Ringing Group. By 1981 this group was disbanded since many of its members had left the region, including Clive Minton (who had emigrated to Australia), or lost interest. Nevertheless, ringing at Drakelow was continued by Dave Budworth and new people, such as school friends Tim Bagworth and Michael Williams, became involved. Dave Budworth also initiated ringing at Elvaston Castle Country Park in 1974 and trained the park gardener, John Potts, as a ringer. The activities at Elvaston had declined by the early 1980s but Ivan Webb (from 1984), and later his wife, Pauline and son, Kevin, took up the interest and there was a period of resurrected ringing studies in the park which also involved the warden, Keith Carvell and colleague, Keith Grimes. This continued for several years and resulted in the formation of the Souder Ringing Group. The old gravel pit known as 'Elvaston Quarry' near Draycott was another valuable site for this group but this was unfortunately filled with fly-ash during the 1990s. Ringing was carried out at this latter site when roosts of Yellow Wagtails were still a regular autumn event, along with large Swallow roosts, attracting the attention of some of the first known breeding Hobbies in the county. During the breeding season the location supported what was probably then the largest Reed Warbler colony in Derbyshire. Activities within Elvaston Castle Country Park had declined once more by the late 1990s but other locations in the south were now being studied by Peter Marks and his daughter Catherine (both trained by Ivan and Pauline Webb) from 1996 to 2000 in their home village of Breaston as well as at the Derbyshire Wildlife Trust's Golden Brook Nature Reserve nearby.

By the late 1950s larger scale ringing in the county was also being conducted in the north-east and new ringing groups were being launched. In the Sheffield area Ray Hawley, who had been trained by the late Harold Hems of Dronfield, was carrying out ringing studies and was beginning to involve new people in a training programme. In those years the ringers around Sheffield also included David Wilson, who left the area in 1959 to work for the BTO in Oxford. The Sorby Ringing Group (SRG) thus became established under the auspices of the Sorby Natural History Society, while Michael Wareing, with David Blackmore, had begun a long-standing ringing initiative on his land at Breck Farm near Staveley in the late 1960s. In 1970 these two groups of ringers decided to join forces to become the Sorby Breck Ringing

Group (SBRG), which continues under the secretarial influence and overall leadership of Geoff Mawson. This group continues to thrive, with up to 30 active ringers in recent years, and is generally responsible for the great majority of birds ringed in the county annually, though the ringing area also extends into parts of South Yorkshire and Nottinghamshire. Long-time stalwarts include David Atkinson, Ray Knock, Alan Peachey, Brian Smithson and David Williams, who assist in diverse activities, such as the Constant Effort ringing at Williamthorpe Nature Reserve (since the inception of the scheme), to autumnal tape-luring of migrant Meadow Pipits on Peak District moors. The group has shown a very wide area of expertise, from excellent nest-finders such as Norman Barker, who also pioneered the technique of 'flick-netting' to catch Swifts, to species specialists like Harry Vilkaitis, who has missed very few broods of Swallows in recent years, and Anthony Messenger, who has probably ringed more Hobby pulli than anyone else in the UK. The group has also assisted with graduate and undergraduate studies at Sheffield University. For many years when Michael Wareing lived at Breck Farm, the group also provided an annual local training course, so as to attract a larger number of people and to give opportunities for ringers from other parts of the country to learn, and pass on experiences and skills.

Just over the county border at Warsop, Nottinghamshire, Bob Jones was beginning his ringing activities from 1966 in the Birklands and Clumber Park. It was at this time that Dave Budworth became involved with ringing studies and, together with Bob Harrison and Fred Mapletoft, they formed the new Birklands Ringing Group (BRG) in 1970. The BRG and SBRG recorded movements of birds between their ringing locations: in particular many Bramblings moved between Breck Farm and the Birklands. In the early 1970s a Whitwell man, John Ellis, joined the BRG and began ringing in Whitwell Wood, using his exceptional nest-finding skills to concentrate on nestling ringing. Since Ellis's death in 1997, ringing at this site has been under the auspices of the SBRG, and is currently led by Eleanor Wilkins.

In the north-west region of the county, the South Pennine Ringing Group (SPRG) operated from 1973, its members including Ted Robson, Bill Underwood, Phil Holland, Ron Dean and Adrian Blackburn. The group had a particular interest in raptors and this continues, although most of the early group members departed the region leaving, for a time, Bill Underwood, Paul Stafford, John Haydon and Logan Steele to continue the studies. From the mid-1970s, an ongoing special study was conducted by the late Derek Yalden on the upland breeding populations of Common Sandpiper and Golden Plover and ringing became a part of this work. In 1983 the group rearranged their activities, changing the name to the Dark Peak Ringing Group (DPRG) and, with the increasing interest in raptor studies in the north of the county, SBRG and DPRG organized themselves between the east and west regions, so as to not overlap and duplicate effort.

In addition to the three ringing groups mentioned above, and the Wassell–Whipple partnership, there have occasionally been 'solo' ringers operating in the county. These include Stephen Moores, who has had considerable success with a Barn Owl nest-box scheme in the Peak District.

By the end of the twentieth century the ongoing ringing activities in the county were still essentially centred in the north-west (DPRG), north-east (SBRG) and the south (Souder Ringing Group). These groups continue to carry out ringing studies in their respective areas and this has served to provide long-term information about the changes in populations, survival data, cause of death, migration and many other more detailed biological features of the various species.

Since the 1980s there have been many changes instigated by the BTO alongside the expanding role that ringing has provided in assisting with bird conservation. The work is financially supported by the Joint Nature Conservation Committee as well as the Country Wildlife Agencies. In return, the resulting database of information is used in many planning decisions affecting wildlife and environmental impacts of major civil and landscape projects. Over this period in particular, the training system has become more rigorous to ensure that data is gathered in a standardized manner and that the welfare of the birds is maintained. It is of no value to collect data by different ringers if their methods produce variations that mask the underlying statistical trends. Furthermore, and probably much more important, the ringing process cannot provide usable information if the bird's normal activities are seriously disrupted by the actual ringing. Correct handling and measuring leaves the bird in its normal condition within a few minutes of release after ringing. There is plenty of evidence to support this, such as a released bird in spring immediately flying to a song-post and beginning to sing or a bird caught at a feeding station returning to feed shortly after its experience of being handled. Indeed the whole daily life of a wild bird is one of avoiding threats from predators and then continuing with normal activity once the danger has passed.

Our knowledge of ageing and sexing techniques has expanded greatly and this has all added to the set of skills and methods to be learned by new ringers. In the earlier years it was essentially the pattern of the plumage which was used to determine a bird's age. Since then the knowledge has widened from the experiences of the many ringers worldwide pooling their findings. The colours and textures of soft parts can now be used to indicate age in some species. The development state of the skull structure of a young passerine bird is such that the colour of the bone showing through the skin is pink in a youngster and turns white as the bird ages into its first year. Feather shape and wear have been studied in great detail over the years and these characteristics now provide very confident indication of a bird in its first year.

Before the 1970s, for example, a free-flying bird was either aged as juvenile (Juv); a first year (1Y) if there was a plumage feature to enable this separation; post-juvenile (PJ) for species which could not be aged after the first autumn moult; and adult (Ad) for species which could be easily separated between first year and beyond, such as the Blackbird.

Nowadays, the scheduling of age is according the numbering system adopted by the European Ringing Committee (EURING). This uses a number, from 1 onwards but generally up to 6 for small passerine species. The number is applied in relation to the calendar year such that all the odd numbers indicate that the bird's actual year of birth is known. For example 1, for nestling or pullus implies that it was specifically ringed as a chick – thereby its birthplace is also known. An age number of 3 is used for birds known to have been born some time in the current year – a bird with juvenile plumage or a bird still showing juvenile characteristics of its first calendar year of life. A 5 category is for a bird known to have been born some time in the previous calendar year and so on.

The even numbers are used to indicate a generally unknown birth-year except that one can be sure that it was born at least before a specific calendar year. If the bird is showing characteristics verifying that it is not an age class 3 and that one can be sure that it was therefore born before the current calendar year, then it is aged with number 4. At certain times of the year when, with knowledge of a species' annual moulting sequence, one can verify that the bird was born before the current year and furthermore, before previous year, then the age number is 6. The age class 2 is used for when one has no idea of the bird's year of birth.

This even and odd numbering system can be applied indefinitely and some of the raptors and gulls, which have definable plumage characteristics in their third and fourth years or beyond, can use larger numbers to define their age class.

In the earlier years, the sexing of a bird could only be applied to a species where there is an obvious dimorphic plumage difference between the sexes. Other sexing techniques are now used which can be applied to species that are alike in plumage, for example, the Dunnock. In the breeding season it can be determined whether the bird is an incubating female by the presence of a large brood patch. At the same time of the year, a male develops a protuberance of its cloaca which is quite obvious when the feathers are blown aside.

The sex of a bird can often be determined when in the hand but not in the field (unless of course it is a singing male). Such species as the Corn Bunting and the Cetti's Warbler are sexually dimorphic on size. Wing-length measurement is thereby a means of deciding upon the bird's sex.

Results

The details of selected recovery information, which have resulted from ringing studies in the county since 1909, are given within the text for each of the species throughout the Species Accounts.

The term recovery is used to describe a bird which has been ringed and caught again, away from the place of ringing, or a bird which is subsequently found dead.

It is this data that has exposed subtleties of the intriguing phenomenon of bird migration across continents. The same data has shown how some species make annual long-distance migration movements while others partially migrate over shorter distances under the influence of weather. In addition, not all populations making up a species behave in the same way. Recent research has shown that the broad south-west autumn migration of Chaffinches across the lowlands of Europe is made up of populations from two separate breeding areas. These two populations maintain separate parallel routes across Germany and France and as such, any major human activity in either of these areas may affect one population and not the other. Such findings are another example of how ringing studies are an indispensable tool for conservation.

The longevity of individuals of the various species has been established by the fitting of a long-lasting, uniquely numbered ring to a bird. Species crashes have been highlighted by the re-trap proportions of birds within populations. The classic example of this was the demise in 1969 of the Whitethroat and more recently the decline in numbers of some of the thrushes and finches. This population change can also be seen from field observations in some instances, but ringing provides precise information about individual birds. For example one can often witness a regular occurrence of Blue Tits visiting a garden feeding table and assume that they are the same birds. However, by trapping and ringing these birds, one then finds that wandering flocks are involved and different individuals visit the garden on a daily basis.

Throughout the 1980s and 1990s many ringers have been carrying out ringing at so called Constant Effort Sites (CES). This method was developed by Mike Boddy and launched in 1982 and is a technique by which the breeding performance of each species at a site can be measured and compared from year to year. A number of visits to the site are made throughout the breeding period at approximately two-week intervals, allowing for weather restraints. On each site visit the mist nets used to catch the birds are erected in the same places at the same time of day on each occasion and left for the same numbers of hours. These latter requirements minimize any bias from the trapping position and time when catching, and the same parameters are maintained between years. Other factors such has habitat changes are monitored by a recognized habitat recording method. The ringing from year to year then produces figures of adult birds caught annually along with the proportion of young birds for the year. This comparative monitoring of breeding performance is maintained over several years and the same ringing programme operating in other regions enables differences across the county to be exposed.

The Constant Effort ringing regime and the commitment to regularly operate at a chosen site is very demanding on time, especially over a number of years, but there are nevertheless schemes still operating after 30 years. For these reasons, however, many ringers are unable to participate in this scheme, and so in 1999 the BTO developed another methodology for a project named Ringing Adults for Survival. This provides different results from those of the CES but gives more flexibility to suit the needs of the participating ringers. It uses more flexible timing methods and targets a selected species with the object of catching all adults of the given species in the study area. Obviously it cannot be applied to all species, but the Swallow is an ideal example. For this example, the study area might be a number of farms over an area and visits would be made to trap the birds breeding at each farm. The chicks would also be ringed to provide information on survival success. Subsequent trapping each year will then provide data on the adult survival, the breeding success to fledging and the later success of the offspring. These continuing projects will provide ongoing information and give a baseline against which to measure future trends.

Another BTO national project to which ringing contributes is the Nest Records Scheme, which began in 1939. This is simply the gathering of nesting statistics for all of our breeding species (and Derbyshire has made a substantial contribution here). Ringers are able to further contribute to this by the fitting of rings to nestlings of known age and known birthplace. The re-trapping or recovery of these individuals thereby provides more precise data on the species' breeding successes and dispersal.

A General Description of the County of Derbyshire

Introduction

Derbyshire is one of Britain's medium-sized inland counties (2550km^2) lying in north-central England, as indicated on the map below. It presents both a scenic and a cultural link between the Midlands and the north of England. The City of Derby (87km^2) has been a separate unitary authority since 1998, but for the purposes of this book is deemed to be included in the county, making a total area of 2637km^2 under consideration. Derbyshire falls almost entirely in the Ordnance Survey 100km square SK, except for very small areas in the north and west which are in SE and SJ respectively.

Boundaries and divisions

Since Whitlock's *Birds of Derbyshire* was published in 1893, there have been many changes to the county boundary, some more significant than others (see 'Changes to the County Boundary', p. 21). The county is bounded by the new unitary authorities and counties of Kirklees (formerly part of West Yorkshire) on the north; by Barnsley, Sheffield and Rotherham (formerly part of South Yorkshire) on the north-east; by Nottinghamshire on the east; Leicestershire on the south-east; Staffordshire on the south-west; Cheshire on the west; and by Stockport, Tameside and Oldham (formerly part of Greater Manchester) on the north-west. For convenience, generally the text refers to the former metropolitan counties, but when dealing with ringing the recording areas are as defined in Balance and Smith (2008). Apart from the City of Derby, the county contains eight borough or district councils as shown on the map: High Peak, West Derbyshire, North-east Derbyshire, Chesterfield, Bolsover, Amber Valley, South Derbyshire and Erewash.

Scenery and land use

Derbyshire is a county of wide scenic diversity, ranging from high peat bogs and gritstone moors, through limestone pastures and enchanting dales, to lowland river valleys, ancient woodlands and industrial dereliction. The variety of attractive scenery in its northern part was the prime reason for the creation of the Peak District National Park in 1951, which lies mainly within Derbyshire and covers over half of the county.

Land use in the county consists of approximately 65% farmland, 13% moorland and 10% urban/suburban areas. The remaining 12% is occupied by broad-leaved, coniferous and mixed woodland, as well as quarries, landfill and wasteland, and areas devoted to industry. Most of rural Derbyshire remains fairly sparsely populated.

The southern part of the county is very fertile and agriculture includes cereals, root crops and dairy farming. The north is rugged and mountainous and mainly supports sheep farming.

For more detail of the county's scenery and land use, see 'The Natural Areas', p. 25.

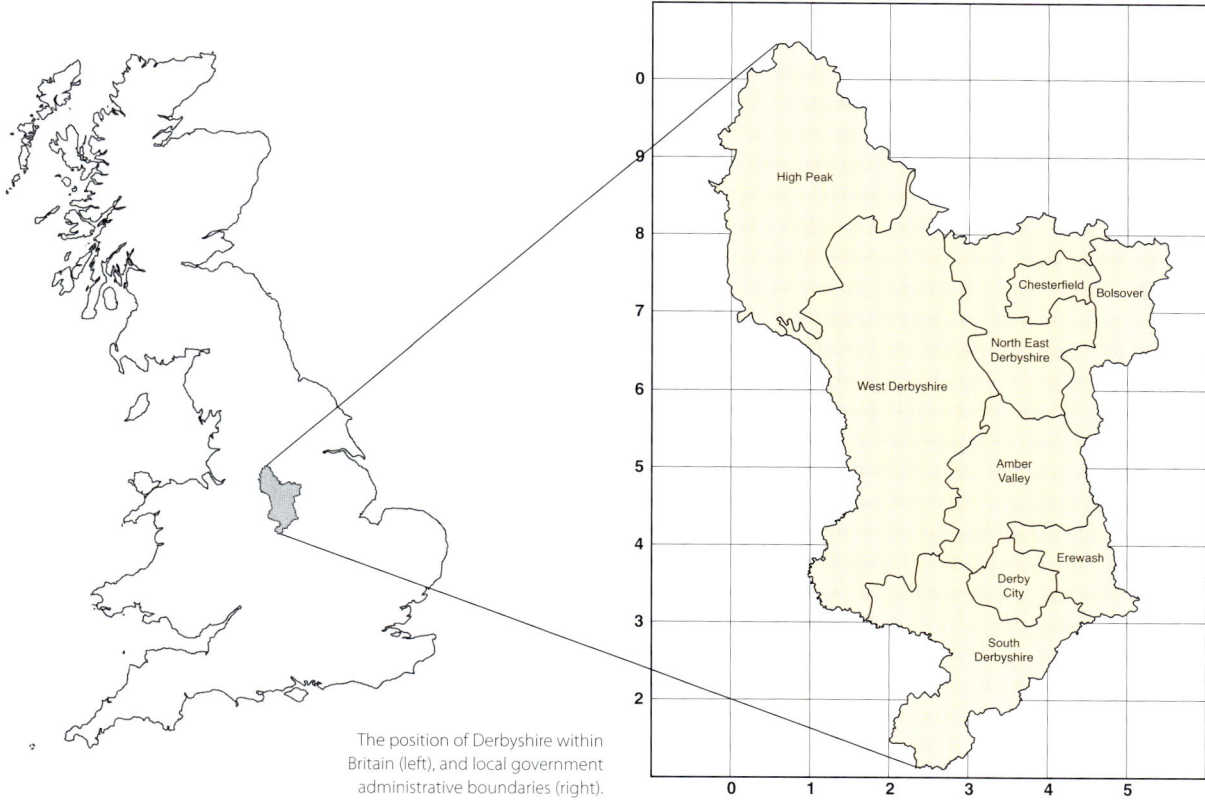

The position of Derbyshire within Britain (left), and local government administrative boundaries (right).

Population and urbanization

The county includes the towns of Matlock (the county town at the geographical centre), Glossop, Chapel-en-le-Frith, Buxton, Bakewell, Dronfield, Chesterfield (the largest town excluding Derby), Ashbourne, Wirksworth, Belper, Alfreton, Ripley, Heanor, Ilkeston, Long Eaton, Coalville and Swadlincote. Thirteen of these 17 towns have between 10,000 and 100,000 inhabitants, compared with Derby which has 248,700 (2011 census). Three-quarters of the population of Derbyshire (1,018,400 at 2011 census) live in about one-quarter of the area, concentrated mainly in the east and south-east.

Hydrology

Apart from in the far north-west and north-east of the county, all the main river systems drain to the south or south-east and ultimately flow into the River Trent, which forms part of the county's southern boundary. Derbyshire's major rivers are the Derwent, Dove, Erewash and Rother. Apart from its Wye tributary and a short stretch of the river in the Matlock area, the Derwent catchment predominantly drains and flows through the northern and central non-limestone area. The Dove forms a large section of the western county boundary with Staffordshire and is the main drainage network of the limestone White Peak. The Erewash flows south draining the south-eastern part of the county, while the Rother rises near Pilsley and flows north into Rotherham to join the Don. North-western rivers, principally the Goyt and Etherow, eventually flow into the Mersey basin.

In the north-east, the Chesterfield canal heads north into Nottinghamshire to join the Trent at Stockwith near Gainsborough. A long-term restoration is currently underway on the Derbyshire section, with the southern section from Chesterfield to Staveley now navigable. Restoration of the Cromford Canal is also a long-term project but at the time of writing only short sections were navigable. In March 2005, the short north-west Derbyshire section of the Peak Forest Canal, which runs from Whaley Bridge, ultimately to link with the Mersey network, was reopened after extensive restoration. The Trent and Mersey Canal in the south is the only major navigable Derbyshire waterway and provides a link between the Dove and Derwent Valleys.

Industry

Industries of the county include the manufacture of aero engines, chemicals, paper, textiles, hosiery, lace, porcelain, plastics, and electrical and mining equipment. Quarrying in the Peak District is very important with limestone being extracted in huge quantities and increasingly hauled out by rail, but smaller amounts of gypsum, lead, zinc, marble, sandstone and pipeclay are also mined. The coal industry, so very important in the eastern part of the county, hugely declined in the latter part of the twentieth century.

With large industrial, heavily populated areas to the east, west and south, together with its suitable topography and rainfall, parts of Derbyshire are ideally positioned for the capture and storage of water. In the first half of the twentieth century, reservoir creation began in northern and western areas of the Dark Peak, where steep-sided valleys and high rainfall in the Upper Derwent, Goyt and Longdendale areas were ideal to meet the demand from nearby industrial conurbations. Postwar projects were mainly in south-eastern areas with the creation of Staunton Harold Reservoir (79ha), Foremark Reservoir (88ha), Ogston Reservoir (80ha), Church Wilne Reservoir (30ha) and Carsington Water (300ha). As a general rule, these newer, more southerly, reservoirs support more aquatic flora and fauna, and hence are more attractive for birds. This is partly due to natural factors such as the older dams being at higher altitudes and fed by acidic peaty water, neither of which is particularly attractive to a wide diversity of wildlife, and partly because more recent developments by water companies have included positive measures to conserve and encourage wildlife in and around their reservoirs.

Along the length of the Dove–Trent Valley, from Hilton in the west through Egginton, Willington, Barrow upon Trent, Swarkestone and Aston-on-Trent as far as Long Eaton in the east, a mixture of operational and worked-out gravel-extraction pits predominate the wide, shallow valley. Several of the pits are no longer in commercial operation and have been, or are in the process of being, made into nature reserves. This corridor of almost continuous gravel pits, together with the river, has created an ideal and productive environment for water-based birds, both resident and migrant.

The River Trent, not only along its Derbyshire stretch but also onwards into Nottinghamshire and Lincolnshire, together with nearby coal supplies, was ideally sited for power stations. Although several of these have been decommissioned, their legacy has been supportive of bird and other wildlife with good use being made of undisturbed areas containing cooling towers (nesting Peregrines) and water bodies. The owners of the now-demolished Drakelow Power Station had sufficient foresight to create an on-site nature reserve. Consequently, this southern part of Derbyshire, despite having a landscape very much influenced by human economic activity, has managed to retain, and maybe even enhance, bird-rich environments.

Communications

Communications in the county are good in the south and east. The M1 motorway passes down the eastern side and there are many good A-roads. This is less true in the north-west where the Pennines are still a serious impediment to movement especially in the winter. Like the road system, the rail network is best in the south and east with the Midland Mainline connecting Derby, through Chesterfield to Sheffield and the north of England, although traffic increased markedly on the Sheffield–Manchester line through the Hope Valley following closure of the Woodhead route.

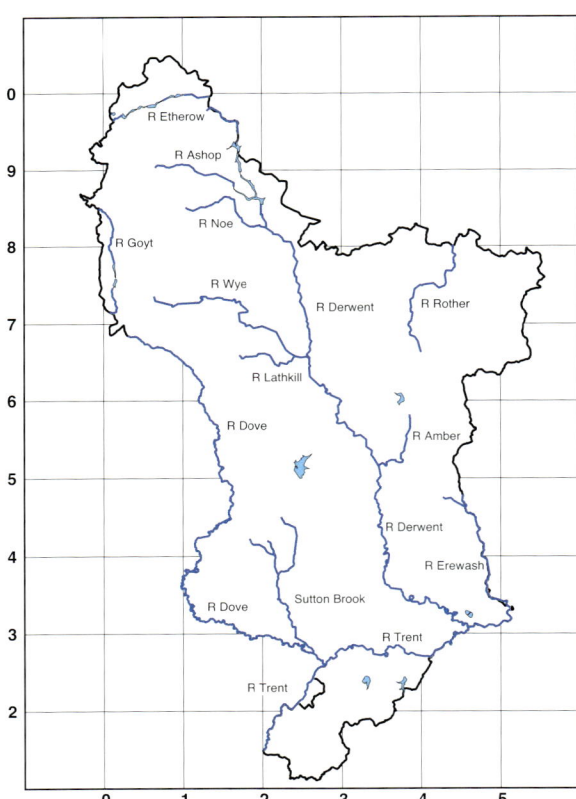

The main watercourses in Derbyshire.

Geology

Geology, climate and human economic activity have created a rich diversity of scenery and wildlife. Geology influences topography, soils and vegetation; climatic variations add another dimension; economic activity has produced the most recent and rapid changes. And all these factors influence birdlife.

In the same way that several English names for birds have been recently changed by the British Ornithological Union, many formerly common names for rock strata have been renamed by the British Geological Survey. Keuper Marl, for example, is now known as the Mercian Mudstone Group. The old names were often based on lithology (rock type) and have been retained here for simplicity and continuity.

North and west upland areas contrast markedly with the lowlands of the south and east. Within these two major regions are several areas of notable geographic diversity. The geology of all but the county's southern area consists of layers of limestone overlain by shales and sandstones and topped with Coal Measures. Tectonic movements uplifted and folded this configuration along an anticline running north to south. The upper layers fractured and eroded leaving the underlying limestone dome exposed, with the sandstones and Coal Measures remaining to the east and west.

Upland Derbyshire's geology dates back to the early Carboniferous period, 325 million years ago. At that time, Britain lay just south of the equator and had a tropical climate. Marine life flourished in a shallow lagoon covering 700km^2 of central Britain where shells and skeletons of marine creatures accumulated on the seabed. Rock formed in the shallower lagoons around the edge of these seas contains many marine fossils, the most abundant of which are crinoids or 'Derbyshire Screws'.

The characteristics and composition of limestone vary throughout the region depending on the conditions under which it was laid down and the extent of any subsequent volcanic activity. The whitest, most pure limestone was formed in clear, undisturbed tropical seas and contains few fossils. A few reefs developed on the edge of deep water that consisted of fine-grained lime-mud, possibly created by calcareous algae, which trapped limy sediment. Today they appear as hills because their composition has left them less susceptible to erosion than the surrounding limestone. Chrome Hill and the adjacent Parkhouse Hill are the most obvious examples of such reefs.

This period of geological activity eventually produced a large dome of Carboniferous Limestone lying at what became the southern end of the Pennines. Sediments, up to 600m thick, became the underlying limestone bedrock of what is now the White Peak. Within the county, the western limestone boundary is the River Dove and its eastern edge is the River Derwent. North to south, limestone reaches from the Hope Valley to Ashbourne, giving a total area for the White Peak of approximately 560km^2. Structurally this region is a plateau which slopes gently from an altitude of 450m in the north-west to 350m in the south-east. Unlike many other northern areas of England, Derbyshire limestone was not scraped clean by glaciation and so has virtually no exposed pavement, its surface being almost entirely covered by soil and vegetation. The plateau surface is an open landscape of small drystone-walled fields almost all of which are given over to pasture supporting sheep and cattle. Occasionally, small copses are to be found, planted as shelter belts around isolated farms and villages. The plateau has a monoculture and the fields themselves do not support a huge variety of birdlife. Some diversity of habitat is provided by the stone walls and quarries, but the very different nature of the dales (valleys) with their rivers, crags and woodland means that the White Peak becomes a significant area for the county's birdlife. The plateau is heavily dissected by these dales that were created by river erosion. They have relatively wide, gentle-sided headwaters, but steep, rocky sides further downstream. Over time, many have become dry, their water having percolated their riverbeds to flow underground through extensive cave systems. Some of the gorges, such as

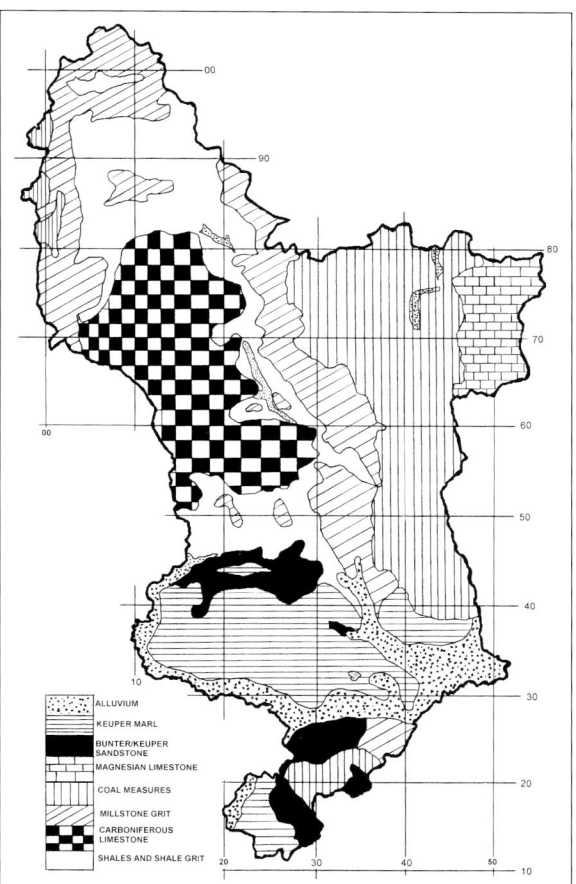

The simplified solid geology of Derbyshire.

Cave Dale near Castleton, are believed to have been formed from collapsed caves. After heavy rainfall, which temporarily raises the water table, some sections of dry valley beds contain running surface water. The upper Lathkill and Cressbrook, both tributaries of the Wye, frequently alternate between dry valley and river conditions, particularly during winter. Castleton, Buxton and Matlock are all sited close to extensive, accessible cave systems, some of which are open to the public as show-caves. They provide excellent conditions for studying the area's geological history.

Some Carboniferous Limestone has been modified by a variety of processes. Dolomitization, where magnesium replaces some of the calcium to produce Dolomitic Limestone, has occurred in the area north and west of Brassington. Here, Rainster and Harboro Rocks are of this form. Weathering of this rock has sculpted small tors and pinnacles, the surfaces of which are often riddled with small finger-sized pockets. Volcanic activity has been another modifier of the original limestone. Occasional periods of such activity gave rise to lava intrusions in the form of basalt. Known locally as 'toadstones', basalt up to 30m thick occurs in Tideswell Dale and Miller's Dale. Marble was formed through metamorphosis where hot volcanic activity met the limestone, and evidence of this can be seen in Tideswell Dale, Great Rocks Dale and at Peak Forest. None of these occurrences are sufficiently extensive to have warranted commercial extraction. At Ashford-in-the-Water, however, black marble proved especially popular in Victorian times. It was used for table tops, washstands and ornamental vases in wealthy households and in churches. Ashford black marble is not a true marble because the limestone has not undergone the metamorphosing heat treatment of marmorization, which tends to remove all evidence of fossils. It is a dark-grey limestone containing finely dispersed organic matter which, when polished, produces a black surface and frequently contains small fossils such as crinoids.

Hydro-thermal vents resulted in a variety of mineral deposits: galena (lead ore), fluorspar, calcite, chalcopyrite (copper ore) and baryte. All of these have been mined in modern times. Evidence of lead mining, in the form of crude ingots dating back to Roman times, has been found near Matlock.

After farming, man's biggest impact on the White Peak landscape has been limestone quarrying. Limestone was the dominant geological feature before a period of uplifting and folding to the north gave rise to the Scottish Highlands. From this elevated region large rivers flowed south into a shallow sea which covered much of what is now the Pennines and Peak District. Sedimentary deposits ranging from mud and silt to sand and pebbles were laid down in the form of deltas on this seabed. Ultimately, ferns and tree-ferns began to colonize the shallower fringes of this sea, which created extensive fen land with swamps and vegetated mud-flats. Occasionally, earth movements caused changes in the direction and flow of the material-bearing rivers, resulting in inundations and swamping of the vegetation by more sediments. This buried vegetation eventually formed Coal Measures.

Muddy sediments consisting of fine particles became compressed into shales, examples of which surface at Mam Tor and in the Alport Valley. Here, lubricated by water percolation and topped by layers of harder rock, instability caused huge landslips at Mam Tor as recently as the 1970s. The Edale Shales are the oldest of these rocks. They lie directly on top of the limestone and form the basis of the Edale and Hope Valleys.

Millstone Grit is the local name for compressed sandstone containing well-cemented small pebbles of quartz and feldspar. It has been widely used in Derbyshire domestic building, for drystone walls and as grindstones in the Sheffield steel and cutlery industries. Circular millstones in various states of completion can be found throughout the area, indicating sites of past quarrying. Along the northern county boundary Millstone Grit is in excess of 300m thick and surfaces as escarpments ('edges') up to 25m high. Nowadays, the edges are popular with rock climbers and offer some of the world's most difficult technical climbing.

The high, horseshoe-shaped Millstone Grit plateau, known as the Dark Peak, dominates the northern part of the county. It creates a well-defined boundary. In the west, from the Goyt Valley towards Glossop, the moors arc north via Axe Edge and then curve eastwards through the highest part of the county: Bleaklow (633m amsl) and Kinder Scout (636m amsl). From there, the edges run south down the eastern side of the Derwent watershed and form the inside of the horseshoe.

Variations of grain size and compactness of rock give rise to subdivisions in Millstone Grit classification. Kinder Scout Grit forms the margins of the Kinder plateau, Derwent Edge and Bamford Edge, whereas Stanage, Froggatt, Gardom's and Chatsworth Edges are made of Chatsworth or Rivelin Grit. Ashover Grit, while forming less spectacular outcrops than its northern counterparts, underlies the south-eastern leg of the horseshoe.

The high moorland of Kinder Scout, Bleaklow, Derwent Edge and the Longdendale moors contains large areas of exposed peat. Soils are very acidic and nutrient poor which, combined with their altitude, makes for large treeless areas of cotton-grass, heather and peat. On the highest moors the peat is 3–4m deep with many meandering rivulets and streams cutting through to the bedrock, producing a maze of twisty corridors, or groughs, across the plateau. While providing insufficient shelter and nutrition for many birds, this harsh environment is ideally suited to upland breeding species such as Red Grouse and Golden Plover.

Rivers cutting through the gritstone-rimmed edges of these upland plateaux have created rocky and stony valley sides in their upper reaches. Lower down, the gentler slopes and more favourable climate make for bracken-covered hillsides with occasional small oak and birch woodlands adorning both valley sides and bottoms. Padley Gorge is a good example of the landscape below Millstone Grit escarpments.

Overlying the Millstone Grit series in east Derbyshire lie Coal Measures, broadest in the north along the South Yorkshire border. They dip gently away to the east and continue into Nottinghamshire and Leicestershire. An equivalent matching geological structure in the west gives rise to the North Staffordshire and Lancashire coalfields. Industrialization and urbanization has been the major geographical consequence of Coal Measures, in the north around Chesterfield, Alfreton, Ripley, Heanor and Ilkeston and in the south at Swadlincote. Where land was not built on, the rural landscape is a mixture of low sandstone ridges interspersed with shale-based valleys. Poorly drained valleys tend to be used for permanent grassland, whereas the better-drained sandstone ridges support some arable farming. Subsequent to the decline of coal extraction, however, potentially derelict industrial areas have benefited from measures designed to regenerate both urban and rural landscapes through the creation of industrial estates, particularly in those areas with ready access to the M1, and also environmental projects, the most recent being the creation of nature reserves at Carr Vale and Pleasley Colliery.

In the Permian period, about 250 million years ago, a small, narrow area (approximately 106km^2) of Magnesian Limestone was formed when a shallow tropical sea slowly evaporated to leave magnesian-rich deposits. Within the county this area lies in the north-east. Its western edge lies on the fringe of the Coal Measures, between the Rivers Rother and Doe Lea (approximately along the line of the M1 motorway) while the county border with Nottinghamshire and South Yorkshire forms the other boundary. Hardwick Hall and Bolsover Castle, both prominent landmarks visible from the M1, stand on the escarpment which then dips gently to the east. This Magnesian Limestone is softer and more porous than its Carboniferous counterpart and has weathered into a more rounded landscape. Occasionally small crags and caves have been produced, the best known being at Creswell, where Neanderthal tools and animal remains dating back 45,000 years were discovered by Victorians. In 2003 cave paintings were discovered, increasing Creswell's significance as an archaeological site and visitor attraction.

Lowland Derbyshire, roughly to the south of a line between Ashbourne and Belper, is an area formed from younger Keuper rocks, particularly Keuper Marls, which consist of clays and thin bands of sandstone. In places sandstones have resulted in hills and ridges such as in the area around Hulland where sandpits are still being worked at Mercaston. Also within this region are isolated deposits of gypsum (to the south-east of Derby) which also occur just outside the county, east of the Staffordshire town of Tutbury. Within this southern area other small geological variations are found such as Bunter Sandstone which outcrops near Repton and again south of Ashbourne. The area immediately north of the southern Coal Measures at Swadlincote provides a microcosm of Peak District geology: Millstone Grit produces a small outcrop at Carver's Rocks by the inlet to Foremark Reservoir and Carboniferous Limestone was once quarried nearby at Ticknall. The River Trent has a major influence on the geography of the south where it has cut into glacial deposits that overlay Triassic sandstones and has created extensive floodplains swathed with sand and gravel terraces.

Topography

Topography depends primarily on the underlying geology but other influences have modified this basic picture. Glaciation, glacial retreats and warmer interglacial periods over one to two million years have further shaped the landscape. The most recent Devensian glaciation reached no further south than North Yorkshire but Derbyshire, on the fringe, was subject to frost action which is believed to be the origin of large blocks and boulders fractured from and now resting beneath many of the Millstone Grit edges. Southerly flowing outwash from the ice sheets is responsible for the deposits of sands and gravels of the lower Wye and Trent Valleys. Many of the steep-sided dales and cave networks owe their origins to the erosive power of glacial melt waters.

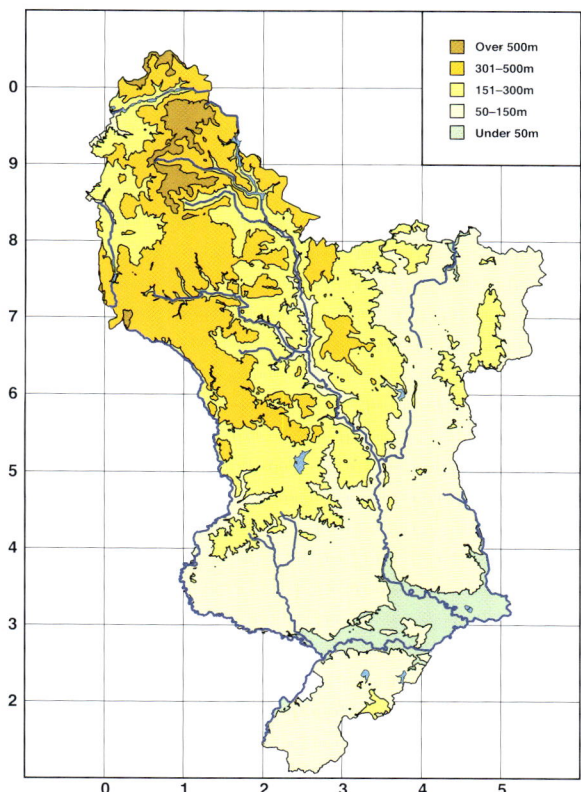
Altitude across the county of Derbyshire.

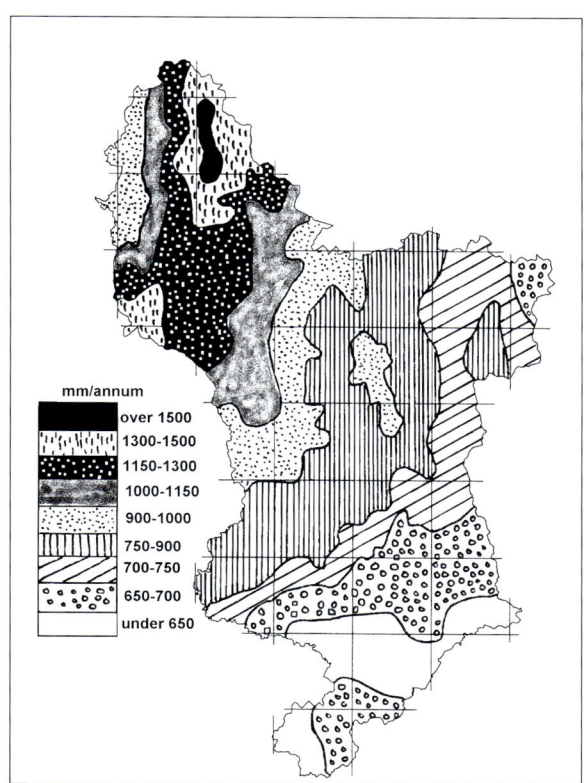
Average rainfall in Derbyshire, 1980–2007.

Climate

Lying in the north of the English Midlands, Derbyshire has contrasting climatic characteristics ranging from the wet and colder north of the county (located on the southern end of the Pennine chain) to the more mild and drier areas further south, where the climate is more typical of the Midlands and parts of East Anglia.

Temperatures in Derbyshire follow a similar north to south gradient, Buxton's annual mean being 7.8°C (compared with Scotland at 8°C), with Wirksworth and Derby recording 9.8°C and 10.9°C respectively, both of which are higher than the average for England of 9.5°C. Derby's mean temperature for January is 3.1°C, and for July is 16.3°C, while Buxton's mean January and July temperatures are 1.9°C and 14.3°C respectively. These compare with English means of 3.3°C and 16.1°C.

Due to the topography of the county, rainfall varies enormously, as can be seen by comparing the altitude and rainfall maps above. As an example, Buxton, in the north-west of the county, has a mean annual rainfall of 1290mm, which is 50% higher than the English average of 820mm (and approaching the averages for Wales and Scotland of 1350mm and 1430mm respectively). Mean annual rainfall for Wirksworth (in the centre of Derbyshire) and Derby itself are 779mm and 605mm, which are well below the English average. The county's wettest place is Bleaklow with average rainfall of 1600mm.

Snow lies on fewer days than it actually falls in southern Derbyshire (as it does in most of England) because ground temperatures often remain above freezing point and the snow melts as it falls. In the north of Derbyshire this trend is reversed, with days of snow lying slightly exceeding days of snowfall.

Wind speed is less variable in Derbyshire, ranging between an annual average of 15km/h in the south, to 19km/h in the north, where the UK's prevailing south-westerly winds are altered by local topography, which often increases wind speed and modifies its direction.

Habitats

Apart from coastal, Derbyshire encompasses virtually every wildlife habitat found elsewhere in Britain. Within an hour's drive, landscape and climate can range from harsh uplands to gentle lowlands, from woodlands to large inland water bodies and from ancient and modern industrial areas to agricultural and wild rural environments. As a consequence this environmental variety supports a richness of flora and fauna rarely found in a county of comparable size. For detailed descriptions of the habitats, see 'The Natural Areas' (p. 25).

A Summary of Derbyshire Statistics

Position in UK
Central, medium-sized county.

Population (2011 census)

Total	per km²	per mile²	per acre
1,018,400	386	1000	1.56

Approximate limits

	Latitude	OS grid line
Northern	53°32'	SE05
Southern	52°41'	SK11

	Longitude	OS grid line
Western	2°2'	SJ97
Eastern	1°12'	SK54

Highest point	Kinder Scout	636m amsl	2088 feet amsl
Lowest point	Trent Valley (at Nottinghamshire border)	27m amsl	88 feet amsl

Bordering Local Government Authorities

North	Kirklees (West Yorkshire)
North-east	Barnsley, Sheffield and Rotherham (South Yorkshire)
East	Nottinghamshire
South-east	Leicestershire
South-west	Staffordshire
West	Cheshire
North-west	Stockport, Tameside and Oldham (Greater Manchester)

Area

	km²	miles²	acres
Total Area	2637	1018	651,520

Administrative divisions (approximate areas)

	km²	miles²	acres
High Peak	578	223	142,720
West Derbyshire	672	259	165,760
North-east Derbyshire	274	106	76,840
Chesterfield	73	28	17,920
Bolsover	189	73	46,720
Amber Valley	268	103	62,920
South Derbyshire	383	148	94,720
Erewash	113	44	28,160
Derby City	87	34	21,498

Land use (approximate main types and areas)

	km²	miles²	acres
Moorland	343	132	84,480
Coniferous woodland	25	10	6400
Broad-leaved woodland	62	24	15,360
Mixed woodland	83	32	20,480
Farmland (all types)	1681	649	415,360
Urban	261	101	64,640
Industrial	67	26	16,640
Quarries and landfill	32	12	7680
Water bodies	32	12	7680
Roads, railways, other	52	20	12,800

Natural Areas (as named for this publication; approximate areas)

	km²	miles²	acres
Dark Peak	576	221	141,440
South West Peak	68	26	16,640
White Peak	560	217	138,880
Peak Fringe	271	105	66,965
Coal Measures	371	157	100,324
Magnesian Limestone	106	41	26,240
South Derbyshire Claylands	305	118	75,367
Trent Valley and National Forest	293	100	63,753
City of Derby	87	34	21,498

Changes to the County Boundary

This section has been included because the text in the Species Accounts often mentions records of birds in areas now lost to the county (for example Rother Valley Country Park).

From just prior to, and since Whitlock's *Birds of Derbyshire* was published in 1893, there have been many changes to the county boundary. The most important ones are listed, but not those that only affected the present City of Derby, as they do not affect the 'outer boundary' of the county.

The various legislation (statutory instruments, giving the dates when the legislation came into force, as shown) concerned with these changes is not cited, but may be inspected for more detail (together with large-scale maps) at Derbyshire County Offices, Matlock, by appointment (telephone 01629 536579).

1889
Appleby: The ancient parish, lying partly in Derbyshire and partly in Leicestershire, was abolished and two civil parishes were created, both called Appleby, one in each county.

Disley: A Cheshire parish, part of which lay in New Mills urban sanitary district, the rest of which lay in Derbyshire. The part in New Mills was transferred to Derbyshire.

Stapenhill: Part of the civil parish was transferred to Burton upon Trent county borough and the remainder transferred to the Derbyshire parishes of Bretby and Drakelow.

Winshill: Part of the civil parish was transferred to Burton upon Trent county borough and the remainder was transferred to the parish of Newton Solney, Derbyshire.

1894
Newton and Furness Vale: Transferred from Cheshire to Derbyshire.

1895
Croxall: The ancient parish included the townships of Croxall (part of which lay in Derbyshire and part in Staffordshire) and Catton (which lay in Derbyshire). The portion of Croxall civil parish (formerly township) was transferred to Staffordshire.

Pinxton: A small part of the parish lay in Nottinghamshire. Parts of the civil parish were exchanged with Kirkby-in-Ashfield, and Pinxton lay entirely in Derbyshire thereafter.

1897
Appleby: The Derbyshire civil parish was abolished and the area transferred to Leicestershire.

Chilcote: Transferred to Leicestershire.

Measham: Transferred to Leicestershire.

Netherseal: Transferred from Leicestershire to Derbyshire.

Oakthorpe and **Donisthorpe**: Transferred to Leicestershire.

Overseal: Transferred from Leicestershire to Derbyshire.

Stretton-en-le-Field: Transferred to Leicestershire.

Willesley: Transferred to Leicestershire.

Woodville: A civil parish created by the union of part of Hartshorne (in Derbyshire) and Ashby Woulds and Blackfordby (in Leicestershire) transferred to Derbyshire.

1901
Beauchief: Part transferred to Sheffield county borough.

Norton: Part transferred to Sheffield county borough.

1903
Rolleston-on-Dove: Considered in the nineteenth century and earlier to be entirely in Staffordshire, but a small part with no population later deemed to be in Derbyshire. The latter area was transferred to Marston-on-Dove in Derbyshire and the remainder of Rolleston was thereafter entirely in Staffordshire.

1929
Derwent: Part transferred to Sheffield county borough.

Dore: Part transferred to Sheffield county borough.

Hathersage: Part transferred to Sheffield county borough.

Outseats: Part transferred to Sheffield county borough.

Totley: Part transferred to Sheffield county borough.

1934
Beauchief: Abolished and its area transferred to Sheffield county borough.

Dore: Abolished and its area transferred to Sheffield county borough.

Norton: Abolished; part transferred to Sheffield county borough (the remainder added to Coal Aston parish, Derbyshire).

Totley: Abolished; part transferred to Sheffield county borough (the remainder added to Holmesfield parish, Derbyshire).

Bretby: Part transferred to Burton upon Trent county borough.

Ludworth: Transferred to Cheshire.

Mellor: Transferred to Cheshire.

1936
Hartington Upper Quarter: Part of the Cheshire parish of Taxal (aka Taxall) was added and therefore transferred to Derbyshire.

New Mills: Parts exchanged with the Cheshire parish of Disley.

Whaley Bridge: A Derbyshire civil parish created in 1936 by the union of parts of four Cheshire parishes (Yeardsley and Whaley, Disley, Kettleshulme and Taxall) and parts of the two Derbyshire parishes of Fernilee and Chapel-en-le-Frith.

1965
Breaston: Part of the Staffordshire civil parish of Lockington-Hemington was added to Breaston.

Melbourne: Part of the area lost to Breedon-on-the-Hill and parts exchanged with Castle Donington, both in Leicestershire.

Shardlow and **Great Wilne**: 20ha lost to Lockington-Hemington and parts exchanged with Castle Donington, both in Leicestershire.

Weston-on-Trent: Part transferred to Castle Donington, Leicestershire.

1967

Beighton: Abolished and part transferred to Sheffield county borough, part to Aston-cum-Aughton (West Riding of Yorkshire), part to Eckington and Killamarsh (both Derbyshire).

Dronfield: Parts exchanged with Sheffield county borough.

Eckington: Part transferred to Sheffield county borough.

Holmesfield: Parts exchanged with Sheffield county borough.

Killamarsh: Part transferred to Sheffield county borough.

1974

Tintwistle: Rural district transferred to Derbyshire.

1991

Netherseal: A very small area lying to the south of the River Mease (in SK2812) transferred from Derbyshire to Leicestershire.

Clifton Campville: An area (about 80ha) north of the River Mease (SK2511/12 and SK2611/12) lying alongside the Seal Brook, transferred to Derbyshire from Leicestershire.

Woodville: An irregular-shaped area (SK3218) lying south-east of Woodville and to the south of the former A50 road (now A511) transferred to Leicestershire. (The proposal for a transfer of a large area near Albert Village, Leicestershire (SK3018) to Derbyshire, at the same time, was never implemented.)

South Wood: A large woodland (SK3619/20) transferred to Derbyshire from Leicestershire.

King's Mills–Derwent Mouth: The boundary between Leicestershire and Derbyshire running along the centre of the River Trent between King's Mills and Derwent Mouth (approximately 6km) moved to the north bank.

Borough Holme: A large area known as Borough Holme (SK2016) and two smaller parcels of land to the north (not named) and south (Cherry Holme), all lying on the west bank of the River Trent to the south-east of Barton-under-Needwood, transferred from Derbyshire to Staffordshire.

Rivers Dove, Trent and Mease: Some 36 very small parcels of land exchanged between Staffordshire and Derbyshire to adjust the boundary to the centre of the rivers.

1991

Egginton: Approximately 1km² of land on the south-west side of the River Dove transferred to Stretton Parish, Staffordshire, rationalizing the boundary between Derbyshire and Staffordshire to the River Dove for about 4km.

1992

North-west Derbyshire: A fairly large number of small areas (in the parishes of Charlesworth, Chisworth and Tintwistle exchanged with Greater Manchester (Tameside) in order to rationalize the boundary.

1993

Long Eaton/Toton: A fairly large area to the north-east of Long Eaton (SK5033/34) adjacent to the River Erewash transferred from Nottinghamshire to Derbyshire.

Toton Railway Sidings: An area to the north of Long Eaton (SK4834 and SK4934), containing a small part of Toton railway sidings, transferred to Nottinghamshire from Derbyshire.

Ilkeston: An area to the east of Ilkeston (SK4742), lying between the River Erewash and the Erewash Valley Railway route transferred from Nottinghamshire to Derbyshire.

Sandiacre–Steetley: Some 16 small but complex exchanges along the whole length of the boundary between Nottinghamshire and Derbyshire, many along the course of the River Erewash. The most significant were to make Langley Mill flash (SK4548) fall mainly in Derbyshire while Brinsley flash (SK4450) was lost entirely to Nottinghamshire.

Langwith: A small area to the east of Langwith (SK5269 and SK5270/5370) transferred to Nottinghamshire.

Whaley Thorns: An irregular-shaped area to the east and north-east of Whaley Thorns (SK5370 and SK5371) transferred to Nottinghamshire.

Steetley Quarry: The maps originally published showing proposals for a complex exchange of land between Derbyshire, Nottinghamshire and South Yorkshire (Rotherham), centred around Steetley Quarry (SK5379, SK5479, SK5579, SK5378, SK5478 and SK5578) were not implemented; modified proposals later were (see Ordnance Survey Explorer Map 270 for eventual arrangement).

Attenborough Nature Reserve: An area to the east of Long Eaton (SK3351), part of the Attenborough Nature Reserve and straddling the River Trent, transferred from Derbyshire to Nottinghamshire.

1994

Rother Valley Country Park: The boundary running through the central lake at Rother Valley Country Park moved south to run along the northern edge of the built-up area of Killamarsh (SK4581), thus transferring an area from Derbyshire to South Yorkshire (Rotherham).

North-east Derbyshire: Several exchanges of land between South Yorkshire (Sheffield and Rotherham) and Derbyshire to rationalize the long boundary, the most important of which was to move the boundary from the centreline of Pebley Pond to the north bank, thus making all of this water lie in Derbyshire.

Nether Langwith: A very small parcel transferred from Nottinghamshire to Derbyshire.

Place-names and the History of Birds in Derbyshire

Place-names provide an interesting additional insight into the former avifauna of the county. Many names date back to the periods when Anglo-Saxon and Norse settlers were first arriving to settle and farm the countryside, about 1500 and 1200 years ago respectively, though of course the names might have been conferred at any time since then. Typically place-names contain two elements, often a noun and an adjective or a noun and a possessive element, sometimes two nouns – like 'crane moor'. Over the centuries, names have been much corrupted, and should not necessarily be read with a modern eye. Eagle Stone, Curbar, seems indeed to refer to a stone that an eagle once frequented, but Eagle Tor, Stanton is a corruption of 'eccles tor', or church rock. Crowden is 'crow valley', but Crowdecote is 'Cruda's cottage'. This last example highlights another problem, that place-names sometimes might be referring to a person named after the animal, rather than the animal itself. For example, Hraefn was sometimes a personal name, perhaps of someone who had black hair, or a deep croaking voice.

The accompanying list is not intended to be complete, but it presents a comprehensive selection of Crane, Raven and hawk names, assembled by Simon Boisseau, plus a small selection of other obvious bird-related names. The Crane names have been published previously by Boisseau and Yalden (1998).

Evidently Cranes were moderately frequent and conspicuous in the county, but not so obvious as Ravens. A few eagle place-names, associated particularly with the high and remoter parts of the Peak District, might refer to Golden Eagles rather than White-tailed Eagles, though the latter is much more common in archaeological sites and is implied by many of the place-names, nationally, which are often near water.

The source for this work is the county volumes of the English Place-name Society (Cameron 1959); and because field names are not listed in their index, the relevant volume and page numbers are cited where possible.

Place-name	Grid reference	Vol:Page	Status*	Language**	Meaning
Conksbury	SK2065	27:107	1	OE cranuc, OE burgh	Fort frequented by Cranes
Corley Farm	SK2147	29:533	1	OE corn, OE leah	Crane's clearing
Craine Moor	SK3474	28:207	3	OE cran, OE mor	Crane moor
Crake Low	SK1753	28:410	2	OE crake, OE hlaw	Crow hill
Cranbury	SK2071	27:140	3	OE cran, OE burh	Fort frequented by Cranes
Cran Moor	SK3378	28:245	3	OE cran, OE mor	Crane moor
Cronkston Grange	SK1165	28:365	1	OE cranuc, OE dun	Crane hill
Crowden	SK0799	–	2	OE crawe, OE denu	Crow valley
Crowden Clough	SK1086	27:87	2	OE crawe, OE denu, OE cloh	Crow valley ravine
Crowden Tower	SK0987	27:87	2	OE crawe, OE denu, OE	Crow valley
Crowshaw	SK1368	27:101	3	OE crawe, OW sceaga	Crow wood
Eagle Stone	SK2673	27:81	2		
Glead Hill	SK0791	27:127	2	OE gleoda, OE hyll	Kite hill
Haukeland	SK3871	28:236	3	OE hafoc, OE land	Land frequented by a Hawk
Haukeresdol	SK3833	28:427	3	OE hafocere, OE dal	Share in a field frequented by a Hawk
Hauke Springe	SK3582	28:289	3	OE hafoc, OE spring	Hawk wood
Havekenestesike	SK4165	28:335	3	OE hafoc, OE nest, OE sic	Hawk's nest stream
Hawkeshaw Piece	SK1647	28:335	3		
Hawkesworth Gate	SK3825	29:643	3	OE hafoc, OE worðign	Hawk's enclosure
Hawk Lane	SK4374	28:305	3		
Hawks	SK1781	27:49	3		
Hawk Sike	SK1683	–	3	OE hafoc, OE sic	Hawk's stream
Hawks Low	SK1756	28:404	2	OE hafoc, OE hlaw	Hawk hill
Hawksmoor	SK2350	28:377	3		
Hern Clough	SK0994	27:127	2	OE earn, OE cloh	Eagle ravine
Hern Side	SK1692	27:127	2	OE earn, OE side	Eagle side
Hernstone Lane Head	SK1179	27:160	2	OE earn, OE stan	Eagle stone
Hern Stones	SK0995	27:127	2	OE earn, OE stan	Eagle stone
Lapwing	SK3825	29:643	3		
Le Corlechefla	SK2350	28:377	3	OE corn, OE laec, ON flat	Flat ground by a stream frequented by cranes

* 1 = a major place-name (settlement); 2 = a minor place-name; 3 = a field name.
** OE = Old English; ON = Old Norse; OW = Old Welsh; OSC = Old Scandinavian.

Place-name	Grid reference	Vol:Page	Status*	Language**	Meaning
Ouzleden Clough	SK1590	27:128	2	OE osle, OE denu, OE cloh	Blackbird valley ravine
Ramshaw Farm	SK3776	28:319	1	ON hrafn, ON haugr	Raven's hill
Ramsley Wood	SK4026	29:642	2	OE hraefn, OE leah	Raven's clearing
Rauenesbroc	SK4665	28:273	3	OE hraefn, OE broc	Raven's brook
Ravencarr Farm	SK4279	28:250	2	ON hrafn, OE kjarr	Brushwood frequented by a Raven
Ravenhill	SK3750	29:567	3		
Ravenhow Stones	SK4132	28:464	3	OE hraefn, OE haugr, OE stan	Stone on a Raven's hill
Raven Meadow	SK1683	–	3		
Ravenscliff	SK1950	28:344	1	OE hraefn, OE clif	Raven's cliff
Ravensclogh	SK2958	28:394	3	OE hraefn, OE cloh	Raven's ravine
Ravensclough	SK1294	27:128	2	OE hraefn, OE cloh	Raven's ravine
Ravensdale	SK1773	29:597	3	OE hraefn, OE dael	Raven's valley
Ravenslack	SK0085	27:152	1	ON hrafn, OSC slakki	Shallow valley frequented by a Raven
Ravens Leach	SK0085	27:152	1	OE hraefn, OE laec	Raven's stream
Raven's Low	SK0172	28:373	2	OE hraefn, OE hlaw	Raven's hill
Ravensmere	SK1831	29:563	3	OE hraefn, OE mere	Raven lake
Ravensnest	SK3461	28:194	2	OE hraefn, OE nest	Raven's nest
Ravenstard	SK2118	29:668	3		
Raven's Tor	SK1573	27:173	2	OE hraefn, OE torr	Raven's rocky peak
Raven's Tor	SK2867	28:417	2	OE hraefn, OE hlaw	Raven's hill (cf Raven's Low above)
Ravenswall	SK2572	27:43	3	OE hraefn, OE wella	Raven's spring
Ravynswall	SK1653	28:400	3	OE hraefn, OE wella	Raven's spring
Redcarr Hillside (formerly Houkneste Hylls)	SK3665	28:331	2	OE hafoc, OE nest, OE hyll	Hill with Hawk's nest
Roystone Grange	SK2054	28:343	1	OE hraefn, OE stan	Raven's stone
Throstle Meadow	SK2168	27:37	3		
Throstle Nest	SK2380	28:377	3		

*   1 = a major place-name (settlement); 2 = a minor place-name; 3 = a field name.
** OE = Old English; ON = Old Norse; OW = Old Welsh; OSC = Old Scandinavian.

The Natural Areas

Introduction

The county is described in this book using English Nature's Natural Areas concept. The agency ceased to exist following a review by Lord Haskins, enacted in the Natural Environment and Rural Communities Act 2006. It was integrated with parts of both the Rural Development Service and the Countryside Agency from 1st October 2006, to form a new body called Natural England. The two names are used synonymously in this publication.

In the late 1990s, English Nature divided the country into 120 Natural Areas, eight of which are partly or wholly within Derbyshire. The boundaries are based on the distribution of wildlife, natural features, land use patterns and human history of each area and do not follow any administrative boundaries. Instead, they relate to variations in landscape character. They are not designations.

For the purposes of this book, the concept has been slightly modified as shown in the map. The boundaries of these areas are not exact, being regarded as several kilometres wide in places, and consequently the areas of each as stated in the table are approximate. In addition, some area names have been changed to titles more appropriate to Derbyshire. Moreover, we have integrated the very small part of the Urban Mersey Basin which lies in Derbyshire into The Dark Peak, while another very small area around Snelston and Norbury in English Nature's Area No. 50 (the Churnet Valley and the Potteries) has been included in the South Derbyshire Claylands. Finally, English Nature included in their Coal Measures Natural Area a separate area some 15km to the south-west around Swadlincote, but for the purposes of this book this is treated as part of English Nature's Area No. 33, the Trent Valley, which is herein called the Trent Valley and National Forest.

The City of Derby is discussed separately (but its area is included within the 2637km^2 in the table), as it falls awkwardly within four natural areas (the Peak Fringe, the South Derbyshire Claylands, the Coal Measures and the Trent Valley) and its urbanization has changed its character so profoundly from any of them that it might be described as an 'unnatural' area.

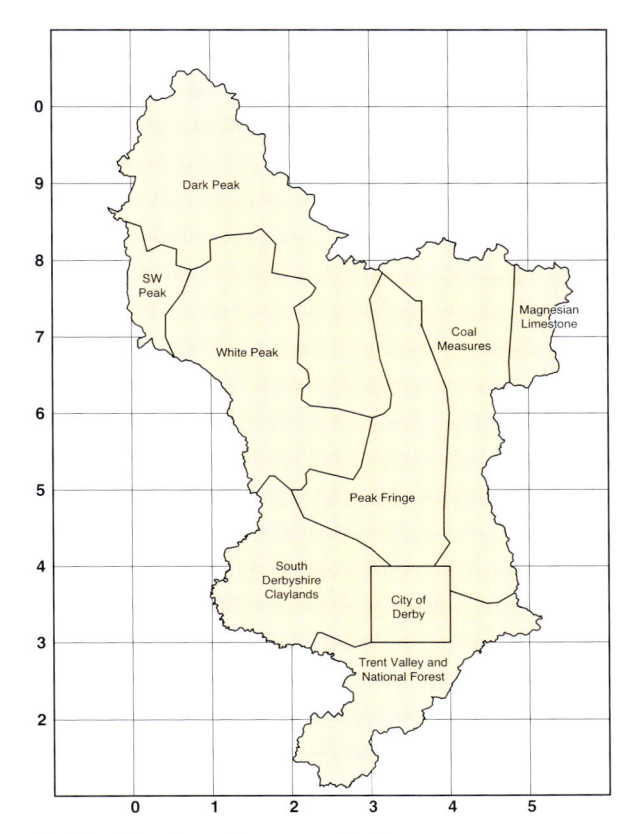

The Natural Areas (boundaries are approximate).

English Nature Natural Area	Nomenclature in this book	Area (km^2)
No. 25 The Dark Peak	The Dark Peak	576
No. 29 The South West Peak	The South West Peak	68
No. 30 The White Peak	The White Peak	560
No. 31 Derbyshire Peak Fringe and Lower Derwent	The Peak Fringe	271
No. 24 The Coal Measures	The Coal Measures	371
No. 23 The Southern Magnesian Limestone	The Magnesian Limestone	106
No. 40 Needwood and South Derbyshire Claylands	The South Derbyshire Claylands	305
No. 33 The Trent Valley and Rises	The Trent Valley and National Forest	293
n/a	The City of Derby	87
	Total	2637

The Dark Peak

The Dark Peak Natural Area (part of English Nature's Area No. 25) extends from Black Hill, the northernmost point in Derbyshire, south to the A6 road between Disley and Chapel-en-le-Frith, along the A625 across to Hope, and then southwards to Matlock to include the Eastern Moors. For the purposes of this account, a small region including Glossop and land west of there has been included; this was placed by English Nature in their Natural Area No. 26, the Urban Mersey Basin – a decision that was not popular with some observers living in the Glossop area. It thus covers approximately 576km^2 of northern Derbyshire (21.8% of Derbyshire, and the largest Natural Area), roughly corresponding to the High Peak District, with a finger just over 20km long extending southwards. At the heart of the area are the high Millstone Grit plateaux, collectively including Kinder Scout, the highest point in the county at 636m amsl, Bleaklow at 633m, the Derwent Edges and the Longdendale moors. The largest settlement is Glossop, with a population of over 34,000, followed by New Mills and Matlock, each with some 11,000–12,000 residents. At the latter town this Natural Area reaches its lowest altitude at about 90m amsl.

The rough sandstones of the high plateaux are extremely acid and nutrient poor. Consequently, they support a rather poor but specialized flora and, because they are also impervious, they retain water, leading to waterlogging and the development of a thick blanket of peat. The peat is largely composed of the undecayed remains of bog-moss, *Sphagnum*, now almost absent from the moors because three centuries of industrial pollution from the surrounding towns has killed it. In places the peat is as much as 5m deep, but is more usually 2–3m, and covers over 14,000ha of the Dark Peak (Anderson & Tallis 1981). It covers an earlier woodland vegetation which it buried as it formed at various times in the last 5000 years. Tree stumps eroding out from under the edge of the peat include mainly oak, pine and birch, often showing signs of burning and severe browsing. It is possible that human interference in this woodland, to encourage grazing herbivores for hunting or farming, may have tilted the water balance of the moorlands and promoted the start of peat formation. Now, the usual vegetation cover is a very uniform expanse of hare's-tail cotton-grass *Eriophorum vaginatum*, interrupted by a low heath of crowberry *Empetrum nigrum* and bilberry *Vaccinium myrtillus* in eroding areas. This provides nesting habitat for important Golden Plover and Dunlin populations, as well as small numbers of Red Grouse, Curlews and Redshanks. In winter, relatively few birds are found on these higher moors, but Ravens, sometimes in small flocks, can usually be seen and occasional Hen Harriers, Peregrines and, on rare occasions, Rough-legged Buzzards might be present. Snow Buntings are sometimes seen but are less regular now than formerly. Much of this blanket-bog was severely eroded bare peat caused by overgrazing, severe summer fires and air pollution. Since 2003, the Moors for the Future partnership has overseen an extensive programme of revegetating these areas, so that most of the bare ground on Bleaklow and Black Hill is now covered in nurse grasses, young heather and mosses. The Kinder plateau is currently (2012–13) being treated. How this affects their bird populations is yet to be determined.

On the better-drained, sloping lower ground that surrounds the high plateaux, the usual vegetation is heather *Calluna vulgaris*. Created by burning management to support the Red Grouse populations, and therefore the sport of grouse-shooting, the heather moorlands are economically, scenically and ornithologically the most important habitat here, covering about 10,500ha of Derbyshire (Anderson & Yalden 1981). Heather burning on a 7–10 year cycle is important for Red Grouse. It creates a mixture of young plants, which are more nutritious, and leaves older ones to provide cover for both the adults and especially the broods of young grouse. Other species also benefit from the cover for nesting – Merlins, Hen Harriers (at least in 2006) and Short-eared Owls among them. The Twite, too, was a characteristic nesting bird of this habitat, but it relied for feeding on the adjoining hay meadows; these have declined alarmingly over the last 20 years, and the bird with them. The most abundant bird is the Meadow Pipit, providing food for the predators, and occasionally, these days, a nest-host for Cuckoos. Where sheep-grazing has been too severe, the heather has been replaced by a tight sward of grasses and stunted bilberry, or, in even worse conditions, by broken turf and eroding ground. This suits few birds, but Wheatears benefit from these conditions, and Meadow Pipits and Skylarks prefer grassy moorlands.

Particularly along the western side of the Eastern Moors, but also along the north side of Kinder Scout, the gritstone plateaux finish, not in gently sloping moorland, but in the steep edges which are so popular with rock climbers. They also are popular with the increasing populations of Ravens and Peregrines that have recolonized the Peak District over the last 40 years. The tumble of boulders and areas of bracken *Pteridium aquilinum* below the edges, and on steeper hillsides elsewhere, often provide Ring Ouzels as well as Wheatears, Whinchats and Stonechats with their cover.

Growing concern over the detrimental impact on breeding Ring Ouzels of rock climbing at Stanage Edge, together with other environmental issues, led to the creation of the Stanage Forum in 2000. Among a variety of measures, interested parties, including the Peak District National Park Authority, the Royal Society for the Protection of Birds (RSPB) and the British Mountaineering Council, have managed to reach a compromise resulting in well and clearly marked areas of voluntary climbing restrictions during the breeding season. Although the measures have not afforded the birds complete protection, they have raised awareness among rock climbers, the majority of whom have abided by the scheme.

The Eastern Moors stretch from Totley Moss in the north almost to Matlock in the south, and are generally flatter and lower than the northern moors. Here a large area of land which once belonged to the Severn Trent Water Authority before being sold to the National Park Authority is now being managed by the Eastern Moors Partnership, a consortium of the RSPB and the National Trust. In 2010 a baseline survey of 19.85km^2 of Big, Ramsley, White Edge and Clod Hall Moors as well as Leash Fen was carried out by Frost and Taylor (2011). Like much of the Eastern Moors region, the area is basically mixed moorland, dominated by heather and purple moor-grass *Molinia caerulea*, with boggy hollows and flushes, areas of scattered trees, and some peripheral oak and birch woodland. Meadow Pipits, unsurprisingly, were numerically dominant, but not many Red Grouse were present: few of these moors have been managed for grouse-shooting since 1945. Total numbers of territories included 27 Curlews, 19 Snipe, 92 Tree Pipits, 23 Whinchats, 19 Redstarts, 158 Willow Warblers, 11 Grasshopper Warblers, 33 Lesser Redpolls and 65 Reed Buntings. The consortium has some interesting plans for the area, including the re-wetting of parts of Leash Fen by blocking drains. The whole of the Eastern Moors area is well watched by birdwatchers seeking wintering raptors such as Peregrines, Merlins and Hen Harriers, as well as migrant Dotterels in spring. In recent years, this has also been the most regular wintering area in Derbyshire of Great Grey Shrikes. In some autumns the birchwoods of the area may support very large numbers of Siskins, Lesser Redpolls and winter thrushes.

In places, remnants of the old deciduous woodland, oak with birch and rowan, occupy the clough sides and slopes below the edges. The best remnants include also hazel, bird cherry, crab apple and honeysuckle, and are carpeted in early summer by bluebells. These woods provide the typical habitat in the High Peak of Redstarts and Pied Flycatchers, but they are small patches of a rather rare habitat, and hopes of expanding them in various conservation schemes now being promoted should benefit these species. The best-known site for these two birds is Padley Gorge, where up to 16 territories of each have been recorded. Shire Hill Wood near Glossop is a deciduous woodland, most of which was scheduled by Bevan et al. (1992) as semi-natural ancient woodland. A Common Birds Census (CBC) of 42ha undertaken in 1994 only by Anne Shaw showed Willow Warbler to be the most numerous species with 26 territories, equivalent to 61.9 pairs per km^2. This was followed by Robin (21: 50.00), Blue Tit (17: 40.48), Blackbird (11: 26.19) and Great Tit (9: 21.43). Other migrant breeders included Wood Warbler, Pied Flycatcher and Redstart, with three, two and one pairs.

Much more extensive are the coniferous woodlands, usually of sitka spruce, with areas of Scot's pine, Norway spruce, and hybrid larch, planted either by the Forestry Commission or by the water companies to protect the water-gathering grounds for their reservoirs, notably in the Longdendale, Snake and Ladybower–Derwentdale areas. Chaffinches and Coal Tits are among the most numerous species in these woods, and Siskins and Crossbills have taken to them, along with Great Spotted Woodpeckers and Goldcrests, while Firecrests have been present in several recent breeding seasons. Wood Warblers frequent the beech compartments in particular but are currently declining. Nesting Goshawks and, increasingly, Buzzards also take advantage of the large areas of woodland provided, along with Sparrowhawks and a very few Long-eared Owls. When in their young stages, these plantations provided temporary habitat for birds of seral scrub, notably Tree Pipits, Whinchats and Black Grouse, but these have been lost, the last almost completely despite a reintroduction programme, as the forests have matured. Further south there are several large areas of coniferous woodland, especially at Chatsworth and Matlock Forest. These hold similar birds to the woodlands further north, and additionally have long been the headquarters of the county's very small Nightjar population. These have traditionally nested in restocks but there has been a very recent and encouraging spread of birds onto open moorland nearby.

The valley bottoms are occupied by upland rivers that often run in spate. Storms are as likely in midsummer as they are in winter, creating wide shingle banks and cutting through rocky gorges, for example, along the River Ashop. This is the habitat of three typical birds: Common Sandpiper, Dipper and Grey Wagtail. Further south, where the rivers are wider and more slow-flowing, such as the River Derwent below Ladybower and the Wye south of Bakewell, Goosanders and Mandarin Ducks also breed, with Sand Martins in the very few places where suitable nesting banks are present.

However, most of the larger northern valleys have been impounded by reservoirs for drinking-water supply. Three reservoirs have been created in the Upper Derwent Valley: Ladybower, flooded in 1943, 210ha; Derwent, 1916, 74ha; and Howden, 1912, 64ha. Others are Kinder Reservoir (16ha) on the Sett, and five on the Etherow in Longdendale, namely Bottoms, Rhodeswood, Valehouse, Torside and Woodhead Reservoirs. Nearby Arnfield Reservoir lies just outside the Etherow Valley. These last six were created between 1853 and 1877 and occupy about 206ha in total. The streams around Glossop feed the smaller Hurst and Swineshaw Reservoirs (4ha each). Most of these reservoirs are routinely frequented by Common Sandpipers, Pied Wagtails and Mallards in the breeding season, and by increasing numbers of Canada Geese. Cormorants are frequent visitors, and rarer ducks, such as Teal and Red-breasted Merganser, sometimes breed, as do Little Ringed Plovers and Oystercatchers, if conditions of summer drawdown allow. Woodhead Reservoir developed the largest colony of Black-headed Gulls in the county, peaking at some 600 pairs in 1997. The colony disappeared temporarily in the early 2000s, possibly due to the presence of mink, but has recently re-formed, with 226 nests in 2011. Goldeneyes and Goosanders can be found on some of these reservoirs in winter. On the Eastern Moors, Barbrook (12ha) and Ramsley (4ha) Reservoirs formerly provided small water bodies, attractive to roosting Goosanders and an excellent variety of migrant waders when some mud was exposed. These included Derbyshire's first Baird's Sandpiper in 1983, three Grey Phalaropes and no fewer than six Purple Sandpipers, as well as migrant Rock Pipits in greater numbers than anywhere else in the county. However, because of concerns about the structural integrity of the retaining walls, the reservoirs were emptied and the dam walls breached in 2002. An ornithological history of Barbrook Reservoir was given by Frost (2003). Unfortunately, the pools created in mitigation at both of these sites have attracted very few birds.

In and around these features, the majority of the land is pasture, frequented mostly by sheep with some cattle. Much is rather poor and rush-infested and once was home to numerous breeding Curlews, Snipe and, especially, Lapwings. These are increasingly rare, and the patches where they occur now notable: the Padfield Reservoir fields, Cown Edge and Cowms Moor are examples. In autumn, and again in spring, some of these fields also serve the passing flocks of Golden Plovers, Fieldfares and Redwings, along with the local corvids at any time, but they are generally bereft of birds in midwinter. Breeding waders, such as Golden Plovers and Curlews, may also feed here, flying in from the nearby moors. Regular dosing with nitrate fertilizers, cutting for silage and heavy grazing pressure have improved these fields agriculturally, but impoverished them ornithologically. Sheep numbers in the Derbyshire moorlands increased from 63,000 in 1968 to 118,000 in 1993 (Defra June census figures, see Anderson et al. 1997), and this biomass dominates all the Dark Peak habitats, except where specifically fenced out. Under Defra's Dark Peak Environmentally Sensitive Area scheme, subsidy is paid to reduce density overall, and particularly to reduce wintering stocks, as well as to provide fencing for regeneration schemes. Changes resulting from these actions are beginning to show as positive effects on the vegetation, and at least on Red Grouse numbers, but not yet for other birds.

Two farmland CBCs were carried out in the Dark Peak during the 1990s. At Broadhay Farm, Hathersage a survey of 49.6ha, conducted by Mrs V.B. Stokes and others, began in 1967 and continued until 1995. The land was used mainly for grazing but also included small copses, standing and running water, a farmstead and a few houses and gardens. The 1990s data showed Chaffinch to be the most numerous species with an average of 16.2 territories, equating to 32.6 territories per km^2. Second was Wren (13.50: 27.2), followed by Blue Tit (10.3: 20.8), Dunnock (9.8: 19.8), Willow Warbler (9.7: 19.5) and Great Tit (6.0: 12.1). Surprisingly, Redstarts were as numerous as Blackbirds, being seventh equal (5.3: 10.3). There was a single pair of Pied Flycatchers in the final three years, and Tree Pipits varied between two and six pairs, but Skylarks were absent. Further north, an area of 67.7ha at Farfield Farm, Hope was surveyed until 1999 by Peter Phillipson, the late Roy Smith and others. This farm was mixed but predominantly grazing, with copses, a farmstead and a small number of houses and gardens. Ten years of data, from 1990 to 1999, showed the two most common species to be the same as at Broadhay Farm: Chaffinch with an average of 15.2 territories, which gives a figure of 22.5 per km^2, and Wren next with 14.9 pairs, giving 22.0 per km^2. These were followed by Robin (11.0: 16.3), Blue Tit (10.7: 15.8), Blackbird (10.3: 15.3), Willow Warbler (4.9: 7.2) and Great Tit (4.7: 6.9). Redstart was only in sixteenth position and Skylark and Tree Pipit were absent.

Some concern has been expressed about the potential detrimental ecological impact of the 2000 Countryside and Rights of Way Act (CRoW). It came into force in Derbyshire in 2004 and is of particular interest in the Dark Peak as much of the land here is 'unimproved' and thereby qualifies as 'open access land'. Some human intrusion is possible into a few previously inaccessible areas. However, the wet and rugged nature of the terrain in much of this upland area is probably sufficient to deter major intrusions into sensitive areas, though hill-running across blanket bog and gulley-scrambling up hill streams remain potential threats. On the positive side, surfacing of the Pennine Way across blanket-bog between Mill Hill and Snake Summit has reduced the 70m-wide trampled zone to a narrow 1m-wide path. Having retreated 200m from this zone, Golden Plovers and Dunlin have recolonized the blanket-bog ridge that is their prime habitat. One notable change in the CRoW is that it is now a criminal offence to 'recklessly' disturb wild birds whereas previously it was only considered an offence where disturbance was intentional. So now, people legally entering bird-sensitive areas will have to be more aware of the danger of disturbing rare and breeding birds and could possibly stand a greater risk of prosecution.

The South West Peak

The part of the South West Peak Natural Area (part of English Nature's Area No. 29) covers only 68km² within Derbyshire (2.6%). This includes the small towns of Whaley Bridge, with some 6000 inhabitants and Chapel-en-le-Frith (over 10,000), together with the ornithologically important areas of the Goyt Valley, Axe Edge, Combs Moss and Combs Reservoir. The altitudinal range is from about 170m amsl at Whaley Bridge to 559m at Shining Tor.

Geologically and ecologically, the South West Peak is a smaller version of the Dark Peak. Formed of acidic Millstone Grit sandstones and shales of Carboniferous age, with some inliers of the slightly younger Coal Measures, the highest parts on Axe Edge, Danebower Moss and the Shining Tor–Cat Tor ridge have a cover of peat and small areas of blanket bog vegetation. However, the large areas of cotton-grass seen in the Dark Peak are here much less extensive, and less monotonous, while the heather moorlands on the lower slopes are also much smaller. Golden Plovers breed in small numbers, perhaps 20 pairs, and Curlews are very conspicuous breeding birds, but only the occasional pair of Dunlin have ever been recorded on the highest parts of Axe Edge. This ridge used to be a local breeding stronghold of Twite, which fed on the nearby meadows across the A53, but these have lost their wild flowers, and thus the birds their food supply. The heather moors still support a sufficient number of Red Grouse to sustain two shoots, and therefore the essential management of the moors, and other moorland birds, such as Ring Ouzel, Merlin and Short-eared Owl, also frequent these areas. More significantly, on a well-publicized occasion in 1997, these moorlands hosted the only Hen Harriers to nest in Derbyshire in the twentieth century; wardening by RSPB staff and volunteers from the Derbyshire Ornithological Society and other organizations enabled many to see these magnificent birds fledge four young. Another pair nested in 2011 but, despite wardening again, failed at the egg stage.

As in the Dark Peak, the moors slope down into steep cloughs containing remnant upland oakwoods, with their Redstarts, Pied Flycatchers and Tree Pipits. Black Grouse graced the conifer plantations into the 1980s, but no longer. Coal Tits, Goldcrests and Siskins, though, have benefited, while a pair of Firecrests nested in 2002 and Nightjars have sometimes bred in very young plantations. Dippers and Grey Wagtails are regular breeding birds along the area's principal watercourse, the River Goyt, and also the Black Brook. Two large reservoirs have been constructed on the Goyt, namely Fernilee (35ha) in the 1930s and Errwood Reservoir (32ha) in the 1960s. They support 10–15 pairs of Common Sandpipers and sometimes Little Ringed Plovers. During the 1990s, a large population of Canada Geese built up, breeding around Errwood Reservoir. Combs Reservoir (25ha), near Chapel-en-le-Frith, which was opened in 1803 as a feeder for the Peak Forest Canal, is a shallower, more open reservoir in a wider valley, which regularly hosts over 100 Canada Geese in winter (and over 300 on rare occasions), presumed to be the Goyt Valley population. Passing gulls, ducks, terns and waders often call here, while it provides Great Crested Grebes and Coots with one of their rare breeding sites in the High Peak. Nearby Toddbrook Reservoir (14ha), also a canal feeder, has a less attractive, steeper, shoreline.

Most of the lower land in this part of Derbyshire is silage grass or pasture, with sheep and some cattle as the main grazers. Reflecting its proximity to Greater Manchester and its commuter links there, horses are also conspicuous, while golf courses and sailing clubs indicate similar pressures on land use. Lightly grazed cattle pasture near Combs Reservoir used to support nesting Lapwings and Yellow Wagtails. Now part of the golf course, it has lost these. Suburban land use is not particularly encouraging to birdlife, but Rooks and particularly Jackdaws thrive. Swifts and House Martins haunt the summer skies round the houses, as well as Swallows in the more rural areas. Collared Doves are as conspicuous as Woodpigeons, while the common garden birds include Greenfinch, Goldfinch and Chaffinch as well as Long-tailed, Coal, Blue and Great Tits, and still some House Sparrows. Shrubberies support Blackbirds and Song Thrushes, as well as attracting Waxwings and winter thrushes in certain years. Sparrowhawks and Tawny Owls are the most obvious predators.

The White Peak

The White Peak is English Nature's Area No. 30, and it occupies 560km², which is 21.2% of the county's total area, slightly smaller than the Dark Peak Natural Area. In Derbyshire, its outline stretches from Castleton and Rushup Edge in the north, south through Buxton to follow the River Dove, which is the county boundary with Staffordshire, to Thorpe before running roughly north-east to Wirksworth and then between north and north-west through Matlock Bath to Bakewell and thus back to Castleton. Part of the Natural Area lies beyond Derbyshire, in neighbouring Staffordshire. To the north, west and east, the White Peak is bounded by gritstone areas and to the south-east by the lower-lying Peak Fringe Natural Area. The largest settlements are Buxton, with a population of 21,000 and Bakewell, with 4000. Altitudinal extremes are 477m amsl near the disused Slitherstone Mine and 80m by the River Derwent at Cromford. The area takes its name from its geology in the form of the grey-white Carboniferous Limestone, which is seen in the frequent outcrops and the drystone walls and buildings of the plateau. The limestone was laid down during the Carboniferous period (about 360–300 million years ago) on the bed of a large, tropical sea. Later, volcanic activity and intrusion penetrated many of the cracks and cavities in the limestone, where a range of minerals accumulated including fluorspar (calcium fluoride), calcite (calcium carbonate), baryte (barium sulphate), galena (lead sulphide), chalcopyrite (copper-iron sulphide), sphalerite (zinc sulphide) and a unique, coloured variety of fluorspar called Blue John. The harder, reef limestones have survived as today's cliffs and crags, with the numerous dales and dry valleys created by glacial meltwater. Complex cave systems have been formed by underground drainage during the last two million years, creating modern tourist attractions, notably around Castleton, where there are more than 15km of passages and various sinkholes, such as the famous Eldon Hole. The area's caves, like some of those in the Magnesian Limestone Natural Area, have produced important fossil bird remains, which are described in 'Fossil Species' (p. 43).

The White Peak is basically a gently rolling, elevated plateau of sweeping vistas, lying mainly between 275m amsl in the south and 477m in the north, and dissected by numerous steep-sided dales, the latter being the epitome of Derbyshire to many people. A lack of woodland emphasizes the open nature of the plateau, with shelter belts around the farmsteads often the only significant arboreal feature. This was not always the case. Neolithic men (6500–4200 years ago) were farmers rather than hunter-gatherers, and found the lightly wooded White Peak plateau easier to clear than most other areas. It is rich in archaeological features from this period, including the celebrated henge at Arbor Low and chambered barrows, as at Five Wells and Minninglow. Slowly, the activities of Neolithic man brought about the deforestation of the plateau, and impoverishment of the soil resulted in leaching, so that by 2500 years ago, heathland had developed over much of the southern area, though its northward spread was much slower. Much later, in parts of the latter area, the Norman kings established the Peak Forest to serve as a royal hunting ground for boar and deer, forbidding cultivation, though the resulting habitat was heathland and scrub rather than mature forest. This gradually dwindled and the heaths largely disappeared after enclosure during the eighteenth and nineteenth centuries. Heathland still remains rare in the Natural Area.

Today the White Peak plateau is largely given over to pastoral farming, and both sheep and cattle are reared. The vast majority of the fields have been improved with fertilizers, leaving few rich in grasses and flowers. Almost all are bounded by the characteristic pale drystone walls, and many contain small dewponds, created as a source of drinking water for the animals. Skylarks are the most common birds, with Meadow Pipits found in some of the more unkempt fields, and along road and track verges. Lapwings and Curlews are scarcer since improvement, though the former may find bare fields temporarily to their liking at times of reseeding. Flocks of Jackdaws and Rooks visit the pastures from their breeding colonies in villages and rock-faces to feed, while especially in early spring Fieldfares, Redwings and Starlings may congregate in high numbers prior to emigration. Little Owls and Wheatears nest in the drystone walls, where the holes and cavities offer an abundance of sites. Some cereals are grown at lower altitudes and formerly held Corn Buntings, now all but extinct throughout Derbyshire, and Yellow Wagtails, which are also in serious decline. The same might be said of those intriguing finches, Twites, which nest only in a very few local quarries, and feed on sorrel and dock in nearby fields. With many hay meadows recently converted to silage and also because of higher stocking rates, the future of the Twite as a breeding bird in the county looks very uncertain. The last local three-figure counts of this bird occurred during 1987–90 on the western edge of the White Peak in the Doveholes–Batham Gate–Peak Dale area, where flocks of 100–160 were attracted to rough fields with thistles.

There are small remnant areas of heathland, notably at Longstone and Bradwell Moors. These are believed to have bird populations similar to those on the gritstone moorlands, with breeding Red Grouse, Curlews, Meadow Pipits and possibly Snipe, but relatively little is currently known about their numbers and densities.

The limestone dales, with their majestic crags, scree slopes, semi-ancient woods, botanically rich grasslands and crystal-clear rivers, are among Derbyshire's wildlife gems. English Nature recognized this by designating five of them as the Derbyshire Dales National Nature Reserve, totalling over 300ha. In decreasing order of size, these are Lathkill, Cressbrook, Monks, Biggin and Long Dales. The Derbyshire Wildlife Trust (DWT) also owns part of Chee Dale and has two other fine reserves on the slopes of the Wye Valley, at Miller's Dale Quarry and Priestcliffe Lees. The charity Plantlife owns the large Deep Dale near Sheldon, one of many 'dry' dales in the region, while the National Trust owns the area between Dove Dale and Wolfscote Dale, and the adjoining Biggin Dale. The rivers, both at the sites mentioned above and elsewhere, are clear enough to support excellent trout-fishing and the Dove Dale area will be forever associated with Izaac Walton and his book, *The Compleat Angler*, while the River Lathkill is clean enough to supply adjacent villages with their drinking water. However, some of the area's rivers and streams are winterbournes, and only the Wye and the Dove always flow throughout their length. Both of these rivers rise in the Axe Edge area: the Wye flows for 41km on an east to south-east course to join the River Derwent at Rowsley, while the Dove runs for 31km through the White Peak (and then for a further 42km before it meets the River Trent at Newton Solney). Little Grebes, Mallards and Moorhens breed widely on the area's watercourses, with Coots and, less commonly, Tufted Ducks on some of the wider stretches, while more recently Mandarins have colonized some of the rivers, especially the Dove. Goosanders, too, breed here but may not be universally welcome. Dippers and Grey Wagtails are very typical species, nesting under bridges, behind waterfalls and in similar sites. The former are resident and their population seems quite stable, with Foster (1994) estimating 39 pairs in the White Peak Natural Area, very similar to the findings of Shooter (1970). They are thought to have suffered from excessive human disturbance in one area, following which camouflaged plastic tubes have been installed in an attempt to allow them to nest away from the more popular spots. Grey Wagtails might be found on the rivers all year but a proportion of the population moves away after breeding, and this species is prone to declines following severe winters. Common Sandpipers are more shy and are now rare breeding birds in the White Peak.

Ash and hazel dominate the wooded slopes of the dales, and many are regarded as ancient, semi-natural woodlands, though species such as beech and sycamore and conifers have been planted here and there. Chaffinches, Wrens and Willow Warblers are among the most numerous birds. Redstarts are relatively common, and may nest in crevices in rock-faces where natural tree holes are scarce. Spotted Flycatchers have greatly decreased but can still be found, often hawking insects above the rivers. Pied Flycatchers breed in a few places but Hawfinches, at one time thinly but widely scattered in the dales, seem now to be absent. Areas of mature beech form the most likely sites for Wood Warblers, while Coal Tits, Goldcrests and Siskins favour coniferous woodland. Buzzards and Sparrowhawks and, very scarcely, Goshawks are found in these woodlands and Hobbies have recently nested in one of the dales. In a few nearby areas, such as Hucklow and Longstone Edges, there are patches of scrub where Tree Pipits and Redstarts can be found and where Willow Tits and Long-eared Owls have bred in the past. However, little seems to have been published on overall bird populations in the White Peak, either on the plateau or in the dales. In 1999 and 2000, Carrington (2000, 2001) carried out a total of 56 visits at all times of year to 12ha of Slinter Wood, which is north-facing and dominated by ash. Seventeen species were proved to breed, of which the most numerous were Wren, Blue Tit, Robin and Blackcap. Another very useful assessment, based on three successive visits, was made by David Gosney in 1993 in the dales of SK17, which includes Wye, Chee, Miller's, Monsal, Tideswell, Monks and Cressbrook Dales. Though there are no figures for the most common species, Gosney produced totals of, among others, 55 territories of Redstarts, 52 each of Blackcaps and Goldfinches, 39 Garden Warblers, 37 Spotted Flycatchers, 20 Treecreepers, 18 Coal Tits, 13 each of Nuthatches and Marsh Tits and 9 Tree Pipits. Some of these species are in serious decline, both locally and nationally, and it would be interesting to have up-to-date figures for comparison.

The grassy higher parts and heads of the dales may hold Meadow Pipits and Whitethroats, and Redstarts and Wheatears nest in rocks and scree, but Whinchats may now be gone completely from such areas. The rock buttresses have breeding Kestrels, Stock Doves and Jackdaws, now joined by small numbers of Peregrines and Ravens in places where they are not unwittingly disturbed by climbers. The activities of the latter may be the reason why most of the White Peak's rock-nesting House Martins are nowadays on quarry faces rather than natural cliffs.

Formerly, the Peak District was famous for its lead mines, but today it is limestone that is quarried in huge amounts, especially around Buxton, where some of the quarries are among the largest in Europe. In the main they are undisturbed and hold all the species found on natural cliffs. For Peregrines and Ravens in particular they provide safe havens, and productivity at such sites is often notably higher than elsewhere in the Peak District. Wheatears frequent many of the quarries and Twites are a recent and unexpected addition, nesting in very small numbers on grassy ledges and behind overhangs. Some of the quarry floors hold wet areas where Little Ringed Plovers breed, and Black-headed Gulls currently nest in two colonies in the Buxton area, sometimes on near-vertical cliffs well above the water bodies. The large Doveholes Quarry has a series of lagoons and wet areas, popular with loafing gulls and ducks, with Shelducks breeding successfully in 2008–09, and one of the few Sand Martin colonies in the area is found here. Another wetland area at Peak Dale is now more overgrown than formerly, when it produced a few waders including a Purple Sandpiper. The small ponds north of Bradwell are heavily fished but usually support a few water birds, and have attracted rarities such as Whooper Swan, Long-tailed Duck and Grey Phalarope.

The most productive wetland site in this rather 'dry' area, however, is at 335m amsl at Middleton Moor, where lagoons were constructed in 1970 to take the tailings from nearby fluorspar mines. As these lagoons have filled and later solidified, others have been created. Currently, there are two lagoons, though one is now largely a reedbed. The other, known as 'No. 4 lagoon', is at the head of Coombs Dale and may be viewed from an adjacent rough lane or from the hide at its southern side. Ducks are usually present in only small numbers, though Teal have exceeded 100 and Shelducks have attempted to breed. Gulls find the site attractive for both daytime loafing and night-time roosting: the Lesser Black-backed Gull roost has reached almost 4000, while Black-headed Gulls nest in the thick vegetation. Lapwings and Little Ringed Plovers breed and Oystercatchers are often present in the breeding season but have not yet been proved to nest. There is usually a Curlew roost in early spring, which peaked at 167 in 1985, but the former large late summer and autumn gatherings of up to 4500 Lapwings and 1130 Golden Plovers no longer occur. The site is, however, still renowned for its migrant waders and 35 species had been recorded by May 2013 (a number equalled only by Ogston Reservoir). These include Stone Curlew, American Golden Plover, Grey and Red-necked Phalaropes, Purple and Pectoral Sandpipers and Least Sandpiper, a Derbyshire first, in 1988. Other rarities seen here include Blue-winged Teal and Sabine's Gull. The future of this very interesting area is uncertain because of the vagaries of economic demand but the site has new owners (as of 2013) and it is to be hoped that the lagoons will remain in a state that is attractive to water birds.

The Peak Fringe

The Peak Fringe and Lower Derwent (English Nature's Area No. 31) covers 271km^2, which is 10.3% of the county and is the only Natural Area that falls entirely within Derbyshire. Lying between the rural landscapes of the Dark and White Peaks to the west and the industrial urban areas of the Coal Measures to the east, it runs from Holmesfield in the north in a narrow finger to the west of Chesterfield, Clay Cross and Ripley as far as the northern outskirts of Derby. It extends westwards to cover southern Matlock, Wirksworth, Belper and Duffield and runs near to, but not as far as, Ashbourne and north of, and roughly parallel with, the A52 along its south-western edge, where it adjoins the Claylands Natural Area.

The area has an altitudinal range of just over 250m, from its lowest point at around 50m amsl by the River Derwent north of the Derby boundary, to 314m amsl at Alport Height (with its breathtaking vista). This pleasant and picturesque region is regarded as the foothills of the Pennines and is characterized by numerous ridges and intervening steep-sided valleys. In the north and south these ridges are formed by underlying shales, gritstones and sandstones. Sandwiched in the centre are more ridges and valleys but these are based on Carboniferous Limestone. In terms of geology, scenery and natural habitats the Peak Fringe can therefore be seen as a microcosm of the larger Dark and White Peak regions lying to the west. The largest towns wholly within the Natural Area are Wirksworth, with 9000 inhabitants, and Belper, with 21,000.

Rivers and brooks are major features in this largely agricultural landscape. Towards the north, small fast-flowing watercourses, such as the Holme Brook, Barlow Brook and the River Hipper run eastwards from the Eastern Moors of the Dark Peak into the River Rother in urban Chesterfield. Some of these were dammed in the past to provide water power for local mills and to create small drinking-water reservoirs. The open water bodies of the rivers and reservoirs, together with occasional small valley mires and swamps, provide important habitats for wildlife. Of particular ornithological interest are the three small, closely linked reservoirs at Linacre constructed between 1854 and 1911 and occupying an area of some 14ha. They are no longer used for water supplies, except in emergency, and have become a popular amenity area. The reservoirs are one of the county's main sites for breeding and wintering Mandarin Ducks, with winter flocks of up to 156 recorded in recent years. Being small, they are not attractive to some of the wintering wildfowl found elsewhere but Goosanders are regularly seen in winter and Common Scoters and Long-tailed Ducks have been recorded. The enclosing mixed conifer and deciduous woodland has a maturity which is attractive to a variety of woodland birds including all three woodpeckers and Pied Flycatchers. West and south of Chesterfield are two small former reservoir areas, at Crowhole and Press (together about 8ha), and a small lake at Stubbing Court which produce a few water bird records and sometimes hold Mandarins and Goosanders. A Red-necked Phalarope at the latter site in September 2009 was a reminder that unusual birds can turn up almost anywhere.

The river valleys of the Derwent, Ecclesbourne and Amber have a dominant influence on the landscape. The largest watercourse is the River Derwent which flows southwards through the central area, forming a pronounced, deep valley with ancient woods such as Shiningcliff Wood and Crich Chase that are excellent for birds. Wood Warblers, Redstarts, Pied Flycatchers and all three species of woodpecker can be found in these and other woods in the area though, typically, Lesser Spotted is likely to be the hardest to find. A CBC of 44ha of Shiningcliff Wood, dominated by sessile oak and birch, but with some sycamore and ash, has been carried out by Michael and Shirley Cross. In the ten years from 1990 to 1999 they found Wren the most common species, with an average of 25.2 territories a year, equivalent to 114.6 territories per km^2. The tits were also well represented with Blue Tit second (21.0: 95.5) and Great Tit fifth (9.1: 41.4). Third and fourth were Robin (13.2: 60.0) and Chaffinch (12.5: 56.8). The most common migrant breeders were Willow Warbler and Redstart in eighth and tenth positions.

Away from the River Derwent the remaining semi-natural woodland is varied, representing a transition from upland to lowland habitats. The former extensive cover of woodland has declined over many centuries such that most ancient woodland is largely restricted to the steeper valley sides, where much comes into the category of upland oakwood. Some of this woodland has been replanted with other species including conifers, notably on Cromford Moor, though recent felling here might prove beneficial to Nightjars. Other woods with large areas of conifer woodland include those in the Cordwell Valley, the Holymoorside complex, near Wingerworth, Rough Pitty Side, Handley Wood and Drum Hill. Goshawks and Siskins are among the species which have increased due to coniferous afforestation. Small areas of wet woodland dominated by alder mixed with ash, birch and hazel, characteristically occur on low-lying wet ground in the valley bottoms. Semi-natural wet woodland in the floodplains is particularly restricted, having been almost completely removed for agriculture and, in this predominantly pastoral landscape, the hedges at these lower altitudes make a significant contribution to the character of the area.

The River Derwent itself, while maintaining a fairly consistent width of 15–20m between Matlock and Derby, flows through a variety of landscapes and supports birds ranging from Dippers and Grey Wagtails to Goosanders and Cormorants. On its western bank near Belper is the DWT's 8ha Wyver Lane Reserve, which has open water, marshland and grassland. Its main interest is water birds and its list includes Pectoral Sandpiper (two together in 2003) and Great White Egret. Nearby, the Belper River Gardens may hold interesting wildfowl in severe weather, while Peregrines nested for the first time in 2012 at the adjacent East Mill (which houses the offices of the DWT).

The region also contains a variety of flowing and standing water habitats, reflecting the transition from those with a generally nutrient-poor, upland character to more enriched, lowland types. Many small streams flow into the main rivers of the Derwent, Amber and Ecclesbourne. The Ecclesbourne is typical of a group of rivers with a mud or silt substrate and clear water. It has steep banks, lined with alders for much of its length, and has developed meanders in its wide valley. An 8km section of the disused, but still watertight, Cromford Canal between Cromford and Ambergate is popular among birdwatchers, with Kingfishers, Little Grebes and Grey Wagtails regularly seen, together with a good variety of species in the adjoining woodland. Although not linked to a water presence, the area around Cromford Canal wharf and the nearby church is the most reliable winter site in Derbyshire for Hawfinches. The Natural Area also contains many ponds; though far fewer than formerly, they range from small garden ponds to large millponds on some of the rivers.

The Peak Fringe also contains the large reservoirs at Ogston and Carsington, two of the county's prime sites of ornithological interest, both of which lie in pleasant, gently undulating pastoral countryside. Ogston Reservoir was created in 1958 when the River Amber was damned near Ogston Hall, flooding a total of 83ha. The reservoir banks are natural, those on the northern and western sides shelving gently, while those on the east are much steeper. The water level usually falls in the summer and autumn periods, exposing muddy margins. Recreational sailing, which was introduced soon after the reservoir was flooded, takes place over much of the existing water area and there is trout-fishing from March to October. The main interests for birdwatchers at Ogston are the gull roost, wintering wildfowl (though numbers in recent years have generally been rather low) and, especially when water levels are low and muddy margins revealed, migrant waders. The site is arguably the best-watched in the county and boasts a bird list of 242 species (to the end of 2012), of which about 85 are known to breed or have bred. The most notable rarities recorded here include: Green-winged Teal, Ferruginous Duck, Fulmar, Leach's and Storm Petrels, Cattle and Great White Egrets, Purple Heron, Glossy Ibis, Corncrake, Crane, Kentish Plover, Pectoral, Purple and Spotted Sandpipers, Wilson's and Grey Phalaropes, Pomarine and Long-tailed Skuas, Sabine's, Bonaparte's and Laughing Gulls, Caspian, Whiskered, White-winged Black and Roseate Terns, Alpine Swift, Red-rumped Swallow and Citrine Wagtail. Roads running along the northern and western sides give good views over the reservoir and there are three bird hides, two of which are owned by the Ogston Bird Club and one, accessed from the western car park, that is open to the public. A few woods adjoin the reservoir banks, including Carr Wood, which has a heronry usually in the region of 15–20 pairs and is a good site for wintering Woodcock. The wood was until recently a DWT reserve but is now back in private hands.

Carsington Water (300ha) is the largest area of open water within the county and the ninth largest reservoir in England. Built as a regulating reservoir for the River Derwent, it has rapidly become a major site of ornithological interest since construction was completed in 1991. Like Ogston Reservoir, it has its own dedicated bird club with a large species list of 222, including 80 breeders. A CBC was carried out in different parts of the recording area in 2003–07 and documented by Carrington (2008). Unlike some of the county's older reservoirs, Carsington was created with environmental and conservation considerations in mind and, as a result, habitat areas favourable to wildlife were incorporated in the construction, while its larger size means that fishing and sailing activities cause less disturbance than at Ogston Reservoir. As at the latter site, the shallower western side of the reservoir is more attractive to birds than the steeper, eastern bank, and there are seven islands which offer relatively safe breeding sites to birds such as Oystercatchers. The site is undoubtedly the most important in Derbyshire for wintering wildfowl. As it is over 30 years younger than Ogston, its species list is shorter but nevertheless includes county rarities of the calibre of Great White Egret, Green-winged Teal, Ferruginous and Ring-necked Ducks, Fulmar, Manx Shearwater, Leach's Petrel, Crane, Baird's and Purple Sandpipers, Grey and Red-necked Phalaropes, Pomarine Skua, Bonaparte's Gull, Roseate Tern, Bearded Tit and Shore Lark. Recent years have produced sizeable gull roosts including up to 10,000 Lesser Black-backed Gulls, a county record total, as were counts of 766 Pochards in 1999, 107 Little Grebes in 2007, four Great Northern Divers in both 2008 and 2011, and 2175 Coots in 2008. There have also been some very unexpected occurrences, including a summering Black-throated Diver in 2003 and likewise a Long-tailed Duck in the following year. There are four hides, all of which are open to the public, along the reservoir's western banks.

While not on as large a scale as in the adjoining White and Dark Peak Natural Areas, widespread historic quarrying of limestone and gritstone has left its mark on the landscape and wildlife habitat is well provided for with many workings now heavily overgrown. Some of these sites hold breeding Peregrines and Ravens and, more rarely, Barn Owls.

Sheep and cattle pasture dominates the land use, and modern agricultural practices such as replacing hay with silage, drainage of wet grasslands and use of fertilizers and herbicides have had negative impacts on birdlife in some areas. In the more upland parts, particularly in the west where the land is less intensively farmed, more favourable bird habitats in the form of rough and damp pastures have survived to such an extent that Lapwings and Curlews still breed. Many field boundaries have not succumbed to extension or fencing and consequently the Peak Fringe is characterized by small fields bounded either by mature hedges, often of ancient origin and with holly a frequent constituent, in the lower areas or by drystone walls at higher altitudes, in both the limestone and gritstone areas. Such boundaries provide nesting habitats for the likes of Yellowhammers and Wrens, with occasional Little Owls and Wheatears in the stone walls.

The Coal Measures

This Natural Area (English Nature's Area No. 24) stretches southwards from the Derbyshire–South Yorkshire border into the south-east of the county, averaging about 10km in width. In the west it borders Natural Area No. 31, the Peak Fringe and Lower Derwent. Its eastern border is the interface with the Magnesian Limestone Area (Natural Area No. 23) and the Nottinghamshire border, and in the south its boundary lies roughly along the A52 road between Derby and Nottingham. The Coal Measures total approximately 371km², representing about 14.1% of Derbyshire's surface area.

The Coal Measures area is characterized by sandstone ridges and clay valleys, generally running north to south. In the south, the River Erewash drains most of the area on its way to the River Trent while in the north, the northward-flowing Rother is the principal river. Altitude varies from about 280m amsl near Holmesfield to about 40m by the Erewash at Sandiacre. The largest towns are Chesterfield, with a population of around 104,000, followed by Ilkeston (38,000) and then Heanor, Dronfield and Ripley, each with populations between 21,000 and 23,000. There are rather few areas that could nowadays be described as scenic, though some parts, such as the Moss Valley and around Dale Abbey, are reminders of how attractive at least parts of the area must have been before the advent of heavy industry.

Three-hundred-and-fifty million years ago the area was on the edge of a warm, tropical sea. It was covered in extensive swamps, crossed by rivers and dotted with lakes. Vegetation thrived in this lush environment, but occasional subsidence and changes in sea level meant the sea flooded in, killing the plants. As sediment built up to sea level, plants were able to grow again. The remains of the dead plants eventually formed the coal that has been so economically important to the area; the sediment from the sea and the mud from the lakes formed bands of clay and mudstone.

After the last ice age, trees slowly colonized this Natural Area until most of it was covered by thick woodland. This remained untouched for thousands of years and many animals and plants slowly evolved to take advantage of this stable environment. These original wildwoods had been largely cleared for cultivation by the time of the Domesday survey of 1086. Much of the woodland that remained was exploited as wood pasture in which livestock was allowed to graze. By medieval times, this was mainly an area of hamlets and farmsteads, with most of the farmland given over to grass, though arable crops were grown on the better soils. Many of the woodlands were managed as coppices to supply fuel to the small-scale iron and lead industries. Coal was dug where it outcropped or lay close to the surface, but not until the advent of canals and railways was the county able to compete with the volumes of coal produced elsewhere. Eastern Derbyshire then became transformed into a well-populated, industrial area, with large companies such as those founded at Butterley, Stanton Ironworks and Clay Cross.

By 1800 there were some 86 active coalmines in Derbyshire and mining flourished for over a century thereafter. At the time of nationalization in 1947, about 60,000 people were employed in over 100 collieries. By 1960, this had almost halved and by 1977 just 11 collieries remained. The last of these, Markham, closed in 1994. Other industries associated with coal, such as the ironworks and brickworks, are all but gone too, but the high population density remains. As well as deep mining of coal, much of the area has also been affected by opencast mining creating large but temporary quarries, and this continues on a smaller scale. After removal of the coal the land is usually reinstated as farmland, though in places amenity woodlands have been planted. Notably at Poolsbrook, the tips and marshy areas once associated with the former Ireland Colliery have been transformed into a country park, which is best known for the excellent views it affords of large numbers of gulls which come from nearby feeding areas to bathe and rest. Not far away, at Arkwright, a small wetland area has been created and can hold good numbers of waterfowl, particularly Wigeon, and five species of waders have bred.

All of the collieries produced waste, which formed the spoil heaps so distinctive of the region, ranging from small, conical hills to flatter areas that might cover scores of hectares. Some had lagoons that attracted a few water birds, including breeding Little Ringed Plovers. Most of these tips have now been levelled and top-soiled. Some are now industrial parks, almost always lacking in aesthetic appeal, and others have been turned into woodland, grassland or other amenity areas. A pair of Woodlarks was found at one of these recently planted sites in June 2008, though breeding was not proved, and three of these sites in north-east Derbyshire have held breeding Long-eared Owls.

One very beneficial aspect of deep coalmining has been the accidental formation of subsidence lakes, known locally as 'flashes'. Though we have nowhere as large as certain similar areas in Yorkshire, some have proved very productive. Two of these, at Westhouses and Sutton Scarsdale, have long been drained, and their loss lamented by Frost (1971a) and Gould (1985). Some important subsidence wetlands remain, however. One at Carr Vale by the River Doe Lea near Bolsover is a DWT reserve, and a popular and intensely watched site (31st December 2012 saw it complete 4665 consecutive days of coverage, by which time the bird list stood at 211). Its 12ha includes areas of open water and lacustrine vegetation including a *Phragmites* bed of recent creation. Good populations of water birds occur throughout the year, including regular nesting Tufted Ducks and Gadwall (out of seven species of duck that have nested) and this is the only site in the county where Garganey has been proved to breed, in 1990. Water Rails also breed and five species of waders have done so, while Common Terns and Black-headed Gulls have taken advantage of the recently installed rafts. Cetti's Warblers were seen nest-building in 2012. Twenty-eight species of waders have been recorded overall, including Pectoral Sandpiper and Lesser Yellowlegs. Other considerable rarities on the Carr Vale list include Ring-necked Duck, Eider, Great White and Cattle Egrets, Black Kite, Corncrake, Red-rumped Swallow, Shore Lark, Yellow-browed Warbler and Common Rosefinch, but arguably the most stunning sighting of all was of a fly-over flock of nine Little Auks in October 1995. Another ornithologically valuable area, managed jointly by the Derbyshire and Nottinghamshire Wildlife Trusts, is the Erewash Meadows Reserve on either side of the river near Langley Mill. It contains similar habitats to those at Carr Vale but is not nearly so well watched, so its bird list is shorter. However, this includes Purple and Night Herons, Red-rumped Swallow and the county's first American Wigeon in November 2002. A little further south, another important area spanning both sides of the Derbyshire–Nottinghamshire border is Bennerley Marsh, where some impressive counts of Golden Plover and Snipe have been made, and rare species here included Sabine's Gull in 1994 and Alpine Swift in 1995.

The Coal Measures Natural Area contains many bird-rich wetlands in addition to those mentioned above. One with direct connections to mining is the Williamthorpe Local Nature Reserve, which was created as a reservoir for the local colliery. This ceased production in 1970 but water from several other collieries, as far away as Thoresby in Nottinghamshire, is still pumped out here. This runs through one of the largest reed-beds in Derbyshire into the reservoir and is at a constant 16°C, meaning that the reservoir does not readily freeze. Large numbers of water birds, especially Teal and Snipe, may winter here and Water Rails and Jack Snipe can be relatively numerous. Four species of ducks breed and migrant waders sometimes visit. Nearby, the DWT has created its Avenue Washlands Reserve on land formerly belonging to the Wingerworth Coalite Plant, and this holds breeding and wintering wildfowl, with Snipe present also in the latter season.

There are also some interesting marshlands in this area, though the largest of all, at Killamarsh Meadows, was opencasted during the 1970s and 1980s and the site now forms part of the Rother Valley Country Park, the Derbyshire element of which was transferred to South Yorkshire in 1994. Further south, Poolsbrook Marsh is a varied area of reed, reedmace and willows with a pool. Water Rails and Reed and Sedge Warblers breed; Cetti's Warblers have probably nested and the site attracted singing Marsh Warblers in 1985 and 2009. There are good numbers of Reed and Sedge Warblers further south along the Doe Lea Valley, where the county's largest-known roosts of Reed and Corn Buntings have occurred. There are other interesting marshy areas in the Natural Area, especially elsewhere in the Staveley area and around Ilkeston.

There are four canals in the region, namely the Cromford, Nutbrook (these two now partly derelict), Erewash and Chesterfield, of which the last is ornithologically the best known. All have birds tolerant of humans, including Mallards and Moorhens, with Mute Swans and Coots in places. Three of these canals have long-existing reservoirs to service them. Pebley Pond (see Natural Area No. 23, 'The Magnesian Limestone') was built for the Chesterfield Canal, and Butterley Reservoir was constructed around the beginning of the nineteenth century to supply the Cromford Canal. Its 17ha are bisected by a heritage steam railway. For a long time Butterley was the main site for Derbyshire's breeding Great Crested Grebes and several pairs still nest there. Wildfowl populations are usually small but the site attracted the county's first Ferruginous Ducks, in 1950 and 1964. Mapperley Reservoir covers 8ha and was created in 1821 to feed the Nutbrook Canal. Few bird records come from this site now, though Common Terns nested on a raft in 2010. There are small, wet areas between Mapperley and Shipley Lake near the site of the former Woodside Colliery, where DWT are developing their recently purchased 74ha Woodside Reserve, the largest reserve in the county outside the Peak District National Park.

The 12ha Shipley Lake was originally an ornamental attraction connected with the now demolished Shipley Hall. Mining and silting degraded the site, which later became part of the Britannia Park and then the American Adventure theme park. It still attracts water birds, however, and in early 2008 a Ferruginous Duck joined the flock of diving ducks here. Two other ornamental lakes are found close to opposite ends of this Natural Area. In the south, Locko Park Lake (4ha) often holds good numbers of Greylag and Canada Geese, and was the site of Derbyshire's first breeding Gadwall in 1957. In the north-east, the private Renishaw Park Lake (7ha) is excellent for water birds, and holds the county's record Gadwall flock, of 255 in October 2009. Mallard, Tufted Duck, Teal, Wigeon and Coot may also exceed three figures and Shoveler, Goosander and Cormorants are regular, as are large flocks of Canada and Greylag Geese, which are sometimes joined by rarer geese. Grey Herons breed here and in 2012 a pair of Cormorants made an unsuccessful nesting attempt.

Two sewage farms in the north-east have proved ornithologically productive in the past, though both are now difficult to access. Staveley Sewage Farm is now largely modernized but there are still open wet areas at Old Whittington Sewage Farm, which may hold ducks, wintering Snipe and sometimes Jack Snipe. There are numerous other small wetlands scattered throughout the region, and the value of watching these was emphasized in 2010 when a Great Reed Warbler was found at Straw's Bridge near Ilkeston; its stay of over six weeks proved to be the longest ever by this species in the UK.

The Natural Area's other major habitats are not so well known as its wetlands. Since the area's industrialization, woodland is now scarce and many areas have been fragmented by opencasting. The larger woodland concentrations are around Renishaw Hall, where Marsh Tits and all three species of woodpecker are present; in the Moss Valley area between Eckington and Dronfield; and in the Sheepbridge–Unstone area. Elsewhere in the north-east, woodlands of ancient origin include Broomridding Wood and Astwith Dumbles, while West Wood, near Staveley, contains large areas of peripheral scrub attractive to the threatened Willow Tit and other small birds. Further south, Carnfield, Lady, Morleyhayes and Spondon Woods are all believed to be ancient woodlands, but few records come from any of these sites. As with so many woods in Derbyshire and elsewhere, many species have declined and Woodcock, Turtle Dove and Hawfinch may all now have gone completely as breeding birds from this Natural Area, while others that were formerly widespread in the region, such as Tree Pipit and Lesser Redpoll, seem to have very largely retreated to higher ground.

There are areas of wet woodland along the rivers of the area, for example in the Ford Valley, although most are relatively small and many have developed in the oxbows that remain, for example at Erewash Meadows. This habitat is also associated with canals, subsidence flashes and other mineral extraction sites. Some of the derelict railway lines in the Natural Area have been preserved by the county council as walkways, such as the Five Pits Trail, and areas of hedges, trees and scrub alongside have become nesting areas for certain woodland and farmland species.

Farmland birds too have declined. This may be confirmed by perusal of the late Michael Wareing's chronological account of the birds at Breck Farm, Barrowhill in the book *Birdwatcher's Year* (Batten *et al.* 1973). Breck Farm might be regarded as typical of many farms in this region and of much of lowland Derbyshire, though the low-lying fields near the River Rother regularly flooded, as they still do, following very heavy rainfall. Wareing later moved to farm at Shottle with his son, partly because of problems that he believed were caused by pollution from nearby heavy industry and also because much of his land was due for opencasting. However, his account is now a valuable legacy, since it highlights the changes that have taken place in the 40 years since then. In 1973, breeding birds at Breck Farm included Turtle Dove, Yellow Wagtail, Spotted Flycatcher and Corn Bunting; none of these are there today. On 6th November 1972, a flock of birds in a kale field included 500 Linnets, 500 Greenfinches, 200 Tree Sparrows and 50 Corn Buntings, all of which would currently be considered exceptionally large gatherings. The declines are not confined just to breeding birds as in December 1972 some 6000 Starlings, no doubt very largely winter immigrants, were counted in a field sprayed with animal slurry, a figure rarely reached even in the biggest Starling roosts of recent years

Industrial areas can hold scarce and interesting species, however. The former large ironworks sites at Staveley and Stanton-by-Dale now contain extensive 'brownfields', with Lapwings, Little Ringed and sometimes Ringed Plovers nesting in stony areas, away from water. Even temporary sites can hold surprises, as in 2008 when Ringed and Little Ringed Plovers reared young in northern Chesterfield, in an area where factories had been cleared to make way for Chesterfield Football Club's new stadium. If grassy vegetation is present, Meadow Pipits and Skylarks may also breed. Stanton Ironworks has also produced several records of Black Redstarts and has a colony of Sand Martins in the spoil heaps.

After Derby, Chesterfield is Derbyshire's second largest settlement but is less endowed with large parks and open spaces. The most interesting of these is Queen's Park (rated as one of the most attractive county cricket grounds in England), which has a small lake where feral Bar-headed Geese bred during the 1990s. As at Derby and Belper, Peregrines can now be seen in the town centre, usually on the famous Crooked Spire. The grounds of this church contain a number of holly trees where up to 370 Goldfinches have roosted and, a few hundred metres away, similar numbers of Pied Wagtails have used laurel bushes in a car park as their roost. Three small lakes on the fringes of the town attract water birds. To the south, Birdholme Wildfowl Reserve sometimes supports nesting Great Crested Grebes and often holds winter Goosanders. In the north-west, the lake in Holmebrook Valley Park also attracts Goosanders, and Red-breasted Merganser, Eider and Whooper Swan have been recorded, while Walton Dam on the western outskirts is known for breeding Mandarins and even has two Fulmar records to its name. There have been many sightings of Dippers, presumed to be wanderers from the Holymoorside area, on the River Hipper close to Walton Dam (where breeding was proved in 1993) and at times these birds have even been seen further down the same watercourse, close to the town centre. Kingfishers and Grey Wagtails are also regularly seen along this section of the Hipper.

The Magnesian Limestone

This section (English Nature's Natural Area No. 23) of approximately 106km² (4.0% of the county) occupies the extreme north-eastern part of Derbyshire and corresponds approximately with the borough of Bolsover. The western boundary is roughly the courses of the Rivers Doe Lea and Rother at the foot of the west-facing scarp slope between Hardwick in the south and Barlborough in the north. The other boundaries are the county borders with Rotherham and Nottinghamshire. Altitudinal limits are 184m amsl at Palterton and 43m at Killamarsh. Bolsover is the largest town, with a population of over 11,000.

Magnesian Limestone is rare in the UK, being found in a single, narrow band running northwards from the vicinity of Nottingham to the River Tyne. It was formed some 255 million years ago during the Permian period when a shallow, tropical sea slowly dried up to leave a residue of magnesian-rich deposits of Magnesian Limestone. This is a relatively soft, porous rock that has weathered to form gently rounded hills dissected by small valleys and in places these contain crags and caves. The mineral-rich soils are among the most agriculturally productive in the county and arable farmland dominates the landscape. Cereals predominate, but potatoes, oil-seed rape, kale, sugar beet, elephant grass and other crops are also grown.

There can be no doubt that overall bird populations have declined in this area as farming has become more efficient. In the past 35 years, many hedgerows, clumps of trees and small thickets have been removed, increasing the 'open' appearance of the region. Three species, namely Quail, Turtle Dove and Corn Bunting, have traditionally been more numerous here than anywhere else in the county. Quail are subject to wide annual fluctuations in numbers, but few years pass without at least one being heard in the area, and in 2011 about 19 singing males were heard at 11 sites, including five at Barlborough Common. The other two species are in steep decline and are in danger of extinction, not only from this region but from Derbyshire overall. Turtle Doves, which are specialist feeders on the seeds of arable weeds, are becoming much scarcer. The best evidence of this comes from a census of 'purring' males at Scarcliffe Woods; here the maximum was 25 in 1981, which had reduced to five or fewer by the late 1980s, and with no more than a single since 2006. Similarly, the number of singing Corn Buntings has fallen dramatically to an average of under one a year and the large winter roosts in the Doe Lea Valley have long gone, though recent years have seen wintering flocks at Creswell and Pebley Pond. Lapwings breed very sparingly in spring-sown cereals and other crops, while a very few pairs of nesting Yellow Wagtails still add colour to the cereal fields. A very welcome addition to the list of breeding birds is the Hobby, which has been nesting here since at least 1992, with several pairs now breeding annually.

In winter, flocks of Skylarks, various finches, Yellowhammers, Reed Buntings, sometimes Meadow Pipits and, more rarely, Corn Buntings can occasionally be found in weedy stubbles, areas of set-aside, or fields containing unharvested crops. Otherwise the fields are home to few small birds at this season, though there may be flocks of Woodpigeons, Stock Doves, gulls and, especially close to release sites, Grey and Red-legged Partridges. At one time, large numbers of Golden Plovers overwintered, but these birds are now best known as spring migrants, albeit still often in large flocks.

Some ornithologically important woodlands are found in this natural area, the best known of which are at Whitwell and Scarcliffe. The latter parish contains three large woods, namely Scarcliffe Park and Langwith and Roseland Woods, totalling around 284ha. These were predominantly broad-leaved (and at one time renowned for their hazel coppice) until the 1960s when the landowners undertook a large-scale reforestation programme planting blocks of conifers, particularly Corsican pine. However, plenty of deciduous woodland survives here, while more recently some stretches have been clear-felled and allowed to regenerate naturally. Sadly, the Hawfinches at Scarcliffe, thought to number some 50 pairs in the early 1960s, have almost gone and are rarely seen in this area now. Since the early 1970s there have been regular counts of both breeding and wintering birds in Scarcliffe's woodlands, which were described by Frost (2008a).

Since the mid-1990s, the same sort of fieldwork has been conducted at Whitwell Wood (142ha), which is excellently managed for both wildlife and timber production by Forest Enterprise with the assistance of the Whitwell Wood Natural History Group. This has involved the widening of drives, coppicing, charcoal burning, the creation of ponds and the siting of nest-boxes. However, Whitwell Wood is perhaps best known for the research into the breeding biology of Woodcocks, carried out here in 1978–91 by the Game Conservancy Trust (now the Game & Wildlife Conservation Trust). Further south, Pleasley Park (73ha) is also under the management of Forest Enterprise, but is not nearly so ornithologically well known as the woods at Scarcliffe and Whitwell.

There are several smaller woods in the area, including the oak-dominated Bradshaw Wood and an adjoining area of hawthorn scrub, which formed part of the 14ha Shirebrook CBC site straddling the county boundary with Nottinghamshire. The results were documented by Frost (1993). At Hollinhill and Markland Grips, both of which are Sites of Special Scientific Interest, yew is a frequent constituent of the semi-natural woodland bordering the small ravines. Small woodlands in the Belph-Creswell area have provided several records of winter Hawfinches, doubtless involving birds from the adjacent Welbeck Estate in Nottinghamshire, which regularly holds one of the largest wintering flocks in Britain.

The region's coniferous woodland holds a very few pairs of Long-eared Owls, and Firecrests have been found in spring and summer, but not proved to breed. Siskins may also nest, at least occasionally, but Lesser Redpolls are currently rare breeders, as they are in most lowland parts of the county. Buzzards are the most frequently seen raptors now, a situation mirrored in much of lowland Derbyshire.

As the limestone overlies Coal Measures, large collieries, all now defunct, were created at Glapwell, Pleasley, Shirebrook, Langwith, Creswell, Whitwell and Bolsover, with attendant settlements becoming established or greatly enlarged as a result. The colliery spoil heaps remain, though most have been transformed into plantations of amenity woodland and grassland, with ponds replacing the former slurry lagoons. One of the most attractive of these is at Pleasley, which is now a Country Park. Here, Derbyshire County Council has created an attractive area of deciduous woodland, open grassland, small reedbeds, a central lagoon of some 2ha and smaller ponds attractive to breeding water birds including Ringed and Little Ringed Plovers and Redshanks. Interesting species recorded here and at other colliery sites include Dotterel, Temminck's Stint, Wryneck, Woodlark, and a Shore Lark that stayed for eight weeks. Nottinghamshire County Council and Forest Enterprise have combined to create similar habitats to those at Pleasley at nearby Shirebrook, where the colliery spoil heap extended into both Derbyshire and Nottinghamshire, though most of the woodland is of Corsican pine rather than deciduous. At first, in the mid-1990s, the very young plantations here attracted large numbers of breeding Skylarks and Meadow Pipits, with smaller numbers of Lapwings and Yellow Wagtails but, as the plantations have matured, very few of these remain, and warblers and finches have taken their place. The ponds here are mainly in Nottinghamshire, and are attractive to breeding water birds, while large numbers of Reed Warblers nest in the peripheral reed-beds.

Magnesian Limestone also makes an attractive building stone, which has been used as far away as the Houses of Parliament. There are extensive quarries at Bolsover Moor, Whitwell and Steetley. The last, although partly infilled with colliery waste, was until very recently much the most valuable to birds. It regularly held breeding Little Ringed and Ringed Plovers, Redshanks and up to 14 pairs of Lapwings, while Jack Snipe wintered in small numbers. However, since 2010 industrial development has greatly diminished its attraction to many birds, and the area created in mitigation shows no sign of reversing the losses. Nevertheless, some areas of open water remain, particularly a deep lagoon that does not readily freeze in cold weather. Great Crested Grebes and other waterfowl still breed in small numbers and rarer visitors have included Red-necked, Slavonian and Black-necked Grebes, Ferruginous Duck and Velvet Scoter.

This is a predominantly dry area, which is largely drained by two small rivers, the Meden and the Poulter, and their tributaries. Both flow eastwards into Nottinghamshire. Grey Wagtails breed by these rivers and the Meden has produced several sightings of Dippers, including one in the spring of 2009 and 2010, which are presumed to be wanderers from the Peak District. There are few open water bodies and of these the most productive is Pebley Pond which, despite its name, was created in the 1770s as a reservoir to feed the Chesterfield Canal. Great Crested Grebes are regular breeders here and wildfowl numbers are usually small, although rarer species have included Ring-necked Ducks on two occasions. There are also three small lakes: the Great Pond and Miller's Pond, both to be found in the ornamental park at Hardwick, and Butcherlawn Pond in Barlborough Park. Smaller waters are found in several places, including very small subsidence flashes at Pleasley and Creswell. Of the various birds found on them, one of the most interesting is the Gadwall, which is believed to have colonized the area from the nearby Dukeries, while Shoveler and Teal have also bred at the Creswell site. The two flashes have also produced records of a few scarcer migrants, including Garganey, Curlew Sandpiper, Little and Temminck's Stints and Rock Pipit.

Finally, mention must be made of the caves of the area. Creswell Crags is a World Heritage Site, internationally famous for its evidence of prehistoric man and the fossilized remains of birds, fishes and mammals, the latter including spotted hyena, woolly rhinoceros, reindeer and mammoth. Similar finds were made in a little-known cave at Langwith. In a sense, these caves retain a link with the past, since the Swallows that sometimes breed in them remind us where these birds must have nested before man created artificial sites for them.

The South Derbyshire Claylands

The Needwood and South Derbyshire Claylands together form English Nature's Area No. 40. The former lies in Staffordshire; the Derbyshire element covers an area of some 305km^2 (11.6% of Derbyshire), stretching from Derby in the east to the River Dove in the west and south. The northern boundary lies a few kilometres north of, and parallel to, the A52 Derby to Ashbourne road and forms a small spur of land north of the latter town. English Nature include a very small area around Snelston and Norbury in their Natural Area No. 50, the Churnet Valley and the Potteries, but it is included in this section, especially since the geology and geomorphology are very similar to the rest of the Claylands.

The extreme north-west of this area, north of Ashbourne, rises to around 200m amsl, and south-south-west of the town to 184m at Roston Common. Otherwise most of the Claylands area is low-lying, particularly in the south where the River Dove forms the county boundary, in the region of the 50m contour. Away from the Dove Valley and its floodplain, the majority of the area, although low-lying, is gently undulating. It is dominated by underlying rocks of the Triassic age, dating from 240 million years ago, which consist of Bunter and Keuper sandstones and Keuper Marls. The Keuper Marl is both the thickest and most extensive of the Triassic deposits in the area, giving rise to a subdued and generally low-lying landscape. Although the Natural Area was almost certainly covered by glaciations in the early Quaternary (the last two million years), there is little landform evidence of this. The land is characterized by a managed, rectilinear landscape of fields, straight roads and small woodlands. Remnants of ridge and furrow agriculture and the earthworks of deserted settlements, such as Hungry Bentley and Barton Blount, indicate that the area was once more densely populated.

Away from the western reaches of Derby, the Claylands remains an essentially attractive, rural area. The small market town of Ashbourne, with around 7000 inhabitants, is much the largest settlement. Almost all of the rest have populations in the hundreds, rather than thousands, and among them are some of the most attractive villages in the county, such as Marston Montgomery and Somersal Herbert. Only three major roads cross the area, though these include the busy A50, constructed during the 1990s to link Stoke-on-Trent to the M1 motorway.

Traditional agriculture represents the main land use, comprising pasture fields enclosed by large hedgerows with scattered trees (especially oaks) and farm ponds, though many of the latter have been lost. Sheep flocks and cattle herds are the main occupants, with many farmers recently changing from dairying to beef production. Increasingly, there has also been a shift to the production of silage and to arable cultivation, especially in the east around Hoon and Hatton, and in parts of the west, where much oil-seed rape and maize are grown. However, several small farms, financially assisted by various government incentives, have retained traditional management techniques, thereby maintaining examples of the unimproved hay meadows that were formerly much more typical of the region. The few large woods are all in the west of the area. The major wetlands are the lakes associated with the historic parks at Kedleston (14ha), Osmaston (7 ha) and Sudbury (6ha), though there are several others, such as the gravel workings at Hilton, of more recent creation. Most of the small streams flow south to join the River Dove and, since they drain a largely pastoral landscape, nutrient levels are low.

A CBC on farmland at Culland, south of Brailsford, was carried out by B.C. Potter from the 1980s to 1993. The site comprised 57.9ha of mixed, but mainly pastoral farmland, with a farmstead and a house with garden. Data for the final four years shows that the most numerous bird was the Wren, with an average of 26.6 pairs a year, equating to a figure of 45.9 pairs per km^2. Second was the Chaffinch (22.8: 39.4), followed by

Blackbird (19.2: 33.2), Robin (18.8: 32.5) and Dunnock (15.2: 26.3). The most numerous migrant breeder was the Willow Warbler, in ninth place with an average of 6.6 pairs a year, a density of 11.4 pairs per km^2. The Tree Sparrow was as high as twelfth (4.20: 7.3) but the Skylark was very scarce, the average of only 1.2 pairs a year (1.7 pairs per km^2) putting it as low as thirtieth overall. Both Grey and Red-legged Partridges were present but Lapwing and Curlews were irregular and not recorded in every year.

There is no reason to think that farmland bird populations elsewhere in the Claylands would be greatly different from those in the Culland area. Quail are occasionally heard and a farm at Rodsley has the distinction of being the last certain breeding site of Corncrakes in the county, albeit as long ago as 1962 (with the exception of a rather vague late 1960s report from the Baslow area in the Peak Fringe). Yellow Wagtails might now be confined to the fields of the Dove flood plain. Little Owls are still relatively numerous in the region, preferring pastoral areas where they can obtain food from cow-pats, among other sources. Stock Doves are quite common, and may occur in three-figure flocks in winter. Hobbies breed throughout the area, nesting in isolated hedgerow trees and at woodland edges. This was one of the first regions to be colonized by Buzzards during their recent, dramatic return to the county as breeding birds, and tree-nesting Ravens are now becoming established: one pair, unusually, has bred in a monkey-puzzle tree. Tree Sparrows are reasonably widespread, especially in the eastern part of the area.

For birdwatchers the two best-known sites in the region are the parks at Osmaston and, particularly, Kedleston. The latter, which contains one of the finest stately houses in Derbyshire, was owned by the Curzon family for over 800 years and is now administered by the National Trust. The park contains large areas of unimproved grassland, deciduous woods, scattered veteran trees and a series of narrow lakes along the course of the Markeaton Brook. Hole-nesters are well represented, with owls, numerous Nuthatches and all three species of woodpecker. Good numbers of wildfowl breed and, in terms of national importance, formerly Kedleston Park was second only to Holkham Park in Norfolk for its Canada Goose population. Currently, numbers are lower but may still exceed 500 in winter. Several pairs of Greylag Geese also nest and over 250 have been counted in winter. Goosanders are regular outside the breeding season and up to 80 Mandarins have been recorded in winter. Recent additions to the list of breeding birds include Shelduck, Oystercatcher and Raven.

Osmaston Park, to the south-east of Ashbourne, is in private ownership though the Manor no longer exists, having been demolished in the 1960s. It lies in hillier countryside than Kedleston Park and is well wooded. Shirley Park is an ancient woodland which has been very largely replanted with larch and pine. Ravens, Long-eared Owls and Grey Herons have occasionally nested and numbers of Crossbills have occurred in some invasion years, and while Derbyshire's first breeding Firecrests were found here in 1981, rather surprisingly none has been found here since. The lakes held another new breeding species for the county when Ruddy Ducks were proved in 1975. Mandarins breed and this was the only known breeding site of the Wood Duck, with broods of young seen in 1984–86, following a series of releases here. Other interesting birds released on the estate have included Golden, Silver and Reeves's Pheasants, though none are thought to remain. Goosanders and Wigeon are often present during the winter months. Oystercatchers have nested by the lakes and on adjacent farmland, while Grey Wagtails often nest by the waterfall alongside the picturesque sawmill. Some of the woodland has a dense understorey of rhododendron and in some winters large numbers of Chaffinches, Bramblings and Greenfinches roost therein.

A little to the north-east of Osmaston Park is Bradley Dam (3ha), which is a renowned site for Mandarins, with up to 251 recorded during the last few years. The dam is the second most important site for this species in the UK, with only the lakes of the Forest of Dean (Gloucestershire) regularly supporting more. There are also usually good numbers of Mallards here, and often other species of wildfowl. Much further south in the Dove Valley, Sudbury Lake, owned by the National Trust, may also hold a good variety of breeding and non-breeding wildfowl, and Reed Warblers breed in the beds of reedmace. A better-known site nowadays is Dove Valley Lake (3ha), between Hatton and Foston, which was created in the 1990s in association with the A50 road construction. Little Grebes, Tufted Ducks and Oystercatchers breed and good numbers of Wigeon graze the open, grassy banks in winter. Rarer visitors have included Black-necked Grebe, Velvet Scoter, Ruff and Mediterranean Gull. Another wetland area of recent creation is Sutton Brook Lakes, which also has a wintering Wigeon flock and has attracted Little and Great White Egrets. There are several other recently formed lakes scattered throughout the area and though created for fishing, they may hold small numbers of breeding wildfowl including Tufted Ducks and Greylag Geese. The small lakes near the Toyota factory, by the A38 road south-west of Derby, have become important for breeding Reed Warblers.

Of much longer existence is the DWT's 29ha reserve at Hilton Gravel Pits, which is now known as Hilton Gravel Pits Nature Reserve. The area was quarried during the 1940s to leave a mosaic of lakes, pools, marsh, willow carr, scrub and woodland including areas of pine. Great Crested and Little Grebes are among the breeding waterfowl and the provision of rafts has enabled up to nine pairs of Common Terns to nest. The reserve is an important breeding site for the declining Willow Tit, and all three species of woodpecker can be seen, while two Firecrests were present early in 2003. Other rarities have included Storm Petrel, Black-necked and Slavonian Grebes and Bearded Tit.

The principal river draining the area is the Dove, which cuts a wide shallow valley, initially curving south-westwards and then south-eastwards to join the River Trent at Newton Solney. Undisturbed stretches of the Dove provide valuable stopovers for migrating waders and wintering wildfowl. Along much of its length the river has a broad floodplain of low-lying wet meadows, mainly now improved for agriculture but still supporting a few pairs of breeding wading birds, especially Lapwing. Birds with long bills, such as Snipe and Curlew, cannot feed unless the soil is wet enough to allow them to probe for invertebrates and they have undergone a significant decline locally, associated with drainage of the meadows. Snipe are now probably absent from the Claylands as breeding birds although Curlews may just cling on and they both still frequent these pastures in winter. Wild swans are occasional, but the area is not well watched except by one renowned observer, who makes regular observations from the Staffordshire banks of the river in the Fauld area.

Woodland occurs mainly as small woods and copses, often dominated by oak on the drier ground with alder and willow in wetter areas. Small stands of wet woodland, such as Tinker's Inn Bog (near Clifton) and Radbourne Roughs, occur on low-lying ground and in valley bottoms throughout the area. The Norbury area has for some decades supported a heronry, though the birds have moved sites twice because of tree-felling. Large woodlands of ancient origin remain at Eaton Wood (about 35ha), on an escarpment east of the River Dove, and Sudbury Coppice, but there are very few recent bird records from such sites and virtually nothing is known about them ornithologically. The same could almost be said for much of the South Derbyshire Claylands area, which is widely regarded by many, and not merely birdwatchers, as Derbyshire's 'quiet corner'.

The Trent Valley and National Forest

English Nature's Natural Area No. 33 is the Trent Valley and Rises, and is very large, extending across six counties. The Derbyshire section is only a small part of the Natural Area and for the purposes of this publication is amalgamated with the former coalmining area around Swadlincote. This town is near the centre of the new National Forest so our area is called the Trent Valley and National Forest. Its boundaries are at Catton in the south-west, north-east along the River Trent, which forms the border with Staffordshire, to just south of Burton upon Trent, and rejoining the river after the town. It goes as far north as a line (roughly the A52 road) between Derby and Nottingham, and from Sandiacre follows the lower Erewash, which forms the Nottinghamshire border, to its junction with the Trent. Its southern border is the county boundary with Staffordshire in the west and Leicestershire in the east. As well as the lower Erewash Valley, this area also includes the Dove Valley east from Hatton and the Derwent Valley east of Derby. Though English Nature's Natural Area includes a sizeable part of the latter city, this has been dealt with in a separate area that we have called the 'City of Derby'. This region covers some 293km², which is 11.1% of the county's surface area. Long Eaton and Swadlincote, with populations of 44,000 and 36,000, are by far the largest Derbyshire towns in the area. Altitudinal limits are 27m amsl by the Trent at Long Eaton and 186m at Pistern Hill.

The Trent Valley's geology is rather complex, but is dominated by a broad expanse of Triassic Mercia Mudstones and clay over glacial and alluvial deposits, which give the area a rich and fertile soil and a considerable source of gravel. It is England's third longest river at around 275km and the second largest in terms of average flow. It rises at 280m amsl on Biddulph Moor in Staffordshire and on its way to the River Humber falls 270m, of which 180m are in the first 32km. Its total length in Derbyshire is 47km. Water quality has improved in recent decades and, in its Derbyshire stretches, it is now rated as grade 2 by the Environment Agency, benefiting from its contributions from the Rivers Dove and Derwent. Also, the three power stations that stood on its banks, at Drakelow, Willington and Castle Donington (the last on the Leicestershire bank) were all closed between the mid-1990s and 2003, leading to reduced pollution from their outflows. Apart from Burton upon Trent, there are no large settlements along the valley until Long Eaton, though there are several pleasant villages and hamlets, such as Newton Solney, Repton and Twyford. The flood plain is on average 2.5–5km wide and the river is still prone to occasional spectacular floods. It flows mostly between steep banks up to 3m or so in height, which are attractive to breeding Kingfishers and Sand Martins. The river itself supports areas of riparian vegetation, especially common clubrush, favoured by nesting Great Crested Grebes, Mute Swans, Coots and Moorhens. Other wildfowl that have recently bred on the Trent include Egyptian Goose, Shelduck and Goosander. Especially at times of low flow, shingle beds are exposed and it was on one of these that pupils of the Repton School Field Club found the county's first breeding Little Ringed Plovers, in 1950.

The surrounding landscape is mainly improved pasture, though with arable in places. Some stretches can be popular with fishermen but there are few walkers, except in one or two places, such as around the intriguing small caves known as Anchor Church. There is no boat traffic upstream from Shardlow as parts of the river are too shallow, which is why, in around 1777, the Trent and Mersey Canal was constructed to run close to and roughly parallel with the river. There are numerous small oxbow lakes, some of which have dried out but others, such as those by the River Dove at Marston-on-Dove, and at Sawley, are attractive to wildlife, including breeding Little Grebes and warblers. As a result of improved drainage in recent years, there are few other remnant wetlands of any size. The most interesting marshland area in the area is the DWT's 8ha Golden Brook Storage Lagoon Reserve at Breaston, which was constructed in the 1960s to alleviate flooding downstream. Here are small pools backed by a large reedswamp, which was the first proven breeding site of Cetti's Warblers, in 2010. Elsewhere, there are numerous small clumps of trees, especially willows, and Grey Herons nest in at least three such sites.

The Trent is currently not well watched by birdwatchers except at a few easy viewing points, such as Newton Solney and Twyford. It comes into its own as a birdwatching locality only in exceptionally harsh weather, when adjacent large water bodies are frozen, but since the creation of three large reservoirs nearby in the 1960s and 1970s, this has hardly ever happened. Things were different in the unforgettably severe winter of 1962/63, however. While virtually everywhere else for a long way around was frozen for many weeks, the Trent, kept open by warm water returned from the power stations, remained ice-free and was a haven for water birds. These included flocks of up to 700 Mallard, 1000 Wigeon, 400 Tufted Ducks, 50 Goldeneye, 117 Goosander, 8 Smew, 9 Shelduck, 19 Whooper Swans and 11 Bewick's Swans, with smaller numbers of rarer wildfowl, such as White-fronted Geese, Garganey, Scaup, Velvet Scoter and Red-breasted Merganser. Waders, too, were well represented and included Oystercatcher, Ringed Plover, Common and Green Sandpipers, Ruff, Knot and Sanderling. While the winter of 1978/79 was also very cold overall, there were occasional slightly milder spells and the new reservoirs of the region usually retained some open water, so the birds along the River Trent were neither so numerous or so varied as 16 years earlier. They did, however, include Red-throated Diver, Red-necked Grebe, a flock of 26 Brent Geese, Red-breasted Merganser and groups of up to six Smew. The lower reaches of the Dove and the Derwent can also be interesting for water birds, again, especially in hard weather; for example, there were White-fronted Geese, Scaup and 650 Wigeon at Ambaston in late December 2010.

The gravel terraces of the Trent have been quarried for sand and gravel for many decades, especially on the north bank. The gravel is usually overlain by alluvial soils and may be 6m or more in depth. During excavation the water is pumped out, though shallow pools often remain and these may attract breeding waders including Oystercatchers and Ringed and Little Ringed Plovers. After pumping ceases, the gravel pits usually flood and in time may develop peripheral vegetation and willow carr. However, until relatively recently, the life of most gravel pits was limited as they were filled, either with domestic rubbish or, more often, with pulverized fly ash produced at the local power stations. Following such filling, the topsoil which had been stored nearby was added and the land returned to agricultural use. To look back to the situation of some 50 years ago confirms the transitory nature of many gravel pits. Around that time, those in the Willington–Egginton–Hilton area were numbered for convenience. Of the seven duly treated in this way, only one remains as a wetland today: Hilton No. 6 Gravel Pit, as it was then, is now known as Hilton Gravel Pits Nature Reserve and is owned by the DWT. This site is on the boundary between this Natural Area and the South Derbyshire Claylands Natural Area and is described there. Clay Mills Gravel Pits were ornithologically productive in the 1960s and 1970s but these were also subsequently reclaimed.

Even some of the gravel pits that were attractive to birds and birdwatchers between the 1970s and early 1990s no longer exist. These include sites at Etwall (part of Egginton Sewage Farm), east of Shardlow, Elvaston (north of Wilne Lane) and at Swarkestone, north of the lane from the village to Ingleby. A large lake still remains south of the latter lane, but the islets that held breeding Black-headed Gulls and Common Terns here during the 1980s have now gone and the site is used for sailing and fishing.

There are currently five major gravel pit complexes in the Trent Valley, of which the most westerly two are DWT reserves. At Drakelow, upstream from Burton upon Trent, the first site covers 31ha and began life as a series of pits in the 1960s. Under the ownership of the Central Electricity Generating Board it was called Drakelow Wildfowl Reserve, but it has been known as Drakelow Nature Reserve since 2007. Most of the pools now have well-vegetated perimeters and the site attracts waterfowl, rather than waders. Up to 109 pairs of Cormorants and 23 pairs of Grey Herons have nested in trees, and up to ten Little Egrets have used these same trees for roosting. The site's bird list is of around 224 species, among which were six new to Derbyshire in the shape of Ruddy Duck in 1963, Ring-necked Duck in 1977, a Savi's Warbler that sang for over a month in 1987, a Little Bunting at a feeding station in 1994, Gull-billed Tern in 1995 and a short-staying Cetti's Warbler in 1999. Other considerable rarities on the site list include Green-winged Teal, American Wigeon, Ferruginous Duck, Great White Egret, Kentish Plover, Pectoral Sandpiper, Pomarine and Long-tailed Skuas, Caspian and Roseate Terns, Golden Oriole and Nightingale.

Willington Gravel Pits is among the most regularly watched sites in the county. The whole area covers 74ha, part of which is a DWT reserve. The pits were created during the 1970s, though there is a much more recent excavation, known as the 'canal pit', which lies between the railway line and the canal. The main access is from a rough lane (frequently flooded after heavy rain) that runs south-west from Willington Bridge; along this lane a series of platforms give good views over the pits to the north. Those to the south are now private fishing lakes. Though some of the pits have quite steep shorelines, there are usually some areas of mud and shingle, including a long spit. Wildfowl are usually present in reasonable numbers. Waders are more dependent on water levels, but if these are suitable they can be both numerous and varied. The extensive reed-beds and other marsh areas hold breeding Water Rails, Cetti's Warblers and the largest colony of Reed Warblers in Derbyshire, with 70 singing in 2004. The spit has held good numbers of breeding Common Terns and Black-headed Gulls, joined in 2009 by an ultimately unsuccessful pair of Mediterranean Gulls. This is a good site for watching Hobbies taking dragonflies on fine summer days. The bird list was of about 218 species at the end of 2012. This includes many extreme rarities: new to the county were Blue-winged Teal in 1995, Pallid Swift in 1998, Spotted Sandpiper in 1999, a UK record flock of 11 Whiskered Terns in 2009 and Franklin's Gull in 2010. The list also includes Ring-necked Duck, Glossy Ibis, Red-footed Falcon, Kentish Plover, Pectoral Sandpiper, Grey and Red-necked Phalaropes, Bonaparte's Gull, Caspian Tern and Golden Oriole.

In the central Trent Valley a smaller, private area of gravel pits, part of which is still being worked, is found south-west of Barrow upon Trent. This area is not so well watched as most of the other sites but has produced Great White Egret, Velvet Scoter and in 2004 the county's only Bufflehead. Also private is the large complex known as Aston-on-Trent Gravel Pits, sometimes referred to as Witches Oaks Gravel Pits. Excavations began here in the 1990s and resulted in a series of lakes now owned by Severn Trent Water, which can be used as a water supply in times of shortage. Some of these have shallow fringes and therefore this is an important site for migrant waders. The 31 species recorded include Baird's Sandpiper and, new to the county in 2004, Broad-billed Sandpiper. An Ortolan Bunting in 2000 and a Tawny Pipit in 2003 were also additions to the Derbyshire list. It is also a very good site for Smew, which peaked at an impressive 17 in February 2011.

The most easterly gravel pits in the county are at Long Eaton, and they are an extension of the large complex of pits that form the Attenborough Nature Reserve, one of the best-known sites in Nottinghamshire. The area is accessed from Meadow Lane. The older, more vegetated pits are to the east of the lane and are used for fishing and occasional windsurfing. Those to the west and south are newer, including the shallow 'conservation pit', and more are being created. There are usually good numbers of wildfowl, especially Wigeon, in winter and sometimes large flocks of Greylag Geese. Migrant waders are regular, as are passage terns, and Common Terns from the Attenborough Nature Reserve often gather here. The two rarest visitors, however, were passerines: these were a Bluethroat that sang for 13 days in 1992, and a Woodchat Shrike in 2006. Other notable species seen here include Ring-necked Duck, Pectoral and Purple Sandpipers, and White-winged Black and Whiskered Terns. There are more gravel pits planned for the eastern Trent Valley, though safety constraints may have to be placed on those near the East Midlands Airport to reduce the chances of bird strike.

There are much smaller gravel pits at Ambaston, and south of Draycott is St Chads Water, where Common Terns nest on efficacious rafts. A small lake at Elvaston Castle Country Park also supports water birds but the site is better known for parkland and woodland birds. Woodland in the Trent, lower Dove and lower Derwent Valleys is otherwise decidedly scarce. However, an area of wet woodland at King's Newton held 48 occupied nests of Grey Herons in 1998, the largest colony ever known in the county, though it has subsequently declined.

Egginton Sewage Farm, nowadays often called Etwall Farm, has a long history of bird recording, stretching back to the 1890s. It was constructed to take effluent produced in Burton upon Trent's breweries. The open large irrigation fields held numerous shallow pools, often rather hidden among tall vegetation, and these were very attractive to waders, of which 32 species were recorded. Among these, a Killdeer in 1964 and a Sociable Plover in 1993 constituted first sightings for the county. Other rarities that have graced the area (including a small area quarried for gravel in the 1980s) include Cattle Egret, Red-footed Falcon, Great Snipe, Pectoral and Purple Sandpipers, Aquatic Warbler and a Lesser Grey Shrike, another species new to the county, in 2004. The site's former importance for farmland birds is sometimes forgotten, but the weedy fields held very large numbers, including maxima of 3500 Linnets, 2000 Greenfinches and 1000 Tree Sparrows, counts that seem unlikely to be exceeded in Derbyshire in the foreseeable future. Large flocks of Golden Plovers were often present, especially in spring and good numbers of Corn Buntings bred. Now, apart from the presence of a sludge treatment works and waste composting site, Egginton Sewage Farm resembles 'ordinary' arable farmland. Nearby, another small sewage farm by the river just east of Willington produced many wader records before its demolition in the 1970s.

Church Wilne Reservoir lies immediately west of Sawley and close to the Trent–Derwent confluence. It was flooded in the early 1970s and is in two parts with the upper section separated from the lower part by a walkway. The upper section covers 33ha and has vertical concrete sides, whereas the similar-sized lower part, which is used for water sports, has largely natural banks and some waterside vegetation. The reservoir is private and cannot be adequately viewed from public roads. Its main interest lies in its waterfowl, which can be numerous between midsummer, when Tufted Duck numbers start to increase (maximum 775 in September 2009) and winter, when the number of species is usually greater, especially in cold weather. In the early days, Wigeon were very numerous, with up to 1634 counted in 1985, but this is no longer the case. The gull roost is composed very largely of Common and Black-headed Gulls, with 30,000 of the latter estimated in 1985 and 2011. Migrant terns are regular, and Little Gulls reasonably so – the flock of 32 in May 1990 remains a county record. Rarer species have included Ferruginous and Ring-necked Ducks, Red-footed Falcon, Grey and Red-necked Phalaropes, Long-tailed Skua and Little Auk.

The quietly pleasant area between the Trent and the coalfield around Swadlincote is sometimes referred to as the Melbourne Parklands. It is a region of varied geology, which includes Carboniferous Limestone, Millstone Grit and sandstones. The ornamental Melbourne Pool, where Grey Herons now nest on an island, was the largest water body in the area until 1964, when Staunton Harold Reservoir was flooded. It occupies some 85ha and its banks are natural and gently sloping, so waders can sometimes be found, especially if the water level is low. Coarse fishing and sailing take place on the northern two-thirds of the water area. Wildfowl can be numerous, especially in winter. There is a rather erratic gull roost, but terns are regularly seen, including a Derbyshire record count of 220 Black Terns in September 1992. Other notable species have included Purple and Pectoral Sandpipers, Pomarine Skua, Roseate and White-winged Black Terns, Razorbill and Little Auk. The three car parks give good views over the reservoir and one of these, by Calke village, has a Tree Sparrow feeding station.

Situated just over 3km west of Staunton Harold Reservoir, the 93ha Foremark Reservoir was flooded in 1977. It has natural but rather steep banks and is used for trout-fishing and sailing. Car parks at the north-eastern end give reasonable views over the whole site. Winter is the best season for birdwatchers, when waterfowl can be very numerous; for example, both Great Crested Grebe and Goosander numbers have reached 200. There are many records of all three divers and the rarer grebes. Equally interesting in recent years has been the gull roost, which involves large numbers of birds that feed during the day at a refuse tip just inside Leicestershire at Albert Village. The most numerous are Black-headed Gulls, with up to 30,000 counted, and Lesser Black-backed Gulls with up to 4000, but good numbers of all the expected inland species occur, including regular 'white-winged' gulls. Arctic Redpolls in 1995/96, Derbyshire's first Surf Scoter in 2005, Franklin's Gull and Little Auk are among the rarities recorded here.

The Melbourne Parklands has some large and attractive woodlands. The superb Calke Park is the county's only lowland National Nature Reserve. Owned by the National Trust, it covers 80ha, including large areas of wood pasture. It contains large numbers of venerable and ancient trees, including two oaks thought to be over 1000 years old. The invertebrate fauna is extremely rich – for example, over 350 species of beetles have been identified – and there are some nationally rare fungi. The stag-headed oaks are full of holes appreciated by nesting Kestrels, Jackdaws and Barn and Little Owls, while Mandarins have recently started to breed on the park's chain of small ponds. Nearby, South Wood is a fine area of ancient woodland, dominated by oaks, but with areas of mature beech and some recent coniferous plantation. It is a good site for all three woodpeckers and Marsh Tits among a wealth of woodland birds. Spring Wood, by the southern end of Staunton Harold Reservoir, is a DWT reserve but lies largely in Leicestershire. Some large flocks of migrant Lesser Redpolls have been seen in the birches here. West of Melbourne there are ancient woodland sites at Robin Wood and Repton Shrubs. The latter was once renowned for its rare lepidoptera, but both woods were very largely felled and replanted with pines. South of the coalfield area, the ancient Grange Wood is also entomologically interesting but is private and not often visited by birdwatchers. Goshawks have displayed in spring over at least one of these woods, and Buzzards and Sparrowhawks are numerous throughout.

The coalfield is based upon the Swadlincote area, where coal was mined as far back as the thirteenth century. In 1955 there were five collieries in this area, of which the last, at Cadley Hill, shut down in 1988 and the potteries, pipeyards and brickworks that were established in connection with the area's coal and clay have also closed. This, and opencast coalmining, led to huge areas of derelict land. Now the area is at the centre of the National Forest project, an ambitious scheme to link together the ancestral forests of Needwood in Staffordshire and Charnwood in Leicestershire. Woodland creation began in the 1990s and around 19% of the area is now under trees, the eventual target being to increase this to around a third. Though most of the new woodlands are in the former coalfield area, others are outside, north to Melbourne and south to Coton-in-the-Elms. Garton (2005–07) wrote an interesting series of articles describing the physical characteristics and birds of these woods. A good variety of both broad-leaved and coniferous trees have been planted, and areas of open grassland and many ponds have been created. The early stages of a new woodland are often among the most interesting and Meadow Pipits, Skylarks, Yellow Wagtails and Yellowhammers were among the first colonists. As the plantations began to mature some of these species moved out, to be replaced by, among others, warblers including Grasshopper Warblers. Willow Tits and Tree Sparrows have also been found at some sites. The ponds have held breeding Little Grebes, Tufted Ducks, and Reed and Sedge Warblers, and a former opencast site north of Overseal has had several records of migrant waders. Another area with marshy pools, known as Nadin's, was created in the same way and has held a few migrant waders, Ring-necked Duck, Glossy Ibis and a roost of up to 10,000 Swallows, but is being developed as a golf course. Outside the breeding season, Short-eared Owls and a Great Grey Shrike have been seen in the new woodlands.

The reddish-soiled farmland to the west and south-west of Swadlincote has, like so many areas, suffered from hedgerow removal and in consequence now has some of the biggest fields in the whole of the county. Because of this and other modern practices, farmland birds in general have declined here and Corn Buntings, at one time tolerably common, have gone altogether. This area and the Melbourne Parklands are traditional areas for Quail with many records over the decades from sites such as Grangewood, Ingleby and Milton.

The City of Derby

The City of Derby lies across the junction of four of English Nature's Natural Areas (the Peak Fringe, the Claylands, the Coal Measures and the Trent Valley), and so has been treated here as a separate unit.

Having a population of 248,700 (2011 census), the city covers 87km^2 (3.3% of the county) and, apart from approximate areas of 2km^2 and 3km^2 in the north-west and east respectively, is contained within and almost completely occupies Ordnance Survey 10km square SK33. The site of the water tower in Allestree, a few metres inside the north-west city boundary, is the highest point at 135m amsl and the lowest altitude is 34m amsl in the east, where the River Derwent leaves Derby.

Since 1990, 188 species, plus a further 21 in the escaped or released category, have been recorded within the city (SK33 and the few city sites that lie outwith SK33, the most notable being Allestree Park, although all species recorded in this park have occurred elsewhere in the city).

Although Derby lies across the junctions of four Natural Areas, the influence on wildlife habitat is dominated, in the main, by the urban built environment. As with most urban areas, it is the domestic gardens, golf courses, public parks and open spaces that provide some of the most attractive bird habitats. There are over 300 public parks and open spaces within the city, covering 700ha, which equates to approximately 9% of its land area. While some of these are small (for example, children's playgrounds) offering little habitat for birds, Derby has three large public parks to the north and west of the centre, namely Markeaton (84ha), Allestree (129ha) and Darley Parks (32ha), and Alvaston (34ha) to the east. Additional to the usual open grassed areas associated with urban parks, which are somewhat unattractive to birds, these parks all have extensive mature deciduous woodland either within the park or along their fringes. Markeaton and Allestree Parks both contain significant-sized lakes, while Darley Park is bounded by the River Derwent. Allestree Park in particular has a long history of bird recording, with Velvet Scoter and Black-throated Diver among its more unusual species. In more recent times it has held over 50 Mandarins on occasions and often supports winter Goosanders, while Lesser Spotted Woodpecker and, until a few years ago, Hawfinches were targets for visiting birdwatchers. Markeaton Park often hosts three-figure flocks of Canada and Greylag Geese, and Great Crested Grebes sometimes breed. Presumably the same wandering geese are sometimes found at Alvaston Park. Although not so well endowed with woodland, this site provides attractive bird habitat in having a lake and being adjacent to the River Derwent. It too can hold good numbers of geese and, for an urban site, good numbers of ducks which have included up to 65 Shovelers and up to 90 Pochard. Goosanders now breed regularly on the River Derwent, with broods of young seen in various sites in the city in all but one year during the period 2000–11.

In places, natural features have some bearing on habitat. In particular, the immediate environs of most of the length of the River Derwent which flows into Derby from the north-west, and through the city centre before meandering to join the River Trent 6km south-east of the city, are in a fairly natural state and lined with mature trees, mainly alders and willows. Upstream from the city centre, the river occupies an unbuilt floodplain ranging in width from 400m to 1km and it is not until the final kilometre into the city centre that the banks are built upon. Again, because of the unsuitability of the floodplain for building, the downstream stretch of the river enters now largely unbuilt territory within 1km of leaving the city centre. In the past this downstream stretch was more urbanized with industry, such as gravel extraction, locomotive, chemical and gas works. These industries are now either gone or operating on a much smaller scale with the land left derelict at worst or consciously converted to nature reserves. The most significant of these wildlife habitat initiatives involving the city authorities, local businesses and wildlife groups, was the creation of a 10ha wildlife reserve within Pride Park, a business park of 80ha created on brownfield sites in the 1990s. The site, formerly a gas works tip, was heavily contaminated but had developed naturally into a 'grassland waste' and was becoming attractive to ground and scrub-nesting birds. Following a lengthy decontamination programme, the 'Sanctuary' has retained its bare, treeless character and been complemented by creating bare gravel and wet areas together with a Sand Martin bank. The 105 species recorded in or flying over the Pride Park area include several that might be unexpected within 3km of a city centre, the most notable being a grounded Manx Shearwater and a Curlew Sandpiper, both in September 2004, and a wintering Dartford Warbler from January to March 2005.

Across the river from Pride Park, a former area of gravel extraction at Chaddesden Sidings held until recent years good numbers of breeding Lapwings, Little Ringed and sometimes Ringed Plovers, while its rarity list included Red-breasted Merganser, Sanderling, Black Tern and Water Pipit. To the east of here and on the north bank of the river, there were many records of water birds from Derby Sewage Farm from the late 1960s to the 1980s. At that time the lagoons were particularly good for ducks, especially Teal, with up to 550 recorded. Migrant waders were regular, while the 20–40 pairs of breeding Black-headed Gulls were, for a time in the 1970s, the only ones known in the county. A well-watched Night Heron was found on the river-bank here in May 1995. There are few records from the sewage farm nowadays as the lagoons have largely dried out and access is difficult. However, Cetti's Warblers are now regular there and are often audible from the opposite river-bank, near which the DWT is developing a reserve to be known as Derwent Meadows. Many of the wildfowl that were flushed from the sewage farm retreated to the industrial lagoon at the adjacent Acordis Works. Again, access problems have led to a recent dearth of records here, though there is known to be a sizeable winter Cormorant roost. That classic bird of industrial areas, the Black Redstart, bred at the factory here (when it was known as British Celanese) in 1978; the only other confirmed breeding record in the city was at the ABB works at Pride Park in 1994, though singing males have since been found elsewhere in 2000, 2005 and 2006.

Another city-centre highlight has been the successful breeding of Peregrines on Derby cathedral each year since 2006 and the raising of 19 young in the seven years to 2012. The creation of a dedicated website incorporating live webcam transmissions has generated a worldwide interest. Their choice of avian prey items has included many species that are scarce or difficult to find locally and is believed to result from their nocturnal hunting of migrant species illuminated by the city's lights.

Wildlife has access to many city centre sites via several relatively quiet corridors linking central areas to rural habitats. The most obvious route is the course of the River Derwent as mentioned above, but narrower, less pronounced links are provided via smaller water courses such as Markeaton Brook entering the city from the north-west. A man-made corridor has been provided inadvertently by the disused Great Northern Railway line running from the old Friargate station out to Mickleover and continuing beyond the city to the west. The former Friargate station, in the city centre, has become a haven for all manner of wildlife, and butterflies in particular. Not to be outdone, the site has also hosted some interesting birds, such as Wood Warbler, Wheatear, Black Redstart and Spotted Flycatcher. Having been converted to a mixture of sensitively managed footpath and cycle route, the edges of the old line have been allowed to develop natural vegetation ranging from grasses and flowering plants through to scrub and saplings which are now becoming mature trees.

For almost its entire length, the city boundary separates suburban housing from farmland of a mainly arable or improved pasture character. To the south of the city, the River Trent and the Trent and Mersey Canal run to within 1km of the city boundary. Consequently, nearby gardens frequently record farmland birds such as Reed Bunting and also woodland birds such as Nuthatch and all three woodpecker species visiting from hedges, trees and coppices found on adjacent farms. A striking example of urban and rural contrast is the triangle-shaped Moorway Lane Pond. One side is bounded by a road and housing estate while the other two shores are on agricultural land and incorporate a length of the city boundary. Seventy-five species have been recorded here with a preponderance of waders, wildfowl and farmland species. Urban gardens in general have increasingly grown in importance over recent years, with many more households feeding birds with specialist bird foods and Derby is no exception.

Despite being the UK city furthest from the sea, Derby has three recent records of Kittiwake, four more Manx Shearwaters in addition to the one mentioned above, and a 1997 record of two fly-over Gannets, in addition to one of an exhausted bird found in brambles less than 2km from the city centre.

A Chronology of Additions to the Derbyshire List

The following table is a chronological list of the rarer species for which there are acceptable records. Historical data is sometimes vague, with even the year uncertain in some cases, let alone the actual date. Where there are no dates, the species have been listed in British Ornithological Union order. Doubtless many of the species listed were present in the county from time to time prior to the records indicated, but went unnoticed, unidentified or certainly unrecorded. Where dates are not shown, they are not known. It is assumed that the more common species have been present for tens of thousands of years, and so are not listed.

Records of Snow Goose, Golden Pheasant, Lady Amherst's Pheasant and Ring-necked Parakeet are not included, despite all four species having been seen at large, since the likelihood of their being of wild origin is very much in doubt. The date of the Lesser White-fronted Goose strongly suggests a bird of captive origin, but the record was accepted by British Birds Rarities Committee as the ninety-seventh for Britain.

Species	Date	
Golden Eagle		1668
Water Rail		1700s
Hooded Crow		1700s
Wryneck		1700s
Quail	24th August	1761
Nightjar	1st September	1761
Red Kite	7th November	1765
Snow Bunting	11th December	1767
Bittern		1768
Crossbill		1768
Grey Phalarope	26th September	1770
Red-backed Shrike	22nd August	1772
Raven	18th September	1772
Great Grey Shrike	16th November	1772
Dotterel	27th April	1774
Waxwing	10th December	1774
Woodlark		1774
Osprey	28th May	1779
Rose-coloured Starling	October	1784
Merlin	prior to	1789
White-fronted Goose	prior to	1789
Barnacle Goose	prior to	1789
Honey Buzzard	prior to	1789
Marsh Harrier	prior to	1789
Rough-legged Buzzard	prior to	1789
Black Grouse	prior to	1789
Oystercatcher	prior to	1789
Little Tern	prior to	1789
Puffin	prior to	1789
Long-eared Owl	prior to	1789
Hawfinch	prior to	1789
Little Bustard		1797
White Stork	early	1800s
Glossy Ibis	mid	1800s
Bean Goose		1800s
Spotted Crake		1800s
Corncrake		1800s
Storm Petrel		1800s
Spotted Redshank		1800s
Green Sandpiper		1800s
Kittiwake		1800s
Black Tern		1800s
Goshawk		1800s
Greylag Goose	circa	1810
Baillon's Crake	8th November	1821
Snowy Owl		1825
Great Northern Diver		1826
Eagle Owl		1828
Nightingale		1828
Hobby	prior to	1829
White-tailed Eagle		1836 or 1837
Firecrest		1838
Woodchat Shrike	19th May	1839
Dartford Warbler	winter	1840
Brent Goose	January	1841
Golden Oriole	25th May	1841
Arctic Tern	May	1842
Peregrine		1843
Little Auk		1843
Avocet	prior to	1844
Red-throated Diver		1844
Red-necked Grebe		1844
Bar-tailed Godwit		1844
Two-barred Crossbill	21st November	1845
Fulmar	25th October	1847
Spoonbill		1847
Little Gull	22nd January	1851
Sooty Tern		1852
Velvet Scoter		1853
Egyptian Goose		1855
Roller	3rd May	1856
Purple Heron	1st July	1856
Black Redstart	2nd November	1856
Slavonian Grebe		1860
Black-necked Grebe		1860
Night Heron		1860s
Hoopoe	prior to	1863
Long-tailed Duck	prior to	1863
Pallas's Sandgrouse		1863
Red-legged Partridge	circa	1865
Leach's Petrel	prior to	1867

Species	Date	
Little Bittern	August	1872
Squacco Heron	17th May	1874
Gannet	27th April	1878
Bee-eater	4th May	1879
Manx Shearwater		1879
Arctic Skua		1879
Cirl Bunting		1881
Whiskered Tern	autumn	1883
Wood Sandpiper	September	1885
Sandwich Tern	May	1888
Sanderling	circa	1888
Little Stint	21st September	1890
Grey Plover	late	1890
Purple Sandpiper	late	1890
Red-breasted Merganser		1890
Stone Curlew		1890
Shag	28th October	1891
Great Snipe	12th October	1892
Sabine's Gull	26th August	1894
Bearded Tit	summer	1896
Black-throated Diver	January/February	1897
Pomarine Skua	early October	1898
Montagu's Harrier	late April	1903
Curlew Sandpiper		1905
Turnstone	1st June	1906
Ruddy Shelduck	18th April	1913
Gadwall		1920
Black-tailed Godwit	25th August	1928
Great Skua	14th October	1934
Eider	circa	1936
Red-footed Falcon	May	1939
Ferruginous Duck	mid-December	1950
Little Ringed Plover		1950
Black-browed Albatross	21st August	1952
Water Pipit	16th November	1953
Kentish Plover	18th September	1959
Red-crested Pochard	27th July	1960
Collared Dove	autumn	1961
Pectoral Sandpiper	12th August	1962
Ruddy Duck	12th January	1963
Mandarin	14th December	1963
Killdeer	29th February	1964
Rock Pipit	6th March	1965
Roseate Tern	18th June	1965
Wilson's Phalarope	23rd June	1965
Mediterranean Gull	18th July	1965
Cattle Egret	12th July	1966
Lapland Bunting	26th October	1966
Iceland Gull	25th November	1966
Little Egret	18th May	1967
Temminck's Stint	25th September	1967
Glaucous Gull	28th January	1968
Caspian Tern	3rd June	1968
White-winged Black Tern	23rd August	1968
Razorbill	18th October	1970
Shorelark	18th October	1971
Great White Egret	19th May	1974
Lesser White-fronted Goose	8th June	1976
Aquatic Warbler	20th August	1976
Green-winged Teal	14th November	1976
Ring-necked Duck	27th December	1977
Long-tailed Skua	5th October	1978
Laughing Gull	29th November	1980
Red-necked Phalarope	3rd July	1981
Yellow-legged Gull	28rd January	1982
Parrot Crossbill	30th October	1982
Baird's Sandpiper	9th September	1983
Red-throated Pipit	20th May	1985
Marsh Warbler	30th May	1985
Black Kite	5th June	1985
Red-rumped Swallow	15th November	1986
Bonaparte's Gull	17th February	1987
Savi's Warbler	26th April	1987
Crane	14th June	1987
Richard's Pipit	26th October	1987
Least Sandpiper	17th July	1988
Yellow-browed Warbler	4th October	1988
Ring-billed Gull	16th December	1989
American Golden Plover	12th October	1990
White-throated Needletail	3rd June	1991
Bluethroat	19th April	1992
Sociable Plover	17th April	1993
Little Bunting	11th March	1994
Gull-billed Tern	25th June	1995
Blue-winged Teal	25th September	1995
Arctic Redpoll	10th December	1995
Black-throated Thrush	3rd January	1997
Serin	6th May	1997
Common Rosefinch	3rd June	1998
Pallid Swift	3rd August	1998
Lesser Yellowlegs	22nd August	1998
Alpine Swift	1st September	1998
Caspian Gull	2nd December	1998
Cetti's Warbler	26th May	1999
Spotted Sandpiper	28th September	1999
Pallas's Warbler	30th October	1999
Ortolan Bunting	6th May	2000
American Wigeon	3rd November	2002
Tawny Pipit	5th October	2003
Bufflehead	20th June	2004
Lesser Grey Shrike	11th July	2004
Broad-billed Sandpiper	18th July	2004
Surf Scoter	9th November	2005
Great Reed Warbler	12th May	2010
Citrine Wagtail	28th August	2010
Franklin's Gull	28th October	2010
Black Stork	21st April	2011
Western Bonelli's Warbler	2nd July	2011

Fossil Species

It is an unfortunate perception that birds rarely fossilize, that their bones are difficult to identify, and that we therefore know little of their longer-term history. It is true that bird bones are more fragile than those of mammals, and that the lack of teeth, very hard and well-fossilized organs that make mammals so well studied, makes birds harder to study. There are also about three times as many breeding birds in Britain as breeding mammals, so there is more scope for confusion. Even so, bones such as the humerus and tarsometatarsus (upper arm and elongated foot bones), are actually quite distinctive. Equally, there are many species which are so distinctive in size and morphology that their identification, given the right bones, is relatively straightforward. Among those of current concern, Red Grouse and Ptarmigan overlap in size, though Ptarmigan are somewhat smaller and more slender. The surface ducks, waders and several groups of passerines also cause difficulties because there are many similar species in those groups.

Derbyshire is fortunate to have two cave-containing areas, the Magnesian Limestone in the east and the Carboniferous Limestone of the White Peak, which have yielded good avian subfossil faunas. The caves of Creswell Crags, shared with Nottinghamshire, have long interested archaeologists, and Jenkinson (1984) has summarized their faunas. The White Peak areas, shared with Staffordshire, have some good faunas from Fox Hole and Dowel Caves near Earl Sterndale. Similarly, caves in the Manifold Valley, including Ossom's and Ossom's Eyrie, should not be ignored because they are only 5km from the county boundary, and surely reflect also the contemporary fauna of Derbyshire. Derbyshire is also fortunate in that the one British bird archaeo-osteologist of note during the 1960s and 1970s, Don Bramwell, lived in Bakewell all his life. He was responsible for identifying the bird bones from many sites across Britain, not only those from the Peak District, and he also supervised himself many careful excavations in Peak District caves, thereby ensuring that bird bones were not ignored. His lists (Bramwell 1978) remain the basis of this account. They have been updated and corrected by reference to accounts published since. Where a question mark follows a species it means that the identification was not certain.

Late Pleistocene, Last Glacial Maximum, around 25,000–15,000 years ago

A time when ice sheets covered northern Britain, and the south, including the Peak District, was bare tundra. By modern analogy, bird faunas would have been sparse. Dating of the deposits at Pin Hole Cave, Creswell Crags is uncertain, and faunas may be mixed, but Red/Willow Grouse and Ptarmigan are prominent, and geese (Barnacle, Greylag or Pink-foot) were breeding, because eggshell fragments were found (Jenkinson 1984).

Late Glacial, 15,000–11,000 years ago

The climate started to improve, and palaeolithic people at Creswell Crags were hunting mountain hares, reindeer and similar northern mammals. From Robin Hood's Cave at Creswell Crags, we have a fauna that has a northern, Scottish or Scandinavian, appearance:

Mallard: *Anas platyrhynchos*
Goldeneye: *Bucephala clangula*?
Goshawk: *Accipiter gentilis*
Kestrel: *Falco tinnunculus*
Red/Willow Grouse: *Lagopus lagopus*
Ptarmigan: *Lagopus mutus*
Black Grouse: *Tetrao tetrix*
Plover sp.:   Charadriidae
Short-eared Owl: *Asio flammeus*
Great Spotted Woodpecker: *Dryocopus major*?
Ring Ouzel: *Turdus torquatus*?
Fieldfare: *Turdus pilaris*
Large Bunting/Finch sp.:   Emberizidae/Fringillidae
Jay: *Garrulus glandarius*?
Magpie: *Pica pica*
Jackdaw: *Corvus monedula*

Early Postglacial, about 10,000 years ago

This saw the end of the ice age, and a sharp increase in temperature by about 8°C. Open-ground birds had been joined by some northern woodland species. From Dowel Cave, we have:

Kestrel: *Falco tinnunculus*
Red/Willow Grouse: *Lagopus lagopus*
Ptarmigan: *Lagopus mutus*
Black Grouse: *Tetrao tetrix*
Capercaillie: *Tetrao urogallus*
Teal: *Anas crecca*
Little/Baillon's Crake: *Porzana parva/pusilla*
Lapwing: *Vanellus vanellus*
Knot: *Calidris canutus*?
Short-eared Owl: *Asio flammeus*
Great Spotted Woodpecker: *Dryocopus major*?
Tit: *Parus/Cyanistes* sp.
Wren: *Troglodytes troglodytes*?
Fieldfare: *Turdus pilaris*
Pipit/Wagtail sp.:   Motacillidae
Bullfinch: *Pyrrhula pyrrhula*
Jay: *Garrulus glandarius*
Jackdaw: *Corvus monedula*

Contemporary with this is a small bird fauna from Wetton Mill Rock Shelter, Manifold Valley, which also includes Black Grouse, Capercaillie, Red/Willow Grouse and Ptarmigan (Bramwell 1976). From about the same time, or perhaps a little later, from Demen's Dale Rock Shelter, near Miller's Dale (Bramwell & Yalden 1988), we have an interesting mixture of woodland, wetland and open-ground species. These might indicate that the fauna accumulated over some 2000 years, or that the combination of dale and plateau generated an odd landscape with a mixed fauna. The unmistakeable large metatarsal of the Eagle Owl and the equally distinctive lower jaw of the Hawfinch are the most interesting specimens. The rallids (Bramwell 1978) have been reidentified as ducks (Coot, Moorhen) and Snipe (Corncrake).

Mallard: *Anas platyrhynchos*?
Teal/Garganey: *Anas crecca/querquedula*
Shoveler: *Anas clypeata*?
Gadwall/Wigeon: *Anas strepera/penelope*
Goldeneye: *Bucephala clangula*
Goosander: *Mergus merganser*
Kestrel: *Falco tinnunculus*
Ptarmigan: *Lagopus mutus*?
Black Grouse: *Tetrao tetrix*?
Grey Partridge: *Perdix perdix*
Grey Plover: *Pluvialis squatarola*?
Snipe: *Gallinago gallinago*
Dunlin: *Calidris alpina*
Knot: *Calidris canuta*?
Ruff: *Calidris pugnax*?
Eagle Owl: *Bubo bubo*
Tawny Owl: *Strix aluco*
Blackbird: *Turdus merula*?
Hawfinch: *Coccothraustes coccothraustes*
Jay: *Garrulus glandarius*

Late Neolithic or Beaker Age of Dowel Cave, about 4000 years ago

From this period we have a fauna that would not be out of place now. Interestingly, though, the most numerous species were woodland ones, Great Tit contributing 39 of 86 passerine bones identified: this is rather different from the limestone grassland fauna now, in which Meadow Pipits and Wheatear are the common species. Some passerine bones have been restudied since Bramwell (1978) listed them, and the Red-backed Shrike is a notable and distinctive addition.

Mallard: *Anas platyrhynchos*
Teal: *Anas crecca*
Goshawk: *Accipiter gentilis*
Kestrel: *Falco tinnunculus*
Grey Partridge: *Perdix perdix*
Sandpiper sp.: Scolopacidae
Tawny Owl: *Strix aluco*
Skylark: *Alauda arvensis*
Swallow: *Hirundo rustica*
Great Tit: *Parus major*
Blue Tit: *Cyanistes caeruleus*
Wren: *Troglodytes troglodytes*
Blackbird: *Turdus merula*
Fieldfare: *Turdus pilaris*
Song Thrush: *Turdus philomelos*
Redwing: *Turdus iliacus*
Robin: *Erithacus rubecula*
Chiffchaff: *Phylloscopus collybita*
Goldcrest: *Regulus regulus*
Dunnock: *Prunella modularis*
Meadow Pipit: *Anthus pratensis*
Pied Wagtail: *Motacilla alba*
Starling: *Sturnus vulgaris*
Hawfinch: *Coccothraustes coccothraustes*

Greenfinch: *Carduelis chloris*
Linnet: *Carduelis cannabina*
Bullfinch: *Pyrrhula pyrrhula*
Chaffinch: *Fringilla coelebs*
Bunting sp.: Emberizidae
Tree Sparrow: *Passer montanus*
Red-backed Shrike: *Lanius collurio*
Jay: *Garrulus glandarius*?
Magpie: *Pica pica*
Jackdaw: *Corvus monedula*
Crow/Rook: *Corvus* sp.
Raven: *Corvus corax*

From Fox Hole Cave, about the same age, we have:

Golden Eagle: *Aquila chrysaetos*
Black Grouse: *Tetrao tetrix*
Capercaillie: *Tetrao urogallus*
Skylark: *Alauda arvensis*
Nuthatch: *Sitta europaea*
Blackbird: *Turdus merula*
Fieldfare: *Turdus pilaris*
Mistle Thrush: *Turdus viscivorus*
Robin: *Erithacus rubecula*
Finch/Bunting sp.: Fringillidae/Emberizidae
Jay: *Garrulus glandarius*?
Magpie: *Pica pica*
Jackdaw: *Corvus monedula*
Crow/Rook: *Corvus* sp.

Additional records from the same age include:

Hindlow Barrow
Black Grouse: *Tetrao tetrix*
Long-eared Owl: *Asio otus*

Tideslow Barrow
Little/Baillon's Crake: *Porzana parva/pusilla*
Mistle Thrush: *Turdus viscivorus*
Hawfinch: *Coccothraustes coccothraustes*

Green Low Barrow (Alsop Moor)
Mallard: *Anas platyrhynchos*
Raven: *Corvus corax*

Green Low Barrow (Aldwark)
Blackbird: *Turdus merula*
Finch sp.: Fringillidae
Jay: *Garrulus glandarius*

Post-Roman layers at Ossom's Eyrie Cave, Manifold Valley

From here we have a large bird fauna (Bramwell *et al.* 1990), in which Black Grouse was the most common and Raven and other species were also prey fed to a young Golden Eagle, which failed to fledge. A varied small bird fauna, perhaps prey of Barn Owls, was recovered from later levels. It included also Swallows and House Martins, probably breeding in the cave, as a reminder of the nest sites that they must have used before houses and other structures became their more usual homes.

Wetland

Willington Gravel Pits is a DWT reserve and one of Derbyshire's most ornithologically productive sites.

The River Trent, looking upstream from Willington Bridge. With its tributaries, the Trent drains nine-tenths of the county and is a major attraction to migrant birds.

Goosanders are common in the Trent Valley in winter, and now also breed along the river.

Bitterns occur in the county every winter, with up to four present recently at Willington Gravel Pits.

A fine male Long-tailed Duck at Long Eaton Gravel Pits.

Little Egrets are regularly seen in Derbyshire, especially in the Trent Valley, and future colonization seems likely.

Opposite: Kingfishers breed widely along the county's rivers and streams.

Wetland

Carsington Water is the county's largest reservoir and attracts large numbers of water birds, especially when the water level is low, as shown here.

Ogston Reservoir has the longest bird species list of any site in the county.

Wetland

The largest recorded herd of Whooper Swans was this one, of 81 at Mapperley Reservoir in March 2013.

Carr Vale Flashes, now a DWT reserve, were originally formed by mining subsidence.

Ospreys are regular migrants at reservoirs and elsewhere. This individual, photographed in September 2012, had been ringed as a nestling near Inverness, Scotland, two months earlier.

Garganeys have been proved to nest only at Carr Vale, but breeding has also been suspected in the Erewash and Trent Valleys.

Snipe are common at many wetlands but are now restricted as breeding birds to upland areas.

The Jack Snipe is a regular migrant and winter visitor in small numbers at marshy sites throughout the lowlands.

Cromford Canal, seen here near High Peak Junction, is a very popular site for birdwatchers, with wintering Hawfinches a major attraction.

Wetland

This Hawfinch was an unexpected visitor to a Curbar garden.

Kedleston Park is one of several fine lowland parks with ornamental lakes.

Great Crested Grebes are typical breeding birds of parkland lakes and other wetlands.

The rapidly increasing Mandarin now breeds widely, especially in south-west Derbyshire and along rivers in the Peak District.

Stock Doves breed in a wide variety of habitats including parkland, farmland and quarries.

Urban and Industrial

The River Derwent in central Derby, the county's largest conurbation. Peregrines have nested on the nearby cathedral in recent years.

A Peregrine at Derby Cathedral.

Great Rocks Dale and Tunstead Quarry. The quarries are the breeding sites of Peregrines, Ravens and House Martins, with Twites in certain areas.

Once moorland breeders, Twites are now restricted to breeding in a very few of the Peak District's quarries.

Willington Power Station, following demolition of most of its buildings. Little Ringed and Ringed Plovers often breed at such sites.

Urban and Industrial

Ringed Plovers breed in small numbers in industrial areas as well as at gravel pits and reservoirs.

Following the closure of the coalmines, most of the attendant spoil heaps have been reclaimed but that at Pleasley is now a Local Nature Reserve, featuring a shallow central lagoon.

Farmland

A view near Marston Montgomery in a traditionally pastoral area, though conversion to arable is increasing.

A medieval ridge and furrow field system in the Carboniferous Limestone area near Tissington.

Harvesting near Whitwell on the Magnesian Limestone plateau, once the county stronghold of birds such as Turtle Dove and Corn Bunting.

Farmland

Barn Owls have shown a very welcome increase recently, which is believed to be mainly the result of nest-box schemes.

Grey Partridges have shown a considerable decline, both nationally and locally.

A rare photograph of a Quail on set-aside. The numbers of this migrant vary considerably from year to year.

Turtle Doves were once common in the county but may now be heading for local extinction.

Corn Buntings may just be clinging on as breeding birds in Derbyshire.

Flocks of Golden Plovers can be seen on farmland on passage and during the winter.

Woodland

Ancient deciduous woodland at South Wood, part of the National Trust's Calke Estate.

Woodcock have shown a recent contraction of range but still breed in many of the county's woods.

The oak woodlands at Padley Gorge are renowned for their Wood Warblers, Redstarts and Pied Flycatchers.

Redstarts are typical of the Peak District's hanging oakwoods.

Pied Flycatchers have greatly benefited from the provision of nest-boxes in many parts of the Peak District.

Woodland

Matlock Forest has a mixture of old and young plantations, supporting Goshawks, Long-eared Owls, Nightjars, Crossbills and sometimes Firecrests.

Crossbills are believed to breed in most, if not all, years in the Matlock Forest and Derwent areas.

Long-eared Owls are rare breeding birds of upland coniferous woodland.

Most of the county's Nightjars are found in the Matlock Forest complex.

Limestone Dales

Little Owls in the Peak District nest mainly in rock outcrops and drystone walls.

Most of the county's Wheatears breed in the Carboniferous Limestone area.

Upper Cressbrook Dale is one of many dry dales in the Peak District National Park. Such areas support Little Owls and Wheatears.

Lathkill Dale forms part of Natural England's Derbyshire Dales National Nature Reserve and holds breeding Dippers and Grey Wagtails.

Dippers are resident on the Peak District's streams and rivers.

Grey Wagtails nest in similar areas to Dippers but many winter away from their breeding areas.

Moorland

Cotton-grass dominates the moorland at Ringinglow Bog, where breeding birds include Golden Plovers and Dunlins.

Golden Plovers breed in some numbers on the higher moors.

Dunlins are scarce breeding birds of higher, wetter moorland areas.

Curlews breed throughout much of the Peak District, in both gritstone and limestone areas.

Hen Harriers bred successfully in 1997 and 2006 but other recent attempts have ended in failure.

A small but declining breeding population of Merlins remains in moorland areas.

Moorland

Short-eared Owls are largely confined to higher moorlands.

Wintering Great Grey Shrikes may occur in almost any open area, but most are seen on moorland, like this one at Beeley.

Cuckoos in moorland areas are believed to mainly parasitize Meadow Pipits.

Bamford Edge, looking towards Ladybower Reservoir and the lower slopes of Win Hill. The rocky edges hold Ring Ouzels, Stonechats and Whinchats.

Ring Ouzels are found on rocky edges and in some of the quieter cloughs.

Moorland

Recent cold winters have taken a toll on the county's Stonechats.

One of a springtime trip of six Dotterels at Stanage Edge.

The Peak District moors can be very quiet for birds in cold winters, although Red Grouse and Ravens are always present.

Red Grouse are common on heather moorland.

Ravens have spread from the Peak District to much of the county, including lowland areas.

A Selection of Derbyshire Rarities

A first-summer female Red-footed Falcon at Breaston in 2011.

The county's second Squacco Heron, an immature, was seen by the River Erewash at Long Eaton in 2011.

Derbyshire's first Franklin's Gull was at two sites in the Trent Valley in autumn 2010.

Three of a UK record flock of 11 Whiskered Terns at Willington Gravel Pits in 2009.

A male Ferruginous Duck visited two sites in the Erewash Valley in early 2008.

The county's second Common Rosefinch was trapped and ringed at Uppertown in 2003.

A Woodchat Shrike stayed for three days at Long Eaton Gravel Pits in 2006 before it was relocated in Cumbria.

A Selection of Derbyshire Rarities

This immature White-winged Black Tern was at Long Eaton Gravel Pits in 2006.

This fine Rose-coloured Starling remained in suburban Sinfin for a week in 2002.

A male Blue-winged Teal was at Monsal Dale for seven weeks in 1997.

The county's first Black-throated Thrush was a first-winter male in a Hollingwood garden in 1997.

The UK's second Black-browed Albatross became entangled in telegraph wires at Staveley in 1952 before being released on the Lincolnshire coast.

The Breeding Bird Survey

Background

Breeding bird survey work was carried out in Derbyshire for the BTO Atlases of 1968–72 and 1988–91, prior to the Derbyshire Ornithological Society (DOS)'s own survey of 1995–99. During the first period, 27 10km squares were allocated to Derbyshire, but this number was subsequently reduced to 23 as shown on the map, the four former squares being indicated by lighter shading.

In the Species Accounts these 23 squares are referred to as the 10km 'core' squares. As will be seen, large areas of the county lay outside the core (particularly in the 1988–91 period) and the survey work for those was co-ordinated by adjacent counties. This was not the case for the DOS 1995–99 survey for which all 724 tetrads (occupying all or part of 40 10km squares) lying within the geographical county boundary were surveyed. Any very small areas of the county which lay outside these tetrads were ignored. However, records received for SK03Y were included with those in SK13D as the area of Derbyshire in tetrad SK03Y amounts to only some 8ha. It was felt more expedient to do this, particularly as this area was dealt with as Staffordshire in the earlier BTO surveys.

Object, survey area, survey unit and time period

The object of the survey was to determine the distribution and status of the breeding birds of the county.

The Derbyshire county boundary used was as defined on the 1:50,000 scale Ordnance Survey maps (Landranger Series) current at the time, and although there were some minor boundary changes subsequently, these did not affect the survey. It should be noted that the City of Derby was included in the survey although it is now administratively separate from the rest of the county.

The survey unit upon which all the systematic observations were recorded was the tetrad, a 2km square based on the Ordnance Survey national grid. Each tetrad is recognized by a five character code: the first two are letters which designate the 100km grid square, followed by two numbers which designate the 10km square within it. The final character indicates one of 25 tetrads within that 10km square using the letters of the alphabet (except the letter 'O') as follows:

E	J	P	U	Z
D	I	N	T	Y
C	H	M	S	X
B	G	L	R	W
A	F	K	**Q**	V

So for tetrad 'SK37Q', which contains Queen's Park just south of Chesterfield town centre, the precise 2km square would be as highlighted above.

It was planned to gather data from all the tetrads falling wholly within the county, together with all those on the periphery that have some part of the county which could be identified in the field (except for some extremely small areas). For the peripheral tetrads, only the part within the county boundary was surveyed, but for the purpose of calculating the percentages of tetrads in which breeding was determined (confirmed, probable or possible), a figure of 724 tetrads was used as defined by the 'tetrad enclosing boundary' indicated by the orange line on the map.

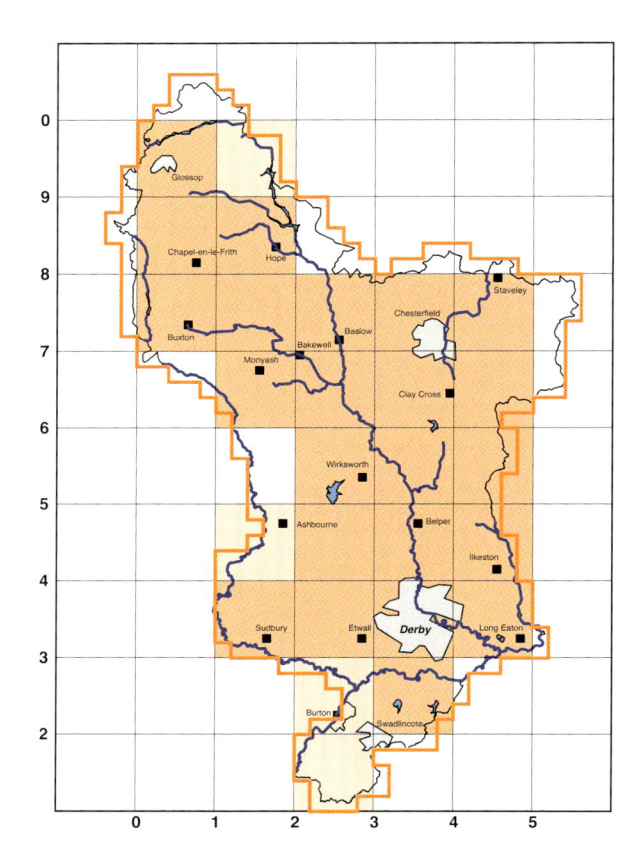

It should be noted that 724 tetrads equates to 2896km^2, which is considerably more (about 10%) than the true area of Derbyshire at 2637km^2 as determined by the geographical county boundary.

The survey period was from 1995 to 1999 inclusive. The breeding season was not specifically defined but was generally taken to mean from late March through to early August. However, participants were reminded to be watchful for early breeders such as herons, owls and resident thrush species, and to continue monitoring the late breeders such as finches, some hirundines and doves.

Taxonomy and names

For the purposes of all the paperwork involved in the survey, the systematic order and scientific names used were as in Cramp *et al*. (1977–94) and Voous (1977).

Recording categories

A series of codes was used, arranged to represent the sequence of events, which together make a complete breeding record. They ranged from a species being present in a tetrad to recording fledged young of that species in the same tetrad, as follows:

Status	Code	Description
Possible breeding	P	Species present within the tetrad during the breeding season, and in suitable habitat
Probable breeding	S	A singing/displaying male in suitable habitat
	C	A species pair in suitable habitat, showing possible territorial behaviour, or male displaying
	N	Bird visiting possible nest site; nest building; anxiety calls, distraction display; recently used nest
Proved (confirmed) breeding	F	Bird carrying food, possibly to nestlings; adult with faecal sac
	E	Nest with eggs or young; adult bird sitting on nest
	Y	Recently fledged young or downy nidifugous chicks

The most basic code of 'present' was framed to obtain the fullest possible picture of birds present during the breeding season. It was expected that some returns would include observations of lingering winter visitors. The expertise and opinion of the stewards allocated to each 10km square was relied upon to place these records in the context of the survey. Inevitably elements of subjective judgement were also required for other species such as Swift, and species recorded later in the survey, for example young Lapwing, Mistle Thrush and Rook, which can disperse widely.

No attempt was made in the fieldwork to count the number of individuals. The reasoning was that it would make the survey overcomplicated, and would deter many of those who would otherwise wish to take part from doing so. The survey was therefore, deliberately, kept simple and straightforward.

Organization of fieldwork

The overall organization of the fieldwork was carried out by Dave Budworth for the south and Oliver Biddulph for the north of the county. This responsibility corresponded with their respective roles as Regional Representatives for the BTO during the period of the survey.

A small steering group prepared the survey material and the fieldwork instructions. A steward was appointed for each of the 10km squares within the county. They, in turn, were requested to arrange coverage by individual observers for each tetrad within their area. Due to the large number of tetrads within the county, there was a need to involve as many people as possible. It was recognized that it would be unlikely that the membership of the DOS could undertake the full survey unaided, and therefore there was a need to involve as many non-members and local bird clubs and societies as possible. As additional benefits, it was hoped that, through the survey work, new members might be attracted to join the Society, and that overall bird recording in the county would be promoted and improved.

For the first year, 724 A5-size Tetrad Cards were prepared, each showing on the front a 1:25,000 scale map of the tetrad, together with a small 10km square grid annotated with the 25 letters, with the particular tetrad highlighted. This was designed to help the observer clearly identify the boundary of their survey responsibility, to see the different habitats within their tetrad, and to allow for plotting routes, to ensure comprehensive coverage. It also gave the name, address and telephone number of the square steward, and on the reverse, instructions to the fieldworker of how to find their tetrad.

Submission of records

Records could be submitted using either a Tetrad Recording Card or a Casual Records Card. Tetrad Recording Cards were designed to record the status of all occurrences, for one year for a particular tetrad. Casual Records Cards enabled ad hoc records to be made for anywhere in the county, and, as the name suggests, catered for the recording of isolated unsystematic casual records.

Survey volunteers were supplied with Tetrad Cards, recording cards and instruction sheets. The instructions contained sections on the aims of the survey, who would do it, how long it would take, the coding of records, how a tetrad should be surveyed, and how to complete both recording cards. There were also sections on codes of conduct and the need to seek access permissions, as well as advice on recording rarities and the provisions for confidentiality.

Tetrad Recording Cards

These were also A5-size cards, and sections on the front of the card gave details of the tetrad code and year of the survey, details of the observer, activity code descriptions, and eight spare entry spaces which were for species not named on the reverse of the card. The reverse carried sections for tetrad code and year details, brief reminders of the code definitions followed by a list of the 92 species thought to be most representative of the county avifauna. There were seven squares at the side of each species to allow recording of the sequence of codes.

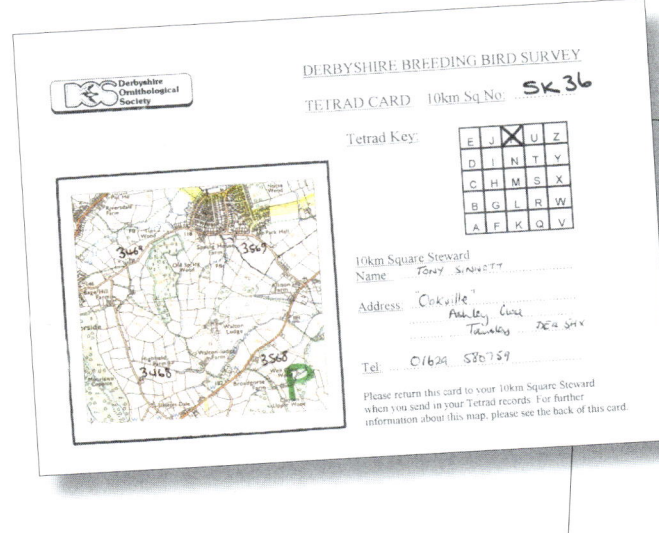

Tetrad Card.

Casual Records Cards

Sections on the front of the card gave details of the year the records were collected, observer details, a summary of the activity codes followed by a grid for recording data. Each entry comprised the species name followed by seven columns, one for each of the sequence of codes. The next column was for the name of the locality where the bird was seen followed by a 1km grid reference and the date of the sighting. The purpose of asking for locality and a grid reference was in recognition of the possibility that different observers might know the same place but by different names. The 1km grid reference would therefore help pinpoint the record and minimize confusion. The reverse of the card contained the same framework, allowing for the submission of 29 records in total per card.

Collecting the data

All the Tetrad Recording and Casual Records Cards were collected at the end of each year. New cards were issued for the following year of the survey, and in the case of Tetrad Recording Cards, the most developed records from the previous year(s) were marked on each card. Tetrad surveyors were then requested to ignore species for which they had already proved breeding, and to concentrate their efforts on developing incomplete records and finding new species for their squares.

At the end of the penultimate year of the survey, a position statement was produced for each tetrad that showed the most developed record for each of the 92 core species. The steering group then made a value judgement of each square by comparing the range of species identified with habitat, and by this broad-brush method arrived at a shortlist of squares where coverage would be better targeted in the final year of the survey. For areas of the county where coverage had been particularly poor, 'hit squads' were formed to provide some coverage in the final year and thereby avoid gaps in the survey, but this was considered to be only partially successful.

Tetrad Recording Card.

Casual Records Card.

Other sources of records

At the time the survey began, the DOS was still gathering county records using a paper-based system of recording slips, which was not then computerized. It was recognized at the outset that important data would be overlooked unless something was done to include information on these record slips in the Breeding Bird Survey. This was because it would be unrealistic for the membership to be expected to keep parallel records of sightings on recording slips and casual record cards. And yet ironically, if the problem was not overcome, the Breeding Bird Survey would not be informed by an important data set in the possession of the Society! The problem was solved by the Society moving, during the period of the survey, to a computerized form of maintaining county records.

Once the computerized system was up and running, the paper records for the years of the survey were trawled and any records of breeding activity were computerized in a form compatible with the programmes used for the recording of the Breeding Bird Survey data.

Confidentiality

It was accepted at the outset that some contributors might wish to keep their records confidential and not submit them through the steward network or the survey organizers. Provision was therefore made for records to be sent direct to the DOS Rare Breeding Birds Recorder. The amount of information supplied was left to the discretion of the contributor. However, the survey instructions pointed out that under these circumstances the observer should be prepared to supply additional information, and possibly complete the Society's Rare Bird Form, if requested by the Recorder.

The survey instructions also included reference to the way information on rarities would be presented in the avifauna. The summaries would be prepared by the DOS Rarities Sub-committee and would not include distribution maps. It would therefore be possible to give details of the incidence and activity of rare birds without disclosing locality.

Provision was made for a review of methods and materials after the first year of fieldwork. All the comments received were positive and consequently there was no need to make any adjustments.

Data processing and record checking

All records were computerized from the outset using Microsoft Excel software. Data was then translated into species maps using DMAP software. For the purpose of the species maps the seven recording categories were condensed into 'Possible', 'Probable' and 'Proven Breeding' status. Records were cumulative and therefore a species might not have been recorded in every year of the survey.

Accuracy and errors

Errors may have occurred for the following reasons:

- species recorded when not actually present
- species recorded in the wrong activity category
- species recorded in the wrong tetrad, where the details of a casual record may have led to problems of identifying location and/or the wrong co-ordinates had been supplied
- incorrect data entry.

The quality of records will have varied depending on the expertise of the observers, their hearing ability and quality of vision, and the duration and timing of field visits. Those missed are more likely to be the nocturnal, the less vocal or less easily observed, and the more skulking species. Clerical error may have led to a species being recorded in the wrong category. It is also likely that some possible and probable breeders may have actually bred, but may not have been recorded as such due to a bias of fieldwork towards the early part of the breeding season. Alternatively, records gathered towards the end of the season may have been of fledged birds dispersing into an area where there was no breeding, and mistakenly being recorded as proof of breeding for that species.

No space was provided on the survey cards for the observer to record the amount of time spent in the field or, in the case of tetrad surveyors, the date of their visits. Requests were made after the first year for the latter to make a note on their cards of the dates and time spent in the field but the response was patchy. The purpose of the request was to help with verification of records and, possibly, to account for omissions and underrecording.

Misidentification of species may have been a problem, but scrutiny of records by the square stewards and the authors of the individual species accounts helped to minimize this.

Overall it was felt that underrecording was likely to have been the biggest problem, and while there may have been some confusion over records, it is felt that, overall, this did not detract from the survey.

The Species Accounts

Sequence and nomenclature

The order of the list of species and English and scientific names are those presented in the forty-first report of the British Ornithologists' Union Records Committee (2013). By 31st December 2011, 319 species of bird had been reliably recorded in Derbyshire since systematic record-keeping began. This excludes birds known only from fossilized remains, such as Capercaillie, which are dealt with in 'Fossil Species' above. Earlier published records which are now, for various reasons, deemed unacceptable, are listed in 'Unacceptable Historic Records' below.

Status

As taken from the 2011 *Derbyshire Bird Report*, the number of species in the various categories is as follows:

Prior to the formation of the DOS	Not recorded since 1954	7
Extinct	Not recorded since 1992, but reintroduced	1
Very rare	Fewer than ten records ever	79
Rare	Ten or more records, but less than annual	51
Scarce	Fewer than ten birds occurring or pairs breeding annually	33
Uncommon	Between ten and 100 birds occurring or pairs breeding annually	48
Fairly common	Between 100 and 1000 birds occurring or pairs breeding annually	53
Common	Between 1000 and 10,000 birds occurring or pairs breeding annually	38
Abundant	More than 10,000 birds occurring or pairs breeding annually	9
TOTAL		319

Breeding species

Information about the 135 regular, more occasional (and in one case former) breeding birds of the county is based mainly on the data obtained from the Derbyshire Breeding Bird Survey (BBS) of 1995–99, and also from records submitted to DOS in the normal way during that period. The distribution maps of 116 of these species are shown at tetrad level. Eleven more erratic and occasional or former breeders are not mapped, while for a further nine rare and vulnerable species, presence is shown centrally in a 10km square.

While 1995–99 is now some time ago, the majority of the information is likely to be little changed for the majority of species. However, the numbers and distribution of some species have indeed changed since 1999, in certain cases markedly so. Some, such as Buzzard and Mandarin Duck, have increased: rather more, for example, Turtle Dove and Corn Bunting, have shown worrying declines. For 30 of these species, we include comparative maps for the periods 1995–99 and 2007–11, where those for the earlier period are essentially the tetrad maps repeated at 10km level. The 2007–11 maps were compiled by Dave Richardson from all records submitted to DOS during the period, and using the same criteria for presence and probable and proven breeding as in 1995–99. It should be remembered that 2007–11 was the period chosen by the BTO for its third Atlas. Many DOS members participated in the latter survey and hopefully fieldwork in the county may have been more intensive and thorough as a result.

The DOS survey was regarded as a considerable success. Taking the almost ubiquitous Wren as an example, this species was found in 697, or 96%, of the county's 724 tetrads.

The BTO's Common Birds Census (CBC) scheme ran from 1962 and had largely petered out by 2000, having been replaced by its BBS. The former gave invaluable insights into the bird densities of specific areas. In this book we have used a good deal of information from the six CBCs that continued into the 1990s. There were three such woodland censuses, at Shirebrook in the Magnesian Limestone Natural Area, Shiningcliff Wood in the Peak Fringe and Lower Derwent Natural Area and Shire Hill Wood in the Dark Peak Natural Area. Two of the three farmland CBCs were in the Dark Peak Natural Area, at Farfield Farm, Hope and Broadhay Farm, Hathersage. The other was at Culland, in the South Derbyshire Claylands Natural Area. All of these CBC sites are described in greater detail in the relevant Natural Area sections.

A census of the birds breeding on water authority land surrounding Carsington Water was attempted by members of the Carsington Bird Club in 2002, but the results were deemed unsatisfactory because of insufficient volunteers. Consequently, the area was divided into five compartments and were then worked sequentially in 2003–07.

Another valuable source of information derives from the BTO's Waterways Bird Survey, which was pioneered in our area by members of the Sheffield Bird Study Group (SBSG), along the Rivers Derwent and Noe in particular.

Other census work has concerned specific birds, such as Red Grouse and Golden Plover, while certain areas have been surveyed to produce indications of overall populations, as occurred with the EMP moors in 2010.

All data pertaining to rare breeding species is submitted annually to the Rare Breeding Birds Panel for their annual report, which is published in the journal, *British Birds*.

It has not been possible to include estimated county populations of most breeding species, save for some of the scarcer ones which are monitored annually (such as Peregrine and Ringed Plover), or those of specialized habitat (such as Common Sandpiper and Golden Plover). Attempts were made, using various methods, to produce county totals for common species but the results were so widely disparate that this was abandoned.

Data in tables

Where data has been presented in periods these have generally been of ten-year duration, but in order to accommodate data for the last two years the final period has been made 12 years long, for example:

Period	Records	Birds
1950s	–	–
1960s	1	1
1970s	1	24
1980s	12	22
1990s	21	38
2000–11	18	41
Totals	53	126

Non-breeding birds

The *Derbyshire Bird Reports* and monthly *Bulletins* for 1955–2013 are the principal sources of information for non-breeders. Generally 31st December 2011 is the cut-off date for inclusion but very important records have been included as close to the publication date as possible, for the sake of completeness.

Histograms (charts) showing occurrence by month or half-month are given for some species. These figures are based on the first sighting of any individual concerned.

The mean maximum Wetland Bird Survey (WeBS) counts of the wildfowl that regularly winter in the county are shown from September to March for the years 1986/87 to 1999/2000. It must be said that in very recent years these counts have been less comprehensive than at previous times and that even certain well-known sites, such as Ogston Reservoir, have not always received regular coverage.

Authentication of records

All records of species that come under the jurisdiction of British Birds Rarities Committee (BBRC) have been accepted by that body. Likewise, species which are considered by the DOS Rarities Sub-committee are only included if accepted by it. BBRC was formed to consider post-1958 records, and that of DOS in the 1960s. Relevant records prior to these periods have generally been determined by the editors, though in certain cases the DOS Rarities Sub-committee has been consulted for an opinion. For very old (pre-nineteenth-century) claims we have invariably gone along with the judgement of the Reverend Francis Jourdain; we are indeed fortunate that he took such an interest in Derbyshire's birds.

Since 1980 it has been standard practice to publish an account of first occurrences for the county in the *Derbyshire Bird Report*. In recent years the majority of these accounts have been provided by Rodney Key in his role as chairman of the county Rarities Sub-committee.

Ringing information and nomenclature

Information on ringing recoveries from the inception of the national ringing scheme until about 2000 was supplied by the BTO. This has been updated in certain important cases. In the information about ringing in particular, but also in the remaining text, the new unitary authorities of Rotherham, Barnsley and Sheffield are referred to under the collective name of the former metropolitan county of South Yorkshire. Foreign countries are generally spelt in an English format, for example, the spelling 'Estonia' is used, not 'Estoniya'. Again, these may differ from the information as supplied by the BTO in its ringing data.

Length of accounts

As far as possible all relevant information about each species is included, but this has resulted in markedly differing length of accounts, largely as the result of certain species (such as Peregrine, Common Sandpiper or Rook) having been the subject of intensive studies. No attempt has been made to equalize the lengths of the accounts.

Species distribution ranking

Where mention is made of a particular species' distribution ranking, in terms of how widespread it is in the county, this has been calculated on the basis of the number of tetrads in which it was found in the Derbyshire BBS (1995–99). Please refer to the 'Table of Breeding Species in Order of Frequency of Occurrence' (p. 343) for further information.

County boundaries

We publish all relevant records which relate to the county of Derbyshire, based upon modern political boundaries prevailing at the time. Thus we include, for example, records from the Rother Valley Country Park up to the year 1994, when it was transferred to Rotherham Borough and thus became part of South Yorkshire.

Rivers form the boundary between Derbyshire and some other counties. Records of birds in such locations are therefore treated as common to both counties (such as the 1852 Sooty Tern on the River Dove).

Observers

It goes without saying that a work such as this draws upon the records of a great number of observers and it would be an impossible task to attribute records to individuals. However, DOS has always believed that observers' names are an integral part of all published records (and not just rarities). Readers wishing to know more are therefore referred to the relevant *Derbyshire Bird Reports* and monthly *Bulletins* produced by the Society.

Mute Swan
Cygnus olor
A fairly common resident but rare in the Peak District.

Whitlock said that 'in former days' this bird was kept very numerously on the upper reaches of the River Trent, while Jourdain likened them to Canada Geese in existing in a semi-domestic state on ponds and ornamental waters. Some were not pinioned and so were able to move along the valleys of the county's three chief rivers. Both authorities quote Edwin Brown (in Mosley & Brown 1863), who said that their numbers had to be reduced because of damage to mowing-grass. Brown had seen as many as 50 within a quarter of a mile of the river at Walton-on-Trent. Frost said that they were fairly common in central and eastern Derbyshire but most bred in the Trent Valley with its greater abundance of aquatic habitat, and he considered the population to be reasonably stable.

Nesting Mute Swans in Derbyshire use a wide variety of sites including reservoirs, lakes and ponds, gravel pits and other industrial lagoons, and canals, rivers and streams. Breeding success was notably low during the 1970s and 1980s when many were affected by lead poisoning, which was particularly bad on the Trent (Hunt 1977). Since 1987, when anglers were banned from using lead shot weighing more than 28gm, productivity has shown a marked improvement, though other factors, such as improved water quality and an increase in breeding habitat, may also be involved.

The chart shows the number of successful breeding pairs from 1980 to 2011. The Derbyshire BBS (1995–99) found this species in 166 tetrads. Of these, breeding was proved in 95 tetrads, while it was probable in 17 and possible in a further 54 tetrads. Breeding was confirmed in 15 of the 10km core squares, compared with 13 in the 1988–91 Atlas and 16 in the 1968–72 Atlas.

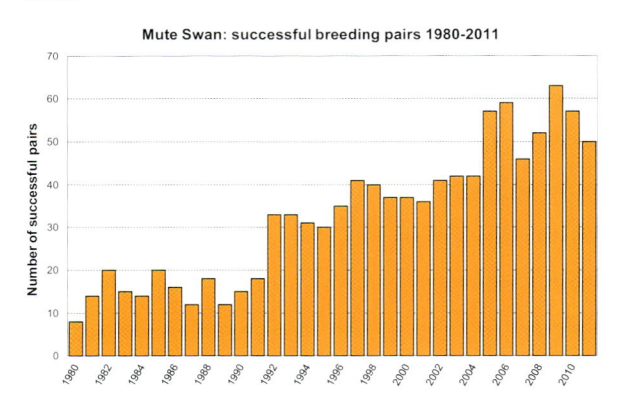

The survey map confirms the traditional preference for lowland waters, and the only breeding success in north-west Derbyshire during the recent survey was at Buxton Pavilion Gardens in 1999. Breeding was previously reported at this site in 1990 and 1994, and subsequently in 2001, 2005 and 2009. Pairs bred at Water-cum-Jolly-Dale in 1982 and 2009, Arnfield Reservoir in 1994 and at Monsal Dale in 2003. A nest on the River Lathkill in 2009 was the first breeding attempt on that river for 28 years.

Testimony to the Mute Swan's scarcity in the Peak District came from Combs Reservoir, where one from March to December 2001 was described as the first to take up residence there since the 1955/56 winter, while one at Chinley in November 2008 was described by two seasoned observers as their first in the 10km square SK08.

At Walton Dam in 2009 a pair hatched three white cygnets, of the so-called Polish morph, two of which survived to become fully grown.

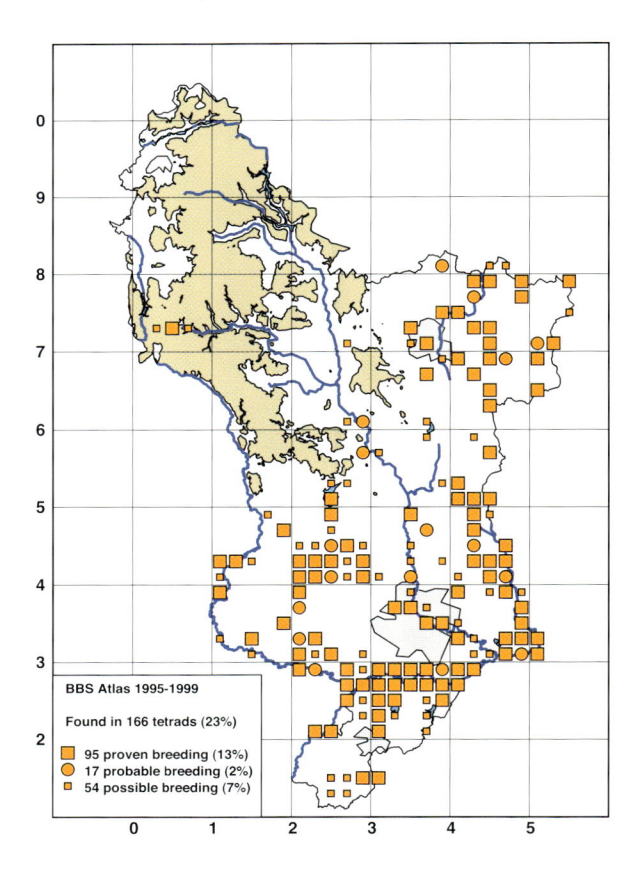

The burgeoning breeding population has produced a commensurate increase in the overall numbers present in the county, exemplified by the number of large herds recorded. The largest flocks known to Frost were both of 78, at Sawley Bridge in January 1958 and Swarkestone Lake in October 1971. Although herds of over 50 were noted occasionally in the 1980s, they became more regular during the 1990s and since the millennium have been reported from at least five sites every year. With the exception of the Straw's Bridge area and Carsington Water, all have been in the Trent or lower Dove Valleys. The table shows the number of sites where over 50 birds have been seen since 1980.

Year	Sites
1980	1
1981	–
1982	–
1983	–
1984	–
1985	–
1986	–
1987	1
1988	1
1989	1
1990	3
1991	1
1992	3
1993	2
1994	1
1995	–

Year	Sites
1996	–
1997	1
1998	3
1999	6
2000	8
2001	8
2002	7
2003	6
2004	6
2005	5
2006	8
2007	9
2008	8
2009	9
2010	10
2011	7

The most notable herd was near Catton, where 197 were counted on 4th January 1993. This was more than double the previous largest counts, of 92 at nearby Walton-on-Trent on 3rd April 1990 and 91 in fields at Church Wilne on 13th February 1999. Frost found that the average county maxima of the National Wildfowl Counts in the five winters from 1969/70 to 1973/74 was 136. This had risen slightly to 143 for the period 1986/87 to 1999/2000, though it is believed that the observer coverage in the latter period was inferior.

Mute Swans have occasionally been found in strange places, such as the central reservation of Derby's very busy outer ring-road on 3rd December 1996. Even stranger, in 1989 an adult was found in a butane gas-tank enclosure measuring about 10m by 21m at the Reckitt and Colman (now Reckitt Benckiser) factory, Sinfin, Derby. This enclosure holds six 20-tonne tanks and is surrounded by a 2m-high wire fence. Over the tanks is a sprinkler system and the only place the bird could have landed was a small gravel area. It was rescued by the RSPCA and was found to be uninjured.

The Mute Swan is probably one of the birds most familiar to the general public and as such it is very likely to be investigated if found dead or injured. This interest has provided 674 records of birds in the county which have been found dead or have been identified from ringing. Many of these reports have been multiple sightings of the same bird from year to year or in different locations. The addition of identifying tags such as colour-rings that can be read from a distance, is a great asset to detailed studies of a species and the large water birds are prime examples.

The majority of the records associated with Derbyshire (64%) have involved birds which have moved between 10km and 50km. Long-distance movement reports to and from the county have been very few at only 7% of the total records. The remaining individuals have only moved up to 10km from their place of ringing and these have not all been young inexperienced birds. Indeed, the oldest Derbyshire record was an adult ringed in 1977 at Attenborough, Nottinghamshire and found dead 20 years later at Draycott, only 8km away.

Regular ringing of the Mute Swan winter flock near Burton upon Trent has produced no fewer than 97 subsequent reports, but nearly all of these have been from elsewhere along the Trent Valley and its tributaries. The greatest distance movement from the Burton site was of one found dead at Ironville in 1966.

The earliest ringing recovery in the county was in 1958 and the longest movement was an adult bird ringed in Caernarvon, Gwynedd, in February 1982, which was found at Shardlow (200km east-south-east) 13 months later.

Bewick's Swan
Cygnus columbianus
An uncommon, but regular, passage migrant and winter visitor.

This species was not separated from the slightly larger Whooper Swan until 1830, and the first documented record in Derbyshire was of a herd of 11 birds by the River Trent in February 1845 (Whitlock). There were two further occurrences in the nineteenth century and only five in the first half of the twentieth century (Frost).

However, since March 1954, when a herd of 76 was seen at Combs Reservoir, Bewick's Swans have become regular passage migrants and winter visitors to the county, recorded in every year except 1975 and 2005. The highest numbers are usually seen during spring passage and a gathering of 100 birds on 28th March 1956, also at Combs Reservoir, remains the largest flock ever recorded. A herd of 87 over Long Eaton on 27th February 1976 is the largest seen in the Trent Valley. Several other flocks of over 50 birds were reported throughout the 1970s, particularly from the Longdendale complex of reservoirs and other waters in the north-west. Their flight directions suggest that they were birds en route to breeding grounds on the tundra of Arctic Russia from wintering grounds at Slimbridge, Gloucestershire and the Somerset Levels.

Period	Sites
1970s	149
1980s	95
1990s	78
2000–11	64

The figures in the table indicate that since the 1970s Bewick's Swans have been seen annually at fewer sites. There has also been an even more significant decrease in the total number of birds reported. Since 1980, flocks of over 30 have been recorded on only ten occasions, with a maximum of 54 at Staunton Harold Reservoir on 6th March 1992, although 68 (in separate flocks of 27, 28 and 13) visited Carsington Water on 27th October 1991. Since March 1996 there have been only six double-figure flocks of 11(2), 13, 16, 24 and 27. In 1999 no more than two birds were found at just four sites, prompting the comment in the *Derbyshire Bird Report* that this species was becoming 'very scarce', and there has been little change since the millennium, with none at all recorded in 2005. Almost all recent records relate to fly-overs, or birds staying only briefly. This downward trend, other than a small improvement in 2011 (illustrated by

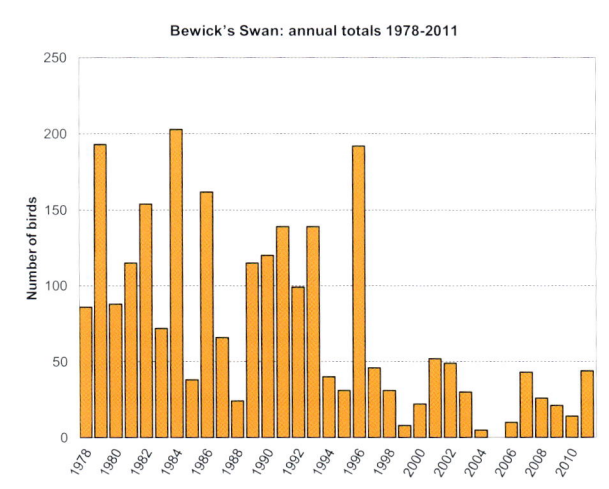

Bewick's Swan: annual totals 1978-2011

the chart, which gives the number of birds recorded from 1978 to 2011), may be explained in terms of changes in favoured wintering grounds elsewhere in England.

Although Slimbridge formerly attracted the biggest gatherings, the Ouse Washes on the Cambridgeshire–Norfolk border currently holds the largest wintering population of Bewick's Swans in Britain, while numbers have also been increasing in Lancashire. The decrease in Derbyshire may also be connected with the partial drainage of the River Idle washlands in north Nottinghamshire, where up to 174 wintered in the 1970s. It is believed that some of these birds moved into Derbyshire, particularly the Trent Valley, when these waters became frozen.

The first autumn arrivals are usually in October, and the earliest date is 2nd October (1977), when seven flew south-west over Elvaston Quarry. The majority normally depart by the end of March, although one appeared at Drakelow Nature Reserve on 4th May 1992, and another associated with Mute Swans on floodwater near Shardlow from 8th April to 11th May 1969. An exceptionally long-staying individual, which remained at Swarkestone Lake from 24th January to 8th August 1970, was able to fly but was considered to be sick.

The Wildfowl and Wetlands Trust introduced a regular ringing programme in 1967 and at least ten colour-ringed birds have been seen in Derbyshire, mostly in the Trent Valley, but also at Ogston Reservoir on two occasions (in 1982 and 1994). Among a flock of 48 at Borough Holme, Catton on 3rd January 1993, one bird was wearing a blue neck-collar which had been fitted in August 1991 or August 1992 in the Pechora Delta, Nenetski, Russia. One of a pair which was seen in the Trent Valley from 5th January to 6th March 1998 and again from 8th December 1998 to 3rd January 1999 had been ringed as an adult in August 1992 on Kashin Island, Korovinskaya, Russia. More recently, a colour-ringed bird was on the River Trent at Weston Cliff on 22nd December 2009, at Lowes Lane in the same month and Swarkestone in January 2010. It had been ringed at Murei Island in the Pechora Sea, Russia in August 2005 and was seen no fewer than 50 times before it was found in Derbyshire, having previously wintered in Germany, Belgium and Holland. It had been seen in the last country 11 days before its arrival in Derbyshire. Finally, one found dead at Rowlee Pasture on 7th February 2011 had been ringed at Arnhew, Holland on 16th December 2007.

Whooper Swan
Cygnus cygnus
An uncommon passage migrant and winter visitor.

Whitlock reported that he had never seen any wild swans in Derbyshire, but that Pilkington, Briggs and Brown considered them to be fairly regular on the Rivers Trent and Derwent. He believed that certain reports of wild swans referred to Mute Swans, some of them domesticated birds frozen out of their usual haunts. Frost said that Whooper Swans had been more regular than Bewick's throughout the first half of the twentieth century at least, but from 1958 to 1992 the smaller species was usually more numerous, with Whooper Swans again more frequent since 1993.

Period	Sites
1970s	46
1980s	56
1990s	108
2000–11	205

As the figures in the table indicate, this species has been recorded at far more sites since 1990 than in the 1970s and 1980s. This trend may be a consequence of a significant increase in the number of Whooper Swans wintering in Britain in the closing years of the twentieth century and in the early twenty-first century.

The incidence of large herds also confirms this increasing trend. Before 1993, herds of over 30 had been seen only twice, with 60 at Barbrook Reservoir in 1934 or 1935 and 50 at Fernilee Reservoir in December 1957 (Frost). There were three herds of over 30 during 1993–99, and 20 in 2002–11. Carsington Water claimed two of these earlier records with 56 (also seen over Chaddesden earlier in the day) on 25th March 1993 and 42 on 8th February 1997. The other record was of 64 moving north-north-east over Carr Vale on 4th February 1995. All but four of the flocks in excess of 30 since 2002 have occurred in March and are believed to relate to birds returning to Iceland from their wintering grounds on the Ouse and Nene Washes. Sixty flew north at Sutton Scarsdale on 14th March 2002, and 54 moved north-west at Netherthorpe on 13th March 2003. There was a very noticeable passage in March 2006, beginning with 49 (in flocks of 35 and 14) flying north-west at Stonebroom on 18th, 56 at Howden Reservoir (that had earlier flown over Grindleford) on the next day and culminating on 22nd when flocks of 50 and 66 moved north over Carr Vale. The larger of the two flocks had been observed earlier over Pleasley Colliery and was seen later at Pools Brook Country Park. In 2007, a herd, counted as 68 and 70, was seen at Baslow and Grindleford on 23rd March, and 70 were over Pleasley Colliery on 1st April 2009.

Although four swans over Bennerley Marsh on 20th September 1995 were thought to have been Whoopers, the earliest confirmed arrival was on 29th September 2011, when two were at Renishaw Park. The latest spring record came from Carsington Water, with a single bird on 18th–19th May 1996. There is also a midsummer record of a badly injured bird with a Mute Swan on the River Trent at Drakelow Nature Reserve on 13th July 1996.

Other interesting records are of two which stayed in an upland stubble field, well away from any open water, at Upper Loads for 12 days from 28th October 2002, and one with a yellow Darvic ring at Staveley in December 1996 and 2002. A colour-ringed bird seen at Willington Gravel Pits in October 2009 had been ringed two years previously at Martin Mere, Lancashire and had been seen in south-west Scotland, Cambridgeshire and back at Martin Mere again in the intervening period.

Bean Goose
Anser fabilis
A rare, usually feral, vagrant.

The earliest reference to Bean Goose came from J.J. Briggs, writing in 1849–50, who noted that they were occasionally seen on the River Trent; a further nineteenth-century record was of three shot on the River Trent in December 1890 at Anchor Church, Twyford and Repton (Whitlock). All 25 subsequent records have occurred since 1977, involving 77 birds, as follows:

Year	Location and date
1977	Kedleston, one from 27th January to 13th February
1977	Drakelow Nature Reserve, one from 19th to 27th April
1985	Newton Solney, one on 6th May
1987	Ogston Reservoir, eight on 15th January, arrived from the south in the early afternoon, and departed to the south-east, but returned later and remained until dusk
1988	Drakelow Nature Reserve, one on 9th January, arrived from the north-east
1989	Swarkestone Lake, two on 19th–20th May
1990	Wyver Lane, one from 14th January to 26th March and believed to be the same at Ogston Reservoir on 18th February
1995	Staveley Flash, one on 20th January, arrived from the north and departed eastwards
1995	Middleton Moor, one on 9th November
1995	Swarkestone Lake, two on 14th December, three from 15th December to 10th January 1996, four (briefly) on 31st December. Seen also at Weston-on-Trent and Barrow upon Trent
1995	Williamthorpe Nature Reserve, one flew east on 17th December
1999	Butterley Reservoir, 16 on 28th October, comprised two flocks (11 and five), which flew north-west/west without landing
2000	Pools Brook Country Park, two departed to the west on 4th January
2004	Ogston Reservoir, one on 9th October, and believed to be the same bird at Langwith on 13th October and Stonebroom on 19th November was considered to belong to the race *A.f. rossicus*, the Tundra Bean Goose
2005	Staunton Harold Reservoir, one on 27th December was considered to belong to the race *A.f. rossicus*, the Tundra Bean Goose
2008	Leash Fen, two on 16th November, departed to the north-west
2009	Ogston Reservoir, five on 22nd March
2009	Aston-on-Trent Gravel Pits, one on 19th December
2010	Ogston Reservoir, five on 18th December were considered to belong to the race *A.f. rossicus*, the Tundra Bean Goose
2010	River Dove, Scropton, four from 17th to 19th January and then at Dove Valley Lake on 23rd January
2011	Whitwell Quarry, three flew south on 11th November
2011	Long Eaton Gravel Pits, one flew east on 13th November
2011	Renishaw Park, two adults and two juveniles on 14th–15th November
2011	Willington Gravel Pits, six on 17th November and seven on 18th–19th November, also seen at Newton Solney on the latter date
2011	Long Eaton Gravel Pits, four flew in briefly from Nottinghamshire on 23rd November

Apart from the sighting of two at Swarkestone Lake in May 1989, those records involving more than one bird are the most likely to relate to wild birds.

Analysis by periods and months is shown in the tables:

Period	Records	Birds
1950s	–	–
1960s	–	–
1970s	2	2
1980s	4	12
1990s	6	24
2000–11	13	29
Totals	25	77

Month	Records	Birds
January	7	18
February	–	–
March	1	5
April	1	1
May	2	3
June	–	–
July	–	–
August	–	–
September	–	–
October	2	17
November	7	21
December	5	12
Totals	25	77

Pink-footed Goose
Anser brachyrhynchus
A common winter transient and scarce vagrant.

The evocative sight and sound of skeins of Pink-feet passing noisily overhead in classic V-formation has brightened many a local birdwatcher's day. It is likely that most of these sightings occur as a result of the regular transfer of birds between their major English wintering grounds in west Lancashire and south Lincolnshire and Norfolk. The great majority of this movement takes place from late September until March, and Derbyshire, particularly the northern half, lies on the main flight path. The largest numbers are usually recorded between October and January, often on clear and relatively calm mornings, with the majority of skeins, which sometimes comprise several hundred birds, reported north of a line from Buxton to Ilkeston. During the autumn period (September–November) passage is predominantly in an east to south-easterly direction, whereas from January to March it is generally west to north-westerly. The earliest ever such record was on 8th August (1954) when 60 flew south-east over Totley Moss. The latest spring record was of 320 moving north at Netherthorpe on 3rd April 2008.

In the late nineteenth century, Whitlock was aware of only occasional flocks of Pink-feet which flew over the upper reaches of the River Trent, but Frost commented that this may have been merely a reflection of the lack of observers elsewhere in Derbyshire at that time and was uncertain if any great change in status had actually taken place since Whitlock's day. However, increasing numbers (1980–2011) of this species have been recorded in recent years, as may be seen in the chart.

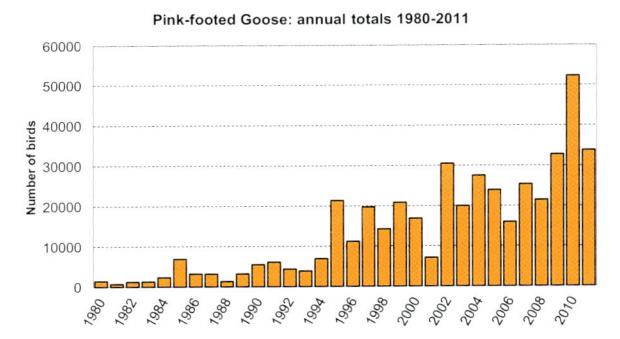

Pink-footed Goose: annual totals 1980-2011

Although some skeins may have been reported more than once, the data in the chart excludes all records of 'grey geese', the majority of which would almost certainly have been Pink-feet, and also skeins which were heard but not seen. Moreover, where a range of numbers was given for the size of the flock, the lowest figure has always been taken and the overall totals should therefore be regarded as conservative estimates. This does not disguise the spectacular rise in numbers from 1995 onwards, which has also coincided with a marked increase in the population wintering in Britain. For instance, on 13th December 2004, 152,514 were present in Norfolk, which represented over 50% of the world's population of this goose.

During prolonged spells of cold weather from January to March 1979, a combined total of about 1000 Pink-feet was reported, while from mid-November to mid-December 1985, a passage of 5000 birds was noted across the county. At the time these were considered to be exceptional numbers, but they have been dwarfed by counts in recent winters. In January 2002, an unprecedented passage, predominantly westerly or north-westerly, involved nearly 20,000 birds and, in January 2005, almost 25,000 were counted. The highest recorded counts at individual sites were of 3270 to the north-west at Strines Top on 21st January 2009, 3040 moving east-south-east at Ramsley on 13th October 2005, 3000 to the west/north-west at Beeley on 29th January 2005 and 2865 to the north-west over Pleasley Colliery on 27th January 2002. In the south of the county, the largest recorded movement was of 2000 flying west in nine skeins over Drakelow Nature Reserve on 29th February 1995.

Despite the greater frequency of sightings, instances of flocks alighting in the county remain unusual. The largest numbers have been 200 on 15th November 2011 at Renishaw Park (with Canada Geese, six White-fronted Geese and four Bean Geese), and 160 which fed on open moorland on Big Moor on 12th November 1998 before departing to the south-east. Such visits are normally short-lived, although (exceptionally) a flock of up to 17 Pink-feet remained at Barbrook Reservoir from October to December 1953.

The only other occasions when a group of more than ten wild birds has stayed overnight was in February 1984 when up to 16 were present on pasture adjacent to Leash Fen; December 2008, when a flock of up to 84 stayed at Carr Vale from 13th to 28th, feeding on farmland to the west of the reserve; January 2010 when 90 stayed in fields from 8th to 16th at Carr Vale and in the same month 48 on 17th–18th, reducing to 38 by 27th January, at Scropton.

The incidence of presumed feral or escaped birds has also risen significantly since 1980. These have been reported in all months at an average of a dozen sites each year, including a maximum of 21 localities in 1995, mainly in the Trent Valley and north-east Derbyshire. Up to seven have been seen together, though most records refer to one or two individuals, quite often associating with Canada Geese. Interestingly, two birds on the banks of Ogston Reservoir on 25th January 2005, which might have been considered to have been most likely feral, rose to join a flock of 250 flying north-west.

One of only two ringing reports for the county concerns a feral Pink-footed Goose, presumed to have been caught during the annual round-up of Canada Geese at Kedleston in June 1983, which was found dead at Ironville three months later. The more interesting recovery is of a wild bird ringed in Iceland as a juvenile in August 1951 which was found dead near Shardlow in February 1952, having covered a distance of 1635km.

A pair of Peregrines was observed to chase a skein of Pink-feet flying south over Crowden on 18th October 1998. The male successfully singled out one goose, which was then pursued by the female, although a direct strike was not made. On 13th October 2005, a skein of 90 landed at Barbrook Pools, apparently in response to the presence of a female Peregrine, and stayed there for 40 minutes.

White-fronted Goose
Anser albifrons
A rare winter visitor and transient. Most records probably refer to feral birds.

Whitlock regarded the White-fronted Goose as an occasional visitor to the Trent Valley. Occurrences usually coincided with severely cold weather, and even prior to 1789 it had been identified at Sinfin Moor and on the River Trent. These early records would almost certainly have related to wild birds, as would flocks of 65 flying east over Glossop on 21st January 1946 and 100 at Etwall on 20th February 1954.

Period	Records	Birds
1950s	2	101
1960s	10	31
1970s	23	90
1980s	39	442
1990s	53	314
2000–11	27	59
Totals	154	1037

This species has been recorded almost annually since the 1960s and with increasing regularity at the end of the twentieth century, but falling off again in the early twenty-first century, as indicated by the figures in the table. However, the majority of sightings have involved only one or two birds, and these are most likely to have been of feral or captive origin. A possible exception to this general observation concerns two adults with two Pink-footed Geese at Carr Vale from 10th to 12th January 1997 that were noted as being extremely wary and two first-winter birds at the same site on 28th December 2008. Presumed feral or escaped birds have been found in Derbyshire in all months of the year, but records of White-fronted Geese considered to refer to genuinely wild birds have all occurred in the winter period, between the extreme dates of 8th October (1972) and 20th February (1988). Despite the greater frequency of sightings, parties of more than ten birds are still exceptional. Since 1955 there have been 14 such instances, with only four involving over 50 birds.

Much the largest flock was one of 250 which passed south-south-east over Drakelow Nature Reserve on 15th January 1989. Two skeins totalling 100 birds headed west over Matlock on 24th December 1995, 80 flew north over Ogston Reservoir on 24th January 1986 and a party of 54 arrived at Carsington Water in mid-afternoon on 16th February 1996 (and were still present on the reservoir at dusk). These records probably all relate to movements of the wintering flock at Slimbridge, Gloucestershire, which comprises birds of the European race *A.a. albifrons*.

Unlike Pink-footed Goose, most flocks of this species have been recorded in the south of the county, and they are more likely to be seen on the ground. Although feral birds have sometimes remained for more than a month, including an individual at Willington Gravel Pits from 27th January to 14th June 1999, visits by wild birds are normally short-lived. However, on two occasions a party of over ten birds has frequented the Trent Valley for a few weeks in midwinter. In 1988 up to 12 were present from 8th January to 20th February, mainly at Swarkestone Lake, and 14 birds stayed at the same locality from 9th December 1995 to 7th January 1996.

The distinctive Greenland race *A.a. flavirostris* has occurred three times. One seen at Renishaw Golf Course and Breck Farm in April 1979 and two on Shipley Lake in February 1981 were probably feral, but three which briefly circled Willington Gravel Pits on 31st December 1992 were more likely to have been wild birds.

Lesser White-fronted Goose
Anser erythropus
A rare vagrant. All records probably refer to feral birds.

There have been about 18 records, believed to involve about 14 individuals. All are presumed to refer to escapes, as follows:

Year	Location and date
1976	Swarkestone Lake, an adult briefly on 8th June before it departed to the south-west
1978	Elvaston Quarry, an adult on 7th May
1984	Melbourne Pool/Swarkestone Lake, one from 30th September to 11th October
1984	Markeaton Park, Derby, one from 26th October to 24th May 1985 (possibly same as above)
1985	Drakelow Nature Reserve, one on 31st May and 2nd June
1986	Swarkestone Lake, an immature on 29th August and 1st September
1987	Drakelow Nature Reserve, one from 24th April to 16th June, and from 19th October to 13th December
1987	River Trent, Newton Solney, one on 18th December
1988	Drakelow Nature Reserve, one from 9th to 31st January
1990	Elvaston Quarry, an immature on 7th January
1993	Locko Park, one on 18th July
2006	Sutton Brook Lakes, an adult from 21st to 26th February
2008	Renishaw Park, one in January, February and October
2008	Pebley Pond, one on 28th October
2008	Scropton, one on 13th December
2009	Renishaw Park, a resident feral adult in February, and October to December

Year	Location and date
2010	Renishaw Park/Pebley Pond, a resident feral adult in February and November
2011	Renishaw Park, a resident feral adult in February, October and November

The 2008–09 records, with the exception of that at Scropton, are believed to involve a single bird. Analysis by period and month is as shown.

Period	Records
1950s	–
1960s	–
1970s	2
1980s	7
1990s	2
2000–11	7
Total	18

Month	Records
January	2
February	2
March	–
April	1
May	2
June	1
July	1
August	1
September	1
October	5
November	–
December	2
Total	18

Greylag Goose
Anser anser
A fairly common resident and uncommon breeder.

The earliest reference to Greylag Geese in the county came from Sir Oswald Mosley who stated that he found them plentiful on the River Dove around 1810 (Mosley & Brown 1863). There were, however, a few nineteenth-century records and Whitlock considered the species to be a very scarce visitor. The only other twentieth-century records of wild birds prior to 1978 were flocks of 43 over Taddington on 25th April 1946 and 87 at Hurst Reservoir on 14th March 1976 (Frost).

Although the Greylag is the only indigenous goose in Britain, the native wild population is now confined to north Scotland and the Western Isles. Since the late 1950s, reintroduction schemes have been undertaken in some regions, and feral populations have become established in many areas, most notably eastern England. An individual present at Kedleston Park for four months in 1957 represented the first occurrence of a feral bird in Derbyshire. There have been records in every year since 1961 with a marked increase from the 1970s onwards, predominantly, though not exclusively, from the south of the county.

Kedleston Park was also the location of the first proven breeding in Derbyshire. This took place in 1977 and broods of Greylag have been reported here in most subsequent years with a maximum count of 36 goslings in May 1999. Successful breeding was also noted at Allestree Park in 1980, but an attempt at Swarkestone Lake in the following year ended in failure due to disturbance. Renishaw Park has been the only regular breeding site in north Derbyshire, and it was first recorded here in 1988. During the 1990s, pairs also bred for the first time at Osmaston Park, Locko Park, Wyver Lane, Carsington Water, Holme Nook, Long Eaton Gravel Pits and Windley Lime Kilns. In addition, there were failed breeding attempts at Steetley Quarry and on the River Dove at Fauld. In 1992, at Staunton Harold Reservoir, an adult Greylag Goose accompanied by an adult Canada Goose was seen with seven hybrid young and in 2005 one paired with a Barnacle Goose and produced two hybrid young at Osmaston.

In the Derbyshire BBS (1995–99) it was found in only 21 tetrads; breeding was confirmed in 12 of these, while it was found to be probable in two others. The distribution map reveals the concentration of sites in the region of parklands to the north-west of Derby. Most of the confirmed breeding records derive from observers seeing pairs of adults with goslings, though birds can sometimes be seen sitting on their nests, usually on islands.

The protected environment of the estate parklands, with extensive areas of open water and restricted public access, obviously suits the species. Large numbers of feral birds have congregated at such sites most notably at Locko, Kedleston and Osmaston, all of which have held more than 100 individuals. The highest annual counts from each of these three localities between 1990 and 2011 are listed in the table.

Year	Locko Park	Kedleston Park	Osmaston Park
1990	70	8	7
1991	94	15	8
1992	48	15	23
1993	57	15	37
1994	125	5	66
1995	159	9	124
1996	60	41	142
1997	53	64	90
1998	104	108	143
1999	91	178	215
2000	49	190	206
2001	30	57	220
2002	60	114	248
2003	59	150	159
2004	114	200	100
2005	88	200	96
2006	180	253	15
2007	100	203	83
2008	118	203	–
2009	189	253	–
2010	180	190	–
2011	148	303	–

Recently, gatherings of over 100 birds have also been recorded at Drakelow Nature Reserve, Staunton Harold Reservoir, Renishaw Park and Long Eaton Gravel Pits. Smaller numbers may now be found at many other sites throughout most of the county, and, since 1992, Greylags have been reported from at least 30 localities each year, with a maximum of 61 in 2010.

The breeding population has continued to thrive in the twenty-first century, and pairs with young have been observed for the first time at locations which have included Sutton Brook Lakes, Swarkestone Lakes, the Trent–Derwent confluence, Barrow Gravel Pits, Darley Abbey, Bradley Hall, Pools Brook Country Park and Langwith. In 2003, a pair was reported to have nested in a sycamore at Osmaston Park. The maps for 1995–99 and 2007–11 show how the breeding range has expanded, particularly in the eastern half of the county.

The largest flock seen in Derbyshire was 561 at Long Eaton Gravel Pits on 13th October 2010. Large skeins were also reported in 1995 when 150 flew east over Two Dales on 2nd November and 200 flew east over Darley Dale on 24th December. A flock of 150 was seen flying north over Longdendale on 1st

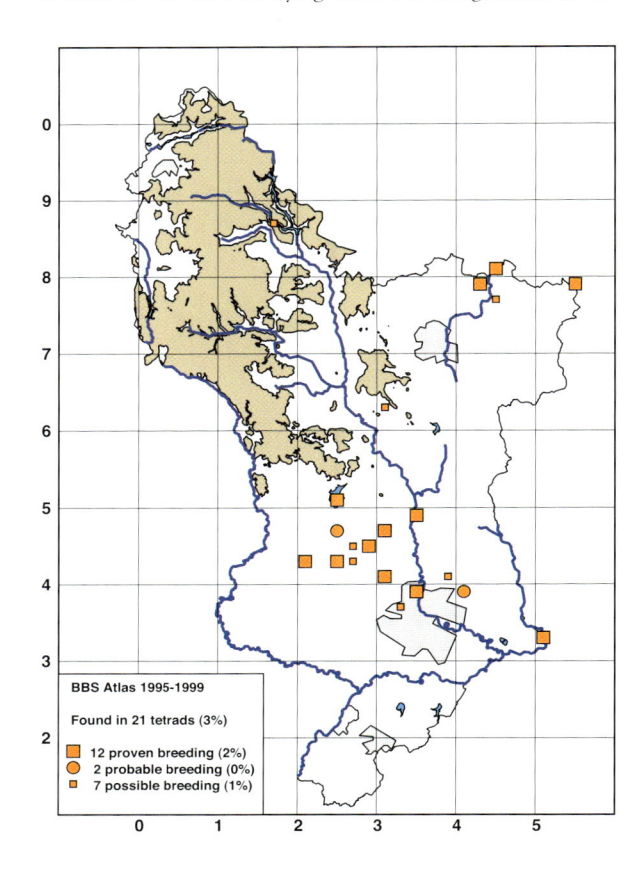

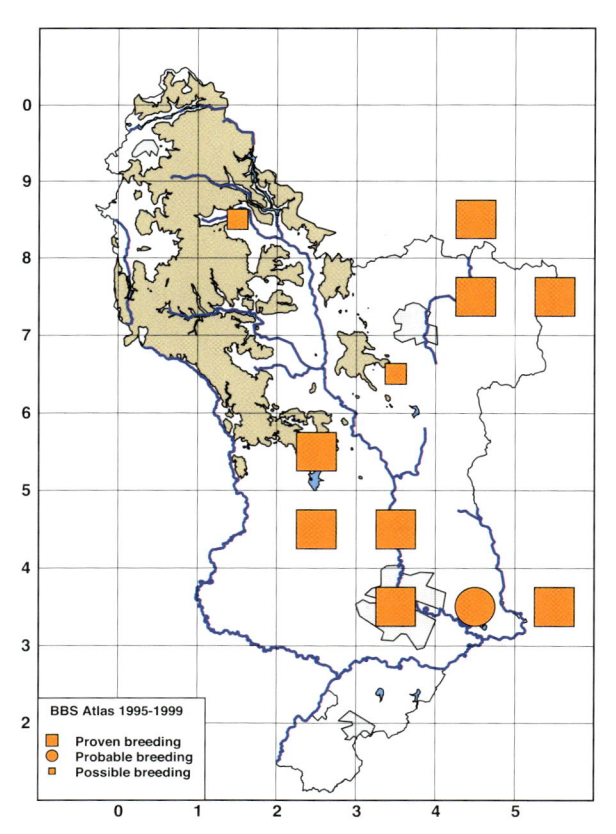

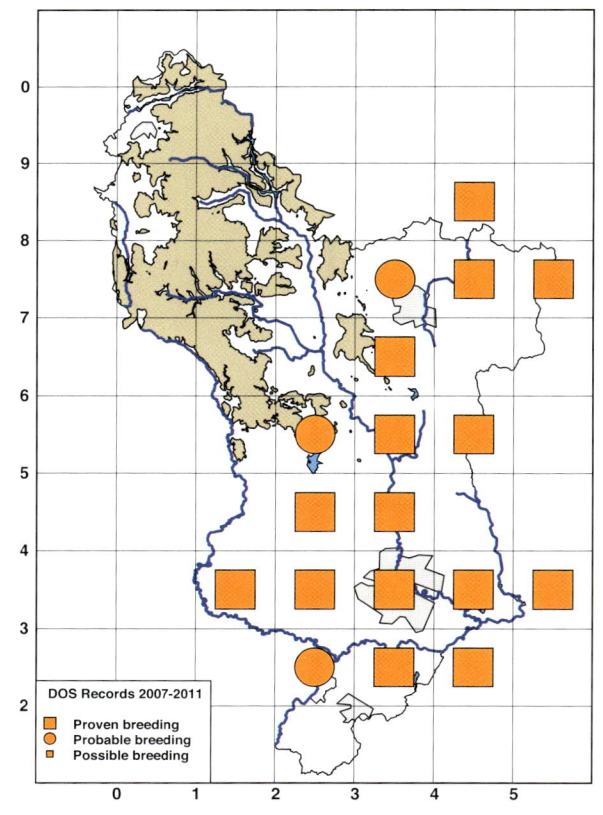

November 2003. These sightings may relate to the passage of wild birds across the county rather than local movements of the resident feral population.

All ringing records for Derbyshire have involved feral birds, usually caught during other trapping activity such as the annual round-up of Canada Geese at Kedleston. Four birds ringed here in 1981–82 were subsequently found dead, all within 18km of Kedleston. Two were goslings which died within two years, whereas the other two, both adults, lived for another four and seven years respectively. Other recoveries include an individual ringed near Brailsford in June 1970 which was controlled near Tatenhall, Cheshire the following year, and one that had been ringed at Tamworth, Staffordshire in June 2002 which was found injured at Coton Park in October 2003.

Canada Goose
Branta canadensis
A common resident.

This ubiquitous goose was first brought to England from its native North America as long ago as the seventeenth century. According to Jourdain it was extensively introduced to many of Derbyshire's waters around 1820–30, while Whitlock knew of large flocks at Chatsworth and Kedleston, with smaller numbers at several other sites. Although the Chatsworth colony became extinct, the population at Kedleston thrived and comprised the majority of the county's total of 900, as calculated by the Wildfowl Trust, in 1967–69 (Frost). This represented one of the largest groups in Britain at the time, and subsequent counts at this locality have included 1400 in September 1976, 1800 in September 1982 and a record total of 2000 in September 1987. Numbers here are much lower during the breeding season: for example, there was a total of 376 birds (which included 123 young) in June 1990 and subsequent counts have been much lower still.

Frost commented that, in addition to Kedleston, Canada Geese nested at many other parks, lakes and gravel pits in south Derbyshire. Elsewhere, even by the late 1970s, the species was still uncommon north of a line from Ashbourne to Belper, breeding only erratically at a handful of sites. Since then there has been a steady and sustained increase in the number of breeding localities recorded annually, which is summarized in the table.

Period	Average number of breeding localities per year
1975–79	7
1980–84	18
1985–89	25
1990–94	33
1995–99	30
2000–04	35
2005–11	40

The seemingly relentless expansion in range of this large, vocal and conspicuous goose is most clearly illustrated by a comparison of the findings from the 1968–72 and 1988–91 Atlases. The original census found breeding in only ten of the 27 10km core squares, whereas in the later survey it was proved in 18 squares. Furthermore, the most recent and also most detailed study, the Derbyshire BBS (1995–99), revealed its presence in every one of the 10km squares, and totalling 226 tetrads. Confirmation of breeding was obtained for 130 tetrads, while it was considered probable in another 35, and possible in a further 61.

The colonization of north-west Derbyshire has been well documented. Successful breeding first took place at Combs Reservoir in 1975, in the Goyt Valley (at Errwood Reservoir) in 1979 and in Longdendale in 1982. By the late 1980s, pairs were nesting at approximately eight sites, mainly reservoirs, each year and, in 1991, two pairs bred in the Upper Derwent Valley, at Howden Reservoir. Yalden (1999) commented on the very high survival rate of not only young birds but also overwintering birds in the Dark Peak, and suggested that the management of surrounding moorland by gamekeepers reduced the potential for predation. Shoreline surveys of Ladybower, Derwent and Howden Reservoirs, carried out annually since 1991, have charted the rapid increase in the local breeding population. Despite the intensive recreational pressures here, this had reached a combined total of 731 birds (including 187 young) in June 2004, with the relatively undisturbed Howden Reservoir holding by far the greatest number. Recent culling around the Upper Derwentdale reservoirs has had a significant impact on numbers with 178 adults and 47 goslings counted in 2010 and 161 adults and 100 young in 2011.

Moorland breeding in the Peak District was first recorded on Big Moor in 1986 and has subsequently been reported from several sites, often well away from any water, and at altitudes of up to 500m amsl.

The marked increase in the county's breeding population since the 1970s has also been reflected, to some extent, in the

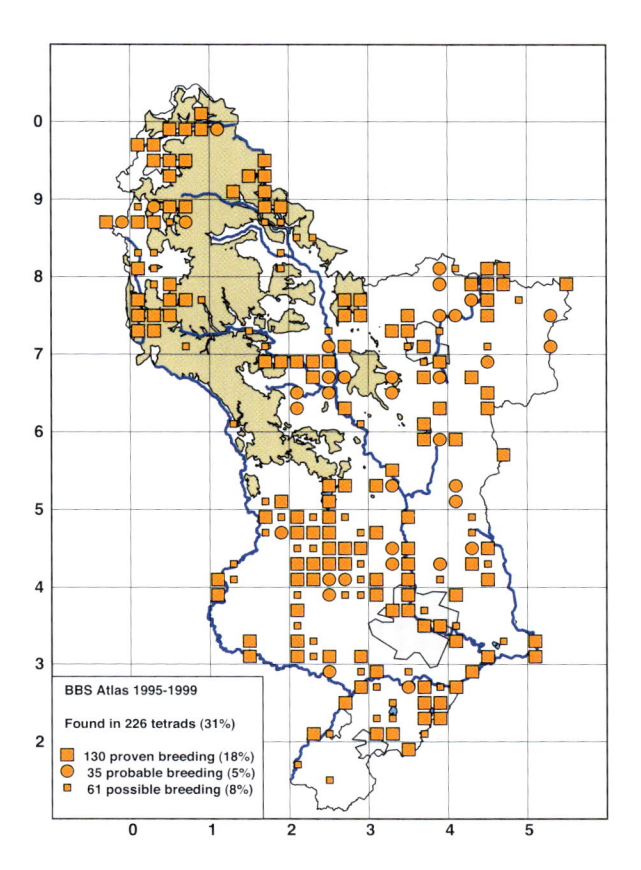

BBS Atlas 1995-1999

Found in 226 tetrads (31%)

- 130 proven breeding (18%)
- 35 probable breeding (5%)
- 61 possible breeding (8%)

monthly wildfowl counts between September and March over the same period. Frost revealed that the average maximum winter count from 1969/70 to 1973/74 was 1034, whereas from 1986/87 to 1990/91 it had risen to 2282, with a highest total of 2642 in November 1990. The average maximum during the four winters of 2000/01 to 2004/05 has been the slightly lower figure of 2158, though this might be partly as a consequence of poorer coverage of countable waters. However, the size of flocks at Kedleston has certainly decreased since the late 1980s, with the maximum count in all following years being 900, in December 1995. In common with Kedleston, Drakelow Nature Reserve attained its highest ever total in 1987, when 1300 were counted in January, but has hosted no more than 700 birds in any subsequent winter.

It is quite possible that overcrowding at these principal localities has been relieved by migration to other, more recently created sites. Since its completion in the early 1990s, Carsington Water has attracted increasingly large numbers of Canada Geese, including a peak count of 1084 in January 2005. Other locations in Derbyshire which have held over 750 birds are Osmaston Park (900 in October 1998) and Markeaton Park (800 in January 1983). In the Peak District, the biggest gatherings in winter are usually at Combs Reservoir where up to 300 have been recorded in recent years.

There have been at least 15 records, involving 21 birds in total, attributed to the smallest race of Canada Goose, *Branta hutchinsii*, otherwise known as Cackling Goose or Lesser Canada Goose, which breeds in coastal areas of western Alaska. The majority occurred from 1982 to 1986, with other records in 1992, 1995 and in 2008–09, when there were up to four together at Carsington Water and at several sites in the Trent and lower Dove Valleys. In addition, up to three of the race *B.h. leucopareia* were at Dove Valley Lake in January and April 2009, with one of the race *B.c. parvipes* at the same site in January 2009.

There have been over 1000 ringing records for this species and, in common with the Mute Swan, this high figure is partly attributable to the use of large colour-rings which also enable non-ringers to submit sightings. More than 30% of all reports have involved birds recovered within 1km of the ringing site, which has invariably been Drakelow Nature Reserve or Kedleston. However, there have also been 96 records of Canada Geese moving between southern Derbyshire and the Beauly Firth, Inverness. This undoubtedly relates to the well-developed pattern of moult migration undertaken each year by some populations from the north Midlands to this coastal region of north Scotland. The record for longevity is held by an individual which was ringed as an adult at Harewood Park, Leeds, in June 1968 and shot near Brailsford over 30 years later, in December 1999.

Barnacle Goose
Branta leucopsis
A recent resident, breeding in 1994 and from 2002 onwards. Most records probably refer to feral birds.

According to Whitlock, the first record of this attractive goose concerned an individual shot at Barlborough some time prior to 1789. The same author also documented a few occurrences in the nineteenth century, as did Jourdain. The next sightings believed to involve genuinely wild birds were of a flock of 25 flying south-east over Glossop on 20th October 1940 and a party of five on ploughland at Sutton Scarsdale from 20th to 22nd March 1969 (Frost).

Since 1958, escaped or feral birds have been recorded with increasing regularity and in growing numbers throughout Derbyshire. They have been reported annually from 1969 onwards, and at all times of year, with the majority noted in the southern half of the county, particularly the Trent and lower Derwent Valleys. The most frequented localities have been Drakelow Nature Reserve, Swarkestone Lake, Kedleston and Osmaston Park, and latterly Carsington Water. During the 1980s, this species was found at an average of five sites each year. The average had risen to ten in the 1990s and included sightings at no fewer than 21 localities in 1996.

Year	Location and date
1981	Drakelow Nature Reserve, nine with Canada Geese from 21st April to 1st May, when they departed to the north
1986	Swarkestone Lake/Barrow Gravel Pits, a flock of 18 was seen at both localities on 26th October
1987	Drakelow Nature Reserve, 53 arrived from the north on 13th November and at least 60 were present on the following day
1991	Rother Valley Country Park (now in South Yorkshire), four on 12th February were very timid and stood well out on the frozen lake
1994	Swarkestone Lake, 12 arrived from the north-east on 8th January, but departed within two hours. What was believed to be the same flock was found next day at Drakelow Nature Reserve, where 11 birds remained until 7th March
1995	Drakelow Nature Reserve, 19 arrived on 14th December, and 11 stayed until 7th January 1996
1996	Shipley Country Park, 17 flew south-east on 7th February
2005	Ogston Reservoir, 45 arrived from the north-east on 30th October and left to the south-east ten minutes later
2006	Ogston Reservoir, 40 on 14th January
2011	Carsington Water, one colour-ringed as a first-winter on 8th February 1999 at Caerlaverock, Dumfries and Galloway, was with the feral flock from 9th March to 7th May

Although it has become more difficult to distinguish the occurrences of wild stock from those birds of feral or captive origin, the following ten records are considered to be the most likely ones to refer to wild Barnacle Geese since 1978.

All of the above sightings have occurred between late October and early May, with the flocks in 1986 and 1987 thought to comprise birds from the north Russian breeding population, which usually winters in the Netherlands. These were believed to be en route to Bittell Reservoirs, Warwickshire, which was apparently a staging post on their journey to Skomer Island in Pembrokeshire. It is possible that the Ogston records of 2005 and 2006 merely related to the wandering of the Carsington Water flock.

Feral birds have bred sporadically in widely scattered parts of Britain for many years, although the population is not yet considered to be self-sustaining. In Derbyshire a pair bred at Kinder Reservoir in 1994, rearing one youngster; a further breeding attempt was made here the following year, but the outcome was unknown. An individual was also seen paired with a Canada Goose at Derwent Reservoir in 1997, and a Barnacle x Greylag Goose pairing produced two hybrid young at Osmaston in 2005.

Successful breeding has taken place at Carsington Water since 2002, when a pair raised two young. Numbers reached a maximum of seven pairs with 22 young in 2005, declining to only two pairs and five young in 2006. These birds are part of a feral population thought to have originated from Rocester, Staffordshire in January 2002 which has now become resident. The flock at Carsington Water initially numbered 15 birds, but by 2004 was in excess of 30 with a maximum of 58 in October 2005, but no young were raised in 2010 or 2011.

Hybrids have been reported on several occasions, usually singly, but five were seen together at Drakelow Nature Reserve in October 1988. A Barnacle x Canada Goose hybrid present at Osmaston Park in 2000 resembled a Lesser Canada Goose, as did two birds seen at Renishaw Park and Pools Brook Country Park in 1996 and 1997.

The only ringing recovery (other than the Carsington Water bird above) concerns an individual caught at Drakelow Nature Reserve in June 1985 and found long-dead at Allestree in August 1987, a movement of 22km north-east. In May 1997 an adult and two colour-ringed immatures were reported from Queen's Park, Chesterfield.

Brent Goose
Branta bernicla
A rare visitor. Most records probably refer to feral birds.

Pilkington (1789) said that Brent Geese had occasionally been seen on Sinfin Moor and Jourdain and Whitlock knew of three nineteenth-century records in the Trent and lower Derwent Valleys. Frost quoted four records from the first half of the twentieth century, including six birds on 11th February and ten on 23rd February 1947 at Newton Solney. The next appearance was a single bird at Ogston Reservoir on 14th March 1964, and since then there have been a further 63 records involving a total of 134 birds. The table highlights how much more regular this species has become since the 1980s.

Period	Records	Birds
1950s	–	–
1960s	1	1
1970s	1	26
1980s	12	21
1990s	21	35
2000–11	29	52
Totals	64	135

Almost half of the records have come from the Trent Valley, particularly Willington and Swarkestone Lake, and Foremark Reservoir. Carsington Water has become the most favoured site in the county with eight occurrences, while single birds have visited Ogston Reservoir six times and Carr Vale on four occasions. Brent Geese have also been recorded at Allestree, Bennerley Marsh, Middleton Moor, Staveley and Alport Castles.

This species has occurred in all months from September to June, with extreme dates of 16th September (2011) to 3rd June (1993 and 2001). However, all sightings in October and from April to June have involved single birds, and it is highly likely that many relate to individuals of feral origin.

The earliest autumn date concerning undoubtedly wild birds is 7th November 1994 when seven (including one juvenile) were present in the afternoon at Foremark Reservoir, while the latest spring date is 22nd March 1992 when two adults and three immatures were seen at Staunton Harold Reservoir.

The largest flock ever recorded in Derbyshire was a party of 24 birds which landed in a field near Willington on 18th February 1979. They were observed cropping grass, and had presumably been driven inland by the severe blizzard conditions affecting much of Britain a few days earlier. A skein of 21 flew east over Church Wilne Reservoir on 3rd October 2005. Apart from a party of nine which arrived and fed with Wigeon at Staunton Harold Reservoir on 12th March 1983, all other records have been of one to four birds. The majority of visits are short-lived, especially those involving more than one bird. The longest stay concerns an individual, which was probably injured or sick, present at Middleton Moor from 15th May to 3rd June 1993.

On those occasions when Brent Geese have been ascribed to a specific race (approximately half of all records) all but one has been identified as the dark-bellied form, *B.b. bernicla*. The exception was one of the pale-bellied race, *B.b. hrota* which flew south-west with Greylag and Canada geese at Long Eaton Gravel Pits on 21st December 2008.

Month	Records	Birds
January	9	10
February	8	34
March	8	22
April	6	6
May	2	2
June	2	2
July	–	–
August	–	–
September	1	1
October	6	26
November	11	18
December	11	14
Totals	64	135

Egyptian Goose
Alopochen aegyptiaca
An uncommon resident of feral origin.

Egyptian Geese were first imported into England over 200 years ago, but the species was not admitted to the British List until 1971 following the establishment of a viable breeding population, mainly in north Norfolk. Several were seen in the Trent Valley during the nineteenth century (Whitlock; Jourdain) and Frost gave details of three further sightings prior to 1940. The next occurrences were in the spring of 1966 when four birds were at Westhouses Flash and one was at Ogston Reservoir. Since 1970, records have become more frequent and, apart from the three-year period from 1993 to 1995, Egyptian Geese have been seen annually in Derbyshire.

The figures in the table indicate that the total of records and birds remained fairly constant during the last three decades of the twentieth century, although numbers can only be approximate as birds often wander between sites. However, reports of this species have increased significantly in recent years.

Period	Records	Birds
1950s	–	–
1960s	2	5
1970s	32	43
1980s	30	31
1990	27	47
2000–11	92	255
Totals	183	381

Egyptian Geese have been found throughout the county, but the Trent Valley has provided most of the sightings, and records from the north and west are still relatively uncommon. Birds have occurred in every month of the year, usually singly, though up to ten have been seen together on a few occasions. The highest numbers have usually been at Long Eaton Gravel Pits, with a maximum of 12 on 1st October 2007. This equalled the previous largest flock of 12 birds, possibly released, in a field near a farm at Weston Underwood on 4th August 1998.

For many years Egyptian Geese have bred at Attenborough Gravel Pits in Nottinghamshire. Therefore it came as no great surprise when breeding was confirmed for Derbyshire in 2008 when a pair nested in a hole in a dead ash tree at Long Eaton Gravel Pits. This was followed by nesting attempts at the same site in 2009 (two attempts) and 2010–11; unfortunately all of these failed. However, in the latter year a pair was seen with eight goslings on the River Trent near Twyford in August, and they bred successfully at Barrow Gravel Pits in 2009 and 2010.

Ruddy Shelduck
Tadorna ferruginea
A scarce feral visitor.

The first record was of one killed at Weston-on-Trent on 18th April 1913 (Frost). The next sighting was not until 1975 when two were present at Drakelow Nature Reserve from 11th to 19th May. The analysis by periods is shown in the table and the chart shows, for the same periods, numbers of birds per month based on the dates of arrival.

Period	Records	Birds
1970s	4	7
1980s	9	14
1990s	15	25
2000–11	21	22
Totals	49	68

Four adults were seen at Ogston Reservoir on 21st August 1999. Groups of three were recorded at Swarkestone Lake on 17th September 1978, at Combs Reservoir (flying north-west) on 31st August 1999 and at Willington Gravel Pits (all juveniles) on 4th September 2006. All other reports have concerned one or two birds. Ruddy Shelduck have been recorded in every month. Most sightings are from the Trent Valley with Drakelow Nature Reserve particularly favoured. Elsewhere, Ogston Reservoir has been visited on six occasions, Carsington Water three times, and Carr Vale two. There are single records from Birdholme Wildfowl Reserve, Kedleston Park, Markeaton Park, Queens Park and Rother Valley Country Park (now in South Yorkshire).

Although genuinely wild birds occur in northern and western Europe, including Britain, especially in 'invasion years' such as 1994, most records of Ruddy Shelduck are attributable to escapes from captivity and their descendants (Vinicombe & Harrop 1999). This is presumably the case with those occurring in Derbyshire.

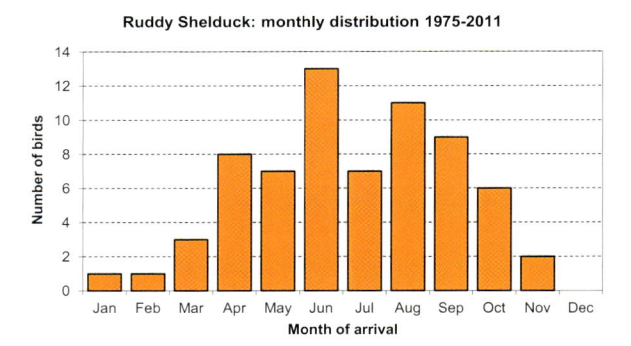

Shelduck
Tadorna tadorna
An uncommon, but regular, winter visitor, passage migrant and summer visitor. A scarce breeder.

Shelduck are colourful and conspicuous ducks which have occurred on many waters, both large and small, throughout the county. They may be found at all times of the year, not only as winter or summer visitors, but also as passage migrants. In the nineteenth century, Whitlock considered them to be occasional visitors, whereas by 1978, Frost regarded Shelduck as quite regular migrants. He commented that probably most occurred in late summer, and flocks of up to 50 flying east over Glossop at that time of year were believed to be birds on moult migration from Cheshire to the Heligoland Bight. However, apart from late summer flocks of up to 35 birds at Barbrook Reservoir, Frost thought there were few other records to suggest that such movements took place on a significant scale across Derbyshire.

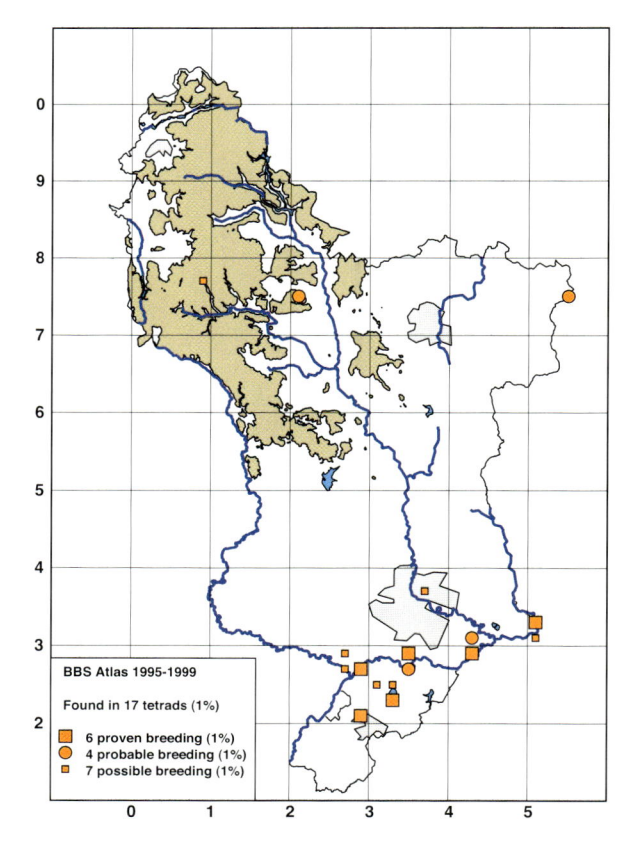

Shelduck have undoubtedly become much more widely reported in recent decades. During the 1970s this species was recorded at an average of 15 localities each year. Throughout the 1980s the average was 26, and in the 1990s it had risen to 30, including a maximum of 38 sites in 1994. Although the majority of sightings still involve single-figure counts, gatherings of 15–25 birds are not uncommon. The largest numbers now tend to occur between March and June, most notably at gravel pits in the Trent Valley. Surprisingly, there have been only three instances of flocks in excess of 35 birds from 1970 onwards, as follows:

Year	Location and date
1970	Staunton Harold Reservoir, 50 flew south-west on 7th November
1981	Ogston Reservoir, 36 arrived from the west on 7th November
2004	Aston-on-Trent Gravel Pits, maximum of 37 on 16th May

In July 1966 a pair with ducklings on the River Trent at Twyford constituted the first breeding record. Successful breeding was not proved again until 1981, but has taken place in most subsequent years, with a highest total of six pairs in 1990 and 1993, and seven in 2004. The advent of breeding in the county mirrors the greatly increased population of Shelduck recorded throughout England between the two BTO Breeding Atlas surveys. Increased population size and saturation of original estuary and shore habitats, as well as local habitat changes such as nutrient enrichment of lakes and pools, have made inland sites more suitable (1988–91 Atlas).

With the exception of Kedleston Park, Middleton Moor, Doveholes and Whitwell Quarries and Shirebrook Colliery, all breeding attempts have occurred within the Trent Valley, where gravel pits have always been the most commonly frequented breeding habitat. Aston-on-Trent Gravel Pits has been the most productive locality, with broods of young seen in ten years between 1998 and 2011. Other locations where Shelduck have bred are Willington, Long Eaton, Swarkestone and Barrow Gravel Pits, Catton, Newton Solney, Elvaston Quarry and Church Wilne Reservoir. This relatively limited distribution is reflected in the findings in the Derbyshire BBS (1995–99) as illustrated by the map, showing it was found in only 17 tetrads, with breeding proved in just six and probable/possible in a further 11.

Nest sites in Derbyshire have been situated within tree roots and the burrows of rabbit and badger, while prospecting birds have been seen among concrete boulders. However, confirmed breeding records usually come from the sighting of adults with ducklings from late May onwards.

Birds return to breeding areas between December and early spring.

Mandarin
Aix galericulata
A fairly common but localized resident. An uncommon breeder.

This exotic duck is a native of China, Japan and eastern Russia. It was admitted to the British List in 1971, having established a feral population, based largely in south-east England, which was descended from escapes and birds deliberately released from captivity. Frost defined its status as that of a rare vagrant and gave details of all six occurrences in Derbyshire up to December 1977, including the first record which was of a male on a pond at Repton on 14th December 1963. There was a further sighting in March 1978 and a total of about 30 records during the 1980s. However, since the early 1990s, Mandarins have been reported from at least 20 locations each year, and in markedly increasing numbers, mostly on wooded pools, streams or rivers in western and central areas of the county.

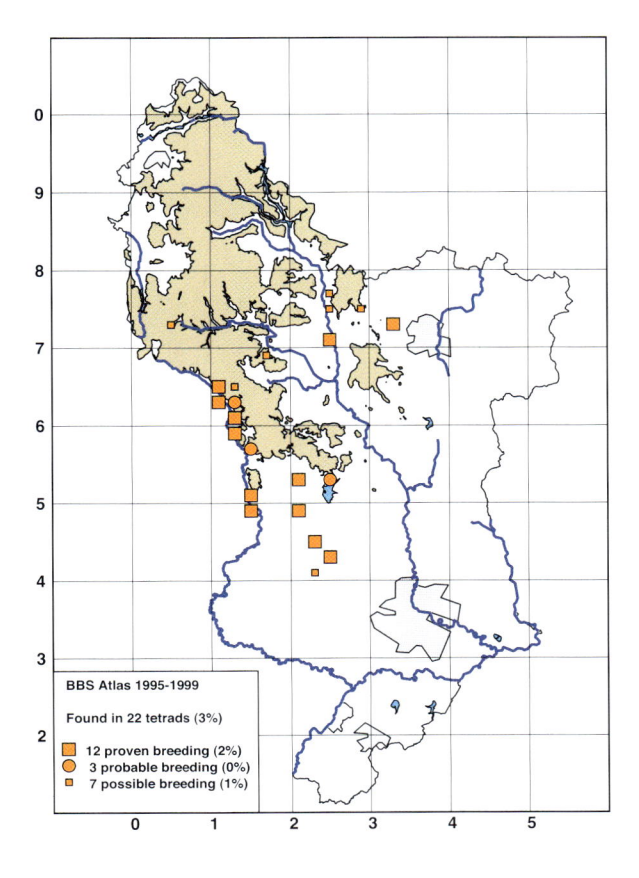

It is virtually certain that Mandarins bred in Osmaston Park during 1983–86 following numerous releases at this site since 1980, although the first 'wild' young were not discovered until June 1986, on a small lake about 1km from Osmaston (Frost 1987). The next proven breeding was on the River Dove near Hartington, when a female was seen with at least five young in July 1991, and further broods have been found in almost every year since 1995, increasing to about 30 by 2011. This shy and secretive nature of the species during the breeding season undoubtedly leads to underrecording, and broods may have been missed on some watercourses, especially the smaller streams. Nests, especially in woodland, are very difficult to find, but there are several records of birds seen at the entrances to tree holes. At Linacre Reservoirs in 2011 a female was found on nine eggs in an owl nest-box.

The Derbyshire BBS (1995–99) revealed proven breeding in 12 tetrads, probable breeding in three and possible in seven. The distribution map shows that all evidence of confirmed breeding was obtained from sites in the western half of central Derbyshire, particularly along the River Dove between Crowdecote and Thorpe.

In the twenty-first century, there has been a considerable expansion of the breeding range. In addition to the Rivers Derwent, Wye and Dove, breeding has occurred at Stoke Brook, Bradford Dale, Monk's Dale, Linacre Reservoirs, Walton Dam, the Ecclesbourne Valley, Kedleston Park, Calke Park, South Wood, Ticknall Limeyards, Dimminsdale and Ogston Reservoir. The maps show how the number of 10k squares with confirmed breeding has more than doubled between 1995–99 and 2007–11.

There have been occasional reports of male Mandarin mating with female Mallard. Frost gave details of two failed breeding attempts in 1973 at Walton Dam, Chesterfield, while in 1999, on the River Bradford, a male was seen with a female Mallard and five ducklings, which were possible hybrids. In addition, a female Mandarin was believed to be paired with a male Wood Duck at Kedleston Park in 2004.

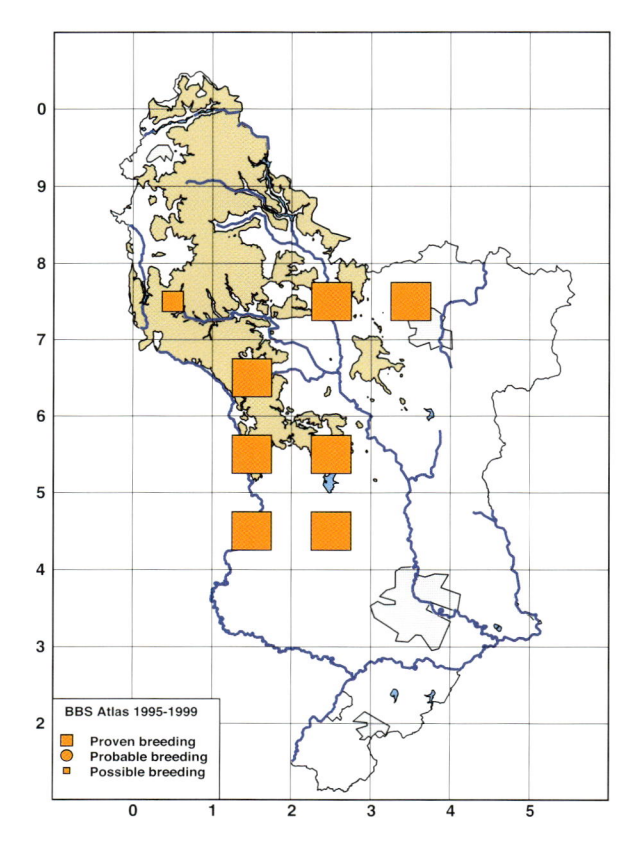

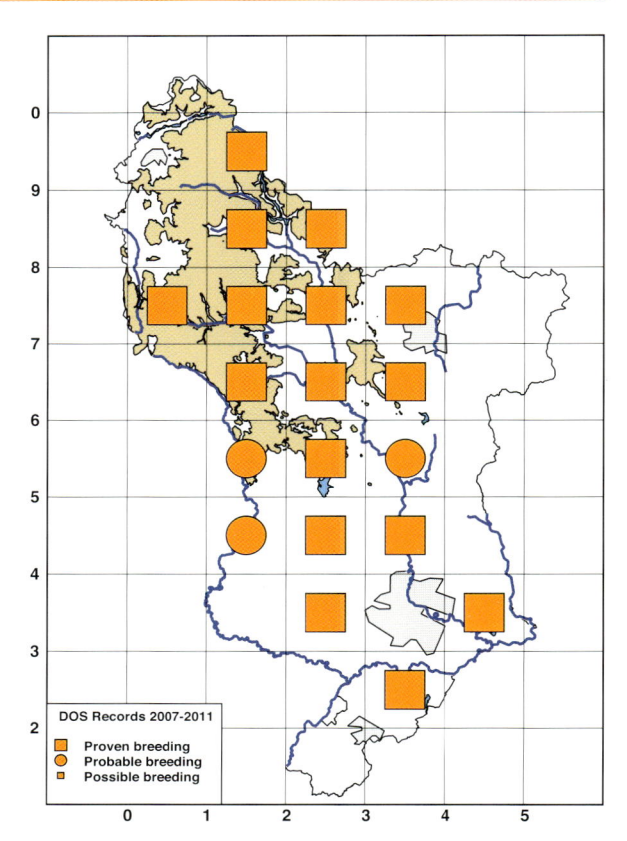

BBS Atlas 1995–1999	DOS Records 2007–2011
■ Proven breeding ● Probable breeding ▪ Possible breeding	■ Proven breeding ● Probable breeding ▪ Possible breeding

Prior to the mid-1990s, although this species was likely to occur outside the breeding season on any water, from small ponds to large reservoirs, it was invariably present in only small numbers, with groups of more than four being exceptional. However, there has been a dramatic upsurge in recent years, most obviously at Bradley Dam, which has become not only the county stronghold for this duck, but also one of its most important wintering sites in Britain. The first significant count here was of 89 in December 1996, with subsequent gatherings of over 100 occurring since 2003, including a current maximum of 251 in January 2008. The table shows the maximum count for all months from September to March at this site.

Despite such impressive numbers, birds at Bradley Dam can be elusive and they apparently readily disperse to other ponds, rivers and streams in the vicinity. Elsewhere, the trio of redundant reservoirs at Linacre held a maximum of 156 in November 2010; the River Derwent at Froggatt had 91 in December 2002; and the River Wye at Rowsley had 76 in February 2010.

Kedleston Park, Wyver Lane and Allestree Park have respective maxima of 80, 44 and 43, while other sites that have held over 25 Mandarins are the River Wye near Bakewell, Chatsworth Park, Norbury, Ednaston Dam and Thornbridge Hall Pond.

The female of a pair at Allestree Park in April 2004 was an albino. Another unusual report was of one found as a raptor kill in Chatsworth Park on 5th April 1996.

Month	Max count
September	55
October	124
November	200
December	176
January	251
February	95
March	74

Wigeon
Anas penelope
A common visitor and passage migrant, especially in the south. Rare in summer.

Flocks of Wigeon are a familiar sight and sound, mostly between September and April, at a number of reservoirs, flooded gravel pits and lakes throughout the county. These birds form a small proportion of the internationally important British and Irish population, which may, at peak times, account for more than half of those wintering in north-west Europe (1984–88 Winter Atlas).

Whitlock considered Wigeon to be fairly common winter visitors to Derbyshire in the late nineteenth century, reporting flocks of up to 100 in the Trent Valley. Apparently the Longdendale reservoirs were regular haunts, as were some of the wet moors and streams near Castleton. Wigeon now visit the north-western waters only infrequently and are no longer found on wet moorlands. Numbers in the first half of the twentieth century appear to have been relatively low, with no more than 24 together until 1948 when 200 were reported from Repton

(Frost). Since then, far greater observer coverage has produced more detailed information, enabling a much clearer pattern of occurrence to be established. Although sizeable flocks of Wigeon winter every year in relatively few places, small numbers winter at, or pass through, numerous other sites throughout the county. Larger numbers may congregate in the Trent Valley in severe weather, most notably in February 1963 when possibly as many as 2000 were present on the River Trent.

Throughout the 1960s, Ogston and Staunton Harold Reservoirs often hosted flocks of over 100 birds but, shortly after its creation in the early 1970s, Church Wilne Reservoir became the most important wintering site. During the 1980s, gatherings of over 1000 birds were not infrequent here, with highest counts of 1634 in March 1985, 1520 in January 1986 and 1523 in January 1987. This concrete-sided reservoir has provided a safe roosting area for birds feeding in the nearby Trent, Derwent and Soar Valleys. However, since the late 1980s, numbers at this site have gradually declined, and in recent winters much higher counts have come from other Trent Valley sites, such as Willington, Barrow and Aston-on-Trent Gravel Pits, and elsewhere, at Carsington Water.

The maximum counts at all sites which have recorded gatherings of over 300 birds since 1990 are as follows:

Site	Date	Max count
Carsington Water	November 2003	1411
Barrow Gravel Pits	January 2003	800
Dove Valley Lake	January 2005	750
Church Wilne Reservoir	January 1996	734
River Derwent at Ambaston	December 2010	650
Aston-on-Trent Gravel Pits	December 2003	600
Willington Gravel Pits	January 2003	560
Long Eaton Gravel Pits	January 2006	440
Staunton Harold Reservoir	February 1996 and December 2000	400
River Derwent at Draycott	December 2010	370
Ogston Reservoir	January 1990	323
Foremark Reservoir	March 2002	303

A few other sites outside the Trent Valley region, such as Scropton, Wyver Lane, Bennerley Marsh, Lower Hartshay, Carr Vale and Renishaw Park have held three-figure flocks on several occasions since 1990.

The earliest birds sometimes appear in July, but are more likely in August, with a steady build-up of numbers thereafter. The highest totals usually occur between December and February, as indicated in the table. The figures represent the mean maximum monthly counts obtained during the WeBS throughout Derbyshire in all winters from 1986/87 to 1999/2000.

Month	Max count
September	44
October	184
November	453
December	792
January	731
February	806
March	558

Numbers decrease in March and the last flocks are seen in April. Lingering birds can often be found in May, and although breeding has yet to occur, there have been several instances of individuals or pairs remaining throughout the summer, though sometimes these are known to be injured stragglers from the winter. A pair summered at Howden Reservoir in 1949 but there was no evidence of breeding. However, a pair present at Barbrook Reservoir between March and June 1990 probably attempted to breed; copulation was noted and the female disappeared for long periods, though neither nest nor young were seen. A pair also frequented the same site during April and May in the following year. Birds seen in summer at other sites have shown nothing to suggest breeding.

Wigeon have nested on two recent occasions within 2km of the county boundary at Redmires Reservoir, South Yorkshire, and future breeding in Derbyshire must be considered possible, particularly as the British population is currently increasing both in numbers and range.

One ringed at Loch Leven, Perth and Kinross, Scotland in March 1982 was shot at Stoneyford in January 1986.

American Wigeon
Anas americana
A very rare vagrant.

For a long time this duck had been predicted to occur within Derbyshire, especially in view of records in all peripheral counties, but it was not until 2002 that this happened. In that year, a male was present on 3rd and 4th November at Langley Mill Flashes, a site that straddles the Derbyshire–Nottinghamshire border. It then moved some 5km south along the Erewash Valley to Bennerley Marsh, where it remained with a small flock of Wigeon from 8th to 14th November. It was thought to have been present at Langley Mill Flashes from at least 17th October, but was very elusive and not positively identified there; Key (2003a) wrote an account of the event. The second county record was of an adult male at Drakelow Nature Reserve from 1st to 6th November 2006. The third record was in 2010 when a female was found in the company of five Eurasian Wigeon at Long Eaton Gravel Pits on 15th October. It was photographed and watched for 25 minutes before flying off south-west with the small flock of Eurasian Wigeon.

This species breeds in Canada and the northern USA, and winters south to Central America. Records were considered by BBRC up to 2001, by when there had been about 350 UK records.

Gadwall
Anas strepera
A fairly common winter visitor and an uncommon resident.

Gadwall are largely found on eutrophic waters, often with abundant waterside and submerged vegetation, and are a familiar sight at wetlands in lowland Britain. The wintering and breeding populations have both increased and expanded in range, especially since about 1975. The first breeding took place in Norfolk in the 1850s, when a wild-caught pinioned pair was set down. Although known previously as a wintering bird in small numbers, it is thought that the offspring from this pair gave rise to the substantial East Anglian population from which more widespread colonization occurred (Taylor *et al*. 1999).

In Derbyshire, the first record was of three females at Hardwick Park on 23rd October 1920. A single bird was at Osmaston in 1936 and one or two visited the south-west of the county each year from 1943 to 1948. One was shot at Catton in 1954 and since 1956 the species has been recorded annually. In 1957 a pair bred successfully at Locko Park, raising eight young. No further breeding took place until 1979, but from that date Gadwall have bred annually, in generally increasing numbers.

Frost considered this species to be a relatively scarce visitor, which might appear on almost any stretch of water mainly in winter. He also suggested that numbers had been boosted as a result of releases by wildfowling associations and shooting clubs. In the late 1970s, Gadwall were reported from about 20 sites each year, but since the mid-1990s the average has risen to over 40.

The mean maximum monthly counts as recorded during WeBS between September and March for Derbyshire between 1986/87 and 1999/2000 are as follows:

Month	Max count
September	35
October	41
November	54
December	61
January	53
February	52
March	42

Although Gadwall can be found throughout the county, they are uncommon in the Peak District and their main wintering sites are in the south, predominantly within the Trent Valley, and the north-east. Church Wilne Reservoir has for a long time been attractive to this duck. This pumped and entirely enclosed raw-water storage reservoir does not, at first sight, appear to be an ideal habitat for Gadwall, but flocks of more than 50 birds have often been observed feeding close to the vertical concrete walls. The maximum here was of 105 in January 1994. Other southern sites where large numbers have been counted are Drakelow Nature Reserve, where the largest gathering has been of 162 in January 2005; St Chads Water, where there were 140 in February 2006; and Aston-on-Trent Gravel Pits, with 185 in September 2010. In the north-east, the greatest numbers have been reported from Renishaw Park, which holds the current county record of 255 in October 2009, and at Carr Vale, where there were 144 in October 2005. The only other site to support three figures is Carsington Water, where there were 131 in December 2006.

The Derbyshire BBS (1995–99) obtained proven breeding in 13 tetrads, and probable or possible breeding in 14. The map indicates a pattern of distribution which, in common with the wintering population, has concentrations both in the north-east and in the south.

The county breeding stronghold in recent years has been the north-east, where regular breeding sites are Carr Vale (which had eight broods in both 2003, 2004 and 2009), Renishaw Park, Belph and Creswell. Pairs have also nested at least occasionally at Scarcliffe, Shirebrook, Steetley Quarry, Whitwell, Williamthorpe, Staveley, Poolsbrook Marsh, Arkwright and Old Whittington Sewage Farm. In the south, breeding has been recorded at numerous sites, from small sewage farms to large reservoirs and gravel pit complexes. The maps show how breeding birds have spread between 1995–99 and 2007–11.

Despite some fluctuation in numbers, the breeding population of Gadwall in Derbyshire steadily increased throughout the 1980s and 1990s, and reached a record total of about 17 to 22 broods seen in 2000, 2009, 2010, 2011 and 2012. The most recent examples of range expansion were of broods seen at Erewash Meadows in 2002, Butterley Reservoir in 2004, Carsington Water and Codnor in 2006, the Avenue Washlands in 2010 and Pebley Pond in 2011.

At Willington Gravel Pits in July 2009, an observer recorded a group of five Gadwall ducklings with seven Tufted Duck ducklings, accompanied by two adult female Tufted Ducks.

A male Gadwall x Teal hybrid was at Swarkestone Lakes on 26th January 2003.

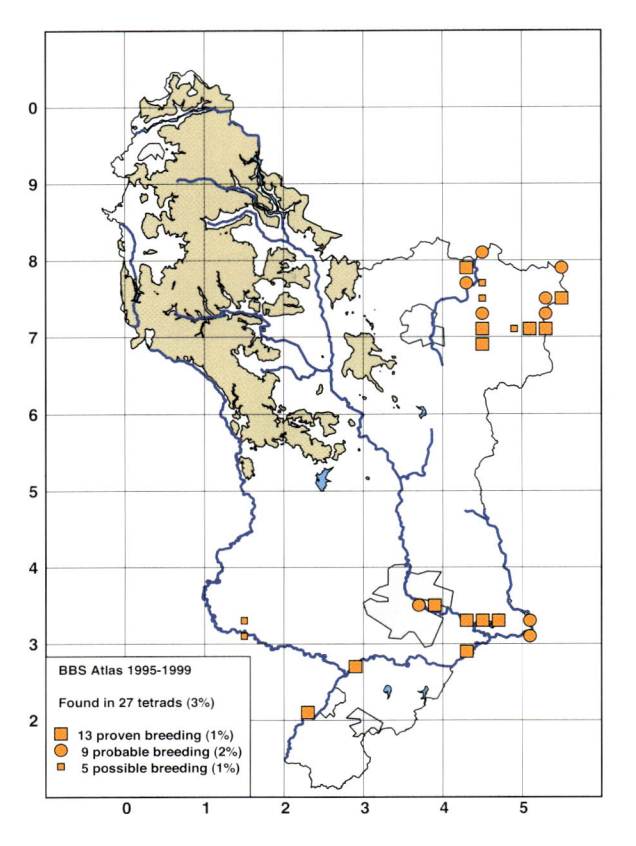

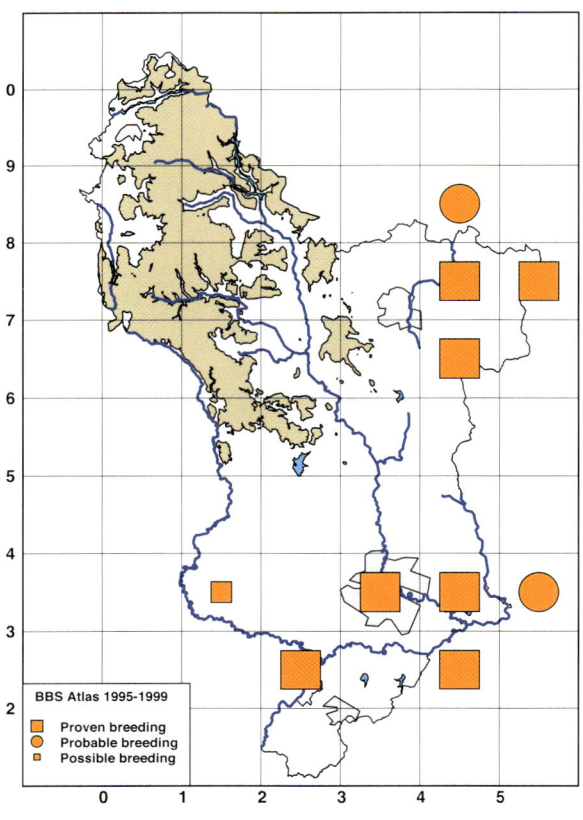

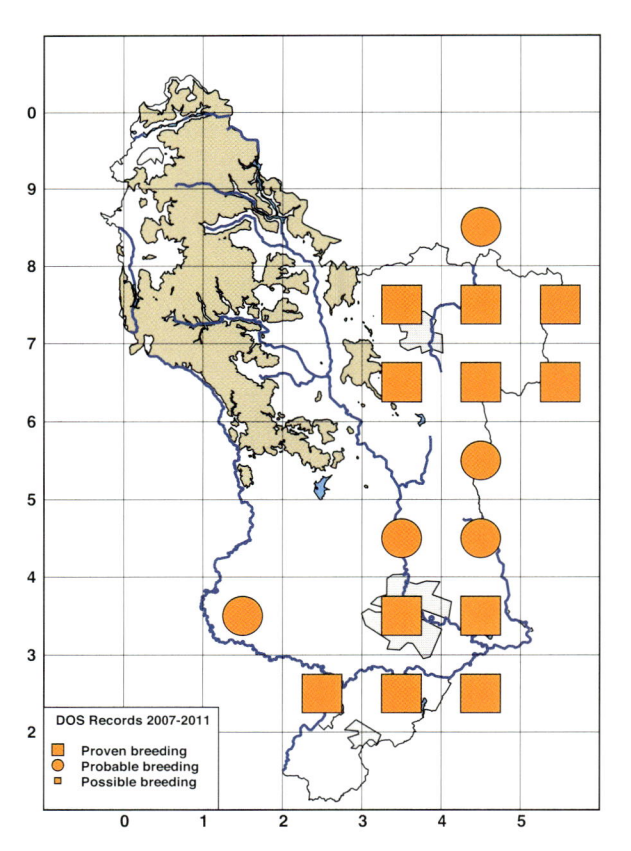

Teal
Anas crecca
A common winter visitor especially in the south and east. A scarce breeder, mainly in the Peak District.

Teal have been common winter visitors to Derbyshire since the nineteenth century at least, and may be encountered at almost any wetland habitat, frequenting not only lakes, gravel pits and large reservoirs, but also rivers, streams and even small marshy areas. They are a familiar sight at many waters throughout the county, particularly from September to April, and are always more prevalent in lowland regions.

This species has undoubtedly become less widespread as a breeding bird since the middle of the twentieth century. Whitlock and Jourdain quoted several instances of likely breeding from the Trent Valley, Sutton Scarsdale, Castleton and on moorland above the Upper Derwent Valley. A few pairs were also believed to be nesting in the Etherow Valley in 1916, while in the 1940s breeding was reported from at least eight localities, including 'fair numbers' in the Derwent area (Frost). However, as evidence of a diminishing population, it was said that hardly any pairs still bred here by the mid-1950s.

Frost remarked that since the 1950s just a few pairs had nested annually, with only four instances of breeding at lowland sites. Although at least eight pairs bred in the county in 1988 and at least ten in 1989, in all other years since the 1970s no more than five broods have been recorded. Very occasional nesting has still occurred in lowland regions, mainly in the Staveley area during the 1980s, but the only subsequent attempt, at Carr Vale in 1995, ended in failure as the female was found dead. Virtually all other breeding records have come from localities in the Peak District. Longdendale, where Torside Reservoir is the main site, has produced many breeding records, and four or five pairs bred here in 2000 but with none since. Other formerly regular breeding sites at Chatsworth Park and Howden Reservoir recorded their last broods in 1992 and 1999. The most regular breeding site since 2000 has been Barbrook, where young have been seen in four of these years, and the draining of the reservoir seems to have had no effect in this instance. Nearby, broods have also been seen in recent years at Ramsley Pools, Jack Flatt and Leash Fen; it is hoped that Teal might be one of the species to benefit from the re-wetting of the last site.

Nest sites in Longdendale and Derwentdale have usually been located close to the reservoir shores, but elsewhere nesting has sometimes taken place in the vicinity of small pools on heather moorland, such as Big Moor. Riparian vegetation has also been used, and at a lowland site a nest with eggs was found among dense, rough grassland with scattered hawthorn.

In the Derbyshire BBS (1995–99) evidence of breeding was found mainly in the High Peak. Breeding was proved in nine tetrads, was probable in six, and possible in a further 12. By contrast, the map for 2007–11 shows that breeding was confirmed only in SK27.

The secretive nesting habits of this small shy duck, and the remote upland areas in which it may be located, make it difficult to obtain an accurate assessment of breeding numbers. For instance, in most recent years, pairs have been present at several suitable locations between May and July, and even though intensive monitoring has sometimes been carried out, more conclusive proof of breeding has rarely been achieved. Broods of young have been seen on very small pools and narrow drains on moorland, and readily secrete themselves in dense vegetation.

From late spring to midsummer, numbers at individual sites do not often reach double figures, despite a slight increase in July. Apart from a total of at least six females with 26–32 young at Torside Reservoir in June 1989, the largest count has been of only 22 birds at Middleton Moor in July 2011. Teal become more widespread in August, while a substantial arrival of wintering birds generally occurs from September onwards.

Month	Mean maximum
September	239
October	396
November	563
December	832
January	913
February	690
March	338

Frost stated that the largest count was usually made in February, with 625 the average maximum for the count from the winters of 1971/72 to 1975/76. Since then, the mean maximum monthly counts (September–March) recorded during WeBS in Derbyshire from 1986/87 to 1999/2000, and shown in the table, indicate that the greatest numbers of Teal have been present in December and January.

The highest count of all remains 2282 in December 1968, which also includes the largest single-site total, of 1250 on the River Trent between Catton and Drakelow. Subsequently, the highest monthly counts have been of 2117 in January 1991, 1869 in February 1991 and 1643 in January 1990. In the Trent Valley area, gatherings of over 500 birds have been recorded on a few occasions, with maxima of 900 at Drakelow Nature

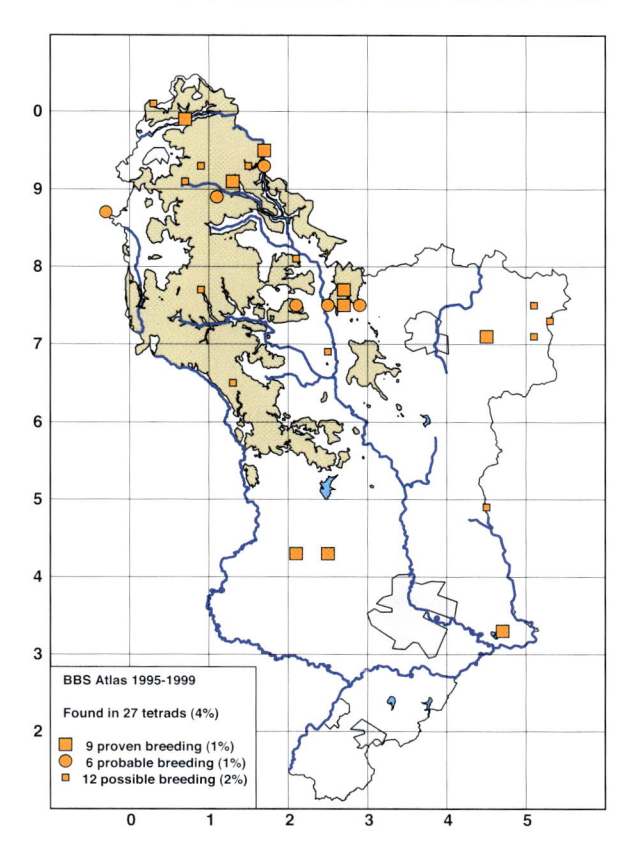

BBS Atlas 1995-1999
Found in 27 tetrads (4%)
- 9 proven breeding (1%)
- 6 probable breeding (1%)
- 12 possible breeding (2%)

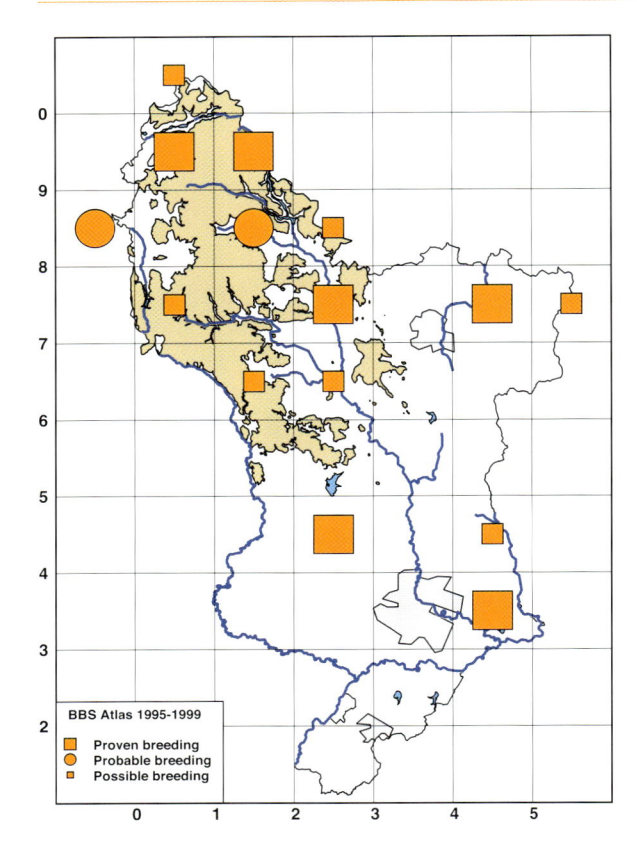

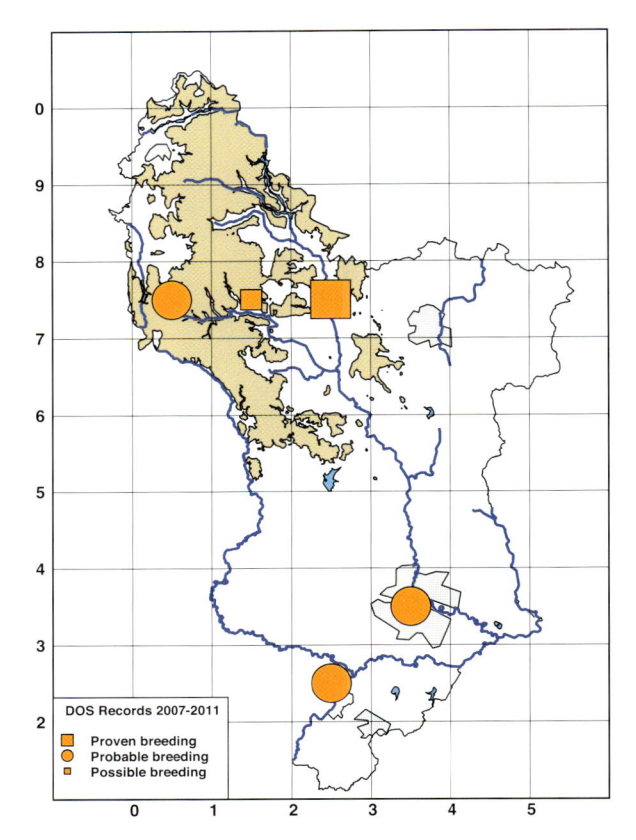

Reserve in December 1989, 863 at British Celanese Lakes Nature Reserve in February 1991, 702 at Church Wilne Reservoir in February 1992 and 634 at Derby Sewage Farm in January 1993. Elsewhere, Carsington Water has attracted the largest numbers, most notably 779 in January 2004. However, even though several lowland waters regularly hold well over 100 birds each year, overall numbers have been lower since the mid-1990s, possibly as a result of milder winters. Middleton Moor is the only site in the Peak District to have held three-figure flocks, and had a highest count of 283 in December 1991. In Longdendale, the greatest number was 90 at Bottoms Reservoir on 8th April 1986. The only other flock of more than 50 Teal in the High Peak was of 60 at Ladybower Reservoir in September 1975.

In common with other wildfowl, most recoveries of Teal concern birds which have been shot, either in Britain or elsewhere in Europe. There have been over 30 reports, spanning several decades, the earliest of which both relate to birds ringed near Milford Haven, Pembrokeshire in December 1938 and shot ten days later at Littleover and a year later at Radbourne. The greatest distance concerns one ringed at Ogston Reservoir in October 1991, which was shot in Kotlassky District, Russia in March 1995, a movement of 3020km. There have been 15 instances of birds being shot within 100 days of being ringed, and on each occasion the ringing date has been between September and January. It is interesting to note that 13 have arrived in Derbyshire from an easterly direction, including two from the Netherlands, which were recovered in winter at Walton-on-Trent and Hathersage, denoting movement from Continental breeding grounds to wintering quarters in Britain.

One with a lime-green bill-saddle was noted at Carsington Water on 9th October 2011, which had been ringed at La Grande Mare, Normandy, France in January of the same year; another noted on 7th and 29th December 2011 with a bill-saddle marked 'A02' had also been ringed in Normandy, in winter 2009.

Green-winged Teal
Anas carolinensis
A rare vagrant.

The Green-winged Teal was formerly considered to be the Nearctic race of the Teal, until it was given species status by the BOU in 2001. Records were assessed by BBRC until 1990. It breeds across northern North America, wintering south to Central America and the West Indies. There have been 14 records involving 15 birds, all since 1976, and involving seven sites, as follows:

Year	Location and date
1976	Ogston Reservoir, a male from 14th to 22nd November
1989	Drakelow Nature Reserve, a male on 26th December
1991	Egginton Sewage Farm, a male on 26th January to 6th April, was joined by a second male from 20th to 24th February
1991	Drakelow Nature Reserve, a male on 27th January
1991	Willington Gravel Pits, one on 10th March
1991	Drakelow Nature Reserve, a male on 27th October
1991	Willington Gravel Pits, one on 24th November
1993	Willington Gravel Pits, a male on 16th and 18th April
1996	Valehouse Reservoir, a male on 29th March
2000	Abbey Hill Floods, a male from 22nd to 25th March
2002	Carsington Water, a male on 27th January
2002	Ogston Reservoir, a male on 8th April
2006	Carsington Water, a male from 10th to 21st December
2009	Carsington Water, a male on 1st November

Mallard
Anas platyrhynchos
A very common or abundant resident and winter visitor.

The ubiquitous Mallard is, and probably always has been, a very common bird in the county. In the nineteenth century, Whitlock considered the species to be fairly common as a breeding bird, but gave little detail about its presence in winter, mentioning only that large numbers were found on the Longdendale reservoirs. Jourdain, writing in 1903, thought that the bird was increasing as a consequence of recent legislation, and stated that considerable numbers bred, especially on the banks of the River Dove. Paradoxically, because it was so numerous, very little mention was made of Mallard during the first half of the twentieth century, though by the mid-1950s three-figure flocks were reported from about five places. The construction of new reservoirs since then has, at least in part, been responsible for further increases.

Mallard will readily nest in all types of wetland areas, with reservoirs, gravel pits and other riparian habitats generally holding the greatest densities. Lakes and ponds in both urban and rural environs are also favoured, and nesting often takes place well away from water, not uncommonly in woodland. The widespread nature of this duck as a breeding species was confirmed in the BTO Surveys (1968–72 and 1988–91) which established its presence within every 10km square of the county. Greater detail was obtained in the Derbyshire BBS (1995–99), with proven breeding in 357 tetrads, probable in 61 and possible in a further 85 tetrads. However, the map reveals some gaps in distribution, largely corresponding to upland areas of limestone pasture and gritstone moorland in the north and west. Other absences relate to pockets of higher ground in the south-west, north-east and central regions, and also to urban districts in Derby, Swadlincote and Chesterfield. In the latter areas breeding is usually confined to parks and river-banks.

The main breeding season is from March to August, although broods of young have been recorded in every month of the year. Since 1980, the greatest number of broods reported at any site have all been at Chatsworth Park, with maxima of 46 broods in 2006 and 36 in 2003 and 2005. The only other sites where over 20 broods have been seen are Queen's Park, Chesterfield, with 26 in 1995, and Carsington Water, where there were 22 in 2007 and 2009, and 21 in 2011. Frost thought the breeding population in the 1970s 'must be of at least several hundred pairs'. An estimate of current numbers cannot be more specific, though a total well in excess of 1000 pairs is quite probable.

Long-term wildfowl counts have provided more precise figures for wintering birds. The average county maximum from 1971/72 to 1975/76 was 2630, with a highest total of 3382 in November 1970. The mean monthly counts (September to March) from 1986/87 to 1999/2000 are shown in the table.

Month	Mean maximum
September	3411
October	3783
November	3913
December	3871
January	3551
February	2501
March	1652

The highest combined totals during this period were 5637 in October 1987 and 5339 in October 1989. These figures would appear to signify a steady increase in the wintering population, but since the early 1990s counts have generally been lower and have only once exceeded 4000. This also mirrors the national trend, where an annual decrease was registered in ten of the 12 years between 1988 and 1999 (Pollitt *et al*. 2000).

Regular counting has established that Mallard numbers build up each year from August onwards, and tend to reach their highest levels between October and December, although they do not fall markedly until March and April. While counts are generally lowest from May to July, flocks of over 100 are not unusual at this time of year. The most notable examples are of 505 in July 2003 and 465 in July 1996, both at Chatsworth Park (these counts being bolstered by the young of that year). Concentrations in spring and summer may also be accounted for by a greater proportion of birds being unable to establish territories after low 'overwinter loss' following years of high production of young (1988–91 Atlas).

Frost noted that one of this species' favourite haunts was Staunton Harold Reservoir where up to 1200 birds had occurred, but since 1980 Drakelow Nature Reserve has regularly held the largest gatherings, including the current county record of 1500 in October 1981. Numbers here, as elsewhere in Derbyshire, have declined in recent years and counts of over 500 are rare nowadays. Nevertheless, several sites continue to host sizeable flocks on a regular basis, such as Chatsworth Park (maxima of 805 in November 1987 and 798 in November 1996) and the River Wye at Bakewell (maximum of 715 in September 2004). Totals of 300 or more birds have been recorded in most recent winters at Kedleston Park (maximum 503 in November 1997) and Ogston Reservoir, and occasionally at Carsington Water, Carr Vale and Bradley Dam. Three-figure counts continue to be reported each year from at least 20 localities widely distributed throughout the county.

There have been numerous ringing recoveries of Mallards involving Derbyshire. The furthest concerns one ringed at Kangasala, Finland in July 1968 that was shot in December of the same year at Yeaveley, 1812km to the west-south-west. Another ringed at Enanger, Sweden in August 1962 was shot at Hardwick Park 14 months later, while other birds recovered in the county had been ringed in Denmark (four individuals), Germany and the Netherlands. Mallards ringed in Derbyshire have subsequently been recovered in Denmark and Norway. There are numerous recoveries within the UK, including no fewer than nine ringed at Slimbridge, Gloucestershire that later moved to Derbyshire.

BBS Atlas 1995-1999

Found in 503 tetrads (69%)

- 357 proven breeding (49%)
- 61 probable breeding (8%)
- 85 possible breeding (12%)

Pintail
Anas acuta
An uncommon passage migrant and winter visitor. Rare in summer.

Pintail are undoubtedly much more regular visitors to the county than formerly. Whitlock described them as being of 'uncertain appearance' and knew of only a few occurrences in the nineteenth century. These invariably coincided with severe weather and were usually in the Trent Valley, though others had been killed at Borrowash, Kedleston Park and Sutton Scarsdale. There were no further records until 1942, but since 1959 this graceful duck has become established as an annual winter visitor, with at least a few birds usually present, even during the mildest of winter conditions.

Although most Pintail wintering in Britain frequent coastal localities, particularly large estuaries, the 1984–88 Winter Atlas also revealed a discernible pattern of distribution along the course of the River Trent and its associated gravel workings. Therefore, in Derbyshire, it is not surprising that many sightings have come from the reservoirs and gravel pits within the Trent Valley. Elsewhere, Carsington Water and Ogston Reservoir have been visited on a regular basis, and nowadays Pintail might occur on any sizeable water body, marsh or flooded area within the county. This species was recorded at a maximum of 23 sites in 1995.

Pintail have been seen in every month of the year, but are rare between May and July, and uncommon in August. From September, small numbers are reported moving into the county, or on passage. The most notable examples of autumn migration are a flock of 24 flying west over Williamthorpe Nature Reserve on 18th September 1989 and a total of 55, nearly all flying west, at Middleton Moor on four dates between 30th August and 1st October 1995. However, it is usually later in the winter that the largest numbers are recorded, and these are associated with influxes that often occur between December and March. On many occasions Pintail have arrived in the Trent Valley very soon after flooding of the area.

Much the largest flock was of 120 birds that circled Church Wilne Reservoir briefly on 31st January 1982 before flying off east. There have been five other flocks of 40 or more birds as follows: Drakelow Nature Reserve, 46 flew over on 1st March 1972; Breck Farm, 40 on 26th December 1981; Church Wilne Reservoir, 43 on 12th February 1984; Ogston Reservoir, 47 on 5th March 1986; and Swarkestone Lake, 46 on floodwater on 11th February 1990.

Since 1990 there have been no further instances of such large influxes. The only subsequent flocks of over 20 birds have been of 28 at Carsington Water on 24th February 1992, and the same number at Willington Gravel Pits on 6th December 1992. Despite the greater frequency of visits, it would appear that Frost's comment that 'any gathering of double figures is noteworthy' is still valid now.

In Britain, Pintail are rare and sporadic breeders, mainly in Scotland, although feral pairs have also bred in several English counties. In Derbyshire, there have been very occasional summer sightings, but there has been no suggestion of breeding.

A male Mallard x Pintail hybrid was at Drakelow Nature Reserve in May and September 1985.

Garganey
Anas querquedula
A scarce passage migrant and summer visitor. A scarce breeder.

This small and beautiful dabbling duck is unique in being the only species of wildfowl that is a summer visitor to Britain. It is therefore surprising that Garganey were considered by Whitlock to be very uncommon winter visitors to the county. However, neither he nor Jourdain ever saw the species, and between 1893 and 1944 there were only two records, at Repton in October 1920 and Kedleston in August 1934.

There would appear to have been a significant change in status during the second half of the twentieth century as Garganey have become scarce, but regular, passage migrants and summer visitors, recorded annually since 1962. The table summarizes their occurrences in recent periods.

Period	Records	Birds
1950s	5	10
1960s	71	124
1970s	99	177
1980s	50	76
1990s	91	136
2000–11	105	150
Totals	421	673

Garganey are nowadays recorded in spring between March and June, often in pairs, with an earliest arrival date of 2nd March 2010 when a pair was at Carsington Water. Return passage normally occurs from July to September and usually involves rather more birds. Occasional stragglers have been reported in October, and there are four records for November: one at Ogston Reservoir on 22nd November 1968; a male at Drakelow Nature Reserve on 11th November 1992; an immature male that stayed at Carsington Water from 16th to 22nd November 2003, and likewise from 29th October to 16th November 2009. The first modern winter record was of a female which frequented the River Trent at Newton Solney for at least a week during the severe weather in January 1963. More recently, an immature male was at Drakelow Nature Reserve from 24th January to 16th February 2009, though it visited Willington Gravel Pits on 6th and 7th February, and what was presumed to be the same individual (now adult) was at the Drakelow site again on 24th December 2009 and 30th February 2011.

The majority of passage birds occur in the south and east. Higher ground is largely avoided and the only Peak District records in 1980–2011 were five from Middleton Moor and singles at Barbrook, Combs and Arnfield Reservoirs. The sighting on 30th March 1997 of a pair accompanying a Blue-winged Teal in Monsal Dale, a site hardly renowned for its wildfowl, was quite exceptional. Smaller water bodies, such as flashes, with their shallow water and marginal vegetation, are often favoured, particularly in spring. The largest count was of seven at Ogston Reservoir on 14th August 1970, and at least six were also seen here in July 1994. Six birds were also recorded at Aston-on-Trent Gravel Pits in August 2002, while five or six were at Brinsley Flashes in August 1971. All other sightings have concerned up to four birds.

The Garganey has a scattered distribution as a breeding bird in Britain, although most pairs occur in central and south-east England. It is a notoriously difficult species for which to prove breeding, largely due to its highly secretive habits when nesting. In 1944, a pair was present at Repton in April and May, and display was seen. Four ducklings were seen in June, but the observers were not completely certain that they were of this species. Frost said that there were strong suggestions of breeding in the Trent and Erewash Valleys from 1962 onwards, but absolute proof was lacking. In 1982, a pair was suspected of breeding at Carr Vale, but it was speculated that the eggs were lost, possibly as a result of flooding (Adams & Frost 1983). However, in 1990, a nest containing ten eggs was found in a field of rye grass some 450m away from the main lake on 16th May and two small ducklings were subsequently seen on 13th June (Irons 1991). Further breeding attempts have been recorded at Carr Vale in 1991, 1992, 1999 and 2000 but each one was either presumed or known to have failed. In addition, breeding was suspected at Willington Gravel Pits in 1991 and 2000.

Blue-winged Teal
Anas discors
A very rare vagrant.

There have been three records, the first two records having been documented by Topliss (1996) and Fisher (1997) respectively, and all involving single birds as follows:

Year	Location and date
1995	Willington Gravel Pits, a female from 25th September to 11th October
1996	Middleton Moor, male in eclipse plumage from 24th to 27th August and presumably the same bird on 10th–11th November
1997	Monsal Dale, a male from 2nd March to 20th April

The Blue-winged Teal breeds in North America, south of the Arctic circle, and winters from the southern USA south to Peru and Brazil. This is one of the more common species of Nearctic wildfowl to be recorded in the British Isles and up to the end of 2010 a total of 240 had been seen (Hudson *et al.* 2011). Although good numbers occur in western Britain, this species has been seen widely throughout the country, mostly between mid-August and mid-November, with peak occurrences from mid-September to early October. A secondary, and much smaller peak occurs between early April and late June (Dymond *et al.* 1989). Interestingly, all three Derbyshire records have fallen within or very close to these peak periods.

The male that was at Middleton Moor in August and November 1996 could, in the intervening period, have moved to either Greater Manchester, where a male was at Pennington Flash from 19th September to 13th October, or into Staffordshire, where a male was at Blithfield Reservoir from 21st to 29th September. The Monsal Dale bird is likely to have been the Middleton Moor individual of the year before, since the sites are only 3km apart.

Shoveler
Anas clypeata
An uncommon visitor. A scarce breeder.

Shovelers, whose name derives from the huge spatulate bill and filter-feeding technique, are dabbling ducks which have a strong preference for shallow water margins. Small numbers have been known to winter in the county since at least the nineteenth century, mainly in the south and east. They have been seen on all kinds of waters such as open reservoirs, flooded gravel pits, fishing lakes, rivers, subsidence pools and ornamental waters. A few are usually to be found throughout the summer months as well, though this species has always been a rare and erratic breeder in Derbyshire.

They are highly migratory and the arrival in Britain of post-breeding birds from the Continent leads to a marked increase in local numbers during the autumn period. The largest gatherings often occur in September and October, although peaks are sometimes later in the winter, possibly as a result of cold weather influxes. The mean maximum monthly winter counts (September–March) recorded during WeBS covering Derbyshire between 1986/87 and 1999/2000 are shown in the table.

Month	Mean maximum
September	36
October	39
November	28
December	26
January	18
February	19
March	13

During the 1970s, Staunton Harold Reservoir often held the most significant numbers, notably 81 in September 1979, but the county record at that time was 92 at Foremark Reservoir in February 1978. The latter water, unlike nearly all others in the Trent Valley, usually remains unfrozen during spells of severely cold weather. However, the premier site for Shoveler since 1980 has been Drakelow Nature Reserve, which has frequently attracted flocks of between 40 and 60 birds. Maximum counts here have been of 131 in October 2004 and 118 in October 2008. However, the count of 131 has recently been exceeded at two other sites: there were 144 at Long Eaton Gravel Pits in February 2009, and 133 at Aston-on-Trent Gravel Pits in November 2008. Other locations where more than 50 birds have been recorded are Willington Gravel Pits, which had a maximum of 60 in November 1990, Breaston Nature Reserve, which hosted 54 in January 1995, and Alvaston Lake, which recorded 65 in December 2010.

In recent years there have been gatherings of over 25 birds elsewhere in the Trent and lower Derwent Valleys region, including Long Eaton Gravel Pits, Church Wilne Reservoir, Derby Sewage Farm and Alvaston Lake. Away from this area, the highest counts have been made at Carsington Water, Ogston Reservoir, Carr Vale, Renishaw Park and Shipley Lake. Shovelers are relatively scarce on upland waters, and parties of more than six birds are exceptional. The majority of occurrences in the Peak District have been at Middleton Moor lagoons and Arnfield, Combs and Barbrook Reservoirs.

Whitlock thought this duck might sometimes nest in the county, but neither he nor Jourdain knew of any conclusive records, and the first definite breeding was not until 1928. According to Frost, confirmed breeding took place in only 13 years between

1928 and 1976 and never involved more than two pairs in any year. The earlier records were exclusively from the Heath and Whitwell areas, with later reports from Kedleston, Ingleby, Westhouses, Staunton Harold Reservoir and Staveley. From 1977 to 1999, breeding attempts were made in 15 years, most successfully in 1981 at Brinsley Flashes where three pairs raised 22 young, although one nest had been found by a shooting club member who hatched the eggs in an incubator and later released eight young. All other sites were in the Trent Valley (at Shardlow, Swarkestone and Willington Gravel Pits, Foremark and Staunton Harold Reservoirs, Breaston Nature Reserve and Drakelow Nature Reserve) or in north-east Derbyshire (at Carr Vale and Williamthorpe).

In the Derbyshire BBS (1995–99), probable breeding was reported from the Peak District, although this related to display by a solitary male Shoveler which frequented the River Wye at Bakewell for several years. There was probable breeding at the nature reserves at Williamthorpe and Breaston, while possible breeding was suspected at Swarkestone Lake. All three are locations where successful breeding has occurred in the past. Proven breeding was established only at Willington Gravel Pits and in the Carr Vale area. One or two pairs were seen at the latter site every summer during the five-year survey, with four pairs present in 1997. Whereas breeding attempts were successful in the first two years, they all failed in the remaining three years, largely due to farming activities.

Since the completion of the survey, the only broods recorded have been at Creswell and Aston-on-Trent Gravel Pits, both in 2003, Carr Vale in 2007 and Willington Gravel Pits in 2011, although pairs have been observed each year at other suitable localities in the county during spring and summer.

Red-crested Pochard
Netta rufina
A scarce visitor. Most records probably refer to feral birds.

The first record in Derbyshire was of a female seen at Locko Park from 27th July to 12th October 1960. There were only two further occurrences in that decade but, as the figures in the table indicate, there has been a significant increase in numbers from the 1980s onwards. With the exceptions of 1992, 1994 and 1998, this species has been recorded annually since 1984. Note that the table excludes all records from Carsington Water which is considered separately.

Period	Records	Birds
1950s	-	-
1960s	3	3
1970s	9	10
1980s	18	24
1990s	15	22
2000–11	43	58
Totals	88	117

Other than at Carsington Water the largest gatherings were all of six birds, at Church Wilne Reservoir on 5th October 1993 and from 20th to 28th November 2010 (also seen at the nearby St Chads Water on 20th), and at Long Eaton Gravel Pits on 13th and 15th October 2011. All other records in the twentieth century were of one or two birds, reported in every month apart from May and June, although predominantly between September and January.

Although it is the most recently created large reservoir in the county, Carsington Water has already become established as the premier site for this species. The first record here was of an immature male which remained from 2nd September to 5th November 1999, and subsequent sightings have become very regular and have involved increasing numbers of birds. However, as it is believed that feral Red-crested Pochards commute between Carsington Water and J.C. Bamford Lakes at Rocester, Staffordshire, and apparently roost at the latter (R. Carrington *pers comm*), Carsington Water records are omitted from the previous table of county records.

The maximum monthly counts at Carsington Water during 2000–11 were as follows:

Month	Max count
January	8
February	7
March	1
April	2
May	2
June	2
July	7
August	6
September	9
October	8
November	5
December	8

Elsewhere, Long Eaton Gravel Pits has had over 25 records, followed by 12 at Drakelow Nature Reserve, ten at Willington Gravel Pits and six at Ogston Reservoir. As well as more open water bodies at gravel pits and reservoirs, Red-crested Pochards have been reported from a wide variety of aquatic habitats, including well-vegetated pools and flashes. In addition to the locations previously mentioned, this duck has been recorded on one or two occasions from more than 20 other waters throughout the county. These have included Alvaston Park, Aston-on-Trent and Barrow Gravel Pits, Belph, Bradley Dam, Bretby Park, Brinsley Flashes, Carr Vale, Derby River Gardens, the River Derwent (at Bamford, Hathersage and Shatton), Elvaston Castle Country Park, Elvaston Quarry, Fairholmes car park, Foremark Reservoir, Hilton Gravel Pits Nature Reserve, Kedleston Park, Melbourne Pool, Moorway Lane Pond, Pebley Pond, Pools Brook Country Park, Pools Head Ponds, Renishaw Park, Rother Valley Country Park (now in South Yorkshire), Queen's Park, Shipley Lake, St Chads Water, Staunton Harold Reservoir and Toddbrook Reservoir.

The male Red-crested Pochard, with its orange-red head and crimson bill, is a striking bird and this no doubt accounts for its popularity in wildfowl collections. The species breeds readily in captivity and it is thought that a considerable number of ducklings avoid pinioning. Frost stated that a captive pair bred in south Derbyshire in the 1970s and that fledged young were allowed to disperse. There seems little doubt that many of the birds seen in the county are of captive or feral origin.

Individuals which were considered to be hybrids have occurred at Shipley Park in January 1988, and at Drakelow Nature Reserve from October 1988 to February 1989 and in September 2001. Leucistic birds have been noted at Willington Gravel Pits in July 1997 and on several occasions at Carsington Water.

Pochard
Aythya ferina
A fairly common winter visitor and passage migrant. A scarce breeder.

This diving duck is found predominantly on reservoirs, gravel pits and lowland lakes, often in association with the closely related Tufted Duck but, unlike that species, it is only a sporadic breeder in the county. Although breeding may have occurred in Derbyshire in 1941, the first conclusive proof was not obtained until 1972 when three broods of young were seen on a pond near Bradley (Frost). In 1976, six young were reared at Brinsley Flashes in the Erewash Valley. Confirmed breeding was next recorded on an annual basis from 1988 to 1995, with broods seen at Steetley Quarry, British Celanese Lakes Nature Reserve, Drakelow Nature Reserve, Carsington Water and Willington Gravel Pits. This raised expectations of gradual colonization but, even though birds have been present in suitable locations during late spring and early summer in subsequent years, the Derbyshire BBS (1995–99) found proven breeding in only two tetrads and probable in another two. Two further broods were found in 2000, at Steetley Quarry and Netherthorpe Pool, but no young have been seen in the county since then.

Since there is no shortage of apparently suitable breeding habitat, such as disused gravel pits, subsidence flashes and other shallow waters with submergent weeds and dense marginal vegetation, the Pochard has proved to be less adaptable than the much more prolific Tufted Duck. Inhibiting factors may include a greater sensitivity to disturbance, water-level fluctuations and nest-site competition, as well as a generally low survival rate of progeny due to predation. Significantly, the only two confirmed breeding records during the entire period of the Derbyshire BBS (1995–99) were both unsuccessful. At Steetley Quarry a nest with eggs failed and, at Willington Gravel Pits, a brood of five small ducklings all disappeared within a few days.

As a winter visitor, the Pochard is nowadays fairly widespread and numerous, and in Whitlock's time the species was apparently quite common in south Derbyshire. However, in the first half of the twentieth century, although small numbers were reported on many waters, the largest flock was of only 58 at Butterley Reservoir in March 1949 (Frost). Since 1950, the construction of five large reservoirs (Ogston, Staunton Harold, Church Wilne, Foremark and Carsington Water) and the permanent flooding of several gravel pits in the Trent Valley have provided ideal wintering sites for Pochard, resulting in a marked increase in numbers.

Ogston Reservoir, the oldest and most northerly of these 'new' reservoirs, hosted the first flock of over 100 birds in December 1958, with a subsequent maximum of 391 here in January 1977. By the 1970s, counts of more than 200 birds had also been reported from Staunton Harold Reservoir, Shipley Lake, Drakelow Nature Reserve, Clay Mills and Egginton Gravel Pits, while Church Wilne Reservoir held the county record of 420 in February 1978. The creation of Foremark Reservoir had a lesser impact, with a peak count of 154 in January 1979.

Since 1980, substantial numbers have also occurred at other localities, such as British Celanese Lakes Nature Reserve (274 in December 1994), Rother Valley Country Park (now in South Yorkshire; 260 in November 1987) and Willington Gravel Pits (253 in October 1994). However, following its completion in the early 1990s, Carsington Water immediately became established as a premier site for wintering Pochard, with 285 present in March 1992. Several counts in excess of 300 birds have been made here in recent years, most notably the current county record of 766 in December 1999.

Gatherings of over 100 birds have now been documented at a total of at least 20 sites in Derbyshire, including 118 on the relatively small lake at Stubbing Court in November 1995. The only three-figure flock in the Peak District was of 108 at Combs Reservoir on 1st March 1994, and the highest counts at other waters in the High Peak are 50 at Derwent Reservoir in January 1985 and 42 at Ladybower Reservoir in December 1984.

The mean maximum monthly counts (September–March) as recorded in WeBS between 1986/87 and 1999/2000 are shown in the table.

Month	Mean maximum
September	54
October	174
November	339
December	348
January	369
February	317
March	187

These figures are largely in accordance with Frost's comment that maximum numbers occur between November and March. Pochard have always been much scarcer from April to June and gatherings of more than ten are exceptional at this time of year. Numbers increase from July onwards, although before October they rarely exceed 50 at any one water. The highest individual site count for August is 140 at Staunton Harold Reservoir in 1972 and for September is 200 at Carsington Water in 2000.

The wintering population in Britain increased considerably until the mid-1970s, and then stabilized at lower levels in the 1980s and 1990s. The average maximum for the county during the winters from 1971/72 to 1974/75 was 625 (Frost), whereas the comparative totals for 1990/91 to 1994/95, and 1995/96 to 1998/99 were 416 and 445 respectively. This would appear to conform with the long-term national trend, but since coverage at countable waters has been as low as 50% in some years, it is difficult to achieve an accurate assessment of overall numbers.

A large proportion of the *Aythya* hybrid birds identified in Derbyshire involve this species, and the broods reared at Drakelow Nature Reserve in both 1993 and 1994 were considered to be such. There have also been records of unusually plumaged birds, including a male at Mapperley Reservoir in February 1976 that was completely black apart from a brown neck and head, and a female summering at Williamthorpe Nature Reserve in 1995 that had a largely white head with a little dark flecking.

There are just two ringing recoveries of this species: a male ringed at Blunham, Bedfordshire in January 1979 was shot at Langley Mill in October of the same year and a female ringed at Engure Lake, Latvia in May 1989 was, rather surprisingly, killed by a cat at Swarkestone in January 1990. One at Carsington Water on 1st August 2007 had a bill-saddle, which had been fitted at Saint-Philbert-de-Grande-Lieu, France in October 2006.

Ring-necked Duck
Aythya collaris
A very rare vagrant.

Ring-necked Ducks breed across northern North America, wintering south to Central America and the West Indies. Although the first British record did not occur until 1955, it is now the most frequent of all the Nearctic ducks occurring in Britain, and was removed from the list of species assessed by BBRC after 1993. There have been ten records in Derbyshire, all of single birds, as shown in the table.

It is surprising that there has been only one recorded at Carsington Water, which usually holds the county's largest concentrations of *Aythya* ducks, and none at Ogston Reservoir, and yet the small and under-watched Pebley Pond has attracted two individuals.

Year	Location and date
1977	Drakelow Nature Reserve, an adult male on 27th December
1982	Pebley Pond, a male on 9th–10th February
1994	Willington Gravel Pits, a male from 27th April to 7th May was seen displaying to a female Pochard
1999	Church Wilne Reservoir, an adult male on 21st November
2000	Pebley Pond, a first-winter male on 4th–5th December
2001	Church Wilne Reservoir and Trent–Derwent confluence area, a male on 20th–21st January
2004	Long Eaton Gravel Pits, a male present from 27th October to 23rd January 2005, and believed to be the same bird at St Chads Water on 25th–26th January
2005	Carsington Water, a first-winter, on 8th November
2007	Nadin's, Newhall, a male from 9th to 15th April, and believed to be the same bird at Drakelow Nature Reserve from 19th to 21st April
2007	Carr Vale, a male from 6th to 8th and 14th May. Pools Brook Country Park, believed the same bird on 14th May

Ferruginous Duck
Aythya nyroca
A rare vagrant.

There have been 16 records, all since 1950, involving 19 birds, as follows:

Year	Location and date
1950	Butterley Reservoir, a pair from mid-December to late March 1951
1964	Butterley Reservoir, an adult female from 29th February to 7th March
1964	Ogston Reservoir, an adult male on 8th March
1972	Drakelow Nature Reserve, an adult male from 6th to 27th February
1973	Drakelow Nature Reserve, a male from 31st January to 11th March
1975	Egginton Gravel Pits, an immature on 9th November
1976	Shipley Lake, a pair on 25th January
1979	Church Wilne Reservoir, a pair on 3rd January
1987	Williamthorpe Nature Reserve, a male on 22nd January was seen later in the day at Ogston Reservoir
1988	Church Wilne Reservoir, a female on 17th April was relocated at Elvaston Quarry on 1st May and last reported from Church Wilne Reservoir on 3rd May
1993	Ramsley Reservoir, an immature male departed to the east on 9th October
1999	Carsington Water, an immature male from 3rd October to 9th December
2003	Willington Gravel Pits, a first-winter on 17th October
2005	Carsington Water, a male on 2nd January
2008	Shipley Lake, Loscoe Dam and Straw's Bridge, a male from 19th January to 9th February
2008	Steetley Quarry, a female or first-winter from 6th to 10th February

Analysis by period and month is indicated.

Period	Records	Birds
1950s	1	2
1960s	2	2
1970s	5	7
1980s	2	2
1990s	2	2
2000–11	4	4
Totals	16	19

Month	Records	Birds
January	5	7
February	4	4
March	1	1
April	1	1
May	-	-
June	-	-
July	-	-
August	-	-
September	-	-
October	3	3
November	1	1
December	1	2
Totals	16	19

This attractive species breeds discontinuously from Spain eastwards to China, and winters from North Africa and the Mediterranean into India. It is commonly kept in captivity but Owen *et al.* (1986), and later Vinicombe (2000), believed that most records were of genuine vagrants. There is no reason to suspect that this is not the case with the Derbyshire records.

Tufted Duck
Aythya fuligula
A fairly common resident and winter visitor.

This familiar diving duck first bred in the county at Osmaston in 1854 (Whitlock), although it had been confirmed as a breeding species in Britain only five years earlier (Brown & Grice 2005). Subsequently, the Tufted Duck rapidly colonized much of the country, nesting at sites such as park lakes, millponds and the quieter reaches of river systems. Jourdain believed it was established as a regular breeding bird in Derbyshire by the end of the nineteenth century, and in 1906 a total of 15 pairs was known to have bred at just two sites, namely Osmaston Park and Ashford Lake (Frost). The local population steadily increased and became more widely distributed throughout the first half of the twentieth century, while in the 1950s and 1960s the construction of reservoirs and the proliferation of gravel pits provided plenty of new breeding sites. By the 1970s, Frost believed that numbers had stabilized, with between 40 and 50 broods of ducklings reported each year. Since then, a broadly similar pattern has emerged, as revealed in the table, which gives the mean number of sites and broods in each five-year period from 1980 to 2009.

Period	Mean number of sites	Mean number of broods
1980–84	18	38
1985–89	16	30
1990–94	23	44
1995–99	21	45
2000–04	24	56
2005–09	24	65

The most detailed information concerning the distribution of this species within the county has been obtained by the Derbyshire BBS (1995–99). During this five-year study, breeding was proved in 86 tetrads, probable in 59 tetrads and possible in a further 67. Evidence of breeding was reported in virtually every 10km square, though more sparsely in some upland areas.

The highest number of broods at a single locality has been recorded recently at Carsington Water, which had totals of 20 in 2007, 24 in 2009 and 29 in 2010. Counts of ten broods or more have also been registered at Drakelow Nature Reserve (maximum of 15 in 1969), Willington Gravel Pits (maximum of 13 in 1995), Chatsworth Park (maximum of 12 in 1971), Shirebrook Colliery (12 in 2009) and Findern Lake (ten in 2005 and 2006). One to four broods have been reported at the majority of breeding locations, although between five and nine have occurred at Kedleston Park, Ogston Reservoir, Osmaston Park, Woodhead Reservoir, Wyver Lane and several sites in the Trent Valley. Post-breeding gatherings of Tufted Duck build up in July and August, and flocks of over 100 are nowadays found in most years, mainly at the larger waters. Over 400 were at Carsington Water in August 2003 and August 2004. There were 520 at Staunton Harold Reservoir in August 1973 and a record count for this month of 657 at Church Wilne Reservoir in August 2006.

During the autumn, birds (which presumably originate from breeding grounds elsewhere in Europe) arrive in the county and remain through to the early spring. Even though this duck has been a relatively common winter visitor to Derbyshire since at least the nineteenth century, it was not until 1943, at Shipley, that the first three-figure count was recorded (Frost). In subsequent years, many waters have held such numbers, although flocks rarely exceed 500, except in severe weather. A total of 800 birds was counted on the River Trent on 22nd January 1963 and a similar number were present on the warm-water fly-ash lagoons at Drakelow Nature Reserve in a spell of freezing conditions in January 1979, with 1000 at the same locality, also during a period of very cold weather, on 17th January 1982.

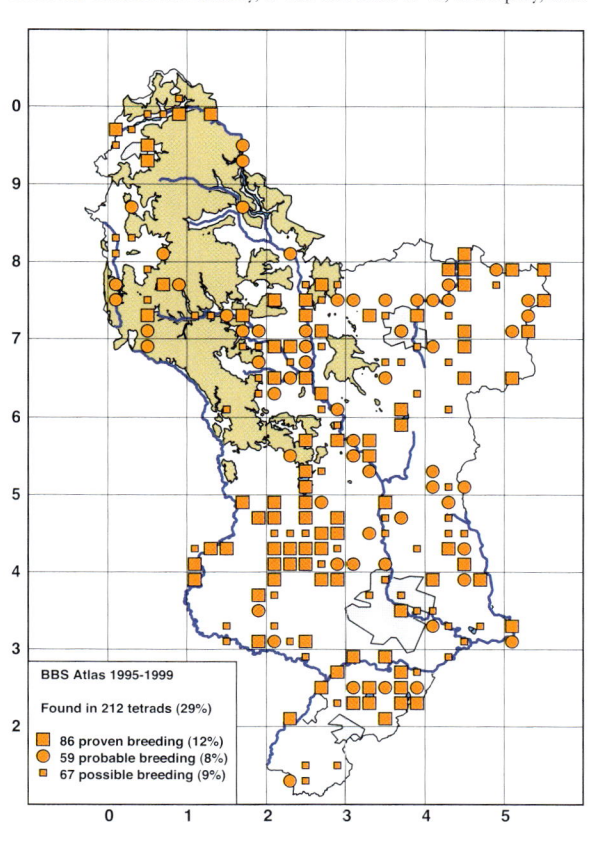

In the 1990s, a decade of relatively mild winters, the largest congregation was 423 at Carsington Water in September 1999. This site has also provided the most recent maxima, with 578–879 birds present from September to December 2010 and the county record of 1248 in December 2005. In addition to those waters already mentioned, the highest counts at all others where there have been counts in excess of 300 Tufted Duck since 1980 are tabulated below:

Site	Date	Max count
Church Wilne Reservoir	September 2009	775
Staunton Harold Reservoir	September 2010	769
Foremark Reservoir	December 2010	660
Swarkestone Lake	February 1989	400
Aston-on-Trent Gravel Pits	December 2009	380
British Celanese Lakes Nature Reserve	December 1990	304

With the exception of Ogston Reservoir, which held 124 birds in December 2002, and Renishaw Park, which also held 124 in December 2009, all other flocks in excess of 100 have been recorded at localities in the southern half of the county. In the north and north-east, although numbers are generally smaller, gatherings of 50 to 100 birds have often been reported at Linacre Reservoirs, Pools Brook Country Park and occasionally at Chatsworth Park, Derwent Reservoir, Crowhole Reservoir and Pebley Pond, while Steetley Quarry held 154 in January 2010. This species is much scarcer in the north-west and even double-figure counts are infrequent. Surprisingly, one of the most regular haunts is the small Bennetston Hall Pond, near Chapel-en-le-Frith, where there was a maximum of 18 in January 1987.

The mean monthly maximum counts (September–March) as recorded in WeBS between 1986/87 and 1999/2000 are as follows:

Month	Mean maximum
September	536
October	546
November	655
December	787
January	741
February	623
March	578

Since the average county maximum between 1971/72 and 1975/76 was 921 (Frost), this suggests a downward trend, which is contrary to a more stable situation at national level during the 1980s and 1990s (Pollitt et al. 2000). However, a decrease in the proportion of local waters covered throughout this period may account for the apparent discrepancy.

The longest-distance recovery involves a first-winter bird ringed at Foremark Reservoir in November 1980, which was shot near Inta, north Russia, in September 1982, representing a movement of 3724km. There have also been two records of birds ringed in Denmark and Latvia in May and June, which were subsequently recovered in Derbyshire in midwinter. In 1980–81, as part of a study to examine the effects of recreation on waterfowl, a special effort was made to catch birds at Foremark and Staunton Harold Reservoirs. As a result, 11 recoveries were obtained (out of a county total of 18) including that of a bird ringed at Slimbridge in December 1977. In 2010 and 2011 there were several sightings of birds with colour bill-saddles which had been ringed in France and the Czech Republic.

BBS Atlas 1995-1999
Found in 212 tetrads (29%)
- 86 proven breeding (12%)
- 59 probable breeding (8%)
- 67 possible breeding (9%)

Scaup
Aythya marila
A scarce but regular winter visitor and passage migrant.

Month	Records	Birds
January	62	99
February	37	67
March	16	30
April	22	31
May	16	24
June	5	9
July	16	24
August	16	23
September	33	38
October	46	64
November	64	105
December	56	86
Totals	389	600

In the nineteenth century, Whitlock considered Scaup to be occasional winter visitors, most likely to appear in times of hard weather such as the great frost of 1890/91. However, he knew of only one occurrence away from the Trent Valley, at Bakewell. This species was subsequently recorded in 1904, 1912, 1924, 1928 and on three occasions in the 1940s (Frost).

Since the 1950s, Scaup have become regular visitors in small numbers not only in winter, but also on passage, and have been recorded annually since 1961. The five-yearly totals of records and birds in the period 1950–2011 are as follows:

Period	Records	Birds
1950–54	2	3
1955–59	6	6
1960–64	21	44
1965–70	31	55
1970–74	50	74
1975–79	50	81
1980–84	29	35
1985–89	22	34
1990–94	38	75
1995–99	45	57
2000–04	34	47
2005–11	61	89
Totals	389	600

Although Scaup have been found in the county in every month, their presence is most pronounced from late November to February, reflecting the national trend of peak numbers in British coastal waters at this time of year (Owen *et al.* 1986). Increased sightings inland in April and May, and also in September and October, presumably denote passage birds.

This duck has been reported from over 50 localities in Derbyshire, with the majority in the Trent Valley. Church Wilne Reservoir, Drakelow Nature Reserve and the gravel pits at Clay Mills, Swarkestone and Willington have all been visited on at least a dozen occasions. The most frequented site, however, is Ogston Reservoir with well over 30 records, while Scaup have already become established as almost annual visitors to Carsington Water since its creation in 1992. Occurrences in the Peak District are significantly fewer than elsewhere in the county, and have been documented most often at Barbrook and Ladybower Reservoirs. Since 1980, this species has been recorded in Derbyshire at an average of over five localities each year, with a maximum of ten sites in 1991 and 12 in 2009, but only one in 1984 and 1986.

Most records involve one to three birds, but there have also been several instances of four or five together. Groups of seven were seen at Ladybower Reservoir on 13th February 1991, Long Eaton Gravel Pits on 7th May 1991 and Willington Gravel Pits on 19th November 1993. A party of nine arrived at Staunton Harold Reservoir on 31st January 1976, joining a lone female. The largest gathering was a flock of 17 (seven males and ten females) which arrived at Ogston Reservoir on 26th December 1963 and, with slightly fluctuating numbers, remained into spring 1964. This location also held three males and five females/immatures on 1st November 2010.

Smaller groups have wintered in the county on other occasions, with up to four birds at Staunton Harold Reservoir from January to March 1965, and up to five at Church Wilne Reservoir from November 1975 to April 1976. Two females which arrived at the latter site on 17th January 1988 were joined by a male on 5th March and all three remained until 17th April. Other long-staying individuals have included a female at Stubbing Pond from 26th November 1972 to 26th April 1973 and presumably the same bird from 14th October 1973 to 4th May 1974. More recently an immature male was present at Willington Gravel Pits from 26th December 1993 to 12th April 1994. Even though birds have often remained for a few weeks, the majority of visits are of only one to three days. One which summered in the Derwentdale area in 1985 was known to be injured.

Eider
Somateria mollissima
A rare visitor.

The Eider is reputed to be Britain's most abundant sea duck, having an exclusively coastal distribution, except for birds occasionally blown inland during rough weather (Lack 1986). Considering this species' essentially maritime nature, there are some impressive records for land-locked Derbyshire.

The species was first recorded in the county 'about 30 years prior to 1966' at Derwent (Frost). The next record related to two birds at Clay Mills Gravel Pits on 25th April 1971. Including this sighting, there have been 19 records involving 107 birds, as follows:

Period	Records	Birds
1950s	–	–
1960s	–	–
1970s	2	32
1980s	7	15
1990s	9	44
2000–11	1	16
Totals	19	107

The largest number of records has been during the months of October, November and December, which perhaps suggests movement due to adverse weather, but only two records have been attributed to such a cause, and these were in February 1986 and May 1997. Moreover, the arrival of Eiders at four different sites in the county in early December 1982, including a party of seven at Swarkestone Lake, occurred in conditions described as 'mild, ordinary weather'. At the same time, other birds were noted in the adjacent counties of Leicestershire, South Yorkshire and the West Midlands. Nor was unusual weather mentioned as a factor contributing to an amazing influx of short-staying birds on 31st October 1993.

Comprising flocks of 26, including five males, at Carsington Water and seven, including one male, at Arnfield Reservoir, this influx accounts for the high incidence of birds in October shown in the chart. A party of 16, including five males, also visited Carsington Water on 21st April 2003, but the largest flock ever recorded in Derbyshire was of 30 (including five males) at Ogston Reservoir on 23rd November 1975; these departed to the south-west in groups of 17 and 13 within 15 minutes of each other. Such occurrences are exceptional, as the majority of records have involved single birds, although there have also been a few instances of up to four birds seen together.

Apart from two occasions, Eiders have always remained for a maximum of three days. In 1993, one individual from an original party of four (including three males), which arrived at Ladybower Reservoir on 7th November, stayed until 6th December. Some members of a group of seven birds which were found at Swarkestone Lake on 5th December 1982 remained for several weeks, most notably an immature male which was last seen on 9th May 1983, representing a stay of over five months.

Eiders have been found predominantly at reservoirs and gravel pits, with the highest number of records from Carsington Water, Ogston Reservoir, Foremark Reservoir and Elvaston Quarry (two each). Other sites visited include British Celanese Lakes Nature Reserve, Carr Vale, Derwent Reservoir, Holmebrook Valley Park, Langley Mill Flashes and Staunton Harold Reservoir.

It is seldom possible to establish the origin of these visitors, but a bird found exhausted (which later died) at Langley Mill Flashes on 8th February 1986 was carrying a ring from Arnhem, Holland. The bird was an adult male and its remains were given to Wollaton Hall Museum, Nottingham.

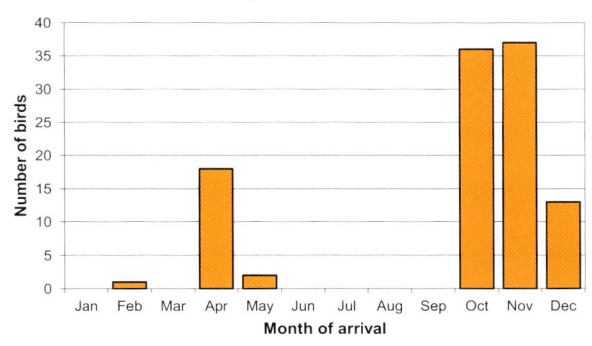

Long-tailed Duck
Clangula hyemalis
A rare visitor.

One of the most attractive and numerous of the sea ducks, the Long-tailed Duck has a distinctly coastal distribution during the winter months. However, a few individuals or small groups may occasionally stray inland.

Whitlock regarded this species as an occasional visitor to the Trent Valley. He quoted Pilkington (1789), who said that examples had been obtained at Sinfin Moor; and Glover (1829) who said that it had been seen on the Rivers Trent and Derwent. Mosley said that a specimen in Sir John Crewe's collection had been obtained at Twyford (Mosley & Brown 1863), while J.J. Briggs said that Long-tailed Ducks occasionally visited the Trent in hard winters. There were no more records until December 1943 when an immature was seen at Shipley Reservoir (Frost). Twenty years later, an immature was seen at Barbrook Reservoir on 17th November 1963, to be followed by a female at Ogston Reservoir on 29th December 1963. Since the 1943 record, there have been 43 records involving 53 birds:

Period	Records	Birds
1950s	–	–
1960s	7	7
1970s	11	13
1980s	8	11
1990s	11	16
2000–11	6	6
Totals	43	53

Records usually concern solitary birds (85%) although two females were at Barbrook Reservoir on 26th November 1972, and two immatures were at Church Wilne Reservoir from 4th November 1979 to 6th January 1980. Church Wilne also held two birds on 19th February 1989, while two remained at Linacre Reservoirs from 20th November to 10th December 1990. A party of three appeared at Ogston Reservoir on 30th October 1988, and the same water currently holds the county record of five birds, which were present on 7th May 1991.

Since most Long-tailed Ducks arrive in northern British waters during October, subsequent southerly movements are indicated by a distinct November peak in the monthly distribution of arrivals in Derbyshire (1960–2011), as shown in the chart. A similar pattern is apparent in the West Midlands (Harrison *et al.* 1982).

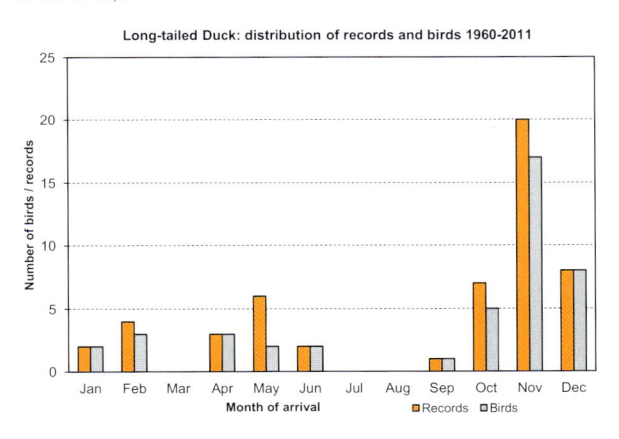

A small number of records refer to late spring or early summer migrants. A summer-plumaged male was found at Barbrook Reservoir on 28th May 1973; a party of five (four males and a female), as previously mentioned, visited Ogston Reservoir on 7th May 1991 and frequently engaged in display; and a summer-plumaged male was present at Willington Gravel Pits from 26th June to 1st July 1993. A female was at Carsington Water from 15th June to 19th September 2004.

Most birds have stayed for one day only, but a small number have remained for more than a month. An immature male frequented Ladybower Reservoir from 7th November 1987 to 24th April 1988 and was latterly seen displaying to Goldeneye and Red-breasted Merganser. An adult female remained at Church Wilne Reservoir from 16th February to 26th April 1992. At Carsington Water, a female was present from 18th November 2003 to 15th February 2004, and the 2004 long-staying bird (June–September) has already been mentioned. A first-winter male was at Williamthorpe Nature Reserve from 27th November 2007 to 3rd February 2008. However, the longest reported stay concerns two birds at Church Wilne Reservoir, one of which lingered for exactly six months, from 4th November 1979 to 4th May 1980.

Sites not mentioned above where this species has occurred are the River Trent at Ingleby; Aston-on-Trent, Clay Mills, Willington, Swarkestone and Long Eaton Gravel Pits; Foremark, Staunton Harold, Crowhole, Ramsley and Combs Reservoirs; Brinsley Flash, Carsington Water, Rother Valley Country Park (now in South Yorkshire) and Brough Clay Pits.

Common Scoter
Melanitta nigra
An uncommon but regular visitor and passage migrant.

This distinctive species is recorded more frequently inland than any other sea duck, and in Derbyshire it is an uncommon but regular visitor, particularly to the larger reservoirs. Even in Whitlock's day, Common Scoters often occurred in the Trent Valley and he thought it probable that a few small flocks migrated annually across the county to the south-west. Frost commented that they may appear 'at any time of year, but peak numbers are in April, July and August, with fewest records for January and February'. Since 1953, birds have been recorded in all years except 1959, the highest yearly totals being 89 in 1994 and 109 in 2004, and the lowest being three in 1955. The increasing frequency of occurrence over recent periods is revealed in the chart.

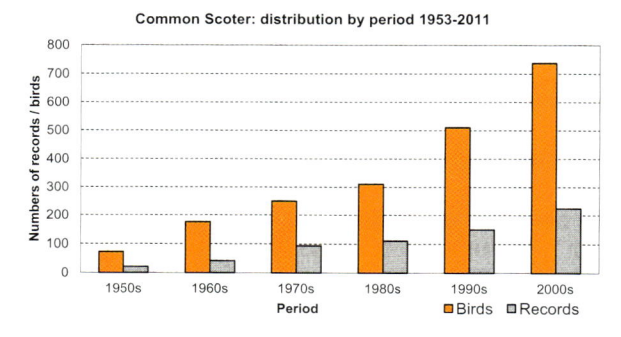

Month	All birds	Males	Females and immatures	Unknown sex
January	16	4	2	10
February	7	4	–	3
March	92	51	18	23
April	344	132	67	145
May	178	70	70	38
June	158	60	20	78
July	463	180	40	243
August	248	96	40	112
September	136	23	19	94
October	95	16	27	52
November	227	7	101	119
December	51	13	26	12

Common Scoter: distribution by period 1953-2011

Various studies have established a clear pattern of purposeful overland passage and moult migration, with distinct peaks in April–May, July–August and October–November (Spencer 1969; Hawker 1970). Key (1983) analysed all records of Common Scoter in Derbyshire from 1954 to 1982 and concluded that there was significant movement through the county from April to September inclusive, and also in November. The monthly table showing breakdown by gender and covering 1954–2011 reinforces and extends his findings to more recent years. Males feature strongly on spring migration, most notably in April. However there is an even greater predominance of males in July and August, which is probably indicative of birds on moult migration to coastal waters in western Britain. This contrasts with the movements in late autumn, particularly November, which involve almost exclusively female or immature birds.

Although records of single birds are the most common throughout the year, small parties of two to five also occur fairly regularly during the passage months. Groups of more than five are relatively infrequent and there have been only eight flocks comprising 20 birds or more, as follows:

Year	Date	Location	Sex (if known)
1960	5th August	Fernilee Reservoir	19m 1f
1971	26th July	Howden Reservoir	27m 1f
1989	14th June	Foremark Reservoir	21
1992	9th August	Arnfield Reservoir	14m 7f
1995	6th November	Carsington Water	35f/immatures
1998	3rd July	Ladybower Reservoir	25m 1f
2001	18th July	Barbrook Reservoir	23m 6f
2004	29th July	Middleton Moor	75
2005	19th August	Carsington Water	47

The record flock at Middleton Moor flew low to the south-west over the lagoons at dusk. Apart from the flock at Carsington Water in November 1995, these large groups have all occurred between mid-June and early August. In common with the vast majority of sightings at any time of year, they were recorded on one day only. Common Scoters rarely remain for more than a few days and usually single birds are involved. A notable exception was a pair which remained at Church Wilne Reservoir from 31st March to 23rd April 1990.

This species is found at an average of six localities each year, predominantly on the larger water bodies in the county, as shown in the chart. Carsington Water is the most regular site, having been visited annually since its creation in 1992. Ogston Reservoir has records in every year since 1960, but far fewer than Carsington Water. Barbrook Reservoir had been the most frequently visited upland locality, with sightings in 28 years since 1954, but just one since it was largely drained in 2002. In the Trent Valley, Church Wilne Reservoir is the most favoured site (records in 22 years since its creation in 1971), although there have been occurrences at Foremark Reservoir in nearly all years since 1990.

Common Scoter: major sites 1950-2011

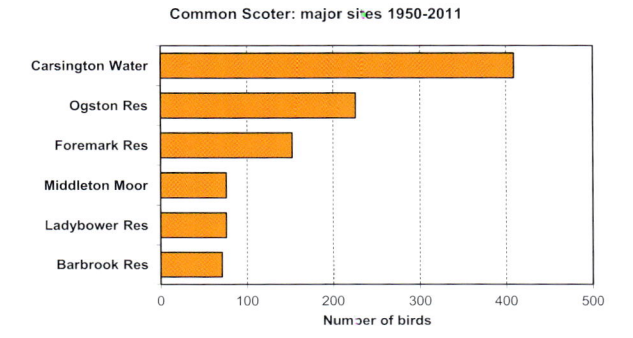

Site	Number of birds
Carsington Water	~410
Ogston Res	~230
Foremark Res	~160
Middleton Moor	~80
Ladybower Res	~80
Barbrook Res	~70

Less frequently visited locations include the gravel pits at Barrow, Drakelow, Long Eaton, Swarkestone and Willington and reservoirs in north-west Derbyshire. Occasionally, birds have been seen on the River Trent and also at relatively small waters such as Flash Dam (nowadays greatly reduced in size and surrounded by building development), Allestree Lake, Alvaston Lake, Wyver Lane, Steetley Quarry, Holmebrook Valley Park, Pleasley Colliery, Carr Vale and even floodwater by the River Dove at Mapleton.

An unusual record concerns an injured female, picked up in a garden at Spondon on 1st January 1982, that was taken into care and subsequently released on the east coast. Another interesting sighting was a flock of 11 birds flying north over a suburban area at Newbold, Chesterfield on 28th April 1993.

Surf Scoter
Melanitta perspicillata
A very rare visitor.

Surf Scoters breed across northern North America, and winter on the Pacific and Atlantic coasts south to Mexico. They were once regarded as great rarities in Britain, but records have increased considerably, with a total of 376 between 1958 and 2002. Fraser and Rogers (2005) said that records now averaged some 10–20 a year. Because of increased frequency, records were not considered by BBRC after 1991.

Nevertheless, inland records remain exceptional. The sole Derbyshire sighting concerns a juvenile at Foremark Reservoir on 9th November 2005. It was found among a flock of Tufted Duck and was present for most of the day, during which it was seen by over 100 observers. It was only the seventh inland record of this maritime duck, the others being in Cambridgeshire (twice), Warwickshire, Oxfordshire, Lancashire and Worcestershire (Key 2006a).

Velvet Scoter
Melanitta fusca
A rare visitor.

Each of the four records before 1950 concerned birds shot at localities in the south of the county. Whitlock quoted records of one killed on the Derwent at Draycott in 1853 and another at Willington prior to 1860. Frost revealed that two others on the River Trent had suffered the same fate. The first was shot by a farmer at Ingleby on 16th November 1932. The second had been present for over a week before it was shot at Catton Park on 26th December 1935. It dived and was not recovered but its remains were later found in nearby Walton Wood, perhaps taken there by a fox.

Since 1950 there have been 22 records, involving 48 birds. Note the short stays in each instance, with the exception of the 1953 bird.

Year	Location and date
1953	Allestree Lake, one from 13th to 15th December
1955	Fernilee Reservoir, a male on 18th February
1963	River Derwent at Duffield, an immature male on 21st January
1963	River Dove at Newton Solney, a male on 26th January, joined by a female on 29th
1963	Weston-on-Trent, two on 4th February
1963	Ladybower Reservoir, a male on 6th October
1965	Ogston Reservoir, a female on 10th January
1965	Butterley Reservoir, a male on 30th November
1966	Ogston Reservoir, a female on 13th February
1966	Ogston Reservoir, a male on 20th November
1968	Butterley Reservoir, a female on 26th December
1974	Ogston Reservoir, a male and an immature female on 13th October
1976	Old Whittington Sewage Farm, an adult male flew south-south-east on 10th January
1979	Ogston Reservoir, 16, including 14 males, circled the site before departing to the north-east on 10th May
1985	Ogston Reservoir, a first-winter male on 11th February
1985	Foremark Reservoir, a second-winter male on 16th–17th February was taken into care but died later
1987	Youlgreave, a female on a pond on 24th January was found dead the next day
1989	Ogston Reservoir, two females and an immature male on 8th April
1992	Foremark Reservoir, four immature males on 20th April
1996	Carsington Water, an adult male and three immature males on 2nd May
2002	Barrow Gravel Pits, an immature male on 25th March
2008	Dove Valley Lake, a female or immature on 12th September

Analysis by period and months is as follows.

Period	Records	Birds
1950s	2	2
1960s	9	11
1970s	3	19
1980s	4	6
1990s	2	8
2000–11	2	2
Totals	22	48

Month	Records	Birds
January	5	6
February	5	6
March	1	1
April	2	7
May	2	20
September	1	1
October	2	3
November	2	2
December	2	2
Totals	22	48

Bufflehead
Bucephala albeola
A very rare vagrant or possibly feral visitor.

In Britain, Buffleheads are major rarities, with only 14 records accepted by BBRC up to the end of 2010 (Hudson *et al.* 2011). The majority of these have occurred since 1994, and this may be linked to an increase and spread in the eastern population. This recent surge in records has also coincided with a general upward trend in the number of Nearctic ducks seen in Britain (Fraser & Rogers 2005). However, the numbers of this species kept in captivity increased significantly after 1980, and the likelihood of Buffleheads seen in Britain having a captive origin has become much greater (Knox 2001).

There has been one Derbyshire record, documented by Key and James (2005a). A male was at Barrow Gravel Pits on 20th June 2004; it had been ringed, strongly suggesting that it was an escape from captivity. This was presumed to be the same bird that was also seen at locations in Staffordshire, Warwickshire and the West Midlands from 24th May to 25th June, although that individual was said to be unringed. There were two further Buffleheads seen in Britain in the spring of 2004: a male in Greater Manchester and West Yorkshire; and another male on the Outer Hebrides. The arrival of these three birds might reflect a small influx in spring of that year which, however, lends weight to the possibility that they were of wild origin (Rogers *et al.* 2005).

Goldeneye
Bucephala clangula
A fairly common winter visitor and passage migrant. Rare in summer.

Although sometimes regarded primarily as a sea duck, the Goldeneye is commonly encountered on a variety of inland water bodies throughout Britain. At the end of the nineteenth century this species was generally considered to be a regular winter visitor to southern Derbyshire (Whitlock). However, the only authenticated occurrences in the north were of one shot at Sutton Scarsdale in 1882, and an undated record from Baslow, quoted by Jourdain. The scarcity of sightings from northern Derbyshire was remarked upon in *British Birds*, when two were reported from Combs Reservoir in March 1927. This elicited a response from A.W. Boyd who had seen Goldeneye at Derwent in January of the same year and believed they were often to be found on Pennine reservoirs outside the county (Frost). The species undoubtedly became more widespread later in the twentieth century, as Frost commented that they 'may visit any sizeable stretch of water in the county, including reservoirs, lakes, gravel pits, and the larger rivers', while the biggest flock was of about 50 birds on the River Trent at King's Mills in January 1963.

Since 1980, this duck has been recorded on average from around 30 sites each year, and usually from a diversity of wetland areas. Such localities may be as wide-ranging as Arnfield and Howden Reservoirs in the north-west, Pebley Pond in the north-east, Ogston Reservoir, Carsington Water and Osmaston Park in central areas, and Catton Park (situated by the River Trent) in the extreme south. Nevertheless, in common with most other wildfowl, the well-watched reservoirs and gravel pit complexes concentrated in the Trent Valley invariably produce the most records and the largest counts. Currently the highest number is 72 at Drakelow Nature Reserve in January 1998, closely followed by 71 at Church Wilne Reservoir in February 2001. Other sites with maxima of over 50 are Foremark Reservoir (62 in February 1987), Willington Gravel Pits (54 in February 1986) and Aston-on-Trent Gravel Pits (69 in February 2010). Elsewhere in this area, gatherings of 20–49 birds have been recorded at Swarkestone Lake and on several stretches of the River Trent.

The largest flocks outside the Trent Valley are one of 40 on the River Derwent at Draycott in December 1996, while further north, Carsington Water held a maximum of 41 in January 2011, and the greatest number at Ogston Reservoir was 26 in November 2000. In the Peak District, the highest counts are mostly from Ladybower Reservoir, which had a maximum of 20 in January 2001. Barbrook Reservoir was another regular haunt of wintering Goldeneye, with a highest count of 13 birds in December 1995, but very few have been reported since it was largely drained in 2002. An unusual record of 12 on the very small Crowhole Reservoir on 2nd April 1986 probably involved passage birds. Up to ten have been present at many other waters throughout the county.

Further evidence that Goldeneye are more numerous nowadays is proved by the long-term national wildfowl counts, carried out on a monthly basis from September to March. The average maximum for Derbyshire in the winters from 1971/72 to 1975/76 was 52 (Frost). During 1990/91 to 1994/95 this figure had risen to 86, and although the subsequent five-year period indicated a decrease to 73, in line with national trends, this may have been attributable to a lack of observer coverage at important local waters. The mean maximum monthly counts as recorded by WeBS from 1986/87 to 1999/2000 are shown in the table.

Month	Mean maximum
September	–
October	3
November	37
December	57
January	76
February	69
March	61

As a rule, the first Goldeneye arrive in October, but there have been at least ten September records. The earliest date is 16th September (in 1975, 1979 and 1984) although a bird seen on 30th August 1993 at Church Wilne Reservoir was present simultaneously with another individual which had summered there. The average date of arrival from 1955 to 1979 was 18th October, whereas from 1978 to 2011 it was 10th October. Numbers build up steadily during November and December, and normally reach a peak between January and March. Counts are still relatively high in April, and no doubt include passage migrants returning to breeding areas. Since pair-formation takes place on wintering grounds, male Goldeneye are often seen displaying to potential suitors, especially in early spring, and in March 1995 copulation was observed at Drakelow Nature Reserve.

The average date of departure (1978–2011) is 29th April. While Frost commented that 'stragglers have been seen in all of the summer months', records of Goldeneye summering in Derbyshire have become progressively more frequent. They have occurred in most years since 1990, though some of these birds have been known to be injured. Most notably, a pair (of which the female had a damaged wing) was present for seven consecutive summers (2000–06) at Pebley Pond, but there was no evidence of breeding. Frost also gave details of an interesting observation concerning an adult female which made short, circular display flights over Barbrook Reservoir on 13th June 1954. The Goldeneye became an established breeder in Scotland during the 1970s and the British population has subsequently increased and expanded its range, encouraged in some areas by nest-box schemes. Future breeding within the county would appear to be a possibility, and nest-boxes have been erected in one area in the hope that this might occur.

Smew
Mergus albellus
A scarce winter visitor.

According to Whitlock, visits of this small and attractive sawbill were not infrequent, and usually occurred during the most severe winters. He knew of only two records away from the Trent Valley area: a female shot at Staveley in 1774 and a male seen at Osmaston in 1855. Frost commented that 'there has probably been little change in status since Whitlock's day' and that the arrival of Smew in Derbyshire largely coincided with the onset of cold weather 'when a few birds may be driven on to the unfrozen River Trent and other waters in the south of the county'.

The species undoubtedly remained a rare winter visitor until the last two decades of the twentieth century, almost invariably in small numbers, with peak counts of six at Repton in March 1947, about 24 at King's Mills in March 1955, at least nine in the Newton Solney area between January and March 1963, and six at Drakelow Nature Reserve in January 1979.

Since 1980, with the exception of 1983, Smew have been recorded annually and with generally increasing frequency. The five-yearly totals of records and birds between 1950 and 2009 are revealed in the table.

Period	Records	Birds
1950–54	–	–
1955–59	2	25
1960–64	8	22
1965–69	6	6
1970–74	1	1
1975–79	10	17
1980–84	8	16
1985–89	26	40
1990–94	20	25
1995–99	52	142
2000–04	60	92
2005–09	26	39
Totals	219	425

During the winter of 1996/97 an exceptional influx occurred throughout the Midlands and southern England as large numbers of Smew were forced by freezing conditions to leave their traditional wintering areas on the Continent at the end of the year. Even allowing for possible duplication of records (as a result of regular local movements), a total of 50 birds may have been present in Derbyshire, including a flock of 12 at Long Eaton Gravel Pits on 8th January 1997 and 11 at Drakelow Nature Reserve on 20th February 1997.

In subsequent years, there have been site counts of up to 17 birds, predominantly from the south of the county, although the majority of records are still of only one or two birds. As well as an increase in the number of sightings, even during relatively mild winters, there has been a greater tendency for Smew to remain for longer periods. This is most evident at Drakelow Nature Reserve and Aston-on-Trent Gravel Pits where there have been several instances of individuals or small groups staying for over four weeks. The longest stay concerns a first-winter male which remained at the Drakelow site for over four months, from 24th November 1993 to 26th March 1994. Long-staying birds have also been present at Willington Gravel Pits and Carsington Water on a few occasions. In recent years, Aston-on-Trent Gravel Pits has become established as the county's premier site for this species, with an impressive peak of 17 on 6th February 2011.

However, perhaps uniquely among all the wintering ducks that are not vagrants to the county, this species has never occurred during the summer months. The earliest arrival was on 27th October 2003 at Drakelow Nature Reserve, while the latest occurrence was at Church Wilne Reservoir on 10th April 1988. Frost stated that most records were in November, but since 1980, Smew have appeared more frequently in December and January, as shown in the table, which summarizes all records between 1980 and 2009 by month of arrival.

Month of arrival	Birds
October	3
November	28
December	93
January	134
February	60
March	13
April	3
Total	334

Sightings have predominantly related to 'redheads' (females or immatures), with adult males comprising little more than 20% of all individuals identified in recent decades. The exceptional flock of 12 birds at Long Eaton Gravel Pits in 1997 was also noteworthy as it contained nine adult males.

Although Smew have become more regular visitors, occurrences continue to be concentrated in the Trent Valley, with Drakelow Nature Reserve, and Aston-on-Trent and Willington Gravel Pits particularly favoured. Other gravel pit complexes have been visited on several occasions including those at Elvaston, Hilton, Long Eaton, Shardlow, Swarkestone and, more recently, Barrow. This species prefers fairly large water bodies and has been found in most recent years at Church Wilne, Foremark and Staunton Harold Reservoirs, as well as Findern Lake. Conversely, sightings on the River Trent have become less common, though this may be related to the fact that nearby reservoirs have rarely frozen over since the mid-1980s.

Away from the Trent Valley, Carsington Water has already become the most frequented site, hosting up to five birds in some years. Ogston Reservoir has been visited on eight occasions, including a party of four birds in December 1997. There have also been occasional sightings of this duck on smaller waters, usually in lowland areas. Such sites have included Belper River Gardens, Bretby Park, Ednaston, Loscoe Dam, Manor Floods, Melbourne Pool, Osmaston, Renishaw Park, Shipley Lake, Williamthorpe Nature Reserve and Yeldersley. The only records from upland regions have been of single 'redheads' at Combs Reservoir on 3rd January 1996 and 14th February 2006, and Arnfield Reservoir on 22nd March 1984, with two birds at the latter locality on 29th–30th November 2003.

It may be that the creation of reservoirs and the plethora of flooded gravel pits in recent years, has been of benefit to the Smew. The earlier arrival dates and longer stays suggest an expansion of normal wintering range, rather than severe winter weather driving birds to our inland localities.

Red-breasted Merganser
Mergus serrator
A scarce winter visitor and passage migrant. A scarce breeder, mainly in the Peak District.

In the nineteenth century a few individuals of this sawbill were shot on the Rivers Trent and Derwent, and also on the lakes which then existed at Sutton Scarsdale (Whitlock; Jourdain). This duck was regarded as a rare visitor to the county, found only in winter, and Frost revealed that the first record in the twentieth century was not until 1940, with hardly more than a dozen further sightings in the following 30 years. Apart from one seen in September 1969, all dated records were between November and April, but since 1971 Red-breasted Mergansers have occurred annually, with increasing frequency, and at all times of year.

During the 1970s, birds summered on several occasions on reservoirs in north-west Derbyshire, and proof of breeding was first obtained on 1st July 1973, when a female with ducklings was seen in the Goyt Valley. Two pairs also bred at the same locality in 1978, while successful breeding was reported in the following year at Ladybower Reservoir. These instances were undoubtedly connected with the species' colonization of north-west England which had taken place since 1950. Except for 1985 and 2003, breeding was proved annually in the county until 2006, since when there have been no breeding records. Although it is unusual for more than three broods to be reported in any year, a total of at least nine broods in 1994 was exceptional, and included a minimum of seven at Ladybower Reservoir. Successful breeding has been reported at this site in most years from 1979 to 2005, but not subsequently, and also on eight occasions on the adjacent Derwent and Howden Reservoirs.

The Derbyshire BBS (1995–99) discovered evidence of breeding in 19 tetrads (eight proven, nine probable and two possible) and it provided clear evidence that the stronghold of the population is situated in Upper Derwentdale.

Birds normally arrive in this area from March onwards, though in some recent years it has been as early as January. A female was seen with seven ducklings at Derwent Reservoir on 5th May 1986, but most broods are found in June and July, and young birds are sometimes still present until September. Pairs are also regularly reported in spring and early summer on other upland waters, and along several stretches of the River Derwent between Bamford and Chatsworth Park, although breeding attempts here seem to be rare. A brood was reported on the River Dove near Ilam Rock in 2002. The only confirmed breeding in south Derbyshire occurred at Willington Gravel Pits in 1993 and 1995, and involved a single pair. Birds summered at this locality in the intervening year and were present in the Trent Valley in 1996 but no further proof of breeding was obtained.

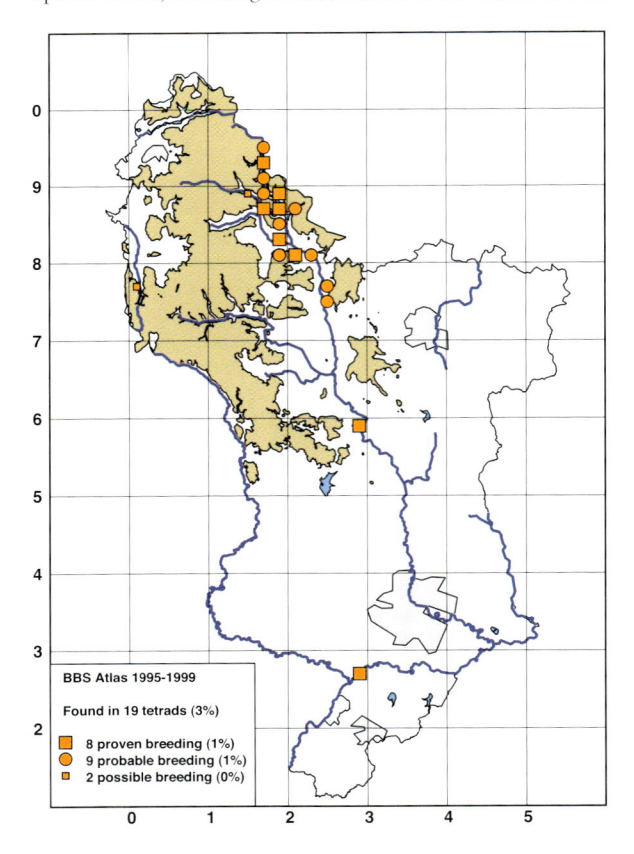

The table reveals the total number of broods reported in each period from 1980 to 2009 inclusive, although none were seen in 2007–11 which suggests a downturn in fortunes since 1995. Having an almost exclusively piscivorous diet, this species (and its congener the Goosander) may well have suffered from persecution by the fishing fraternity. However, there seems no natural reason to prevent the population from proliferating in the future, especially as the habitat requirement for breeding is far less restricted than that of the largely tree-nesting Goosander.

Period	Total broods
1980–84	5
1985–89	10
1990–94	19
1995–99	7
2000–04	6
2005–09	4

Outside the breeding season, sightings of Red-breasted Mergansers are more sporadic and less predictable. Passage migrants and winter visitors can turn up at a variety of waters anywhere in the county, most often in ones or twos, although greater numbers may appear in cold spells. An exceptional influx occurred during prolonged severe weather from January to March 1979, when several parties of up to five birds were found in the Trent Valley. The largest counts in the autumn and winter periods have been of 21 on the River Derwent between Bamford and Hathersage on 7th September 1991, 15 at Chatsworth Park on 17th February 1991, and 12 at Ladybower Reservoir on 16th October 1988. The majority of visits are short-lived, often lasting no more than a day or two, though occasionally individuals have remained at the same site for over a month. The longest recorded stay concerns a first-winter male which was at Drakelow Nature Reserve for over four months, from 18th November 1980 to 2nd April 1981.

In the Trent Valley, most gravel pits have been visited at least once, but the majority of sightings have been at Foremark, Staunton Harold and Church Wilne Reservoirs. Elsewhere, Ogston Reservoir has been the most frequently visited site with records in at least 15 years since 1980 alone. In recent winters, other, more diverse localities have included Dove Dale, Lathkill Dale, Monsal Dale, Holmebrook Valley Park, Renishaw Park, Carr Vale, Williamthorpe Nature Reserve, Stubbing Court, Birdholme Wildfowl Reserve, Bennerley Marsh and Markeaton Park.

BBS Atlas 1995-1999
Found in 19 tetrads (3%)
- 8 proven breeding (1%)
- 9 probable breeding (1%)
- 2 possible breeding (0%)

Goosander
Mergus merganser
A fairly common winter visitor and passage migrant, and an uncommon breeder.

Goosanders have always been the most frequent of the sawbills in Derbyshire. Whitlock quoted several records, dating back to 1774, and towards the end of the nineteenth century he believed Goosanders could be found on an almost annual basis. They were more likely to be encountered in hard weather, particularly on the River Trent, but were occasionally seen at other sites. Frost described a broadly similar pattern of occurrence, except that Staunton Harold Reservoir had become the most favoured haunt and held a regular wintering flock in the 1970s which peaked at 49 in March 1974. However, at this time, the River Trent still tended to host the largest gatherings in prolonged cold weather. The most notable examples were flocks of 125 in January 1952 and 117 in January 1963, both reported in the Newton Solney area. Virtually all records of Goosander were from September to May inclusive, and summering birds in 1963, 1974 and 1975 were considered to be sick or injured.

The first evidence of a significant change in status was obtained during the spring of 1982, when a female was discovered in a nest hole within an area of ancient oaks in Chatsworth Park. Two years later, on 5th June 1984, a female was observed brooding several small ducklings by the River Derwent near Chatsworth House (Shaw & Shooter 1985). Breeding was proved again in 1986 on the same river, though much further downstream, in the vicinity of the Cromford Canal.

The establishment of a breeding population in the county represents a further stage in the colonization of Britain by this species, which first bred in Scotland in 1871, reached England (Northumberland) by 1941, and continued to spread southwards through Lancashire and Yorkshire during the 1970s.

The Derbyshire BBS (1995–99) found the species breeding in 43 tetrads, all of which were situated within the immediate environs of the four rivers, as illustrated in the distribution map, and almost exactly equally split between proven and probable/possible as shown on the legend.

Since 1988 Goosander have bred annually, with usually five to ten broods reported, but at least 14 were found in 1991 and possibly as many as 22 in 1995. Therefore, despite approximately a decade's head start by the Red-breasted Merganser as a local breeding species, the Goosander has been the more successful of the two large sawbills, but for reasons unknown, numbers subsequently declined to only five to seven broods in some years.

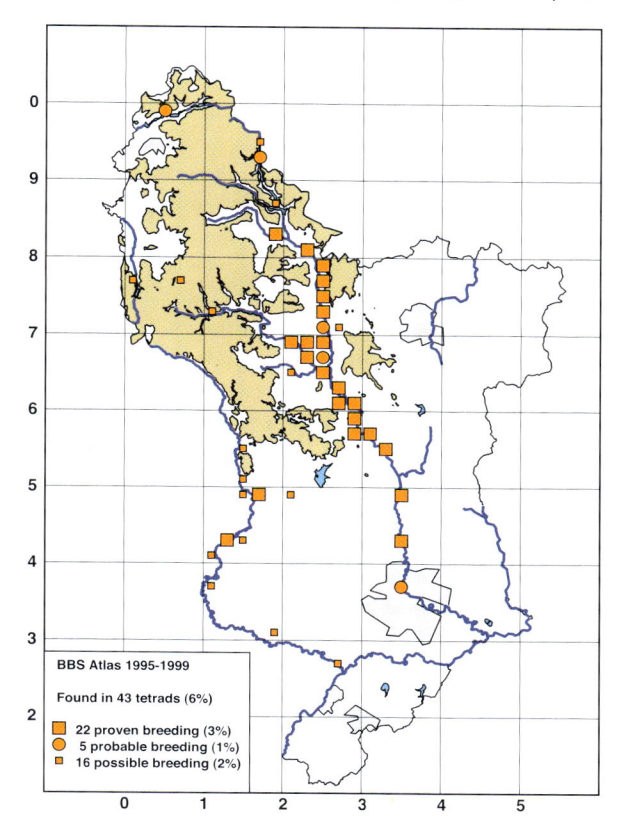

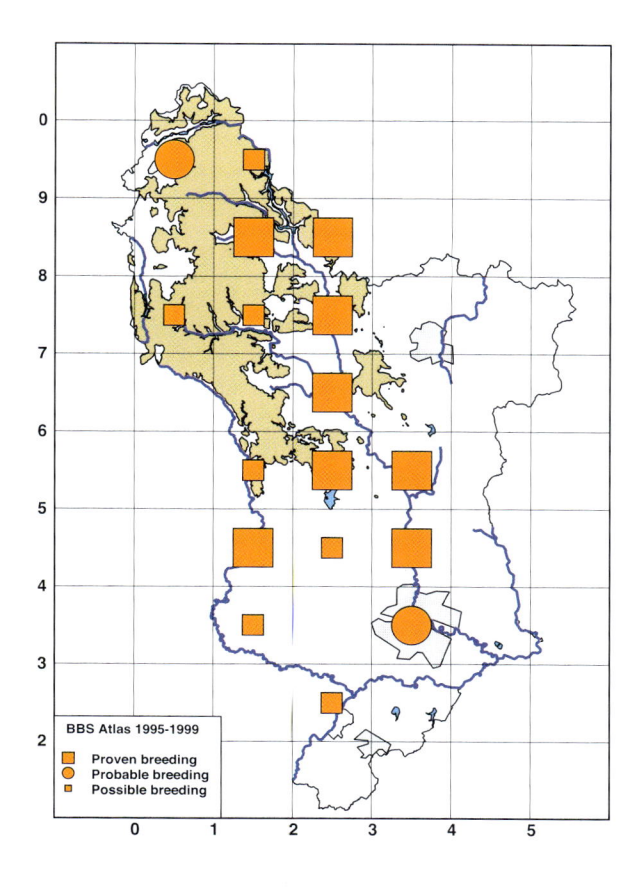

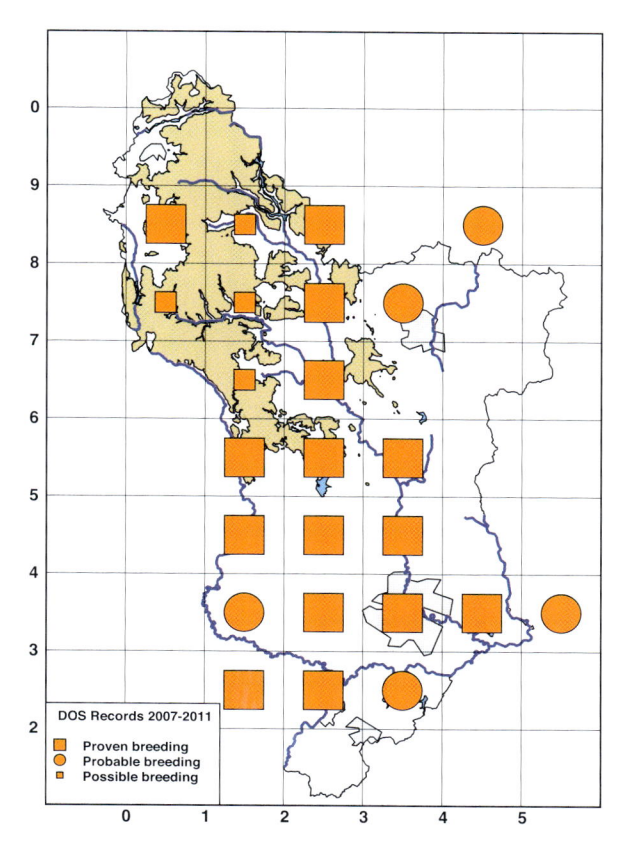

However, there has since been a partial recovery, with 11 broods seen in 2007–08 and 12 broods in 2010.

The Derwent has been by far the most important river for this species, with about 140 broods seen in 1988–2011. This figure includes many seen in the southern lowlands of the county since 1995, when two broods of ducklings were found between Duffield and Allestree. Young were seen on the same river at Darley Park in 2000 and breeding has been proved inside Derby City boundary and further south as far as Ambaston, in most years since then. Breeding was recorded on the River Wye in 11 years between 1990 and 2010, totalling 18 broods, and on the Dove, as far downstream as Marston-on-Dove, in most years during 1991–2010, involving 23 broods in all. Three broods were seen on the River Noe during 1992–96. The River Trent had its first breeding record in 2006 at Ingleby and in 2009 likewise the River Goyt at New Mills. A female with young was seen at Ogston Reservoir (which lies on the River Amber) in 1997. There were further extensions of range in 2010, when a brood was reported from the River Ecclesbourne below Idridgehay, while a female was seen to leave a presumed nest hole in a tree at Longford. Of the 12 broods seen in 2010, most were in the southern lowlands of the county. This range extension is shown clearly in the comparison maps for 1995–99 and 2007–11.

The largest brood recorded was of 17 young at Dovedale on 18th May 2002. Other interesting sightings have included two newly hatched youngsters, possibly abandoned, some 400m from the river at Chatsworth in May 1992 and a female with 12 ducklings crossing the A6 in rush-hour traffic at Cromford in May 1994. Most broods have been found between May and July, but in recent years a few have been reported in mid-April.

Studies by Meek and Little (1977) have shown that Goosanders often do not move far from their breeding areas in winter and this may to some extent explain the far greater numbers found in Derbyshire since the 1980s. Until it was largely drained in 2002, Barbrook Reservoir was a very important site for this duck, where throughout the 1990s a sizeable roosting flock built up from late summer or early autumn, and reached a maximum of 97 in November 1995. Birds were usually present here in significant numbers from August until April.

This species has undoubtedly become more widespread, with birds nowadays recorded each winter at well over 50 localities throughout the county. Flocks of more than ten are commonly reported, especially in the south, and from time to time on various upland reservoirs, including those in the Goyt and Upper Derwent Valleys and in the Longdendale complex. Goosanders may also be found on smaller waters, particularly lakes and ponds, even in suburban areas. Recent examples have included sightings in Derby at Allestree, Alvaston and British Celanese Lakes Nature Reserve, and in Chesterfield at Holmebrook Valley Park and Walton Dam.

The highest overall numbers usually occur in January and February, as is apparent in the table This summarizes the mean maximum monthly counts, between September and March, established by WeBS from 1986/87 to 1999/2000, and contrasts markedly with the average maximum count of only 28 during the corresponding periods between 1969/70 and 1973/74, as revealed by Frost.

Month	Mean maximum
September	3
October	11
November	43
December	73
January	107
February	105
March	76

Since the late 1970s, Foremark Reservoir has replaced Staunton Harold Reservoir as the premier site, and also hosts the largest gatherings in severe weather rather than the River Trent. Flocks in excess of 125 have been reported here in seven winters, including the current county record of 275 on 3rd February 1996. Other locations which have held three-figure flocks are Swarkestone Lake (maximum of 140 on 11th February 1996), and Willington Gravel Pits (maximum of 105 on 15th March 1991), while Carsington Water and Long Eaton Gravel Pits both had 100 in January 1997. Goosander have also been regular visitors over many years to Ogston Reservoir, which has a highest count of 68 in February 1997.

There have been no ringing recoveries to date, but a female at Barbrook Reservoir on 16th September 1992 had been wing-tagged during the previous month, while in moult, on the Eden Estuary in Fife. What was presumed to be the same individual was reported again at the same site on 23rd September 1993 and at Dove Dale in December 1993, March 1994 and January 1995. A wing-tagged male was also seen with this bird in Dove Dale, on 19th March 1994.

Ruddy Duck
Oxyura jamaicensis
Formerly an uncommon resident.

This native of North America rapidly became established as a breeding species in Britain following the escape of several unpinioned birds from the headquarters of the Wildfowl Trust at Slimbridge, Gloucestershire in the late 1950s. Ruddy Ducks first bred in the wild at Chew Valley Lake, Avon in 1960 and within a few years began to colonize Midland counties. Their prodigious increase and spread made it inevitable that birds would soon reach Derbyshire, and by the 1990s they could be found throughout the year in a wide variety of wetland habitats. These ranged from small subsidence pools and gravel pits to the larger reservoirs such as Carsington Water.

The species was first recorded in the county on 12th January 1963 when two males were shot on the River Trent at Drakelow. Single birds occurred briefly in November 1965, July 1966,

February 1969 and September 1971, and the next record was of a male which remained at Ogston Reservoir for over a month, from 26th December 1972 to 5th February 1973 (Frost). There were no sightings in 1974, but from 1975 onwards the number of reports and birds began to rise sharply. In January 1977, up to eight were seen together at Staunton Harold Reservoir, while the first double-figure count was in January 1979 at Foremark Reservoir, where a flock of 26 built up during cold weather.

The preferred breeding habitat of this pugnacious but charismatic stiff-tail duck is small lakes and pools with dense peripheral vegetation, and many such waters exist in lowland Derbyshire. The first instance of confirmed breeding came from Osmaston, where adults were seen with young in September 1975 and 1978. Ruddy Ducks bred annually thereafter, with pairs present at more than 20 suitable localities between May and August in most years from the mid-1980s onwards. However, breeding was usually proved at only five to ten sites each year, as indicated in the table. The figures represent the mean numbers for five-year periods from 1980 to 2004 and also include the average number of broods reported.

Period	Mean number of localities (pairs present)	Mean number of localities (breeding proved)	Mean number of broods
1980–84	10	4	6
1985–89	21	5	6.5
1990–94	26	8	13
1995–99	22	8	12
2000–04	20	6	13

This species bred at about 47 localities in all. The majority of these sites held only one or two pairs, with the largest numbers at Renishaw Park, where there were seven broods in 1992 and five in 1998, and at Carr Vale where five or six broods were recorded each year from 2001 to 2003. These two sites, together with Carsington Water, Ednaston, Osmaston and Williamthorpe Nature Reserve have been the most regular breeding locations in the county.

The distribution map produced by the Derbyshire BBS (1995–99) revealed a virtual absence of the species in the north-west of the county and also south of the River Trent. During this period, breeding was proved in 15 tetrads and probable/possible in 20.

Sightings from upland areas in the county were quite rare, and in the Peak District the only instances of more than one bird were of a pair at Errwood Reservoir in January 1981 and two immatures at Barbrook Reservoir in August 1999.

The 'bubbling' display of the male was recorded between the extreme dates of 8th March (1998) and 14th November (1995). An individual in female or immature plumage was observed 'bubbling' at Williamthorpe Nature Reserve on 1st April 1998 and a male was seen displaying to a female Pochard at Hardwick on 17th April 1989. This duck was a relatively late nester, and broods were commonly reported in August and September. There was an instance of much earlier breeding, which was at Loscoe on 29th April 1990, when two adults were seen with four chicks.

The highest counts in the summer months occurred at the more productive breeding sites, such as 34 at Carr Vale in July 2002, 56 at Renishaw Park in August 1992 and 59 at Carsington Water in August 1999. However, in the winter period, the biggest gatherings were at the larger reservoirs. Foremark Reservoir held up to 50 birds in December 1981 and January 1982, and 68 in March 1985, while Church Wilne Reservoir hosted the first three-figure flocks in Derbyshire, with 107 present in February 1996 and January 1997. In later years, Carsington Water became the most important wintering site, recording annual maxima of 118 in January 2001, 161 in January 2002 and 199 in December 2003. It is believed that Carsington Water has the unwanted distinction of being the last British site to support a three-figure flock. Such large gatherings, which were of significance at national level, provide an interesting comparison with the much lower mean maximum monthly bird counts (September–March) as recorded in WeBS from 1986/87 to 1999/2000, shown in the table.

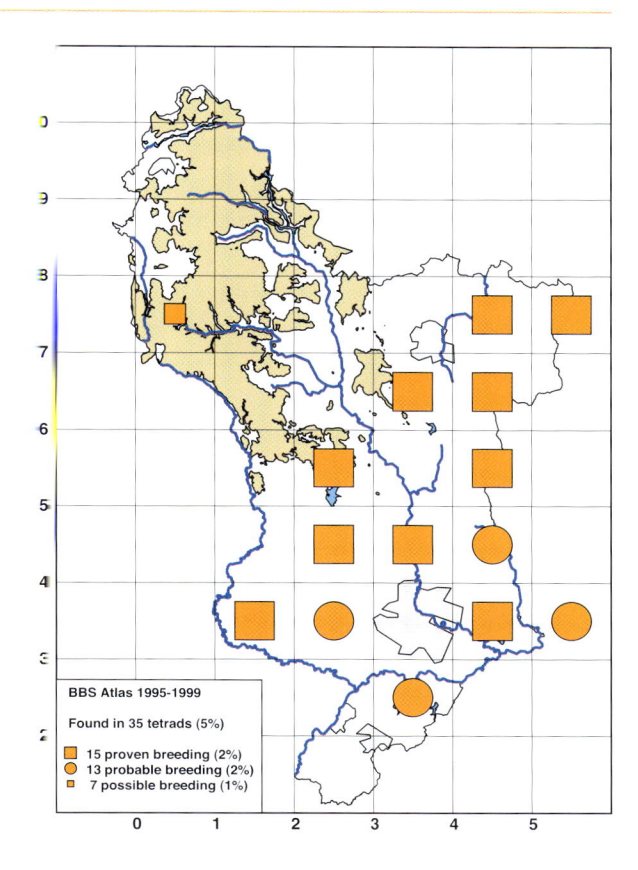

Month	Mean maximum
September	31
October	21
November	13
December	14
January	14
February	19
March	24

Interesting observations included one of a female described as 'all dark except for pale chin and belly', which summered at Williamthorpe Nature Reserve from 1995 to 1998; and an individual which was found on a road in Chellaston, Derby in December 1991. It was taken into care and later released on the River Trent.

The culling of the UK Ruddy Duck population was undertaken in an attempt to stop the species hybridizing with the White-headed Duck *Oxyura leucocephala* in Europe. Locally, this has involved shooting the birds, both at breeding and wintering sites. Because of disagreement with the cull, and in common with some neighbouring societies, the DOS has not published any site information on this species since 2004. It is also known that some observers, upset at what they have witnessed from the shooters, have perhaps understandably withheld information from the Society. It now appears that this controversial and widely unpopular cull has been largely successful, though whether total elimination will result remains to be seen. Breeding took place in Derbyshire in 2011 and there were thought to be up to ten birds in the county in hard weather during the 2011/12 winter.

Quail
Coturnix coturnix
A scarce and erratic summer visitor and passage migrant.

Quail are diminutive and secretive birds of open countryside. They usually occur in large, arable (especially cereal) fields, but are not uncommonly found on uncultivated land. Very few are seen and almost all records result from recorders hearing the male's unmistakable and far-carrying triple-song. While the song is often heard by day, it is most frequently uttered at dawn and dusk, and sometimes into the night. Because of this, Quail are undoubtedly underrecorded and, especially as a result of difficulties in accessing their nesting areas, breeding is particularly difficult to prove, with very few confirmed records for the county.

Quail have clearly always been scarce birds in Derbyshire, and being migrants (they are the only non-resident gamebirds) their numbers are prone to wide annual variations. Both Jourdain and Whitlock thought them most numerous in the southern half of the county, while Frost considered the most favoured areas were the Magnesian Limestone plateau and certain areas south of the River Trent. Although these areas are still among the most attractive to Quail, more recent records have shown a wider scatter, across many parts of the county. There are very few records of confirmed breeding, however, and the most recent of these were in 1994, in the Coton-in-the-Elms and Cauldwell areas.

By far the earliest ever Derbyshire record was of one flushed from a cereal field at Cutthorpe on 13th April 2011. Although there were also records on 1st May from Carr Vale in 1997 and Arleston in 2001, Quail have usually been first heard from mid-May onwards. The frequency of first records for the years 1979–2011 is summarized in the table:

Period	Records
11th–20th April	1
21st–30th April	–
1st–10th May	4
11th–20th May	11
21st–31st May	9
1st–10th June	3
11th–20th June	3
21st–30th June	2

The latest record in recent years is of one found in a garden in Burton upon Trent on 16th October 1982, which died on the following day. A wing of this species was found beneath the Derby Cathedral Peregrine site on 12th October 2005, and one was flushed by a dog at Dethick on 24th September 2007. However, at one time, winter records of Quail in England were more frequent (Brown & Grice 2005), and Whitlock reported that singles were shot near Tutbury on 22nd February 1847 and 15th December 1856. Although Tutbury lies just inside Staffordshire, presumably Whitlock was satisfied that these were Derbyshire records.

Frost reported that there had been a long-term decline in the number of birds visiting the county throughout the twentieth century, but nationally by the time of the 1988–91 Atlas the number of 10km squares in which Quail were recorded was almost double those recorded in the 1968–72 Atlas. Numbers vary so much from year to year that it is difficult to say for certain if there is a more recent population trend but cumulative records suggest an increase from 1980 until the end of the century. Thereafter numbers fell significantly in the 2000–04 period, followed by a rise in the following five years. The table refers to the number of singing males recorded within each period.

Period	Birds
1980–84	27–31
1985–89	48–49
1990–94	58–62
1995–99	81
2000–04	25–26
2005–09	64–66

In the county, 1975 was the most recent year in which no Quail were recorded. The best recent years were 1989, when about 29 were heard, and 1997, with about 27. Singing males may be unmated and roaming birds but, not uncommonly, groups of Quail are heard singing in a small area. Such gluts include up to 11 at Grangewood in 1977, six at Alderwasley in 1983, in the Palterton area in 1998 and at Elton Common in 2009. These clusters may have amalgamated to increase the chances of attracting receptive females. It is also possible that they involve birds which have been reared earlier in the same year in North Africa and Iberia, and subsequently moved north. Such birds can reproduce when as young as three months old.

The group at Elton Common was in lupin fields but most farmland records are from cereals, especially barley. However, there are several records from uncultivated ground, such as at Egginton Sewage Farm and the site of Pleasley Colliery, and there are many records, usually short-lived, from open moorland in the Peak District. A curious sighting of one eating seed in a Tupton garden on 7th August 1992 may relate to an escaped cage-bird. Some were said to have been released by shooters near Combs Reservoir in 2010.

An enterprising ringer caught three birds in the Elton Common group in June 2009 and was rewarded when one of these, an adult male, was shot less than two months later in August at Aliud, Spain, 1277km to the south. This was only the fourth recovery of a Quail ringed in Britain.

Red-legged Partridge
Alectoris rufa
A fairly common resident.

The Red-legged Partridge was first introduced into Britain from France in the late eighteenth century, giving rise to its colloquial name of the French Partridge. At first its spread was slow but it was aided by further introductions, including one on the Derbyshire–Leicestershire border in 1849: a pair nested here in their first year of liberty. By 1893, Whitlock reported that it was not uncommon in the lowlands, especially the Trent Valley. Frost described it as a scarce resident, with its strongholds in the Trent Valley and that part of the county south of there, the Magnesian Limestone plateau and the Moss Valley; it was also present in parts of the Peak District.

Nationally, the 1968–72 and 1988–91 Atlases showed an increase of 32% in occupied squares between 1972 and 1991, although Game Conservancy Trust (now the Game & Wildlife Conservation Trust) data suggested a marked decline since 1985. Of the 10km core squares in Derbyshire, breeding was proved in six in 1968–72 and 13 in both 1988–91 and 1995–99. The map, relating to the latter survey, shows that they were found in 252 tetrads, with breeding proved in 86 of these, and probable or possible breeding in a further 166. Most records were from lowland areas but they were also found to be widespread in certain hillier areas, including SK24 and SK26. Most records of proven breeding resulted from the sightings of adults with young, since nests are well hidden in undergrowth. This species has an interesting breeding strategy, with most females laying two clutches, one of which she incubates and the male incubates the other: the two broods are then raised separately. Nevertheless, the nests are frequently predated.

The position in the last quarter of the twentieth century was complicated, not only by the regular introduction by shooting interests of captive-bred and reared birds, but also because some of these releases were of both full-blooded Chukars and Red-legged Partridge/Chukar crosses. Hybrids lay more eggs than Red-legs and are well suited to captivity. In the wild, however, they are less productive and since no licences to release hybrids have been issued since 1992, this complication no longer occurs. Sightings of Chukar and hybrids were recorded in a number of years but, since observers were only generally alerted to their presence in 1987, many Red-leg records may also refer to Chukars or hybrids. Birds recorded as true Chukars were recorded in 1979, 1988 and 1992–94; hybrids were reported in 1987, 1990–91 and 1993–95. There have been no claims of either since the latter year.

Red-legged Partridges prefer arable farmland to grassland. The only farmland 1990s CBC plot to feature this species was that at Culland, where there was an average of 1.20 pairs a year, representing 2.40 pairs per km^2. They also breed on barren land and there have been many records from such sites as colliery spoil heaps, quarries and industrial wasteland. Most sightings are therefore in the lowlands but there have been regular records from Peak District localities, mainly in upland farmland but also on moorland. The highest record was of two at 470m amsl at Cracken Edge in January 1981. There are also several records from built-up areas, including gardens and in 1994 a pair nested in a Bretby garden alongside the busy A50 road, while in 2011 a nest with 11 eggs was found in a suburban garden at Midway.

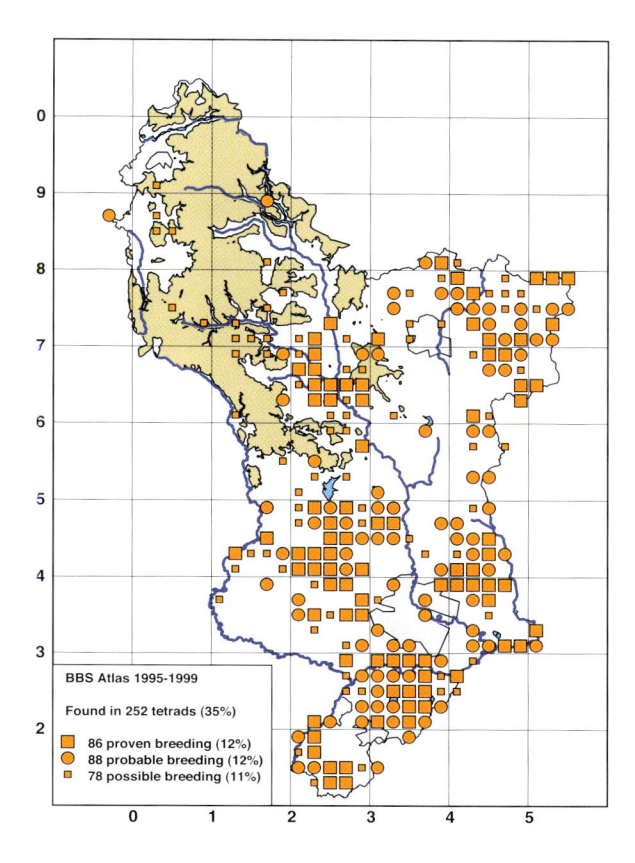

BBS Atlas 1995-1999
Found in 252 tetrads (35%)
- 86 proven breeding (12%)
- 88 probable breeding (12%)
- 78 possible breeding (11%)

This species perches far more readily than the Grey Partridge and there are numerous records of them on the roofs of houses and farm buildings. Perhaps the most unusual such sighting was of two roosting at 0100hrs on a workshop roof in the Derby Locomotive Works complex in October 1984. Another interesting record concerned 15 inside beech woodland at Upperdale in October 1984.

A very unusual nest site was found at Brailsford Hall in 1990, when a workman trimming ivy growing on a wall discovered a nest with eggs at least 4m above ground level. Two photographs of this site featured in the *Derbyshire Bird Report* for that year.

Flocks of up to 20 birds probably concern family groups, which often amalgamate in the autumn at places where feeding conditions are suitable. The largest count known to Frost was of 60, but there are many more recent counts well above this number, including 80 in the Moss Valley in September 1986, 200 at Bretby in September 2000, 90 at Windley in October 2003, and 250 in sugar beet at Langwith in October 2003 with a similar count there in October 2011. Nearly 600 were shot at Foremark Hall on two dates in October 2010.

Indicative of this bird's reluctance to take flight was one running down an Ingleby lane in 2001 and 'clocked' by a following car at 29kph, an impressive 12.4 seconds for 100 metres.

Red Grouse
Lagopus lagopus
A common resident of the high moorlands of the Peak District.

No single bird species has more influence on the natural history of the county. Conservation of the moorlands, so that Red Grouse can be shot in the autumn (12th August to 12th December each year), provides not only this species, but many others, with appropriate habitat. It is, moreover, only this activity that has provided a balance against the economic forces of forestry and sheep grazing that would otherwise have seen the moorlands converted to other habitats during the twentieth and twenty-first centuries.

Whitlock and Jourdain regarded Red Grouse as common moorland birds, from the northern limits of the county southwards to the Matlock Moors in the south-east and Axe Edge in the south-west. This is still essentially true, though they have gone from the Matlock Moors. A survey of the Peak District moorlands in 1969–72 found the bird in 503 1km squares, and it was later suggested that these might represent around 10,000 pairs, about 5600 of them in Derbyshire (Yalden 1972). The resurvey of moorland birds by the JNCC (Brown & Shepherd 1991) found essentially the same main distribution, and reported the species still present in 483 1km squares. However, they confined their surveyors to main moorland blocks, prompting a survey of the smaller peripheral moorlands in 1993–94, repeated in 2008–10. Both numbers and presence of Red Grouse in these areas had declined significantly, from presence in 90 squares to 64 and 57 squares, and in density from 7.09 grouse per km^2 to 2.16 and 2.60 grouse per km^2 (Yalden 1994 & *pers obs*). Among areas showing a decline were the few small areas of moorland on limestone (Longstone and Bradwell Moors) and small areas of partially isolated moorland such as Offerton Moor, Eyam Moor and Win Hill. However, there were a few sites where numbers of grouse had recovered as a consequence of improved moorland management. Notably, the National Trust has improved the control of grazing by sheep on its Kinder Estate, and where there was just acid grassland in Broad Clough in the 1970s, there is now about 50ha of heather, and with it a grouse population of 20–30 pairs (Anderson & Radford 1994). Similarly, the summit of Lantern Pike had about 17ha of moorland and a dozen grouse in 1993, where there had been neither in 1969. These examples show that it is possible to reinstate moorland, and the moorland bird community with it, given appropriate management. Compared with the 1990 survey, the 2004 survey initiated by Moors for the Future (Carr & Middleton 2004) suggested a dramatic increase of 2337 to 5416 grouse counted, following increased moorland management.

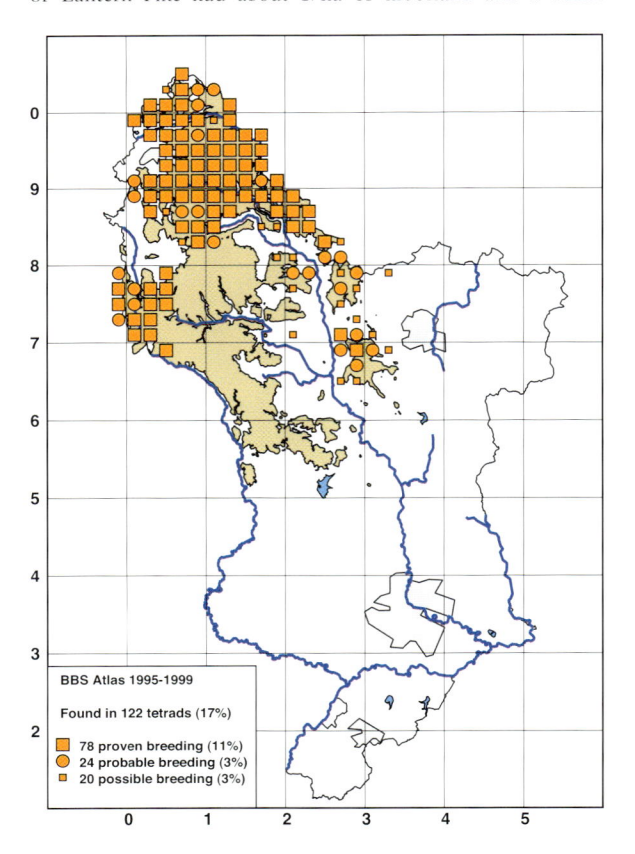

The overall results from the Derbyshire BBS (1995–99) are shown on the map, with the species being found in 122 tetrads, of which 78 were proven, 24 probable and 20 possible.

Red Grouse depend almost entirely on heather for food and shelter. It is the gamekeepers' main duty to ensure this provision by burning the heather in small strips in a 7–10 year cycle. Young heather shoots, preferably 3–4 years old, are the main food, being dense enough to sustain the birds' feeding activity, and rich enough in elements such as nitrogen and phosphorus in particular. Older heather is poorer in nutrients, but provides suitable cover, for adults, nests and young. Since grouse are reluctant to feed further than about 15m from this cover, new heather has to be provided in small patches. Control of predators of eggs and young, particularly foxes, mustelids and corvids, is also an important duty, ensuring that enough grouse nests and then young survive until August to sustain driven shooting. This requires at least 60 grouse per km^2 in August (Hudson 1992). In the past, the zealousness of gamekeepers meant that many predators, which are nowadays protected, were also killed, and there is concern that such persecution of raptors still occurs (both locally and nationally). The important work on the interactions of Hen Harriers, Peregrines and Red Grouse populations on the Langholm Estate in Scotland shows that predators can indeed kill so many grouse as to ruin the economics of grouse-shooting, with gamekeepers losing their jobs as a consequence (Redpath & Thirgood 1997).

Away from the moorlands, Red Grouse are rarely seen unless really deep snow has displaced them. There was one in a Hartington garden in mid-December 1981, with two nearby on 21st December. One was found dead at Sheldon Moor, well away from any known breeding sites, in September 1985, while Red Grouse records from pasture on Ladder Hill above Combs on 23rd February and nearby in the Goyt Valley on 2nd March 1986 are probably the most recent examples from this habitat. However, this was not always the case and there are several historical records of Red Grouse, sometimes in packs, in lowland parts of the county. The winter of 1860/61 produced many sightings between Derby and Burton upon Trent; these may have come from Cannock Chase, Staffordshire, where the species had been reintroduced (Jourdain).

In recent years, the largest counts have been of 400 on East Moor in September 1980 and 300 at both Beeley Moor in October 1986 and Abbey Clough in October 1994. There are very occasional reports of Red Grouse attacking hill walkers, and one even flew onto an observer's shoulder at Derbyshire Bridge in April 2003.

A walk on the moorlands of the Peak District in winter finds an almost birdless landscape, but the toughness of the Red Grouse and its equally tough food source ensure that at least one species is always present. If ever we fail to hear that unwelcoming 'go-back, go-back' call on our favourite hill, we will know that we have lost much more than just this species.

BBS Atlas 1995-1999
Found in 122 tetrads (17%)
- 78 proven breeding (11%)
- 24 probable breeding (3%)
- 20 possible breeding (3%)

Black Grouse
Tetrao tetrix
Formerly a scarce resident of the Peak District. Became extinct locally but reintroduced from 2003.

The Black Grouse was once a widespread bird of moorland and heathland throughout Britain, but by the start of the twentieth century had already been lost from most southern counties from Cornwall across to Sussex and north as far as Norfolk. By this time, the Peak District was on the edge of the range, but Whitlock thought it still nested in at least four areas in Derbyshire. As late as the 1960s, flocks of up to 18 were still being recorded in the Goyt and Derwent Valleys. Through the 1970s and 1980s, numbers slowly declined, only two males being seen in 1987. There was only one record for Derbyshire from the 1990s, of a male and female together near Ladybower Reservoir on 2nd May 1992, and in nearby Staffordshire the last sighting for the Peak District (prior to reintroduction) was of a female on Swallow Moss in February 2000.

The decline of the bird locally has been relatively well documented, though poorly understood. The Workers' Educational Association class at Alfreton Hall, tutored by P. Shooter, summarized the records available for all the Derbyshire localities, and the Peak District population as a whole was discussed by Lovenbury *et al*. (1978) and Yalden (1986a). Because the birds do not form pairs or occupy territories, and as females are so secretive, it is usual to rely on counts of males on the lekking grounds to indicate the sizes of population. Abney Moor had a population of up to two males in the 1930s, and three in 1940, but none was seen in 1941 or 1943. A female with three young in 1944, a solitary female in 1945 and one heard in 1966 were the last records here, with the exception of rumoured sightings in 1976 and 1977. On Matlock Moor (Litchfield 1977a & b) the species had been common enough for organized shooting in the 1910s; by 1955 the bird was still being regularly recorded, but after six were reported in 1956, only singletons were occasionally seen. A possible record of a female with four young in 1971 is the last for that area. In the Goyt Valley, numbers were high enough during the 1960s for flocks of 10–20 to be seen regularly, and it is reported that 18 brace were shot in 1966. A flock of 18 was reported there in October 1968, but numbers dwindled through the 1970s from a peak of eight in 1973 to singles in 1980–84 (Kitchen 1978; Lovenbury *et al*. 1978; Yalden 1986a). A female seen on 16th March 1985 was the last sighting here (Yalden *pers obs*). The Upper Derwent Valley and the adjoining moors to the south-east, as far as Longshaw and Big Moor, had what were initially regarded as separate populations. Flocks of 18–20 females were reported from Big Moor in 1930, and up to three were still being reported in the early 1960s (Litchfield 1977a & b). In the Ladybower area, numbers increased from the 1950s into the 1960s, when there were about 14 attending two leks (Kitchen 1978). However, one of the leks was abandoned in 1968, and in the early 1970s numbers dwindled to two to four males. A short-lived increase up to 1976 saw an estimated 11 males at two leks, but numbers then dwindled again, and there have been no sightings since 1992.

Elsewhere in the Peak District, Cheshire lost its breeding birds in 1960. Birds along the Yorkshire side of the Derwent Edges probably belonged to the Ladybower population, and there were in any case few records. In Staffordshire, the population lasted longer than in Derbyshire; there were around 55 males reported in a specific count in 1973–75, and still 20 in 1985 at four lek sites. Although numbers increased slightly from eight to a maximum of 15 males at the main lek site in 1990, other lek sites were abandoned by then, and numbers declined slowly through the 1990s. The last (pre-reintroduction) sightings of any Black Grouse in the Peak District were of a pair on 20th February 1999, with single females on 23rd February and 19th March that year, and a female on 6th February 2000 (Poyser & Yalden 2009).

As the Derbyshire population has been isolated by at least 80km from its nearest neighbours since at least the 1960s, there was no chance that Derbyshire would be repopulated without human involvement, and Severn Trent Water financed a reintroduction scheme that began in 2003, with 26 birds released in Upper Derwentdale. By 2007, 210 had been released, and another 360–400 birds were due for release in 2008–09. A few birds have been recorded since then, mainly in the Moscar, Upper Derwent and Goyt Valley areas but also in Cheshire and Staffordshire, emphasizing the unsuspected dispersal ability of this species. Assessing the success or otherwise of the scheme will only be possible after a few years but the signs are not encouraging, and by 2009 it was generally feared to have been a failure. In 2011 there was just one record for the county, of a single bird at Derbyshire Bridge in March.

Black Grouse are not strictly birds of moorland, rather of the moorland edge. They like tall, old heather for roosting and perhaps for some of their feeding, but they also need short pasture for the lek sites, to allow good visibility of both rivals and approaching predators. Additionally, they require scrubby woodland, of birch and rowan with bilberry understorey, to provide food, particularly in autumn and winter. There has been some discussion about the reasons for the loss of the species locally (Kitchen 1978; Yalden 1986a) and two factors seem to be critical. One is the agricultural intensification of the area, particularly increased sheep stocks but also drainage and pasture intensification. This has resulted in the habitat mosaic being broken up and, in particular, in the loss of bilberry which is far more sensitive to overgrazing than heather. The other is that this is only a woodland bird in the sense that Whinchats, Short-eared Owls and Hen Harriers are woodland birds: young plantations are favoured because, for a while, they provide the scrubby woodland and ungrazed bilberry that the Black Grouse needs. It seems clear that the modest increases in populations recorded at all the Derbyshire sites in the 1950s and 1960s were associated with new plantations. Once these closed over, the birds lost their habitat and slowly declined, but their longevity and mobility served only to confuse what was happening.

Although Whitlock made no mention of sightings well away from breeding areas, Jourdain said that stray birds from the populations in Needwood Forest and Cannock Chase (both in Staffordshire) had been recorded in southern Derbyshire, but by 1903 they were hardly ever met with. A female was shot at Yeldersley in winter, probably 1896 (Jourdain additions). Whitlock, however, mentioned a Pheasant x Black Grouse hybrid that was shot near Melbourne in February 1854, and Jourdain said that the same hybrid had been killed at Breadsall Moor. A male that was seen at Mapperley Wilderness, in the eastern lowlands of the county, on 31st October 1976 is widely considered to have been a released bird.

Grey Partridge
Perdix perdix
A fairly common resident.

Both nationally and locally, there has been a huge decline in numbers of the Grey Partridge, which was formerly one of the most abundant farmland birds. The reasons for its demise are related to farmland changes including increased specialization and intensification, the widespread change from spring to autumn sowing of cereals with a consequent loss of wintering stubbles, and greater application of herbicides and insecticides. Derbyshire has not been immune from such changes.

The decrease is considered to have become most noticeable since about 1970, but both Whitlock and Jourdain, writing around the end of the nineteenth century, hinted at its former abundance. Whitlock said that, except on moorland, it was found throughout the county but was most numerous in southern grain-growing areas where game was preserved.

The 1968–72 and 1988–91 Atlases both showed confirmed breeding in 21 10km core squares, and the Derbyshire BBS (1995–99) proved breeding in all 23 such squares. In all it was found in 339 tetrads, and breeding was confirmed in 128 of these, with probable and possible breeding in 115 and 96. Comparable figures for the Red-legged Partridge were 252, 86, 88 and 78. Grey Partridges in growing crops in spring can easily be missed but the crowing calls of territorial males may betray their presence.

Numbers of this species are released every year, but at far fewer sites than the Red-legged Partridge. Perhaps because of this and the fact that it is native and declining, it engenders more interest among birdwatchers. It might also be perceived as an underdog, struggling to survive against a non-native species. Since the turn of the century, records of confirmed breeding have remained fairly constant around a mean of 12 sites, with lows of eight in 2001 and a high of 19 in 2006. The maps comparing the 1995–99 results with sightings in 2007–11 are believed to be far too pessimistic.

Grey Partridges frequent both pasture and arable farmland, usually below 350m amsl, so numbers are greatest in the lowlands, with breeding densities probably at their highest in the north-east. Of the farmland CBCs carried out during the 1990s, it was absent from Farfield Farm at Hope; at Broadhay Farm, Hathersage there was a single territory in 1990 only; and at Culland there were single territories in two of the five years. Conversely, in a single 1km square (SK4476) at Staveley on 16th May 1987 there was an impressive count of 16 pairs and two singles. In 1997 an observer commented that numbers around Holbrook were much reduced since some of the hay meadows were converted to pasture.

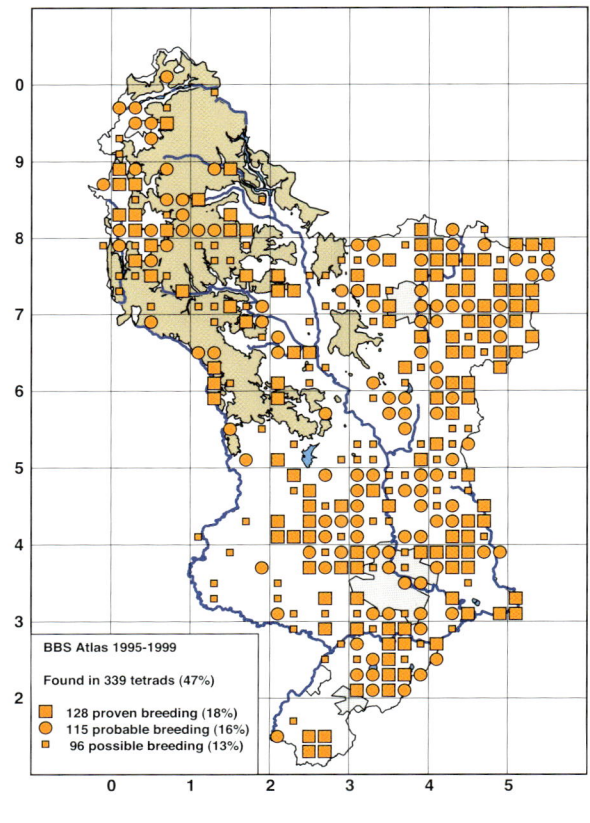

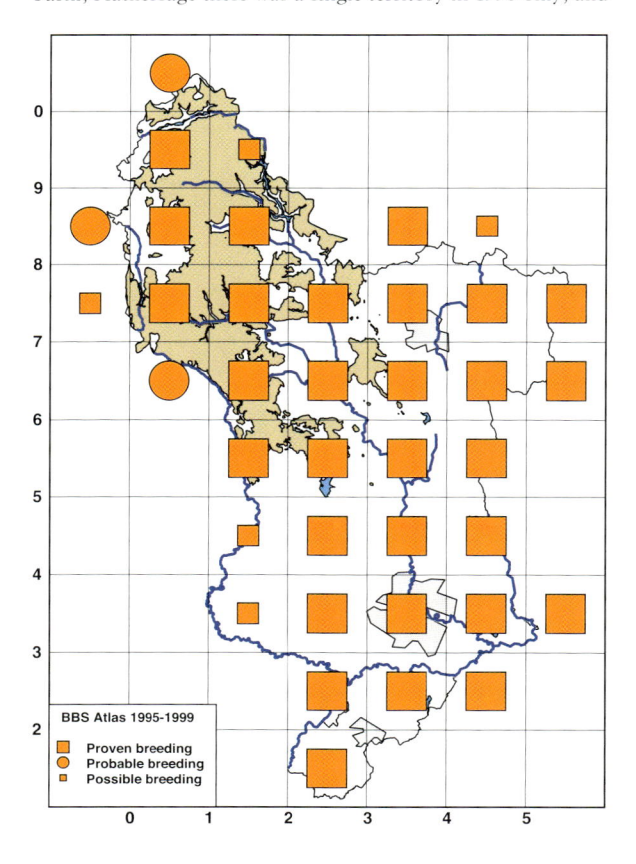

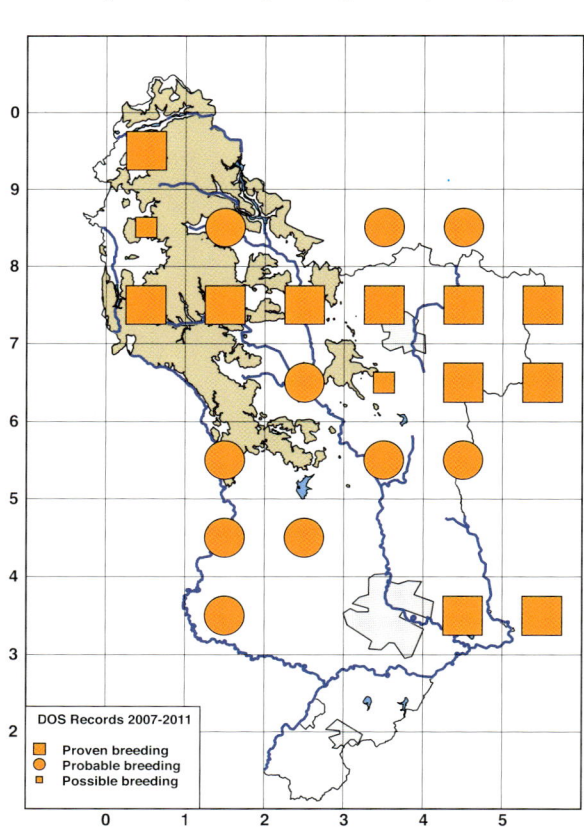

BBS Atlas 1995-1999
Found in 339 tetrads (47%)
- 128 proven breeding (18%)
- 115 probable breeding (16%)
- 96 possible breeding (13%)

BBS Atlas 1995-1999
- Proven breeding
- Probable breeding
- Possible breeding

DOS Records 2007-2011
- Proven breeding
- Probable breeding
- Possible breeding

The species can be found breeding in upland areas, generally in rough grassland but if there is sufficient heather cover it is replaced by the Red Grouse. As with the Red-legged Partridge, there have also been many records of breeding in relatively bare sites such as areas of colliery waste and industrial sites, the latter including Derby gasworks. Such areas may be visually unappealing but they have plenty of weed seeds and insects which are to some extent lacking on modern farmland. Many are now derelict and difficult to access, and as a result some have become, in effect, nature reserves.

Numbers at particular localities fluctuate greatly because, along with other gamebirds, shooting interests may release several hundred hand-reared birds at a time. Particularly high counts were made at Shirebrook during the 1980s, with 300–320 counted in October 1980 and 385 in October 1984, while at nearby Langwith, 110 in October 2003 was the most recent three-figure count recorded in the county. Most of the higher counts are made before, or early in, the shooting season, so a covey of 44 at Barlborough in January 2000 was noteworthy.

Although regarded as a bird epitomizing open, rural habitats there are several records of Grey Partridges being found in unexpected places, such as two birds by the side of the Derby ring road near the Kingsway Fire Station in March 1982, while an adult female was found dead by the roadside at Boythorpe, Chesterfield in October 1998. A covey of 34 graced the gravel drive of a house in Buxton in December 1988 and bizarrely, seven birds flew in front of a hearse as it drove through the built-up area of Brampton in October 1989.

This species has been subject to various status changes within the British ringing scheme over the years. There was a period when it could not be ringed, since it was classed as a gamebird and populations considered artificial. As the decline of the species became apparent, however, this ban was lifted. Nevertheless, the species is not ringed in large numbers and it is not particularly targeted as part of any ringing projects. The ring can only be fitted to a free-flying bird and its association with open habitat means that any caught are almost by accident. There are four local recoveries, all during the 1970s and early 1980s. All but one were subsequently shot very close to the ringing site. The only bird that moved far was ringed at Doe Lea in June 1980 and shot at Spondon, 30km south-south-west, in October 1981. The longest-lived recovery was a Melbourne-ringed bird that avoided the gun for over five years.

Pheasant
Phasianus colchicus
A fairly common resident.

The status of the Pheasant is greatly modified by the annual rearing and releasing of many thousands on numerous large estates, with lesser numbers on ground leased by small shooting syndicates. The tetrad map, based on the Derbyshire BBS (1995–99), shows them to be present in every major 10km square and in almost three-quarters of the entire county: 197 tetrads had proven breeding, with 143 probable and 191 possible. They are easy birds to find, especially in spring when the colourful males, often with their harems of females, can be noisy, but nests are well hidden. In most years only a handful of breeding records are submitted, the most in the last decade being seven. Other records are generally of unusual numbers, behaviour, localities or plumage, reflecting a general lack of enthusiasm among birders for species which are released, non-native, or both.

Pheasant-shooting has been popular for a very long time and the practice of using domestic hens to incubate their eggs and rear the chicks was widespread by the nineteenth century. Whitlock described the majority of released birds as 'mongrels between the Persian and Chinese species'. In more recent times, released birds have included pale buff 'Bohemian' types, males with pale blue backs (sometimes known as Michigan Bluebacks) and a strikingly dark variety, of which the males are bluebottle-blue and the females, chocolate-brown. Albinos are quite often reported and there are two records of single birds that showed both male and female plumage, at Radbourne in 1986 and Chatsworth in 1989.

Whitaker recorded that a Pheasant x Black Grouse hybrid was shot near Melbourne in February 1854, and Jourdain knew of a similar bird at Breadsall Moor.

Pheasants are most typical of well-wooded countryside in arable areas. However, they can be found in a wide variety of habitats including moorland (up to 480m amsl at Derwent Edge), marshes and even gardens. Bird-table visiting has been recorded with increasing frequency since 1987. Though they may be initially cautious, these garden visitors can become very tame, and even demanding. In December 2003, a male at Chaddesden Sidings met an unusual end in the talons of a Harris's Hawk.

Pheasants are often seen at sites well away from known release areas and there are undoubtedly some wild and self-sustaining populations in the county. Most nest in woodland or below rank hedgerows, and nests have also been found on heather moorland at Longstone and Strines Moors. More unusual nest sites have been in reed canary-grass *Phalaris arundinacea* in a marshy spot at Pebley Pond and on a pile of roof tiles at Osmaston. Some choose seemingly unsuitable nest sites such as road verges, while those in gardens make predation of the young by cats almost inevitable. A deserted nest in long grass at the roadside at Sutton Scarsdale village in April 1994 contained two Pheasant and two Red-legged Partridge eggs.

Breeding density is very variable, but at the CBC plot in mixed farmland near Brailsford there was an average of 12 pairs per km^2 during the five-year period from 1990 to 1994, making this the ninth most common species in that area.

As a gamebird, this species has hardly been ringed in the UK, with only 17 ringed up to 1987. These included an adult female ringed near Eckington in June 1978 that was shot at the same site four months later.

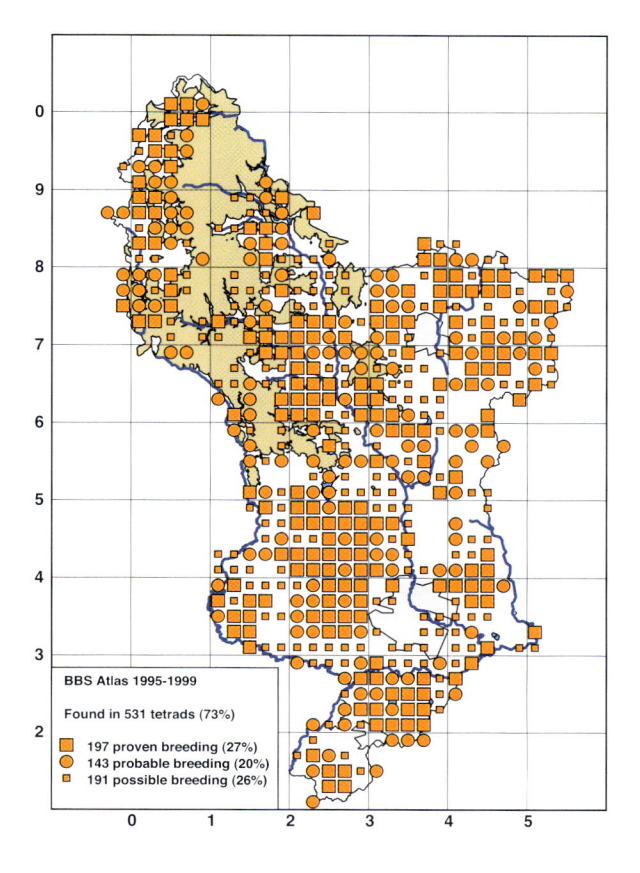

BBS Atlas 1995-1999
Found in 531 tetrads (73%)
- 197 proven breeding (27%)
- 143 probable breeding (20%)
- 191 possible breeding (26%)

Red-throated Diver
Gavia stellata
A rare visitor, usually in winter.

Inland, Red-throated Divers are rare, mainly winter visitors, and were formerly the most commonly occurring diver in Derbyshire. Whitlock stated that one was killed during severe weather conditions on 31st January 1848, but he gave no locality. He also stated that during this period many occurred on the River Trent, including 'quite a little flock not far from the county border'. There were three further records up to the formation of the DOS in 1954, but since then there have been a further 40 records involving 45 birds, all occurring between September and May. The earliest of the four September records was at Ogston Reservoir from 13th to 15th September 1974, while the latest was of two winter-plumaged adults flying along the River Trent near Walton-on-Trent on 23rd May 1994. Although it is generally thought of as a winter visitor the occurrence of birds in April/May and September/October leads to the idea of a small cross-country migration of this species, a situation mirrored in the West Midlands (Harrison & Harrison 2005). The monthly distribution of the records since 1954 may be seen in the chart.

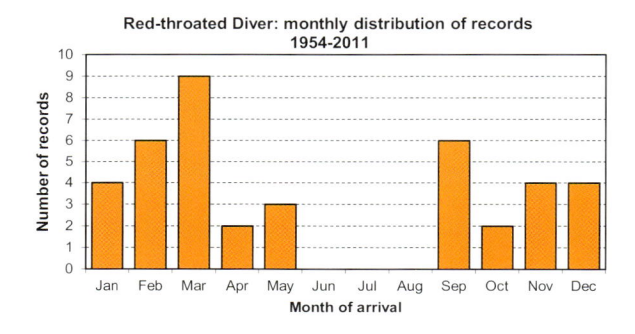

The largest number seen together was four, at Howden Reservoir on 25th March 2006, and there have been two records of two birds together: at Foremark Reservoir on 15th February 1985 and at Walton-on-Trent in May 1994. Most of the birds seen in the county are either adults in winter plumage or immature birds, although there have been at least six records of birds seen in full summer plumage.

Almost half of the records refer to birds being seen on a single date. The longest recorded stay was of 36 days, when one remained at Swarkestone Lake from 20th February to 26th March 1996. The next-longest stay was of 29 days, at Foremark Reservoir from 18th January to 15th February 1985.

The chart shows the distribution by periods from 1950 to 2011. There is an obvious peak in the 1990s when a total of 14 birds was seen. Surprisingly, the most seen in one year was in 1969, with four birds seen from a total of six in that period. Three were recorded in both 1993 and 1996.

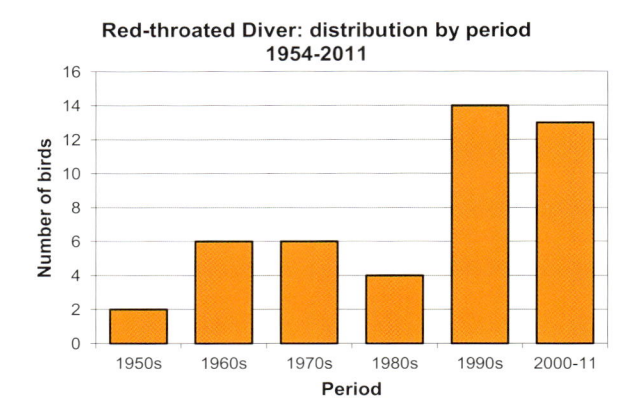

Predictably, the most favoured localities are the larger reservoirs. Of these, the Derwentdale complex has recorded nine birds, Ogston Reservoir six birds, Foremark Reservoir and Carsington Water five each, while Staunton Harold Reservoir and Swarkestone Lake have both recorded three.

Four have been picked up dead: at Ramsley Reservoir on 19th January 1947; below telephone wires at Farnah Green in November 1953; at Osmaston on 3rd March 1965 and at Ashford-in-the-Water on 30th March 1969. One found exhausted in December 1988 on a school sports field in Sheffield and subsequently released at Ladybower Reservoir is excluded from the above totals.

Severe blizzards in February 1979 brought six Black-throated Divers to the county but only two Red-throated Divers, both on the River Trent, at Shardlow and Weston Cliff.

Black-throated Diver
Gavia arctica
A rare visitor, usually in winter.

Frost states that the first Derbyshire record was at Combs Reservoir in January or February 1897. Further records followed: Beauchief Dam, Sheffield in February and March 1938, Staveley on 3rd April 1947 and Buxton in November 1951. From 1955 to 2011 there have been a further 39 records involving 44 birds. All have occurred between October and May, though surprisingly none have arrived in April. The monthly distribution is shown in the first chart.

The October records relate to a bird present for 'several days' at Bakewell in 1955, one at Carsington Water on 26th October 2001, and one at Combs Reservoir from 29th October to 13th November 1975. There have been six May records, which suggests a cross-country migration for this species. Birds seen in May are usually in full summer plumage and birds in this most attractive of plumages were seen at Howden Reservoir from 1st to 3rd May 1978, and also on 17th May 1988, and at Barbrook Reservoir on 4th May 1981.

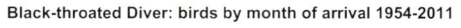

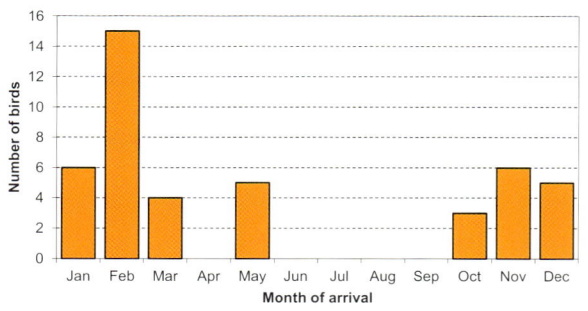

The second chart shows the distribution by periods of all birds since 1954. The obvious peak in the 1970s and 1980s can be partly explained by severe winters of 1979/80, when six birds were found in the county between 16th and 21st February and of 1985/86, when four were again found in January and February. However, they have undoubtedly become more frequently recorded with the recent increase in coverage.

Most records refer to single birds, but in 1979 three were at Staunton Harold Reservoir on 18th February. In addition, there have been three instances where two birds have appeared together. The first of these was at Staunton Harold Reservoir, where an adult and an immature stayed from 15th to 17th February 1983, when the adult moved to Foremark Reservoir. Interestingly, both birds were heard to call, a most unusual winter occurrence. There were also two at Swarkestone Lake from 22nd to 30th November 1985 before one bird departed, the other remaining until 3rd December when it left to the west. Finally, at Carsington Water, two were present from 18th February to 15th March 1994, with one bird remaining until 23rd April.

Most birds are only seen for a short time, but the longest staying was the first-summer bird at Carsington Water, which although appearing unhealthy when it arrived, remained for a period of 120 days, from 9th May to 5th September 2003. This is the only bird to have summered in the county and for part of its stay it was flightless as it underwent moult.

As might be expected, Black-throated Divers have occurred on all of the large waters in the county, with Carsington Water recording seven birds, Ogston and Staunton Harold Reservoirs recording six each, followed by Foremark Reservoir with four. More unusual localities to record this species are Allestree Lake, Bakewell, Barbrook Pools, and the River Derwent at both Calver and Alvaston.

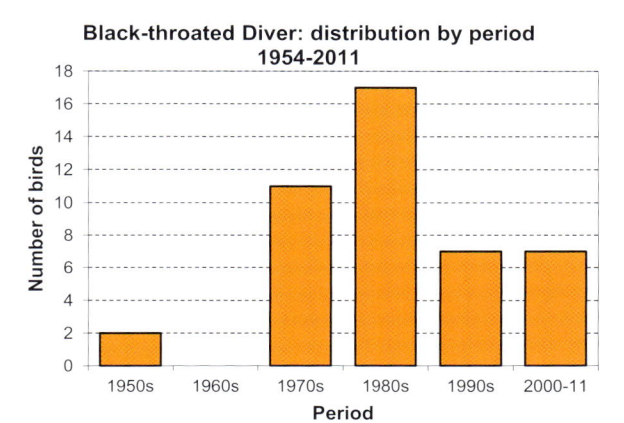

Black-throated Diver: distribution by period 1954-2011

Great Northern Diver
Gavia immer
A rare visitor, usually in winter.

Frost stated that there were five dated records for Great Northern Diver from the nineteenth century, with several other possible occurrences. These were from the River Trent and lower reaches of the Rivers Dove and Derwent, Darley, Ockbrook, and between Peak Forest and Tideswell. He also quoted two records before 1954, at Williamthorpe in December 1931, and on the River Derwent at Rowsley in January and February 1942. There was then a long period before the first modern record, at Staunton Harold Reservoir from 15th to 23rd May 1968. Since then there have been 47 records involving 56 birds. They have been seen in all months between September and February, with single records in May and in June, the latter an adult in full summer plumage at Ogston Reservoir on 30th June and 1st July 1989. The peak time is November and December, and probably involves birds brought in by autumn gales, most being immatures.

The charts show the distribution of records involved during each month and periods from 1954 to 2011.

Many of the Great Northern Divers seen in Derbyshire have remained for long periods and the average stay is about 20 days. One was seen at Carsington Water from 26th October 2008 to 10th May 2009, a total of 197 days but, since up to four were seen here during the period, there is no evidence that the original individual remained throughout. The earliest autumn record was of an adult at Barbrook Reservoir on 3rd–4th September 1984.

They were recorded in the county in 28 years between 1978 and 2011. In 2006 six individuals were seen in the county between 28th November and the year end; part of a marked influx into the central and southern Midlands from late November. The years when more than one was recorded were 1978, 1983, 1984, 1989, 1998, 2005, 2006, 2007 and 2009. In the last year, four remained from 2008 during the early months and six were recorded between 15th October and the year end, five of them at Carsington Water. This site has attracted Great Northern Divers annually between 1998 and 2011, with the exception of 2004, with records of four simultaneously in 2008 and 2011.

It is apparent that, unlike the Black-throated Diver, there have not been any influxes into the county as a result of severe weather.

The largest group seen together was at Carsington Water in 2008, when four birds were seen on 11th November and between 5th and 11th December. Other records of more than one bird were in 1993 at Foremark Reservoir and Carsington Water in 2006 and 2007.

This species usually occurs at the largest waters in the county and the most favoured is Carsington Water, where 27 birds have been recorded, followed by Ogston Reservoir, with nine and Foremark Reservoir where there have been seven.

The only unexpected locality for this species was Pools Head, Brailsford, where an adult in summer plumage was present from 16th to 18th October 1983. Surprisingly, there has been only one record from a gravel pit complex, at Swarkestone, where a first-winter was seen from 5th to 18th December 1999.

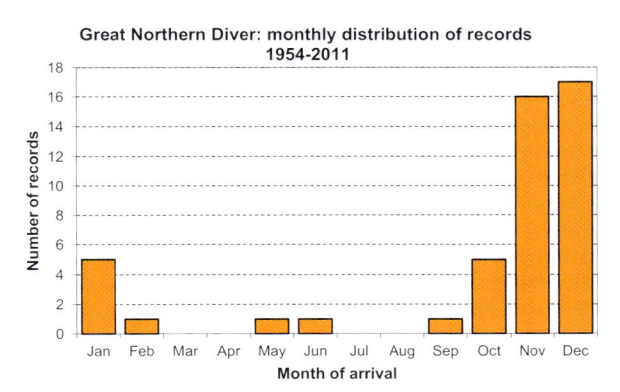

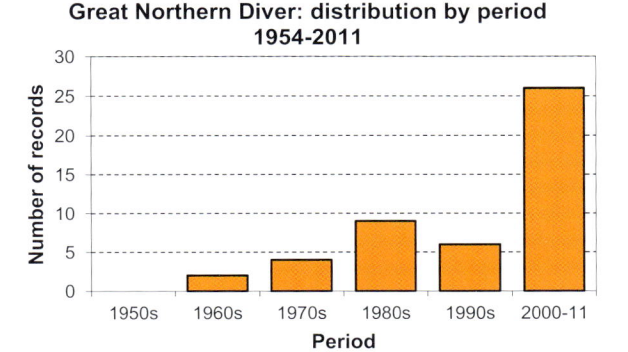

Great Northern Diver: monthly distribution of records 1954-2011

Great Northern Diver: distribution by period 1954-2011

Black-browed Albatross
Thalassarche melanophris
A very rare vagrant.

By the end of 2011 there was a total of 27 accepted records in Britain of this vagrant from the southern oceans (Hudson *et al.* 2012). Unusually, the first two records were of birds found inland, the first being in Cambridgeshire in 1897. The Derbyshire record constituted the second ever and was of a bird captured at Staveley, a few days prior to 21st August 1952, after it had become entangled in telephone wires. Thought to be exhausted, it was captured by an RSPCA officer and taken by rail to Skegness, Lincolnshire, where it was released. It was recorded in square brackets in *DAJ* 'because of the possibility of it having been caught by a sailor and released in home waters'. However, the record was fully accepted by the national ornithological bodies (Macdonald 1953) and a recent review by BBRC found that it was still acceptable as the second British record.

Fulmar
Fulmarus glacialis
A rare vagrant.

The only nineteenth-century county record was of one shot at Melbourne on 25th October 1847 (Whitlock). Another was found in Lathkill Dale on 18th December 1949, but died that night (Frost). Since then, there have been a further 20 records involving 21 individuals.

Year	Location and date
1973	Ogston Reservoir, one on 23rd–24th June, departed to the south
1974	Walton Dam, two on 16th January
1974	Walton Dam, one on 6th July
1978	Woodthorpe, Staveley, an adult was picked up on 3rd July and ringed before being released on the Pembrokeshire coast
1980	Poolsbrook, one flew south on 12th July
1984	Derwentdale, one, found dead in a conifer plantation on 12th February, may have been killed by a Goshawk
1984	Foremark Reservoir, one flew east on 22nd May
1985	Ogston Reservoir, one on 21st May
1986	Arnfield Reservoir, one found dead in March
1988	Ogston Reservoir, one flew north-west on 14th June
1990	Willington Gravel Pits, one flew north on 17th May
1991	Middleton Moor, one on 14th June
1994	Foremark Reservoir, one on 21st May
1998	Foremark Reservoir, one on 19th May arrived from the west and departed to the south
2000	Ogston Reservoir, one on 4th April circled for an hour and departed to the north
2003	Carsington Water, one on 18th April
2008	Aston-on-Trent Gravel Pits, one flew north-east on 19th April
2009	Ogston Reservoir, one on 31st May
2010	Ogston Reservoir, one flew north-west on 30th May
2010	Ogston Reservoir, one on 10th June

Seven records have been from the well-watched Ogston Reservoir while, surprisingly, the small Walton Dam, Chesterfield, has had two records (in the same year) and the only record of two together.

Analysis by periods is shown in the table.

Period	Records	Birds
1970s	4	5
1980s	6	6
1990s	4	4
2000–11	6	6
Totals	20	21

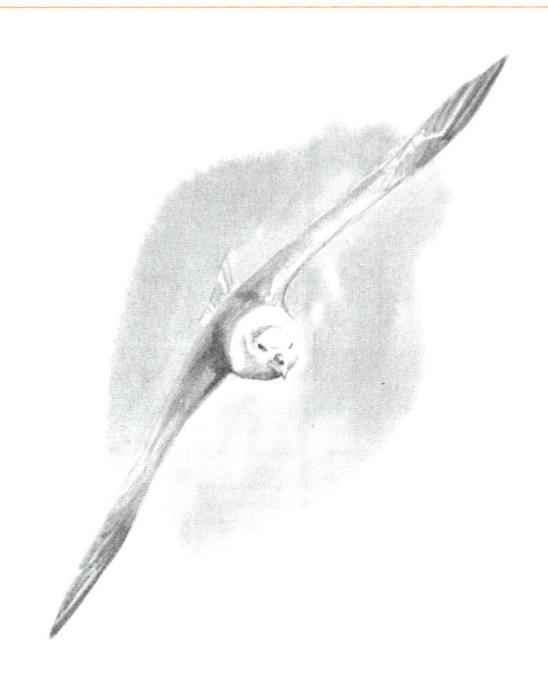

Analysis by months is shown in the chart.

Fulmar: monthly distribution 1973–2011

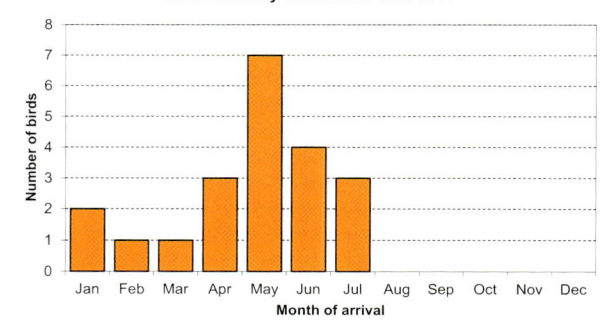

Month	Number of birds
Jan	2
Feb	1
Mar	1
Apr	3
May	7
Jun	4
Jul	3
Aug	0
Sep	0
Oct	0
Nov	0
Dec	0

It is surprising that more than half of the birds (14 of the 21) have been found in the period May to July, when they would be expected to be on their breeding grounds, and when, generally, the weather is more settled. A similar pattern has, however, occurred in the West Midlands region, where of the last 22 records there, at least eight have been found in the same period with a further four records in the autumn (Harrison & Harrison 2005).

Manx Shearwater
Puffinus puffinus
A rare, usually storm-blown, vagrant.

The status of this species has changed very little during the last two centuries, and it remains an occasional vagrant to Derbyshire. Most birds have arrived during, or immediately following, westerly gales and nearly always have been exhausted, dying or dead. There have been 41 records in total, all involving single birds, and 24 of these have occurred since 1950 (22 since the formation of the DOS) as detailed in the table:

Year	Location and date
1950	Chesterfield, an immature on 28th September
1953	Quarndon, an adult picked up exhausted on 28th September later died
1963	Eckington, one found dead in woodland on 7th September had been ringed in County Down on the previous day
1967	Sawley, an immature on 6th September, taken into care but died
1967	Riddings, one on 6th September had been ringed six days earlier as a nestling in Pembrokeshire. It was released on the Dee estuary
1970	Raynesway, Derby, one on 1st September, taken into care and later released on Hilbre Island, Wirral
1979	Drakelow Power Station, one found in a car park on 13th September, taken into care and released locally
1982	Raynesway, Derby, one on 27th August, taken into care and later released at Gibraltar Point, Lincolnshire
1985	Boylestone, one found dead on 5th September
1988	Oakwood, Derby, one on 3rd September, taken into care and later released at Gibraltar Point, Lincolnshire
1988	Tintwistle, one found dead by the A628 road on 4th September
1988	Allestree, Derby, one on 6th September, taken into care and later released in Norfolk
1989	Drakelow Nature Reserve, one flew west on 23rd September
1989	Swanwick, one was picked up alive on 23rd September in the grounds of a hotel. After being examined by a vet it was released the following day at Gibraltar Point, Lincolnshire
1992	Carsington Water, one on 31st August was present all day
1994	Carsington Water, one on 11th September was present from early afternoon to dusk
1998	Barlborough, one on 11th September was picked up on a road and later released at Rother Valley Country Park (now in South Yorkshire)
2003	Froggatt Bridge, one found dead on 17th July
2004	JJB Sports, Pride Park, Derby, one found behind a board on the six-a-side football pitches on 13th September. It was taken to the RSPCA, and released that evening on the south coast
2004	Sandiacre, one found on a garden patio on 15th September. It was taken to the Ranger Centre at Elvaston Castle County Park, and then to a bird hospital for later release on the east coast
2004	Butterley Reservoir, one until dusk on 18th September
2004	Carsington Water, one found near the Visitor Centre on 10th October. It was taken into care and later released on the Welsh coast
2006	Toyota site, near Derby, one was found exhausted on 8th September and was taken into care, but died in Norfolk on 10th September
2010	Little Hayfield, a headless corpse was found on 23rd September

Analysis by period and months for records since 1950 is as follows:

Period	Records	Birds
1950s	2	2
1960s	3	3
1970s	2	2
1980s	7	7
1990s	3	3
2000–11	7	7
Totals	24	24

Month	Records	Birds
July	1	1
August	2	2
September	20	20
October	1	1
Totals	24	24

Apart from a bird found dead at Froggatt on 17th July (2003), all have been found between 27th August and 5th October. This is when most young Manx Shearwaters are fledging. At this time of year they often meet very strong westerly gales which drive the weaker birds inland, where they are picked up either dead or exhausted. Of the Derbyshire records, 17 fall into this category.

Between 1950 and 1971, there were four Derbyshire ringing recoveries, all of birds ringed in colonies in Wales. There was an additional bird, which had been ringed as an adult on Copeland Island, County Down, Ireland in September 1963, which was found dead at Eckington the next day. One of the Welsh birds showed a similar rapid movement eastwards into Derbyshire; it had been ringed as a chick on Skokholm, Pembrokeshire in September 1967, and was found alive six days later at Riddings. Obviously, this bird was on the verge of fledging when initially caught.

It is strange that there have been no more recent reports, since ringing has continued at these breeding colonies.

The Sawley bird, in 1967, developed blisters on its feet and suffered from trembling spasms before dying in the early hours of 10th September. The corpse was sent for analysis by B.C. Potter to J.W. Macdonald, who found symptoms suggesting puffinosis, a viral disease (Harris 1968).

Storm Petrel
Hydrobates pelagicus
A rare, usually storm-blown, visitor.

There have been 16 Derbyshire records with most birds found exhausted or dead following severe gales. Whitlock quotes five undated records and Jourdain added three more. One was obtained at Whitwell in the early years of the twentieth century and one was picked up in 1919 in Derby on the curious date of 14th June (Frost). Since then there have been six records, all of single birds, as follows:

Year	Location and date
1967	Clay Mills Gravel Pits, one on 11th September
1972	Buxton golf course, one found dead on 27th May
1980	Little Rowsley, one on 5th October
1980	Ogston Reservoir, one on 12th October
1983	Edale, one found dead on 20th October
1989	Church Wilne Reservoir, one on 29th October

Five of the six modern records have occurred in September and October, when this species is sometimes driven inland by very strong westerly or south-westerly gales. The record of May 1972 is curious, although again, the bird had apparently been driven inland by adverse weather conditions: two Great Skuas were seen nearby in the Goyt Valley on the same date.

Interestingly, on the same day that a Storm Petrel was at Church Wilne Reservoir in October 1989, a Leach's Petrel was also present in the county at Ogston Reservoir, 28km to the north.

Leach's Petrel
Oceanodroma leucorhoa
A rare vagrant.

There have been at least 27 records in the county. There were sightings on the River Trent at Walton before 1863, at Markeaton Park and Draycott in November 1881, and two in the Erewash Valley in December 1888, although the latter may relate to Nottinghamshire (Whitlock; Jourdain additions). One shot at Etwall in September 1924 was accidentally omitted by Frost. The next came in 1952 when a nationwide wreck in the final days of October produced sightings in nine localities, scattered throughout the county, from Spinkhill to Swadlincote. All were dead or picked up in a weakened condition (Frost). Since then there have been 14 records.

Year	Location and date
1957	Fernilee Reservoir, one on 14th–15th and probably 17th September
1978	Langley Mill, one on 30th September
1978	Arnfield Reservoir, one on 30th September
1980	Hilton Gravel Pits Nature Reserve, one flew off east on 12th October
1980	Clay Mills Gravel Pits, one on 12th October was possibly the bird seen at Hilton Gravel Pits Nature Reserve
1983	Etwall Brook, one flew south-east on 17th October
1988	Netherseal, one was found freshly dead in a garden on 10th January
1989	Ogston Reservoir, one on 29th October
1993	Chatsworth Park, one caught near the cricket pitch on 25th January. Placed under cover as protection from predators but was dead three days later
1994	Carsington Water, one on 12th September
1994	Ogston Reservoir, one which flew south on 12th September was possibly the bird seen at Carsington Water
2006	Ogston Reservoir, one picked up dead on the east bank on 6th December
2006	Duffield, one picked up dead in a garden on 9th December
2007	Carsington Water, one on 9th November

Apart from the five winter records, all recent sightings have occurred between mid-September and late October, usually following severe weather, when migrating birds may be forced inland by strong north-westerly winds and bad weather. The four winter records, two in December and two in January, were of birds found either dead or moribund. The two found in 2006 were part of a large wreck of at least 2600 birds which were initially brought into the west and south-west of the country by gales and storm-force westerly and south-westerly winds (Gantlett 2007). These particular birds may have been weak and therefore had little or no resistance to strong westerly gales and were blown inland.

Analysis by period and months for records since 1950 is shown in the tables.

Period	Records	Birds
1950s	10	10
1970s	2	2
1980s	5	5
1990s	3	3
2000–11	3	3
Totals	23	23

Month	Records	Birds
January	2	2
September	5	5
October	13	13
November	1	1
December	2	2
Totals	23	23

They have been found in a variety of places, although most were seen at open waters. The strangest record came from Netherseal, where in January 1988 a corpse was found by a householder picking Brussels sprouts in his garden for his evening meal.

Gannet
Morus bassanus
A rare vagrant.

There have been 56 records, of which eight were in the nineteenth century and a further 11 in the first half of the twentieth century. There was also one at Sudbury on 21st September 1954. Some of these birds were picked up exhausted, but several were seen in flight, including two birds together over Fenny Bentley in April 1919 and Parwich in December 1943.

Since the formation of the DOS there have been 36 records involving 40 individuals, as follows:

Year	Location and date
1955	Buxton, an emaciated immature on 12th October. It was taken into care and later released at Blackpool, Lancashire
1965	Chatsworth Park, one on 19th April was taken into care but died next day
1967	Ladybower Reservoir, an immature on 5th November
1968	Great Longstone, one on 25th March was taken into care but died
1968	Darley Dale, one on 21st–22nd November was taken into care and later recovered
1970	Chesterfield, an immature on 21st September was taken into care and released in early October on the Yorkshire coast
1976	Clay Mills Gravel Pits, a first-year bird flew south-west on 17th October
1977	Eckington, an adult on 25th May
1980	Catton Hall, an immature on 15th October, died the next day
1986	Ogston Reservoir, an adult arrived on 2nd February, and was present until 11th February when it was rescued after the reservoir froze over. It was released the next day at Gibraltar Point, Lincolnshire
1992	Brailsford, an immature flew east on 7th October
1992	Ogston Reservoir, an adult circled for five minutes before departing north on 22nd November
1996	Beeley, two immatures flew west-south-west on 19th September
1997	Chaddesden, two immatures flying south-east on 18th September were also seen at Sinfin later in the day
1998	St Chads Water, a second-year bird on 11th–12th September. It roosted overnight and departed to the north-west
1998	Carsington Water, a first-winter for five minutes before it left to the west on 22nd September
2000	Carsington Water, a first-winter for 25 minutes before it left to the east on 20th October
2001	Staunton Harold Reservoir, a juvenile circled the southern arm before it left to the south on 21st September
2001	South Head Farm, Kinder, a juvenile was picked up alive and taken into care on 22nd September
2001	Near Wheston, an adult flew south on 30th December. This was during relatively calm, frosty conditions
2002	South Derbyshire, one flew into the county from Trent Valley Pits, Leicestershire on 27th October
2004	Chesterfield, one picked up, exhausted in a garden on 22nd September. Later released on the east coast
2004	South Derbyshire, three flew into the county from Trent Valley Pits, Leicestershire on 6th October
2004	Aston-on-Trent Gravel Pits, one, associating with Mute Swans on the evening of 16th October until the next morning
2006	Repton, an immature flew west along the River Trent on 7th October
2006	Big Moor, an immature flew west on 21st October
2006	Combs Reservoir, an immature flew east on 4th December
2007	Parcel Terrace, Derby, an adult was found exhausted in a bramble bush behind 2m-high railings on 18th June. Later collected by the RSPCA and taken to a sea-life rescue centre in Norfolk
2007	Howden Reservoir, a juvenile was found on 6th October and remained until 10th, when it was taken into care and subsequently released at Carsington Water
2007	Carr Vale, a juvenile on 13th October, and presumably the same bird at Doe Lea 15 minutes later
2007	Litchchurch Lane, Derby, one on a factory rooftop on 2nd November
2008	Shipley Country Park, one on 23rd October
2009	Foremark Reservoir, a third-year on 16th and 17th July
2009	Carsington Water, an adult on 23rd and 24th November
2011	Shirebrook, an adult flew south on 31st May
2011	Carsington Water, a fourth-winter on 13th September

It is considered that the Howden Reservoir/Carsington Water bird in October 2007 may have been the same as that subsequently at Carr Vale and Doe Lea.

Analysis by periods 1955 to 2011 is shown in the table.

Period	Records	Birds
1955–59	1	1
1960s	4	4
1970s	3	3
1980s	2	2
1990s	6	8
2000–11	20	22
Totals	36	40

Analysis of birds by months is shown in the chart.

Gannet: monthly distribution 1954-2011

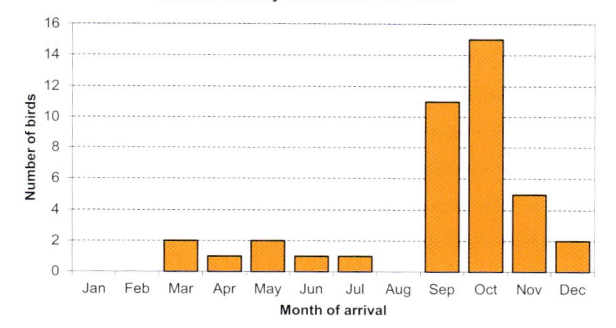

Cormorant
Phalacrocorax carbo
A fairly common and increasing resident, passage migrant and winter visitor. First bred in 1998.

In the nineteenth century, Cormorants were regarded by Whitlock and Jourdain as irregular visitors to south Derbyshire, usually in the autumn. Numbers began to increase by the second half of the twentieth century, with 13 at both Church Wilne Reservoir in November 1971 and at Newton Solney in December 1977 being the largest gatherings known to Frost, who said that regular overwintering began in 1970/71.

The 1980s saw the start of a dramatic increase in the county, mirroring the national trend, with the first three-figure count being of 105 at Drakelow Nature Reserve in February 1985. Although not confined to the south of the county, the majority of birds were, and still are, found along the Trent Valley, with three-figure counts made at several sites. Smaller numbers are recorded further north. They can now be found on water bodies of almost any size, with reservoirs and gravel pits being particularly favoured, and are commonly seen on the rivers of the county, with even small ones such as the River Erewash (only 4m in width) being used for feeding. Cormorants might be seen over open countryside almost anywhere in the county as they travel between their feeding grounds and roosts. Birds from Derbyshire have been known to use roosts at Attenborough Gravel Pits (Nottinghamshire) and King's Bromley (Staffordshire). From 1998, roosts developed at Drakelow Nature Reserve and from 1999 at Ogston Reservoir, from where previously the birds had departed for the Attenborough roost. Also a small roost has become established at Carsington Water.

Illustrating the increase in numbers and the progressive reduction in more northerly areas, the table shows annual maxima for 1990–2011 at two mid-county sites (Carsington Water and Ogston Reservoir) and four Trent Valley sites (Drakelow Nature Reserve, Willington Gravel Pits, Church Wilne Reservoir and Aston-on-Trent Gravel Pits).

Records in the far north of the county, especially in the Derwentdale reservoir complex, show that the increase here is less marked with up to only 17 recorded, while up to 12 have been seen at the Longdendale reservoirs. These lower numbers are presumably due to the lower fish densities in these upland, acidic waters. The first instance of wintering in Derwentdale was in 1987/88, when up to three birds were present.

The increase in population has almost inevitably led to breeding taking place. Mild display had been recorded at many sites and it was Willington Gravel Pits that hosted the first confirmed breeding, when four pairs nested on an electricity pylon in 1998. This was this first recorded use of one of these structures in Britain. Seven young were reared, but no breeding was attempted here in 1999 (James & Key 1999). However, at Drakelow Nature Reserve, a remarkable 24 to 26 pairs nested successfully in 1999, rearing around 60 young. This colony has gone from strength to strength, peaking at 109 occupied nests in 2008. The birds breed very early, with young often seen in the nest in March, while in 2005 two pairs both apparently reared two broods of young (Cockburn 2006). The only other record of

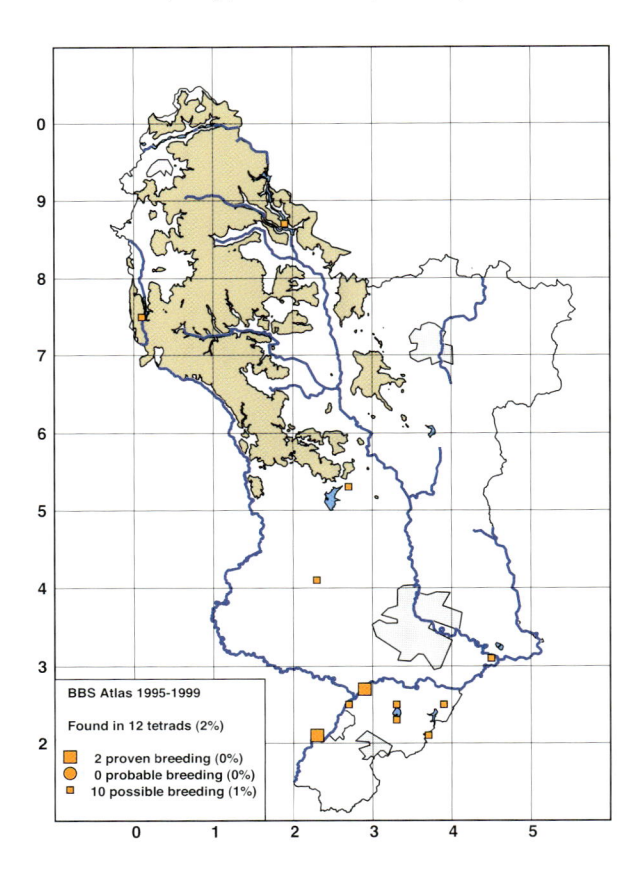

Year	CW	OR	DNR	WGP	CWR	AoT
1990	–	35	55	20	–	–
1991	–	28	85	40	33	–
1992	12	22	51	80	25	–
1993	36	44	30	90	23	–
1994	65	17	120	96	33	24
1995	74	26	47	90	15	–
1996	77	39	140	100	28	–
1997	70	39	138	109	24	18
1998	39	25	132	91	17	39
1999	30	35	115	64	11	50
2000	56	53	144	97	45	48
2001	94	36	210	89	61	117
2002	62	71	227	97	127	79
2003	52	71	276	53	30	60
2004	46	70	322	80	114	96
2005	72	59	308	78	51	50
2006	51	55	303	40	33	59
2007	60	100	423	127	40	174
2008	62	81	333	80	37	95
2009	60	69	280	54	109	83
2010	67	70	351	33	140	97
2011	45	70	305	65	32	47

BBS Atlas 1995-1999

Found in 12 tetrads (2%)

- 2 proven breeding (0%)
- 0 probable breeding (0%)
- 10 possible breeding (1%)

attempted breeding was by the River Wye at Bakewell in March 2007, when a pair was seen nest-building and at Renishaw Park in 2012. At Drakelow Nature Reserve, four pairs raised second broods in 2010. Breeding was proved in only two tetrads and possible in ten in the Derbyshire BBS (1995–99).

The Continental subspecies, *P.c. sinensis*, is now regularly recorded in the county, and it is thought that a large proportion of inland-breeding Cormorants in Britain are of this race.

One was seen to drown a Black-headed Gull at Ogston Reservoir in November 1994.

The presence of large numbers of Cormorants roaming between sites throughout the year tends to mask any true migration, but there are many records that suggest that birds move through the county to the west and north-west in the spring.

Most recoveries of Cormorants within Derbyshire have concerned birds ringed as nestlings at Besthorpe Gravel Pits near Newark by the North Nottinghamshire Ringing Group. These represent movements along the Trent Valley by inland populations and it would suggest that the source of Derbyshire breeding colonies is Besthorpe, resulting from juvenile dispersal. Others seen in the county had been ringed as chicks in Holland (four), Denmark (two), County Dublin (Ireland), Strangford Lough (Northern Ireland), northern Scotland (two), Puffin Island (Anglesey, Wales) and Cumbria.

Shag
Phalacrocorax aristotelis
A rare visitor, usually in winter.

Whitlock listed four nineteenth-century sightings and records remained sparse to the end of the 1960s. In the period from the 1970s to the 1990s there was quite a notable increase, but by the 2000s numbers had fallen off again. The table shows the analysis by periods for the years 1950–2011.

Period	Records	Birds
1950s	1	1
1960s	11	12
1970s	20	24
1980s	16	20
1990s	25	40
2000–11	14	16
Totals	87	113

Shags have been recorded in every month of the year, and the chart gives the monthly totals for birds in the period 1978–2011.

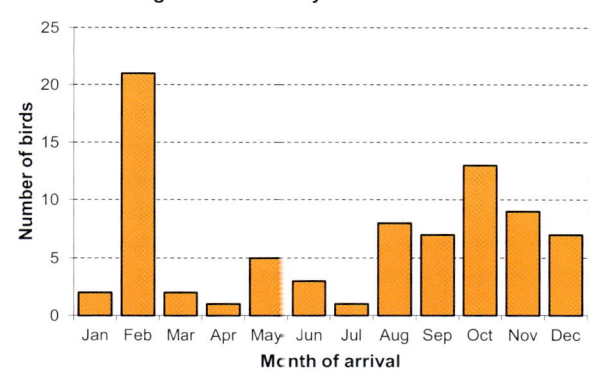

Shag: distribution by month 1978-2011

The only recent years in which this species was not recorded were 1997, 1999, 2000, 2005 and 2011. During this period, a little over half of all records have come from the Trent Valley reservoirs and gravel pits complexes, but there have been records from many sites, including some of the High Peak reservoirs.

At William's Clough on 2nd November 1986, one was 'gently walked' onto the adjacent Kinder Reservoir, where it remained until 10th January 1987.

The longest-staying bird was another in the north of the county, in the upper Derwent complex, where an adult was seen on all three of the reservoirs between 20th June 1994 and 18th February 1995, a stay of 244 days.

Multiple counts of Shag remain very rare in Derbyshire. Most records involve one to three birds, so that a record of 11 (seven adults and four immatures) at Ogston Reservoir on 1st February 1993 was a notable event, and this remains the largest flock seen in the county. These were part of a Midlands-wide influx of birds during the first few days of February 1993 and, on the same day as the 11 at Ogston Reservoir, there was an amazing record of 56 Shags some 12km to the east on a small suburban lake in Nottinghamshire. Four others were seen in Derbyshire around the same time. In addition, four immatures were at Willington Gravel Pits on 23rd August 1992.

Some birds have proved to be very approachable. For example, the bird at William's Clough and also an immature at Shardlow Gravel Pits on 16th October 1983 were both watched down to just over one metre. Records have come from unusual localities, such as the buttress of a road bridge over the River Derwent at Cromford where an immature roosted from 4th to 17th October 1989. Another first-winter frequented two small pools in a wooded valley at Two Dales from 1st March to 2nd May 1993, while a second-winter bird was on a small fishing pool at Wilne Church from 23rd to 26th February 1996.

Any inland recoveries of Shag are obviously the result of storms or disorientation taking the birds away from their coastal haunts. Many adult birds tend to stay in the vicinity of their breeding grounds after the young have fledged and it is the latter, the inexperienced birds, which generally meet an early death, away from the colony.

Of the three recoveries in the county, all were found dead. Two of these had been ringed as chicks on the Isle of May in Fife, Scotland in June 1992, and died in Derbyshire in the following spring. The older record was of one ringed as a chick on the Farne Islands in Northumberland in June 1953, which was found at Ambergate in the following February.

Bittern
Botaurus stellaris
A scarce autumn and winter visitor.

Whitlock and Jourdain knew of some 30 nineteenth-century records of Bitterns, the former mentioning that the Wilne area had been a regular wintering site. Both authorities thought this species may have bred formerly in the county, since one was shot near Staveley in July 1768. Frost was aware of a further 19 records in the period 1924 to 1977. Since then there has been an upsurge, with about 104 recorded between 1978 and 2011. It is thought that this is tied in with Continental birds moving into Britain, because numbers seen in winter away from the traditional breeding areas are much larger than the UK's small breeding population.

All records have been of single birds apart from the following: two at Ogston Reservoir on 15th March 1993, which were seen to depart south together in the early evening of 17th March; two at Willington Gravel Pits on 1st January 2010 and four on 17th December 2010, then up to three until 31st December and two between 1st January and 8th February 2011 including a maximum of three on 4th and 8th January; and two at Swarkestone Causeway on 13th January 2010. By far the best year for Bitterns in Derbyshire was 2010, involving 25 birds of which 13 were in the first winter period and 12 in the second.

Of the 104 birds seen since the formation of the DOS, about half were in the Trent and Lower Derwent Valleys, while elsewhere there have been multiple records from several sites. The most frequented sites, 1954 to 2011, are shown in the first chart.

Records from the Peak District are very rare. One was shot at Chatsworth in the 1890s; one found in an exhausted state at Hope Cement Works in January 1985 was later released at Leighton Moss. Others were seen at Combs Reservoir in November 1989 and at Monsal Dale in December 2010.

Bitterns have been recorded between 2nd August (2009), when one was at Willington Gravel Pits and 15th April (2010), when a late bird was at the same location. The monthly first-arrivals from 1954 to 2011 are shown in the second chart.

The preponderance of records for December to February is probably accounted for by easier observation conditions in harsh weather, a point emphasized by the record of a bird on snow-covered ground on 17th February 1991 at Dale Abbey, which allowed observers to approach within 4m. The longest stay was by the one at Willington Gravel Pits from 2nd August 2009 to 15th April 2010. Prior to that, one remained at Brailsford for 58 days from 19th December 1996 to 14th February 1997.

A Bittern was ringed as a nestling at Minsmere, Suffolk in 1950 and had moved to Walton-on-Trent by October of the same year. The circumstances of the recovery are not clear but the bird appears to have been released in a poor condition.

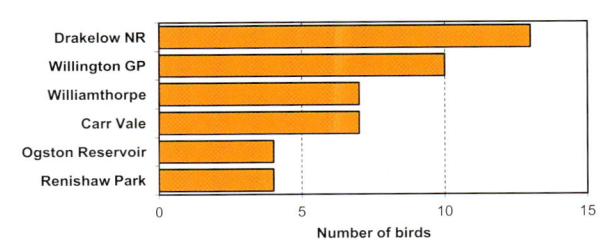

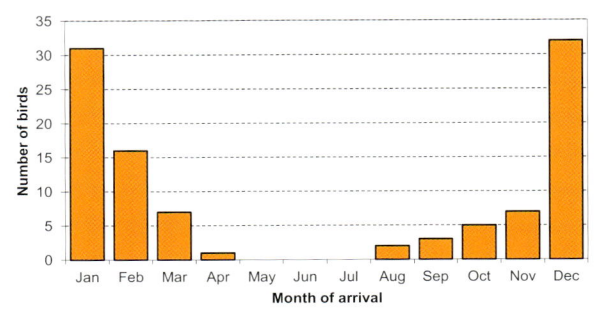

Little Bittern
Ixobrychus minutus
A very rare vagrant.

There are only two satisfactory records. In August 1872 a female was flushed from reeds by the canal at Draycott; it alighted on a hedge and was shot (Whitlock). The same fate befell one at trout ponds at Langwith in the spring of 1889 (Jourdain). This declining species breeds across Europe to western Asia and Africa, wintering in the latter region. There are other populations in the Indian subcontinent and in Australia. Breeding took place in South Yorkshire in 1984. Hudson *et al.* (2012) recorded a total of about 486 in Britain up to the end of 2011.

Night Heron
Nycticorax nycticorax
A very rare vagrant.

Records of this almost cosmopolitan species were considered by BBRC until 2002 but, with 436 occurrences between 1952 and 2002, it was then removed from the list. Many Night Herons are kept in zoos and wildlife parks, and it has become increasingly difficult to differentiate between escaped and wild birds.

In Derbyshire there have been five or six records. An adult was shot at Combs Reservoir in the early 1860s (Jourdain) and another at Castle Donington in 1846, but the latter would probably have been in Leicestershire (Whitlock) and is listed in Hickling (1978). On 13th June 1931, an adult was killed on the Derbyshire side of the River Dove between Norbury and Calwich Abbey.

There have been four modern records:

Year	Location and date
1976	Langley Mill, an immature on 9th–10th September and presumed to be the same bird at nearby Brinsley Flashes on 2nd October
1976	Shipley Country Park, one on 28th November. Presumed to be the Langley Mill bird
1995	River Derwent, Alvaston, a first-summer bird roosted in riverside trees on 7th–8th May
2006	Morris Croft, Caldwell, an adult on a private pool on 7th May

The bird at Alvaston was one of five seen nationally during May 1995, two of the others also occurring between 6th and 11th May. The 2006 bird was one of about 35 birds seen in March to May of that year, mainly in the south and west of the UK.

Squacco Heron
Ardeola ralloides
A very rare vagrant.

Up to the end of 2011 a total of 149 of these attractive, small herons had been seen in Britain (Hudson *et al.* 2012). Records are well scattered, but mainly in southern and eastern England. They occur mostly in spring from early April to early July with small numbers in August, September and October. Squacco Herons breed from Iberia to south-west Asia, and in Africa, where the European population winters.

There are two Derbyshire records. Whitlock records a male shot on the banks of the River Dove on 17th May 1874. This was also recorded for Staffordshire by Harrison and Harrison (2005), who give the locality as Coton-in-the-Clay. The Dove forms the county boundary with Staffordshire for most of its length and it is usual to treat records such as this as common to both counties. The nearest Derbyshire locality is Scropton.

The second record concerns a juvenile seen at Long Eaton from 28th October to 6th November 2011. This bird frequented the River Erewash, which here forms the county boundary; though it spent most of its time on the Nottinghamshire side, it was frequently seen in Derbyshire. Gauton (2012) documented the occurrence. Only three others had by that time been seen in the UK in November.

Cattle Egret
Bubulcus ibis
A very rare vagrant.

Based on colonization of new breeding areas, the Cattle Egret is one of the most successful birds in the world. It breeds in Europe, Asia, Africa, Australia and the Americas, which it colonized in the twentieth century. It was formerly a very rare UK vagrant but is now seen annually, and breeding occurred in Somerset in 2008.

There have been six records of this egret in Derbyshire, the last two sightings almost certainly involving only one individual:

Year	Location and date
1966	Egginton Sewage Farm, an immature on 12th July
1968	Shardlow, an adult from 15th to 17th September
1986	Hurst Reservoir area, one on 16th December. Relocated on 20th December in the Thornsett–New Mills–Watford Lodge area, remaining until 7th January 1987, when it moved to Doxey Marshes in Staffordshire
1996	Swarkestone area, one from 19th to 21st December. This was the individual that was at Moorends, South Yorkshire from 11th October to 27th December, except on the above dates
2009	Carr Vale, one arrived from the north on 25th October
2009	Ogston Reservoir, one, which left to the south-west, on 28th October

Little Egret
Egretta garzetta
A rare, but greatly increasing, vagrant.

The Little Egret has undergone a major change of status in the UK in recent decades. Once a rare vagrant, it is now a regular breeder, with a large and widespread non-breeding population. Breeding took place for the first time in Dorset in 1996 and by 2009 there were 701–800 breeding pairs in England and Wales (Holling *et al.* 2011). The driving force behind the expansion has been a post-breeding dispersal, leading birds to winter in new areas, and then stay to breed (Lock & Cook 1998).

It was the second half of the twentieth century before the first Little Egret was recorded in Derbyshire: an adult in summer plumage was on a backwater of the River Trent, near Repton, from 18th to 24th May 1967. Twenty years passed before another was recorded, at Swarkestone Lake on 23rd August 1987. A further three were seen in August 1989, part of a notable influx into Britain that year. They remained rare and irregular in their occurrences during the early 1990s but since 1998 they have been annual visitors. From 2002 numbers have increased dramatically, cumulating in peaks of 59 birds in 2003, 124 by 2008 and 252 in 2011, as shown in the table.

Year	Birds
1987	1
1988	–
1989	3
1990	–
1991	–
1992	–
1993	2
1994	3
1995	3
1996	1
1997	–
1998	1
1999	6

Year	Birds
2000	3
2001	5
2002	23
2003	59
2004	15
2005	48
2006	46
2007	78
2008	124
2009	122
2010	194
2011	252

Little Egrets have now been seen in Derbyshire in every month of the year. The monthly distribution up to 2007 as indicated in the chart (after which birds were so numerous that monthly analysis was discontinued in the *Derbyshire Bird Report*) shows a small peak in May suggesting overshooting migrants, followed by a major influx in late summer, which is no doubt due to post-breeding dispersal. This usually commences in July and continues into September, with August being the peak month for arrivals, accounting for about one-third of the total number of birds seen in the county. Most of these leave during the autumn, but a few are now seen each winter, though their occurrences are sporadic.

Little Egret: monthly distribution 1987-2007

A long-staying individual was present on streams around Longford from 15th December 1993 to 7th January 1994, before moving to Shirley Mill, where it remained into April.

Most of the records have come from the Trent Valley corridor, especially at the gravel pit complexes at Barrow upon Trent, Aston-on-Trent and Willington, and also the confluence of the Rivers Trent and Dove at Newton Solney. Further north, the well-watched Ogston Reservoir is also a regularly visited site. There have been six records from the Peak District: at Combs Reservoir on 13th August 2002; the Bowers Hall–Haddon Hall area on 28th August 2002; Freebirch on 18th May 2009; Harp Edge on 1st August 2009; Bakewell from 23rd December 2009 to 3rd January 2010; and at Chatsworth Park, up to two between 19th July and 3rd August 2010. The table shows the most productive sites for Little Egrets up to 2007.

Location	Birds
Aston-on-Trent Gravel Pits	15
Barrow Gravel Pits	14
Willington Gravel Pits	10
Ogston Reservoir	9
Newton Solney	9
Long Eaton Gravel Pits	7
Drakelow Nature Reserve	6

Sightings of single birds account for the majority of the records, but following the dramatic increase in numbers seen in the county from 2002, small groups have become more common. The first county double-figure count (11) was recorded at Drakelow Nature Reserve on 16th August 2007, and the largest counts were both of 14 at Aston-on-Trent Gravel Pits on 21st August 2010 and at Willington Gravel Pits on 2nd September 2011. Other large counts have been of 11 at Aston-on-Trent Gravel Pits on 3rd and 8th October 2011, and ten at Long Eaton Gravel Pits on 20th July 2011. Also, there have been counts of six to nine birds at Newton Solney and Ambaston Gravel Pits.

Interestingly, at Drakelow Nature Reserve, a Little Egret roosted with a Great White Egret on several occasions during August and September 2003, an unusual occurrence for an inland site.

Great White Egret
Egretta alba
A very rare vagrant.

The recent Derbyshire records of this cosmopolitan egret have occurred at a time of national increases in Britain and western Europe. In 2003, BBRC accepted 42 records for this species, making it the second-best year nationally (Rogers *et al.* 2004). A feature of recent records is that, as with the bird seen at Drakelow Nature Reserve in 2003, many have been long-staying individuals.

Until the end of 2005, a total of 310 had been recorded in Britain, with most records coming from the south and east coasts (Fraser *et al.* 2007). Thereafter this species was removed from the list of species assessed by BBRC.

There have been 16 Derbyshire records, shown in the table. The 1974 individual was only the eleventh to be recorded in Britain and Ireland, and the first since 1951. What was presumed to be the same bird was later seen at Scaling Dam, North Yorkshire from 28th May to 6th June. The long-staying bird in 2003 was also seen in Staffordshire, at Blithfield Reservoir and Whitemoor Haye; Cockburn (2004) gave an account of its stay at Drakelow Nature Reserve. The records from Drakelow and Barrow in 2009 almost certainly related to the same bird.

Year	Location and date
1974	Newton Solney–Clay Mills area, one on 19th May
2003	Drakelow Nature Reserve and River Trent near Walton-on-Trent, one intermittently from 21st August to 10th October
2004	Wyver Lane, an adult in breeding plumage on 10th June
2007	Leash Fen, one flew north-east on 26th September
2007	Drakelow Nature Reserve, one on 10th and 22nd November
2007	Barrow Gravel Pits, one, which left to the west, on 1st December. Presumed to be the Drakelow bird
2008	Ogston Reservoir, one on 4th June
2008	Harewood Moor, one flew south-east on 14th June
2008	Carsington Water, one present briefly before it left to the south-east on 7th December
2009	Sutton Brook Lakes, one from 6th to 14th February
2009	Willington Gravel Pits, one on 28th June
2009	Drakelow Nature Reserve, one flew north-east on 27th September
2009	Barrow upon Trent, one from 28th to 30th September
2010	Manchester Playing Fields, Long Eaton, one flying over on 17th March
2011	Carr Vale, an adult from 12th to 14th June
2011	Barrow Gravel Pits, one from 29th October to 5th November

Grey Heron
Ardea cinerea
A fairly common resident and winter visitor.

Grey Herons are currently widespread in most of Derbyshire and might be expected at any wetland area that contains fish or amphibians. They occur by running water, ranging from tiny streams to large rivers, and at still waters of all sizes. Not infrequently these include garden ponds in built-up areas where some owners have discovered, to their chagrin, reduced numbers of their pond-fish. A garden visitor at Whaley Bridge in 1990 was even seen standing on a car roof. They are not confined to wetlands, however, and take a wide range of food, including small mammals and invertebrates, so they are sometimes recorded feeding in dry areas.

For much of the year, Grey Herons are solitary birds but considerable numbers can assemble at favourite feeding areas. The largest gathering known to Frost was of 39 in August 1962 at Ogston Reservoir. The same site hosted the largest subsequent count, of 70 in June 2002.

The Derbyshire BBS (1995–99) showed proven breeding in 27 tetrads and probable breeding in a further six. There were a further 283 tetrads where Grey Herons were recorded during the breeding season. However, these are not shown on the map as the overwhelming majority are believed to relate to non-breeders (they do not breed until two or three years old) or to birds commuting between nesting and feeding sites, which may be many kilometres apart.

Most nests are in tall trees, especially deciduous, in relatively undisturbed areas. Single nests or very small colonies can easily be overlooked, especially in coniferous woodland, where it can be difficult to distinguish between old and new nests in dense canopy. Sometimes single pairs, or very small colonies, have been found only when the clattering calls of the nestlings were heard. At Poolsbrook a few pairs have bred in the 2000s in willow carr.

The lattice steel structure of an electricity substation at Spondon formed a very unusual nest site for two pairs in 1948, while there was an unconfirmed 1993 report of a pair nesting on a pylon between Arkwright and Carr Vale.

Whitlock knew of only one active heronry in 1893, at Kedleston Park, where there had been 20 pairs in 1884. The colony at Sutton Scarsdale, which held about 12 nests in 1884, was defunct nine years later; likewise, it was believed, the colony at Eaton Wood. Both Whitlock and Jourdain stated that Grey Herons suffered high levels of persecution by fishing interests. Frost said that breeding information was far from complete, but he knew of only one then regular colony, at Norbury, which held about 15 nests in 1976.

Although occasional persecution is still suspected today, the Derbyshire Grey Heron population is higher now than ever previously recorded. The national picture is also a rosy one, with an increase of 24% between 1970 and 2008 (Eaton *et al.* 2010). Likely reasons include improved water quality, reduced persecution, and the increase of well-stocked fisheries, both large and small. Unfortunately, nest counts at the colonies have been rather irregular and even some of the largest are not monitored annually. Coverage was best in 2003, coinciding with a year of the BTO's national census of this species, when there were about 151 nesting pairs in 11 colonies in the county.

Since 1900, only 11 colonies are known to have reached double figures. The Kedleston Park colony existed from 1876 to at least 1910, with 15 pairs in 1901; occasional nesting has taken place there in more recent years. The colony at Catton Park was in a wood known as The Rough and was present from 1933 to 1971, peaking at 20 pairs in 1947. In 2002 and 2003, eight pairs nested some 700m from the original site but then abandoned it, possibly due to disturbance. It is possible that the deterioration of the beeches in which they nested (in Serpentine Wood), as well as disturbance, may have been the reason for the demise of the heronry at Calke Park, which was known from 1941 to 1964, possibly 1967. There were 44 pairs here in 1944 (W. Cove *pers comm*) and this was the largest single count for Derbyshire until it was superseded in 1998 by the 48 pairs nesting near the River Trent at King's Newton. This colony, in tall willows, was discovered in 1985 and is still in use, though recent numbers show a substantial decline. Two other heronries have recently been established close to the Trent. The heronry at Repton dates from 1996 and held 13 nests in 2007. The other, at Drakelow Nature Reserve, began in 1998 and reached a maximum of 23 pairs in 2007. Here the birds nest on mature willows and sycamores fringing one of the larger water bodies and now have nesting

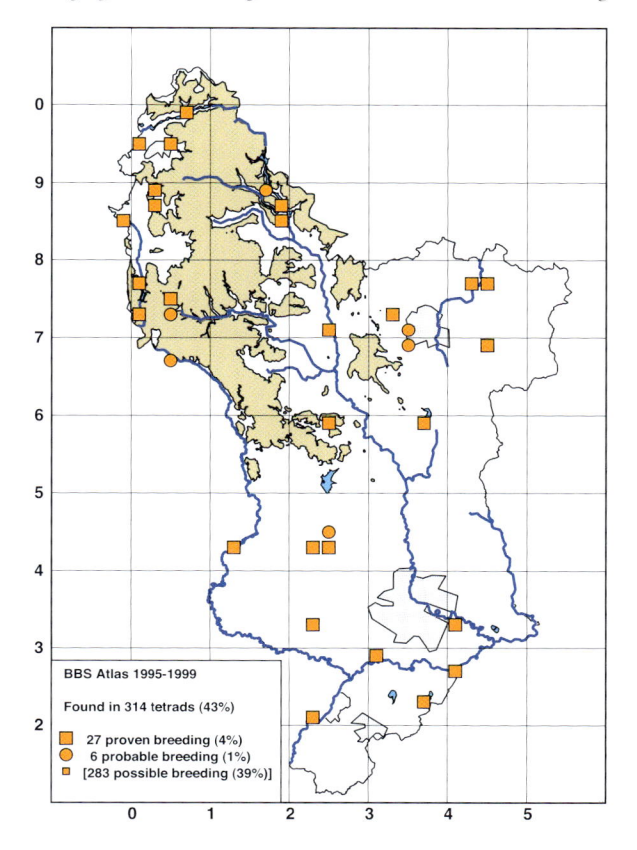

BBS Atlas 1995-1999
Found in 314 tetrads (43%)
- 27 proven breeding (4%)
- 6 probable breeding (1%)
- [283 possible breeding (39%)]

Cormorants as neighbours. There were 12 nests at Elvaston Castle Country Park in 2011.

The remaining five heronries are much further west or north. The colony at Norbury, in the Dove Valley, was first recorded in 1968 and still exists, though the actual site has changed twice because of felling. The current colony is in coniferous woodland and held 24 nests in 2005. The heronry at Carr Wood, close to Ogston Reservoir, has been in existence since 1976. Most nests are in larches, close to the woodland edge, and the highest count was of at least 20 pairs in 1991. There are less than annual counts of the colony in a conifer plantation at Chatsworth Park, which was first recorded in 1992, with 12 or more nests in 1997 and 2003. Near Ladybower Reservoir there is a colony at Win Hill, which was discovered in 1986 and held 11 pairs in 1987, 1992 and 1999. Finally, a site at Old Glossop was in use from 1991 and reached ten nests in 2005, but there is no subsequent information from here.

Additionally, there have been many smaller colonies or sometimes single pairs, widely scattered through the county. Nest sites in 2000–09 alone were found at Egginton Chase (destroyed by housing development), Osmaston Park, Anchor Church, Scropton, Melbourne Pool, Willington Gravel Pits, Elvaston Castle Country Park, Poolsbrook Marsh, Renishaw Park, Birleyhay, Linacre Reservoirs, Barlow, Ashford-in-the-Water, Derwent Reservoir, Abbey Bank, Doctor's Gate, Combs Reservoir and Torside Reservoir.

Melanistic birds were seen at Sawley Water Meadows in 1985 and at Carr Vale in 1996.

Though sometimes thought of as a strictly resident species, there are occasional records of birds that appeared to be on passage. An interesting example was in the Goyt Valley on 14th December 2008 when nine flew north in formation, rose on thermals to well over 600m and moved off west.

The earliest recovery of a Grey Heron in Derbyshire was of a chick ringed in Poland in 1934 and found the following spring in Bakewell. Other foreign recoveries have been from Germany, Denmark, France, Holland, Sweden and Norway, involving a total of nine birds.

Of the 39 birds ringed in Britain and Ireland, and recovered in Derbyshire, five had moved up to 10km, 22 up to 100km and 12 more than 100km. Of the long-distance records, nearly all of these have moved to Derbyshire from East Anglia. By contrast, over half of the birds which had travelled between ten and 99km, had originated from Staffordshire in the south-west.

Purple Heron
Ardea purpurea
A very rare vagrant.

From 1958 to 2002, 745 Purple Herons were recorded in Britain, making this species the most commonly occurring of the rarer herons (Fraser & Rogers 2005).

Whitlock recorded that a male was killed on the River Trent (apparently on the Derbyshire bank) at Wetmore on 1st July 1856, and another was shot at Newton Solney prior to 1881. Since 1950 there have been six records involving six or possibly seven birds.

Purple Herons breed widely across Europe, and in southern Asia and East Africa; European birds winter in sub-Saharan Africa. The first UK breeding took place in Kent in 2010.

In the UK, Purple Herons mainly occur in spring, with a peak from mid-April to early June. In the autumn young birds disperse from their European breeding colonies and there is a secondary peak in August. Four of the six Derbyshire records occurred during the spring peak period, while the other occurred during the autumn peak period.

Year	Location and date
1968	Shardlow, an adult on 18th–19th April
1975	Sawley Water Meadows, an adult on 27th August flew off west
1977	Brinsley Flash and Langley Mill, one (possibly two) from 2nd to 4th May
1977	Shipley Country Park, one flew south-east on 15th May
1985	Old Whittington Sewage Farm, one, probably first-summer, on 26th May
2011	Ogston Reservoir, a first-summer on 8th May, which arrived from the north and later departed north-east

Black Stork
Ciconia nigra
A very rare vagrant.

Black Stork is a widespread, but uncommon, species that breeds in the warmer parts of Europe (predominantly in central and eastern regions) and across temperate Asia to the Pacific. There is a small population in Iberia and another in southern Africa. They winter south of the Sahara, and in India and south-east Asia. There was a UK total of 212 by the end of 2011 (Hudson *et al.* 2012). Although records extend from April through to November, most (about 80%) have occurred between May and August, and it seems very likely that most birds seen are wandering subadults.

The spring of 2011 saw a small influx of birds into Britain, and Derbyshire was graced by possibly two birds. The first was watched for about five minutes soaring, just south-east of Beeley 'Triangle' on 24th April 2011 before it flew off in a south-easterly direction (Moulden 2012). The second was seen drifting slowly westwards over Hall Dale Wood near Two Dales on 24th June 2011 (Smith 2012). These were the first and second records for Derbyshire, though it is possible that only one individual was involved.

White Stork
Ciconia ciconia
A very rare vagrant.

White Storks breed in much of Europe, north-west Africa, the Middle East and central Asia, and Western Palearctic birds winter in Spain and Africa. Between 1958 and 2002 a total of 657 birds was recorded in Britain, with increasing regularity since the early 1970s (Fraser & Rogers 2005). However, it is not easy to distinguish between wild birds and those that have escaped or wandered from captivity.

Whitlock reported that several had been seen or shot on the River Dove, according to Robert Garner in his *Natural History of Staffordshire* (1844). More recently there have been 15 records, all of single birds with the exception of the 2004 record.

It is possible that some of these records relate to birds that may have wandered from the small feral population at Harewood House, Leeds. Key (2003b) thought that most of the four in 2002 were probably of feral origin. However, the two birds seen in 2004 were almost certainly the same individuals that arrived in South Yorkshire on 14th April and then moved to Horbury Wyke, Wakefield, where they attempted to build a nest on a small electricity pylon, before being discouraged by the utilities services. One of these birds had been ringed in Belgium, while the other was from a French reintroduction scheme. They had also been seen in Warwickshire on 12th April and had been reported flying over the A50 between Derby and Uttoxeter in Staffordshire on 13th April. One of the 2002 birds was notable for its long stay of nearly four months, and its well-monitored departure in early April.

One seen in Wingerworth on 22nd November 2011 was considered to have been an escape. It was believed to be the individual that wintered at Sookholme, Nottinghamshire and later built a nest on a restaurant roof there. It was seen to be wearing an avicultural ring.

Year	Location and date
1978	Ambergate, one in a meadow by the River Derwent on 8th–9th April
1986	Tideswell Moor, one on 19th May
1988	Parsley Hay, one flew north-west on 3rd April
1998	Sudbury, one on 10th–11th July
1999	Willington Gravel Pits, one on 16th–17th April, was also seen over Swarkestone Lake, Melbourne, Aston-on-Trent Gravel Pits, and Sawley on the latter date before departing west
2000	Goyt Valley, one flew north-west on 14th May
2002	One at Littleover and Mickleover on 7th and 9th January and then between Littleover and Findern, where it remained until 2nd April. It was seen over Mickleover on 1st April and Allestree on 2nd April. Later on 2nd April, it was seen flying north over Barbrook Reservoir, then over Ringinglow Bog, before flying south-east over Newhaven Crossing. It was last seen flying east over Hathersage on 3rd April
2002	Rosliston, one on 29th June
2002	Tideswell–Windmill area, one on 10th July
2002	Cavendish Mill, one on 11th July was presumed to be the Tideswell bird
2002	Ticknall, one on 26th July
2004	Chatsworth Park, two soaring along the ridge east of Chatsworth House on 14th April before flying off to the north
2005	Pools Brook Country Park, one flew north-north-west on 14th November
2008	Glapwell, one flew south-east on 5th July
2011	Willington Power Station, one on 20th April

Glossy Ibis
Plegadis falcinellus
A very rare vagrant.

In Europe the Glossy Ibis breeds in France and Spain but mainly in the Ukraine, Romania and the Balkans; it winters in East Africa. In the UK there were some 340 records of this species before 1950 and then 226 from 1950 to 2011 (Hudson *et al.* 2012). Most occurrences are in spring and autumn, but they can occur at almost any time of the year.

There have been eight Derbyshire records, four of which were in the nineteenth or early twentieth century. One was shot near Derby railway station in February 1842. One was shot at Walton-on-Trent 'many years ago' according to Whitlock; Smith (1938), quoted in Harrison and Harrison (2005), said this was in 1847 or 1848. One passing at immense height over Chellaston, probably in the 1850s, was shot and injured. It then lived in captivity for some months, feeding chiefly on young frogs (Whitlock). Additionally, one was shot at Sawley on 24th January 1923 (Frost).

The fifth sighting was at Nadin's, Newhall, where one was flushed during the morning of 17th September 2006. It returned to roost that evening and was present until late morning on the next day when it flew off north-west; it was later seen flying north-west over Burton upon Trent, Staffordshire. This may have been the bird first seen on 7th September at Radipole Lake RSPB Reserve, Dorset, and later present at various locations in Lancashire from 20th September to 15th December 2006 (James 2007).

Two were recorded in 2009, part of a record influx of at least 38 in Britain in September and October, and a further 23 in Ireland; a number of these were colour-ringed, showing their origins as Spanish breeding colonies (Hudson *et al.* 2010). The first flew north over Ogston Reservoir on 27th September, and was almost certainly the individual that had been seen earlier that morning at Langford Lowfields, Nottinghamshire and which arrived later at Hatfield Moors in South Yorkshire. The second sighting was at Willington Gravel Pits on 18th October, when one circled the area before leaving to the east-north-east. This may have been the individual present at Drayton Bassett, Staffordshire around that time. A fuller account of these two 2009 records is given by Key (2010a). None were seen in 2010 but one was recorded in 2011 on 12th November at Willington Gravel Pits.

Spoonbill
Platalea leucorodia
A rare vagrant.

In the UK Spoonbills are regular visitors, most of which are thought to come from an increasing population in Holland. Small numbers have also bred recently in southern Scotland and East Anglia.

In Derbyshire there were two nineteenth-century records. Whitlock was informed of birds killed at Butterley Reservoir on an unknown date and in the Erewash Valley in winter 1847; the latter was said to be 'opposite Toton' (in Nottinghamshire) which places it in the Long Eaton area. In 1942, three flew over Lea on 'Whit Monday' (Frost).

Since then, there have been 16 records, involving 22 birds. The two on 5th May 2008 were believed to be the two present at Alvecote, Warwickshire on 5th–6th May.

Year	Location and date
1966	Willington, an adult by the River Trent on 18th June
1969	Ogston Reservoir, an immature on 9th November
1978	Elvaston Quarry, three arrived from the south and departed south-south-west on 10th June
1979	Swarkestone Lake, an adult flew west on 14th May
1979	Twyford, an immature on 1st June
1980	Long Eaton, two flew over the town at 1930hrs on 11th August
1980	Elvaston Quarry, two immatures, presumed to be the Long Eaton birds, roosted each evening from 11th to 13th August
1980	Drakelow Nature Reserve, two immatures on 16th August, which left to the north-east. Probably the same birds as above
1988	Langley Mill Flashes, an immature from 20th to 22nd September
1995	Brinsley Flashes and Bennerley Marsh, an immature on 17th, 25th, 26th and 28th July
1998	Willington Gravel Pits, an adult arrived from the east and departed to the south-west on 21st August

Year	Location and date
2008	Willington Gravel Pits, two first-summer birds flew east on 5th May
2008	Carsington Water, one present for 30 minutes before departing to the north on 29th May
2010	Willington Gravel Pits, a immature on 29th May
2011	River Trent, King's Newton, one on 15th May
2011	Ogston Reservoir, one on 19th May, which arrived from the north and departed south-west

Analysis by period and months since 1960 is shown in the tables.

Period	Records	Birds
1960s	2	2
1970s	3	5
1980s	4	7
1990s	2	2
2000–11	5	6
Totals	16	22

Month	Records	Birds
May	6	7
June	3	5
July	1	1
August	4	7
September	1	1
November	1	1
Totals	16	22

Little Grebe
Tachybaptus ruficollis
A fairly common resident but scarce in the north-west.

Little Grebes are found throughout Derbyshire's lowlands, wherever ponds, gravel pits, lakes, reservoirs, canals and slow-moving rivers provide suitable breeding habitat. They attach their floating nests to fallen logs, tree roots, marginal vegetation or anything that will provide sufficient support. Where the water margins are thickly vegetated, Little Grebes can be self-effacing and sometimes overlooked, but their distinctive trilling song often betrays their presence. Later, any family groups are often located by the hunger-calls of the young. However, population figures published annually in the *Derbyshire Bird Report* are likely to be underestimates.

The number of breeding pairs in the years 1979–2011 is shown in the chart.

The Derbyshire BBS (1995–99) proved breeding in 115 tetrads, with probable and possible breeding in a further 29 and 48 tetrads respectively.

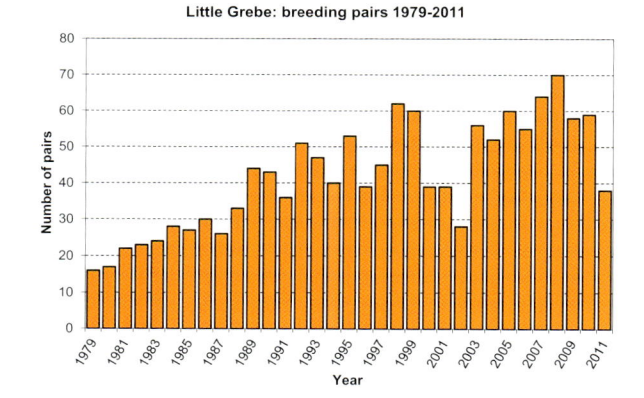

Little Grebes are scarce in the west and north-west of the county, due to a lack of suitable breeding sites. However, good numbers breed on rivers in the limestone dales of the Peak District. Whitlock said that the bird was common in the county and very common around Bakewell, which is still largely true of the current situation. They are often quick to colonize relatively new water bodies, presumably in response to the availability of small fish and other food. Many are resident at their breeding sites, leaving only if the waters freeze.

In Derbyshire, most Little Grebes breed between May and July, but young have been seen in the first few days of April, while dependent young are often recorded into October and on rare occasions into November, as late as 13th.

The Species Accounts

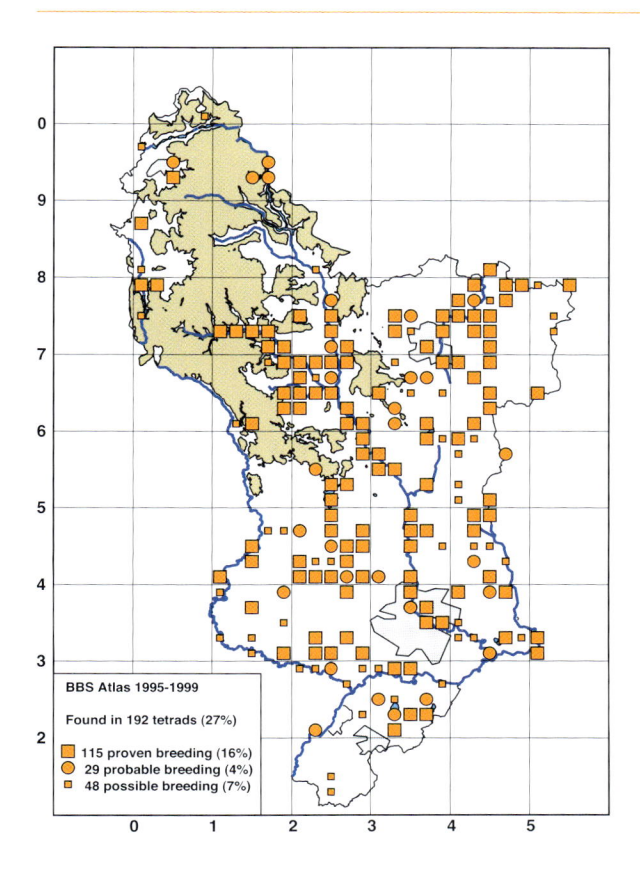

The largest counts of Little Grebes are usually made in late summer and autumn. The highest at this time were both of 43, at Elvaston Quarry in October 1978 and Chesterfield Canal in July 1999, followed by 38 at Drakelow Nature Reserve in October 2005. In winter the largest counts were of 37 in Cressbrook Dale in January 1978 and 35 at Williamthorpe in January 1981. However, these have recently been eclipsed by substantial numbers at Carsington Water, where there was a maximum of 107 in November 2007. This is the only large reservoir in the county where high numbers have been recorded. Unfortunately, a Yellow-legged Gull at this site in recent years has specialized in killing and eating Little Grebes.

The table shows the average of the monthly winter counts made during the period 1986/87 to 1999/2000. These are likely to considerably underestimate the population since this species inhabits many smaller sites where counts are not carried out.

Month	Birds
September	86
October	78
November	61
December	51
January	45
February	51
March	46

There are occasional sightings of migrants from non-breeding sites, such as some of the upland reservoirs. A quite exceptional record was of 13 at Kinder Reservoir on 2nd April 2002.

One was found dead at Coldwell Bridge on the River Dove in February 1980 with a fish, believed to be a bullhead, wedged in its throat. At Ogston Reservoir in August 1981 an adult was seen running along the road, vainly trying to become airborne.

Great Crested Grebe
Podiceps cristatus
A fairly common resident and passage migrant, mainly in the south and east.

Great Crested Grebes breed on lakes, reservoirs and gravel pits and, since 1981, on southern rivers. They are found mainly in the south and east of the county, but are scarce in other areas because of a lack of suitable habitat. Some of the breeding sites are deserted in winter.

Whitlock stated that these grebes were mainly passage migrants or winter visitors in Derbyshire, with very few breeding pairs. Jourdain believed that the three pairs at Shipley in 1900–01 constituted the entire breeding population of the county. However, there was a rapid increase from this low point, with breeding birds established on many lakes and ponds in central and southern Derbyshire by 1914, while the first northern nesting record was at Combs Reservoir in 1918. With better protection from persecution the population increased steadily thereafter, as shown by the following census results. The numbers are of individuals and not pairs.

Year	Breeding adults	Sites	Source of information
1931	42	14	National Census
1953	80–84	16	S.J. Weston *
1954	96	18	S.J. Weston
1958	71	15	S.J. Weston *
1965	91–98	18	National Census
1972	186	31	P.J. Bacon *
1975	134	25	P.J. Bacon *

* private surveys

The increase between 1958 and 1975 is likely to be due to the increased amount of open water in the form of new reservoirs and gravel pits. Since then the population has been relatively stable; during the 1990s it fluctuated between 58 and 75 pairs, and in 2000–11 between 50 and 70 pairs. However, numbers in the south of the county have declined, possibly due to increased boating and other leisure activities at some breeding sites.

Broods of young have been reported from early April to late November, with most seen between May and September. The chart shows the breeding population from 1990 to 2011.

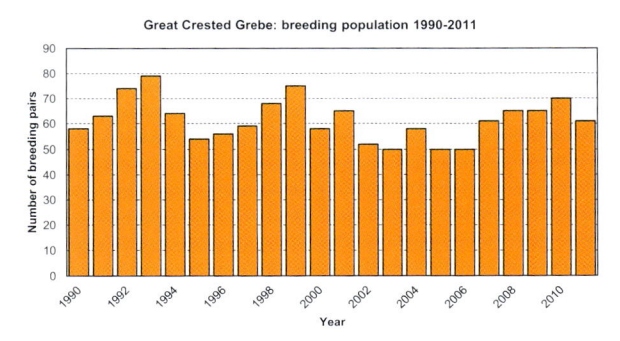

Interestingly, Butterley Reservoir was said by 1933 to be the main breeding site in the county; it is still a major site today. In the north-west of the county the most regular breeding site is Combs Reservoir, where up to six pairs nested in the 1990s, while the first breeding record at the Derwent Valley reservoirs came from Ladybower in 2002. Riverine breeding was first recorded on the Trent at Twyford in 1981 and is now regular on this river and on the lower River Derwent.

The Derbyshire BBS (1995–99) proved breeding in 71 tetrads, with probable in 12 and possible in a further 22, showing that they were found in 105 tetrads in total. Breeding is easily proved, as nests are usually quite conspicuous and the noisy young are dependent on their parents for 10–11 weeks.

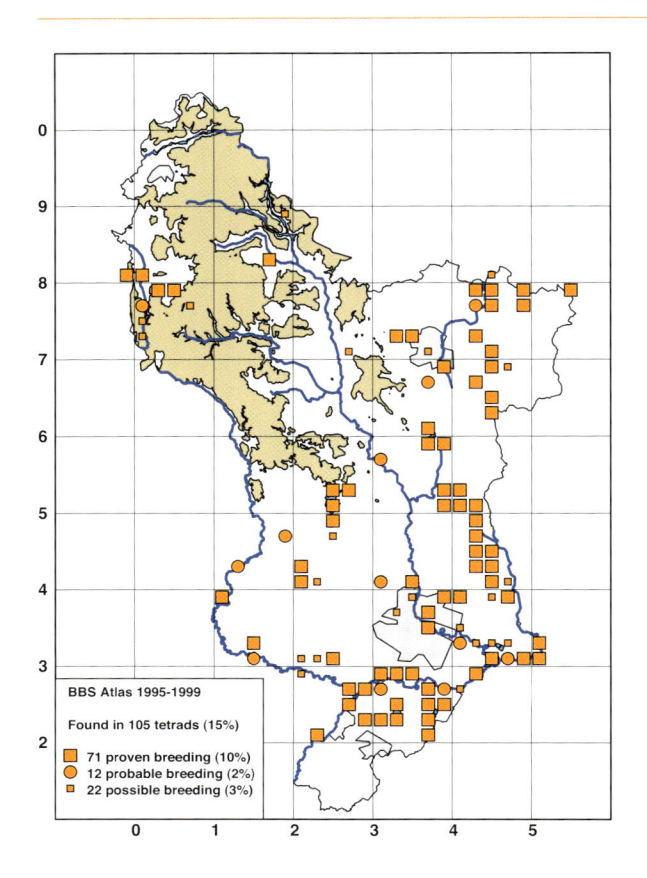

Although some birds remain throughout the year at breeding sites, especially the larger reservoirs, most other Great Crested Grebes in Derbyshire return in late winter and early spring. Early nests and young are frequently lost because of inclement weather and fluctuations in water levels. For example, at some of the larger water bodies, nests have often been washed out by strong wave action. At Carsington Water, several pairs nest on the ground on small islands in an apparent response to this problem. In 2002, 10–13 pairs nested successfully at this site.

Broods of young have been reported from late March until late November, with most seen between May and September.

The winter population is prone to considerable fluctuations, mainly in response to weather conditions. The table shows the average monthly counts during the period 1986/87 to 1999/2000.

Month	Birds
September	169
October	141
November	111
December	104
January	116
February	137
March	163

The first count of more than 100 was at Staunton Harold Reservoir in August 1971. The highest counts of all have come from southern reservoirs with about 200 at Foremark Reservoir in February 1991, 178 at Church Wilne Reservoir in September 1988, and 164 at Staunton Harold Reservoir in September 1974. The only other sites where more than 50 have been counted are Carsington Water, where there was a maximum of 95 in December 2010; Long Eaton Gravel Pits, with 77 in October 2008; and Butterley Reservoir, which held 51 in September 1985.

Red-necked Grebe
Podiceps grisegena
A rare winter visitor.

Whitlock quoted two nineteenth-century records: one shot on the River Derwent near Derby about 1844, and another on the River Trent between Burton upon Trent and Stapenhill in April 1849. Jourdain added a third record, of one shot on a brook near Chapel-en-le-Frith around 1887. The next sighting was in 1922, and the first DOS record concerned one at Ogston Reservoir from 11th to 27th February 1966, followed by a further eight up to 1977 (Frost). Since then, there have been a further 48 records involving 54 birds. Of these, no fewer than 19 occurred during the early months of 1979, when, following blizzards in mid-February, 17 were found in the county between 17th February and 10th March, although some of these were later found dead. One bird from this influx was picked up alive in Newton Solney on 17th February and released on the 'old River Trent' at Repton. These birds were part of a national influx, which were thought to have originated in the Baltic. A further six birds occurred between 26th January and 25th March 1996.

The distribution of records by period may be seen in the table, and the paucity of records since 2000 would suggest that this species may be reverting to being a rarity again in Derbyshire.

Period	Birds
1950s	–
1960s	1
1970s	26
1980s	12
1990s	16
2000–11	8
Total	63

The earliest record was of one at Carsington Water from 20th to 22nd September 1997, while the latest date was 8th May 2000, when one in full summer plumage was seen on the water-ski pit at Church Wilne Reservoir.

There is a winter peak of records between December and February, with 50 of the 63 birds having occurred during this period. February is the most favoured month, with no fewer than 33 birds being found then, although this total is somewhat distorted by the 1979 influx. The monthly distribution of records is given in the chart.

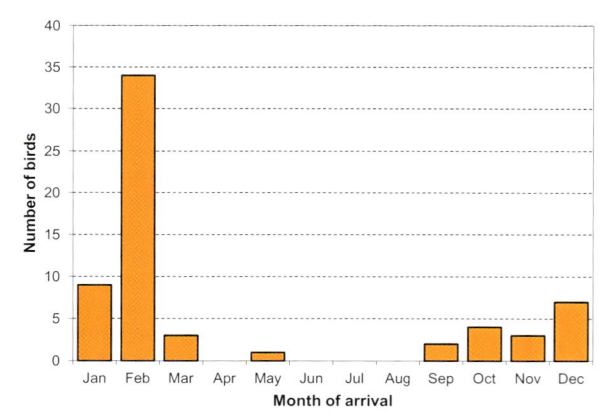

Most records relate to single birds, although two were seen together at Staunton Harold Reservoir from 17th to 20th February 1979, at Church Wilne Reservoir on 23rd February 1979, and Carsington Water from 15th to 19th February 2010.

The largest gathering was of three, at Ladybower Reservoir on 18th–19th February 1979, although all of them had been found dead by 1st March. Most birds stay only for a short time but there are occasional lingerers, which include singles at Carsington Water from 29th December 1997 to 15th March 1998, and another from 17th November 2005 to 17th April 2006. Another remained at Staunton Harold Reservoir from 25th December 2002 to 4th January 2003, and was then recorded at nearby Foremark Reservoir from 6th January to 3rd May 2003. The latter site also hosted one from 8th February to 3rd April 2009.

As is to be expected, most records have come from the large reservoirs within Derbyshire. The most productive sites are shown in the chart.

A surprising number have also been found on the river systems, mainly in the south of the county. They have occurred on the River Derwent at Alvaston, Milford and Ambergate, the River Trent at King's Mills and Trent Lock, and at the confluence of the Rivers Trent and Dove at Newton Solney. They are very rare birds in the far north-west, where the only record was one at Torside Reservoir from 19th to 23rd February 1979; it was found dead on the latter date. Other unusual sites where this species has occurred are Wyver Lane, Butterley Reservoir and Steetley Quarry.

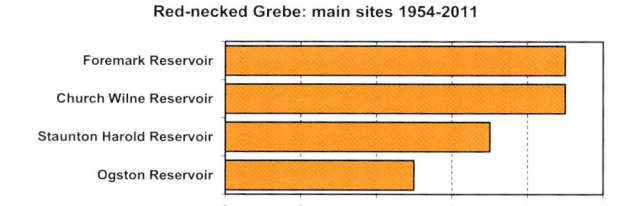

Red-necked Grebe: main sites 1954-2011

Slavonian Grebe
Podiceps auritus
A rare winter visitor and passage migrant.

The Slavonian Grebe is the rarest of the three smaller grebes to occur in Derbyshire. Frost quotes two nineteenth-century records of single birds shot at Newton Solney in 1860 and at Allestree in 1898. There were another four records up to 1954 and since then a further 63 birds have been recorded in the county.

The table shows the number of birds seen in each period.

Period	Birds
1950s	–
1960s	1
1970s	12
1980s	11
1990s	24
2000–11	15
Total	63

The high total of 24 birds in the 1990s is partly due to an influx of ten during January and February 1996, and a further two in both March and April as birds moved through the country. Normally, only one or two are seen each year, but the total in 1996 was 15. The next best years were 1985, when six were found and 1972, which had five.

The chart shows the monthly distribution of birds. From this, it can be seen that Slavonian Grebes are winter visitors and passage migrants to the county, with peak numbers found in November and January.

Slavonian Grebe: monthly distribution 1954-2011

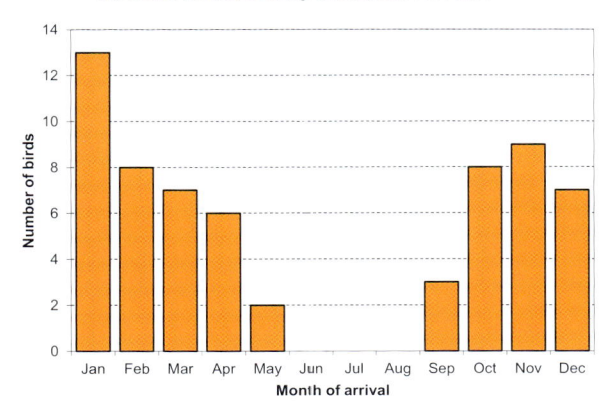

The extreme dates range from 19th September (2001) at Foremark Reservoir to 5th May (2007), when a summer-plumaged adult was at Church Wilne Reservoir. This range mirrors that found in the West Midlands (Harrison & Harrison 2005).

Most records are of single birds, but there have been three instances of two together, at Ogston Reservoir on 13th October 1973, and at Staunton Harold Reservoir on 26th January 1985. At Foremark Reservoir on 22nd November 2002, two were found together during the morning and had been joined by a third bird in the afternoon.

Most birds have remained for up to three days. The longest-staying bird was one at Steetley Quarry from 16th February to 12th April 1996, a stay of 57 days, while one was at Foremark Reservoir for 44 days from 19th September to 1st November 2001.

The large reservoirs account for the vast majority of the records, with 12 birds recorded at Carsington Water and 11 at Church Wilne Reservoir. Foremark Reservoir has had nine, Ogston Reservoir seven and Staunton Harold Reservoir five birds. More unusual sites have been Combs Reservoir in the north-west, which has recorded three birds, Hilton Gravel Pits Nature Reserve, which has had two, Steetley Quarry and Barlow Fish Ponds. Slavonian Grebes have also been seen on the River Trent at Drakelow Nature Reserve, the River Erewash at Long Eaton, and on the River Derwent at Wilne and Belper, as well as the gravel pit complexes at Willington, Barrow upon Trent, Swarkestone and Long Eaton.

Black-necked Grebe
Podiceps nigricollis
A rare, but nearly annual, passage migrant. Possibly attempted to breed in 1983 and 1994.

Whitlock knew of only one sighting in the county, at Draycott in 1860. The next records were in 1924, 1943 and 1947. Since 1954 there have been a further 117 records involving 175 birds. The table shows the number of records and birds in each period.

Period	Records	Birds
1950s	2	3
1960s	12	16
1970s	12	14
1980s	15	23
1990s	31	54
2000–11	45	65
Total	117	175

It is clear that this species is becoming more common, as 119 were seen between 1990 and 2011. This can probably be explained by the increase in the British breeding population, which has risen from 50 pairs in 1993, to 65–70 pairs in 2000–02, but had declined to 38–49 pairs by 2010 (Holling *et al.* 2010). With a large portion of this population breeding in Cheshire and Greater Manchester, and others breeding in Nottinghamshire, the passage birds occurring in Derbyshire may well involve birds from these localities. The chart shows the monthly distribution of records.

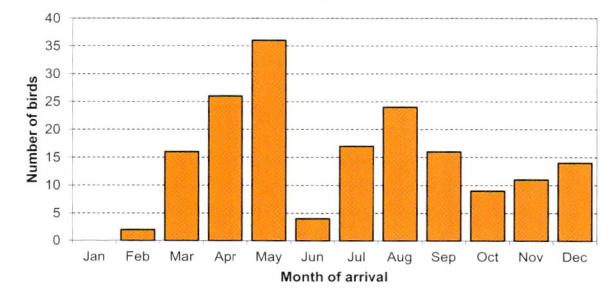

Black-necked Grebe: monthly distribution 1954-2011

The earliest arrival was one at Aston-on-Trent Gravel Pits from 17th February to 1st March 2007, while the latest was at Foremark Reservoir on 23rd December 1996. The spring peak is obvious from the chart, with 37 birds being found in May. There is a second peak in late summer and autumn, with adults, perhaps failed breeders, being seen in July, followed by the dispersal of young birds from their breeding sites. It is surprising that none have arrived in January, especially in view of the number seen in November and December. This situation is mirrored to a certain extent in the West Midlands (Harrison & Harrison 2005). There have now been three instances of wintering at Carsington Water: in 2004/05 one stayed for 79 days from 22nd December to 19th March, while in 2005/06 two birds, thought to be a pair, were present from 20th December to 18th March, a stay of 86 days.

Most birds occur singly, especially in autumn, but four were at Ogston Reservoir on 11th December 1968 and three at Howden Reservoir on 8th November 1981. In spring, up to three birds are normal and four birds were seen at Carsington Water in May 1992, May 2004 and April 2005, Aston-on-Trent Gravel Pits in May 1994 and Church Wilne Reservoir in March 1995.

Spring birds rarely stay for long, but some of the autumn migrants have remained for extended periods. At Church Wilne Reservoir an adult remained for 63 days, from 20th August to 21st October 1972, and at the same site, one was present from 18th August to 14th October 1973, a total of 58 days.

Black-necked Grebes have occurred at many suitable locations in the county including the Peak District reservoirs of Combs, Fernilee, Howden, Ladybower and Barbrook. The most productive lowland sites are shown in the chart.

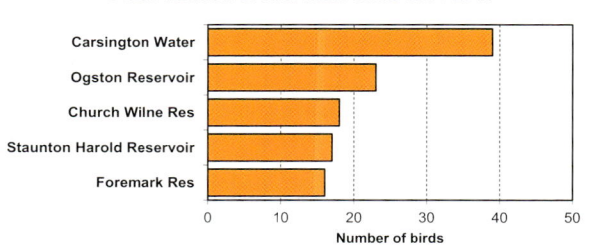

Black-necked Grebe: main sites 1954-2011

Unlike the other two rarer grebes, none have been recorded on the county's river systems, presumably because they are rarely displaced by cold, icy conditions, Ashbourne Hall Pond being an unusual locality for one on 10th November 1988.

There have been two instances of possible breeding attempts in the county. In 1983 a pair was present at Poolsbrook Marsh in May. They were seen to enter dense marginal vegetation and one of the pair was observed chasing off Little Grebes and Moorhens. This pair may have nested but they disappeared when the site became highly flooded on 1st June. At Aston-on-Trent Gravel Pits in 1994, a single bird was present on 1st May and four were seen on 29th May, when display and copulation were recorded, but only one remained on 1st June. Future breeding in the county must be likely as Black-necked Grebes have bred or are currently breeding in every county surrounding Derbyshire.

Honey Buzzard
Pernis apivorus
A rare passage migrant and non-breeding visitor.

S. J. Roberts Sep '99
John Roberts

Honey Buzzards feed predominantly on the larvae, pupae, adults, and even combs and nests of social hymenoptera, including wasps, bees and hornets, though they will also eat other food items, such as amphibians and pigeon squabs. Because of their specialized dietary requirements, they are strictly summer visitors and passage migrants to Britain and much of Europe, spending the winter in Africa. In the UK they breed in small numbers in lowland deciduous or mixed woodland, and also in upland conifer forests.

Frost listed seven Derbyshire records between the eighteenth century and 1958. Since 1970 there have been a further 63 records. Until 2000, all were of singles, except for two seen with seven Buzzards over Killamarsh on 12th September 1999.

The table shows the number of records and birds for each period from 1970.

Period	Records	Birds
1970s	4	4
1980s	5	5
1990s	14	15
2000–11	40	50
Total	63	74

The year 2000 was an exceptional one for this species, both nationally and in Derbyshire. County-wise, there was a total of 11 records involving 20 birds and all but one of these occurred between 22nd and 29th September. They were part of a notable influx of mainly juvenile birds, displaced from their usual migration route from southern Sweden across the narrow strip of water into Denmark. Classic anticyclonic conditions existed which encouraged the birds to migrate and once in flight they met a strong easterly airstream, which pushed them westwards across the North Sea. They then encountered an occluded front, moving east across the area, which subsequently slowed down and started to return westwards. Birds caught on the 'wrong side' of the front were swept in a south-westerly direction to make landfall on the east coast of Britain from 20th September. It was thought that some 500–700 birds were involved in this movement (Gantlett & Millington 2000; Key 2001a).

The Derbyshire records included three over the former Derby Racecourse on 22nd September, four over Foremark Reservoir and two over Big Moor on 23rd September, two over Etwall on 25th September, and three over Ogston Reservoir on 28th September. Others were claimed during this period but unfortunately were never substantiated. Since 2000, numbers have returned to normal and all records have again been of single birds, except for two on 14th September 2008 at Carr Vale.

Honey Buzzards have now become more regular as genuine passage migrants, particularly in the autumn, and migrants now account for the great majority of the birds seen in the county since 1970. However, seven sightings that came from locations in the north-east (at Scarcliffe, Sutton Scarsdale, Creswell Crags, Belph (three), and Upper Langwith) almost certainly relate to wandering by birds which were breeding in the Dukeries, Nottinghamshire, close to the county boundary. On one occasion a bird was watched flying directly from the breeding site into Derbyshire. The only records which might suggest possible breeding in the county were of singles in different areas of upland forest in early June 2006 and 2007, and in early August 2009.

Honey Buzzards have been seen in Derbyshire between late April and early October though, as might be expected, few migrants are seen in the county in the summer months. The earliest records were from Ogston Reservoir and Hognaston on 22nd April 2005 and believed to involve the same bird, and the latest record was of one over East Moor on 12th October 1990.

The table shows the monthly distribution of records since 1970.

Month	Records	Birds
April	2	2
May	8	8
June	6	6
July	6	6
August	12	12
September	27	38
October	2	2
Total	63	74

The majority of locations where Honey Buzzards have been recorded are in the northern half of Derbyshire and, apart from the birds seen during the influx of September 2000, the only localities in the south to produce modern records are Willington Gravel Pits, Aston-on-Trent Gravel Pits, Drakelow Nature Reserve and Hilton Gravel Pits Nature Reserve. There are much older records from Aston-on-Trent (prior to 1789) and from Allestree, Melbourne and Osmaston between 1904 and 1936.

Black Kite
Milvus migrans
A very rare vagrant.

Black Kites breed throughout most of Continental Europe, where their range is expanding, and winter in Africa, south of the Sahara. They are annual vagrants to Britain, with 345 records to the end of 2004 (Rogers *et al*. 2005). Most occur in April and May, with a predominance of records from East Anglia, the south-east and the southern coastal counties to the Isles of Scilly (Evans 1994).

There have been three Derbyshire records, all of short-staying birds. Broome (1986) wrote an account of the 1985 record, and Beevers (1998a) that of 1997.

Year	Location and date
1985	Chisworth, one flew north-east on 5th June. Also seen in Greater Manchester
1987	Burnaston, one on 26th May
1997	Carr Vale, one, which flew off high to the north on 22nd April

Red Kite
Milvus milvus
A rare vagrant.

In 1789 Pilkington regarded the Red Kite as one of the county's more common birds of prey and 40 years later Glover (1829) stated that it was the best known and 'most ignoble' of the falcon tribe. Nevertheless, by 1863 the breeding population had been persecuted to extinction and Whitlock said that occurrences in Derbyshire were as rare as those of the Golden Eagle. Whitlock believed that the Red Kite's Derbyshire headquarters had been in the wooded parts of the Peak District, the Buzzard replacing it in lowland areas.

The same situation prevailed throughout England, though a tiny population survived in Wales. In the period 1900–77 only six individuals were seen in Derbyshire: one in 1913, two in the 1960s, and three between 1970 and 1977 (Frost). A further record occurred in 1979 and there were nine in the 1980s.

With the population in Wales growing only slowly, and because the species was globally threatened, the Nature Conservancy Council (now Natural England) and the RSPB instigated a programme to reintroduce Red Kites into England and Scotland. The first English release area was the Chilterns, from 1989, followed by Rockingham Forest, in the East Midlands, from 1995 and the Harewood Estate in Yorkshire, from 1999. Red Kites very quickly bred in these areas (Brown & Grice 2005). The scheme has been highly successful and there can be no doubt that this is the main reason for the great increase in sightings in Derbyshire.

Although there was no immediate increase in records (for example, only three in 1998 and four in 1999) the 2000s have seen a great upsurge. 2002 saw the first double-figure total of records (13) and this increased rapidly to no fewer than 128 in 2011. Sightings have been from all parts of the county, and in a variety of habitats. Most have been seen on one date only, but there have been many records of birds lingering for several days. The first sighting of two together was at Osmaston in February 2002; in 2009, records of two together came from eight localities and three were seen at Ripley on 23rd May 2010.

The analysis of records by periods is shown in the table, while that by months is in the chart. It can be seen that most records are between March and June, with fewest in winter.

Period	Records
1960s	2
1970s	4
1980s	9
1990s	26
2000–11	324
Total	365

Red Kite: monthly record distribution 1954-2011

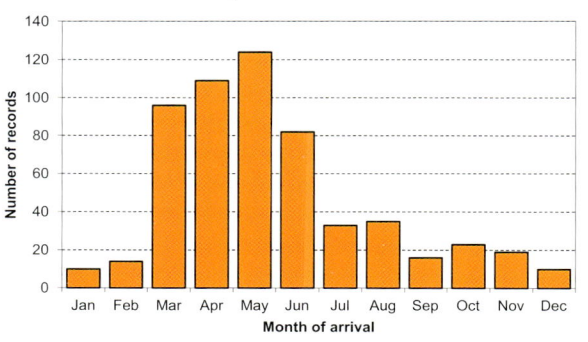

Many of the reintroduced birds and their progeny have been wing-tagged and there have been several Derbyshire sightings of some of these, with the first at Ashover in 1998. Not all tags have been identifiable but others have related to all three English release areas. One at Bretby in April 2000 had been ringed in the Rockingham Forest region, probably in 1999 and one at Carr Vale, also in April 2000, had been marked in the Chilterns the year before. One at Kedleston in April 2006 was a second-year bird from the Yorkshire release area. Another wing-tagged bird at Beeley Moor in April 2011 was a ten-month-old bird from Northamptonshire. By contrast, one found long-dead near Dale Abbey in March 2009 had been ringed as a chick near Llandovery, Dyfed, Wales in July 2007 and had travelled 198km to the east-north-east.

With the success of the reintroduction programme, there is a distinct possibility that the Red Kite could once again become a Derbyshire breeding bird. The county's habitat mosaic of upland moors and sheep-walks, wooded valleys and mixed lowland farms ought to provide ideal habitats for this spectacular raptor.

White-tailed Eagle
Haliaeetus albicilla
A very rare vagrant.

Jourdain said that this magnificent bird was 'a not uncommon winter visitor to the Derbyshire moors'. The opinion was based on his and Whitlock's knowledge of eight individuals and two further probable individuals. All of the eight above were shot between 1836 and 1891, five of them in the Derwent area and the others at Cuckoostone Moor, Hathersage and Strines. The Cuckoostone bird unwisely attacked a gamekeeper's dog.

In the twentieth century, an immature was at Derwent from 20th December 1920 to 8th February 1921, when it was killed by Lord Fitzallan's gamekeeper. Another gamekeeper, E.H. Peat, who later submitted many useful ornithological records, was presented with a pair of binoculars by the RSPB for his efforts to protect this bird. An immature frequented the Derwentdale area from 9th to 17th March 1939. In addition, eagles seen in the Kinder area in 1933 and Derwent again, in 1940, would most likely have been White-tailed Eagles (Frost).

A first-year bird was found by two observers at Beeley Moor on 29th January 2005 and was seen during the following hour by three others. To the delight of the now-assembled masses it then briefly reappeared about 90 minutes later. This individual had appeared in Norfolk in December 2004 and was then tracked through Cambridgeshire, Northamptonshire and Shropshire prior to its arrival in Derbyshire. It was subsequently seen in Lincolnshire and South Yorkshire until March 2005. Its initial appearance in Norfolk suggests a bird of north European rather than Scottish origin. Taylor (2006) documented the occurrence.

Marsh Harrier
Circus aeruginosus
A scarce, but increasing, passage migrant.

Although Frost mentions only occasional sightings in the eighteenth and nineteenth centuries, as well as ten in the twentieth century, the Marsh Harrier has become an annual visitor to the county since 1983, with a generally increasing number of sightings. Its status has been revised from 'a rare passage migrant' since 1994. In 1990–99, 78 individuals were seen; in the 2000–11 period there were 250. The increase is likely to be connected with the northern extension of the Marsh Harrier's breeding range in Britain, with, for example, many now nesting in Lincolnshire and Yorkshire, while Nottinghamshire had its first breeding record in 2009.

Most Derbyshire records fall between April and September, with extreme record dates of 2nd January (2008) at Hillstown, and 11th December (2005) at Pools Brook Country Park.

Most records are of single birds, but there are records of two at Carr Vale on 1st and 3rd May 1988 (and three on 12th May 2010); Willington Gravel Pits on 14th May 1999; Big Moor on 23rd–24th August 2008; Harewood Moor on 31st August 2009 and Barbrook Pools on 16th August 2010. Most birds are identified as 'cream-crowns' or all-dark immatures. The records are widely distributed throughout the county.

Most Marsh Harrier records are of 'fly-throughs', but some have roosted or attempted to roost: in 1993 a subadult male roosted on 12th and 13th May at Willington Gravel Pits, and at Carr Vale on 13th May an immature male roosted in a barley field. In 1994, a subadult male was seen to roost on Totley Moss on 29th April. On 16th April 1996, a male Marsh Harrier attempted to roost at Willington Gravel Pits, but was mobbed by corvids and departed north at 1925hrs.

The longest-staying birds have been an immature male at Carr Vale from 2nd to 8th June 1992, and a 'cream-crown' from 14th to 19th May 1999 at Willington Gravel Pits. Only one bird has been recorded with a kill: a female on 28th April 1996 with a Black-headed Gull at Willington Gravel Pits. In 2001, one at Carr Vale was believed to have killed at least one Great Crested Grebe.

In 1996, a wing-tagged second-summer male was observed at Carr Vale on 25th April, and possibly the same bird was observed the following day at nearby Shuttlewood. This was one of 11 tagged in Scotland in 1994. One ringed in June 1983 at Knardijk, Zuid Flevoland, Netherlands, was found sick, but later released, at Axe Edge in May 1984.

Hen Harrier
Circus cyaneus
A scarce or uncommon winter visitor and passage migrant, mainly in the Peak District. Bred in 1997 and 2006 and attempted to breed in 2003, 2008 and 2011.

The Peak District contains large areas of habitat suitable for Hen Harriers and Whitlock and Jourdain both suggested that there was evidence to show that the bird was once common and widespread throughout Derbyshire. However, from the 1830s persecution of this species increased nationally with the intensification of game preservation, and numbers of Hen Harriers began to decrease. Holloway (1996) documented the declines, first on the lowland breeding sites and then extinctions in many areas as a consequence of both habitat loss and persecution. He suggested that by the 1850s breeding was generally recorded only on grouse moors; intensive keepering on these was responsible for the final decline from around 1850. Until the isolated breeding records in 1997 and 2006, the only previously recorded nest with eggs in Derbyshire was one at Drakelow in 1870.

However, Hen Harriers continued to visit the county in the period between late autumn and early spring, and the larger number of observers in recent years has contributed to a much greater increase in reports. Frost remarked that 1963 was the last year when the species was not recorded. Hornbuckle and Herringshaw (1985) also noted the steady increase in the number of Hen Harriers reported, most records coming from the Eastern Moors, possibly because this area is better watched than other upland areas further north.

Numbers passing through the county in late autumn are generally greater than those that overwinter. Frost reported at least two August records, but arrival dates are usually in mid to late September. The earliest recent arrival dates are 15th July 2001 at Pike Low, and 2nd August 2005 at Highshaw Clough. The average arrival date for the period 1978–2011 was 17th September.

Most sightings relate to gritstone moorland and adjacent upland farmland, while lowland records are less frequent but increasing. In most years only single birds have been seen at any one time, but up to six individuals have been identified on the Eastern Moors in many years, latterly in 1998, during the winter period. Most birds have departed from the area by mid to late April (the average date in the period 1978–2009 is 20th April), although some may linger until May and occasionally June.

Outside the breeding season, they are known to use communal roost sites and there is a pattern of enormous increase in reported discoveries of regular communal Hen Harrier winter roosts in England since the mid-1970s (Clarke & Watson 1990). In the winter of 1979/80, roosting Hen Harriers were seen at a moorland site near Harland Edge on several occasions, probably peaking at four grey males and two females on 27th December. The site was regularly watched in December and January, and numbers fluctuated without any apparent relationship with weather conditions (Hornbuckle 1980). There were no further reports of communal roosting in Derbyshire until 1986, when a newly discovered roost of up to three 'ring-tails' was reported in late December on Bamford Moor. Since then up to five have roosted communally in various parts of the Eastern Moors.

During the early 1990s, there was an interesting series of records involving wing-tagged birds. All these had been ringed in Scotland as part of the RSPB Harrier Survey, co-ordinated by Brian Etheridge. The first reports were in 1991, when immature male birds were recorded on Beeley Moor from 16th to 18th October and north of Longdendale on 10th November. The first bird had been tagged as a pullus earlier in the year at a nest in Perthshire, a movement of 410km south-east, while the second bird had been tagged earlier in the year in Ayrshire, representing a movement of 380km south-east. In mid-October 1992, there was another immature male on Beeley Moor that had been tagged as a pullus earlier in the year at a nest site in the south-east Sutherland–Easter Ross area, a movement of 540km south-east. In 1993 a 'ring-tail' was seen on various dates between 27th February and 27th March in Upper Derwentdale. A first-winter female, it had been tagged as a pullus in summer 1992 in Argyll and Bute, a movement of 395km south-east, while a wing-tagged 'ring-tail' was observed on 27th October at Castle Naze, but no further information was received on this bird. A wing-tagged female recorded at Cutthroat Bridge on 30th April 1995 had been tagged as a chick in summer 1992 in Dumfries and Galloway. A wing-tagged male sighted in the latter part of October 1998 on the Eastern Moors related to the Langholm Project, co-ordinated by Redpath and Thirgood (1997), and was tagged at Langholm on 4th July 1998. A female on Leash Fen in October 2006 had been wing-tagged in Bowland, Lancashire in 2005.

Although there were records of Hen Harriers displaying in north Derbyshire in 1993 and 1995, and of two birds in 1994, no evidence of breeding was obtained. However, on 23rd May 1997, a pair of Hen Harriers breeding in the Goyt Valley was reported to the RSPB. A public nest-watch was set up (the first of its kind in England) and, with volunteer help and funding for three wardens, the birds were able to breed successfully, raising three (possibly four) young from a clutch of five eggs. This constituted the first confirmed breeding record in the county since 1870.

The event was particularly significant, since there were only seven other known successful Hen Harrier nests in the whole of England in 1997 (Hudson 1998). Although Hen Harriers were reported from the Goyt Valley in 1998, with a grey male on 22nd May and single 'ring-tails' in June and July, no nesting attempt was made.

More recently, a 'ring-tail' was seen carrying nesting material in north Derbyshire in 2000, and displaying birds were seen at two sites, also in north Derbyshire, in 2002, although no breeding took place. In 2003 a pair attempted to breed in the Goyt Valley and laid two eggs, but no further progress was made. There was a strong possibility of human interference and a spent gun-cartridge was found near the nest. Also in 2003, an adult female spent eight days in May and June in a possible breeding area in north Derbyshire.

In early April 2006, a nesting pair was discovered just outside the Derbyshire border in Stainery Clough (a short tributary of the River Derwent) in South Yorkshire, and towards the end of the month a second pair was found about 2km further up the Derwent Valley, in Barrow Clough. A protection scheme was mounted by the National Trust, Natural England and the RSPB, with additional funding from the British Association of Shooting and Conservation and support from the moorland tenant. Funding was sufficient for Natural England to employ four full-time wardens, and local bird clubs and other organizations provided a pool of about 40 volunteers prepared to make the long walk to both sites. All went well until 31st May, but by 2nd June both males had suddenly and mysteriously disappeared. Urgent action was needed and the wardens took the decision, approved by Natural England, to provide supplementary food to the nests. At Stainery Clough, where the breeding attempt was more advanced, the female took little advantage of this, but the Derbyshire bird did so readily. Her nest contained six eggs, from which five young fledged (the South Yorkshire bird fared likewise), and four of these had wing-tags and radio transmitters fitted. There were subsequent sightings or trackings of some of these birds elsewhere in Derbyshire, and in 2007 one of them bred successfully in the Yorkshire Dales. A detailed account of the event was given by Messenger and Taylor (2007), and of the supplementary feeding by Heath and Armstrong (2008).

In 2008 a male and female were seen in Upper Derwentdale in late April and 'sky-dancing' display, copulation and nest-building were observed. On the evening of 3rd May the female went to roost at the nest site and was never seen again: the male remained and attracted a second female, with the above activities recorded until 19th May, after which there were no further sightings of the female. Both females were believed to have been illegally killed. The male was last seen on 21st June.

In 2011 a male and two females were present during the spring in north-west Derbyshire. Copulation and the carrying of nest material were observed but the initial attempt failed. However, the male and a female remained and a second nesting attempt was made a few hundred metres from the first site. The nest was visited and contained seven eggs. Dawn to dusk watches were carried out but on the next nest visit it was clear that the female had been killed or predated and the eggs had been smashed. Police enquiries proved inconclusive.

Montagu's Harrier
Circus pygargus
A rare passage migrant.

The first county record of this species was in late April 1903, when a bird was shot in the Big Moor area. There were six records in the period 1940–56 including, in 1953, a male and two females at Ringinglow Bog, which nested on the Yorkshire side of the county boundary. Birds returned to the site in 1954, but did not breed; neither, apparently, did a pair that summered at Whitwell in 1955, and a female summered at Derwent in 1956 (Frost). Subsequent records are:

Year	Location and date
1961	Big Moor, a male on 27th May
1966	Eastmoor, a 'ring-tail' on 12th May
1971	Ladybower Reservoir, an immature on 13th August
1976	Lightwood–Combs Moss, a male on 10th June
1982	Eastmoor, a first-summer male from 10th June to mid-August
1986	Eastmoor, an adult male from 20th to 25th August
1988	Tideswell Moor, an immature on 25th August
1993	Middleton Moor, an immature on 30th–31st August
1994	Middleton Moor, a 'ring-tail' on 24th July
1997	Berry Clough, a 'ring-tail' on 3rd June
2000	Shardlow, a first-summer male on 13th May, seen flying towards Shardlow from Leicestershire
2000	Longstone Edge and Middleton Moor, a first-summer male on 13th May
2000	Ringinglow Bog, a 'ring-tail' on 20th June
2001	Tibshelf, a juvenile on 10th September
2006	Bolsover Moor, a female flew west on 25th May
2008	Ogston Reservoir, a juvenile arrived from the east and drifted south on 7th September
2010	Eastern Moors, an adult male from 26th April to 23rd May was seen displaying on 11th May
2010	Ogden Clough, a female on 15th May

Analysis by periods from 1960 is shown in the table.

Period	Records and birds
1960s	2
1970s	2
1980s	3
1990s	3
2000–11	8
Total	18

Goshawk
Accipiter gentilis
A scarce resident, mainly in the Peak District.

The historic information regarding this bird's status in Derbyshire is rather vague but both Whitlock and Jourdain were happy to accept a record of one shot at Ashover on an unspecified date, believing it to be the individual from the Jebb collection in Derby Museum. There was a probable record of one that was slightly injured when attacking an aviary at Bakewell in 1893.

However, this much-vilified raptor has been breeding in the county since at least 1966 and probably for some years before this, although its provenance is suspect because of either falconers' escapes or deliberate releases (Frost).

The Derbyshire population's stronghold has historically been in the forests of the Derwentdale complex, but in recent years there has been a slow but progressive spread southwards. Only 22 tetrads held Goshawks in the Derbyshire BBS (1995–99); breeding was proved in seven of these, and regarded as probable in six others and possible in the remaining nine. Nests are situated in a variety of woodlands and may be in broad-leaved or coniferous trees. Successful nests have been found as close as 1.25km apart.

Most Goshawk sightings are fleeting glimpses of hunting birds or longer views obtained in late winter or early spring when these birds display spectacularly over their nesting territories, their undulating display flight attracting birdwatchers from far and wide. They also display on fine days in autumn. A few are seen well away from known breeding areas in most years.

The Derbyshire population may be in the region of 18–25 pairs. This would no doubt be much higher if it were not for the malevolent interest of oologists and a minority of game preservers. The one-time threat of the illegal taking of young by unscrupulous falconers seems to have diminished since the introduction of DNA sampling.

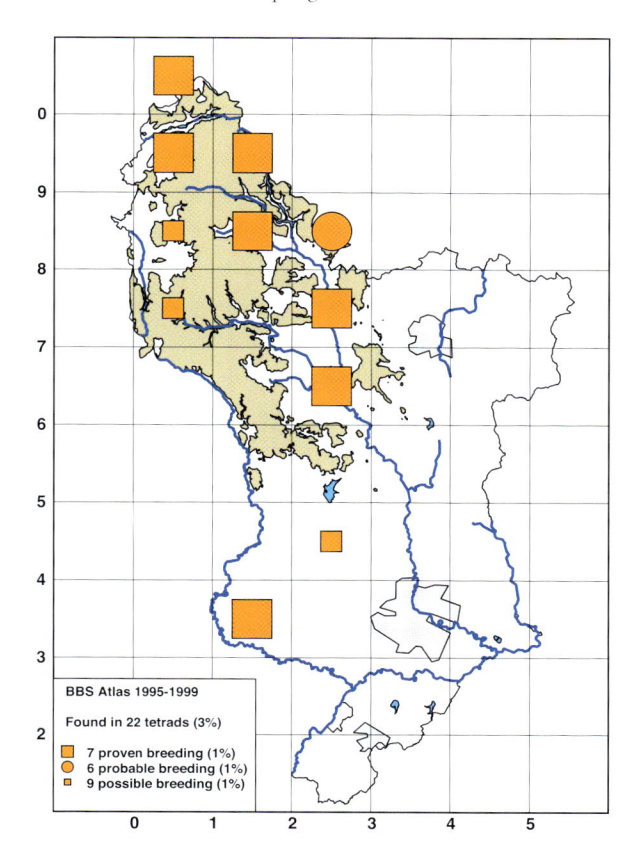

BBS Atlas 1995-1999
Found in 22 tetrads (3%)
■ 7 proven breeding (1%)
● 6 probable breeding (1%)
▪ 9 possible breeding (1%)

The table shows the known breeding in the period 1998–2009 and is based upon intensive fieldwork by members of the South Peak Raptor Study Group and the Peak District Raptor Monitoring Group.

Year	Sites	Successful	Young fledged
1998	13	5	14
1999	10	5	9
2000	17	8	17
2001	12	10	17
2002	13	10	26
2003	17	at least 10	at least 23
2004	16	at least 8	at least 16
2005	17	12	at least 21
2006	19	12	at least 25
2007	23	14	at least 26
2008	21	11	at least 27
2009	18	9	20
2010	22	12	at least 25
2011	21	8	18

Prey items have included some interesting species other than its favoured victim in this area, which is Woodpigeon. These range from birds as small as Siskin and Green Woodpecker (the remains of which were found in a pellet), to ducks. There are three reports of Mallard being attacked, and a female Goshawk was seen attempting to lift a Goldeneye from the surface of an upland reservoir. In the Peak District, Goshawks are frequently seen hunting over open country, especially moorland.

The ringing of this species in Derbyshire has to be done under special licence and a small number of recoveries has resulted since the 1970s. Most recoveries have involved only short distances. Longer journeys have been by one ringed near Bamford in June 1991 that was found long-dead in Kielder Forest, Northumberland (218km north-north-west) in June 1997, and one ringed near Matlock in June 1997 that was found dead 36km to the east-north-east at Clumber Park, Nottinghamshire in August 1998.

Sparrowhawk
Accipiter nisus
A fairly common resident and winter visitor.

Nowadays, Sparrowhawks are likely to be encountered virtually anywhere within the county, from Peak District woodlands to lowland farmland, parks and gardens. Garden bird tables, in even the most urban situations, will occasionally be visited by this tenacious raptor as it hunts, oblivious to its man-made surroundings.

It was not always so. Although Whitlock and Jourdain wrote about the high levels of persecution of the Sparrow Hawk, both said it was widespread, though not common. Alongside many other birds of prey, however, this species was greatly affected by the organo-chlorine pesticide poisoning of the 1950s and 1960s. Such was its decline that only one nest was reported in the county in 1966–67. However, with stricter pesticide control, numbers started to increase from 1971 onwards, with six nests found in that year. This increase continued and accelerated through the 1980s. For example, in 1984 11 pairs nested in the Wingerworth area, while in the following year there were no fewer than 465 dated records submitted to the *Derbyshire Bird Report*.

Most large areas of woodland in Derbyshire now hold breeding Sparrowhawks, while small copses may be regularly occupied if there are no suitable alternatives. If available, conifers are the preferred nesting trees, but otherwise a wide variety of deciduous trees may be used. The map shows 199 proven, 53 probable and 235 possible breeding tetrads.

It is likely, due to the secretive nature of this species, particularly in conifer plantations, that many of the possible breeding tetrads relate to breeding pairs. Most records of proven breeding result from observers hearing the squealing hunger calls of fledglings. The map also shows clusters of tetrads in the south and north-east. At the time of the last avifauna in 1978, the Sparrowhawk was considered primarily a bird of the Peak District. While the Peak District population has undoubtedly increased, the main range expansion has occurred in lowland Derbyshire.

Much of the success of the Sparrowhawk has been due to its adaptability in nest site selection. For example, the species has successfully colonized areas of north-east Derbyshire where opencast mining has reduced the amount of mature woodland and nesting is now regular in the scrub areas alongside the disused railway lines that once served the collieries.

Until very recently, when it was usurped by the Buzzard, the Sparrowhawk was regarded as the most numerous raptor in the county and had probably been so since the mid-1980s.

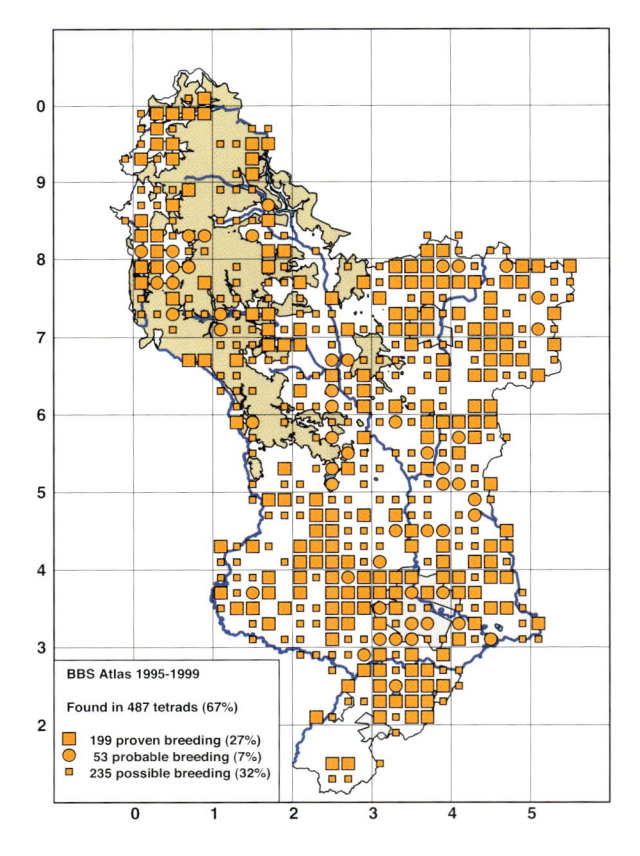

BBS Atlas 1995-1999
Found in 487 tetrads (67%)
■ 199 proven breeding (27%)
● 53 probable breeding (7%)
▪ 235 possible breeding (32%)

The current county population may be in the region of 600 breeding pairs, although some tetrads in prime areas will hold multiple pairs, so this might represent an underestimate. Most large counts of Sparrowhawk are made in spring in areas of high breeding density when the birds display above the woodland canopy. Derwentdale often produces the largest counts with at least ten on 26th March 1994 and nine on 30th March 1996.

Along with other opportunistic raptors, the Sparrowhawk takes a variety of prey. The majority are the more common woodland passerines such as Blackbird, Robin, Blue Tit and Chaffinch. More unusual prey species recorded in Derbyshire include Red Grouse, Green Woodpecker, Woodcock, Snipe, Cuckoo and Little Ringed Plover. One was seen raiding House Martin nests below the eaves of Cressbrook Mill on 15th June 2000. One caught in a mist net in Renishaw Park on 14th December 2002 had a house mouse in its talons, while a male was seen to kill a brown rat at Alfreton on 27th February 2005. Most bizarrely, a female took a large black water-snail from a Brailsford garden pond on 1st October 2006. A male mobbing a Peregrine on Big Moor in August 1997 made the wrong decision, as it was last seen disappearing over White Edge in the talons of the larger bird.

There are many reports of Sparrowhawks pressing home attacks in urban areas, in some cases despite human intervention. Two of the more interesting reports include one unsuccessfully attempting to catch a Pied Wagtail on the cricket pitch at Queen's Park, Chesterfield during the Derbyshire versus Gloucestershire match on 5th August 1994, while at Brockwell, Chesterfield on 3rd March 1986, a male caught a Blackbird within 1m of the observer's back door, defied her when she tried to frighten it into dropping the prey and finally flew off with the unfortunate prey still screaming.

There are several records which suggest that this species occurs as a migrant through the county. In some years, increased numbers have been recorded on the well-watched Eastern Moors in October. Six at Jeff's Wood between 24th September and 4th October 2004 all moved between west and north-west, while a 'loose flock' of seven flew south at Carr Vale on 16th April 2005.

This bird of prey has suffered various strains on its populations over the last 50 years, and shooting, trapping and poisoning have taken their toll. As a result, there are records of 152 recoveries from ringing effort starting in the 1940s. Of these only 3% concerned birds declared shot and these are all of the early records from the 1940s. A further 3% were reported as having been shot during the late 1970s and early 1980s and 1% of the recoveries were reported to be the direct result of poisoning. The major known cause of death, including 23% of the recoveries, is collision with glass and 88% of these were inexperienced birds in their first year. Of the remaining records, some 41% have been reported with no known cause of death; the birds simply being found dead.

The majority (72%) of recoveries have been within 20km of their ringing site although one individual provided the longest-distance recovery of 270km between Longdendale and Bramley, Surrey, some ten months after being ringed as a nestling. There were four other recoveries of birds moving in excess of 100km and of these the quickest individual moved 185km from Swineshaw Reservoir to Longtown, Cumbria in 71 days. Again, this had been ringed as a nestling and became a road casualty. The longer-lived birds have all been individuals that have not ventured far from their birthplace, the longest period being almost eight years.

Buzzard
Buteo buteo
A fairly common and increasing resident, passage migrant and winter visitor.

The recent dramatic resurgence of the Buzzard is a very welcome sight in the Derbyshire countryside. This raptor is now well established in almost all of the county, which would have been unthinkable even as recently as the early 1990s.

The Buzzard was described by Whitlock as a common breeder in the Peak District prior to removal of much of the forest. After that it was seemingly restricted to the south of the county where it remained common until the end of the nineteenth century, when it gradually declined and became almost extinct. Sir Oswald Mosley wrote in 1863, that about 50 years earlier he had seen upwards of 20 soaring over Egginton Heath and Etwall Common (Mosley & Brown 1863). In the twentieth century there were hundreds of records but breeding was confirmed only in 1922, during the myxomatosis years of the 1950s, 1964–65 and 1975 (Frost). There was no great improvement in the 1980s with, for example, just five records for the whole of the county in 1985 and likewise nine in 1989. The situation did not markedly improve until the late 1990s.

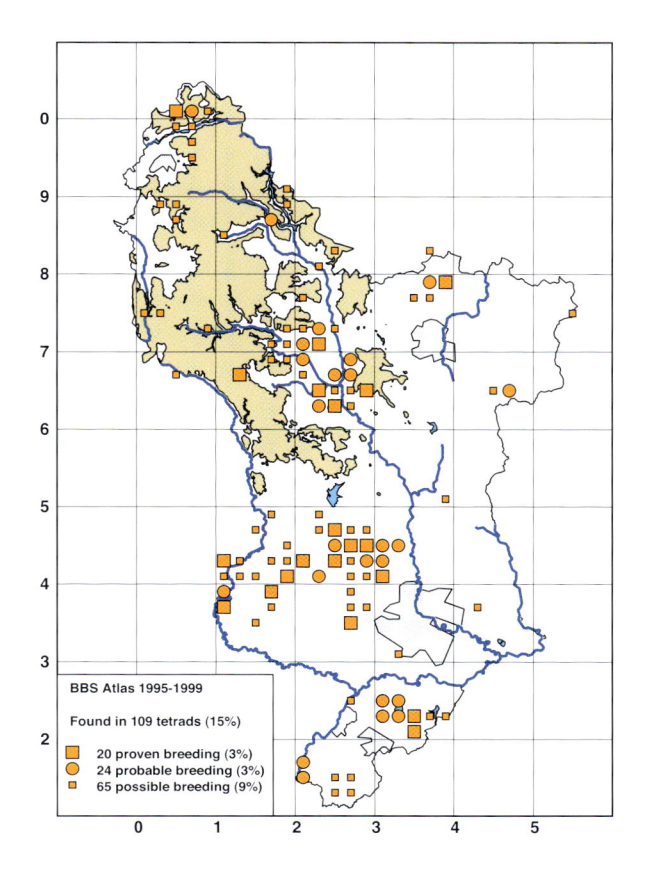

Buzzards are found in open country, especially farmland, where they do most of their hunting. They are easily seen when hunting or soaring, but can be surprisingly inconspicuous when perched. They usually nest in woodland, although occasionally they have been known to use small copses, lines of trees and even isolated farmland trees. The display, which involves steep dives and sometimes talon-grappling, may be seen as early as February in favourable conditions, as territories and pair-bonds are re-established, but it is most frequent during March and April. Buzzards can be quite elusive when incubating but are much more obvious when feeding young and the latter, with their far-carrying hunger calls, are dependent on their parents for several weeks after fledging.

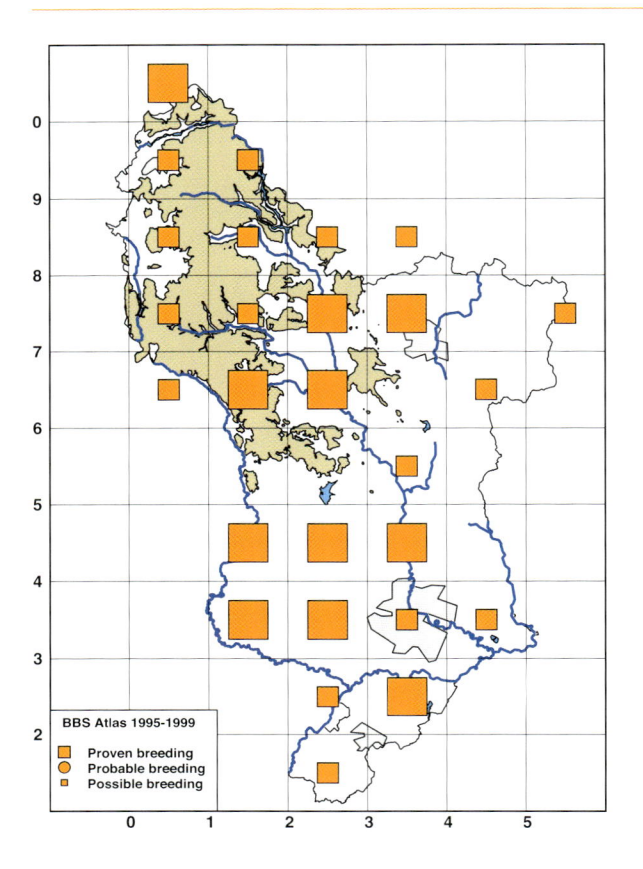

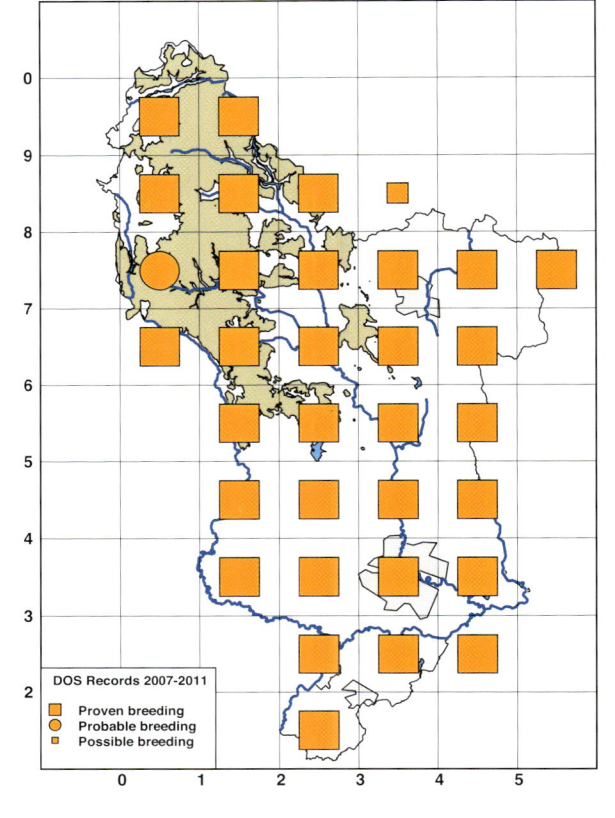

The tetrad map, based on the Derbyshire BBS (1995–99), shows 89 tetrads containing either possible or probable breeding Buzzards, with 20 revealing proven breeding.

The largest population was in the southern half of the county with a smaller concentration in central Derbyshire. Only six 10km squares show no records of Buzzard at all during 1995–99 (in contrast, the map for the 1968–72 Atlas showed no probable or proven breeding records at all, while that for the 1988–91 Atlas had two squares with probable breeding records). The extensive Coal Measures Natural Area only contained one tetrad of proven breeding with none at all on the Magnesian Limestone. There were also surprisingly few records for the White Peak area with its well-wooded scenic valleys. This area is very popular with tourists, so disturbance could be a limiting factor, or it could simply be that this particular region is currently underrecorded. Most breeding sites were between 80m and 250m amsl.

Since 1994 there has been an increasing number of breeders, which has led to a few raptor enthusiasts making a concentrated effort to establish more accurately the size of the breeding population. In 1999, it was found that there were at least 30 pairs in the county and, of these, 19 pairs were proved to breed successfully. The number of pairs proved breeding in the period 1990–99 is shown in the table.

By 2001, the population had risen still further. Lacey and Messenger (2002) found 81 occupied territories and proved breeding in 68 of these. A total of 66 pairs were successful, fledging a minimum of 113 young, representing a mean of 1.71 young per successful pair.

The maps show the contrast in the breeding situation in 1995–99 and 2007–11.

There have probably been a number of factors which caused the number of breeders to be suppressed in the past, including destruction of woodland, persecution and, with other raptors during the 1950s and 1960s, pesticide poisoning. The pesticide problem is now all but eradicated and, as many of the successful breeding Buzzards are found on keepered estates, there is believed to be very little persecution of this relatively harmless raptor. The only exceptions to this are the Upper Derwentdale and Longdendale areas, where it is suspected that human interference is still taking place. In other areas there were records of successful nests as close as 500m apart by 2009.

In line with increasing numbers of breeders the largest aerial gatherings have been recorded since about 2005, usually in early spring when pairs congregate to dispute boundaries, or in late summer when a number of family parties may interact. The largest recorded gatherings were of 20 at Willington Gravel Pits on 18th March 2011 and 18 at Ockbrook on 26th September 2011.

During the winter months, most Derbyshire Buzzards appear to remain on their breeding territories, but it is not known to what degree numbers are swelled by immigrants. However, before breeding became widespread there was undoubtedly a regular annual passage of birds, with a small spring movement

Year	Pairs
1990	–
1991	2
1992	2
1993	1
1994	1
1995	4
1996	9
1997	6
1998	10
1999	19

mainly during March and April, and a more marked passage during August to October. The origins of these migrants is unknown. More recent records suggesting migrants were of 12, all apparently dark juveniles, moving west at Marston-on-Dove in five hours on 28th August 2008, and an impressive 26 moving north at Carr Vale on 21st March 2010.

There are two relevant ringing recoveries. One ringed as a nestling near Matlock in July 1980 was found injured, 112km to the south-east, at Peterborough in October 1981, and one ringed at Attenborough, Nottinghamshire in March 1984 was found in poor condition near Matlock ten months later and temporarily taken into care before being released.

Rough-legged Buzzard
Buteo lagopus
A rare winter visitor and passage migrant.

In the nineteenth century, Rough-legged Buzzards were said to be regular in Derbyshire each time an invasion to Britain took place. John Wolley of Matlock saw at least a dozen during the winter of 1839/40, although some of these may have actually been in Nottinghamshire. Other nineteenth-century records, usually of birds killed, came from Derby, Kinder Scout, Longdendale, Derwent, Curbar and Monsal Dale. There were only eight records, involving nine birds, in the twentieth century up to 1977 (Frost). These were at Ashford-in-the-Water, Curbar, 'near Sheffield', Lumsdale, Derwent, Leash Fen and Beeley. There were no more until 1982, since when there have been 32 records as shown in the table.

Period	Records	Birds
1980s	7	8
1990s	14	15
2000–11	11	11
Totals	32	34

The increase in numbers of records may be related to greater observer activity. The gritstone uplands of the Peak District are the favoured area, with most of the recent records from that area. Upper Derwentdale is the most regular site, possibly because of the availability of mountain hares as prey items. Most birds specifically aged have been first-winters.

Analysis of records since 1982 by month of arrival is shown in the chart.

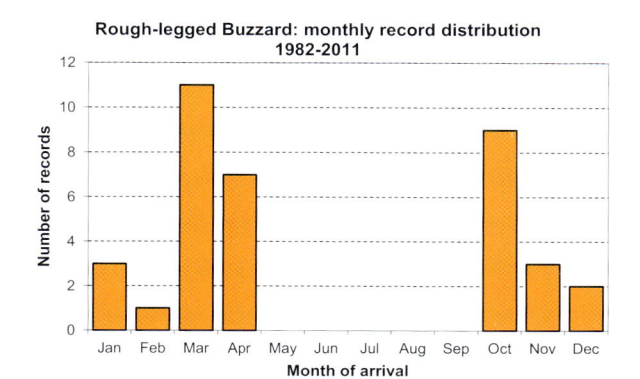

The earliest autumn records are of one flying south over Leash Fen on 10th October 1976 and one flying south at Ashover on 10th October 2004. The latest spring records are of singles in the Heyden Brook area from 27th to 29th April 1996 and in Upper Derwentdale on 29th April 2004.

The pattern of records suggests that most of the Rough-legged Buzzards seen in Derbyshire are moving through. Of the occurrences since 1982, only in 1984/85 was there evidence of overwintering, when an adult in the Derwent area on 10th November was joined by a first-winter bird from 8th December, with both still present by 1st January 1985 and one remaining until 10th March. In 1986 the remains of one found in the Goyt Valley were thought to be of the bird that had been seen in that area from 7th to 29th December 1985.

Golden Eagle
Aquila chrysaetos
A very rare vagrant.

Jourdain stated that 'there is no record of the golden eagle having bred in any English county south of the Lake District, with the exception of Derbyshire'. This remains the case. Willughby described a nest found in the Woodlands near the Derwent in 1668 as 'made of great sticks, resting one end on the edge of a rock, the other on two birch trees, upon which was a layer of rushes, and over them a layer of heath, and upon the heath rushes again, upon which lay one young one and an addle [*sic*] egg, and by them a lamb, a hare and three heath poults. The nest was about two yards square and had no hollow in it. The young eagle was black as a hobby, of the shape of a gos-hawk, of almost the weight of a goose, rough footed or feathered down to the foot, having a white ring about the tail'. This was quoted in Pilkington (1789) and is the only certain breeding record for the county.

In 1720, one was taken on Kinder Scout in an exhausted state, and eagles seen at Hardwick in 1759 and 1782 may have been of this species. A bird which was definitely a Golden Eagle was shot near Cromford in 1823, and what may have been one was at Matlock in 1843 (Whitlock; Jourdain).

A Golden Eagle was reported at Derwent in April 1952 following a probable sighting in December 1948.

Only one modern record has been accepted, at Holme Moss on 11th April 1982, when an immature flew south into Derbyshire from South Yorkshire, before returning to the north. It was independently identified by two experienced observers, stationed several kilometres apart. Mather (1986) gave further details of this sighting.

Osprey
Pandion haliaetus
A scarce migrant.

Ospreys have long been visitors to the county's water bodies. The first record was of one shot at Staveley in May 1779 and Whitlock knew of many other records, mainly in the Trent Valley, where favourite localities were Melbourne Pool and the Trent near Weston Cliff, where the river was wide and sluggish, and always well stocked with fish. Frost knew of only ten records in the period 1900–69 but numbers have increased steadily since the start of the 1970s, and markedly since the 1990s. There were far more records in the 2000s than in the previous 40 years combined. Though poorer years have still occurred, records are still showing an upward trend and reached a maximum of 67 in 2009. This may well reflect the burgeoning breeding population in Scotland but is also very likely to involve birds from the release scheme at Rutland Water in Leicestershire.

The number of records by period is shown below.

Period	Records
1960	2
1970s	31
1980s	31
1990s	107
2000–11	343
Total	514

Inevitably, for a bird which feeds almost exclusively on fish, most of the records are from the larger reservoirs and gravel pits.

Ogston, Foremark, Staunton Harold and Carsington Water are the most favoured reservoirs, while Willington and Swarkestone are the preferred gravel pits in the Trent Valley. Much smaller waters are sometimes visited and transient birds are occasionally recorded crossing open countryside.

Ospreys usually occur singly, but there are at least five records of two seen together, the latest in 2009.

All records in the period 1978–2011 fall between March and November, although there are older records from Derwent on 4th January 1947, and during February to April 1952. As the chart shows, spring passage is heavier than that in autumn.

Osprey: monthly record distribution 1978-2011

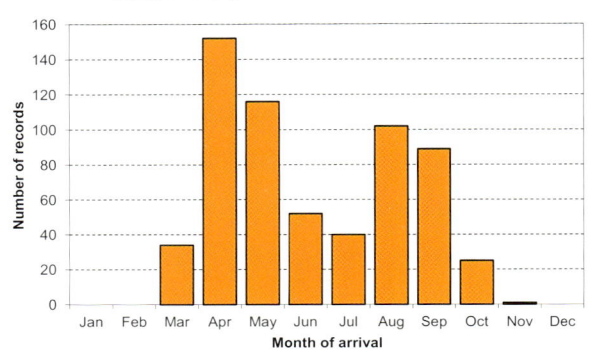

Extreme dates during the period 1978–2011 are 23rd March (1991) when one flew north-west at Chatsworth and 23rd March (2010) when one was at Butterley Reservoir; and 19th November (1978) in the Goyt Valley, where a bird had lingered from 22nd October. Individuals summered at Ogston Reservoir in 1979 and at Chatsworth in 1982.

The satellite tagging of Scottish birds has produced some very interesting records involving the county. In 2010 a male left Dumfries and Galloway on the morning of 9th October and flew south along the Derwent Valley as far as Belper later that day. A colour-ringed bird at Carsington Water on 5th and 6th May 2011 had been ringed at Loch Ussie, Highland in June 2009. A tagged ten-year old male left Aviemore, Highland on the morning of 7th September 2011 and by 1300hrs it was at Ladybower Reservoir, and two hours after that, at Carsington Water.

Frost believed that the Osprey was a potential future colonist, and recent breeding in Leicestershire, resulting from the Rutland Water release scheme, must give further cause for optimism. With this in mind, nest platforms have been erected in several areas.

Kestrel
Falco tinnunculus
A fairly common resident and partial migrant.

Kestrels can be found throughout Derbyshire in a wide range of habitats, but are most typically seen hunting over open areas, such as farmland, rocky edges, moorland and roadside verges.

Whitlock, Jourdain and Frost all considered this the most numerous diurnal raptor in the county, enjoying a widespread distribution but with the largest numbers in the Peak District. There were few indications of any change in status until the mid-1950s, when Kestrels suffered, as did most other raptors, from the organo-chlorine pesticide problem which caused a sudden and drastic decline in numbers. Totals remained low until the mid-1960s when a recovery began and the population was believed to be fairly stable until recent years when some experienced observers have commented on declining numbers.

This is also suggested by Eaton *et al.* (2010) who detected a 20% decrease based on BBS figures for 1995–2008.

The tetrad map shows their wide distribution, with a slight bias in proven breeding records from the north-east and south of the county. A total of 617 tetrads was found to be occupied, with proven breeding in 252, probable breeding in 64 and possible breeding in the remaining 301. There is no evidence of any change in distribution between either the 1968–72 or 1988–91 Atlas, for which it was found in every 10km square. Although the Derbyshire BBS (1995–99) shows the Kestrel to be more widespread than the Sparrowhawk (ranked fifteenth and thirty-second respectively), it is likely to be the less numerous of the two, as Sparrowhawks are harder to locate because of

The Species Accounts

BBS Atlas 1995-1999
Found in 617 tetrads (85%)
- ■ 252 proven breeding (35%)
- ● 64 probable breeding (9%)
- ▪ 301 possible breeding (42%)

Breeding numbers and success vary in some habitats depending on food supply and weather. For example, numbers are highest in upland areas during 'vole years', when clutches of up to six eggs have been recorded. In late summer and early autumn, good numbers can be seen hovering over west-facing moorland edges, especially when the wind shows a westerly vector. Up to eight were regularly seen over favoured sites such as Harland Edge, while 12 were counted on nearby East Moor on 20th August 2002. The most ever recorded in such a situation was 23 over a mile-long ridge in Longdendale on 2nd August 1980.

In some years, a few observers have commented on an increase in the number of birds seen during early autumn, suggesting an influx of possibly Continental birds. Many Derbyshire birds also clearly leave the county after the breeding season and there are usually relatively few in high upland areas in winter.

Particularly interesting records were of four interacting with four Hobbies and a Merlin, all chasing moths on Beeley Moor on 28th June 1993. At Hathersage, during September 1991, one was seen with white wing-flashes from shoulder to carpal joints on each wing. Another unusual record was of five on a street lamp at Shuttlewood on 23rd November 2000. At Mugginton on 4th June 2008, an adult female was carrying a dead male Kestrel, which was believed to be a road casualty.

There are 210 recovery records of Kestrels relating to Derbyshire, the earliest being from 1944. The longest distance recorded involved an early record from 1959 when a bird ringed in Flakatrask, Sweden was captured and released in Swadlincote, 1718km south-west, in the same year. This was the first Swedish-ringed recovery of the species in Britain. The longest interval between ringing and recovery is 19 years and concerned a bird ringed near Burton upon Trent in 1981, found dead near Ashbourne in 2000. The majority of the recovery information (62%) concerns birds within 50km of their place of ringing; 81% of these were ringed as nestlings and 70% were found within 20km of their birthplace. This statistic is common to many species but serves to illustrate that the birds spend a significant amount of time in their natal area during their more vulnerable months, just after fledging. Others have travelled further: there have been two recoveries in France and others as far south as Sussex, Kent and Wiltshire, and as far north as Durham.

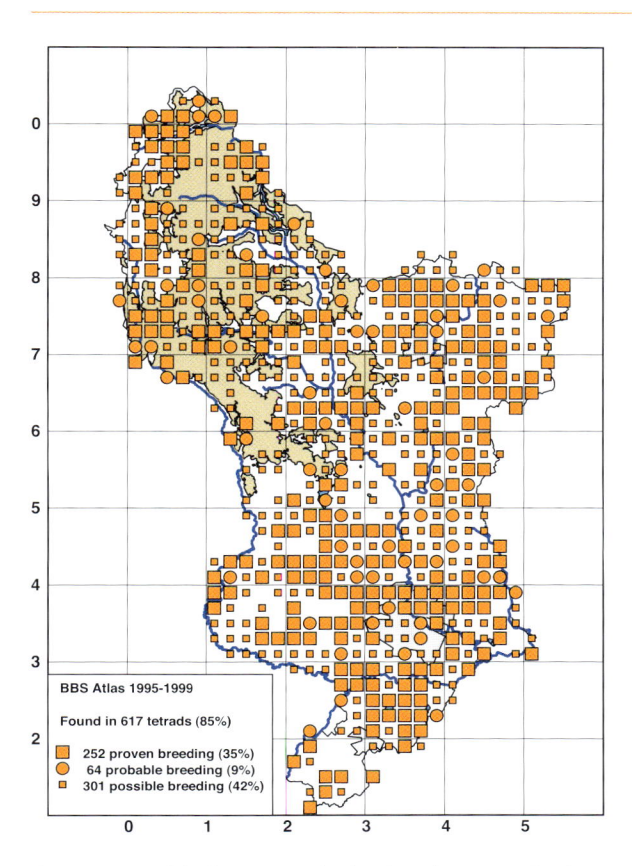

their more stealthy hunting methods. Kestrels are easy birds to find, as many nest sites are used annually, and large nestlings and recently fledged young can be noisy.

Nest sites include holes in trees, holes and ledges in buildings, electricity pylons, natural and man-made rock-faces, and disused corvid nests. They breed in urban and industrial sites as well as rural localities, and there are recent records of breeding in nest-boxes in large gardens at Stanley and Holmewood. In 1971, two pairs nested 15m apart on an electricity pylon at Staveley, although both were unsuccessful.

Red-footed Falcon
Falco vespertinus
A rare vagrant.

Red-footed Falcons breed from eastern Europe to Mongolia and winter in southern Africa. They are annual vagrants to the UK, mainly in spring. With some 740 records by the end of 2005, BBRC removed it from the list of species under its jurisdiction.

There was only one Derbyshire record of this attractive small falcon prior to 1950. A male was shot in early May 1939 on moorland in the Peak District (Frost). There have been 14 subsequent records, all involving single birds, as follows:

Year	Location and date
1969	Great Hucklow, a female on 14th June
1969	Egginton Sewage Farm, a male on 21st–22nd June
1973	Chelmorton, a female on 28th May
1975	Church Wilne Reservoir, an immature on 6th and 9th July
1977	Upper Derwentdale, an adult male on 28th May
1978	Eastmoor, a female on 7th June
1979	Beeley Moor, a female flew north on 1st July
1979	Beeley Moor, a female flew south on 24th July (probably a different bird from the above)
1990	Unstone, a female, probably adult, from 21st to 27th May
1990	Langley Mill, a female on 16th–17th July (probably the same bird as above)
2000	Crowden, a first-summer male from 29th June to 2nd July

Year	Location and date
2008	An adult male flew into the county from Brinsley (Nottinghamshire) on 9th May
2008	Ingleby–Barrow area, a first-summer female from 19th to 26th May, and presumably the same bird at Willington Gravel Pits on 23rd June
2011	Breaston, a first-summer female on 22nd June, had probably been present since 17th June having previously been seen at Ledbury, Herefordshire (about 130km south-west) from 8th to 11th June

Analysis by period and months is shown in the tables.

Period	Records	Birds
1960s	2	2
1970s	6	6
1990s	2	2
2000–11	4	4
Totals	14	14

Month	Records	Birds
May	5	5
June	5	5
July	4	4
Totals	14	14

Merlin
Falco columbarius
An uncommon breeder and an uncommon passage migrant and winter visitor.

Merlins have been present for centuries on the county's uplands, but during the nineteenth and first half of the twentieth century they suffered much persecution from shooting interests. Whitlock thought that they were 'pretty plentiful' at the end of the eighteenth century but by 1893 only a few pairs remained. He wrote with evident bitterness about the game preservers who instructed their keepers to destroy both old and young Merlins. Jourdain also complained about their being shot or trapped at the nest and predicted their imminent disappearance as a Derbyshire breeding species.

The birds managed to hang on, however, and with more enlightened attitudes and a reduction in keepering during and after the Second World War, were again nesting quite commonly by the early 1950s on suitable heather moorland in the Peak District. But by the late 1970s, they had declined to a very low level, considered to be of fewer than five pairs. This was mainly due to the effects of organo-chlorine pesticides, from which they seemed slow to recover, and to a lesser degree, habitat loss (Frost). From the early 1980s a partial recovery began which continued into the 1990s, and at the present time the population appears to have stabilized at about 15–25 pairs, though with some yearly fluctuation between the main breeding areas.

The table shows the known population and productivity in the years 1998–2011, based on fieldwork carried out by members of the South Peak Raptor Study Group and the Peak District Raptor Monitoring Group (although certain information from 2003, and productivity figures for 2008 and 2009, are unavailable and the 2010–11 data may be incomplete).

Year	Sites	Successful	Young fledged
1998	23	14	at least 48
1999	21	15	at least 55
2000	15	7	23
2001	10	7	24
2002	14	8	33
2003	at least 6	at least 4	at least 17
2004	21	11	39
2005	13	9	35
2006	17	10	38
2007	17	10	32
2008	21	14	56
2009	20	–	–
2010	16	at least 5	21
2011	at least 11	at least 3	–

This species is still threatened by egg collectors and unscrupulous falconers; clutches and young have been lost to both during recent years. Despite this, the main threats to the continued welfare of the species are degradation of heather moorland from overgrazing by sheep, and in some areas red deer, and increased recreational access to previously private areas.

Breeders return to their moorland sites from late February onwards, and most are on territory by early to mid-April. They are fiercely territorial, and will chase and harass corvids and other raptors intruding into their domain. Most nests are in deep heather at altitudes between 350m and 400m amsl. They are usually bare scrapes, although rudimentary grass-lined structures have been noted. A few pairs sometimes use old tree nests of other species, usually corvids, especially in grassland 'white moor' areas. In 2000 a nest suffered an unlikely fate when the female and three young were killed by an Arctic fox, which had escaped from a nearby zoo.

The tetrad map shows Merlins were found in 36 squares between 1995 and 1999, with breeding proved in 13 and probable in 23.

Eggs are usually laid during the first half of May and incubation takes 28–32 days, with the young birds being fledged by late July. Some youngsters become independent very quickly, and at one site a 37-day-old fledgling was seen to take a Meadow Pipit unaided. Most breeding sites are vacated by early August. Small passerines, especially Meadow Pipits, form the majority of the diet during the breeding season, but they are not averse to taking wader chicks, moths (mainly emperor and northern eggar), butterflies and the occasional small mammal.

From September through to April, passage migrants and wintering birds may be seen in open countryside almost anywhere in the county, although the Eastern Moors remain a popular area. Merlins can sometimes be seen 'waiting on', ready to take prey flushed by other raptors such as Hen Harriers.

Most of our wintering birds are thought to be immigrants from further north or abroad. Since 2003, there have been several records of birds showing some characteristics of the Icelandic race *F.c. subaesalon*.

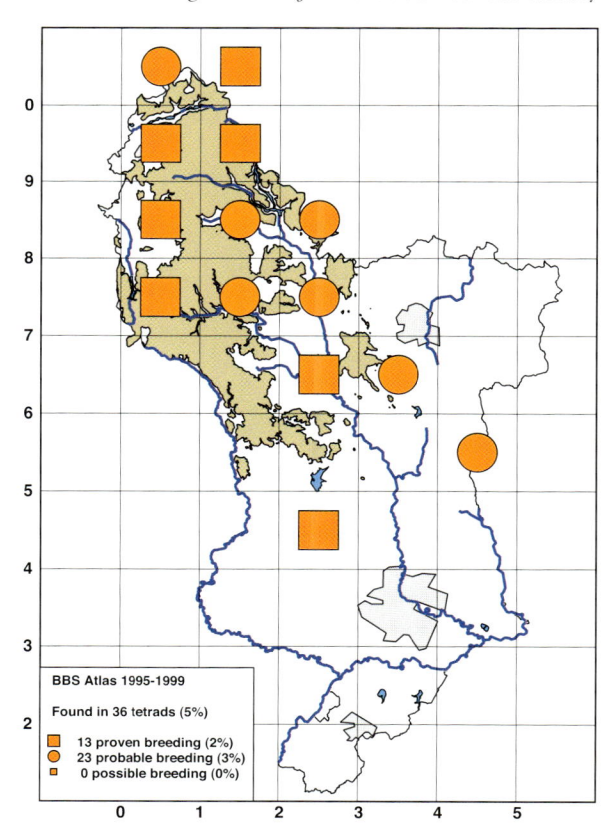

Recoveries of Derbyshire-ringed pulli suggest an easterly bias to dispersion, with several records from counties between North Yorkshire and Cambridgeshire, with others as distant as Wiltshire. One ringed on 28th June 1998 became a road casualty near Louth, Lincolnshire on 25th July 1998, having travelled approximately 100km east-south-east in less than a month. This and several other first-year recoveries illustrate the high mortality rate among young birds. A bird ringed on 1st July 1989 was found dead on the road near Biarritz, southern France on 15th February 1991, a distance of 1115km, while one ringed as a nestling at Hrafnabjorg, Iceland in July 1986, died on 1st April 1987 when it collided with wires at Findern, 1582km away.

The earliest ringing recovery concerning Derbyshire was that of a nestling ringed in 1920 and being reported from Longshaw Moors two years later in circumstances not known. A chick ringed in the Tayside Region in 1991 provided the longest UK movement record of 415km, when it killed itself by hitting a glass window near Ashbourne, some two months later. The female of a pair killed on the nest by a mammalian predator in June 1991 had been ringed as a pullus in Northumberland in July 1990.

Hobby
Falco subbuteo
An uncommon breeding summer visitor and passage migrant.

The Hobby has classic good looks, breathtaking aerial agility and a degree of scarcity, which means that, for most observers, even a brief glimpse of this superb falcon is noteworthy. Traditionally thought of as birds of southern heaths and downs, in Derbyshire breeding Hobbies favour mixed farmland, where they nest most often in single trees but also in clumps or lines of trees, and less often in woods. Hobbies are as synonymous with farmland in Derbyshire as Grey Partridge and Yellowhammer. However, the casual observer is more likely to encounter the species at the local gravel pit or reservoir, chasing hirundines or effortlessly catching insects on warm summer days. Sometimes they are seen taking insects, especially northern eggar moths, over moorland, where up to four have been seen together, mainly on the Eastern Moors. Occasionally, they have been reported hunting insects over the higher moors, with a notable record of three first-summer birds at almost 600m amsl near the Bleaklow summit on 24th July 1991. Some birds regularly hunt over towns; a pair has displayed and held territory within the city boundary of Derby. The largest gathering was of eight over Staunton Harold Reservoir on 2nd June 2006.

The combined researches of Whitlock, Jourdain and Frost revealed just three definite breeding records in the county: at Goyt's Bridge in 1894, Tansley in 1902 and Newton Park in 1926. Additionally, nesting was said to have taken place around Melbourne in the mid-nineteenth century, and there were probable breeding records at Howden in 1891 and the Goyt Valley in 1938. The first breeding record after the formation of the DOS was in 1975 in the Trent Valley.

However, the main northward spread and population increase of Hobbies in Britain began to be noticed in Derbyshire in the early 1980s. Numbers steadily increased, and by 1990 the number of sightings became too numerous to be listed individually in the *Derbyshire Bird Report*. Since 1984 breeding has occurred annually.

The earliest arrivals in the county were both on 13th April: in 2006 at Drakelow Nature Reserve and in 2008 at Raynesway, with the earliest date for a pair on territory being on 21st April (1996). The main arrival is in late April to early May, when pairs begin displaying high over their breeding grounds, sometimes indulging in spectacular aerobatics.

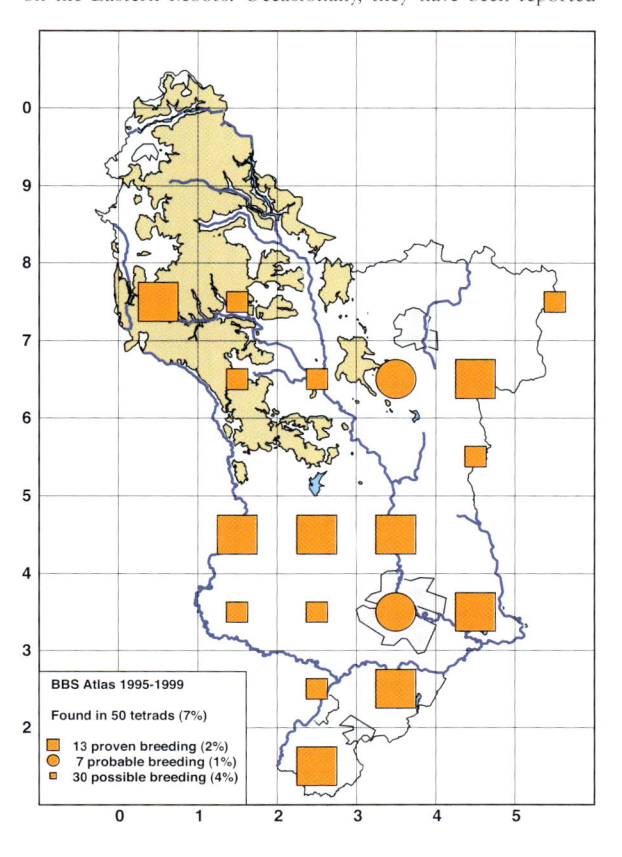

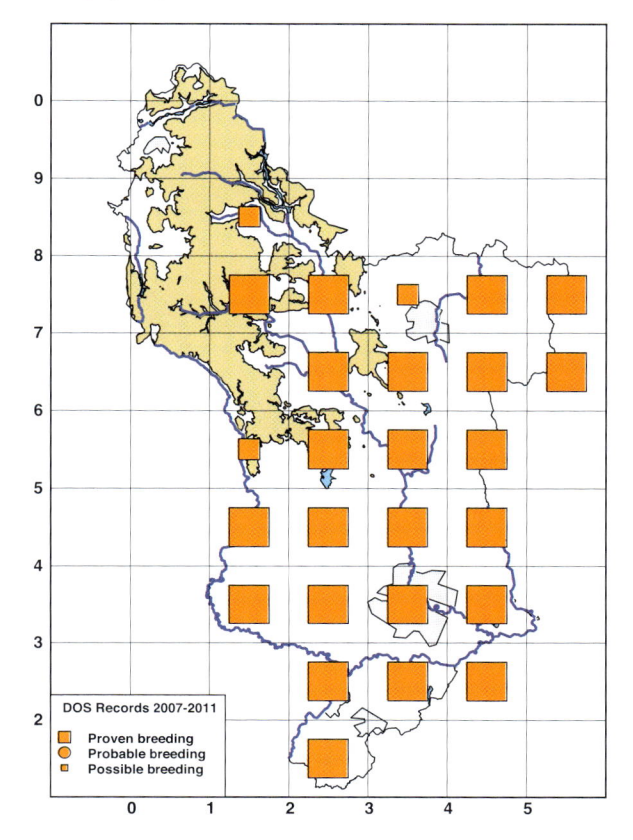

In the Derbyshire BBS (1995–99), breeding was proved in 13 tetrads, and was probable and possible in a further seven and 30 respectively. Hobbies hunt over a wide area, often at considerable distances from their breeding sites, and it is likely, therefore, that the 31 possible tetrads exaggerated the breeding population of the county in the late 1990s. Because of concerns for the species' welfare, registrations are plotted centrally in their 10km squares.

During a ten-year study (1992–2001) of 412km^2 of lowland farmland in Derbyshire, Messenger and Roome (2007) found that the number of breeding pairs ranged from seven to 18, giving a mean density of 3.06 pairs per 100km^2. At least 35% of nesting ranges were occupied every year and of 126 breeding attempts, only seven failed. There were few predators in the area and the birds tolerated motor vehicles, so were thus able to breed undisturbed on modern, highly mechanized farms, as well as close to roads. The main factors preventing even higher success seemed to be occasional and unintentional human disturbance, predation by Carrion Crows and grey squirrels, and entanglement of the nestlings in baler twine used by the crows in their nests. The average distance between adjacent nesting pairs was 4.55km but breeding pairs have nested as close as 1.5km apart. Interestingly, several successful pairs have involved females which have bred in their first year. The mean first clutch size during the study was 2.96 across a sample of 67 nests, with a mean number of 2.44 young fledged per successful pair.

Oak is the preferred tree species for nesting and accounted for 79% of total nests found during the study. Electricity pylons have also been used. When old nests of other species are selected, Carrion Crow is most often favoured, but there have been several nests in rookeries.

The main breeding area of Derbyshire's Hobbies remains the southern lowlands, but intensive fieldwork by members of the South Peak Raptor Study Group in particular has shown that many pairs nest annually in central and north-eastern areas, and recently breeding has been proved in at least seven sites in the Peak District. In the latter area, Frost (1983) showed a link between occurrences on the Eastern Moors and the biennial flights of northern eggars.

The number of territorial pairs, proven breeding pairs and fledged young known in the whole of the county since 1992 are tabulated.

After the young have fledged, family parties generally stay together until around late September, when most adults seem to leave. However, there have been several recent October records, as late as 30th (2011) at Rowsley.

Of the recoveries, all involving birds that were ringed as nestlings, the least expected concerned one ringed in South Derbyshire which landed on a boat near the Azores during a subsequent February. The longest distance movement within Britain is of a bird ringed near Duffield in August 1995 and found the following spring 334km away in Devon. It was found in a poor condition during violently windy weather but later released after being kept in captivity for about a month. One ringed near Heanor in August 1994 was found injured a year later at Abergavenny, Monmouthshire, 163km south-west, while another ringed in August 1994 was found in Kent in June 1995. Colour-ringing of local Hobby nestlings has resulted in two particularly interesting sightings. One ringed near Swadlincote in 2007 was photographed in Cambridgeshire in May 2008, while earlier, one colour-ringed in Leicestershire in August 1995 was photographed 78km away as a breeding female in South Derbyshire 3281 days later, in August 2004. This is one of the greatest longevity records for this species.

Year	Pairs on territory	Pairs proved to breed	Young fledged
1992	15	14	38
1993	12	7	12
1994	11	7	16
1995	14	14	30
1996	17	13	25
1997	17	9	22
1998	23	17	39
1999	25	23	57
2000	25	22	47
2001	20	16	37
2002	24	22	at least 45
2003	28	25	55
2004	23	17	at least 41
2005	35	32	72
2006	40	at least 32	at least 73
2007	44	28	55
2008	35	25	61
2009	39	28	66
2010	41	28	61
2011	41	33	70

Peregrine
Falco peregrinus
An uncommon breeder, passage migrant and winter visitor.

Although it is probable that the Peregrine attempted to nest at suitable sites in the northern parts of Derbyshire throughout much of the nineteenth century, there are very few old records of eyries. Whitlock did not cite definite evidence of breeding and Ratcliffe (1980) repeated that there are remarkably few old records of eyries and also said that game preserving had virtually extinguished the Peregrine as a regular nester in the Peak District well before 1900. Frost believed that there were more or less annual attempts at breeding in one or more of three different sites from 1919 to 1954 or 1955, but gamekeeper vigilance nearly always ensured failure, and in many cases one or both of the pair were shot. After 1957 the Peregrine virtually disappeared from the county, in common with much of England, due to the well-documented effects of toxic chemicals, with very few sightings recorded, and those were not even annual occurrences. However, the two national censuses of the species in 1971 and 1981 (Ratcliffe 1972 & 1984) established that a marked recovery in numbers was taking place nationally, and it was only a matter of time before the Peregrine would return to Derbyshire as a breeding bird.

In 1981 a pair nested at a traditional site in the north of the county, but heavy snow in late April caused desertion. Although a pair returned to the site in 1982 and 1983, the nest was robbed of eggs in both years. In 1984 a protection scheme was mounted using the resources of the DOS and SBSG, and, despite a further unsuccessful attempt to rob the nest, three eyasses fledged from the site in late June (Hornbuckle 1985). A further wardening scheme operated at the site in 1985 and four young fledged in late June. This site has continued to be successful in several, but by no means all, years since then. At a second site in the north-west of the county, pairs were intermittently successful in the mid and late 1980s, and in 1990 a third pair fledged two young from a quarry site in the north of the county. The three Derbyshire pairs fledged a total of seven young in 1990 and Grimshaw (1991) documented this increase in breeding success.

During the Derbyshire BBS (1995–99), Peregrines were proved to breed in 19 tetrads, with 12 probable and 34 possible.

The population has continued to grow and the Peak District is currently thought to hold 25–35 territorial pairs. The table shows the situation in this region in 1998–2011, and is largely based on fieldwork by the South Peak Raptor Study Group and the Peak District Raptor Monitoring Group, with further information from Holling *et al.* (2010 & 2011).

Year	Sites	Successful	Young fledged
1998	15	9	24
1999	18	8	18
2000	14	7	16
2001	17	7	14
2002	21	11	23
2003	19	13	26
2004	21	13	32
2005	22	12	33
2006	26	15	35
2007	31	13	29
2008	25	at least 15	at least 33
2009	20	at least 17	at least 31
2010	23	16	33
2011	23	18	50

The present situation at long-established and traditional moorland sites in the High Peak is precarious. Ratcliffe (1980) observed that the higher moorlands and precipitous edges between Sheffield and Manchester provided scope for at least 11 pairs of Peregrines. He concluded that the prospects for the species becoming firmly established in the Peak District were rather slender, due to constant disturbance by rock climbers and the vigilance of the gamekeeping fraternity. By the second edition of his monograph (1993), he commented that it was gratifying to see that the birds had returned to the Peak District in some numbers, with at least seven pairs in the High Peak.

All of the Peregrine eyries in the High Peak are on, or adjacent to, grouse moors and their breeding success is markedly lower than at sites elsewhere in the county, while there has been a noticeable recent decline in the number of pairs present. For example, in the Upper Derwent area up to three pairs nested in the early 2000s, with a fourth pair just beyond the county boundary. By the mid to late 2000s, the number had reduced to one pair and human interference is strongly suspected.

Breeding in one of the quarries of the White Peak was first recorded in 1990, and these sites now hold the bulk of the county population. Ratcliffe (1980) stated that quarry sites were able to provide many of the same features and attractions as natural cliffs, many providing a wide outlook with sheer, clean-cut faces, often with ledges with enough fine material for the birds to scrape a nest hollow. Additionally, many quarries now hold Ravens, whose old nests offer extra scope. The quarry nests generally have a good success rate, and those in working quarries are especially safe as the employees ensure their protection. Nevertheless, there remain occasional incidents, suggesting a small degree of persecution (possibly by pigeon-fanciers) at a few of these sites. Since 2001, up to two pairs have nested in most years in lowland quarries in the county.

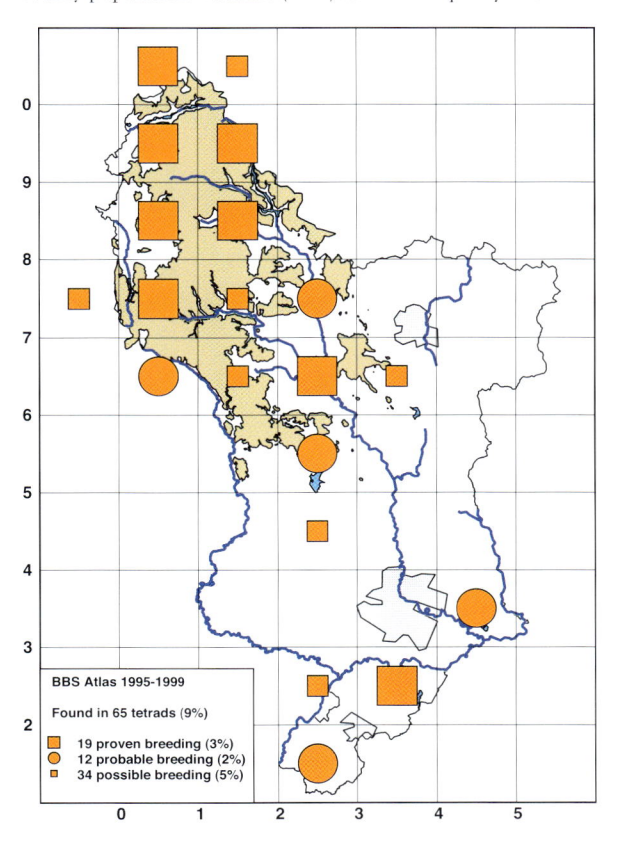

Grimshaw (1991) also documented the presence of Peregrines roosting at Drakelow Power Station in the south of the county. T. Cockburn (*pers comm*) believes that the birds bred at this site from 1984, but access problems made this difficult to prove. The cooling towers have since been demolished. At Willington Power Station a nest platform was erected initially on a cooling tower and was subsequently moved lower down onto a boiler house, resulting in successful breeding there in most years during 1993–99, and possibly since.

Peregrines were first noticed on Derby Cathedral in 2004. A pair was present in 2005 and in the following year took readily to the installation of a wooden platform lined with gravel, on the east side of the tower, rearing a total of 19 young in 2006–11. Webcams on the nest created a huge amount of interest worldwide with over 200,000 'hits' during April to July 2007 alone, and over two million by 2011. However, the most interesting aspect of these birds' behaviour concerns their food. Brown (2007) cited 53 species of bird identified from prey remains and a single brown rat seen via the webcams being fed to the young. The birds ranged in size from Robin to Mallard and included some locally scarce species, such as Waxwing, Cuckoo, Arctic Tern, Quail, Corncrake and Budgerigar, plus 12 species of wader. The Arctic Tern had been ringed as a chick in June 2002 on an island off south-west Sweden; its remains and ring were found on the nave roof in August 2007.

The presence of species such as Quail, Corncrake, Woodcock and Water Rail suggested that the Peregrines must have been hunting at night, using the floodlighting around the cathedral, especially at times of migration. This was proved when a webcam video recording made at 2300 hours on a December night in 2009 showed one of the birds bringing in a still-struggling Woodcock. By early 2013 the list of wader kills stood at 51 each of Golden Plover and Snipe, 38 Woodcock, 40 Lapwings, ten Redshank, eight Knot, seven each of Dunlin, Jack Snipe and Turnstone, three each of Whimbrel and Black-tailed Godwit, and two Bar-tailed Godwits (N. Brown *pers comm*).

In 2012 a pair of Peregrines nested unsuccessfully on the East Mill at Belper. Future breeding on other tall urban and industrial structures elsewhere in the county must be a distinct possibility. Perhaps significantly, one took up residence on Chesterfield's famous Crooked Spire from the end of 2009 onwards, with two there more recently. The remains of Dunlin and Snipe have been found nearby and it is likely that nocturnal hunting also happens at this site. Other prey items have included Golden and Grey Plover and Swift.

Inevitably, sightings of Peregrines throughout Derbyshire are now regular at all times of the year. On the Eastern Moors in late autumn, flocks of migrant Woodpigeons are often attacked; on one occasion a large flock rose spectacularly into a low cloud in an attempt to avoid a pursuing Peregrine.

Grimshaw (1991) recorded close nesting of Peregrines and Kestrels at a site in the north-west of the county in 1989, with nest sites only 150m apart. Regular conflict, usually initiated by the Kestrel pair, was observed early in the season, but later when the Peregrines had small young, the tiercel would harass the Kestrels on occasion. Later still in June, shortly before fledging when the eyasses were active on the eyrie ledge, the male Kestrel was able to hunt immediately in front of the eyrie, a distance of no more than 50m and was not harassed by either Peregrine, although both birds were present close by.

A male nestling, ringed in May 1988, was found shot in Lancashire four years later, 71km north-west, while one found long dead at Chapel-en-le-Frith in July 1995 had been ringed as a nestling four years earlier at Sedburgh, Cumbria. One female ringed as a nestling in June 1984 was found dead by the M62 motorway near Warrington in July 2004; at over 20 years old it exceeded the previous oldest ringed bird (as quoted in *BWP*) of 15 years 9 months.

Water Rail
Rallus aquaticus
A scarce winter visitor and passage migrant. A rare breeder.

Water Rails are usually highly secretive and are therefore probably underrecorded. They frequent a variety of wetland sites with thick vegetation including watercourses, reed-beds, marshes, sewage farms and gravel pits. Fortunately, they are also vocal, often betraying their presence with loud calls, some of which have been likened to pigs squealing. As passage migrants or winter visitors they are recorded annually, usually between September and March, from numerous wetland sites in the county. Most records are of single birds but there have been double-figure counts from Williamthorpe Nature Reserve (ten in 1987), 12 at Drakelow Nature Reserve in 1998 and 2005, and a highest ever count of 17 at Willington Gravel Pits in November 2007. Most are seen in the lowlands, but a few are recorded at Peak District sites in most years. Numbers peak in November and December and there is some indication of an increase in the last decade; the minimum number of birds recorded in Derbyshire during these two months during the period 1992–2011 is shown in the table.

with open mud, and always expanses of tall emergent vegetation (1988–91 Atlas). The species may be faithful to one site for several years and then not be recorded there again for a long period. In Derbyshire, breeding has been proved in most recent years. Sites where breeding has taken place since 1980 are Aston-on-Trent Gravel Pits, Brinsley Flashes, Breaston Nature Reserve, Carr Vale, Drakelow Nature Reserve, Elvaston Castle Country Park, Erewash Meadows, Middleton Moor, Netherthorpe Flash, Poolsbrook Marsh, Wyver Lane, Willington Gravel Pits, and the Osmaston area. Breeding has been suspected at several further sites.

There were five proven, three probable and four possible breeding tetrads from the Derbyshire BBS (1995–99). Three of the proven sites were in the 23 10km core squares, compared with one each in the 1968–72 and 1988–91 Atlases. Breeding is not easily proved for such a skulking bird and very few nests have been found in the county.

Whitlock said that this species was more common than the Spotted Crake and stated, as a measure of its abundance, that an observer at Repton School trapped 11 in the winter of 1884. He knew of breeding records from the Melbourne area and Longdendale, while Jourdain added Sudbury, the Henmore Brook between Hognaston and Kirk Ireton, and Haddon (Jourdain additions). Frost knew of only three recent breeding sites, all in the period 1969–76, at Hilton Gravel Pits Nature Reserve, Killamarsh and Mapperley, and it seems that, while still localized, Water Rails have become more widespread breeders than for some time.

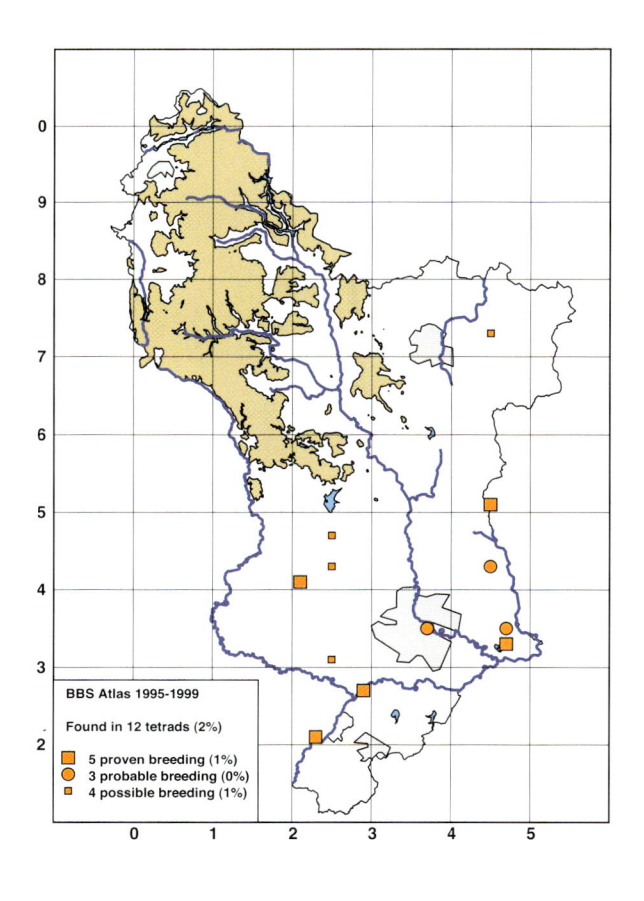

Year	November birds	December birds
1992	11	9
1993	12	10
1994	16	15
1995	14	23
1996	21	25
1997	16	19
1998	26	24
1999	19	25
2000	17	28
2001	35	36
2002	23	31
2003	19	12
2004	21	20
2005	30	18
2006	27	19
2007	39	32
2008	31	20
2009	21	27
2010	25	19
2011	17	16

Even though numbers in the table may reflect under-recording, far fewer nest in the county than are present in November and December. Water Rail breeding territories usually embrace a mosaic of static or slow-moving freshwater normally

BBS Atlas 1995-1999
Found in 12 tetrads (2%)
■ 5 proven breeding (1%)
● 3 probable breeding (0%)
▪ 4 possible breeding (1%)

Spotted Crake
Porzana porzana
A rare passage migrant.

Whitlock and Jourdain considered Spotted Crakes to be regular breeders in the valleys of the lower Dove, Trent and Erewash in the nineteenth century. Nests were reported from the Old Trent at Repton and near Derby. One killed in October 1897 on the River Lathkill was probably a migrant. There are two early-twentieth-century records of birds: one killed at Little Eaton in 1900 and one near Derby in October 1903. There were no further sightings until 1963, since when there have been 17 further records, involving 20 birds.

Year	Location and date
1963	Willington Gravel Pits, one found exhausted on 23rd August and died later
1965	Egginton Sewage Farm, one from 1st to 9th October
1966	Egginton No. 4 Gravel Pit, one was caught and released on 27th August
1971	Killamarsh, one from 18th to 22nd September
1977	Drakelow Nature Reserve, one in June
1977	Drakelow Nature Reserve, up to four from 14th August to 16th September
1978	Drakelow Nature Reserve, one from 25th August to 15th September
1982	Drakelow Nature Reserve, one on 5th August
1984	Sandiacre, one found dead on 11th August
1991	Middleton Moor, one on 10th October
1994	Drakelow Nature Reserve, one on 27th–28th August
1998	Willington Gravel Pits, one from 4th to 9th September
2000	Willington Gravel Pits, one on 19th–20th September
2002	Willington Gravel Pits, one from 26th August to 5th September
2003	Drakelow Nature Reserve, one from 18th to 29th March
2005	Ambaston Gravel Pits, one from 14th August to 1st September
2010	Willington Gravel Pits, one on 3rd, 4th, 9th and 11th September

The most bizarre record concerns that at Egginton No. 4 Gravel Pit in 1966, when strange noises were traced by an observer to a tin can floating in a lagoon. They came from a Spotted Crake, which he extricated and released.

The presence of one in June and four in August at Drakelow Nature Reserve in 1977 might suggest breeding, but the recorder doubted this. This has been the best recent site for the species, with six records involving nine birds. The Willington–Egginton complex, where there have been seven birds, is also a favoured area.

As can be seen from the tables, the majority of the records are of autumn passage migrants with 12 birds being found in August. Most of these were juveniles. The March record from Drakelow Nature Reserve in 2003 is notable because of the very early date.

Period	Records	Birds
1950s	–	–
1960s	3	3
1970s	4	7
1980s	2	2
1990s	3	3
2000–11	5	5
Totals	17	20

Month	Records	Birds
March	1	1
June	1	1
August	9	12
September	4	4
October	2	2
Totals	17	20

Baillon's Crake
Porzana pusilla
A very rare vagrant.

This species breeds very patchily from Iberia east to Japan, and south to Australia and southern Africa. It is a very rare visitor to Britain, with only 81 records up to 2009, of which 65 occurred prior to 1950 (Hudson *et al*. 2010). The only Derbyshire record is of one that was killed at Spondon on 8th November 1821 (Whitlock; Jourdain additions).

Corncrake
Crex crex
A very rare summer visitor and passage migrant.

The decline of the Corncrake in Britain has been well documented and is strongly correlated, first with the advent of mechanical hay-cutters and then with the replacement of hay meadows with rye-grass, cropped for silage. By 2009, targeted conservation efforts had increased the UK population to 1167 singing males, overwhelmingly in north and west Scotland (Holling *et al*. 2011).

Whitlock reported that the bird was plentiful throughout the county and especially so in the lush lowland valleys. His book contains a photograph of an almost completely white bird that was shot at Kedleston in September 1892. By 1940, however, every occurrence was significant enough to be recorded. Throughout the 1950s, 1960s and 1970s there were records of calling birds in most years but this species is notoriously difficult to see and breeding was only confirmed in 1952 (at Walton, Chesterfield), 1956 (Burbage), 1962 (Rodsley) and in the Baslow area in the 'late 1960s' (Frost). Since 1980, the decline has progressively worsened, with only 11 records of single birds as follows:

Year	Location and date
1982	Swarkestone Lake, one flushed from waist-high grass and nettles on 27th September
1983	South Normanton, one calling on 15th–16th June 1983
1983	Blackwell–Westhouses area, one calling on 23rd August
1987	Brailsford, one on 24th May
1988	Kilburn, one calling in June
1988	Dronfield, one flushed several times on 9th October
1998	Middleton Moor, one flushed on 5th August
2000	Hartington, one calling from 8th to 12th July
2000	Calow, a juvenile found dead on 10th October
2010	Furness Vale, one calling on 10th July
2011	Middleton Moor, one calling on 23rd April

Analysis by periods and months since 1950 is shown in the tables:

Period	Records	Birds
1950s	21	26
1960s	16	17
1970s	8	8
1980s	6	6
1990s	1	1
2000–11	4	4
Totals	56	62

Month	Records	Birds
April	2	2
May	11	12
June	22	27
July	8	8
August	5	5
September	4	4
October	3	3
November	1	1
Totals	56	62

Moorhen
Gallinula chloropus
A common resident.

It seems unlikely that the recent status of the Moorhen has changed to any great degree. Whitlock said that it was extremely common throughout the county, and mentioned that it bred on all of the quieter streams of the Peak District. Its eggs were sought-after as human food. Frost said that it frequented waterways in all parts of Derbyshire, from narrow streams and ditches to the largest rivers, and could be found in some numbers at sewage farms, ponds and lake margins.

This is still the case today and, of all county breeding wildfowl, only the Mallard is more widespread. The Derbyshire BBS (1995–99) found it present in 479 tetrads, and breeding was proved in 376 of these. It was present in all of the 10km squares, as it was in the 1968–72 and 1988–91 Atlases. The map shows absences in parts of the north and north-west, where many of the rocky and fast-flowing streams are unsuitable for it. In these areas it breeds on still waters and has bred occasionally at upland sites such as Howden and Barbrook Reservoirs. Other apparent absences, such as those in parts of western Derbyshire, might be attributable to mink, which are widespread there.

Breeding is easily proved for this species since the nests, although better hidden than those of the Coot, are usually easy to see and juveniles are readily distinguishable from adults. Also, Moorhens can be quite tame, especially those breeding on lakes and water courses within built-up areas. The breeding season is a long one, with two or three broods regularly reared, and young have even been recorded during the winter months. Small young are often seen on 'brood nests', which are thought to be built to save them from predatory fish.

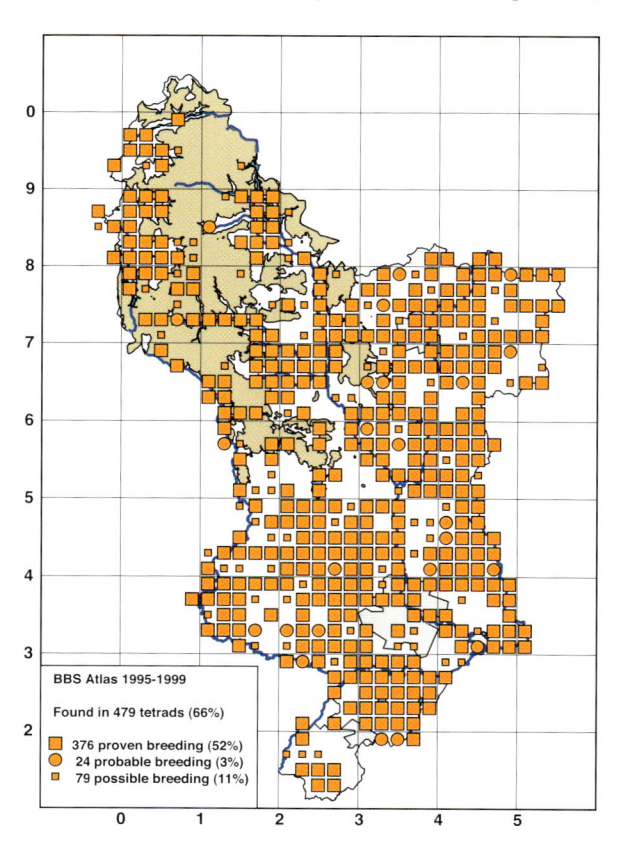

Most nests are situated in waterside vegetation, such as rushes and reedmace, and many have also been found in waterside trees. Jourdain found one near the River Dove at a height of some 5m in a chestnut tree, while Frost recorded a nest inside a dustbin trapped in river silt at Cressbrook and another in the glove compartment of a car that was partially submerged in a gravel pit at Egginton.

The most important source of information on breeding densities of Moorhens has been the Waterways Birds Survey carried out by the the SBSG. Falshaw *et al*. (1999) and Falshaw (2005) gave details of annual censuses of the River Noe and the River Derwent between Bamford and Beeley, a combined total of 24.1km. There were 93 pairs in 1978, but only 51 in 1979, following a severe winter. The population rose to 95 pairs by 1995, falling to 82 pairs by 2003. Useful counts of breeding birds elsewhere include 41 pairs at Carsington Water between 2003 and 2007, and up to 32 pairs (in 2005) on the Chesterfield Canal between Tapton and Staveley.

Moorhens are largely sedentary, with pairs defending their territories throughout the year, though severe winter weather may lead to concentrations at favoured feeding areas. There are numerous records of over 100 birds, with the largest counts being of 160 on the River Wye at Bakewell in February 1998; 154 at Westhouses Flash in September 1967; and 140 at Carsington Water in December 2003.

Other interesting records were: 17 eating berries in hawthorns at Scarcliffe in November 1984; at Carr Vale, 20 climbed into low bushes during a thunderstorm in August 2004; and one roosted overnight on a crane inside a tyre factory in Chesterfield on 9th January 1991.

It is known that some Moorhens of Continental origin winter in Britain but there is only one relevant record for Derbyshire. A ring on the skeleton of a Moorhen picked up at Whitwell in April 1976 had been placed on the bird 687km away in Jutland, Denmark in the previous May. All of the remaining recoveries are from records of the 1950s and 1960s, the earliest being of a bird ringed at Repton in 1955 which was found dead locally four years later.

BBS Atlas 1995-1999

Found in 479 tetrads (66%)

- 376 proven breeding (52%)
- 24 probable breeding (3%)
- 79 possible breeding (11%)

Coot
Fulica atra
A common resident and winter visitor.

Around the end of the nineteenth century the Coot was a very localized breeding bird in Derbyshire. It nested at southern lakes such as those at Bradley, Osmaston and Sudbury, and in the north-east at Sutton Scarsdale, while in the north-west it was known only at the Longdendale reservoirs (Whitlock; Jourdain).

Little more was recorded of the Coot's status until the 1940s, since when the population has shown a great increase, to such an extent that the Derbyshire BBS (1995–99) found that it was our third most numerous species of wildfowl, after Mallard and Moorhen. It was present in 274 tetrads, with breeding proved in 222 (81%). Breeding was confirmed in all of the 23 10km core squares, compared with 20 and 21 in the 1968–72 and 1988–91 Atlases.

There can be no doubt that the increase, which was 83% nationally between 1970 and 2008 (Eaton *et al.* 2010), has resulted from the creation of numerous water bodies, including reservoirs, gravel pits, ornamental lakes, and so on.

Although often breeding near to Moorhens, Coots prefer larger areas of open, preferably shallow, water with peripheral and submerged vegetation. Proof of breeding is easily obtained since most nests are readily visible and family parties make little attempt at concealment. The breeding season is a long one: for example, in 2009 one was sitting on a nest in Lathkill Dale on 23rd February while, eight months later on 30th October, a pair was seen with four tiny chicks at Butterley Reservoir.

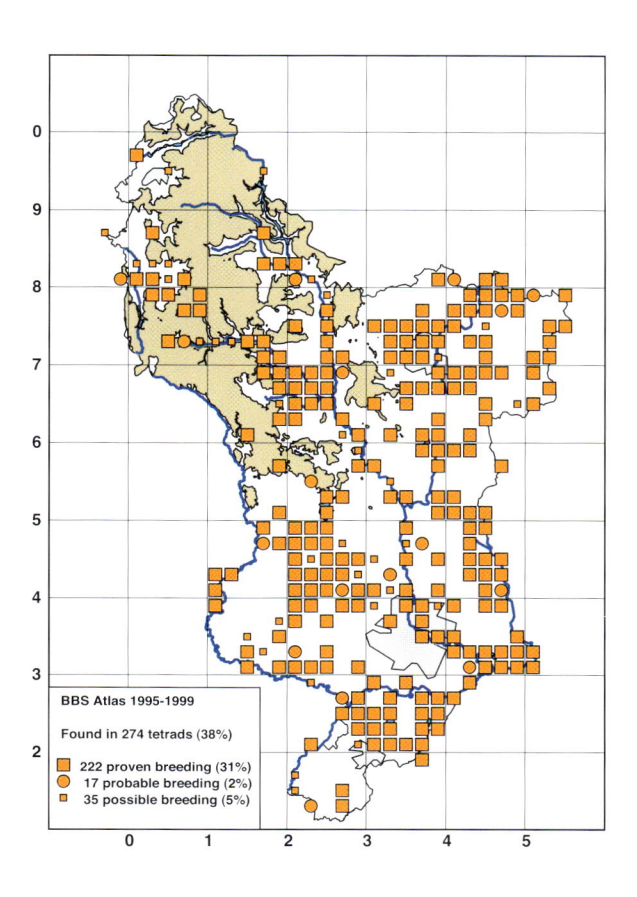

Coots obtain most of their food by diving, but also graze on suitable shorelines. They are not shy birds and inhabit suitable water bodies within built-up areas. They also breed on canals and rivers, including some slow-flowing ones in the Peak District. On the River Noe and on the River Derwent between Bamford and Beeley, this was a scarce species in the 1970s. A regular breeding population was not established until the early 1980s, after which numbers escalated to 36 pairs by 1996, but fell back to 21 pairs by 2003 (Falshaw *et al.* 1999; Falshaw 2005). However, they are still scarce breeders in the High Peak. For example, the only recorded nesting at the Derwent Valley reservoirs was by a pair at Ladybower Reservoir in 1997. The presence of five nesting pairs at Arnfield Reservoir in 1997 was attributed to suitable water levels.

Two unusual nesting records concern first, a pair with young in July 2001 at a pool at Topley Pike Quarry that was described as totally devoid of vegetation and secondly, at Yeldersley in 1999 where a nest was on the branch of a beech tree a metre above the water level.

Coots are believed not to breed until two years old, so site counts of pairs during the breeding season may exceed the number of pairs actually nesting. Numbers may show considerable annual variations, as shown by the counts of the number of pairs in the breeding season at Kedleston Park:

Year	Pairs	Year	Pairs
1984	12	1994	11
1985	15	1995	19
1986	13	1996	21
1987	16	1997	22
1988	15	1998	7
1989	29	1999	–
1990	25	2000	27
1991	24	2001	–
1992	23	2002	6
1993	18		

Breeding birds often overwinter where they have nested. Some though may move to larger waters in autumn, where they join resident birds and therefore large numbers may be present between September and March. The highest counts were: at Swarkestone Lake, 721 in November 1980; Staunton Harold Reservoir, 1133 in November 1972; Foremark Reservoir, about 450 in January 1986; and Carsington Water, 2175 in November 2008.

The average of the monthly wildfowl counts in Derbyshire in the period 1986/87 to 1999/2000 is as follows:

Month	Mean
September	1117
October	1249
November	1422
December	1588
January	1294
February	966
March	740

Variation in numbers throughout the year can be demonstrated by monthly counts at two well-watched sites, Drakelow Nature Reserve and Carsington Water. Peak monthly counts averaged over a year in the period 1995–2008 are shown in the table:

BBS Atlas 1995-1999
Found in 274 tetrads (38%)
- 222 proven breeding (31%)
- 17 probable breeding (2%)
- 35 possible breeding (5%)

Year	Drakelow	Carsington
1995	57	100
1996	56	83
1997	58	108
1998	31	216
1999	22	332
2000	23	370
2001	–	514
2002	48	617
2003	41	781
2004	45	767
2005	72	873
2006	40	913
2007	34	837
2008	37	850

The average monthly maximum counts at the same two sites in the period 1995–2008 are as follows:

Month	Drakelow	Carsington
January	47	929
February	38	340
March	35	209
April	28	89
May	20	46
June	36	100
July	30	259
August	55	471
September	71	862
October	85	958
November	73	1090
December	73	1165

Carsington Water has become by far the most important site in the county, as indicated in the table, which shows the peak count for each year from 1997 to 2011:

Year	Peak count
1997	293
1998	467
1999	797
2000	1005
2001	1558
2002	1332
2003	1818
2004	1805
2005	2048
2006	2136
2007	1785
2008	2175
2009	1845
2010	1783
2011	1340

Although it is known that some Coots wintering in Britain are of Scandinavian and Russian origin, there are no such ringing records involving Derbyshire. Most of the 12 recoveries resulted from shooting. The furthest distance travelled was by one ringed at Market Deeping, Lincolnshire in September 1974 that was found dead in Derby, 79km west-north-west in March 1975. Other movements were 42km from Blithfield Reservoir, Staffordshire to Breaston, and 20km from Staunton Harold Reservoir to Swithland Reservoir, Leicestershire.

Crane
Grus grus
A very rare vagrant.

Frost listed this species in an appendix of unacceptable records saying 'Glover included the bird in his list, saying that it was rarely found in the county. Whitlock thought the record may have referred to the Heron.'

The first authenticated county record was from Middleton Moor in June 1987, and since then there have been a further ten records, all of birds overflying, apart from the Ringinglow Bog and Lower Hartshay birds. Hatfield (1989) and Hornbuckle (1989) documented the 1987 records and all records have been of one or two birds except the five at Ogston Reservoir on 3rd May 2010.

The one moving north-north-west at Carsington Water in March 2002 was almost certainly the individual seen at Old Moor RSPB Reserve, Barnsley, the next day, and was part of a mid-March influx noted mainly along the east coast of Britain, from Kent to Moray. Cranes now breed regularly in East Anglia, South Yorkshire and more recently at the Somerset Levels, and so a future increase in records might be expected. Elsewhere they breed from central Europe to eastern Siberia, with many wintering in France, Iberia and north Africa.

Year	Location and date
1987	Middleton Moor, one flew north-east on 14th June and was seen to land on Ringinglow Bog (11km north-east) 25 minutes later
1988	Ogston Reservoir, two flew north-north-west on 12th April
1995	Ogston Reservoir, one briefly on 7th September
1996	Lower Hartshay, one roosted on 21st–22nd October. It arrived from the north-east and left to the south
2002	Carsington Water, one flew north-north-west on 16th March
2006	Breadsall Hilltop, one flew south on 1st April and presumably the same bird at Kirk Ireton on the same date
2009	Willington Gravel Pits, two flew north-east on 14th May and the same at Aston-on-Trent Gravel Pits 30 minutes later
2010	Beeley Moor, and East Moor, one flew north-north-east on 2nd March
2010	Carr Vale, two circled and departed to the north on 9th April
2010	Ogston Reservoir, five arrived from the north-east and left to the north-west at 1107hrs on 3rd May. Presumed same as the five over Sunk Island, East Yorkshire at 0845hrs on the same date
2011	Mickleover, one flew south on 2nd April

Little Bustard
Tetrax tetrax
A very rare vagrant.

This species is nowadays a very rare visitor to the UK; formerly it was more regular. In Europe it breeds from Iberia east to southern Russia and Kazakhstan. There were 111 records of this species in the UK by 2002, of which only 19 occurred after 1957 (Rogers *et al.* 2003). Whitlock reported that a female was shot on Etwall Common in 1797, and another female was killed by a farmer at Middleton Top, near Youlgreave, on 14th May 1901 (Jourdain).

Stone Curlew
Burhinus oedicnemus
A very rare vagrant.

The first confirmed record was of one shot near Overton Hall, Ashover in 1890 (Whitlock). The same authority regarded Glover's statement in 1829 that this species bred on some of the Derbyshire moors to be possibly correct. However, Jourdain was more sceptical and Frost commented that the claim must be regarded as unproven, since there appear to be no instances of this species breeding on upland moors elsewhere. Frost also gave details of an individual killed in October 1922 which almost certainly came from Shardlow, and a probable sighting of one over Findern on 7th November 1954.

Subsequently there have been four accepted records, as shown in the table. The individual at Middleton Moor was a juvenile which had been ringed as a chick at Icklingham, Suffolk in June 1987.

Year	Location and date
1961	Beighton (now in South Yorkshire), one on 2nd September had been flushed from a large landfill site at Woodhouse shortly beforehand
1971	Big Moor, one in tussocky moorland on 22nd May
1987	Middleton Moor, one on 29th August was relocated on 4th September and found dead on 20th September
2010	Beeley Moor, one on 17th July

Avocet
Recurvirostra avosetta
A rare visitor.

Whitlock documented four nineteenth-century records, one from the Dove Valley and three from the Trent Valley, all of which occurred between 1800 and 1859. This striking black-and-white wader was not recorded again in the county for almost 100 years, although this period largely corresponded with its absence as a breeding species in Britain. Since 1956 there have been 35 records, involving 91 birds:

Year	Location and date
1956	Egginton Sewage Farm, five on 6th September, one remaining until 9th September
1960	Shardlow, eight flew south-east on 3rd April
1969	Clay Mills Gravel Pits, one on 30th–31st May
1975	Elvaston Quarry, two from 11th to 13th May
1976	Elvaston Quarry, one on 9th May
1977	Egginton Sewage Farm, two from 1st to 3rd June
1983	Shardlow Gravel Pits, one on 19th–20th May
1983	Elvaston Quarry, one on 22nd May, possibly the same bird as above
1984	Drakelow Nature Reserve, four departed to the north-east on 24th March
1984	Barbrook Reservoir, two on 24th March
1987	Willington Gravel Pits, one arrived from the west and flew off east on 26th April
1992	Church Wilne Reservoir, 15 arrived from the west and flew off north-east on 20th April
1993	Long Eaton Gravel Pits, two on 13th May
2001	Ogston Reservoir, one on 4th April
2003	Sawley, two on 21st April
2004	Ogston Reservoir, one on 27th March
2006	Carr Vale, one on 14th March
2007	Willington Gravel Pits, one on 15th April
2008	Carsington Water, two on 15th March
2008	Willington Gravel Pits, three on 28th March
2008	Ogston Reservoir, two on 20th April
2008	Carsington Water, two on 29th April
2008	Willington Gravel Pits, one on 7th May
2008	Willington Gravel Pits, three on 18th May
2008	Aston-on-Trent Gravel Pits, one on 20th May
2009	Carsington Water, five on 2nd April
2009	Willington Gravel Pits, three, which departed south-east on 9th April
2009	Willington Gravel Pits, three flew south on 10th April
2009	Aston-on-Trent Gravel Pits, two on 12th April
2009	Carsington Water, one on 26th April
2010	Ambaston Gravel Pits, two on 5th April (also circled Aston-on-Trent Gravel Pits)
2010	Willington Gravel Pits, two on 5th and 10th April
2010	Carr Vale, two seen mating on 25th April (also seen at Sutton Scarsdale and Pleasley Colliery)
2011	Wyver Lane, five on 15th April
2011	Overseal, one departed to the north on 22nd May

An analysis by periods is shown in the table.

Period	Records	Birds
1950s	1	5
1960s	2	9
1970s	3	5
1980s	5	9
1990s	2	17
2000–11	22	46
Totals	35	91

Apart from the first occurrence, in September 1956, subsequent sightings of Avocets have been exclusively during the spring passage period, mostly in April and May. The earliest date of arrival is 14th March (2006) and the latest is 3rd June (1977).

The half-monthly pattern of occurrence from 1950 to 2011 is shown in the chart.

Avocet: half-monthly distribution 1950-2011

The majority of Avocets have been present on one day only, while the longest visit is that of four days by one bird at Egginton Sewage Farm, from 6th to 9th September 1956. The appearance of two birds at Barbrook Reservoir in snowy conditions in March 1984, individuals at Ogston Reservoir in March 2004 and Carr Vale in March 2006, represent the only records outside the Trent Valley.

The largest group has been of 15 birds which arrived at Church Wilne Reservoir from the west on 20th April 1992. Remarkably, the entire flock alighted on the reservoir and spent approximately 15 minutes swimming around and feeding by pecking at the water's surface before flying off to the north-east.

As can be seen from the earlier table, the increase in records in the 2000s is notable, there being more than in all the previous periods combined. This seems likely to be connected to increasing breeding populations in eastern England. As well as the long-established colonies in East Anglia, there are now colonies in Lincolnshire and along the River Humber, while breeding has recently taken place in several inland counties including Nottinghamshire and Leicestershire.

Oystercatcher
Haematopus ostralegus
An uncommon passage migrant and scarce winter visitor. A scarce breeder, mainly in the south of the county.

To hear the clamorous, excitable calls of Oystercatchers is to be instantly reminded of the coast and its pebble beaches or rock-strewn shorelines. However, occurrences in land-locked Derbyshire of this conspicuous wader have been documented for well over 200 years. The earliest example was of one shot near Derby prior to 1789, and there were a few records elsewhere in southern Derbyshire in the nineteenth century (Whitlock), but they were considered to be accidental visitors. After 1904 there were no further sightings until 1944 and 1949, and nine in the 1950s (Frost).

This species has now been recorded annually since 1959, predominantly at wetland sites in lowland regions and most frequently in the Trent Valley. It was reported with increased regularity throughout the period 1980–2009, the vast majority of birds occurring between February and August. Another significant development in recent years is that this 'seaside bird' has become established as a scarce breeder in the county. Oystercatchers had been observed prospecting for nest sites since 1969 at gravel pits and riverside beaches, although breeding was not confirmed until 1972 when a pair with a chick was seen at Egginton Gravel Pits (Frost). Unfortunately, this breeding attempt and another made at Clay Mills Gravel Pits in the following year were both thought to have been unsuccessful. There was no further proof of breeding until 1985, when a pair nested at Sawley Water Meadows, but this effort also ended in failure. The first successful breeding eventually took place in 1987, when a pair raised one youngster at Egginton Sewage Farm.

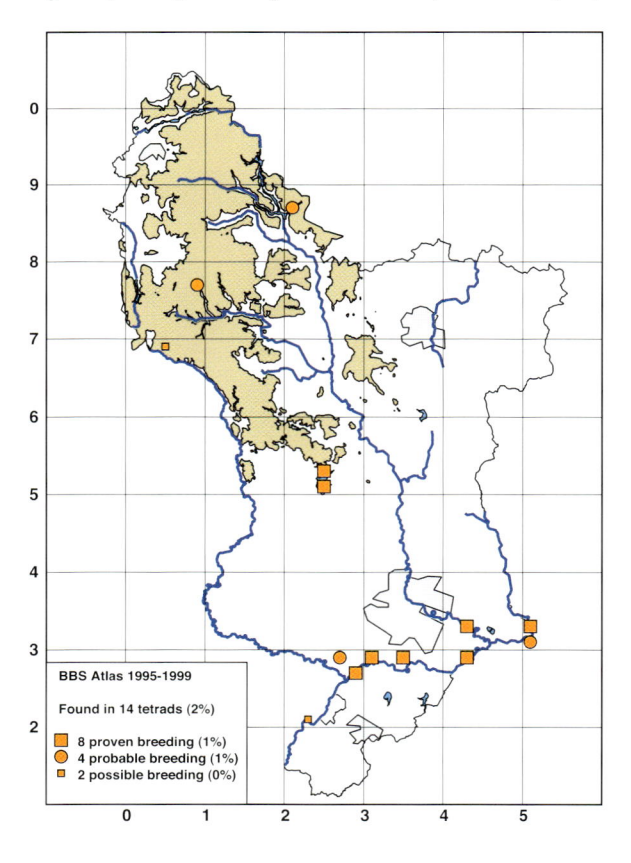

A widespread range expansion inland across central England by this wader was highlighted in the comparative results of the 1968–72 and 1988–91 Atlases. This trend was thought to have been triggered by behavioural changes rather than human pressure on coastal nest sites (1988–91 Atlas). Although breeding has been confirmed almost annually in Derbyshire since 1985, it was not until the late 1990s that more than one or two pairs were reported and any degree of success from nesting attempts was achieved. In 1999, at least five out of 11 pairs were successful, and in every subsequent year to date several young have been fledged. In both 2007 and 2010 there were 18 pairs present at 12 sites, though with fewer in 2008, 2009 and 2011. The total number of breeding pairs recorded in each period from 1985 to 2011 is set out in the table.

Period	Total pairs	Average pairs per year
1985–89	4	0.8
1990–94	7	1.4
1995–99	25	5.0
2000–04	46	9.2
2005–11	101	14.4

A key factor in the recent growth of the local population has been the establishment of a regular breeding colony at Carsington Water, where the large islands provide safe nest sites. Since 1997, between two and seven pairs have bred every year at the county's newest and largest water body, and a high proportion are known to have reared young successfully. The distribution map, which summarizes the findings of the Derbyshire BBS (1995–99), reveals that Carsington Water was the only locality outside the Trent Valley where breeding was confirmed during this period, and that there was proof of breeding in eight tetrads, probable in four and possible in two.

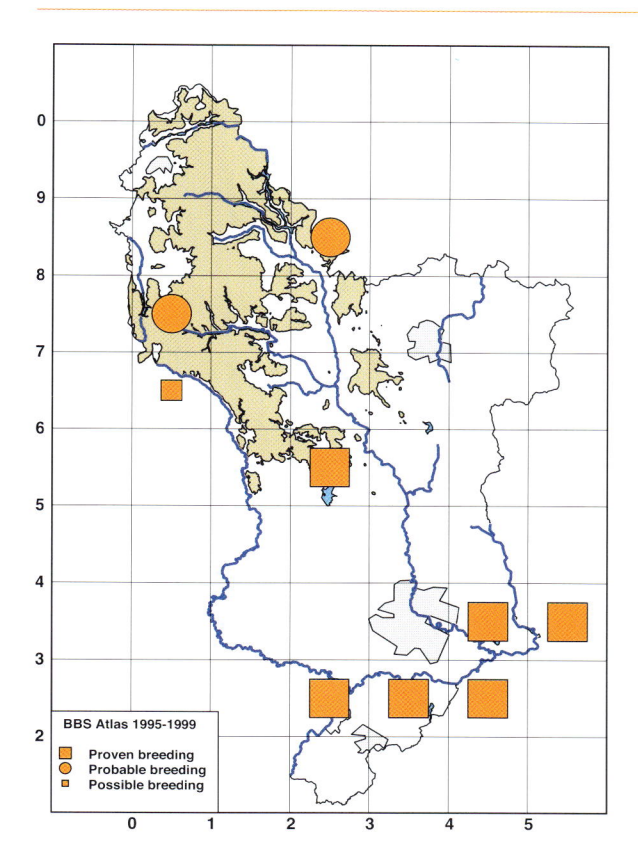

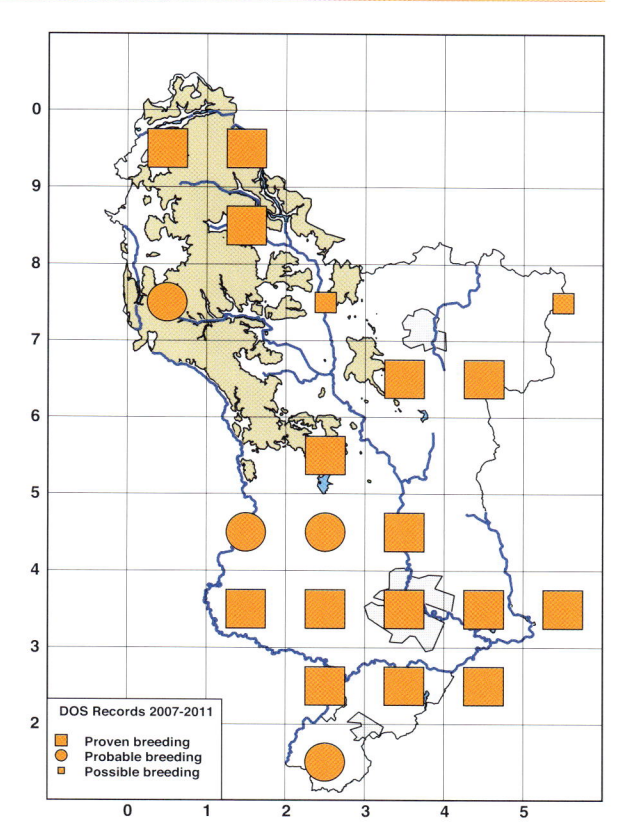

Even though probable breeding is indicated on the map at Ladybower Reservoir and near Buxton, the only proof of breeding in the Peak District came in 2004, 2006, 2007 and 2011, when a pair nested in Longdendale, successfully in the two latter years. There was an attempt at Ogston Reservoir in the same year. The first breeding records in the north-east were at Carr Vale in 2005 and Arkwright in 2006, and in the latter year a nest in maize stubble near Ashbourne was the first breeding record for the west of the county. Favoured nesting areas in the Trent Valley have been closely associated with gravel pits, although the specific locations have not been revealed in the *Derbyshire Bird Report* from 1993 onwards for reasons of security.

The maps show the increased range of breeding Oystercatchers in 2007–11 compared with 1995–99. As a direct result of the burgeoning population, double-figure counts of Oystercatchers have been regularly reported in recent summers, especially at Carsington Water and Willington Gravel Pits. Until the late 1990s, gatherings of more than ten had been exceptional and always involved birds on spring or autumn migration. Another consequence of successful colonization is that it has become more difficult to obtain an accurate picture of the occurrences of passage birds. While spring migrants are generally first reported in February, the majority almost certainly pass though during March and April. In the twentieth century the largest parties were 11 at Drakelow Nature Reserve on 5th April 1987 and the same number at Willington Gravel Pits in February 1999.

Frost suggested that autumn migration took place mainly from July to September and normally peaked in August. He quoted an unusual sighting of 30 over Hathersage on 22nd September 1967. Since 1980, the largest flocks on return passage have been 19 at Ogston Reservoir on 1st August 1989 and 14 at Middleton Moor on 28th July 1984, and the next highest September count was seven, at Barbrook Reservoir in 1984. There is invariably a significant reduction in numbers after August, although this could also be attributable to the fact that adults as well as young have usually vacated their breeding grounds in the county before the end of the month.

Nationally, the majority of our breeding birds spend the winter around coastal areas of Britain, where they may be joined by immigrants (1984–88 Winter Atlas). In Derbyshire, occurrences between October and January have always been infrequent, averaging fewer than three each winter over the period 1980–2009. The number of sightings and birds recorded in these months are summarized in the table.

	October	November	December	January
Years recorded	10	10	10	17
Total records	18	24	14	38
Total birds	21	28	23	64

With the notable exception of nine at Foremark Reservoir on 18th December 1997, nearly all other records have been of one or two birds. There has not yet been any instance of overwintering, though an individual was present at the Pleasley Colliery site from 13th November to 25th December 2004.

Throughout the year, Oystercatchers are most likely to be found at gravel pits, reservoirs and other wetland sites, but there have been occasional sightings of this species flying over localities well away from water, such as moorland regions; these almost certainly involve passage migrants. Nocturnal movement has also been reported a few times, mainly over urban areas.

A remarkable observation was made in July 2003 at Carsington Water, where an adult was seen to raid a Coot's nest and feed the eggs to its own young (Carsington Bird Club 2004). Another unusual sighting was witnessed at Draycott on 17th August 2001, when a bird swam across the River Derwent.

There has been a solitary ringing recovery which concerned an individual shot on 29th August 1968 at Holymoorside. This bird had been ringed only four days earlier at Heacham in Norfolk, and was presumably transferring from the Wash to an estuary on the west coast of Britain. This pattern of movement across England and Wales has been well documented in subsequent recoveries.

American Golden Plover
Pluvialis dominica
A very rare vagrant.

There have been two accepted records of this North American vagrant. The first was of a juvenile at Rother Valley Country Park (now in South Yorkshire) on 12th and 15th October 1990. The next was of a first-summer bird, discovered with the Golden Plover flock, at Middleton Moor on 19th August 1995, which was present on most days until 30th August. It was believed to be the individual subsequently present at South Anston, South Yorkshire, from 31st August to 6th September, and at Besthorpe, Nottinghamshire, from 17th September to 5th October. Further details were given by Gould (1997a).

This species breeds in the Arctic tundra region of North America and winters in central South America. It is one of the more common Nearctic waders in the UK and by the time it was removed from the list of species considered by BBRC in 2005 there had been 277 accepted records (Fraser *et al*. 2007).

Golden Plover
Pluvialis apricaria
A fairly common summer visitor to the Peak District moorlands. A fairly common passage migrant and winter visitor elsewhere.

The Golden Plover is a fairly common breeding bird on the Peak District moorlands, and one of the characteristic birds of that community. Two three-year research projects and three status surveys also mean that it is one of the better-studied species. Wintering flocks are also quite common, usually in lowland areas, and migrating flocks mix with returning breeding birds on the hill pastures in late winter and early spring.

Whitlock said that it bred on all Derbyshire high moorlands, though nowhere was it very numerous. A survey in 1970–72 estimated a Derbyshire contingent of about 250 pairs in a Peak District National Park population of perhaps 432 pairs (Yalden 1974). Regular annual counts centred on a section of the Pennine Way from Snake Summit to Mill Hill suggested a decline during the 1980s (Yalden 1986b). Although a partial survey by the RSPB in 1981 found that overall numbers were rather similar, at 159 pairs where there had been 183 pairs (Campbell 1982), there was some redistribution from southern to more northern moors. This heightened fears that recreational disturbance might be affecting the local population, prompting a study of this problem (Yalden & Yalden 1990) and a resurvey by the JNCC (Brown & Shepherd 1991).

Despite the evident continuation of disturbance, numbers actually recovered during the late 1980s and 1990s, although surfacing of the Pennine Way has concentrated, and therefore greatly reduced, the impact of this factor (Finnegan *et al*. 2005). Arguably, a series of cold winters was a more likely cause of the decline in the 1980s, with subsequently milder winters facilitating the recovery (Yalden & Pearce-Higgins 1997). A restoration in the population level was confirmed in another survey of the Peak District National Park, carried out in 1991, which found an overall total of 456 pairs, including about 232 in Derbyshire. This study also concluded that some retreat in the south-west of the region had been balanced by some expansion in the east (Brown 1993). In 2004 the totals were 424 pairs, about 298 of them in Derbyshire (Carr & Middleton 2004).

Frost identified the main breeding grounds of Golden Plover in the county as being centred on Bleaklow, though stating that they also bred elsewhere in north-west Derbyshire and on the Eastern Moors, from 350m amsl to the highest tops. This is broadly the range established by the Derbyshire BBS (1995–99) in which breeding was confirmed in 27 tetrads, probable in 26 and possible in 13.

Although specific breeding densities were not ascertained in this five-year survey, weekly censuses between Snake Summit and Mill Hill showed up to 49 pairs in 1997, while about 53 territorial pairs were located on Alport Moor in June 1999. At least seven pairs were found between Axe Edge and Goyt's Moss in July 1996 and an extensive survey of the Eastern Moors (Beeley to Strines) revealed eight territories in 1996. Surveys in the Big Moor area revealed four pairs in 1990 and one in 2004, but none in 2010. Pairs were found principally in tetrads that combined extensive cotton-grass swards, the most favoured nesting habitat, with adjoining crowberry/bilberry heaths which are the preferred feeding areas for the older chicks.

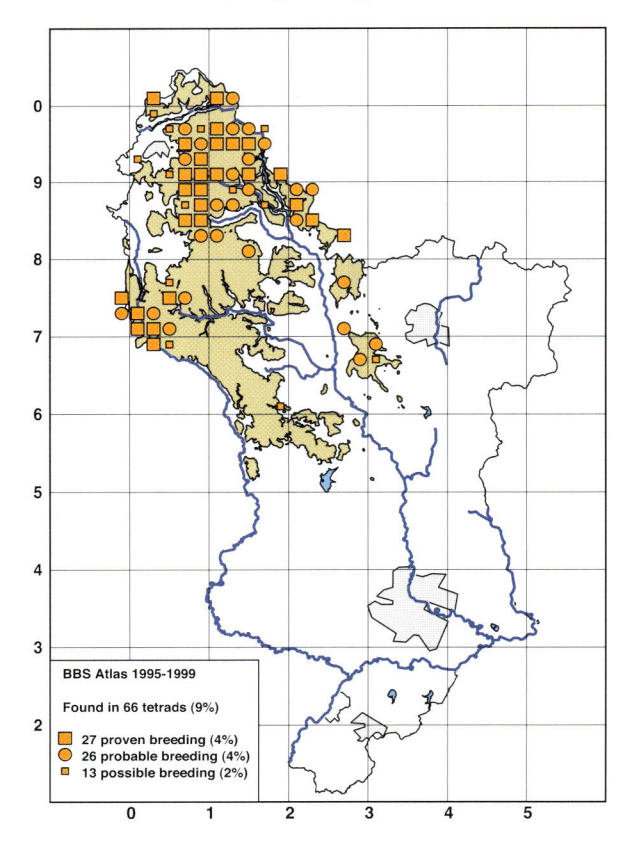

Egg-laying normally takes place in April, though exceptionally clutches are started in late March. Belated wintry weather can cause significant losses of eggs or young, as happened as a result of heavy snowfall in late April 1981. Golden Plovers are rather secretive before and during incubation, but when the eggs hatch, usually around mid-May, the parents' behaviour changes and they will alarm and call, long and repeatedly, while any intruder is near their young. Although this makes these waders easier to count and to confirm breeding, it is much harder to find the chicks since they scatter and hide. Until the young have grown and become fully fledged, approximately six to seven weeks after hatching, the adults will maintain this very vocal behaviour. Rare late clutches may mean that alarming parents are sometimes reported on breeding grounds throughout August, but the majority of families have left the moors by mid-July and have started to congregate on nearby hill pastures. Middleton Moor used to be a favourite site for such post-breeding gatherings during the 1980s and early 1990s. Flocks numbering several hundreds were regularly recorded here in autumn, frequenting nearby pastures during the day and assembling at the lagoons to roost. Now the site is almost completely deserted, the most recent three-figure gathering here being recorded in autumn 1995.

By September and October, larger numbers build up in lowland areas of Derbyshire, often in association with Lapwings. However, the biggest flocks are usually recorded in the period between November and February, as revealed in the table. This specifies the highest counts in any locality in each winter (September–April) from 1979/80 to 2010/11 inclusive.

Winter	Month	Max count	Location
1979/80	Dec 1979	1250	Stoneyford
1980/81	Jan 1981	800	Hilton–Hatton area
1981/82	Apr 1982	900	Carr Vale
1982/83	Jan 1983	1250	Burnaston Airport
1983/84	Dec 1983	1000	Burnaston Airport
1984/85	Nov 1984	1130	Middleton Moor
1985/86	Sep 1985	800	Middleton Moor
1986/87	Nov 1986	1000	Breaston Nature Reserve
1987/88	Jan 1988	1000	Church Wilne area
1988/89	Dec 1988	2000	Rother Valley Country Park (now in South Yorkshire)
1989/90	Nov 1989	2000	Church Wilne area
1990/91	Dec 1990	1300	Bennerley Marsh
1991/92	Mar 1992	1100	Carsington Water
1992/93	Mar 1993	1500	Sawley Water Meadows
1993/94	Jan 1994	2200	Bennerley Marsh
1994/95	Jan 1995	2400	Bennerley Marsh
1995/96	Dec 1995	1309	Bennerley Marsh
1996/97	Feb 1997	1400	Bennerley Marsh
1997/98	Apr 1998	840	Egginton Sewage Farm
1998/99	Dec 1998	5200	Bennerley Marsh
1999/2000	Feb 2000	2000	Aston-on-Trent Gravel Pits
2000/01	Feb 2001	2000	Aston-on-Trent Gravel Pits
2001/02	Feb 2002	1280	Bennerley Marsh
2002/03	Dec 2002	2650	Bennerley Marsh
2003/04	Dec 2003	809	Egginton Sewage Farm
2004/05	Feb 2005	2184	Egginton Sewage Farm
2005/06	Dec 2005	1100	Hardwick
2006/07	Dec 2006	1500	Aston-on-Trent Gravel Pits
2007/08	Nov 2007	1460	Aston-on-Trent Gravel Pits
2008/09	Oct 2008	1000	Pleasley Colliery
2009/10	Oct 2009	700	Scarcliffe
2010/11	Nov 2010	600	Carr Vale

Since 1980, flocks of more than 1000 have been recorded at over 20 different sites. Previously, co-ordinated monthly surveys in January 1977, and from November 1977 to February 1978, produced a highest combined total of just over 2200 birds in the county (Shaw 1978). It is quite probable that milder winters, particularly since the late 1980s, have enabled larger numbers to remain. Wintering Golden Plovers can be very mobile and will readily respond to severely cold conditions by heading southwards. The heaviest visible passage in these circumstances was witnessed at Ogston Reservoir on 30th December 1981 when a total of 706 flew south. Gatherings in excess of 1000 birds were regularly reported at Bennerley Marsh throughout the 1990s, with an unprecedented count of 5200 on 26th December 1998. The apparent increase in the wintering population has occurred in spite of the loss of some traditional haunts through the redevelopment of former wasteland, such as that at Tibshelf in the 1970s, or the more intensive management of pasture.

The precise origins and composition of wintering flocks are hard to determine, though they almost certainly contain a mixture of local birds and those which breed in Scandinavia and Iceland. Members of this northern population (formerly regarded as a separate race *P.a. altifrons*) have a much stronger contrast between the white fringe and the black bib and belly when in summer plumage. The magnitude of wintering flocks in recent years indicates a high proportion of these 'northern' birds, because they easily outnumber the local breeding population. However, some of the latter clearly do not winter far away, since mild weather can see them back on the moors even in January or February, although a gathering of as many as 50 on Ringinglow Bog on 1st January 1989 was exceptional.

During March, Golden Plovers which breed in the Peak District reassemble on upland pastures near to their nest sites and are sometimes accompanied by northern-race birds. The latter become distinguishable as they moult into their more striking summer plumage, occasionally frequenting such areas until May. By this time the local birds are well into their breeding cycle and now using the same fields for feeding purposes. Frost considered springtime gatherings would be predominantly, if not entirely, made up of northern-race birds. He also commented that the biggest flocks of the year usually occurred in March and April, occasionally numbering over 2000, but this has rarely been the case since 1980.

There have been only three ringing recoveries of this species to date. An adult which had been colour-ringed on Black Ashop Moor in June 1997 was controlled later that year on 14th September at Sunderland Point on the Ribble Estuary, Lancashire, and was sighted in the same area on 21st October. One of a brood of three chicks which hatched on the Snake Summit on 29th May 1987 was found freshly dead at Eyam almost two months later, on 23rd July. This provided the first positive evidence that Peak District breeding birds contributed to the large flocks which gathered in the Tideswell–Middleton Moor area at that time. The remaining record concerned a pullus ringed in June 1974 near Ladybower Reservoir that was found dead at the same locality four months later. This individual may have succumbed some time previously, possibly as a result of becoming ensnared.

Grey Plover
Pluvialis squatarola
A scarce passage migrant.

The first positive identification of this species in the county was made by Whitlock when examining skins in Derby Museum. He found a specimen which had been shot at Egginton Sewage Farm during the winter of 1890 and was previously considered to be a Golden Plover. Whitlock believed that Grey Plovers were occasional visitors to the Trent Valley and gave details of another recently shot bird in 1893.

There were only three records in the first half of the twentieth century: in 1917, 1946 and 1947. However, during the period 1950–2011 there were 321 records involving a total of 452 birds. The figures for each period are shown in the table, and reveal a progressive increase in occurrences throughout this period until the twenty-first century, when it has been reversed.

Period	Records	Birds
1950s	3	6
1960s	19	26
1970s	40	61
1980s	79	117
1990s	100	151
2000–11	80	91
Totals	321	452

Grey Plovers have been found annually since 1967, though numbers have sometimes fluctuated quite markedly from year to year. This is demonstrated in the table which shows the annual totals of birds from 1980 to 2011.

Year	Birds	Year	Birds
1980	5	1996	23
1981	16	1997	6
1982	18	1998	6
1983	16	1999	4
1984	12	2000	13
1985	7	2001	9
1986	9	2002	6
1987	5	2003	5
1988	14	2004	4
1989	15	2005	6
1990	37	2006	5
1991	7	2007	3
1992	8	2008	5
1993	17	2009	8
1994	22	2010	12
1995	21	2011	15

The year with most records was 1990 when 37 individuals were seen, although there have been many years in which fewer than ten have occurred. Since 1980 this wader has been reported at an average of six localities each year.

Although it is primarily a passage migrant, there have been sightings of Grey Plover in all months, as evidenced in the chart, which represents the half-monthly distribution of all records between 1980 and 2011. The figures indicate that spring migration usually peaks in May, with larger numbers encountered on autumn passage, particularly in September, and to a lesser extent in October and early November. While this pattern of occurrence largely corresponds with that described by Frost, there appears to have been a slight increase in the number of winter records, especially for December and January, over recent years.

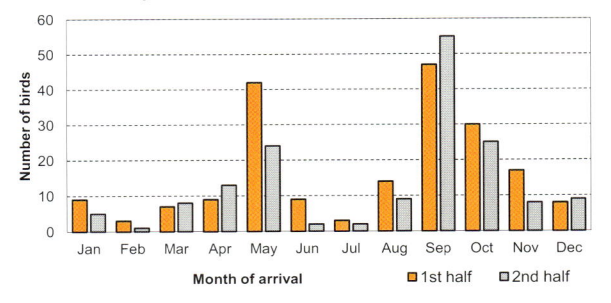

In common with virtually all other scarce waders in Derbyshire, the majority of records (approximately 80%) have involved single birds. Parties of up to five have occasionally been sighted, most recently at Carsington Water on 5th September 1996. The only larger flocks in autumn have been nine that flew west over Ramsley Reservoir on 28th September 1972, and 14 which circled Egginton Sewage Farm and flew off north-west on 12th September 1990. The biggest gatherings in spring have been ten at Foremark Reservoir on 7th May 1981 and seven at Willington Gravel Pits on 15th May 1994.

Although most visits are short-lived, there have been several instances of individuals remaining for more than a week. The longest stay has been that of a summer-plumaged bird at Willington Gravel Pits from 12th May to 1st June 1993. Adults in breeding plumage have been recorded on at least 17 other occasions since 1980, mainly on spring migration in May, but sometimes on return passage in July and August.

The distinctive call of the Grey Plover has facilitated the identification of birds in flight. This has happened most often at reservoirs, gravel pits and other wetland sites, but there have also been a few sightings over built-up areas, which have included Bolsover, Chesterfield, Derby, Melbourne, North Wingfield and Ticknall, as well as one over open moorland at East Moor.

This species has been recorded at more than 50 sites in the county, though these are predominantly in the south and east. Willington Gravel Pits has been visited most regularly, with records in 20 of the 32 years from 1980 to 2011, and a surprisingly high proportion in spring. Drakelow Nature Reserve, which lies only 8km to the south-west, has records in 15 years since 1980, mainly involving autumn migrants. The most favoured haunts outside the Trent Valley have been Ogston Reservoir and Middleton Moor, with visits in 19 and 16 years respectively. A single bird at Derwent Reservoir on 2nd June 1985 constitutes the only occurrence to date in the High Peak area.

There have been three recorded instances of single Grey Plovers associating with flocks of Golden Plover, as follows: at Wardlow Mires on 31st August 1985, at Bennerley Marsh from 4th to 19th February 1997, and at the nearby Bennerley Coal Plant on 15th April 2001.

An interesting record from 1993 concerns an individual which was first seen at Middleton Moor on May 17th, and last seen on May 27th when it was taken by a Peregrine.

Sociable Plover
Vanellus gregaria
A very rare vagrant.

An adult in summer plumage was found at Egginton Sewage Farm on the afternoon of 17th April 1993. Its calls, as it was initially mobbed by a territorial male Lapwing, drew the observer's attention to it. It was then seen well in a ploughed field, where it allowed approach to 50m. However, it could not be relocated in the evening nor the next morning. It was believed to be the individual that appeared at Cley-next-the-Sea, Norfolk, four days later, and was subsequently seen at other sites in Norfolk and Lincolnshire until 12th June (Thornhill 1994).

This declining species breeds across the steppes of southeast Russia and west central Asia, and winters from Sudan to Pakistan. This sighting represented the thirty-seventh record for Britain and only a further six had occurred by 2007 (Hudson *et al.* 2010).

Lapwing
Vanellus vanellus
A common but decreasing resident, passage migrant and winter visitor.

This species, commonly known in former days as the Peewit or Green Plover, has been the most widespread wader in the county since the nineteenth century at least. It was regarded by both Whitlock and Jourdain as a very common resident, which bred extensively throughout low-lying areas, and also up to the moorland fringes, where it was considered to be most abundant in the Peak. While Frost believed that this was still a reasonably accurate description of its status in the late 1970s, he also commented that there had undoubtedly been a considerable decrease in numbers. He thought this had first become apparent in Derbyshire around the middle of the twentieth century and had particularly affected birds on farmland in lowland regions.

Evidence of breeding was recorded in all 10km squares in both 1968–72 and 1988–91 Atlases, and also during the Derbyshire BBS (1995–99). There was confirmed breeding in 255 tetrads, probable in 135 and possible in a further 114, indicating that it was found in no less than 504 tetrads.

This might perhaps suggest that there has been no contraction in range in recent decades, yet a long-term reduction in numbers is indisputable. One example quoted by Frost concerned an area of farmland between Clay Cross and Stretton that held 121 pairs in 1950, but only 79 by 1958. Subsequently, the number of pairs found in the same 10km² of land had fallen to 22 by 1984. Similarly, 39 pairs nested in 36.5ha of ploughed land at Calton Pastures, near Bakewell, in 1976, declining to only eight or nine in 1981, and none at all by 1993. Nationally, a survey of breeding Lapwings in 1998 revealed a reduction of almost 50% in England and Wales in only 11 years (Wilson *et al.* 2001). Locally, the highest density recorded during CBC studies has been 1.38 pairs per km², on a mixed lowland farm in the central southern area of the county. One impressive lowland concentration in the last few years was at Arkwright, with up to 22 territorial pairs (in 2010) on farmland recently reinstated from opencast coalmining.

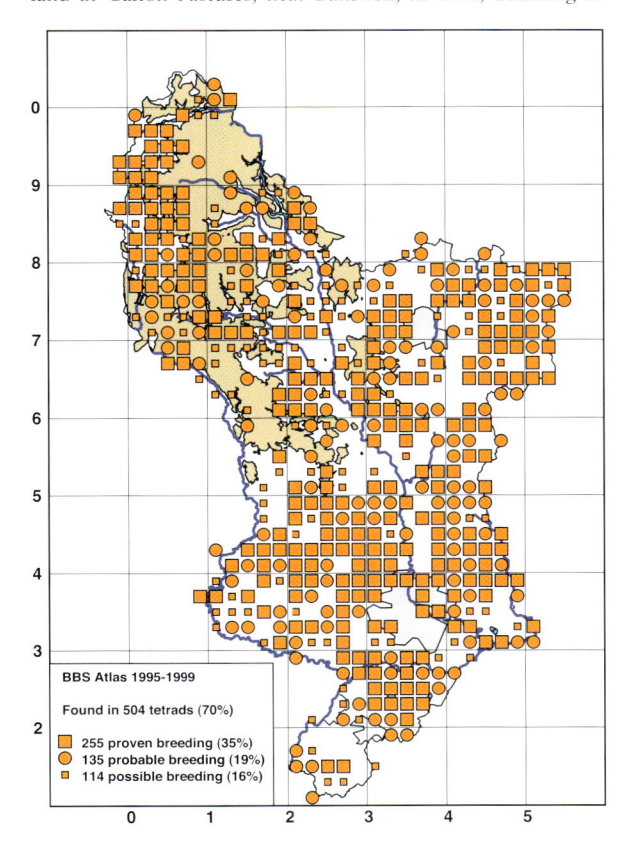

Lapwings prefer to nest in fields cultivated in spring, and ideally those adjacent to rough grassland, as this provides the best habitat for rearing chicks successfully. The widespread loss of mixed farmland, combined with a change from spring to autumn sowing and the conversion of rough grazing to improved grassland, appear to have been the major reasons for the steep decline in the population (1988–91 Atlas). In Britain, the stronghold of this species is now the uplands of northern England, of which the Peak District National Park represents the southernmost region. Worryingly, the tetrad map reveals that, in Derbyshire, Lapwings may have already disappeared from many upland areas, although there was an impressive count during the survey period of about 40 territories in fields at Cown Edge in 1997.

The most recent information on the Peak District population resulted from a 2002 survey organized by the RSPB and carried out mainly by local observers (Sugrue 2002). This was largely a survey of upland farmland in the National Park and adjacent area. It revealed a population of approximately 469 pairs in Derbyshire out of a total of 1213 pairs in the Peak Park District, with notable concentrations in the Rowarth–Cown Edge–Chisworth area with approximately 97 pairs, and the Harewood Moor area where there were 59 pairs. The most important habitats for nesting Lapwings were unimproved pasture, which held 259 pairs, and rush-pasture with 89 pairs. Initial results from a recent survey in 2007 show an estimated population in the Peak District overall of 500–600 pairs, suggesting a decline of around 50% in five years (Pearce 2009a).

Low productivity on the breeding grounds has also been identified as a contributory factor in the general decline in numbers. Bolton *et al.* (2007) found that Lapwing breeding productivity was twice as high on sites managed under agri-environment schemes (Entry Level and Higher Level Stewardship) as on unmanaged sites. A recent example in north-west Derbyshire was a report of over 30 pairs nesting at Glossop in 2000 which were thought to have fledged a total of only 12 young, owing to predation by Carrion Crows and cats. Similarly, in the Trent Valley, some 40 pairs were present at Egginton Sewage Farm in 1997, but virtually all nests and young were destroyed by machinery in May and June. Further losses were sustained in the following year, while in 2000, crop-spraying activities were believed to have caused the desertion of all 20 nesting pairs after egg-laying. Both of these scenarios are believed to happen on a widespread scale.

Lapwings usually return to their breeding grounds in March, when the males perform their acrobatic and vocal display flights. The earliest date that display has been noted in any year since 1980 is 28th February (1994), at Carr Vale. The main period for

BBS Atlas 1995-1999
Found in 504 tetrads (70%)
- 255 proven breeding (35%)
- 135 probable breeding (19%)
- 114 possible breeding (16%)

egg-laying occurs from late March until early May, although chicks have occasionally been reported in July and there is a late record of a female with unfledged young on 4th August (1993), at Tupton.

Post-breeding flocks start to build up at favoured sites, occasionally before the end of May, but normally during June, when gatherings of several hundreds have been recorded. During the years from 1980 to 2011, the highest count in this month has been 1050 at Flagg Moor on 29th June (1982). Larger numbers are invariably present from July onwards, possibly augmented by the arrival of Continental birds. Throughout the 1980s, Middleton Moor regularly hosted gatherings of over 1000 birds in the late summer and early autumn period, including maxima of 3086 in July 1983 and 4500 in August 1989. Since the early 1990s, Willington Gravel Pits has often witnessed the biggest post-breeding assemblies, most notably 4600 in July 1992. Flock sizes have, not surprisingly, diminished in recent years and the only four-figure counts in any month from June to September since 1997 have been of 1500 at Botany Bay Farm, near Coton-in-the-Elms on 26th September 2000, 1048 at Aston-on-Trent Gravel Pits on 17th September 2006 and also 1000 on 3rd September 2007.

A similar pattern of decreasing numbers in winter is also evident in the table, which specifies the highest counts at any site between October and March in each winter from 1979/80 to 2010/11 inclusive.

Winter	Max count	Location
1979/80	4000	Shardlow
1980/81	9000	Burnaston Airport
1981/82	3000	Burnaston Airport
1982/83	5000	Burnaston Airport
1983/84	2500	Burnaston Airport
1984/85	6000	Breaston
1985/86	5000	Elvaston Quarry
1986/87	5000	Breaston Nature Reserve
1987/88	1200	Ogston Reservoir
1988/89	7000	Chaddesden Sidings
1989/90	5000	Swarkestone Lake
1990/91	7400	Chaddesden Sidings
1991/92	5500	Chaddesden Sidings
1992/93	3500	Chaddesden Sidings and Willington Gravel Pits
1993/94	4600	Breaston Nature Reserve–Church Wilne Reservoir
1994/95	1600	Bennerley Marsh
1995/96	1678	Bennerley Marsh
1996/97	800	Ogston Reservoir
1997/98	1400	Bennerley Marsh
1998/99	1300	Nadin's, Newhall
1999/2000	1000	Bolsover, Aston-on-Trent Gravel Pits and Hatton
2000/01	1318	Aston-on-Trent Gravel Pits
2001/02	1000	Dove Valley Lakes
2002/03	1200	Barrow Gravel Pits
2003/04	1000	Chaddesden Sidings
2004/05	2250	Egginton Sewage Farm
2005/06	1075	Willington Gravel Pits
2006/07	1246	Church Wilne Reservoir
2007/08	2600	near Eaton Wood
2008/09	1250	Willington Gravel Pits
2009/10	700	Willington Gravel Pits
2010/11	815	Willington Gravel Pits

All of these highest winter counts were recorded at lowland sites, mainly in the Trent Valley, and usually in December or January. Relatively low maxima since the mid-1990s contrast sharply with those of previous years, most notably 7400 at Chaddesden Sidings in December 1990, approximately 9000 at Burnaston in January 1981, and an earlier example quoted by Frost of an estimated 13,000 in the Erewash Valley between Ilkeston and Alfreton in November 1961.

An interesting observation was of 250 on an office roof at Pride Park on 13th February 2006; this is the first local record of such behaviour, which is commonly seen in parts of north-west England.

In mild weather, Lapwings generally remain in the county throughout the winter, but harsh conditions will precipitate movement of birds, usually between south and west. Such instances have included 2140 flying south over Staveley on 30th December 1981, and an exceptional passage of 10,000 flying south-west over the Church Wilne area on 25th November 1986. Conversely, a heavy easterly passage over Drakelow Nature Reserve, totalling more than 6000 birds from 21st to 23rd February 1979, indicated a swift return when conditions had ameliorated after a period of severe weather. A combination of mild winters and declining numbers in recent years has resulted in very few large-scale movements, and none involving over 1000 birds since 1986.

A leucistic bird was present at Staunton Harold Reservoir on 28th August 1982, while another was identified at Willington Gravel Pits on 18th July 1998. An individual with pale cinnamon upperparts, a dark breast band and reddish under-tail coverts was seen at Carsington Water in August 1998.

There have been 45 ringing recoveries involving Derbyshire birds, all except four having been ringed as chicks. This is doubtless because nests and young are easily located, whereas adults are much more difficult to trap, and probably also explains why virtually all reports have been of dead birds rather than 'controls'. The earliest record is of a pullus ringed at Kettleshulme, Cheshire in June 1932, which was shot exactly six years later at Kinder Reservoir. Over half of the recovered birds have been found within 10km of the place where they were ringed. Since a large proportion of such recoveries have occurred at least a year or more after ringing, this suggests quite a high fidelity to the natal area. However, there have been foreign recoveries of locally ringed birds, in Spain and the Ukraine, as well as one ringed in Finland in June 1963 which was found dead at Pilsley (near Alfreton) in 1971. There were also eight recoveries in Ireland between 1956 and 1985, all relating to birds shot in winter, including one ringed as a chick at Glossop in May 1970 which was killed in Galway in February 1985. Such examples support the belief that many Lapwings reared in northern Britain overwinter in Ireland (1984–88 Winter Atlas). Since the mid-1980s almost all records have involved only local movements, averaging 20km, with the greatest distance being 123km. This concerned an individual ringed in May 1986 at Markeaton Park, Derby that was shot at North Somercotes, Lincolnshire in February 1996.

Little Ringed Plover
Charadrius dubius
An uncommon summer visitor and passage migrant, mainly in the south and east.

Pupils of Repton School were the first observers of these delightful small waders in Derbyshire, when they found a pair nesting on a shingle bank of the River Trent at Repton, on 30th May 1950; young were thought to have fledged in July. It had taken just 12 years for this species to reach the county from its Hertfordshire bridgehead. There were no further sightings in the county until 1955, but in 1956 breeding was confirmed at two sites in the Trent Valley and has occurred in this region ever since. Little Ringed Plovers have also bred regularly in north-east Derbyshire since 1958, and more sporadically in the Peak District from 1970 onwards. The county population reached double figures for the first time in 1964 and by 1970 it had risen to at least 31 pairs.

After this initial period of consolidation and range expansion, there appear to have been significant variations in the size of the population. For example, in 1973 only 22 pairs were found in the county during a national census organized by the BTO, yet in 1979 a total of 55 pairs was located in a survey carried out by R.A. Frost. Another national census conducted by the BTO in 1984 indicated a marked decrease, with an estimated local population of 30 pairs. Information published in the *Derbyshire Bird Report* suggested that numbers had declined to fewer than 12 pairs in 1986. In contrast, at least 20 pairs have been present in every subsequent year, peaking at 57 in 1999. The specific annual totals (1990–2011) are revealed in the table, and provide further illustration of short-term fluctuations.

rapidly become partially, or even completely, deserted. A classic example of this sequence of events occurred at Chaddesden Sidings in Derby. This complex of gravel pits and refuse tips held a single pair in 1989, and yet by 1993 there were 12 breeding pairs, representing the highest concentration ever recorded in the county. In subsequent years, as landfill operations recommenced and conditions became less attractive, numbers swiftly declined (Messenger & Roome unpublished).

Frost stated that most bred either in gravel pits or on colliery waste tips. More specifically, following the completion of the national census of 1984, in which he was the co-ordinator for Derbyshire, Frost identified three main areas of population: in the Trent Valley, where these small waders nested predominantly at gravel and sand quarries; in north-east Derbyshire, where colliery waste areas were favoured; and in the High Peak, where they were found almost exclusively along the chain of reservoirs in Longdendale. Other habitats which held Little Ringed Plovers included limestone quarries, a subsidence flash, an industrial refuse tip and an area of waste ground (Frost 1985).

A broadly similar pattern of distribution was established by the Derbyshire BBS (1995–99), during which breeding was proved in 32 tetrads, was probable in 18, and was considered possible in a further 16 tetrads.

It would appear that ongoing gravel extraction in the Trent Valley, by providing new habitat to balance the loss of former haunts, has enabled this species to maintain a relatively widespread presence in this region. Despite the reclamation of many colliery waste sites, the other breeding stronghold centred around traditional mining areas in the north-east of the county has also been retained. The continuing existence of opencast workings and industrial wasteland may well prove essential for the future prosperity of these waders in this area. The cluster of confirmed breeding records in central Derbyshire depicted on the map corresponds to Carsington Water, where a maximum of eight pairs has been reported. Low water levels at reservoirs are of crucial importance, not only because potentially large

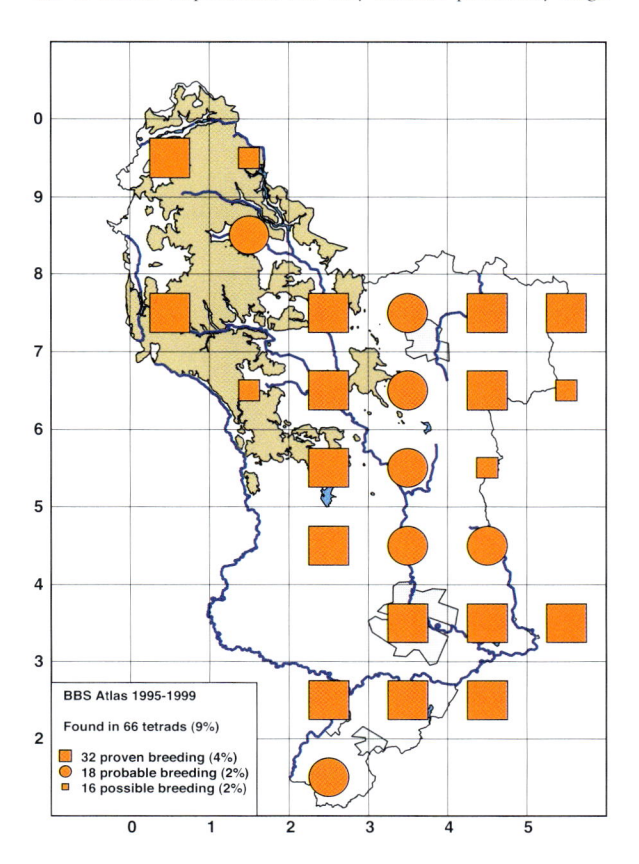

Year	Pairs	Year	Pairs
1990	26	2001	32
1991	20	2002	34
1992	28	2003	40
1993	48	2004	34
1994	25	2005	38
1995	28	2006	22
1996	22	2007	30
1997	20	2008	35
1998	34	2009	25
1999	57	2010	38
2000	41	2011	41

Since Little Ringed Plovers are essentially summer visitors, annual variations in numbers could be regarded as normal, though sharp declines are almost certainly a consequence of temporary or permanent loss of suitable breeding habitat. This species is highly dependent on man-made sites for nesting, and only 3% of all British records obtained during the national survey of 1984 related to natural habitats (Parrinder 1989). These birds are opportunistic breeders and many of their chosen sites, such as gravel pits and opencast workings, are relatively transient, which inevitably produces a great deal of instability. Locally, some sites have been favoured by several pairs for a few seasons while prime breeding habitat has existed. However, if this is degraded as a result of being permanently flooded, overgrown, landscaped or subject to disturbance, these localities may

BBS Atlas 1995-1999

Found in 66 tetrads (9%)

- 32 proven breeding (4%)
- 18 probable breeding (2%)
- 16 possible breeding (2%)

numbers of territorial pairs can be supported, but also because successful breeding is more likely to occur. The majority of nest sites found in the Peak District have been on reservoir shores, especially those in Longdendale. Since 1970, breeding has also been confirmed, or strongly suspected, at Barbrook, Combs, Derwent, Errwood and Ramsley Reservoirs, the lagoons at Middleton Moor and Peak Dale, and in certain limestone quarries.

Little Ringed Plovers are normally among the first summer visitors to appear, and have been recorded as early as 5th March, at Drakelow Nature Reserve in 1991 and at Carr Vale in 2000; the average date of first arrival during 1978–2007 was 15th March. Spring passage, which takes place mainly between mid-March and mid-May, is generally light, and any flocks of more than ten are noteworthy. Gatherings of 17 birds at Shirebrook on 26th April 1988, 18 at Willington Gravel Pits on 10th April 2008 and the same number at Ogston Reservoir in April 2011 are the largest recorded at this time of the year. Throughout both migration periods, birds may turn up at a wide variety of wetland sites, but predominantly those situated in lowland parts of the county.

Although males may be seen performing their fluttering, Greenfinch-like display flights before the end of March, some breeding birds may not settle into their territories until late May. The largest annual counts are often recorded during midsummer, and most frequently in July, which is the month when adults and young from the local breeding population, as well as early returning migrants, may all be present. Parties of over 20 have been reported on several occasions. The current county maximum is 43 (including unfledged young) at Ogston Reservoir in June 2011, and otherwise the highest counts recorded outside the Trent Valley have been 27 at Carr Vale on 10th July 1999 and 24 at Carsington Water on 3rd July 2002. Autumn migration is usually heavier than spring passage, and is most pronounced in July and August, with comparatively few birds seen in September. The average date of final departure over the period 1978–2007 is 22nd September. There have been only 12 October records since 1980, all of one or two individuals and none since 1998. The latest ever sighting was of one at Church Wilne Reservoir on 22nd October 1977.

The first ringing recovery in Derbyshire dates back to July 1972 when a bird that had been ringed when already fully grown in August 1970, at Kings Lynn in Norfolk, was controlled at Drakelow Nature Reserve. The longest-distance record concerns an adult ringed at Drakelow Nature Reserve in July 1981 that was shot three months later at Berrechid in Morocco, a movement of over 2200km south-south-west. One ringed as a chick at Barrow Hill in July 1986 was controlled the following month at Stuivekenskerke, Belgium.

There have also been several controls and sightings of colour-ringed individuals, mostly within the county, generated by a nine-year project carried out by A.P. Messenger and M. Roome. This was designed to look at site fidelity of birds breeding in the Derwent and Trent Valleys near Derby. The study established that male Little Ringed Plovers were faithful to the same site (most notably for as long as five years), provided it remained suitable, and that they often enticed females to nest within a few feet of a previous scrape. Pair fidelity was also recorded, with one particular pair known to have returned to the same territory for three consecutive years. During the study period, no evidence was found of double-brooding, but if the nest was robbed, some pairs would abandon their territory and a replacement clutch would then be laid elsewhere. On one occasion a pair was known to have moved a distance of 15km for this reason.

An interesting record was of two nests, each containing two eggs, which were discovered only 1.34m apart on a sloping colliery tip at Whitwell in 1979. An adult was seen sitting on each nest at different times, before adopting the lower one.

Ringed Plover
Charadrius hiaticula
An uncommon passage migrant and scarce breeder. Rare in winter.

According to Whitlock, Ringed Plovers were annual visitors to Derbyshire in the nineteenth century, occurring in small numbers on both spring and autumn migration, and he gave details of occurrences dating as far back as 1786 when one was shot at Derby. While Frost similarly defined the status of this species as that of a scarce passage migrant, he also commented that there had been records in all months of the year, though sightings in winter were rare.

From 1980 to 2011, Ringed Plovers were reported on only seven occasions in January. Two were present at Aston-on-Trent Gravel Pits on 26th January 2003, but all other records have been of single birds. The first spring migrants are usually seen before the end of February, generally in small numbers, with a maximum of ten at Willington Gravel Pits on 28th February 1999. The movement of passage birds through the county gains momentum during March and April, and invariably peaks in May, although even in this month any gathering of over 20 is noteworthy. Prior to 1980, the maximum count had been of 31 at Barbrook Reservoir on 28th May 1974, but this was exceeded on 15th May 1994 when 37 were present at Middleton Moor.

Exceptional numbers were reported at Aston-on-Trent Gravel Pits in 2004, including 65 on 20th May, 82 on 21st May (the current county maximum) and 31 on 6th June. Many of these were believed to be of the race *C.h. tundrae*, which breeds in northern Scandinavia and Russia. Individuals belonging to this slightly smaller and darker subspecies have been identified on several other occasions, mainly in spring, though nearly all such records have involved fewer than ten birds.

Return passage, which normally commences in July, is generally heaviest during August, with a maximum count of 36 on 17th August 1970 at Ogston Reservoir. Since 1980, the largest gatherings have been of 30 at Rother Valley Country Park (now in South Yorkshire) on 17th August 1983 and the same number at Willington Gravel Pits in August 1993. Sizeable flocks are occasionally found in September, most notably 25 at Staunton Harold Reservoir on 7th September 1990 and 20 at Carsington Water in September 1996. The majority of birds have usually departed by the end of September with only a very few lingering into October.

Throughout both spring and autumn migration, Ringed Plovers are most frequently recorded at major wetland sites in lowland areas, with gravel pits and reservoirs especially favoured. The most regularly visited upland localities are the lagoons at Middleton Moor, where there have been sightings in every year since 1980, and the reservoirs at Barbrook and Combs where these waders have been found on several occasions. However, occurrences elsewhere in the Peak District are relatively scarce. An unusual record was of a juvenile by a small pond at Derbyshire Bridge in the Goyt Valley on 26th July 1985. Another interesting report concerned a bird feeding on a manure heap near Ashbourne on 30th May 1979.

Ringed Plovers are rarely recorded anywhere in Derbyshire in November, and there were only eight instances from 1980 to 2011. With the notable exception of 12 at Ogston Reservoir on 21st November 1994, all other occurrences have involved single birds. December sightings are rarer still, with only two since 1980.

Frost considered Whitlock's account of possible breeding at Long Eaton in 1889 to be unconvincing. However, he suggested that future colonization was imminent, since territorial behaviour and display had been observed in the mid-1970s and Ringed Plovers had also begun to breed regularly in five out of six neighbouring counties. Prater (1989) established that between 1973 and 1984 the inland population nesting in England had more

Period	Total pairs	Average pairs per year
1980–84	18	3.6
1985–89	26	5.2
1990–94	32	6.4
1995–99	38	7.6
2000–04	42	8.4
2005–11	41	5.9

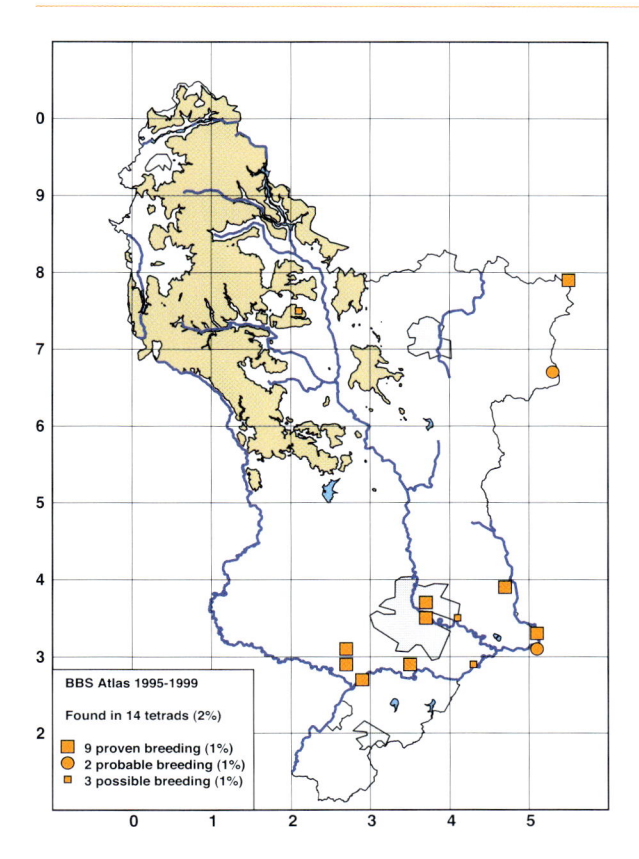

BBS Atlas 1995-1999
Found in 14 tetrads (2%)
- 9 proven breeding (1%)
- 2 probable breeding (1%)
- 3 possible breeding (1%)

than doubled. This development was associated with an increase in the number of gravel pits, lakes and reservoirs, and may also have been assisted by low water levels in prolonged dry weather (1988–91 Atlas).

Breeding was first confirmed in Derbyshire in 1978 at Killamarsh Meadows, which had recently been opencasted, leading to the accidental creation of many pools. A nest was found in May and young were subsequently observed. The following year a pair bred successfully in the Trent Valley at Swarkestone Lake (Frost 1980). Since 1980 the population has gradually increased in size, as indicated in the table, which gives the total number of pairs recorded in each period from 1980 to 2011.

Since 1980, pairs have been recorded almost annually at localities in both the north-east and the south of the county, with the majority usually found in the Trent Valley. The information obtained during the Derbyshire BBS (1995–99) largely confirmed this pattern of distribution, which is illustrated by the map. Eleven of the 14 tetrads where the species was found were located within the Trent Valley, while two were situated along the north-east border and one in central Derbyshire. In the Peak District, the only evidence of breeding has come from Longdendale, where there were single pairs in 1995 (believed successful), 2003 (failed) and 2005 (outcome unknown).

The highest number of breeding pairs in any year has been 16, which were reported from a total of eight sites in 1999. Although the population has steadily consolidated, many breeding attempts have failed for a variety of reasons including human disturbance, natural predation and the activities of egg collectors. In 2000, two nests at a locality in south Derbyshire were destroyed as a result of ploughing. Ringed Plovers have bred most regularly at gravel pits and reclaimed colliery sites, though precise locations have not been disclosed in the *Derbyshire Bird Report* since 1993 in order to help safeguard nest sites. Breeding has also been documented at other habitats such as sewage farms, arable farmland, reservoir shores, landfill sites and industrial wasteland. It is possible that a very few Ringed Plovers have been overlooked in these latter areas, as certain sites have not been accessible to birdwatchers.

A short-term colour-ringing scheme, conducted by A.P. Messenger and M. Roome in the Derwent and Trent Valleys near Derby, revealed that site fidelity was strong in males, whereas females might breed at different locations in successive years. Evidence of this behaviour was obtained in May 1993 when the female of a pair at Chaddesden was trapped and found to have been ringed as a breeding bird at Long Eaton Gravel Pits in June 1992. This is the only ringing recovery to date.

Killdeer
Charadrius alexandrinus
A very rare vagrant.

One frequented the open fields of Egginton Sewage Farm from 29th February to 22nd March 1964. The presence of this bird precipitated the first major 'twitch' in Derbyshire, and it was seen by a large number of observers, despite being very elusive at times.

Killdeers breed across North America and in the Caribbean, and winter south to Peru. Uniquely among Nearctic vagrants to Europe, Killdeers have appeared more regularly in winter than in autumn, with the majority of sightings in south-west Britain. Records from inland counties remain extremely rare. The Derbyshire record constituted only the sixteenth for Britain and Ireland. By 2011, this total had risen to 55 (Hudson *et al.* 2012).

Kentish Plover
Charadrius vociferus
A very rare vagrant.

Frost referred to an unsubmitted report of one seen by the distinguished ornithologist, Ian Newton at Ogston Reservoir on 18th September 1959. Since then there have been six records, all of single birds, as shown in the table. This small plover once bred in very small numbers in England but is now a scarce passage migrant, with around 30 records a year, largely between March and June, and lesser numbers occurring between July and October (Brown & Grice 2005).

Year	Location and date
1968	Westhouses Flash, an immature on 23rd July
1979	Drakelow Nature Reserve, an adult male on 7th May
1980	Elvaston Quarry, an adult male on 3rd September
1990	Ogston Reservoir, a female on 16th–17th May
1991	Willington Gravel Pits, a male on 9th–10th May
1997	Willington Gravel Pits, a male on 25th–26th April

Dotterel
Charadrius morinellus
A rare passage migrant, mainly in spring.

Whitlock and Jourdain considered this species to be a regular spring migrant to the Peak District in the nineteenth century, with gatherings of up to 40 birds sometimes reported. Occasionally Dotterels lingered for a few weeks though no evidence of breeding was ever found. However, there was a considerable decline in numbers which became apparent by the early part of the twentieth century. A trip of seven birds was seen at Dore Moor in 1916, but there were only four further records during the next 55 years, including two birds at Alport Stone on the early date of 18th April 1946 (Frost).

The table indicates that occurrences became more frequent during the 1980s and 1990s, but decreased quite noticeably again in 2000–11.

Period	Records	Birds
1950s	2	4
1960s	–	–
1970s	7	14
1980s	11	30
1990s	16	41
2000–11	10	25
Totals	46	114

The marked increase in the Scottish breeding population during this period (1988–91 Atlas) is presumably a significant factor, although the more intensive study of moorland areas, particularly in late April and early May, has undoubtedly contributed to the upsurge in sightings in the county. However, even though there have been at least three occurrences in some years, with a maximum of five records relating to 21 birds in 1996, Dotterels are by no means annual visitors. There have been blank years in each decade and a five-year absence from 1998 to 2002 inclusive.

The chart of half-monthly figures (all occurrences, 1950–2011) reveals an obvious predominance of sightings in May, concentrated in the first half of the month. The earliest spring passage record during this period is 9th April 2011 (at Beeley Moor) while the latest is 5th June 1991 (at East Moor).

Dotterels are distinctly rare in autumn, with only six records since 1950. All were in upland areas, with extreme dates of 21st August 1977 (at East Moor) and 24th October 1976 (at Beeley Moor).

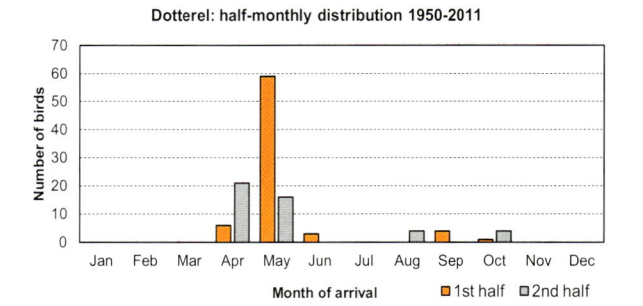

Dotterel: half-monthly distribution 1950-2011

The majority of the more recent sightings have been on stretches of *Calluna* moorland, burnt for grouse management purposes. The well-watched Beeley Moor, where Dotterels have been recorded in 12 years since 1980, has far more records than any other site in Derbyshire. However, Dotterels have also been recorded on the high moorland plateaux of Kinder Scout and Bleaklow on six occasions. At all these sites, as elsewhere in Derbyshire, birds usually move on within a couple of days. These delightful and enigmatic waders have very occasionally been found on farmland, most notably a party of up to six birds in spring-sown cereals at Spancarr, Kelstedge in May 1996.

Whitlock knew of two lowland records, of singles shot near the River Trent at Twyford and near the River Dove in the Tutbury area. There have been only four subsequent records away from upland areas, which are shown in the table:

Year	Location and date
1976	Stanton-by-Bridge, a female on farmland on 21st May, joined by a male on 23rd May. Both departed on 27th May
1979	Ashbourne Airfield, one on 27–28th May 1979
1986	Williamthorpe, four males and three females on reclaimed colliery waste-ground on 2nd May
1995	Pleasley Colliery, one on 9th May

The stay of six days by the female at Stanton-by-Bridge is the longest recorded in recent decades. The party of seven at Williamthorpe represents the largest gathering since 1916, although groups of four to six birds have been at moorland sites on several occasions.

Whimbrel
Numenius phaeopus
An uncommon passage migrant.

Whitlock stated that Whimbrels were regular migrants through the county, with flocks appearing every year in the Trent Valley. He believed that they had been overlooked by previous writers. Only once had he seen one on the ground, feeding by the River Trent at Long Eaton on 15th April 1892.

Frost suggested that the status of this species had not altered significantly since Whitlock's day and thought it likely that a considerable amount of migration took place nocturnally. Frost also revealed that the biggest flocks in the first half of the twentieth century had been 50 over Shardlow on 16th September 1924 and 'an even larger flock' there at the end of the same month. During the second half of the century, this wader has been recorded annually since 1959 and, as the figures in the table (1950–2011) indicate, far more frequently in the most recent decades. This trend may be as much a reflection of greater observer coverage as that of a genuine increase in occurrences.

Period	Records	Birds
1950s	13	28
1960s	59	136
1970s	86	143
1980s	207	507
1990s	329	818
2000–11	402	815
Totals	1096	2447

The highest number in any year has been 144 in 1998, coinciding with peak counts of Whimbrel registered at national level by WeBS. In contrast, only 11 birds were seen in 1982. The annual totals from 1980 to 2011 are listed in the table.

Year	Records	Birds
1980	21	100
1981	20	33
1982	10	11
1983	14	20
1984	16	44
1985	19	52
1986	27	76
1987	28	82
1988	30	46
1989	22	43
1990	29	47
1991	33	59
1992	22	46
1993	32	111
1994	36	94
1995	33	79
1996	41	88
1997	41	113
1998	37	144
1999	25	37
2000	31	53
2001	28	97
2002	37	80
2003	36	79
2004	30	71
2005	32	51
2006	25	45
2007	31	71
2008	31	43
2009	36	73
2010	47	89
2011	38	63

Frost documented the earliest arrival as 22nd March (1938), which was equalled in 1996 when one was heard over Drakelow Nature Reserve and exceeded by one at Long Eaton Gravel Pits on 20th March 2005. There has been only one other record in this month, of a single bird at Middleton Moor on 23rd March 1982.

The chart summarizes the half-monthly distribution of all occurrences from 1950 to 1999.

Spring migration is generally concentrated into the six weeks from mid-April to the end of May. The small, but evenly spread, number of reports in June bridges the gap between the two migration periods, but the first returning birds are usually noted in July.

Autumn migrants are most numerous in August but are quite scarce by mid-September. The latest sightings were at Egginton Sewage Farm on 6th October 1968 and 7th October 2006, and at Carr Vale on 13th October 2006. This wader has yet to be recorded in winter.

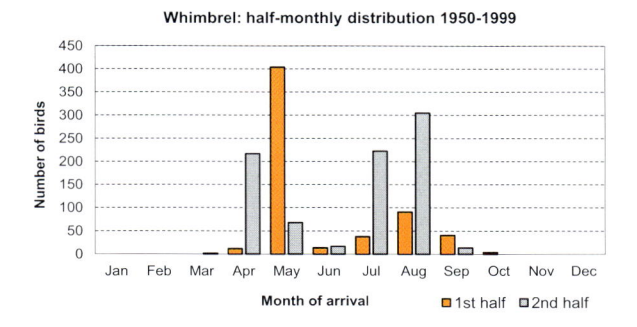

The majority of records (approximately 60%) have involved single birds, though small groups of up to nine are not uncommon, and double-figure flocks have been noted on more than 20 occasions since 1980. The largest was an exceptional flock of 70 which flew in low at Ogston Reservoir, and then departed to the west, on 13th August 1998. All other double-figure counts since 1980 have been of no more than 30 birds, usually in July or August. The largest number in spring was 21 at Ogston Reservoir on 1st May 2011.

Apparently, Whimbrels occasionally stayed for a few days on the fields of Egginton Sewage Farm (Frost), and there were also several instances in the 1980s and 1990s of birds lingering at favoured sites, such as Middleton Moor, Willington Gravel Pits and Carsington Water. This species has sometimes been found roosting with Curlews, invariably at upland locations, and most notably in 1987 at Middleton Moor, where 19 were observed on 22nd July and up to 30 at the end of the month. The longest stay at any site has been of ten days, when a solitary bird remained at Drakelow Nature Reserve from 24th April to 3rd May 1988. However, throughout both spring and autumn migration, visits are normally short-lived and many records still concern Whimbrels seen or heard only in flight.

Whimbrels have been reported from a wide variety of localities throughout the county, including at least 100 sites since 1980. There have been occasional records from dry sites, such as upland pasture. The distinctive and far-carrying flight-calls have sometimes revealed their movement at night over Derby, Chesterfield and other urban areas, while passage has also been noted on several occasions over high ground within the Peak District.

At well-watched wetland sites, Whimbrel have often been observed 'on the ground'. Ogston Reservoir has been visited most consistently, having records in several years prior to 1980 and in every subsequent one, except for 1995 and 2006. This species has also been reported regularly at Middleton Moor in 27 recent years, and annually at Carsington Water since 1992. In the Trent Valley, where occurrences in spring usually outnumber those in autumn, the most favoured locality has been Willington Gravel Pits, which has been visited in 21 recent years, including annually from 1990 to 2004 and again from 2007 to 2011. Drakelow Nature Reserve, where this wader was occasionally reported in the 1970s, has also been visited in 15 recent years.

An interesting bird, which had a dark rump and a small amount of white on its back, was observed at Willington Gravel Pits on 30th April 1994. A detailed description was forwarded to John Marchant, an acknowledged expert on wader identification. In his opinion this individual was unlikely to have belonged to the North American race *N.p. hudsonicus* and could not be assigned with any certainty to the Siberian race *N.p. variegatus*. He concluded that it may well have been an 'intergrade', since there is no discontinuity between the breeding ranges of the Palearctic races of this species (Roome & James 1995).

Up to early 2013, three had been found as Peregrine prey items at Derby Cathedral.

Curlew
Numenius arquata
A fairly common summer visitor to the uplands, but scarce in the lowlands. Fairly common on passage, but scarce in winter.

The Curlew is a very welcome harbinger of spring to the upland areas of the county, when its bubbling calls and wide-ranging song-flights advertise its return to traditional breeding sites. Although often associated with moorland, and surveyed along with the other moorland specialists, it is more catholic in its choice of habitat, and common also on wetter upland farmland and river valley pasture. This seems to be a twentieth-century change: Whitlock regarded it as a typical, though sparsely distributed, breeding bird in the Dark Peak, and it expanded into the White Peak during the 1920s and 1930s.

An attempt to estimate the population of the county in 1973–75 was only partly successful; the bird is so wary, and was so thinly yet widely spread, that a full count was difficult to achieve. However, Anne Shaw (*pers comm*) received counts that totalled over 300 pairs, widely spread across the moors and down the Dove as far as Fenny Bentley. The partial survey of moorland birds by the RSPB in 1981 found evidence of only 18 pairs, and concluded that it was not so much a bird of moorland as of the nearby grasslands. The resurvey by the JNCC (Brown & Shepherd 1991) found only 25 pairs in the same areas, and an overall figure for the Peak District of 338 pairs, about 140 of which were in Derbyshire. They noted that the territories tended to be around the edges of the moorlands, and pointed out that the main moorland areas of Kinder Scout and Bleaklow were largely bereft of them. However, this moorland/moorland peripheral population is only about half the total; the current Biodiversity Action Plan for the species in the Peak District guessed that the total population would be around 1000 pairs, half on moorland and half on pasture. On this basis, the Derbyshire population ought to be around 600 pairs.

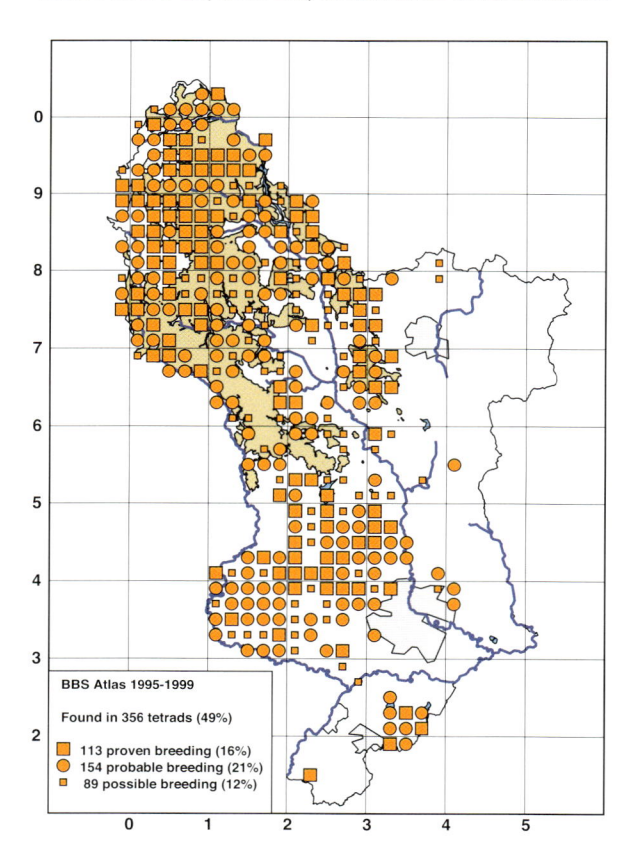

The RSPB-organized survey of 2002 located 264 pairs in the Peak District National Park, of which only 77 pairs were in Derbyshire. The repeat survey of 2007 showed an overall Peak District total of 335 pairs (Pearce 2009b). The 2010 survey of the EMP moors produced a total of 27 pairs (15 of them on Big Moor), an increase of seven since 2004.

The 267 confirmed and probable breeding tetrads found by the Derbyshire BBS (1995–99) were divided equally: about 133 in the White Peak and further south, and 134 in the High Peak (though not necessarily on the moorlands).

One would expect an average of at least two pairs per tetrad. Notable, though, is the scarcity of the species on the eastern side of the county, where agricultural pressures leave little suitable habitat.

Adult Curlews feed largely on earthworms, and are thus limited to wetter areas. Ground that drains very readily, or is artificially drained, becomes too hard in summer, and earthworms burrow deeply or aestivate. Agricultural intensification is therefore inimitable, and there is concern that the population is currently declining. Certainly areas such as Rushup Edge and Edale, where Curlews were prominent in spring, along with the Lapwings, in the 1970s, are now deserted. Hence, one aim of the Biodiversity Action Plan is to reverse these losses. The diet of the chicks is more catholic, but being so large they require good feeding areas. Even newly hatched Curlew chicks are large enough to be able to thermoregulate, so do not usually need brooding. However, poor weather results in poor food supplies, and Curlew chicks may starve in cool weather (Yalden & Yalden 1989). Moorland provides good cover, but may be poor feeding habitat, and parents may lead their chicks off the moorland as they get older.

The first returning migrants usually appear in February, although the main arrival is invariably in March. It is normally during this month that the largest gatherings of the year are recorded, often at communal roosts. Since 1980, Middleton Moor has regularly hosted assemblies of over 50 birds, including maximum counts of 167 on 20th March 1985 and 135 on 7th March 1998. Combs Reservoir has been another favoured haunt, with highest counts of 120 on 22nd March 1980 and 110 on 15th March 2006. The only other upland sites where more than 90 birds have been reported are Arnfield Reservoir, where there were 100 on 27th March 1983, and Peak Dale, with 94 on 27th March 1985.

In lowland areas, the greatest numbers at this time of year occur in the Trent Valley. Willington Gravel Pits has often witnessed the most impressive gatherings, such as 132 on 11th March 1999, and 120 on both 3rd March 1995 and 11th March 1998. However, the maximum count for this region is 140 at the nearby confluence of the Rivers Trent and Dove on 4th March 2002. Curlews may sometimes be encountered on passage over non-breeding areas, although flocks are usually small, and none has exceeded the exceptional sighting, quoted by Frost, of 130 over Belper on 1st March 1974.

Breeding birds quickly take up territories, and although adverse weather may force them to descend temporarily from the moorlands, eggs are usually laid in April. For such a large wader, an incubation period of 29 days is relatively short, and consequently chicks are often seen from mid-May onwards. They grow rapidly and normally fledge within 32–38 days of hatching. Feeding flocks may be seen on recently cut fields in June, most notably a total of 31 near Beeley Moor on 23rd June

BBS Atlas 1995-1999

Found in 356 tetrads (49%)

- 113 proven breeding (16%)
- 154 probable breeding (21%)
- 89 possible breeding (12%)

1992, while 45 were in the area of Gladwin's Mark–Harewood Moor on 15th June 2005. By mid-July the majority of Curlews have left their breeding grounds to assemble on pastureland or at the sites where they congregate in spring.

Post-breeding and autumn gatherings are, surprisingly, generally not as large as those in spring. A total of 76, which roosted in stubble at Sutton-on-the-Hill in September 1979, exceeded the previous maxima of 60, at Drakelow and at Egginton Sewage Farm. Since 1980, the highest counts have been of 160 at Mercaston Sand Pits on 15th September 1980 and 93 at Middleton Moor on 21st August 1987. However, there have been relatively few records of over 50 in this period, and in several years flocks have numbered no more than 25 birds.

This species is scarcest in Derbyshire during December and January, and in some winters has been completely absent in one or both of these months. Normally only a few individuals occur, and any double-figure count at this time of year is exceptional. The largest number recorded in midwinter since 1980 has been 16 near Catton on 2nd January 1995.

Nationally, Curlews have an essentially maritime distribution in winter, preferring large estuarine mud-flats for feeding, and are most widespread along western coasts and throughout Ireland (1984–88 Winter Atlas). The precise wintering grounds of a locally bred bird was established when a chick ringed near Bamford in June 1971 was shot near Pembrey, Carmarthen, in December 1972, a movement of over 250km south-west. Similarly, an adult trapped at Drakelow Nature Reserve in March 1977 was controlled at Bangor, Gwynedd in October 1982. A long-living individual, ringed at the same locality in Wales in September 1974, was found as a road casualty near Carsington Water almost 18 years later. The earliest recovery relates to a pullus ringed in 1959 at Penistone, South Yorkshire, which was shot at Hartington five years later.

An albino was present among roosting birds at Arnfield Reservoir in March 1989 and was known to have bred locally. Another interesting observation was of an individual with a broken bill (only about 25mm long) at Shardlow Gravel Pits on 11th April 1997.

Black-tailed Godwit
Limosa limosa
An uncommon passage migrant. Rare in winter.

Whitlock accepted that Black-tailed Godwits had occurred occasionally in Derbyshire in the nineteenth century. He summarized the information and evidence provided by five different authorities, but Jourdain was not wholly convinced of the validity of any of these claims. Frost stated that a female shot at Egginton Sewage Farm on 25th August 1928 must therefore be regarded as the first acceptable record. There were very few further sightings of this species until the 1970s, by which time it was described as a rare but regular passage migrant. This wader has occurred annually in the county since 1978, with a dramatic rise in numbers by the end of the twentieth century. This trend is apparent in the respective aggregates of records and birds for each period as shown in the chart. During the period 1950–2011, there were 631 records, involving a total of 3391 individuals, excluding (since a number was not given) a 'large flock' at Carsington Water on 1st April 2007.

Prior to 1978, a maximum of six Black-tailed Godwits had occurred together (Frost), though the following year a group of 18 was seen at Swarkestone Lake on 29th April 1979. This was exceeded by a flock of at least 23 at Drakelow Nature Reserve on 30th August 1982, but the next double-figure flock was not until 1991, when 12 flew west over Middleton Moor on 25th August. Then 60 departed from Willington Gravel Pits to the east on 16th April 2008.

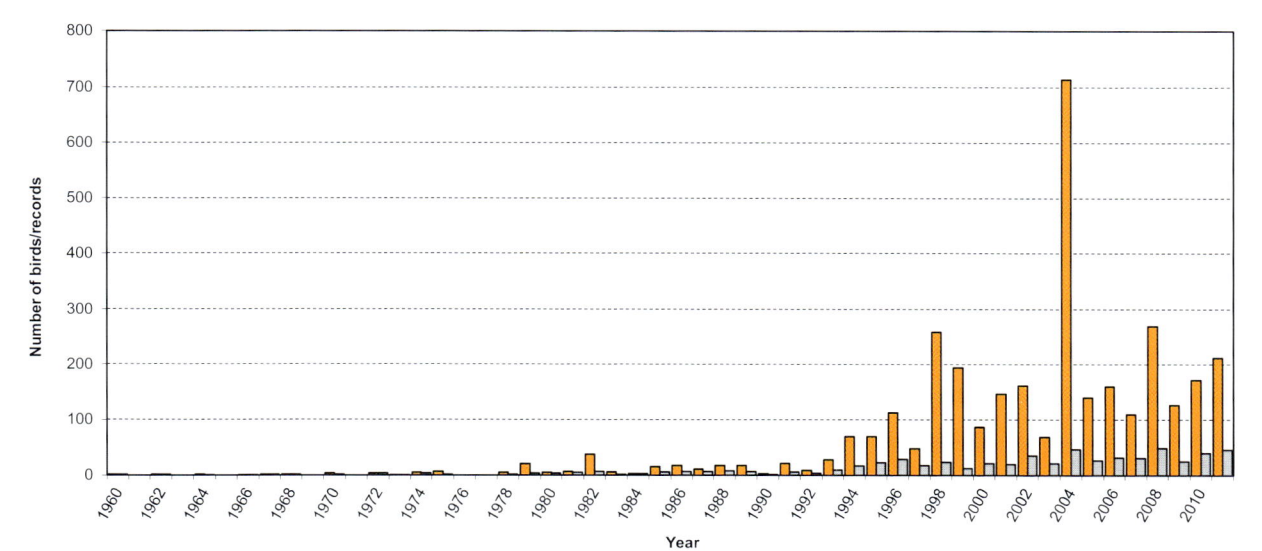

Black-tailed Godwit: annual totals of birds and records 1960-2011

Period	Records	Birds
1950s	3	7
1960s	10	11
1970s	19	47
1980s	56	140
1990s	146	816
2000–11	397	2370
Totals	631	3391

The table of records since 1980 reveals that the most significant increases have occurred since 1993 (although with occasional reversals of trend).

Year	Records	Year	Records
1980	4	1996	29
1981	5	1997	18
1982	7	1998	24
1983	2	1999	13
1984	3	2000	22
1985	6	2001	20
1986	7	2002	36
1987	7	2003	22
1988	8	2004	47
1989	7	2005	27
1990	2	2006	32
1991	6	2007	31
1992	4	2008	49
1993	10	2009	25
1994	17	2010	40
1995	23	2011	46

An exceptional flock of 132 birds flew south-east over Carsington Water on 22nd April 1998, thus surpassing the previous county record of 29 in April 1994. However, in the following spring, the record was broken again when 150 were noted at Willington Gravel Pits on 23rd April 1999. The largest groups of all occurred on 20th April 2004, when a remarkable flock of 170 landed at Ogston Reservoir in the evening, while at Carsington Water, 138 were counted at dusk and up to 60 had been seen in flight earlier in the day. The majority of birds moving through Derbyshire are thought to be those which breed in Iceland (*L.l. islandica*), and the recent increase in numbers may perhaps be a reflection of a growth in population in that country.

Another significant change in status has become apparent in recent years, as there have been occasional sightings of this wader during the winter period. Until the mid-1990s, it had never occurred in the county any earlier than March or any later than October. The first records in winter comprised a flock of 12 flying north at Poolsbrook Country Park on 8th December 1995, and a party of seven which roosted overnight at Ogston Reservoir on 22nd–23rd November 1996. Subsequent sightings have encompassed all months between November and February, although these have involved only single birds, except for four at Carr Vale on 27th November 2004, two at Dove Valley Lake and five at Aston-on-Trent Gravel Pits on 17th and 28th December 2006 respectively, and five at Carsington Water on 1st January 2010.

The first spring migrants normally appear in March, but by far the greatest numbers are encountered during the second half of April, and all four of the flocks of over 100 birds previously mentioned have occurred between 20th and 23rd April. By contrast, until recently, the largest party recorded in May was just seven. This pattern is evident in the chart, which shows the half-monthly distribution of records from 1960 to 2011.

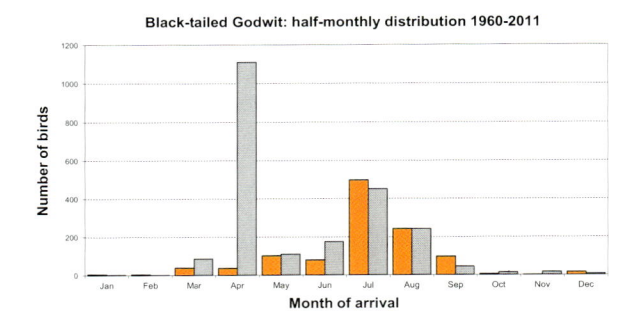

Black-tailed Godwit: half-monthly distribution 1960-2011

While the division between the end of spring passage and the start of autumn passage is not always clear cut, returning birds are usually noted from mid-June onwards. Black-tailed Godwits are recorded more regularly throughout July and August, but relatively few appear after mid-September.

During both spring and autumn migration, the majority of sightings are of singles, although gatherings of up to six birds are not uncommon. Larger groups have occurred more frequently in recent years, with flocks of more than ten recorded on over 50 occasions since 1991. In most instances these have involved parties of up to 30 birds on return passage. However, with the exception of 109 which flew north-west over Carsington Water on 21st July 2004, all other flocks of over 100 birds have comprised spring migrants. The highest day count is from Carsington Water, where flocks of 60 and 138 flew over on 20th April 2004.

There have been records of summer-plumaged birds in most years, mainly during the spring migration period, though sometimes in July and August. An adult, still in breeding plumage, was present at Elvaston Castle Country Park for just over a month, from 10th September to 12th October 1989. This relatively late occurrence also represents the longest stay by any individual in the county. The majority of visits are short-lived, especially those involving larger numbers, and there have been very few instances of birds remaining for more than a week.

Since 1980, Black-tailed Godwits have been reported at about 40 localities, approximately half lying within the Trent Valley. Willington Gravel Pits has become the most favoured site with records in 25 recent years, including an unbroken sequence of sightings in at least three months of every year (with the exception of 2005) from 1991 to 2011. Elsewhere, Ogston Reservoir and Carsington Water have also been visited in most recent years, while in the Peak District, Middleton Moor has records in 21 years in the period 1981 to 2011. However, this species is rarely encountered at other upland sites, and the only occurrences in the north-west of the county have been at Arnfield Reservoir, Combs Reservoir and in the Goyt Valley, with no more than three birds ever seen together. An unusual upland occurrence was of one feeding in a very small marshy area at Screetham Lane on 5th May 2007.

While this elegant wader has been observed almost exclusively at wetland sites in Derbyshire, one notable exception was a flock of 38 flying west over farmland at Alkmonton on 30th August 2001. Even more surprising was the discovery of the remains of a Black-tailed Godwit at a Peregrine nest site in the Peak District in September 1984, while by early 2013, three had been found as Peregrine prey items at Derby Cathedral.

Bar-tailed Godwit
Limosa lapponica
An uncommon passage migrant. Rare in winter.

An individual shot at Swarkestone in 1844 was the earliest of three nineteenth-century records (Whitlock; Jourdain). The first known occurrence in the following century was of a single bird at Barbrook Reservoir in September 1953. There were three further sightings in the 1960s and since 1973 this wader has been recorded annually in the county. During the period 1950–2011 there were 217 records in total, involving 406 birds, with the figures for each period listed in the table.

Period	Records	Birds
1950s	1	1
1960s	3	3
1970s	33	54
1980s	37	95
1990s	62	102
2000–11	81	151
Totals	217	406

There has been an undoubted increase in occurrences of Bar-tailed Godwits in recent decades, though annual numbers fluctuate quite significantly, as revealed in the table of yearly totals (1980–2011).

Year	Records	Birds
1980	2	3
1981	1	2
1982	2	6
1983	4	18
1984	9	22
1985	3	3
1986	2	2
1987	3	4
1988	7	24
1989	4	11
1990	4	5
1991	3	6
1992	4	4
1993	10	17
1994	13	26
1995	9	17
1996	9	11
1997	5	7
1998	2	2
1999	3	7
2000	10	10
2001	5	7
2002	9	16
2003	3	6
2004	5	7
2005	7	22
2006	6	8
2007	7	7
2008	5	7
2009	5	6
2010	9	26
2011	10	29

In 1984, 1988, 1994, 2005, 2010 and 2011, over 20 birds were recorded, whereas in others there have been only two or three individuals (such as 1985 and 1986). There may even be a cyclical pattern to these peaks and troughs, similar to that of Grey Plover, with which it partially shares both wintering and breeding areas. The overall population of Bar-tailed Godwits in Britain during the winter months tends to fluctuate markedly from year to year and this has been linked to predation levels on the breeding grounds (Pollitt *et al.* 2000). This could account for variations in numbers on passage in Derbyshire.

There are records for every month except February, although this wader is only occasionally found in the period between mid-October and mid-April. The majority of such sightings have been in March, and may relate to movements of wintering birds rather than early spring migrants. The chart, showing the half-monthly distribution of all records from 1950 to 2011, reveals that spring passage is usually heaviest during the first half of May, but does not extend beyond the end of that month.

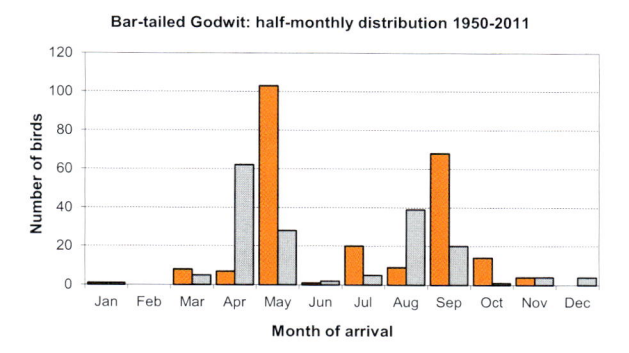

A bird which remained at Middleton Moor from 3rd May to 16th June 1984 (a stay of 44 days and a county record), appeared lethargic and was thought to be sick. The only other Bar-tailed Godwits seen in June have been singles at Carsington Water from 9th to 13th June 1996 and at Egginton Gravel Pits on 28th June 1973.

This wader is sometimes noted on return passage as early as the first half of July, but the largest numbers move through the county between mid-August and mid-September. There have been a few sightings in October, and even in November, most recently one at Carsington Water on 15th November 2011, with a latest date of 22nd November (1969) at Ogston Reservoir.

The only winter records in the twentieth century both concerned single birds at Ogston Reservoir, on 6th January 1985 and 17th December 1986 respectively. However, one was also seen flying south-west at this site on 21st December 2000, and was possibly the same bird that was found exhausted in a garden at Bakewell a week later. This individual was taken into care but died shortly afterwards. A single bird was also present at Carsington Water on 26th December 2001.

Almost half of all records have been of single birds, but parties of up to seven have been reported on several occasions, usually on return passage. The largest flock in spring was of 18 at Middleton Moor on 7th May 2011. All other double-figure flocks have occurred in the autumn: at Middleton Moor, where there were 17 on 4th September 1979, 13 on 14th September 1983 and 15 on 29th August 1988; at Pleasley Colliery, where 12 were seen on 3rd July 2005; and at Carsington Water, with ten on 9th September 2010.

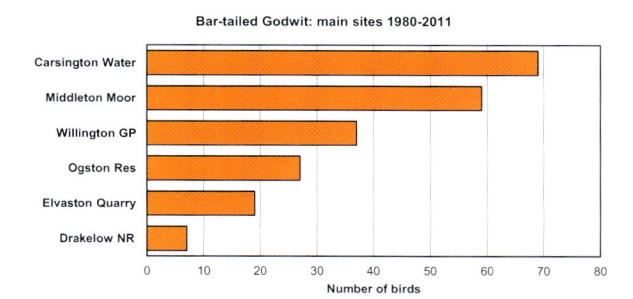

A few birds have appeared in fine summer plumage, invariably in April or May, but the vast majority have been in the much drabber non-breeding or immature plumage.

Since 1980, Bar-tailed Godwits have been found at about 30 localities in the county. Approximately half of these lie within the Trent Valley, where Willington Gravel Pits is the most regularly visited site, having records in 13 of the years from 1980 to 2011. Elsewhere, Ogston Reservoir has had records in 17 years, including 13 since 1980, while Carsington Water has been visited on an annual basis following the first sighting here in March 1994. However, the most favoured location since 1980 has been Middleton Moor with records in 15 years. The number of individuals recorded at six principal sites from 1980 to 2011 are shown in the chart. The only other occurrences in upland areas have been at Arnfield and Barbrook Reservoirs, over Eastmoor and at Peak Dale.

Two Bar-tailed Godwit corpses have been found as Peregrine prey items at Derby Cathedral.

Turnstone
Arenaria interpres
An uncommon, but regular, passage migrant.

This species was first reported in Derbyshire in unfortunate circumstances, as three birds were killed when they flew into telegraph wires at Longcliffe on 1st June 1906 (Frost). This was followed by records in 1927, 1943, 1946, 1949, 1951, 1952 and 1957, since when they have been found annually on migration, predominantly at gravel pits, reservoirs, and other well-watched wetland sites.

Records and birds for 1950–2011 are tabulated.

Period	Records	Birds
1950s	6	6
1960s	34	45
1970s	58	108
1980s	69	100
1990s	88	150
2000–11	113	218
Totals	368	627

The table reveals a sustained increase in sightings throughout the period, which has resulted in a change of status from 'rare' to 'uncommon' passage migrant, a trend which is consistent with that of several other waders.

The specific totals for each year from 1980 to 2011 are listed in the table. While the annual average over this period was 15 birds, numbers were particularly low from 1981 to 1983, and each record was of single birds. Conversely, at least 30 were seen in 1990 (mainly in autumn, including five parties of three or four), 32 in 2009 and 34 in 2011. Larger numbers than usual also appeared in 1994, though almost all were on spring migration.

Year	Records	Birds
1980	7	17
1981	4	4
1982	2	2
1983	5	5
1984	10	16
1985	7	7
1986	7	11
1987	11	17
1988	6	6
1989	10	15
1990	15	30
1991	8	12
1992	6	9
1993	7	17
1994	9	23
1995	6	8
1996	13	18
1997	7	13
1998	11	11
1999	6	9
2000	11	20
2001	5	10
2002	14	27
2003	9	14
2004	5	6
2005	6	14
2006	7	15
2007	12	24
2008	13	18
2009	12	32
2010	4	4
2011	15	34

The table depicting the half-monthly distribution includes all records from 1950 to 1999 and reveals that Turnstones have occurred in every month, although only rarely earlier than mid-April or later than mid-September. In some years, the first migrants have appeared in the last week of April, but spring passage is largely concentrated in the first half of May, with very few birds in June. In the twentieth century, the largest groups recorded on spring migration were a party of six at Swarkestone Lake on 3rd May 1980 and a flock of the same number which flew north-east over Barbrook Reservoir on 15th May 1994. More recently there were flocks of eight birds at Carsington Water on 13th May 2002, 11th May 2005 and 15th May 2009, and seven at Aston-on-Trent Gravel Pits on 14th May 2006.

Returning migrants move through the county from July to September, but are most often encountered in August. During autumn passage, as in spring, parties of more than three are still noteworthy. Frost referred to gatherings of 15 at Ogston Reservoir on 22nd August 1970 and of ten at Church Wilne Reservoir on 31st August 1975 as 'exceptional'. Since the 1970s, despite an increase in sightings, the largest groups recorded in the autumn migration period have been of just five birds at Ogston Reservoir on 26th July 1986, Middleton Moor on 11th August 1993 and Carsington Water on 24th August 2011, and six at Pleasley Colliery on 28th August 2007.

Occurrences between October and March have always been infrequent and involved solitary birds, with the exception of a remarkable flock of 12 at Middleton Moor on 30th December

Month	Records	Birds	Percentage of records per month
January	1	1	0.5
	–	–	
February	–	–	1.0
	2	2	
March	–	–	0.5
	1	1	
April	1	1	5.0
	12	21	
May	60	90	35.0
	29	44	
June	4	5	1.5
	–	–	
July	6	6	11.5
	23	32	
August	43	66	31.5
	37	77	
September	20	34	9.0
	3	4	
October	2	2	1.0
	–	3	
November	3	2	2.0
	2	3	
December	2	2	1.5
	2	13	
Totals	253	409	

1979. A Turnstone at Combs Reservoir on 4th and 5th January 1996 was a rare sighting in north-west Derbyshire, and also constitutes the only record for this month. Another unusual report was of a bird first seen during a heavy storm on the evening of 3rd October 1996, by the River Derwent at Draycott, which was still present the following day, feeding along a nearby shingle path.

Turnstones rarely remain for more than a few days at any time of year, with the majority recorded on one day only. The longest stay to date involved a single bird which was present at Ogston Reservoir for at least two weeks in September 1989. More recently one remained at Carsington Water from 18th to 30th April 2003.

This species has been found at almost 30 different sites in the county since 1980, including about a dozen in the Trent Valley. Within this region, Willington Gravel Pits has been visited most regularly, with records in 17 years since 1988. Elsewhere, Ogston Reservoir has provided the largest number of sightings, with reports in ten years before 1980 and in 17 since then, while the more recently created Carsington Water has been visited almost annually from 1992 onwards.

The number of birds recorded at the principal sites in the period 1980–2011 are shown in the chart.

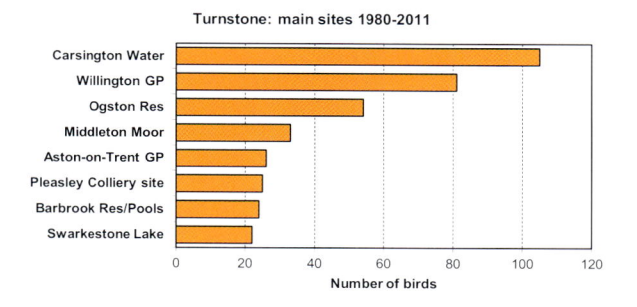

Turnstone: main sites 1980-2011

- Carsington Water
- Willington GP
- Ogston Res
- Middleton Moor
- Aston-on-Trent GP
- Pleasley Colliery site
- Barbrook Res/Pools
- Swarkestone Lake

Number of birds

There have been very occasional sightings at the reservoirs at Arnfield, Combs and Torside, and at comparatively small waters in lowland areas, including those at Carr Vale, Shirebrook Colliery, Staveley, Williamthorpe and Wyver Lane. However, by early 2013 no fewer than seven had been found as prey items of the Derby Cathedral Peregrines.

Knot
Calidris canutus
A scarce passage migrant, mainly in autumn. Rare in winter.

Whitlock considered this wader to be an occasional visitor in the nineteenth century, and gave details of four individuals that had all been shot in 1891 in the south of the county. In the first half of the twentieth century there were occurrences in 1930, 1946 and 1949, including a party of five at Egginton Sewage Farm in May 1946. There were records in only six years in the 1950s, but since 1963 Knot have been found annually, largely on autumn migration. During the period 1950 to 2011 there were 289 records in total, involving 410 birds. The respective figures for each period are listed in the table, which shows a marked increase in numbers in the 1960s, and another significant rise in the 1980s, with numbers maintained into the 2000s.

Period	Records	Birds
1950s	13	9
1960s	28	35
1970s	31	34
1980s	65	88
1990s	57	89
2000–11	95	155
Totals	289	410

The respective totals for each year from 1980 to 2011 are specified in the table, and show a maximum of 54 birds in 2011.

Year	Records	Birds
1960	2	2
1961	1	1
1962	0	0
1963	4	7
1964	2	2
1965	4	7
1966	6	7
1967	2	2
1968	2	2
1969	5	5
1970	1	1
1971	2	2
1972	3	4

Year	Records	Birds
1973	6	6
1974	2	2
1975	1	1
1976	4	5
1977	5	5
1978	2	3
1979	5	5
1980	8	8
1981	3	6
1982	4	5
1983	8	8
1984	7	10
1985	9	18
1986	2	2
1987	14	16
1988	6	9
1989	4	6
1990	4	5
1991	5	6
1992	3	6
1993	12	27
1994	5	5
1995	9	15
1996	5	6
1997	5	6
1998	7	11
1999	2	2
2000	17	22
2001	10	12
2002	7	7
2003	3	14
2004	4	4
2005	10	11
2006	5	5
2007	7	7
2008	11	11
2009	4	4
2010	4	4
2011	13	54

While the annual average over this period was eight birds, only two individuals occurred in both 1986 and 1999. A lack of suitable habitat due to high water levels at most favoured haunts may have been the major factor in 1986.

This species has been found at all times of year, though most often in August and September. The chart showing the half-monthly distribution of all records in 1960–2011 indicates that spring migration is relatively light. Moreover, sightings in March probably concern British wintering birds rather than early migrants. The highest numbers in spring have been nine flying north-east over Willington Gravel Pits on 22nd May 1993, and an earlier record quoted by Frost of six at Staunton Harold Reservoir on 11th June 1966. The most recent large flock, and the county maximum, was of 25 birds at Middleton Moor on 7th May 2011.

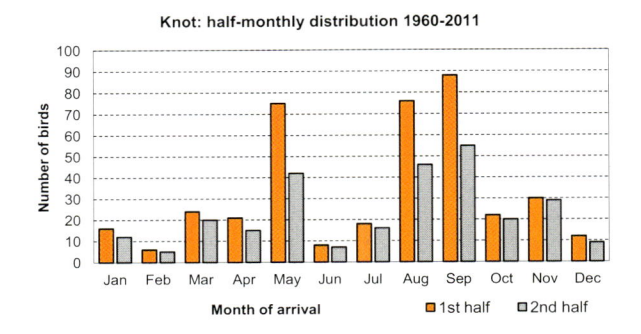

Knot: half-monthly distribution 1960-2011

Return passage takes place from early July, and reaches an obvious peak between mid-August and mid-September. The largest gatherings in autumn have all occurred within this period, as follows: seven at Middleton Moor on 25th August 1985, five at Willington Gravel Pits on 1st September 1993 and 17 at Carsington Water on 26th August 2011.

There has been a significant proportion of records in October and November (almost 20% in total). Four birds flying south at Foremark Reservoir in a blizzard on 13th December 1981 represented the first record for that month, though subsequently there have been three further instances, possibly involving later autumn stragglers rather than wintering birds. Frost listed January as one of the peak months, yet since 1977 there have been only two sightings, both occurring in late January 1987.

The majority of reports (80%) throughout the year relate to solitary birds. Visits are normally short-lived and rarely exceed a week. Exceptions have been an individual which remained at Sutton Scarsdale from 17th to 27th September 1979, one at Ogston Reservoir from 14th to 21st August 1992, and another which was present at Carsington Water from 1st to 16th November 2003. Knot are mostly encountered in their somewhat drab non-breeding plumage, but a few have been seen in the far more colourful breeding attire, mainly in May but occasionally as late as August. At least 20 summer-plumaged individuals have been recorded in Derbyshire since 1980.

The vast majority of Knot have been observed on the ground, with only a handful of birds identified purely in flight. Since 1980, Ogston Reservoir has been the most favoured location for this species with records in 20 years, followed closely by Middleton Moor with records in 18 years. Willington Gravel Pits is the most regularly visited site in south Derbyshire with sightings in 15 years.

Although this wader has been noted occasionally at several other localities in the Trent Valley, exclusively gravel pits, sewage farms and reservoirs, this region has only about one third of the overall total of about 30 sites where Knot have been found since 1980. Carsington Water has been visited in most years since 1994, while there have been records from at least ten waters in north-east Derbyshire. Apart from those at Middleton Moor, the only recent Peak District sightings have been at Barbrook Reservoir, Peak Dale, Bakewell (see below) and Combs Reservoir, although Frost also referred to earlier occurrences at Bakewell and Chinley.

An interesting record concerns the mostly skeletal remains of a first-winter Knot, probably killed by a predator, which were discovered in a field near Ashbourne Sewage Farm on 19th March 1979. Another was found dying as a road casualty at Bole Hill, near Bakewell, on 23rd September 2008.

Ruff
Calidris pugnax
An uncommon passage migrant. Rare in winter.

Evidence of Ruffs occurring in Derbyshire has been documented as far back as the eighteenth century. Writing in 1789, Pilkington stated that they had been found on Sinfin Moor, although this tract of marshland was apparently drained soon afterwards. Whitlock believed that this species would have been encountered fairly regularly on migration along the Trent Valley in what he referred to as 'former days'. However, he thought that they had been rarely seen in the nineteenth century and gave details of only two such occasions. The first concerned a pair killed near Burton upon Trent in the summer of 1857, while the second was of a female shot at Egginton Sewage Farm in 1892.

During the first half of the twentieth century, sightings remained relatively infrequent, but since 1955 this wader has been reported annually, predominantly on passage, and almost exclusively at wetland sites in the county. In the period 1950–2011 there were 885 records in total, involving 2024 birds, and the respective figures for each decade are shown in the table.

Period	Records	Birds
1950s	26	49
1960s	125	363
1970s	167	324
1980s	186	419
1990s	179	487
2000–11	202	382
Totals	885	2024

The table reveals a dramatic rise in numbers in the 1960s, followed by a steadier, but largely sustained increase in subsequent periods before a decline in the 2000s. The Ruff became re-established as a breeding species in Britain during this period, although the proliferation of sightings locally is probably far more attributable to much greater observer coverage, particularly at reservoirs and gravel pits.

The data in the table of annual occurrences from 1980 to 2009 provides a more detailed analysis, revealing considerable fluctuations within a comparatively stable long-term trend. In certain years, some interpolation has been necessary, as a number of records in the *Derbyshire Bird Report* have been summarized. Although the annual average in this period has been approximately 43 birds, in 1998 there were at least 89 individuals, including the largest gathering in the county to date, when 44 birds were present at Willington Gravel Pits on 2nd September. Ruffs are usually reported from about eight localities each year, but in 1992 there were only nine records, involving a total of 29 birds, all of which were seen at either Willington Gravel Pits or Carsington Water. 2005 accounted for even fewer, with only seven records totalling 13 birds, after which the situation improved somewhat.

The chart, representing the half-monthly distribution of all records during 1950–99, indicates that, although there have been sightings at all times of the year, this wader is primarily a passage migrant which is most numerous in autumn.

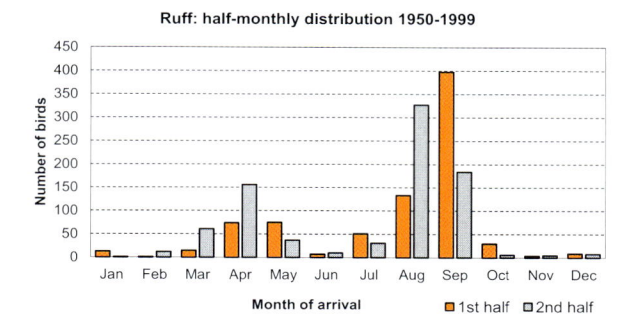

Year	Records	Birds
1980	22	50
1981	19	36
1982	17	28
1983	14	26
1984	18	40
1985	17	77
1986	15	26
1987	25	76
1988	19	27
1989	20	33
1990	25	62
1991	17	51
1992	9	29
1993	16	54
1994	21	56
1995	20	31
1996	27	46
1997	19	28
1998	14	89
1999	11	41
2000	28	65
2001	17	45
2002	25	65
2003	17	32
2004	19	24
2005	7	13
2006	10	21
2007	13	20
2008	12	19
2009	11	15
2010	36	48
2011	7	15

Ruff: half-monthly distribution 1950-1999

Ruffs on spring migration are usually first reported during the second half of March and their numbers tend to peak about a month later. The remainder have normally moved through by the end of May, but on a few occasions one or two individuals have been seen in June. The biggest gathering of spring migrants was 36 at Middleton Moor on 18th April 1985, whereas the next largest was 13 at Willington Gravel Pits on 19th April 1999. Smaller parties of up to seven Ruffs have been noted in most years and there was an exceptional influx in April 1987 when over 40 birds in total were reported throughout the county.

Return passage, which commences in July and often continues through to October, is usually at its most intense between mid-August and mid-September. Almost 40% of all records, and nearly 45% of all birds, have occurred within this specific period. However, even though passage is undoubtedly much greater in autumn, flock sizes are, on average, only slightly larger than those in spring. Apart from the previously mentioned county maximum of 44 in September 1998, there have been relatively few double-figure counts and none of more than 20 birds.

Despite a slight, but perceptible, increase in occurrences between November and February in recent years, this species is still only a rare winter visitor to Derbyshire. While most sightings have been of one or two birds, at Willington Gravel Pits six were present on 15th January 1995 and eight were recorded on 18th November 2000. Up to three Ruffs were also reported fairly regularly at this site from December 2000 until March 2001, although such instances of overwintering at a specific locality are exceptional. What may have been the same group of six was at Carr Vale on 31st December 2005, and at Butterley Reservoir and Aston-on-Trent Gravel Pits on the following day.

Visits at any time of year have always been relatively brief, normally lasting no more than two or three days. Very occasionally birds have lingered for over a week, including two at Willington Gravel Pits from 26th August to 10th September 1993. However, the longest continuous stay has been that of exactly a month by an individual at Drakelow Nature Reserve, from 14th August to 14th September 1972.

Since 1980 this wader has been found at about 40 sites in the county, with a predictable concentration of occurrences in the Trent Valley. Historically, Frost suggested that Egginton Sewage Farm, 'where the wet fields have formed an ideal habitat for them', was the locality most often frequented by Ruffs. Despite significant changes in land use over recent decades, sightings have continued here, though far less regularly. From 1981 to 2011, Willington Gravel Pits has become established as the most favoured location, having been visited annually. Outside the Trent Valley, Ruffs have been reported most often at Ogston Reservoir on several occasions prior to 1980 and in 19 of the following 27 years. Carsington Water, since its establishment in 1992, has had records in every year except 1998 and 2009.

With the notable exception of Middleton Moor, which has had records in 17 years in the period 1980–2009 (but none since 2002), sightings at upland waters are unusual. Arnfield and Barbrook Reservoirs and the lagoons at Peak Dale are the only other wetland sites where Ruffs have been reported, although singles were seen on pasture at Peak Forest on 3rd September 1979 and at Alicehead on 23rd March 1996. Another occasion when this species was found away from water was on 17th April 1987, when a party of six frequented Ashbourne Airfield.

An unusual event was witnessed at Ogston Reservoir on 18th May 1973 when a reeve, having been flushed by a fisherman, flew almost 100m out into the reservoir and swam for 20 minutes with Mallards.

Broad-billed Sandpiper
Calidris falcinellus
A very rare vagrant.

Broad-billed Sandpipers are annual visitors to the British Isles, particularly to the east coast in spring. By the end of 2011 there had been 239 British records (Hudson *et al*. 2012). The only Derbyshire record was of a worn, moulting adult which accompanied six Dunlin at Aston-on-Trent Gravel Pits on 18th July 2004. After 30 minutes observation the waders were flushed by a party of Common Terns, and the Broad-billed Sandpiper and a Dunlin departed to the north-west. This was one of seven national records for 2004 and also the second seen in the Midlands that year (Key & James 2005b).

Curlew Sandpiper
Calidris ferruginea
An uncommon passage migrant.

This attractive wader was first recorded in the county in September 1905 at Egginton Sewage Farm. The next sighting was not until 1952, and although there were further records in 17 of the following 25 years, occurrences were still irregular (Frost). Since then, Curlew Sandpipers have appeared in every year, with the exception of 1983, 1984, 1986 and 2005. During the period 1950–2011 a total of 158 records, involving 394 birds, was documented and the respective figures for each period are shown in the table.

Period	Records	Birds
1950s	4	8
1960s	16	39
1970s	16	26
1980s	24	68
1990s	65	177
2000–11	33	76
Totals	158	394

These figures reveal a significant increase in numbers towards the end of twentieth century, although this trend was not sustained in the 2000s. A more erratic pattern of occurrences latterly is evident in the annual totals from 1980 to 2009.

Year	Records	Birds
1980	4	5
1981	1	12
1982	3	5
1983	–	–
1984	–	–
1985	3	13
1986	–	–
1987	4	5
1988	6	24
1989	3	4
1990	10	32
1991	10	31
1992	2	2
1993	7	14
1994	1	1
1995	7	17
1996	15	49
1997	1	1
1998	6	13
1999	6	17
2000	4	10
2001	5	13
2002	3	5
2003	4	4
2004	3	10
2005	–	–
2006	4	8
2007	1	1
2008	3	3
2009	1	1
2010	2	4
2011	3	17

The migration route of this species can be significantly influenced by adverse weather conditions, most notably strong westerly winds, and this may explain its absence or extreme rarity in certain years. For instance, there were no records in 1986, when the turbulent remains of hurricane 'Charley' affected Britain during the autumn. By contrast in 1996, 49 Curlew Sandpipers were recorded in the county, the majority occurring during anticyclonic conditions in September. This also coincided with a strong passage of Little Stints along the east coast of England (Nightingale & Allsopp 1997).

In the UK and Derbyshire, this wader is encountered almost exclusively on autumn migration. The chart, which represents the half-monthly distribution of all records in 1950–99 in Derbyshire, reflects the national trend.

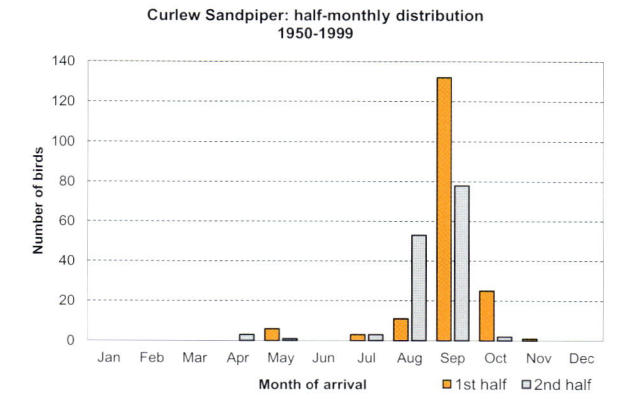

Curlew Sandpiper: half-monthly distribution 1950-1999

Less than 7% of all sightings were in spring, with an earliest arrival date in that period of 17th April (1963), when three were seen at Ogston Reservoir. All other spring records were in May and involved short visits by single birds.

During this period, autumn passage was noted between the extreme dates of 13th July (1963) and 17th November (1991). The majority of occurrences were in September, with a distinct peak in the first half of the month. The largest gathering was of 16 at Clay Mills Gravel Pits on 19th September 1967. The only other double-figure flocks were 12 at Middleton Moor in September 1981 and 11 at Egginton Sewage Farm in September 1996. Parties of up to nine were not uncommon, although nearly half of all records were of single birds.

Curlew Sandpipers have sometimes remained in the county for several days in the autumn. The longest stay involved an individual present at Derby Sewage Farm from 2nd to 29th September 1979. On a very few occasions, adults in their stunning brick-red breeding plumage have been reported, either on spring passage or as early return passage migrants in July, but from August onwards virtually all sightings have been of immature birds.

This species has been recorded at the following 20 sites in Derbyshire: Ambaston Gravel Pits, Aston-on-Trent Gravel Pits, Barbrook Reservoir, Carsington Water, Clay Mills Gravel Pits (now in Staffordshire), Derby Sewage Farm, Drakelow Nature Reserve, Egginton Sewage Farm, Elvaston Quarry, Long Eaton Gravel Pits, Middleton Moor, Ogston Reservoir, Pleasley Colliery site, Pride Park Sanctuary, Rother Valley Country Park (now in South Yorkshire), Sawley Water Meadows, Staunton Harold Reservoir, Swarkestone, Westhouses Flash and Willington Gravel Pits.

Although the majority of the above sites lie within the Trent Valley, Ogston Reservoir and Middleton Moor have been the most regularly visited locations since 1980, with 14 and 13 records respectively since 1980. In the Trent Valley, Curlew Sandpipers have been found most often at Willington Gravel Pits, particularly since the late 1980s. The chart shows the total numbers for each of the five main sites, 1980–2011.

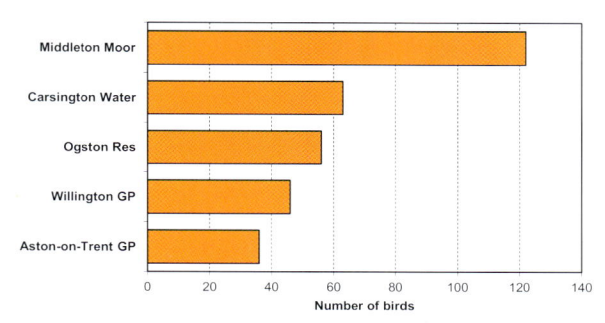

Curlew Sandpiper: main sites 1980-2011

An unprecedented sequence of spring passage records occurred at Aston-on-Trent Gravel Pits from 2000 to 2003, involving eight individuals between the extreme dates of 8th April (2003) and 2nd June (2002).

Temminck's Stint
Calidris temminckii
A rare passage migrant, mainly in spring.

There have been 23 records, involving 27 birds, as follows:

Year	Location and date
1967	Westhouses, one on 25th September
1969	Breaston, two on 25th–26th May
1971	Drakelow Nature Reserve, one from 25th to 28th May
1974	Drakelow Nature Reserve, one from 16th to 18th May
1975	Ogston Reservoir, an adult from 16th to 21st August
1979	Drakelow Nature Reserve, one on 11th May
1980	Creswell, one on 14th May
1981	Drakelow Nature Reserve, one on 31st May
1985	Staveley, one on 15th May
1993	Shirebrook Colliery, one on 24th May
1994	Ambaston Gravel Pits, one on 13th May
1994	Willington Gravel Pits, two, which departed to the north-east on 18th May
1998	Carsington Water, one on 11th–12th May
1999	Pleasley Colliery, one on 19th May
1999	Willington Gravel Pits, one from 20th to 22nd May
1999	Willington Gravel Pits, one on 27th May
2004	Aston-on-Trent Gravel Pits, one on 20th May
2005	Aston-on-Trent Gravel Pits, one on 14th May
2005	Aston-on-Trent Gravel Pits, one on 17th May
2005	Carsington Water, one on 18th May
2006	Aston-on-Trent Gravel Pits, one on 7th–8th May
2008	Willington Gravel Pits, two on 27th–28th May
2009	Pleasley Colliery, two from 13th to 15th May

Analysis by periods and months is shown:

Period	Records	Birds
1950s	–	–
1960s	2	3
1970s	4	4
1980s	3	3
1990s	7	8
2000–11	7	9
Totals	23	27

Month	Records	Birds
January	–	–
February	–	–
March	–	–
April	–	–
May	21	25
June	–	–
July	–	–
August	1	1
September	1	1
October	–	–
November	–	–
December	–	–
Totals	23	27

Although the first sighting was in autumn, on 25th September (1967), this small and unobtrusive wader has subsequently been recorded almost exclusively on spring passage to its breeding grounds in northern regions, with a notable concentration of occurrences between 7th and 21st May. The majority of visits have been short-lived, and it may be no coincidence that the only other autumn record also involves the longest stay by a Temminck's Stint, an adult at Ogston Reservoir from 16th to 21st August (1975). Just over half of all records have come from gravel pits in the Trent Valley.

Sanderling
Calidris alba
An uncommon passage migrant, mainly in spring. Rare in winter.

Whitlock thought that Sanderlings seldom appeared as far inland as Derbyshire, but felt able to include the species on the county list on the strength of three individuals shot at Walton-on-Trent on an unspecified date in the 1870s. Frost commented that there were many records from 1943 onwards and that Sanderlings had occurred annually since 1960, especially in spring. During the period 1950–2011 there were 450 records in total, involving 944 birds. The table reveals that numbers rose sharply in the 1960s and that the upward trend continued steadily and perceptibly to the end of the twentieth century and has been maintained in the 2000s.

Period	Records	Birds
1950s	8	13
1960s	36	101
1970s	53	114
1980s	88	143
1990s	118	264
2000–11	147	309
Totals	450	944

Approximately half of all records have concerned single birds, although groups of up to five are not uncommon. Larger numbers are still relatively infrequent, and the county maximum remains 25, which were seen together in a flooded field at Breaston on 23rd May 1969. In the majority of years, fewer than 30 birds in total are recorded, though at least 73 appeared in 1994. This featured an exceptional occurrence of over 50 Sanderlings on 15th May, including flocks of 24 at Middleton Moor and 17 at Willington Gravel Pits. In stark contrast, only five individuals were seen in 1992. The table, which lists the yearly totals from 1980 to 2011, provides a more detailed account of the annual fluctuations which are contained within the overall trend of increasing numbers.

Year	Records	Birds
1980	11	15
1981	5	6
1982	7	11
1983	3	3
1984	7	15
1985	7	15
1986	6	8
1987	18	35
1988	12	12
1989	12	23
1990	6	11
1991	16	32
1992	4	5
1993	10	21
1994	15	73
1995	18	36
1996	14	22
1997	10	25
1998	12	19
1999	13	20
2000	11	28
2001	8	27
2002	18	35
2003	11	18
2004	11	36
2005	11	14
2006	9	26
2007	8	11
2008	14	32
2009	16	30
2010	10	19
2011	20	31

The chart, which summarizes the half-monthly distribution of all occurrences from 1950 to 1999 inclusive, indicates that Sanderlings are primarily birds of spring passage in Derbyshire, most likely to be encountered during May, and just over half of all records have been in this month, including almost every party of more than five birds.

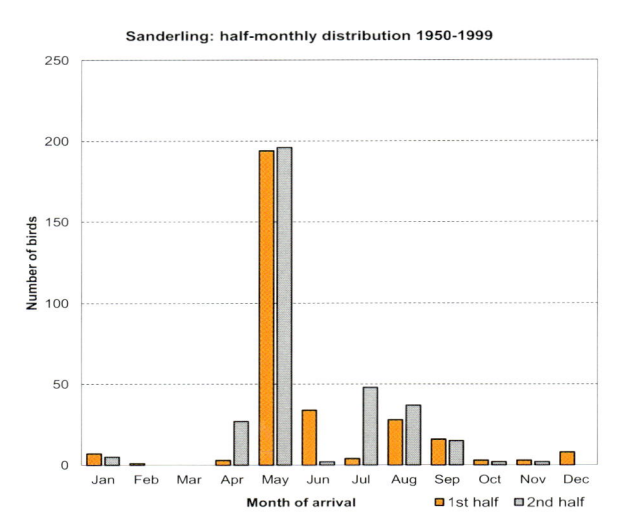

Return passage is much less evident and tends to peak as early as the second half of July, possibly as a result of this wader's short breeding season in the high Arctic. Even by September, autumn migrants are quite scarce, with only very occasional stragglers appearing in October.

There have been a small number of occurrences between November and February, most notably a party of seven at Middleton Moor on 1st December 1985. Although March was the only month without any sightings throughout the second half of the twentieth century, there have already been two records since the millennium: one was present at Willington Gravel Pits on 11th March 2002 and another was seen at Aston-on-Trent Gravel Pits on 30th March 2003.

In keeping with their habit of appearing always to be in a great hurry, these energetic waders rarely linger for more than a day or two. However, the longest documented stay is of ten days, by one at Carsington Water from 10th to 19th April 1996.

Frost commented that Drakelow was the most regular calling place in the county for Sanderlings, but during the period from 1980 to 2011 Middleton Moor has proved to be the most favoured location, with records in all except four years. However, the majority of sightings are still at wetland sites in lowland areas, especially those in the Trent Valley. Approximately half of the 27 locations where this wader has been found since 1980 lie within this region, including Willington Gravel Pits which has been visited in 20 years since 1980. Elsewhere, following the first occurrence in December 1991, there have been records almost every year at Carsington Water from 1994 onwards, and regular appearances at Ogston Reservoir also. The number of birds recorded at the principal sites are shown in the chart.

The first record in north-west Derbyshire was at Arnfield Reservoir in May 1986, and there have been two subsequent sightings there and also three at Combs Reservoir. The remaining sites outside the Trent Valley where Sanderlings have been seen since 1980 are Barbrook Reservoir, Carr Vale, Errwood Reservoir, Pleasley Colliery, Poolsbrook, Rother Valley County Park (now in South Yorkshire), Shirebrook, Staveley and Williamthorpe.

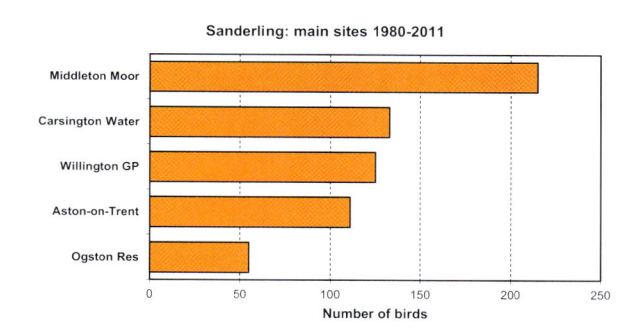

Dunlin
Calidris alpina
A scarce summer visitor to high moorland in the Peak District. A fairly common passage migrant and winter visitor elsewhere.

The Dunlin is a scarce breeding bird of the wetter Peak District moorlands, but it is also a fairly common visitor to wetlands elsewhere on migration and in winter, most often to gravel pits and reservoirs in the Trent Valley.

Although Whitlock suspected that it bred in or near Derbyshire, this was not proved until the mid-1930s, and its numerical status as a breeding bird in the county remained uncertain for many years thereafter (Frost). A survey of the Peak District moorlands in 1970–72 estimated a Derbyshire contingent of about 93 pairs in a population of about 158 pairs (Yalden 1974). Regular annual counts along a section of the Pennine Way from Snake Summit to Mill Hill suggested that there were generally about eight pairs there during the 1980s (Yalden 1986b), but a partial survey of moorland birds by the RSPB in 1981 found evidence of some decline, to 48 pairs in areas where the earlier survey had found 75 pairs (Campbell 1982). It was not clear whether this represented a genuine decline, or was a consequence of different surveyors being involved.

Dunlins are very secretive when breeding, being much harder to survey than the Golden Plover, with which they often associate. However, a resurvey by the JNCC (Brown & Shepherd 1991) found only 32 pairs in the same area, and an overall figure for the Peak District of 88 pairs, of which only 38 pairs were in Derbyshire. Carr and Middleton (2004) found 67 pairs in the Peak District in 2004 (only 24 of them in Derbyshire); a decline of 24% from 1990 and 58% since 1974. Annual counts along the Pennine Way also found fewer pairs in the 1990s than formerly, usually three to six pairs, but ranging from none in 1997 to ten in 1993, and 11 in 2001 and 2004.

The Dunlin has always been associated with the wetter expanses of cotton-grass, from the Ashop Valley northwards across Bleaklow to the Longdendale Moors, and the most likely explanation of the decline is that a series of drought years, notably 1975, 1976, 1995 and 1996 have reduced the pools along with cranefly populations on which the birds depend. Sites such as Axe Edge and Ringinglow, never host to more than a few pairs, have been affected by drainage schemes, although these may now be reversed under schemes financed by the Environmentally Sensitive Area programme.

This is essentially the range and status determined by the Derbyshire BBS (1995–99). During this five-year period, breeding was proved in only three tetrads, probable in seven and possible in a further two tetrads.

While the level of coverage may have been less intensive than during the earlier surveys, the decline of this species over recent decades seems to be confirmed by its findings. The only other area where breeding has been strongly suspected since 1980 is Big Moor, in 1982 and 1984, although a bird in breeding plumage was seen on Beeley Moor on 12th June 1985.

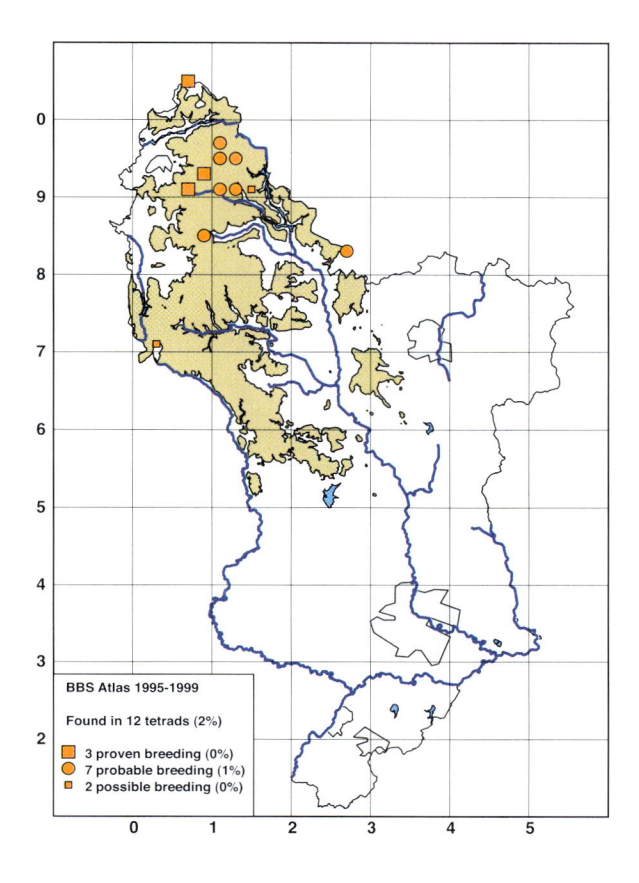

Frost commented that 'there are occasionally records from breeding sites as early as February and as late as November'. During recent years, the earliest date that display has been observed is 8th April (1995) involving two birds on Axe Edge, while the latest record on high moorland was at Upper Derwent on 15th October (1994). Nevertheless, the breeding season is rather short, since Dunlins do not normally appear on the moors until late April (when Golden Plovers are already well into incubation) and they have usually left by mid-July. However, both species have chicks for a relatively brief period in late May and early June, and this is when Dunlins earn their traditional nickname of 'plover's page' as they frequently stand close to alarming Golden Plovers and follow behind them when they fly. It is assumed that the Dunlins are taking advantage of their neighbour's watchfulness, but their attentions are certainly resented, and while they have young chicks in particular, the plovers strive to drive the Dunlin away. It is not clear whether they are seen as endangering the plover chicks by advertising their presence (the plover parents do this very effectively themselves) or as rivals for the chicks' food (Yalden & Yalden 1990).

Outside the breeding season, and particularly during the main passage periods, this wader may be encountered at a wide variety of wetland sites across the county, favouring those with muddy expanses or margins. Dunlins are generally most numerous on autumn migration between July and November, with the largest flocks usually comprising 20 to 30 birds. Paradoxically, some of the biggest gatherings have occurred in spring, including 90 at Staunton Harold Reservoir on 25th April 1969. This phenomenon is also apparent in the list detailing reports of flocks of more than 50 recorded since 1980.

In addition, 71 were recorded at Middleton Moor on 28th August 1993 but this relates to a series of flocks and groups moving through the site over several hours.

Year	Date	Birds	Location
1982	3rd May	59	Middleton Moor
1984	23rd March	103	New Mills
1999	10th December	250	Swadlincote
2000	8th March	350	Swadlincote

Although nationally the Dunlin is the most abundant of our shore waders in winter, it is undoubtedly scarcest in Derbyshire from December to February. In each of these months only a handful of birds may be recorded, and occasionally none at all. Small parties may sometimes turn up during spells of cold weather, but any double-figure count in winter is noteworthy. The flock of 250 at Swadlincote in December 1999 was therefore exceptional. Prior to that, the highest winter count was of 62 in several parties along the River Trent between Newton Solney and King's Mills in severe weather on 19th January 1963.

Individuals believed to be of the race $C.a.$ $alpina$ have been reported on several occasions on spring migration, mainly in May, although a party of 17 at Drakelow Nature Reserve on 7th March 1982 were probably wintering birds. Some of the population of this nominate race, which breeds in northern Scandinavia and Russia, is known to spend the winter around coastal areas of Britain, whereas the subspecies $C.a.$ $schinzii$ which nests in Britain, migrates to wintering grounds further south, probably in West Africa (1984–88 Winter Atlas). Evidence of such movement was apparent in one of only two ringing recoveries to date. This concerned a Dunlin ringed on Snake Summit in May 1974 that was taken by a bird of prey at the Coto Doñana in southern Spain in November 1980.

Purple Sandpiper
Calidris maritima
A rare passage migrant, mainly in autumn.

There are three nineteenth-century records documented by Whitlock. Writing in 1893, he knew of a specimen which had been killed 'some years ago' at Egginton Sewage Farm, two shot at the same site in the latter part of 1890, and a further bird shot on the River Doe Lea near Sutton Scarsdale in March 1891.

There were no known occurrences during the first half of the twentieth century, but beginning in 1955 there have been 22 records, all involving single birds, as follows:

Year	Location and date
1955	Ramsley Reservoir, on 30th October
1965	Barbrook Reservoir, on 22nd August
1972	Peak Dale, on 16th September
1974	Staunton Harold Reservoir, on 22nd–23rd September
1974	Barbrook Reservoir, on 5th October
1976	Long Eaton Gravel Pits, on 4th November
1977	Ogston Reservoir, on 13th–14th November
1980	Elvaston Quarry, on 3rd and 6th September
1986	Rother Valley Country Park (now in South Yorkshire), on 23rd November
1989	Egginton Sewage Farm, from 15th to 18th October
1990	Egginton Sewage Farm, an immature on 7th, 11th and 13th September
1990	Barbrook Reservoir, on 13th–14th September
1990	Church Wilne Reservoir, on 18th September
1991	Ogston Reservoir, on 29th September
1995	Middleton Moor, on 8th May
1996	Staunton Harold Reservoir, from 8th to 10th September
1997	Barbrook Reservoir, an immature on 10th September
1997	Ogston Reservoir, on 15th October
2000	Willington Gravel Pits, an immature on 20th August
2000	Barbrook Reservoir, an immature from 8th to 10th September
2001	Long Eaton Gravel Pits, on 11th September
2002	Carsington Water, on 8th–9th November

Analysis by periods and months is shown:

Period	Records/Birds
1950s	1
1960s	1
1970s	5
1980s	3
1990s	8
2000s	4
Total	22

Month	Records/Birds
January	–
February	–
March	–
April	–
May	1
June	–
July	–
August	2
September	11
October	4
November	4
December	–
Total	22

The only individual recorded on spring passage in Derbyshire was chased off by Lapwings soon after its arrival at Middleton Moor during the early evening of 8th May 1995, departing to the west. Autumn passage has been noted between the extreme dates of 20th August (2000) and 23rd November (1986) with a clear majority of sightings in September. Most visits have been very short-lived, but an immature was present at Egginton Sewage Farm for nearly a week in September 1990. Before it was largely drained in autumn 2002, Barbrook Reservoir was the most favoured site, with five records. The bird at this site in 2000 was initially found dozing on the road leading to the site, several hundred metres from the water body.

Baird's Sandpiper
Calidris bairdii
A very rare vagrant.

There are three records of this vagrant. It breeds in north-eastern Siberia, across the Arctic region of North America and in north-western Greenland, and winters in southern South America. There were 238 records in Britain to the end of 2011 (Hudson *et al*. 2012). An adult was present at Barbrook Reservoir from 9th to 12th September 1983 and was seen by many observers. Another adult, seen by two observers, was at Carsington Water on the evening of 23rd July 1996; and an adult in breeding plumage was likewise seen by two observers at Aston-on-Trent Gravel Pits on the evening of 7th June 2006.

Little Stint
Calidris minuta
An uncommon passage migrant, mainly in autumn.

The first authenticated record was of one shot by Whitlock on 21st September 1890 near the mouth of the River Erewash. There were subsequent reports in 1905, 1908 (including a flock of 12 at Egginton Sewage Farm on 26th September: Jourdain additions), 1922, 1933, 1940, 1952 and 1953 (Frost). Since 1957 this delightful little wader has occurred in every year, with the exception of 1971, 1982 and 2005. It is recorded in Derbyshire almost exclusively on return passage from breeding grounds in the Arctic tundra, with the largest numbers invariably appearing in September. During the period 1950–2011 there were 287 records, involving 727 birds, and the respective figures for each period are shown in the table.

Period	Records	Birds
1950s	8	17
1960s	28	62
1970s	58	115
1980s	60	107
1990s	82	355
2000–11	51	71
Totals	287	727

These figures reveal a trend of increasing sightings throughout the second half of the twentieth century, with a particularly high number of birds in the 1990s. In contrast, annual totals in the opening years of the twenty-first century have all been relatively low.

The data in the table of annual occurrences from 1980 to 2011 highlights 1996, when there was an unprecedented movement of Little Stints through the county during September. This peaked on September 21st when there were 17 at Ogston Reservoir, 28 at Egginton Sewage Farm, 31 at Middleton Moor, and a record flock of 49 birds at Carsington Water. There were still good numbers present at other sites two or three days later, including ten at Foremark Reservoir and 16 at Willington Gravel Pits. Virtually all of these birds were juveniles, and the exceptional numbers in Derbyshire were a reflection of autumn passage across Britain that was described as probably the best ever known for this species (Nightingale & Allsopp 1997).

There have been only two other occasions to date when more than a dozen Little Stints have been seen together. A party of 23 was at Ogston Reservoir on 18th September 1990 and a flock of 37 was at Willington Gravel Pits on 5th September 1998.

Year	Records	Birds
1980	9	11
1981	9	18
1982	–	–
1983	7	22
1984	3	4
1985	6	12
1986	5	7
1987	5	5
1988	9	15
1989	7	13
1990	15	44
1991	5	5
1992	1	3
1993	10	30
1994	10	14
1995	7	17
1996	12	165
1997	4	5
1998	14	68
1999	4	4
2000	6	8
2001	6	10
2002	4	4
2003	3	4
2004	5	10
2005	–	–
2006	4	6
2007	7	13
2008	1	1
2009	1	1
2010	6	6
2011	8	8

Although this wader is most often encountered in September, return passage has been recorded between the extreme dates of 21st July (1997) and 28th November (1997). The latter date also constitutes the latest ever sighting and was of a solitary bird at Willington Gravel Pits. Occurrences after mid-October are rare and have always involved single birds. This is evident in the chart, which depicts the half-monthly distribution of all records from 1950 to 2011.

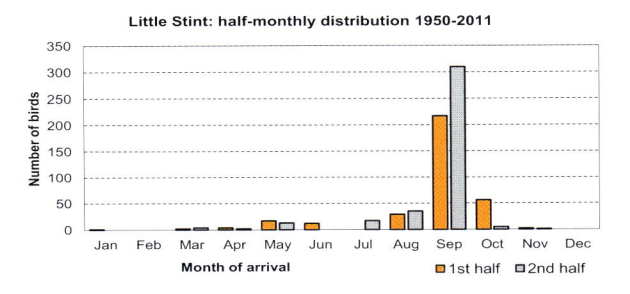

A recent winter record of one at Ogston Reservoir on 3rd January 2008 was quite exceptional. This species is also rarely found in March and April, the earliest date being 8th March (1964) when one was present at Egginton Sewage Farm. Even though most spring migrants have been reported in May there were only 13 records for this month, involving 24 birds, during the second half of the twentieth century. Interestingly, all June occurrences have been at either Carsington Water, Aston-on-Trent Gravel Pits or Middleton Moor. The latest date relating to birds on spring passage is 11th June (1995), when two were seen at the latter site.

Little Stints hardly ever remain for longer than a day or two in spring, and even in autumn very few birds stay for more than a week. However, in 1996 this species was recorded continuously from 14th September to 26th October at Carsington Water. Throughout most of this period three to six were reported, but between 18th September and 1st October at least 19 birds were present. The longest stay by an individual is of three weeks, at Egginton Sewage Farm from 24th September to 14th October 1990.

This wader has been found exclusively at wetland sites, with Middleton Moor the most regularly visited locality, having records in 17 years since 1980. Willington Gravel Pits is also a favoured haunt, with records in 16 years since 1980. During this period, Little Stints were reported at a total of 26 different sites in the county, almost half of which lay within the Trent Valley. Elsewhere, Ogston Reservoir has been the most visited location, with reports in several years prior to 1980 and in 13 since then, while the more recently established Carsington Water has had sightings of this species in virtually every year from 1994 onwards.

The numbers of individuals at the main sites from 1980 to 2011 are shown in the chart.

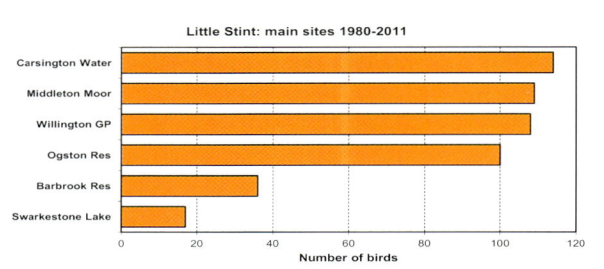

Occurrences in the Peak District, apart from those at Middleton Moor, have been documented only at Barbrook Pools and Peak Dale Quarry. Little Stints have occasionally appeared at relatively small waters in lowland areas, including Carr Vale, Old Whittington Sewage Farm, Poolsbrook, Steetley Quarry, Williamthorpe, Wyver Lane and Arkwright, Markham, Pleasley and Shirebrook Colliery sites.

Least Sandpiper
Calidris minutilla
A very rare vagrant.

Least Sandpipers breed across North America and winter from the southern USA to central South America. A moulting adult was found at Middleton Moor on the morning of 17th July 1988 and remained until 19th July. Very unusually for waders at this site, the bird favoured the grassy margins of the large lagoon, rather than the mud deltas. On the final day it spent a long time apparently dozing on a concrete block situated 3m out in the water. This was the twenty-ninth record for Britain and Ireland of this diminutive wader (Frost & Gould 1989). The total to the end of 2011 was 36 (Hudson *et al*. 2012).

Pectoral Sandpiper
Calidris melanotos
A rare vagrant, mainly in autumn.

Pectoral Sandpipers breed on the Arctic tundra of North America and northern Siberia, wintering in southern South America and Australia. They are the most common Nearctic waders occurring in the UK and they bred in Scotland in 2004.

There have been 19 Derbyshire records, all but one of single birds, as follows:

Year	Location and date
1962	Egginton Gravel Pits and Sewage Farm, one from 12th to 24th August
1975	Shipley Lake, one on 1st September
1976	Drakelow Nature Reserve, one on 25th September
1976	Elvaston Quarry, one on 26th September
1979	Sutton Scarsdale Flash, an immature from 20th September to 5th October
1983	Drakelow Nature Reserve, an immature from 25th to 29th September
1984	Elvaston Quarry, one on 7th October
1987	Middleton Moor, one on 6th May
1991	Egginton Sewage Farm, an adult male which departed to the west on 4th July
1995	Long Eaton Gravel Pits, one from 2nd to 6th August
1996	Staunton Harold Reservoir, one on 1st–2nd September
1999	Willington Gravel Pits, an immature on 12th September
2003	Wyver Lane, two immatures from 12th to 20th September
2003	Carr Vale, an immature on 16th September
2003	Ogston Reservoir, an immature on 17th September
2004	Sawley, one on 7th September, had flown in from Trent Valley Pits, Leicestershire
2005	Ogston Reservoir, an adult on 14th–15th July
2005	Carr Vale, an adult on 29th July
2010	Willington Gravel Pits, a juvenile from 19th to 25th September

Analysis by periods and months is shown.

Period	Records	Birds
1950s	–	–
1960s	1	1
1970s	4	4
1980s	3	3
1990s	4	4
2000-11	7	8
Totals	19	20

Month	Records	Birds
January	–	–
February	–	–
March	–	–
April	–	–
May	1	1
June	–	–
July	3	3
August	2	2
September	12	13
October	1	1
November	–	–
December	–	–
Totals	19	20

Approximately half of the records have been of birds present for only one day, although some individuals have remained for over a week. The longest stay was of 16 days, from 20th September to 5th October, by an immature at Sutton Scarsdale Flash in 1979.

The predominance of autumn sightings, particularly in September, corresponds with the national trend for this largely transatlantic vagrant. Extreme dates at this time of year are 2nd August (1995) and 7th October (1984). The cluster of records in September 2003, including the only instance of two birds together, at Wyver Lane, was part of an unprecedented influx of Pectoral Sandpipers throughout Britain and Ireland. Lees and Gilroy (2004) provided a summary of this invasion and speculated that the routes and wintering grounds used by this species may be more dynamic than had been previously acknowledged. Their argument also lent weight to the theory that individuals seen in spring may originate from the eastern Siberian population, possibly wintering somewhere in Africa, and this might account for occurrences in the county in May (1987) and July (1991).

Wilson's Phalarope
Phalaropus tricolor
A very rare vagrant.

Wilson's Phalaropes breed from western Canada to California and throughout the American Midwest, and winter in South America. They are rare vagrants to Britain, with 238 records up to the end of 2011 (Hudson *et al.* 2012).

The only county record was of an adult female in breeding plumage that was found at Ogston Reservoir on the evening of 23rd June 1965. It was accidentally flushed from the western bank and flew around for over ten minutes, chasing and being chased by two Snipe before resettling, to the relief of the two observers. It was seen by several other birdwatchers until early afternoon on 24th. This constituted the eighteenth British and Irish record. It was thought very likely to have been the same bird that was at Scaling Dam, Redcar and Cleveland on 20th–21st June 1965.

Red-necked Phalarope
Phalaropus lobatus
A very rare vagrant.

There have been six records of this small northern wader.

Year	Location and date
1981	Middleton Moor, an adult on 3rd July
1990	Church Wilne Reservoir, an immature from 18th to 23rd August
2000	Willington Gravel Pits, an immature briefly on 24th September
2001	Carsington Water, an immature on 10th September
2009	Stubbing Pond, an immature on 26th September
2011	Middleton Moor, a female on 24th May, before departing to the north-west

Stubbing Pond is an unlikely location for a rare wader but phalaropes obtain most of their food while swimming and have no need of muddy margins. They are pelagic for most of the year, chiefly in the tropics. A very small population breeds in north and west Scotland but otherwise they have a circumpolar breeding distribution, which includes Europe.

Grey Phalarope
Phalaropus fulicarius
A rare vagrant.

Grey Phalaropes breed throughout the Arctic tundra region. They are pelagic in winter, with most Western Palearctic birds being found off West Africa. They are usually late autumn migrants, and therefore often get caught up in storms that drive them inland. This would account for two-thirds of the Derbyshire records having occurred in September and October. They rarely linger, and only five recent birds have remained for more than one day, with one at Ladybower Reservoir from 20th to 24th September 1989 being the longest-staying individual. An unusual old record is of one that remained for a fortnight on the Cromford Canal in September 1935. The other older records came from Staveley in 1770, Little Eaton in 1861 and Draycott and Swarkestone, where two were shot on the same date, 17th October 1891. One was seen on a pond at Winster in 1906 and two on an unknown date at Heeley, Sheffield (Whitlock; Jourdain additions).

Since 1950 there have been 22 records, all of single birds.

Year	Location and date
1950	Bradwell, one on 17th September
1951	Barbrook Reservoir, one from 31st August to 2nd September
1968	Egginton Gravel Pits, one on 28th September
1969	Barbrook Reservoir, one from 30th October to 2nd November
1972	Barbrook Reservoir, one from 26th to 28th October
1973	Church Wilne Reservoir, one on 21st October arrived from the south-east and departed to the north-west
1975	Church Wilne Reservoir, one on 30th August
1981	Belper River Gardens, an adult on 11th October
1984	Ogston Reservoir, an adult on 4th November
1984	Ogston Reservoir, one on 1st December
1987	Ogston Reservoir, an immature on 16th October
1987	Middleton Moor, an immature from 18th to 21st October
1989	Ladybower Reservoir, one from 20th to 24th September
1998	Foremark Reservoir, one on 31st January
2001	Carsington Water, a first-winter from 2nd to 5th October
2001	Williamthorpe Nature Reserve, a first-winter on 6th November
2003	Codnor Park Reservoir, on 14th October
2003	Carsington Water, on 15th–16th October (possibly the same bird as above)
2004	Aston-on-Trent Gravel Pits, a winter-plumaged adult on 24th October
2007	Carsington Water, one on 10th November
2008	Carsington Water, a first-winter on 6th September
2008	Ogston Reservoir, a first-winter on 27th October

The monthly distribution of records since 1950 is:

Month	Records
January	1
August	2
September	4
October	11
November	3
December	1
Total	22

Common Sandpiper
Actitis hypoleucos
An uncommon summer visitor, mainly to the Peak District. A fairly common passage migrant. Rare in winter.

The Common Sandpiper is one of three species that are typical breeding birds on upland rivers, and therefore typical of Peak District bird communities. Long-term studies, involving colour ringing of the population inhabiting the Ashop–Alport river system, mean that it is also one of the better-known local breeding birds.

As a breeding bird, this wader favours rivers with extensive shingle beds and undercut banks, which are produced by winter spates on the hill streams. Limestone rivers rarely meet these criteria, and Common Sandpipers are much scarcer in the White Peak (in contrast to Dippers, which show the reverse preference). However, the reservoirs of the Dark Peak are even more suitable, primarily because, while full in winter and subject to wave action which undercuts the banks, drawdown in summer produces similar shingle shorelines which provide good feeding areas, while undercut banks and boulders provide hiding places for chicks. A survey of all reservoirs and rivers in the Peak District National Park in 1977–80 suggested a total Derbyshire population of about 136 pairs (Holland *et al.* 1982). More were on the reservoirs than along the rivers (77 pairs compared with 59), and only four pairs were on limestone rivers (Wye and Dove). Strongholds were the Goyt, upper Longdendale and Derwent Valleys, with their reservoir complexes. Recent maxima were 85 territories at the Derwent Valley reservoirs in 2007 and ten pairs at the Goyt Valley reservoirs in 2006.

This is essentially the breeding distribution recorded in the Derbyshire BBS (1995–99), which discovered definite breeding in 34 tetrads, probable in 11 and possible in a further 37, but it is evident that the population has shrunk, particularly from the fringes of its range.

Many traditional territories have been abandoned and this is particularly obvious along the Noe and Derwent, which have been censused for the Waterways Bird Survey (WeBS, for the BTO) since 1973. Where there were typically 7–9 pairs up to 1986, numbers then dwindled and by 1996 there were none (Falshaw *et al.* 1999). This pattern is matched by the studied population in the Ashop–Alport Valleys. There were around 21 pairs in 1977–79 when the study started, but severe late April snowstorms in 1981 affected the returning birds, just as they were reoccupying their territories, and only 14 pairs bred that year. Numbers recovered during the 1980s, but another severe snowstorm in April 1989 caused a further slump (Holland & Yalden 1991) and numbers did not recover in the 1990s; there were only eight pairs in 2000, with a partial recovery to 15 pairs by 2005 and 11 in 2006, but in 2009, three pairs represented the lowest ever number here.

The cause of the decline is not understood, but it is part of a national trend detected both in national breeding atlases and by WeBS. Derbyshire is typical in that it takes the form (and especially so) of a retreat from the periphery of the breeding

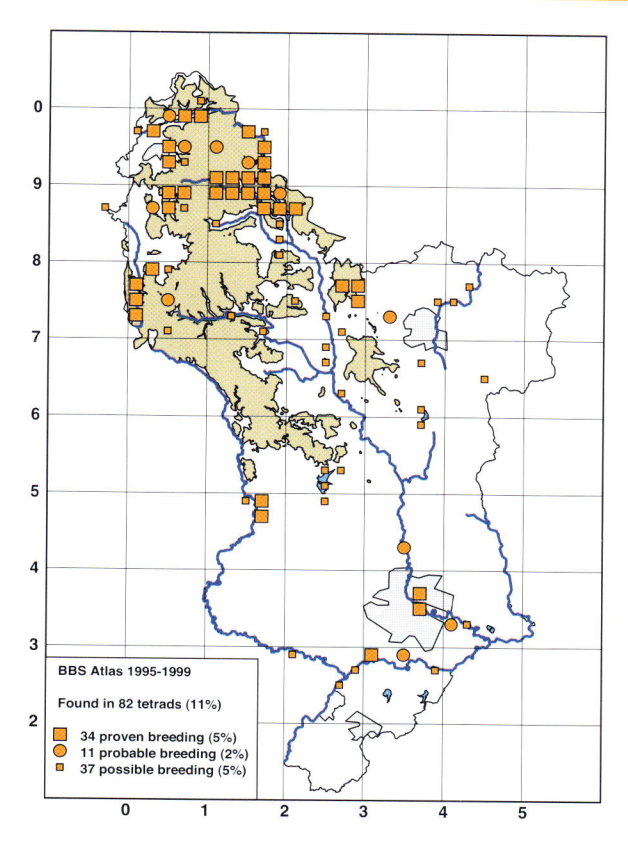

BBS Atlas 1995-1999
Found in 82 tetrads (11%)
- 34 proven breeding (5%)
- 11 probable breeding (2%)
- 37 possible breeding (5%)

range. Studies around Ladybower Reservoir have shown that the bird is sensitive to recreational disturbance, avoiding in particular the main angling beaches (Yalden 1992). In some cases, birds have retreated to breed in the forestry plantations, even rearing their chicks there. The detailed studies suggest that adult survival and breeding success have been as good in the 1990s as earlier, but recruitment of new adults has been insufficient to replace the losses. Whether this indicates that breeding elsewhere (that is, the source of Derbyshire recruits) or overwintering of younger birds in Africa has been poorer, remains to be ascertained.

The only confirmed breeding in upland Derbyshire, away from the main population in the north-west, as indicated on the distribution map, was on the River Derwent at Chatsworth, and the reservoirs at Barbrook and Ramsley. A very few Common Sandpipers breed in most years at sites outside the Peak District, usually at gravel pits within the Trent and lower Derwent Valleys. During the five-year period of the Derbyshire BBS (1995–99), evidence of breeding was obtained in such environs at Willington, Ambaston, Chaddesden Sidings and Barrow upon Trent, as well as on the lower Dove at Mapleton. Pairs have occasionally made breeding attempts in central and north-east Derbyshire, most recently at Williamthorpe in 2004, although these have nearly always been unsuccessful. A notable exception was at Carsington Water in 1992, when two pairs raised eight young. However, all sites in lowland areas seem to have been used irregularly and by no more than three pairs in any one year.

Frost revealed that evidence of overwintering by this species was first obtained in the late 1950s, and one or two birds had been found in most subsequent winters, predominantly in the Trent Valley. Similarly, since 1980, Common Sandpipers have occasionally been encountered between November and March, usually singly, with a highest count of three together, at Willington Gravel Pits in January and March 1991.

In the period 1978–2011, the average date of arrival of the first individuals considered to be genuine migrants (rather than overwintering birds) is 8th April. Spring passage is most regularly recorded at lowland reservoirs, rivers and gravel pits from early April until late May. Parties are relatively small, normally consisting of up to four birds, although eight were present at Chaddesden Sidings Gravel Pits on 30th April 1995 and at Willington Gravel Pits in May 1993.

The more significant return passage occurs from June onwards and is generally heaviest in late July and August. However, autumn birds also tend to migrate in small groups, perhaps involving family parties, rather than in the larger flocks which are favoured by some other waders. Nevertheless, double-figure counts are reported almost every year at one or two localities in southern Derbyshire. The largest gathering since 1980 has been of 25 at Aston-on-Trent Gravel Pits on 27th July 2003, while counts of 20 or more were made at Willington Gravel Pits on four separate occasions between 1989 and 1995. Outside the Trent Valley, the greatest number at a single site in recent years has been 18 at Carsington Water on 18th July 2011. There is an earlier maximum of 21 at Ogston Reservoir on 25th July 1971, but the largest count of passage birds in the county was of 30 at Drakelow Nature Reserve in August 1965. Although overall numbers diminish during September, Common Sandpipers are still relatively widespread throughout this month, but only a few individuals linger into October.

There has been a relatively large number of ringing recoveries of this species. Almost all of the 36 records to date have resulted from the long-term breeding studies conducted by Drs P.K. Holland and D.W. Yalden. A programme of colour-ringing of birds in the main study areas has generated many sightings and recoveries. While most of the 'controls' have occurred close to the original place of ringing, there have been several reported from much further afield. In addition to an unfortunate locally ringed juvenile which was taken by a raptor at Twyford, Berkshire, all foreign recoveries have been in accordance with a southerly migration to wintering grounds in Africa, with two recoveries in France and one each in Portugal and Spain. The longest distance recorded has been just over 2000km and involved an adult ringed at Glossop in July 1977, which was trapped almost two years later at Nador, Morocco. The record for longevity is currently held by a 15-year-old bird, which was ringed as a chick in 1992 on the northern arm of Ladybower Reservoir, colour-ringed in the Ashop in 1993, and resighted every year to 2007 on the western arm of Ladybower Reservoir.

An unusual sighting was of a bird which landed briefly on the back of a Mute Swan at Ogston Reservoir on 10th May 1979.

Spotted Sandpiper
Actitis macularius
A very rare vagrant.

There have been three records, all relatively recent. A lone observer found a juvenile at Willington Gravel Pits on 28th September 1999 at 1500hrs, but it was flushed by a vehicle at 1545hrs and not seen again (Key 2000a).

An adult in summer plumage was seen by many observers along a short stretch of the River Derwent immediately below Chatsworth House from mid-afternoon until late evening on 30th May 2000, and was the only sighting of the species in Britain during that year. Another adult, also in summer plumage and similarly well witnessed, visited Ogston Reservoir from 30th April to 1st May 2003.

Spotted Sandpipers breed throughout North America, wintering from the southern USA to central South America. There were 180 British records by the end of 2011 (Hudson *et al.* 2012).

Green Sandpiper
Tringa ochropus
An uncommon winter visitor and passage migrant, mainly in autumn.

This species is most often encountered when flushed, uttering its musical call and revealing a distinctive white rump which contrasts sharply with the almost jet-black wings. According to Whitlock, in the late nineteenth century Green Sandpipers were seen nearly every year in the Trent Valley, usually as passage migrants in July and August. Occurrences in winter were apparently also fairly regular, although there were only occasional sightings in spring. Frost stated that in the days of both Whitlock and Jourdain the majority of birds frequented rivers and streams, whereas by the second half of the twentieth century they were more likely to be found at gravel pits and sewage farms, with lesser numbers at reservoirs and other wetland sites. This species appears to favour relatively small and enclosed areas in preference to the more open shorelines of larger waters and has sometimes also been recorded at ponds and floodwater pools.

Throughout the year, the majority of birds are found within the Trent Valley, but sightings are also reported annually at several widely scattered localities in central and north-east Derbyshire. In the Peak District, where they have always been rather scarce birds, Barbrook Reservoir/Pools has been the most regularly visited site. The principal wader haunt in this region, the lagoons situated at Middleton Moor, has produced surprisingly few records of Green Sandpipers, presumably because the habitat is too 'open' for them. Other occurrences in upland areas have been mainly at reservoirs in the north-west of the county. A most unusual report concerned an individual which was flushed from a puddle on a footpath on Howden Moor, during heavy rain and in low cloud on 8th July 1988.

The majority of the Green Sandpipers which breed in Europe, mainly in the boreal regions of Fennoscandia, migrate in autumn to the Mediterranean basin and to sub-Saharan Africa, returning northwards in the spring. However, a small proportion of the population spends the winter in Britain, mostly at inland rather than coastal localities and Derbyshire lies on the northern fringe of this range (1984–88 Winter Atlas). Although this wader has been known as a regular winter visitor to the county for more than 100 years, instances of overwintering do not appear to have become commonplace until the 1970s. Subsequently, several birds have been seen throughout each winter, but it is virtually impossible to obtain an accurate estimate of the numbers involved, as individuals can be extremely mobile, moving readily from one site to another, especially in spells of hard weather.

In recent years, during the period from November to February, Green Sandpipers have been recorded at an average of about 20 separate localities. They are invariably found in lowland areas and reported most regularly at gravel pit complexes adjacent to the River Trent. Single birds are most often encountered, and there have been relatively few winter sightings of more than three birds together. A notable exception was the occurrence of four at Staveley Sewage Farm during the winters of 1987/88 and 1988/89. Since 1980, the maximum count has been six, at Willington Gravel Pits in February 1982 and at Aston-on-Trent Gravel Pits in January 1997.

There is normally a perceptible rise in numbers in March and April, which may be as a result of the arrival of early spring migrants before the departure of wintering birds. However, spring passage is not heavy, and the largest gatherings during these two months have been only seven, at Egginton Sewage Farm in March 1991 and Willington Gravel Pits in April 1999. This species is undoubtedly scarcest in May, being completely absent in some years, and with no more than two seen together in this month in recent years.

Green Sandpipers often appear on return passage slightly earlier than most other migrant waders. The first birds, which may well be failed breeders, usually move through the county in late June. Frost commented that the highest numbers for the year were reached in August and September, and that the sewage farms at Willington and Egginton had sometimes attracted as many as 20 birds. An even larger total was reported at Derby Sewage Farm on 21st August 1978 when at least 25 were present. However, during the period 1980–2011 the maximum count has been of 18 at Willington Gravel Pits on 23rd July 2007. The greatest number found at any site in each of these years is specified in the table. This reveals that double-figure counts have been achieved in most years, although the maximum in 2001 was only seven. The highest numbers have been recorded most often at Willington Gravel Pits, including every year from 1993 to 2002 and again in 2007–08. While August remains the peak month, the largest gatherings have sometimes occurred in July.

Year	Max count	Month	Location
1980	13	August	Drakelow Nature Reserve
1981	11	July	Drakelow Nature Reserve
1982	11	August	Willington Gravel Pits
1983	9	September	Willington Gravel Pits
1984	13	July	Drakelow Nature Reserve
1985	14	August	Derby Sewage Farm
1986	12	July	Willington Gravel Pits
1987	16	August	Derby Sewage Farm
1988	12	August	Derby Sewage Farm
1989	8	August	Egginton Sewage Farm
1990	13	July	Egginton Sewage Farm
1991	12	August	Sawley Water Meadows
1992	8	August	River Derwent at Church Wilne
1993	13	August	Willington Gravel Pits
1994	12	July/August	Willington Gravel Pits
1995	9	July	Willington Gravel Pits and Long Eaton Gravel Pits
1996	8	July	Willington Gravel Pits
1997	10	August	Willington Gravel Pits
1998	10	August	Willington Gravel Pits
1999	10	August	Willington Gravel Pits
2000	10	August	Willington Gravel Pits
2001	7	August	Willington Gravel Pits
2002	15	August	Willington Gravel Pits
2003	8	July	Aston-on-Trent Gravel Pits
2004	12	August	Barrow Gravel Pits
2005	6	August	Aston-on-Trent Gravel Pits
2006	10	July	Aston-on-Trent Gravel Pits
2007	18	July	Willington Gravel Pits
2008	11	August	Willington Gravel Pits
2009	11	July	Drakelow Nature Reserve
2010	14	August	Aston-on-Trent Gravel Pits
2011	5	August	Willington Gravel Pits

Although it is not readily apparent in these annual figures, there seems to have been a decline in the overall numbers of return passage migrants recorded in recent years. Fewer Green Sandpipers are currently reported in September than previously, which may possibly be indicative of lower levels of productivity during the breeding season. Nevertheless, in autumn this species is still found far more widely across the county than in spring or winter, and virtually all sightings in the Peak District have been made at this time of year. Since 1980, up to three birds have occasionally been recorded at wetland sites in upland areas, with an exceptional seven at Barbrook Pools on 8th August 2004, following an earlier record of nine at Ramsley Reservoir on 15th August 1976.

There is a remarkable record of a pair which summered at Willington Gravel Pits in 1999. Display and song were first noted on 23rd April, shortly after dusk, and were witnessed again in late May and June. Other behaviour also indicated that the pair was apparently 'holding territory' although no conclusive evidence of nesting was obtained before the birds were last seen at the end of July (Jackson 2000). In the same year, breeding was proved in Scotland in the Highland region and was suspected in Aberdeenshire (Ogilvie et al. 2001). The only previous confirmed breeding records of Green Sandpipers in Britain had been in Inverness-shire in 1959 and in Westmorland in 1917.

Spotted Redshank
Tringa erythropus
A scarce passage migrant, mainly in autumn. Rare in winter.

The earliest reference to this elegant wader is an undated nineteenth-century record from the River Dove (Whitlock). A specimen in the possession of Derby Museum was believed to have been obtained from the River Trent near Derby in 1905. The only other records during the first half of the twentieth century were of an individual shot in 1924 and three occurrences in the 1940s (Frost). There were five further records in the 1950s, but since 1961 this species has been recorded annually, principally on autumn migration.

During the period 1950–2011 there were 366 records involving 524 birds. The chart shows a dramatic rise in the 1960s and 1970s, followed by a steady decrease in occurrences over the next three decades.

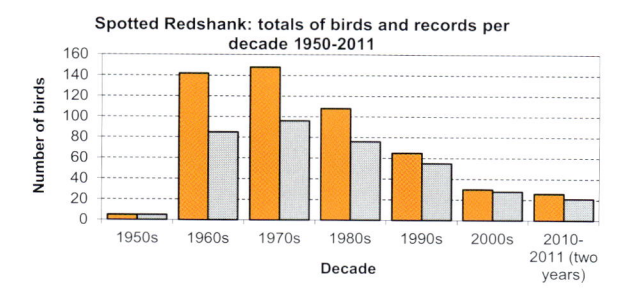

The peak year was 1978, when a total of at least 35 Spotted Redshanks was recorded. This included the largest gathering in the county, of eight birds at Sawley Water Meadows on 14th September. Until 2010 no more than 11 individuals had been reported in any year since 1982, and only single birds in 1993 and 2009, and none at all in 2007, but there was a very welcome increase with 13 birds recorded in each of 2010 and 2011.

There have been sightings in all months of the year, but this wader is rarely encountered in winter. The only instance of overwintering at one site in the county was at Drakelow Nature Reserve, where a bird remained from 10th November 1968 to 1st April 1969, although another appeared intermittently at various sites in the Trent Valley from January to April 1974. The three subsequent winter records have each involved single birds seen briefly at Newton Solney on 18th December 1977, Sinfin on 4th January 1990 and Willington Gravel Pits on 1st February 2003.

Frost commented that spring migrants, usually in April and May, had become more regular in recent years. While this trend continued during the 1980s, it has since been reversed, with only five records of spring passage in the 1990s, and none in the twenty-first century. Apart from a group of five at Rother Valley Country Park (now in South Yorkshire) on 6th April 1986 and up to four at Willington Gravel Pits in May 1967, virtually all other sightings at this time of year have involved single birds. The earliest arrival date since 1980 is 28th March (1998); before that, one was at Staunton Harold Reservoir on 20th March 1969.

Movements from mid-June onwards are more likely to relate to birds on return migration, and sometimes feature adults which are still in their resplendent 'dusky' breeding plumage. The chart showing the half monthly distribution of all records between 1960 and 2011 indicates that autumn passage is normally heaviest between mid-August and mid-September. This was most evident in the 1960s and 1970s, particularly in the Trent Valley, when parties of up to five were not unusual and the previously mentioned record gathering of eight birds occurred, in 1978, at Sawley Water Meadows. Since then the highest number at this time of year has been five at Willington Gravel Pits on 20th September 1997.

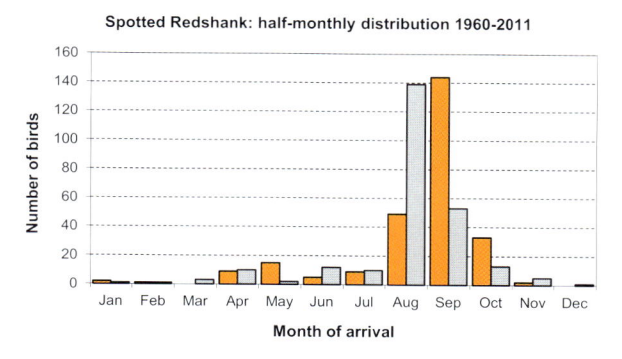

Occasionally, Spotted Redshanks continue to move through the county in October, but records in November are rare. The latest sighting in recent years is of one which was present at Egginton Sewage Farm from 22nd to 27th November 1998. Even in autumn, individuals rarely remain for more than a few days, although an immature stayed at Ogston Reservoir for over a month from 19th September to 26th October 1989.

Since 1980, this wader has been reported from over 30 localities in Derbyshire, with a predictable concentration of sightings in the Trent Valley, and especially at well-watched wetland haunts such as gravel pits and reservoirs. Willington Gravel Pits has been visited most regularly, having records in 18 recent years. In the Peak District, Middleton Moor has records in 13 years since 1980, but Barbrook and Ramsley Reservoirs are the only other upland sites where this species has been found. Elsewhere in the county, Ogston Reservoir, which has been visited fairly regularly since the early 1960s, has records in 11 recent years and Carsington Water has been visited in 12 years since its creation in 1992. The remaining localities outside the Trent Valley where Spotted Redshanks have occurred are Belper, Carr Vale, Codnor, Langley Mill Flashes, Mercaston Sand Pits, Netherthorpe Flash, Pleasley Colliery site, Rother Valley Country Park, Staveley, Sutton Scarsdale Flash, Williamthorpe and Wyver Lane.

Greenshank
Tringa nebularia
An uncommon passage migrant, mainly in autumn. Rare in winter.

Whitlock, who gave details of several records in the nineteenth century from various parts of the county, regarded Greenshanks as occasional visitors. Frost commented that increased observation had revealed these elegant and rather vocal waders to be regular passage migrants in both spring and autumn. While this remains a generally valid description of their occurrence, there has been one significant change in status in recent years. Until the mid-1990s, this species had been recorded in winter on only two occasions: one frequented the Trent Valley from December 1968 to February 1969, another was seen at Brailsford on 8th February 1976 and two were present at Sawley Water Meadows on 9th December 1990. Following the next sighting, at Hurst Reservoir on 18th January 1995, one or two Greenshanks have been found annually in winter, almost exclusively at gravel pits and reservoirs in the Trent Valley, and often commuting between adjacent sites.

This development may have been encouraged by a succession of mild winters. It is now believed that the bulk of the population which breeds in Scotland also overwinters in Britain and Ireland, having a predominantly westerly distribution and favouring estuaries and small creeks in coastal areas (1984–88 Winter Atlas). Since 'Scottish' Greenshanks have usually returned to their breeding grounds by early April, it is likely that the spring migrants occasionally seen in Derbyshire in March are drawn from this population. However, the main movement through the county takes place from late April to early June and doubtless involves birds migrating to Scandinavia.

During the period to 2011, Greenshanks have been reported on spring passage at an average of about six localities per annum. In several years fewer than ten have occurred, but in 1992 and 2000 over 30 birds were recorded. At this time of year, most visits are short-lived with many birds observed flying over, their distinctive and far-carrying calls often attracting attention before they are seen. Parties of more than three are unusual and the largest spring gatherings since 1980 have been of nine birds at Carsington Water and Willington Gravel Pits in May 2000. These equalled the previous maximum recorded at Egginton Sewage Farm on 31st May 1963.

Return passage is invariably much heavier and occurrences are more widespread. Since 1980 this species has been reported at an average of 20 localities in the county each autumn. The first sightings are often made in late June, although numbers do not normally peak until August or September, with only occasional stragglers found in October and November. Autumn migration is a more leisurely affair and gatherings are generally larger than those in spring. While there are regular reports involving three to six birds and occasionally parties of up to 12, higher counts are exceptional. There have been only six such instances since 1980: at Ogston Reservoir, 13 on 8th August and 17 on 25th August 1984; at Aston-on-Trent Gravel Pits, 13 on 31st August 1998; at Ogston Reservoir, 19 on 21st September 1999; at Middleton Moor, 13 on 20th September 2000; and at Willington Gravel Pits, 15 on 15th August 2010.

During this period, Willington Gravel Pits and Carsington Water were the only other localities where gatherings of more than ten birds were reported. The largest total anywhere in the county, that of 19 at Ogston Reservoir in September 1999, was equal to the previous maximum in autumn, which was recorded near Burton upon Trent in August 1976 (Frost).

Throughout both spring and autumn migration, the majority of Greenshanks occur in lowland areas of east and south Derbyshire, being found most often at gravel pits and reservoirs in the Trent Valley area. They may also be encountered alongside rivers and at relatively small waters, such as those created by subsidence or flooding. Sightings in the Peak District have been made at several widely scattered wetland sites, but most frequently at Middleton Moor. Other localities within this region which have been visited on a regular basis are Barbrook Reservoir/Pools, where a maximum of five birds has been recorded, and Combs Reservoir, where up to three birds have occasionally been present in autumn.

An individual at Drakelow Nature Reserve was observed to catch 22 small fish during a 20-minute feeding spell on 24th September 1985. Another interesting record is of a bird at Derby Sewage Farm, which frequently uttered snatches of song on 4th September 1987.

Lesser Yellowlegs
Tringa flavipes
A very rare vagrant.

Lesser Yellowlegs is one of the more regularly occurring Nearctic waders to visit the British Isles, with 328 records by the end of 2011 (Hudson *et al.* 2012). Most have occurred between August and October. It breeds in Alaska and Canada, and winters in the southern USA and in Central and South America.

There have been two Derbyshire records. The first was of a moulting adult, which was discovered at 0830hrs on 22nd August 1998 at Carr Vale, and was seen by many observers until it departed to the north-west at 1905hrs on the same day. This record represented approximately the eleventh for the Midlands region (Beevers 1999a).

The second record concerned one that was observed for about five minutes at Willington Gravel Pits on 29th May 2011. This bird was relocated at Uttoxeter Quarry, Staffordshire (close to the Derbyshire border) later on the same day and remained there until 31st May.

Wood Sandpiper
Tringa glareola
A scarce passage migrant, mainly in autumn. Very rare in winter.

The only record from the nineteenth century was of an immature shot near Breadsall in September 1885 (Jourdain additions). The next occurrences were not until the 1940s (two records) and the 1950s (five records), but since 1962 Wood Sandpipers have been reported annually (Frost). During the period 1950–2011 a total of 268 records, involving 336 birds, was documented and the respective figures for each period are shown in the table.

Period	Records	Birds
1950s	5	5
1960s	35	54
1970s	42	43
1980s	61	91
1990s	47	59
2000–11	78	84
Totals	268	336

The specific numbers for each year from 1980 to 2011 are listed in the table. This reveals that in the majority of years fewer than ten birds are reported, but occasionally larger numbers occur, most notably a total of 30 individuals in 1980.

Year	Records	Birds
1980	12	30
1981	3	3
1982	5	5
1983	2	3
1984	4	4
1985	6	8
1986	3	3
1987	11	16
1988	4	5
1989	11	14
1990	5	5
1991	7	10
1992	3	3
1993	2	2
1994	8	8
1995	6	6
1996	4	6
1997	4	11
1998	4	4
1999	4	4
2000	9	10
2001	6	6
2002	11	13
2003	6	6
2004	4	6
2005	3	3
2006	6	6
2007	4	4
2008	8	9
2009	6	6
2010	7	7
2011	8	8

The chart represents the half-monthly distribution of all records from 1950 to 1999 and shows clearly that spring passage is concentrated in May.

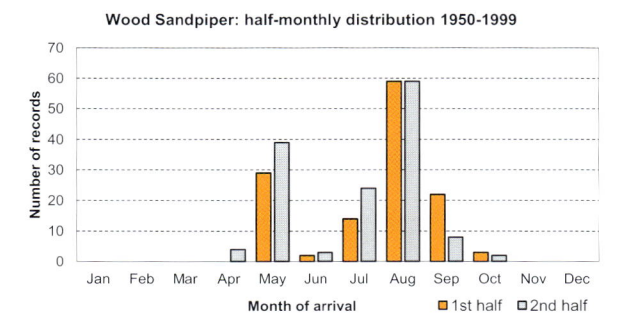

Wood Sandpiper: half-monthly distribution 1950-1999

During this period there were few arrivals before May. One was at Elvaston Quarry on 27th April 1984, while in 2003 there were three occurrences (at Carr Vale, Nadin's (Newhall) and Willington Gravel Pits) between 24th and 26th April. One was at Pleasley Colliery from 27th to 29th April 2009, and in 2011, single birds were at Langley Mill on 18th April and Aston-on-Trent Gravel Pits on 30th April.

The majority of records at this time of year relate to solitary Wood Sandpipers pausing briefly on their long northward migration. Very occasionally two or three occur together, but seven at Egginton Sewage Farm on 19th May 1997 was exceptional. One of a party of three birds at Swarkestone Lake on 15th May 1987 was heard to give a short snatch of song, while another individual at Langley Mill on 24th May 1977 was seen in display flight.

Return passage takes place mainly from July to September, with an obvious peak in August (see chart). This month has nearly half of all sightings, including a remarkable party of 13 birds at Elvaston Quarry on 17th August 1980. However, as in spring, one or two birds at any site is the norm, and the only other instance of more than five together was a gathering of six at Willington Sewage Farm in September 1965. Wood Sandpipers sometimes linger for several days in autumn, and at Carsington Water one was present for almost a month, from 12th August to 9th September 1996.

Occurrences in October have always been rare, and an immature which frequented Egginton Sewage Farm from 31st October to 2nd December 1998 constituted the latest county record at that time. Incredibly, what was probably the same individual returned to this site on 25th October 1999 and remained until early May 2000, by which time it had acquired breeding plumage. This was the first occasion that this species had over-wintered in Derbyshire, although a wintering bird (possibly the same individual again) was seen at both Egginton Sewage Farm and Willington Gravel Pits in January and February 2001.

The majority of reports since 1980 have been from gravel pits, sewage farms and reservoirs in the southern half of the county. As indicated in the chart showing the number of individuals, Willington Gravel Pits has been visited most regularly, with records in 18 years, including annually from 1993 to 2003, while Egginton Sewage Farm has records in nine of the last 25 years. Away from the Trent Valley, Wood Sandpipers have occurred most often at Ogston Reservoir. There were sightings here in seven years during the 1960s and 1970s, and further records in eight years since 1980.

The number of birds recorded at the principal sites in the period 1980–2011 are shown in the chart.

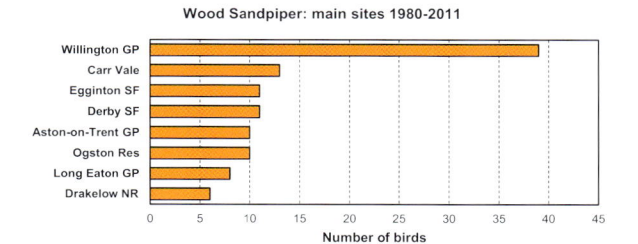

Wood Sandpiper: main sites 1980-2011

Subsidence 'flashes', several of which existed in the Coal Measures Natural Area, were also a favoured haunt of this species, but this habitat has now largely disappeared from the landscape. Carr Vale is a notable exception and was visited 13 times in the period 1980–2011. This wader is rarely found in the Peak District, which has a combined total of 13 records since 1980, the majority at Middleton Moor, with no more than two birds ever seen together. Arnfield, Barbrook, Combs and Ramsley Reservoirs are the only other sites in this region where Wood Sandpipers have been recorded.

An interesting observation was of a bird on return passage which flew south-south-west over Chesterfield, calling continuously, shortly before midnight on 27th July 1994.

Redshank
Tringa totanus
An uncommon breeder, passage migrant and winter visitor.

Whitlock considered that these vociferous waders first became established as breeding birds in Derbyshire at some point in the 1870s or 1880s. By the end of the nineteenth century, they had apparently bred at many sites in the Trent Valley and were also regular breeders in the Dove Valley. Throughout the early part of the twentieth century their range extended northwards and by the 1930s, breeding pairs could be found in some moorland areas and even 'the barren country round Peak Forest' (Frost). The population almost certainly peaked during the 1940s but then collapsed dramatically following the severely cold winter of 1962/63 which badly affected this species and led to a significant fall in the number of inland breeding Redshanks in Britain.

Frost suggested that locally the continuing drainage of suitable wetland sites had hindered any subsequent recovery, and estimated annual totals of 30–50 nesting pairs in the mid-1970s. These were found largely at subsidence flashes, gravel pits and water meadows in the south and east of the county, with a few still present on the damper stretches of moorland in the Peak District. A sequence of cold winters from the late 1970s until the mid-1980s may well have contributed to further setbacks. Since then, milder winters have generally prevailed, and despite the progressive loss of ideal breeding habit, primarily to land redevelopment and agricultural intensification, the population appears to have at least stabilized, if not increased, averaging somewhere in the region of 12 to 20 pairs.

Although there were marked fluctuations in the size of the population during the second half of the twentieth century, the overall presence of this wader had until very recently been fairly consistent. Redshanks were proved to breed in ten of the 23 10km core squares in the county during 1995–99. The 1968–72 and 1988–91 Atlases showed proven breeding in eight and seven squares respectively. In the Derbyshire BBS (1995–99) they were found in 31 tetrads, with breeding proved in 19, probable in four and possible in eight.

The map indicates that the distribution is very similar to that described by Frost, showing a predominance of records from the Trent Valley region and north-east Derbyshire. In both of these areas there have been significant changes in habitat in recent decades and this has inevitably affected breeding Redshanks. One example was the drainage of Sutton Scarsdale Flash in 1984, causing the complete desertion of a site that in previous years had been a county stronghold for the species, and where six pairs had raised 17 young in 1982. In the period 1978–2011, up to three nesting pairs were reported at about a dozen other localities in north-east Derbyshire, including several reclaimed colliery sites. Similarly, the dynamics of gravel extraction in the Trent and lower Derwent Valleys have created many transient sites for these waders. Willington Gravel Pits has proved to be the most enduring, with breeding activity recorded here in nearly all years since 1989. However, at another favoured locality, Sawley Water Meadows, six pairs were present in the spring of 1985, but no breeding occurred, possibly as a result of overgrazing or flooding. Findern Lake, with its grassy spits and islands, attracted up to five, and possibly seven, breeding pairs in the mid-2000s but has since been destroyed as a suitable habitat by the conversion of the site into a marina.

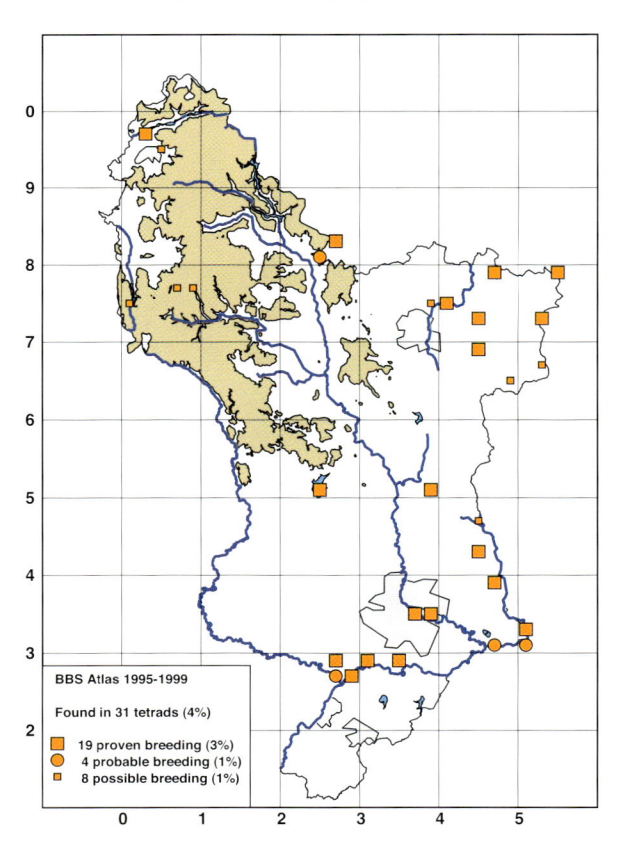

Upland breeding has persisted in the county, but appears to have become largely restricted to two sites in the Longdendale area. Since 1980 the only confirmed nesting elsewhere in the Peak District has been on Beeley Moor in 1981, on Ringinglow Bog in 1984, and at Middleton Moor in 1988. A small population has become established around Carsington Water, holding up to five pairs in recent years. The maps represent the breeding situation in 1995–99 compared with 2007–11, and show how the range has contracted during this time.

Redshanks normally return to their breeding grounds in Derbyshire from late February onwards. Their impressive 'switchback' display flights, accompanied by a distinctive yodelling song, may be observed as territories are secured in late March and April, although there is an early breeding record of a pair with three juveniles at Poolsbrook on 21st April (1992). The majority of young birds are reported in May and June with occasional late broods in July. Territories are usually vacated by August, and although local post-breeding birds, as well as passage migrants from further afield, can be found at a variety of wetland sites in autumn, numbers are generally low. Counts of more than six at any locality in August or September have always been rare, and since 1980 the most notable have been 20 at the lagoons at Middleton Moor on 28th August 1986, and 27 at Carsington Water on 22nd September 2000.

There has been a dramatic rise in the number of birds recorded during recent winters, particularly in the Trent Valley. Prior to 1998 there had been few double-figure counts in any month from October to February, with a maximum since 1980 of 24 at Rother Valley Country Park (now in South Yorkshire) in January 1991, although Frost quoted an earlier record of 30 at Rowthorne in February 1977. By contrast, in every winter from 1998/99 to 2005/06 at least 20 were regularly reported at Willington Gravel Pits, with up to 45 present here in January and February 2001, although winter numbers have declined since 2005. Notable counts at other sites have included 34 at Barrow Gravel Pits in November 2002, and up to 28 at Egginton Sewage Farm in November and December 1998. While milder weather in recent years may have encouraged this trend, this species is undoubtedly more vulnerable than many other waders to spells of cold weather and sharp reversals could still occur. The majority of Redshanks which winter in Britain are thought to be birds of the subspecies *T.t. robusta* which breeds mainly in Iceland (1984–88 Winter Atlas).

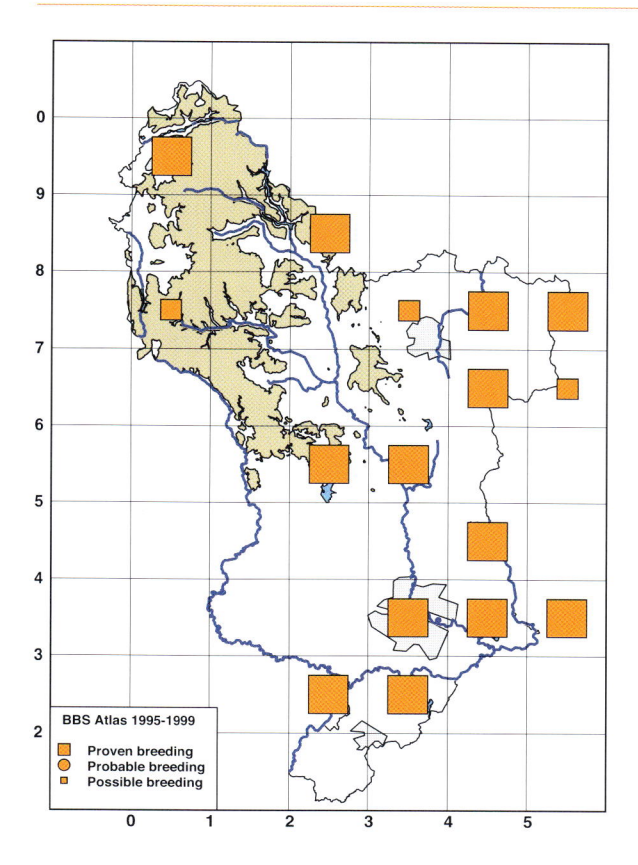

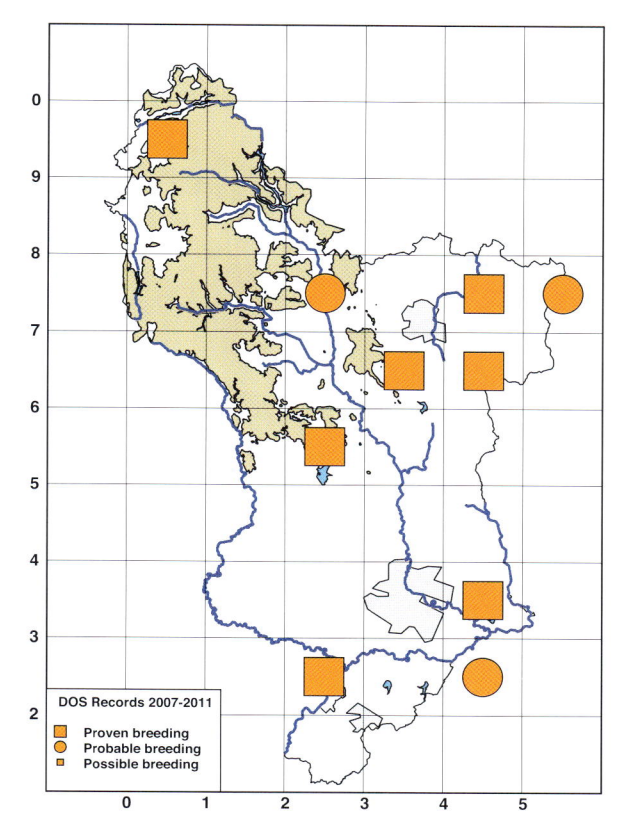

The largest gathering in the county to date, that of 54 at Willington Gravel Pits in March 1999, may well have consisted predominantly of birds wintering locally, augmented by the arrival of some spring migrants. Even though these waders are fairly widespread on spring migration, as in autumn, passage is relatively light. The greatest number ever found in April or May was recorded at Carsington Water on 18th April 1997 when, in addition to six breeding birds, a flock of 32 northward-bound migrants was also briefly present.

The first ringing recovery was of an adult ringed at Staveley in May 1968 which was shot on the River Severn in Gloucestershire in January 1970. The next record concerned a chick ringed at Whitwell in June 1972 that was caught on the Wash in Norfolk in August 1975. Another example of a locally bred bird migrating to a coastal estuary involved a nestling ringed at Willington Gravel Pits in May 1994 that was 'controlled' on two occasions on the Taff Estuary, near Cardiff, during the following winter period. Furthermore, an adult ringed on the Exe Estuary in Devon in September 1978 was found dead at Hulland Ward, near Ashbourne, over five years later (in April 1984), and may well have been a local breeding bird which regularly wintered along the south coast of Britain. The only foreign recovery related to one, ringed as a chick at Sutton Scarsdale in June 1983, which was found dead the following March in a coastal region of Brittany in north-west France, a movement of 550km south-south-west.

Jack Snipe
Lymnocryptes minimus
A uncommon winter visitor and passage migrant.

The French name of *Bécassine sourde* – the deaf snipe – admirably suits this small, secretive wader which flushes at the last moment, often not until it is almost trodden on, to fly only a short distance before dropping suddenly into the marsh. It is found in a variety of marshy places, including bogs, sewage farms, reed-beds, wet grassland and vegetated water margins.

Jack Snipe normally arrive in Derbyshire from the second half of September into October. Between 1978 and 2007, first dates ranged from 9th September to 22nd October, with a mean date of 29th September. The earliest ever was on 15th August (1964) at Willington No. 1 Gravel Pit. Numbers usually increase to their highest level of the year in late October and November, before declining as part of the population moves elsewhere.

Relatively small numbers winter in the county: during the 20 winters from 1989/90 to 2008/09, numbers present between mid-November and mid-March varied from about 20 to 61, with an average of 37. However, bearing in mind the bird's secretive nature, it is almost certain that the true number will be somewhat higher than this.

A small spring passage is detected in late March and April in most years. Between 1978 and 2007, the last recorded dates have ranged from 24th March to 4th May, with a mean of 20th April. The latest ever was on 5th May (1973) at Killamarsh.

Frost considered that there had been little change in status since the days of Whitlock and Jourdain. More recently, overall numbers seem to have declined in the last 35 years or so, as suggested by Frost (1986). Nevertheless, some of the largest recorded counts are quite recent, including the highest ever site count of about 30 on the irrigation fields of Egginton Sewage Farm on 24th December 1996, with up to 16 there later in the same winter. Other high counts were of 21 at Bennerley Marsh on 19th March 1995, 19 at Drakelow Nature Reserve in January 1995, and 18 at both Willington No. 1 Gravel Pit on 17th November 1962 and Staveley on 30th October 1972.

Most of the Jack Snipe seen in the county are in the lowlands of the south and east, but sightings from boggy areas in the lower Peak District are not uncommon. There are two records of single birds at 480m amsl, in the Upper Derwent area: on 3rd February 1993 and near Barrow Stones on 21st November 1994. One was seen several times in a Kelstedge garden in severe winter weather in early 1979. Another was seen on the road at Axe Edge on 20th November 2006, and one was brought in, dying, to a house in North Wingfield by the householder's cat on 3rd February 1989. The remains of seven individuals had been found at the Derby Cathedral Peregrine site by early 2013.

There is a single ringing recovery involving Derbyshire, of an individual ringed at Killamarsh in December 1968 that was shot some 1463km to the east at Kaliningrad, Russia, in the following October.

Woodcock
Scolopax rusticola
An scarce winter visitor and resident, breeding mainly in the northern half of the county.

Standing on a woodland ride at dusk or dawn in spring and early summer gives an observer the best chance of locating breeding Woodcock. At these times the male birds fly just above treetop level in their so-called roding flights, uttering quiet croaking and almost sneeze-like calls. Sometimes roding birds meet and a noisy chase may ensue before they separate to resume their search for females.

Roding activity has been recorded between 10th February (2007) and 24th July (1986) but is more usual between mid-March and mid-July. In the 1990s, the mean dates for first and last recorded roding were 14th March and 14th July. Interesting records from Scarcliffe Woods were of one roding as early as 1725 hours in bright sunshine on 31st May 1971 and of one uttering both forms of its roding calls from the ground on 17th March 1992. Another unusual observation at the same site was of one flushed from the horizontal bough of a beech, 4m above the ground, on 24th May 1992.

Between the late 1970s and the early 1990s, the Game Conservancy Trust (now the Game & Wildlife Conservation Trust) carried out a great deal of research into the Woodcock's breeding and wintering biology, much of this undertaken at Whitwell Wood and the surrounding area. This locality was chosen mainly because of the exceptional nest-finding abilities of John Ellis who, with other members of the Whitwell Wood Natural History Group, was able to give much practical help to the researchers, the latter including Drs G.J.M. Hirons and A.N. Hoodless. Many nests were found and chicks ringed: for example, 16 nests and 64 chicks ringed in 1988. In addition, many adults were caught and some had radio transmitters fitted.

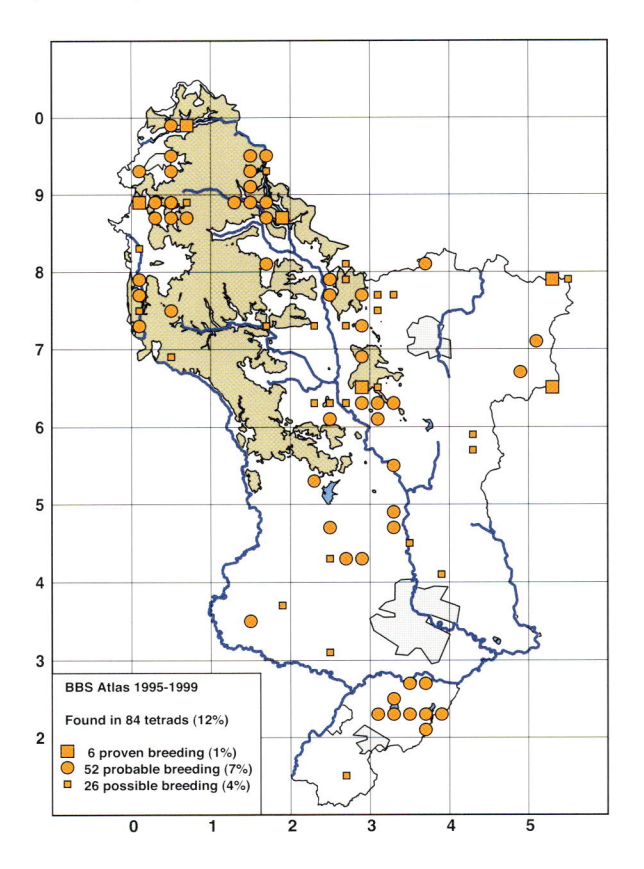

As a result, far more is known about the Woodcock's breeding system. Hoodless (1995), in a succinct précis of this research, stated that most first-year males do not rode, and that a dominance hierarchy becomes established among older roding males. Dominant males roded for the longest periods and obtained all the matings with females, which were accompanied for three or four days before being deserted when the male resumed his display flights in search of other receptive females.

Hirons believed that in a single breeding season up to 100 roding males might visit Whitwell Wood, most remaining for only short periods, before seeking mates elsewhere. Females might also wander. In May 1980, a radio-tagged female with chicks in Whitwell Wood quickly lost her brood during drought conditions and disappeared from the local population. Ten days later, she was tracked (initially from a light aircraft) sitting on eggs 10km away in Clumber Park, Nottinghamshire (G. Hirons *pers comm*).

BBS Atlas 1995-1999

Found in 84 tetrads (12%)

- 6 proven breeding (1%)
- 52 probable breeding (7%)
- 26 possible breeding (4%)

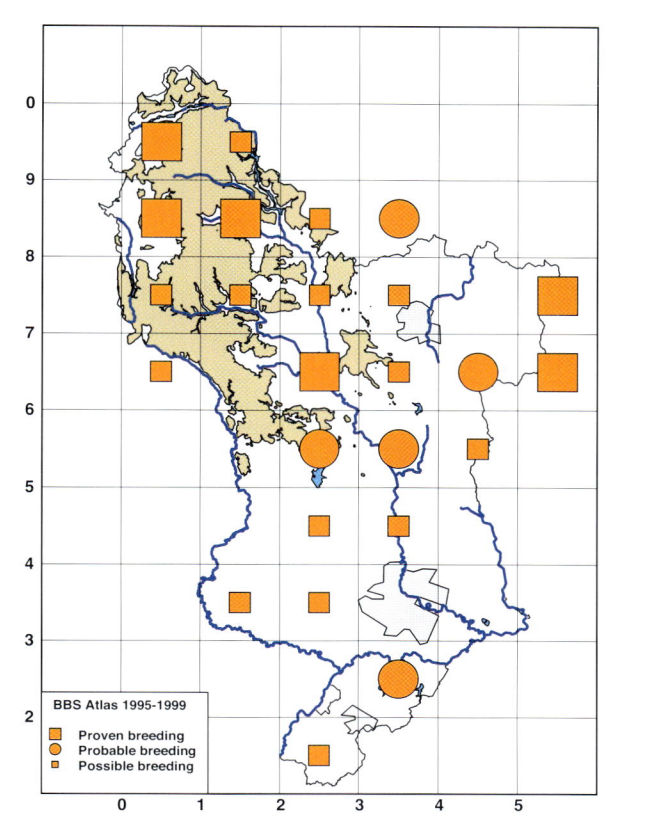

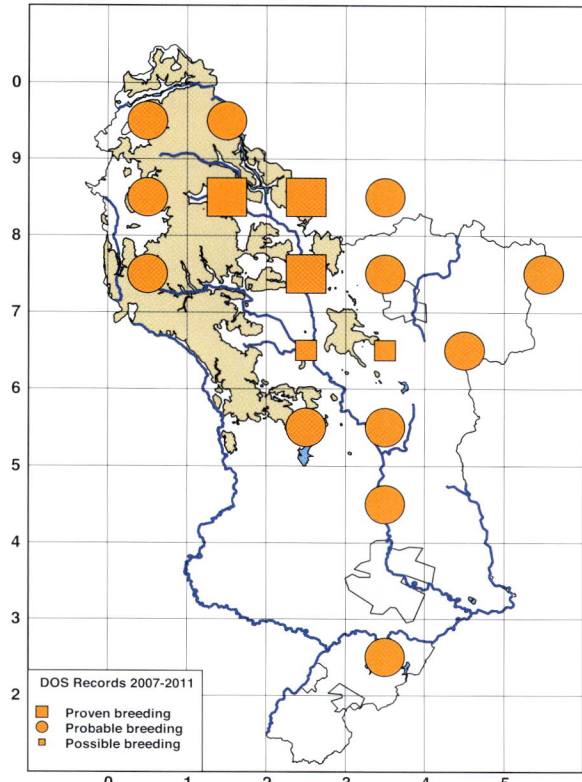

The Species Accounts

BBS Atlas 1995-1999
- Proven breeding
- Probable breeding
- Possible breeding

DOS Records 2007-2011
- Proven breeding
- Probable breeding
- Possible breeding

In the Derbyshire BBS (1995–99), the number of probable breeding records (52), based almost entirely on sightings of roding birds, considerably exceeded the combined total of the possible (26) and proven (6) categories shown on the tetrad map. Breeding is difficult to prove, since the incubating or brooding female relies on her cryptic colouration, remaining crouched and still until the last possible moment. Broods of young are rarely seen, except occasionally when crossing roads or woodland rides.

Breeding birds may use coniferous, deciduous or mixed woodland of any size, though larger blocks are preferred. Nests have also been found in moorland areas, including Combs Edge in 1987 and 1992. Both were in dead bracken fronds on steeply sloping ground at 400m amsl, well away from the nearest trees. Earlier nest sites mentioned by Frost include the grounds of a school at Taxal and a hole in the bank of a quarry at Pebley.

As the tetrad map shows, Woodcock are widely but thinly scattered through much of Derbyshire. There are striking absences from the Carboniferous Limestone plateau and the Coal Measures area. This is surprising, since both contain areas of woodland. Woodcock were similarly absent from the limestone area in the 1988–91 Atlas, but were proved to breed on the Coal Measures then. Comparison of probable and proven breeding between 1988–91 and 1995–99 shows gains by two 10km squares, but losses in five. This apparent decline accords with the national situation (Hoodless 1995) and is quite recent, the causes apparently unknown. The maps of breeding distribution in 1995–99 and 2007–11 demonstrate the range contraction.

Frost stated that breeding Woodcock were relatively scarce in the county until 1930–45, when a very large increase occurred. The population in 1978 was considered to be stable.

After the cessation of roding, very few Woodcock are seen until the arrival of immigrants, in annually varying numbers, from the Continent in late October and November, these remaining until the following March. During the arrival period, birds are sometimes found in unusual localities such as built-up areas. One of the most bizarre records concerns a live bird found in a factory toilet at Sinfin at 0645hrs on 4th November 1995. During the winter months, Woodcock are still found mainly in woodland, as they are in summer, but may also occur in smaller clumps of trees or bushes, by hedgerows and on moorland and elsewhere. They roost in such places by day, leaving at dusk to feed on farmland, especially pasture. The largest count of all concerned some 36–44 found at night by powerful torchlight on fields near Whitwell in February 1990. Up to 13 have been seen leaving Carr Wood at dusk. Otherwise, the largest winter counts are usually of birds disturbed by shooting parties, such as 12 at Scarcliffe in January 1980 and likewise at Ednaston in November 1995. An interesting record from Derby Sewage Farm was of one that wintered there in 1982/83 and 1983/84, which was in precisely the same spot whenever the observers visited the site. By early 2013, no fewer than 38 had been found as prey items of the Derby Cathedral Peregrines.

Most of the ringing recoveries concerning Derbyshire have resulted from the studies at Whitwell Wood, where large numbers of these birds have been trapped. Many of them were lured into mist nets by a russet-coloured bantam (named Spiteful), which was mistaken as a female Woodcock by roding males in the fading light. Three such birds ringed here in spring were found in Counties Dublin, Killarney and Mayo in Ireland in winter. Two others ringed at Whitwell Wood in March were found in the summer of the same year at Vijlandi, Estonia and Hallefornas, Sweden, and one ringed as a chick in April was shot seven months later at Plesidy in France. Another ringed at Lemland, Finland in November 1979 was shot in the same month, 11 years later at Combs, while the oldest record concerns one ringed at Skrunda, Latvia in July 1932, which was found at Belper in December 1933.

Snipe
Gallinago gallinago
An uncommon summer visitor to gritstone moorland, but now scarce as a breeding species in the lowlands, where it is a fairly common winter visitor and passage migrant.

The exhilarating sight and sound of a male Snipe in its drumming display, or the insistent 'chuck-er chuck-er' calls emanating from boggy areas, are usually the first indicators of the presence of breeding Snipe. Much of the Snipe's breeding and feeding activity takes place very early or late in the day and it is possible that some birds, especially in more remote areas, are overlooked as a result. Furthermore, nests are difficult to find and adults with chicks are only rarely encountered. Significantly, the map shows that breeding was proved in only 11 tetrads, compared with more than three times as many (37) where it was thought probable. It can, however, be assumed that the probable records almost certainly relate to definite breeders. There were also 26 tetrads in which breeding was thought possible.

Breeding Snipe require soft, organic soils which they can probe for worms and other invertebrates with their long bill, and tall grasses, sedges or rushes for nesting. Increasingly these conditions are met only in upland areas, either on moorland or in unimproved pastures with wetter areas containing marshy vegetation.

In lowland Derbyshire, Snipe were proved to breed in a mere five tetrads in the Derbyshire BBS (1995–99), with probable breeding recorded in six more. Had the start of the survey been delayed, it is possible that there would be no confirmed instances of lowland breeding, since none have been reported in the *Derbyshire Bird Report* since 1995. There were a handful of instances of birds drumming on single dates in lowland areas in 2000–05, but all of these, except possibly birds at Mercaston and Pleasley Colliery, were believed to be wintering or migrant birds on the point of departure. The maps show the contraction of breeding range between 1995–99 and 2007–11.

This decline is not a new phenomenon. Jourdain said that very few bred in the south of the county, while Frost reported an ongoing decline in lowland areas, attributed to changes in farming practices. Even as recently as 1979, no fewer than ten were heard drumming and chipping at Brinsley Flash, while in 1993–95, displaying birds were still present at three or four lowland sites. Improved drainage, allied to the increasing conversion of pasture to arable land, has led to the loss of feeding and nesting areas and, even where pastures remain, higher stocking rates lead to the loss of tall vegetation and increased likelihood of nests being trampled on.

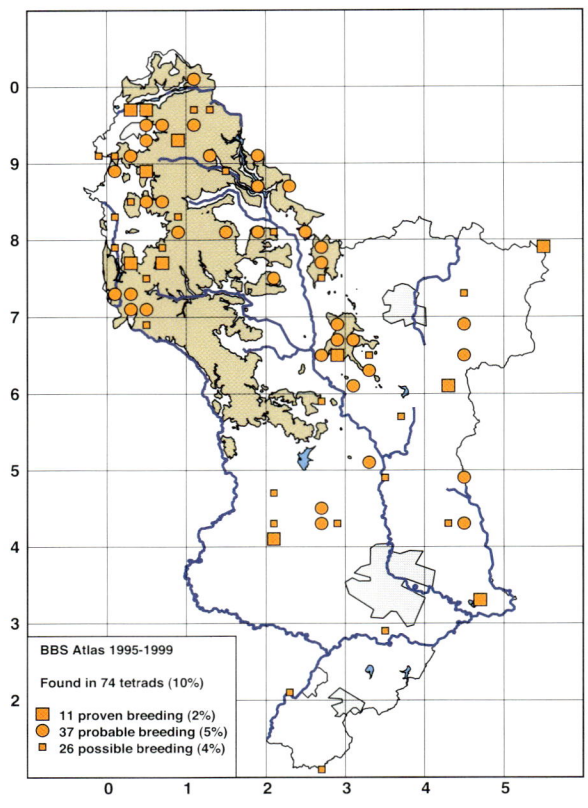

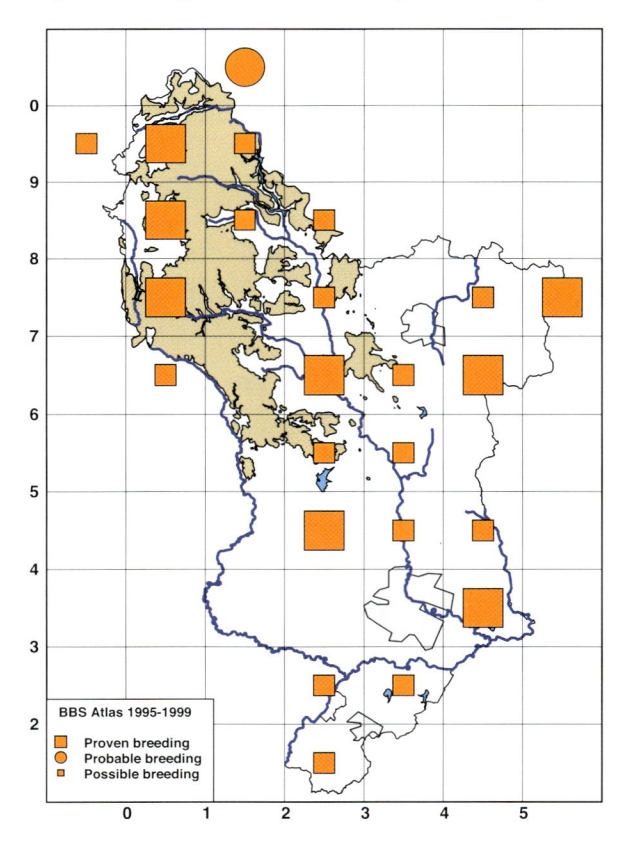

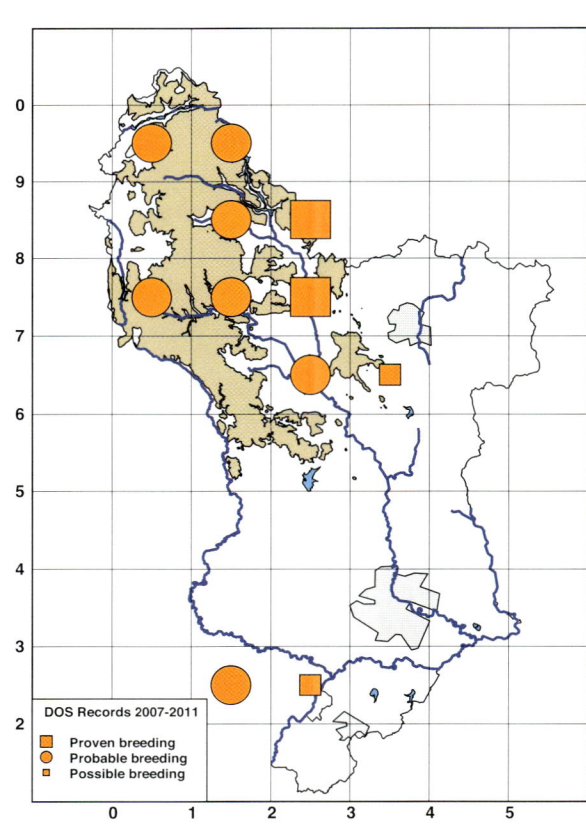

Assessing the trend in the Snipe breeding population of upland areas is less easy, but recent improvements to much upland pasture can only have led to a decline. Recent surveys in the Peak District are thought to have underestimated the numbers because of surveying difficulties (Pearce 2009b). The EMP moors survey of 2010 revealed 19 'pairs', five more than in 2004 but this increase might be explained by a change in methodology (Frost & Taylor 2011).

Even on moorland, it seems highly likely that there has been a decrease. Frost said that in this habitat a dozen or so might be seen in simultaneous display in early spring; such a number would be exceptional now. This is a cause of some concern, particularly as many moors seem, at least to human eyes, to be unaltered. Birds have been found breeding as high as 550m amsl (at Barrow Stones in 1983). At Stanage Edge on 13th June 1986, an adult with chicks nearby was alarming from the roof of a car.

The winter distribution of Snipe is markedly different from that of the breeding season. Upland breeding Snipe are generally present from late March until autumn, very few remaining beyond the onset of cold weather; in the lowlands, winter numbers are augmented by spring migrants from late February to early April. Returning birds are found in very small numbers from late June or July, increasing until November or even December. Wintering and passage birds may be found in a variety of wetland sites, including the margins of reservoirs and lakes, flooded farmland, sewage farms and so on.

The largest counts of wintering and passage birds may be made at any time between October and March. The highest count was in December 1981 of 500 at Drakelow Nature Reserve, which equalled the highest previous count, from Willington No. 2 Gravel Pit in the 1960s. Drakelow Nature Reserve usually produced the highest counts until the early 1990s, with regular three-figure maxima. Since then, counts of over 200 have come from Williamthorpe, where 250 were seen in December 2002, and Bennerley Marsh, which held a maximum of 240 in December 2001. Other sites which have held 100 or more Snipe since 1978 are Brinsley Flash, Elvaston Quarry, Sawley Water Meadows, Wyver Lane, Egginton Sewage Farm, Ogston Reservoir and Carsington Water. Overall wintering numbers have declined since the early 1980s.

The table shows the highest counts in each winter (between November and March) from 1979/80 to 2010/11. At Willington Gravel Pits, 141 birds were disturbed by reserve management work on 21st September 2008, which was a surprisingly large number for such an early date.

In severe weather, birds may occur in unusual places in their search for feeding areas. Five were seen in various built-up areas in heavy snow in December 1981 and one was at the Friends Meeting House in Chesterfield in similar conditions in February 1991.

There are seven records of birds showing the characteristics of the race *G.g. faroensis*, which breeds in the Faroes, Shetland, Orkney and Iceland. Singles were seen at Williamthorpe on 25th August 1989, 29th September 2002, 7th September 2003 and 4th February 2010 (ringed), with others at Ogston Reservoir on 16th and 19th October 2007 and 16th March 2010, and at Carsington Water on 15th November 2008. A leucistic bird was at Drakelow Nature Reserve from January to March 1982.

There have been over 50 ringing recoveries of Snipe associated with Derbyshire, although these all relate to efforts made during the 1960s and early 1970s. The longest distance movement concerned a bird ringed near Etwall in September 1968 that was shot at Archangel, Russia two years later, 2727km east-north-east. Other examples of locally ringed birds migrating eastwards have included recoveries from Denmark, Norway and Poland. A bird ringed near Etwall in October 1971 was shot two months later in Ireland, thus providing evidence of westerly migration. Southerly movement has also been confirmed by recoveries from Cornwall, France, Spain and Portugal. In addition, there have been instances of individuals ringed in Sweden, Germany and the Netherlands that have been subsequently recovered within the county. The record for longevity is held by a bird ringed near Etwall in October 1966 that was shot in the same area almost nine years later.

Winter	Max count	Month	Location
1979/80	150	Dec 1979	Drakelow Nature Reserve
1980/81	250	Feb 1981	Drakelow Nature Reserve
1981/82	500	Dec 1981	Drakelow Nature Reserve
1982/83	180	Jan 1983	Drakelow Nature Reserve
1983/84	100	Dec 1983	Sawley Water Meadows
1984/85	130	Jan 1985	Drakelow Nature Reserve
1985/86	170	Dec 1985	Drakelow Nature Reserve
1986/87	85	Mar 1987	Egginton Sewage Farm
1987/88	84	Jan 1988	Middleton Moor
1988/89	100	Jan 1989	Belper
1989/90	123	Mar 1990	Bennerley Marsh
1990/91	116	Jan 1991	Bennerley Marsh
1991/92	130	Jan 1992	Bennerley Marsh
1992/93	160	Dec 1992	Drakelow Nature Reserve
1993/94	130	Mar 1994	Bennerley Marsh
1994/95	210	Nov 1994	Bennerley Marsh
1995/96	212	Mar 1996	Bennerley Marsh
1996/97	120	Mar 1997	Egginton Sewage Farm
1997/98	107	Feb 1998	Ogston Reservoir
1998/99	76	Feb 1999	Lower Hartshay
1999/2000	58	Feb 2000	Aston-on-Trent Gravel Pits
2000/01	90	Dec 2000	River Trent, Twyford
2001/02	240	Dec 2001	Bennerley Marsh
2002/03	250	Dec 2002	Williamthorpe Nature Reserve
2003/04	130	Nov 2003	Carsington Water
2004/05	165	Jan 2005	Ogston Reservoir
2005/06	70	Nov 2005	Williamthorpe Nature Reserve
2006/07	60	Dec 2006	Willington Gravel Pits
2007/08	200	Feb 2008	Williamthorpe Nature Reserve
2008/09	106	Jan 2009	Willington Gravel Pits
2009/10	100	Nov 2009	Avenue Washlands
2010/11	41	Feb 2011	Tibshelf

Great Snipe
Gallinago media
A very rare vagrant.

Whitlock was convinced that the Great Snipe had occurred in Derbyshire, while conceding that some of the available information was rather vague. Joseph Whitaker of Rainworth had two that were shot in the vicinity of Derby well before 1893 in his collection (later given to the Mansfield Museum). Jourdain states that one was killed at Bolsover on 12th October 1892 and several were shot in the county in January 1902. The *Zoologist* stated that these were in the 'low country around Derby'.

Frost provided details of three subsequent occurrences. A male was shot at Egginton Sewage Farm on 11th August 1928 (Frost) and one suffered the same fate at Spondon Sewage Farm (now known as Derby Sewage Farm) on 11th September 1933; and one was seen in a marshy field by the River Dove at Ashbourne on 8th December 1941.

This declining species breeds in Scandinavia, and in central and eastern Europe and western Siberia; the wintering grounds are in sub-Saharan Africa. The decrease is shown by the fact that, of 695 British records by 2011, no fewer than 532 occurred prior to 1950 (Hudson *et al.* 2012).

Pomarine Skua
Stercorarius pomarinus
A very rare vagrant.

A skua was obtained in an exhausted state near Burnaston on 23rd September 1854 after it was mobbed by Rooks. It was recorded as this species by J.J. Briggs and accepted as such by Whitlock, but Jourdain had doubts that it was a correct identification. Therefore, the first acceptable record was of one killed on moorland on the county boundary at Strines on 6th October 1898 (Jourdain additions).

There have been six subsequent records, all of single birds. The bird at Ogston Reservoir in 1981, which was accompanied by an Arctic Skua, was part of an inland wreck of seabirds during 25th–26th April during north-easterly gales and heavy snowfalls. As a result of the storm, a total of 14 skuas was found inland but this was the only Pomarine Skua recorded in the country (Nightingale & Sharrock 1982).

The only winter record was of a very approachable individual at Staunton Harold Reservoir in February and March 1983, which spent much of its stay on the east bank and fed on pilchards that were thrown to it. The latest records have occurred at the peak time for northbound passage for this species off the west coast of Britain.

Year	Location and date
1977	Drakelow Nature Reserve, an adult flew south on 20th September
1981	Ogston Reservoir, a dark-phase adult on 25th–26th April
1983	Staunton Harold Reservoir, an immature from 28th February to 3rd March, when it departed to the south
1985	Howden Reservoir, one flew south on 10th November
1993	Carsington Water, a pale-phase adult arrived from the north-west on 15th May
2005	Derby, a pale-phase adult, being chased by crows, flew north-west over the Derbyshire Royal Infirmary on 7th May

Arctic Skua
Stercorarius parasiticus
A rare vagrant.

This is the most frequently recorded skua in Derbyshire, with a total of 42 records involving 64 birds. Whitlock knew of two undated records of birds killed near Burton upon Trent and another one found near Mickleover in 1879 or 1880. Frost stated that the next records were not until 1948, when a flock of nine flew over Ashover on 25th March and two were at Hardwick on 25th May. All of the records may be summarized as follows:

Period	Records	Birds
pre-1900	3	3
1940s	2	11
1950s	2	4
1960s	3	3
1970s	10	15
1980s	10	13
1990s	8	11
2000–11	4	4
Totals	42	64

Since 1900, the monthly distribution pattern has been as shown in the table.

Month	Records	Birds
January	–	–
February	–	–
March	1	9
April	2	3
May	3	4
June	–	–
July	2	2
August	9	13
September	15	20
October	3	3
November	3	6
December	1	1
Totals	39	61

There is a clear peak of records from mid-August to September, with 55% of all birds seen during this period. Many of the birds seen in the county at this time have been associated with gales, and they may have been following similarly displaced groups of *sterna* terns.

Most records have been of single birds, but there is one of nine, already mentioned, while four, and possibly five (two, two and a probable fifth), flew south at Ogston Reservoir on 10th November 1985. Groups of three have been seen on three occasions.

Virtually all of the records relate to birds seen on single dates only. The only birds to remain longer were a dark-phase immature bird at Ogston Reservoir on 27th–28th December 1985 and another immature bird, also at Ogston Reservoir on 3rd–4th September 1995. Since the first modern-day records in 1948, when 11 birds were observed, the most seen in any year is six, in 1974 and 1985, and five in 1995.

Of those that were aged, 76% were adults, while the proportion of pale-morph birds to dark-morph birds was precisely equal, contrasting with the situation in the West Midlands where dark-morph birds predominate (Harrison & Harrison 2005).

Most records have come from the county's largest reservoirs as indicated in the chart.

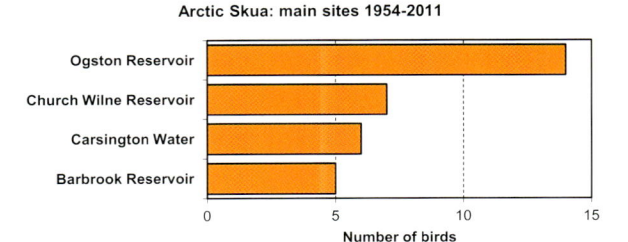

Arctic Skuas have been seen over open countryside at Ramsley Reservoir, Harland Edge and Fairfield, and singles have been seen over built-up areas at Ripley and St Mary's railway goods yard in Derby.

Long-tailed Skua
Stercorarius longicaudus
A very rare vagrant.

Whitlock and Jourdain both mention Sir Oswald Mosley's statement that this species was said to have been shot near Burton upon Trent, but neither authority was willing to accept this species onto the Derbyshire list, as the information was too vague.

A bird found in an emaciated condition at Derby in 1922 and published in Frost as the only Derbyshire Long-tailed Skua record, was more recently reidentified from the skin in Derby Museum as an Arctic Skua.

Therefore, the first record was in 1978, and is one of six records, all of single birds recorded during the main autumn passage period for this species in the UK.

Year	Location and date
1978	Middleton Moor, an immature picked up dead on 5th October
1982	Ogston Reservoir, an immature on 18th–19th September, which departed to the north on the latter date
1988	Church Wilne Reservoir, a pale-phase immature on 21st August
1988	Drakelow Nature Reserve, an adult flew east on 9th October
1990	Pilsley Green, a pale-phase immature on 30th September
2010	Solomon's Temple, Buxton, an exhausted immature on 5th September, was subsequently identified from a photograph

The corpse of the 1978 bird was taken to a meeting of the Yorkshire Naturalists' Union, where it was identified by John Mather. The bird at Pilsley Green was found in a pasture, where it waddled about in an ungainly fashion catching craneflies.

Great Skua
Stercorarius skua
A rare vagrant.

Frost quoted a first record of an exhausted bird standing on a road near Sheldon on 14th October 1934, following a violent north-westerly gale. Since then, there have been 21 records, involving 24 birds.

Year	Location and date
1971	Church Wilne Reservoir, one on 26th September
1972	Goyt Valley, two flew south on 27th May
1974	Ogston Reservoir, one on 12th–13th April, which departed to the north-west on the latter date
1974	Egginton No. 7 Gravel Pit, one on 2nd September
1978	Foremark Reservoir, one on 3rd December
1984	Temple Normanton, one found dead on 27th March
1985	Swarkestone Lake, one departed to the west on 6th January
1988	Crich Common, an immature was picked up exhausted on 29th September, but it later died
1991	Swadlincote, one flew east on 3rd November
1992	Carsington Water, an adult arrived from the south and departed to the west on 3rd October
1994	Staunton Harold Reservoir, an adult on 14th September
1997	Carsington Water, one on 2nd–3rd November
1998	Near Buxton, one flew north on 27th September
2001	Carsington Water, one from 18th to 20th September
2001	Willington Gravel Pits, one on 18th September
2002	Carsington Water, one on 1st–2nd August, which departed to the south
2002	Carsington Water, a juvenile on 29th August
2002	Carsington Water, two on 9th September, one of which remained until the following day
2004	Carsington Water, an adult and a juvenile on 10th August
2005	Long Eaton Gravel Pits, one on 22nd August
2006	Carsington Water, an adult on 11th April

The pattern of records and birds by period from 1954 is shown in the first chart.

It appeared that this species was becoming more regular, with eight records involving ten birds between 2000 and 2006, more than in any of the previous periods. However, there were none in 2007 to 2011.

The pattern by months of the 21 occurrences of 24 individuals from 1954 is shown in the second chart.

There is an obvious peak in August and September, which is believed to concern storm-blown birds, although it is possible that there may be a small cross-country movement then, as there may be in spring. There have been five birds between March and May, though the two in the latter month (in 1972) occurred at a time of westerly gales.

Most records involve birds seen on one date only, but at least four birds have roosted overnight, and one at Carsington Water in 2001 roosted for two nights before departing on the third day.

Carsington Water has become the favoured locality for this species and ten of the 24 birds have been seen there. No other site has recorded more than one bird. All but five birds have been on or over water bodies, the exceptions being two found dead or exhausted and three flying over open countryside.

The one at Ogston Reservoir was seen to kill and eat a Coot, while at Carsington Water the bird present in September 2001 killed and ate a Lesser Black-backed Gull, and at the same locality on 2nd August 2002, one was seen to drown and eat a male Mallard.

One ringed as a chick on Foula, Shetland (where there is a large breeding population) in July 1983 was found dead near Temple Normanton in the following March, a movement of 772km south.

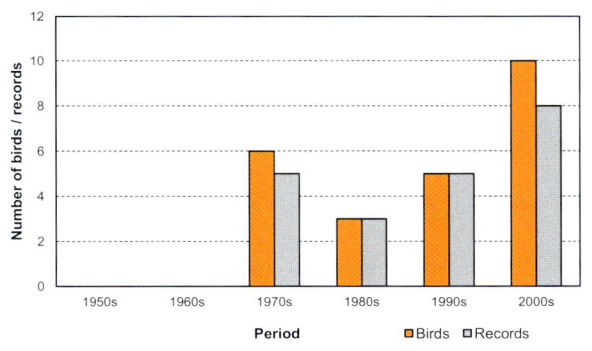

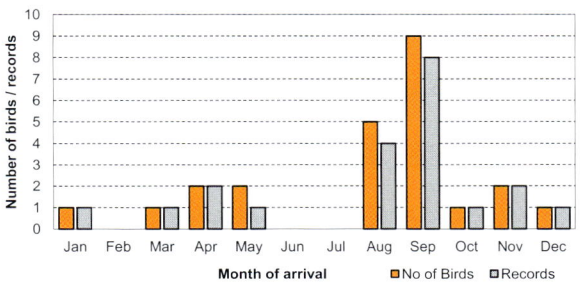

Puffin
Fratercula arctica
A very rare vagrant.

One was shot near Derby before 1789 (Whitlock), and one was found on the River Derwent at Derby in November 1907. Doubts arise over the next report, of a juvenile at Markham Colliery on 13th July 1952: since the bird could not fly, it was thought to have been brought from the coast by humans (Frost), but this record may have been given more credence by the 2001 Holymoorside record (see below).

The last six reports are more authentic. Four involve birds picked up sick or dead and come from Chesterfield on an unspecified date in 1954, Fernilee Reservoir on 7th July 1963, Old Whittington on 26th October 1969, and Monsal Dale on 20th October 1970 (Frost). One, probably exhausted, was picked up on the sixth floor of the cement works at Hope on 17th March 1980 and later released at Hornsea, East Yorkshire.

The most recent record concerns a juvenile found in an orchard at Holymoorside on 18th July 2001 and taken to a wildlife rescue centre at Shirebrook. It seems quite probable that it originated from a colony in north-east England, as there were exceptionally strong north-easterly winds on the night of 17th July, and it is customary for young Puffins to make their maiden flight at night. After further care at a specialist rehabilitation centre in Cheshire, it was released in Anglesey on 17th August (Hattersley 2002).

Razorbill
Alca torda
A very rare vagrant.

The only record concerns an adult which stayed at Staunton Harold Reservoir from 18th October to 13th November 1970. Inland records of this auk are exceptional, and the length of its stay is also noteworthy. Britain holds about 110,000 pairs out of the world's estimated population of 610,000–630,000 pairs, all of which breed in the North Atlantic (Brown & Grice 2005).

Little Auk
Alle alle
A rare vagrant.

There were about five reported from the south of the county in the nineteenth century (Whitlock; Jourdain), and approximately 20 in widely scattered localities during the first half of the twentieth century, of which about 12 occurred between 25th January and 18th February 1912.

Since 1950 there have been 15 further records, involving 23 birds, as follows:

Year	Location and date
1958	Clay Cross, one found dead on 11th November
1958	Miller's Dale, one found dead on 18th November
1959	Risley, one picked up exhausted and later died on 2nd November
1967	River Derwent, Curbar, one found injured and taken into care on 31st October
1968	Rosliston, one found dead on 5th November
1976	Staunton Harold Reservoir, one from 25th to 27th December was ultimately killed by Carrion Crows
1978	Church Wilne Reservoir, one from 31st December to 1st January 1979
1983	Sandiacre, one picked up exhausted and taken into care on 29th October
1984	Milford, one taken into care on 6th November and later released at Gibraltar Point, Lincolnshire
1987	Derwent Reservoir, a badly decomposed body picked up on 22nd March
1989	Walton Dam, Chesterfield, one on 30th October, flew off west
1995	Carr Vale, a flock of nine flew north on 31st October
1995	Williamthorpe Nature Reserve, one flew south-west on 29th October
1995	Foremark Reservoir, one on 4th November was taken into care
1996	Ashgate, Chesterfield, one picked up exhausted on 12th November was released at Flamborough Head, Yorkshire the next day

As the table shows, Little Auks in Derbyshire are usually picked up dead or dying, at sites often unconnected with water and not infrequently in urban areas. Nearly all occurrences are associated with severe weather, particularly coastal gales. The flock of nine birds at Carr Vale in October 1995 was exceptional. The gap of 16 years without any records between 1997 and 2011 is surprising.

Analysis by period and month is shown in the tables.

Period	Records	Birds
1950s	3	3
1960s	2	2
1970s	2	2
1980s	4	4
1990s	4	12
2000s	–	–
Totals	15	23

Month	Records	Birds
Unknown	*1	*1
October	5	13
November	7	7
December	2	2
Totals	15	23

* This bird was 'long-dead' when found on 22nd March 1987, so cannot be accurately assigned to a particular month of arrival.

Sooty Tern
Onychoprion fuscata
A very rare vagrant.

This species breeds throughout the tropics and is otherwise pelagic.

Whitlock stated that one was killed on the River Dove near Tutbury, Staffordshire, in 1852 by a stone thrown by a deaf-and-dumb boy called Ault. It was at first believed to be a Gull-billed Tern and was exhibited by Yarrell at a meeting of the Linnaean Society in February 1853 before ending up in the collection of Sir Henry des Voeux at Drakelow Hall. This was the first record for Europe. As the River Dove forms the county border between Derbyshire and Staffordshire, it is usual to treat such records as common to both counties.

There is some confusion about the date of the record. Mosley (Mosley & Brown 1863) said it was killed in summer, while both Whitlock and Jourdain said 'about October'. A note in the *Zoologist* of 20th December 1852 said 'killed about four months ago'. Because of this uncertainty and the circumstances surrounding the record, Harrison and Harrison (2005) have queried its authenticity.

Little Tern
Sternula albifrons
A scarce passage migrant.

Although there were a few sightings in the eighteenth and nineteenth centuries, as well as the first half of the twentieth century (Frost), the Little Tern has become an almost annual visitor to the county since 1960. The last year without a record was 1984. The table shows a total of 106 occurrences, involving 143 birds, recorded in the period 1960–2011. While far more intensive study of all waters during this period has undoubtedly contributed to the greater frequency of sightings, it is worth remembering that the increase has actually taken place despite a long-term decline in the number of breeding pairs around the shores of Britain (*BWP*).

Period	Records	Birds
1960s	9	12
1970s	18	26
1980s	13	18
1990s	22	32
2000–11	44	55
Totals	106	143

About 70% of the records have been of single birds but there are 14 instances of two, and seven of three together, while a party of four was seen at Willington Gravel Pits in May 1994. Visits are generally brief, although birds have twice roosted overnight, and singles have stayed for three days on three occasions. In 2007, a juvenile stayed for four days at Carsington Water.

The chart for the period 1960–2011 clearly shows the predominance of spring birds, especially in the first half of May. In contrast, autumn passage is small.

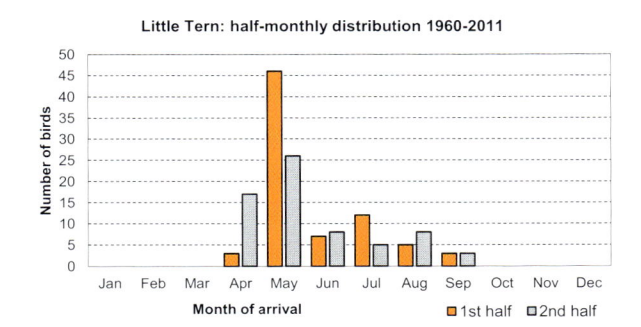

Extreme dates of occurrence are 9th April (1948) on the county boundary near Calwich, Staffordshire and 29th September (1944) at Mapperley. More recently, extreme dates have been 11th April (2009) and 22nd September (1975).

The Trent Valley has provided the majority of sightings, with Willington Gravel Pits particularly favoured in recent years. Elsewhere, Ogston Reservoir has been visited on 19 occasions, and there have also been records from several small waters along the eastern boundary of the county. However, occurrences at upland sites are very rare, with the only Peak District records being from Barbrook Reservoir, Combs Reservoir and Middleton Moor, where three were recorded on 7th May 2011.

Gull-billed Tern
Gelochelidon nilotica
A very rare vagrant.

The only record of this species concerned an adult at Drakelow Nature Reserve on 25th June 1995. It was found at an ash-lagoon with a small group of Black-headed Gulls and was watched at distances down to 30m for five minutes before it flew off northwest (Cockburn 1996a). This may have been the individual seen at Slimbridge Wildfowl Reserve, Gloucestershire on 28th July and Seaforth Docks Nature Reserve, Liverpool, on 30th–31st July. This tern breeds discontinuously from Iberia to China and in North America. European birds winter in West Africa. By the end of 2011 there had been 340 British records (Hudson *et al.* 2012).

Caspian Tern
Hydroprogne caspia
A very rare vagrant.

These large and powerful terns occur as vagrants in Britain in most years but, unusually, most are seen in midsummer, especially July, rather than spring or autumn. Up to the end of 2011 there had been 292 British records (Hudson *et al*. 2012). They breed discontinuously in Eurasia, Africa, Australasia and North America. The closest population to the UK is in the Baltic; birds from here winter in West Africa.

There have been seven Derbyshire records, all involving single birds present on only one date.

Year	Location and date
1968	Egginton No. 7 Gravel Pit, one which flew off south-west on 3rd June, was seen later that day at Stanford Reservoir, on the Leicestershire–Northamptonshire border
1976	Drakelow Nature Reserve, one on 10th October
1977	Ogston Reservoir, one on 19th June
1988	Ogston Reservoir, one which departed to the south on 26th June was at Neumann's Flash, Cheshire later that day
1988	Rother Valley Country Park (now in South Yorkshire), one flew north on 29th July
1993	Willington Gravel Pits, one on 11th May. It was presumed to be the individual reported from Dosthill Lake, Warwickshire on 10th May, Lound Gravel Pits, Nottinghamshire on 12th May, and Southfield Reservoir (then Humberside), on 13th May
2007	Willington Gravel Pits, a second-summer bird on 11th June

The bird seen at Drakelow Nature Reserve in 1976 is the third latest to be seen in Britain.

Whiskered Tern
Chlidonias hybrida
A very rare vagrant.

One was shot on the River Trent near Barrow in the autumn of 1883 (Whitlock), and this remained the sole record until the remarkable events of April 2009.

At Willington Gravel Pits a flock of 11 was seen to arrive at 1245hrs on 24th April 2009 and all were still present at dusk. Eight remained on the following day; at midday they left to the south but returned ahead of a weak rain belt. They were still present on 26th before departing in the presence of a Peregrine and a Hobby. Two duly returned and stayed until dusk, and one was present on 28th, the last sighting at this locality. What was presumed to be one of this group was seen in the late afternoon of 26th April at Long Eaton Gravel Pits. There was a further record of a single at Ogston Reservoir on 30th July, which was watched for 45 minutes in the early morning before it left to the north-east.

The flock of 11 at Willington Gravel Pits was the largest ever seen in Britain and was one of the national ornithological highlights of the year. This flock accounted for sightings at Croxall Lakes in Staffordshire, Rutland Water in Leicestershire, and Rutland and Paxton Pits in Cambridgeshire between 26th and 28th April, while the Ogston Reservoir bird was believed to be the individual seen at Fiskerton Fen, Lincolnshire, three days later. The sequence of events was documented by Key (2010b).

There were 204 national records by the end of 2011 (Hudson *et al*. 2012). This tern breeds discontinuously in Europe, Africa, Asia and Australia, and those from western Europe winter in West Africa.

Black Tern
Chlidonias niger
An uncommon passage migrant

Since the formation of the DOS in 1954, this attractive tern has visited the county every year except 1960, and in recent decades it has been recorded with increasing regularity during the main passage periods of spring and autumn. In the period 1950–2011 there were over 900 records involving well over 3000 birds, as shown in the table.

Period	Records	Birds
1950s	24	69
1960s	89	299
1970s	177	467
1980s	175	449
1990s	240	1391
2000–11	239	687
Totals	944	3362

The Black Tern was apparently 'pretty regular' in the nineteenth century, although it was only known as a spring visitor (Frost). The increase in the frequency of sightings throughout the second half of the twentieth century, and particularly over the last 30 years, is almost certainly a reflection of far greater and more effective observer coverage throughout the county and the creation of many large water bodies.

There appears to be a strong connection between easterly airflows and the presence of Black Terns in Derbyshire, especially in spring. As the birds migrate to their breeding grounds in Continental Europe from wintering areas to the south-west, they are sometimes diverted over Britain by easterly winds, and this can lead to their appearance far inland in relatively large numbers. There have been three notable examples of such movements, all in early May. The first took place in May 1988 when approximately 100 birds were reported, including a flock of 30 at Church Wilne Reservoir. However, in May 1990, there was a phenomenal passage of Black Terns noted both locally and nationally. In Derbyshire about 400 individuals were reported, with several flocks of over 40 seen in the Trent Valley, and the largest gathering was again at Church Wilne Reservoir, where 62 were seen on 2nd May. More recently, there was a concentrated movement through the Midlands on 3rd May 1997, with nearly 100 birds found across southern and central Derbyshire, including a maximum of 62 at Carsington Water. Such influxes are exceptional and the average flock size in most years is much lower, with parties of over ten birds fairly unusual.

In autumn, the influence of anticyclonic conditions is also significant, although the arrival of Black Terns is often more directly linked to the occurrence of frontal systems. Not surprisingly, this return passage includes both adult and juvenile birds, and although it is generally on a slightly smaller scale (there have been very few gatherings of more than ten birds during return passage), there have been several years in which total numbers in autumn have exceeded those in spring. The most spectacular example of this happened in 1992 when over 350 birds were recorded between 9th and 11th September. A flock of 45 was seen at Combs Reservoir, and a remarkable 220 gathered at Staunton Harold Reservoir. There were exceptional numbers in Leicestershire at the same time, including 650 at Rutland Water and 400 at Eyebrook Reservoir. This remained an unprecedented autumn influx, as the largest movement in any other year was 27, passing through Ogston Reservoir on 5th September 1987 and another five on 6th September, until the first week in October 2001 during which a total of at least 33 were recorded at Carsington Water. One of these was killed by a Peregrine.

The chart illustrates the half-monthly totals of all birds for the period 1950–2011. Almost 50% have occurred in May, while some 23% have appeared in September and 16% in August. The extreme dates of occurrence are 12th April (1992) at Church Wilne Reservoir and 28th October (1984) at Swarkestone Lake.

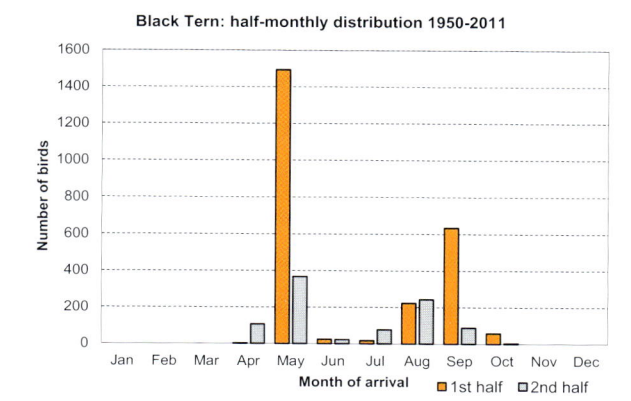

The geographical distribution of records for Black Tern is broadly similar to that of the other 'regular' terns, with a predominance of sightings from the Trent Valley, where it is an almost annual visitor to Church Wilne and Staunton Harold Reservoirs. In recent years Willington and Long Eaton Gravel Pits have also been visited regularly. Ogston Reservoir has produced the greatest number of records for a single locality, while Barbrook Reservoir was the most favoured upland site prior to its partial draining. Carsington Water, the largest and most recently established reservoir in Derbyshire, has already become a reliable site. Black Terns are also quite likely to be encountered at relatively small waters in the county; such habitats are presumably more attractive to this marsh tern than the more essentially marine members of the tern family. Unfortunately, these visits are nearly always short-lived, although occasionally one or two birds, usually immatures, have lingered for a few days in the autumn.

White-winged Black Tern
Chlidonias leucopterus
A very rare vagrant.

There have been six Derbyshire records, all of single birds in autumn. Five of these were immature birds.

The dates and locations are shown in the table. The Barbrook Reservoir bird in 1997 occurred on the same day as a Sabine's Gull at Ogston Reservoir.

White-winged Black Terns were removed from the list of species assessed by BBRC after 2005, by which time there had been 871 records nationally. They breed from eastern Europe to China, and European birds winter in sub-Saharan Africa.

Year	Location and date
1968	Staunton Harold Reservoir, an immature on 23rd–24th August
1976	Ogston Reservoir, a winter-plumaged adult on 30th August
1987	Ogston Reservoir, an immature on 5th September
1988	Staunton Harold Reservoir, an immature on 24th–25th September
1997	Barbrook Reservoir, an immature on 29th August
2006	Long Eaton Gravel Pits, an immature on 13th September

Sandwich Tern
Sterna sandvicensis
A scarce, but regular, passage migrant.

According to Whitlock, J.J. Briggs said that this species often occurred in the Melbourne area in spring and during stormy weather. Whitlock rather doubted this, on the grounds that he had only seen one locally, on the River Trent between Barton Ferry and the confluence with the River Soar on 14th May 1888. Jourdain's copy of Whitlock says that one was in Mr Cockburn's collection from Chesterfield, dated 1880.

There was a surprisingly long gap until the next record, of two flying south-west over open countryside at Staveley on 24th September 1967 (Frost). However, since then, there have been 149 occurrences involving 260 birds. The last year without a record was 1985, and nowadays the Sandwich Tern seems to be established as a scarce but regular visitor to Derbyshire. A steady increase in the number of pairs breeding around Britain's coasts in recent decades, together with much more intensive observer coverage throughout the county, probably accounts for such a significant change in status.

Period	Records	Birds
1960s	9	23
1970s	19	33
1980s	17	37
1990s	40	66
2000–11	65	103
Totals	150	262

Up to 2011, nearly half of the sightings were of single birds, almost one-third involving two birds, while there were 21 instances of three or four together, and one of five. The largest groups recorded were of six at Ogston Reservoir in July 1969 and Carsington Water in August 2005. There are records for all months between March and October with extreme dates of 28th March (1989) at Howden Reservoir and 24th October (1983) at Ogston Reservoir.

The chart shows the half-monthly distribution pattern of birds in 1950–2011. A ringing recovery in November, see below, is omitted from the figures as it is not known how long the bird had been dead.

Sandwich Tern: half-monthly distribution 1950-2011

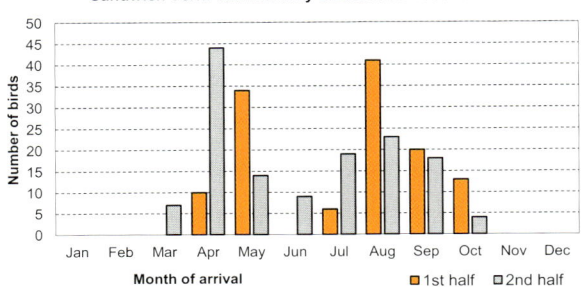

A concentrated spring peak in late April and early May is quite obvious, with a slightly larger, but more evenly spread, number of sightings from mid-July until late September, especially in early August. While the majority of observations have been made within the main spring and autumn passage periods, there is still insufficient evidence to prove a deliberate overland migration of Sandwich Terns, equivalent to that already described for Kittiwakes (Hume 1976). However, with over 50% of records coming from the Trent Valley, including several from the River Trent itself, it is quite likely that many birds seen in Derbyshire are following the course of this major waterway through the Midlands. Away from this area, Ogston Reservoir has been the most frequented site, providing around a quarter of all records, although the more recently established Carsington Water has already produced 19 records. The remaining sightings have come mostly from upland waters in the north-west, including Arnfield, Howden and Combs Reservoirs, with just a few occurrences along the Erewash Valley and in north-east Derbyshire. Visits are almost always fleeting or short-lived, and Sandwich Terns have hardly ever been known to stay overnight in the county. An exception was a bird that remained at Combs Reservoir from 23rd to 29th April 1992.

There is a single Derbyshire recovery for this species of a chick ringed in the Republic of Ireland in 1963 and found dead, possibly shot, near Monyash on 13th November 1970.

Common Tern
Sterna hirundo
An uncommon breeder, mainly in the Trent Valley. An uncommon but regular passage migrant.

Even in the nineteenth century Common Terns were known to be quite regular at migration times (Whitlock). Since the 1950s they have been recorded annually, both in spring and autumn, with a marked increase in the frequency of sightings over the last 30 years. During the same period the number of reports in the summer months has risen even more significantly as the Common Tern has become established as a breeding species in the county.

The earliest arrival date is 26th March (1964) on the River Trent at Long Eaton, with only four other records for this month, two of them on 29th March 2005. Over the 30 years from 1978 to 2007 the average first date was 12th April. The main passage takes place in May. Although the overall number of birds in most years probably exceeds that of Arctic Tern, the size of Common Tern flocks is generally smaller, with groups of over 30 birds fairly rare. The largest spring gatherings were of 100 at Church Wilne Reservoir on 2nd May 1990 and 55 at Willington Gravel Pits on 23rd April 1994.

Nowadays, Common Terns seen in June and July are most likely to be birds breeding locally rather than passage migrants, which have always been rare at this time of year. This species first nested in Derbyshire in 1956 (Frost), but it was not until the 1970s that the breeding population began to consolidate, though it remained exclusively within the Trent Valley until 1990. The total number of breeding pairs for each period since 1970 is shown in the table.

Period	Pairs
1970–74	5
1975–79	38
1980–84	48
1985–89	50
1990–94	138
1995–99	77
2000–11	270
Total	626

As indicated on the map, proven breeding came from 18 squares, probable six and possible 19, all information gleaned from the Derbyshire BBS (1995–99).

The map reveals the preponderance of nest sites in the Trent Valley, which are usually on small islands within flooded gravel

BBS Atlas 1995-1999

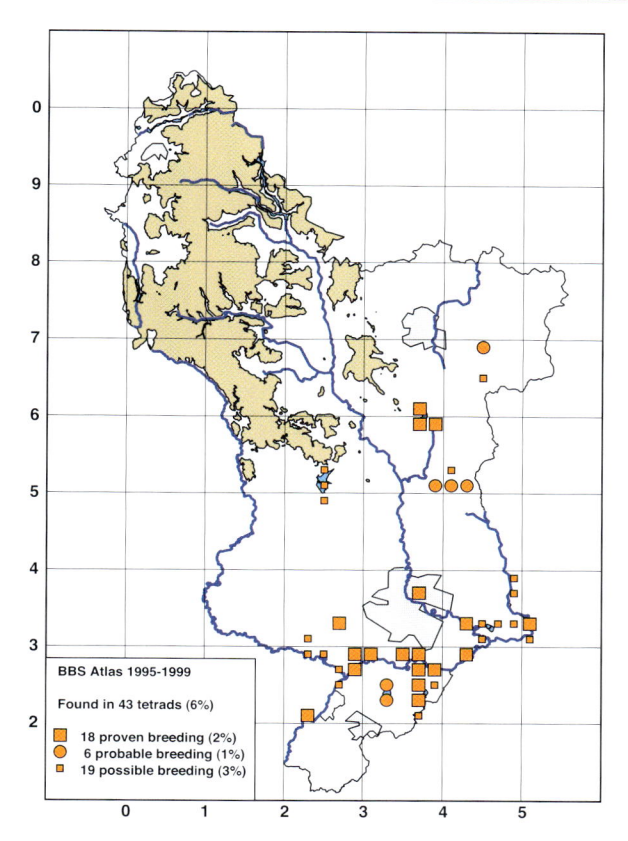

Found in 43 tetrads (6%)

- 18 proven breeding (2%)
- 6 probable breeding (1%)
- 19 possible breeding (3%)

pits. While workings at Willington Gravel Pits have usually held the largest and certainly the longest-established colony, the often transient nature of such habitats inevitably provides an element of instability. For example, Elvaston Quarry, the most favoured site for almost a decade, with up to eight pairs nesting, was deserted once infilling operations began in the late 1980s. The colony at Swarkestone Lake, which had existed since the mid-1970s and had built up to about 20 pairs, suddenly collapsed in 1993 and never re-established itself. This particular loss largely accounts for the sharp drop in the overall population from a record high of 38 pairs in 1992 to only five pairs in 1996. In recent years there has been a partial population shift to the eastern end of the Trent Valley, where conditions at Aston-on-Trent and Ambaston Gravel Pits have sometimes been suitable for Common Terns to nest.

A welcome extension of range in 1990 was encouraged by the provision of rafts at Ogston Reservoir which enabled two pairs to raise young. Successful breeding continued to 1995, and a pair was successful in 2001 following a failure in the previous year, and in 2009, 2010 and 2011 breeding resumed. Purpose-built nesting platforms have also been provided at Carsington Water, with successful breeding in 2001, 2002, 2006 and 2008–10, but failure in 2011; Staunton Harold Reservoir with up to six pairs; Hilton Gravel Pits Nature Reserve with a pair in 2001–05, three pairs in 2006, two in 2007, six in 2008–09, seven in 2010 and nine in 2011; and Carr Vale, where a pair bred in 2006 and two pairs from 2007 to 2009. In the latter year, one of the adults was attacked by a Coot and seriously injured. In 1995, a pair bred at Higham Fish Ponds, a very unusual locality, and in 2010 a pair bred at Mapperley Reservoir.

Despite a partial recovery in numbers at the end of the twentieth century and an increase in the 2000s, future prosperity is by no means guaranteed. The Common Tern is vulnerable to both disturbance and predation and these factors have certainly limited its breeding success in the past. The provision and maintenance of nesting rafts is likely to be crucial to the continued breeding success of this species in Derbyshire.

At the end of the breeding season in late summer, numbers tend to be slightly higher than in spring as returning migrants, often in family parties, augment those adults and young reared locally. The largest autumn flocks were of 72 at Church Wilne Reservoir on 22nd August 2003, 70 at Willington Gravel Pits on 23rd August 2002 and up to 49 roosting on buoys at Church Wilne Reservoir in August 1984. Autumn passage is quite leisurely, with birds regularly lingering for several days. By September numbers dwindle noticeably, and the average date of the last sighting in 1978–2011 is 29th September. A few stragglers have been seen in October, with the latest ever date being 28th October (1967) at Staunton Harold Reservoir.

The Common Tern is undoubtedly the most widespread tern to be found in Derbyshire, with sightings from around 30 localities per annum during the 1990s. Not surprisingly, most originate from the Trent Valley, with several also from other lowland sites. Peak District records are not uncommon, and occasional observations have been made of birds in flight over rural and urban environments.

There are four ringing recoveries of this species, all from the late 1980s and early 1990s. Two ringed as chicks at Egginton and Ogston Reservoir both moved to Seaforth Docks Nature Reserve, Liverpool where their rings were read in the field; one seven weeks and one nearly three years after ringing. Another, ringed as a chick in the Menai Straits in Anglesey in July 1989, was found freshly dead near Glossop a month later. The fourth bird was a local recovery, from Attenborough Gravel Pits, Nottinghamshire to Long Eaton.

Roseate Tern
Sterna dougallii
A very rare vagrant.

Mosley and Brown (1863) claimed that this species had occurred in the Tutbury and Burton districts and James Harley of Loughborough included it in a list from the River Trent. However, both Whitlock and Jourdain were unwilling to accept it on the Derbyshire list on the evidence available.

The first acceptable sightings were in 1965 and in all there have been only seven confirmed records involving ten birds, which reflects the rarity of this species inland. Interestingly, the two seen at Carsington Water in 2006 were part of a small inland passage of up to five birds seen in the Midlands, as one was seen at Blithfield Reservoir, Staffordshire and two were at Pitsford Reservoir, Northamptonshire on the same date.

In addition, a bird believed to be a hybrid Roseate x Common Tern was seen at Ogston Reservoir from 1st to 6th June 1996. This may have been the bird reported in the Trent Valley region of Nottinghamshire in 1992–95.

Year	Location and date
1965	Staunton Harold Reservoir, four on 18th June
1965	Swarkestone Lake, four on 22nd June were presumed to be the same birds as the above
1967	Clay Mills Gravel Pits, one on 14th May
1968	Ogston Reservoir, one on 15th May
1978	Drakelow Nature Reserve, one flew west on 16th May
1979	Church Wilne Reservoir, one on 10th June
2006	Carsington Water, two on 7th May, which left to the north-east

Arctic Tern
Sterna paradisaea
An uncommon or fairly regular passage migrant.

This renowned long-distance traveller has been recorded in the county every year since 1964, and is established as a fairly regular passage migrant, especially in spring. During the period 1960–2011, there were just over 1000 records with almost 7300 individuals identified. An analysis of the figures into the respective periods reveals that the average rose steeply from just ten to over 280 birds per annum in the 1990s, but fell back again to just under 200 per annum in 2000–11.

Period	Records	Birds
1960s	44	104
1970s	112	567
1980s	190	992
1990s	301	2837
2000–11	419	2788
Totals	1066	7288

In sharp contrast to the relative abundance of recent sightings, there were hardly any authenticated records prior to 1960. This apparent change in status would not seem to have been caused by any alteration in the breeding sites or numbers of Arctic Terns in northern Europe, which have remained reasonably stable, during the twentieth century at least. A more likely explanation may be found in terms of the undoubted increase in observer coverage, particularly at lowland reservoirs, most of which have been created since the 1950s. Another factor may well be the considerable improvement in the standard of optical equipment and field guides featuring new identification criteria, enabling more frequent and accurate separation from the closely related Common Tern. A closer study of the number of Arctic Terns seen each year in the period 1980–2011 reveals some significant fluctuations in annual totals, with certain years, especially 1991 and 1998, having considerably more than others, as shown in the chart.

This is probably not an entirely new phenomenon, as Frost suggested that influxes occurred during the nineteenth century. As documented by Kramer (1995), there is growing evidence to support the theory that large numbers of Arctic Terns regularly fly over inland regions in spring. The most notable passage took place from 1st to 3rd May 1998 when an estimated 800 birds were recorded, including flocks totalling 300–400 birds at Carsington Water, and about 200 at Long Eaton Gravel Pits. Large influxes also occurred in 1996, 1991, 1983, 2004 and 2009, each time coinciding with inclement weather in the first week of May. There have been records of up to 100 birds on several occasions during the last decade, usually from Ogston Reservoir and Carsington Water, but also at localities in the Trent Valley, particularly Church Wilne Reservoir and Willington Gravel Pits.

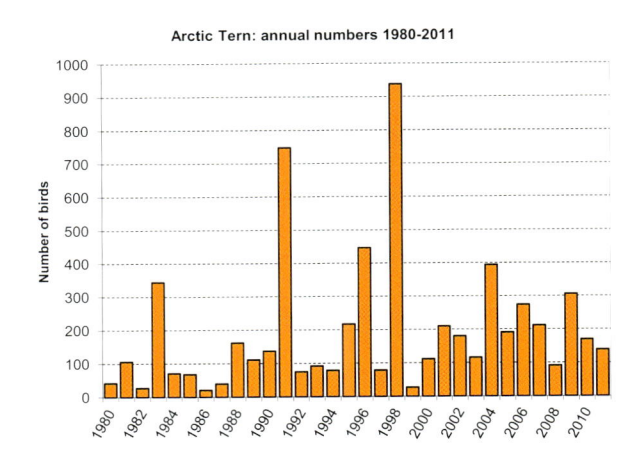

However, Arctic Terns are mainly found in parties of fewer than 20 birds during the spring. Visits are usually very brief, although 17 stayed overnight at Willington Gravel Pits in April 1997. During the autumn, even smaller numbers normally occur, with the only records of more than a dozen birds being 30 on 1st October 1977 at Ogston Reservoir and 16 at the same site on 9th August 1993. Like the Common Tern, movements of Arctic Tern during the return passage involve both adults and immatures, with some birds occasionally remaining for a few days.

The half-monthly distribution pattern for the period 1960–2011, based on all available information, is shown in the table.

The extreme dates of occurrence are 4th April (1994) at Catton and 12th November (1967) at Pebley Pond.

Between 1960 and 2005, Arctic Terns were found at over 50 localities throughout the county. Ogston Reservoir and Carsington Water are particularly favoured, being visited almost annually, while reservoirs and flooded gravel pits in the Trent Valley are also regularly frequented. Sightings in the Peak District are fairly unusual, although Barbrook Reservoir has provided records on several occasions, prior to its partial drainage.

Half-month	Birds	Half-month	Birds
April	95	August	103
	1890		140
May	4371	September	137
	218		55
June	60	October	59
	47		2
July	41	November	1
	69		–

Sabine's Gull
Xema sabini
A very rare vagrant.

This beautiful gull breeds around the Arctic, and winters at sea in the Pacific and Atlantic oceans. There is one nineteenth-century record, of a young bird shot at Chaddesden on about 26th August 1894 (Frost). There were five twentieth-century records, all since 1980 and all involving single birds.

Year	Location and date
1980	Elvaston Quarry, a first-winter on 15th and 16th September
1983	Ogston Reservoir, an adult in summer plumage on 9th October
1994	Bennerley Marsh, a juvenile on 15th September
1995	Middleton Moor, a juvenile, which left to the north-west at 1810hrs on 17th September
1997	Ogston Reservoir, a juvenile on 29th August

Inland sightings of this small, maritime gull usually occur after strong westerly or south-westerly winds, which may drive them close inshore and sometimes inland. The 1994 bird was one of 66 seen in Britain during the first half of September; the only other one inland was a juvenile at Upton Warren, Worcestershire from 13th to 15th. The 1995 bird occurred after heavy rainstorms, and was conceivably the individual that had flown west from Rutland Water, Leicestershire and Rutland, just over three hours earlier. The final bird, in 1997, occurred on the same day as a White-winged Black Tern at Barbrook Reservoir.

Kittiwake
Rissa tridactyla
An uncommon, but regular, passage migrant.

This is the most maritime of the gulls to be seen regularly in the county, but its status has changed dramatically. Whitlock considered Kittiwakes second only to Black-headed Gulls in their regularity in the county, the two species often consorting together. He stated that they were 'pretty regular' in the Trent Valley, being found almost daily in March and April. At other times of the year they were thought to be storm-blown vagrants. Jourdain agreed largely with this statement and went even further by stating that they were met with more regularly than Black-headed Gulls. However, this species was not then recorded in Derbyshire until 1946, 41 years after the publication of the *Victoria County History*. Only four were seen in the 1950s, all dead or dying birds (Frost), as was the second-winter bird resulting from the 1957 wreck found in an Ashbourne garden on 29th January. Thereafter, records became more regular and have been annual since 1964.

Nowadays, the greatest numbers of Kittiwakes occur between February and May when an undoubted migration takes place. Some large flocks have been found at this time. The largest of these were: approximately 120 during a period of very strong north-west winds at Church Wilne Reservoir on 29th March 1980, all adults, the majority of which roosted; and 130, which roosted in wet and windy weather at Ogston Reservoir on 27th February 2000. A flock of 120 alighted on Derwent Reservoir on 19th March 1994 and another flock of at least 98 birds settled on Howden Reservoir in a severe snowstorm on 12th March 1988. Further large flocks have been seen at Foremark Reservoir, where about 100 birds settled at 1430hrs on 12th February 1996; most had moved on by 1500hrs, although 11 remained to roost. At Rother Valley Country Park (now in South Yorkshire) a total of 89 birds flew south in two flocks on 19th May 1992. At Carsington Water a flock of 74 arrived at 1730hrs on 8th March 2003 and roosted, but only two were present on the next day. Although the flock at Church Wilne Reservoir may have been displaced by strong winds, it is more likely that this and the other birds were 'grounded' by the severe conditions on their normal cross-country migration.

Key (1982) plotted the monthly distribution of Kittiwakes recorded in Derbyshire from 1954 to 1981 and found the peak numbers occurred in March, with smaller numbers in April. Comparative figures, showing some large variations, for the periods 1954–81, 1982–99 and 2000–11 may be found in the table.

Although the peak numbers still occur in March, it can be seen that the cross-country movement nowadays starts much earlier in the year, with larger numbers recorded in February. The period 1982–99 showed a secondary peak in May, but this has recently reduced. In addition, small but regular numbers are now being found in midwinter, mainly at gull roosts. The 1984–88 Winter Atlas stated that more birds were now wintering around harbours and fish-docks and this accounted for the increase in wintering records found during that survey. Key discovered that birds were returning earlier to breeding colonies, although this varied from colony to colony. However, he found the number of inland records of this maritime gull surprising, and difficult to explain. Most were in England and he attributed them to birds displaced in bad weather, commenting that some were found dead. A surprising number have been found dead or moribund in Derbyshire, including at least six in moorland localities. Among these was the mummified corpse of an adult in winter plumage found at Nether Reddale Clough on 16th May 1981 sitting in a roosting position, untouched by scavengers. One was also killed by a Peregrine in north Derbyshire during early April 1987 and one was found freshly dead at 430m amsl on the Derwent Moors on 15th April 1994.

Kittiwakes have been recorded at all of the county's larger reservoirs, with some surprisingly high numbers in the Derwentdale complex. Nowadays, this species might occur almost anywhere, although occurrences at landfill sites are exceptional, the only instances being of one at Barrow Hill on 6th March 1988 and an adult at Staveley on 13th March 1999. This species is also very scarce in the extreme north-west of the county, with just a few records from the reservoirs in Longdendale.

Long-staying birds include an immature (ringed in France in 2009) seen at Pleasley Colliery on 16 dates between 27th June and 3rd November 2010, and 38 dates between 13th January and 24th October 2011. This individual was also recorded at Carr Vale and Carsington Water.

Occasionally, birds will rest in fields, if they cannot find anywhere more suitable. An adult was sitting in a ploughed field near Swarkestone Lake on 6th March 1993 and another adult was found with a flock of about 100 Black-headed Gulls in fields at Windy Harbour on 23rd March 1996. On 15th May 1994 an adult was seen standing on a road at Shirebrook until it was flushed by a car.

Month	1954–81	1982–99	2000–11
January	8	47	46
February	6	162	146
March	193	668	203
April	55	69	33
May	16	126	14
June	1	23	3
July	6	4	–
August	10	7	4
September	8	4	5
October	5	12	5
November	7	27	42
December	25	37	9

Bonaparte's Gull
Chroicocephalus philadelphia
A very rare vagrant.

There have been six records of this species, all in the late twentieth century and involving single birds. Calladine (1989) provided an account of the 1987 sighting.

The first inland record of this rare gull was at Barn Elms Reservoir, London in 1983. Since then there have been many records inland, though no other county has had six such occurrences. The UK total to the end of 2011 was 188 (Hudson *et al.* 2012). It breeds in Canada and winters on the Great Lakes and from coastal USA south to the Caribbean and Mexico.

Year	Location and date
1987	Ogston Reservoir, an adult roosted from 17th to 19th and from 22nd to 26th February
1995	Lea, Matlock, a winter-plumaged adult on 13th December. This bird roosted at Ogston Reservoir from 14th to 16th December
1995	Ogston Reservoir, a first-winter roosted on 29th December
1996	Willington Gravel Pits, a first-summer on 5th May. This may have been the individual that was classed as a first-winter at Blithfield Reservoir, Staffordshire between 27th and 30th April
1996	Carsington Water, a first-summer, briefly, on 26th June before it departed south
2000	Ogston Reservoir, an adult roosted on 26th–27th December. This bird was also seen at Pools Brook Country Park on the latter date

Black-headed Gull
Chroicocephalus ridibundus
An abundant winter visitor and passage migrant. A fairly common breeder in the south and the north-west.

The first breeding record in the county came from Leash Fen in 1918 and this site held over 100 pairs in some years until military operations caused the birds to desert in 1944. Between 1920 and 1944 gulleries were recorded on Big Moor (maximum 56 pairs), near Hathersage (up to 200 pairs), Egginton Sewage Farm (200–300 pairs) and British Celanese Lakes Nature Reserve (200 pairs). Smaller numbers bred elsewhere in the county. They colonized Willington No. 2 Gravel Pit in 1956 and bred until 1961 when the 100 pairs present were very unsuccessful and subsequently deserted the colony. In the period 1955–78 small numbers bred at four sites in the Trent Valley, as well as on Ringinglow Bog and in Longdendale (Frost).

From 1978 to 1986 only small numbers bred in the county, mainly in the Trent Valley, but from 1982 the colony in Longdendale, which had been deserted for the previous ten years, became re-established and by 1988 approximately 200 pairs were breeding at Woodhead Reservoir. This colony held some 600 pairs by 1997, but in 1999 only about 200 pairs bred due to higher water levels. By 2004 this site was deserted following two years of low success, possibly due to the presence of mink, but breeding was recorded again in 2007, 2009 and 2010 with 110 nests in the latter two years, and 226 nests in 2011. Some of the birds may have moved to Waterswallows Quarry, where there were 105 nests, many with small young, on 29th May 2005. By 2007 there was only one nest here, but 63 pairs nested at the nearby Doveholes Quarry, with 60 nests in 2008, 35 in 2009, 43 in 2010 and 46 in 2011. Single pairs have also nested at Topley Pike and Peak Dale Quarries since 2000. Middleton Moor saw the establishment of a new colony in 2000 with seven nests, and numbers had risen to 40–60 nests by 2010. At Carsington Water, up to seven pairs nested in 2007–11 on rafts intended for terns. The first breeding at Carr Vale was in 2010 (one successful pair), and in 2011 a nest was predated. The Trent Valley saw just one breeding attempt in 2011 when a nest was abandoned at Willington Gravel Pits.

In the south, numbers started to increase from 1988 with a colony at Derby Sewage Farm, which peaked at 95 pairs in 1989. Willington Gravel Pits then became the main site in this area, reaching about 150 pairs in 1995 and still having around 100 pairs in 1999. In 1996, a maximum of approximately 170 pairs nested here, but the season was disastrous as only small numbers of young were seen, none of which fledged; this was thought to be due to a very cold May with frosty nights. This site has also experienced much disturbance due to habitat changes, and in 2002 to 2008 held only a few pairs of Black-headed Gulls before at least 40 pairs nested, with a low success rate, in 2009. By 2011 just one pair attempted to nest here. For a while, Aston-on-Trent Gravel Pits became the main breeding site in the south with over 60 nests in 2002 and at least 204 in mid-May 2003. Many had small young by the end of the month, but, because of a lowering of water levels due to quarrying activities, no young fledged, most falling victim to foxes. Since 2004 the numbers attempting to breed have been very small, with none in the last few years. In 2000 at nearby Ambaston Gravel Pits, nearly 100 fledged and unfledged young were present in late June, but again,

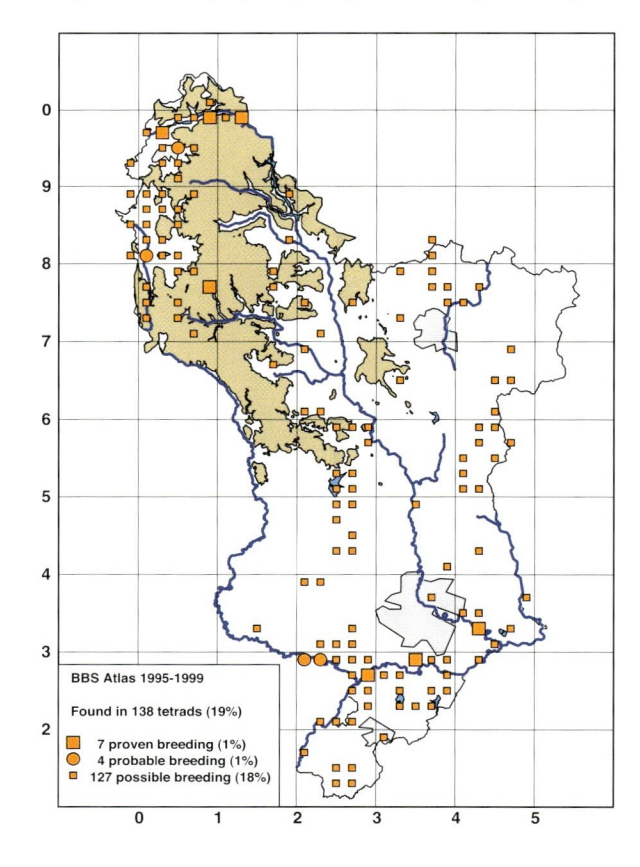

BBS Atlas 1995-1999
Found in 138 tetrads (19%)
- 7 proven breeding (1%)
- 4 probable breeding (1%)
- 127 possible breeding (18%)

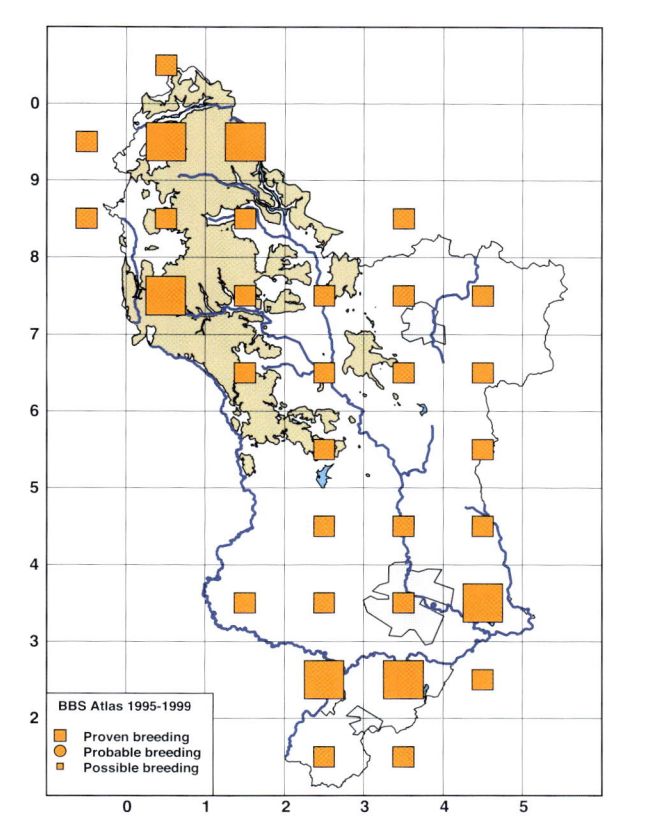

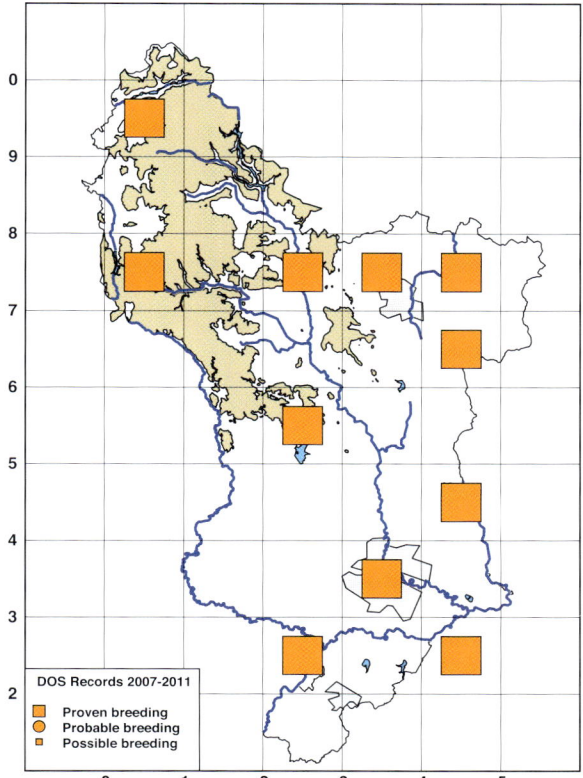

fluctuating water levels have meant that this site has also been almost abandoned.

During the Derbyshire BBS (1995–99) this species was found to have bred in seven tetrads, with probable breeding in four more. Well over 100 sightings of birds moving to and from such sites have not been mapped as 'possible', as it was considered that this distorted the overall picture. Unfortunately, the southernmost sites are at working gravel pits and these are normally very quickly returned to their former status when extractions are complete.

The maps show confirmed breeding areas in 1995–99 and 2007–11.

In winter, Black-headed Gulls have increased greatly. Whitlock found this species to be the most common gull in the county and he often recorded flocks of up to 40. By 1955 the largest recorded gathering had risen to 300. But today, four-figure counts are common at the roosting sites, and five-figure counts are the norm now at the main roost at Church Wilne Reservoir. The peak count from here was a massive 30,000 on 13th and 20th January 1985 and in December 2011, with counts of 20,000 recorded in most years. Foremark Reservoir held 15,000 in November 2001 and December 2007, and numbers here doubled to 30,000 by the end of 2009 probably because of the proximity of a large landfill site at Albert Village in north-west Leicestershire. Ogston Reservoir held a maximum of 8300 in January 1993. Up to 6000 have roosted at Staunton Harold Reservoir and 7000 at Drakelow Nature Reserve, although the latter is now defunct as a roost site. This species will sometimes roost on floodwater in the Trent Valley, for example near Elvaston Quarry with 5000 on 12th February 1984 and 4500 on 8th December 1984. At Church Wilne Reservoir on 23rd January 1990, 'hundreds' were flying round the works buildings at 2330hrs, presumably after being disturbed at the reservoir. At Derby Locomotive Works on 8th July 1984, a flock of 12 landed in an empty car park at 2300hrs and roosted until disturbed at 0330hrs the following morning.

Away from the roosts, big flocks have been noted at landfill sites during the day, with 4350 at Doe Lea on 31st December 1993 and about 4000 at Ambaston on the same date being noteworthy. Floodwater often attracts good numbers of loafing birds, with 3000 at Darley Fields on 2nd November 1998 and 2000 at Repton on 23rd November 1992 being the largest recorded gatherings. This species is an opportunist feeder and can be found anywhere, especially in winter, even coming into gardens to feed on scraps. For example, about 20 were noted feeding on hawthorn berries at Willington Gravel Pits on 10th October 1982, and at Shirebrook, two took acorns from the crown of an oak on 24th October 1981.

The most conspicuous movements are of birds flying to roost in winter. Examples involving birds using the Ogston Reservoir roost include: 3225 leaving Doe Lea landfill site on 31st December 1992; 3000 over Pilsley on 31st December 1993 and 3360 flying south at Carr Vale on 21st January 2000. True migration is usually noted between March and May, with birds moving north and east. The return movement is from July as birds migrate westwards through the county.

Albinistic and leucistic birds have been noted in most recent years at a wide variety of sites, but mainly in the roosts at Church Wilne, Foremark and Ogston Reservoirs, with a maximum of three leucistic birds at the latter in January 1995. A bird at Rother Valley Country Park (now in South Yorkshire) on 6th–7th February 1989 had all-violet plumage, while a melanistic bird was at Elvaston Quarry on 20th July 1986. An all-grey immature bird was at the Trent–Derwent confluence on 29th November 1982 and at Elvaston Quarry landfill site on 4th December 1982. Occasional wing-tagged and colour-ringed birds have been noted.

At Aston-on-Trent Gravel Pits on 29th April 2003, one was noted as having a largely decurved bill, 50% longer than normal.

There are almost 100 recovery records for the county dating back to the early 1960s. Of these, some 33% have been of birds moving more than 500km. Among the more interesting were: one ringed at New Mills in August 1962 and recovered at Braslav, Vitebsk, Russian Federation, 1872km to the east in July 1966; one ringed at Alvaston in January 1987 that was controlled at Wolgast, Rostock, Germany 1030km east in July 1990; and birds ringed as chicks at Bromolla, Kristianstad, Sweden and Kretuonas, Svencionys, Lithuania that were shot at Clay Cross and Long Eaton in subsequent springs. The oldest record is of a bird ringed at Beighton in the winter of 1963 which was caught and released in Denmark, 21 years later.

Little Gull
Hydrocoloeus minutus
An uncommon passage migrant. Rare in summer and winter.

Little Gull: monthly distribution 1960-2011

In Derbyshire, at least three were reported seen or killed on the River Trent during the nineteenth century (Frost). The next record was not until 1962, when a first-summer bird was at Barbrook Reservoir on 7th August and one, perhaps the same bird, was at Ogston Reservoir on 13th August. Although there were no records in 1963, this species has occurred in the county every year since. Up to 1983 no more than ten had been seen in any one year, but in 1984 a total of 56 was recorded, followed by a staggering 92 in 1990. Other years with high numbers were 1991, 1996 and 2009.

The five-year totals are given in the table. Since 1980 the totals for the five-year periods are fairly consistent apart from 1990–94 and 2000–04.

Period	Birds
1960–64	3
1965–69	18
1970–74	38
1975–79	26
1980–84	77
1985–89	50
1990–94	156
1995–99	106
2000–04	168
2005–09	179
2010–11	35
Total	856

Little Gulls have been recorded during every month of the year. The largest numbers have occurred in April and May, with a much lower peak in August and September as shown in the chart.

The greatest numbers have occurred in late April and early May, with flocks at Church Wilne Reservoir of 32 on 3rd May 1990, 26 on 30th April 1984 and 24 on 16th April 2009. At this time of year, this species often occurs with Black Terns.

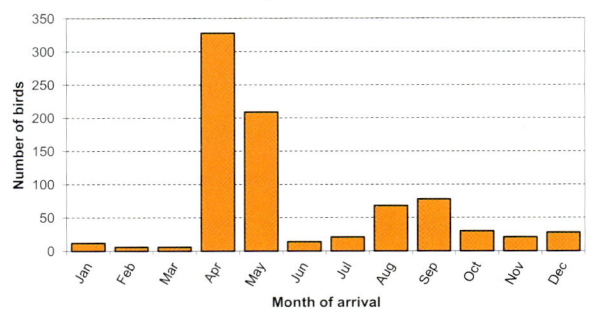

Surprisingly, the next largest parties both occurred in winter when 11, all adults except for one first-winter, roosted at Foremark Reservoir on 20th December 1996, while another group of seven was present at Bennerley Marsh on the same date.

The first bird to be found in winter was an adult at Foremark Reservoir on 19th January 1983. Since then, Little Gulls have occurred in 11 more winters, mainly at the well-watched roosts at Ogston, Church Wilne and Foremark Reservoirs. It may be that small numbers are blown inland at this time of year by gales in their offshore wintering grounds.

From 1962 to 2011, of a total of 856 birds seen in the county, 266 were recorded as immatures, with a further 302 aged as adults. Adults are certainly more liable to be recorded in spring, and the three large flocks noted then were mainly adults, including 24 of the 26 on 30th April 1984 and all of the 24 on 16th April 2009.

This species has been recorded from 40 localities throughout the county, five large reservoirs accounting for a minimum of 600 out of the total. Church Wilne Reservoir is the favourite site, with at least 302 birds having been recorded. Staunton Harold Reservoir has 57 records and 86 have been seen at Ogston Reservoir. Carsington Water has hosted 119 birds. Away from the reservoirs a total of 58 has been seen at Willington Gravel Pits. It is no coincidence that most of the favoured sites are in the Trent Valley, a noted migration route. This species is decidedly rare away from the southern and eastern lowlands, with eight being recorded at Barbrook Reservoir, five at Combs Reservoir and 12 at Middleton Moor lagoons, these all being relatively upland sites.

Unusual records concerned an immature found in a field of winter wheat at Etwall Brook on 27th March 1986; an adult in winter plumage flying north-east over Sinfin Lane, Derby on 9th September 1989; a first-winter watched, preening, close to nightfall in car headlights down to 4m at Pools Brook Country Park on 20th January 1995; three flying south near Hardwick Park on 2nd September 2003, and a first-winter hawking insects on the River Wye at Bakewell on 11th October 2003.

Laughing Gull
Larus atricilla
A very rare vagrant.

Laughing Gulls breed in Nova Scotia and south along the eastern seaboard of the USA, in the Caribbean, and from Central America to Venezuela. Northern breeders move south within this area. They are rare vagrants to Britain, although they have become more frequent in recent years, with 193 British records up to the end of 2011 (Hudson *et al*. 2012). Unusually for a Nearctic species, records have been spread throughout all months of the year and show a surprisingly wide geographical scatter.

There have been two Derbyshire records. A second-winter bird roosted overnight on 29th–30th November 1980 at Ogston Reservoir, and a first-summer bird entered the county at Sawley, flying north-east from Trent Valley Pits, Leicestershire on 5th July 1995.

Franklin's Gull
Larus pipixcan
A very rare vagrant.

This handsome small gull breeds in the American prairies and winters along the Pacific coast of South America. By the end of 2011 there had been 67 UK records (Hudson *et al.* 2012).

An adult was seen at Willington Gravel Pits on 28th–29th October and 2nd November 2010, and was found in the gull roost at nearby Foremark Reservoir on most evenings between 28th October and 5th November. It may well have been the individual seen in Staffordshire at Chasewater and Gailey Reservoirs in July and August of the same year. Oulsnam (2011) described the event.

Mediterranean Gull
Larus melanocephalus
A scarce, but increasing, winter visitor and passage migrant. Attempted to breed in 2009.

The first Derbyshire record was of a second-summer bird at Westhouses on 18th July 1965, which was one of the first birds ever seen in the Midlands region. The next record was not until 1978, when a first-winter bird was at Ogston Reservoir on 29th October. Since then, these fine gulls have been recorded in every year except 1979, 1981 and 1986. The table gives the numbers recorded in five-year periods, and the increase in records from the mid-1990s is clearly indicated. This correlates with an increase in breeding pairs in the UK as reported by the Rare Breeding Birds Panel.

Period	Birds
1965–69	1
1970–74	–
1975–79	1
1980–84	6
1985–89	12
1990–94	47
1995–99	165
2000–04	106
2005–11	172
Total	510

There may be some duplication in these numbers as birds seen at roosts disperse during the day to be recorded at other localities. Most records come from the well-watched gull roosts at Ogston, Foremark and Church Wilne Reservoirs. Away from the roosts, they have been mainly reported in the Trent Valley and the north-east of the county, usually in the vicinity of landfill sites. However, three of the first 11 Derbyshire records were from the north and north-west, with an adult at Arnfield Reservoir on 7th April 1984, a first-summer at Middleton Moor from 27th to 29th May 1984, and a second-summer at Peak Dale on 10th July 1988. Since then, only seven more have been seen in upland areas. Most are seen during the periods January to March and October to December, but there are records for all months, with June and August having the fewest.

The first record of this species in a breeding colony of Black-headed Gulls occurred when two summer-plumaged adults were at Willington Gravel Pits on 16th June 1992 before they flew off west.

The latter was the site of the first breeding attempt in the county, in 2009. Four individual adults were identified between 15th and 24th March, but there were no further sightings until 30th April, when a pair was seen in the Black-headed Gull colony on a low, gravel island densely covered with docks. Display, copulation, nest building and actions suggestive of egg-turning were subsequently observed. The nest was about 1m from the water's edge. Unfortunately, all of the 40 or more nests of Black-headed Gulls were deserted for unknown reasons in early June and there were no more sightings of the pair of Mediterranean Gulls. The island was visited on 21st September, when at least 20 long-dead Black-headed Gulls were found. An account was given by James and Roome (2009).

Other June records were all of summer-plumaged adults, at Ogston Reservoir on 22nd June 1996, Bennerley Marsh from 30th June to 2nd July 1997 and Carsington Water on 21st June 2009. The monthly distribution of all 510 birds is shown in the chart.

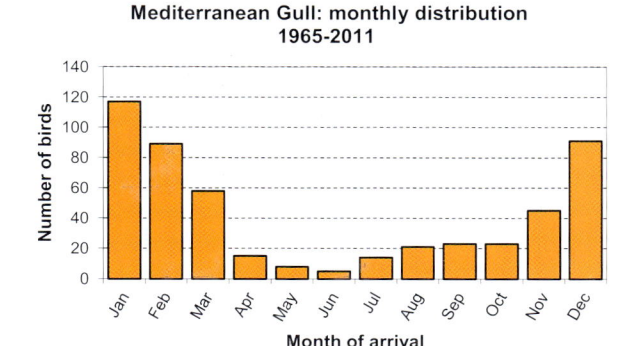

Adults and first-year birds have been recorded almost equally (40% adults and 42% first-years), but there have been nine records of birds aged as juveniles moulting into first-winter plumage, the first of which was at Pools Brook Country Park on 18th August 1994.

Records of hybrids showing characteristics of both Mediterranean and Black-headed Gulls were at Pools Brook Country Park on 8th February 1997 and Long Eaton Gravel Pits on 31st January 2005.

Common Gull
Larus canus
A fairly common winter visitor and passage migrant. Scarce in summer. Attempted to breed in 2008.

Whitlock described this species as a frequent visitor to Derbyshire in small numbers. This statement holds true today with usually only small numbers being seen away from the large southern reservoirs, where this species roosts in big numbers throughout the winter months. Since its construction, Church Wilne Reservoir has held fairly large numbers of roosting Common Gulls with up to 100 recorded by the late 1970s. Since 1980, numbers have increased considerably with regular roosting counts of up to 570, and maximum counts of 1500 on 29th December 2000 and again in December 2009 and 2011. Smaller numbers roost at Foremark Reservoir, where there are usually up to 100, but 750 were present there in January 2011, while at Carsington Water 800 roosted on 22nd March 2006. Up to 100 have roosted at Staunton Harold and Ogston Reservoirs. The diurnal whereabouts of these roosting birds at the southern reservoirs is something of a mystery, as only small numbers are seen at local landfill sites and elsewhere.

Another area where large numbers may be recorded in winter is the north and north-west of the county. About 240 were at Little Hucklow in December 1996 and 300 at Sparrowpit in December 1998, feeding on limestone grassland. They use flooded quarries to rest during the day before moving off, probably to the roosts in the Greater Manchester area.

Passage occurs from late February to April as birds move across the county towards their breeding areas. In the north and north-west, the largest counts have been of 297 at the Bakewell Showground on 21st February 2006, 215 at Peak Dale on 12th March 1999, 200 at Bradwell on 7th March 1986, and about 200 at Combs Reservoir on 3rd March 2002. Smaller numbers have been recorded in the north-east. At Ogston Reservoir on 14th May 1981, 150 flew east with Black-headed Gulls and 242 moved north-east in two hours on 2nd March 2011. A total of 140 was recorded at Pools Brook Country Park on 23rd December 2001. At Carsington Water in 2009, 177 flew north on the afternoon of 16th March, and 365 moved north-west in two hours on the afternoon of 23rd March. Only small numbers are usually seen during June and July, increasing from August to October.

That Common Gulls should attempt to breed in the county was rather unexpected. In 2008, a pair built a nest on one of the tern rafts in Shiningford Creek at Carsington Water but this was destroyed by a Coot. A second breeding attempt was then made on the adjacent Horseshoe Island but this also failed (Carrington & Bradley 2009).

A melanistic second-winter bird was on Derby Racecourse on 10th January 1986.

An unusual record was of two near a compost heap during harsh weather at Stonebroom on 25th December 1981.

Ring-billed Gull
Larus delawarensis
A very rare vagrant.

This is the most numerous of the small American gulls occurring in the UK. Between the first record in 1973 and 1985, no fewer than 449 were seen (Dymond *et al.* 1989) and it was removed from the list of species considered by BBRC after 1987.

The table lists all the 17 Derbyshire records.

Year	Location and date
1989	Ogston Reservoir, a second-winter from 16th to 18th December
1993	Ogston Reservoir, a first-winter roosted on 2nd December
1994	Ambaston landfill site, a first-winter on 16th–17th February and a first-winter which roosted at Church Wilne Reservoir on 9th March was presumed to be the same bird
1994	Ogston Reservoir, an adult on 1st November
1995	Ogston Reservoir, a first-winter on 10th December
2001	Carsington Water, a first-winter on 18th February
2001	Carsington Water, a first-summer on 21st April
2003/04	Carsington Water, an adult roosted intermittently from 15th November–17th December 2003 and between 10th November and 25th December 2004
2004	Ogston Reservoir, an adult roosted on 1st January
2004	Wyver Lane, an adult on 30th November
2006	Carsington Water, an adult roosted on 12 dates between 4th November and 20th December
2007	Carsington Water, an adult roosted on nine dates between 9th November and 6th December
2008	Long Eaton Gravel Pits, a first-summer on 23rd April
2008	Carsington Water, an adult roosted on nine dates between 7th November and 1st December
2009	Aston-on-Trent Gravel Pits, a first-winter on 31st January
2009	Carr Vale, a first-winter on 5th February
2009	Carsington Water, an adult roosted on 16 nights between 31st October and 6th December

It is probable that the records of the adult roosting at Carsington Water in 2003, 2004, 2006, 2007 and 2009, and the Wyver Lane bird of 2004 all relate to the same individual. Mann (1990) gave an account of the 1989 sighting.

This species breeds across North America, and winters south to Central America and northern South America.

Lesser Black-backed Gull
Larus fuscus
A common non-breeding summer visitor, passage migrant and winter visitor.

Recent taxonomic changes mean that there are three recognized races of Lesser Black-backed Gull. The nominate race, *L.f. fuscus*, sometimes called the Baltic Gull, breeds around the Baltic Sea, in northern Fennoscandia and into the far north-west of the Russian Federation. The race *L.f. intermedius* breeds throughout southern Scandinavia, while *L.f. graellsii* breeds throughout the rest of this species' range, which includes the British Isles, where it breeds around much of the coast, as well as at several inland colonies.

Whitlock considered this species a migrant to the Trent Valley, but only storm-driven to other parts of the county. Jourdain agreed with this, and it remained scarce in the first half of the twentieth century with few records. An increase was noted from 1951, and by the mid-1950s flocks of up to a few hundred became quite common, especially in the east of the county, at landfill and opencast mining sites. Most of the birds that were summering were identified as subadults and immatures by Rayner (1963). He also found evidence of a southward movement from July to September and a heavy west-north-west spring passage, which still holds true today. Lesser Black-backs are at their scarcest in the period April to May. A pair held territory at Middleton Moor from 3rd to 8th April 1982, before moving away.

However, a major recent change has been the increase in wintering birds, with several hundred noted in the roosts in the 1970s. This trend has continued with other large counts as follows: Church Wilne Reservoir, with 1400 in November 1980; Staunton Harold Reservoir, with 2500 in November 1974; and Foremark Reservoir, with 2300 in November 2004, 2000 in November and December 2009 and 4000 in December 2010. Between 2750 and 2800 roosted at Ogston Reservoir in November and December 2006. However, Carsington Water is nowadays by far the most important site in Derbyshire for this species: 4000 roosted there in November 1994; 6000 in January 2000, January 2001 and October to December 2001; 7000 in October 2002, November 2005 and September 2011; and 10,000 on 15th November 2003.

Numbers usually decrease at the roosts with the onset of winter, and the large flocks in November may consist of birds still migrating southwards through the county. Large numbers in the late summer and autumn roosts at Middleton Moor and Barbrook Reservoir from the 1960s and 1970s onwards were considerably reduced by the early 2000s, probably by the 'capture' by Carsington Water and later by the destruction of Barbrook as a reservoir. Middleton Moor held 3989 in August 1998 and Barbrook Reservoir 3223 in September 1997, evidence of just how many birds move southwards over Derbyshire in autumn.

Away from roosts, this species may occur in large numbers at landfill sites and on farmland. The largest non-roost counts include: approximately 5000 at Cauldwell on ploughland on 8th September 1996; 3000 flying south-west at Hasland on 13th October 2010; 2500 at Highoredish on 17th October 2010; 1440 at Brassington in a large field that was being harrowed on 7th September 2005; 1050 flying south over Carr Vale on 31st August 2003; 1000 at Bolsover Moor on 18th September 2005; 1000 in a pre-roost gathering at Ambaston Gravel Pits on 20th August 1991; 800 at Victory Quarry, Doveholes on 1st September 1990; and 900 at Pools Brook Country Park in November 1999. In 2000, there were three records of flocks of 1000 away from roosts: at Pikehall on 11th January, Elton Common on 11th September and on flooded fields at Allestree on 12th and 19th November. At Whitwell Quarry, 1000 flew west on 3rd October 2010 while 1100 flew west at Drakelow Nature Reserve on 19th July 2011.

A pale leucistic bird, thought to be an adult, was at Foremark Reservoir on 30th January 1994. At a distance this bird looked very much like an immature Iceland Gull. Another bird at Barbrook Reservoir on 22nd November 1995 and Ogston Reservoir on 25th and 27th November 1995 was basically pure white with a lot of black mottling on the underparts, some on the upper wings and solid black on the inner wing, with an adult's bill.

For many years the *Derbyshire Bird Report* listed details of sightings believed to refer to Scandinavian race birds, *L.f. fuscus*. It is now known that this bird is an exceptionally rare visitor to the UK. Evans and Proctor (1997) knew of fewer than 20 acceptable records. Most, if not all, of these dark-backed gulls are now considered to be of the race *intermedius*, which breeds in southern Scandinavia. Small numbers, sometimes reaching double figures, occur regularly in Derbyshire, especially in autumn.

Between the 1960s and the 1980s there were several records of paired birds apparently holding territory for a few days in spring at Barbrook Reservoir and Middleton Moor. On 10th April 2009 up to four birds were calling around Derbyshire Royal Infirmary and two at Bass's Recreation Ground, Derby. This may be significant as this species is increasingly nesting on tall buildings in many English towns and cities, and future breeding in Derbyshire must be a possibility.

Of the 66 ringing recoveries of this species, all but five concerned movements around Britain. The earliest record is of a bird moving from Lancaster to Chesterfield in 1958, and the longest lived was one ringed as a chick on Walney Island in 1964 and shot at Barrow upon Trent in 1985. Two ringed as pulli in Iceland were found dead in Derbyshire in subsequent autumns; likewise, two ringed at the same age at Vest-Agder, Norway were found in the county in subsequent summers. Others had travelled to the county from their natal ringing sites in Stirling (Scotland), Pembrokeshire (Wales), Cumbria, Suffolk and Gloucestershire.

Herring Gull
Larus argentatus
A common winter visitor. Uncommon in summer.

The Herring Gull is the familiar 'seagull' commonly found around much of the coastline of Britain and Ireland. The race involved, *L.a. argenteus*, is also resident in Iceland, Faroes and along the western seaboard of the Continent. The nominate race, *L.a. argentatus*, breeds in Fennoscandia and the Baltic. A yellow-legged race, *L.a. omissus*, breeds in Finland and Estonia. The species has a Holarctic range and the whole question of the so-called Herring Gull/Lesser Black-backed Gull complex is currently under review with the possibility of some of the subspecies being regarded as full species in the future.

Historically, this has always been the most common of the large gulls in Derbyshire, and Whitlock regularly reported flocks moving north over the Trent Valley in spring. In November 1905, a flock of over 150 gulls in the Dove Valley were thought to be mainly Herring Gulls. However, from then to 1952 no double-figure flocks were reported in the county. From 1953 onwards, an increase was apparent, with a flock of 210 at Dale Abbey landfill site on 1st April 1958. The first gathering in excess of 500 was of 510 at Beighton on 9th December 1961. From 1963 gulls began to use Ogston Reservoir as a roosting site and, with the creation of other large reservoirs at Staunton Harold and Church Wilne, this species became numerous in winter, with the largest flocks being 3000 at Ogston Reservoir in January 2004 and 1700 at Church Wilne Reservoir in December 1981. Smaller numbers have roosted at Carsington Water, with a maximum of 1210 in December 2004; Foremark Reservoir, with maxima of 1200 in January 2003 and 1510 in December 2010; and Staunton Harold Reservoir, with a maximum of 1050 in November 1985. Since the early 1990s, numbers have fallen drastically at both Church Wilne and Staunton Harold Reservoirs, leaving Ogston and Foremark Reservoirs as the two main roosts in the county. The reason for this decline is that there are no working landfill sites nowadays near Church Wilne Reservoir (and Staunton Harold Reservoir is only a short distance from Foremark Reservoir). 1510 were recorded at the Foremark Reservoir roost in December 2010.

Away from the roosts, many large gatherings have been recorded at or near landfill sites in the north-east of the county, and presumably comprised birds roosting at Ogston Reservoir. At Carr Vale, 4690 flew north on 22nd January 2005, and at Staveley landfill site 2100 were present on 4th January 1998 and 2000 on 9th January 1999, while there were three separate flocks totalling 2400 in that area on 3rd January 2008. The Glapwell landfill site held 1500 on 13th January 1986 and 1400 on 11th January 1995; Breck Farm, 1500 on 5th January 2005 and 10th January 2007; Barrow Hill Tip, 1300 on 2nd January 2007; Unstone, 1000 on

20th October 1981, with the same number at Staveley Works on 4th and 19th January 2003; while Duckmanton had 2000 on 1st February 2000 and 1500 on 8th January 2008. Nearby, there were 1200 on the site of Markham Colliery on 17th January 2008.

This species is scarce in most parts of the Peak District, a situation that seems to have changed since the late 1970s when Frost stated that it was common, with flocks of over 500 in winter, and three-figure counts even in summer.

Albino birds have been seen in at least six years in the roosts at Ogston and Church Wilne Reservoirs and, in January 1977, one which roosted at Ogston Reservoir was also noted at Wyver Lane. Leucistic birds were recorded at Ogston Reservoir, one in January 1981, an adult at Ogston Reservoir and Glapwell landfill site in January 1995, Church Wilne Reservoir on 1st January 1997 and Ambaston landfill site on 2nd January 1997, and Carsington Water on 6th February 2000.

Although most birds seen in the county are of the race *L.a. argenteus*, a good proportion probably belong to the nominate race *L.a. argentatus*. This mirrors the situation in winter in northern England and Scotland as shown by ringing recoveries (Coulson *et al.* 1984). In Derbyshire, these larger, nominate-race birds have been identified at the main roosts and at Willington Gravel Pits. Two colour-ringed birds at Staveley landfill site on 2nd January 1999, both of which belonged to this race, were respectively 18 years and 20 years old. An immature bird at Church Wilne Reservoir on 20th and 22nd December 1992, probably a third-winter bird, was thought by the observers to belong to the race *L.a. taimyrensis* (Key 1993). This subspecies is now thought to be a race of Heuglin's or Siberian Gull *L. heuglini*.

A probable hybrid Lesser Black-backed Gull x Herring Gull was noted at Willington Gravel Pits from 10th to 12th December 2011.

All 14 ringing recovery records for this species are from places within Britain, with the furthest distance being from Fife in 1967. All but one have been ringed as chicks within colonies in the south-west, Wales, the Isle of Man, the north-east and in the Firth of Forth area. The longest-lived bird was ringed as a chick on Anglesey in 1968 and lived for 6.5 years, before being found dead near Dove Holes. Indeed, all the recovery circumstances are of dead, mainly shot, birds except for a house-top chick ringed in Bristol which was caught and released at Middleton Moor after being colour-marked. A third-winter female at Drakelow Nature Reserve on 15th March 2010 had been colour-ringed as a first-winter at Tor Reservoir, Somerset in 2007.

Yellow-legged Gull
Larus michahellis
An uncommon, but increasing, autumn and winter visitor.

Frost stated that Herring Gulls with yellow legs and dark mantles, indicating a southern race, had been seen on occasions. In 1980, there was an almost certain sighting at Elvaston Quarry on 12th October, but the first record to be accepted was of an adult at Ogston Reservoir on 28th January 1982, followed by occasional records until the late 1980s. The big increase in the late 1990s and in 2002–09 is partly due to the awareness by local observers of the identification criteria for this species, together with a genuine increase and more widespread distribution in Britain. Much of the local increase is due to intensive scrutiny of the Foremark Reservoir gull roost by dedicated watchers. The table indicates this trend.

Year	Birds	Year	Birds
1982	1	1997	88
1983	1	1999	122
1984	10	2000	74
1985	10	2001	61
1986	4	2002	176
1987	11	2003	145
1988	12	2004	104
1989	12	2005	150
1990	28	2006	346
1991	35	2007	252
1992	33	2008	248
1993	56	2009	583
1994	59	2010	312
1995	59	2011	277
1998	121	Total	3471
1996	81		

The Derbyshire monthly distribution shows that small numbers start to arrive in June and increase from July, reaching a peak in November. Numbers then reduce gradually until January, followed by a more rapid fall, with only small double-figure counts for April and May.

Month	Birds
January	319
February	124
March	75
April	30
May	23
June	56
July	293
August	393
September	452
October	459
November	739
December	507

The vast majority of the birds which have been aged have been adults.

The largest roost counts were of 18 at Foremark Reservoir on 13th November 2009 and 20 at Carsington Water on 16th October 2010. The upland roost at Middleton Moor held a maximum of 13 on 4th August 2007. Up to 13 have roosted at Ogston Reservoir and six at Church Wilne Reservoir. Away from roosts, the largest count was of ten at Pools Brook Country Park in October 2006.

A colour-ringed adult at Middleton Moor on 22nd July 2007 had been ringed at the Stoke Orchard landfill site in Gloucestershire on 27th November 2004, and was resighted at the latter on three dates in 2005.

Yellow-legged Gulls have occasionally stayed for a considerable time. At Carsington Water, a third-winter arrived on 18th October 2007 and stayed until 3rd February 2008. The same bird, believed to be a male, returned on 30th June 2008, and it (or perhaps another) returned on 12th July 2010 and remained until 25th February 2011 before returning again on 3rd July 2011 and remaining into 2012. It was seen to catch and eat numerous Little Grebes. At Ogston Reservoir, a third-winter bird was seen on an almost daily basis between 17th June and 30th October 2004.

Caspian Gull
Larus cachinnans
A rare, but increasing, autumn and winter visitor.

Caspian Gulls breed mainly in the Caspian and Black Sea areas and in Kazakhstan, but have recently spread to Poland, with occasional records from Germany. This species is now a scarce visitor to western Europe and to the southern half of Great Britain, where it is recorded mainly in an area from Essex through Cambridgeshire to the East Midlands.

Twentieth-century records are shown in the table.

Year	Location and date
1998	Ogston Reservoir, an adult on 2nd December
1999	Ogston Reservoir, a first-winter on 18th February
1999	Pools Brook Country Park, a first-winter from 12th to 14th March
1999	Ogston Reservoir, an adult on 9th November
1999	Willington Gravel Pits, an adult on 28th November
1999	Ogston Reservoir, a first-winter on 10th December

From 2000, records increased (but not steadily) and are summarized in the table.

Year	Records
2000	13
2001	5
2002	8
2003	18
2004	19
2005	64
2006	111
2007	36
2008	62
2009	62
2010	64
2011	44

As more observers became aware of the identification criteria of this species, the numbers found in Derbyshire generally increased, with more birds being recorded in each successive year until 2006 (since when records have been more stable). The increase mirrors that in more south-eastern counties, especially Cambridgeshire.

Birds may now be seen from January to April, the latest being a first-summer which roosted at Carsington Water on 24th April 2006, and again from June to December, with the earliest a first-summer at Aston-on-Trent Gravel Pits on 6th June 2003 that year. It is thought that the summer influx coincides with the movement of non-breeding Lesser Black-backed Gulls through the county.

Caspian Gulls may now be expected in the well-watched roosts at Ogston and Church Wilne Reservoirs, Carsington Water and especially Foremark Reservoir. The latter site currently hosts Derbyshire's largest gull roost due to its proximity to the large landfill site and adjacent lake just over the Leicestershire border at Albert Village.

Pools Brook Country Park and Carr Vale, in the north-east, attract birds which are loafing or moving from roost sites to nearby landfill sites. In the Trent Valley, Aston-on-Trent Gravel Pits has proved to be a good site, especially in June–September, with a maximum of seven (two adults, a third-summer and four second-summers) on 12th July 2008. Foremark Reservoir held a maximum of six (four adults and two second-winters) on 17th December 2009, while Ogston Reservoir has had a maximum of four birds, in 2004, 2005 and 2006.

Iceland Gull
Larus glaucoides
A scarce winter visitor.

There are thought to be three races of Iceland Gull, of which at least two have occurred in Derbyshire. Most records refer to the nominate race, *L.g. glaucoides*, which breeds in Greenland. There are two distinct populations of this race: the one from the west of Greenland remains there throughout the year, while the eastern population, which is thought to winter mainly in Iceland, provides the birds that occur in Britain. Thayer's Gull, *L.g. thayeri*, breeds in Arctic Canada and is thought to be a rare vagrant to Europe, with at least one claimed for Derbyshire. The race *L.g. kumlieni*, Kumlien's Gull, breeds in north-east Canada and is a transatlantic vagrant to this country. Although this race is regarded by some authorities as a full species, there is a modern train of thought that it may actually be an intergrade between Thayer's Gull and the nominate Iceland Gull.

The first Derbyshire record was of a second-winter bird at Beighton on 25th November 1966, with the next being a first-winter bird which roosted at Ogston Reservoir on 6th and 7th March 1968. Since then Iceland Gulls have been recorded every year except 1971 and 1979, with most birds being seen at the main gull roost sites of Ogston, Church Wilne and Foremark Reservoirs, and Carsington Water. Ogston Reservoir has recorded some 52% of all birds seen in the county. Increasingly, Iceland Gulls are found at refuse dumps, especially in north-east Derbyshire, as a result of greater observation. The most seen together was four at Ogston Reservoir on 22nd January 1984, 28th February 1996 and between 25th and 27th January 2007.

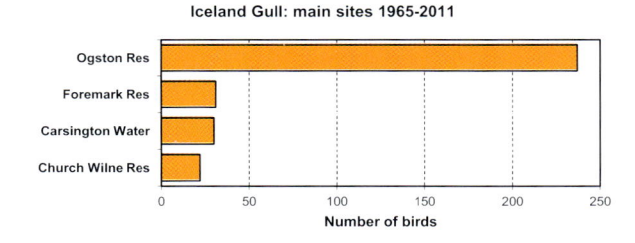

Up to the end of 2011 this species has been recorded at 37 localities in the county. Almost all are in the Trent Valley or the eastern half of the county. There are only three records from the north-west, of single birds at Combs, Fernilee and Torside Reservoirs.

At least 476 have been seen in Derbyshire, with all ages being identified. Typically, the majority (220) have been identified as first-winters, with a further 101 being noted as adults. The analysis is given in the table.

Age	Birds
First-winter	220
Second-winter	102
Third-winter	22
Fourth-winter	5
Adult	101
Unaged	26
Total	476

Thus 46% were aged as first-years, 21% as second-years, 5% as third-years and 22% as adults or subadults. These figures are very comparable with those from Yorkshire (Wilson & Slack 1996).

The periodic distribution is shown in the table. The peak years were 1996, 1997 and 2007 when a minimum of 37 birds was recorded in each of these years.

From this, it is immediately obvious that there was a dramatic upsurge in numbers from 1995 to 1999, a feature mirrored in Norfolk (Taylor et al. 1999). There is no apparent reason for this, although Evans (1996) states that the average incidence in Great Britain is between 30 and 50 wintering birds, but in severe winters numbers may be swollen with further arrivals from Arctic waters and numbers can increase to as many as 400 birds.

Most have been seen in the period December to March, with January being the peak month. The extreme dates are 6th

Period	Birds
1965–69	5
1970–74	15
1975–79	19
1980–84	27
1985–89	34
1990–94	40
1995–99	140
2000–04	65
2005–11	131
Total	476

November (2003), when an adult was at Pools Brook Country Park, and 13th April (1969), when a first-winter bird was at Drakelow Nature Reserve.

There have been at least three records of Kumlien's Gull. At Ogston Reservoir, an adult roosted on most nights from 14th to 24th February 1996 and another adult roosted on 27th January 1997; both of these records were accepted by BBRC. At Carr Vale, there was a second-winter on 29th and 31st January, and 2nd, 4th and 6th February 2007, which was accepted by the DOS Rarities Sub-committee (after it was removed from the BBRC list on 1st January 1999). In addition, at Ogston Reservoir, a second-winter bird that was thought to show some characteristics of this race, roosted on six nights between 15th and 31st December 2007, again on 12th and 19th January, and on 3rd February 2008. This latter bird was also seen at Pools Brook Country Park on 22nd January 2008.

There has been one record of a possible Thayer's Gull, from Pools Brook Country Park from 16th to 18th February 2008. This bird had previously been at Dix Pit, Oxfordshire from 4th to 31st December 2007, and was subsequently at Wheldrake Ings, Yorkshire on 23rd February 2008 (Hallam & Lewington 2007).

Glaucous Gull
Larus hyperboreus
A scarce winter visitor.

Whitlock had little doubt that Glaucous Gulls sometimes occurred in the county as he often saw light-coloured gulls which he could not certainly identify, but there was a 75-year wait for the first definite record of a third-winter bird which roosted at Ogston Reservoir on 28th January 1968. This was quickly followed by two more records later in the same year: a first-winter bird at Willington No. 1 Gravel Pit from 2nd to 31st March, and a first-winter bird at Ogston Reservoir on 30th–31st December. Since then the species has been recorded annually with 495 records up to the end of 2011.

The periodic distribution is shown in the table.

Period	Birds
1965–69	12
1970–74	46
1975–79	50
1980–84	60
1985–89	64
1990–94	32
1995–99	60
2000–04	66
2005–11	105
Total	495

The peak years were 1977 and 1980, similar to the situation in Yorkshire (Wilson & Slack 1996), and 1997, 2000, 2007 and 2008. The decrease in numbers in the early 1990s, followed by an increase in the late 1990s and early 2000s, was a trend also apparent in Norfolk (Taylor et al. 1999). Numbers fell briefly but started to increase again between 2006 and 2008, although 2009,

2010 and 2011 were poor years with only five to seven records in each.

Glaucous Gulls have been recorded from 44 localities in Derbyshire, with the vast majority (at least 255) in the well-watched winter gull roost at Ogston Reservoir. Church Wilne Reservoir has had far fewer, with 32 birds (but none since 1992), and 24 have been recorded at Carsington Water. Although it has never held an established gull roost, there have been nine sightings at Drakelow Nature Reserve, but interestingly none since 1999.

Glaucous Gull: main sites 1965-2011

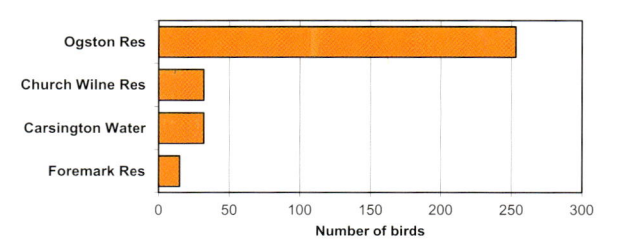

Away from the roosts, landfill sites are well represented with a total of ten recorded at Elvaston Quarry and numerous records from the tips in the Staveley area since 2000. Pools Brook Country Park and Markham Colliery have become popular localities where birds wash and loaf. Only six have been seen away from the southern and eastern lowlands: at Ladybower Reservoir, Monsal Dale, Middleton Moor, Barbrook Reservoir, Sharplow and Moorhall. The most seen together was at Ogston Reservoir, with four in the roost from 11th to 15th February 1980, and five on 22nd January 2008.

Glaucous Gulls have been seen in all months from October to April, with the extreme dates being 8th October (1974), when an adult was at Drakelow Nature Reserve and 22nd April (1969), when one was at Staunton Harold Reservoir. Most are seen between December and March, with the peak in January, when at least 130 birds have been recorded.

An analysis of ages is given in the table.

Age	Birds
First-winter	304
Second-winter	75
Third-winter	22
Fourth-winter	–
Adult	66
Unaged	28
Total	495

No fourth-winter birds have been identified, presumably because the few traces of immature plumage still present would be difficult to pick out in a roost.

During the night of 10th/11th March 1984 a first-winter bird, thought to be sickly, was killed by a fox at Ogston Reservoir.

In Iceland, a proportion of the population consists of Glaucous x Herring Gull hybrids. The first to be seen in Derbyshire was a first-winter bird at Church Wilne Reservoir on 24th December 1979, with 19 subsequent records to 2011, seven of which were at Ogston Reservoir. All have been immature birds, apart from single adults at Doe Lea Tip on 21st, 24th and 26th–29th January 1995, and at Foremark Reservoir on 2nd February 2009.

Thirteen birds have been seen which remained unidentified as either Glaucous or Iceland Gulls.

Great Black-backed Gull
Larus marinus
A fairly common winter visitor. Rare in summer.

Both Whitlock and Jourdain found that this gull was only an occasional visitor to the county, with no more than five ever seen together. This situation continued through the first half of the twentieth century and Frost stated that only single figures were recorded up to 1964. Numbers then started to build up, with flocks of 13 in 1965 and 15 in 1966. The main increase in this species has taken place since the late 1960s, with significant numbers coming inland during the winter. This trend may well have been fostered by two developments: the proliferation of landfill sites, which produce a regular food supply, and the creation of many large reservoirs, which provide ideal roosting sites.

Not surprisingly therefore, the biggest gatherings are generally recorded at roosts and landfill sites. The Ogston Reservoir roost has held the largest numbers, with annual maxima of 1190 in December 2007, 1065 in January 2008 and 1000 in January 2004. Church Wilne Reservoir held 680 on 7th December 1980 and more than 600 in December 1981, with Foremark Reservoir holding 500 on 16th January 1987 and in January 1991, and 550 in December 2010. A total of 300 roosted at Carsington Water in April 2007. The largest numbers noted at or very near to landfill sites were: 525 at Staveley on 4th January 1998; 405 at the Markham Colliery site on 22nd January 2008; 400 at Glapwell on 11th January 1986; 362 at Pools Brook Country Park on 8th March 2008; and 300 at Doe Lea on 1st February 1995.

Birds will often use farmland for daytime loafing but the fields are generally near landfill sites, as exemplified by a flock of 165 at Elvaston Quarry on 5th January 1986, 150 near Ambaston on 21st January 1995, 200 at Carr Vale on 22nd January 2000, and 200 at Duckmanton on 1st February 2000.

Numbers start to build up in November, peaking in December to February, before falling rapidly from late February into March, as birds move back to their breeding grounds on the coast.

Most movement in the county can be attributed to birds moving from roosts to landfill sites, but occasional large movements have been noted at Drakelow Nature Reserve, with 258 flying west on 1st January 1999 and a further 166, also flying west, on 19th January in the same year.

At Carsington Water in 2005, 600 roosted in April and 300, mainly juveniles, in May. Such numbers must relate to spring movement through the county.

This species becomes scarce between May and October, with generally only single figures noted, but they can be seen almost anywhere in the county at this time of the year. Flocks of 30 at Elvaston Quarry on 25th September 1978, 50–60 at Peak Forest on 23rd September 1984, 60 at Middleton Moor on 26th October in the same year, 35 at Drakelow Nature Reserve on 4th May 1988, 53 at Staunton Harold Reservoir on 20th October 1999 and 30 immatures at Arkwright Town on 25th May 2004, represent the peak numbers seen during this period.

Great Black-backed Gulls are noted predators of other birds. At Ogston Reservoir on 30th December 1990, one killed and ate a first-winter Black-headed Gull. At Ambaston Tip on 1st December 1994, an adult seized a Golden Plover by the leg, severely injuring the bird, but then discarding it.

It is thought that most of our winter visitors originate from Norway and also the Russian Federation, an example of which was a bird found dead at Shirland in Spring 1967 that had been ringed on Great Ainov Island in the Murmansk region. More recently, a colour-ringed first-winter seen at Pools Brook Country Park in February 2008 had been ringed as a pullus at Glana, in Vest-Agder, Norway (a movement of 761km) in July 2007.

Pallas's Sandgrouse
Syrrhaptes paradoxus
A very rare vagrant.

One of the ornithological events of the nineteenth century was the widespread invasion of Europe in 1863 by this species, which has a breeding range normally extending from central Asia east to Manchuria and China. A further massive irruption occurred in 1888, involving some 3000 birds, in every English county and breeding attempts were reported from Morayshire, Suffolk and Yorkshire. Since 1909 its status has reverted to become a very rare vagrant (Brown & Grice 2005). In Derbyshire, two birds were shot in 1863 'on our northern borders' (Whitlock) and Jourdain's additions state that the site was near Fox House. In May 1888, one was found dead in a garden at Breaston and others were said to have been seen or shot, though not preserved, including one killed at Shardlow (Whitlock). Two were shot near Parwich in June 1888. Both Whitlock and Jourdain gave the date as July 1889 but this was subsequently corrected in the *Zoologist* (1909). Jourdain thought he saw three near Ashbourne in May 1900, but later withdrew the record.

Rock Dove
Columba livia
A common resident.

The Rock Dove, or Feral Pigeon, is a familiar resident of towns and cities, and yet it goes largely unrecorded by the county's ornithologists. This descendant of the wild Rock Dove, breeds in a variety of sites in built-up areas including shops, factories and churches, and under road and railway bridges; in a rural setting, active and disused quarries are favourite haunts.

The tetrad map shows a distribution centred on the main areas of human habitation, with Derby and Chesterfield easily identifiable, along with the industrial areas of north-east Derbyshire. In the Derbyshire BBS (1995–99), breeding was proved in 93 tetrads, and was possible or probable in a further 218. It is likely that some were not recorded by observers who deemed them to be 'unworthy'.

Although the distribution map shows a clear eastern and southern bias, the Feral Pigeon is a hardy bird, capable of surviving in moorland districts provided that suitable nesting and roosting sites are present. For instance, one or two pairs were usually present on the dilapidated boat-house at Barbrook Reservoir on Big Moor before its demolition. They have certainly been present in such areas for long time, since Whitlock stated that they bred in such sites in the Peak District, for example near Bakewell, and Frost mentioned Kinder Downfall, at 600m amsl, as a known site for this species.

The large number of possible breeding tetrads in the north-west of the county perhaps relates to homing pigeons crossing open country. To what extent these birds supplement the breeding population of Feral Pigeon is unknown, but it may be significant.

This species has a protracted breeding season, and it is not unusual to see young on nesting ledges in October and November, while display takes place throughout the winter months.

The largest flocks are recorded on arable farmland, especially stubble fields, in autumn, with flocks of up to 300 not uncommon. The largest recorded flocks are of 1300 at Drakelow Nature Reserve on 4th November 1984, and over 1000 at Sinfin on 29th November 1985. In recent years, the highest counts have been lower and since 2000, only two flocks have reached 400: at Drum Hill on 9th December 2003 and at Drakelow Nature Reserve in December 2005. A reduction has been noted at sites in central Derby since Peregrines began nesting on the cathedral.

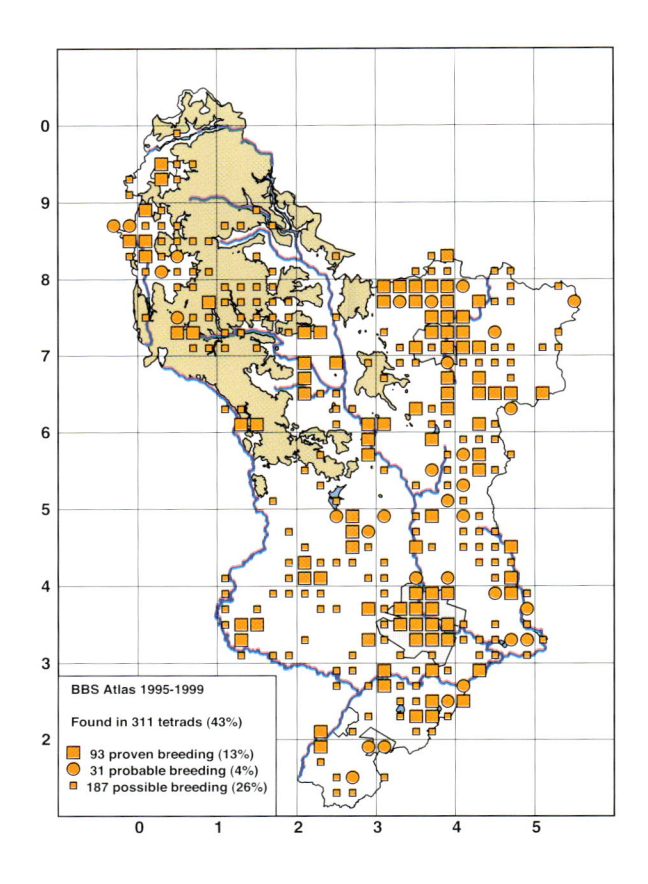

Stock Dove
Columba oenas
A fairly common resident.

Stock Doves are unobtrusive birds, usually first located at their breeding sites by their trisyllabic cooing, or by the circling display flight, during which the wings are clapped above the back. In the breeding season they are found mainly in parkland, well-timbered farmland and quarries, and sometimes extend into built-up areas. Their nests are in holes and crevices and are not easily seen. In Derbyshire, these are typically in holes or epicormic growths in trees, but the birds use a wide variety of other sites, including cliff faces, buildings (often ruined ones) and walls, and under bridges and aqueducts. More unusual sites have been rabbit burrows, under grass tufts and between straw bales in a barn, while there are several records of breeding in boxes erected for owls, sometimes in large gardens. Stock Doves have a long breeding season, and unfledged young have been found in late October.

During the Derbyshire BBS (1995–99), proof of breeding was obtained in only 104 tetrads (26% of the tetrads where the species was found). The rather low figure results from the difficulty in seeing the nest, and probably because adults and juveniles are not easily told apart. Probable breeding was recorded from 141 tetrads, mainly based on records of display flight, and birds entering and leaving likely nest sites.

Stock Doves feed predominantly on grain and arable weeds and are therefore strongly associated with farmland at all times of the year. The map shows a strong bias towards lowlands in the south and east of the county, but substantial numbers also breed in the White Peak, where quarries offer an abundance of nest sites. They are almost absent as breeding birds from the higher gritstone areas of the Peak District.

The only CBC site to regularly hold this species was Culland, where the 1990s average of 2.2 territories equates to a density of 3.8 pairs per km². Otherwise, almost all information on breeding numbers comes from cliff sites. Ten pairs were thought to be nesting in the limestone ravine at Creswell Crags in 1978, though an increase in public access means that this site is now less favoured. The nearby Whitwell Quarry held 18 pairs in April 1995, in which year 11 pairs raised young at Bennerley Viaduct. There were considered to be 15 pairs in an area of unspecified size at Darley Abbey in 1992. In recent years, a box-nesting population has been studied in South Derbyshire, based at five sites at

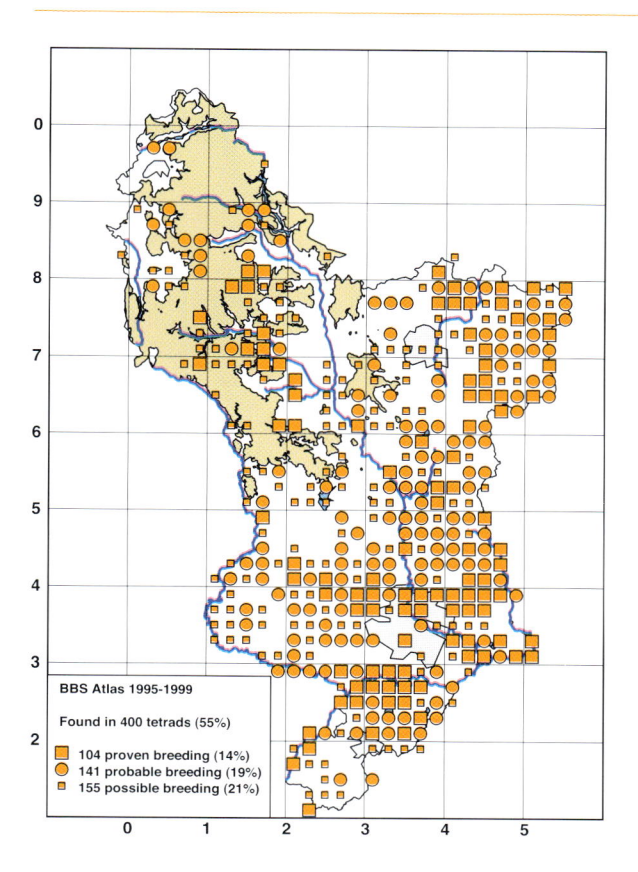

Caldwell, Catton, Coton-in-the-Elms, Drakelow Nature Reserve and Foremark Reservoir. The highest success was seen in 2009, with 79 breeding attempts at 43 nests and 75 young ringed.

There has probably been little change in the distribution of Stock Doves since the 1988–91 Atlas. In that period, breeding was recorded in SK27 but the Derbyshire BBS (1995–99) map shows presence in just one tetrad here. However, it is hardly credible that there were none in the large quarries in this 10km square.

Both Whitlock and Jourdain considered Stock Doves to be fairly common, and this seems to have been the case for a long time, except during the 'pesticides era' of the 1950s and 1960s. This species is believed to be largely sedentary, and the size of winter flocks is probably a good indicator of population trends. Averaging the size of the largest flock recorded annually in the *Derbyshire Bird Report* since 1970 gives figures of 333 for the 1970s, 235 for the 1980s and 189 for the 1990s, but rising again to 209 in the 2000s. By far the largest flock recorded in Derbyshire was of 950 at Creswell in November 1978. Even if this year is omitted from calculations, the 1970s average remains the highest at 264. These figures suggest that Derbyshire Stock Doves have undergone a decline, which is contrary to the national trend.

There are very few records to suggest that these birds are migrants through the county. Birds have often been seen flying in a north-westerly direction over Big Moor in late summer, but these may merely be flights between different breeding and feeding areas. Very small numbers may occasionally be seen accompanying the migrant Woodpigeon flocks moving over the moors in late autumn.

There are five ringing recoveries concerning Derbyshire and in four of these only short distances were involved. The other recovery was of one ringed in August 2005 as a chick at Drakelow Nature Reserve that was shot 561km away just south of Le Mans, France in January 2006.

Woodpigeon
Columba palumbus
An abundant resident and passage migrant.

This handsome but destructive bird proved to be the fourth most widespread bird in Derbyshire (together with Blue Tit) during the Derbyshire BBS (1995–99). It was found in every 10km square, as it was in both the 1968–72 and 1988–91 Atlases. Only on the highest gritstone moorlands are the blanks on the map likely to be genuine. It is an easy species for which to prove breeding as nests are easily seen, and hatched eggshells are often found on the woodland floor. Breeding was proved in 410 tetrads, with probable breeding recorded in a further 168 and possible in 105.

The breeding season is a lengthy one, extending from early spring until the autumn, with records of adults feeding fledglings in February and November.

It was present in all of the six CBC plots censused during the 1990s and, coincidentally, was the eighth most common species on five of these, but only eighteenth at Broadhay Farm, Hathersage. Woodland densities ranged between 5.1 pairs per km² at Shiningcliff Wood to 41.67 at Shirebrook. On farmland the range was from 2.69 at Broadhay Farm to 18.31 at Culland.

Both Whitlock and Jourdain implied that Woodpigeons were restricted to woodlands as breeding birds but they may now nest in almost any site containing trees, including moorland cloughs, hedgerows and in towns, even alongside busy roads. They can become very tame in built-up areas. One was singing by a street lamp in Bolsover at 2230hrs on 11th April 1996. Nests as low as 1m above ground level have been found in bushes and saplings. A very unusual nest site with eggs and young, was found under a clump of heather in Span Clough, near Glossop in May 1992.

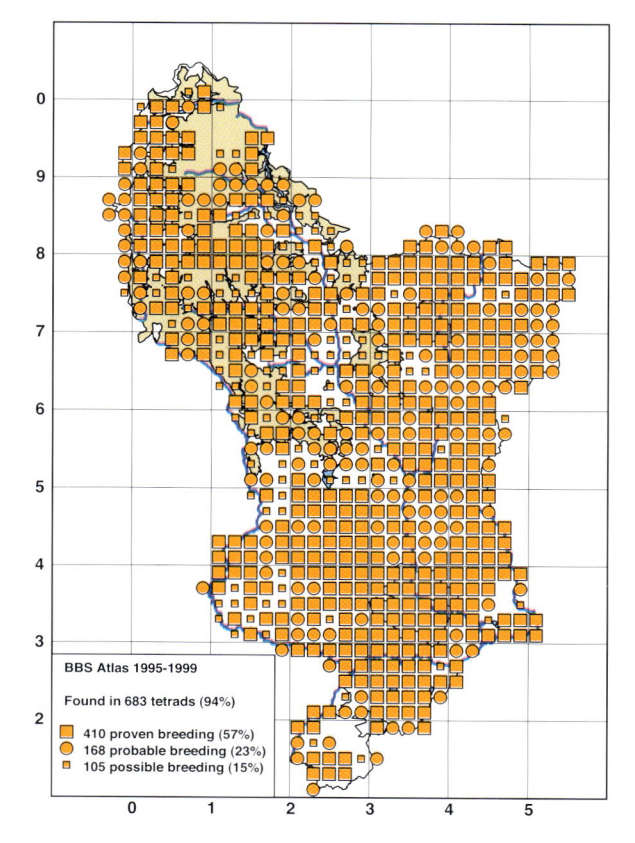

Although Woodpigeons eat natural woodland food such as berries and nuts, they feed mainly on farmland, where they may cause a great deal of damage to crops such as brassicas and oil-seed rape. Although apparently abundant in the county for a long time (Frost), it is likely that the conversion of large areas of farmland to arable has enabled them to increase their numbers. Very large flocks may descend on favourable areas, including 5000 at Breck Farm, Staveley in November 1993, and 8000 between Branston and Walton-on-Trent in January 1994. However, the largest annual counts are often of communal roosts in woodland. These included 10,000 at Smeekley Wood in January 1985 and 7200 at Barlborough Park in November 1985.

A south to south-westerly movement of Woodpigeons takes place in late autumn and can be quite spectacular. Passage is normally recorded for about a month from mid to late October onwards. The highest counts have been at Ramsley, where there have been 18 records of over 10,000 birds in a day, with maxima of 26,170 on 4th November 2004 and 21,770 on 29th October 2009. Other five-figure counts have come from Ashover Fabric, with a maximum of 18,680 on 6th November 2010 and Barbrook, where 10,060 moved through on 8th November 1996. However, the most impressive of all was at Upper Loads, where 28,730 were counted on 6th November 2011; at nearby Cupola Ponds, the 21,880 seen on the same date undoubtedly included many of the same flocks, and the same day saw 11,140 moving over Ogston Reservoir. Counts of over 4000 have also come from Strines Top, Totley Moss, Hare Edge, Bottom Moor, Highoredish Hill, Crich Stand, Alport Heights and Mickleover (the only southern locality), where 5000 passed through on 1st November 1998. A migrant flock over Big Moor in November 1997 deliberately flew up into low cloud in an attempt to avoid a pursuing Peregrine.

Unfortunately, there are no ringing recoveries to indicate the sources of this impressive movement, but the fact that it is most evident on the Pennine fringe and is predominantly in a southerly direction, suggests that the birds originate from further north in England and perhaps Scotland, rather than from Continental Europe.

The earliest recovery for this species was a bird ringed in 1955 at Repton and shot at Stretton, Staffordshire, three years later. The longest-lived bird was one ringed in Whitwell Wood in 1978 which was shot at Barlborough in 1985. The species is generally sedentary with 64% of the recoveries within 20km of ringing and of those that moved further, only 18% exceeded 50km. The bird covering the longest dispersal was ringed as a chick in July near the Snake Inn and shot near Tewkesbury, Gloucestershire in the following February.

The Derbyshire ringing dataset suggests that a large proportion of chicks born later in the year are well able to survive their first winter. There are recovery records of 25 chicks ringed between August and September of which 54% had been shot after the following summer, indicating that at least this proportion had survived their first winter with the potential to expand the breeding population.

Collared Dove
Streptopelia decaocto
A common resident.

The Collared Dove is associated with human habitation throughout the county, from parks and gardens in urban Derby to the smallest Peak District villages. It is now such a familiar resident that it is easy to forget its relatively recent arrival.

Collared Doves first bred in Britain in 1955 following a rapid north-westerly expansion across Europe, which commenced in the 1930s. The first Derbyshire sightings were at Brailsford in 1961, and Youlgreave and Great Longstone in 1962. The first confirmed breeding took place at Spondon in 1963. A dramatic increase meant that by the 1970s, the Collared Dove was a common bird established throughout much of the county. There is very little quantitative data on this species, although the number of entries in the *Derbyshire Bird Report* increased markedly in the 1990s, which is probably due to more thorough reporting. Although Eaton *et al.* (2010) record an increase of 403% between 1970 and 2008, there is no evidence of any great change in status in Derbyshire since the 1970s, and certainly the highest annual counts have remained fairly stable. The greatest counts have been: 280 at Whitwell on 23rd August 1974; 200 roosting in the Pavilion Gardens, Buxton in 1975; 200 in the Moss Valley on 10th October 1975; 200 at Stubley Hollow on 22nd September 2003; and 199 at both Stenson Fields on 1st September 1998 and Tupton on 14th October 2008.

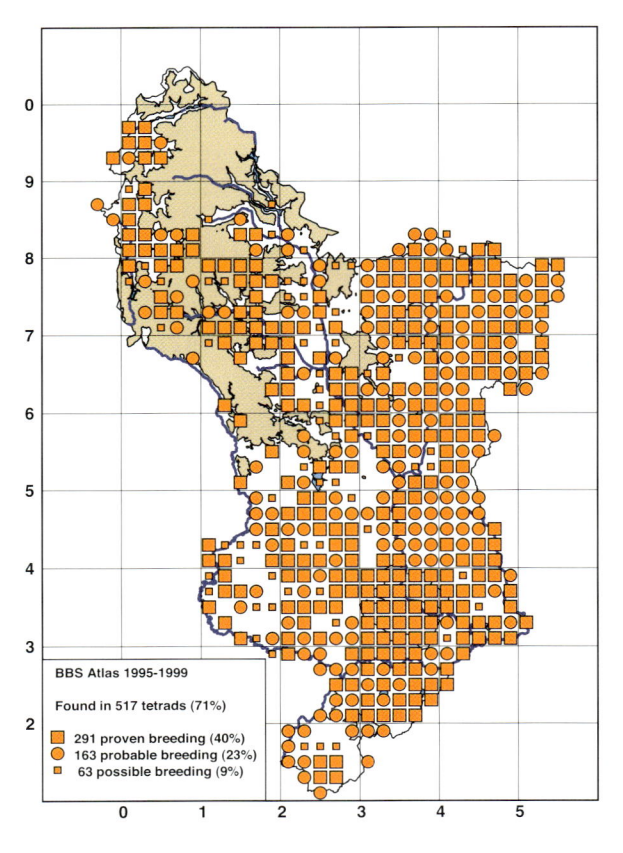

Breeding was confirmed in all but one of the 23 10km core squares for the 1988–91 Atlas. The map, based on the Derbyshire BBS (1995–99), shows 291 proven, 163 probable and 63 possible breeding tetrads. Though nests are usually well hidden, often in evergreen trees, the birds draw attention to themselves by their song and display flight, and their tameness. South Derbyshire, especially around Derby, has the greatest concentration of occupied squares and may therefore hold the densest population. The band of probable tetrads through mid-Derbyshire perhaps relates to the large areas of mixed farmland where the species is present, but at a lower density than in some of the urban areas. This species is conspicuously absent from large areas of north-west Derbyshire; an area of high altitude consisting predominantly of moorland and rough grassland with very little arable farming and few settlements.

In common with other members of the pigeon family, this species may breed at almost any time of the year. Nest-building has been noted as early as 1st January, while at Newbold, a pair had a nest with two eggs on 22nd January 1999. In the same year a pair had a nest with eggs in a Mickleover garden on 28th December. In January 2000 the moving of a Christmas tree at New Square, Chesterfield had to be delayed as it contained a nest with young. The great majority nest in trees and shrubs, with conifers particularly favoured. Nests in farm buildings are occasionally reported. Unusual sites have included a satellite-television bracket and under the junction of steam pipes at a factory.

Every year small numbers of birds are reported crossing the Peak District moorlands, usually from visible migration watch-points such as Ramsley and Barbrook. These are presumably the result of local movements and are usually in a westerly or south-westerly direction. Unusual records include a pair that flew over the Goyt Valley, landed in heather and appeared to settle to roost, unperturbed by a hunting Hen Harrier, on an unspecified date in 1997, and a pair at 420m amsl in a young conifer plantation at Derbyshire Bridge on 11th July 1990.

BBS Atlas 1995-1999
Found in 517 tetrads (71%)
- 291 proven breeding (40%)
- 163 probable breeding (23%)
- 63 possible breeding (9%)

The earliest county ringing recovery is of one ringed at Coal Aston in 1977 and found dead at Dronfield in the winter period five years later, apparently having starved to death. Although the species has exhibited remarkable dispersal behaviour in the way that it has colonized Europe, the Derbyshire ringing data indicates a sedentary population, with the exception of one ringed at Aston-on-Trent in January 1992 that was shot 152km away at Blackpool in the following October.

Turtle Dove
Streptopelia turtur
A scarce summer visitor.

Turtle Doves are typically birds of arable farmland, feeding on weed seeds and breeding in tall hedgerows, spinneys and woods. Unfortunately, these attractive birds are declining rapidly in Derbyshire and their range is contracting to the east and southeast, mirroring the national situation. This is well illustrated by comparing the distribution in terms of 10km squares. In the 1968–72 Atlas they were found in 23 squares; in the 1988–91 Atlas only 15 were occupied and by 1995–99 the Derbyshire BBS located them in just ten. Historically, Turtle Doves did not begin breeding in Derbyshire in any numbers until late in the nineteenth century but were common in lowland areas by 1893 (Whitlock). Although some observers detected a decline in the period 1949–54, this was apparently reversed by the end of the decade. Twenty years later, Frost said that numbers were subject to some annual variation but with no long-term trend.

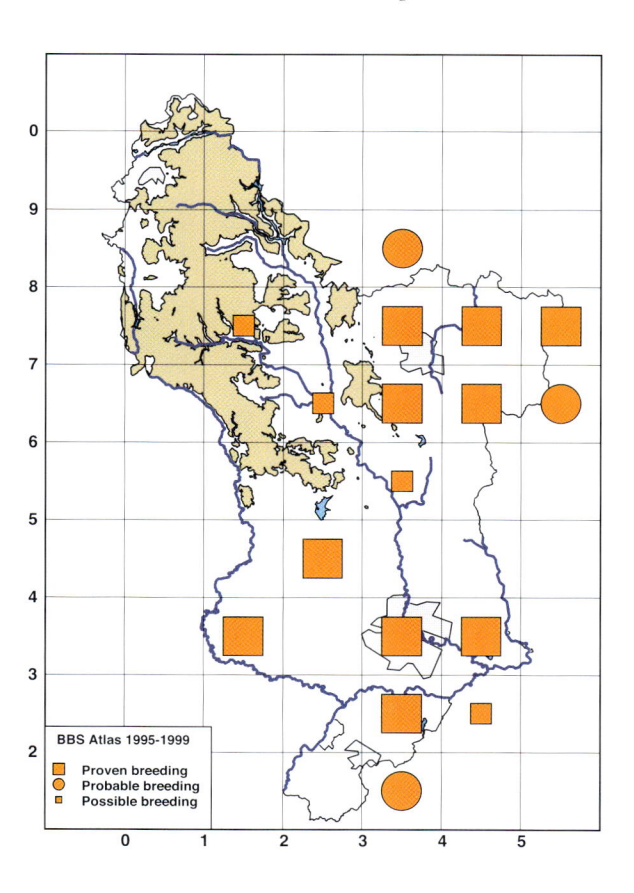

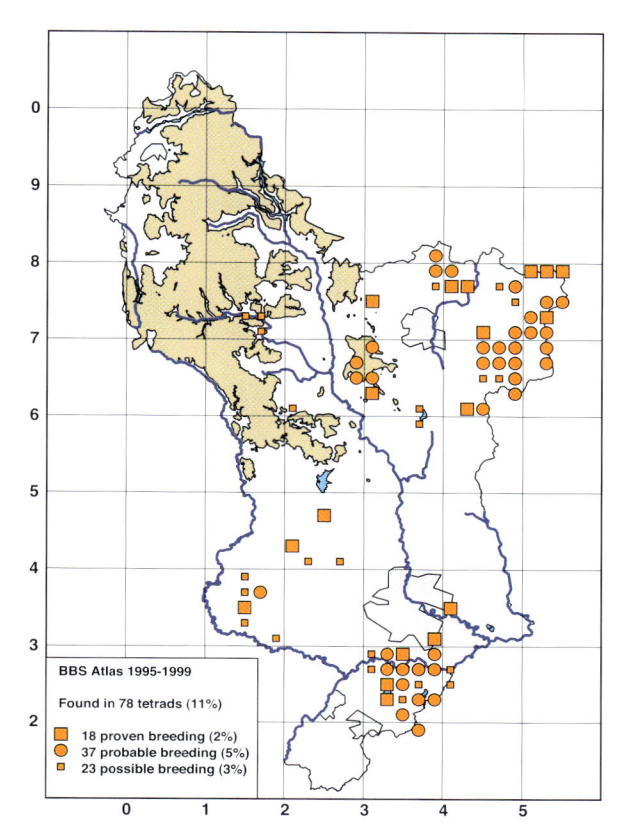

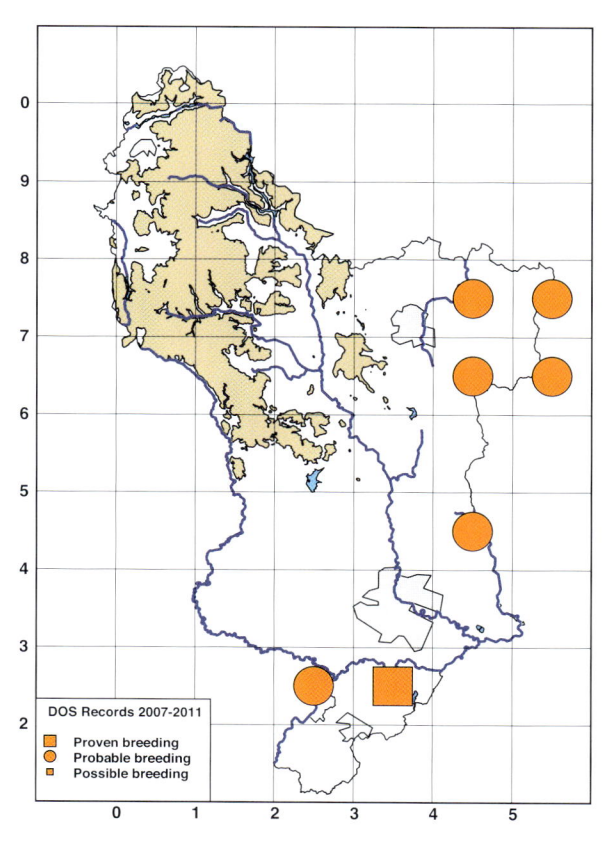

The Derbyshire BBS revealed that 78 tetrads held Turtle Doves and of these only 18 (23% of the tetrads in which found) had confirmed breeding. This is not easily obtained for this species, which generally builds well-hidden nests in trees and tall bushes, and feeds its young by regurgitation. Probable breeding was noted in 37 tetrads (47% of the tetrads in which found), a figure based largely on recording the distinctive 'turring' song, with possible breeding in a further 23 (29% of the tetrads in which found).

The county population of the late 1990s was probably in the region of 50–100 pairs. A worrying decline has continued since then and there may be fewer than 20 pairs breeding in Derbyshire in the late 2000s. During 2007–11, Turtle Doves were reported from eight to 15 sites in each year. The maps demonstrate the rapid withdrawal of range to the south and east between 1995–99 and 2007–11.

Increased use of herbicides, and the loss of tall hedges and spinneys are possibly the main causes of the decline, although losses on migration and in their wintering ground could be significant. One of the main breeding areas in the county is the Magnesian Limestone plateau. Here, Scarcliffe Woods held 25 singing males in 1981 but no more than six by the late 1990s, with an average of only three in 2000–05 and one in 2006–08. Nearby, the Shirebrook CBC plot held up to three territories in 1978–91. The other area still holding a very small but regular population is the Trent Valley and the well-wooded farmland to the south, especially the Repton–Ticknall–Melbourne area; six were singing at Foremark Reservoir in May 1998. More surprisingly, a small outlier existed at around 300m amsl in the pine plantations of the Matlock Forest area, where up to nine territories were occupied during the 1990s, but these are now believed to have gone.

The national decline in 1970–2008, as documented by Eaton et al. (2010), was of a catastrophic 89% reduction.

After the breeding season Turtle Doves may form small flocks. At Whitwell, 87 were counted on 16th August 1971; there were 42 at Poolsbrook an hour after a heavy thunderstorm on 19th June 1982; and 32 at Elmton on 21st August 1986. The largest gathering in the period 1995–99 was of only nine at Firbeck Common on 31st August 1999 and, since 2000, the largest counts were of five at Foremark Reservoir on 21st August 2002 and at High Moor on 8th September 2003. This is further evidence of the scale of the decline.

The earliest spring arrival was on 10th April 1945 at Whitwell. Most return in late April and May, with 26th April the average first date in the period 1978–2011. The last ones are normally recorded in September, with 13th the average last date in the above period. October sightings are (or rather, were) not rare, however, with the latest of all on 22nd (1995) at Carr Vale.

Only small numbers of Turtle Doves have been ringed in Derbyshire and these have produced one interesting recovery: one, ringed as a chick in Dronfield in July 1952, was found dead near Seville, Spain in the following May.

Ring-necked Parakeet
Psittacula krameri
A scarce visitor and breeder.

Ring-necked Parakeets (also known as Rose-ringed Parakeets) were first recorded in the wild in Britain in 1969 (Hudson 1974). The first occurrence in Derbyshire was only four years later when one was seen at Shardlow in January 1973.

There were four further records of singles in the 1970s, including one observed flying south-west over Big Moor in November 1974. Since then, this brightly coloured and noisy bird has been reported with increasing regularity, as indicated in the table, with a maximum of eight records in 2002:

Period	Birds
1970s	5
1980s	12
1990s	23
2000–11	61
Total	101

Ring-necked Parakeets have appeared in all months, usually singly, although on a few occasions two have been seen together, and three were present at Staveley in December 2001. The majority of records emanate from the south and north-east of the county, with very few from elsewhere, and the largest gathering was of eight, at Ringwood Park on 24th November 2005.

Although there is a naturalized and thriving British population, principally in south-east England, it is most likely that all individuals seen locally are free-flying 'homing' birds which have failed to return to their aviaries or have escaped from pet shops.

The first breeding in Derbyshire occurred in 2003 and 2004 when a pair nested at Ringwood Park, Hollingwood, although the outcome was unknown. This followed rumours of small numbers having been released in the area. Two juveniles were seen at the nearby Hollingwood Estate in March 2004. As this species is adaptable and surprisingly resilient to harsh weather, there is a strong possibility that it will in the future be able to establish and maintain a breeding population within the county.

Cuckoo
Cuculus canorus
A fairly common summer visitor.

Cuckoos were considered very common by Whitlock, especially in parts of the Peak District. Frost said that Cuckoos had probably declined, but that the male's song was still frequently heard in most rural areas of the county. This is still the situation, but there has undoubtedly been a further decrease in numbers since 1978. Eaton et al. (2010) found a national decline of 58% between 1970 and 2008. Suggested reasons include declines of some host species and habitat loss (1988–91 Atlas).

The Derbyshire BBS (1995–99) recorded Cuckoos in 431 tetrads, a surprisingly widespread distribution. Of these, breeding was proved in only 28, probable breeding in 285 (largely on account of the male's unique song), and possible breeding in 118. This is a notoriously difficult species for which to obtain conclusive proof of breeding, one of the main problems being that young are often not seen until well into July, when observer effort is likely to be lower.

Only 11 males in total were found by the Eastern Moors surveys of 1998 and 2010, although in other years there have been more moorland than lowland records. At least six were singing on Ramsley Moor on 5th May 2008 and the same number in Upper Derwentdale on 12th May 2011. The maximum breeding density on any of the CBC surveys was 6.94 pairs per km^2 on the 14.4ha plot at Shirebrook, which consisted of woodland, hawthorn scrub and two small fields. Counts at Scarcliffe Woods give an indication of the scale of the decline: there was a largest count of eight males and four females in 1981, but no more than two males recorded in 2000–06, though there were four in 2008 (Frost 2008a). The maps show the breeding situation in 1995–99 and 2007–11.

Females are thought to be very largely host-specific, each laying between ten and 25 eggs (1988–91 Atlas). Meadow Pipits are the dominant host species in upland areas, with Dunnock

The Species Accounts

and Pied Wagtail their lowland counterparts. Other host species recorded in Derbyshire include Tree Pipit, Wren, Whinchat, Blackbird, Song Thrush, Grasshopper Warbler, Lesser Whitethroat, Sedge Warbler, Reed Warbler, Spotted Flycatcher, Greenfinch, Linnet, Yellowhammer and Reed Bunting. An interesting record in 1984 came from the Chatsworth Garden Centre, where a fully grown chick was in a Dunnock's nest in a container-grown cupressus tree which was for sale. Hopefully, it was not sold before the chick fledged.

Exceptional gatherings of Cuckoos have been recorded on three occasions, all of them on Beeley Moor, where they are believed to have been attracted to concentrations of the large, hairy caterpillars of the northern eggar. About 30 were seen on 28th May 1978, about 14 on 3rd and 4th July 1980, and 16 on 1st June 1984 (the last double-figure count in Derbyshire).

There are seven records of hepatic females: at Alport Moor in June 1966; Williamthorpe Nature Reserve in May 1995; both Arkwright Colliery and Locko Park in May 1996; Hasland in May 2002; and Willington Gravel Pits and Ramsley Moor, both in May 2010. Albino birds were noted at Tansley Common in June 1956 and Lumsdale in May 1961.

The earliest ever Cuckoo in the county was at Pilsley (near Clay Cross) on 24th March 1977. Otherwise, the first records are invariably in April with a mean first date of 13th during 1978–2011. Adults tend to leave from July onwards, and the latest ever singing bird was heard on 12th July 1978 at Ogston Reservoir, but juveniles may stay until September, with 5th being the mean departure date during the above period. Birds were noted on 7th October 1977, 1st October 1985, and 3rd and 4th October 1998, but the latest date of all was for a juvenile which stayed in a Cutthorpe garden, where it took caterpillars from cabbage plants, until 17th October 1996.

This species is ringed in only very small numbers throughout the UK, with probably equal numbers of adults and chicks. There is only one Derbyshire recovery of interest: one ringed as a chick at Totley, Sheffield (then in Derbyshire) in July 1960 was recovered near Stowmarket, Suffolk, a month later.

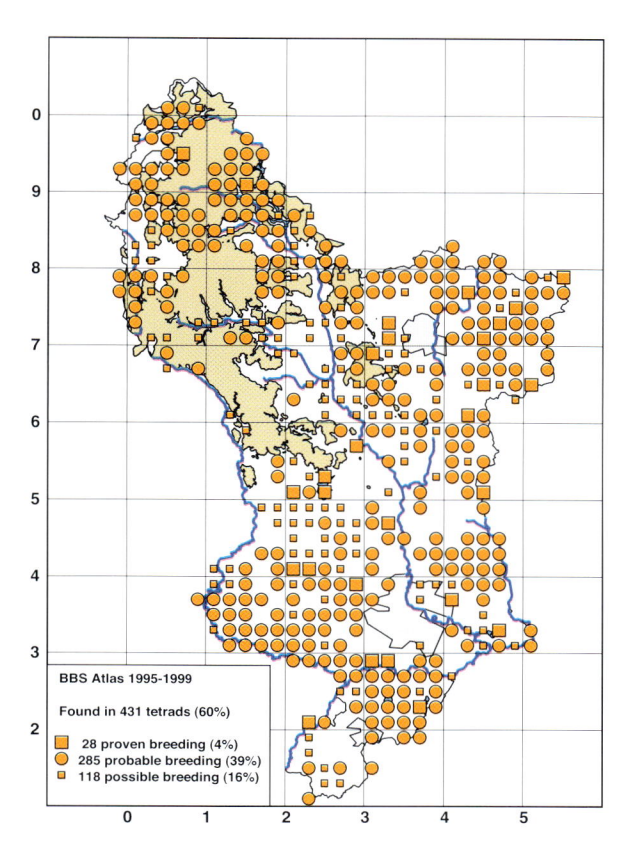

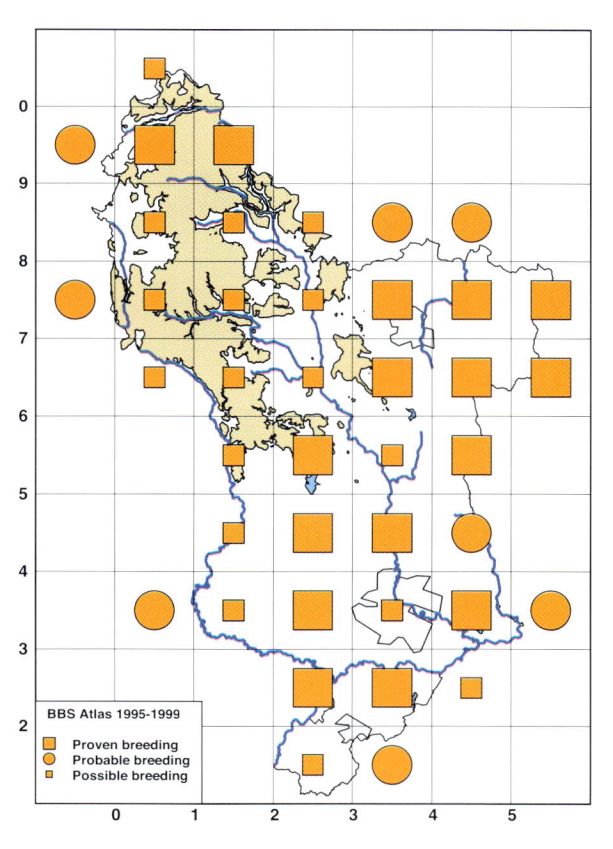

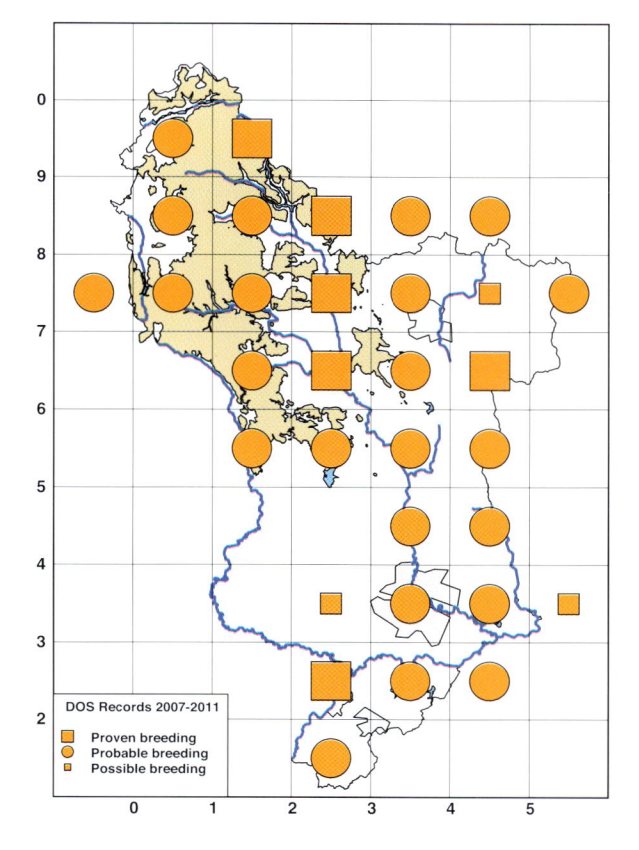

Barn Owl
Tyto alba
An uncommon resident.

Once a familiar sight in the lowlands, especially as a ghostly moth-like figure hunting at twilight over damp meadows and fields, the Barn Owl was until very recently considered to be the rarest of the five species of owl breeding in the county. In contrast, Whitlock stated that they were more common than Tawny Owls in southern Derbyshire in the nineteenth century although persecution, especially by shooters, was causing a reduction in their numbers.

Nationally, a major decline seems to have set in from the early part of the twentieth century. This was believed to have been largely due to agricultural intensification, combined with the loss of many suitable breeding sites in old trees and barns. The downward trend was undoubtedly accelerated from the middle of the century by the widespread use of pesticides. Moreover the Barn Owl, unlike the more adaptable and aggressive Tawny Owl, does not cope well with prolonged adverse weather conditions and is more limited in its choice of nest sites. It also seems to be more prone to being injured or killed by motor vehicles because of its habit of hunting along roadside verges.

In Derbyshire, the Barn Owl had disappeared from some of its traditional haunts by the 1940s, becoming scarce within a further decade, and it was not until the early 1990s that the fortunes of this most attractive bird began to show any signs of the recovery that has continued into the present century: in 1999, Barn Owls were recorded at 27 sites in Derbyshire, with breeding proved at only one, whereas by 2010 this had increased to 85 sites with 36 pairs proved to breed.

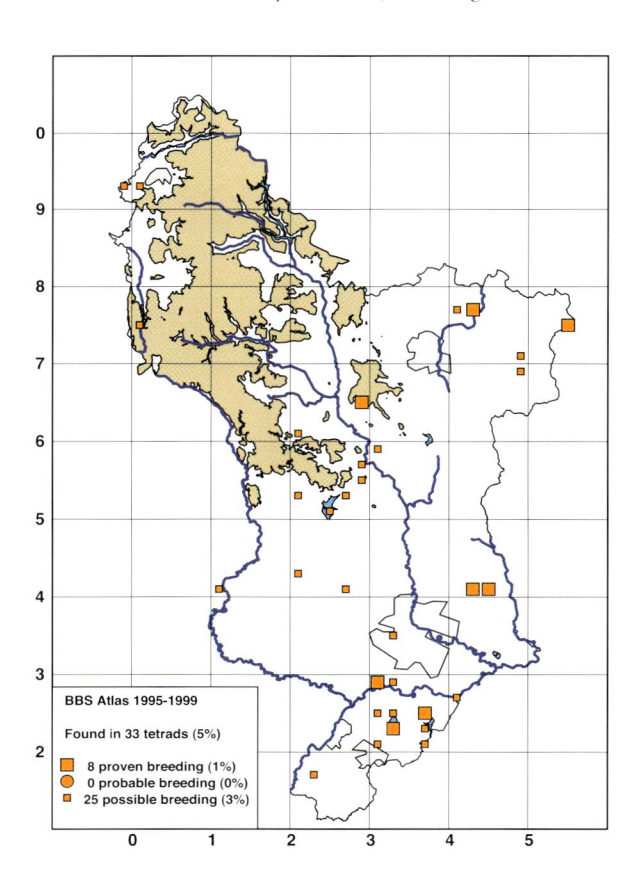

This recent revival may have been prompted by the restrictions on the use of pesticides, and reintroduction schemes undertaken by licensed breeders. For example, between 1995 and 1997, a total of 39 Barn Owls were released at two sites in the county. Milder winters may also have been beneficial and nest-box schemes in southern Derbyshire and parts of the Peak District have met with considerable success.

The table reveals the total number of sites per year at which birds were recorded and the number of breeding pairs, in five-year periods from 1980 to 2011.

Period	Sites	Breeding pairs
1980–84	71	7
1985–89	over 24	3
1990–94	87	14
1995–99	113	10
2000–04	149	19
2005–11	362	117

In the Derbyshire BBS (1995–99), breeding was proved in only eight tetrads, relating to four 10km squares, and included just one in the Peak District. A further 25 tetrads were found to contain possible breeders, though there were no probable records. This is significantly different from the 1968–72 Atlas, when breeding was confirmed in 14 10km squares, with probable and possible breeding in five others. In the 1988–91 Atlas, breeding was proved in six 10km squares and probable breeding in four more.

However, it is possible that there are more pairs than is currently known, as breeding has recently been recorded in limestone quarries, of which there are many in the county. Such habitat is not extensively visited by birdwatchers – certainly not nocturnally – nor indeed is farmland, compared with other habitats. As the Barn Owl population in Britain is slowly recovering from its lowest levels, its future at the start of the twenty-first century seems brighter than for some time.

Barn Owls are largely sedentary and the majority of adults remain paired throughout the winter, often roosting together in the vicinity of their breeding area. It is therefore not surprising that the 1984–88 Winter Atlas revealed a very similar distribution pattern to that produced by the 1968–72 Atlas. In Derbyshire, this species has occasionally been observed roosting with, or close to, other owls. One was found roosting with Long-eared Owls in the north-east in January 1989, and another roosted in a hole in the same tree as a pair of Little Owls at Ticknall in 1989. A Barn Owl roosted within four metres of a Tawny Owl in a tree at Langwith in December 1997 and January 1998.

Sightings of individuals at unusual localities have included one in Chesterfield town centre over the former Chesterfield Football Club ground on Saltergate in October 1980 and one roosting in the bathroom of a partly built house at Bretby in September 1982. They are very occasionally seen in remote upland areas, one instance being as high as 600m amsl at Kinder Downfall in May 1997.

There are 55 recoveries of Barn Owls affecting Derbyshire, dating back to 1937. The majority were ringed as nestlings and 69% of these had died within a year. Thirteen per cent survived for more than three years, but some of these were nevertheless traffic casualties: experience apparently does little to improve their chances of avoiding a road death. The oldest bird was also the furthest travelled: it was ringed in a nest at Great Hucklow in

July 1970 and found dead at Aberystwyth in Ceredigion, 190km away in January 1978. Others ringed in Derbyshire moved to East Lockinge in Oxfordshire, Runcorn Bridge in Halton, Rochdale in Greater Manchester, Bransholme in Kingston upon Hull, Thurlby (near Bourne) in Lincolnshire, Little Steeping in Lincolnshire and Rugeley in Staffordshire. One ringed as a chick at Rimac dunes on the Lincolnshire coast in June 1987 was found dead at Borrowash six months later.

Little Owl
Athene noctua
A fairly common resident.

Birdwatchers in most parts of the county will be familiar with the squat form of the Little Owl as it sits prominently on an exposed perch in broad daylight or suddenly flushes with strongly undulating flight from a hidden roost.

Birds of Continental origin were first released in Britain in Yorkshire in 1843 and extensively elsewhere during the second half of the nineteenth century. Many of the release schemes failed, but two concerted efforts, from the 1870s in Kent and in the 1880s in Northamptonshire, are believed to have resulted in the successful naturalization of Little Owls in Britain (Holloway 1996). The first Derbyshire record was of one shot at Hartshorne in 1888, and the first known breeding occurred at Sinfin Moor in 1909. Numbers built up quickly and by 1918 they had reached the Peak District. They were said to be common around Buxton by 1932, although it took a further six years before they were seen in the Glossop area. By then these owls were apparently well distributed and quite common in the county (Frost).

Little Owls are found in a wide variety of habitats including industrial wasteland, quarries, moorland and parkland, but are most numerous on lowland farmland, especially where dairying predominates. Here they find an abundance of food in the pastures and plentiful nest sites in hedgerow trees and pollarded stream-side willows. In other parts of the county, nests are often in drystone walls and buildings, rock-faces and, more rarely, nest-boxes may also be used.

Little Owls are very vocal early in the breeding season and can be very conspicuous as they sit outside their future nest holes in late winter and early spring, so it is likely that the distribution map, based on the Derbyshire BBS (1995–99), is the most accurate for any of the owls. The map shows 394 tetrads in which Little Owls were found, with breeding proved in 171 tetrads, and probable and possible breeding in a further 57 and 166 tetrads respectively. Breeding was confirmed in all 23 of the main 10km squares, compared with 17 in the 1968–72 Atlas and 19 in the 1988–91 Atlas.

Roworth (1981) found the birds to be most numerous in the eastern and southern lowlands but scarce in the Magnesian Limestone, White Peak and Dark Peak upland regions. This is still broadly the situation today, except that the Magnesian Limestone region holds plenty of Little Owls: for example, birds were recorded at 13 sites around Bolsover in 1992, with breeding proved in five of them, while at Whitwell Common in 1981, two nesting pairs were only 180m apart. Elsewhere, the position also seems relatively healthy, although Eaton *et al*. (2010) described a decline of 38% in the period 1970–2008. In 1983 there were believed to be 12–14 pairs in the Moss Valley. In the early 1990s up to six pairs bred at both Shipley Park and nearby West Hallam, and there were thought to be about 12 pairs in the Dale Abbey area. No fewer than 21 were heard in the Shipley Park area between midnight and 0745hrs on 1st January 1992. Further south, 12 pairs were proved to breed at Calke Park in 1999. In north-west Derbyshire in 1987, they were described as fairly common in moorland-edge fields bounded by drystone walls. Ten years later there were three territories around Lantern Pike and six in the Hayfield–Sett Valley area.

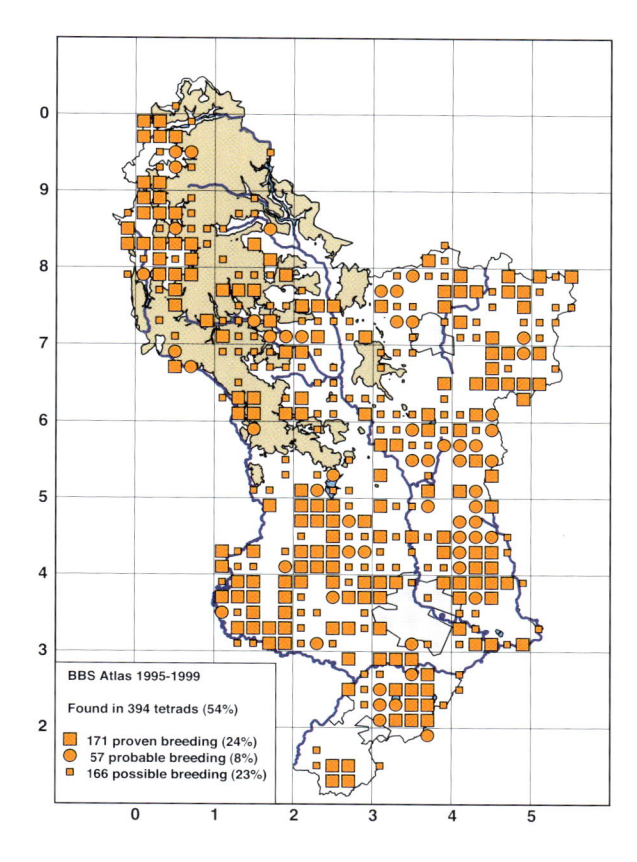

Hollick (1982) described the vulnerability of Little Owls to prolonged severe weather, during which they roosted in gardens, including her own in the centre of Ashbourne. Eight were found dead in Cubley during the long hard winter of early 1940.

Records of interesting prey items involve a snake (presumably a grass snake) carried by a bird at Rowthorne in July 1980; a dead adult Lapwing at a nest site at Arnfield Reservoir in 1984; one which ate five broods of Swallows at Markland Grips in June 1998; and in 2008, one was said to have taken all of the nestling Blackbirds from two, possibly three, nests in Horsley Woodhouse.

A bizarre sighting was of one taking a peanut from a garden feeder towards its nest in a nearby box at Botany Bay in June 2001.

Of the nine recovery reports for this species, five were found within 4km of their ringing site and of the remaining four birds only one moved more than 7km. There was a single wanderer, ringed as a chick at Unstone in August 1986, that was a road casualty at Bawtry, Nottinghamshire, 39km east-north-east, five months later. Although the species is quite sedentary, the ringing results suggest that they can expect to survive an average of 2.8 years, despite this being from the small sample of nine birds. Of these, the longest lived was 8.8 years.

Tawny Owl
Strix aluco
A fairly common resident.

The Tawny Owl, aptly named the Wood Owl in the past, is largely nocturnal and is rarely seen during daylight hours. The haunting, far-carrying hoot of the male is, however, familiar to most people. In Derbyshire it is present in woods of reasonable size, whether coniferous, deciduous or mixed. It also inhabits small copses and sometimes dense hawthorn scrub and lines of conifers. It may be found well within urban areas where there are mature trees and even in remote upland valleys with stunted trees. This adaptability explains why this species is by far the most widespread owl, rivalled only perhaps in places by the introduced Little Owl. Historically, the Tawny Owl was persecuted, as were so many other birds of prey, which kept numbers down, but there has been a widespread increase since the early twentieth century. Nationally, there was very little change in the breeding population between the 1968–72 and 1988–91 Atlases, although Eaton *et al*. (2010) state that it declined by 18% between 1970 and 2008. Whitlock stated that the Tawny Owl was 'fairly diffused' throughout the county, though outnumbered by the Barn Owl in the south. Jourdain thought it likely to be the county's most common owl overall, especially in hilly country. By the mid-twentieth century it was by far Derbyshire's most common owl, as it remains today, with no suggestions of any decline, except on a very localized basis.

By far the most frequent encounter is with calling birds. The highest recent counts were: 16 at Shipley Park on 14th October 1977 and ten at the same site between midnight and 0745hrs on 1st January 1992; six males and four females calling in the South Wood area on 7th February 1985 and nine hooting before dawn in the same area on 27th November 1994; and ten in the Elton–Kenslow area on 3rd March 2007. Two males were calling at each other from the chimney-pots of adjacent houses, less than one mile from Chesterfield town centre, in the early morning of 8th December 1984. There has been only one record of hunting during broad daylight, at 1300hrs at Killamarsh on 27th December 1985. More unusual prey items have included grey squirrel, Woodcock, a Woodpigeon squab, Swallow, Magpie, Blackbird and Nuthatch, the last of which was identified from a ring found in a pellet. A bird was seen apparently hunting Snipe at Barbrook Reservoir on a number of dates in September 1979.

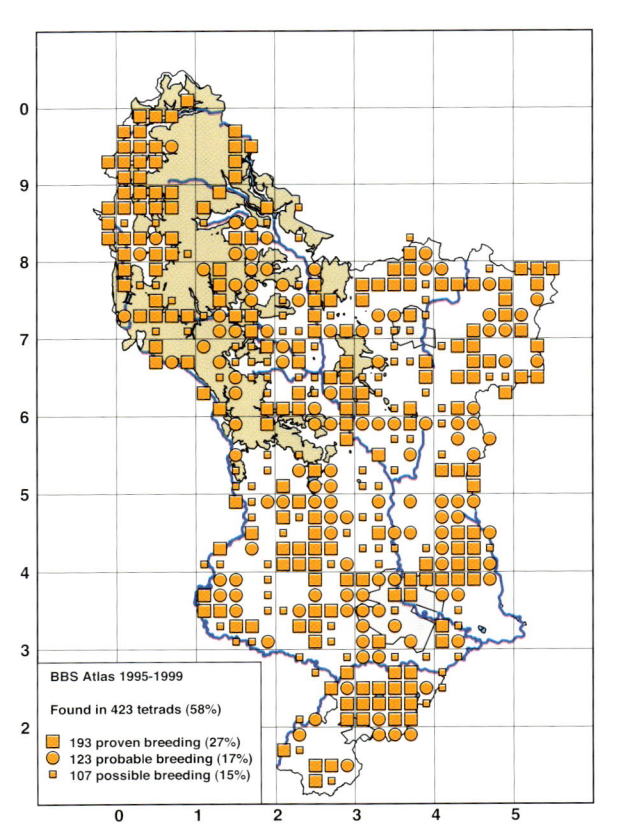

The Tawny Owl is adaptable in its choice of breeding site, which is mainly in tree holes or old nests of other birds such as Carrion Crow or Woodpigeon, or in old squirrel dreys, but there are local nesting records for rabbit burrows, rock ledges, on the ground and among hay bales in a barn. They also take very readily to barrels or nest-boxes put up for them, or intended for other species such as Kestrels. They have been known to usurp the nest holes of Little Owls. The highest altitude recorded for a nest site is 420m amsl in an old oak on the Upper Derwent Moors on 18th April 1994.

The tetrad map shows a total of 193 proven breeding tetrads, with a further 230 tetrads containing probable or possible breeding birds. There are no 10km squares with more than 25% of their area falling within the Derbyshire boundary that do not have proven breeding records. In the 1968–72 and 1988–91 Atlases, Tawny Owls were also confirmed as breeding in virtually all the 10km squares.

It is likely that the population in the far south of the county will increase, as large areas are being planted with trees to form part of the National Forest.

The Tawny Owl has not, however, been very well represented on either the three woodland or three farmland CBC plots. It was recorded on one of the woodland and two of the farmland sites. This is almost certainly to do in part with its nocturnal habits, since most CBC visits are made during daylight hours. Moreover, being at the top of the food chain, it would be expected to be at relatively low density. In the mixed woodland plot at Shiningcliff, there was an average of well under one territory per annum, representing 0.91 pairs per km^2. On the farmland plots, an average density of 2.07 pairs per km^2 was recorded at Culland, and a much lower density of 0.34 pairs per km^2 at Broadhay Farm, Hathersage.

Unusual roost sites have been within a hawthorn in a reed-bed at Carr Vale on 1st January 1994 and on the roof of a busy factory in Chesterfield on 27th April 1979.

There are 202 ringing recoveries for this species, but it is generally very sedentary with only 20% moving more than 10km from the place of ringing and of these, 10% managed to venture more than 40km. The furthest was ringed as a chick at Hayfield in May 1995 and was found dead at Leeds, 54km north-north-east, in January 1996. Another ringed at Arnfield died 32km away on the M1 Motorway at Barnsley and one moved 36km from Chisworth to Worsborough, Barnsley. A bird found dead at Glossop had been ringed at Earby, Lincolnshire, 53km away. By far the greatest percentage of the birds stay in the area in which they were born and 36% of the whole dataset have been later found still within 1km. By contrast, the species is relatively long-lived with 31% of birds (most ringed as nestlings) surviving for at least two years and 60% of these exceeding four years. Indeed, two of the records are for birds ringed as chicks in the Glossop area that were found dead, close to the ringing sites, almost 17 years later.

In the north-west of the county, the Dark Peak Ringing Group has erected barrels and ringed birds annually at these and at natural nest sites since, at an average rate of more than 100 per year. The most productive year was 1993 when 167 were ringed.

Of the generally sedentary owl species, the number of Tawny Owl recoveries far exceeds those for Little Owl, Barn Owl and Long-eared Owl. This implies that more Tawny Owls have been ringed over the years but of these there are far fewer pre-1970 records (4% of total) than for the other three species (respectively 44%, 20%, 15% ringed before 1970). This is surprising, since all species are easy to ring as nestlings, so even though their breeding densities differ, the data suggest that less effort was made to find and ring other owl species during these earlier years. Nevertheless, there is a single very early record from 1919 of a bird ringed in Staffordshire that was found dead at Norbury eight months later.

BBS Atlas 1995-1999
Found in 423 tetrads (58%)
- 193 proven breeding (27%)
- 123 probable breeding (17%)
- 107 possible breeding (15%)

Long-eared Owl
Asio otus
A scarce resident and winter visitor.

This beautiful and enigmatic owl is not as strictly nocturnal as the Tawny Owl, but it is nevertheless rarely observed during daylight hours, apart from a few weeks in midsummer when birds are feeding young; at this time it can be confused in flight with the Short-eared Owl.

The best time of day to watch this owl is the two-hour period after sunset, especially in February and March, when pairs are indulging in courtship. Despite the sometimes intense cold, listening to the soft hooting of the males and watching the pair float over the future nest site, vigorously wing-clapping, is one of the joys of early spring.

In Derbyshire, Long-eared Owls are found in a wide variety of habitats, from hawthorn hedges on lowland farmland, to isolated conifer stands on upland heather moors. However, coniferous woodland is the most favoured habitat: in 1991, of 21 sites, 15 (71.4%) were in conifers, with the remainder divided between hawthorn scrub, three (14.3%); deciduous woodland, two (9.5%); and open moorland, one (4.8%) (Roome 1992). More unusual sites have included a scrub-covered embankment alongside a major railway line, isolated hedgerow oaks, and ledges on quarry faces. In the Peak District, where ground-nesting still occurs occasionally, all sites are on, or adjacent to, large areas of rough grassland or moorland. This reflects the hunting preferences of this species. Nest sites have ranged in altitude from 55m to 390m amsl, with over half being between 100m and 200m.

Long-eared Owls are thinly distributed across the north and north-west, while breeding south of the River Trent is very rare. There was a 60-year absence from 1945, when a pair bred at Repton Shrubs, to 2005 when two pairs reared young in the area. By contrast, in 1991, the north-east was quite well populated, holding over 50% of the breeding population. In this area, a few pairs had taken advantage of the planting of colliery spoil heaps with conifers, colonizing these sites when the trees were only 3–5m tall.

Whitlock thought that a few pairs bred in 'Peakland' woods and elsewhere, and believed that the species had previously been much more numerous. Although Frost also believed that a long-term decline had taken place, Scott (1997) concluded that the population in his study area in neighbouring counties had increased by 10–15% since the mid-1950s. In Derbyshire the population appears to be stable at around 20 known pairs. However, this is almost certainly an underestimate, as most pairs are found on hearing the food-begging calls of the owlets in midsummer, leaving failed and non-breeding birds unrecorded. Breeding was confirmed in three of the 10km core squares in the 1968–72 Atlas and 11 in the 1988–91 Atlas. The results of Derbyshire BBS (1995–99) are summarized on the map.

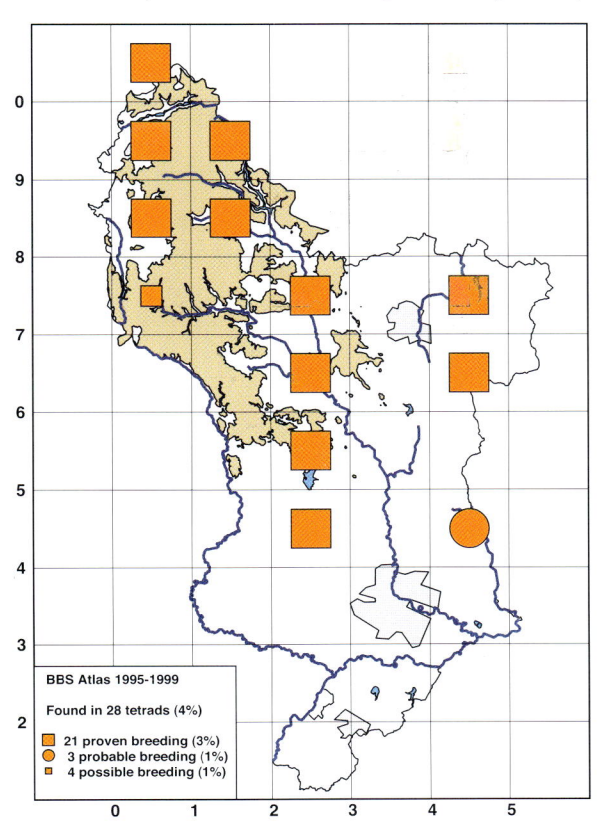

Not all pairs breed every year. Some display, mate and even sit on nests, without laying eggs. This behaviour is probably associated with fluctuations in food availability, as Long-eared Owls rely to some extent on a good supply of small mammals, notably voles, during the breeding season. Even Derbyshire's small population shows that the peak in successful pairs correlates with high vole numbers. Such peaks were evident in 1980, 1984, 1988, 1991, 1993, 1995 and 1999, coinciding with an apparent three to four year cyclical pattern of vole numbers. During 1991 at least 36 young fledged from 15 nests, an average of 2.4 young per successful nest. In four monitored nests, all lost one owlet, but there was no record of a complete brood being lost (Roome 1992). Breeding numbers have been generally lower in the 2000s than in the 1990s.

In 2008, a nest in the north-west of the county was visited in early April and was found to have collapsed, with a broken egg and a dead youngster under the tree. However, one of the adults was brooding a surviving youngster on the ground. The nest was rebuilt and the young bird duly fledged from it.

Until recently, the best opportunity for birdwatchers to see Long-eared Owls in the county was at well-established and relatively well-known communal roosts. Unfortunately, wintering numbers have crashed from the highs of the late 1980s and early 1990s, when there was an average of over 30 birds each winter spread over six traditional roosts in north-east and south Derbyshire. In the period 1996–2005 there was an average of just three birds at only one or two roost sites per winter including a maximum of five at Willington Gravel Pits in early 2000. Subsequent numbers were higher, with two roosts holding up to five and six birds from 2006 to 2009 and a small scatter of ones and twos elsewhere. The reasons for the overall decline are not known, but human disturbance may have been a factor. In north-east Derbyshire in 1975–76, up to 12 birds frequented an area of conifer trees and scrub, and in 1988 and 1989 a maximum of 13 were recorded at another site (which is now in Rotherham), while in south Derbyshire up to 14 were at a winter roost in the late 1980s and early 1990s. One was found roosting in a yew at Bemrose School, Derby on 7th March 1979, a very unusual suburban record. One roosted with a group of six Short-eared Owls at Elvaston Quarry in late December 1991 into January 1992.

An interesting record is of a male singing in sunshine at 1300hrs on 31st March 1997 at Scarcliffe.

The earliest recovery for this species was in 1926, relating to a bird moving between Buxton and Chapel-en-le-Frith after fledging. Most of the recoveries have come from the years since the late 1970s and all concerned quite short distances. A relatively long-distance record was reported for one ringed as a nestling at Great Longstone in 1990, which moved 97km south-east to become a road casualty at Uppingham, Rutland in May 1999. All but three of the reports have concerned chicks ringed in the nest, the birds having generally only survived to about 18 months. The oldest record was one such bird ringed at Markland Grips which was found freshly dead at Unstone almost three years later. One ringed as a chick near Baslow in June 1996 was found as a road casualty at Barlborough six months later.

BBS Atlas 1995-1999

Found in 28 tetrads (4%)

- 21 proven breeding (3%)
- 3 probable breeding (1%)
- 4 possible breeding (1%)

Short-eared Owl
Asio flammeus
A scarce summer visitor to the Peak District moorlands. A scarce passage migrant and winter visitor.

The Moor Owl, as it is sometimes known, favours upland moorland for breeding, and Derbyshire is blessed with large areas of such habitat (over 300km²) in the gritstone region of the north and north-west of the county. This interesting owl is the only regular British breeding species of owl to nest exclusively on the ground and is also the most likely to be seen hunting diurnally, especially when it has dependent young.

Short-eared Owls usually arrive on their Derbyshire breeding grounds in March, but an early pair was seen on a known territory on 1st February (1997). Vacation of breeding grounds seems to begin around August. The number of breeding Short-eared Owls fluctuates from year to year due to their dependence on short-tailed voles which form the bulk of the diet. However, many well-watched breeding sites are known to be occupied in most years, although the level of breeding success varies, presumably because of fluctuations in prey abundance. The minimum numbers of pairs present and where breeding was proved on approximately 12km² of well-watched moorland in the Upper Derwentdale area in the period 1993–2011 are shown in the table.

Year	Pairs present	Pairs breeding
1993	6	3
1994	6	3
1995	3	2
1996	4	2
1997	6	1
1998	4	3
1999	6	5
2000	4	4
2001	4	3
2002	7	3
2003	4	2
2004	4	4
2005	5	2
2006	4	–
2007	4	–
2008	4	4
2009	3	–
2010	–	–
2011	–	–

Most nests are in heather, but they are occasionally in rough grass. Short-eared Owls seem to favour areas above 350m amsl on the higher and wetter moors of the far north and north-west of the county, and are scarce on the Eastern Moors, as shown by the tetrad map. Successful breeding is fairly easy to detect as the species is readily seen in daylight hours when feeding young. However, they are very difficult to locate early in the breeding cycle, and thus the number of failed pairs is hard to determine. Close nesting between adjacent pairs has been noted in good years; in 1999, for example, two nests were only 600m apart. Human persecution of breeding birds is still suspected in some areas.

The map shows breeding was proved in 14 tetrads, with a combined total of 20 tetrads in which breeding was probable or possible.

These findings are broadly similar to those of the 1968–72 and 1988–91 Atlases. Nationally, the number of proven breeding pairs fell by 30% between the two Atlas periods, but there was no marked peak in vole numbers during the latter survey (apart from local exceptions in 1991), so this could be misleading. The last year in which there were no proven breeding records in the county was 1981, while the highest number of successful pairs was 12 in 2003. This is a marked improvement on the situation in 1978 when Frost considered that they bred only in years of small mammal abundance: there were breeding records in only 11 years in the period 1905–77, although in 1893 Whitlock stated that a few pairs bred annually on the 'Peakland' moors but were subjected to persecution.

In Derbyshire, Short-eared Owls are more widely reported while on passage or in winter, where they can turn up at almost any site that harbours voles. Most are seen between October and March, mainly in lowland areas, where they have also been known to exploit alternative food sources, including frogs at Manor Floods, Ilkeston in March 1989 and a rabbit at Willington Gravel Pits in January 1993. Nationally, numbers are known to fluctuate widely, and wintering birds in Britain are made up of both breeders, which have remained to overwinter, and immigrants from the Continent. The total number of birds is difficult to ascertain in any year because of the species' nomadic tendencies. They often travel great distances in search of good hunting grounds and move on when the supply is exhausted. Consequently, there is a strong likelihood of wintering records being duplicated within the same, or even across a number of counties during the course of a winter.

Frost referred to an exceptional glut of records in the winter of 1974/75, including a flock of up to nine at a gravel pit at Elvaston Quarry. Based on pellet analysis, G.P. Mawson considered that this group fed mainly on small passerine birds. There was an even greater influx in 1978/79 when over 50 birds were

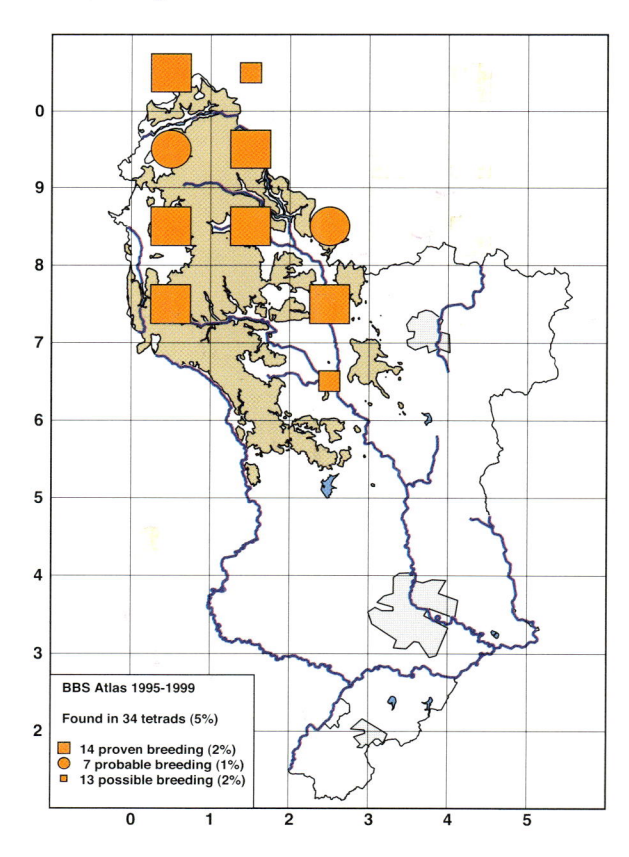

BBS Atlas 1995-1999
Found in 34 tetrads (5%)
- 14 proven breeding (2%)
- 7 probable breeding (1%)
- 13 possible breeding (2%)

reported from more than 30 localities, mainly in the south, with no fewer than 11 together at Staveley in February 1979. Since then, the numbers of Short-eared Owls recorded in the county each winter have ranged from peaks of 36 in 1982/83 and 33 in 1991/92 to lows of only three in 1997/98 and two in 2003/04. Events in 2008 showed the erratic occurrences of wintering birds: there were none in the early months but between October and December they were seen at eight sites, with up to seven at Leash Fen and five in the Beeley Moor area.

The earliest recorded lowland post-breeding migrant in the period 1978–2003 was one at Long Eaton Gravel Pits on 2nd July 1994, while the latest wintering birds seen in non-breeding habitat were singles on 20th May at Elmton in 1992 and Ogston Reservoir in 1996, and Brinsley Flash on 29th May 1975.

Owing to their habit of hunting over open terrain, sometimes diurnally, Short-eared Owls are more prone to harassment from birds than are other owls. Species observed mobbing them include Hen Harrier, Kestrel, Hobby, Peregrine, Curlew, Magpie (30 in pursuit, on one occasion) and Raven. An interesting record was of a bird hiding prey on two occasions at Little Longstone, on 2nd December 1978.

Based on ringing recoveries, Short-eared Owls have undertaken the longest movements of the county's five owl species. Most, if not all, leave the moors after the breeding season. All of the six recoveries were of birds ringed here as nestlings and all were recovered in their first year except for one ringed at Woodhead in May 1988 that was found dead at Harrogate, North Yorkshire in March 1990. There was a second record of one moving from Longdendale to Lofthouse, North Yorkshire, while others ringed in the Woodhead area were found dead 221km away at Hirwaun in Rhondda-Cynon-Taff (Glamorgan) and 796km away at Deux-Sèvres in western France.

Nightjar
Caprimulgus europaeus
A rare summer visitor.

According to Whitlock, in the nineteenth century the Nightjar was a regular spring visitor to Derbyshire, and was thought to be common in some areas of the High Peak. During the twentieth century an almost continuous fall in its numbers has occurred. The long-term decline in breeding pairs and contraction of range in Britain is well documented, with the 1988–91 Atlas revealing that the formerly widespread Nightjar population of the north Midlands had been reduced to scattered pockets. Frost considered there were fewer than 20 pairs left by the 1970s and predicted that the species was likely to become extinct as a Derbyshire breeding bird before the end of the century. However, the Nightjar has managed to retain a foothold, with a maximum of ten pairs or singing males recorded in each summer since 1979, and always in the northern half of the county. The occasional sightings in the southern half of the county in recent decades have involved passage birds, usually in May, and breeding is not thought to have taken place there since the early 1960s.

During the 1980s and 1990s, breeding sites have been concentrated in the Matlock Forest–Beeley Moor area, although at least one pair was reported in most years from 1989 to 1995 in the Goyt Valley region. Formerly, a few pairs bred in areas of bracken below gritstone edges, but the last record from such habitat was of a pair below Curbar Edge in 1985. Otherwise, until 2008, Nightjar territories have been exclusively in newly planted or recently clear-felled conifer plantations. This extremely limited distribution was confirmed by the findings of the Derbyshire BBS (1995–99) and, despite extensive coverage, no new sites were discovered. However, since 2008, Nightjars have also been found on open heather moorland, albeit close to coniferous woodland. In 2011 they were present at three such sites, with breeding proved at two of them. The overall total for the latter year was five pairs and five singing males. In the previous year, churring Nightjars were also found in the Cromford area and in the north-west of the county. Current trends are encouraging.

Frost remarked that many old Nightjar sites, particularly in the Peak District, remained unoccupied, probably due to human disturbance or climatic changes.

While the status of the Nightjar is undoubtedly precarious, recently there have been some grounds for optimism. A national survey in 1992 concluded that the British population had made a partial recovery since 1981 (Morris *et al*. 1994). A study in North Yorkshire revealed a significant growth in population between 1981 and 1996, probably as a result of an increase in the available area of suitable nesting habitat due to forest management (Scott *et al*. 1998). Nightjars have adapted successfully to clear-fell areas within commercially grown forests, and the sympathetic management of such areas may well prove crucial for the future survival of this intriguing bird.

Nightjars are generally the last of the regular summer visitors to arrive, usually being reported first in the second half of May. The earliest return to the breeding area in the county is 5th May (1995) although there is an exceptional record of one

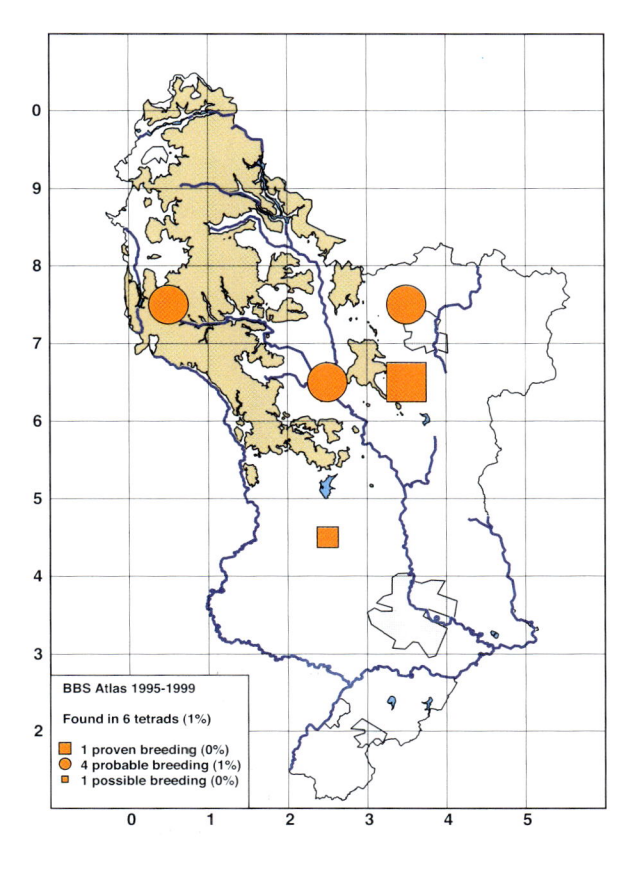

BBS Atlas 1995-1999
Found in 6 tetrads (1%)
- 1 proven breeding (0%)
- 4 probable breeding (1%)
- 1 possible breeding (0%)

on 6th April (1904) at an undisclosed locality. They normally depart in August, though 'churring' birds have been heard occasionally towards the end of the month and one was present at a breeding site until 10th September 2000. Exceptionally, one was seen hawking insects at Foremark Reservoir on 21st September 1995, while the latest date is 20th October (1949) at Meynell Langley.

A male ringed at Williamthorpe on 6th June 1991 was presumably a late migrant. Other migrants in the period 1980 to 2011 have been at Brailsford, Crich, Drakelow, Foremark, Ilkeston, Stanton Ironworks, Staunton Harold Reservoir, Torside and Twyford Greens. A well-watched and photographed immature bird, the second latest record, roosted on an urban garden fence at Codnor from 23rd to 30th September 2011.

Few birds of this species have been ringed within Derbyshire and the only recovery relates to a juvenile ringed near Curbar on 12th August 1975 which was killed a week later by a car at Widnes, Lancashire, 74km to the west (Frost).

Needle-tailed Swift
Hirundapus caudacutus
A very rare vagrant.

The only record of this extreme rarity, surely one of the least expected birds ever to be seen in Derbyshire, was of one flying over Belper at 1530hrs on 3rd June 1991. When it appeared, the observer was watching and sketching Swifts moving between west and south-west over agricultural land. It was in view for about three minutes, latterly passing about 6m from her to be lost from view behind houses. This was presumed to be the individual which visited Kent on 26th May, Blithfield Reservoir, Staffordshire on 1st June and Noss, Shetland from 11th to 14th June. The Derbyshire bird was accepted as the tenth British record and an account was given by Thorpe (1996).

This swift breeds from western Siberia to Japan and winters in Australia. Of the eight previous British records, six had occurred in the period 26th May to 20th June.

Swift
Apus apus
A common summer visitor and passage migrant.

Swifts are among the last summer visitors to arrive in Derbyshire, usually not appearing until the third week in April. Numbers then build up rapidly during the first half of May, when screaming display flights announce their presence over towns and villages. The earliest ever recorded arrival date is 3rd April (2005) at Matlock, although the average first arrival date between 1978 and 2011 was 22nd April. Birds start to leave their breeding sites from July onwards and most have gone by the end of August, leaving only a few individuals which stay into September. However, even though the average last departure date in the 30 years between 1978 and 2011 is 24th September, there are several records for October, and three for November (on 9th in 1985, 12th in 2000 and 21st in 1976). A remarkably late individual was seen at an unnamed Derbyshire locality on 21st December 1888 (Witherby *et al.* 1938–41), which might still be the latest British date.

Frost believed there had been little alteration to the status of the Swift since the start of the twentieth century at least. Nationally, this would also appear to be the case, with hardly any long-term change in population, though there may have been some short-term variation in numbers. In recent years growing concern has been expressed about the loss of traditional nest holes in older buildings following demolition and renovation work. To try and address this problem, in 2005 the DOS commenced a survey of the species in the county, and the results have been incorporated herewith.

The Derbyshire BBS (1995–99) reported proven breeding in 161 tetrads, probable breeding in 63 tetrads and possible breeding in a further 329. Breeding was confirmed throughout most of the county, the main exception being the high moorland areas, which although providing useful feeding areas, have little in the way of suitable nest sites.

The distribution map reflects the predominance of breeding records from the main areas of human habitation. Swifts nest mainly inside the eaves of houses and also in crevices in taller structures such as factories, mills and railway viaducts. There have been no instances of this species using natural nest sites, such as trees or rock-faces, since the 1930s, when they were discovered breeding in crevices at Raven's Tor on the Staffordshire side of the Dove Valley (Frost). Egg-laying usually commences about 20th May with a hatching date around 10th June (1988–91 Atlas). Evidence of a large variation in laying dates was obtained on 18th July 1991 when four nests were examined in a factory roof in Derby. Two of the nests contained young close to fledging, while the other two contained eggs which were still being incubated. In 1978 many birds remained well into October, as late as 21st, including over 30 at Hadfield on 8th October and young were still in the nest at Bradwell on the exceptionally late date of 7th October.

The highest counts of Swifts are usually recorded at large water bodies, although large flocks are often seen over arable farmland, especially fields of oil-seed rape, later in the breeding season. On 25th July 1999, 1600 were present at Foremark Reservoir, while up to 1000 have occurred at Ogston Reservoir (May 1986, May 2005 and May 2006), Drakelow Nature Reserve (August 1988), Unstone (May 1996) and Carsington Water (June 2001). Heavy passage movement has been observed in late summer, with notable counts of 3000 to the west on 15th July 2001 at Drakelow Nature Reserve; 3000 to the south-west

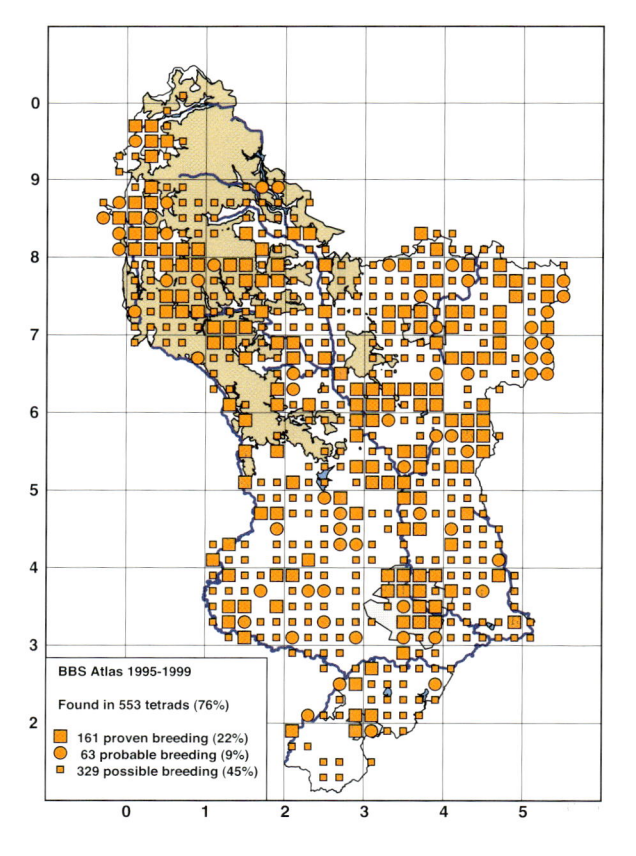

BBS Atlas 1995-1999
Found in 553 tetrads (76%)
- 161 proven breeding (22%)
- 63 probable breeding (9%)
- 329 possible breeding (45%)

in three hours on 8th August 1993 over Darley Abbey; at Pebley Pond 2500 to the south-west in only 30 minutes on 13th August 1999 and 1500 south-west in two hours on 1st August 2006; and 2650 between west and south-west in two hours at High Moor on 5th August 2005.

There are two records of partial albinism: an individual at Long Eaton Gravel Pits on 25th May 1998 had a distinct white belly-patch, and one at Ogston Reservoir on 12th June 1995 had white upper and under-tail coverts as well as a blotchy white back.

An interesting report concerns two birds seen fighting on the road at Darley Dale on 24th April 1957. Surprisingly for a species which spends virtually all its life on the wing, Swifts are by no means immune from capture by domestic cats. On 3rd August 1989 a young bird at Calver Mill was retrieved from the works cat and subsequently released. There are also two instances of birds ringed in the 1980s in Dronfield which, in both cases, were killed by a cat nine years later, at the same site or nearby.

Large numbers of Swifts have been ringed as adults because of the ease by which they can be caught in mist nets by the technique of 'flicking'. This consists of a pair of observers holding the net horizontally before moving it quickly to a vertical position to intercept passing birds. It is notable that the recoveries have all resulted from ringing since the 1960s. Before then, mist nets were not available and the nest sites of the species do not usually permit easy access for the ringing of nestlings. Indeed, of over 160 recoveries involving the county, only two were ringed as nestlings.

More than 60% of the recoveries have been 'controls', that is, birds caught by another ringer. This is a potentially long-lived species, with two local birds known to have survived to about 11 years, and some 75% of all recoveries have occurred more than three years after ringing.

There have been recoveries from many areas of England, as far south as Sussex and north to Cleveland, and there are five from overseas. Two came from Morocco, both in September, two from Zaire in September and November and, furthest of all, a ringed bird travelled 8108km from Eckington to Tanzania where it was killed in December (1976).

Pallid Swift
Apus pallidus
A very rare vagrant.

The only record is of one at Willington Gravel Pits during the late afternoon and early evening of 3rd August 1998. It was initially seen and identified while flying alone, before it joined up with a flock of up to 40 Swifts and was seen intermittently until the last definite sighting at 2015hrs, when the flock was lost to view over Repton. By this time, several other observers had seen the bird. An account of the event was given by Hutchinson (1999). BBRC accepted this bird as the fourteenth record for Britain. By 2011, this total had risen to 79 (Hudson *et al*. 2012). They breed in the Mediterranean region and the Middle East, wintering mainly in central Africa.

Alpine Swift
Apus melba
A very rare vagrant.

Alpine Swifts are fairly regular overshooting migrants to Britain between March and November, with peaks in May to early June and late September (Dymond *et al*. 1989).

There have been three county records. Tomlinson (1999) gave an account of the Bennerley Marsh sighting. The 2006 bird is believed to have roosted overnight on Ogston Hall.

Year	Location and date
1998	Bennerley Marsh, one was present for ten minutes on 1st September
2000	Littleover, Derby, one flew south-east on 14th May
2006	Ogston Reservoir, one on 27th–28th April

Alpine Swifts breed across Eurasia east to Turkestan, in India, and in eastern and southern Africa. Most winter in sub-Saharan Africa. There had been about 575 records nationally by the time it was removed from the *British Birds* Rarities List after 2005.

Kingfisher
Alcedo atthis
A fairly common resident.

Kingfishers are quite widespread on suitable rivers, streams and canals throughout much of Derbyshire and are regularly seen at larger water bodies such as reservoirs and gravel pits. They require reasonably clear water in which to catch fish and, in the breeding season, suitable banks in which to excavate their nest hole. They occasionally nest a little way from water and will do so in the banks of grossly polluted rivers, provided there are suitable feeding areas nearby, as at Shuttlewood in 1994–95, when a pair reared young by the River Doe Lea, at the time one of England's filthiest waterways.

Human persecution, particularly by fishing interests, was a serious threat to the well-being of this species in the nineteenth century. Whitlock wrote of their incessant persecution and noted several instances of birds being caught in 'the deadly hanging-net, a most fateful trap for this beautiful species.' Nevertheless, in May 1888 he recorded a dozen pairs during a long row up the River Trent, almost to Burton upon Trent. In 1905, Jourdain reported a recent increase in numbers, which he connected with protection measures introduced by the county council. In more recent times, the two factors most influencing population levels appear to be harsh winter weather and water pollution. Kingfishers are particularly vulnerable to prolonged periods of severe cold when rivers and streams may freeze, but their long breeding season, in which up to three broods may be reared, may facilitate a rapid recovery in numbers. Frost commented that the population fully recovered within six years from the heavy mortality suffered in the exceptionally cold winter of 1962/63. The series of relatively cold winters from the late 1970s to the mid-1980s also caused a significant decline, but subsequently, again aided by a succession of generally milder winters, the population was fully restored: for example, in 2001 this species was recorded at 175 sites. Its prospects have undoubtedly been

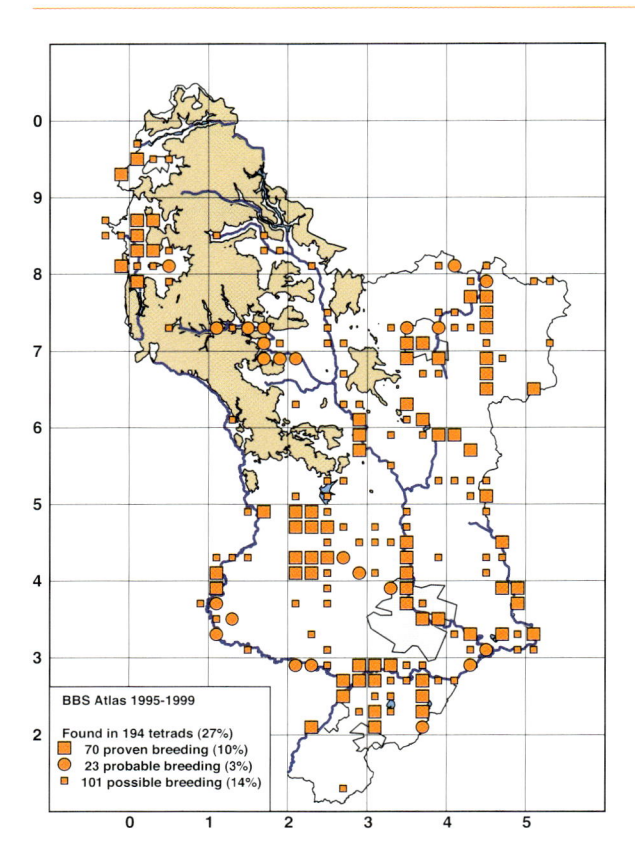

BBS Atlas 1995-1999
Found in 194 tetrads (27%)
■ 70 proven breeding (10%)
● 23 probable breeding (3%)
▪ 101 possible breeding (14%)

further improved by legislation to enforce higher standards of water quality.

The Derbyshire BBS (1995–99) revealed a predominantly lowland distribution in the south and east of the county, with another concentration in the north-west along the river systems of the Goyt and Etherow. Breeding was confirmed in 70 tetrads, probable in 23 and possible in a further 101. It is likely that many of the 'possible' tetrads held breeding pairs, as this is not an easy species for which to prove breeding, owing to difficulties of access to river-banks in some areas and the large size of Kingfisher territories. Breeding was confirmed in 17 main 10km squares, compared with 12 in the 1968–72 Atlas and 14 in the 1988–91 Atlas.

Counts of up to six birds are not uncommon at gravel pits and lakes, especially in the Trent Valley area. Higher counts were of eight at Willington Gravel Pits in August 1990, and nine along the River Dove between Sudbury and Newton Solney in September 1982.

There are occasional records of Kingfishers at upland waters well away from known breeding sites, including Barbrook and Ramsley Reservoirs in September 1990, Derwent Reservoir in March 1999 and Ladybower Reservoir in June 2002, while another wanderer was seen at 270m amsl on East Moor in September 1996. There are numerous other records of birds in unlikely situations, one of the most bizarre involving a bird surrounded by heavy traffic as it sat on a kerbstone on a traffic island at Little Eaton in October 1980. Others have wandered almost to the centres of Derby and Chesterfield and there are now numerous records of individuals visiting garden ponds. Kingfishers have also been reported in flight well away from water, in villages, over open farmland and along a woodland ride.

Examples of particularly interesting behaviour include one seen diving from an 11m-high power cable into the River Trent at Newton Solney in December 1976, and one diving through thin ice to successfully catch a fish at Birdholme Wildfowl Reserve a month later. At Drakelow Nature Reserve in May 2005, one caught and attempted to swallow a 150mm perch before discarding it several minutes later.

There have been 13 ringing recoveries of this species involving Derbyshire, most of them very close to the ringing site. Since it is not usually possible to ring chicks in the nest, all except one were birds ringed as adults. This exception was ringed as a chick in an accessible nest at Whitwell in June 1974 and found dead at Pitsmoor, Sheffield, 12 months later. Among the 13, two long-distance travellers moved 123km, from Renishaw to Wisbech, Cambridgeshire, and 62km from Birdholme to Rugeley, Staffordshire.

Bee-eater
Merops apiaster
A very rare vagrant.

Among the most spectacular and colourful European birds, Bee-eaters are annual vagrants to Britain, with records ranging from mid-April to early November. Most occur in spring and there is a distinct peak in records from late May to early June (Dymond *et al*. 1989). They were removed from the *British Birds* Rarities List after 1990, by which time there had been some 478 records. Bee-eaters breed from Spain to northernmost India and beyond, and in southern Africa, wintering in sub-Saharan Africa.

Whitlock recorded that one was shot in the gardens of Stainsby House, near Mapperley, on 4th May 1879 and another also at Mapperley on 10th June 1879. A third was also rumoured to have been shot in the same area around that time.

There have been three recent records. One flew west on 22nd July 1984 at Edale Cross (four days after a Roller was found in the county), two were watched for 15 minutes on the evening of 5th July 1991 at Elvaston Quarry, and one was heard calling as it flew south on 10th June 2006 over Codnor Park.

Roller
Coracias garrulus
A very rare vagrant.

Rollers breed from Spain to western Sinkiang and winter in sub-Saharan Africa. They are rare vagrants to Britain, with few records from inland counties. By 2011 there had been 311 UK records, of which 196 were prior to 1950 (Hudson *et al*. 2012).

There have been two Derbyshire records. One was seen by a Derby optician by the River Derwent, between Duffield and Darley, nearly opposite Allestree Hall on 3rd May 1856 (Whitlock). More recently, a local veterinary surgeon found an adult at Morley on 18th July 1984. It remained in the area until the following evening at least, and spent much of its time on telephone wires in open countryside. This was the only record in the UK in that year and was found four days before a Bee-eater was seen in the county.

Hoopoe
Upupa epops
A rare vagrant.

Frost gave details of six records from the nineteenth century and there were three further occurrences prior to 1950. There have been 26 subsequent records involving 30 birds, summarized by periods in the table. The only year with more than two records of this handsome species in Derbyshire is 1988, when five individuals were seen at four localities. The predominance of spring sightings is revealed in the half-monthly occurrence chart.

The earliest arrival was of a bird found on 17th March 1996 at Rowthorne, while the latest date is 8th November 1993 at Burnaston. Hoopoes have rarely stayed longer than a day or two, although one individual remained at Overseal from 22nd June to 2nd July 1978. Two birds have been seen together on three occasions: at Drakelow in June 1973, Belper in May 1983 and Staveley Sewage Farm in October 1988. The majority of sightings have been in the south and east of the county, and the only records from the north-west concerned singles at Arnfield Reservoir in April 1981 and May 2004. Other localities where Hoopoes have been found since 1950 are Netherseal, Catton Hall, Drakelow Nature Reserve, Egginton Gravel Pits, Woodville, Hilton, Breadsall, Little Eaton, Belper, Hulland Ward, Carsington Water, Stretton, Hardwick Park and the Rowthorne Trail, near Haddon Hall, Scarcliffe, Chatsworth Park, Bolsover and Old Brampton.

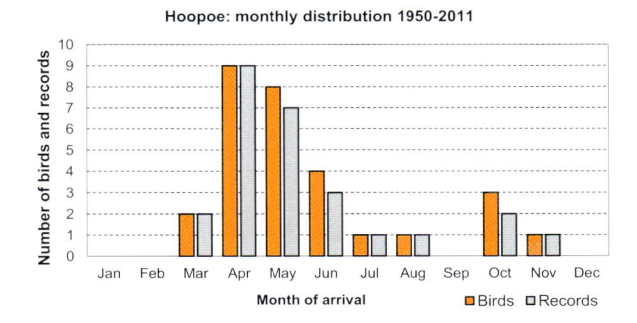

Period	Records	Birds
1950s	1	1
1960s	5	5
1970s	6	7
1980s	8	10
1990s	4	4
2000–11	2	3
Totals	26	30

Wryneck
Jynx torquilla
A rare passage migrant.

The Wryneck is a scarce passage migrant in England, occurring in variable numbers each year, mainly on the east coast in autumn. It is especially associated with easterly winds (Brown & Grice 2005). Unfortunately, this species is now virtually extinct as a British breeding bird following the long-term decline and eventual demise of its population in England and Wales, although very small numbers have attempted to breed in Scotland since 1969.

According to Jourdain and Whitlock, Wrynecks were local spring and summer visitors to Derbyshire in the nineteenth century, frequenting woods and parks in the south, south-west and north-east of the county, while one or two pairs nested in the Upper Derwent Valley.

Frost gave details of the first sighting in the twentieth century, which did not occur until 27th August 1966. There have been 43 records in total, summarized by periods in the table.

Period	Records
1960s	3
1970s	15
1980s	10
1990s	3
2000–11	12
Total	43

The upsurge in records in the 1970s may be explained in terms of increased observer activity, although the subsequent decrease is almost certainly a reflection of its genuine scarcity. The only year with more than three records is 1976 when five birds were found between 26th August and 25th September. Mirroring the national trend, the preponderance of early autumn occurrences is apparent in the monthly chart.

All records since 1966 have involved singles with the exception of possibly two birds at Wyver Lane in August 1983. The earliest of only five spring records was of one in a garden at Chinley on 17th April 1987, while the latest autumn sighting was of one by a railway line at Etwall on 16th October 2000. Wrynecks have rarely stayed more than a day, although one remained in a birdwatcher's garden at Duffield for four days in September 1994 and there was one in another birdwatcher's garden at Crich for three days in 1993; likewise at Willington Gravel Pits there was a rather elusive bird for the same length of time in September 2003.

Other modern records of birds in gardens are from Allestree, Brailsford, Crich, Duffield, Kirk Langley and Long Eaton, where the bird was found dead. An unusual record was that of a bird which had become trapped in the apex of a house roof at Nottingham Road, Derby in September 1986. The 1966 bird was caught in a farm building at Tibshelf and released. Three individuals have been trapped and ringed; at Old Whittington Sewage Farm, Markland Grips and Whitwell Common.

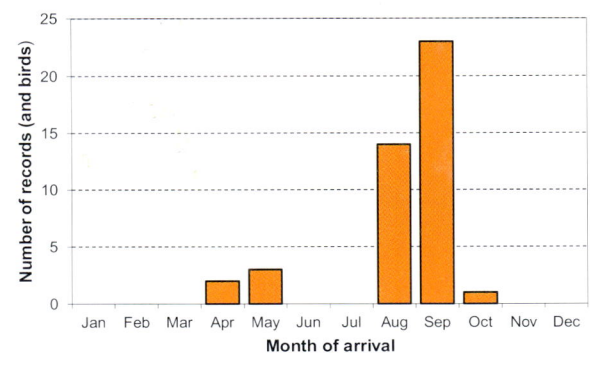

Drakelow Nature Reserve and Hilton Gravel Pits Nature Reserve are the only sites where Wrynecks have been seen on two occasions. The other sites of modern records, not mentioned above, are Abney, Arnfield Reservoir, Bolsover, Brackenfield, Carr Vale, Carsington Water, Clay Mills Gravel Pits, Corbar Wood, Derby, Dronfield, Egginton, Errwood, Heanor, Long Eaton Gravel Pits, Mam Tor, Netherseal, Normanton, Oker, Palterton, Pleasley Colliery, Ramsley, Shottle Hall Farm, Sinfin and Sutton Scarsdale.

Green Woodpecker
Picus viridis
A fairly common resident.

According to Whitlock, writing in 1893, the Green Woodpecker was by far the most common of its family in Derbyshire and, with the exception of moorland areas, could be found throughout the county. Although it has been outnumbered by the Great Spotted Woodpecker since the 1940s (Frost), this species is currently widespread and locally quite common. However, because it is largely a ground-feeder and therefore susceptible to extended periods of frost and snow, the Green Woodpecker has suffered periodic reversals of fortune. Frost observed that the severe winter of 1962/63 drastically reduced the population and in many places it was very slow to recover, apparently still being absent from some of its traditional haunts even in the mid-1970s. It continued to be regarded as scarce and thinly distributed until the early 1990s. Subsequently (and mirroring the national trend) the Green Woodpecker population has flourished, and this increase has presumably been facilitated by a succession of relatively mild winters. Eaton *et al*. (2010) reported a national increase of 123% between 1970 and 2008. Since 1998, the species has been reported annually from over 100 sites in the county, and at no fewer than 251 in 2001, though the number fell to 91 in 2009.

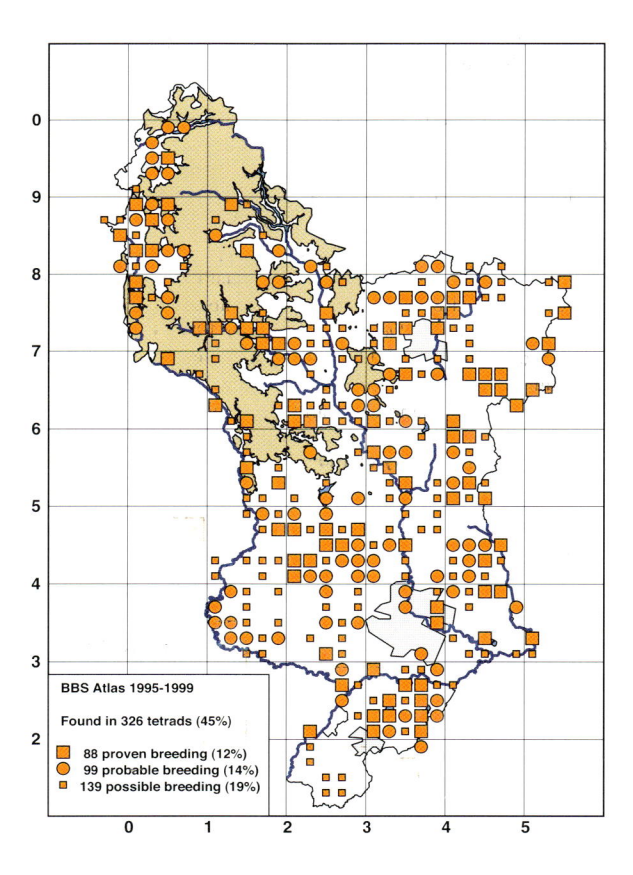

A comparison of confirmed breeding in the 10km core squares recorded in the three major surveys of recent decades provides further evidence of this species' revival: 1968–72 Atlas, five squares; 1988–91 Atlas, 14 squares; Derbyshire BBS (1995–99), 21 squares. Based on a national average of nearly ten pairs per 10km square this would suggest a current population of over 200 pairs in the county, and it may well be considerably higher.

The tetrad map, produced from the findings of the latest survey, reveals an extensive distribution, with absences only in the centre of large urban areas and high moorland where suitable breeding habitat is lacking. More specifically, breeding was proved in 88 tetrads, probable in 99 tetrads and possible in a further 139. Most of the records in the latter category derive from observers hearing the far-carrying 'yaffle' song.

Only two of the six CBC plots surveyed during the 1990s held Green Woodpeckers. There was a single territory in two years at Shiningcliff Wood, and in one year at Shire Hill Wood. This species occurs in mature deciduous and mixed woodland, well-wooded farmland and parkland. The birds forage mainly on open ground where the sward is short enough. In Derbyshire they are most regularly recorded in the limestone dales of the Peak District, the gravel pit region of the Trent Valley, the Cromford Canal area and Padley Gorge. They are nowadays also increasingly reported on industrial wasteland, and golf courses are also a favoured habitat. Green Woodpeckers seldom visit the centre of large towns or areas of extensive moorland, and on such occasions they are usually noted flying over. The largest numbers tend to involve family parties of up to five birds, but there are several higher counts than this, including an impressive 12 at the Shirebrook Colliery site in October 2006. An interesting report was of four adults in one tree at King's Newton in March 1978.

There have been several instance of this species being attacked by other birds, most notably Sparrowhawk. One individual was chased by a Buzzard at Darley Dale in February 1997, and another was harassed by a Black-headed Gull at Carr Vale Nature Reserve in December 1993. Conversely, Green Woodpeckers have been observed acting aggressively towards other species, with a record of a vigorous tussle between one and a Great Spotted Woodpecker at Booth's Wood, Holbrook in January 1994, where both birds were seen to fall to the ground, locked together, before disappearing from sight. One was reported as 'squaring up' to a mink at Kedleston Park in March 2005.

At Eckington in August 1984 a dead immature had a broken upper mandible which is presumed to have prevented its feeding. Another interesting record was of one in 'classic pose' on a rockface at Fairbrook Naze 625m amsl and a mile from the nearest trees on 2nd August 2010.

The species is only caught occasionally with a typical annual national total of about 300 birds throughout the 1990s. The total of recoveries for the species since the start of the ringing scheme was 191 as at 2000 and just one of these is accredited to Derbyshire. This bird was ringed at Fernilee, Whaley Bridge in 1961 and was shot at Stretton, near Cannock, Staffordshire, 18 months later.

BBS Atlas 1995-1999

Found in 326 tetrads (45%)

- 88 proven breeding (12%)
- 99 probable breeding (14%)
- 139 possible breeding (19%)

Great Spotted Woodpecker
Dendrocopos major
A fairly common or common resident.

Great Spotted Woodpeckers may be found in almost any habitat containing trees. Although deciduous woodland and parkland is preferred, they will breed in much smaller clumps of trees and in coniferous woods, while they are increasingly regular visitors to mature suburban gardens. They feed mainly on invertebrates extracted from dead or dying timber, but also on a wide variety of seeds, such as beech.

Within the county, as in most of Britain, the species is widespread and fairly common, showing great adaptability, which largely explains the steady increase in its population through most of the twentieth century. However, according to Whitlock, the Great Spotted Woodpecker was much less numerous than the Green Woodpecker in the previous century and he described it as 'local but fairly common where it occurs'. It was known to breed in the north-east and the High Peak, but was said to be most common in south Derbyshire. By the 1940s, it was undoubtedly the most common of its family (Frost), a status which has been maintained into the twenty-first century, despite indications of a slight decline in the 1970s, possibly caused by habitat destruction, the spread of grey squirrels and the usurping of its nest holes by Starlings.

Overall, numbers have certainly increased in recent decades, though doubtfully by as much as the 348% increase recorded nationally in 1970–2008 by Eaton *et al.* (2010). At Scarcliffe Woods, Frost (2008a) found an increase of 160% between the mid-1970s and the mid-2000s. Between 1998 and 2011 it was reported from between 80 and 211 sites in Derbyshire each year: the latter figure was for 2001, the same year as the largest reported number of sites for the Green Woodpecker. The loss of nest sites to Starlings is no longer thought to be a problem in view of the latter's decline as a woodland nester.

The findings of the Derbyshire BBS (1995–99) demonstrated the relatively dense and widespread distribution of this species (ranked thirty-ninth) throughout the county. The only absences were in the midwestern and high moorland areas of the Peak District, and the urban centres of Derby and Chesterfield. Breeding was proved in 219 tetrads, was probable in 79 tetrads and possible in a further 145. Breeding was confirmed in every one of the 23 main 10km squares, compared with 22 in the 1988–91 Atlas and 12 in the 1968–72 Atlas. The species is relatively easy to locate on account of its loud, staccato call and its far-carrying drumming. While it is rather quiet when the nest has eggs, the young keep up a continuous hunger call, enabling easy location of breeding sites.

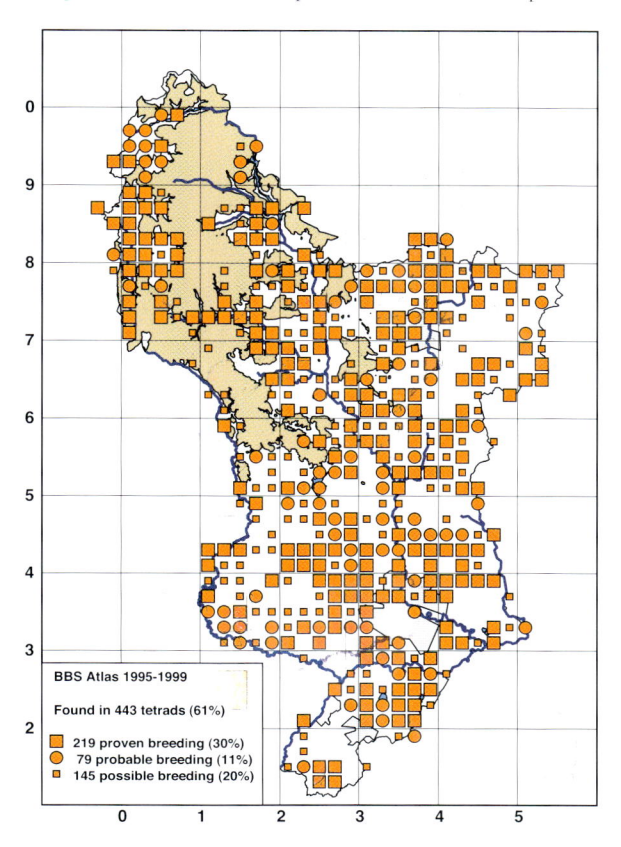

CBC data for the 1990s revealed an average of one pair per year at Shirebrook and 1.5 at Shiningcliff Wood, giving densities of just below seven territories per km^2 at both. Great Spotted Woodpeckers were found on all of the three farmland plots studied, but averaged less than a pair per year on each. Additionally, in 1988, 1992 and 2002, an area of mainly mixed deciduous woodland of approximately 2km^2 at Scarcliffe held seven territories during censuses in May, producing an abundance figure for the site of about 3.5 pairs per km^2. Within the county a clear preference for oak-dominated woodland is apparent, with farmland being less favoured, and the number of pairs per hectare is slightly below the national mean abundance range for the species.

Two particularly interesting breeding records concerned two pairs nesting only 150m apart at Manners Wood in 1991, both successfully raising young; while in 2008 a pair reared young in the totem pole at Fairholmes car park. In 2010 a pair bred in the same tree as a pair of Barn Owls at Breadsall.

The highest counts since 1980 were of 11 at Ogston Reservoir in January 2004 and at Hardwick Wood in January 2007; nine at Scarcliffe Woods in December 2008 and nine territories there in May 2010, and at Drakelow Nature Reserve in March 2009; and eight at Shipley Park in April 1993 and at Osmaston Park in March 2007. Interesting records include five Great Spotted Woodpeckers seen together in a tree at Darley Abbey in February 1981, and four birds in the same tree as two Lesser Spotted Woodpeckers by Cromford Canal in January 1984. One was observed fly-catching from the perimeter fence of Drakelow Nature Reserve on 29th August 1999. This species sometimes extracts pine seeds by wedging the cones in a crevice. The discarded cones then gather below and a pile of some 300–400 that accumulated in a Tansley garden in January to March 1962 was attributed to this species.

Drumming is heard occasionally during the winter months, but most frequently in the spring. There have been several instances of Great Spotted Woodpeckers drumming on wooden posts, nest-boxes, the metal capping of telephone poles and the steelwork of an electricity pylon. Their habit of visiting bird tables and feeding stations in suburban gardens was first recorded in 1952 (Frost), and has been regularly reported since the 1980s, predominantly in the winter period. Sightings in the centre of urban areas are still quite exceptional; one flying over Chesterfield town centre on 9th October 1987, one in a supermarket car park at Sinfin on 15th October 2011 and one near Clay Cross town centre on 20th October 2010 represent the only recent examples.

In 1978, Frost commented on autumn and winter records of birds found well away from known breeding areas, such as over open moorland, and speculated that some could be of Continental origin. Although there have been further suggestions of migration, most notably in the autumns of 1985, 1997, 1998 and 2004, it may be equally likely that these involve the movements of local birds since this species, despite being largely sedentary, wanders more widely than the other woodpeckers. However, one near Scropton on 15th December 2008 was believed to be of the northern race *D.m. major*. A bird found dead in heather on Derwent Moor on 17th May 1986 was thought to have been killed by a raptor.

There are seven recovery records for the county, none of which involved a movement of more than 10km from the place of ringing. One ringed at Warsop, Nottinghamshire was found dead in Whitwell Wood. The earliest record was of a bird ringed at Repton in the winter of 1958, which was shot at Foremark a few months later. The longevity record, which exceeds three years, was for a bird ringed at Glossop and found dead 1117 days later, 5km from the ringing site.

BBS Atlas 1995-1999
Found in 443 tetrads (61%)
- 219 proven breeding (30%)
- 79 probable breeding (11%)
- 145 possible breeding (20%)

Lesser Spotted Woodpecker
Dendrocopos minor
An uncommon resident.

Lesser Spotted Woodpeckers prefer open broad-leaved woodland, spinneys, parkland and areas of mature willow and alder carr. Coniferous woodland is generally avoided. They forage on the branches and the foliage of trees or scrub and will also catch insects in the air. Nest holes are often excavated on the underside of branches rather than in the trunk, and decayed wood is preferred, presumably since it is easier to work.

Throughout much of the year these diminutive birds are relatively quiet and unobtrusive, generally frequenting the upper branches of trees, and are consequently very easily overlooked. However, in spring they become very vocal, uttering their high-pitched and repetitive calls and drumming regularly. They are essentially sedentary, with little evidence of wandering, so that one seen flying north-east over Crich, until lost to sight, in April 2001 was quite unusual. In winter they are often seen in the company of roaming tit flocks.

In 1978, Frost stated that Lesser Spotted Woodpeckers 'are thinly scattered throughout Derbyshire in most well-wooded areas, including the Peak District, but are certainly most numerous in southern districts.' He concluded that it was unlikely that there had been much change in the species' status during the preceding 100 years. However, in the Derbyshire BBS (1995–99), only one confirmed breeding record was found in the western half of the county (in SK07). In this survey, breeding was confirmed in nine 10km core squares compared with 11 in the 1988–91 Atlas and only three in the 1968–72 Atlas. Overall, breeding was confirmed in only ten tetrads, and was probable and possible in a further 21 and 25. Detail down to tetrad level is as shown on the map.

Nationally, after a slight increase in the 1970s, this species has declined markedly since 1980 with the spread of Dutch elm disease considered to be a major contributing factor. Another possibility is increased competition from the thriving population of Great Spotted Woodpeckers. In Derbyshire it is probable that Lesser Spotted Woodpeckers are less numerous than in 1978, and that they are now largely confined to the lowland regions of the south and east. Although they have been reported from about 30 localities each year on average during the 1980s and 1990s, including a maximum of 39 in 1994, this may be a reflection of greater observer coverage. In 2000–11 the number of localities varied between 17 and 40 per year. The 10km square maps for 1995–99 and 2007–11 also reinforce the notion of ongoing losses in western Derbyshire.

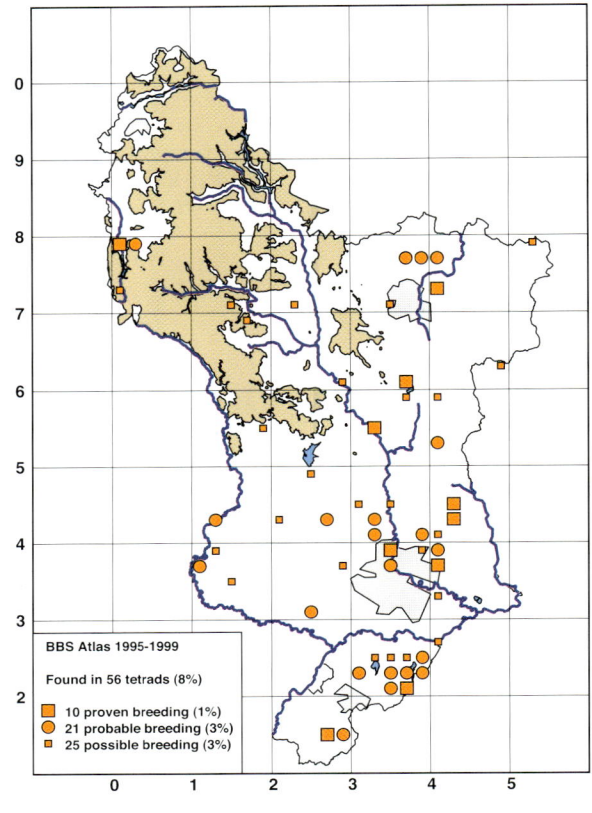

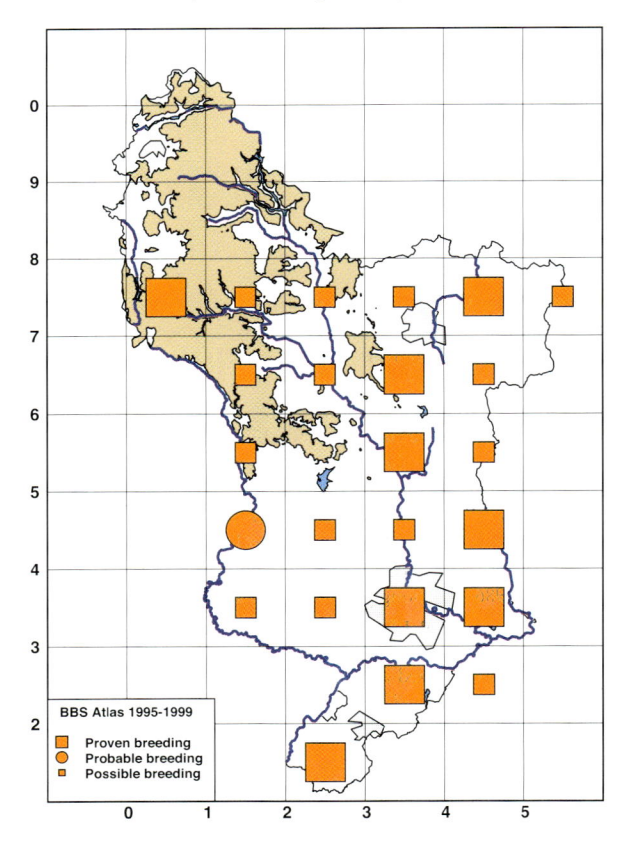

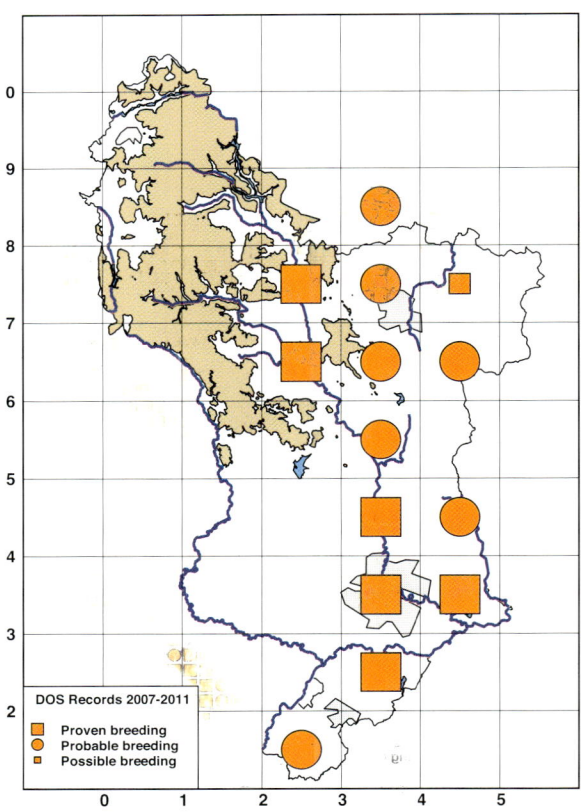

Whereas Great Spotted Woodpeckers were found in five of the six CBC plots studied during the 1990s, Lesser Spotted Woodpeckers were present only at the farmland site at Culland which held 0.69 pairs per km². This is well below the national mean breeding density of 1–3 pairs per km² in suitable woodland (1988–91 Atlas), perhaps suggesting that this species is scarcer in Derbyshire than in some other counties. An example of how uncommon it can be concerns a sighting in Scarcliffe Woods in December 1992 which was the observer's first at this site for over 31 years.

The highest number of birds seen together in recent years is four at Allestree Park in March 1993. With the exception of the Cromford Canal area, this site provides the most regular sightings of this species in the county. There are signs of an increasing tendency to visit suburban areas with a few reports of birds seen in gardens in Derby, Chesterfield, Long Eaton, Spondon and Dronfield, with adults observed feeding fledged youngsters at the last two sites and at Belper in 2011. At Allestree one regularly took woolly aphids from a garden crab-apple in June and July 2007.

Although Great Spotted Woodpeckers have been known to use the nest holes of their smaller relative, the record of a pair taking over the feeding of a brood of Lesser Spotted Woodpeckers in 1987 at Lea Wood is exceptional.

Golden Oriole
Oriolus oriolus
A rare vagrant.

Golden Orioles are rare breeding birds in Britain. Their breeding range is virtually confined to the East Anglian fen basin, where, since the late 1960s, they have nested in very small numbers, almost exclusively in poplar plantations. They are also rare passage migrants, mainly in the southern counties.

The first Derbyshire record concerns a female shot at Egginton on 25th May 1841, about which it was stated that 'from the ruffled state of the feathers on her breast, she appeared to have been recently disturbed from her nest'. A male was seen there at the same time, and Whitlock believed that there was little doubt the descriptions related to a breeding pair. Whitlock also mentioned one killed near Burton upon Trent in 1871, but this was found to be a Staffordshire record (Jourdain additions). There is an undated record of one killed at Kirk Ireton, and a male was shot at Creswell on 13th May 1889 (Whitlock; Jourdain additions).

Frost considered the only acceptable record in the first half of the twentieth century to be that of a pair seen in 1910 at Cratcliffe Tor where, unfortunately, a 12-year-old boy killed the male, which had earlier been 'bullied by Jackdaws'.

Since 1950, 16 individuals have been seen in the county, with 2002 being the only year in which more than one has occurred.

The bird in 2009 was found by an observer looking for the Marsh Warbler which had been found earlier that day.

Despite their bright yellow and black plumage, adult male Golden Orioles can be surprisingly difficult to see, the duller females and first-summer males even more so. It is no coincidence, therefore, that many of those seen in Derbyshire have been singing males, which were initially located by their melodic and fluty song.

Golden Orioles are relatively late migrants to Britain, with most arriving along the coasts from Cornwall to Suffolk in early May before filtering northwards to their breeding sites. Many of these are likely to be first-year males, which frequent a wide range of arboreal habitats. It is noteworthy that there has been an upsurge in Derbyshire records since 1993, while during the same period there has been a decline in numbers in the species' breeding population in East Anglia. In Derbyshire 13 (81%) have been seen in May and June and are no doubt wandering birds, since none have been recorded on more than one day.

The tables show the analysis by month, number of records and number of birds.

Year	Location and date
1951	North-west Derbyshire, one on 24th July
1976	Bretby Park, a singing male on 13th June
1978	Mercaston, a female on 6th August
1979	Ingleby, a male near the River Trent on 12th May
1980	Wye Dale, one on 14th August
1984	Poolsbrook, a female or immature on 28th May
1993	Sawley, one seen to fly into the county from Leicestershire on 22nd June
1994	Scarcliffe, one on 31st May
1999	Drakelow Nature Reserve, one, probably an immature male, singing on 6th June
2000	Pools Brook Country Park, one, probably an immature male, singing on 25th June
2002	Drakelow Nature Reserve, one singing on 2nd May
2002	Willington Gravel Pits, a singing male was seen and heard on 16th May before it departed to the south-west
2003	Kedleston Park, one was heard singing and seen twice on 26th May
2004	Linacre, one was heard to sing four times on 12th May
2007	Carr Vale, a female or first-year male on 31st May
2009	Poolsbrook Marsh, a singing immature male present for seven hours on 16th June

Period	Records	Birds
1950s	1	1
1960s	–	–
1970s	3	3
1980s	2	2
1990s	3	3
2000–11	7	7
Totals	16	16

Month	Records	Birds
May	8	8
June	5	5
July	1	1
August	2	2
Totals	16	16

Red-backed Shrike
Lanius collurio
A former breeder and now a very rare vagrant.

Red-backed Shrikes were common and widespread breeding birds in Britain in the nineteenth century, but declined drastically thereafter and are now only very occasional breeders, although they remain regular passage migrants in both spring and autumn.

Whitlock believed that this species was a regular breeder in small numbers in south and east Derbyshire, principally south of Derby, though breeding was also reported from Sutton Scarsdale. Jourdain said they bred below the 150m contour, penetrating along the Rivers Dove and Derwent as far north as Thorpe and Curbar respectively. In the first half of the twentieth century, they were reported as breeding in the Dovedale area, Spondon, Repton, Cromford, the Matlock area and Parwich. The last nest was found in 1942, close to Cromford railway station.

There was a record of a male at Robin Wood, Ingleby in the 1950s, and since then there have been a further 12 records, all involving single birds. These are shown in the table.

Year	Location and date
1951	Lumsdale, a male on 1st July
1960	Masson Hill, a male on 8th August
1962	Sawley, a male on 3rd June
1975	Langley Mill, a female on 27th May
1976	Taddington, one on 26th October
1988	Rother Valley Country Park (now in South Yorkshire), an immature caught and ringed on 22nd August
1989	Bolsover, a female on 25th May
1993	Chesterfield Canal, Brimington, a male on 4th August
1994	Wollen Meadow, Creswell, a male from 21st to 28th August
1997	Shipley Country Park, a male on 28th–29th June
2005	Milton, a female on 19th June
2009	Carr Vale, a male on 7th June

The tables show the analysis by period and months.

Period	Records
1950s	1
1960s	2
1970s	2
1980s	2
1990s	3
2000–11	2
Total	12

Month	Records
May	2
June	4
July	1
August	4
October	1
Total	12

Lesser Grey Shrike
Lanius minor
A very rare vagrant.

The only Derbyshire record was of one found in a field of unripened wheat at Egginton Sewage Farm around 2000hrs on 11th July 2004. It caused much consternation to a pair of Yellow Wagtails, but was ignored by nearby Skylarks and Whitethroats. It was seen again briefly at 1815hrs on the following evening in cool, wet and windy conditions (Key 2005).

There were three other Lesser Grey Shrikes seen in Britain in 2004, all in autumn, and this was only the fourth ever record for the Midlands. Hudson *et al.* (2012) state that there were 185 British records to the end of 2011. It breeds from France and Germany eastwards to Afghanistan and Turkestan, wintering in sub-Saharan Africa. The European population is undergoing a serious long-term decline.

Great Grey Shrike
Lanius excubitor
A scarce winter visitor and passage migrant.

With its striking appearance, and a degree of scarcity and unpredictability, the Great Grey Shrike is something of a birdwatcher's bird. Its status as a scarce winter visitor and passage migrant is unlikely to have changed to any great extent over a long time. Both Whitlock and Jourdain mention the fact that Francis Willughby said in his *Ornithology* (1676) that it 'is found in the mountainous parts of the north of England as, for instance, in the Peak of Derbyshire'. The first dated record relates to one shot by the Reverend Francis Gisborne of Staveley on 16th November 1762, and described as a 'Great ash-coloured butcher bird'. Both Whitlock and Jourdain knew of several subsequent records.

There were nine twentieth-century records before the formation of the DOS in 1954. The only subsequent years without any records were 1958, 1959, 1961, 1963, 1986, 1987, and 1998. Frost said that in some years perhaps 20 individuals might be seen, but the only years when this figure was approached were 1973 and 1975. The 1970s was by far the best decade for sightings, with around 120 seen. There were about 35 individuals in the county during the 1980s, followed by a large reduction to about 20 in the 1990s and then a resurgence to some 55 in the 2000s. The most in any year since 1978 was about 11, in 2004.

The chart shows the approximate number of individuals each year from 1980 to 2011.

Great Grey Shrikes show a diverse taste in habitats, which includes moorland (especially with scattered trees), farmland, woodland edges, sewage farms, reservoir hinterlands and limestone dales. This species needs a perching or vantage point from which to hunt for its food, which includes birds, mammals, insects and lizards. All of the areas mentioned have this requirement in the form of scattered trees, bushes, fence posts and the like. There are several records of birds heard singing.

Some birds stay for only a short time, but others take up a winter territory, which can apparently cover a large area. Overwintering occurs sometimes, as at Carsington Water from November 2004 until April 2005, in the Catton Park–Walton-on-Trent area from October 2005 until April 2006, and in the Wragg's Quarry area from October 2010 until February 2011 and from October 2011 to March 2012. In some years, birds have stayed on the Eastern Moors from late autumn until driven out by adverse weather nearer the end of the year.

The main time for autumn arrivals is in early to mid-October, with a few first seen during November and December. The earliest arrivals were two seen on 30th September; at Ramsley in 1972 (where one was singing and attacking Jays) and at Barbrook Reservoir in 1984. There is sometimes a small flurry of records during March which may involve returning passage birds from further south and west. A few have stayed into April, with the latest being one that lingered in the Parwich–Brassington area until 5th May 1983.

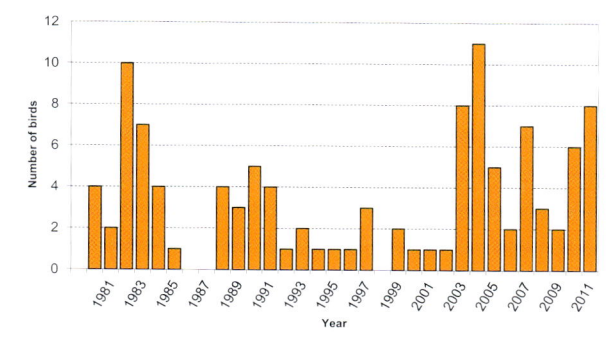

Woodchat Shrike
Lanius senator
A very rare vagrant.

There have been three records, all in southern Derbyshire in spring. One was recorded in the Melbourne district on 19th May 1839, eating a Yellowhammer, which it had impaled on a thorn (Whitlock). Another was seen at Clay Mills Gravel Pits on 20th April 1968 (two days after a Purple Heron arrived at Shardlow), and a first-summer bird was seen by a large number of observers at Trent Meadows, Long Eaton, from 1st to 3rd May 2006. The last individual was relocated approximately 200km north-west at Torver Low Common near Coniston Water, Cumbria on 6th May 2006, remaining there until 12th May.

This shrike breeds discontinuously from north-western Africa and Iberia through the Near East to Iran, and winters in sub-Saharan Africa. It is a regular visitor to the UK in spring and autumn, and was removed from the list of species assessed by BBRC after 1990, though that body still deals with records of *L.s. badius*, the race that breeds on islands in the western Mediterranean.

Magpie
Pica pica
A common or abundant resident.

An opportunistic and very adaptable species, the Magpie is a controversial bird. Admired by some for its handsome looks and bold behaviour, it is despised by others for its perceived effect on songbirds, though the evidence is that they do not adversely affect populations (Brown & Grice 2005). It inhabits many types of farmland, especially where spinneys and tall hedgerows are present. It is also found in woods of various types, including both broad-leaved and coniferous, wherever glades, clearings, or more open stands occur, especially near natural or cultivated grasslands and croplands. It is almost omnivorous and eats a wide variety of soil invertebrates. Nowadays, it is common in urban areas, where it can be seen in parks, gardens and on industrial sites. Human intervention in spreading suitable mixed habitats has contributed to the advance of this species.

Historically, Magpies were not always so common, probably as a result of human persecution. In 1893, Whitlock considered that the species was declining within Derbyshire, though it was still not uncommon in some areas. Jourdain stated that Magpies were uncommon only in those districts where game was strictly preserved, including the grouse moors, and that it was often very numerous where undisturbed. Frost stated that there had been no indication of population change until the late 1940s and 1950s, when an increase in numbers was reported, most likely as a result of diminished persecution and by 1978, the species had become fairly common in residential areas. It is less likely to be controlled in built-up areas than in rural ones, where many are shot or taken in Larsen traps.

Nationally, Magpies underwent a rapid increase from 1970 until the late 1980s, when the population stabilized (Brown & Grice 2005). Eaton *et al.* (2010) stated that there was an increase of 94% between 1970 and 2008. This trend has been associated with increases in breeding performance and earlier laying, and probably reflects the benefits of its generalist strategy under changing environmental conditions. Reduced control by gamekeepers may also have helped Magpies (Marchant *et al.* 1990). In Derbyshire, a significant increase from 1978 has been apparent and the species is now very common or abundant throughout most of the county.

CBC data from 1990 to 1994 shows a density of 10.42 pairs per km^2 at Shirebrook, 3.18 at Shiningcliff Wood and 3.02 at Broadhay Farm, Hathersage. At Farfield Farm the density was 1.31 per km^2, but it was absent from Culland and Shire Hill Wood.

These data conform to some degree with a mean of ten pairs per km² for woodland and five pairs per km² on farmland (1988–91 Atlas). In the 1968–72 Atlas, Magpies were proved to breed in 21 of the 23 10km core squares, and in all 23 in the 1988–91 Atlas. The Derbyshire BBS (1995–99) confirmed that the species still bred in all 10km grid squares. Breeding, which is easy to prove as most nests are built before leaf-break and newly fledged family groups are noisy and conspicuous, was confirmed in 498 tetrads, was probable in 60 tetrads and possible in a further 108 tetrads. This gave a total of 666 tetrads, making it the eighth most widespread Derbyshire bird. The Carrion Crow was found in 667 tetrads, just one more than the Magpie.

Unlike Carrion Crow and Rook, the Magpie has not yet adapted to nesting in pylons, but a pair nested on a mobile-telephone mast at Alfreton in 2001.

An interesting historical record from Jourdain concerned a wild female Magpie that paired with a feral male Jackdaw at Fenny Bentley in 1899. The pair built a nest together, but no eggs were laid.

Magpies do not usually venture onto the high moorland tops, although several records exist of birds at quite high altitudes in the Peak District. In the Westend Valley in 1990, two were seen at approximately 400m amsl on 4th–5th May and were the first and only birds the observer had seen in the area. In the same year on 29th September and 14th October in Upper Derwentdale, up to three birds were seen at 300m amsl and were higher up the valley than the observer recalled seeing the species before.

BBS Atlas 1995-1999
Found in 666 tetrads (92%)
- 498 proven breeding (69%)
- 60 probable breeding (8%)
- 108 possible breeding (15%)

Magpie: maximum annual counts 1978-2011

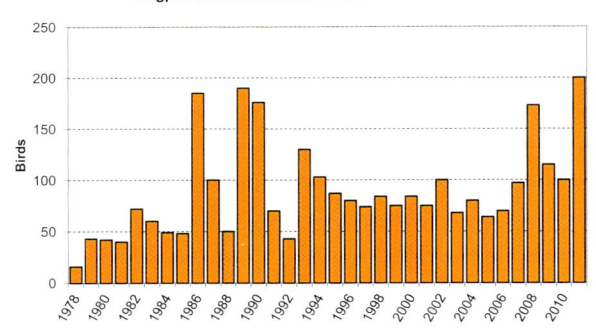

The Magpie is a gregarious species, with many reports of large gatherings, especially at roosts, which are often in thorny scrub. The chart shows maximum annual counts and they have generally increased since Frost published records of 100 in a stubble field at Grindleford in January 1964 and 100 at a Hathersage roost in 1967. Three-figure flocks have been reported in many years since then, with the largest being 190 at Bradwell Ponds on 20th January 1989, 176 at New Mills on 10th February 1990, 173 at Drakelow Nature Reserve on 22nd November 2008, and 200 at Chinley on 24th October 2011.

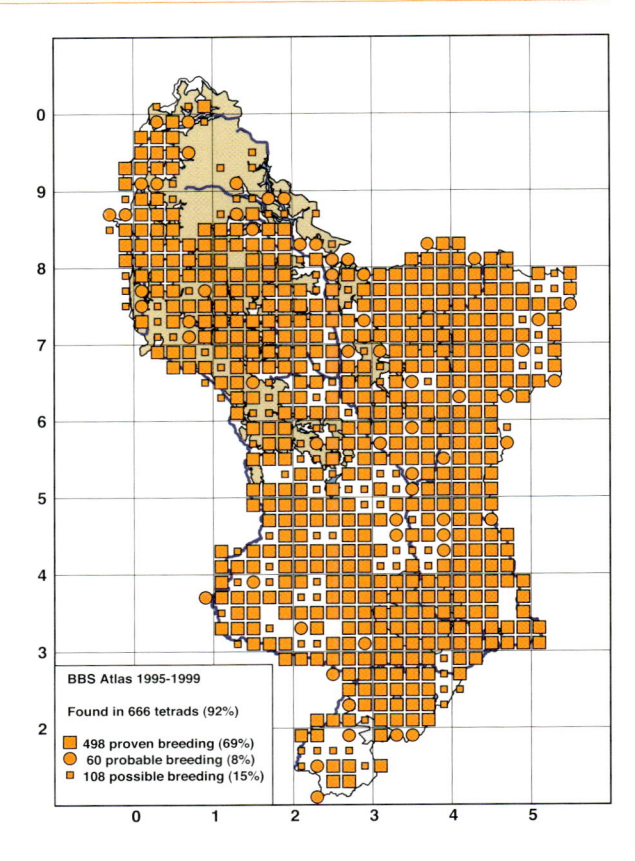

There are several records of Magpies exhibiting aberrant plumage. These include an albino bird in a flock of 12 at Long Eaton on 6th November 1978, and a fawn bird at the same site on 23rd June 1981. A buff-and-white bird was shot near Ashbourne in April 1985 and a well-watched, light buffish-brown bird was seen regularly in the Etwall–Egginton–Willington area between 1991 and 1993. Another, at Quarndon on 11th November 1992, had a horn-coloured bill and white tail, with other normally black areas of plumage a milky-brown colour.

National ringing information indicates that British Magpies are very sedentary, and virtually all movements have been of under 10km. The Derbyshire data show 34% of birds were recovered at the place of ringing and 78% within 5km. Of the remaining five birds, four were recovered within 20km, but one travelled 42km south-east from Holmesfield, where it had been ringed in April 1988, to near Newark, Nottinghamshire, where it was killed by a cat in May 1992. One ringed on 9th December 1961 at Marple, Cheshire, was also killed by a cat near Dove Holes, a distance of 17km to the south-east, on 16th March 1971.

Jay
Garrulus glandarius
A fairly common resident.

Jays are strongly arboreal, and are at home in a fairly dense cover of trees, scrub, and woody undergrowth, especially in oak and beech woods. They will also inhabit other broad-leaved and coniferous woodland and can be found in smaller, outlying woods, spinneys and copses, and even in urban and rural parkland and large gardens. Jays may visit garden feeding stations but only if there is sufficient tree cover nearby, since they are generally shy and secretive birds. They have a close association with oaks and a mixed diet, although acorns are the staple food in most months (1988–91 Atlas).

There was formerly a difference of opinion regarding this bird's status in the county. Whitlock stated that while Jays were previously common, by 1893 only a few lingered in wooded districts; but Jourdain, in 1905, described them as fairly numerous where woods existed. Frost thought that numbers had increased, especially from the 1940s and 1950s, possibly as a result of diminished persecution from sporting estates; he said that by 1978, although nowhere really common, the species was found in most sizeable woods, especially those of oak or at least partially of conifers. Presently, Jays can be described as widespread and fairly common with an apparently stable population. This is supported by Eaton *et al.* (2010), who recorded an increase of 3% between 1970 and 2008.

The results of the Derbyshire BBS (1995–99) showed the species to breed fairly evenly over the county, except in the centre of towns and on high moorland, with notable absences in some northern upland areas, in the central west and in the Derby area. Breeding was proved in 105 tetrads, was probable in 58 tetrads and possible in a further 185. Breeding is harder to prove than for other corvids on account of the bird's secretive habits, while the nest is relatively small and well hidden.

Twenty-one of the 23 10km core squares contained proven breeding, compared with 15 in the 1968–72 Atlas and 20 in the 1988–91 Atlas.

CBC data from 1990 to 1994 shows that there were 6.94 pairs per km^2 at Shirebrook and 5.91 at Shiningcliff Wood but only 1.04 and 1.01 respectively on the farmland plots at Hathersage and Culland, with none at Farfield Farm; their absence from Shire Hill Wood was surprising. At Scarcliffe Woods there were up to five territories (in 1986, 1987 and 1993) in a 36-year study period (Frost 2008a), though it is likely that some were overlooked.

Small gatherings of Jays are not uncommon, although it is the only local corvid which does not form large, communal roosts. Recently, numbers have been lower than in the early 1980s. Winter counts at Scarcliffe Woods have shown a decline from a maximum of 15 (and a further eight recently killed and hanging from a gibbet) on 24th December 1985, to six in 1998 and usually fewer than five through to 2007, although there were counts of 11 in 2002 and nine in 2007. Other large flocks of Jays have included a remarkable record of 100 at Brinsley Flashes on 1st January 1982, 16 in an oak in the Goyt Valley on 15th November 1984, 20 in a hedgerow at Mickleover on 6th January 1985, and 19 at Repton Shrubs on 29th August 1988. During the 1990s and 2000s, the largest counts (other than wandering birds in autumn) were of 15 at Halldale Wood on 29th October 2006, 16 in Derwentdale on 20th October 2010, and 14 at Hardwick Wood 20th January 2011.

Jays are dependent to a large extent on acorns, and collect and bury them in autumn in large numbers. In those autumns of low productivity of acorns, or where there is a total failure of the crop, wandering Jays may be quite noticeable. The most notable movements have occurred at Ramsley and (at least since 2000) considerable numbers have occurred biennially in 2001, 2003, 2005, 2007 and 2009. In 2001, 124 moved south-west on four dates between 28th September and 9th October, with a maximum of 54 on 4th October. In 2005, 54 flew west on 24th September, and 47 mainly south on 29th September, while on 30th September 2007, small flocks totalling 54 moved in random directions. Smaller counts of wanderers have been recorded at other sites, including Carr Vale, where 12 flew south on 24th August 2009 and 13 likewise on 24th September 2009. The origin of such birds is unknown, but they are almost certainly British, although in autumn 1983 there was a huge invasion of Continental Jays, mainly into southern Britain. The most interesting Derbyshire record at this time was of 35 moving south over Dronfield in one hour on 11th November.

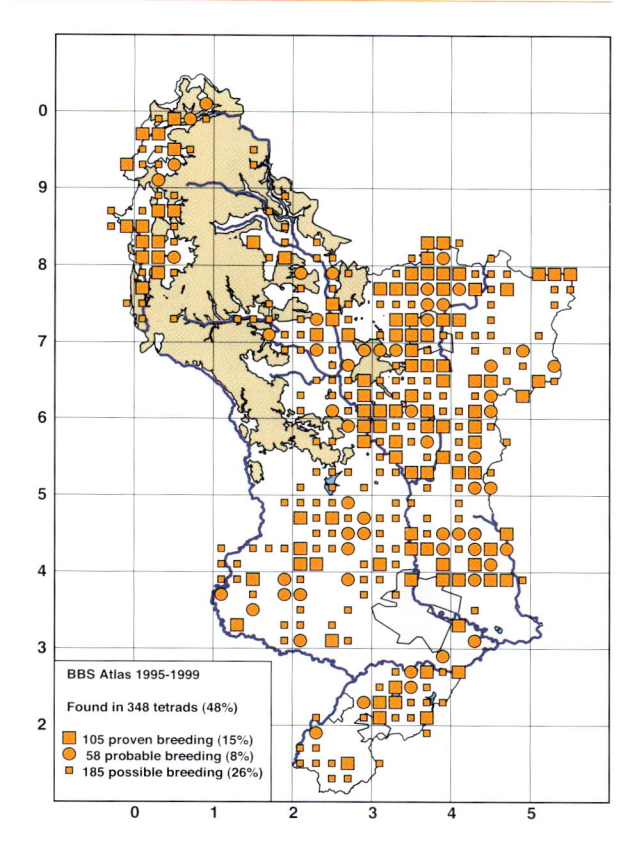

BBS Atlas 1995-1999
Found in 348 tetrads (48%)
- 105 proven breeding (15%)
- 58 probable breeding (8%)
- 185 possible breeding (26%)

Unusual records for the species include rare sightings over the high moors: on 17th April 1982, one was seen over treeless moorland on Birchinlee Moor at about 450m amsl; on 19th March 1991, a bird was seen at Westend Valley (about 320m amsl); and on 26th September 1993, one was seen in a small clough in the Upper Derwentdale area, a long way from the main areas of woodland.

There was an interesting record of a nesting pair attacking passers-by at Chaddesden Park during the 2010 breeding season.

There have been 41 ringing recoveries: all but one had been shot, with the remaining bird a road casualty. The records show that only two Jays have travelled more than 20km from their ringing sites: one ringed at New Mills in August 1963, which was shot 34km west-south-west at Northwich, Cheshire six months later; and another, ringed at Whitwell Wood in August 1977, was shot at Chatsworth, 27km west-south-west in January 1979. The longevity record concerns a bird ringed as a nestling at Dronfield an 31st May 1957, which was shot at Barlow on 11th July 1964.

Jackdaw
Corvus monedula
A common resident.

Jackdaws are among the most gregarious of birds, often nesting, feeding and roosting together. They exploit a range of breeding habitats, nesting in trees, holes in rocks and in buildings (often in chimneys). Parkland, where clumps of old hole-ridden trees are interspersed with open grassland, is ideal for them. They also nest in natural crags and many of Derbyshire's quarries contain large nesting colonies.

They are adaptable birds and have generalist feeding habits, readily exploiting many types of food. Jackdaws usually feed on open ground, preferring pasture to croplands and, in common with Rooks, may fly long distances to exploit food resources of varying types. They can also be seen taking insects on the backs of sheep and other livestock, foraging in trees for acorns and fruits, and hawking high-flying insects.

Nationally, the Jackdaw is undergoing a moderate increase in numbers that began in the 1960s (along with Magpies, Rooks and Carrion Crows). Eaton *et al.* (2010) showed a gain of 107% in the period 1970–2008. In Derbyshire, it is a common and widespread species, most abundant in the western half of the county, though it is largely absent from the high moorland parts of the north-west and shuns heavily urbanized areas. Historically, the Jackdaw has always been common in the county: Whitlock said that the species was extremely common in many parts, and abounded in some of the Peak District dales. Frost stated that the species nested virtually throughout Derbyshire and that the largest colonies were probably in the Carboniferous Limestone region, due to the increase in the number of quarries that provide cliff-nesting areas.

The Derbyshire BBS (1995–99) results show that breeding was proved in 292 tetrads, was probable in 54 tetrads and possible in a further 186, giving an overall total of 532 tetrads. Breeding was proved in all of the 10km core squares, as it was in the 1988–91, while the figure for the 1968–72 Atlas was 20 10km squares. Breeding Jackdaws are relatively easy to locate on account of their tame and noisy nature.

BBS Atlas 1995–1999

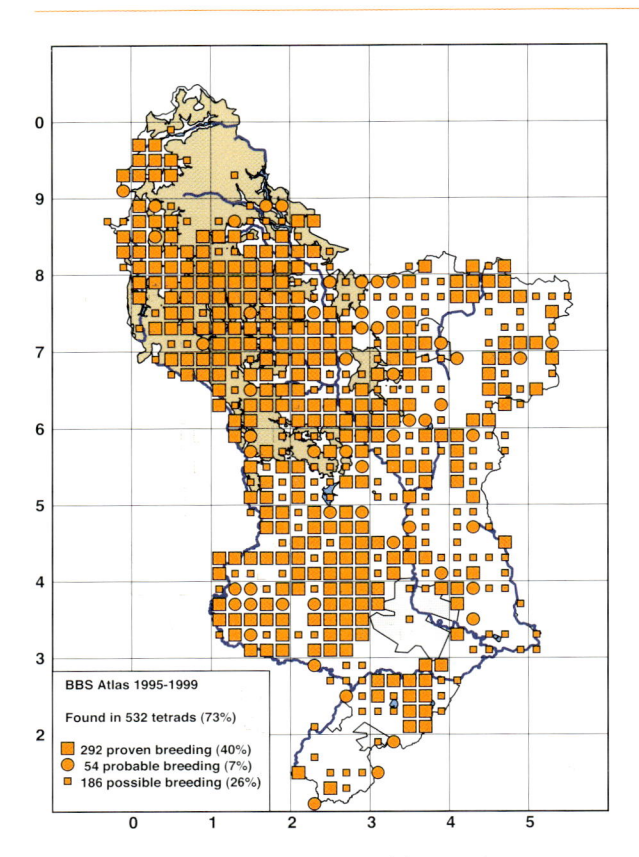

Found in 532 tetrads (73%)

- ■ 292 proven breeding (40%)
- ● 54 probable breeding (7%)
- ▪ 186 possible breeding (26%)

The only CBC sites to support Jackdaws in the 1990s were the mixed farmland site at Culland, with a density of 2.76 pairs per km², and Broadhay Farm with 0.34 pairs per km².

During winter, in keeping with their sociable nature, they roost in large flocks with Rooks and sometimes Carrion Crows, and there are numerous records of flocks of up to 900 birds. Larger counts, usually involving roosting or pre-roosting assemblies, include one of about 5000 flying east over Big Moor on 2nd November 1980, and a similar-sized flock at Renishaw Park on 11th January 1981. In 1986, flocks of about 2200, about 2000 and about 1000 were seen at Matlock Forest (25th December), Owler Bar (26th October) and Beeley Moor (20th November) respectively. At Ramsley, 2000 flew south from a roost in Ecclesall Woods, Sheffield in November 2006, and at least 1000 left a roost at British Celanese Lakes Nature Reserve on 19th November 2000. At Big Moor, 2500 flew west on 22nd October 2011. In the north-west, 1000 were at New Mills in early March 2002, and in the same year about 2000 flew north-west along the Etherow Valley at Chisworth soon after dawn on 17th October. A total of 1300 went to roost at Raynesway, Derby on 13th December 2010, and 1200 at Spondon on 25th January 2011, while 1000 were noted at Darley Dale on 7th February 2011.

In 2003, a mottled grey-and-white bird was reported at Intake Quarry on 19th January, and an almost white bird was at Bakestone Moor on 5th February. Other partial albinos have been recorded at various sites in the county. One with russet-brown primaries and secondaries was seen at Rother Valley Country Park (now in South Yorkshire) on 27th February 1988.

Birds showing characteristics of the nominate Scandinavian race *C.m. monedula* occurred at the Erin Landfill site on 16th March 2006, Picory Corner on 6th and 10th January 2007 and Brackenfield on 1st January 2010, while one at Ogston Reservoir on 29th December 2011 showed some characteristics of the eastern race *C.m. soemmerringii* and may have been from the area where this intergrades with *C.m. monedula*. Perusal of large Jackdaw flocks in winter would probably produce similar records to these.

Jackdaws show only a small distance dispersal in Britain, and this is borne out by the dataset for Derbyshire. The majority of the 13 recoveries in the county have been within a short distance of the ringing locality, but one ringed as an adult at Barrow Hill on 22nd February 1978 was found dead near Pocklington, East Yorkshire, on 10th April 1980, a distance of 89km north-north-east. A shorter movement in a similar direction was made by a bird ringed as a pullus at Great Longstone in June 1979 and caught 37km away and three months later, near Rotherham, South Yorkshire.

Rook
Corvus frugilegus
A common, but possibly declining, resident.

Rooks are largely birds of agricultural land, preferring areas of mixed farming. Breeding depends to a large extent on the availability of fairly tall trees in which to site their rookeries. These may be on the edges of woodland, in groves, clumps or linear forms, but fronting open fields of pasture and arable land. Rooks tend to avoid dense woodland, anywhere with dry, hard, and rocky surfaces, and wetlands and tall dense vegetation. They may breed in towns and villages if adjacent countryside is readily accessible (*BWP*; 1988–91 Atlas).

Both Whitlock and Jourdain considered the Rook to be an extremely common bird in Derbyshire. In 1931, a rookery on the Staffordshire side of Dovedale held 800 nests, whereas the largest Derbyshire colonies in the survey years of 1966 and 1975 were of 271 and 279. In 1980, the largest rookery, of 320 nests, was at Renishaw Park, while the Coalite complex near Bolsover held 220 nests in 2002 and 222 in 2005.

In Derbyshire, the Rook is still a common, but possibly declining, resident. Away from their main food sources they are generally absent from the centres of towns, industrial areas and the high moorlands, although a few birds can be seen in suburban areas, foraging on school playing fields and grassy areas.

In the Derbyshire BBS (1995–99), breeding was proved in 312 tetrads, was probable in 20 tetrads and possible in a further 161 tetrads. Unsurprisingly, there was a marked correlation with the areas of arable land in the county. Breeding was confirmed in all of the 23 10km core squares, as it was in the 1968–72 and 1988–91 Atlases.

The Rook is one of the most studied of Derbyshire's birds, with several important surveys carried out since 1929. The results of these surveys are shown in the table, indicating a general decline in the number of nests since the peak in 1944. However, Marchant and Gregory (1999) documented a national increase of 40% during 1975–96, and there is evidence of the number of Derbyshire rookeries and nests increasing slightly between 1980 and 1998.

The Species Accounts

Recent data, however, suggest that the decline has halted or slowed down, or that numbers have fluctuated. For example, in 10km grid square SK23, there was a peak of 547 nests in 2000, which had fallen to 442 in 2005 before recovering to 510 nests in 2008, only to reduce in number again to 466 nests in 2009. In SK46, there was a steady rise in the total number of nests from 107 in 1980 to 270 nests in 2001, falling to 220 in 2007 and 202 in 2009. The fluctuation in the SK23 data in later years may be due to relocation of the Burnaston House rookery (caused by the Toyota car factory development) to two new rookeries nearby but just outside the 10km square. Studies by M.R. Hopton and D.A. Richardson (unpublished) have shown that rookeries can spontaneously split and relocate for reasons unknown, and it is not thought the impact of the car factory was significant. For example, a small rookery in SK23 (Etwall) split into two new rookeries approximately 900m apart following the loss of all nests in a January gale.

The number of nests and the number of nests per rookery in the period 1980–2009 are shown in the charts. SK23, in the south-west, lies on Keuper Marl and is a sparsely populated, mainly agricultural area. It is largely pastoral in the west and more mixed in the east. By comparison, SK46 which lies in the north-east of the county is largely on the Coal Measures, with Magnesian Limestone in the east. It is more heavily populated than SK23 and large parts have a postindustrial landscape.

Since 1995, the trend towards more but smaller rookeries in SK23 has resulted in a reduced number of nests per rookery, whereas SK46 has a higher and more stable mean number of nests per rookery. The number of rookeries in SK46 has remained

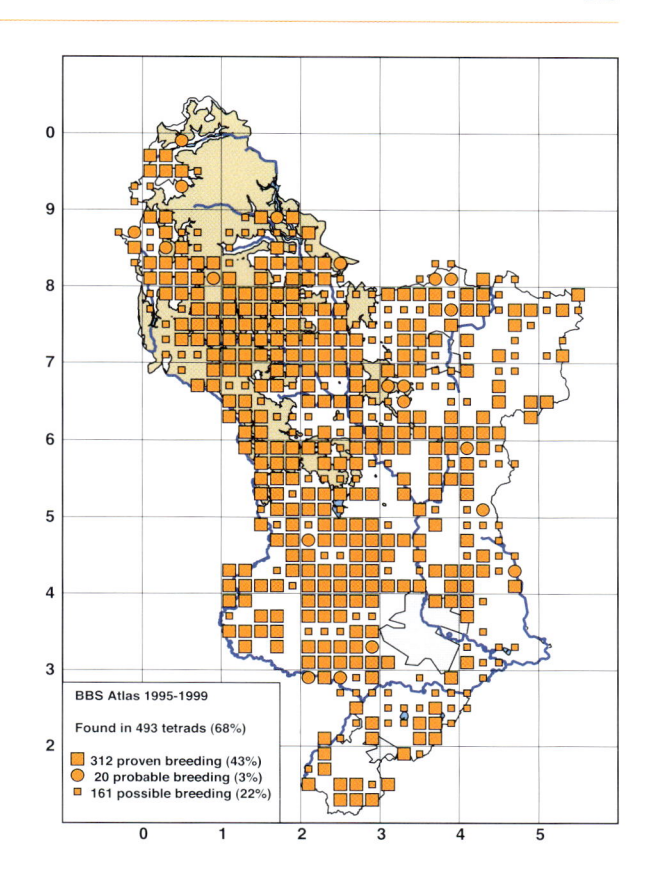

BBS Atlas 1995-1999
Found in 493 tetrads (68%)
- 312 proven breeding (43%)
- 20 probable breeding (3%)
- 161 possible breeding (22%)

Author	Year	Rookeries	Nests	Mean nests per rookery	Nests per km²
Roebuck (1933)	1929	240	10,620	44	4.0
Roebuck & Waud (unpublished)	1944	371	16,114	43	6.1
Lomas (1968)	1966	440	12,630	29	4.8
Cockburn (1976)	1975	320	9713	30	3.7
Mawson (1981)	1980	270	7389	27	2.8
Hopton & Richardson (unpublished)	1998	313	8500	27	3.2

Rook: number of nests in SK23 and SK46 1979-2009

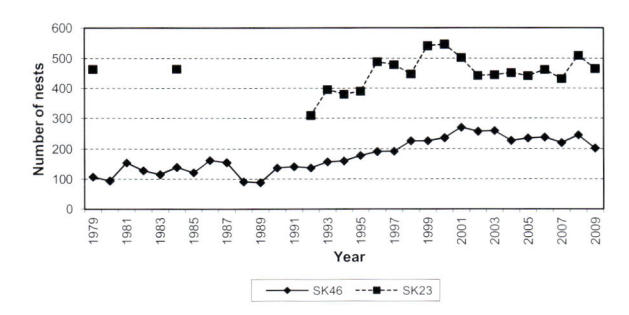

Rook: frequency plot - Nests per Rookery for Derbyshire Surveys, 1975, 1980, 1998

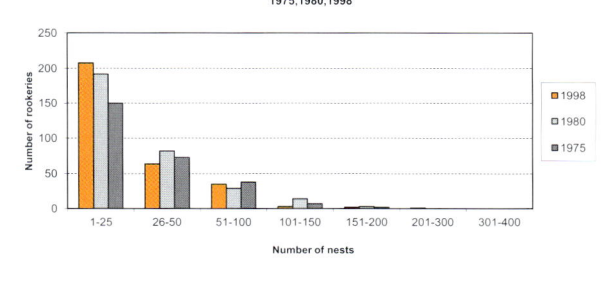

Rook: Nests per rookery in SK23 and SK46 1979-2009

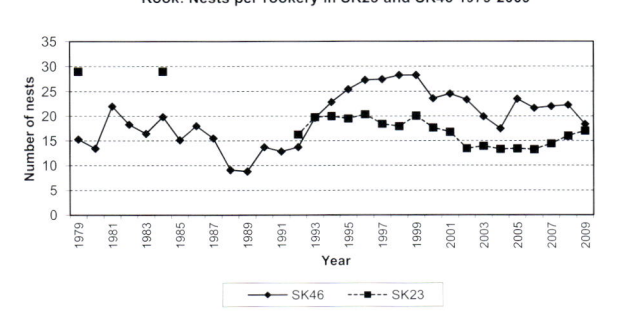

Rook: altitude range of rookeries (m amsl)

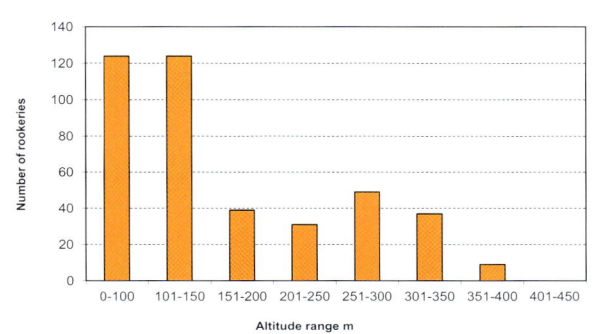

almost constant while the number of nests has increased, though with a more recent decline.

The trend towards smaller rookeries is also illustrated by the chart which shows the number of nests per rookery for three county surveys carried out since 1929 compared with data collected by Hopton and Richardson in 1998 (unpublished).

According to BWP, Rooks breed in England up to 450m amsl. However, in Derbyshire, the highest known rookeries occur at approximately 380m amsl at Brierlow Grange just south-east of Buxton with the majority below 150m.

Alsop (1987) wrote an interesting account, based on nest counts, of the Rook population of the parishes of Whaley Bridge and Chapel-en-le-Frith between 1965 and 1986. In the first year there were 1041 nests, rising to 1128 in 1968. Thereafter, there was a pronounced and regular decline to just over 600 nests in 1975, followed by a period of stabilization, with 635 nests in 1986, the final year. Discussing possible reasons for the decline, Alsop considered agricultural changes, cold winters and the organized shooting of fledglings but could find no obvious causes.

The first record of Rooks nesting on electricity pylons was at Drakelow Power Station in 1976, and this has subsequently been seen at many other sites. In 1984, three of seven colonies in SK46 were on pylons, and three pairs used pylons in Longdendale in 1996. In the late 1980s, a few pairs nested on a 49m-tall flood-light tower at Arkwright Colliery.

During the winter months, Rooks can be seen in large flocks with Carrion Crows and Jackdaws in favoured feeding areas and especially at roosts. One of the largest roosts was at Renishaw Park, where a mixed flock of 12,000 Rooks and Jackdaws was observed on 7th February 1980, and on 28th January 1983 an exceptionally large Rook flock of 7000 was seen here. Other sites where very large winter flocks have been recorded include Ogston Reservoir, Owler Bar, Drakelow Nature Reserve and Upper Loads. In the 2000s, flock sizes have generally been smaller, with most only numbering a few hundred.

Populations of Rook in Britain are very sedentary, with only two records of birds moving to the Continent, although there are more reports of foreign-ringed birds coming to Britain (Wernham et al. 2002). There are 13 recoveries for Derbyshire, of which 77% were within 11km of their ringing locations. The three furthest concerned two ringed at Great Budworth, Cheshire, on 16th January 1936 and 6th January 1939, which were found at Bradley (66km) on 17th April 1937 and Woolley Moor (74km) on 30th April 1948, respectively. The other bird was ringed in May 1980 in Wragby, Lincolnshire, and was recovered 63km away in Barlborough a year later.

Carrion Crow
Corvus corone
A common resident.

Carrion Crows are common in almost all parts of Derbyshire, breeding in small woods, spinneys and isolated trees, on farmland and moorland and in built-up areas, although generally avoiding dense woodland. They also nest on electricity pylons. They are almost omnivorous, and refuse-tips, manured fields and sewage farms are favoured feeding areas.

Whitlock said that the Carrion Crow managed to exist in most parts of the county, but that its chief breeding grounds were in the Peak, in those areas where game preservation was not strictly practised. Jourdain stated that it was decidedly common in one or two districts, such as the Dove Valley between Thorpe and Hartington. Frost thought that the species was most numerous on higher ground but still locally numerous in the south, and gave examples of 400 birds at Egginton Sewage Farm, with 100 there in midsummer. Three-figure roosts could be found in many parts of the county, as occurs nowadays.

Nationally, the current status of Carrion Crow is that the species has undergone a moderate increase from around 1980. This trend has been associated with increases in nesting success and earlier laying, perhaps as a result of climate change. It also probably reflects the adaptability of the species to changing habitats as well as the exploitation of ephemeral food resources and intensive agriculture (Crick et al. 1997). A reduction in gamekeeping is likely to have led to increased numbers of Carrion Crows. Some of these factors may explain the increased numbers of Magpie, Jackdaw and Rook. Eaton et al. (2010) stated that Carrion Crows increased nationally by 82% between 1970 and 2008.

The Derbyshire BBS (1995–99) showed Carrion Crow to be present in all the 10km core squares in the county, as it was in the 1988–91 Atlas, though not in the 1968–72 Atlas when it was, very surprisingly, not proved in the two western squares of SK24 and SK25. Breeding was proved in 481 tetrads, with probable and possible breeding in a further 70 and 116 tetrads respectively, a total of 667 tetrads. This confirmed its distribution ranking of seventh, just ahead of the Magpie, which was found in one tetrad fewer. Carrion Crows and their nests, usually built before the trees are in leaf, are both conspicuous.

CBC data from 1990–94 show the species as most numerous at Shiningcliff Wood, with 5.45 pairs per km², and slightly lower with 5.09 pairs at Farfield Farm. Figures for Broadhay Farm, Culland and Shire Hill Wood were lower, at 4.03, 3.80 and 2.38 respectively, and there was an absence from Shirebrook.

Paul Tooley (*pers comm*) made a study of the nesting biology of the species in the Alton–Uppertown area, examining 130 nests in 1982–91. Sycamore, beech, birch and oak were the most frequent of 12 tree species used, and nest heights varied from 3.3 to 20m. Clutch sizes were between two and six, with about half having four eggs. The observer commented that many nests were in or close to farmyards, which would not have been tolerated in the past.

Unusual nest sites for this species include a 1991 nest with three eggs only 1.5m above ground level in a birch at Ringinglow.

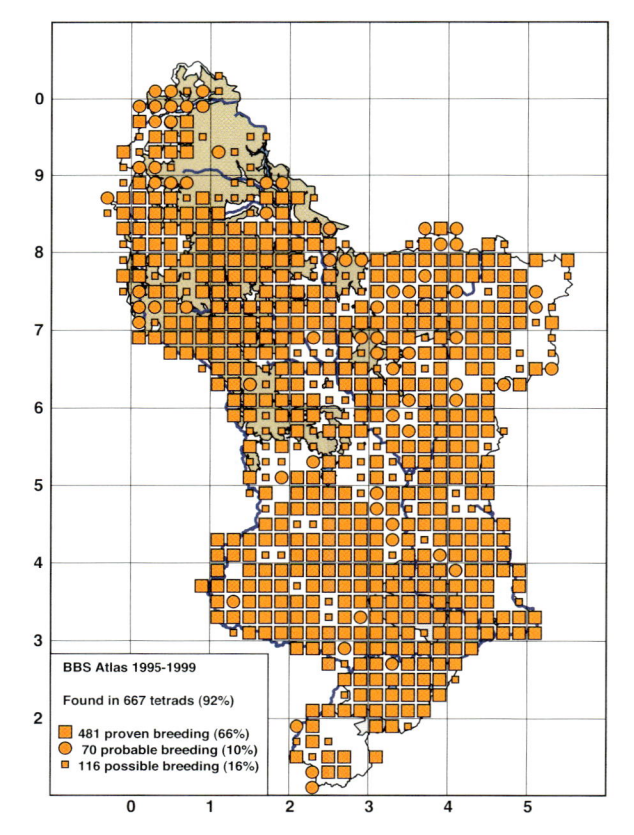

Near Buxton, in May 1995, a nest with three eggs was located 2m from the top of a 15m-high, east-facing cliff and another nest was found on a quarry ledge at Doveholes Quarry in 2007.

Although thought of as solitary, Carrion Crows are gregarious and can be seen in flocks throughout the year. The largest counts are usually of communal roosts, which may be purely of this species, or mixed with Rooks and Jackdaws. The table shows the largest flocks and the average largest recorded during five-year periods since 1980.

Period	Max count	Average max count
1980–84	650	436
1985–89	500	300
1990–94	624	457
1995–99	800	460
2000–04	500	282
2005–09	450	351

The largest roosts were of 800 at Hardwick Park on 16th November 1998, and 650 at Smeekley Wood on 22nd December 1980. The biggest diurnal gathering was of 600 at Clay Mills on 6th February 1983.

There are many records of Carrion Crows with aberrant plumage. Birds with white wing-stripes have been seen on many occasions. Wholly albino birds are much less common, though a completely white individual was seen from 1997 to 2003 in the Owler Bar–Totley Moss area. A pale 'washed-out' brown bird was recorded at Foremark Reservoir in November 1991.

There are several records of Carrion Crows taking frogs, toads and newts, including an incubating bird that flew down from its nest to take a toad at Staunton Harold Reservoir in 1990. At Drakelow Power Station, Carrion Crows were regularly observed taking freshwater mussels during 1995 and 1996, opening them by dropping them from a height of 6m onto tarmac. Similar behaviour has also been observed at Willington Gravel Pits. Perhaps most unusual was a record of one at Chaddesden Brook in Derby on 30th January 1997, seen standing in the water, turning stones to find and consume caddis-fly larvae. There are numerous records of Carrion Crows killing and eating smaller birds (as large as Magpie) and small mammals. An interesting behavioural record was of one harassing a hang-glider near Mam Tor on 22nd May 1995.

Of the few ringing recoveries, those of most interest include a bird ringed as a nestling at Blythe Bridge, Staffordshire in May 1951, which was shot in January 1953 near Derby in January 1953, a distance of 30km east-north-east. Another, ringed as a nestling at Combs Reservoir on 31st May 1962, was killed at the same site on 8th March 1974. A first-year bird ringed at Drakelow Nature Reserve on 8th June 1975 was shot at Radcliffe-on-Trent, Nottinghamshire, 46km to the east-north-east, on 22nd May 1980.

Hooded Crow
Corvus cornix
A rare or very rare winter visitor and passage migrant.

Hooded Crows were once regular, if local, visitors to Derbyshire. Both Jourdain and Whitlock described them as numerous on the lower Trent, and not uncommon around Sutton Scarsdale and on some of the Peakland moors. They were still numerous on the Eastern Moors in the 1920s and E.H. Peat said that to shoot 30 in an evening at a roost in Longshaw was not uncommon at that time (Frost). Whitaker (1929) said that Hooded Crows could be seen almost daily during the colder months of the year. A marked decline began shortly afterwards, as shown in the table.

Period	Records
1920s	'Numerous'
1934–49	10
1950s	1
1960s	10
1970s	24
1980s	3
1990s	2
2000–11	1

The 1970s saw an upsurge in records with no fewer than 24, including one record of three individuals together. An unusually concentrated passage involving six individuals was witnessed between 11th and 16th October 1975. Frost stated in 1978 that Hooded Crow was 'a rare winter visitor and passage migrant' based on the historical records and the observed passage in 1975. Since then there has been a significant change in status in the county and Hooded Crow is now a rare or very rare winter visitor with records of single birds in 1981, 1985, 1986, 1995 and 2007, and a 1998 record of one described as a 'Hooded Crow type'.

The decline of this bird as a visitor to the county is commensurate with a decrease throughout England: this is believed to be because an increasing proportion of the population in northern and eastern Europe is becoming resident in those areas (Brown & Grice 2005).

The 1985 and 1986 records are of particular interest: a very tame bird was reported from Mickleover on 28th December 1985 and possibly the same bird was reported from a public-house car park, again in Mickleover, on 23rd January 1986. The 1995 record was of a bird flying from a tree in the observer's garden in Smalley on 31st October. The last Derbyshire record of the species was of a bird at Carsington Water on 21st October 2007.

All the recent records since 1980 are for the period October to January and probably relate to migrating birds. This autumn/early winter pattern fits that observed by Frost in the 1970s when there were far more records.

In 1915, a pair nested in Dovedale on the Staffordshire side of the River Dove, very close to Derbyshire (Frost). Hybridization with Carrion Crow was recorded in both 1959 and 1960 when a female Hooded Crow paired with a male Carrion Crow at Hardwick and three of their six progeny had Hooded Crow markings.

Raven
Corvus corax
An uncommon resident, breeding regularly since 1994.

The Raven was once a common bird in Derbyshire and there are many, well-scattered places that include its name, illustrating a former widespread distribution. Both Whitlock and Jourdain confirmed its former presence in upland areas, with known nest sites as far east as Ashover and south to Clifton. However, the most graphic account of its abundance, and the reasons for its decline, are provided by Lovegrove (2007), who examined churchwardens' accounts. He found that several Derbyshire parishes took a heavy annual toll of Ravens: these included Hartington and Hathersage, and, in particular, Wirksworth. The latter village was responsible for a quite remarkable total of 1775 Ravens killed between 1707 and 1724.

Regular breeding took place until about the 1860s, after which Ravens were only occasional vagrants in the county, until September 1966, when a pair appeared in the Bleaklow area and bred at Alport Castles in 1967–68. However, it was believed that these may have been released birds (Frost). For much of the following two decades the Raven remained a rare vagrant, averaging fewer than one record per year. Meanwhile, numbers in Wales were increasing rapidly, and breeding resumed in Worcestershire in 1997 (Harrison & Harrison 2005) and Cheshire in 1991 (Norman 2008). Recolonization of Derbyshire began in 1992, when a pair bred in a quarry in Longdendale, followed in 1994 by another successful pair in a Wirksworth quarry. Breeding has since taken place annually. By the time of the Derbyshire BBS (1995–99), a quite rapid colonization was well underway, with presence in 82 tetrads, as the map shows.

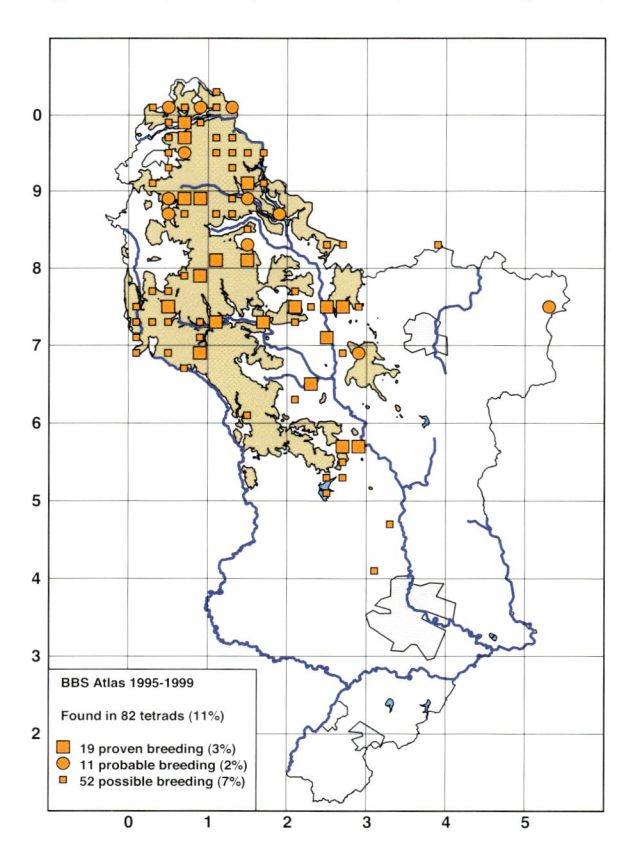

The tetrad map shows 19 proven, 11 probable and 52 possible breeding tetrads. Ravens do not join the breeding population until three or four years old (Ratcliffe 1997) and while immature they wander widely, so a large proportion of the possible breeding tetrads will refer to these wandering immatures. It is also not uncommon for these non-breeding birds to pair and hold territory. Occasionally they will build a nest, even though no serious breeding attempts take place. Often full breeding occurs in the following year. The tetrad map has overestimated the size of the gritstone population because several confirmed breeding tetrads include alternative sites used by the same pair.

Since 1999 the breeding population has continued to increase and expand its range, with nesting now taking place in the southern and eastern lowlands of the county as illustrated on the maps for 1995–99 and 2007–11.

Initially, the recent breeding population nested almost entirely on cliffs, especially in quarries. However, as the population has grown and extended its range, tree-nesting has become much more frequent. Such sites are much harder to locate than those on cliffs and it is likely that a number are overlooked, especially in the south. Allowing for this, the current county population is believed to be well over 60 pairs. The number of nesting pairs found in the period 1992–2011 is shown in the chart.

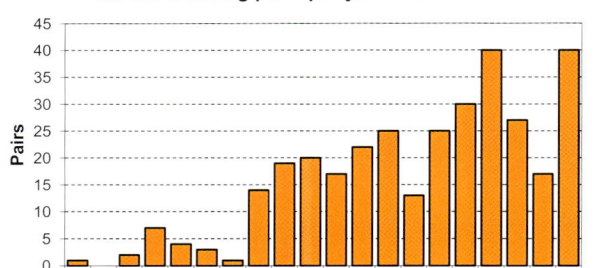

Pleasingly, several natural crag sites in the limestone dales now support breeding Ravens, despite human pressure at some of these locations. However, many modern nest sites are in limestone quarries where the birds generally find quieter, unworked faces away from the main quarrying activity. Ravens have fared less well on the gritstone moorlands where their increase has been slower, and successful nesting less frequent. In contrast, pairs breeding in lowland areas recently have been particularly successful. During 2006 and 2007, a pair nested successfully on a metal gantry at an electricity substation in the Trent Valley and since then, other industrial structures have been used in the south of the county and perhaps elsewhere.

Ravens are known to form large, communal winter roosts but none have yet been located in Derbyshire. However, 35 moving south-east over Whaley Bridge in December 2009 were believed to be flying to roost. Otherwise, the largest recent counts were of 27 drifting northwards at Win Hill on 27th September 2003, 74 (perhaps with some duplication) between Crowdecote and Hartington on 14th December 2005, and 40 at Monk's Dale on 11th February 2007.

There is considerable future potential for the Raven to both expand its breeding range and to increase its breeding density in areas that it has already colonized.

National ringing information suggests that post-fledging dispersal of Ravens may lead young birds to travel up to 100km, but more typically 30km, in their first six months. After this period, the birds tend to move back towards their natal area and begin breeding after about three years (Wernham *et al.* 2002). Two of the three county recoveries have shown long-distance movements. One ringed as a nestling near Ludlow, Shropshire in April 1996 was shot at Bamford Edge (123km) in May 1998, and another ringed near Austwick, North Yorkshire in May 1994, also as a nestling, was shot at Combs Moss, a distance of 98km south, in May 1995.

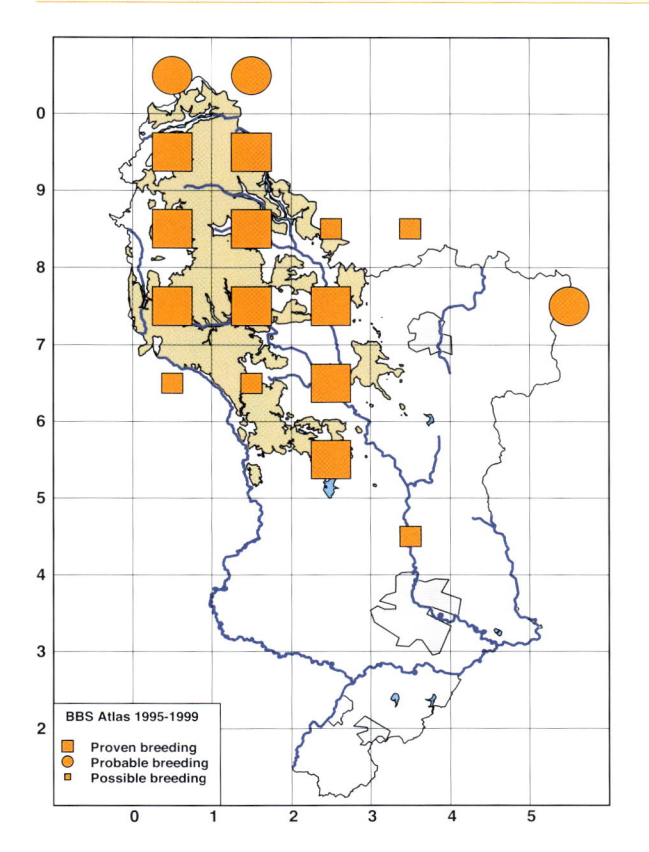

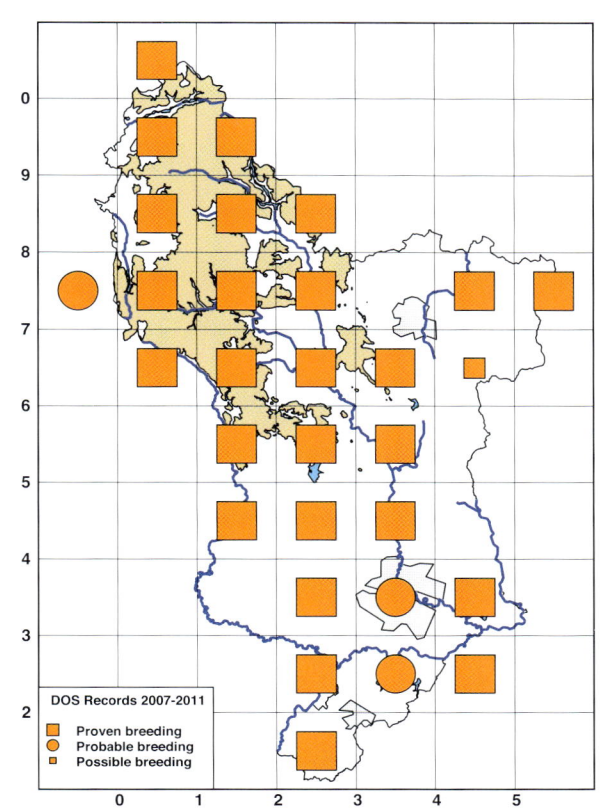

Lacey (2000) stated that five colour-ringed birds have been observed at nest sites in the county and the inscriptions on two of these show that both birds originated from Shropshire. They were three and four years old respectively and probably first-time breeders. Both had been reared in tree nests and had built tree nests in Derbyshire. Lacey believed that many birds in the burgeoning Derbyshire population originated from Shropshire and Wales. He linked the spread of the Raven to that of the Buzzard, with the use of Larsen traps largely superseding the illegal use of poisoned baits. Nevertheless, it was noted that there was evidence of interference at nest sites in the Dark Peak, close to areas of grouse-rearing.

Goldcrest
Regulus regulus
A common resident, passage migrant and winter visitor.

Europe's smallest birds, Goldcrests are familiar, restless sprites of coniferous and mixed woodland, in which the thin, rhythmic song can be surprisingly loud. Hearing this accounted for the majority of the 164 records of probable breeding shown on the tetrad map, being 50% of those tetrads occupied. Breeding was proved in 99 tetrads (14%). Fortunately, newly fledged young attract attention by their rather metallic hunger calls, although nests can be very difficult to see.

Coniferous woods, especially with more mature trees, hold the greatest densities of breeding birds, with spruce clearly preferred to pine. Goldcrests will also nest in mixed woodland, though typically favouring even tiny clumps of conifers in these while the presence of trees with ivy cover allows nesting in purely deciduous areas, especially when populations are high. Likewise, they may nest in gardens and churchyards if yews or other ornamental conifers are present.

Whitlock described the Goldcrest as 'fairly distributed' throughout the county and recorded an unusual event at Melbourne Hall Gardens, where two active nests were found on the same branch of a yew.

In the 1968–72 Atlas, four 10km squares were without this species, whereas the 1988–91 Atlas and the Derbyshire BBS (1995–99) recorded proven or probable breeding in all 10km core squares. As one would expect from their habitat preferences, breeding was rather patchily spread throughout Derbyshire, with the greatest concentrations in the Dark Peak Natural Area and fewest in the White Peak, where coniferous woodland is scarce.

Breeding numbers during the 1990s were considered to be at a high level in many places, doubtless aided by generally mild winters and the maturation of much coniferous woodland. For example, almost annual samples of breeding birds in Scarcliffe Woods revealed an increase from three territories in 1973 to 30 by 1996, though subsequently with no more than 11 by 2008 (Frost 2008a). Goldcrests are not, however, well represented in recent CBC work undertaken in the county. They averaged a pair a year at Shirebrook, equivalent to a density of 6.94 pairs per km^2, but fewer than half a pair per year at Shiningcliff Wood and Farfield Farm, and they were absent from the other sites. The highest counts of territorial birds are usually from northern forestry areas, where 19 were singing between Westend and Slippery Stones in May 2005, and 19 on Win Hill during the springs of 2007 and 2008. The census of 2003–07 at Carsington Water suggested 19 territories.

An influx of birds is noted every autumn, usually between early September and November, and often in areas where they do not breed. In some autumns, especially when westerly winds predominate, as in 1996, the arrival is relatively small. Regular midwinter counts at Scarcliffe Woods showed considerable annual variation and ranged from a high of 77 in 1988 to one

Severe winters, especially when branches and twigs become glazed with hoar frost for any length of time, take a considerable toll, doubtless of both our breeding birds and the Continental immigrants. Numbers in subsequent breeding seasons may then be drastically reduced but Goldcrests have the capacity to recover quickly as they lay large clutches and are double-brooded. The largest counts were of about 200 in Heath Wood on 27th December 1992, 100 in the Upper Derwent Valley on 22nd November 1997, 95 at Westend on 10th October 1992 and 95 at Elvaston Castle Country Park on 21st October 1992, while there was an earlier count of 90 at Shiningcliff Wood on 16th December 1967.

This species, although mainly arboreal, will occasionally feed on the ground. Nevertheless, a count of 50 foraging in mossy clearings at Wooler Knoll on 13th January 1988 was quite exceptional.

Although none of the 12 ringing recovery records in the county data-set relate to birds ringed during the breeding season, they include some interesting recoveries, and illustrate movements both north from and south to Derbyshire, and similarly to and from east and west. The greatest recorded distance travelled concerns a bird ringed at Elvaston Castle Country Park in September 1997, and found in April 1999 at Aberdour, Fife, on the Firth of Forth, 373km to the north-north-west. Another, ringed at Swarland, Northumberland in October 1997, was found 263km south at Rodsley in the following February. Two ringed on the Isle of Man in autumn were found at Swadlincote and Hathersage respectively, in the following late winter, and another also moved east, from Bootle, Lancashire and North Merseyside, to Drakelow Nature Reserve, in the autumn of 1990. A westerly movement involved a bird trapped at Renishaw Park in December 2000 that had been ringed two months earlier at Filey Brigg on the North Yorkshire coast, while others that travelled more than 100km moved from Hathersage to Ditton Priors, Shropshire. and from Uppertown to Spixworth, Norfolk.

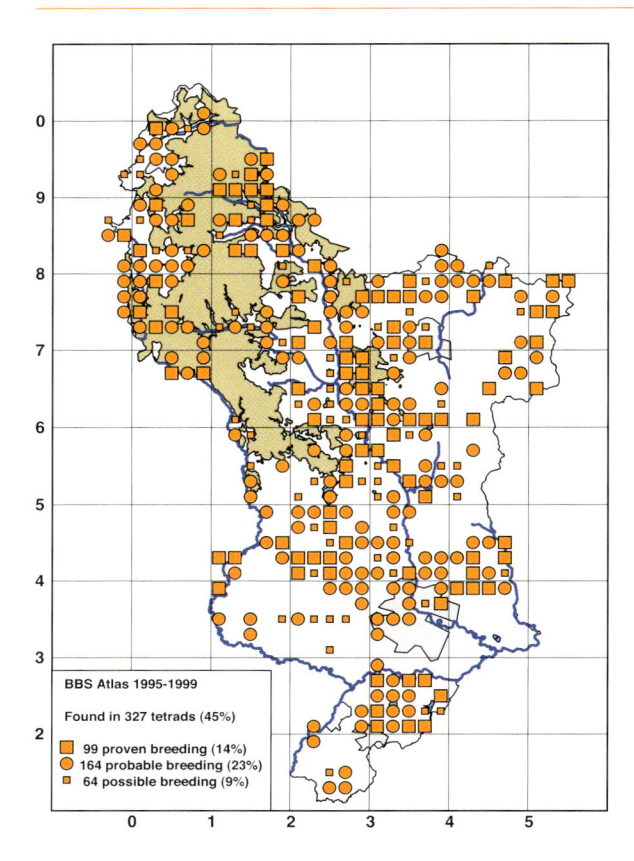

in 2007. The flocks may be purely of Goldcrests, but in other woodland, scrub and gardens they often associate with tits. There is little doubt that most of these birds are Continental immigrants.

Firecrest
Regulus ignicapilla
A rare summer visitor, passage migrant and winter visitor.

The delightful Firecrest is very much a birdwatcher's bird. If seen with the naked eye in treetops or against the light it could be passed off as a Goldcrest but seen clearly it is unmistakable, and the call and song are distinctive to those able to detect the high-pitched sounds. Most of the breeding birds have been recorded in areas containing Norway and sitka spruce and also lodge-pole pine, whereas passage and wintering birds have occurred throughout the county, usually in lowland areas. Scrub and woodland areas have produced most of the records, but others have occurred in such varied habitat as a roadside hedgerow, allotment gardens and a suburban garden.

The first Derbyshire record was of one shot near Melbourne in 1838, and another fell to the gun near Draycott a few years prior to 1893 (Whitlock), while Frost added six further records between 1944 and 1977. Excluding probable or definite breeding birds (see below), a further 65 Firecrests were recorded in the period 1978 to 2011, mostly between November and January, as the table giving the month of first occurrence of individual birds shows.

Month	Birds	Month	Birds
January	9	July	–
February	4	August	–
March	5	September	4
April	7	October	6
May	5	November	11
June	1	December	13

Firecrests first bred in England in the New Forest in 1962 (Adams 1966) but it was a further 19 years before breeding occurred in Derbyshire, when a pair fledged young at Osmaston in 1981 (Frost 1982). None have been seen there since. Thereafter, males were singing at Errwood Reservoir on 18th August 1986 and at Scarcliffe Woods on 29th May 1989. The latter was in a garden near the woodland edge and was presumed to be a late migrant, as was one at Derbyshire Bridge (where the habitat is unsuitable for breeding) on 1st June 2007. Single birds were also found at Scarcliffe Woods in late spring 1993 and 1999, but breeding was not proved and it was the mid-1990s before Firecrests again bred in the county, This was proved in the Derwent area in 1995, when two pairs and one or two unmated males were present (Frost 1996; Roddis 1996). In the following year, a male Firecrest hybridized with a female Goldcrest at Carsington Water and both birds were seen feeding the nestlings. A singing male was also in the Derwent area in June 1996, while a pair nested, probably unsuccessfully, in the Goyt Valley in 2002.

Since 2004, there have been signs of colonization by Firecrests in only two locations. The Derwentdale area held two singing males in June 2004, there were another two during the 2007 breeding season and, in 2008, four were singing in June with juveniles seen in July. This was followed by three singing males in 2009, and single birds in March 2010 and March 2011. In the Matlock Forest area there was a singing male in the summer of 2006, seen with possibly hybrid young on 25th June. Breeding was proved in 2007, when there were at least three singing males at two sites, and in 2008 when a pair and two singing males were present; the only records in 2009 and 2010 were of singing males in May.

Excluding breeding and presumed breeding birds, the chart shows the number of other birds recorded each year. Wintering birds are recorded only for the year in which they were first seen.

While most were recorded on a single day only, overwintering has occurred in eight winters: at Comb's Reservoir in 1974/75; Rother Valley Country Park (now in South Yorkshire) in 1990/91; Carr Vale in 1996/97, 1997/98 and 2002/03; Renishaw Park in 1999/2000; Hilton Gravel Pits Nature Reserve in 2002/03; and Elvaston Castle Country Park in 2003/04.

The great majority of these sightings are of single birds, with the only records of two being: at Rother Valley Country Park for eight days in December 1990; Renishaw Park on 31st January and 8th February 2000; Hilton Gravel Pits Nature Reserve from 12th December 2002 until March 2003; and Elvaston Castle Country Park on 10th January 2004. The latest spring occurrence concerned the individual already mentioned, at Derbyshire Bridge on 1st June 2007. The earliest in autumn was at Ramsley on 6th September 2003.

Finally, and of much potential interest, Mawson (2010) documented an apparent nesting association between Firecrests and Goshawks in the Derwent Valley area.

Firecrest: annual totals 1978-2011

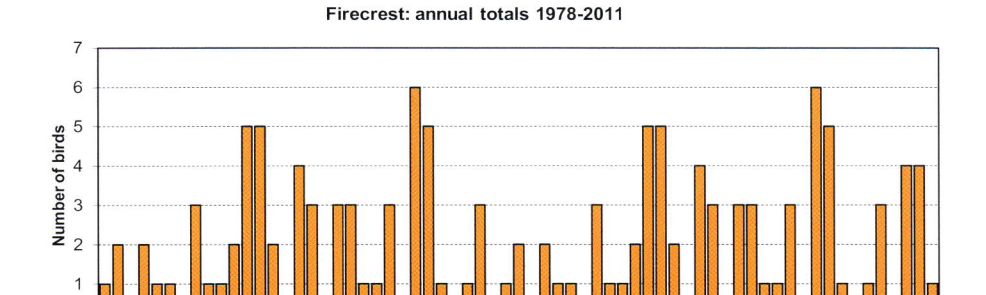

Blue Tit
Cyanistes caeruleus
An abundant resident.

A frequent visitor to gardens everywhere, the Blue Tit is one of our most familiar and popular birds. It also occurs commonly in woods, parks and hedgerows and may be found wherever trees are present. It breeds most commonly in deciduous woodland, especially oak, but occurs in all kinds of woodland if suitable nest sites are available. It uses nest-boxes very readily, but will nest in a variety of situations which, in Derbyshire, have included lamp standards, metal and wooden gateposts, holes in rocks and cliffs, machinery at a railway station, bat-boxes and a House Martin nest on a limestone crag.

There seems to have been little or no change in the Blue Tit's status for a long time, being presently the county's fourth most widespread species (jointly with Woodpigeon). Whitlock said it was abundant throughout the county, adding that flocks arrived in autumn from further north to frequent osier-beds in the Trent Valley. Proof of breeding is easily obtained for this confiding species and the Derbyshire BBS (1995–99) established confirmed breeding in 567 tetrads with a further 70 probable and 46 possible. These were distributed evenly throughout the county and almost to the tree line in the Peak District, as suggested by Frost.

CBC data in the 1990s show that the highest density occurred in mixed woodland at Shiningcliff Wood, where an average of 21 pairs bred annually over the period 1990–99, representing an estimated density of 95.45 pairs per km^2. At two other woodland sites, Shirebrook, consisting of mixed woodland, and Shire Hill, which is dominated by sessile oak, the estimated densities were 59.03 and 40.48 pairs respectively. On three farmland sites, average densities ranged from 10.67 to 18.65 per km^2. Blue Tit densities in woodland were generally around double those for the Great Tit and a little under double in farmland. Elsewhere, at Carsington Water there was an estimated total of 107 pairs in 2003–07. At Whitwell Wood there were up to 29 pairs in the late 1990s, but numbers seemed to have halved since then, possibly because many of the nest-boxes became dilapidated. At Scarcliffe Woods there were up to 35 territories in 1996 and an overall increase of 135% in breeding birds during the study

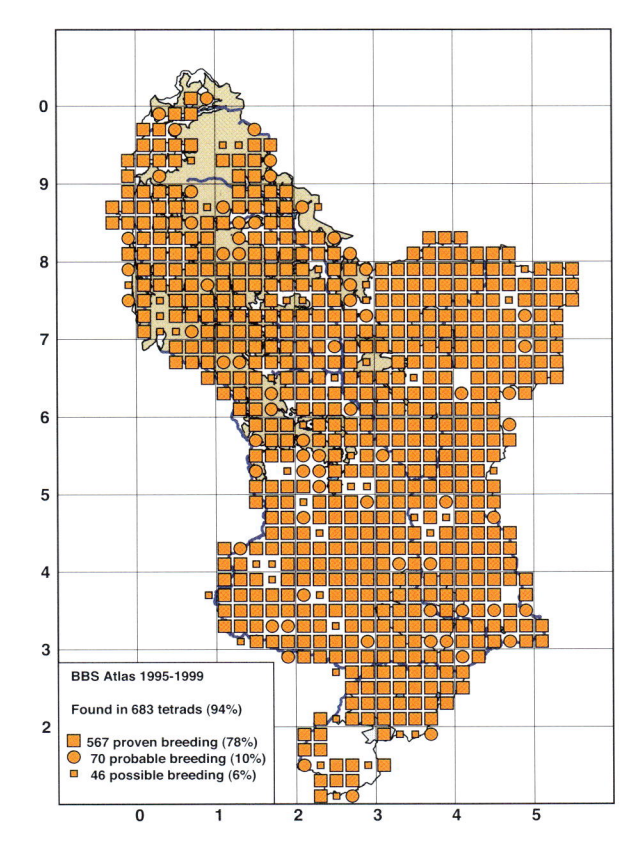

BBS Atlas 1995-1999
Found in 683 tetrads (94%)
■ 567 proven breeding (78%)
● 70 probable breeding (10%)
■ 46 possible breeding (6%)

period (Frost 2008a). Eaton *et al.* (2010) show an increase of 21% in the period 1970–2008, which may well be connected with a series of mild winters and greater provision of food in gardens.

Outside the breeding season, Blue Tits form flocks and may join with other species so that groups of 50–60 are not uncommon. The largest party recorded in the county was of 250 at Chatsworth on 26th August 1976, and interestingly, two of the other largest recorded groups occurred at virtually the same time of year, with 100 at Carsington Water on 27th August 2002 and 100 at Mickleover on 24th August 2004. The largest midwinter counts were of 120 at Scarcliffe Woods on 25th December 1989 and 114 at Creswell Crags on 1st January 1986.

Visible movements have been recorded on only a few occasions. These autumnal sightings include Frost's record of three parties flying over moorland near Barbrook Reservoir on 15th October 1957. Movement was also recorded at Ramsley Reservoir on two dates in September 1986, while 18 flew south-west over moorland there on 17th September 1988.

Because of their density, habitat preference and frequency of nest-box use, Blue Tits are frequently and easily ringed. There are 354 recovery records relating to Derbyshire, 44% being reported within 1km of the place of ringing. Only five birds moved more than 100km, of which the two most remarkable were: one ringed near Newbury, West Berkshire in December 1958 and controlled 161km further north at Breaston in February 1960; one ringed as a pullus in a box at Carr Wood in May 1987 that travelled 119km south-south-west to Evesham, Worcestershire, where it was killed by a car five months later. The longevity record is held by a bird ringed in Bretby Park and killed by a cat seven years later. It is also interesting to note that there are significant numbers of recoveries for this species in each decade since the 1950s, including the period before the introduction of mist nets. This is presumably because of its readiness to use nest-boxes, which enables easy access for the ringing of nestlings and particularly for trapping the brooding adults. It is likely that the reduction in numbers ringed in the 1990s is the result of a considerable rise in ringing costs.

Great Tit
Parus major
A common resident.

Whitlock and Jourdain disagreed over the relative status of Great and Blue Tits, the latter believing the Great Tit to be the more common bird. Frost said that this was not the case, and quoted CBC figures showing an average of 44 territories in eight areas covered, compared with 83 territories for Blue Tit. More recent CBC figures, for the 1990s, confirm that this is still the case and suggest that on farmland and in woodland, Blue Tits are almost twice as numerous as Great Tits. Estimated densities of Great Tits were 41 pairs per km^2 at Shiningcliff Wood, 31.25 at Shirebrook and 21.43 at Shire Hill Wood, whereas for three farmland plots, the estimated densities were 12.1 pairs per km^2 at Broadhay, with 8.98 at Culland and 6.89 at Farfield.

The noisy and tame nature of the Great Tit make it an easy species to find. The Derbyshire BBS (1995–99) located them in 660 tetrads (the ninth most widespread species in the county) with breeding confirmed in 514 (78% of those found). They were distributed virtually throughout Derbyshire, being absent, it was believed by surveyors, only from treeless moorland in the Peak District.

Interesting recent breeding counts include 20 pairs along 2.5km of a disused railway line at West Hallam in May 1994, while at Carsington Water in 2003–07, there were an estimated 82 pairs, 25 fewer than for Blue Tit. At Scarcliffe Woods there was a maximum of 24 territories in 1995, followed by an overall increase of 327% between the mid-1990s and 2004–08 (Frost 2008a). Eaton *et al.* (2010) recorded a 90% increase between 1970 and 2008.

Great Tits and Blue Tits are found in similar breeding habitats including woodland of all types, parks, gardens and hedgerows with trees. Outside the breeding season, they may form small, wandering groups, sometimes with other tits. Areas of beech are especially favoured in good beechmast winters, but these are far from being an annual occurrence in Derbyshire.

Flocks may then be seen feeding on the ground, such behaviour being far more frequent in Great Tits than the other tits. However, the flocks are usually smaller than those of Blue Tits, as evidenced by the largest counts, which were of 130 (in separate groups of 60 and 70) at Elvaston Castle Country Park on 26th September 1993; 107 at Hardwick Wood on 26th July 2007 and 96 there on 20th January 2011; 92 at Hardwick Park on 4th January 2007; 77 at Hardwick Wood on 13th January 2009, and 70 at both Shipley Country Park on 28th November 1976 and Rowsley on 31st August 2011.

The species is very sedentary and even small movements have been reported on very few occasions. Eleven flew west at Ramsley Reservoir on 9th September 1986 and small numbers were recorded moving north-west during several days of high pressure at Strines Top in October 1992. Further unusual

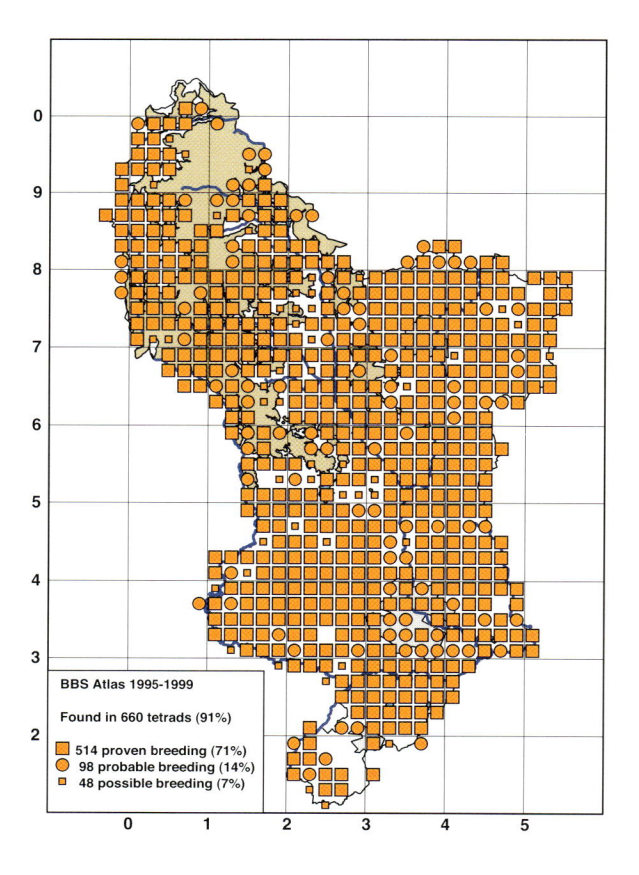

BBS Atlas 1995–1999

Found in 660 tetrads (91%)

- 514 proven breeding (71%)
- 98 probable breeding (14%)
- 48 possible breeding (7%)

sightings were of one feeding on the corpse of a Pheasant at Scarcliffe Woods on 8th March 1982, and of another with a light brown cap, wing coverts and breast-bar, which was ringed at Staveley Sewage Works in July 1985.

Ringing recoveries associated with Derbyshire number 162 and date from as early as 1950, at Repton. Although 59% of the recoveries are from within 5km of their ringing site, this rises to 77% when the range is extended to 20km. Of the remainder, just 8% moved more than 50km and only a single bird travelled further than 100km. This individual was ringed in September 1979 at Dronfield and caught again at Corby, Northamptonshire (104km to the south-south-east) six months later. Other examples include a bird ringed at Shrewsbury, Shropshire in January 1986 and controlled at Thorpe, 76km east-north-east in both April 1986 and February 1987; a bird ringed in the Goyt Valley recovered in Wrexham; and another ringed at Ancaster in Lincolnshire, recovered in Staveley. Long-lived birds have survived for at least six years.

Coal Tit
Periparus ater
A common resident.

Coal Tits are synonymous with coniferous woodlands and it can sometimes seem that they are the only species present in such areas. However, they also occur in mixed and broad-leaved woods and may breed in smaller areas, such as churchyards and gardens, if conifers are present.

Whitlock stated that the Coal Tit's breeding grounds in Derbyshire were in the wooded dales and plantations of the Peak, where it was fairly common in several localities. Interestingly, he said that the Marsh Tit replaced it in the lowlands, but he was writing before the Willow Tit had been classified as a separate species. Frost said that the creation of extensive conifer plantations had aided its increase and no doubt the planting of conifers as garden and amenity trees has enabled a further spread. Eaton *et al.* (2010) recorded an increase of 23% in the period 1970–2008.

The tetrad map indicates that breeding was confirmed in 181 tetrads, with probable and possible breeding in a further 115 and 105 respectively. Concentrations appear in north-west, north and central Derbyshire, but Coal Tits are now also widespread in the lowlands of the south and east, including squares SK22 and SK32, where they were not recorded for the 1968–72 Atlas.

Frost (2008a) reported that the conversion of Scarcliffe Woods from deciduous to largely coniferous woodland had benefited Coal Tits, which showed an increase of 650% (the largest for any species) between the mid-1970s and 2008. On three CBC plots at Shiningcliff Wood, Shirebrook and Shire Hill Wood, estimated Coal Tit densities were 14.09, 13.89 and 11.9 pairs per km^2 respectively. On farmland plots, estimated density was 3.7 pairs per km^2 near Hathersage and 0.66 at Farfield.

Most nests are in holes in trees, often lower than those of other tits and not uncommonly at, or below, ground level among tree roots, while other nests have been found in drystone and concrete walls, wooden and metal gateposts, and holes in grassy banks.

After the breeding season, Coal Tits form flocks, sometimes joining other species. In winter, while still mostly to be found in coniferous woodland, they occur more widely in other habitats and, as with Great Tits, may congregate on the ground to feed on beechmast. Their habit of caching food has been noted on numerous occasions. The largest counts were of 130 in Matlock Forest on 22nd July 2006, following 100 there in August 1987; over 100 at Derwentdale on 17th October 1996; 95 in the Snake Forest on 11th March 1991; and at Scarcliffe Woods, 87 on 25th December 2006 and 136 on 2nd December 2011. At the latter site it was the eighth most common species overall in winter. In Upper Derwentdale in 2009, 322 birds were ringed and a further 44 from previous years were re-trapped.

Apparent movements have been recorded on a few occasions. These include three birds moving north-west over open land at Ashover on 2nd October 1983, five flying south at Highoredish Hill on 5th October 1986, and 12 flying south-west at Ramsley Reservoir on 17th September 1988. At Carr Vale in 1996 small numbers were observed moving south between 15th and 30th September, including a maximum of 10–12 on 27th September. Continental birds are sporadically eruptive after the breeding season (*BWP*) and higher counts in some years may indicate that birds from elsewhere in Europe have reached Derbyshire. However, the only accepted record of one showing characteristics of the Continental race *P.a. ater* was at Shirland on 7th January 1998.

The county ringing recovery data for this sedentary species comprise 21 records, 76% being of birds that travelled less than 10km. There are two records of birds moving more than

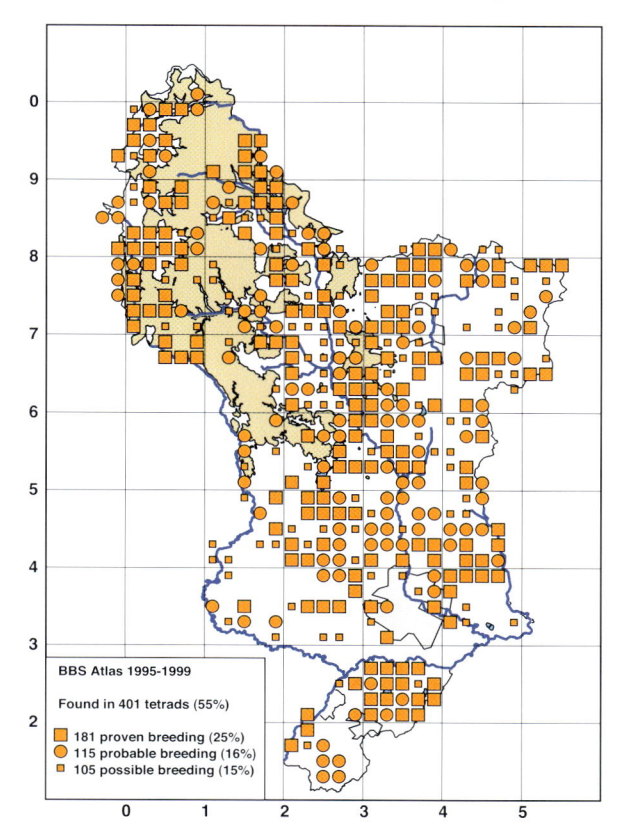

BBS Atlas 1995-1999
Found in 401 tetrads (55%)

■ 181 proven breeding (25%)
● 115 probable breeding (16%)
▪ 105 possible breeding (15%)

100km, both of which were birds of the year, ringed during the breeding season. One moved 109km south from near Wetherby, North Yorkshire, where it was ringed in July 1993, to Littleover, where it was killed by a cat three months later. The other, ringed near Bakewell in June 1966, travelled 120km north-north-east to Malton, North Yorkshire, where in January 1967, it also fell prey to a cat. Survival appears to be such that it is in the year of ringing that most dead Coal Tits are reported, and the record of a bird re-trapped six years after ringing at Hathersage was exceptional.

Willow Tit
Poecile montanus
A fairly common resident.

Willow Tits were not differentiated from Marsh Tits until around 1900 and it was well into the twentieth century before the distinguishing characteristics for their separate identification, both in the hand and in the field, were resolved and made known. The first Derbyshire records were published in 1910 and Frost later described them as fairly common, except on high ground.

Willow Tits prefer damp woodland, willow carr, trees, scrub and hedgerows, and are sometimes found in young coniferous woodland. However, they require rotting wood in which to excavate their nest holes and this is most likely to be found in damp places. Nests are usually low down and are easily overlooked.

The map shows that breeding was confirmed in 85 tetrads, with probable and possible breeding in 47 and 70 tetrads respectively. These were concentrated in the southern and eastern lowlands, but with a scattering across the centre and south-west of the county. There were confirmed records in SK15 and SK16, but very few records, and none of confirmed breeding, in the north-west.

In Derbyshire, Willow Tits are both more widespread and more numerous than Marsh Tits, for which breeding was confirmed in only 22 tetrads. This is the reverse of the national situation, where well over twice as many Marsh Tit territories were estimated in the 1988–91 Atlas. National CBC data also showed on average a 3:1 ratio of Marsh to Willow Tits in woodland and 2.5:1 on farmland. In Derbyshire, the woodland CBC at Shirebrook held an average of 2.5 pairs of Willow Tits to one of Marsh Tits. Neither species was present at the two other woodland CBC plots at Shiningcliff Wood and Shire Hill

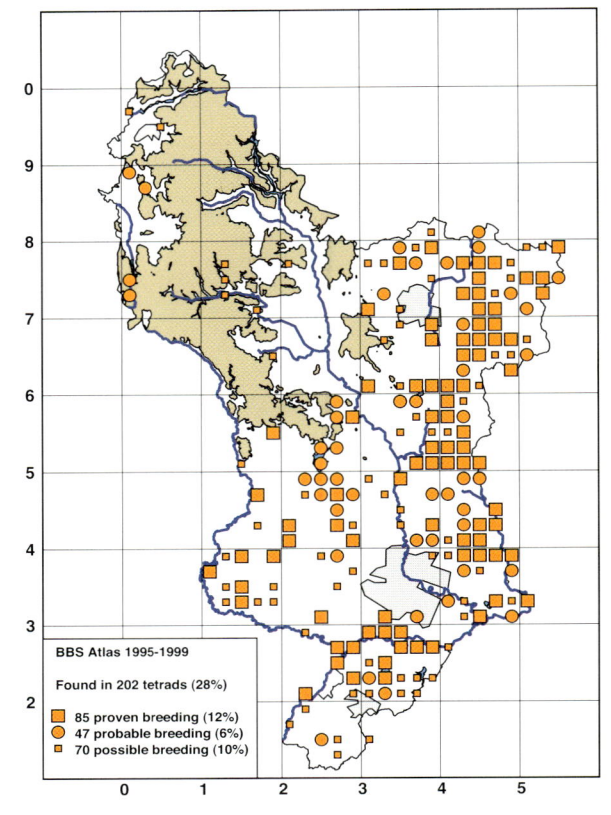

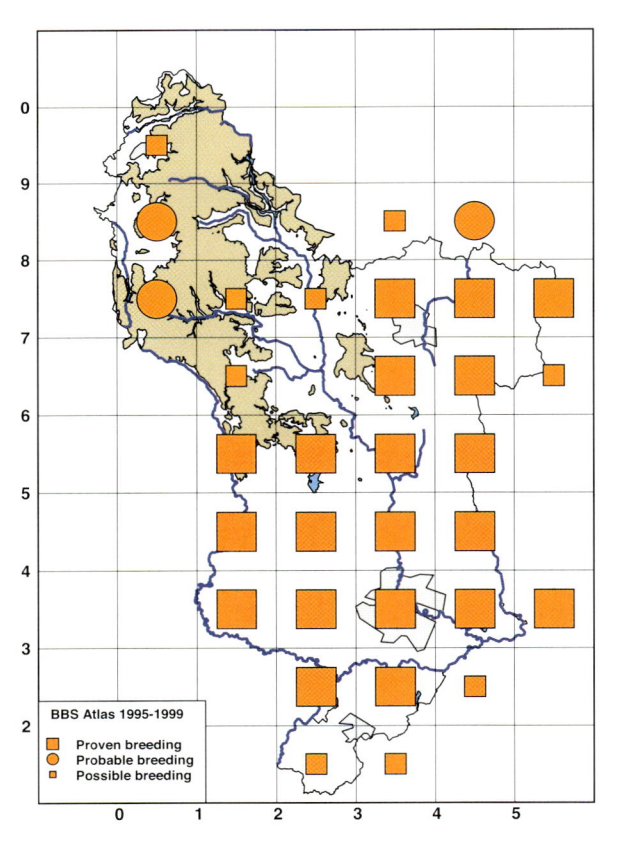

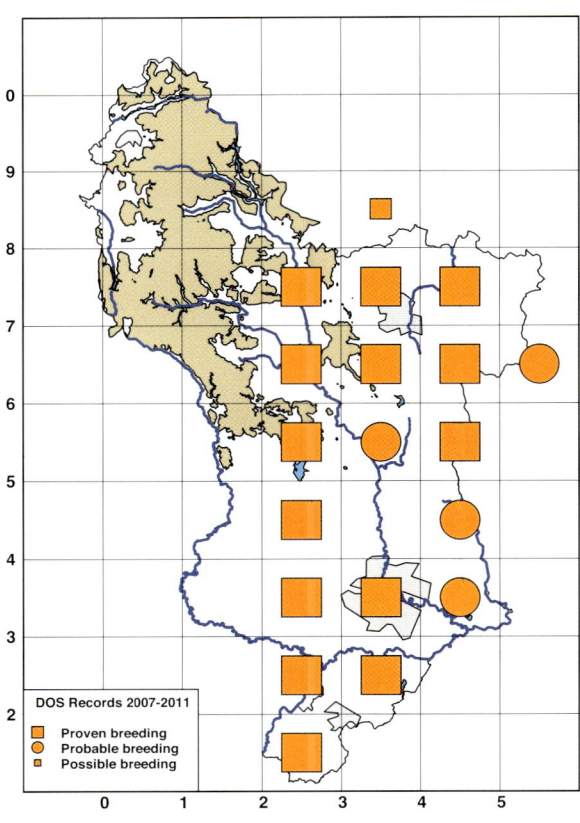

Wood. Regular breeding sites include Carr Vale (up to four pairs), Ogston Reservoir, Mapperley, Wyver Lane, Willington Gravel Pits (up to four pairs) and Scarcliffe Woods, where there was a maximum of six pairs in 1988 but none in 2006 or 2008. There were believed to be four territories at Carsington Water in 2003–07, but none of Marsh Tit.

Nationally, Willow Tits are in decline and this now seems to be the case in Derbyshire, although to a lesser degree than the 91% recorded for 1970–2008 by Eaton et al. (2010). The maps for 1995–99 and 2007–11 suggest that these tits are now absent in the west and north-west of the county.

The decline started much more recently than that of the Marsh Tit, beginning in the late 1980s (Siriwardena 2001). The reasons for this are unclear, and research is being carried out by the RSPB, some of it in the East Midlands. Nest predation by an increasing population of Great Spotted Woodpeckers is a possible cause of the decline.

Outside the breeding season, Willow Tits may be encountered in very small groups, but rarely join with other species of tits. In some suburban areas they are not rare at this time, and will visit bird tables and other areas where they do not breed. The largest counts come from Scarcliffe Woods, with 21 in December 1970 and 14 in December 1979. Elsewhere in the eastern lowlands there were: 15 at Sowbrook Pond and Kirk Hallam in February 1994; 12 at Willington Gravel Pits in August 2002; 11 at Mapperley Reservoir in October and November 1993; and 12 at Carr Vale in December 2011. In the Peak District, a count of ten at Ramsley Moor in November 1983 was noteworthy.

This species is known to be sedentary both during the breeding and the winter period. The dataset of ringing recoveries for Derbyshire comprises 13 birds of which 85% moved less than 7km. The longest movement recorded was of 19km from Drakelow Nature Reserve to Griffydam, Leicestershire, within two months of ringing, in the autumn of 1995.

Marsh Tit
Poecile palustris
A fairly common resident.

The early status of this species is unclear as a result of confusion with the Willow Tit, from which it was not separated until about 1900, and for some time afterwards many observers did not accept that there were two separate species. Whitlock said that they had recently declined for unknown reasons, but also referred to birds excavating holes in pollarded willows in river valleys, which clearly related to Willow Tits. Jourdain said that Marsh Tits were absent from the north of the county.

Its name is misleading, since Marsh Tits are found in mature deciduous woodland, parks and large gardens, but they usually avoid urban areas and coniferous woods. However, they occasionally visit the more rural garden feeding stations.

The map shows confirmed breeding in 22 tetrads with a further 26 probable and 29 possible tetrads. There are concentrations in the White Peak dales, the far south of the county and the north-east, but it is absent from northernmost areas, and parts of central and south-west Derbyshire.

It is perhaps more easily overlooked than some of the other tit species, being quieter and less demonstrative near the nest, which is often sited low down. The Marsh Tit is certainly scarcer in the county than the Willow Tit, the reverse of the national situation: the 1988–91 Atlas estimated 60,000 Marsh Tit territories compared with 25,000 for the Willow Tit. Eaton et al. show a decrease of 66% between 1970 and 2008, thought to have started as early as 1965. Possible causes are falling survival rates and interspecific competition with the increasing populations of Blue, Great and Coal Tits (Siriwardena 2001; Brown & Grice 2005).

The only CBC plot in Derbyshire on which the species was recorded was Shirebrook but the data are insufficient to make direct comparisons possible. However, the population appears to fluctuate, and the number of localities recorded in the annual *Derbyshire Bird Report* declined from 35 in 1995 to ten in 1999. In 2000–09, these varied between 20 and 37. At Scarcliffe Woods there were up to three territories, but Marsh Tits were much more common before felling and restocking changed the woods from deciduous to largely coniferous with, for example, 22 counted in January 1964 (Frost 2008a). A survey in 1993 by the SBSG counted 13 pairs in the dales of SK17, with six pairs in Chee Dale. South Wood is a favoured site of this species, where there were ten singing on 24th May 1994, and five family groups and four other territories on 5th June 2004. Nearby, there were four territories in Ticknall Limeyards on 29th June 2002, while in 2007 a pair nested in a box erected for hazel dormice in Monsal Dale.

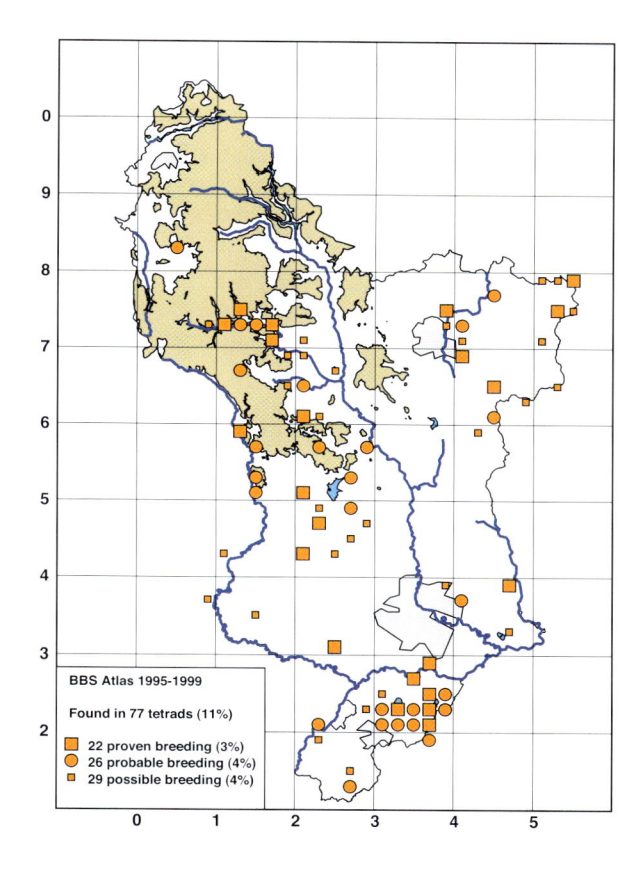

Outside the breeding season they are seen in small parties of up to five and may occasionally join flocks of other species of tits. The highest recent counts have been of 22 on 29th November 1992 and 31st December 1994, both at South Wood. In the Peak District there were ten at both Monsal Dale and Peter Dale in late 1983, and likewise at the lay-by feeding station in the Via Gellia in December 2001.

An unusual record was of a single bird seen on moorland near Barbrook Reservoir in June 1975. As Marsh Tits are rarely seen in urban areas, a bird at Chester Green in April 2000 and two at Pride Park in December 2000 were noteworthy.

There have been no ringing recoveries of this species.

Bearded Tit
Panurus biarmicus
A rare and erratic, autumn and winter visitor and passage migrant.

Bearded Tits are almost always found in large beds of common reed, a habitat that is scarce in Derbyshire, but are sometimes seen in other wetland habitats, such as areas of reedmace. While they are insectivorous in summer, they are almost entirely dependant on the seeds of common reed in winter.

There are three nineteenth-century records, although the details are somewhat vague. Based on the authority of a Mr Emery, Garner (1844) stated that this species had occurred on the River Dove (the county boundary with Staffordshire). Whitlock included a record of one shot in an osier-bed at Toton, which had been recorded in Sterland and Whitaker's *Birds of Nottinghamshire* on the grounds that it was on the Derbyshire–Nottinghamshire border. Thirdly, Jourdain accepted a record of one seen by Captain Henniker in a reed-bed between Marchington and Sudbury in the summer of 1876.

In modern times, they were first seen in Derbyshire in 1974, which was about the time when annual eruptions commenced from East Anglia. Of the Bearded Tits subsequently seen in Derbyshire, 33 (77%) first appeared in October or November, no doubt due to these post-breeding eruptions. Overwintering in 1987/88, 1988/89 and 1998/99 was notable.

Since 1974 there have been 20 records involving 48 birds.

Year	Location and date
1974	Hilton Gravel Pits Nature Reserve, a female on 14th and 21st April
1977	Birdholme Wildfowl Reserve, three on 16th October
1977	Shipley Park, a male on 5th November departed to the south-west
1978	Bolsover, two, a male which was trapped and ringed and a female from 14th February to 4th March
1978	Williamthorpe, two from 19th February to 17th March
1978	Staveley, two on 7th and 9th October
1979	Williamthorpe, two on 2nd January, heard on 5th January, and a female on 16th February
1981	Williamthorpe, one from 13th to 25th February
1982	Breaston, two on 8th, and one on 17th and 19th October
1982	Elvaston Quarry, four (two males and two females) on 17th, and a female still present on 29th–30th October
1984	Bolsover, two on 20th January
1985	Williamthorpe, one on 9th December

Year	Location and date
1986	Elvaston Quarry, six (three males and three females) on 26th and 28th October
1987	Williamthorpe, three from 24th October to 21st March 1988
1988	Williamthorpe, four on 16th October, three from 17th to 30th October, when two were trapped and ringed, remaining until 31st March 1989
1998	Drakelow Nature Reserve, a male was present intermittently from 8th November–25th March 1999, and was trapped and ringed on 29th November 1998
1998	Draycott, a female or immature on 13th December
2002	Willington Gravel Pits, six (three males, two females and a juvenile) on 16th–17th October
2004	Nadin's, Newhall, a male from 15th to 17th October
2010	Carsington Water, a male on 1st November, before departing west

The table shows the analysis by period and months since the first record.

Period	Records	Birds
1970s	7	14
1980s	8	24
1990s	2	2
2000–11	3	8
Totals	20	48

The chart shows the number of individuals in each record, similarly.

Bearded Tit: half-monthly distribution 1974-2011

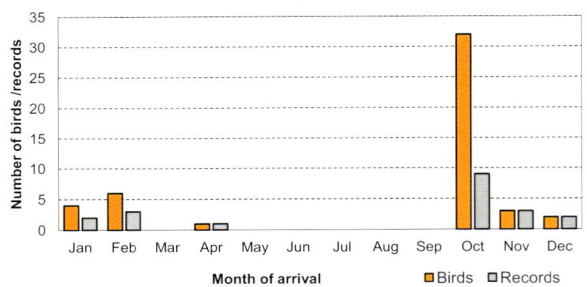

Woodlark
Lullula arborea
A former breeder, now a rare passage migrant or vagrant.

In 1836, Neville Wood of Foston described the Woodlark as tolerably abundant in that area and mentioned some nests found in unusual situations. It was said to be resident throughout the year. J.J. Briggs, writing in 1850, described it as thinly distributed and declining in the Melbourne area. It was said by Sir Oswald Mosley and Edwin Brown in 1863 to be scarce or rare in the Tutbury–Burton area. Whitlock never saw a Woodlark in Derbyshire, while the last nest known to Jourdain was in the Burton district in 1881. Frost gave details of a nest at Whitwell Wood in 1910, the last known instance of breeding in the county.

Since then, there have been only 21 records, involving 24 birds.

Year	Location and date
1958	Longshaw, a singing male on 26th April
1968	Egginton Sewage Farm, one on 13th January
1969	Matlock Forest, two on 3rd December
1971	Ogston Reservoir, one flew over with migrant Skylarks on 8th October
1976	Drum Hill, Breadsall, one on 24th April
1994	Pleasley Colliery, two immatures from 18th July to 1st August
1997	Barlborough Golf Course, one on 8th–9th April
2000	Killamarsh, one on 2nd May
2001	Alvaston Park, one flew north-west on 25th March
2001	Carr Vale, one flew south on 6th October
2001	Carr Vale, one flew south on 25th October
2002	Ashover, one flew south on 1st September
2002	Carr Vale, one flew south-west on 30th September
2003	Mercaston Sand Pits, one on 1st March
2003	Williamthorpe, one flew south-west on 11th October
2008	Poolsbrook, two from 11th to 28th June, including a singing male, at the former Ireland Colliery tip
2009	Foremark Reservoir, one overhead on 26th July
2009	Ambaston Gravel Pits, one flew north-west with Skylarks on 8th November
2010	Ramsley, one circled and departed to east on 30th September
2011	Ashover, one flew south-west on 15th October
2011	Beeley Moor, one flew over on 5th November

The two birds seen at Pleasley Colliery in 1994, one of which was ringed, were almost certainly from the local breeding population in nearby Nottinghamshire. The Poolsbrook birds in 2008 might well have been a breeding pair, but were discovered late in the season and breeding was not confirmed. There was no sign of them in the area subsequently.

Skylark
Alauda arvensis
A common resident and passage migrant.

The pleasant, incessant song of the Skylark is synonymous with spring and summer days on farmland, on moorland and in other open countryside. The song may be heard in January in mild weather but is more typically heard from February onwards, and throughout the breeding season. There is often a small resumption in autumn. Hearing the song accounted for the great majority of the 318 tetrad records (52% of those found) in the probable breeding category. 264 records (43%) were of confirmed breeding, and there were 30 in the possible category. This data also gave it a distribution ranking of sixteenth in the county.

The current distribution of Skylarks in the county is unchanged since the 1968–72 and 1988–91 Atlases, with breeding recorded in every 10km square. Though its absence in some tetrads, as in SK21 and SK26, must have been a consequence of underrecording, the large gaps in SK33 and SK37 show its aversion to built-up areas, in these cases Derby and Chesterfield. Woodland is, of course, also shunned, though Skylarks will nest for a very few years in areas of felled and restocked woodland.

On moorland, Skylarks prefer areas of grass to heather, and breed to at least 580m amsl, though avoiding the eroding peat areas on the highest ground of Kinder Scout and Bleaklow. In 1978, 19 territories were located in the Snake Pass area. The 2010 survey of the EMP moors gave a total of 49 territories, with 31 of these on Big Moor.

The larger, more open fields of lowland Derbyshire are more suited to the species' requirements than the smaller fields of upland areas. None was found on CBC plots in the 1990s at Farfield Farm, Hope or Broadhay Farm, Hathersage, while at Culland numbers were at a low density of 1.73 pairs per km². A more typical density was found at Oxcroft with 22 singing in a 1km square sampled by the BBS in May 1995. At High Low

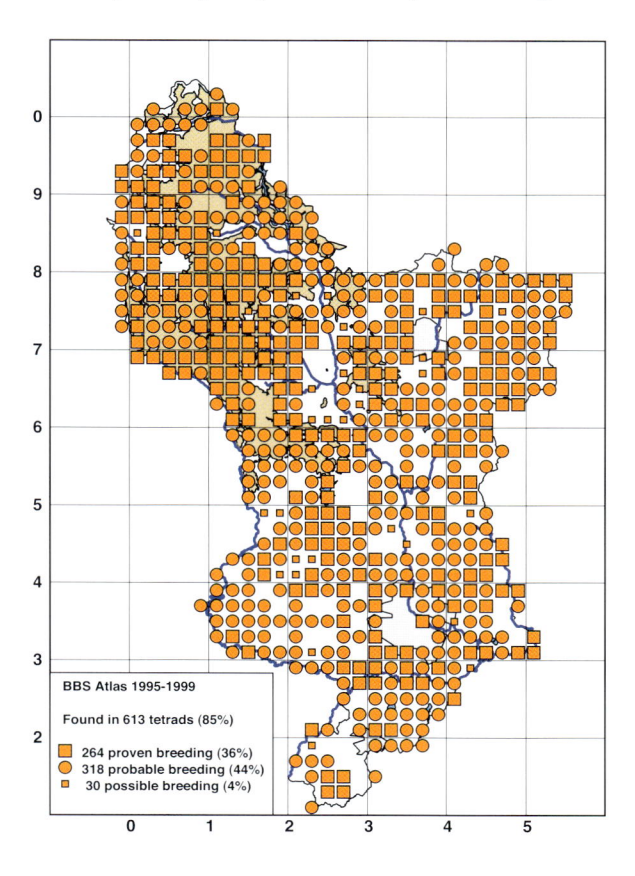

BBS Atlas 1995-1999

Found in 613 tetrads (85%)
- 264 proven breeding (36%)
- 318 probable breeding (44%)
- 30 possible breeding (4%)

in May 2000, 17 territories were found in 16ha of hay meadow, with much lower numbers on pasture where there were four territories in 15ha. Another BBS plot in SK3423 (Ticknall) was given over to mixed farming and held a mean of 5.3 territories in 1994–2008. Conversely, square SK4164 (North Wingfield), dominated by autumn-sown cereals, held an average of just 1.1 territories during the same period. At Egginton Sewage Farm, some 20 pairs nested in 1997, all failing because of water company operations.

Nationally, numbers of breeding Skylarks have fallen considerably in recent decades. Locally, the situation is less clear: both Whitlock and Jourdain regarded them as numerous; Frost alluded to decreases in some moorland areas but made no comment about farmland population trends. The clearest evidence of a local decline was given by Hornbuckle and Herringshaw (1985), who stated that numbers at Breck Farm, Staveley, halved from 28 to 14 pairs between 1970 and 1980, while on higher ground at Tor Farm, Hathersage, five pairs in 1975 were reduced to only one subsequently. Comments on local populations by contributors to the *Derbyshire Bird Report* since 1978 are only marginally in favour of lower numbers. However, Eaton *et al.* (2010) record a decline of 53% between 1970 and 2008.

Set-aside is believed to have helped Skylarks, at least temporarily, but other farming practices have been injurious, in particular the early ploughing of stubbles and the trend towards autumn sowing of cereals. The latter has resulted in crops which, after early spring, are too tall for feeding and breeding Skylarks.

This species also breeds on industrial wasteland, gravel pit margins, golf courses and other open habitats. In the east of the county the reclamation of colliery spoil heaps has resulted in extensive stretches of grassland that are ideal, at least temporarily, for this species. As an example, the former Shirebrook Colliery supported 68 pairs in 2002, though numbers rapidly declined as the plantations on the site matured, with only eight pairs by 2011.

After the breeding season, Skylarks occur mainly in flocks, especially in stubble fields. Three-figure autumnal flocks are not rare and there were impressive counts of 300 at Egginton Sewage Farm in October 2005, and 412 at Firbeck Common in October 2006. The two largest recorded flocks, of about 1000, occurred in severe winter weather at Egginton Sewage Farm on 2nd January 1971, and between Aston-on-Trent and Weston-on-Trent on 11th January 1997. The next largest gathering, of more than 700 at Shipley on 1st January 1992, was an unusually large mild-weather flock. In cold weather, birds may occur in unusual places, including gardens, while one fed at a rubbish bin in a school playground at Alvaston in February 1984. Cold-weather movements are also often recorded, mainly early in the winter. Two of the heaviest were from the same site, at Staveley Hillyfields, where 767 flew south-west in only 35 minutes on 25th December 1970, and 500 moved in the same direction on 1st January 1997. At Ogston Reservoir, 593 flew south-west in 90 minutes on 27th December 1970.

In mild weather, breeding Skylarks sing at lowland sites from January, and return to moorland areas from February, well ahead of the bulk of the breeding Meadow Pipit population. Spring movements are rarely reported and are very small in number. Autumn passage, from the second half of September to November, is much more noticeable and is mainly between south and west. At Egginton Sewage Farm, 500 moved south on 24th September 1990, a very early date for such a heavy passage. Otherwise, the largest movements recorded were 305 at Barbrook Reservoir on 10th October 1957 and 370 at the same site on 5th November 1983, 206 at Totley Moss in two hours on 17th October 1994, and 206 at Morton on 14th October 1997.

Skylarks are usually ringed as nestlings, since their affinity to open ground makes the use of mist nets less effective. They can be caught at night by dragging a net over the ground to trap roosting birds, but this requires the presence of a suitable team of ringers. The species becomes very mobile in the winter period and large numbers often move to coastal areas. The only recovery for the county is of one ringed near Harrogate, North Yorkshire in January 1969 that was found dead 12 days later at Ilkeston, 112km south.

Shore Lark
Eremophila alpestris
A very rare vagrant.

Shore Larks are winter visitors to Britain from their breeding grounds in Fennoscandia. They are found mainly along the east coast, with the majority between the Humber and Thames estuaries, and inland records are rare.

There have been nine records in Derbyshire, involving 15 birds, with all but the long-staying bird of 2002 appearing in October or November, which is when most reach Britain.

Year	Location and date
1971	Abney, three flew west-north-west on 18th October
1973	Church Wilne Reservoir, one on 26th October
1975	Willington No. 2 Gravel Pit, one flew east on 12th October
1996	Carsington Water, two from 24th to 29th November
1997	Barbrook Reservoir, one circled and departed to the north-east on 14th November
1998	Carr Vale, three briefly on 11th November, arrived from, and departed to, the north-east
2002	Pleasley Colliery, one from 21st January to 19th March
2003	Carsington Water, one on 15th November
2006	Butterley Reservoir, two flew west on 20th October

Sand Martin
Riparia riparia
A fairly common summer visitor and passage migrant.

Sand Martins breed colonially in river-banks and other suitable vertical faces. Normally, they will excavate their own nest hole but occasionally they will use existing holes such as drains. This specialized nesting requirement results in a rather patchy distribution in Derbyshire, where there is a strong association with the main river systems, especially in the south of the county, with its river-associated sand and gravel quarries.

In keeping with the species' scientific name, this has been the basic distribution pattern in the county for a long time. Whitlock, Jourdain and Frost all said that most Derbyshire Sand Martins were found along the River Trent and the lower reaches of the Derwent and Dove. Much smaller numbers breed alongside rivers elsewhere, even at some altitude, as on the River Ashop. Away from waterways, it breeds sparingly in sandpits, quarries and other industrial areas, where it is very much an opportunist if sand-piles or similar areas are available.

In the Derbyshire BBS (1995–99), breeding was proved in 62 tetrads, with 83 probable/breeding tetrads. Large colonies are obvious, but very small ones can easily be overlooked. The association with the river systems is very evident from the map.

BBS Atlas 1995-1999

Found in 145 tetrads (20%)

- 62 proven breeding (9%)
- 5 probable breeding (1%)
- 78 possible breeding (11%)

In the 1990s, at least 12 other counts of breeding colonies in excess of 50 holes were reported, but the majority of counts were of fewer than 30 nests. The seasonal variation within sites suggests that this species may not be as site-faithful as Swallow and House Martin; it might also be explained by variation in the availability of sites, particularly in working gravel and sandpits, or the changing numbers of birds returning from wintering quarters each year. Nevertheless, there is significant degree of local and colonial fidelity, with the majority of birds returning to breed within 10km of their birth site (*BWP*).

Unusual breeding sites have included a colony of up to 60 pairs in a basalt slag-heap at Waterswallows in 1995 and 1996, nests in overflow pipes set in a wall in Derby in 1978 and 1980, while 50 pairs bred in steel river-bank supports at Pride Park in 2000. Also in 2000, a pair nested in a crack in a garden wall at Barrow upon Trent. A similar but much earlier site was in a high wall supporting a garden lawn at Bakewell in the late 1800s (Whitlock). Frost mentioned nests in two feet of soil topping a Home Guard shelter. At Osmaston, in 2007, 36 pairs nested in a hole dug as a farm cess pit, while at Melbourne Pool, four were entering holes in a wall in June 2009. There were 65 occupied holes in steel piles at Derby Locomotive Works in 2010.

Sand Martins are the earliest of the hirundines to return from their winter quarters. Average earliest reported dates for the 1970s, 1980s, 1990s and 2000s were 26th, 21st, 11th and 9th March respectively. The average date in the period 1978–2011 was 14th March, and the earliest ever arrival date was 1st March 2008, when one was at Twyford. Length of stay and latest recorded dates were similar throughout the last three decades of the twentieth century, with the average latest date being 2nd October, 26th September and 30th September in the 1970s, 1980s and 1990s respectively. Over the period 1978–2011, the average latest date was 26th September and the latest recorded date was 24th October 1990, at Staveley.

Spring flocks are generally larger than post-breeding gatherings. In 1996, exceptionally large numbers were observed at Willington Gravel Pits, where 2200 roosted on 16th April, and 750 flew east-north-east in 90 minutes during heavy snow on 13th April. Other very large counts were of 1500 at Long Eaton Gravel Pits on 5th April 2006; 1000 at Carsington Water on 19th April 2003 and Ogston Reservoir on 19th April 2010; and 800 at Church Wilne Reservoir on 28th April 2004.

After the breeding season the largest gatherings were usually of communal roosts in reed-beds. These include one estimated at 6000–8000 at Elvaston Quarry in August 1977, dwarfing the second largest count of 2000 at Newhall in July and August 2000. The greatest diurnal gatherings at this time were of 1000 on power lines by the River Derwent at Church Wilne on 14th July 2001, 800 at Church Wilne Reservoir on 31st July 1974 and 700 at Willington Gravel Pits on 8th July 1989.

Much visible migration watching is carried out in Derbyshire, especially during the autumn months and mainly at upland sites. Sand Martins are recorded in only very small numbers at these sites, probably because most have already moved through and also because migrants seems to favour lowland river valleys. The most interesting records of passage include 400 per hour moving south at Staunton Harold Reservoir during an unspecified period on 29th August 1964, and 296 moving south in five hours at Carr Vale on 9th July 2008.

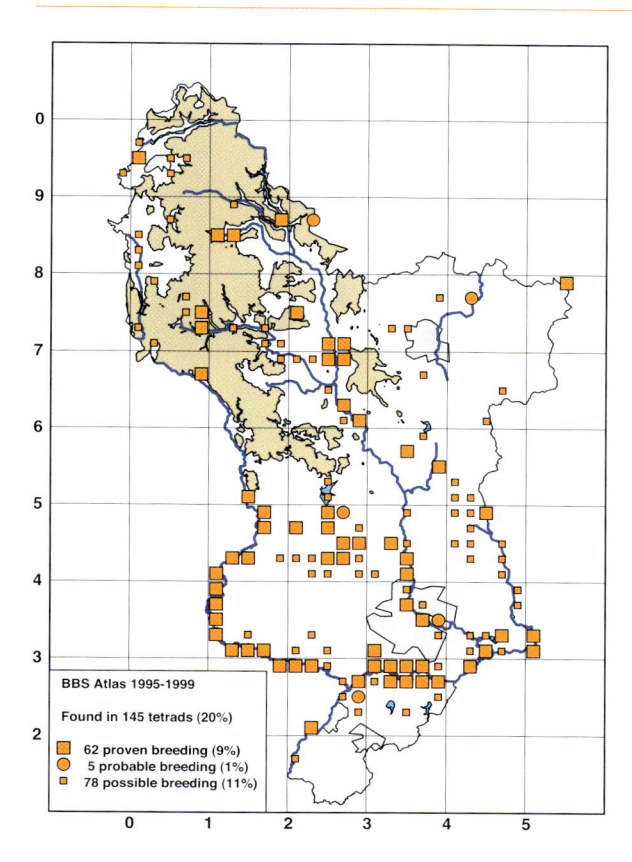

Breeding was proved in 14 of the main 10km squares in the county, compared with 20 and 10 in the 1968–72 and 1988–91 Atlases respectively. This suggests that Derbyshire Sand Martins are more localized than 30 years ago, and this may be related to poor survival rates on the wintering grounds, notably in 1968/69 and 1983/84. However, many colonies have been flooded out in some of the recent wet summers, which has clearly affected breeding productivity.

Frost said that it was doubtful whether colonies of three figures existed, but since then there have been many colonies of more than 100 pairs. These include up to 252 occupied burrows in 1999, 156 in 2002, 227 in 2005 and 202 in 2006, all at Mercaston Sand Pits; 146 at Drakelow Nature Reserve in 1988; 140 at Sawley Water Meadows in 1992; up to 275 nests at Willington Gravel Pits in 2008; and up to 300 at Barrow Gravel Pits in 2000. At Scropton in 2009 there were 82 new holes on 25th April, and a further 75 in May but all were later flooded out. An artificial colony provided for Sand Martins at Pride Park held 50 breeding pairs in 2009.

Breeding numbers may show considerable annual fluctuations, as (available) counts of occupied nest holes at Mercaston Sand Pits show:

Year	Nests	Year	Nests
1982	100	2000	–
1983	16	2001	116
1984	3	2002	156
1985	–	2003	–
1986	26	2004	–
1987	–	2005	227
1995	32	2006	202
1996	35	2007	82
1997	20	2008	–
1999	252	2009	–

In the northern half of the county, the larger recent colonies include up to 84 pairs by the River Derwent at Chatsworth Park in 2006; 90 pairs at Doveholes Quarry in 2006; 65 pairs at Whitwell Quarry in 2008; and 56 pairs at Bolsovermoor Quarry in 2001.

The British populations of this migratory species move south through the western countries of Africa to spend the winter in the Sahel zone. Derbyshire ringing recovery data comprise 126 records, of which 73 relate to the 1960s when, between 1960 and 1968, 400,000 birds were ringed on their wintering grounds. Of all reports involving birds associated with Derbyshire, 94% are controls. This is the percentage for the national data set (Wernham *et al*. 2002). In the late 1960s, a long-term drought in the wintering area reduced survival rates and caused a large population crash. This reflects in the numbers of birds being controlled through the 1970s, 1980s and 1990s; the county records show respectively 6, 12 and 34 controlled birds for each decade.

Autumn passage through Britain funnels through the Sussex coastline, and large-scale ringing at Icklesham and Chichester has involved birds passing through or breeding in Derbyshire. A simple analysis of the 17 Derbyshire–Sussex controls shows that nine of the ten birds ringed in Derbyshire and controlled in Icklesham or Chichester were ringed in the autumn and controlled on their way out of the country several days later. By contrast, of the spring passage via Sussex, none have been caught breeding in the county the same year, but rather they have been caught on autumn passage in later years. This suggests that birds leave the UK via the Sussex coast and return the following spring by a different route. Three records of birds ringed in spring and controlled in Derbyshire in the same season are from the Avon, Wolverhampton and Herefordshire, suggesting that the inward spring route is more westerly.

The furthest distance within the UK concerns a bird ringed at Balchraggan, Highland in August 1981 and controlled at Old Whittington six weeks later. There are three recoveries involving France but by far the longest Derbyshire migratory record (4073km) was of a bird ringed in March 1992 at Djoudj National Park in Senegal and controlled at Shardlow in June 1994.

Swallow
Hirundo rustica
A common summer visitor and passage migrant.

Swallows are common and found throughout Derbyshire (being the tenth most widespread species), breeding in most areas except city and town centres, and some of the higher upland moors of the north-west. They may be found nesting in a wide range of habitats, from isolated farms and villages to the edge of heavily built-up areas and on moorland, but are most numerous on lowland farms, especially those which contain grassland grazed by animals, where the birds can readily find their insect food. They often form large congregations over reservoirs, lakes and rivers. In 1893, Whitlock described Swallows as extremely common, a similar assessment to that of Jourdain. Frost was a little more cautious and considered that by the early 1970s numbers were generally lower, perhaps because of the same African desertification factors which had reduced Whitethroat populations. Recent information shows a national increase of 22% between 1970 and 2008 (Eaton *et al.* 2010).

The Derbyshire BBS (1995–99) showed that breeding was proved in 494 tetrads, and was probable or possible in a further 160. Breeding took place in all of the 10km squares wholly within the county, including the 23 core squares, where it was also proved in the 1968–72 and 1988–91 Atlases. Breeding or probable breeding is easily proved for Swallows since most nest in buildings, which they readily enter in the presence of observers, drawing further attention to themselves with their twittering calls and songs.

In 2007, BBS data showed that 80% of surveyed squares were occupied, where the previous ten-year mean was 69.7%. Nesting is normally associated with structures, especially barns and outbuildings, while other artificial sites regularly include the underside of bridges and bus shelters. More unusual sites have included the outside of buildings (as House Martins), the top of an electric light shade inside a small museum, the end of a punt pole resting against a boathouse wall, and over 5m below ground level in a manhole. A nest inside a temporary shelter at 440m above the Westend Valley suggests that the absence of Swallows from parts of the north-western moors may relate to an absence of nest sites, rather than a lack of food.

Natural sites, mostly in caves and rock-faces in the Peak District and the north-east, have been used in the past. A review by Davies (1986) identified such sites as having at some time had nesting Swallows, though during latter years only two were in use: Giant's Hole in Castleton had a single nest and the caves at Creswell Crags had several nests. Nesting at this latter site continued to be regularly reported until 2001, but probably amounted to only single nests in each year. Occasional cave-nesting occurred at Upper Langwith for a few years from 1989, and at Wolfscote Dale (a site not mentioned by Davies) during 1994 and 1995. At Anchor Church in the Trent Valley, breeding occurred in a semi-natural cave in at least 1990–91. Breeding activity may occur well into the autumn, as in 1991, when adults were still carrying food to a nest on 10th October, while in 1987 young fledged from a nest at Belper on 19th October.

Particularly useful information on Swallow breeding numbers and productivity has come from two ringers working in the extreme south of the county, roughly between Repton and Catton. Here an average of 154 young a year were produced in the period 2003–08, with totals varying between 107 and 224. The latter figure was for 2008, when only six nests failed. In the same area, at least six pairs nested within 500m of Netherseal church in 2004. There were 104 nests (of which 15 failed) in 2009, from which a record 380 young were ringed. Further north, at a site at South Wingfield, four pairs each reared three broods in 1997. Another specialist Swallow-ringer in the north-east of the county found a record nine breeding pairs at a farm at Elmton in 1996, and there were 11 active nests at a single Alderwasley farmhouse in June 2010 and likewise ten at Pentrich in the following month.

As a summer visitor, the Swallow is popularly associated with the arrival of spring. In the period 1978–2011, the earliest arrival was on 17th February 2004 at Starkholmes but the earliest ever was on 11th February 1957 at Somersal Herbert. The first arrival date has become earlier, possibly as an effect of global warming, being 6th April, 31st March, 25th March and 17th February in the 1970s, 1980s, 1990s and 2000s respectively; and a mean arrival date of 27th March for 1978–2011. This is not reflected in the length of stay, which remains unchanged, presumably because earlier arrival allows for fledging of last broods to be completed earlier. Departure commences in August and most birds have left by mid or late October, although

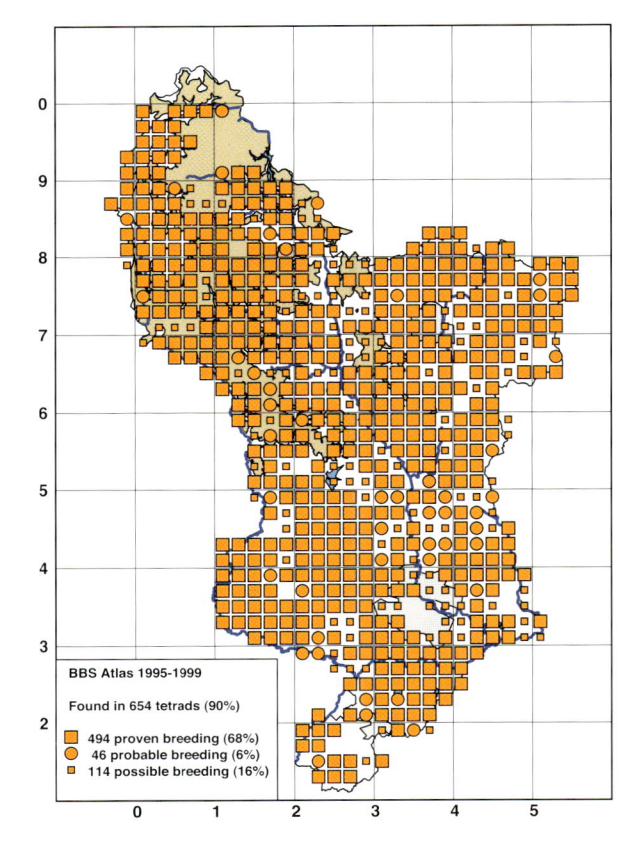

BBS Atlas 1995-1999

Found in 654 tetrads (90%)

- 494 proven breeding (68%)
- 46 probable breeding (6%)
- 114 possible breeding (16%)

November records are not unusual. The average last date in the 34-year period 1978–2011 was 2nd November. There are no fewer than four December records, of which the latest were on 17th December 1967 at Barlborough and 26th December 1968 at Mapperley Reservoir, meaning that January is the only month in which Swallows have not been recorded in Derbyshire.

In April and May, spring feeding flocks often occur over reservoirs and gravel pits. Large flocks of 200–600 have regularly been reported from Ogston Reservoir, with higher counts of 750 on 10th May 1984, 800 on 30th April 1991, 900 on 2nd May 1996, 1000 on 16th April 2009, and 1400 on 19th April 2010, while 726 flew north there in four hours on 11th May 1998. Similarly sized flocks have occurred at other waters, especially Carsington Water where the largest counts have been of 1000 from 2nd to 7th May 1996, 3000 in heavy rain on 3rd May 2001, up to 1100 on 19th April and 1st/2nd May 2003 and up to 600 on 29th–30th April 2004.

Many of the large gatherings between late August and early October are of birds roosting communally, often in reed and reedmace beds. Counts of 5000 have quite frequently been recorded, with higher numbers being 10,000 at Willington Gravel Pits on 27th August 1965, 6000 at Old Whittington in 1977, 10,000 at Williamthorpe on 19th August 1988, 10,000 in reedmace and maize at Carr Vale in the first two weeks of September in 1994, and 10,000 at Nadin's, Newhall on 19th–20th August 2000 and 6th September 2001. Swallows are occasionally recorded roosting in quite dry situations, such as fields of maize and energy willows. More unusual was a roost of 1500 in bracken and heather at Tansley Moor on 15th September 1967, and 250 in bracken at Greaves's Piece on 28th July 1994.

Visual migration is recorded between late August and October and sometimes involves hundreds of birds an hour. Four-figure counts have included 1138 to the south-west at Ramsley on 13th September 1992; 6100 moving west (including 5500 in 40 minutes) at Strines Top on 20th September 1994, and 2700 to the south-west at the same locality on 13th September 1995; 2000 to the south-west at Willington Gravel Pits on 15th September 1999; 1600 to the south in the Goyt Valley on 5th September 2004; 1585 moving south at Carr Vale on 10th October 2007 and 1370 south in 3.5 hours at the same location on 16th September 2011; 3000 south in two hours on 14th September 2008 at Errwood Reservoir; and 2000 south-west in seven hours at East Moor on 2nd September 2009.

Albino and white birds have been recorded in 1972, 1978, 1981, 1982, 1993 and 2010, while a bird at Rowlee Bridge in June 2000 had a white (rather than red) bib and one at Ramsley in September 2006 had white primaries. One in 1922 was described as being almost as bright as a male Yellow Wagtail. In September 1985, a Swallow x House Martin hybrid (with head and wings as in Swallow and belly, rump and tail as in House Martin) was at Ogston Reservoir, and a juvenile Swallow x House Martin hybrid was caught and ringed at Carr Vale on 7th July 2009.

Swallows are ringed in large numbers every year and 41% of the 282 birds in the county recovery reports had been ringed as nestlings, of which about two-thirds were reported within three months of ringing. The remaining one-third which are encountered after their first year are generally found dead. Overall, however, 59% of all age-group reports were of birds trapped and released by other ringers, which corresponds to the proportion nationally (Wernham *et al.* 2002).

It is well established that Swallows winter in the Pretoria area of South Africa and there are six Derbyshire recoveries from that region. One was a juvenile ringed at Williamthorpe in 1995 that was found dead in Cape Province, South Africa in February 1996, a movement of 9709km in 177 days. There is a single report from Guinea Bissau, which is somewhat west of a direct route to South Africa, and other African recoveries have been from Morocco in April and May. European recoveries have been from France and Spain in October and November. A Spanish-ringed bird was trapped at Nadin's, Newhall on 17th September 2006.

As with the young birds of many species, the juvenile dispersal sometimes takes them well away from the route to their wintering area. There are a number of recoveries from other parts of Britain, including several examples of young birds recovered in adjacent counties to the north of their natal area. Two records from much further north, in Norway and Sweden, were of birds in their second and third summers that had been ringed in Derbyshire as juveniles. These were undoubtedly birds passing through Britain from more northerly breeding areas and which had come through Derbyshire on first autumn migration.

The longevity record concerns a bird hatched in 1980, which was caught at roost at Poolsbrook and found dead in the Dumfries region seven years later. This was presumably another example of a bird which had passed through the county on its first autumn passage.

House Martin
Delichon urbicum
A common summer visitor and passage migrant.

House Martins are common in Derbyshire today, as in the time of Whitlock and Jourdain, though they were regarded as more local than Swallows, which still remains the case. Whitlock believed that they were most numerous in the 'rocky dales of the Peak.' They are, however, more likely than Swallows to be found in urban and suburban breeding situations, perhaps because they may be able to feed at higher altitudes.

House Martins are widely distributed throughout the county, as shown by the Derbyshire BBS (1995–99), when breeding was confirmed in 402 tetrads and was probable or possible in a further 151. Comparable figures for the Swallow suggest that the latter is approximately 20% more widespread. In 2007, BBS data showed that 27.4% of surveyed squares in Derbyshire were occupied where the previous ten-year mean was 29.5%.

House Martins breed on a variety of structures, most often under the eaves of houses and farm buildings, but they also nest under bridges and on reservoir dam towers. An unusual internal nest site recorded by Jourdain was among the beams of the rafters in a shed near Mapleton. A number breed on natural cliffs and quarry faces in the Carboniferous Limestone area of the county, especially, according to Frost, in the Wye Valley and around Stony Middleton. In 1975 an incomplete survey of rock-nesting birds revealed 159 pairs. Counts of cliff-nesters at Shiningbank Quarry near Youlgreave were of 72 in 1981, 53 in 1982, 70 in 1986 and 54 in 1987. At Middleton Dale there were 75 in 1981 and Stony Middleton held 100 in 1993. There has been rather little information on rock-nesting birds in recent years, but the areas mentioned still support them, as do other quarries south to Ballidon and west to Tunstead. There are no confirmed breeding records of this species in quarries away from the Carboniferous Limestone area. It is suspected that far more

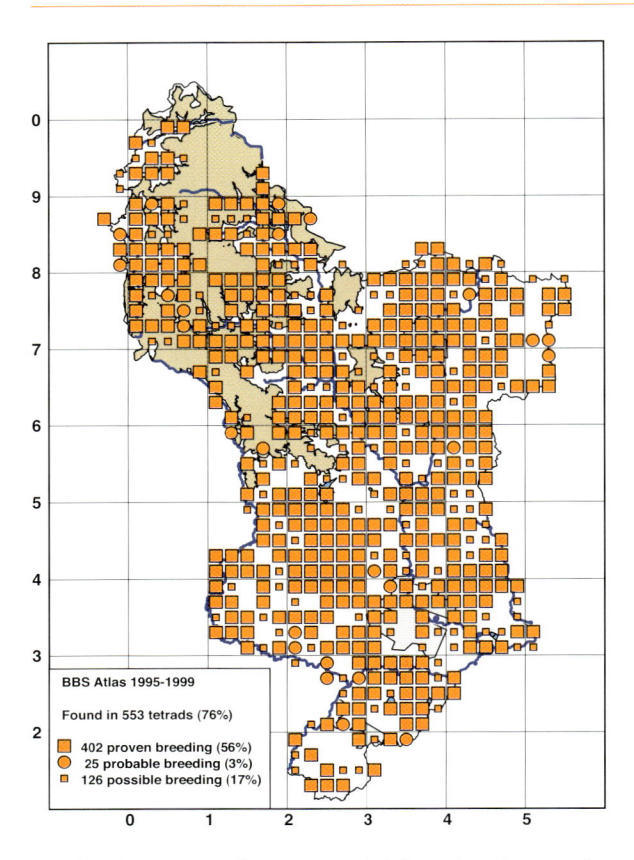

BBS Atlas 1995–1999
Found in 553 tetrads (76%)
- 402 proven breeding (56%)
- 25 probable breeding (3%)
- 126 possible breeding (17%)

now breed in quarries than on natural cliffs, perhaps because the latter suffer a higher level of disturbance.

There have been a few published studies of local House Martin populations, the earliest being Cain-Black (1975), which announced preliminary results of a 1968–69 Derbyshire survey of the species. One of the findings was that over 60% of nests were within 400m of the nearest permanent water supply and, as in Whitlock's day, many were taken over by House Sparrows. With the latter species much reduced in numbers over 40 years on, it is not known whether this situation is still as prevalent. A survey of breeding House Martins in the Dronfield area during the ten-year period up to 1978 showed a fivefold increase in nest numbers coincident with a large increase in housing development. Most of the new breeding locations held but a single pair's nest, but the expansion was achieved despite considerable householder destruction of their nests (Mawson 1979). It is by no means unusual for this species to nest on houses under construction, and muddy building sites can provide ready supplies of nest material.

Smith and Vilkaitis (2000) reported on a survey in the recording area of the Sorby Natural History Society, which includes a large part of northern Derbyshire. The authors reached no firm conclusions about overall population trends but useful details of breeding numbers were given for 30 small towns and villages, stretching from Peak Forest and Hartington in the west to Shirebrook in the east, of which 18 are in Derbyshire. No House Martins were found in three settlements (Taddington, Ford and Two Dales) but the remaining 15 held a total of 242 nests, built on 113 properties.

Monitoring of an established colony in Derby between 1991 and 1999 showed that numbers of nests fluctuated from ten in the initial year to a peak of 38 in 1996, falling to 23 in 1999. At Carsington Water a new colony began with six nests in 1996 and rose to 31 by 2007. A particularly large colony was of 50 nests at Kedleston Hall in 2000. Breeding very frequently extends into September and it is not uncommon for young to be in the nest as late as the latter half of October. The very latest recorded date for this species in the county was of a pair which remained until the extremely late date of 27th November (1836) to rear a brood in Derby.

Most birds arrive from mid-April onwards and well into May. There are a number of March records with the earliest on 15th March 2006, when three were at Netherthorpe. Evidence from the early 1970s suggests that arrival is becoming earlier. The mean earliest arrival dates are: 1970s, 13th April; 1980s, 6th April; 1990s, 30th March; and 2000s, 15th March. The average date for 1978–2011 was 1st April. Like the other hirundines, there is no suggestion that the average length of stay has increased by any more than two to three days. The average departure date in 1978–2011 was 24th October. The latest modern record was on 23rd November 1997 at Drakelow Nature Reserve.

Between April and early June, the largest numbers are mostly recorded from reservoirs and gravel pits, often in bad weather. However, there has been a tendency during the 2000s for flocks to be generally smaller, with the threshold for inclusion in the *Derbyshire Bird Report* being reduced from over 100 to over 50. Large gatherings have been reported from Ogston Reservoir in many years, with 500 counted on 21st May 1994, 2nd May 1996, 17th and 30th May 2006, and 28th May 2007. Elsewhere there are a number of records of flocks of up to 300, and larger gatherings of 600 at Dronfield Sewage Farm on 31st May 1980 and 9th May 1981, 350 at Rother Valley Country Park (now in South Yorkshire) on 7th June 1991, at least 500 at Carsington Water on 20th May 1994 and 400 on 20th June 1997, and 500 at Long Eaton Gravel Pits on 15th May 2001.

From midsummer into autumn, large counts are often made over favourable feeding habitats, which may include farmland, moorland or even open woodland, as well as water bodies. The highest counts at this time are generally higher than those in spring. Again, Ogston Reservoir features frequently in a list of the highest such counts, which included 1600 on 25th September 1982, 1200 on 2nd September 1988, 2000 on 10th September 1993, and 1000 on 20th–21st August 1998, 22nd August 2003, 21st September 1994, 5th September 2009 and 6th September 2011. Counts of 600 or more have been made at many other sites, including 600 at Sudbury on 11th September 1982, 1000 at Hardwick Park on 16th September 1989 and also 1200 there on 9th September 1995, 700 at Lathkill Dale on 11th September 1994, 1000 at Grindleford on 16th September 1995, 600 at Scarcliffe on 21st August 1999, 600 at Bretby on 1st September 2001, 700 at Carsington Water on 13th September 2001, 1000 between Newton Solney and Willington on 21st September 2004, 700 at Creswell on 1st September 2005, and 1000 at Beeley on 15th September 2008.

Unlike the other hirundines, House Martins are only rarely recorded at communal autumn roosts, but there are a very few observations of roosting in trees, including 200 at Chesterfield on 2nd September 1997. Up to 300 roosted on the roofs and vertical walls of two houses adjacent to Holmebrook Valley Park during late August 2005.

Visible migration is usually recorded between late August and October and may sometimes involve movements of hundreds of birds an hour. Counts of over 600 include: 650, mostly to the south-west, at Hardwick Park on 7th September 1992; 3000 to the west at Strines Top on 20th September 1994, with 1858 to the south or south-west in two hours at the same site on 13th September 1995; 646 to the south at Ogston Reservoir on 26th August 1997, with 667 in the same direction there on 19th September 2007; 900 to the south or south-west at Belph on 14th September 1998; 2000 to the west at Wormhill on 29th September 1999; 788 to the south-west in four hours at Moscar on 23rd September 2000; 2500 moving east (an unusual direction) in three hours at Fairbrook Naze on 29th September 2002; 758 moving south-west at Spitewinter on 9th September 2003; 700 to the south in three hours in the Goyt Valley on 21st September 2003; 4000 south in two hours at Errwood Reservoir on 14th September 2008; and 1500 south-west over East Moor in seven hours on 2nd September 2009.

House Martins are not trapped in such large numbers as Swallows and can usually be ringed only as free-flying birds. The ringing of nestlings in artificial nests is permitted, however, and indeed the earliest county recovery is of a chick ringed in Kirkbridge, Cumbria, in 1951, which was found dead in

Chesterfield three months later. The longevity record is of a bird which was controlled 3.8 years after ringing.

All but one of the 41 recoveries have been from within the UK. The same low proportion of foreign recoveries applies also to the national database (Wernham et al. 2002) and therefore adds little to our understanding of the bird's migratory routes into Africa. The only foreign recovery was of one ringed at Palterton in August 1980 that was found dead two years later, 770km away, in Cher, France. Of the 40 British records, nine are of birds involved in movements to and from places north of Derbyshire, the extremes being from Dronfield to Errol, Perth and Kinross, a distance of 361km over 64 days, and a bird found dead at Rowsley in 1988 which had been ringed 302km away at Portland Bill, Dorset, two years previously. The remainder are in various other directions with a bias to the south-west.

Aberrantly plumaged birds include one with white wings at Poolsbrook in August 1990, and albinos at Cressbrook Dale in August 1995 and Glutton Bridge in August 1999.

Red-rumped Swallow
Cecropis daurica
A very rare vagrant.

Red-rumped Swallows breed widely across southern Europe and Asia and more discontinuously in sub-Saharan Africa, which is where European birds winter. There were 511 UK records by 2005, by which time their consideration by BBRC ceased to be necessary. They are rare visitors to Britain, occurring annually, mainly as overshooting spring migrants, with peak numbers usually occurring between mid-April and early June; but, of the seven that have been seen in Derbyshire, only three occurred in this period. Mann (1987) gave an account of the first of these records.

Year	Location and date
1986	Williamthorpe, one flew south on 15th November
1991	Ogston Reservoir, one from 5th to 8th May
1995	Brinsley Flash, one on 1st July
1996	Carr Vale, one flew north on 12th April
2008	Stanton-in-Peak Sewage Farm, one on 7th September
2010	Ogston Reservoir, one on 29th–30th May
2011	Ogston Reservoir, one flew south-south-west on 7th June

Cetti's Warbler
Cettia cetti
A scarce resident.

Cetti's Warblers are skulking birds that usually betray their presence by their explosive, staccato song. They first arrived in Britain in Hampshire in 1961, following a northwards extension of their range from the Mediterranean region. They subsequently colonized many parts of southern Britain and, following a succession of mild winters, singing males were reported from 23 counties in 2002 (Ogilvie et al. 2004), while by 2009 there were 2347 singing males or territories in 40 counties, with strongholds in Kent, Somerset, Norfolk, Suffolk, Essex, Sussex and Hampshire (Holling et al. 2011).

With small breeding populations in Leicestershire, Warwickshire and Worcestershire, occurrences in Derbyshire were predictable, and there were five records to the end of 2009. Key (2000b) wrote an account of the first record.

Year	Location and date
1999	Drakelow Nature Reserve, one on 26th May
2007	Hallcroft Lake, Hilton, one on 5th–6th May
2009	Derby Sewage Farm, two near the north bank of the River Derwent from 14th April to the year end
2009	Carr Vale, one from 6th November to 6th December
2009	Poolsbrook Marsh, one from 13th November to 14th December, and two on 13th December

In 2010 they were reported at seven sites, and at one of these, Breaston Nature Reserve, breeding was confirmed for the first time in the county.

Year	Location and date
2010	Poolsbrook Marsh, two on 7th February and one on 28th February
2010	Derby Sewage Farm/River Derwent, one on 23rd February, increasing to three on 22nd April and four on 23rd April. Present throughout the summer and autumn, and last reported on 5th November
2010	Breaston Nature Reserve, one on 11th May, increasing to four by 25th May, and two on 15th June. A recently fledged juvenile was ringed during the summer, constituting the first confirmed breeding record
2010	Church Wilne Reservoir water-ski pit, one on 24th–25th May
2010	Long Eaton Gravel Pits, one on 6th, 9th and 19th October
2010	Willington Gravel Pits, one from 14th October to 20th November, and two on 30th November
2010	Carr Vale, one on 24th–25th October, and from 1st to 27th November

Following the first proven breeding in 2010, the species made the first tentative steps towards becoming an established resident within the county during 2011. Small numbers were present almost throughout the year, being reported from early February until the end of December.

Year	Location and date
2011	Willington Gravel Pits, first heard on 20th February and present until 29th December, with a maximum of four on 8th November and three on 2nd and 14th October
2011	Breaston Nature Reserve, two were singing on 8th March to the first week in July, and three were singing on 24th March and 24th April, and in a nearby garden in June
2011	Raynesway, River Derwent, one from 14th to 21st March
2011	Carr Vale, one from 21st August to 31st December
2011	Long Eaton Gravel Pits, one on 3rd–4th October

Long-tailed Tit
Aegithalos caudatus
A fairly common resident.

These delightful, acrobatic birds are certainly more numerous than they were a little over a century ago, when Whitlock said that they were thinly distributed in south and north-east Derbyshire but very scarce in the Peak. Nowhere were they common. Jourdain added that the numbers breeding varied considerably from year to year. Seventy-three years later, Frost said that there was no evidence of any great change since then. Pleasingly, the situation is much better today, almost certainly the result of milder winters as severe winters are known to cause considerable mortality within this species.

Long-tailed Tits occur in woodland, scrub, thickets, parks, hedgerows and gardens and may be found throughout the county except on high moorland. The tetrad map shows that they are widely distributed (being twenty-eighth in an analysis of all breeding species), with confirmed breeding in 346 tetrads and a further 163 tetrads having possible or probable breeding. Clearly, they are more widespread in the Peak District than formerly. This is quite an easy species for which to prove breeding on account of its regular contact calls and confiding nature. Many nests, especially in thorn bushes, are constructed before the leaves are out and so are easily seen.

CBC data from the 1990s showed estimated densities of 20.83 pairs per km^2 at Shirebrook and 6.36 at Shiningcliff Wood. Figures for farmland plots were much lower, as would be expected with 2.76 per km^2 at Culland and 3.36 at Broadhay Farm, near Hathersage.

Eaton et al. (2010) recorded an overall increase of 89% in the period 1990–2008, although the BBS trend, based on 1995–2008, was much lower, at 13%. There is relatively little real information on breeding densities in the county, but at Scarcliffe Woods, Frost (2008a) recorded extremes of two pairs in 1984 and 25 in 2000; there was an overall increase of 65% during this 30-year period. Another regular census area, at Whitwell Wood, held up to 14 pairs in 1994–2009; the maximum there was also in 2000. Of four pairs there in 1995, three were nesting in only 0.5ha of scrub. Seven pairs were found at Williamthorpe Nature Reserve in May 2001.

As soon as the breeding season is over, Long-tailed Tits can be found in groups and small flocks, sometimes with other tits. Typically there may be up to 35 or so, but larger counts have been recorded, even in midsummer, including 60 at Drum Hill on 14th June 1999 and 64 at Carr Vale on 20th June 2004. However, the largest counts are normally made in winter. The highest was of 137 at Scarcliffe Woods on 2nd December 2011, and there have been five more three-figure counts at this site, where it was found to be the fourth most common species overall in winter. Other noteworthy records were of 98 at Ogston Reservoir on 1st January 2003; 80 at Loscoe Dam on 5th February 1979; 75 along the River Derwent at Hathersage on 19th January 1999 and at Sinfin Moor on 16th October 2008; three counts of 71, from Calke on 23rd December 1993, Hardwick Wood on 6th January 2000 and Whitwell Wood on 2nd December 2003. In the Peak District, 67 between Errwood Reservoir and Taxal on 8th February 2003 was a high count.

Wandering birds may be seen almost anywhere in the county, including the moorland edge, especially if birches are present. They are sometimes seen moving across moorland and other stretches of open country. They are also much more frequent nowadays in built-up areas, using garden feeding stations as other tits do.

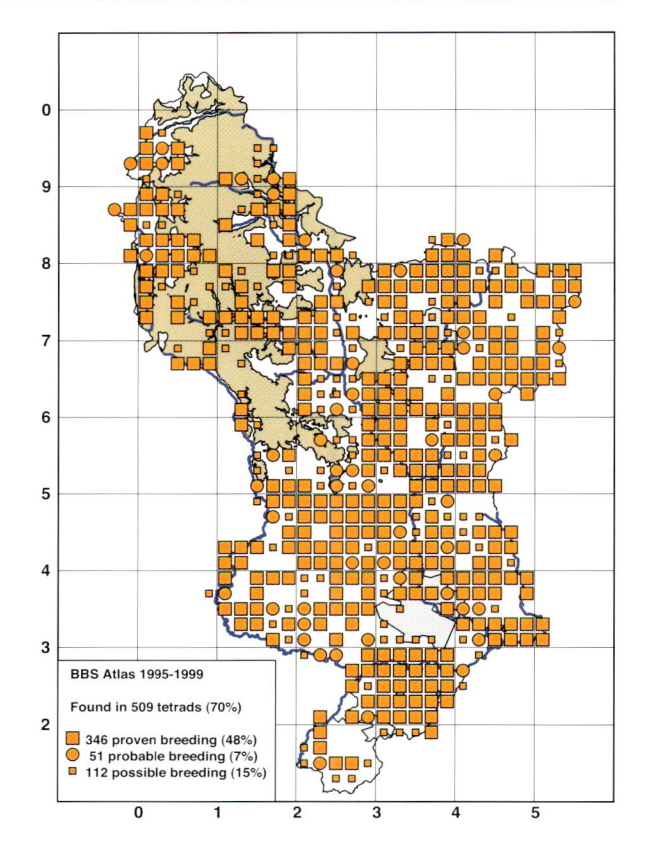

The British race of Long-tailed Tit is sedentary, so it is to be expected that the movements highlighted by ringing recoveries would not involve large distances. There have been no recoveries nationally of foreign-ringed birds found in the UK (Wernham et al. 2002). Nevertheless, there is a Derbyshire record of one ringed at Renishaw Park in October 1995 which moved 90km to Hallaton, Leicestershire, where it was controlled in September 1997. Another moved 78km from Coventry, where it was ringed in November 1973, to Alfreton, where it was found dead in January 1977. A Warwickshire bird, ringed at Whitacre Heath in June 1999 was controlled at Drakelow Nature Reserve in the following March, and one ringed at Retford, Nottinghamshire in August 1999, died at Old Tupton, 33km away, five months later. By contrast, of the county recoveries, 16 (75%) were later found within 10km of their ringing location.

Pallas's Warbler
Phylloscopus proregulus
A very rare vagrant.

Pallas's Warblers breed in Asia and winter in southern China, India and Indochina (*BWP*). They are scarce but annual visitors to England, occurring mainly between late September and mid-November. Most records are from eastern coastal counties and Scilly (Brown & Grice 2005). They were removed from the BBRC list after 1990.

The only Derbyshire record was of one that was ringed after being found in a mist net straddling the stream at Bondhay Common on 30th October 1999. The stream forms the county boundary between Derbyshire and South Yorkshire (Rotherham). It remained in this small, sheltered valley until 1st November, and was usually seen associating with a flock of Long-tailed Tits. An account was given by Fell (2000).

Yellow-browed Warbler
Phylloscopus inornatus
A very rare vagrant.

Yellow-browed Warblers are the most common of the Siberian vagrants to be found in Britain, with most occurring from mid-September to October, although a few late autumn birds have subsequently overwintered. Most sightings have come from the east and south coasts. Numbers seen in the country vary greatly each year, although there has been a sharp increase in annual occurrences since 1984. They breed from the Urals eastwards across Siberia, and winter in southern Asia.

There have been ten Derbyshire records, all of which occurred during the peak period for autumn arrivals of this species. Cross (1989) gave an account of the 1988 record.

Year	Location and date
1988	Breadsall Cutting, one from 4th to 6th October
1993	Ramsley Moor, one caught during the evening of 2nd October and released on the following morning
1999	Carr Vale, one from 19th to 27th October
2005	Etwall, one from 17th to 19th October
2006	Ashover Fabric, one heard calling on 29th September
2006	Carr Vale, one on 29th October
2006	Greaves's Piece, one heard calling on 30th October
2008	Ambaston, one on 28th–29th September
2008	Woodthorpe Hall, Holmesfield, one on 12th October
2008	Wirksworth, one in a garden on 30th October

Western Bonelli's Warbler
Phylloscopus bonelli
A very rare vagrant.

This species breeds in north-west Africa and in western and central Europe east to Austria (*BWP*). It winters in the African Sahel region. By the end of 2011 there were 105 accepted records of this species, and a further 96 that were either this or Eastern Bonelli's Warblers *Phylloscopus orientalis* (Hudson *et al*. 2012).

A male, which initially attracted attention by its song, was found on 2nd July 2011 at Arnfield Reservoir, where it remained until 28th July (Greenall 2012). This is believed to be the longest UK stay by this species. It frequented areas of willow, birch and other scrub by an inlet, often in the company of other small birds.

Wood Warbler
Phylloscopus sibilatrix
An uncommon summer visitor, mainly to the northern half of the county.

Wood Warblers have much more specialized habitat requirements than Derbyshire's other two breeding *Phylloscopus* warblers. They prefer woods with a closed canopy, little secondary growth and sparse ground cover. All layers of the wood are exploited, with birds nesting on the ground, feeding from the canopy and using lower branches as posts, from which they deliver their delightful trilling song.

There has been little change in the distribution pattern over the last 40 years. The tetrad map shows them to be present in 17 10km squares, compared with 16 in the 1968–72 Atlas and 20 in the 1988–91 Atlas, but the Derbyshire BBS (1995–99) indicates a slight contraction in range away from the south of the county, where the species has been decidedly local in recent years. This was not always the case, since Whitlock considered it fairly well distributed throughout the county, while Jourdain said that it was probably most common in the north, but numerous in some southern districts. They were recorded as present in 81 tetrads in the Derbyshire BBS (1995–99), with breeding proved in only 13 of these. Probable breeding, judged mainly by birds singing in likely breeding habitat, was recorded in a further 53 tetrads. The overall picture for the period 1995–99 is as shown on the tetrad map.

Most records of proven breeding resulted arose from adults sighted carrying food to their well-hidden nests. The fledged young seem to spend their time in the upper canopy and are not easy to see.

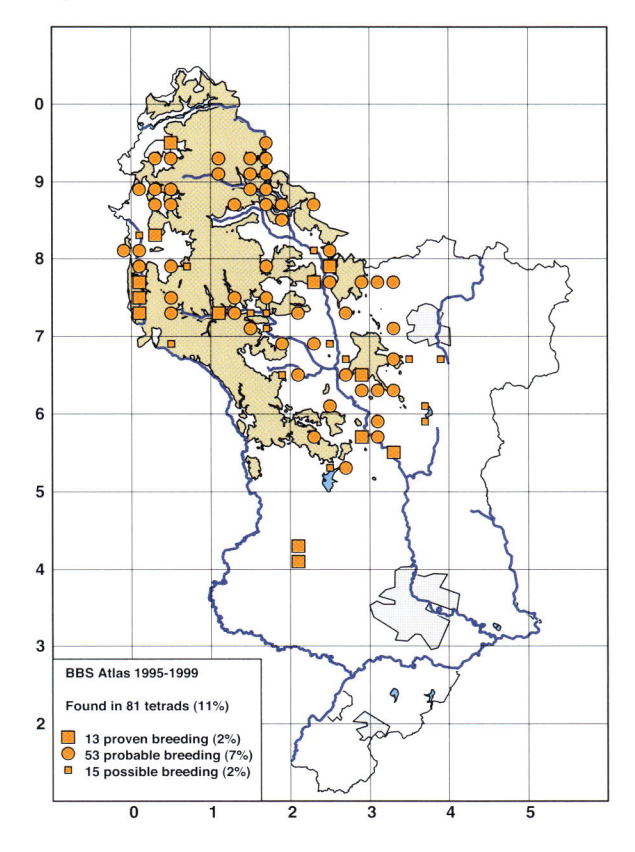

BBS Atlas 1995-1999
Found in 81 tetrads (11%)
- 13 proven breeding (2%)
- 53 probable breeding (7%)
- 15 possible breeding (2%)

The 'hanging' woods of the Peak District, in particular those on Millstone Grit, remain particularly favoured by this species, though a small population is also present in the lightly wooded dales of the Carboniferous Limestone area. They are usually found in deciduous woods, mainly of oak and beech, although recently they have also been recorded regularly in coniferous woodland.

Although numbers vary annually in the county, there was generally an increase in the numbers of singing Wood Warblers recorded in the period from 1980 to 1994. However, there was a marked decline in 1995, when compared with the previous year, with a 40% reduction in both the number of singing males and of sites holding birds. Although there was a nominal recovery subsequently, numbers overall have since continued to decline. This is consistent with the national trend, where the BBS has shown a rapid and significant decline since 1994 (Baillie *et al*. 2007).

The maps for 1995–99 and 2007–11 show a contraction of range between the two periods.

The table indicates sites and numbers of singing males from 1981–2011.

Informal data from two of the most favoured woods reflects these variations and the general decline in numbers. At Manners Wood, Bakewell there was an average of eight singing birds in 1981–93 (with a maximum of 11 in 1981), just two in 1995 and an average of four in 1996–99. Numbers reduced further, to two in 2002, while in 2007, for the first time ever, none were heard, nor in 2008–11. At Padley Gorge, there was an average of six singing birds in 1984–89, three in 1990–99 and two or three in 2000–09, the latter period including one year, 2005, when none were found; but a recovery to four in 2010 and 2011.

In the north-west, the Goyt Valley has long been the most favoured site. Here, the population has also varied widely. There were two singing males in 1980, with numbers rising to a maximum of nine in 1985–87, falling to four in 1992–97 and increasing to eight in 1998 and nine in 2003, with up to eight in subsequent years. Eaton *et al*. (2010) recorded a decline of 61% in numbers recorded by the BTO's Breeding Bird Survey between 1995 and 2008.

The largest spring concentration in the period 1980–99 was of 16 singing males between Black Rocks and High Peak Junction (a distance of 2.5km), on 6th May 1994; such a high number almost

Summer	Sites	Singing males	Largest site count/location
1981	12	27	11 – Manners Wood
1982	15	33	6 – Manners Wood, Shiningcliff Wood and Goyt Valley
1983	19	46	10 – Manners Wood
1984	17	61	7 – Manners Wood
1985	20	about 40	9 – Goyt Valley
1986	21	36	7 – Manners Wood
1987	25	43	9 – Goyt Valley–Taxal area
1988	27	69	9 – Manners Wood
1989	29	74	9 – Manners Wood
1990	20	32 min	6 – Manners Wood
1991	18	40	8 – Goyt Valley
1992	25	50	8 – Manners Wood
1993	24	48	9 – Manners Wood
1994	32	65*	16 – Black Rocks to High Peak Junction
1995	19	41	5 – Ladybower Reservoir
1996	23	34	5 – Manners Wood
1997	21	49	4 – Padley Gorge, Goyt Valley and Black Rock
1998	24	64	9 – Mag Clough
1999	24	45	11 – Upper Derwentdale
2000	31	61	7 – Hall Dale Wood
2001	19	45	10 – Upper Derwentdale
2002	20	75 *	33 – Ladybower South Woods
2003	22	62 *	18 – Ladybower South Woods
2004	21	57	8 – Goyt Valley
2005	25	43	5 – Goyt Valley
2006	14	23	4 – Hall Dale Wood
2007	20	30	5 – Win Hill
2008	19	35	8 – Win Hill
2009	29	54	7 – Derwentdale and Ladybower Wood
2010	25	44	4 – Padley Gorge and Goyt Valley
2011	19	29	4 – Padley Gorge and Mag Clough

* Totals which include exceptional counts

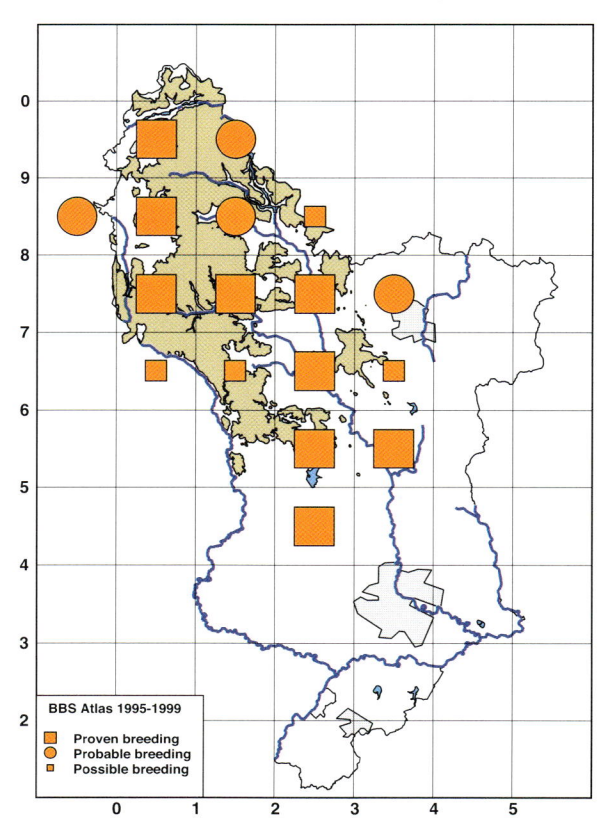

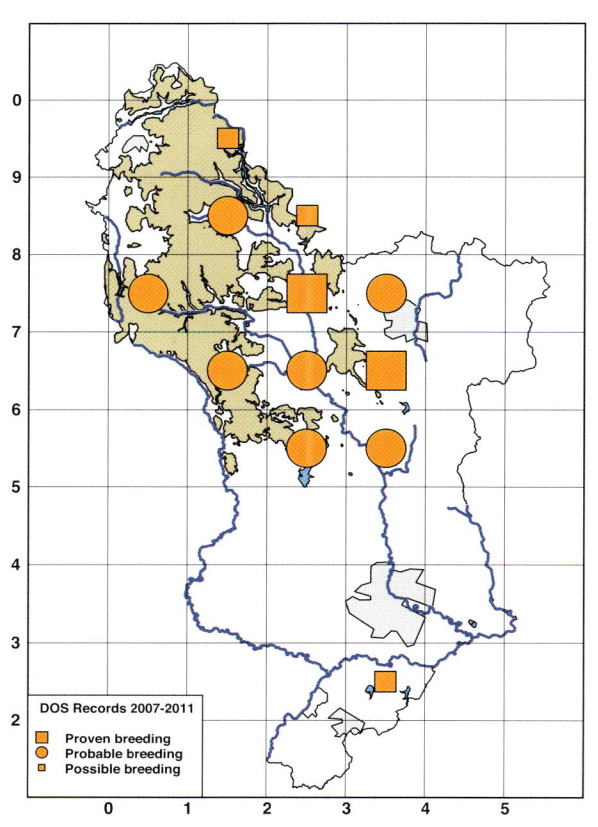

certainly contained many passage birds. Recent records from Upper Derwentdale suggest that this extensive area is their current stronghold. There was a large count of 11 singing males there, between Fairholmes and King's Tree, on 13th May 1999. However, this was exceeded in 2002 at Ladybower South Woods and Win Hill, when 33 singing males were present on 19th May in a parcel of 250ha of mixed, but predominantly coniferous, woodland. On 10th May of the following year, there were 18 singing males in the same area, but such large numbers have not been reported from the area subsequently. Both of these extraordinary counts presumably contained some passage birds. Wood Warblers have previously been found breeding in coniferous woodland, at sites such as Linacre and Matlock Forest.

Away from the Peak District, and particularly in the south of the county, recent breeding records have been extremely scarce and rather erratic. This is likely to remain so given that this species breeds most successfully when in the close proximity of other pairs (Herremans 1993). Also, most lowland deciduous woods have a shrub layer which is too dense for breeding. However, in 1984, a pair bred successfully and raised six young in Carr Wood, and during the Derbyshire BBS (1995–99) breeding was proved in the woods at Osmaston Park. Unfortunately, there have not been any subsequent breeding records away from traditional northern areas.

Numbers of breeding pairs of Wood Warblers are difficult to assess as a proportion of singing males remains unmated, while some paired males will continue singing after pairing, in an attempt to attract a second female, which can result in polygyny (Herremans 1993).

Wood Warblers usually begin to arrive in the county during late April, although many do not arrive until May, with the first dates for the period 1978–2011 ranging from 5th April to 8th May; the April record, of one at Taxal in 1995 constituting the earliest ever county record. The mean first date during 1978–2007 was 21st April. Spring passage birds away from breeding sites are very scarce, averaging fewer than two per year and the majority of these have been found in the south of the county. Most are present for a single day but often sing continuously, as if territorial, before moving on, although in 2003 a passage bird sang at Carsington Water from 21st to 27th April.

Few Wood Warblers are seen once the males cease singing. Therefore, they are rarely observed after July, either on their breeding grounds or on passage. Three passage birds seen at Drakelow Nature Reserve between 8th August and 12th September 1992 were therefore noteworthy.

In the period 1978–2011, the latest sightings were between 16th June and 12th September, with a mean last date during 1978–2011 of 27th July. The latest ever record was of one at Ogston Reservoir on 16th September 1966.

The only ringing recovery concerns one, ringed as a pullus at Dore in July 1962 that was recovered in August 1964 at Mosorrofa, Italy.

Chiffchaff
Phylloscopus collybita
A fairly common summer visitor and a scarce winter visitor.

Chiffchaffs occur throughout much of Derbyshire, where they are found mainly in deciduous and mixed woodland with not too dense a canopy and with well-developed undergrowth, which they require for feeding and nesting. They are particularly fond of areas containing rhododendrons.

The tetrad map shows that, although they are distributed throughout much of the county (being the thirty-fourth most widespread species), their main concentrations are in the lowlands in the east and south. They are absent from the upland areas in the north-west, from much of the Carboniferous Limestone plateau of the White Peak, from open farmland and most suburban areas, as these all lack suitable breeding habitat. The Derbyshire BBS (1995–99) found confirmed breeding in 133 tetrads, probable breeding, based largely on hearing the distinctive song, in 314 and possible breeding in 38 tetrads. The combined total of 485 tetrads is 156 fewer than that of the Willow Warbler.

There has been little change in range over the last 40 years: in the 1968–72 Atlas it was present in every 10km square and in the 1988–91 Atlas it was absent from just one. Chiffchaffs are clearly much more numerous in the county now than they were about a century ago. Whitlock described them as 'fairly diffused over the whole county'. It was said to be missing from the Bakewell area and was mainly an autumn migrant in the Trent Valley. Jourdain described Chiffchaffs as rather local.

Numbers present each year can be extremely variable, with mortality in their wintering quarters almost certainly responsible for these fluctuations. In recent times, Chiffchaff numbers in Derbyshire were at their lowest in the mid-1980s and again in the early 1990s, since when there has been a marked recovery. The largest breeding concentrations of this species are regularly found at Scarcliffe Woods, where informal census data reflects this trend. In the 1980s there were between five and 18 territories, while in the 1990s there were from eight to 31. This latter count was surpassed in 2004 and again in 2008, when 56 singing males were counted. Nearby at Whitwell Wood, there were just five territories in 1993, rising to a maximum of 31 in 2003, but falling to nine in 2009 and recovering to 21 in 2011. Another large recent breeding season count was at Ogston Reservoir, where 51 singing males were present on 22nd May 2004. The combined count for Carsington Water in 2002–07 was of 79 territories.

In the north-west, where the species is rather local, the Goyt Valley held four territories in 1992 and a maximum of ten in 1998, compared with a regular five to seven pairs at the time of the previous avifauna in 1978. CBC plots in mixed lowland woodland tell a similar story: Shiningcliff had just one pair in 1991, increasing to a maximum of four in 1993 and 1995, while at Shirebrook there was just one pair for most of the mid-1980s, rising to five in 1990. In these two survey areas Chiffchaff was the twelfth and eleventh most common species, but they were

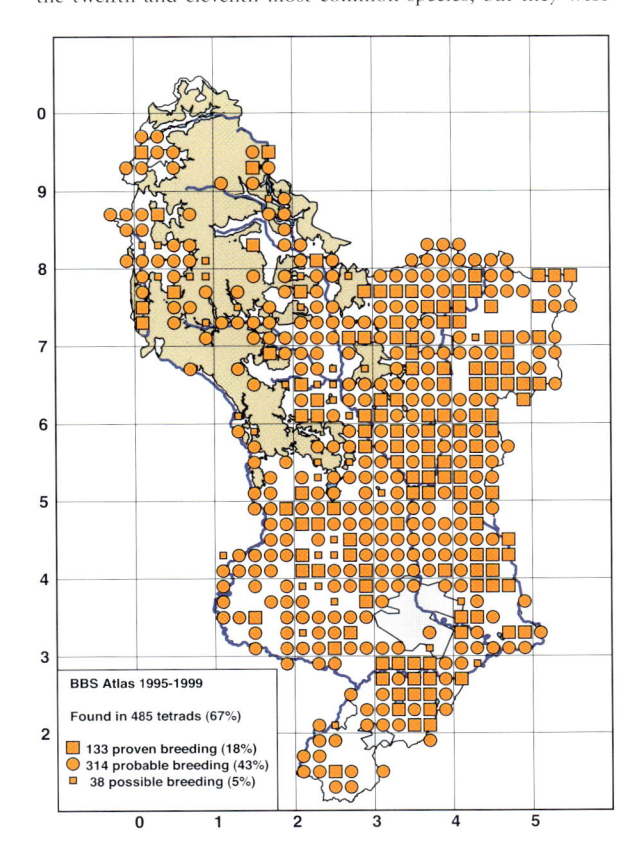

BBS Atlas 1995-1999
Found in 485 tetrads (67%)
■ 133 proven breeding (18%)
● 314 probable breeding (43%)
▪ 38 possible breeding (5%)

absent, however, from both upland and lowland farm CBC plots. They are outnumbered by Willow Warblers at most locations where the two species occur alongside one another. This situation, however, is reversed in mature oak woods in the south of the county such as Calke Park and South Wood, where they are more common than Willow Warblers by an average of nearly four to one. Eaton *et al.* (2010) recorded a national increase of 41% in the period 1970 to 2008; during the same period Willow Warblers declined by the same amount, 41%.

Chiffchaffs are among the earliest summer migrants to Derbyshire, with their appearance in spring greatly influenced by weather conditions. Because of the presence of wintering birds it is sometimes difficult to ascertain when the first spring migrants arrive, but this is usually in mid-March, with spring passage continuing throughout April and some late birds not arriving on territory until early May. Records from Drakelow Nature Reserve, a site where Chiffchaffs have only recently started to breed, reflect this long period as singing birds are often recorded on passage between mid-March and mid-May.

The earliest spring arrival for this species was on 1st March (1972) at Little Eaton, although this may have been a wintering bird, and there have been several records of presumed migrants from the first week of March. The first dates of presumed migrants for the period 1978–2011 ranged from 4th March to 31st March, with a mean first date of 12th March.

Return passage commences in July and continues into October, with some birds remaining almost to the month's end. Passage numbers are usually smaller than those recorded for Willow Warbler and concentrations of more than ten birds are scarce. The largest autumn counts in the period 1980–99 were of 16 at Drakelow Nature Reserve on 17th September 1998 and 14 at Carr Vale on 31st August 1998. There was a particularly large passage in 2002, when several sites throughout the county had counts in excess of 15 birds. The largest numbers were at Williamthorpe Nature Reserve, where at least 50 (including 32 trapped and ringed) were seen on 28th July and at Carr Vale, where 45 were in hawthorn scrub on 28th August. This was repeated in 2003, when large counts included 26 at Ashover on 26th August and an exceptional 105 at Ogston Reservoir on 10th September; the latter count is by far the largest autumn count made in Derbyshire. At Carr Vale, 41 juveniles were trapped and ringed on 25th July 2009.

Some autumn passage birds may be of the race *P.c. abietinus* (from Scandinavia and north-eastern Europe), including one at Drakelow Nature Reserve, on 4th December 1990, and two calling and singing by the River Dove at Scropton from 17th to 23rd September 1996.

The combination of lingering autumn birds and possibly milder winters has led to the species becoming a regular winter visitor to the county. The first such record was as long ago as 5th February 1836, with others on another occasion on 25th February (Whitlock). There were no more wintering records in the next 107 years, until one was seen at Ashbourne on 7th December 1944. Although the next winter record was not until 1969, they have been recorded wintering in the county in every winter since 1979/80, with numbers varying quite dramatically, but with a steadily increasing trend as indicated in the table.

Winter	Birds	Winter	Birds
1979/80	4	1995/96	12
1980/81	5	1996/97	8
1981/82	1	1997/98	6
1982/83	7	1998/99	21
1983/84	5	1999/2000	18
1984/85	11	2000/01	28
1985/86	2	2001/02	24
1986/87	8	2002/03	19
1987/88	1	2003/04	11
1988/89	9	2004/05	25
1989/90	7	2005/06	25
1990/91	6	2006/07	34
1991/92	4	2007/08	29
1992/93	14	2008/09	14
1993/94	4	2009/10	31
1994/95	14	2010/11	1

The presence of just one bird in the 2010/11 winter was almost certainly the result of very cold weather, with heavy snowfall, in December. A full account of Chiffchaffs wintering in the county was given by Staley (2009), and most of the following information derives from his paper. By the end of the 2010/11 winter, there had been a minimum of 404 sightings. Many of the earlier winter records were from Dronfield Sewage Works, but the most regular wintering sites are Carr Vale, where 58 have been seen, Drakelow Nature Reserve, where there have been 33, and Willington Gravel Pits with 35. Nearly all of the winter records have come from the east or south of the county. The map shows the localities of all winter records between 1836 and 2011.

Most winter records are of single birds, present for one or two days, although there have been several occasions where small numbers have been seen together. The largest such concentration was at Avenue Washlands Nature Reserve, where six were ringed on 13th November 2011. At Carsington Water, five were present on 9th November 2002 and four were there on 23rd February 2007. Four were also at Chaddesden Sidings Gravel Pits on 10th December 2000. At Elvaston Castle Country Park, a Chiffchaff controlled in December 1988 had been ringed at that locality the previous May, suggesting that some of our wintering birds remain faithful to the same location throughout the year.

Their monthly distribution indicates that most are seen in November and December, suggesting that Chiffchaffs find it difficult to sustain themselves on their wholly insectivorous diet through the hardest part of the winter and that they therefore either die or move on during the coldest weather. The majority are seen at aquatic habitats such as gravel pits, sewage farms and reservoirs, and there have been 14 records from suburban gardens. The monthly distribution is shown in the table.

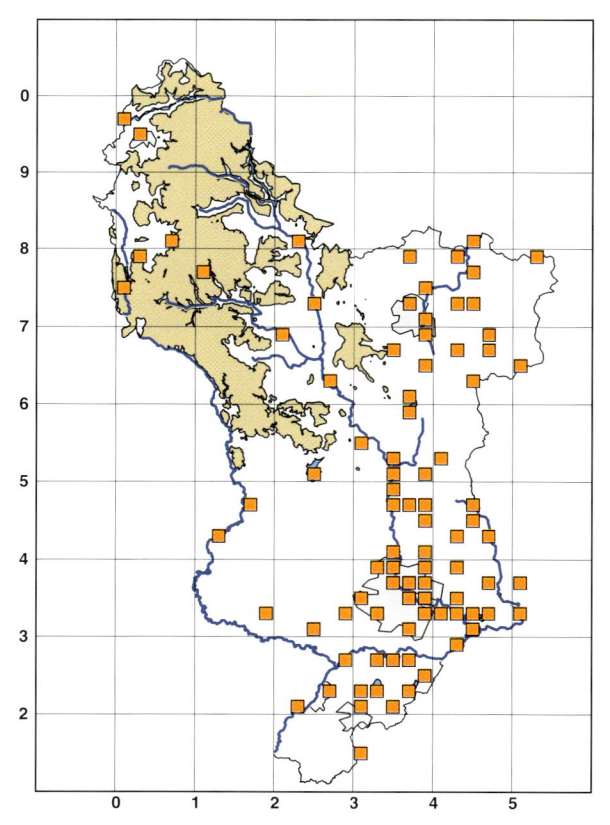

Chiffchaff winter records between 1836 and 2011.

Month	Percentage of records
November	34
December	33
January	19
February	14

In addition to birds of the nominate race *P.c. collybita*, which breeds in the British Isles and much of central, southern and western Europe, there have been nine accepted records of birds showing characteristics of the race *P.c. tristis*, from Siberia, as shown in the table:

Year	Location and date
1997	Carr Vale, one between 23rd November and 8th April 1998
1998	Carr Vale, one between 29th November and 4th December
2000	Carr Vale, one between 1st and 17th December
2000	Carr Vale, one between 28th December and 1st January 2001
2001	Poolsbrook Country Park, two between 31st December and 10th March 2002
2002	Carr Vale, one between 24th December and 24th February 2003
2003	Carr Vale, one in song between 15th and 20th March
2008	Aston-on-Trent Gravel Pits, one between 7th and 14th December
2008	Old Whittington Sewage Works, one between 26th and 27th December

Beevers (1998b) documented the 1997 occurrence. There have also been two unsubstantiated records of *tristis*-type birds, at Melbourne on 24th December 1993 and at Shardlow Sewage Farm, where there were two on 17th January and 11th February 1994.

At Drakelow Nature Reserve, from 12th to 25th May 1995, a Chiffchaff was present which sang the typical songs of both the nominate race *P.c. collybita* and the Iberian Chiffchaff *P.c. brehmii* (now *P. ibericus*) from south-west France and Iberia, and a mixture of both (Cockburn 1996b). Some birds from the overlap zone between the two races give a mixed song which is generally closer to *ibericus*, but with much variation.

The ringing data show 14 recoveries involving Derbyshire, of which 11 were controlled. The longest distance concerns one ringed at Coal Aston in July 1992 that was controlled 4300km south-south-west at Djoudj, Senegal, five months later. Another, ringed at Derby in July 1985, also travelled south-south-west to Safi, Morocco, 2396km away where it was found dead in December 1985. One travelled from Barbrook, where it was ringed in July 1999, to be controlled at Sint-Laureins, Belgium, two months later, and a particularly intriguing record concerned one ringed at Elvaston Castle Country Park in May 1988, that was found in Telemark, Norway, 11 months later. Other recoveries were of birds ringed in late autumn in Kent, Surrey and East Yorkshire which were found at Ogston Reservoir, Elvaston Castle Country Park and Codnor respectively in the following spring.

Willow Warbler
Phylloscopus trochilus
A common summer visitor.

Willow Warblers have less precise habitat requirements than other *Phylloscopus* warblers and may therefore nest in almost any location where there are small trees and bushes. They occur in many habitats, including gravel pits, hedgerows, large gardens, moorland cloughs, farmland, young conifer plantations, scrub, and woodland, where they prefer areas with an open canopy.

Whitlock said that Willow Warblers were among the most numerous spring visitors, being common everywhere and present in a wide variety of habitats; they could be found breeding 'wherever a tree or shrub breaks the monotony of the moorlands'. Frost said that they were the most common of all the summer visitors to Derbyshire. This is probably still the case overall, although it is no longer numerically dominant in many woods where it once was but, bearing in mind the extent of birch woodland (a favoured habitat), especially in upland areas, it probably still retains first overall position in the county.

The tetrad map shows that they are distributed throughout the county with the only significant absences being from the moorland in the north-west and some of the more heavily urbanized areas. They were found in 641 tetrads (making it the eleventh most widespread species) of which 335 had proven breeding and 306 either probable or possible breeding.

There is no evidence of a recent change of range since the 1968–72 and 1988–91 Atlases found them to be present in every 10km square. In the late 1980s and early 1990s, however, there was a decline in numbers of breeding birds in the county, this being particularly noticeable in the south and north-east. This mirrors a similar decline noted in southern Britain, with a high degree of mortality among adult birds thought to be the reason. A further theory suggests that summer migrants fill territorial voids left vacant when numbers of resident species decline following harsh winters. Therefore Willow Warbler numbers may be reducing due to increased densities of resident birds brought about by the recent trend of warmer winters, thus reducing territories available to arriving summer migrants (Marchant *et al*. 1990). Maturation of woodland may also have contributed to their demise.

Birds reach their greatest densities in scrub and deciduous woodland. At Scarcliffe Woods, the number of territories fell from a maximum of 168 in 1976 and 1978, to a low of 45 in 1993, followed by a partial recovery to 80 in 1996, before declining to a minimum in 2008 of 24, an 86% reduction in a 30-year period. Frost (2008a) commented that it would have been unthinkable in 1976, when there were 161 more Willow Warbler territories than those of Chiffchaff, to imagine the latter would be the more numerous 30 years later. On the nearby Shirebrook CBC plot, where it was the most abundant species, there was a maximum of 26 territories in 1987 and 1989, reducing to only 14 indicated by an informal census in 1999. On the 42ha Shire Hill Wood

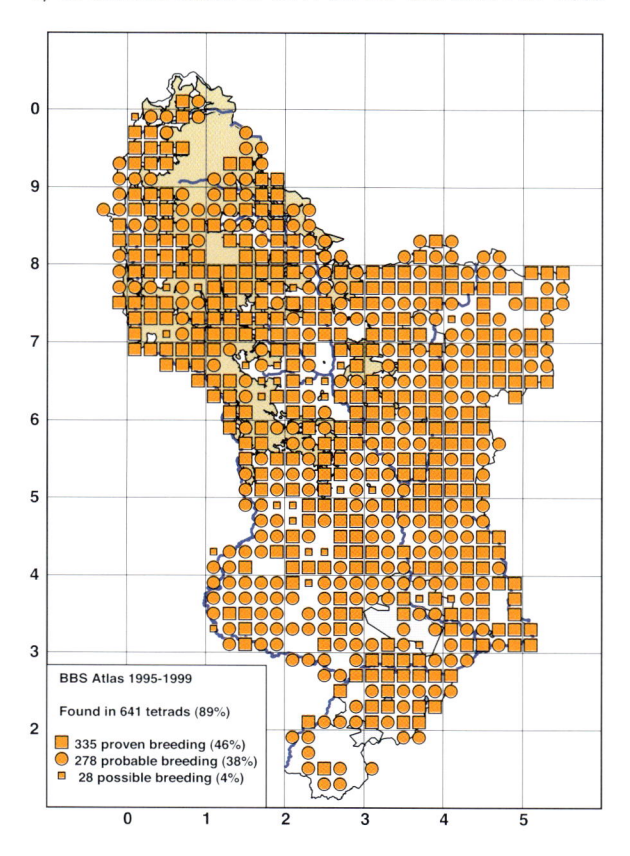

BBS Atlas 1995-1999
Found in 641 tetrads (89%)
- 335 proven breeding (46%)
- 278 probable breeding (38%)
- 28 possible breeding (4%)

CBC plot, which is largely broad-leaved woodland, it was the most numerous species in 1994 with 26 territories, although at Shiningcliff Wood, which is mixed lowland woodland, it was only the ninth most common species, averaging five pairs in 22ha in 1990–99. However, at Williamthorpe Nature Reserve, 73 territories in the summer of 2003 was an excellent number. This last site was planted with trees and shrubs in the 1980s. Similarly, the former Shirebrook Colliery site was afforested in the 1990s and held 49 territories by 2011. The five-year census at Carsington Water, in 2003–07, found 167 territories, though numbers were declining as some of the site's woodland matured. A total of 158 territories was found on the 2010 survey of the EMP moors, where they were particularly associated with areas of birch and willow.

Declining populations have also been noted on both upland and lowland farmland CBC plots. On an upland farmland plot at Broadhay Farm, Hathersage in 1990–95, Willow Warblers averaged just ten pairs in 49.6ha compared with 18 in 1974–75, making them the fifth most abundant species, whereas they had previously been the most common. At the upland Farfield Farm plot near Hope, there was an average of five pairs in 67.7ha in 1990–99, making it the sixth most abundant species. On a lowland farm plot near Brailsford in 1990–94, numbers reduced from 13 pairs in 1990 to only five pairs in 1992, making it the tenth most abundant species. Eaton *et al*. (2010) stated that numbers in the UK had declined by 41% between 1970 and 2008. There was just one singing male at Drakelow Nature Reserve in 2010, the observer commenting that this was almost certainly the first time in about 40 years that this species had not bred there.

At Drakelow Nature Reserve, a bird was heard singing the song of both Willow Warbler and Chiffchaff on several dates in May and June 1992. It usually began as a Chiffchaff and finished as a Willow Warbler, but occasionally sang the other way round. Unfortunately, it could not be seen adequately for positive identification, although at that time Willow Warblers bred on the reserve, while Chiffchaffs did not. Another interesting record was of two pairs breeding successfully just 6m apart alongside a ride in Whitwell Wood in 1976.

Willow Warblers usually arrive in Derbyshire during the first half of April, although between 1993 and 2006 there was a trend for a few birds to be found in the last week of March. Passage birds undoubtedly swell the numbers in the county during April, with many males in song while still on migration. At Monsal Dale about 180 were recorded on 17th April 1982, and at Bennerley Marshes approximately 120 were in song on 15th April 1995, while more recently at Carsington Water there were 90 on 24th April 2000. The first arrival dates for the period 1978–2011 range from 3rd March to 8th April; the record of one at Carsington Water on 3rd March 1997 was the earliest ever in the county. The mean first date during this 34-year period was 27th March.

Return migration takes place from July, continuing until late September or early October. Willow Warblers are commonly seen on passage and are found in a variety of habitats, including on occasions, suburban gardens; 14 passed through a garden in Belper between 28th and 31st August 1993. At Ramsley Moor, 202 were ringed between 12th June and 13th August 1983. The largest autumn count in 1980–89 concerned a 'fall' of about 100 in scrub at Ashover on 9th August 1988, and approximately 50 were recorded at the same location on 17th August 1989. The largest passage numbers in the 1990s were 50 at Bradwell Ponds on 31st July 1993 and 50 at Combs Reservoir on 18th August 1994. In 2000–07 the largest such counts were of 63 trapped and ringed at Hathersage Sewage Farm on 2nd August 2004, and 40 at Jarvis Clough on 13th August 2006.

In the period 1978–2011, the latest sightings for this species have been between 17th September and 21st October, with a mean latest date of 2nd October. The latest ever recorded was on 11th November 1962, when one was taken into care at Tansley; it died five days later. There was another late record in 2008, at Haywood Farm, Grindleford on 1st November.

In addition to birds of the nominate race *P.t. trochilus*, there have been two records of birds showing characteristics of the Scandinavian and eastern European race *P.t. acredula*. One was seen at Ogston Reservoir on 16th May 1984, and the other was caught and ringed at Ramsley on 19th September 1992.

To date there have not been any confirmed records of Willow Warblers wintering in the county. Although some wintering *Phylloscopus* warblers are not specifically identified, it is thought that they are almost certainly Chiffchaffs.

The Willow Warbler is one of the most commonly ringed warblers with a national total of over 9 million birds, of which there are some 2500 recoveries, a mere 0.25%. The Derbyshire dataset holds 59 recoveries, dating from the 1920s when a nestling was ringed at Buxton and reported dead near Warminster, Wiltshire, two years later.

Analysis of the national dataset as reported by Wernham *et al*. (2002) shows an initial early autumn migratory movement from Britain into the Low Countries and France, with a more westerly movement down the Iberian Peninsula by September–October. Recoveries are further reported from Morocco and Algeria, with the general wintering area for the British and Irish birds being the Ivory Coast and Ghana. The intensive ringing project carried out in Senegal in the early 1990s did not find a significant number of Willow Warblers in this area of Africa. It is likely that the birds make their way more directly southward through Mali, and indeed the longest distance record involving Derbyshire was of 4271km, from Fernilee, where one was ringed as a pullus in June 1963, to Mali, where it was killed in April 1964.

There are three other foreign recoveries of Derbyshire-ringed birds, from Spain, Portugal and France and several of long distance, presumably migratory, southerly movements in the UK, including five at Dungeness, Kent. Similarly, there is a record of a bird which was found at Staveley just 14 days after it was ringed on the Isle of May, Scotland in May 1954.

The longest-living bird, a breeding female, was ringed in Whitwell Wood in 1983 and re-trapped at the same place five years later. Of the 59 recoveries for the county, 46% were later reported dead and of these, almost 80% had survived for fewer than two years.

Blackcap
Sylvia atricapilla
A fairly common summer visitor and an uncommon winter visitor.

Blackcaps are found in mature deciduous and mixed woodlands, particularly those containing tall, but not too dense, shrubby undergrowth suitable for nesting. Blackcaps are more often found in parkland and urban areas than are Garden Warblers.

In Derbyshire, both Whitlock and Jourdain considered this species to be well distributed in the lowlands but scarcer in the woods and copses of the Peak District. Both authorities said that it was less common overall than the Garden Warbler. Frost said that this was no longer the case, with the Blackcap the more numerous of the two, though there was insufficient data to say when the change occurred. Counts in three areas suggested a ratio of nearly three Blackcaps to one Garden Warbler.

The tetrad map shows that they are widely distributed (being thirty-first in an analysis of all breeding species). They are most common in the north-east, east and south, while absent from the upland areas of the central north and north-west, and some urban areas, particularly around Derby. The Derbyshire BBS (1995–99) found them in 487 tetrads, and of these breeding was confirmed in 186, probable in 271 and possible in 30. The probable records were mainly based on recorders hearing the

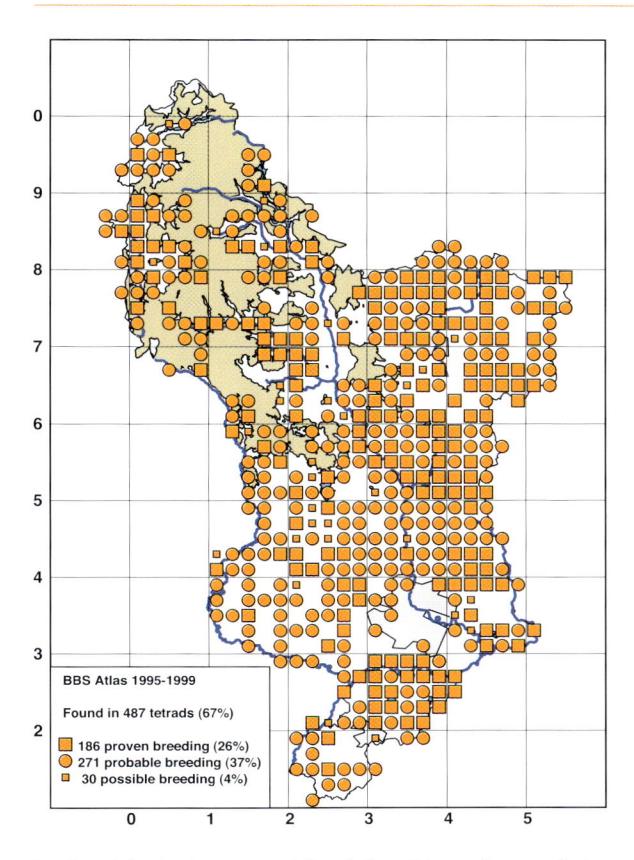

BBS Atlas 1995-1999
Found in 487 tetrads (67%)
- 186 proven breeding (26%)
- 271 probable breeding (37%)
- 30 possible breeding (4%)

loud and distinctive song, while adults with nestlings or fledglings frequently draw attention by their repeated tacking calls.

There is no evidence of any change in range, as both the 1968–72 and 1988–91 Atlases found them breeding, or probably breeding, in every 10km square. Blackcap numbers have risen steadily in the county in recent years, as they have done nationally. It is not clear why this is so, but improved survival rates during winter is a possibility, which may be the result of an increased tendency for the birds to remain in southern Europe rather than cross the Sahara to winter. The local increase accords with a national increase of 156% in the years 1970 to 2008 (Eaton et al. 2010).

The largest reported breeding concentrations regularly come from Scarcliffe Woods. Here, informal census data revealed that there were 19 territories in 1983, rising to a high of 57 in 1989, and falling to 37 in 2004, while 70 recorded in 2010 was the highest ever. The nearby Whitwell Wood also regularly attracts populations of at least 20 pairs, with a maximum of 32 territories in 2000. At Drakelow Nature Reserve, there were seven singing males in 1991, rising to a maximum of 20 in 1999. Similar increases have been recorded on CBC plots at Shiningcliff Wood, which held one pair in 1990, increasing to five pairs in 1997, while on the Farfield Farm plot near Hope there were two pairs in 1992, increasing to six pairs in 1996–97. The Carsington Water census in 2003–07 found a combined total of 106 territories. Detailed information from woodlands around the county, including Scarcliffe Woods, Whitwell Wood and Shirebrook, suggests that Blackcaps outnumber Garden Warblers by a ratio of about 2.5:1 in that habitat, a similar ratio to that noted in the previous county avifauna. As with Garden Warbler, a fairly healthy population exists within the Limestone Dales area in the Peak District. There were 21 singing between Tideswell Dale and Monsal Dale on 27th May 1990, and a breeding season survey of these dales in SK17 in 1993 estimated that 52 pairs were present, totals which were only 1.3:1 in relation to those of Garden Warbler.

Blackcaps usually arrive in Derbyshire during April, with the main influxes occurring between the middle and the end of the month. Although the presence of wintering birds veils the true arrival dates, there have now been records of presumed migrants on 1st April in five years during the 1990s, and the recent trend has been towards earlier arrivals. Their survival during any cold spells in early spring is aided by their ability to feed on berries.

Departure commences in late July, with small post-breeding groups being seen during August and September. In recent years, passage has continued well into October. During passage they supplement their normal diet of insects with fruit, such as those of elder and hawthorn. The largest recently recorded autumn counts have been at Drakelow Nature Reserve, with 20 on 20th August and 22 on 1st September 2001. In the north-east, the largest counts were at Carr Vale on 29th August 1998, when 12 were seen, and Williamthorpe Nature Reserve, with 31 ringed on 22nd August 2010.

Blackcaps have been noted mimicking the songs of several other species. For example, at Drakelow Nature Reserve in 2001 and 2002, a bird was heard to mimic the calls of Reed Warbler, Sedge Warbler, Blackbird and Song Thrush. One at Scarcliffe Woods in 1987–90 had a long, rapid stuttering song, lacking any of the usual warbling quality.

The first record of a Blackcap wintering in the county was of a female shot at Norton (now in South Yorkshire) on 11th December 1881 (Jourdain). In recent years, the most notable change in status has been the dramatic increase in the number of Blackcaps wintering in the county, probably assisted by a succession of mild winters. This was documented by Hattersley (1990). Since 1959, Blackcaps have been seen in the county in almost every winter period, with the average number of birds seen each winter rising from just two in the 1960s, to ten in the 1970s, 25 in the 1980s, up to 41 in the 1990s, and 59 in 2000/11. The chart illustrates how numbers of wintering birds have increased in the county since 1959.

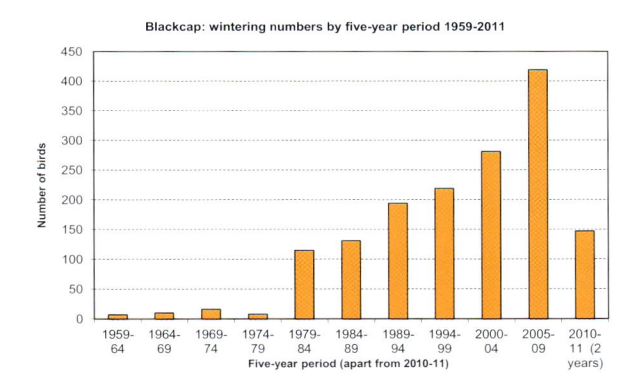

Blackcap: wintering numbers by five-year period 1959-2011

Numbers fluctuate dramatically between winters, with a maximum of 89 being reported during 1995/96, after only 23 in the previous winter. These annual fluctuations are best illustrated in the table.

Winter	Birds	Winter	Birds
1979/80	22	1995/96	89
1980/81	11	1996/97	59
1981/82	11	1997/98	19
1982/83	48	1998/99	29
1983/84	23	1999/2000	56
1984/85	33	2000/01	64
1985/86	25	2001/02	69
1986/87	27	2002/03	50
1987/88	24	2003/04	42
1988/89	22	2004/05	50
1989/90	14	2005/06	55
1990/91	41	2006/07	66
1991/92	23	2007/08	58
1992/93	47	2008/09	67
1993/94	69	2009/10	72
1994/95	23	2010/11	75

January and February are the peak months for records of wintering birds. With the onset of colder weather that is usually associated with these two months, they move from habitats such as woodland, where they feed on natural foods (for example, berries) and are difficult to observe, into mainly urban areas. Here they often frequent gardens, feeding at bird tables and eating bread, fat, nuts, bird seed and even Christmas cake! Their omnivorous habits help Blackcaps to maintain a greater weight in winter than they do in summer (as established from ringing data from the county) and so ensuring a better chance of survival in winter.

Month	Percentage of records
November	11
December	20
January	25
February	21
March	23

Males account for 58% of wintering records, with the majority of records being of single birds, although up to four have been seen together, and five were ringed in a Mickleover garden between 4th January and 23rd March 1996. Most birds are present for just one or two days, although some remain faithful to the same location for several weeks.

Approximately 80% of the winter records come from the eastern half of the county. Significantly, most of the western half of the county lies over 150m amsl, and it has been shown nationally that wintering Blackcaps prefer low altitudes. Additionally, the largest human populations are found on the eastern side of the county. During January and February virtually all reports are from the urban areas, Derby and its suburbs attracting nearly a third of these, with Chesterfield, Matlock, Dronfield and Ashbourne also being favoured towns. It is likely that the Blackcaps wintering in Derbyshire are not our own breeding birds, but migrants from northern and eastern Europe where there has been a considerable growth of breeding populations in recent decades.

There are seven overseas recoveries of Derbyshire-ringed Blackcaps. The furthest concerns one ringed at Ogston Reservoir in July 1981 that was shot 2216km further south at Oulmes, Morocco in October of the same year. There are two other recoveries from Morocco, two from Algeria and singles from Spain and France, while birds ringed in Belgium and Portugal in autumn were found in Derbyshire in the following breeding season.

The only two records relating to wintering birds concern one that was ringed on Bardsey, Wales, in October and found dead at Bamford in December 1987, and one that was ringed at Alvaston in November 1988 and re-trapped in the same area two weeks later.

Garden Warbler
Sylvia borin
A fairly common summer visitor.

Garden Warblers share similar habitats to Blackcaps. Both are found throughout the county in open deciduous and mixed woodland, with a fairly dense and tall scrub or a shrub layer, although there is a slight divergence in habitat between the two species. Garden Warblers are more usually found in woodland fringes, glades and areas of regrowth in clearings, and also in young conifer plantations. Unlike Blackcaps, they are rarely seen close to urban areas, as they are more susceptible to disturbance. Sometimes they may be found in patches of upland scrub, such as the one singing at 335m amsl on Big Moor in May 1997.

Garden Warblers have always been compared with Blackcaps, no doubt at least in part, due to the similarities in their songs. Several early ornithologists, such as Mosley and Brown (1863), considered Blackcaps the more numerous species, but both Whitlock and Jourdain considered Garden Warbler to be the more common. Although Garden Warblers have been less common than Blackcaps for many years now, exactly when the change in relative status occurred is not adequately documented.

The tetrad map, based on the Derbyshire BBS (1995–99), shows that they are distributed rather patchily throughout the county, being somewhat more localized than Blackcap (present in 355 tetrads compared with 487 for Blackcap), although they broadly share the same areas. Breeding was confirmed in 98 tetrads and regarded as probable and possible in 226 and 31 respectively.

They are absent from the upland areas of the north-west and central and northern parts of the county, and from many urban areas. There is little evidence of change in range since both the 1968–72 and 1988–91 Atlases found Garden Warblers breeding, or probably breeding, in every 10km square. Following a decline in the mid-1970s, numbers in the county have steadily recovered, with the population now being relatively stable. Nonetheless, numbers vary annually, which may be linked to mortality on their migration route, which crosses the Sahel region of Africa. A national increase of 3% was recorded by Eaton *et al.* (2010) between 1970 and 2008.

At Scarcliffe Woods, informal census data revealed that there were seven singing males in 1983, rising to a maximum of 27 in 1989, falling to ten in 1991–92 and rising again to 20 in 1994, then reducing to 11 in 2000 and 2004 before rising yet again to 18 in 2010. In the south of the county, at Drakelow Nature Reserve, there were five singing males in 1992–93, rising to 19 in 1995, 17 in 2003 and 18 in 2010. In the Peak District they are concentrated along the wooded river valleys, with a fairly healthy population being present in the limestone dales. There were 17 singing between Tideswell Dale and Monsal Dale on 27th May 1990, and a survey of those dales in SK17 revealed that 39 pairs were present in 1993. The Carsington Reservoir survey of 2003–07 found 53 territories, exactly half the number found for Blackcap.

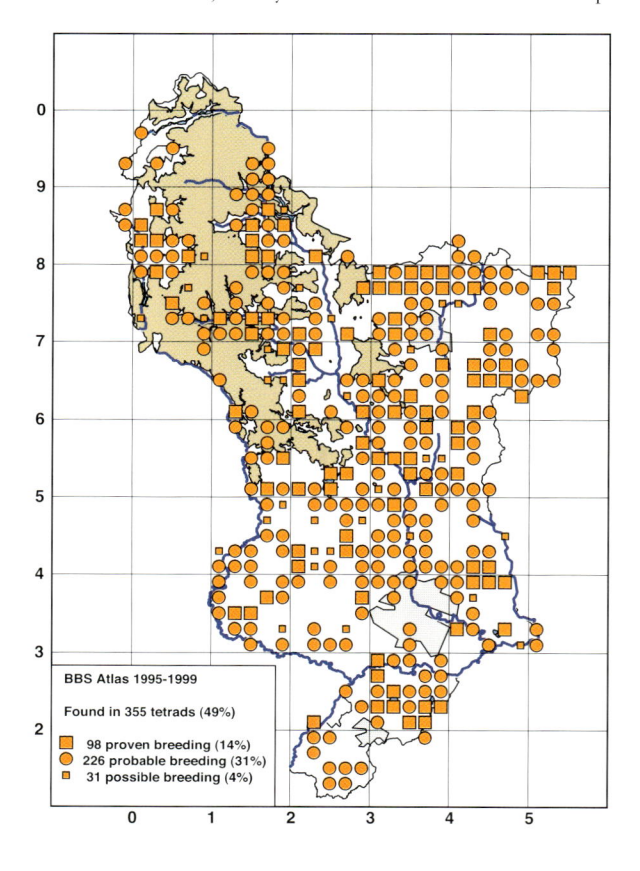

BBS Atlas 1995-1999
Found in 355 tetrads (49%)
■ 98 proven breeding (14%)
● 226 probable breeding (31%)
▪ 31 possible breeding (4%)

The EMP moors survey in 2010 revealed 13 territories, compared with 15 of Blackcap. Garden Warblers are very rarely recorded on farmland CBC plots within the Peak District, although on a lowland farm plot near Brailsford their density at 5.89 pairs per km^2 almost equalled that of Blackcap. At Shirebrook the density was 6.9 pairs per km^2.

Garden Warblers generally arrive in the county during the second half of April, but it may be as late as mid-May before some territories are occupied. The first dates for the period 1980–99 range from 3rd April to 4th May, and this April record, at Darley Park in 1987, constituted the earliest ever record. The mean first date in the 34-year period 1978–2011 was 17th April.

Few Garden Warblers are seen after the breeding season, with most birds departing from mid-July and during August. Passage through the county is unremarkable, with very few birds being seen in September. The maximum autumn passage count during the period 1980–99 was of 12 at Drakelow Nature Reserve on 24th August 1991, with the latest sightings of this species made between 25th August and 26th September. The mean latest date during the period 1978–2011 was 11th September. The latest ever sighting was of one trapped and ringed at Cowers Lane on 28th October 2006.

National ringing data suggest a convergence of departing British birds in autumn onto the Sussex coast (Wernham et al. 2002). The Derbyshire data shows two birds that moved to southern counties. One, ringed at Darley Dale in August 1996, was controlled at Slapton Ley, Devon (350km), 12 days later; and one ringed at Whitwell in July 2000 became a road casualty at Rodwell, Dorset (312km), a month later. A bird controlled at Melbourne in May 1973 had been ringed in Northumberland (241km) in May 1969. There are three recoveries involving much shorter distances.

Lesser Whitethroat
Sylvia curruca
An uncommon summer visitor, mainly to the south and north-east.

In Derbyshire, Lesser Whitethroats are found in areas of tall, dense hedgerows, thickets and patches of tall scrub, especially of hawthorn, blackthorn, bramble and rose, usually enclosing open pastures, where they usually nest higher off the ground than our other *Sylvia* warblers. They are rather skulking and their presence is usually first revealed by their rattling song.

The tetrad map shows that their distribution is somewhat patchy, and restricted almost exclusively to lowland areas, predominating in the farmland of the south and the north-east. Even here, they are fairly localized and never numerous, as their favoured habitat is not particularly common. This is reflected by their presence in just 233 tetrads in the Derbyshire BBS (1995–99), with almost three-quarters of these being in the eastern half of the county. Breeding was proved in 74 tetrads, mostly by seeing adults carrying food, or newly fledged young; the birds draw attention with their nervous 'tacking' calls. Probable breeding, which was judged mainly by birds singing on territory, was noted in a further 130 tetrads.

Their range has increased in recent years, the tetrad map showing them to be present in almost all of the 10km squares, compared with 19 in the 1968–72 Atlas and 22 in the 1988–91 Atlas. This range expansion has mainly been into the north-west of the county, in areas locally within the Peak District, though numbers are still extremely small. This seems to accord with the national trend, which has seen this species expand its range northwards and westward. In most of the Peak District, drystone walls border fields, and as Lesser Whitethroats are generally only found where suitable hedges and thickets occur at lower altitudes, they therefore remain absent from not only the higher land within this region but also from much of the farmland. This is confirmed by results from the farmland CBC plots.

The numbers of Lesser Whitethroats in the county are subject to annual fluctuations, as they have been since the days of Whitlock. These fluctuations are almost certainly caused by adverse climatic conditions in their wintering quarters or along their migration routes. However, as they migrate south-east and winter in Sudan and Ethiopia, their numbers have not suffered the severe crashes affecting species such as Whitethroat, which winter in the Sahel region of Africa. It seems likely, however, that overall numbers have declined in the last 100 years or so. Whitlock said that it was fairly numerous in the cultivated parts of the county, but very local in the Peak District. Jourdain agreed that it was rarer than the Whitethroat, but said that 'sometimes its monotonous little song may be heard in all directions'. Frost described it as a scarce summer visitor and passage migrant.

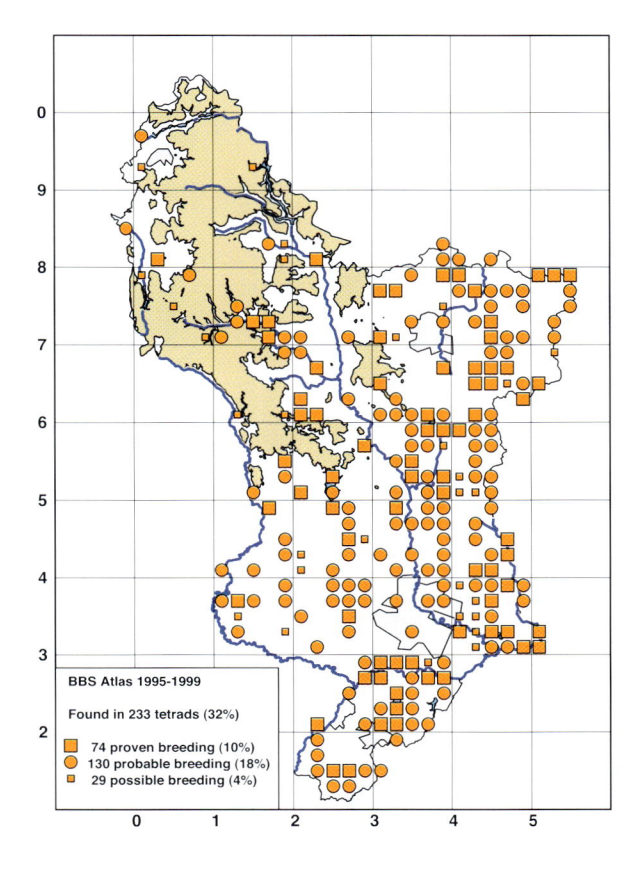

Breeding concentrations of this species are small, being confirmed by the limited data available from both farmland and woodland CBC plots, and suggesting that they require large territories. The largest concentrations of singing males have been nine at Shirebrook in 1984 and at Rother Valley Country Park (now in South Yorkshire) in 1988, although in the 1980s there were up to six singing males present at Etwall Brook. Numbers decreased in the late 1990s, with many observers noting declines, particularly in 1997–98. Carsington Water hosted the largest reported breeding concentration in the 1990s, with a maximum of seven singing males in 1996, but reducing to just three in 1999, though the 2003–07 census suggested six territories. Subsequently, eight singing males were observed at Swarkestone Lake on 6th May 2002. In the north-east at Carr Vale there was a maximum of five singing males in 1992, 1994 and 1996, but only one or two in 1999. Nationally, numbers increased by 20% during 1970 to 2008 (Eaton *et al*. 2010).

In some places this species has colonized industrial sites containing suitable habitat, a good example being the former Willington Power Station, which had up to five pairs in the 1990s. More unusual records were of a pair that bred successfully by the A57 road at Glossop in 1986, and another pair that did likewise on the embankment of the M1 motorway near Poolsbrook in 1988.

An interesting observation concerned a bird at Ticknall in 1988, which was noted singing a strange, garbled song, at twice the normal speed. The observer noted that he had only heard this song previously in central Europe.

Lesser Whitethroats arrive in the county regularly during the third week of April, although sometimes their arrival is delayed until the first week of May. The first arrival dates for the period 1978–2011 range from 10th April to 4th May, with a mean first date of 20th April. The earliest ever spring arrival was on 9th April 1937 at Radbourne.

Departure from their breeding grounds commences in July, with migration usually continuing until the end of September, although a few have been seen in early October in recent years. Migrants are often seen in non-breeding areas, occasionally even in suburban gardens. Passage numbers are usually quite small, so a count of 18 at Poolsbrook on 20th August 1990 was therefore noteworthy. In the period 1978–2011, the latest sightings for this species were between 6th September and 18th November; the latter concerned a bird at Wyver Lane in 1995, and not only constituted the latest ever county record, but also considerably postdated the previous latest record of 8th October (2000). The mean last date during this 34-year period was 25th September.

There has been just one instance of a Lesser Whitethroat attempting to winter in Derbyshire. At Midway, one was seen at a garden nut-feeder on 27th–28th November and 27th December 1998.

This species performs a migration pattern that contrasts with most other British passerine species which move down the Iberian Peninsular into Africa. It travels across Europe to the south-eastern coast of the Mediterranean and into Ethiopia, Sudan and Chad. Ringing recoveries have come from countries along this passage route but very little is known of its wintering area (Wernham *et al*. 2002). One ringed at Kibbutz Kfar Ruppin in Israel in March 1999, was controlled 3741km north-west at Elvaston Castle Country Park six months later. South-south-east movement is evidenced by a bird moving from Cousland, Midlothian, where it was ringed in July 1981, to Long Eaton, where it was controlled a year later; and by one ringed at Williamthorpe in August 1993 that was caught at Dungeness, Kent 12 days later.

Whitethroat
Sylvia communis
A fairly common summer visitor.

In Derbyshire, the favoured habitats of Whitethroats are woodland edges and clearings, in particular those with tangled thickets of bramble and hawthorn, hedgerows, scrubland and waste ground.

It was described by Whitlock as an abundant summer visitor to all low-lying portions of the county and this remained the case until 1968. However, the drought conditions in the wintering grounds, the Sahel region of West Africa, during the winter of 1968/69 were responsible for a 75% reduction in Whitethroat territories in Derbyshire in 1969, with a similar collapse in numbers being reported nationally. Some of our other migrants only pass through the Sahel region, thus avoiding the worst of the droughts, but Whitethroats suffered larger declines than most as they spend the whole winter there, rather than migrating further south. Although there was a sporadic and gradual recovery, the population initially re-established itself in areas of optimal breeding habitat in the county. However, further declines in 1984 and 1991, caused by similar droughts in their winter quarters, once again reduced their abundance. Numbers at a few locations in the county fell to such low levels that Lesser Whitethroats outnumbered them for the first time. Since 1991 numbers have recovered again, but remain much lower than they were before 1969. Eaton *et al*. (2010) record a national decline of 2% during 1970–2008, but this does not take the 1969 collapse into consideration.

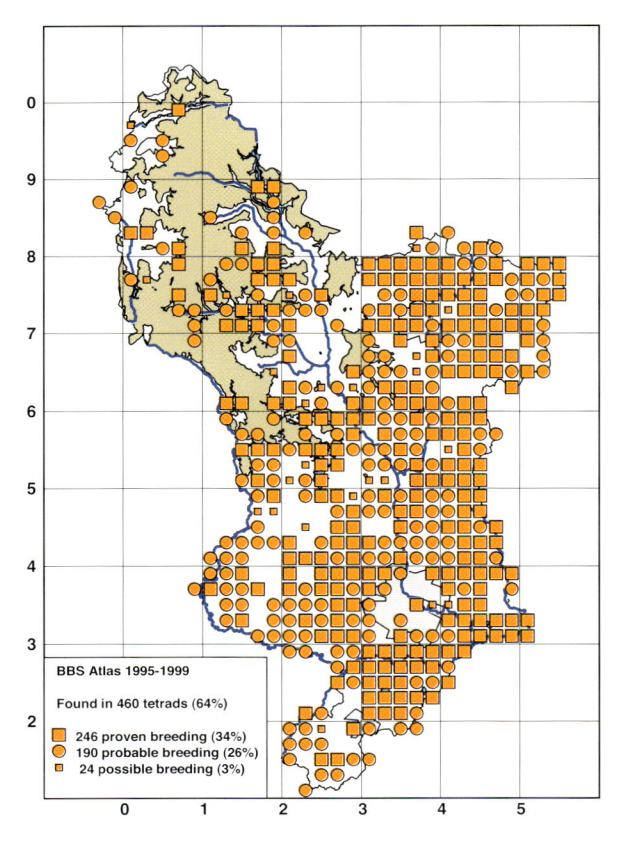

Though often skulking, Whitethroats draw attention to themselves by their scratchy songs, often given in display flight, and their alarm calls are distinctive.

The tetrad map shows a fairly widespread distribution, but with an absence from the upland areas of the central north and north-west, the main population being in the lowlands of the south and east of the county. They were found to be present in 460 tetrads, with proven breeding in 246, probable in 190 and possible in 24. At the 10km resolution the 1968–72 Atlas found them present in every square and they were present in all except two squares in the 1988–91 Atlas. They were missing from only one square (SK19) in the Derbyshire BBS (1995–99).

The small decline in range has been away from the less favoured upland areas in north-west of the county, where Whitethroats have always been localized.

A long-term informal census of Scarcliffe Woods revealed that the number of territories fell from a high of 32 in 1974 to a minimum of two in 1984 and 1992–93, rising again to 20 in 1998. Nearby, at Carr Vale, there were only five territories in 1992, a maximum of 27 in 1996 and eight in 2002. Similar fluctuations

BBS Atlas 1995-1999

Found in 460 tetrads (64%)

- 246 proven breeding (34%)
- 190 probable breeding (26%)
- 24 possible breeding (3%)

were noted at most other locations throughout the county. In 1994 a partial survey of the area north of the A617 road and east of the M1 motorway revealed that there were at least 65 singing males or pairs present, with non-singing birds present at a further 12 sites. The largest reported breeding concentration in the 1990s was at Carsington Water, which had approximately 60 territories in 1997, though by 2003–07 this had reduced to 31 territories, doubtless connected with the maturation of planted woodlands. Densities on lowland CBC plots ranged from 17.4 pairs per km^2 at Shirebrook to 5.9 at Culland.

Their decline in upland areas is confirmed by data from farmland CBC plots within the Peak District at Hathersage and Hope, where none were recorded between 1990 and 1995. The late 1990s have seen birds returning to a few upland areas: at Hollins Cross, three or four were singing at 375m amsl on 22nd May 1998, while at Fernilee, a male singing on territory in May and June 1999 represented the first potential breeding record in the Goyt Valley since 1968. Subsequently, three pairs bred at Curbar Edge in 2001, and within the Peak District, maximum counts of singing males have been of seven at Gratton Dale in 2002 and at Longstone Edge in 2004. Also, in the north-west a pair that bred at Chapel-en-le-Frith in 1995 was the first breeding record in that area for many years.

An interesting observation concerned one at Ogston Reservoir on 6th May 1999 that incorporated a Lesser Whitethroat-like rattle in its song. At Long Eaton Gravel Pits in 2000, a female with dark plumage and lacking a white throat was paired with a normally coloured male and seen feeding young. Plumage variation has rarely been recorded in this species.

Most Whitethroats arrive in the county from mid-April onwards. The first arrival dates for the period 1978–2011 range from 6th April to 25th April, with a mean first date of 15th April. The earliest ever spring arrival was on 27th March 1968, at Clay Mills Gravel Pits.

Following breeding, Whitethroats are quite gregarious and are often seen in small parties, before leaving on migration. At Staveley Sewage Farm, 51 were ringed between June and August 1987, while the largest counts have been of approximately 30 at Elvaston Quarry on 26th August 1991 and 39 (including 17 juveniles) at Carsington Water on 14th July 2003. Most birds depart during August, although a few remain during September and early October. In the period 1978–2011, the latest sightings were between 16th September and 23rd November, with the latter record, at Ogston Reservoir in 1988, not only constituting the latest ever county record, but also postdating any other county record by 51 days. The mean last date during this 34-year period was 25th September.

The Derbyshire ringing data reveal that 83% of young birds returned in subsequent years to within 60km of their ringing site. National ringing data indicate an autumn migratory flight route across the eastern part of the English Channel and southwards along the west side of France into western Iberia. Recoveries further south have been from Morocco, with a few from Senegal and Nigeria. Returning birds in spring take a more easterly route through Spain to northern France (Wernham *et al*. 2002).

Two recoveries from Aston-on-Trent serve to illustrate the varying migration performances of individuals. One had laid down sufficient fat reserves to make a flight into western Spain in 21 days, whereas the other took the same amount of time to fly only to Beachy Head in East Sussex. Another ringed at Broadbottom (on the county border with Greater Manchester) in August 1970 was found at Shoreham, West Sussex six days later. There are two more overseas recoveries involving Derbyshire. One found at Alvaston in May 1958 had been ringed at Leerdam, Holland in the previous August; and one ringed at Zwin, Belgium in September 1993 was controlled at Breaston in April 1996.

Dartford Warbler
Sylvia undata
A very rare vagrant.

A pair was shot off the top of a furze bush, half-covered with snow, at Melbourne Common during severe weather in the winter of 1840 by J.J. Briggs (Whitlock). The same observer wrote to *Ibis* in 1865 to say that he believed that a nest he had recently taken in Derbyshire to be of this species (Jourdain additions).

Although Hickling (1978) knew of no Dartford Warbler records for Leicestershire, Whitlock believed that the extensive tracts of gorse in Charnwood Forest, some 15km to the south of Melbourne, could easily have held a few overlooked pairs of these birds.

The only subsequent record concerns a male at the newly created Pride Park Sanctuary (less than 2km from Derby City centre) from 24th January to 8th March 2005. It frequented an area of rank grassland with scattered bushes and could be elusive, especially in windy conditions, but usually rewarded patient observers. It was heard singing on several occasions and was frequently seen associating with the on-site Stonechats (Key 2006b).

Dartford Warblers were almost confined as breeding birds to central southern England until recently but, following a series of very mild winters, they have colonized areas elsewhere, as far north as Staffordshire. Interestingly, in the 2004/05 winter there were at least four other extralimital birds in the Midlands, with others in Cheshire and West Yorkshire. A male sang on moorland within 1km of the Derbyshire border at Blackamoor, South Yorkshire, during the summers of 2005, 2007 and 2008.

Grasshopper Warbler
Locustella naevia
An uncommon summer visitor.

The Coal Measures and alluvial regions in the east and south of Derbyshire are the Grasshopper Warbler's current strongholds. It occurs in a variety of scrubby habitats, particularly where there is a good cover of long grass, tangled vegetation or bramble, often close to wetlands. Young forestry plantations are a favoured temporary habitat, providing suitable conditions for only a few years before they grow too tall and dense. Moorland records are not rare, while birds have also sung in fields of barley and oil-seed rape, and in allotment gardens.

There has apparently been little change in the status of Grasshopper Warbler since the days of Whitlock and Jourdain, with both authors stressing the erratic nature of this bird's appearances. Jourdain said that in some years they could be found all over the county, even on grouse moors where, at Derwent, he had found breeding pairs at 365–395m amsl. As examples of this irregularity, six or seven pairs bred in the Ashbourne district in 1898 and 1901 but none in the intervening years, while in more recent times, in the Flash Dam area there were eight singing males in 1972 but only one in 1973. Favoured modern-day localities such as Drakelow Nature Reserve, Foremark Reservoir and Carver's Rocks Nature Reserve, and Carr Vale have also experienced the erratic nature of this species and can have several consecutive poor or even blank years. This is exemplified by counts at Foremark Reservoir, where there were up to six reeling males in 1988, four in 1993, seven in 1995, four in 1996, five in 1997, none in 2002, three in 2007, and no more than one in any of the other years. They are still found in small numbers at higher altitudes, such as a male singing from a patch of bilberry in Upper Derwentdale at 400m amsl on 5th May 2007.

The early 1990s saw an increase in numbers compared with the 1980s, especially from 1984 to 1986 when they were at very low ebb. At the start of the twenty-first century numbers again fell, before increasing to 46 'reeling' birds in 2002 and 2003, and reaching 110 by 2011. This increase has taken place in spite of local population instabilities. It is not clear why these occur, but studies have shown that for breeding they require thick cover in which to nest, several suitable song-posts and a source of invertebrate food within 50m of the nest. Possibly, if any one of these criteria is missing when the birds return in spring they will move on to another site. The table shows the totals for the period 1983–2011.

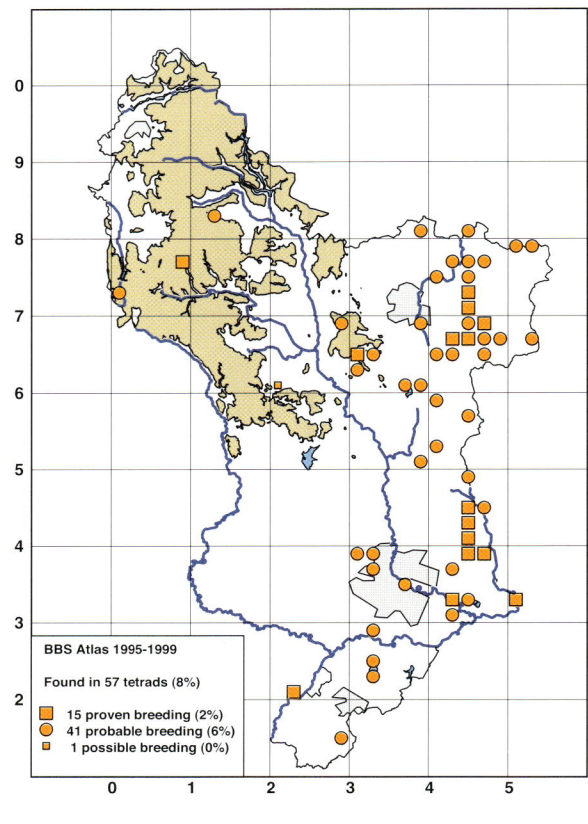

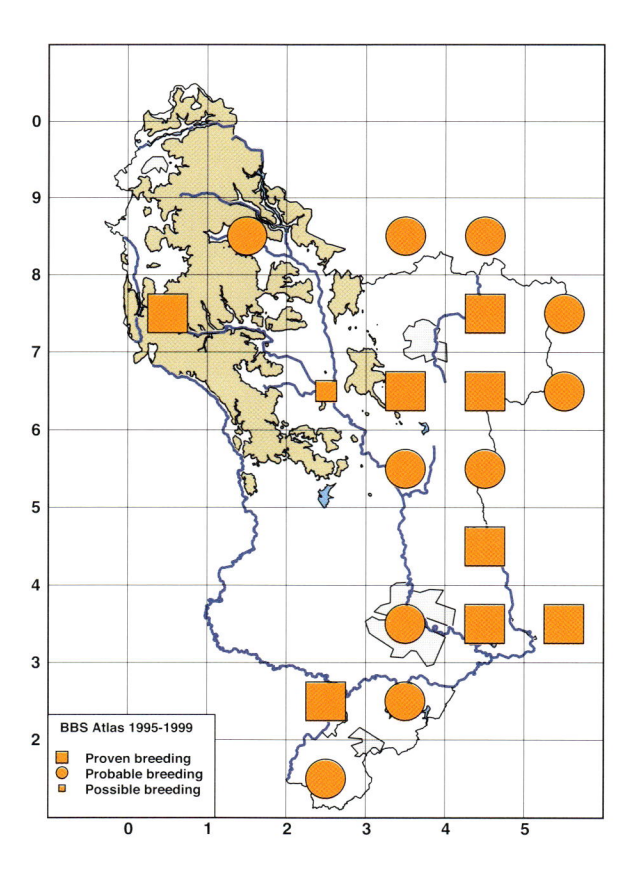

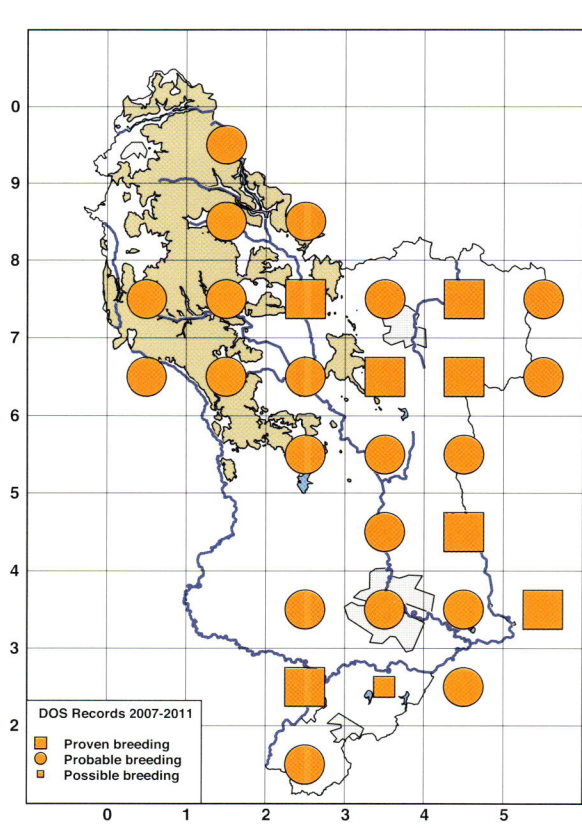

BBS Atlas 1995-1999
Found in 57 tetrads (8%)
- 15 proven breeding (2%)
- 41 probable breeding (6%)
- 1 possible breeding (0%)

BBS Atlas 1995-1999
- Proven breeding
- Probable breeding
- Possible breeding

DOS Records 2007-2011
- Proven breeding
- Probable breeding
- Possible breeding

Year	Birds
1983	12
1984	8
1985	10
1986	7
1987	18
1988	24
1989	17
1990	22
1991	31
1992	27
1993	30
1994	35
1995	27
1996	34
1997	50

Year	Birds
1998	47
1999	24
2000	36
2001	30
2002	46
2003	46
2004	53
2005	60
2006	49
2007	63
2008	54
2009	73
2010	104
2011	110

The Derbyshire BBS (1995–99) found Grasshopper Warblers in 18 10km squares, compared with 22 and 17 in the 1968–72 and 1988–91 Atlases respectively. They were found in 57 tetrads, mainly in the east, in particular in the valleys of the Rivers Doe Lea and Erewash, and to a lesser extent the River Trent, with a wide but very thin scattering elsewhere. Breeding is difficult to prove for such a skulking species, but it was confirmed in 15 tetrads, very largely by seeing adults carrying food or by finding recently fledged young. Probable breeding, based on the male's distinctive song, was recorded in a further 41 tetrads, and it was considered possible in one other. Some individuals seem to sing mainly at night and may therefore have been overlooked.

The largest concentrations of singing birds in recent years included Breck Farm, with up to eight in the area in May 1991, and the Doe Lea Valley (which includes Carr Vale and Poolsbrook Marsh) held up to 11 territories along an 8km section between Doe Lea and Renishaw during 1998, although typically, numbers were much reduced there in 1999. Since 2000, the largest counts have been from an area between Staveley and Renishaw, where there were seven on 21st April 2002; Morton, with seven in newly planted woodland on 6th June 2004; seven at Bondhay Common on 5th July 2009; and nine at Trent Meadows on 28th April 2011. The 2010 survey of the EMP moors produced 11 reeling males, seven of them on Leash Fen. Most were associated with small clumps of willows but two were in areas dominated by greater tussock sedge.

The maps for 1995–99 and 2007–11 show the more widespread distribution in the later period.

Most birds arrive during late April and early May and are almost invariably located by their reeling song. However, average first-arrival dates have become progressively earlier, from 24th April during the 1970s to 15th April during the 1990s. In the period 1978–2011, the mean first date was 17th April, with 3rd April, at Rother Valley Country Park (now in South Yorkshire) in 1992 and Carr Vale in 1993, the earliest of all. Departure commences from July onwards, although some are still heard reeling in August. Records of passage birds are extremely rare, but no doubt many are overlooked. In contrast to the arrival dates, the latest recorded dates have remained quite constant, with 23rd August the average during the period 1978–2011. The latest of all was on 26th September 1964 at Ladybower.

Savi's Warbler
Locustella luscinioides
A very rare vagrant.

Savi's Warblers breed patchily across western Europe and winter in East Africa. There were 603 UK records up to the end of 2011 (Hudson *et al.* 2012). In the 1960s they underwent a moderate range expansion to the north and west, resulting in a first British breeding occurrence in Kent in 1960. This led to the establishment of a small breeding population, mainly in Norfolk, Suffolk, Cambridgeshire and Kent, which reached a peak in 1979. This trend has since been reversed and by 2010 there were only between two and ten singing males or pairs in the UK (Holling *et al.* 2012).

Derbyshire's only Savi's Warbler was found on 26th April 1987, a typical date for an overshooting migrant, in a reed-bed at Drakelow Nature Reserve. It remained until 28th May and was regularly heard singing. Cole (1989) gave an account of the event.

Aquatic Warbler
Acrocephalus paludicola
A very rare vagrant.

One of the most threatened of Europe's breeding birds, the Aquatic Warbler breeds in Germany, Poland and Hungary, east to the Urals, and winters in sub-Saharan West Africa. Most British records of Aquatic Warbler occur in August and September at sites along the south coast. There have been four records in Derbyshire, all at the peak time for sightings in Britain. This species was removed from the BBRC list in 1982.

Year	Location and date
1976	Clay Mills Gravel Pits, an immature from 20th to 26th August, was trapped and ringed on the former date
1989	Williamthorpe Nature Reserve, an immature on 18th–19th September
1990	Etwall Gravel Pits, an immature from 29th September to 7th October
2004	Aston-on-Trent Gravel Pits, an immature on 31st August

Sedge Warbler
Acrocephalus schoenobaenus
A fairly common summer visitor.

The Sedge Warbler is more catholic in its habitat choice than its close relative the Reed Warbler, and is therefore more widespread and common. Although not as colonial as Reed Warblers, several pairs may nest in close proximity, drawing the observer's attention by their prominent song-flight. Marshes and reed-beds, particularly those interspersed with shrubs or small trees, are the main habitat, although they also frequent hedges bordering water and the drier margins of wetlands. Increasingly the species is also able to use drier habitats, such as industrial wastelands, oil-seed rape and cereal fields, young forestry plantations and scrubby woodland edges.

The Sedge Warbler was described by Whitlock in 1893 as 'extremely common, except in the Peak where they nest only in the broad dales', while Jourdain stated that they were common below 1000 feet (305m) amsl and 'exceedingly common in the Trent Valley'. The species declined during the twentieth century, due mainly to wetland drainage, although to some extent this loss has been compensated for by habitat created following mineral extraction, with gravel pits being particularly favoured. The decline accelerated during the late 1960s and early 1970s, in keeping with the national trend, with drought conditions in their African wintering grounds south of the Sahara during this period thought to be responsible (Frost). Although there was a partial recovery during the latter part of the 1970s, a further severe drought in their wintering grounds over the winter of 1982/83 once again drastically reduced the population and numbers again fell to an all-time low. Since then, numbers have again recovered, but to levels below those of the 1960s, and breeding numbers at many locations are still subject to much annual variation. Informal census records from the last three decades of singing males at one of the county's most important sites for this species, Drakelow Nature Reserve, illustrate this point perfectly. In the 1970s there was a maximum of 30 in 1970, but only six in 1974; in the 1980s there were 25 in 1987, and eight in 1988; in the 1990s there were 13 in 1993, and a maximum of 23 in 1994 and 1997; and in the 2000s there was a maximum of 39 in May 2007, but just four in 2009, five in 2010 and four in 2011. Many other important sites experience this annual variation in numbers too. Willington Gravel Pits had a maximum of 25 singing males in 1989, 45 in 2004, and 39 in 2009, but a minimum of just five in 1997 and 1998; Williamthorpe Nature Reserve had a maximum of 25 in 1986 and a minimum of seven in 1997. In the north-east, regular counts of the Doe Lea Valley, which encompasses Carr Vale and Markham and Poolsbrook Marsh, indicate a fairly consistent population of between 20 and 30 pairs.

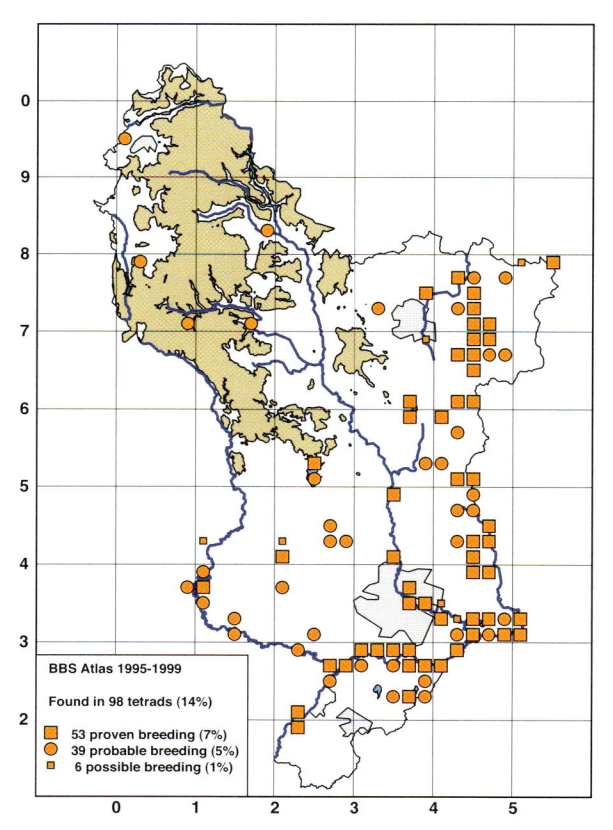

The ability of the species to colonize maturing gravel pit complexes is well illustrated at the recently created Aston-on-Trent Gravel Pit complex, where up to 35 singing males were present in May 1999, although there were only six in 2004 and four in 2011. In most years both Long Eaton Gravel Pits and Swarkestone Lake also attract double-figure counts of singing males. However, when vegetation at gravel pits becomes overgrown, and therefore unsuitable, the numbers of birds can decline quite quickly. Hilton Gravel Pits Nature Reserve, a good example of this, had 26 territories in 1967 but currently does not have any breeding Sedge Warblers. Unfortunately, some sites are still being lost to drainage and reclamation, including Elvaston Quarry, an important breeding site, which held 17 singing birds in 1991.

The tetrad map shows that their current distribution is still strongly centred around the valleys of the Rivers Doe Lea, Erewash, Trent and Derwent in the east and south of the county. They are rare in the Peak District and no longer found in the dales. There was probable or proven breeding in 19 10km squares in the 1968–72 Atlas, reducing to 14 in the 1988–91 Atlas and increasing to 21 during the Derbyshire BBS (1995–99). Over the period of the three surveys, there has been a definite contraction away from the north-west (where they had probably not bred since 1969, until a pair bred at Arnfield Reservoir in 2004) and a consolidation in the south and east. The Derbyshire BBS showed proven breeding in 53 tetrads, with probable breeding in a further 39 and possible in an additional six.

The main arrival starts in the second week of April. During the period 1978–2011 the mean arrival date was 12th April. The average arrival date of 11th April during the 1990s is 12 days earlier than the corresponding arrival date during the 1970s. The earliest recorded arrival was on 31st March 2010 at Long Eaton Gravel Pits. Spring migration and subsequent occupation of breeding sites often takes place quite quickly. For example, at Drakelow Nature Reserve in 2000, the first two birds of the year arrived on 20th April and had increased to 29 by 30th April. Interestingly, this site, which holds the first suitable habitat for spring arrivals moving northwards along the River Trent, hosted the first spring records in the county in six years between 1980 and 1999.

Departure commences in late July, after which only small numbers of birds are generally seen in the county. There was however, an exceptional record of approximately 60 in a loose flock at Elvaston Quarry on 28th August 1991. As with arrivals, the average departure date of 28th September in the 1990s has extended compared with the 1970s, in this case by five days. The Sedge Warbler's length of stay in the county has gradually increased over the last 34 years. The mean final departure date in the period 1978–2011 was 28th September and the latest record of all was on 13th October 1974, when there were still no fewer than eight at Williamthorpe Nature Reserve.

This species is well known for its feat of a series of non-stop autumn migration flights, particularly over the Sahara to its wintering grounds in central and West Africa. Large fat deposits are laid down to enable the bird to cover such vast distances without refuelling. Within Britain, many birds develop the fat reserve in the reed-beds of southern England and south Wales (Ormerod 1990), and the Derbyshire data includes a number controlled in these areas, including Williamthorpe to Dorset, Poolsbrook to Kent, and Sussex to Williamthorpe.

One ringed at Williamthorpe in July 1966 was found at Lavadores, Portugal, 1407km to the south-south-west, two months later. Another moved swiftly from Elvaston Castle Country Park, where it was ringed in September 1996, to Berlare, Belgium, 423km east-south-east, where it was controlled four days later.

Ringing projects have established that in general the males are faithful to their breeding territories between years, whereas the females tend to move to other areas. This was supported by a male ringed in Loire-Atlantique, France in September 1988, which was subsequently controlled in the breeding season at Drakelow Nature Reserve in 1990 and again in 1991.

Marsh Warbler
Acrocephalus palustris
A very rare vagrant.

Marsh Warblers are among the last of the summer visitors to arrive in the UK, usually in late May or early June. All five of the Derbyshire records, which were of singing males, have been in this period.

Year	Location and date
1985	Etwall Brook, one from 30th May to 4th June
1985	Poolsbrook Marsh, one from 9th to 16th June
1995	Williamthorpe Nature Reserve, one on 5th June
2003	Shirebrook Colliery, one on 12th June
2009	Poolsbrook Marsh, one on 16th June was seen carrying nesting material

Marsh Warblers are exhilarating songsters and mimics, and no fewer than 24 species were recorded as being mimicked by these five Derbyshire birds. The sightings in 1985 were documented by Adams and Thornhill (1986).

Marsh Warblers are widespread in Europe, where they breed east to Russia, north to southern Sweden and south-east to Iran. They are very rare British breeding birds with a 2010 population of four to nine pairs (Holling *et al.* 2012). Formerly, they were more numerous and had a stronghold in Worcestershire, where there were up to 95 pairs during the 1960s (Kelsey *et al.* 1989). None breed there now and most of the English population is in the south-east. It is probable that most or all of Derbyshire records relate to birds overshooting their English breeding sites.

Reed Warbler
Acrocephalus scirpaceus
A fairly common and increasing summer visitor and scarce passage migrant.

The Reed Warbler is a habitat specialist, relying primarily on beds of reed and osier, although it will also use reedmace, reed sweet-grass and other lacustrine vegetation, all of which may be found by the margins of shallow lakes, ponds and sluggish rivers. The stands of reeds used for nesting can sometimes be quite small, for example, the reed-beds created at sewage farms as filtration systems. Dense reed-beds tend to be less favoured and it is known that a reed-bed's perimeter length is more important than its area for this species. In Derbyshire this habitat, which is neither common nor extensive, occurs mainly in the south and east, along the valleys of the Rivers Trent, Doe Lea and Erewash. Thus, the main range of this species has probably remained largely unchanged since Whitlock described it as 'local in the area of the Trent and its tributaries' during the nineteenth century, although it is undoubtedly more numerous nowadays. They have occasionally been noted singing in atypical habitats such as fields of cereals and oil-seed rape, and areas of sallows and hawthorn, while one was noted singing from raspberries at Long Eaton on 26th May 1990. Reed Warblers are the most colonial of all our warblers, and therefore in suitable habitats can be reasonably common. They are also fairly common foster-parents of the Cuckoo.

During the Derbyshire BBS (1995–99), the species was recorded in 54 tetrads, with almost all of these in lowland areas. Breeding was confirmed in 35 (64% of those found and less than 8% of the county), while probable breeding occurred in a further 12. Away from the principal areas, proven breeding occurred at a few scattered alluvial or other waterside localities, a small number of which were fairly close to the Peak District, an area where they are very rare and have yet to be proved breeding.

The map indicates proven or probable breeding in 17 10km squares, one more than the total from the 1988–91 Atlas, and exceeding the 11 in the 1968–72 Atlas. This illustrates a genuine increase of the species over the last three decades. One reason for

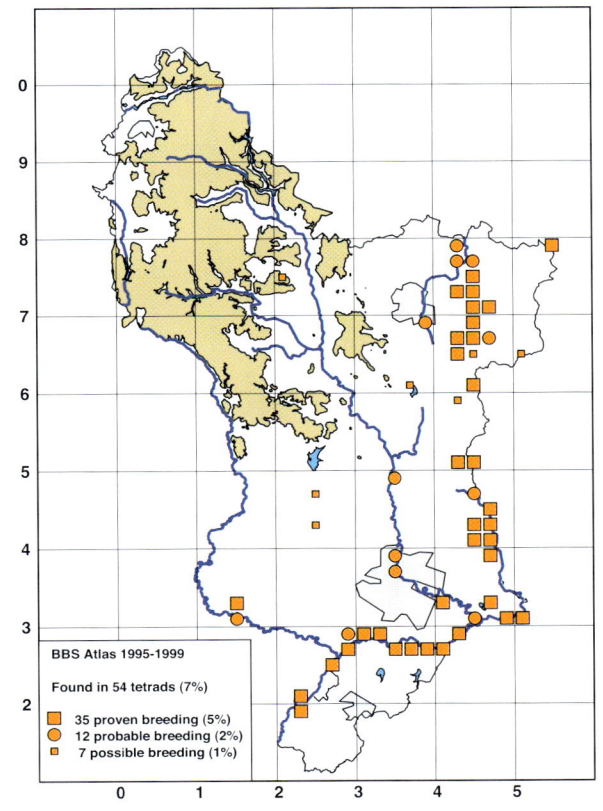

BBS Atlas 1995-1999
Found in 54 tetrads (7%)
- 35 proven breeding (5%)
- 12 probable breeding (2%)
- 7 possible breeding (1%)

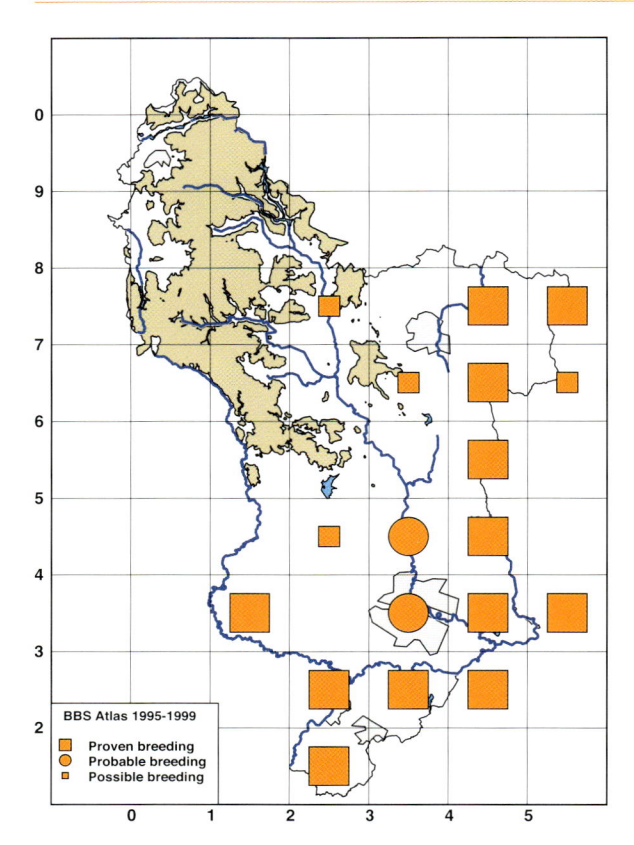

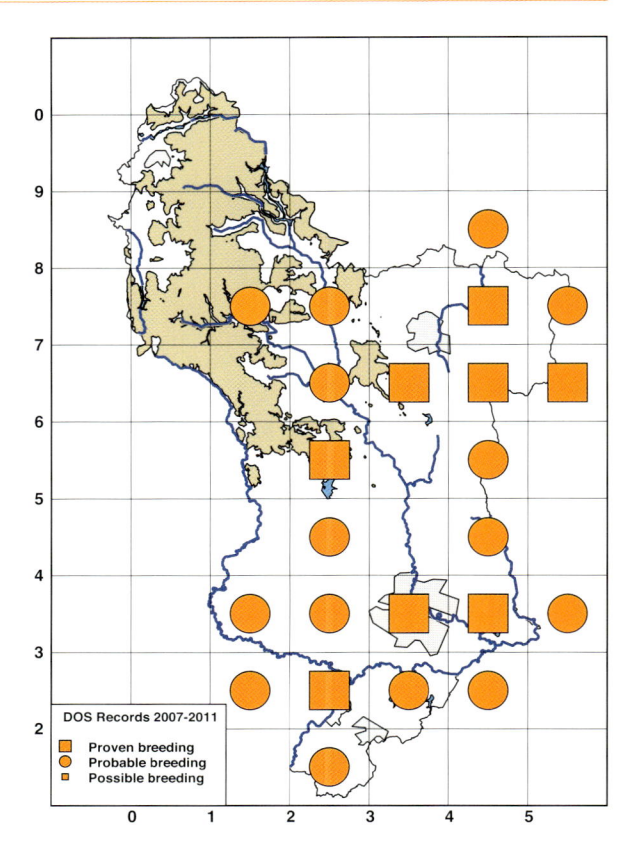

this is that Reed Warblers have not suffered the losses affecting other species that winter in the Sahel region, since they winter further south. Indeed, Reed Warblers were recorded at the highest number of sites during the latest survey, reaching 26 in 1998, but even this was surpassed in 2004 when they were recorded at 29 sites; by 2010, this had risen to 44 sites. The average of 25 sites during 1995–99 compares to just 15 in the previous five years, and only 12 during 1985–89. This increase in sites is likely to be due to habitat creation following mineral extraction activities, especially those of sand and gravel.

Frost believed that the population was in the range of 20–40 pairs, with 14 pairs the largest colony he had heard of, and the Alfreton Workers' Education Association estimated a breeding population of 65–75 pairs in 1981–82. Numbers at the main sites have increased too, presumably as reed-beds encroach upon open shallow water. This is reflected by counts of singing birds at the following localities: Drakelow Nature Reserve held eight in 1986, increasing to a maximum of 40 in 2004; at Williamthorpe Nature Reserve there were 15 in 1984, rising to 23 in 1999, 2001 and 2003; at Willington Gravel Pits the population expanded from five in 1988 to 25 in 1999 and a maximum of 70 in 2004; the Poolsbrook–Markham complex held 17 in 1994 but 31 by 1996.

This population expansion resulted in approximately 160 singing birds in the county in 2006, 185 in 2007 and 2008, 200 in 2009, and 275 in 2011. Unfortunately, some important sites have been lost recently, due to reclamation of wetland areas. One such site, Elvaston Quarry, held up to 15 pairs throughout the 1980s, before being lost after the 1991 breeding season. However, much conservation effort nowadays is put into the creation of reed-beds, and many of the fishing ponds created in recent times have also developed suitable vegetation for Reed Warblers.

The maps show the breeding range at 10km square level in 1995–99 and 2007–11.

Reed Warblers are not often recorded on passage and may well be overlooked, although a few are reported singing from non-breeding sites in most springs. Although migrants are usually recorded at wetland sites, they are sometimes found in drier areas. An unusual record was of one singing in a Newhall garden in May 1972. They are very rare on passage in the north-west, with one at Fernilee in September 1958 being the only documented record from that region until the 1980s. Therefore, migrants recorded subsequently at Combs Reservoir in 1993, 1996 and 2009 are noteworthy.

Evidence from ringing recoveries at the reserves of Williamthorpe and Drakelow has shown that Reed Warblers often exhibit a high degree of site fidelity. Indeed, one bird trapped at the latter site in 1999 had returned for its fifth consecutive year. Post-breeding numbers at favoured sites may be considerable. At Williamthorpe Nature Reserve on 18th August 1990, 51 were ringed and a least a further 30 unringed birds were seen.

Reed Warblers usually begin to arrive in late April, with the majority arriving in early May. In the period 1978–2011, the mean arrival date was 23rd April and the earliest recorded arrival was on 8th April 2011 at Willington Gravel Pits. Most birds probably depart in August and early September, although occasionally adults are seen still feeding fledged young in early September, and so a few remain until late September and early October. The mean latest date in the period 1978–2011 was 2nd October and the latest of all was on 22nd October 2007 at Willington Gravel Pits.

County ringing data for Reed Warblers has come mainly from the reed-beds of the nature reserves at Williamthorpe and Drakelow, and until the time of its reclamation in 1991, Elvaston Quarry, which probably supported the largest breeding population of Reed Warblers in the county. There are 137 reports for the county and all but five of these are birds which have been caught again by another ringer within Britain or abroad. The intensive ringing project at Icklesham, East Sussex has produced 14 records of birds associated with Derbyshire. One ringed near Ashton-in-Makerfield, Wigan in July 1979 was controlled at Williamthorpe ten years later. Overseas recoveries include one ringed at Etwall in July 1969 that was killed in Morocco (2385km south) in April 1972. One ringed as a pullus at Williamthorpe in June 1991 was controlled 4293km south-south-west at Djoudj, Senegal in the following April, and another ringed at Williamthorpe in August 1994 moved 854km south to Mortagne, France, where it was controlled 24 days later. In July 1995 one was trapped at Drakelow Nature Reserve; it had been ringed at Retie, Belgium a year earlier.

Great Reed Warbler
Acrocephalus arundinaceus
A very rare vagrant.

Great Reed Warblers breed across Eurasia to Japan and China, wintering in sub-Saharan Africa. There were some 250 UK records up to the end of 2011 (Hudson *et al.* 2012). Most are found as singing birds in May and June (Brown & Grice 2005). A singing male was found in a small *Phragmites* bed at Straw's Bridge Pond, Ilkeston on 12th May 2010, and remained for 45 days, until 25th June, during which period hundreds of observers saw it. This was the longest stay ever by a UK bird; Key (2011) described the event.

Waxwing
Bombycilla garrulus
A rare winter visitor.

The first documented record of Waxwing in the county was provided by Francis Gisborne, Rector of Staveley, who shot one on 10th December 1774 (Whitlock). There were obviously 'invasions' in the nineteenth century, as Whitlock referred to the appearance of large numbers in 1827, 1829, 1835 and 1850. This pattern has continued throughout the twentieth and into the twenty-first century, with the largest recent influxes in Derbyshire occurring in the winters of 1970/71, 1988/89, 1995/96, 2000/01, 2004/05, 2008/09 and 2010/11. On each occasion flocks of over 100 were reported, the largest being of 400 at Dinting in December 1970 (Frost), 280 in the Hope Valley in January 1971 and, between January and March 2005, 250 at Staveley, 215 at Carr Vale and 203 at Darley Dale, while Shipley Wood produced a flock of 212 in January 2009. However, such flocks are exceptional and most winters produce only a few records.

The table shows the specific totals for each winter from 1970/71 to 2010/11 as well as the respective dates of the first and last sightings. It illustrates not only the marked variation in numbers, but also the occasional sequence of winters when not a single Waxwing has been seen. (Note that the figures during the main influx winters are inevitably only very approximate, since flocks can be highly restless, mobile and unpredictable in their movements.)

While the status of Waxwings as erratic winter visitors is unchanged, they are nowadays far more frequently reported from built-up areas than from rural areas. This is believed to be due to the proliferation of berry-bearing trees and shrubs in urban sites, which have been planted as amenity features in places such as gardens, parks and supermarket car parks. These clearly prove a greater attraction to these opportunistic feeders than the scattered countryside hawthorns which they previously favoured. As well as eating berries, Waxwings can sometimes be seen indulging in bouts of aerial fly-catching activity, especially in spring but also on mild winter days.

The earliest sightings concern three over Big Moor on 22nd October (1979) and seven on 23rd October (2010) on Beeley Moor, but there are relatively few records for this month and the main influxes usually occur in November and December. This was certainly the pattern in 1970/71 and 1988/89, when large flocks had built up in the north-west of the county by mid-December. Most birds had moved on by the end of January, with relatively few seen in February and March.

However, in 1995/96 it was not until 20th January that the first bird was reported in what was then the biggest invasion on record. Owing to the highly mobile nature of Waxwing flocks it is very difficult to assess overall numbers, but quite possibly up to 1000 individuals were involved. For several weeks there were regular sightings of groups containing over 100 birds around Derby, and sizeable flocks were also present in the Ilkeston, Matlock and Chesterfield areas. They were still widespread, though in smaller numbers, throughout April.

The next significant influx occurred in 2000/01 when over 450 Waxwings were recorded in the county. On this occasion there were very few birds on high ground with most being found in the eastern lowlands, including a flock of 112 at Staveley in March.

The winter of 2004/05 witnessed the greatest invasion of Waxwings recorded in Britain to date. In Derbyshire, the appearance of a few birds in late October heralded much larger arrivals throughout the following months, with three-figure

Winter	First record	Last record	Birds
1970/71	26th October	29th March	860
1971/72	28th November	29th March	37
1972/73	23rd November	12th March	6
1973/74	29th November	26th December	13
1974/75	26th October	20th February	94
1975/76	'November'	1st March	21
1976/77	–	–	–
1977/78	'early January'	12th January	2
1978/79	11th January	18th March	12
1979/80	22nd October	22nd October	3
1980/81	–	–	–
1981/82	–	–	–
1982/83	–	–	–
1983/84	–	–	–
1984/85	–	–	–
1985/86	20th January	22nd January	2
1986/87	26th December	16th April	14
1987/88	–	–	–
1988/89	6th November	5th February	400
1989/90	1st January	15th February	3
1990/91	29th October	23rd April	105
1991/92	20th November	21st April	85
1992/93	–	–	–
1993/94	–	–	–
1994/95	–	–	–
1995/96	20th January	28th April	1000
1996/97	16th November	21st March	34
1997/98	1st December	1st December	4
1998/99	24th January	25th February	2
1999/2000	27th November	22nd April	134
2000/01	31st December	2nd May	458
2001/02	–	–	–
2002/03	21st December	5th March	30
2003/04	20th November	2nd May	130
2004/05	26th October	11th May	2000
2005/06	4th December	22nd February	59
2006/07	11th February	11th February	1
2007/08	8th February	18th April	7
2008/09	15th November	20th April	1700
2009/10	–	2nd April	7
2010/11	23rd October	6th May	4000

flocks reported from at least 15 locations between December and April, and with a total of possibly 2000 individuals involved. In addition to the flocks of over 200 previously mentioned, counts of 100 or more were recorded at Hathersage, Eyam, Bolsover, Hodthorpe, Pools Brook Country Park, Chesterfield, North Wingfield, Hilcote, Ripley, Ilkeston, Long Eaton and Swadlincote. This winter also produced the latest sighting in the county, with ten still present in Derby on 11th May. An interesting observation concerned 45 roosting with Bramblings at 350m amsl at Shooter's Clough on 9th February.

Another very memorable 'Waxwing winter' was in 2008/09 when an estimated 1700 were seen, including 212 at Shipley Wood, and flocks of 100 to 130 at Allestree, Heanor and the Avenue Washlands. In the first winter period of 2010/11 up to 270 were at Shirebrook, 200 at Cotmanhay, 167 at Carr Vale, 150 at Long Eaton and 100 at Newhall with many flocks of 20–60, while in the second winter period 250 were recorded at Chesterfield, 150 at Littleover, and 100 at Tapton, Sinfin and Barlborough, harbingers of what was to be the largest county invasion to date.

Ringing has generated specific information regarding the movements of this species in Britain during its periodic eruptions from Scandinavia. For instance, in the invasion of 1970/71, eight Waxwings ringed in Derbyshire were all subsequently recovered within a range of 68km, while one controlled at Dinting had been ringed 35km away, a month earlier, in South Yorkshire. Evidence of birds arriving in Scotland in autumn and later progressing southwards, is provided by three examples. One which had been colour-ringed in Aberdeen in November 1990 was caught 440km further south at Walton, Chesterfield in the following February; an individual colour-ringed at Inverurie, Aberdeenshire on 30th October 2004, was sighted in Chesterfield on 8th March 2005; and one seen at Alvaston, Derby in February 2009 had been ringed in Aberdeenshire.

Nuthatch
Sitta europaea
A fairly common resident.

The range of the Nuthatch in the county has greatly expanded since 1893, when Whitlock described it as a local resident, confined to the north-east, south and south-west of the county; he thought it had declined. Jourdain said that it was very local and bred only in the north-east and south of the River Trent. By 1937 they were thought to be extinct around Derby, but numbers increased through the 1940s and 1950s in the southern part of the county. They were first reported from Chatsworth in 1946 and spread northwards up the Derwent and Wye Valleys during the 1960s and early 1970s, when breeding was recorded in Cressbrook Dale, Miller's Dale and Lathkill Dale. Breeding in the north-west was first recorded in 1962 at Taxal in the Goyt Valley and subsequently has occurred at several other sites in the area. This postwar range expansion was described in detail by Rodgers (1975) and corresponds to a national northward expansion recorded in the 1988–91 Atlas. Frost reported that, by contrast, it had become rare in the east and north-east, and by 1980 it was still described in the *Derbyshire Bird Report* as 'breeding throughout the county except the east', but Nuthatches have since reoccupied this area.

In the Derbyshire BBS (1995–99) the Nuthatch was found in 317 tetrads, with breeding confirmed in 157 of these, spread throughout the county, though with a number of gaps, most of which coincide with areas lacking in deciduous woodland. A total of 160 tetrads were considered to be in the probable or possible category. All but one of the 23 10km core squares had confirmed breeding records, compared with 12 in 1968–72 and 20 in 1988–91. This indicates a genuine spread into much of the county, and Eaton *et al.* (2010) show a national increase of 176% between 1970 and 2008.

As Nuthatches are generally noisy and very territorial birds, they are easily located during most of the breeding season, although nests can be hard to find if high up. Nest-boxes are frequently used. Unusually, a pair nested in a 4m-high hole on Sutton Scarsdale church in 2001, 2003 and 2006, and at Milton there was a nest in a brick-walled building in 2009.

They are predominantly found in deciduous woodland, parks, large gardens and churchyards. Oak trees with their abundant insects, are especially favoured. CBC data showed estimated densities of 5.91 pairs per km² at Shiningcliff Wood and 2.38 at Shire Hill Wood near Glossop. Records of territorial birds or pairs include: seven pairs present in Elvaston Castle Country Park in 1981; 30 present in the Bretby–Hartshorne area in 1986; nine singing in Shipley Park on 29th March 1992; 24, mostly singing, at Elvaston Castle Country Park on 15th April 1992; and eight territories in South Wood in May 1995. A survey in 1993 estimated 13 pairs in the limestone dales of SK17.

Winter counts are normally of small parties, up to seven or eight birds, with the highest totals recorded being 25 at Elvaston Castle Country Park on 9th December 1995, 20 at South Wood

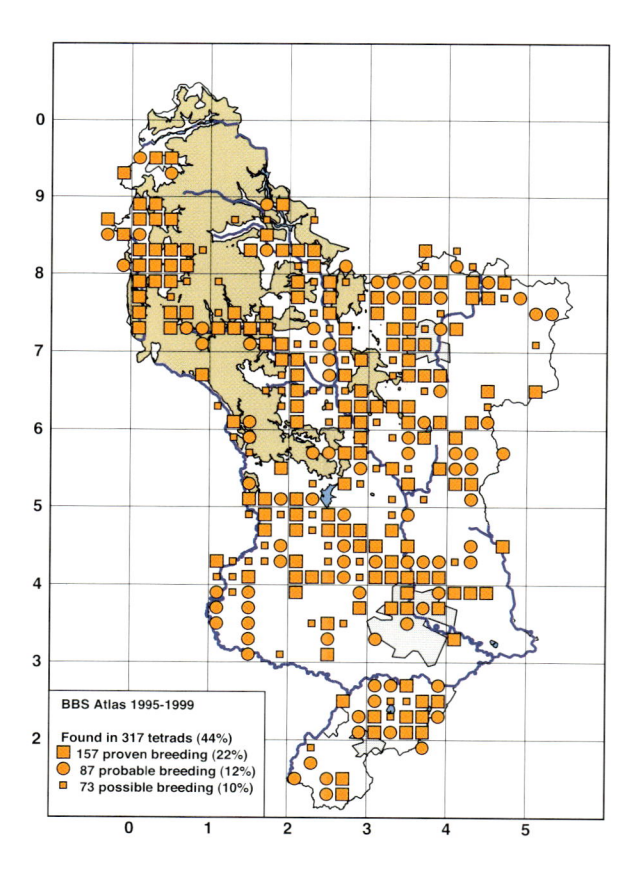

BBS Atlas 1995-1999
Found in 317 tetrads (44%)
157 proven breeding (22%)
87 probable breeding (12%)
73 possible breeding (10%)

on 29th December 1990 and 21 there on 31st December 1994. Nuthatches are more widespread outside the breeding season and are quite frequent visitors to garden feeding stations, even in some built-up areas.

Although they are generally absent from areas of moorland, there are three records from this habitat. One bird was observed on boulders on Stanage Moor on 15th August 1991, one was flushed from bilberry on Mill Hill, on the western flank of Kinder Scout, on 18th June 1997, and another was flushed from heather on Big Moor, 300m from the nearest tree, on 14th September 1998.

Interesting behavioural records include a pair inspecting holes in a limestone quarry near Ashbourne on 15th April 1978, one repeatedly making clumsy flights to take flies from an ivy-clad tree at South Wood in November 1986, and one taking food from a church window at Kedleston in July 1991. Archer (2005) recorded one taking insects in flight by a bare ash in Tideswell Dale in May 2002.

There have been 13 ringing recoveries in the county, all but two of these of birds having been ringed at Elvaston Castle Country Park between 1981 and 1995. The Nuthatch is a sedentary species and 69% of recoveries have been within 5km of their ringing site. Some youngsters have demonstrated a wider post-fledging dispersal, with one moving 15km from Elvaston to Loscoe in 37 days, and another moving 30km from Elvaston to Matlock in 122 days. The ring from an adult female, fitted in May 1987, was found in a Tawny Owl pellet the following winter. The oldest ringed bird was just over two years old.

Treecreeper
Certhia familiaris
A fairly common resident.

There has apparently been little change in distribution since Whitlock described Treecreepers as 'fairly diffused' over the whole county and common in some areas. They are found in both broad-leaved and coniferous woodland, parks and small groups of trees. The tetrad map shows that they occur throughout the county except in the moorland areas of the north. This is a relatively unobtrusive species and its calls, and especially its song, are often unrecognized by birdwatchers. Moreover, its habit of using inconspicuous nest sites in crevices and below flaps of bark, makes it more difficult to confirm breeding. This explains the relatively low number of 165 tetrads where breeding was confirmed, compared with those with probable and possible records at 86 and 142 tetrads respectively. All 23 10km core squares provided records of confirmed breeding; comparable figures for the 1968–72 and 1988–91 Atlases were 15 and 20 respectively.

Numbers in the county seem to be generally stable with only small annual fluctuations. Treecreepers are vulnerable to cold weather and mortality rises during severe winters such as those of 1946/47 and 1962/63, but the population soon recovers. At national level there were few differences in distribution between the two atlas periods, though numbers were reported to be increasing slowly. Eaton *et al.* (2008) suggest a currently stable population in the UK.

There were 22 on a census at Carsington Water on 23rd April 2003, although the CBC of 2003–07 suggested 11 territories there; 13, including seven in song, at Allestree Park on 20th March 2004; six singing at Win Hill on 2nd April and two extra territories on 6th June 2005; and seven singing in Whitwell Wood in May 2000. A survey in 1993 estimated 20 pairs in the limestone dales of SK17. Data from three CBC woodland plots in the 1990s showed estimated densities per km^2 of 8.18 pairs at Shiningcliff Wood, 6.94 pairs at Shirebrook, and 2.38 pairs at Shire Hill Wood. Three farmland CBC plots contained estimated densities of 0.33 pairs, 1.01 pairs and 3.80 pairs per km^2. Variations in the latter figures presumably relate to varying amounts of tree cover on the three plots. At Scarcliffe Woods, Frost (2008a) recorded a maximum of 15 territories in 1996. The overall increase of 63% there between the mid-1970s and the mid-2000s was possibly caused by the maturing of the plantations.

After the breeding season, Treecreepers forage widely away from nest sites, when they may join mixed flocks with tits and Goldcrests. Counts of more than ten birds are unusual but 25 were counted in a 3km stretch of the Moss Valley on 18th March 1984, and 20 were at South Wood on 31st December 1994. There was an exceptional record, from a reliable observer, of 75–100 birds at Chatsworth on 19th August 1977.

Treecreepers have been reported foraging on open rock-faces in Miller's Dale, Chee Dale and Froggatt Edge, and on the walls of buildings. Examples of the latter include a shop in Bakewell on 11th December 1983, Melbourne Church on 18th May 1983 and a house at Hopton in 1994, while one was seen on a stone bridge at Hope in March 2000. There are two records, dating from 1992, of birds climbing telegraph poles, at Cromford and Lower Padley, and one foraging on standard roses at Pastures Hill, Derby in January 1993. Other unusual records involve birds feeding on a peanut-holder, bird tables and window-sill crumbs.

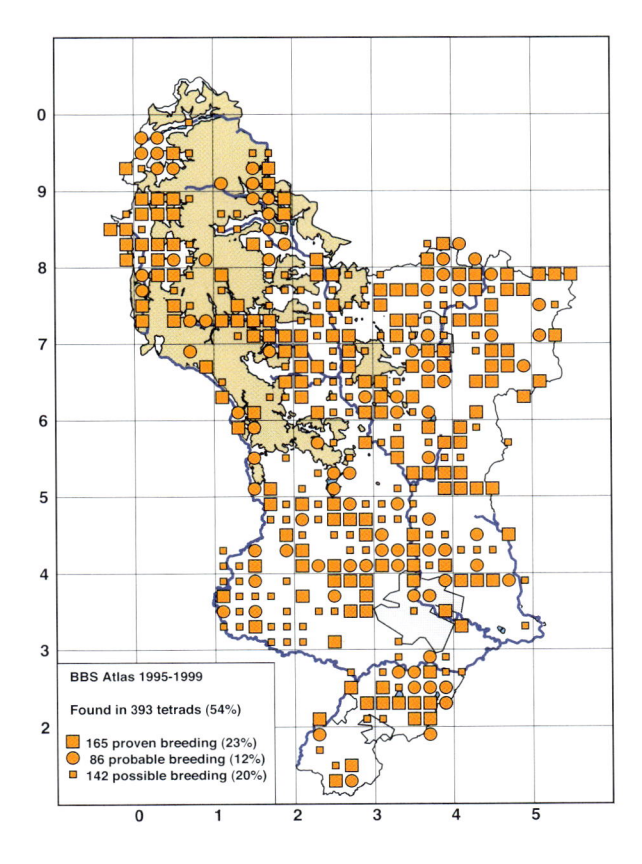

Unusual nest sites have been in crevices of sheds and other buildings, a hole in a shed door jamb, between timbers stacked upright, in a log-covered waste-bin and on the ground at the foot of a Scots pine.

This species is sedentary in Britain and the national ringing data show only five birds that have moved more than 20km. Indeed, 15% of birds have been recorded more than 5km from their ringing location (Wernham *et al.* 2002). There have been only three recoveries concerning Derbyshire: one found near to its place of ringing nine months later; an adult that travelled 11km from Elvaston Castle Country Park to Attenborough, Nottinghamshire, where it was controlled three months later in May 1991; and one ringed at Misson, Nottinghamshire in July 2007 that was controlled 28km south-west at Whitwell Wood two months later.

BBS Atlas 1995-1999

Found in 393 tetrads (54%)

- 165 proven breeding (23%)
- 86 probable breeding (12%)
- 142 possible breeding (20%)

Wren
Troglodytes troglodytes
An abundant resident.

The Wren was found to be the most widespread bird in the county during the Derbyshire BBS (1995–99), occurring in no fewer than 697 of a total of 724 tetrads (96%). This accords with the findings of the 1988–91 Atlas, when it was considered both the most widespread and the most numerous breeding species in Britain. This is due to the Wren's ability to exist in a very wide variety of habitats, such as woodland of all types, farmland, parks, gardens, scrubland, industrial wastelands, marshes and so on. It is found on our local moorlands to at least 500m amsl. Breeding was proved in all of the 23 10km core squares in the county, as it was in the 1968–72 and 1988–91 Atlases. The tetrad map confirms the wide distribution in the county.

This has obviously been the situation for a very long time, since Whitlock described Wrens as numerous residents and said that they were almost as frequent on the moorland edges as in southern woodlands, while Jourdain said that 'even in the wildest parts of the moorlands its cheery little song may frequently be heard'. Neither authority, however, commented on the bird's susceptibility to severe winter weather, unlike Frost, who remarked upon the Wren's capacity to recover its numbers. By 1966, for example, they were back to normal following the 1962/63 winter, which was by far the most severe in recent times.

Archer (2008) censused singing Wrens on a 7.4km transect from Tideswell Dale to Ashford-in-the-Water. He found a very strong correlation between the population and the number of frost-free days in the preceding winter, the latter based on data from the weather station at Weston Park, Sheffield, some 20km from the midpoint of the transect. The highest count, of 66 singing in 1990, followed the mildest winter, when only 14 days of frost were recorded. Conversely, the lowest, in 1986, when only 13 singing Wrens were found, followed the coldest winter in the period, with 61 days of frost.

In the CBC plots in the county, the Wren was the most numerous species at one of the woodland plots, Shiningcliff Wood, where it averaged 25.2 territories a year, at a density of 115 pairs per km². It was likewise the most common species at the Culland farmland plot, with 26.6 territories a year (45.9 pairs per km²). It was the second most numerous species at Farfield Farm, Hope and Broadhay Farm, Hathersage, and third most numerous at Shirebrook, but only sixth at Shire Hill, Glossop. Densities at these four site ranged from 19 to 83 pairs per km². A less intensive survey of Scarcliffe Woods in 1973–2008 (Frost 2008a) showed it to be the fourth most numerous breeding species overall, with territory counts ranging from nine in 1984 to 91 just six years later, and averaging 51. There was an overall increase of 43% during the survey period. Nationally, Eaton *et al.* (2010) show an increase of 55% during 1970 to 2008.

Counts during the 2000s show that numbers were very high, following a sequence of mild winters. Many valuable records of singing or territorial birds have been submitted to the *Derbyshire Bird Report*, though the most useful also gave details of the linear distances or areas involved. For example, 26 were counted along 8km of the Dove Valley between Hartington and Glutton Bridge in May 2002, and 32 along 6.5km of the River Lathkill in May 2003. Numbers of singing males at two well-monitored sites peaked in 2007 and 2008, with 37 at Carr Vale Nature Reserve and 44 at Drakelow Nature Reserve. There were 69 singing at Foremark Reservoir in 2007 and 36 likewise at Win Hill in 2008. At Carsington Water it was the most numerous passerine on the 2003–07 census, with an impressive 194 territories recorded. A useful upland record was of 25 singing on Big Moor in 2004.

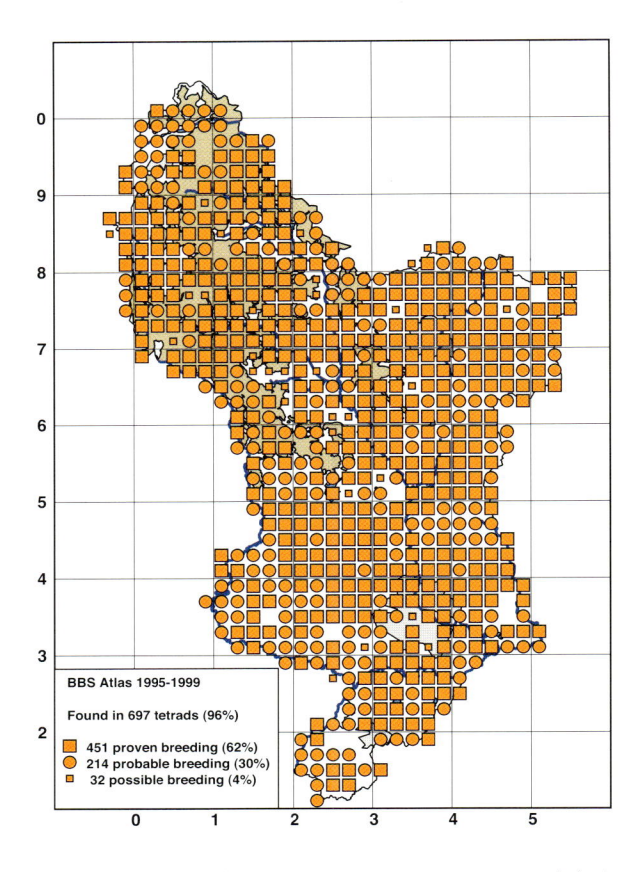

Derbyshire's Wrens have nested in some interesting sites. The more bizarre include the pocket of a pair of denim jeans hanging on a washing-line in a Shirebrook garden, a hanging basket at Dunston Garden Centre and in an old fuse-box on the wall of a ruined farm at Glapwell. There have been several instances of Wrens building on top of an old Swallow nest in barns.

Equally interesting, and endearing has been their choice of communal roosting sites. These range from the eaves of a Dronfield house, where up to 26 roosted in February 1989; ivy (for example 11 at Hayfield in December 1995); nest-boxes; an old Wren nest under a bridge; while a single bird roosted in a discarded tin can at Barbrook Reservoir in December 1998. Wrens obviously roost communally in small spaces for warmth, but a record of 12 found dead in a roost at Bakewell on New Year's Day 1982 is a reminder of just how vulnerable this bird is to very low temperatures.

This small species is usually considered to be sedentary but ringing has shown it quite capable of long-distance migration, with recorded movements to Scandinavia and the Mediterranean. The Derbyshire dataset comprises 22 records, mainly of movements inside Derbyshire or involving adjacent counties. However, one ringed at Hathersage in September 1987 was killed by a cat in the following January at St Neots, Cambridgeshire, 151km away. Twelve of the recoveries within Derbyshire are also of birds which were killed by domestic cats; three were controlled and the remainder simply reported as dead.

BBS Atlas 1995-1999

Found in 697 tetrads (96%)

- 451 proven breeding (62%)
- 214 probable breeding (30%)
- 32 possible breeding (4%)

Starling
Sturnus vulgaris
A common or abundant resident, passage migrant and winter visitor.

The Starling is a common or abundant bird throughout most of Derbyshire, and is equally at home in both built-up and rural areas. Whitlock described it as 'extremely abundant' and wrote of its beneficial qualities in destroying slugs and other garden pests. He quoted W. Storrs Fox of Bakewell, who erected nest-boxes for them in his garden, but the birds were so successful that they caused a lot of damage to his garden plants and finally he 'had to shoot them off'. Jourdain made two interesting observations concerning their breeding, recording hosts of Starlings breeding in Eldon Hole, about 50 to 100 feet below the Jackdaw colony, on 17th July 1903. This suggests that these were second-brood nesters, which are only occasional nowadays. Starlings no longer nest at Eldon Hole, though Jackdaws still do so. Secondly, he also recorded winter breeding, with a nest of large young in January 1898. Frost knew of a similar event in 1975.

Most Derbyshire Starlings nest in houses and other buildings but some nest in trees, though less commonly than before, and in holes in rock-faces, at least in the Peak District. Both Whitlock and Jourdain recorded breeding in Sand Martin burrows, but there are no recent reports of this. An interesting event occurred at Wingerworth in 1984, when a pair reared young in a hole in an elm, a metre below an occupied Tawny Owl nest.

The Derbyshire BBS (1995–99) confirmed that this remains a very widespread species, with a distribution ranking of fourteenth in the county. Breeding was proved in 544 tetrads, with possible and probable breeding in a further 71 and 15 tetrads.

Breeding is most easily proved when the birds are feeding noisy, newly fledged young, usually in the second half of May. Starlings were found in every 10km square in Derbyshire except SK19, which is predominantly moorland, with very little habitation. They were, however, proved to breed in this area in the 1968–72 and 1988–91 Atlases. Recorded absences here and in other upland areas in the north-west of the county are likely to be genuine, but omissions elsewhere suggest that the species has been overlooked.

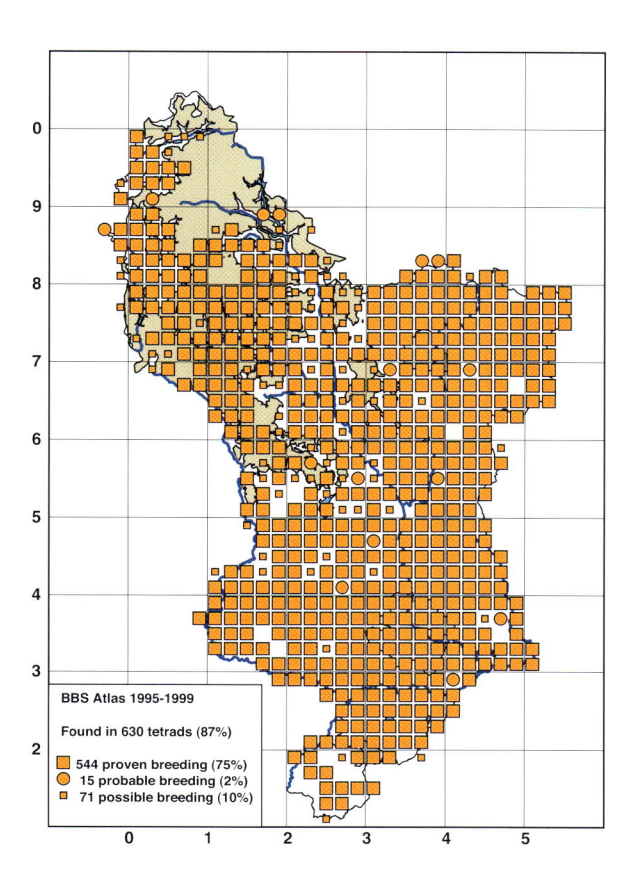

Frost believed that the Starling's status in the county had barely changed since Whitlock's day, but this is no longer the case, as there has been a widespread decline, both in the UK and in Europe. Eaton *et al.* (2010) show an overall UK decline of 76% in the period 1970–2008. There are relatively little quantitative data on this in Derbyshire, but BBS data for the East Midlands showed a decrease of 39% in the breeding population between 1994 and 2004. At Barbrook Plantation none have bred since 1987, where there were three to six pairs in the previous 30 years and populations in woodlands have clearly decreased much further than those in built-up areas. Possible reasons for the decline include a loss of nest sites to building modernization, improvements to pasture, that disrupt the birds foraging for leatherjackets and other invertebrates, and the conversion of pasture to cereals.

The decline in European populations is reflected locally in the lower numbers seen both on autumn migration and in wintering flocks. Passage is recorded in October and November, and while there was little recording of this before the early 1980s, it is significant that by far the largest count of migrants took place then, with 8500 moving south-west at Barbrook Reservoir on 27th October 1984. The biggest subsequent counts were: at Strines Top, where 5200 moved between south-west and west on 15th October 1995, with 3675 moving west there on 23rd October 1995; 2640 flying west over Big Moor on 1st November 1998; and at Ramsley, 3410 moving west on 1st November 2008 and 2860 west on 7th November 2010.

Starlings form large, communal roosts at all times of the year except April and May, when they are breeding. Even in June they may form five-figure roosts, but the largest gatherings are usually in winter, and consist mainly of immigrants. The largest roost recorded in Derbyshire was at Markland Grips, with over a million in the 1959/60 winter, and there were still 300,000 there in February 1963. Since then six-figure roosts have been reported east of Locko Park, with several hundred thousand in December 1963, and presumably the same roost recorded by another observer near Ockbrook during the following month and assessed at 150,000. There were 100,000 at Haddon Plantation in January 1967 and a similar number at Shuttlewood in December 1973. Subsequently, all roosts have been much smaller, with the largest being of 30,000 or more at Hilton Gravel Pits Nature Reserve in March 1983, 50,000 at Willington Gravel Pits in December 1993 and 30,000 at Kirk Ireton in January 2007. Roosts are most commonly in conifer plantations and reed-beds, while other sites have included hawthorn and willow scrub, a tall windbreak of *Cupressus leylandii*, and a maize field.

The table shows the largest roosting flocks in five-year periods since 1980.

Period	Largest flock	Mean largest annual flock
1980–84	30,000	13,400
1985–89	15,000	10,000
1990–94	20,000	10,700
1995–99	15,000	6500
2000–04	18,000	7200
2005–09	30,000	12,800

Many birds have been trapped and ringed at these winter roosts. Starlings were the subject of the earliest ringing studies and indeed the earliest recovery concerning Derbyshire was of one ringed near Cheadle, Staffordshire and shot at Sudbury in 1916. It is of interest that, of the 28 foreign recoveries involving distances greater than 500km, 43% were ringed in the 1950s and 1960s, and 45% of all Starlings ringed in Britain were trapped in this period (Wernham *et al.* 2002). In the 1990s, none of the 41 recoveries involving Derbyshire was further than 62km from

BBS Atlas 1995-1999

Found in 630 tetrads (87%)

■ 544 proven breeding (75%)
● 15 probable breeding (2%)
▪ 71 possible breeding (10%)

the ringing site. There are recoveries of Derbyshire-ringed birds in Germany, the USSR, Finland, Denmark, Sweden, Estonia and Poland, with birds ringed in Russia and Denmark being later found in the county. The two furthest moved from Breaston to Kashin, Russia (2523km east-north-east) and from Beighton to Dmitrov, Russia (2508km east). The oldest bird was found dead in July 1987 at Allestree, over 18 years after it was ringed at nearby Darley Abbey, in February 1969.

Rose-coloured Starling
Sturnus roseus
A very rare vagrant.

The Rose-coloured Starling breeds from south-east Europe east to Iran, and winters in India. Renowned for its periodic irruptions, it was on the BBRC list until 2001, by which time there had been 614 UK sightings.

Whitlock knew of five records. One was shot at Weston Cliff in October 1784, and one was seen near the River Trent at King's Newton on October 1842 by J.J. Briggs. The same observer examined the skin of one killed near Matlock prior to 1845. An immature was killed at King's Newton (again) on 16th September 1854 and one was shot as it ate elderberries at Melbourne in 1866. Jourdain added a record of one at Allestree prior to 1863.

There have been four modern records.

Year	Location and date
2001	Hilton, an adult in a garden on 19th July
2002	Sinfin, Derby, an adult from 10th to 18th June
2002	Shirebrook, an adult in a garden on 12th–13th June
2009	Curbar, an adult in a garden on 3rd May

The years 2000–02 saw record numbers of Rose-coloured Starlings occurring in Britain, with the 2002 total of 182 birds being the largest ever influx. Key (2002 & 2003c) gave accounts of the birds in 2001 and 2002.

Dipper
Cinclus cinclus
A fairly common resident, mainly in the northern half of the county; scarce in the south and east.

The Dipper is a familiar sight on the rivers of the Peak District, occurring on both gritstone and limestone rivers. Moreover, it is relatively tolerant of human presence, making it easy to watch back to its nest to confirm breeding. The fact that it is noisy, both in its song and its other calls, also means that it is not readily overlooked.

It was regarded by Whitlock and Jourdain as similarly widespread on the northern rivers, breeding as far south as Doveridge on the Dove and Ambergate on the Derwent. It may have retreated about 5km up the Dove and 2km up the Derwent since those days, but essentially its distribution is almost identical. The species has been surveyed twice, in 1958–68 by Shooter (1970) and then again by a team of DOS members in 1993 (Foster 1994). Its population changes have also been tracked by WeBS plots on much of the Derwent system (Falshaw *et al*. 1999). The main conclusion of all of these studies is that the Dipper population of the county is remarkably stable. Shooter (1970) thought there might be 107 pairs, and the 1993 survey recorded 112 pairs. The WBS surveys on 18.7km of the Derwent since 1973, and an extra 5.4km of the Noe since 1975, have reported between 14 and 24 pairs, with no long-term trend. However, Eaton *et al*. (2010) record a decline of 31% in the period 1970 to 2008.

Unlike Common Sandpipers, Dippers do not breed around the upland reservoirs, and construction of these must represent a loss of habitat; but Dippers are in any case less abundant on the gritstone rivers. The 1993 survey found that densities along the Derwent, Dove and Wye all averaged 0.48–0.49 territories per km of river. On the Goyt and Etherow, however, densities were 0.32 territories per km, and on the River Hipper there was only one pair in 7km. The Derbyshire BBS (1995–99) suggests that a few pairs nesting in less obvious sites might have been overlooked in the earlier ones, since pairs were found on the Henmore Brook near Ashbourne and on the River Amber near Ashover. There was also a cluster of three tetrads with possible breeding birds lower down the River Derwent near Duffield where it is joined by the River Ecclesbourne. Since some of the 49 possible records may represent non-breeding birds, and densities in the Dark Peak are lower, a county population of about 110–120 pairs seems probable. Foster (1994) was surely correct to conclude that the 1993 survey gave a good estimate of the county population.

Dippers breed early, courtship being recorded from January onwards. Eggs may be laid as early as February, though the peak

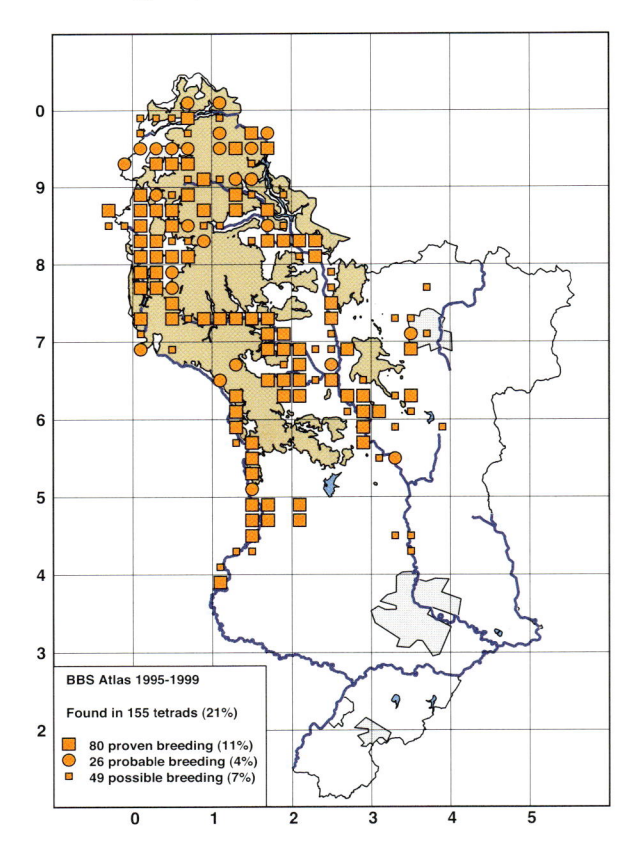

BBS Atlas 1995-1999

Found in 155 tetrads (21%)

- 80 proven breeding (11%)
- 26 probable breeding (4%)
- 49 possible breeding (7%)

is in late March or early April. Second clutches produce a second smaller peak in May. Dippers are resident, and young birds mostly disperse from their natal territories no more than 10km away. Severe winters may also push upland birds downstream, even to the coast. Research in Wales and Scotland shows that Dippers have suffered from acid rain, and the consequent loss of invertebrates such as caddis-fly larvae on which they depend (Tyler & Ormerod 1994). Given that the Peak District has suffered from the industrial output of the surrounding towns for three centuries, it is remarkable that the species has flourished so well, though the limestone rivers will be well buffered. Recreational pressure, from walkers and others on the very popular riverside paths, has also not diminished its numbers. Some security is allowed by its nest sites, often located over deep water, on small cliffs, under overhanging banks or below waterfalls and bridges. In 2009, low water levels in Lathkill Dale was thought to be the cause of five nest failures there. Artificial nest sites have recently been installed at this location and elsewhere in the county.

Jourdain recorded regular nesting by a pair in the roof of a cave known as the Dove Holes, and the same site has been used in subsequent years, even into the twenty-first century. Another very interesting site was the bottom of one of the arches of the railway viaduct spanning Millers Dale, some 18m above ground level.

Though our Dippers are often thought of as strictly sedentary, there are many Derbyshire records at sites well away from breeding areas. The more notable include singles at Drakelow in August 1974, Drum Hill in June 1982 and Etwall Brook in March 1987. Since 1978, other extralimital records have come from Allestree, Avenue Washlands Nature Reserve, Belper, Chesterfield Canal, Clay Cross, Dronfield, Hulland Ward, Hardwick Park, Leesbrook, Ogston Reservoir, Osmaston, Pleasley, Renishaw, Rother Valley Country Park (now in South Yorkshire), Sheepbridge and Williamthorpe. The discovery in 2010 of family parties on the Normanton Brook at Westhouses and on the River Drone at Sheepbridge, came as a considerable surprise.

Derbyshire birds are of the British race, *C.c. gularis*. The only accepted record of the Continental, black-bellied form, *C.c. cinclus*, was of one at Langley Mill on 1st January 1976. Others that may have been of this subspecies were seen at the Pavilion Gardens in Buxton in January 1988 and on the River Derwent at Borrowash in December 1997.

There have been 16 ringing recoveries associated with Derbyshire, all of birds ringed as nestlings. The earliest report was from 1939 of a bird ringed near Hathersage which was found dead near Grindleford almost two years later.

Ring Ouzel
Turdus torquatus
An uncommon summer visitor to the moorlands of the Peak District, and a rare passage migrant elsewhere. Exceptional in winter.

The Ring Ouzel is still a regular summer visitor to the Peak District, typically associated with the gritstone edges, but numbers have declined steadily over the last 30 years, as they have nationally, and research is currently in progress in southern Scotland and elsewhere to try to understand the causes.

It was regarded by Whitlock as a common spring visitor to the Peak District, breeding on the gritstone area as far south as Ashover, and in Dove Dale, Coombs Dale and Lathkill Dale in the White Peak. By the time Alsop (1975) collated the breeding range, it was almost confined to the gritstone of the High Peak. The only breeding reports from the limestone area concerned Dowel Dale, near Buxton, and the marginal sites of Winnats Pass and Treak Cliffs, very close to the gritstone at Mam Tor.

The tetrad map shows that it was found in 69 squares; of these, 30 had proof of breeding, 29 were probable and 10 possible. All were in gritstone areas.

Alsop (1975) remarked that this was a difficult species to survey well, but he estimated, from his own experience, that there might then have been 200–250 pairs. Brown and Shepherd (1991) recorded only 60 territories in Derbyshire, but conceded that by concentrating on the main areas of moorland they may have missed some pairs. Only nine pairs were recorded in English Nature's Eastern Moors survey of 1998. If all 69 tetrads in which birds were mapped in the breeding season (confirmed, probable and possible) contained two pairs, there would be only 138 pairs now, and the decline is not merely caused by range contraction. In his own study area, Comb's Moss, which Alsop regarded as a particularly favourable site, there used to be six to eight pairs regularly but there are nowadays no more than two. Carr and Middleton (2004) revealed a decline of 15% in the Peak District population compared with 1990. Only two, possibly three, pairs were found on the EMP moors survey in 2010.

The nest sites and feeding habitats seem to be unchanged, making the decline hard to understand. National ringing recoveries have identified the wintering grounds as being in southern Spain and northern Africa, where they feed on juniper and other berries. The possibility that these have deteriorated seems negated by the fact that the Scandinavian populations, which winter in the same areas, have not declined to the same extent as the British

BBS Atlas 1995-1999
Found in 69 tetrads (10%)
- 30 proven breeding (4%)
- 29 probable breeding (4%)
- 10 possible breeding (1%)

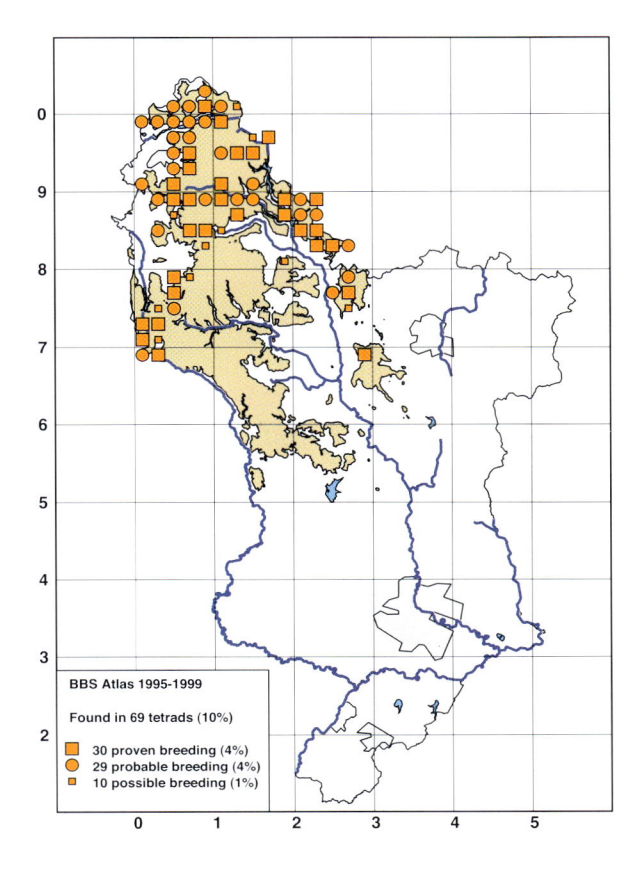

ones. Breeding success here also seems as good as ever. The possibility that post-breeding food for the juveniles, perhaps the berry crops from rowan and bilberry, has declined through overgrazing or other agricultural changes, remains to be explored.

Another possible cause of the decrease is increased human pressure resulting from recreational activities. This is exemplified at Stanage Edge, which is both a traditional breeding area for Ring Ouzels and a site of world renown for rock climbing. There were eight pairs in 2001, when climbing was curtailed by the foot-and-mouth epidemic, but only three pairs since (Atkin & Falshaw 2004). The management plan for the North Lees Estate (PDNPA 2002) took these findings into account, and has promulgated strategies to reduce the disturbance to nesting birds.

Ring Ouzels are associated with the periphery of the moorlands, particularly the rockier slopes where long heather, bracken and boulders provide suitable nest sites. Nests are usually on the ground, though sometimes on small cliffs and exceptionally in trees. However, feeding takes place on nearby pastures, and is concentrated on earthworms. It is not unusual to see Ring Ouzels feeding in fields with Blackbirds or Mistle Thrushes, and once, on 22nd May 1977, five *Turdus* (these three, Fieldfare and Song Thrush) were noted feeding together at Pikenaze, Longdendale (Yalden *pers obs*).

They are among the earlier of summer migrants to return. Alsop (1975) recorded extreme dates at Comb's Moss of 14th March 1965 and 10th April 1966, with 25th March the usual date. In Derbyshire in 1978–2011 the mean first date was 19th March and the earliest ever record was from Holymoorside on 23rd February 1941. Males usually arrive a few days before females, but they take up territory and pair quickly, the first clutches being laid in mid to late April. Incubation lasts for 12–14 days, and fledging takes about the same period, so fledglings appear in mid to late May. The harsh 'chack-chack' of anxious parents, attempting to avoid intruders, but feeding their young at this time, is often the best indication that they are breeding, as song is relatively sporadic. Second clutches are usual, and laid within about nine days of the first broods hatching. Exceptionally, a third clutch in June may follow (Appleyard 1994).

In August and September, family parties and larger flocks may gather in suitable berry-rich areas, particularly rowan and bilberry, fattening up prior to migration. Small numbers are sometimes recorded at the regular migration watch-points, especially Ramsley and Strines Top, with a maximum of nine moving north-east at the latter site on 20th September 1994. The most impressive flock of all was of about 100 at Chunal Moor on an unspecified date (Frost). More recently, the largest autumn gatherings were of 26 in a single rowan at Westend on 15th October 1988, and 22 on Big Moor on 25th September 1999. Departure takes place from September and the latest dates are sometimes as early as this (for example on 30th August 1985, 6th September 1991, and 17th September 1983), but usually there is a straggle of later sightings, frequently in October and not uncommonly in November; there were records in the latter month in six years of the period 2000–11. The average latest date in 1978–2011 is 21st October.

Surprisingly, there are no fewer than seven winter records, all of singles. These were at Longshaw on 9th and 16th December 1979; Derwent on 7th January 1983; Ladybower on 9th December 1995; close to the centre of Ilkeston from 14th to 22nd December 1998; in a Froggatt garden on five dates between 27th January and 20th February, and again on 16th March 1996; a Duffield garden from 21st December 2000 to 4th April 2001; and Stubley Hollow on 8th January 2008.

Away from moorland areas, the Ring Ouzel is a very uncommon passage migrant, occurring from March to May (as late as 20th in 1978) and from August to November. One at Barrow Gravel Pits on 2nd July 2006 was exceptionally early. Spring records in lowland areas are more frequent than those in autumn, but are still erratic. For example, in the springs of 2007 and 2008 there were records from six and eight lowland sites, followed by none at all in 2009. It is possible that some of the sightings at this season, especially the later ones, are of birds moving to Scandinavia. In recent years, however, the two largest spring gatherings were at upland localities. There were 23 at Cracken Edge on 16th April 2006, and 24 males and four females at Crowden on 19th April 2008.

There are two overseas recoveries of birds ringed in the High Peak as chicks that were found in southern France in the following October and March. Another, ringed on Hilbre Island, Cheshire on 30th April 1997, was found at Edale 26 days later.

Blackbird
Turdus merula
An abundant resident, passage migrant and winter visitor.

The Blackbird is possibly second only to the Robin as the most familiar British bird, and it is the third most widespread species in Derbyshire. Its catholic diet and wide choice of nest sites enables it to utilize a great variety of habitats, such as woodland, farmland and built-up areas. At higher altitudes it may be present on the moorland edge, sometimes overlapping with the Ring Ouzel. The tetrad map shows this wide distribution: it was found in 684 tetrads (95% of the whole county) with breeding proved in 558 (82% of those found). It is an easy species for which to prove breeding, since both nests and family parties are readily seen, and the breeding season is a long one.

It ranked between the fourth and seventh most numerous species on the CBC plots surveyed in the county during the 1990s, though densities showed considerable variation. On the three woodland plots these ranged from 65.97 pairs per km^2 at Shirebrook to 26.19 at Shire Hill, while the farmland plots supported 33.16 pairs per km^2 at Culland, down to 10.75 at Broadhay Farm, Hathersage. On all of these plots, however, it was easily the most numerous thrush. The same applies to Scarcliffe Woods, where it was the third most numerous breeding species in 1973–2008, and also the third most common in midwinter (Frost 2008a). In 2003–07 there were 143 probable breeding pairs at Carsington Water. Densities are, however, likely to be much higher in gardens and parks in built-up areas.

The Blackbird has the ability to rear three broods of young in a favourable year. In very mild weather, breeding may begin in late winter: fledged young were seen as early as 7th February in Derby in 1981, with other February fledglings seen on 27th at Glapwell in 1998, and in Derby, again, on 19th in 2005. In Chesterfield, a nest with young a week old was found on 4th February 1981, but apparently failed. This species also shows versatility in its choice of nest sites: unusual examples have included an unlined hollow on a shelf in an outbuilding at Renishaw Park and in a tree hole in Derby, while nests on the ground and in drystone walls are not rare. At Birdholme in 1985, a nest that contained 15 eggs, thought to be the product of only one female, attracted the attention of the local and national press.

Whitlock described the Blackbird as a very common resident, adding that, 'In Derbyshire, immigration is not very apparent, Blackbirds being equally common at all times of the year.' Jourdain made no mention of immigrants in the county.

Only a few Blackbirds are seen during migration watches, with 53 moving south in only eight minutes at Drakelow Nature Reserve on 2nd October 1989 being the most striking record. Most movement is thought to take place nocturnally. Influxes, presumed to be of Continental birds, are regularly recorded during late October and November, and the highest counts of the year are usually made in the latter month, or in December. These include 'several hundreds' at Sinfin Moor on 27th–28th November 1990, 270 at Markeaton Park, including 66 in 100m of hawthorn hedgerow, on 22nd November 1988, and 231 in the Moss Valley on 7th December 1982. At the last site there was also an interesting

BBS Atlas 1995-1999

Found in 684 tetrads (94%)
- 558 proven breeding (77%)
- 97 probable breeding (13%)
- 29 possible breeding (4%)

with a biscuit-coloured body, almost white wings and a pale-yellow bill. Whitlock remarked that the Rolleston Hall collection included one that was pale buff and another with a 'curious chestnut tint.'

The Blackbird is one of the most commonly ringed birds and no fewer than 716 recoveries have been associated with Derbyshire. The earliest record is of a nestling ringed at Hope in May 1912 which was shot in Tipperary, Ireland the following January. The longevity record concerned a bird ringed near New Mills in 1963 that survived for over ten years before being killed by a cat at the same site. As with most passerine ringing recoveries, the bulk are of individuals that have been killed within a short distance of their place of ringing. Indeed, 80% of the 716 reports are of birds moving no more than 10km. By contrast, 17 of the birds moved more than 1000km and all but one of these involved movements to or from Scandinavia. The odd one out was of a bird ringed at a winter roost near Eckington that was found freshly dead two winters later in Vizcaya, Spain, which represents a less likely movement of Blackbirds between subsequent winters. The table shows the numbers of recoveries in each country of birds ringed in Derbyshire, and the numbers of birds ringed abroad and recovered in the county. The pattern closely mirrors the national situation (Wernham et al. 2002), except for the lack of any records from the Baltic countries.

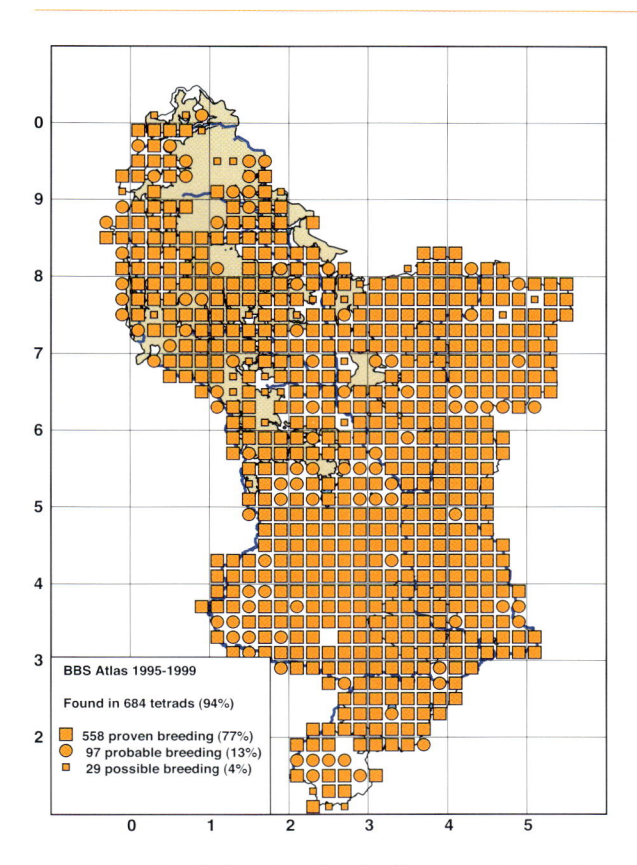

record of 50 disturbed inside a farm building on 19th December 1981, after a period of heavy snow. Many upland breeding sites are abandoned in cold winter weather, while at lower levels Blackbirds may, at least temporarily, desert their territories to take advantage of favourable feeding conditions elsewhere.

There have been many records of partial or full albinos. Leucistic birds are much rarer, but included one at Whitwell in 1992, while at Elvaston Quarry in April 1986 there was one

Country	Ringed	Recovered
Belgium	–	2
Netherlands	5	4
Denmark	4	1
Sweden	10	1
Norway	5	1
Finland	4	–
Germany	5	–
France	1	–
Spain	1	–
Ireland	4	–
Totals	39	9

Black-throated Thrush
Turdus atrogularis
A very rare vagrant.

A first-winter male frequented suburban gardens at Hollingwood, Chesterfield from 3rd January to 24th February 1997. It was found by an observant householder who reported it to a colleague, who was a keen birdwatcher. During its stay, this well-watched bird favoured an apple tree and a line of hawthorn bushes in which it fed and sheltered. It was even seen to feed on mince pies. This constituted the forty-second record for Britain (Key 1998a): by the end of 2010, the total number of records had risen to 70 (Hudson et al. 2011). The species breeds in central Siberia and winters mainly from Iraq to Burma.

Fieldfare
Turdus pilaris
A common winter visitor, passage migrant, and an occasional breeder.

Whitlock described this species as a common winter visitor in fluctuating numbers, which is still the case. The first autumnal arrivals are generally in September, with 17th the mean first date in the period 1978–2011. An exceptionally early flock of 21 was seen at Parwich on 31st August 1978. Most arrive between mid-October and mid-November, when major movements can be witnessed. These have included 7700 west at Strines Top on 2nd November 1986; 7200 moving between south-east and south-west at Ogston Reservoir on 21st October 1990, and 4087 moving north-west at Highoredish Hill on 2nd November 1986. More than 10,000 overflew Ramsley on 22nd October 1990 and other large counts at this site were of 8530 on 2nd November 2006, 6860 on 12th November 2008, 7850 on 10th November 2009, and 10,995 on 14th October 2011.

In late autumn and winter, flocks of up to several hundred may be seen feeding on berries, or seeking food from grassland areas, especially permanent pasture. Very large counts at this time include 3500 at Breck Farm on 15th January 1984, 3500 along the Rowthorne Trail on 6th January 1991, 3000 at Stanley (near Tibshelf) on 25th December 1990, 3000 at Newton on 29th December 1990, 2500 at Cathole on 8th November 1999, and 2500 at Eastmoor on 9th December 1981. However, as with Redwings, the largest counts are usually of communal roosts. These are generally in areas of dense scrub, including hawthorn and willow, and in conifer plantations, though there are also several records of them roosting in heather on moorland. The largest recorded winter roosts were of 10,000–12,000 at High Moor in January 1983 and 8000 at Osmaston in December 1976.

Severe weather and depletion of food sources may cause many Fieldfares to move away, although some will seek food in gardens and built-up areas. Hard weather movement is sometimes recorded but, strangely, the heaviest midwinter movements took place in mild conditions in January 1996: at Carr Vale 13,000 moved south to south-west during 9th–13th January, while at Glapwell 5000 flew south in just 50 minutes on 10th January.

Return passage is recorded in late March and early April, when very large flocks may again be seen. These included 3000 roosting in heather on Big Moor on 5th April 1973, 2000 at Castleton on 5th April 1988, 3500 roosting at Drakelow Nature Reserve in late March 1996, and a notable 7935 roosting at Belper Park on 5th April 1996. Most have departed by the end of April but a few are frequently recorded in early May, even in flocks, such as 120 near Ashbourne on 6th May 1991 and 65 near Wormhill two days later. Song is very occasionally heard from birds in spring, but is far less frequently heard than that of Redwing. The mean last date for the period 1978–2011 was May 10th.

Fieldfares have nested in the county on at least six occasions and have been suspected of doing so in several other years. Frost and Shooter (1983) attempted to clarify the situation. In 1921, Ralph Chislett saw a pair near Hathersage on 1st May and believed them to be the owners of a partly built nest, but after a week the birds had gone. In 1969, a pair was seen regularly taking food to a ditch in a field at Moorfield, Glossop (a bull in the field prevented closer examination). In 1970, an adult with two recently fledged young was seen at Hay Dale. Another family party was seen at Edale in June 1975. Food-carrying was observed in Longdendale in 1978, though a plucked bird was subsequently found at a Kestrel nest. At Foolow, one was watched nest-building on 18th May 1980 and the most recent year when breeding was proved was 1989, when one was carrying food at Heyden Brook at the end of May.

Other than these confirmed breeding records, there have been numerous records, particularly in the Peak District, of Fieldfares in late spring and summer, usually involving only one or two birds, though a flock of 13 was seen at Combs on 13th June 1998. Some of these records might well have been of breeding birds, including five at Wigley in June 1946; a pair was seen at Leash Fen in June 1974, and subsequently a probable used nest was found there; two alarming at a Sparrowhawk at Ladybower in June 1981 were thought to be behaving parentally; one at Blackden Moor on 2nd June 2004 was considered to be engaged in distraction display, and one was at the same site in June 2005. Breeding may have taken place at a site in the west of the county in 2008, when two were seen on 23rd May and one on five dates in early June.

It is generally considered that the birds spending the winter in central and northern Britain have originated from Norwegian populations, whereas birds breeding in Sweden winter in south-east England, Belgium and France. Finnish populations similarly occur in the south-east but also go as far south as Italy (Wernham *et al.* 2002). The ringing data for Derbyshire somewhat modifies this view in that three of the recoveries, of birds ringed in winter, were later found in the breeding season in Sweden and another in Finland. Three others ringed in the county in winter were found in subsequent winters in France, Poland and Italy. There is also a recovery of a bird ringed as a chick in Sweden which was found in Melbourne two winters later.

Song Thrush
Turdus philomelos
A common resident and partial migrant.

Song Thrushes are found throughout Derbyshire, in parks, woods, gardens and almost anywhere that trees, shrubs and bushes grow. They are absent from open moorland but can be found on the moorland fringe in woods and conifer plantations, and in the latter habitat they are sometimes the most numerous thrush. The tetrad map shows their widespread distribution (being nineteenth in the 'league'), with the gaps in the central north and north-western areas considered genuine absences from these upland areas. There is no evidence of a change in range since the 1968–72 and 1988–91 Atlases, when it was also found in every 10km square. Although the Song Thrush was recorded in 579 tetrads in the Derbyshire BBS (1995–99), the Mistle Thrush was, surprisingly, slightly more widespread, its presence in 603 tetrads ranking it two places above the Song Thrush. Nevertheless, there is no question that the latter is the more numerous of the two species overall.

Breeding was confirmed (mostly by observing newly fledged young or adults foraging on the ground for food) in 359 of these, and was probable in a further 174, mainly on account of observers hearing the familiar and far-carrying song.

However, overall numbers have decreased in recent years, as they appear to have done slowly for the past century or more. Whitlock described it as extremely common, even up to the moorland edge. Subsequently, most observers' comments on changed status refer to declines.

Caution must be exercised with numerical comparisons, since Snow (2003) showed that Song Thrushes sing mainly at dawn and dusk, and counts at other times of day may lead to considerable underestimation. Nevertheless, on the Shirebrook CBC plot the number of territories fell from a high of six in 1979–80 to a minimum of one by 1991. Of the 1990s woodland CBC plots, this site had a density of 10.42 pairs per km^2, compared with 6.36 at Shiningcliff and 4.76 at Shire Hill. Densities on the three farmland CBC plots were very similar, at 2.69 to 3.11 pairs per km^2. The six plots combined averaged 10.0 Song Thrush territories in the 1990s; the totals for Mistle Thrush and Blackbird were 7.0 and 63.2. At Scarcliffe Woods the number of territories reduced from 47 in 1974 to 11 in 2002, before a good recovery to 26 in 2008. The 1973–2008 average of 25 territories made it the seventh most numerous breeding species in the woods, well below Blackbird, which averaged 58 territories, but much more numerous than the Mistle Thrush, with an average of just three territories (Frost 2008a). The Carsington Water census of 2003–07 indicated a total of 62 territories.

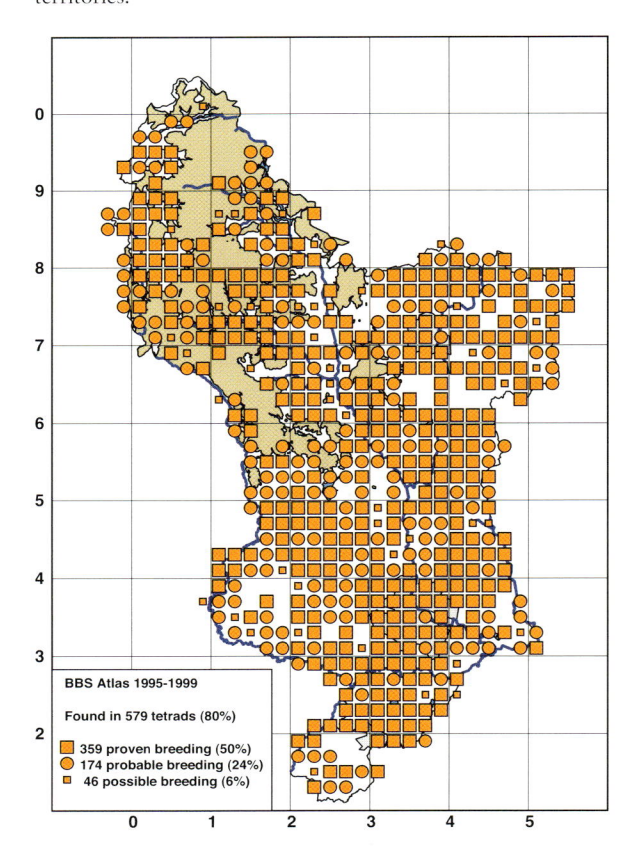

BBS Atlas 1995-1999
Found in 579 tetrads (80%)
■ 359 proven breeding (50%)
● 174 probable breeding (24%)
▪ 46 possible breeding (6%)

Although the middle years of the 2000s witnessed some recovery in Song Thrush numbers, overall declines have been recorded throughout much of the UK since the 1970s. Various reasons for this have been suggested, most of them connected with agricultural changes, including the switch from the spring sowing to autumn sowing of cereals, thereby reducing the amount of tillage available for feeding in spring, and better drainage, which has led to a decline in the availability of worms. The increased use of molluscicides in gardens may also have caused a decline in the numbers of slugs and snails, which are also important food items.

In winter, woodland is largely devoid of Song Thrushes. For example, at Scarcliffe Woods, a regular midwinter census from 1971/72 to 2007/08 showed an average of four birds per visit, compared with 58 Blackbirds. Numbers of Song Thrushes in other habitats at this season are also lower, presumably as a result of emigration.

Influxes of birds presumed to be of Continental stock are recorded in the county in most autumns, usually in September and October, when berry-laden trees and shrubs such as rowan, whitebeam and elder are a particular attraction. The largest recent gatherings were of 60 at Barbrook Plantation on 11th October 1987, and 50 at Darley Dale on 21st October 1979, Riddings Park on 22nd September 1983 and Carsington Water on 5th November 2002. Small numbers are often seen or heard on visible migration, sometimes nocturnally, with an outstanding record of 87 south-west over Strines Top on 10th October 1993. Another particularly interesting record was of 13 flushed at dawn from heather, where they had presumably roosted, at Totley Moss on 16th October 1994.

The species is highly migratory in parts of its range but in contrast most British and Irish populations are strikingly sedentary (Wernham *et al.* 2002). The data for Derbyshire support these findings in that, of the 123 recoveries, only five are from outside the British Isles: in France (three), Portugal and Denmark. Within Britain there have been ringing recoveries south to Cornwall and north to Angus, and including the Isle of Man and Lundy. As with most passerines, however, most recovered birds have been close to their place of ringing, with 58% of the Derbyshire-ringed birds found again within 4km.

Redwing
Turdus iliacus
A common winter visitor and passage migrant.

Whitlock described this species as a common winter visitor, as it remains today. The first autumnal Redwings usually arrive in the latter half of September with a mean first date in the period 1978–2011 of 24th. This is seven days later than the Fieldfare, which is perhaps surprising as the two species often migrate together. The earliest record was on 3rd September 1977 when birds were heard over Barlborough. In some years the first are not recorded until October, and the main arrival is almost always in the period from mid-October to mid-November.

Much Redwing migration takes place nocturnally, and is especially typical of damp, misty, late autumn nights. However, visible diurnal passage, usually between south and west, may be spectacular, though numbers are prone to great annual variation. The premier site has been Ramsley, where the largest counts were of an amazing 41,600 on 27th October 2006, 16,240 on 17th October 2002, and 9770 on 26th October 2005. Other large counts have come from Strines Top, where 6500 moved north on 10th October 1992, 4900 north-west on 14th October 1993, and 4185 west in one hour on 1st November 1989. At Ashover, 7000 passed through on 18th October 2005 and 4250 were counted at Hardwick on 26th October 2005. On 21st October 1990, 4800 flew between south-east and south-west over Ogston Reservoir. There are many other four-figure records of migrating birds.

Wintering numbers also vary considerably from year to year. Sometimes, relatively few are seen in midwinter but in others, flocks of several hundred birds may be found, often feeding on pastures or in woodland and scrub containing berry-bearing trees and bushes, though some forage among the leaf litter below trees. Redwings are very vulnerable to severe weather and many move away in such conditions, though others penetrate into built-up areas and gardens. A flock of 1100 flew over Milford during a snowstorm on 11th February 1983, while in mild weather in January 1996 a southerly movement consisting of thousands of birds was witnessed at sites throughout the county; these were presumed to be moving away from colder conditions elsewhere.

The largest winter counts are generally of birds roosting communally, usually in rhododendrons or hawthorn scrub, and often with Fieldfares. Up to 8000 have been recorded at Hayfield (Frost); 5000 were at Osmaston in December 1976, and 3500 at High Moor in January and February 1983. Large counts away from roosts include 2400 along 3.5km of the Nutbrook Canal in January 1996, over 3000 at Bennerley Marsh in February 1996, and 3000 at Egginton Sewage Farm in January 2003.

By late February, numbers are generally much lower but, like Fieldfare, increase with return passage in late March and early April. Sub-song is sometimes heard from birds at this time as it is, to a lesser extent, in autumn. Most birds have departed by late April, and the average last date in the period 1978–2011 was 24th April. There are occasional May records, the most interesting of which were of a bird in full song at Slagmill Plantation on 18th (1985) and likewise in the Goyt Valley on 17th (2003). Later records were of one at Ladybower in June 1976 (Frost) and on 19th July 2003, at Glossop on 9th August 1990 and 26th June 2008, and another in the latter year at Willington Gravel Pits on 6th July. Other than the singing birds, there have been no signs to suggest breeding.

Frost recorded that one of the Icelandic race *T.i. coburni* was ringed at Hackenthorpe in 1972.

Many Redwings have been trapped and ringed in the county, often when arriving at their roosts. This species readily moves according to the available food supply and winter conditions. It will also move from its breeding grounds to quite different parts of Europe in subsequent winters; indeed the Derbyshire data indicate only two birds which were encountered a second time in Britain after the winter of ringing. More than half of the British-ringed birds are subsequently recovered abroad and where the cause of death was known, 83% of these were a consequence of hunting (Wernham *et al.* 2002). By contrast, albeit from a smaller county dataset (12), 50% of the Derbyshire-ringed birds recovered abroad had been shot. There are five recoveries linking the county with France, three with Italy and Belgium, two with Norway, and singles with Portugal and Spain. Within the UK, Derbyshire-ringed birds have been recovered as far away as Norfolk and Dorset.

Mistle Thrush
Turdus viscivorus
A common resident.

Mistle Thrushes may be found breeding in a wide variety of habitats including open woodland, woodland edges, parkland, well-timbered farmland and built-up areas, especially those close to parks, cemeteries and similar sites. They attract attention by their simple, far-carrying song which is uttered from midwinter onwards. Thus, they are readily found by atlas workers and proof of breeding is quite easily obtained, mainly by observing adults collecting food from grassland areas and by encountering family groups, as the adults are very noisy when they have recently fledged young.

Both Jourdain and Whitlock said that Mistle Thrushes were common in Derbyshire, their numbers varying only according to the severity of the previous winter. Both authorities believed that autumn numbers were swelled by foreign immigrants. Frost considered that there had been little change in status and that cold winter weather affected them less than before.

The tetrad map shows a county-wide distribution, it being the seventeenth most widespread species. The small gaps in the central-west of Derbyshire are considered to be the result of underrecording. They were, unexpectedly, more widespread than Song Thrushes, occurring in 603 tetrads, with breeding proved in 387 and considered probable in a further 145. There was no overall change in distribution from that shown by the 1968–72 and 1988–91 Atlases.

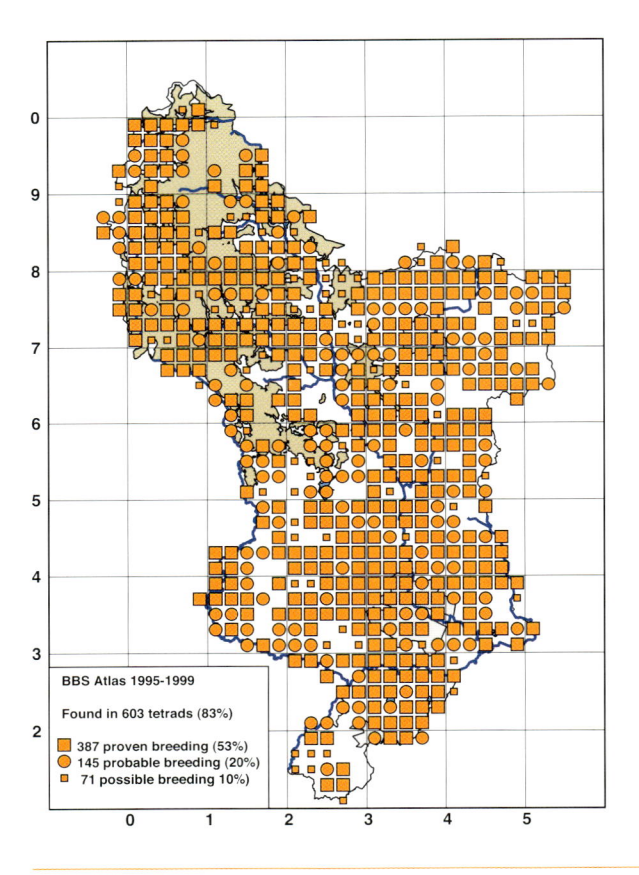

CBC data and counts elsewhere show that this is the least numerous of the four regular breeding thrushes in the county, since it generally occurs at relatively low density. No more than three territories a year were recorded on any CBC plot during the 1990s, and overall densities ranged from 1.04 to 6.94 pairs per km^2. At Scarcliffe Woods there was an average of three pairs in 1973–2008, with never more than seven pairs in a year (Frost 2008a). Other valuable counts of breeding birds include ten pairs proved at Kedleston Park in 2000 and a probable 11 pairs at Carsington Water in 2003–07. A very unusual nest site was in heather at Derwent Moor in 1993. Mistle Thrushes are early breeders, though a record of young fledging from a nest in Derby on 14th February 1989 was exceptionally so.

After the breeding season, Mistle Thrushes often occur in small flocks, frequently feeding on newly mown pasture where they search out invertebrates. Flocks of up to 50 are not rare and some have been much larger, including 180 at Ramsley in September 1973 and 120 at Holymoorside in October 1970, but much the largest flock was of an impressive 500 roosting at Elvaston Castle Country Park in 1972 (Frost). The fact that all these largest flocks (excepting possible wandering birds, as discussed later) were recorded over 40 years ago suggests a decrease in overall numbers and this is given further weight by comparing the average of the largest recorded flock in each year. In 1970–79 this was 130; the equivalent figure in 2000–11 was 52. Since the mid-1970s there has been an overall decline in the English breeding population, though this has been more marked in the east (Brown & Grice 2005). Eaton *et al.* (2010) recorded a national decline of 48% between 1970 and 2008. Possible reasons for this include agricultural changes, and perhaps in particular, the change from pastoral to arable farmland.

Later in the year, Mistle Thrushes are frequently found in berry-bearing areas, but gatherings are rarely as large as those in the late summer and autumn months. Especially in mild weather, flocks may break up by early winter, after which single birds or pairs often defend berry-laden trees and bushes from other species.

Some apparent movement takes place in autumn with occasional records from regular watch-points and elsewhere. These are probably of parties wandering locally in search of food, rather than long-distance migrants. The two largest such totals were of 300 moving west at Egginton Sewage Farm on 22nd October 1994 and 100 flying south-west at Ramsley Moor on 7th October 1995.

According to Wernham *et al.* (2002), the vast majority of Mistle Thrushes in Britain and Ireland are sedentary, with over 98% of the recoveries involving movements of less than 1km. There are 26 ringing reports for birds associated with Derbyshire and of these 88% were recovered within 10km of their ringing site. The only one that moved much further was ringed as a nestling at Hathersage in April 1981 and recovered 188km to the south at Dursley, Gloucestershire in the following January.

BBS Atlas 1995-1999
Found in 603 tetrads (83%)
- 387 proven breeding (53%)
- 145 probable breeding (20%)
- 71 possible breeding 10%

Spotted Flycatcher
Muscicapa striata
A fairly common summer visitor.

The Spotted Flycatcher has recently undergone one of the most serious declines of all widespread birds in Derbyshire. Whitlock described them as abundant in most parts of the county, especially in the Derwent Valley around Cromford and Matlock. He commented that, in July 1892, nearly every dead branch overhanging the river there appeared to be tenanted, the birds frequently flying after insects over the streets of Matlock. Jourdain described them as common, except in bleak upland and moorland areas. Over 70 years later, Frost thought that there had been little change in status, and said that Spotted Flycatchers were most numerous in some of the dales and larger parks.

The latter areas are favoured by these birds nowadays, but they are also found in woods, especially around the edges, and in broad rides and clearings. They often breed close to human settlements, such as in large gardens and in churchyards.

The tetrad map for 1995–99 shows confirmed breeding in 198 tetrads, probable in 51 and possible in 94. Spotted Flycatchers are quite confiding near nest sites and so obtaining proof of breeding is fairly easy. The weak song can be overlooked, however, and most birds are probably first noticed by their eye-catching insect-chasing habits. Of the 343 tetrads in which it was found, the map shows a reasonably even distribution across the county, with concentrations in the White Peak, as noted previously, and in central southern Derbyshire.

Though superficially the distribution at 10km level is unchanged, numbers today are much smaller than in former times, albeit that there is relatively little quantitative information. CBC data from the 1990s showed calculated densities of 2.38 pairs per km^2 at Shire Hill Wood, 0.91 at Shiningcliff Wood and 0.49 at Farfield Farm, Hope. Counts of breeding birds include 12–15 pairs at Chatsworth Park in 1983, and 37 pairs in the limestone dales of SK17 in 1993.

Numbers along less than 1km of the Etwall Brook, centred on the John Port Woods, were unexpectedly high, with ten pairs in 1985, and 20 in 1987 and 1988. Six pairs were at Melbourne Pool as recently as July 1998. At Scarcliffe Woods, there was an average of 12 pairs per year in the mid-1970s, reducing to an average of less than one pair annually in the mid-2000s (Frost 2008a). The 2003–07 survey at Carsington Water revealed six territories. Other indications of its former status include records of four family parties at a farmhouse at Sutton-on-the-Hill in late August and early September 1979, and four nests in a linear 110m at Ashbourne in 1983; similarly, two occupied nests at Chatsworth Park in 1981 were only 40m apart.

The above data give some evidence of the serious decline. Brown and Grice (2005) stated that this began nationally in the mid-1960s, while Eaton *et al.* (2010) recorded an overall decrease of 85% in the period 1970–2008. The reasons for this demise are unclear and suggestions include habitat deterioration on their wintering grounds, the loss of larger trees, including elms (due to disease), and a decrease in their insect food, especially butterflies. There are some indications that the recent declines may be smaller on high ground than in lowland areas. The maps show the breeding situation in 1995–99 and 2007–11.

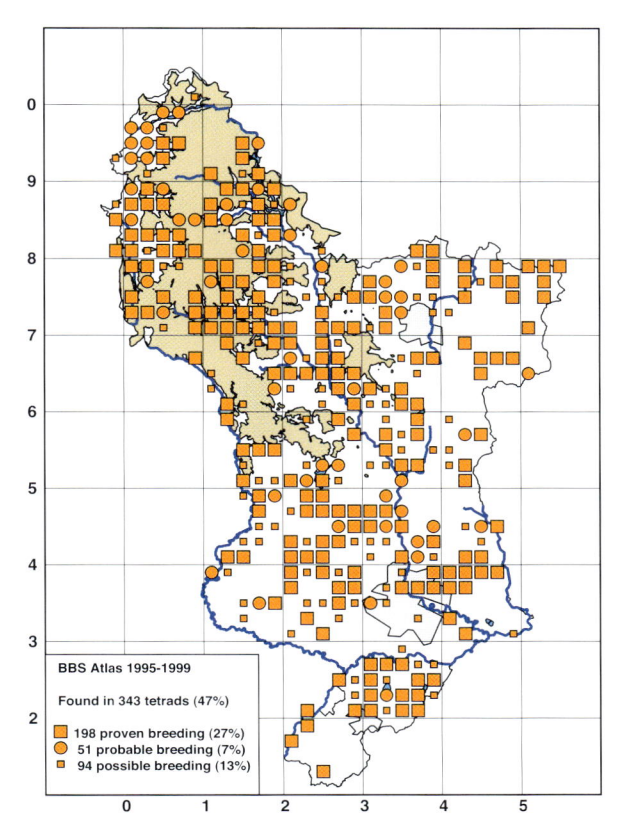

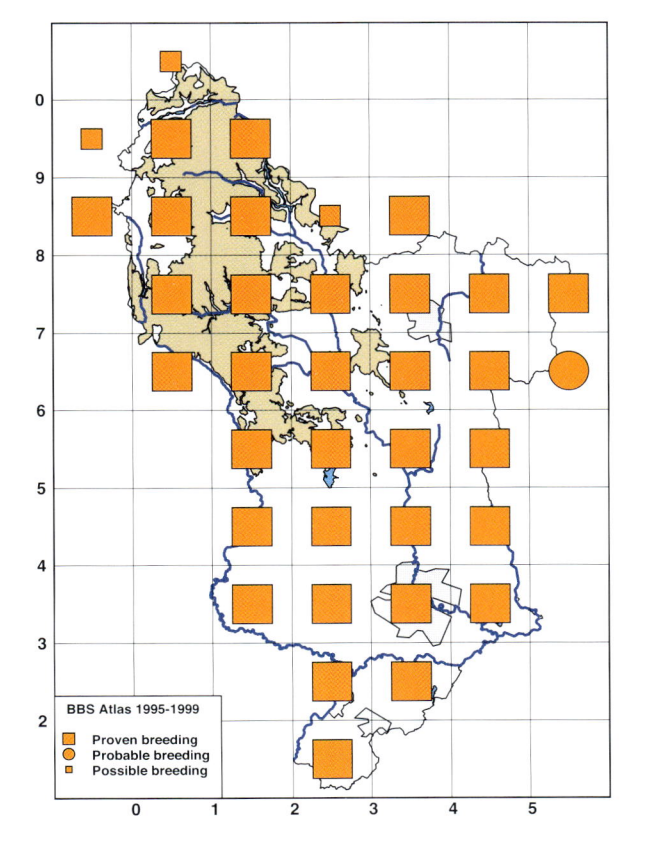

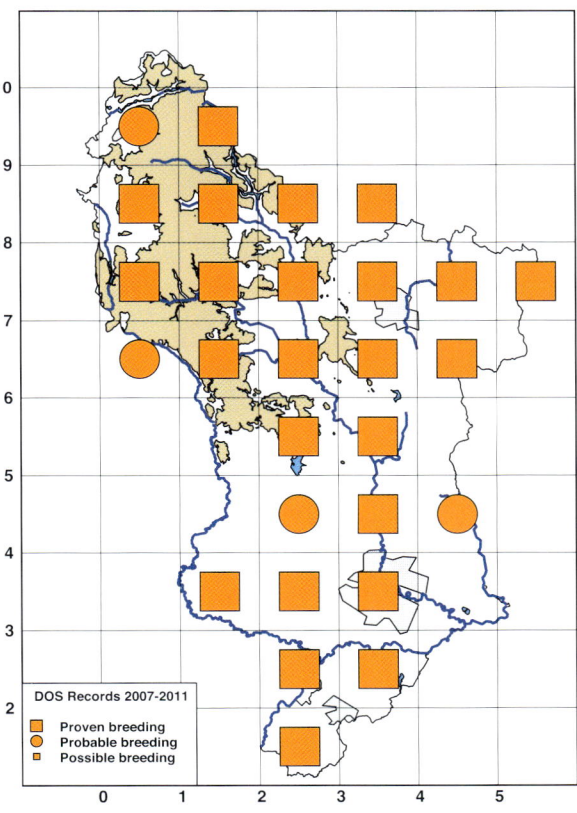

Locally, Spotted Flycatchers have chosen some interesting nest sites. Whitlock recorded nests on wisps of hay deposited by floodwater on overhanging branches along the lower Derwent. In the nineteenth century, a pair nested for 20 years on the branch of a tree nailed to a house wall. Other examples of site tenacity come from Derwent village, where a pair nested in the same small area of drystone wall each year from 1988 to 1991, and from Radbourne, where a door hinge site was used in most years from 1920 to at least 1957 (when the observer moved away). The old nests of other species are often used; these have included Song Thrush, Blackbird, Swallow, House Martin and Hawfinch.

Spotted Flycatchers are usually seen singly, in pairs or, later in the season, in family groups, with parties of 10–12 recorded on several occasions. The largest counts have all been in August: at Hardwick Park in 1978 there were 37 on 20th and in 1989 there were 37 on 21st and 27 on 27th; 22 were at Calke Park on 28th in 1986, 20 in the Hayfield–Kinder area on 25th in 1997, and 20 in Lathkill Dale on 31st in 2003.

This is one of the latest summer visitors to appear, usually arriving in the county in late April or early May. First arrival dates in the period 1978–2011 ranged from 16th April to 13th May, with a mean of 1st May. The earliest ever arrival date was at Darley Abbey on 8th April 1944, an exceptional date.

They leave in late September or early October with the last sightings for the period 1978–2011 falling between 15th September and 9th October; on the latter date in 1995, singles seen at Ashover and Ambergate were the latest ever records for the county. The mean last date over this period was 25th September.

Derbyshire recoveries for this species have largely concerned birds ringed as nestlings (71%) and subsequent recovery has been generally within 50km of the ringing site, in the same or following year. More interesting recoveries include one ringed in June 1961 as a chick at Lowdham, Nottinghamshire, that was killed by a cat 42km west-south-west at Etwall, seven years later; and another ringed as a chick at Drakelow Nature Reserve in July 1993, that was controlled at Finningley, South Yorkshire (Doncaster), a movement of 89km north-north-east, 13 months later.

Robin
Erithacus rubecula
A common resident and a winter visitor.

The Robin can be found almost anywhere that trees or shrubs are present. It nests in hedges and hedge banks, gardens, parks, wasteland, all types of woodland and even on moorland fringes. Its adaptability is exemplified by its wide choice of nest sites. Unusual examples of these include a jam-jar in an apple tree, at Hartshorne in 1984; a motorcycle cylinder, at Bretby in 1986; a clothes-peg bag hanging on an external garage wall, at Shirebrook in 1994; and a compost heap, at Allestree in 1999. Jourdain knew of a nest which contained a large piece of blue paper and a complete page of a French dictionary!

Robins were found in all the complete 10km squares in the county in the 1968–72 and 1988–91 Atlases and in the Derbyshire BBS (1995–99). The tetrad maps shows it to be one of the most widespread species in the county (ranking sixth), being present in 675 tetrads, with breeding proved in 510 of these and probable/possible in a further 165. Though nests are usually very well hidden, proof of breeding is quite easily obtained as a result of the Robin's tameness and the distinctive plumage of the fledglings. Only the higher parts of the Dark Peak are thought to lack breeding Robins. Absences shown on the tetrad map for lowland areas must surely result from inadequate survey coverage.

In the three woodland CBC plots during the 1990s, it was ranked second at Shirebrook, and third at both Shiningcliff Wood and Shire Hill Wood, with densities of between 50 and 87 pairs per km². On the farmland plots, it was the third most common species at Farfield Farm and Culland, and fourth at Broadhay Farm, Hathersage, with densities ranging from 16 to 32 pairs per km². At Scarcliffe Woods it was the fifth most numerous species during the breeding season, but down to 15th in winter (Frost 2008a), suggesting emigration from the woodland to better feeding sites.

It is unlikely that there has been any great change in status, both Whitlock and Frost considering it a common bird throughout the county. However, numbers may fluctuate considerably from year to year, and this species is known to be susceptible to severe winters. The long-term trend, between 1970 and 2008 showed an increase of 52% (Eaton *et al*. 2010). Despite this, nesting has, on rare occasions, been recorded during the winter months.

Robin song is perhaps most frequent in early spring and there were 93 singing in Shipley Park on 8th April 1993. Other large counts of singing or territorial birds include 168 at Carsington Water in 2003–07, and 76 at Foremark Reservoir (including Carver's Rocks Nature Reserve) in May 2007. However, Robins sing for much of the year, exemplified by a record of 23 singing between the hamlet of Alport and Lathkill Lodge on 30th September 1986. Nocturnal singing is nowadays frequently reported and no fewer than 14 were heard on a transect through Matlock at 0300hrs on 29th December 1988.

A Robin photographed at Ramsley on 29th January 2010 was considered to show characteristics of the nominate, Continental form, *E.r. rubecula*.

There are 121 county ringing reports for Robin, including a very early local recovery from 1912. Many Robins do not stray

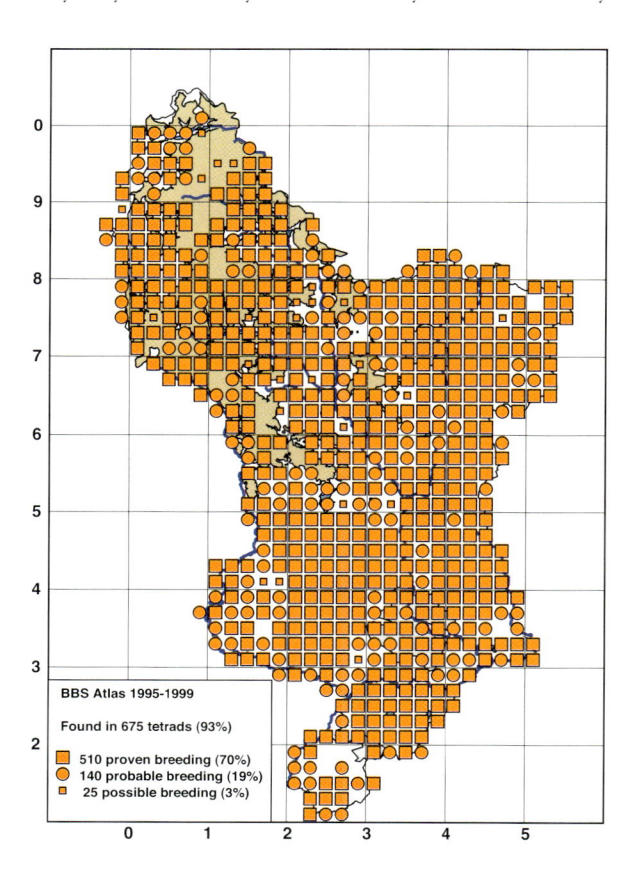

BBS Atlas 1995-1999
Found in 675 tetrads (93%)
- 510 proven breeding (70%)
- 140 probable breeding (19%)
- 25 possible breeding (3%)

far from the area of their birth (for example, one trapped at Drakelow Nature Reserve in 2011 had been ringed there in 2005), although there are some records nationally of birds moving to or from Scandinavia, the Baltic area, lowland Europe, Iberia and Morocco (Wernham *et al*. 2002). The furthest movement in the Derbyshire data is of a first-year bird ringed in April 1984 at Nidingen, Sweden, which was caught in the following January near Staveley, 950km away. A juvenile ringed at Breck Farm in August 1974 was killed by a cat at Oostvoorue, Holland in the following May, while another, ringed as a bird of the year at Awirs, Belgium in October 1991 was caught two months later at Drakelow Nature Reserve. Within the UK there are recoveries involving counties as distant as Dorset. The longest-lived bird is one ringed when it was at least one year old near Sudbury in May 1990, which was caught five-and-a-half years later some 8km away in Staffordshire.

Nightingale
Luscinia megarhynchos
A rare summer vagrant.

Whitlock said that Nightingales were uncertain visitors to Derbyshire, regular only south of Derby and there usually in only small numbers. Occasionally they were found further north in the eastern fringe of the county, mainly close to Sherwood Forest. Jourdain's additional notes comment that a singing bird at Clay Mills attracted hundreds of residents of Burton upon Trent to listen to it, while another at Ockbrook attracted 'crowds of undesirable people'. He also records that Francis Wright of Osmaston Manor attempted to naturalize this species there by releasing a number of birds, but the experiment was not a success.

Frost stated that Nightingales were clearly less regular by 1978, with the only confirmed breeding records from Melbourne in 1911, Clay Cross between 1910 and 1920 and in South Derbyshire in 1947. Extreme dates for records are 22nd April (1944) at Allestree and 31st August (1951) at Matlock.

Since the formation of the DOS in 1954 there have been only 12 records, as detailed in the following table. All refer to singing males, with the exception of the Drakelow 1984 record.

Year	Location and date
1956	Ticknall, one from 5th to 29th May
1963	Foston, one from 10th to 31st May
1963	Coxbench, one on 17th and 24th May
1973	Scarcliffe, one on 27th May
1978	Shirebrook, one from 18th May to 6th June
1982	Shirebrook, one on 5th May
1984	Ecclesbourne Valley, one from 23rd to 29th May
1984	Drakelow Nature Reserve, one on 23rd August
1991	Coton-in-the-Elms, one from 18th to 30th May
1993	Drakelow Nature Reserve, one from 1st to 4th May
1999	Drakelow Nature Reserve, one on 1st May
2011	Ambaston Gravel Pits, one from 1st to 8th May

Bluethroat
Luscinia svecica
A very rare vagrant.

The two Bluethroats which have occurred in Derbyshire were both males of the Red-spotted race *L.s. svecica*, which breeds in Fennoscandia and Siberia. There is a spring peak of occurrences in Britain in mid to late May; surprisingly, both of the Derbyshire birds occurred outside this period.

Year	Location and date
1992	Long Eaton Gravel Pits, a male from 19th April to 1st May
2001	Beeley Moor, a male on 2nd June

Both of these birds were initially located by their song. The Long Eaton bird also defended a territory against other species. Carrington (2002) provided an account of the 2001 record.

There was a report of a male of the Red-spotted race in a Mickleover garden on 23rd May 1977. The record was published in the *Derbyshire Bird Report* and accordingly included in Frost. However, it has not been possible to obtain further details and the record must be regarded as unproven.

Pied Flycatcher
Ficedula hypoleuca
An uncommon, but increasing, summer visitor.

Whitlock stated that there was little reason to doubt that this species had formerly bred 'in the romantic dales of the Peak', and thought it might still breed in the north of the county. He knew of several other sightings, which he assumed were of passage birds. Jourdain was of a similar opinion. He reported two nests at Matlock in 1892, but later used the expression 'believed to have bred'. There were several more records in the twentieth century, but breeding was not proved beyond doubt until 1945, when a pair nested unsuccessfully at Padley Gorge; this area has remained a local stronghold ever since. Breeding was recorded at Ford Hall in 1946 and from 1949 at Chatsworth Park. Frost recorded an exceptional lowland breeding pair at Whitwell Wood in 1948–49. Another favoured area, the Goyt Valley, had its first recorded breeding birds in 1961.

The county population increased to over ten pairs in the 1960s, but apparently declined in the 1970s with, for example, only six pairs or singing males in 1973. In 1982, the Pied Flycatcher was still described as 'a rare visitor, breeding regularly in two restricted areas of the county'. Nonetheless, two years later in 1984, increased fieldwork showed that the species bred in at least 14 sites, which included 14 and nine pairs at two of these. A further steady expansion has continued since then. In the period 1995–2011, 19–34 sites had some 40–91 pairs, as shown in the table.

The low number in 2001 almost certainly resulted in part from lack of coverage, due to foot-and-mouth disease movement restrictions.

The tetrad map shows confirmed breeding in 29 tetrads, with probable breeding in 22 more and possible breeding in a further eight. Most of these are situated in the Peak District with a scattering of records as far south as the Windley area (in SK34).

Padley Gorge, where up to 16 pairs have held territory, is usually regarded as the county's *locus classicus*, but the DWT's Hillbridge and Park Wood reserve, in the Goyt Valley near Taxal, usually holds higher numbers, with eight to 17 breeding pairs in 1995–2009. Other areas holding good populations in recent years include Priddock and Ladybower Woods (16 pairs in 2009), North Lees Estate (15 pairs in 2009), the Hayfield area (ten pairs in 2007) and Froggatt (nine pairs in 1997). In all of these areas, the great majority of birds nest in boxes and are thus easily monitored,

Year	Sites	Pairs
1995	20	74
1996	26	85
1997	24	78
1998	26	80
1999	23	62
2000	31	70
2001	19	40
2002	25	70
2003	26	67
2004	30	74
2005	33	82
2006	20	55
2007	34	83
2008	30	82
2009	33	91
2010	34	88
2011	24	90

but natural tree holes are frequently used. In 1979, a pair nested unsuccessfully in an excavator at Cromford. Occasionally, singing males hold territory well outside the known breeding range, such as at Catton Park from 11th to 29th May 1996.

Most of Derbyshire's Pied Flycatchers nest in sessile oak and other broad-leaved woodland with a sparse shrub layer, allowing them to fly below the canopy. Recent breeding records have come from ash wood sites in the White Peak such as Cressbrook Dale, Miller's Dale and Lathkill Dale. This preference for sessile oak woodland reflects the national trend, but in Continental Europe, Pied Flycatchers breed in nearly all forest types (Lundberg & Alatalo 1992). The 1988–91 Atlas reported a slight national expansion between the two Atlas periods, but the rate of increase within Derbyshire has been greater, which is due to the provision of nest-boxes. This does not accord with the most recent national figures, which show a 50% decline in 1995–2008, based on BBS data (Eaton et al. 2010).

Most sessile oak woods in the Peak District are in nature reserves or SSSIs, and the identification of upland oak and birch woods as a priority habitat in the UK Biodiversity Action Plan has led to further conservation measures and planting schemes to increase the area of oak woods.

Birds usually arrive in mid-April and the earliest ever arrival date was 3rd April 1999 at Lea Wood. First dates for the period 1978–2011 range from 3rd to 27th April, with a mean first date of 16th April. Males usually arrive before females. Over the same period, the mean last date was 16th August, with latest sightings between 21st June and 28th September. The latest of all occurred in a Borrowash garden on 1st October 1962 (Frost). Breeding birds seemingly depart soon after the young have fledged, and most of the later records are believed to refer to passage migrants from farther north.

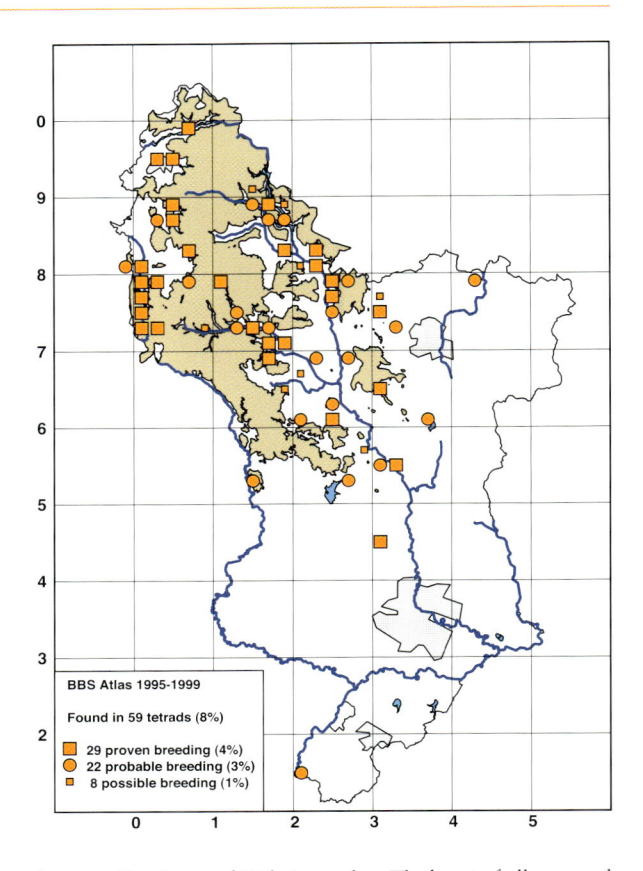

This species is the subject of large-scale nest-box studies and most birds ringed locally have been nestlings. There are about 40 recoveries to date, and of these, more than 50% have been found within 35km of their ringing location. However, there is a long-distance recovery from the Goyt Valley to Souzelas, Portugal, a distance of 1526km; the bird, having made the journey in 84 days, was unfortunately shot. Another very interesting report was of one ringed as a breeding female at Newby Bridge, Cumbria in May 1997 that was controlled, presumably breeding, at Hathersage in May 2002. One ringed as a pullus at Combs Reservoir in June 2003 fell victim to a cat at New Milton, Hampshire, two months later.

Black Redstart
Phoenicurus ochrurus
A scarce breeder, passage migrant and winter visitor.

Whitlock knew of only one record, of two Black Redstarts at Melbourne in November 1856. Frost listed only three more records before the formation of the DOS in 1954, including one of apparent wintering at Findern in 1949/50. Since then, the frequency of records has increased with over 30 in 1960–77 (Frost). In the period 1978–2011, at least 84 migrant Black Redstarts have been recorded, in all months except July, and from a wide variety of habitats. These include reservoirs, gravel pits, water treatment plants, a school, quarries, moorland edges and even a garden manure heap. These 84 records show a clear peak in April, with 26 first seen in that month, followed by 12 in November and 11 in October.

The above records exclude birds seen at known or likely breeding sites. Breeding was first proved at Drakelow Power Station in 1970, and this has remained the favoured site, with breeding proved in ten further years, including three pairs in 1988 and four in 1994. Birds have been seen at Drakelow Power Station or at the adjacent nature reserve in the great majority of the last 30 years. Single pairs bred at British Celanese Works (now Acordis) in 1978; an industrial site near Ilkeston in 1985, 1995 and 1997; at Willington Power Station (now demolished) in

1994 and 1997 and probably also in 1995; and at ABB Limited's Derby premises on Pride Park Way in 1994. The last was the peak year for breeding in the county, with six successful pairs, and a singing male in a limestone quarry at Stony Middleton.

Other records that may well have referred to breeding birds were from various areas of urban Derby in May 1979, May 1985, April and May 2000, March 2005, May 2006, and April and May 2010, at an industrial site at Sheepbridge in May 1986, at Foston in June 2010 and in an industrial area at Wormhill in 2011. Most breeders seem to take up territory in April, but birds have been seen at Drakelow Power Station throughout the year (prior to its demolition in 2005). Unusual records have been of one flitting around rock climbers at Stanage Edge in 2010 and one touching down on a bird-feeder in an industrial area in Wormhill in 2011.

Overwintering was first recorded in 1949/50, and more recently at Drakelow Power Station site in 2004/05 and in early 2007. There was a female/immature at Aston-on-Trent Gravel Pits from 31st December 2000 to 1st January 2001 and another wintering bird at Ashford-in-the-Water from 18th February to 1st April.

In view of the industrial nature of the Black Redstart's breeding habitat and the difficulty of access to many sites, it is quite likely that some breeding pairs have been overlooked. However, urban regeneration and the tidying up of certain industrial areas may have led to a decrease in numbers, which has been recorded in cities in adjacent counties. The problems of how to retain breeding Black Redstarts in the light of the above changes were discussed by Frith and Gedge (2000).

Redstart
Phoenicurus phoenicurus
A fairly common summer visitor, mainly to the northern half of the county.

Whitlock described this beautiful bird as 'pretty well diffused as a breeding species throughout the county'. It was quite common in several parts of the Peak District then, as it is now, both on the limestone and the gritstone. 'Hanging' oakwoods, a habitat shared with Pied Flycatcher and Wood Warbler, are especially favoured but it is also found in coniferous and other broad-leaved woodland. There are good numbers in many limestone dales, especially those with scattered trees or open woodland and rocky outcrops. It is also quite common in other habitats in the Carboniferous Limestone region, such as around Brassington and Bonsall Moor, where it frequents areas of scattered hawthorns and nests in adjacent drystone walls or abandoned buildings. Jourdain found a pair breeding in a Swallow's nest in an outhouse at Ashbourne Hall.

Frost summarized the results of census work undertaken locally in the 1960s and 1970s, which provided a useful indication of population density. Subsequent surveys have produced more specific data. For instance, in 1988 the SBSG located 32 territories in Upper Derwentdale (which compared with an estimated 30–50 pairs in Derwentdale in 1982), and 18 between Castleton and Edale. Directly south of this area, David Gosney found 55 territories in the limestone dales of SK17 in 1993. English Nature's 1998 survey of the Eastern Moors, from Beeley to Strines, revealed a total of 22 singing males. Linear transects along a 16km stretch of the Dove Valley between Hartington and Glutton Bridge, conducted by one observer over a number of years, have yielded maximum counts of 18 territories in 2000 and 2008. Lathkill Dale is a particularly favoured breeding locality, with impressive totals of 21 males in 1998, 22 in 2006, 26 in 2007 and 31 in 2011. Other sites where relatively high counts of singing males have been reported are Padley Gorge in 1986, Longstone Edge in 1987 and Birchen Edge in 1994 (16 in each instance), Monsal Dale in 1994 (when at least 12 were present), Haddon Hall in 2010 (14) and the Via Gellia in 2011 (13).

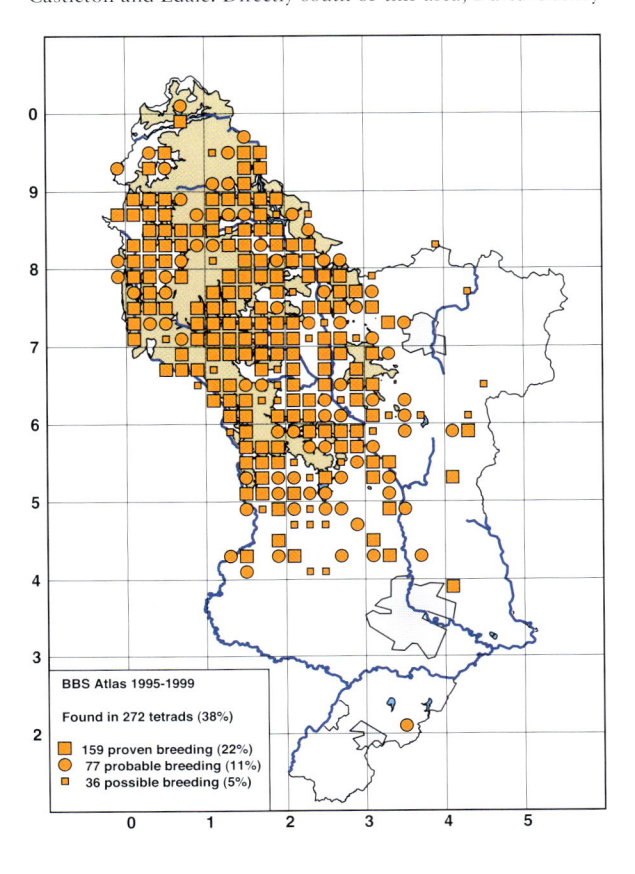

The most detailed information for the county as a whole was obtained in the Derbyshire BBS (1995–99), where proof of breeding was obtained for 159 tetrads, mainly as a result of observers encountering adults carrying food or with recently fledged young. The probable breeding in 77 tetrads was based mainly on observers hearing the distinctive and far-carrying song. There were also 36 possible breeding squares.

The map shows that the Redstart has an almost exclusive northern and western distribution, with only one proven breeding record (in SK44) in the southern third of the county. This and two tetrads in SK45 constituted the only breeding records in the eastern lowlands. Whitlock described it as numerous in some of the southern parklands, such as Calke, Donington and Sudbury, and likewise in the north-east at Sutton Scarsdale, while a few pairs nested in pollarded willows in the Trent and lower Dove Valleys. There are no modern breeding records for the latter sites. Frost spoke of the decrease and contraction in range in the lowlands, and believed that the most likely reason was the felling of mature trees, but the Sahel drought conditions may also have contributed. The 1968–72 and 1988–91 Atlases also confirmed this range contraction, with breeding proved in 13 of the 10km core squares in 1968–72 and 11 in 1988–91. However, the DOS survey revealed proof of breeding in 16 of the squares, a pleasing extension of distribution. Eaton *et al*. (2010) state that there was an increase of 17% between 1970 and 2008. Nevertheless, the Redstart remains rare as a lowland breeder in Derbyshire, with the only confirmed records since the turn of the century at Windley in 2000, and Kedleston Park in 2001 and 2002.

In the three woodland CBC plots in the Peak District and fringes in the 1990s there was an average of almost three pairs at Shiningcliff Wood and a single pair at Shire Hill, while at Broadhay Farm, Hathersage, it was the seventh-equal most common species, with an average of over five pairs, but averaged under two pairs a year at Farfield Farm, Hope. Densities for these sites are between 2.4 and 13 pairs per km^2.

Small numbers of Redstarts may be seen away from breeding sites during both passage periods, but especially in autumn,

BBS Atlas 1995-1999
Found in 272 tetrads (38%)
- 159 proven breeding (22%)
- 77 probable breeding (11%)
- 36 possible breeding (5%)

from July onwards. At such times they occur widely and there have been several records from gardens. Most are seen only briefly but there was a particularly interesting record from Carr Vale in 1998, when a fledged brood of three arrived on 11th July and remained for 48 days until 27th August, moulting into first-winter plumage during that time.

The mean first date in the period 1978–2011 was 11th April, with the earliest ever on 26th March 2005 at Flash Lane. The average last date in the same period was 3rd October, the latest ever being on 14th November 1981 at Carver's Rocks Nature Reserve.

There have been 14 recoveries of Redstart associated with Derbyshire, all but two of which had been ringed as nestlings. Surprisingly, ten of these were ringed before 1970, and most resulted from nest-box schemes in the Goyt Valley area. This led to 1960s recoveries from the French Pyrenees, the Algarve in Portugal, southern Spain and Morocco. The UK recoveries include Derbyshire-ringed nestlings that travelled to Norfolk and Somerset.

Whinchat
Saxicola rubetra
An uncommon passage migrant and summer visitor, breeding mainly in the Peak District.

Whinchats are all but lost as breeding birds in Derbyshire's lowlands. Fortunately, they still breed widely in parts of the Peak District but are in decline here, too, and their long-term survival in the county must be in doubt.

This demise has been taking place over a long period. Whitlock described them as abundant, being 'naturally most common in the rich meadows of the southern portion of the county'. He also believed that they were fairly numerous in upland areas, though almost absent from the moorlands.

Frost said that they were still numerous in parts of the south in 1942 but the decline, if not started by then, was soon underway. By 1948 they had disappeared from the Bretby area, and by 1956 this was also the case in the Ashbourne district and, no doubt, in many more areas. By 1978, few pairs bred south of Derby, while they were localized in eastern lowland areas. Seven pairs bred successfully at Langley Mill in 1979, but just two years later there were only two pairs. Breeding Whinchats were found in eight lowland areas in 1984, but three years later this was reduced to just two. In 1990, traditional breeding sites at Staveley, Breck Farm and Poolsbrook had been abandoned, although a family group, possibly locally bred, was seen at Staveley in August 1993. There were four pairs at the site of Carsington Water in 1992–93, inhabiting a large area of farmland abandoned to the incipient reservoir and a pair bred here during the Derbyshire BBS period, in 1995 and 1996.

This was the most southerly breeding site found during the survey, though it is just possible that a pair with three juveniles at Draycott on 1st August 1997 had nested locally. The same comment applies to a sighting of two adults and four juveniles at Ockbrook Sewage Farm in September 2003. Similarly, no breeding birds were found in the Derbyshire BBS (1995–99), nor since, in the eastern lowlands. Changes in agriculture are believed to be the main cause of the decline, and in particular the general tidying up of rough areas, loss of hedgerows, improved drainage, and crop monoculture. Based on BBS data, Eaton *et al.* (2010) recorded a national decline of 57% in the period 1995–2008.

The distribution map shows graphically the bias to the north-west. Whinchats were found in 113 tetrads, with breeding proved in 61 of these. This is a fairly easy bird to locate on account of its habit of using conspicuous perches, and adults with young can be nervous and noisy.

It can be seen that breeding was confirmed in just nine of the 10km core squares, which compares with 12 in the 1988–91 Atlas and 18 in the 1968–72 Atlas. Few of our breeding species have lost so much ground in recent times. The maps show the breeding distribution in 1995–99 and 2007–11.

Whinchats are still reasonably common in parts of the Peak District. Most moorland Whinchat territories hold heather and bracken, sometimes with occasional small trees and the vicinity of rocky edges is often favoured. New plantations are attractive to Whinchats and their creation has led to localized, but very short-lived, increases. Even in the Peak District, however, most recent records of changed numbers are of declines. In 1965, 32 pairs were found on some 1100ha of moorland centred on Big Moor, and there are certainly far fewer than that today. At Combs Moss Whinchats were absent in 1994 for the first time in over 20 years, though a single pair returned in 1995 and 1996. In 2003–04 there was only one pair at Berry Clough, which had previously supported several pairs and a similar comment was made in 2007 for the Goyt Valley in general, with only one breeding pair there in 2008 to 2011. At Baslow Edge there was a single male in 2005, which was the first time in a decade that the observer concerned had failed to prove breeding there.

In 1998, Natural England's survey of the Eastern Moors located 64 territories between Beeley Moor and Strines, and the species is still found in reasonable numbers in this region. Twenty-three pairs were found on the EMP moors in 2010, with 13 of these around White Edge. The 2004 survey by Moors for the Future found 97 pairs in the whole of the Peak District moorlands. The cloughs and larger valleys of the Upper Derwent area hold several pairs while small numbers may be found in the Longdendale area and other parts of the north-western corner of the county and elsewhere. There are very few recent records from the limestone dales and the last record of a territorial bird in this region was of a singing male in Cunning Dale in 2004. Even allowing for some overlooking of birds in more remote areas, it seems unlikely that the Derbyshire Peak District currently holds more than 100–120 pairs of Whinchats.

The number of Whinchats seen on passage in Derbyshire has also declined markedly over the same period as the demise of breeding birds, but they are still seen at a wide variety of sites in April and May and, usually in greater numbers, from August onwards. Counts away from breeding areas are always small,

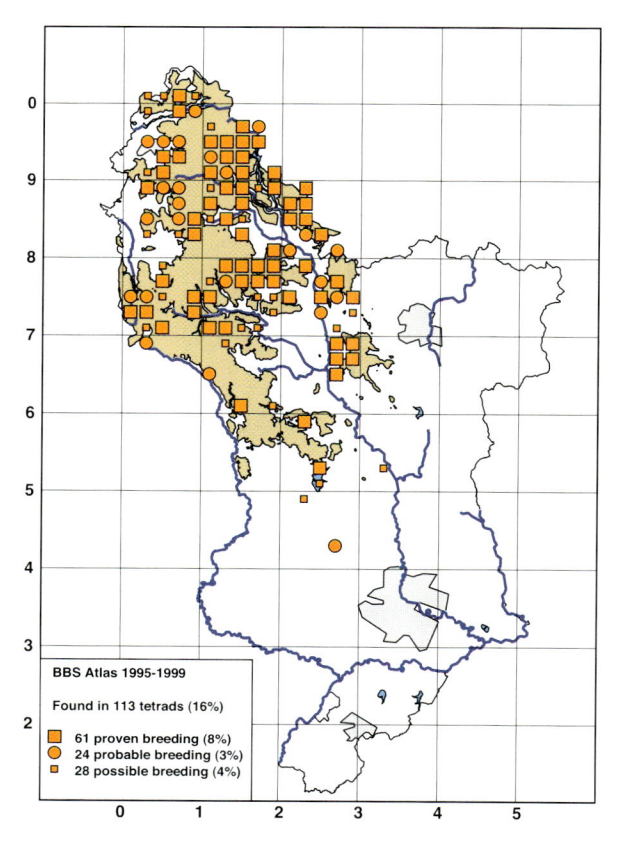

BBS Atlas 1995-1999

Found in 113 tetrads (16%)

- 61 proven breeding (8%)
- 24 probable breeding (3%)
- 28 possible breeding (4%)

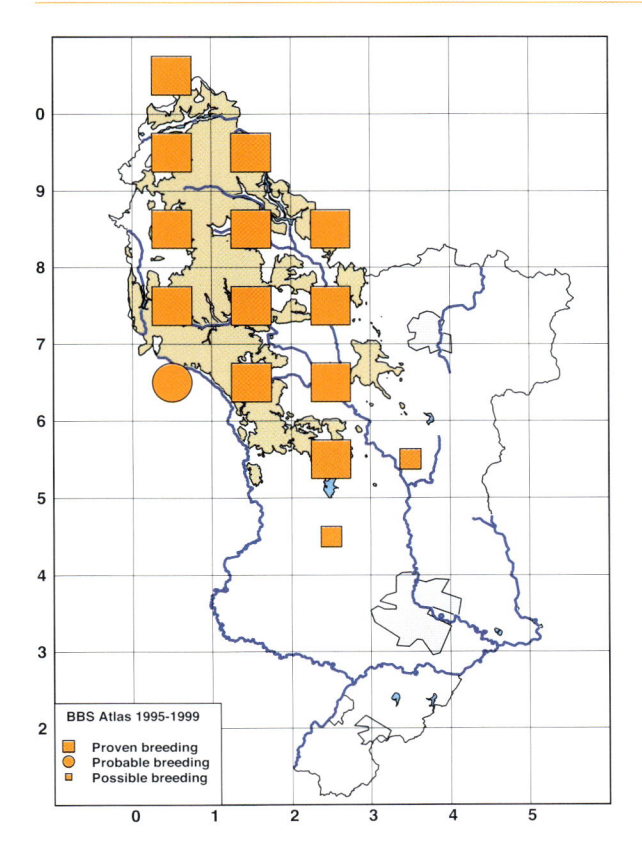

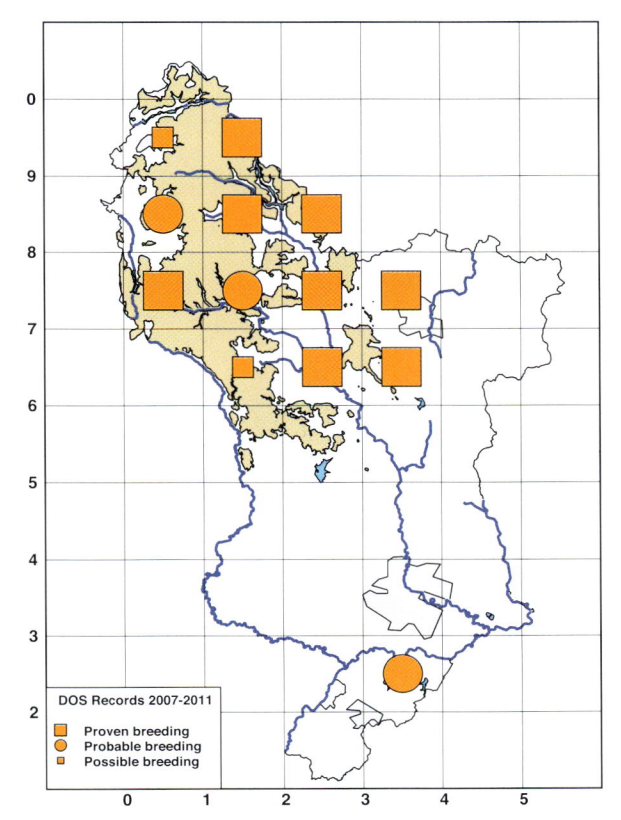

with 15 at Egginton Sewage Farm in September 1998 and 12 at Drakelow Nature Reserve in September 1991 being the highest recent counts. The largest recent moorland count was of 20 at Ramsley on 3rd September 2003.

The earliest ever arrival was of a male on 2nd April 2005 at Cutthroat Bridge. The mean first arrival date in the period 1978–2011 was 19th April. During the same period the mean latest date was 5th October. There have been five November records, with the latest ever at Holmebrook Valley Park on 12th in 1998.

There have only been three recoveries involving Derbyshire. Two of these were of birds controlled near their ringing site. The other was ringed as a chick at Moscar in June 1953 and recovered 1874km away in southern Portugal three months later. The British populations winter in the Sahel zone of Africa and it is considered that birds on autumn migration overfly the Sahara (Wernham *et al*. 2002). As with many migrant species into Britain, their route is down the Iberian Peninsula and is reinforced by this Derbyshire record.

Stonechat
Saxicola torquatus
A uncommon resident, passage migrant and winter visitor.

In 1789, Stonechats were described by Pilkington as common in hilly areas, especially the High Peak. A century later, Whitlock considered them extremely local and attributed the decline to the enclosure of waste land and the destruction of areas of gorse by burning. Jourdain said that they were exceedingly scarce and erratic, but believed that 'a pair or two' might breed near Bakewell and in the upper Dove Valley. Frost stated that the only definite instances of breeding during the first three-quarters of the twentieth century were in 1907, 1916, 1938 and 1975, with three pairs confirmed in the last year.

The next known breeding took place in 1981 (three pairs) and 1983 (one pair), and has been annual since 1994 with the numbers of confirmed pairs as shown in the chart.

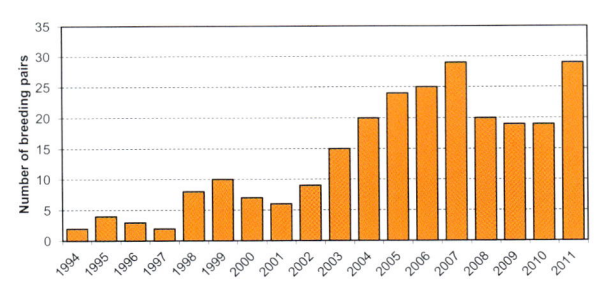

The tetrad map resulting from the Derbyshire BBS (1995–99) shows that the 26 tetrads in which it was found were in the north-western quadrant, where the preferred habitat is heather moorland, usually also containing bracken, sometimes with occasional scattered bushes, bilberry and gorse.

More recent survey work in 2004 revealed 91 pairs in the Peak District compared with just three in the 1990 survey (Carr & Middleton 2004). However, recent cold winters have caused

BBS Atlas 1995–1999

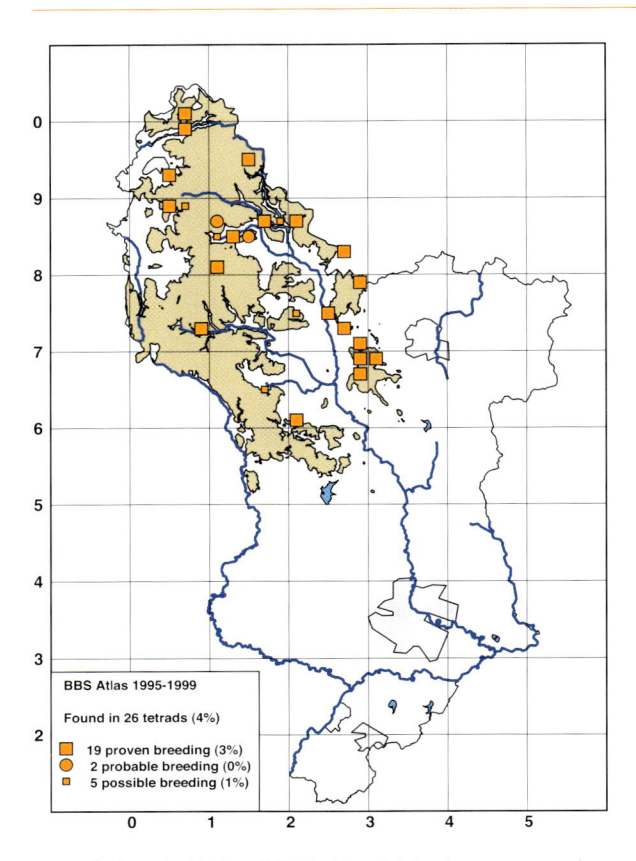

Found in 26 tetrads (4%)

■ 19 proven breeding (3%)
● 2 probable breeding (0%)
▪ 5 possible breeding (1%)

some decline: in 2010 and 2011, 19 and 29 pairs were proved to breed. The EMP moors held six pairs in 2010, which was half of that found in 2004 (Frost & Taylor 2011).

As the Peak District breeding population is presumed to be resident, it is highly susceptible to periods of severe cold weather and might conceivably be eliminated by a single hard winter. If, however, a breeding population remains, Stonechats have the capacity (since a pair might rear three broods in a season) to make good any losses within a few years.

There are few, if any, discernible differences between the habitats used by Whinchats and Stonechats and the two species nest closely together in many places. As with the Whinchat, this is an easy species to locate, especially with recently fledged young.

There are two recent breeding records from the Carboniferous Limestone area: at Eldon Hill, a pair bred in a young tree shelter-belt near the quarry in 1996, and two years later a pair bred in scrub on the slopes of Gratton Dale.

Outside the breeding season, Stonechats are quite a familiar sight. Most occur from September onwards, usually in ones or twos, though larger groups are often recorded. Many move through, but smaller numbers sometimes overwinter until the following early spring. The origins of these birds are unknown and there are no ringing recoveries involving Derbyshire. Their fortunes have changed over the years: they were scarce in the 1960s, but increased during the 1970s with, for example, over 100 reported in 1975 in gatherings of up to ten (Frost). The severe winter of 1978/79 caused a decline and it was not until 1988 that Stonechats returned in any numbers, with reports from 14 sites in the last four months of that year. Since then, passage numbers have been relatively large, particularly in October; for example, in October 2006 a total of 91 birds was seen at 35 sites.

Passage and wintering birds may be found in moorland areas, especially those with bracken beds, and in a wide variety of lowland habitats including rough grassland with scrub, colliery tips, young forestry plantations, railway embankments and wetland margins. The birds are often in pairs and are rarely far apart. The largest upland counts were of 17 at Eastmoor in October 2001 and 14 at Ramsley in September 2009. In the lowlands the highest numbers were nine at both Willington Gravel Pits in October 2006 and Long Eaton Gravel Pits in March 2009, and eight at both Newhall in November 2001 and Darley Moor in March 2008. The number of birds seen in lowland areas has declined since 2009, in line with the reduced breeding population.

Wheatear
Oenanthe oenanthe
A fairly common summer visitor, mainly in the Peak District, and a fairly common passage migrant.

As breeding birds in the county, Wheatears are very largely confined to the Peak District. Formerly, they also bred in some lowland areas, such as the Melbourne district, where enclosure and cultivation caused their demise, probably during the mid-nineteenth century. Whitlock also knew of rare instances of lowland breeding at Repton and Sudbury, and both he and Jourdain suspected that this species may have declined in the Peak District. The only definite lowland breeding records known to Frost were from the Staveley area during the 1950s and 1960s, and Castle Gresley in 1967. Fieldwork for the Derbyshire BBS (1995–99) revealed only one instance of probable lowland breeding, in SK47 at High Moor, where large areas of derelict land and rubble remained after the closure of a colliery.

The recent survey showed that the basic distribution of breeding birds was very similar to that revealed by the 1968–72 and 1988–91 Atlases, when Wheatears were confirmed as breeding in 11 of the 10km core squares, compared with 12 in the Derbyshire BBS (1995–99). This shows that they breed largely in the north-west quadrant of the county. Here, however, their distribution is uneven. They are found mainly in areas of very short vegetation (often grazed by rabbits or sheep), especially at sites that also have rocky outcrops, scree slopes or drystone walls, all of which offer nest sites. Many of the dales fit this description, as do the peripheries of several quarries. These areas are more numerous on the Carboniferous Limestone than on the Millstone Grit. As indications of this, there were 12 pairs at both Long Dale and Cressbrook Dale in 1997, with two pairs and nine singing males at the latter site in April 2005. Conversely, the survey of the gritstone moors between Beeley and Strines by English Nature in 1998 found only 14 territories. Carr and Middleton (2004) gave a total of 45 pairs for the gritstone moors of the whole Peak District. Only two pairs were found in the EMP moors survey in 2010, both at White Edge.

Perusal of both Whitlock and Frost suggests that there has been little change in breeding distribution for over a century, except perhaps for local changes, such as the conversion of old pastures to cereals in some moorland fringe areas. Eaton *et al.* (2010) state that BBS figures indicated a 5% decline between 1995 and 2008.

This is an easy and conspicuous bird to locate on its breeding territory. It was found in 196 tetrads, with breeding proved in 118 of these, and probable in a further 39. It is likely that birds recorded at almost all lowland tetrads were spring migrants; such birds may sometimes show signs of territorial behaviour, and even investigate potential nest sites before moving on.

Wheatears are among the earliest spring migrants to arrive in the county. The first records are almost always in March, with a mean first date of 16th in the period from 1978 to 2011. There have been two February records, the earlier being of one on 19th in 1977 at Drakelow Nature Reserve. Both in spring and autumn, migrants may be seen in any part of the county in a wide variety of situations. Sometimes small flocks are seen, the largest of which were of 39 at Beeley on 30th March 1995 and 30 at Egginton Sewage Farm on 2nd May 1992. Counts of family groups in their breeding areas in summer can also produce impressive numbers, such as 34 in the Greensides Farm area, near Glutton Bridge, in August 2002 and August 2007, and 29 at the same site in July 2004. There were earlier counts of 25 at Barbrook Reservoir in July 1980 and August 1986, and 24 at Haylee, near Combs, in June 1996. Numbers on autumn passage in Derbyshire are usually much smaller than in spring, with a largest lowland count of 20 at Long Eaton Gravel Pits on 8th August 1991. The mean last date for the county in 1978–2011 was 16th October, with the latest of a few November records on 13th in 2011 at Drakelow Power Station.

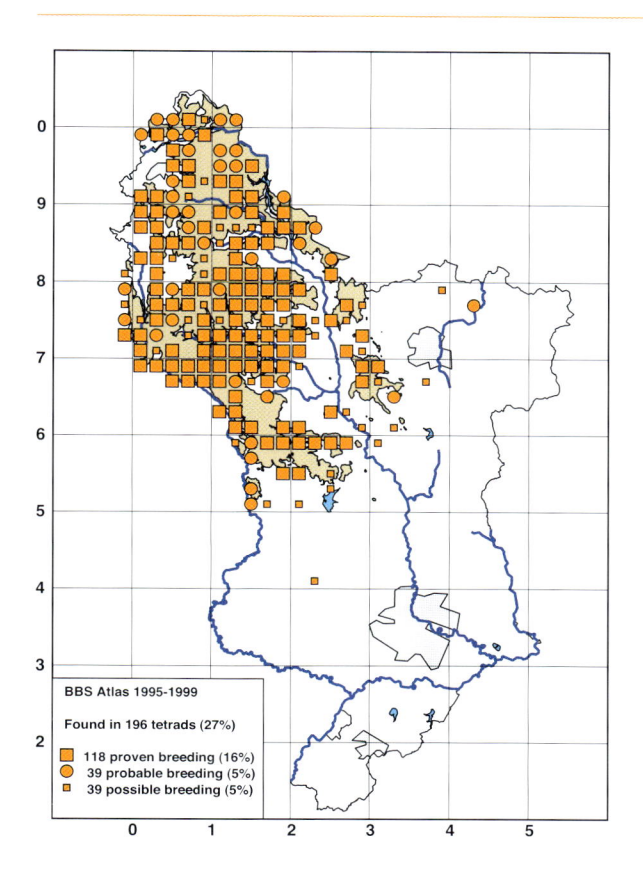

Birds showing characteristics of the race *O.o. leucorhoa*, which is known as the Greenland Wheatear (though it also breeds in Iceland and eastern Canada), are recorded annually, though mainly in spring when they are easier to identify. Spring records span the period 13th April to 15th June, with the majority in late April and early May. Most occur in small numbers, but over 85 passed through the county in the spring of 2009, including 20 at the site of Drakelow Power Station on 20th May, a count exceeded only by 21 at Williamthorpe Nature Reserve on 26th April 1996. Autumn migrants of this race, usually singles, have been identified in the period 21st August to 14th October, with a largest gathering of six at Moorhall on 21st–22nd September 2006.

There are only six recoveries for this species, between 1966 and 1986, all but one of which had been ringed as nestlings. These included one that was recovered at Tudela in north-east Spain in September 1986, two months after it was ringed near Grindleford. This fits the pattern of movement through the Iberian Peninsula into Morocco shown by national ringing recoveries (Wernham *et al.* 2002). Derbyshire-ringed birds have also been recovered in Huntingdonshire and Oxfordshire, both in August. An indication of fidelity to the breeding area is shown by one, ringed as a chick near Fernilee, that was found dead just 11km away, two springs later.

Dunnock
Prunella modularis
An abundant resident.

The Dunnock is present almost throughout Derbyshire, in woods, parks, gardens, farmland, and is ubiquitous where trees and bushes are to be found. It is generally only absent from the higher moorland areas and even here may sometimes be found in bracken beds away from trees. In May 1989, one was recorded as singing at Grinah Stones at 580m amsl. The tetrad map for 1995–99 confirms this widespread distribution having been located in 633 tetrads, with only its absences in the north-western uplands likely to be genuine. Breeding was proved in 381 tetrads and thought probable or possible in 252 others.

It is a common bird in built-up areas and nests in the smallest town gardens, often in low, well-clipped privet hedges, which are unattractive to most species. Overall it was found to be the thirteenth most widespread species in the county.

Historically, there seems to have been little change in the Dunnock's status. Whitlock described it as abundant everywhere and mentioned seeing it on 'the huge masses of fallen rocks on the slopes of Kinder Scout'. Jourdain said it was generally distributed and common almost everywhere, while Frost added that on higher ground it could be found up to 1600ft (488m) amsl.

Despite being one of the most familiar of Britain's birds, it is only in relatively recent times that the Dunnock's complex social organization has been unravelled (Davies 1992). Because of this, it is a difficult species to census. Though many Dunnocks are monogamous, instances of polyandry, polygamy and polygyny (two or three males with up to four females) are not at all uncommon. Males and females form separate territories: those of a male may be shared by another male and both may mate with the same females. Both of the territory-sharing males sing, which may lead to an underestimate of numbers.

It seems very likely that Dunnock numbers in Derbyshire have declined in recent times, as they have done nationally; Eaton *et al.* (2010) recorded a decline of 30% during 1970–2008. At Scarcliffe Woods, Frost (2008a) found a decrease of 73% in the breeding population between 1973 and 2008, while winter counts here also declined drastically from 110 in 1975 to no more than 25 from the 1980s onwards. In the early years of reforestation at this site, Dunnocks almost totally shunned the new conifer plantations and most nested in wood-piles left after felling. Numbers at a nearby CBC site at Shirebrook were far more stable, with the average of seven territories in 1990–91 making it the seventh most numerous species there, at a density of 48.61 territories per km^2. At the Shiningcliff and Shire Hill woodland CBC plots, it was much scarcer, at 1.82 and 4.76 pairs per km^2. Densities on the farmland CBC plots varied from 26.25 pairs per km^2 at Culland (where it was the fifth most numerous species) to 3.7 pairs per km^2 at Broadhay Farm, Hathersage.

Other useful counts during the breeding season were of 18 territories at Williamthorpe Nature Reserve in May 2002. At Carsington Water there were believed to be 110 territories in the five years 2003–07, making it the site's sixth most numerous species. High counts of singing males were: 22 at Stubley Hollow on 11th April 2009 and Foremark Reservoir on 8th April 2010;

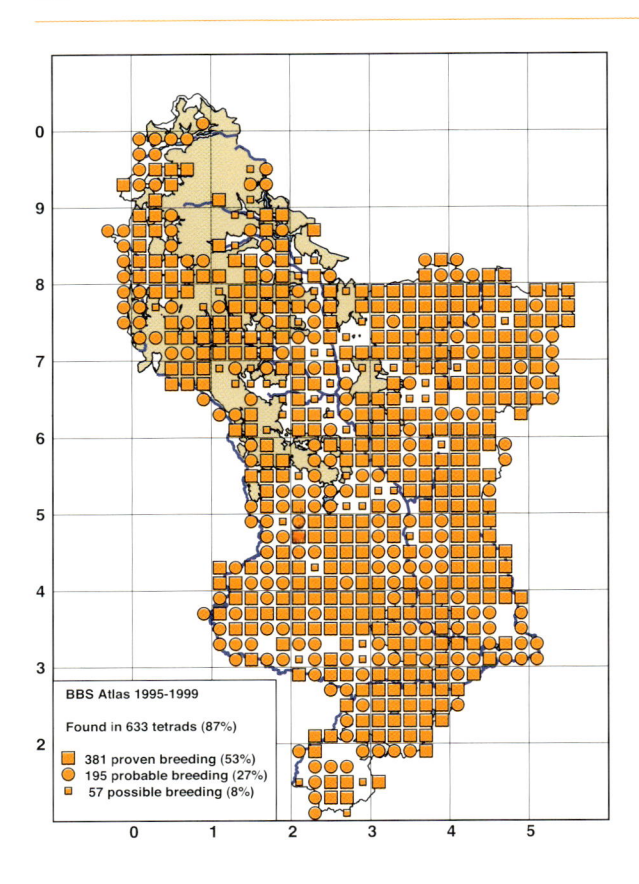

18 at Drakelow Nature Reserve on 18th March 2005; 17 at both Willington Gravel Pits on 25th March 2006 and Ambaston Gravel Pits on 29th March 2009; and no fewer than 42 at Darley Dale on 18th March 2011. In 1998 a Glossop observer commented that there had been a marked decline in the number of Dunnocks visiting her garden in the previous two years.

There have been several records of Dunnocks with aberrant plumage. These range from partial albinos to a cream-coloured bird at Swarkestone in 1982 and a sandy-brown bird at Carr Vale in 1993.

The Dunnock is another species in which the British and Irish races show little or no tendency for migratory movement, whereas the Fennoscandian race migrates southwards during the winter, the weather being the influencing factor. Nonetheless, examples of migratory restlessness in native Dunnocks are recorded in almost every autumn, usually on sunny anticyclonic mornings. Among the more interesting of these observations was a record from Carr Vale on 29th September 1986 when groups of three, four and one moved off to the north-west, while two groups of three flew south at the same site on 18th September 1996. One trapped and ringed at Barrow Hill on 2nd November 1969 was considered to be of the Fennoscandian race *P.m. modularis*.

The majority of long-distance movements in the national database are associated with coastal sites. The Derbyshire data contain no long-distance recoveries and indeed 60 of the 76 reports are of birds reported within 2km of their place of ringing. The furthest distance reported was for a bird moving from Ogston Reservoir to Rotherham, 35km north-north-east. Although the species leads a very sedentary life, some birds are well able to survive for a number of years and the dataset has seven individuals which survived for more than three-and-a-half years after ringing, the longest living for almost five years. This was eclipsed in December 2009, when one re-trapped at Williamthorpe was found to be nine years and four months old.

House Sparrow
Passer domesticus
A common but decreasing resident.

Since 1998 the House Sparrow has been described as a common but decreasing resident in the county. This differs from its status in the late 1970s and 1980s, when it was described as abundant, and reflects the now noticeable decline which this species is experiencing nationally.

Things were very different at the turn of the twentieth century. Whitlock said that it was generally considered too numerous and caused 'much profanity on the part of the Derbyshire agriculturalist'. Mr J.J. Briggs had commented that an attempt to limit numbers had resulted in 4579 sparrows being taken to the Melbourne Club between January and September 1848. Many 'sparrow clubs' were created in the nineteenth century to encourage their destruction (Lovegrove 2007). Both Whitlock and Jourdain said that House Sparrows were found throughout the county.

As a measure of the bird's abundance, Frost reported that, at Bradley in 1965, 54 occupied nests were found in three acres that contained a farmhouse, sheds and trees. He described how, from late summer until the following spring, House Sparrows often formed large flocks, sometimes of four figures, which frequented, first, ripening cereals and then stubble fields, plough-land and other open ground later. While this pattern of behaviour may still be true, the numbers have declined markedly during the period from then until the present time. Nothing was published about House Sparrows in the *Derbyshire Bird Report* between 1978 and 1982. Thereafter, details were published in most years of the largest flocks and analysis of these gives a measure of the decline. In 1983–89 the largest annual flock averaged 275; in the 1990s it was 209; and in the 2000s it had almost halved, at 113. In 2008–11 the only three-figure flock was of 120 at Longford on 21st September 2010. An observer commented that, by 1996, House Sparrows were rarely seen in Derby city centre.

Conversely, a population monitored in a Stonebroom garden showed no significant decline between 1999 and 2011.

This decline was demonstrated nationally by surveys carried out by the BTO. Their Garden Bird Feeding Survey found that most gardens lacking House Sparrows were in rural and upland locations, but that the species was becoming scarce even in suburban localities. It also found that even in the suburbs, flock sizes had reduced by half, and in rural habitats by around one third, during the previous 20 years. The above declines are mirrored in the findings of the CBC for farmland, woodland and special habitats combined for the same period. In Derbyshire in CBCs carried out in the 1990s it was present only at Culland and at Farfield Farm, Hope, but was irregular at both sites, averaging under one territory a year. Overall therefore, it is clear that, although the breeding distribution for the county may not have changed significantly over the last 30 years, the size of the population has clearly reduced. Nationally, Eaton *et al.* (2010) state that the decrease between 1970 and 2008 was 67%.

Reasons for the decline may include more intensive farming methods leading to less spilt grain, fewer soft invertebrate foods in the summer, structural improvements leading to a loss of safe breeding and roosting sites, disease and pollution.

Summers-Smith (1963) described it as 'that ultimate bird commensal of man' and commented that the winter distribution is almost exactly that of the breeding season; both closely parallel to the human population. This is the case in Derbyshire, as in the Derbyshire BBS (1995–99) breeding was recorded in each of the county's 10km squares, with the exception of SK19 (centred on Upper Derwentdale) which is almost devoid of any human settlement. Breeding density appears lower on high ground, no doubt because of reduced habitation in upland areas.

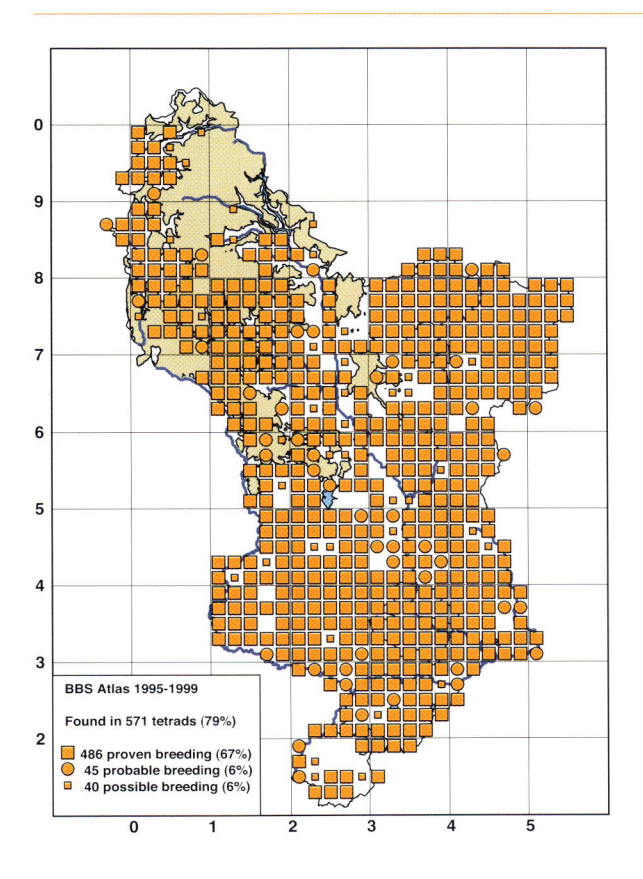

The House Sparrow has a rather surprisingly low distribution ranking, in twenty-first position. It was recorded in 571 tetrads, with breeding proved in 486 (85% of them). As well as the complete absence in SK19, other absences in the north-west, such as those in the east of SK09 and SK08, and in the west of SK18, are likely to be genuine.

Nest sites are usually in holes and crevices in buildings, but are less common now in thick hedgerows. An unusual site was recorded in a Glapwell garden in June 1984 when a colony of about 12 nests was found in a tall Scots pine.

There is little evidence of any movement of House Sparrows, except from breeding areas to farmland to feed, as described earlier. Observers at moorland migration watch-points in autumn now rarely record this species, and even then only in very small numbers, with most moving between south-west and north-west. In this respect, they behave like several other migrant passerines.

From 1970 this species was ringed only when special projects were involved; any casual ringing was discouraged by the levying of a surcharge on rings used. The levy was removed in 1993 as a result of the rapid population decline and ringing of the House Sparrow is now encouraged. Nevertheless, it leads a very sedentary way of life and of the 41 recoveries reported in the county only three had moved more than 10km, with the majority recovered at their place of ringing. The earliest record concerns one ringed at Breaston in 1951 and killed by a cat at the same place six years later. Almost 50% of the grand total of ringed House Sparrows is from the period 1960–69 (Wernham *et al.* 2002).

The long-distance record was of 130km by a bird of the year, which was ringed at Spurn Point in East Yorkshire in June 1967 and found dead in the following February near Peak Forest. The longevity record is held by a bird which apparently lived in the Allestree area for at least seven years.

Tree Sparrow
Passer montanus
A fairly common resident, although uncommon in the Peak District.

The Tree Sparrow occurs largely on farmland and, despite its scientific name, is generally missing from upland regions. It is essentially sedentary and is mainly confined to low-lying areas. During the breeding season it is often loosely colonial, but at other times of the year may occur in flocks in suitable feeding areas.

The tetrad map, based on the Derbyshire BBS (1995–99), shows its widespread lowland distribution. Of the 10km squares largely or wholly inside Derbyshire, it was absent only from the predominantly upland areas of SK19, 18 and 27 and had only a token presence in the nearby areas of SK07, 08 and 09. There were concentrations in the north-east, south-east and central southern parts of the county. This is a clear contraction of range compared with the 1968–72 Atlas, when it bred, or probably bred, in all squares except SK19, but is not dissimilar to the pattern shown by the 1988–91 Atlas, when it was absent from five squares in the north-west.

Breeding was proved in 102 tetrads in the Derbyshire BBS, and was probable and possible in a further 33 and 68. Large, noisy colonies might readily be found but small colonies, or isolated pairs, are very easily overlooked.

Both Whitlock and Jourdain described the Tree Sparrow as local and, while scarcer than the House Sparrow, by no means uncommon in certain areas, though Whitlock implied that they were absent from known breeding areas in the Trent Valley in winter. Frost considered that there had been little overall change in breeding status since then. However, this is no longer so and currently it is a species giving cause for great concern, its UK population having declined by a staggering 93% during 1970–2008. However, BBS counts show a very welcome rise of 55% in the period 1995–2008 (Eaton *et al.* 2008). The reasons for the decline are not currently clear, but as the Tree Sparrow is largely dependent on holes for nest sites, it may have been affected by the loss of hedgerow trees, Dutch elm disease, and the modernization or conversion of farm buildings. Another factor may be reduced summer and winter food due to changes in agricultural methods. Autumn sowing of cereals reduces the availability of weed seeds, and scattered grain in stubbles is reduced by more efficient harvesting.

There are a number of records which illustrate the scale of decline of the species in the county. At Scarcliffe Woods there was a sizeable population before much of the area was felled and replanted. Sympathetic foresters erected boxes for them, and in 1974 40 out of 45 nest-boxes held this species. However, since 1983, no more than two pairs have been found in any year (Frost 2008a) perhaps due, at least in part, to the dilapidation of the boxes. At a CBC site at nearby Shirebrook, there were six pairs in 1978 (the first year) but only one pair by 1981 and

BBS Atlas 1995-1999

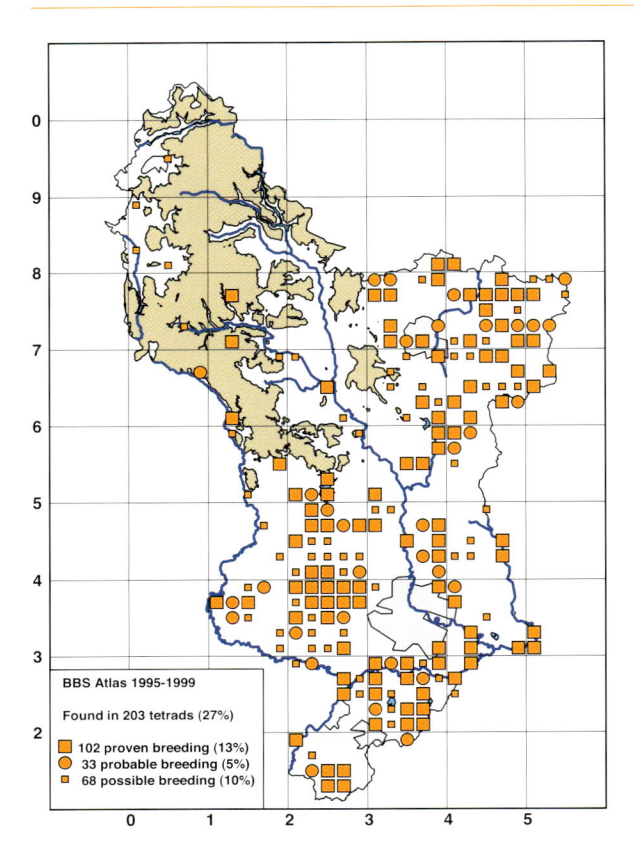

Found in 203 tetrads (27%)

- 102 proven breeding (13%)
- 33 probable breeding (5%)
- 68 possible breeding (10%)

no definite territories thereafter until the survey ended in 1991 (Frost 1993). At other CBC plots in the county during the 1990s, it was absent or present only at very low density with the exception of Culland, where annual numbers ranged from three to seven territories, averaging 4.20 a year, at a density equivalent to 7.25 pairs per km².

Fortunately, Tree Sparrows will readily use nest-boxes and many have been specially installed for them in various parts of the county. Such sites include Carsington Water, where there were considered to be 30 pairs during 2003–07; Cowers Lane, where 482 young were ringed in 2004–08; and the Cauldwell to Coton-in-the-Elms area, with 156 young ringed in 2004–05 and 2007–08. Two valuable records in 1994 were of an estimated 18 pairs at Aston-on-Trent Gravel Pits in April and May, while at Elvaston Castle Country Park, nine pairs bred in gaps in telegraph poles.

The Tree Sparrow remains very much a farmland bird in winter, when it often associates with finches and buntings in stubble fields and at other food sources. In 1978, Frost described winter flocks of 200 as 'not rare' with gatherings of over 500 seen at Pleasley and Dethick, while the highest ever count was of 1000 at Egginton Sewage Farm on 5th December 1970. During the 1970s the average largest annual flock was of 433, but by the 1980s this had tumbled to 172, with a highest count of 400 at Breck Farm in December 1980. The 1990s figure was 99, with a maximum of 160 at St Chads Water in November 1997. Flock sizes were, pleasingly, a little higher in 2000–09 averaging 104, with 150 at Blackwell in November 2002 the largest in that period. In 2010–11, only two flocks over 60 were found: 90 at Glapwell on 22nd November 2010 and 70 at Scarcliffe on 2nd December 2011.

It is to be hoped that this small, apparent upturn in the fortunes of this engaging species will continue. Many people obtain pleasure from seeing Tree Sparrows, nowhere more so than at Carsington Water, where a resident flock has greatly benefited from the provision of nest-boxes and food, and can be watched throughout the year at very close range at one of the hide bird tables. Early signs are that a similar scheme at Staunton Harold Reservoir might be equally successful.

A melanistic bird was seen at Poolsbrook in July 1979, and Tree Sparrow x House Sparrow hybrids were seen on several occasions at Ogston Reservoir during spring 2002, and likewise in a Shirland garden in 2010–11.

Though largely sedentary, Tree Sparrows have very occasionally been seen moving over northern watch-points in autumn, with six moving north-west at Strines Top on 2nd November 1986 being the largest count. The Derbyshire ringing dataset has produced 21 records, of which 33% have involved movements greater than 30km, while 23% of the birds have been recovered at their place of ringing. This contrasts significantly with the 83% of House Sparrow records which had not moved from their original ringing sites. The greatest movements were by one which was ringed at Eckington in July 1975 that was killed near Skipton in North Yorkshire, 90km north-north-west, two years later; one ringed at Nether Padley in August 1968 was controlled 57km west-north-west near Salford six months later; and one ringed at Breck Farm in October 1971 was found dead 50km to the north-west at Slaithwaite, West Yorkshire in April 1972.

Yellow Wagtail
Motacilla flava
Fairly common summer visitor.

Yellow Wagtails, *M.f. flavissima*, are summer migrants breeding in damp areas such as water-meadows and the margins of open water. They are also found well away from water on farmland, particularly in cereal and potato fields.

There are few finer springtime sights than a newly arrived group of Yellow Wagtails, usually dominated by canary-yellow males, feeding along the edge of a reservoir or gravel pit. Unfortunately, in a relatively short period of time, such sightings have become less regular and the groups smaller in number, and there is evidence of a severe decline in the county's breeding population. This is a worrying trend, which is also exhibited by several other summer visitors.

Whitlock described Yellow Wagtails as abundant in all lowland areas, with their headquarters in the Trent and lower Derwent Valleys. They were local in the Peak District, although not uncommon around Hope and in some of the broader dales. Jourdain said that considerable numbers occurred up to 500ft (152m) amsl, with a few pairs in grass or cornfields to 600ft (183m), and added the lower Dove as one of its major breeding areas. In his monograph on the species, Smith (1950) implied that its status was little changed; he added that it was common around Ashbourne and between there and Hartington, but was absent from the areas around Glossop and Shirebrook. Frost believed that there had been little change in lowland populations, but stated that numbers in upland areas had increased: for example, it was by then common around Glossop. It bred in grassland and arable areas to over 1000ft (305m) amsl.

Perusal of survey results shows little change in status, at least at the 10km square level. It was found to breed in 22 of the 23 10km core squares in the 1968–72 Atlas; this was down to 18 by the 1988–91 Atlas, but back to 20 during the Derbyshire BBS (1995–99), in which it was proved to breed in 74 tetrads, with a combined total of 111 probable and possible tetrads.

Breeding was most often proved by the observation of adults carrying food for young, for which they may fly considerable distances from the nest. The map shows concentrations along the Trent and Dove Valleys, and part of the Carboniferous Limestone area, north-east and central west Derbyshire.

The decline is believed to have started in the early 1980s and is ongoing. The reasons for this are unknown. Brown and Grice (2005) believed the losses related to the continuing drainage of damp fields and wetlands, and conversion of intensively managed grassland to arable. However, even at nature reserves, such as Carr Vale and Willington Gravel Pits, which would still seem ideal for this species, only very small numbers breed nowadays. In arable areas it seems possible that the large-scale change from spring to autumn sowing has rendered large areas less suitable for Yellow Wagtails (as it has with Skylarks). It is also probable that changes in the African wintering grounds may be causing problems. Eaton et al. (2010) stated that there was an overall decline of 73% between 1970 and 2008.

Although the decline appears to have spanned the greater part of three decades, there were some local increases during this period. At Williamthorpe there were three or four pairs in 1987, quickly increasing to eight or nine by 1990; none are thought to breed there now. In 1992, numbers at Foolow were stated to be 'up on last year', with six pairs on one farm. But in 1996 the absence of Yellow Wagtails was remarked upon at Brailsford, Cadley Hill and Drakelow Nature Reserve. At Combs in 1999, there were said to be few records of a once-common species. Egginton Sewage Farm has long been a local stronghold of this species and in 1997, 15 pairs nested but all failed because of water company operations. Fortunately, the situation was reversed and in 1999, when at least 30 males held territory, dozens of young were reared as a result of habitat protection, with another very productive season in 2000. However, only seven pairs were found there in 2005, decreasing to none in 2008, when oil-seed rape was grown; the presence of four pairs in 2009 was believed to result from a change to winter wheat. Elsewhere, there have been several records in recent years of breeding on 'dry' farmland, in cereal and potato fields. At the Shirebrook Colliery site, five or six pairs bred in 2000, but all were gone just two years later due to afforestation. A BBS plot at Ticknall held five pairs in 1995, but none by 1999. A very surprising record from 1981 was of a pair raising young on the traffic roundabout at Derby City Hospital; this would be unthinkable today.

Other valuable counts of territorial pairs include: 17 along the Derbyshire side of the River Dove, between Sudbury and Hatton in June 1987; 21 along the River Trent between Newton Solney and King's Mills in June 1988, with 17 in the same area in May 1992; and 29 in a partial survey of north-east Derbyshire (north of the A617 Chesterfield to Mansfield Road and east of the M1 motorway) in 1994. It should be borne in mind that all these counts took place after the start of the decline, which was assessed at 73% during 1970–2008 (Eaton et al. 2010).

The maps comparing the position in 1995–99 with that of 2007–11, show a striking decline in the breeding distribution, especially in the Peak District and in central Derbyshire.

The earliest arrival of a Yellow Wagtail was recorded on 15th March 1961 at Draycott. There have been a few other late March records including 29th in 2011, but the first of the year are usually recorded in early April. The mean arrival date in the period 1978–2011 was 2nd April. Arrival continues into

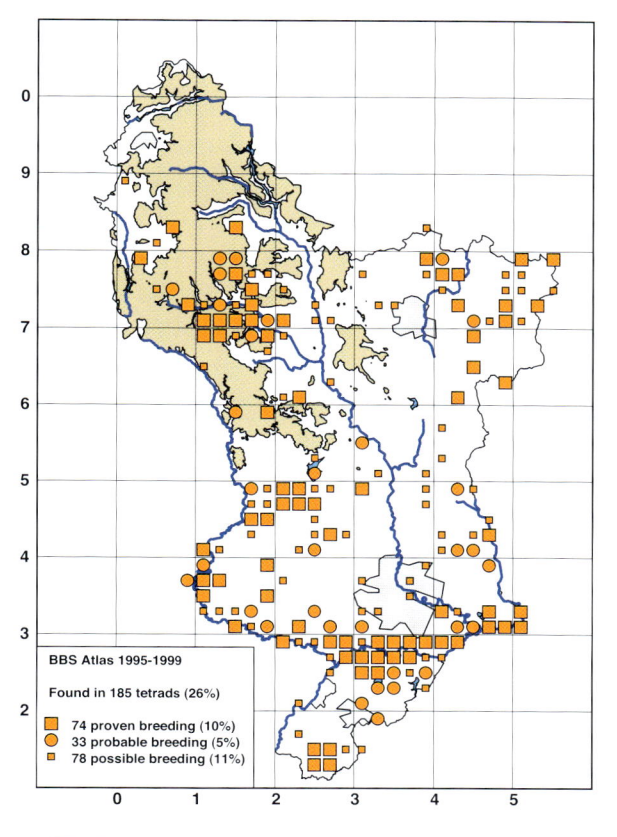

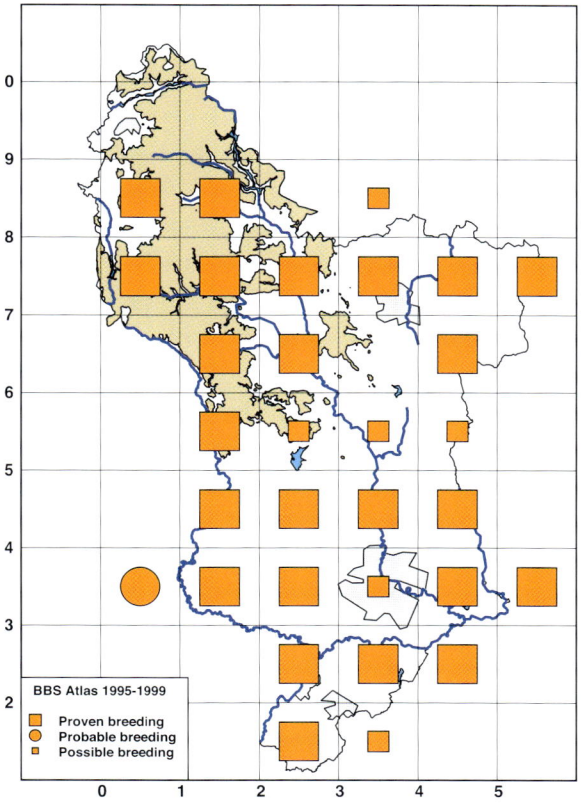

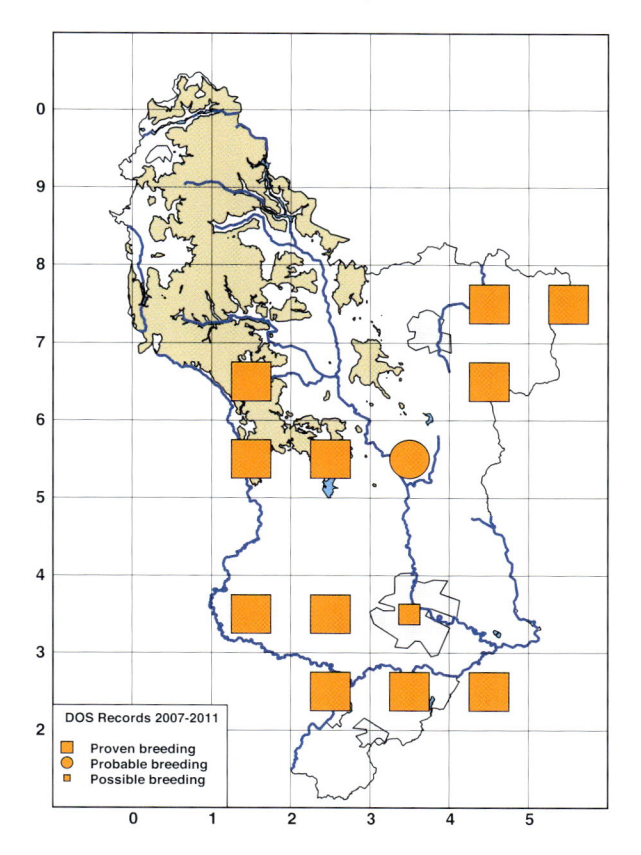

May and flocks seen at this time of the year have occasionally been of three figures, including 117 at Church Wilne Reservoir on 4th May 1985 and 100 there on 23rd April 1988, and 150 at Willington Gravel Pits also 23rd April 1988, with 100 on 29th April and 10th May 1996. Since 2000, the largest spring flocks have been smaller, with a maximum of 52 at Willington Gravel Pits on 2nd May 2004.

Post-breeding flocks are also much reduced nowadays. The largest gathering of all was in September 1971, when 300 roosted at Drakelow Nature Reserve. Since then, gatherings of 100 or more were at Elvaston Quarry with 100 roosting in lacustrine vegetation in August 1983, September 1986 and September 1991; 150 at Willington Gravel Pits on 23rd July 1989 and 117 there on 23rd July 1990; and 200 at Staunton Harold Reservoir on 23rd August 1990. Since 2000, the largest post-breeding gathering was of 50 at Willington Gravel Pits on 15th August 2002.

Visible migration involves only small numbers with double-figure totals now exceptional. In 1994, 50 flew south at Willington Gravel Pits on 7th September and 60 south-east on 18th September. Yellow Wagtails appear to migrate mainly along river valleys and are only seen occasionally at upland migration watch-points.

The average date for final sightings in the period 1978–2011 was 6th October. Records in later months were in 1963 when one (possibly showing some characteristics of Blue-headed Wagtail, *M.f. flava*, which breeds in western and central Europe) was at New Mills Sewage Farm from 27th October to 13th December, during which time it was caught and ringed. In 1970 there was an adult male at Staveley Sewage Farm from 27th November to 3rd December, and a first-winter bird at Brinsley Flashes on 28th November. One was at Shardlow Sewage Farm on 17th January 1976. It is possible that this was the same bird as recorded with a damaged wing at nearby Church Wilne Reservoir on 26th October 1975.

The Yellow Wagtail group is composed of numerous subspecies, some of which can be difficult to identify because of hybridization where their breeding ranges overlap. Furthermore, identification may be complicated by normal variations in plumage and by the presence of unusually pale birds. Three subspecies are believed to have occurred in Derbyshire and of these, the only one of regular occurrence is the Blue-headed Wagtail. The first record was of one killed in Darley Dale in the summer of 1895 (Jourdain) and Frost knew of about nine further occurrences. Since then, Blue-headed Wagtails have been recorded in most, but by no means all, years in very small numbers, almost always in spring. Most sightings have been in the Trent Valley, but there have been records at many sites, including a few in the Peak District. Most have been males, since females are much harder to identify. It is possible that hybridization with Yellow Wagtail *M.f. flavissima* has occurred, as there were breeding season records of male Blue-headed Wagtails apparently paired to female Yellow Wagtails at Shirebrook and Combs Reservoir in 1980, and Williamthorpe in 1989. In 1998 a female wagtail, thought to be Blue-headed, raised young with a male Yellow Wagtail at Willington Gravel Pits.

There have been two accepted records of males with the characteristics of Ashy-headed Wagtail, *M.f. cinereocapilla*, which breeds in southern France and Italy. The first was at Long Eaton Gravel Pits on 18th April 1999, and the second at Ogston Reservoir on 16th April 2005.

The Grey-headed Wagtail, *M.f. thunbergi*, which breeds from northern Scandinavia eastwards into Siberia, has occurred once, when a male was seen at Ogston Reservoir on 18th May 2008.

There have been several sightings of birds resembling Sykes's Wagtail, *M.f. beema*, which breeds in northern Kazakhstan and south-western Siberia, but all are far more likely to have been pale variants of *flava* intergrades between *flava* and *flavissima* (the so-called Channel Wagtail) or aberrants (Alström & Mild 2003). One such bird bred with a female Yellow Wagtail at Ogston Reservoir in 1963. One was present throughout May 1977 at Drakelow Nature Reserve, and one was at Church Wilne Reservoir on 25th April 1987. There was a sequence of records from Long Eaton Gravel Pits in the late 1990s. In 1997, a male paired with what was believed to be a female Blue-headed Wagtail and reared four young; in 1998, this male was again present from 23rd April to 25th May and in 1999 what was described as a possible *flavissima* x *beema* hybrid was seen from 19th to 21st April. A Channel Wagtail was at Egginton Sewage Farm in late June 2003.

There are eight ringing records of Yellow Wagtails concerning Derbyshire, where most have been caught at roosts. The majority were found close to their ringing sites. The exceptions were one ringed at Killamarsh in September 1961 that was controlled in July 1966 at Wakefield, West Yorkshire (47km north-north-west); one ringed at Bretby Park on 8th June 1972 that was controlled at Radipole, Dorset six weeks later (250km south-south-west); and one that was ringed at Hathersage in July 1968, which was found freshly dead at Beira Litoral, Portugal (1594km south-south-west) in September of the same year.

Citrine Wagtail
Motacilla citreola
A very rare vagrant

Citrine Wagtails of the nominate race breed from northern Russia east across Siberia to the Taimyr Peninsula, and south to central Siberia. Small numbers also now breed in the Baltic countries, Belarus and Finland. They winter in Asia, from India eastwards. There were about 263 UK records up to the end of 2011 (Hudson *et al*. 2012). A juvenile, moulting into first-winter plumage, was present at Ogston Reservoir from 28th to 30th August 2010, though its identification was only clinched on the last date. Mann (2011) wrote an account of the occurrence.

Grey Wagtail
Motacilla cinerea
A fairly common resident, mainly in upland areas. A fairly common winter visitor in the lowlands.

This delightful and colourful bird is a familiar sight on Peak District streams, but nests more sparingly in lowland areas, too. However, away from the hills it is best known as a regular winter visitor in small numbers. It is often seen on boulders in the water, flitting up to take insect prey such as mayflies and caddis-flies, though it also consumes insects of arboreal origin, and is therefore most numerous where trees are present along river-banks. Relatively fast-flowing water is required and it is found along most of the river courses in the Peak District, from upland streams on moorland to broader limestone dales, such as those on the Rivers Wye and Dove.

It seems likely that the breeding distribution in the upland parts of the county has been the same for a long time, since it is basically as Whitlock, Jourdain and later Frost described it. In the *Derbyshire Bird Reports* of 1978–79, the county population was estimated at 130–150 pairs, based on notes made by Philip Shooter while working on Dippers, and from the SBSG's work on the BTO Waterways Bird Survey. The latter survey, carried out along a total of 24.1km of the Rivers Noe and Derwent from Bamford to Beeley was documented by Falshaw *et al.* (1999). This showed a marked decline from a peak of 23 territories in the mid-1970s to a mere seven in 1982; but there was a swift recovery to 12 territories in the mid-1980s and a further increase to around 19 in the mid-1990s. The same two rivers held 23 territories in 2002, slightly more than double those of the Pied Wagtail (Falshaw 2005).

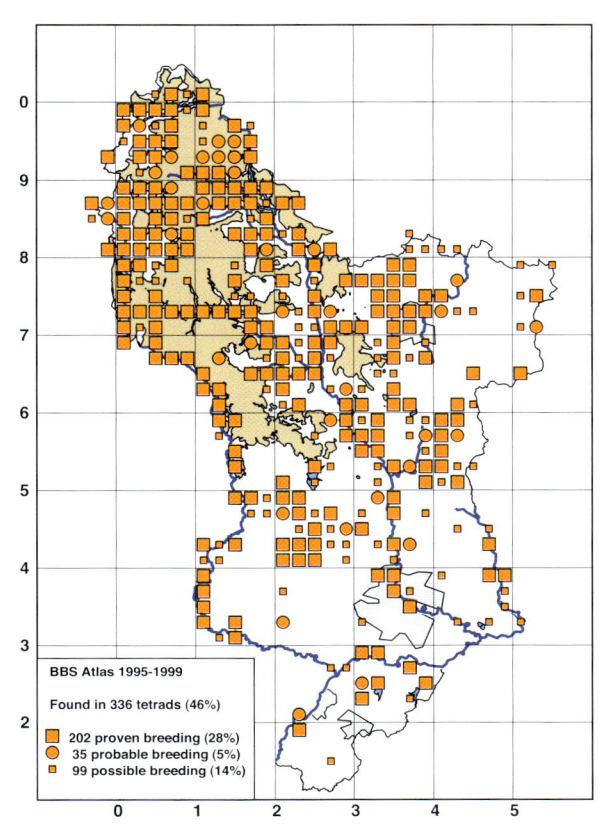

Another valuable survey was undertaken by J. Szczur in 1989, of 50km of the River Wye catchment, including Lathkill, Bradford and Cressbrook Dales. This revealed 30 breeding territories of Grey Wagtails, which were most numerous in the 5km of Chee Dale, where there were seven territories. Also in 1989, the same observer found three pairs in the Via Gellia and five territories in 10km of the Rivers Alport and Ashop, and at least ten pairs bred in that area in 1992. There were ten territories in 9km of the Ashop in 2001. In 1985, five pairs were found at Ladybower Reservoir, compared with 18 of Pied Wagtail. There were eight pairs in the Derwent Valley reservoir complex (Ladybower, Derwent and Howden) in 2000, with seven at Howden Reservoir alone two years later. More recent counts from many parts of the Peak District suggest a healthy population of Grey Wagtails, and as they were recorded from 338 tetrads in the Derbyshire BBS (1995–99), the county population is likely to have at least doubled from the earlier estimate of 130–150 breeding pairs. However, this species is very susceptible to cold winters, and numbers are always subject to considerable declines as a result. The 1962/63 winter caused an almost total desertion of the rivers and streams in much of the Snake area, including the River Ashop, and numbers in much of the Peak District were not considered 'normal' again until about 1971.

Grey Wagtails are by no means confined to upland areas. Whitlock and Jourdain both wrote of a few pairs nesting along the River Trent, the former adding that it rarely bred south of the river. A few pairs were also said to breed near Sutton Scarsdale. Frost recorded lowland breeding at Walton-on-Trent in 1955 and Hartshorne in 1969, and said that they bred at that time on two of the Magnesian Limestone streams, as well as in urban Derby in 1977. Since then, breeding in lowland areas has become much more widespread, as shown by the tetrad map, based on the Derbyshire BBS (1995–99). The only 10km square lacking proof of breeding during that period was SK23 (west of Derby). Of the 23 10km core squares, breeding was proved in 12 in 1968–72, 17 in 1988–91 and 22 in 1995–99. There can be little doubt that the generally milder winters of the 1990s facilitated this expansion of range. Improved river quality may also have helped. Since then, some colder winters, especially that of 2010/11, have led to localized declines, especially in the north of the county. Nationally, numbers declined by 26% between 1970 and 2008 (Eaton *et al.* 2010).

Successful breeding is easy to prove as the adults and fledglings are virtually confined to watercourses in the breeding season.

Lowland breeding sites are generally by rivers, streams or canals, frequently adjacent to weirs, locks and riffles. Grey Wagtails are nowadays often found breeding in built-up areas, and nests are not always sited by watercourses. In central Derby a pair nested in an urban courtyard 500m from the River Derwent in 1994 and at Walton, Chesterfield in 1993 nesting took place in a supermarket car park. In 2004 there were two nests with young just 70m apart on the Henmore Brook in the centre of Ashbourne. A particularly interesting record in June 1999 was of a recently fledged brood and three additional singing males along just 1km of the River Derwent in Derby.

Most Derbyshire Grey Wagtails nest very close to running water. Typical sites include holes in banks and retaining walls, ledges on rock-faces or buildings, and among tree roots. There was an earlier instance of breeding in a 'dry' situation in 1911, when a pair nested on a sandstone bluff by the side of a main road some 400m from the nearest stream. In 1950, a pair at Darley Dale railway sidings nested more than 5m down a wall, less than 2m above water level, while another unusual site was at Coxbench in 1955, when a pair nested 2m high in a climbing rose.

BBS Atlas 1995-1999
Found in 336 tetrads (46%)
- 202 proven breeding (28%)
- 35 probable breeding (5%)
- 99 possible breeding (14%)

Some Grey Wagtails remain all winter by upland rivers and streams but many more are seen in lowland regions, where they are not so restricted to running water as they are in the breeding season. They have been recorded in a wide variety of situations at this time, including urban rooftops, manure heaps, a tiny puddle among builders' rubble and, very occasionally, town gardens, such as one taking mealworms and suet for about two months in 2011 at Sinfin. The largest gatherings outside the breeding season are usually recorded at sewage farms; these include record counts of 32 at Stanton-in-Peak in September 2008, and 24 at High Peak Junction in March 2000. At Hathersage Sewage Farm, 20 were ringed on 20th August 1995 and 45 juveniles were ringed at the same site between 10th June and 22nd August 2004. The largest count of all was of 40 at Baslow Sewage Farm in July 2008.

Grey Wagtails are generally much scarcer than Pied Wagtails and do not form the large communal roosts typical of the latter species. Even small roosts are rarely reported. The larger ones include 13 on a Chesterfield factory roof in November 1976; six in *Phragmites* at Williamthorpe in February 2002; and in laurel bushes at Butterley Reservoir, 11 in November 2004 and 15 in September 2006.

Only small numbers of Grey Wagtails are recorded on autumn migration, usually between late August and October, with almost all being counts of single figures. A very notable exception to this was on 2nd October 1995, when an unprecedented 31 flew south at Bennerley Marsh. The only other double-figure records were of 15, mostly moving south, at Drakelow Nature Reserve on 20th September 1992 and ten to the south-west at Strines Top on 12th September 1994.

This species undertakes partial migration and also altitudinal migration within Derbyshire. Nests are quite easily located, especially when chicks are being fed, and all of the ringing recoveries are of birds ringed as nestlings. Adults can be caught in their breeding territory by mist netting across the rivers, and more recently many have been trapped at sewage farms, as previously mentioned, but most recoveries have been of dead birds. This applies similarly to the six county records, but there was one ringed as a nestling in the Goyt Valley in July 1964 that was controlled near Stockport (then in Lancashire), 19km to the north-west, six months later. The only long-distance record concerns one which had been ringed at Moor House National Nature Reserve, Cumbria in July 1954 that was found dead 184km to the south-south-east at Pilsley (near Chesterfield) in November 1956.

Pied Wagtail
Motacilla alba
A common resident and passage migrant.

This familiar and popular bird frequently lives close to man and is undoubtedly the best known of the wagtails. It occurs in a wide variety of habitats, though it is often most numerous at wetlands, such as the edges of rivers and open water, and also sewage farms, especially those with rotating sprinklers. However, it is often found on drier ground including ploughland and fields of young cereals, farmyards and areas of short grass, such as lawns and sports pitches (often in urban areas), where it can easily obtain insect food.

The tetrad map from the Derbyshire BBS (1995–99) confirms the Pied Wagtail's widespread distribution as a breeding bird, with breeding proved in 450 tetrads, mainly by the recording of adults carrying food or recently fledged young, which are easily distinguishable from their parents. Breeding was regarded as probable or possible in a further 59 and 128 tetrads, with the overall total of 637 tetrads making it the twelfth most widespread species in the county. Breeding was proved in all 23 10km core squares, as it was in the 1988–91 Atlas, with 22 in the 1968–72 Atlas. Eaton *et al*. (2010) stated that the UK population increased by 38% during the period 1970 to 2008.

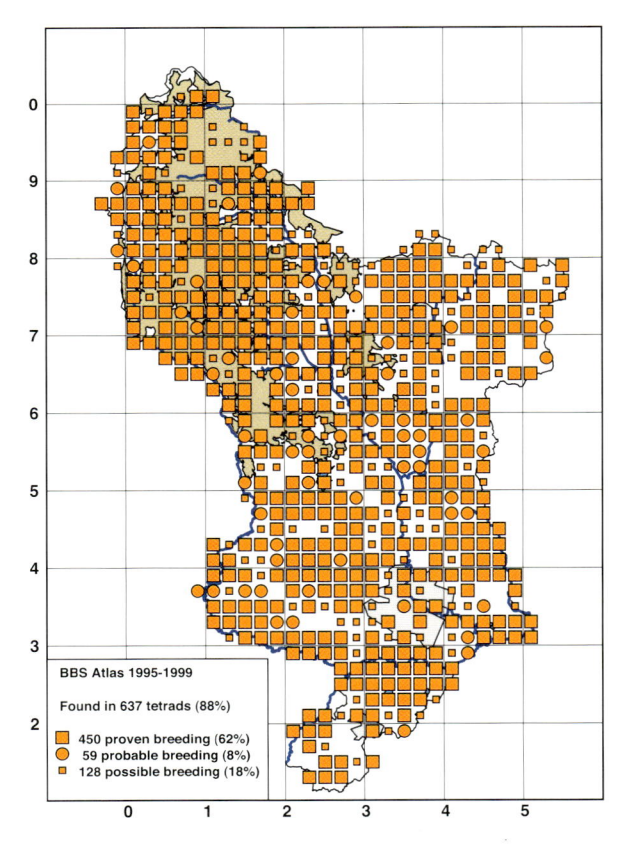

Whitlock described Pied Wagtails as abundant, though mainly as summer visitors between April and September, with relatively few remaining in winter. Frost said that they bred to at least 1500ft (457m) amsl in the Peak District. They occurred on two of the farmland CBC plots studied during the 1990s, with an average of 0.67 pairs a year (0.98 pairs per km^2) at Farfield Farm and 1.17 pairs a year (2.35 pairs per km^2) at Broadhay Farm. Other very useful counts of breeding birds include an estimated 18 pairs at the Derwent Valley reservoir complex (Ladybower, Derwent and Howden) in June 1985, but with only nine there in 2001. Along the River Ashop in 2001, there were three territories compared with ten of Grey Wagtail. Falshaw *et al*. (1999) published combined figures for the River Noe from Townhead Bridge to Mytham Bridge (5.4km) and for the River Derwent from Bamford to Beeley (18.7km). The number of Pied Wagtail territories fell from 28 in 1974 to nine in 1992, before stabilizing at around 15 in the mid-1990s. The same area held 11 territories in 2002 compared with 23 of Grey Wagtail (Falshaw 2005). At Carsington Water the 2003–07 census suggested 26 territories.

Most nests are well hidden on ledges or in recesses in rocks and buildings. Unusual sites have included a rat-trap, inside a locomotive awaiting restoration, in a Wren's nest at a height of 8m on the wall of a gamekeeper's house and in a dumper truck at Drakelow Power Station in 2010.

There has certainly been a change in the status of this species since Whitlock's day, as Pied Wagtails are now numerous at all times of the year. The largest diurnal counts in winter come from sewage farms, which provide favourable feeding sites. Counts of three figures are not unusual and over 200 have been recorded at the Derby Sewage Farm and over 300 at Stanton-in-Peak Sewage Works.

Pied Wagtails roost communally for almost all the year, in a wide variety of habitats. Lacustrine vegetation, such as common reed and reed-mace, is frequently used but, increasingly, roosts are in dry situations, including lines of trees and bushes (both deciduous and evergreen), and on the roofs of large buildings such as factories. The largest recorded roosts were: 1080 at

BBS Atlas 1995-1999

Found in 637 tetrads (88%)

- 450 proven breeding (62%)
- 59 probable breeding (8%)
- 128 possible breeding (18%)

Nadin's, Newhall in October 2003; 1000 at Mansfield Road, Derby in March 2006; 940 at a Darley Dale factory in March 2011; 700 at Swadlincote Tip in September 1988; 641 on the roof of Eastlands House, Derby in September 1989, with 530 there in September 1991; and 500 at Holmewood in February 2002. A count of 500–750 at Bakewell in October 1943 also seems likely to have referred to a roost.

Numbers at well-watched localities usually increase in March and April, as a proportion of the breeding population returns and other migrants pass through. But visible migration is much more noticeable in autumn, lasting from September to November and is usually heaviest in late September and early October. Numbers are relatively small, and the only records of over 100 have been: Strines Top, 118 south-west on 4th October 1993 and 105 likewise on 30th September 1994; Ashover, 178 south on 2nd October 2000; Ramsley, 277 south on 7th October 2004 and 215 south-west on 9th October 2001; and 105 south at Moorhall on 9th October 2008.

White Wagtails of the nominate race M.a. alba are regular spring and autumn migrants through Derbyshire, although in very variable numbers. They are more associated with wetlands than Pied Wagtails, and the majority of records come from reservoirs, gravel pits and other areas of open water. Most sightings are in spring, when subspecific identification is easier, and span the period from 16th February (2009), when two were at Palterton, to the end of May, with a very late one at Wyver Lane on 9th June 1991 and at Carsington Water on the same date in 2010. Autumn birds are harder to identify, but there have been records between 9th July (2003) at Carsington Water and 27th November (2009) at Scropton.

Most White Wagtail records are of single figures and the largest counts have been: 40 at Combs Reservoir on 2nd September 1991; 30 roosting with Pied Wagtails at Staveley on 12th April 1966; 25 at Williamthorpe on 19th April 1987; 25 at Aston-on-Trent Gravel Pits on 18th April 1999; and 24 at Fernilee Reservoir on 19th September 1956.

An aberrant White Wagtail at Stanton-in-Peak sewage farm in March 1995 had an all-white head and bright, creamy-pink legs.

Whitlock expressed little doubt that White Wagtails occasionally bred in Derbyshire and was shown a clutch of eggs taken at Repton by Henry Tomlinson which were said to have been of this subspecies. Jourdain thought they possibly bred occasionally in the Trent Valley. But Frost stated that although 'one or two records suggesting breeding have recently been submitted, none are sufficiently authenticated'. Subsequently, the only evidence of potential breeding concerns a bird apparently holding territory at Ravensnest, Ashover on 14th June 2000.

Of 84 ringing recoveries of Pied Wagtails involving Derbyshire, 15 had been ringed as nestlings of which four had migrated to winter in Portugal. Five caught as birds of the year or older were found in France and one in Spain.

One ringed at a roost on Lewis, Western Isles in August 1981 was found dead at Mickleover, 681km south-south-east on 28th December 1982.

Richard's Pipit
Anthus richardi
A very rare vagrant.

The migratory race of the Richard's Pipit, which breeds from western Siberia eastwards, and winters in India and south-east Asia, is a regular autumn migrant in the UK. The five Derbyshire records have all occurred during this season; Lacey and Frost (1988) documented the first occurrence.

The Catton bird flew from the Derbyshire side of the River Trent to join a second bird at the adjacent Barton Gravel Pits, Staffordshire, before both departed to the south-west.

Year	Location and date
1987	Staveley, one on 26th, 28th and 30th October
1994	Catton, one on 23rd October
1996	Ashover, one flew west-south-west on 17th October
2002	Holmewood, one on 11th November flew towards Williamthorpe, where it was observed on the following day
2010	Screetham Lane, one from 3rd to 10th November

Tawny Pipit
Anthus campestris
A very rare vagrant.

The only Derbyshire record of this species, which is extremely rare inland, was of a first-winter bird at Aston-on-Trent Gravel Pits from 5th to 7th October 2003. It was elusive throughout its three-day stay, spending much of its time in thick vegetation and giving only occasional flight views to most observers. On at least two occasions it was seen to fly over the River Trent into Leicestershire. Key (2004) wrote an account of the occurrence.

The Records Committee of the Leicestershire and Rutland Ornithological Society were unconvinced of the identification, believing that it may have been a Richard's Pipit, which is admittedly more likely in view of the site and date. However, further enquiries of eight or so experienced observers who saw the bird revealed that all remained convinced of the original identification.

Tawny Pipits breed from north-west Africa and Iberia to Mongolia, and winter from Sahelian Africa to India. They were removed from the list of species considered by BBRC after 1982, by which time there were about 620 national records.

Tree Pipit
Anthus trivialis
A fairly common summer visitor.

Though similar in appearance to Meadow Pipits, Tree Pipits are readily distinguished by their song, often given during the conspicuous 'parachuting' display flight, beginning and ending on a tree or bush. This is usually the first indication of its presence in an area and accounted for records of probable breeding in 91 tetrads in the Derbyshire BBS (1995–99), compared with 83 in the other two categories combined. Breeding was proved in 58 tetrads, most readily by seeing birds carrying food, often calling nervously in the presence of observers.

Tree Pipits, as the name suggests, are more linked than Meadow Pipits with arboreal habitats, being birds of large woodland glades or woodland edges, especially of birch or sessile oak, clear-fells, and restocked plantations. Where these habitats adjoin moorland, there may be a small zone of overlap with Meadow Pipits, but Tree Pipits are not found on open, treeless areas of the moors.

In Derbyshire breeding numbers have declined in the past 15 years, particularly in southern and eastern lowland regions. The 1968–72 and 1988–91 Atlases revealed confirmed breeding in 14 and 15 10km squares, but this had reduced to 12 by the time of the Derbyshire BBS (1995–99). This change in distribution is shown in the comparative maps for 1995–99 and 2007–11.

This decline is fairly recent, since Frost considered Tree Pipits fairly common throughout the county, and Whitlock said they were 'very familiar everywhere', while Jourdain said that they were found everywhere except on the moors and the bleakest uplands, being most numerous in the well-wooded valleys of the Rivers Dove and Derwent and on the rising ground in the Trent Valley. Most recent comments on changed status refer to declines. Nationally, Eaton *et al.* (2010) recorded a decrease of 73% between 1970 and 2008.

At CBC plots there were five territories at Shire Hill in 1994 (a density of 11.9 pairs per km^2), there was a single territory at Shiningcliff Wood in 1990 but none subsequently, while at Broadhay Farm there were five or six territories in 1990–93, reducing to two by 1995. In 1998, the Eastern Moors survey located 65 singing males, and in the same year there were at least 20 singing males in the Goyt Valley and eight at Win Hill. Good numbers of Tree Pipits were still present in parts in 2006, with counts of singing males included 15 at Win Hill, 16 in the Ramsley Moor–Greaves's Piece area and five at Alderwasley Park. The Peak District is now the local stronghold, with 92 singing males, for example, in the 2010 survey of the EMP moors, where almost all were associated with birch woodland and scrub.

The situation in lowland areas is very different, with very few records of breeding since 2000, although two were carrying food at Carver's Rocks Nature Reserve in 2007. At Scarcliffe Woods there was a maximum of 17 pairs in 1974, but the population was reduced to single figures by the late 1980s, with none at all since 2002, despite the creation of some apparently ideal habitat following felling (Frost 2008a).

In the period from 1978 to 2011, the mean first arrival date was 8th April, with the two earliest ever records on 27th March at Clay Mills Gravel Pits in 1968 and at Whaley Bridge in 2011. Territories are vacated in late summer and most of the latest sightings of the year are of migrants. The average last date in the same period was 23rd September and the latest of all was at Staunton Harold Reservoir on 26th October 1976. An 1833 sighting (in Whitlock) in November seems to have been based on its moult-pattern, which would not nowadays be considered reliable.

Small numbers are recorded on autumn passage from August to October, their throaty calls distinguishing them from the much more numerous Meadow Pipits. The largest numbers were at Strines Top with 11 moving south-west on 10th September 1995 and seven likewise on 21st August 1992, seven flying south-west at Ashover on 23rd August 1985, and six south at Foremark Reservoir on 22nd August 2001. Some observers consider that passage numbers are smaller than before, in line with the species' reduced breeding status.

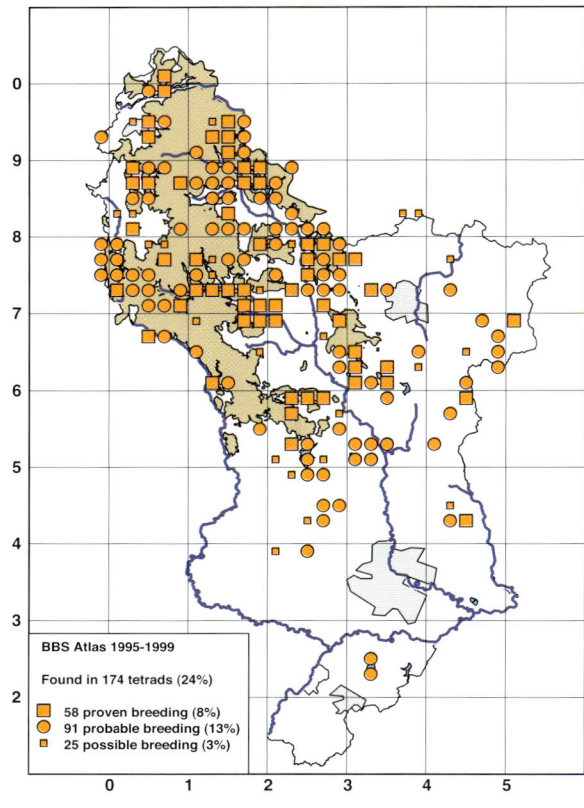

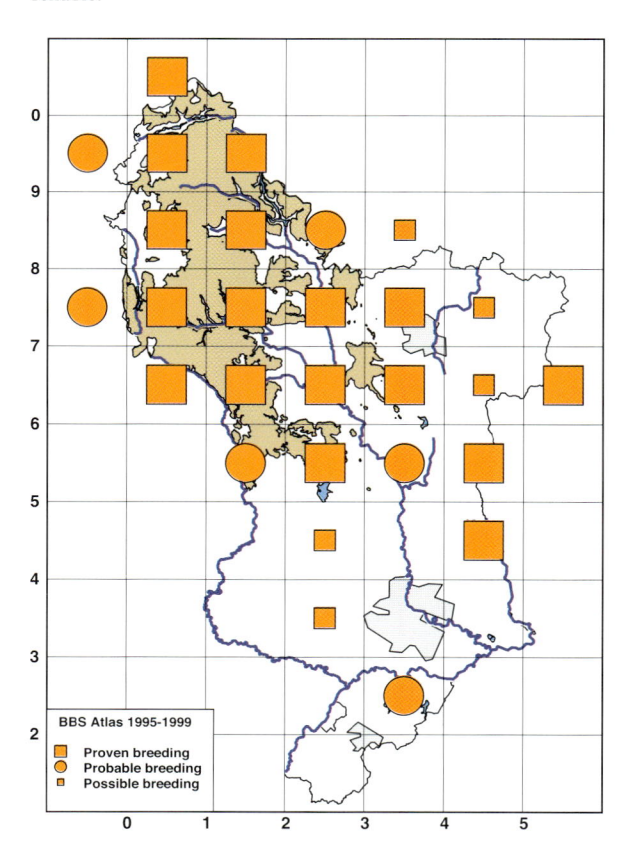

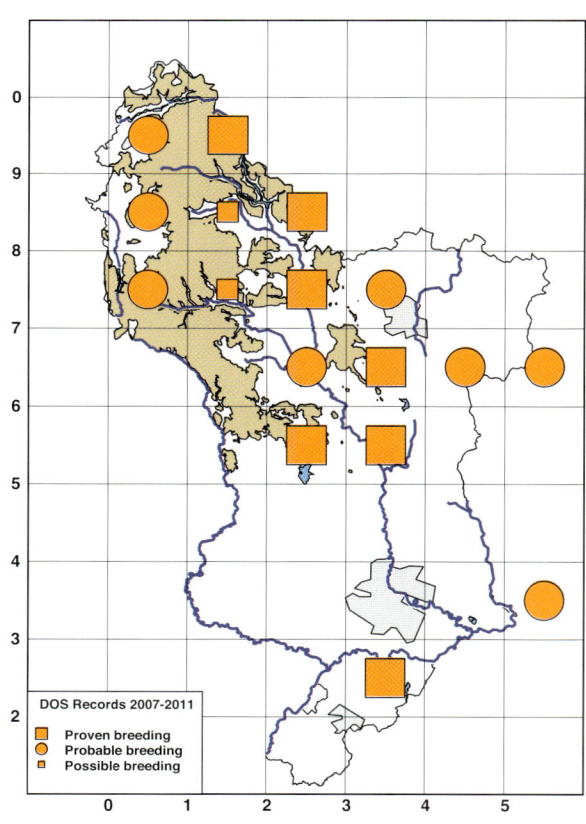

Meadow Pipit
Anthus pratensis
A common summer visitor, passage migrant and winter visitor.

The Meadow Pipit is by far the most numerous breeding species on moorland, and occurs commonly in other upland habitats such as rough pasture and road verges. In lowland areas it is much scarcer, inhabiting uncultivated ground such as industrial wasteland, quarries, gravel pit margins and golf courses. Both Whitlock and Frost considered this a common species, especially on moorland.

Meadow Pipits may begin to return to their breeding grounds in February, if the weather is mild, but it is not until March that they are present in any numbers, and it is often late April before populations are full. Due to difficulties in accurately censusing this species, there is relatively little recent quantitative data on upland breeding densities. In 1979, 67 territories were found in 9km^2 in the Snake Pass area, while in 1998 the combined population of East Moor and Leash Fen was estimated, perhaps conservatively, at 90 pairs. For the 2010 EMP moors survey, the birds were counted on the initial visits. This resulted in a figure of 485, which included pairs and singing and non-singing birds. It was believed that the total population was considerably higher than the 242 pairs that the total might suggest (Frost & Taylor 2011).

In lowland areas there were 11 singing at Bondhay Golf Course in June 1998 and April 2001, while at Drakelow Nature Reserve seven pairs nested in 1979, but only two by 1998. The Shirebrook Colliery site held 31 territories in 2002, reducing to six by 2009 as the plantations matured. The only CBC plot where Meadow Pipits were regularly recorded was at Broadhay Farm, with one to four territories in 1990–95.

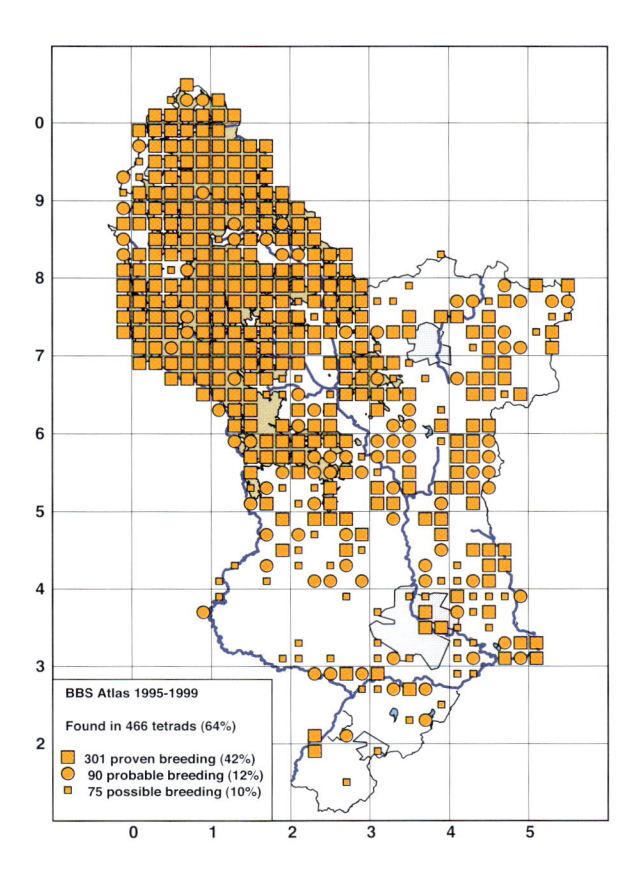

Meadow Pipits are fairly confiding birds and not difficult to locate, especially when the males perform their frequent song-flights. Breeding is also easily proved, especially when they are feeding young, as they may be seen with bills full of food, awaiting the departure of the observer. Of the 466 tetrads which held this species in the Derbyshire BBS (1995–99), 301 had proof of breeding, with probable breeding recorded in a further 90.

The tetrad map shows that breeding was proved in 21 of the 23 10km core squares, compared with 19 in both the 1968–72 and 1988–91 Atlases. However, it seems likely that the increased efficiency in farming has caused a decline, especially the loss of in-bye land and increased conversion to arable. However, there is little information on population trends of local moorland breeders. Nationally, Eaton *et al.* (2010) found that there was a decline of 43% between 1970 and 2008.

In winter, Meadow Pipits are very largely absent from high ground, but are much more widespread in lowland areas, in a variety of open countryside, usually in small parties. Higher concentrations, very occasionally reaching three figures, may occur at favoured sites, such as Derby Sewage Farm, which held 250 on 10th January 1982.

Spring passage is observed mainly in March and April and is mostly between north and north-west. At Alport Dale, 500 flew north on 25th April 1992, and 328 moved north over Carr Vale on 3rd April 1997. Post-breeding flocks build up on moorland and in other upland areas, and may be of some hundreds, with 1000 roosting in heather at Beeley Moor on 19th September 1986 and 1000 counted at Hathersage on 9th September 1991.

Visible migration, usually between south and south-west, is much more evident in autumn than in spring and lasts from August to November, generally peaking in the second half of September and early October. The largest recorded movements were at Strines Top, with 4805 on 14th September 1991 and 2100 on 25th September 1995, and at Ramsley Moor, with 9015 moving south to south-west on 9th October 2001 followed by 3743 five days later and 3447 south on 7th October 2004. At Ashover, 1511 flew south to south-west on 8th October 1988. The heaviest lowland movement was of 1605 south-south-west over Carr Vale on 9th October 2001.

This species offers year-round opportunities for ringing, both on its moorland breeding grounds and also on lower ground in winter, when flocks may include immigrants. The longest movement by a Derbyshire-ringed bird within the UK is 220km, from Hathersage south to Somerset. There are a further 18 recoveries involving the county. Eight of these refer to birds ringed in the Peak District in spring and recovered during the period 12th October to 10th March in France, Portugal (two) and Spain (five). The records show a relatively short life, with the longest-lived bird from the data being just 14 months.

BBS Atlas 1995-1999

Found in 466 tetrads (64%)

- 301 proven breeding (42%)
- 90 probable breeding (12%)
- 75 possible breeding (10%)

Red-throated Pipit
Anthus cervinus
A very rare vagrant.

Red-throated Pipits are annual, but scarce, visitors to Britain, with records almost equally divided between spring and autumn. There is usually an easterly bias and inland records are rare. They breed in Arctic Russia and Fennoscandia, and winter chiefly in sub-Saharan Africa. The British total stood at about 435 by the time it was removed from the BBRC list after 2005.

There have been three Derbyshire records, two of which occurred during the peak time for this species from late April to early June, and the other in September. An account of the 1996 record was given by Gould (1997b).

Year	Location and date
1985	Rother Valley Country Park (now in South Yorkshire), one from 20th to 23rd May
1996	Hillyfields (now known as Pools Brook Country Park), a summer-plumaged bird on 23rd–24th April, departed to the north
2006	Butterley Reservoir, one briefly on 3rd September

Rock Pipit
Anthus petrosus
An uncommon passage migrant and rare winter visitor.

This species, which was formerly regarded as conspecific with Water Pipit, was first identified in Derbyshire as recently as 1965, when one was seen at Westhouses Flash on 6th March. By the end of 1977 over 200 had been seen, mainly on autumn passage, with much smaller numbers in spring, and a few overwintering in the Trent Valley (Frost).

Although very occasionally seen in the winter months, the only evidence of overwintering since 1978 was in 2003/04, when what was considered to be the same individual was seen at Carsington Water and the sewage works at High Peak Junction from November to January. Numbers on passage have been variable, as the chart shows.

It can be seen that the 1970s produced the largest numbers of Rock Pipits visiting the county. Numbers collapsed in 1979, with only five records, and no more than 12 were recorded in any subsequent year until 1997. The period 2000–11 saw this moderate improvement sustained.

Most records come from reservoirs, sewage farms, lakes and subsidence flashes. The stony-sided Barbrook Reservoir was the most productive site and held an exceptional 11 birds on 15th October 1999. Following the reservoir being drained in 2002, it produced only seven sightings in 2003–11. Most records relate to single birds with occasionally up to four seen at any site.

Autumn passage begins in September, with the earliest record being on 9th September 2010 at Carsington Water. October is the main month for migrants, with fewer in November. Spring migrants, in much smaller numbers than in autumn, occur in March and April. The latest ever was at Williamthorpe on the exceptional date of 9th May 1992.

The Scandinavian subspecies *A.p. littoralis* is only distinguishable from the nominate subspecies in fresh spring plumage. It has been identified on 17 occasions in 1969–2011, in the period from 12th March to 17th April. However, it is likely that many, perhaps almost all, of the birds seen in the county at other times are also of this subspecies. Evidence of this comes from a sighting of a colour-ringed bird at Church Wilne Reservoir on 4th October 1988. It had been ringed as a chick on the island of Nidingen, Onsala, Sweden on 30th June that year and was last noted there on 16th September, 18 days before it was seen in Derbyshire.

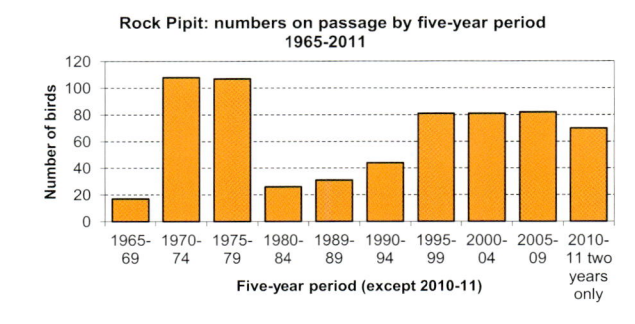

Water Pipit
Anthus spinoletta
A scarce passage migrant and winter visitor.

Three at Press Reservoirs on 16th and 23rd November 1953 constituted the first Derbyshire record of this species. No more were seen until 1965, since when it has been an annual visitor to the county, in very varying numbers. The chart shows the approximate numbers recorded in periods.

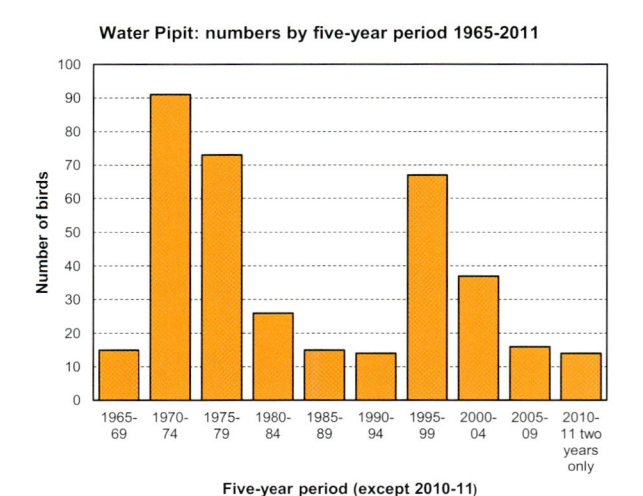

The pattern of occurrences is remarkably similar to that of Rock Pipit, with the highest numbers during the 1970s, a collapse from 1979 and a partial recovery at the end of the 1990s. Numbers have never regained the levels of 1971/72, when Frost stated that at least 20 wintered in the county, including ten at Old Whittington Sewage Farm. More recently, the largest gathering was of six at Willington Gravel Pits on 27th March 1999, and since 2000, five at Willington Gravel Pits in February and March 2010, and four at Egginton Sewage Farm on 21st March 2000. The greatest numbers in recent years have been on spring passage between February and April, with smaller numbers on autumn passage, mainly in October and November. Extreme dates are 27th September 1980 at Drakelow Nature Reserve and 2nd May 2007 at Aston-on-Trent Gravel Pits. Up to five overwintered during the late 1990s, following a gap from the winter of 1985/86 to 1992/93. However, since 2000 there have been only seven individuals recorded in the months of December and January.

Most wintering birds have been seen at subsidence flashes, sewage farms, gravel pits and reservoirs in the eastern and southern lowlands of the county. Passage migrants are more widespread, and Water Pipits have occurred on numerous occasions in the Peak District, mainly at Barbrook Reservoir, but also at Errwood and Arnfield Reservoirs, and elsewhere.

A striking, partially albinistic bird at Willington Gravel Pits in March 2000 was documented by Key (2001b).

Chaffinch
Fringilla coelebs
A common resident, passage migrant and winter visitor.

Chaffinches are among the county's most familiar and widespread birds. They nest wherever trees and bushes occur, in woodland of all types, hedgerows, built-up areas and in scattered trees in moorland cloughs. This species is easily located by its often-confiding nature (at popular picnic sites it is a persistent scrounger of food) and by its loud and familiar song and calls.

The status of Chaffinch has been the same since the time of Whitlock and Jourdain. In 1918, the species was described as being seen and heard everywhere and to be more plentiful than sparrows (*DAJ*).

In the Derbyshire BBS (1995–99) it was found in 695 tetrads, making it the second most widespread species in the county. Breeding was proved in 453 (63% of the total) and was probable in a further 207 (29% of the total). The absences in the extreme north-west of the county, where the highest ground and largest expanses of treeless moorland occur, are likely to be genuine. Apparent absences elsewhere are probably the result of under-recording, as it is inconceivable that there are any such tetrads without breeding Chaffinches. Breeding was proved in all of the main 10km squares, as it was for both the 1968–72 and 1988–91 Atlases.

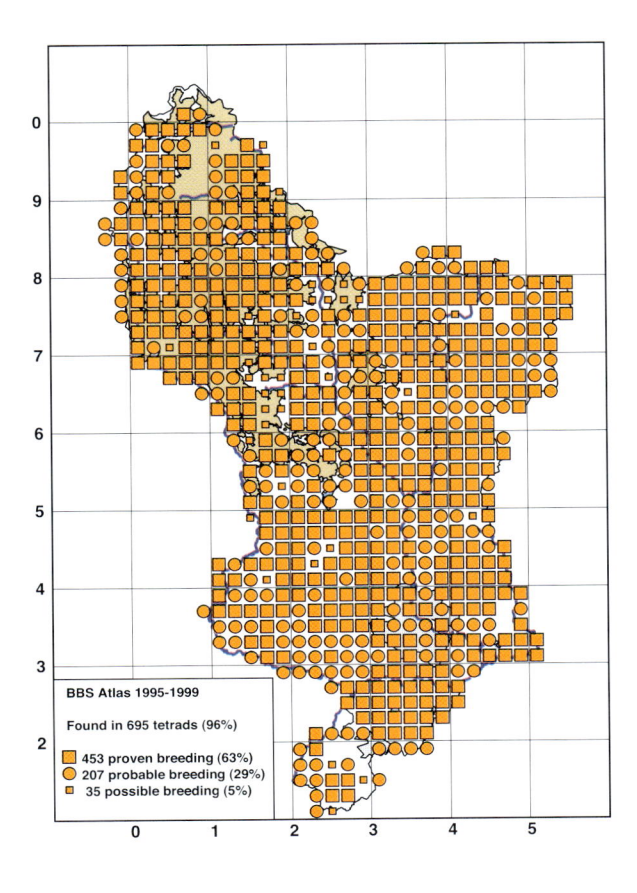

On woodland CBC plots surveyed in the county in the 1990s, Chaffinches were between the fourth and ninth most numerous species, with densities per km^2 ranging from 19.05 to 56.82 pairs. At Scarcliffe Woods (284ha), a study by Frost (2008a) showed that it was the third most numerous species in the mid-1970s, but by 1989 had become the most common, as it was in every subsequent year, with a maximum of 149 singing males in 1994. This increased to 153 in 2010.

Regular counts at Whitwell Wood between 2004 and 2011 recorded a mean number of 50 territories per year with extremes of 68 in 2011 and 32 in 2000. At Ticknall, linear BBS counts in 1km of farmland over the same period of time recorded a mean of 13 singing males per year, with extremes of 20 in 1997 and nine in 2000. It was the fifth most common species at Carsington Water during the 2003–07 survey, totalling 133 territories. There were 67 territories on the EMP moors in 2010, with a third of these on Ramsley Moor.

On farmland CBC plots, the Chaffinch was found to be the most common bird at Broadhay Farm, Hathersage and Farfield Farm, Hope, and second only to Wren at Culland. Farmland densities ranged from 22.48 to 39.38 pairs per km^2. There is little evidence of any large, long-term change in numbers in Derbyshire. Nationally, numbers increased by 34% between 1970 and 2008, according to Eaton *et al.* (2010).

Flocks may be seen shortly after the end of the breeding season, sometimes reaching three figures. A notable count was of 363 moving along Cressbrook Dale in a five-minute period on 7th September 1982.

During the autumn our breeding birds are joined by others of presumed Continental origin. Visible migration is generally recorded from late September to November, with the heaviest movements in October. Easily the most outstanding series of counts has come from Strines Top. Here, the largest counts have been 2440 flying west in three hours on 31st October 1986, 859 flying south-east on 12th October 1992, and 900 which passed on 15th October 1993. Elsewhere, the largest such counts were from Ramsley, where 742 flew south-west on 31st October 2006, 337 flew south-west in 130 minutes on 9th October 1988, 884 south-west on 27th October 2008, and 923 south-west on 4th October 2011. At Ashover Fabric, 587 flew north-west in two hours on 18th October 1986.

In winter, concentrations occur at favoured food sources, such as stubble and manured fields, and flocks of up to 300 are not uncommon. The largest recent counts were of 800 at Hollington in January 1994, and 1000 on beechmast at Ladygrove on 14th January 2003. However, the highest counts are usually from communal roosts in rhododendron thickets, often in the company of Bramblings and Greenfinches. Numbers were at their highest in the 1960s, when there were records of 3000 at Shiningcliff Wood and at least 4900 at Osmaston Park. The largest roosts since 1978 have also been at the latter site, with maxima of 1200 in December 1995 and 1500 in November 2006. A smaller roost at Cordwell reached a maximum of 589 in November 1983.

BBS Atlas 1995-1999
Found in 695 tetrads (96%)
- 453 proven breeding (63%)
- 207 probable breeding (29%)
- 35 possible breeding (5%)

There have been 91 Chaffinch ringing recoveries involving Derbyshire birds. Of these, eight individuals were found elsewhere in Europe and three had been ringed in The Netherlands. Of the remainder, 45% were found within 5km of their ringing site. Some of the more interesting recoveries include a female ringed at Elvaston Castle Country Park on 17th December 1989 that was found at Billingstad, Norway, a distance of 1066km, on 20th December 1992, and a male ringed at Barrow Hill on 26th January 1980 that hit glass in Moss, Norway (1006km) on 10th April 1980. A long-lived bird was a male ringed at Mugginton on 12th January 1985 that hit glass at Hulland Ward (only 5km distant) on 13th April 1993.

Brambling
Fringilla montifringilla
An erratic, but usually common passage migrant and winter visitor. Rare in summer.

Year	Location	Birds	Date
2002	Sir William Hill	450	28th December
2003	Stoke Hall	450	15th January
2004	Goyt Valley	400	31st December
2005	Goyt Valley	500	3rd January
2005	Derwentdale	1220	24th March
2007	Win Hill	500	16th November
2008	Screetham Lane	500	25th February
2008	Upper Derwentdale	1000	5th April
2008	Screetham Lane	500	17th December

Bramblings have for a long time been very variable in number as passage migrants and winter visitors in Derbyshire. Whitlock said they were winter visitors in small numbers from October to March, while Jourdain described them as somewhat irregular, but occasionally seen in large flocks. They frequent a variety of habitats, including farmland, and both coniferous and deciduous woodland, particularly beech if the crop of mast is heavy.

Autumn arrival is usually from late September to early November. In the period 1978–2011, first dates ranged from 19th August to 26th October, with a mean of 29th September. There are two August records, the first concerning a bird at Ramsley Reservoir on 19th August 2002 and the other a road casualty at Lea Hall on 28th August 2005.

In some years, the number recorded moving over the regular visible migration watch-points in autumn has been greater than the number seen during the remainder of the winter. Strines Top has witnessed the most spectacular of these movements, with an outstanding count of 1712 flying south-west in three hours on 31st October 1986, and 900 moving north-west on 15th October 1993, contributing to a total for October 1993 of some 3800 recorded moving over this site. At all of the other watch-points, numbers have usually been much smaller, with the highest counts at Ramsley, where 2381 flew between south and west on seven dates between 20th October and 7th November 2005, with a highest count of 1032 on the latter date, and at Ashover Fabric, where 478 flew north-west in two hours on 18th October 1986.

In the winter months, Brambling numbers may vary considerably from year to year. For example, in 1980–99 the largest count recorded in any winter varied between 80 and 1000, with the highest number in Derwentdale on 1st April 1996. Large numbers have been recorded in 2002–11 and in most of these winters three-figure flocks have been widespread. Flocks of 400 and over are shown in the table.

Many of the largest counts have been of roosts in rhododendron thickets with, in recent years, counts of up to 800 at Shiningcliff Wood, 400 at Cordwell Valley and 300 at Osmaston Park. By far the largest gathering recorded in the county was at the Shiningcliff Wood roost in December 1967, when an unprecedented 5700 were counted.

Hard-weather movement is rarely witnessed, and then only on a small scale. However, cold weather conditions are the most likely to cause birds to feed in gardens, an apparently increasing trend.

Spring movement is recorded between March and early May, though the visible migration as witnessed in autumn is not apparent at this season, and it is possible that much emigration takes place during the hours of darkness. The latest sightings in the period 1980–2011 were between 30th March and 31st May, with a mean last date of 29th April. The latest record was at Cowers Lane on 31st May 2006. Springtime males may sometimes be heard uttering their nasal sub-song.

In summer, singing Bramblings have been recorded in 1956, 1970, 1976 (Frost) and most recently in 1983, when one tried to mate with a Chaffinch at Padley Gorge (Hornbuckle 1984).

There have been 16 ringing recoveries for Derbyshire and four of these have been of foreign movements. A male ringed at Breck Farm on 16th February 1969 was controlled 2103km to the north-north-east in Lappi, Finland in the following July, and a female ringed at the same site in January 1972 was shot at Trier, Germany on 18th October 1972, suggesting wintering in separate areas. One ringed at Drakelow Nature Reserve in April 1995 was controlled at Hareid, Norway, 1157km north-east, in January 1996, while one controlled at Darley Dale in November 1998 had been ringed at Zeeland in The Netherlands, in the previous March.

Greenfinch
Chloris chloris
A common resident.

The familiar wheezy call note of the Greenfinch delivered from atop a tall tree on a balmy summer's day, and its curious song-flight at treetop level on bat-like wings are still common experiences in Derbyshire. They are to be found throughout the county where trees and hedges occur, as they have been since the days of Whitlock and Jourdain. Greenfinches can therefore be found nesting in open woodland, woodland edges, shrubberies and hedgerows, and their close association with man is echoed in their modern preference to live in parks, gardens and churchyards. In winter they frequent farmland and are often seen at garden bird tables.

The tetrad map for 1995–99 confirms their widespread distribution in the county (ranked twentieth). They were present in 572 tetrads, with breeding proved in 326 (57% of these), and probable breeding in a further 185 (32%). They possibly bred in a further 61 tetrads and were found to be absent only from the higher ground and moorland in the north-west, which lacks suitable nesting habitat.

There is no evidence of any change in range, as the 1968–72 and 1988–91 Atlases also found them breeding, or probably breeding, in every 10km square. BTO data suggest breeding levels throughout Britain are stable, though there are concerns whether this will be maintained in the light of evidence of nest failure at the incubation stage and decreasing average clutch sizes nationally. However, Eaton *et al.* (2010) reported an overall increase of 10% between 1970 and 2008.

On woodland CBC plots surveyed in the 1990s, Greenfinches were between the fourteenth and fifteenth most numerous species, although they were absent from Shire Hill Wood. Their densities ranged from 7.27 to 13.89 pairs per km^2. On farmland CBC plots, the Greenfinch was the fourteenth most common species at Broadhay Farm, Hathersage, the seventeenth most common at Farfield Farm, Hope and the thirtieth most common at Culland. Farmland densities ranged from 1.73 to 3.70 pairs per km^2. At Scarcliffe Woods during 1973–2008, numbers varied from two to 17 territories a year (Frost 2008a), while there were ten territories at Carsington Water in the period 2003–07.

Greenfinches eat a wide variety of seeds, and at feeding stations they have developed a predilection for black sunflower seeds and peanuts, which they despatch with their stout bills. Nationally, they are recorded as the sixth most frequent garden-feeding bird species, compared with ninth in the 1970s and are now ahead of Starling and House Sparrow. As a regular food source, oil-seed rape was first recorded in August 1997 at Hardwick Park where 80 birds were feeding, while 600 gathered in oil-seed rape stubble at Ingleby on 23rd August 2002.

Greenfinches flock together in winter in stubble fields and weedy areas, often associating with other species, Linnets and Yellowhammers being the usual companions. The increase in autumn sowing of cereal crops has meant a reduction in stubble fields and this, combined with increased use of selective herbicides, has seen a reduction in the size of winter flocks. Frost said that feeding flocks of up to 2000 had been seen at Egginton Sewage Farm, but since 1978 the largest flock was of 1300 at the same locality on 4th January 1980. During the 1990s the largest recorded annual flocks ranged from 200 to 450, and during the 2000s the range was from 150 to 600.

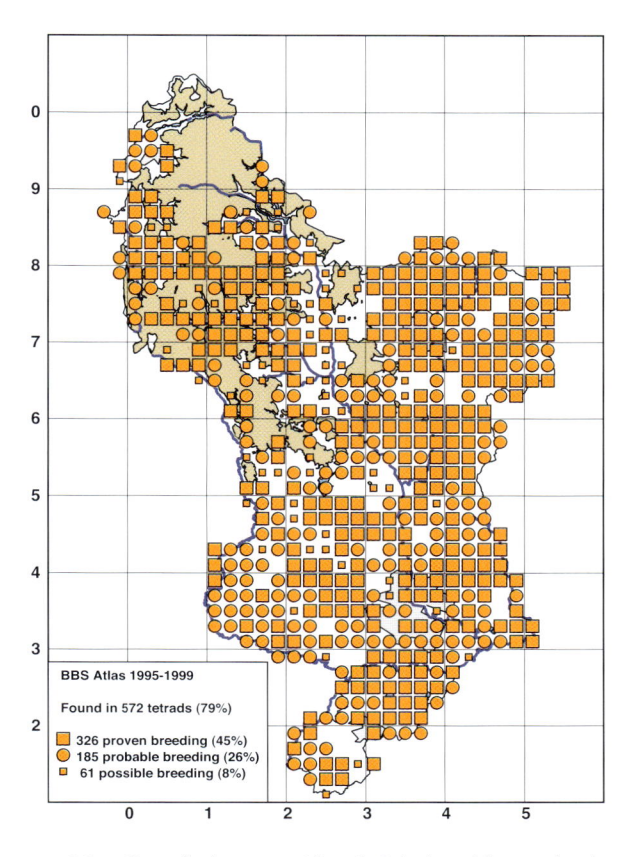

BBS Atlas 1995-1999
Found in 572 tetrads (79%)
- 326 proven breeding (45%)
- 185 probable breeding (26%)
- 61 possible breeding (8%)

Most Greenfinches are resident in Britain, with some hard-weather movements being noted. There is some migration from Britain from October to mid-November, with birds moving to south-west Europe. Migratory movement in the county has been recorded at a number of sites, but most frequently at Strines Top, Ramsley Reservoir and Ashover Fabric. The largest movement recorded in the county was of 1153 birds flying south to south-west at Ramsley Reservoir on three dates from 7th to 26th October 2004, with 856 on the first date. At Strines Top, 270 flew south-west on 15th October 1995, though more usual counts of birds on visible migration watches are of up to 100.

Greenfinches roost communally in winter, often in evergreen vegetation, such as rhododendron thickets. Up to 150 birds have roosted in places such as the Cordwell Valley and Tansley Moor, while the largest roost in recent years was of 450 birds at Osmaston Park on 24th December 1995. However, this cannot compare with the roost of up to 2000 birds that gathered at Shiningcliff Wood in the winter of 1966/67.

There are no fewer than 506 ringing recoveries involving Derbyshire. Of these, 62% have concerned movements of under 20km, and 62% of these were of young birds. The only long-distance movements were by one ringed at Breck Farm in April 1975 that was found dead, 319km west near Dublin, Ireland, a year later, and another that moved 303km north-west from Thorpe, where it was ringed in April 1983, to Stranraer, Dumfries and Galloway, where it was controlled in the following January.

Serin
Serinus serinus
A very rare vagrant.

The only Derbyshire record was of two at Combs Reservoir at 1930 hours on 6th May 1997. They flew, calling, from a grassy bank alongside the reservoir, at a range of 6m from the observer before moving off high in a northerly direction. They were searched for again on the next day without success. The timing fits perfectly with the April to May peak for spring records in Britain (Key 1998b). Serins breed widely in Europe, north-west Africa and Turkey, and winter in southern Europe. In the UK they are mainly scarce passage migrants but have bred on several occasions in southern counties since 1967.

Goldfinch
Carduelis carduelis
An increasingly common resident and summer visitor.

Whitlock said that the Goldfinch was mainly an autumn visitor, with only a few pairs breeding in the south of the county. He stated that it had formerly been far more common, but had declined as a result of enclosure and better cultivation. Numbers have increased since then, quite dramatically in the last 40 years or so, and it is now the eighteenth most widespread species in Derbyshire. Reasons for the increase are believed to include the virtual cessation of large-scale trapping and removal of nestlings by cage-bird fanciers, both of which were widespread activities during the first half of the twentieth century. Also, the Goldfinch's ability to exploit winter food sources in gardens, and the widespread planting of birch and alder as amenity trees (for example, on reclaimed spoil heaps), may have been beneficial. The increase is national, with populations increasing by 81% between 1970 and 2008 (Eaton *et al.* 2010).

Goldfinches can now be found breeding in a wide variety of habitats from urban gardens, parks and shrubberies to trees and large bushes on woodland edges, inside open woodlands, and farmland hedgerows.

This is the eighteenth most widespread Derbyshire species, the tetrad map for 1995–99 showing that it was present in 586 tetrads, with proven breeding in 298 (51% of these), probable breeding in a further 205 (35%), and possible breeding in the remaining 83 (14%).

Nests are not easily found, as they are well hidden and often quite high in trees, but noisy family parties are frequently seen, with young birds easily distinguished from their parents.

Their breeding range has increased since the 1968–72 and 1988–91 Atlases. In 1968–72 they were proved to have bred in 19 of the 23 10km core squares, which increased to 20 in 1988–91, and the Derbyshire BBS (1995–99) proved breeding in all 23. They breed throughout the county, with the exception of the high moorland areas of the north-west.

Goldfinches have a long breeding season and late broods are not unusual. At Swarkestone Lake, a nest with four half-grown young was found on 4th September 1990, and Frost stated that young had been seen in the nest as late as October.

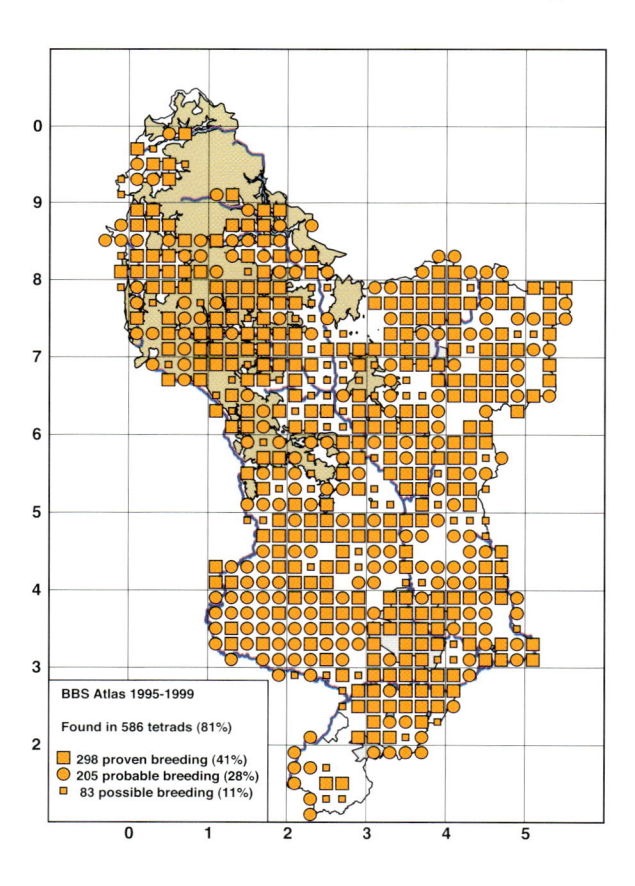

Goldfinches were absent from all of the woodland CBC plots surveyed in the county in the 1990s. However, on farmland CBC plots during the same period they were the twelfth most common species at Farfield Farm, Hope, with a breeding density of 3.77 pairs per km^2, while at Broadhay Farm, Hathersage, they were the twenty-fifth most common, and the thirtieth most common at Culland. Breeding densities at the latter two sites averaged 1.53 pairs per km^2. At Scarcliffe Woods, numbers varied considerably from an average of nine territories a year in the mid-1970s to none a decade later (a period when many seed-eating species declined), but recovering to an average of 11 by the mid-2000s (Frost 2008a). The Carsington Water census of 2003–07 produced 32 territories.

Up to 80% of the British breeding population moves south during September and October to winter in Belgium, France and Spain (1988–91 Atlas), and this is reflected in numbers counted at key visible migration watch-points. For example, at Strines Top, 70 moved south-west on 4th October 1991, and 62 moved south-west on 30th September 1994; at Carr Vale, 137 moved south over 16 dates during October 2001; at Ramsley Reservoir, 153 moved south-west on 27th and 30th October 2006, and a total of 124 flew south on 22nd and 23rd September 2007; at Ashover Fabric, 50 moved south on 2nd October 2007; and at Highoredish Hill, 157 moved west on 4th October 2011.

Numbers in the midwinter months of December to February are usually lower than they are at other times of the year and three-figure flocks at this time are uncommon. Nevertheless, there were counts of 200 at Carr Vale in January 2000, at Long Eaton Gravel Pits in January 2002 and 2003, and 350 at Pleasley Colliery in January 2010. They may occur in mixed finch flocks at these times but most are in single-species flocks. Visits to garden feeding stations have become regular in the last two decades; peanuts and nyjer seed are very attractive to Goldfinches.

During spring and autumn, Goldfinches form parties or flocks, and many three-figure gatherings have been reported over the years, the largest being about 600 at Carsington Water on 17th September 2000. The largest counts clearly show the increase in the Goldfinch population: in 1980–89, the largest annual flock varied between 60 and 200 with a mean of 102; in the 1990s, numbers ranged from 100 to 400 with a mean of 126; and in 2000–09, comparable figures were 150 to 600 and a mean of 275. The large counts were mainly in September, with many fewer in August and October, and only rarely in other months.

Large communal roosts of this species are not often reported, so the following are noteworthy. There were 120 in a single holly in an Ashbourne garden in March 1959, and 200 in alders and hollies at Bradley Dam in March 1964. In the winters of 1998/99 to 2004/05, a roost, which peaked at 370 birds on 13th February 2000, was seen in holly trees in the churchyard of All Saints Church (the Crooked Spire) in the centre of Chesterfield.

There were 240 in a roost in hollies at Grassmoor in February 2010, and 400 in evergreens at Derby in January 2011.

There are 13 ringing recoveries involving Derbyshire birds between 1945 and 2000. Six records are of birds moving less than 10km within a year of ringing and three more are similarly local recoveries, but after longer periods of time. Two birds were found to have moved within Britain on a south-east/west line, suggesting possible movement to the Low Countries. Long-distance migrants have been a female, ringed at Poolsbrook on 28th August 1978, that was reported from Valladolid, Spain, on 6th January 1979, and another female, ringed in Derby on 27th September 1975, that was hunted in Logroño, Spain, on 25th January 1976.

Siskin
Carduelis spinus
A common winter visitor. An uncommon, but regular, breeder in the Peak District.

The sight of Siskins in late winter and early spring, feeding hungrily on the red bag of peanuts hanging from our bird tables may be taken for granted, but this behaviour is of only recent origin, first recorded in Surrey in 1963 and in Derbyshire for the first time as late as the 1971/72 winter (Frost).

Their natural food source is the seed of conifers, especially spruce and larch, but they also eat birch and alder seeds. The increased presence of the Siskin in Derbyshire, both in winter and as a breeding species, is attributable to the increase in afforestation and the maturation of these trees, particularly in the Dark Peak. This trend is mirrored across Britain and Ireland according to the 1988–91 Atlas, where until the mid-nineteenth century, breeding Siskins were confined to the Scottish Highlands.

Whitlock stated that Neville Wood considered Siskins had bred near Foston in 1831 and also in subsequent years. Jourdain had accepted a record of breeding Siskins at Repton, but his diaries suggest he was sceptical and the record cannot be endorsed.

Siskins were seen in suitable breeding habitat in the Peak District in 1962, 1965 and most years after 1970, and in June 1971 fledged young were seen in Derwentdale (Frost). The 1968–72 Atlas showed them present, but without proof of breeding, in only three 10km squares. The first nest to be found in Derbyshire was in Derwentdale in 1977. As is so often the case with this species, proof of breeding success has relied on observing fledglings, as their nests are notoriously difficult to find. Young birds have been seen in most years since 1977, with increasing frequency, probably connected with the maturing of the conifer plantations.

In 1989 Siskins were found to be breeding in only four localities, and the 1988–91 Atlas found them breeding in two 10km squares and probably breeding in a further eight, all in the north of the county. By 1999 they were reported from many areas in the Peak District. Analysis of the Derbyshire BBS (1995–99) showed birds in 43 tetrads, with breeding proved in 13, thought probable in 15 and possible in a further 15. Some probable or possible breeding in tetrads in the south and north-east of the county indicated a possible expansion of the breeding range away from the Peak District. These findings are reinforced by reports of possible breeding at Scarcliffe Woods from 1992 to 1994 and in 1998.

Siskins are gregarious and the males sing not only when breeding but also in late winter and on spring passage, which may continue until mid-April. This may of course lead to a false assumption of local breeding, as birds may in fact be heading to more northerly forests to breed. However, the impressive butterfly-like song-flight is rarely recorded away from known breeding areas. Many of the recoveries of birds ringed in spring in Matlock, for example, have been in the Scottish Highlands in areas perhaps more traditionally associated with breeding Siskins before their afforestation-related spread. However, it is also probable that some of these late birds will stay in Derbyshire to breed, as there is plenty of suitable habitat available.

The autumn passage often now starts in July or August, peaking in late September and October. The first birds are often sighted on visible migration watches. The largest recorded movements have been at Strines Top, with 245 flying south-west in 75 minutes on 19th September 1991, while October 1993 saw south-westerly movements of 200 on 10th and 300 on 14th, followed by movements north-west of 250 on 15th and 140 on 22nd. In some years there are very large numbers involved, notably when alder or birch seed availability is low, leading to noticeable irruptions of birds. In the 2000s, most of the largest movements have been recorded at Ramsley, with most notably 550 on three dates between 5th October and 9th December 2003, and 329 flying south or south-west on five dates between 20th September and 4th November 2007. A total of 525 moved south at Carr Vale in September 2011. Autumn passage used to begin in September but there have been many late summer records in recent years. This was the case in 1997 when influxes were noted from July, continuing until the end of October. Observers at Carr Vale counted 343 Siskins flying south in September alone, with a maximum of 53 on 5th.

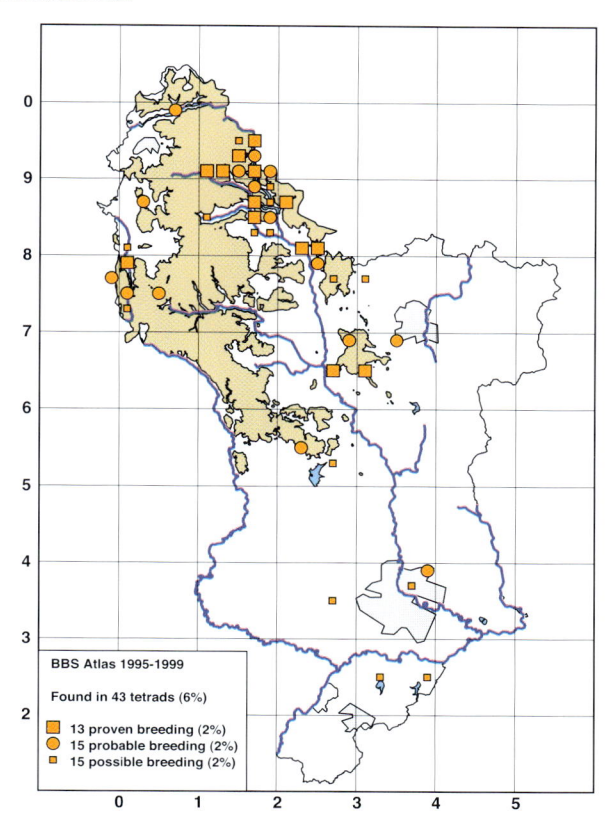

Most Siskins will winter in different areas in successive years and associate with other species, typically Lesser Redpolls. Most flocks are of up to 50 or so, but in good years these numbers may swell considerably. Frost stated that the largest count was 700, in Derwentdale in March 1970. However, this was surpassed by counts of 800 birds, also in Derwentdale, on 11th October 1984 and of over 1000 at the same location on 24th February 2003, with similar numbers on 19th March 2005 and in February and March 2008. In winter they seek out waterside alders as a food supply, supplemented in late winter and early spring by garden feeding. In 1986, another irruption year, Siskins were recorded in 67 gardens across Derbyshire, in flocks of up to ten. These numbers too can swell, and flocks of 50 birds have been recorded in gardens in Matlock from February to April 1997, Lea Bridge from November to December 2002, and an impressive 81 in a Cromford garden in April 2009.

Much information about the movements of Siskins in Derbyshire was obtained from the ringing of birds coming to a garden feeding site in Matlock. Of the recoveries, 50% were of birds moving quickly back to their Highland breeding areas, while others were of birds moving via the east coast of England and the Low Countries to Scandinavia. One bird ringed in Matlock in March 1997 was in Norway two weeks later. The most unusual recovery was of a bird ringed in Matlock in March 1993 and found 2384km away in Greece in March 1995, the first British-ringed bird to be found so far east, though there are single recoveries from Poland, Hungary and the former Yugoslavia.

That there is an established north–south movement within Britain from northern breeding areas in England and Scotland to wintering locations in the Midlands and further south is reinforced by six birds which had been ringed mainly in Scotland north of Inverness during the summer, being re-trapped in Derbyshire from Dronfield south to Elvaston Castle Country Park. Obviously, some birds are moving further south and there have been exchanges with Hertfordshire, Hampshire, Surrey and more easterly to Suffolk. Some individuals are in the process of moving beyond Britain for the winter period, as confirmed by a male trapped at Chapel-en-le-Frith on 19th November 1961 being caught in West Flanders, Belgium, in the following February. Another male ringed at Great Hucklow on 15th November 1970 was found dead in Vasterbotten, Sweden on 8th May 1972, indicating that some wintering or passage birds are arriving from Scandinavia.

Another ringing study of Siskins in his Dronfield garden was documented by Mawson (2006). No fewer than 531 were caught there in the first few months of 2004. These included two that had been ringed in Vest-Agder, Norway and five that subsequently moved to Scotland.

Linnet
Carduelis cannabina
A common resident.

The Linnet is the typical finch of open country and is most numerous on lowland farmland, but it can also be found in other habitats, including industrial wasteland, areas of gorse and in recently planted woodland. On higher ground it is still numerous on bracken-clad slopes on the gritstone moorlands and at a lower density in the drystone wall country of the White Peak. Its only requirements are a supply of weed seeds for food and small trees or bushes for nesting. In autumn, the uplands are vacated and then large flocks can be found on weedy fields, sewage farms and waste ground.

Whitlock said that the Linnet was far less common than formerly, while remaining 'pretty common' in the wilder parts of Derbyshire in particular. He believed that the increase in cultivation was the main reason for its decline, while noting that it was a target of bird-catchers. Frost believed that there were some signs of a slight decrease in numbers during the 1970s, and this appears to have continued through to the present day, especially in farmland habitats. He said that it bred on the moors, sometimes alongside the Twite, up to 1400 feet (427m) amsl.

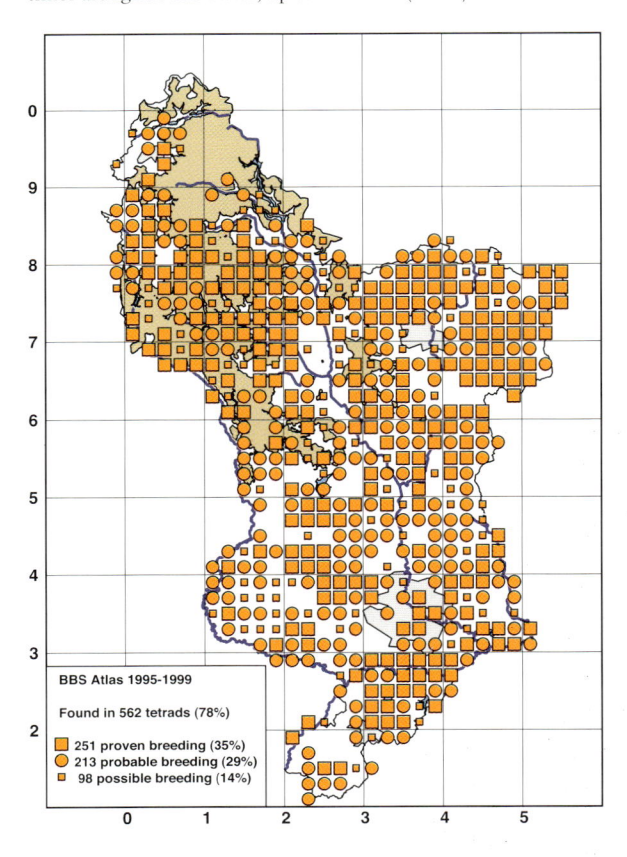

The tetrad map shows a widespread (ranked twenty-second), but patchy, distribution. The area with the highest number of proven breeding tetrads is north-east Derbyshire, with its mixture of arable farming and redundant colliery sites. Overall this species was found in 562 tetrads, breeding in 251 and with 311 probable or possible tetrads. Breeding colonies are quite easy to find but single nesting pairs are easy to miss. Breeding was proved in all of the 23 10km core squares, as it was for the 1988–91 Atlas, compared with 22 in the 1968–72 Atlas.

Disused colliery spoil heaps are often rich in weeds and, even when landscaped, form good habitat with a mosaic of grassland and immature woodland. Linnets are still widespread in the Peak District, found in both the Dark and White Peak, and only becoming scarce on the highest moorlands in the far north-west. On the Eastern Moors, the Linnet bred alongside the Twite until at least the mid-1980s. However, unlike the latter species, the Linnet is still widespread on these lower gritstone moorlands and surrounding rough pasture, especially where patches of gorse grow. In such locations Linnets often nest colonially, defending a small area around their nest, but feeding together in a group. The region south of the Trent has the smallest number of occupied tetrads in lowland Derbyshire and this may represent a genuine decline in this region. Along with other farmland finches and buntings the Linnet has declined since the 1970s due to an intensification of farming practices; a decline in weed seeds is thought to have reduced both breeding success and winter survival rates. Eaton *et al.* (2010) documented a 57% decrease between 1970 and 2008. The comparative maps for 1995–99 and 2007–11 suggest declines in the south, west and north-west of the county.

A census carried out at Scarcliffe Woods showed a population of 34 pairs in 1974, which had declined to four pairs by 1981 and none by 1983, although with four pairs in most years from 1993 to 2008. Here, it was thought that a gradual maturation of the Corsican pine plantations led to the decline (Frost 2008a). In 1998, a survey of the Eastern Moors suggested a breeding population of 64 pairs, and in June 2004 there were 17 territories on Big Moor. The more thorough 2010 survey of the EMP moors revealed 33 pairs, breeding in areas of gorse and bracken (Frost & Taylor 2011). Only seven pairs were found in the combined annual survey of 2003–07 at Carsington Water.

Post-breeding flocks are usually noted from mid-July, particularly on recently cut stubble fields. Flocks of several hundred are recorded each year, the largest recent one being of about 1000 at Williamthorpe Nature Reserve on 17th August 1990. Through the 1990s and 2000s the trend has been for smaller numbers, with the last flocks of 400 being recorded on 30th April 2007 at Upper Loads and 20th September 2009 at Atlow. A flock of 3500 at Egginton Sewage Farm in October 1964

The Species Accounts

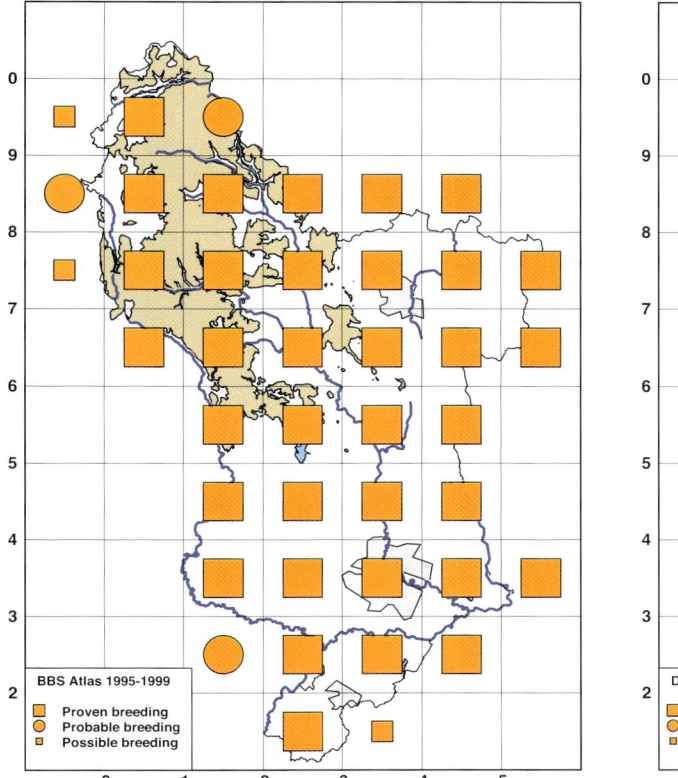

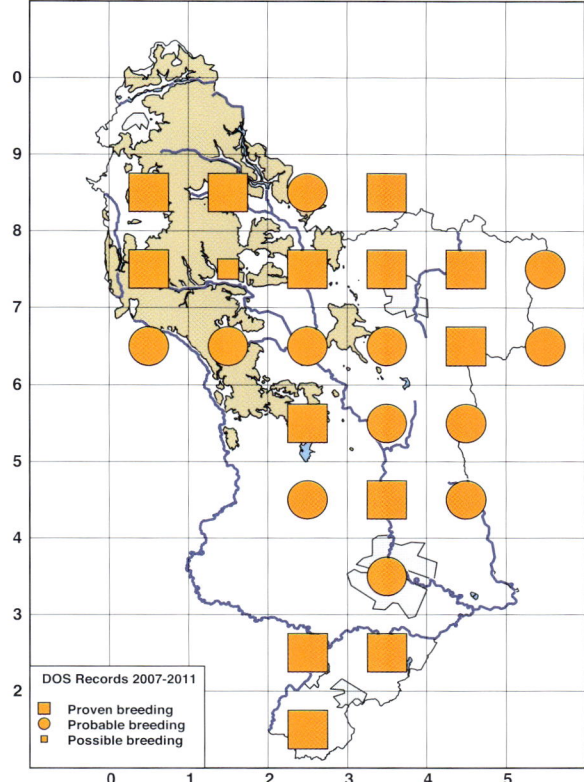

BBS Atlas 1995-1999
- Proven breeding
- Probable breeding
- Possible breeding

DOS Records 2007-2011
- Proven breeding
- Probable breeding
- Possible breeding

remains the largest flock ever recorded. Large communal roosts of Linnets are rarely reported, so a record of 120 roosting in rhododendrons on Beeley Moor in March 2011 was of interest.

While Linnets are present in the county all year, large numbers undoubtedly emigrate in the autumn months. Birds are regularly reported from upland visible migration watch-points, with peak numbers in late September, usually moving in a south-westerly direction. Some of the largest counts of migrating birds originate from Strines Top, where 382 flew south-west on 28th September 1994 and 273 south-west on 25th September 1995. Large numbers were recorded in October 2001 when, over several dates, a total of 1008 flew south or south-west at Ashover Fabric, Ramsley and Carr Vale. Ramsley has been the site of the most frequent visible migration records with a highest count of 278 moving south on 11th October 2003, while at Ashover 202 flew west-north-west on 11th September 2011.

From the national ringing recovery data it is known that, within Linnet populations, some remain in their breeding areas for the winter, while others move south-west to western France, through to central Spain and Morocco (Wernham *et al*. 2002). The county dataset conforms with the national picture and there have been at least four ringing recoveries from Spain and seven from France. Nearly all of the local data show a longevity of less than two years, but a bird ringed near Eckington on 29th January 1972 as a youngster, born in the previous year, was found dead in Landes, France, on 15th February 1976.

Twite
Carduelis flavirostris
An uncommon summer visitor to the Peak District, and a rare passage migrant and winter visitor elsewhere.

This small, brownish finch is a rather nondescript bird which could easily be misidentified as Linnet or Lesser Redpoll were it not for the urgent, nasal 'chweet' call and the metallic twitter. It breeds in moorland and other upland areas, and winters at low altitudes, mainly on the coast.

In England, the southern Pennines hold the only breeding population of Twite, about a quarter of which is in the Peak District National Park. Unfortunately, almost all of these are west or north of Derbyshire. This has not always been the case, however.

Whitlock said that they bred on some Derbyshire moors, particularly around Castleton, and stated that nests had been found as low as Anchor Church and Foston. Frost considered that the bird continued to breed in very small numbers until the mid-1960s, when there was a great increase, with birds nesting in many parts of the western Peak and on all suitable moors in the east. The increase was short-lived; by the end of the 1970s Twite were again in decline in Derbyshire and this has continued to the present day. The Derbyshire BBS (1995–99) found them breeding in only five tetrads, three of which were in the Kinder Scout area, with the others near Doveholes and south of Buxton. No birds were seen on the Eastern Moors, despite a Natural England survey of the whole area in 1998.

The reasons for the decline are believed to be largely unrelated to the state of the moorlands where they nest, but concern adjacent feeding sites. Their diet consists entirely of seeds obtained from hay meadows, lightly grazed pasture and unmanaged ground. It is here that wholesale changes have taken place;

the hay meadows have largely been converted to silage, and the pastures are subjected to heavier grazing, while earlier cutting of roadside verges has also decreased a food source (Brown & Grice 2005). The loss of pioneer saltmarsh in coastal wintering areas on the English east coast may also be significant. New initiatives, including the provision of food close to known breeding sites, have now been put forward to try to reverse the trend.

Since 1995, a small breeding population has been found in limestone quarries in north-west Derbyshire, the birds somewhat unexpectedly nesting on vertical cliff faces. Twite there have been seen in four quarries during the breeding season, and appear at present to nest annually in two of them, with probably no more than ten pairs in total (Frost 2008b).

Most of the Twite now seen in the county are thought to be migrants, probably from the breeding areas a little further north of Derbyshire. Most are seen from August to November, with much smaller numbers from February to May. Winter records are now rare. Most of these birds are seen in upland areas, in rough fields, at reservoir margins or flying over open country. Limestone pastures in the Buxton area dominate the list of gatherings of 50 or above recorded since 1980, as shown (in descending order) in the table.

Migrants are still occasionally seen on the Eastern Moors in late autumn, but numbers never approach the 400 on Big Moor in October 1973, still by some margin the largest flock ever seen in Derbyshire. In lowland areas, where nowadays records are scarce, extreme recent dates are 29th August 1999 at Draycott and 1st May 1988 at Drakelow Nature Reserve.

There have been nine ringing recoveries involving Derbyshire birds. Of these, three have been of nestlings re-trapped or found dead near to their breeding sites. The remaining six highlight the corridor of migration, for birds of the year and adults, from northern Derbyshire to the coast of the southern North Sea, with recoveries from Kent, Essex, Lincolnshire (two) and Belgium. One exceptional record is that of a nestling ringed near Dove Holes on 20th June 1967, that was trapped in Venice, Italy, on 19th November in the same year.

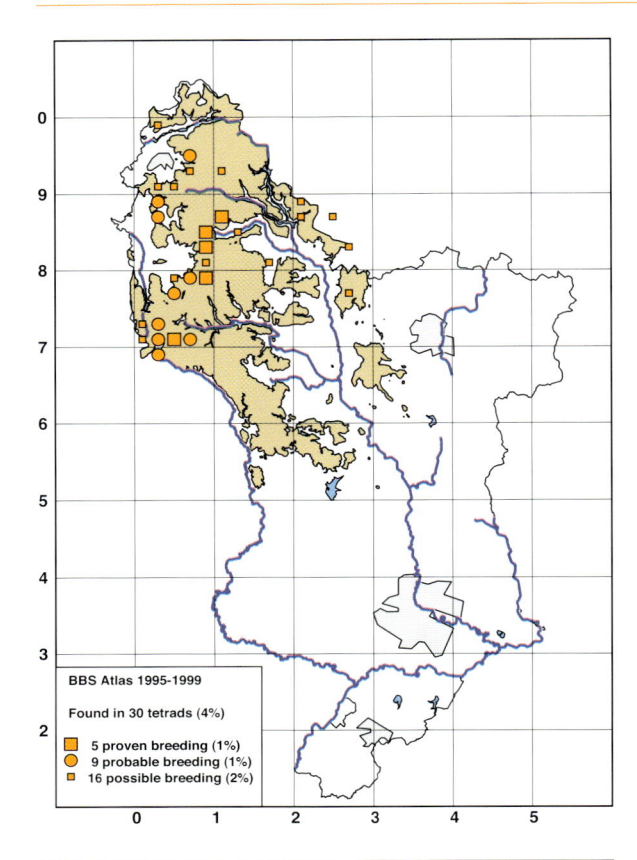

Location	Date	Birds
Batham Gate	late August 1987	160
Small Dale	28th September 1997	150
Peak Dale–Dove Holes area	21st August 1989	130
Dove Holes	28th August 1990	100
West End Moors	4th October 1992	80 (2 flocks)
Drakelow Nature Reserve	27th January 2001	58
Dove Holes	2nd August 2007	50

Lesser Redpoll
Carduelis cabaret
A fairly common, but significantly decreased, resident, passage migrant and winter visitor.

This handsome, small finch is a bird of pioneer woodlands, favouring trees that produce small seeds, such as birch and alder. It is gregarious throughout the year: in winter the sight of a flock foraging in the treetops is always welcome, while in summer several pairs may nest in close proximity, their breeding areas revealed by displaying males giving their buzzing songs.

Whitlock said that Lesser Redpolls occurred in occasional large flocks in winter, and bred in small numbers throughout the county, most commonly in northern woods while, according to Jourdain, it was most numerous in the valleys of the upper Derwent, Ashop and lower Dove. Numbers were maintained during the first half of the twentieth century, with increases recorded around 1908, 1944–45 and between 1960 and 1977 (Frost). By this time it was described as fairly common in a variety of woodland, especially coniferous, and in areas of scattered bushes and hedges on farmland, in gardens, and even in towns.

The late 1970s saw the start of a considerable decline and range contraction. For example, at Scarcliffe Woods a maximum of 38 singing males was recorded in 1976, but only five years later this had reduced to six. There was a resurgence to 12 singing males in 1986 but only five in 1988 and none at all since then (Frost 2008a). Similar declines took place in most other lowland areas of Derbyshire. The Derbyshire BBS (1995–99) showed confirmed breeding in just seven lowland tetrads, out of 19 in this category. Possible and probable breeding were recorded in a further 52 and 50 tetrads respectively. Of the 23 10km core squares, breeding was proved in 11 in the 1968–72 Atlas, 12 in the 1988–91 Atlas and nine in the Derbyshire BBS (1995–99). Breeding evidence is not especially easy to obtain, since nests are usually well hidden and the young are fed by regurgitation.

There were concentrations to the north and west of Buxton, in the upper Derwent and Ashop Valleys, and in the Matlock region. All of these locations have extensive areas of upland birch woodland and coniferous plantation, which would describe the Lesser Redpoll's main breeding habitats today.

There have been no instances of confirmed breeding in lowland areas since 1999 and the withdrawal of a once-widespread species to more upland areas is similar to that shown by Whinchat, Tree Pipit and possibly others. The decline is widespread in the UK: Eaton *et al.* (2010) showed a decrease of 90% between 1970 and 2008. Brown and Grice (2005) believed that this may be due to the maturation of coniferous forest, the successional loss of birch from woodlands and possibly the loss of mature hedgerow trees. The maps for 1995–99 and 2007–11 show the considerable changes that have taken place between the two periods.

Other than at Scarcliffe, there is relatively little detailed information about breeding numbers. The only Derbyshire

CBC plot to register territories during the 1990s was Shire Hill, Glossop, where there were 4.76 pairs per km². There were estimated to be 13 pairs in the Upper Derwent Valley in 1988. In the Sickleholme Golf Course area, Bamford there was evidence of four pairs in 1998 and five in 2006. During surveys in 2010, 33 territories were found on the EMP moors.

Lesser Redpolls remain reasonably common as passage migrants and winter visitors in the county. Though numbers may show considerable annual variation, they have not decreased commensurately with the breeding population. Autumn migrants are usually recorded between August and November, with a peak in October. The largest visible migration totals have nearly all come from the northern watch-points: three-figure counts were of 150 to the south-west at Strines Top on 15th October 1995; at Ramsley on four occasions, with a maximum of 170 to the south-west on 2nd November 2008; at Leash Fen 350 moved west-south-west on 15th October 2008, followed by 150 south-west three days later; 149 flew south at Moorhall on 9th October 2008; at Ashover Fabric, 102 flew south on 16th October 2007; and 208 also flew south at Shirebrook Colliery on 13th October 2011,

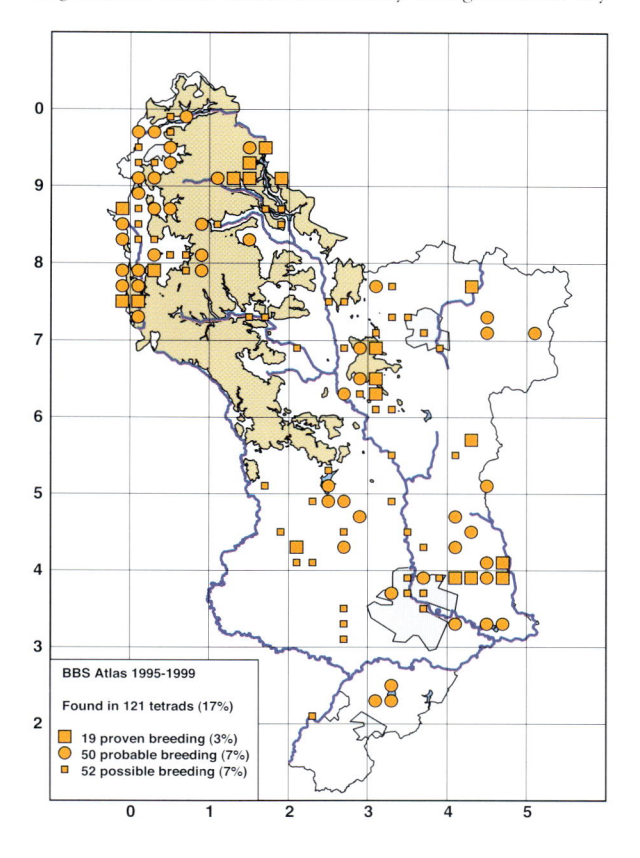

Numbers in autumn 2008 were exceptional. Mawson (2009) said that at Ramsley Moor, where the main attraction was an abundance of birch seed, a remarkable 1619 birds were trapped and ringed on 19 dates between 29th August and 3rd November, with a maximum of 360 on 17th October. He stated that from 8th October some of the birds caught had longer wings, indicating more distant origins than those caught previously. It was estimated that perhaps 5% of all the birds moving through the site that autumn were caught, which would indicate the remarkable overall figure of over 32,000. Many re-traps resulted from the activity including subsequent controls in autumn from Kent, Surrey and Hampshire, and in the following spring from Perth and Kinross as well as Cumbria.

Spring passage is seen from March to May, but in generally smaller numbers than in autumn.

Outside the breeding season, Lesser Redpolls may still occur in coniferous and birch woodland but they may also be found in a wider variety of habitats including alders (especially along river valleys), weedy areas on arable farmland and on industrial wasteland. The largest flocks are generally recorded between October and March. Ramsley Moor, with its abundant areas of birch, is especially favoured, holding a maximum of 1100 on 1st October 2000. Elsewhere, the largest gatherings since 1978 were each of 300, at Derwent in November 1989 and at the site of Shirebrook Colliery in November 2007. Smaller flocks, of 200–250, have been seen at Barbrook Plantation, Smeekley

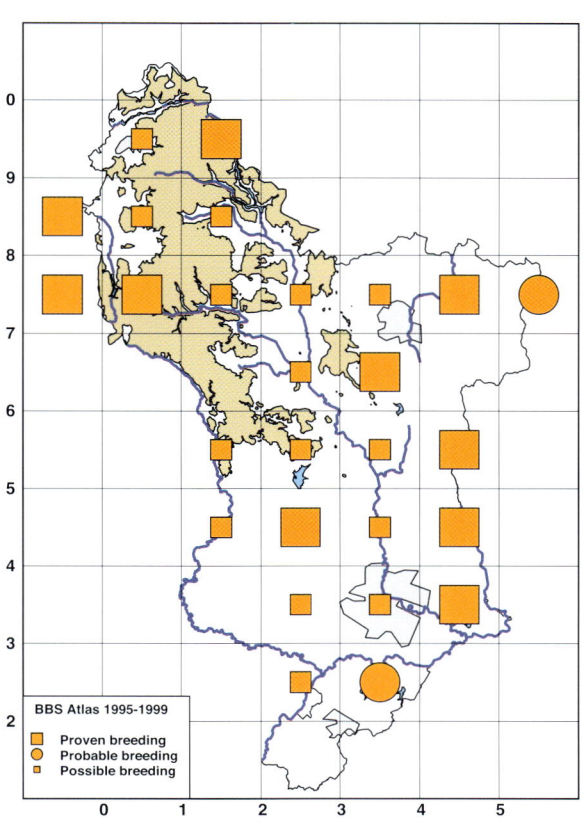

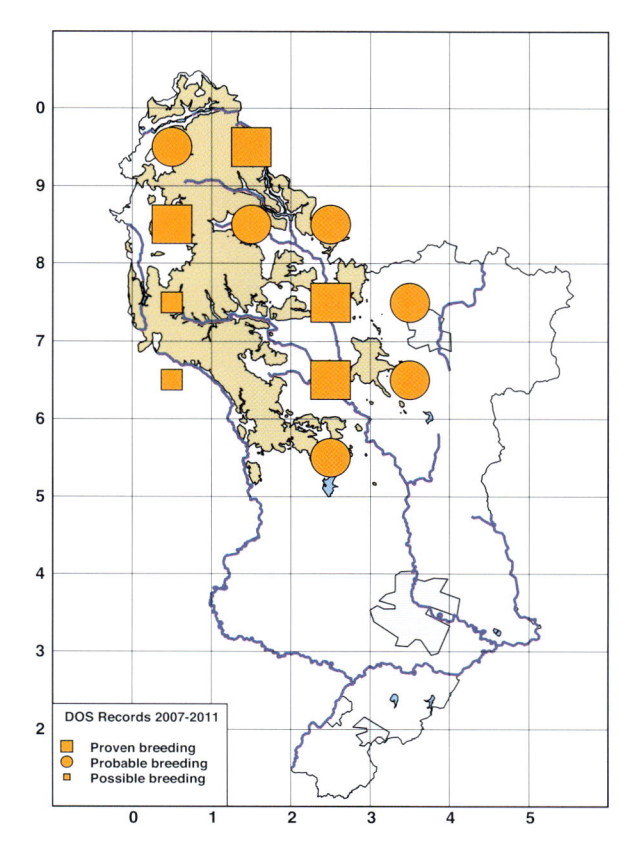

Wood, Ogston Reservoir, Poulter Country Park, Matlock Forest and Sitch's Plantation. The largest flock listed by Frost was of 500, at Spring Wood in February 1971.

Earlier ringing data for this species may also include that for Common Redpoll. Recoveries of birds which were probably breeding in Derbyshire were of two involving Kent and one from Surrey. Another ringed in Northumberland in September 1991 was found at Littleover 11 months later. Overseas recoveries were of one ringed at Mickleover in March 1996 that was controlled at Rogaland, Norway, nine weeks later and one ringed at Melbourne in March 1975 that was found in Zuid-Holland, in the Netherlands in April 1976.

Mealy Redpoll
Carduelis flammea
A scarce but almost annual winter visitor and passage migrant.

Split as recently as 2001, during the reassessment of the Redpoll complex by the BOU, the Mealy Redpoll was formerly known as the Common Redpoll.

Whitlock accepted only one record, of a single killed at Draycott around 1873, and Jourdain knew of no others. Frost stated that 'the larger, greyer, Scandinavian subspecies known as Mealy Redpoll is seen in the county in most winters but only in very small numbers'. Seven at Williamthorpe in December 1972 was the largest recorded gathering at that time.

Mealy Redpolls are still seen in Derbyshire in almost every year; since 1980, only 1982, 1998, 2000 and 2004 are without records. Most sightings are of birds accompanying Lesser Redpolls, usually between October and April. Extreme dates are 5th September (1999) at Ramsley Reservoir and 25th April (1983) at Tansley.

The table shows the numbers of Mealy Redpolls recorded in Derbyshire during the period 1980–2011.

Since 1980, the largest gathering was of 65 at Scarcliffe on 21st March 1985, until the winter of 1995/96, which saw an unprecedented arrival, both in Derbyshire and elsewhere in the UK. Arrival was from early November and the largest flocks were of 200 in the Foremark Reservoir–Carver's Rocks Nature Reserve area in December and January; 170 in the Ramsley–Barbrook Plantation–Clodhall area in December; 130 at Unstone Green in February; and 100 in Derwentdale in March. Smaller gatherings during this winter included 80 at the former Ireland Colliery site, 80 in the Flash Lane area, 65 at Williamthorpe, 60 at Birchen Edge, 50 at Carr Vale and 50 at Ogston Carr Wood. There was a very rapid exodus at the end of March, with no later records.

There was a small influx into southern Derbyshire in the 2001/02 winter, when up to 18 were recorded at Staunton Harold Reservoir and 20 at Carver's Rocks Nature Reserve. The largest subsequent gatherings were of 20 at Upper Moor on 25th March 2007 and 25 at Staunton Harold Reservoir on 2nd January 2011.

	Jan	Feb	Mar	Apr	Sep	Oct	Nov	Dec	Total
1980	1	–	2	–	–	–	–	–	3
1981	–	1	–	–	–	–	–	–	1
1982	–	–	–	–	–	–	–	–	–
1983	1	–	–	1	–	–	–	–	2
1984	–	–	–	–	–	–	–	1	1
1985	–	–	66	–	–	–	–	4	70
1986	3	–	–	1	–	–	–	–	4
1987	–	1	–	–	–	–	1	–	2
1988	–	–	4	–	–	–	–	–	4
1989	–	2	–	–	–	–	2	–	4
1990	–	3	–	–	–	–	–	1	4
1991	–	1	–	–	–	–	–	–	1
1992	–	–	–	–	–	1	–	–	1
1993	–	–	2	–	–	1	–	–	3
1994	–	1	–	–	–	–	–	–	1
1995	–	–	–	–	–	–	47	484	531
1996	350	360	200	–	–	–	–	–	910
1997	–	–	1	–	–	–	–	3	4
1998	–	–	–	–	–	–	–	–	–
1999	–	–	–	–	1	1	–	–	2
2000	–	–	–	–	–	–	–	–	–
2001	–	–	1	5	–	–	–	18	24
2002	10	3	–	23	–	–	–	–	36
2003	–	–	2	–	–	1	6	1	10
2004	–	–	–	–	–	–	–	–	–
2005	–	–	–	2	–	–	6	5	13
2006	5	3	7	4	–	–	–	–	19
2007	1	6	34	–	–	1	4	21	67
2008	1	4	3	14	–	8	–	4	34
2009	–	6	5	5	–	–	–	2	18
2010	8	2	24	2	–	1	4	31	72
2011	58	6	39	–	–	1	–	2	106
Total	438	399	390	57	1	15	70	577	1947

Arctic Redpoll
Carduelis hornemanni
A very rare vagrant.

Arctic Redpolls breed in the high Arctic and make short-distance movements to lower latitudes in winter. Most birds probably winter south of the Arctic Circle. Periodic eruptions have seen many reach Britain as occurred, for example, in the winter of 1990/91.

The winter of 1995/96 however, will be the one remembered for its unprecedented, widespread invasion of Arctic Redpolls, which were often in the company of large numbers of Common Redpolls. No fewer than 431 records between November 1995 and May 1996 were accepted by BBRC (Riddington *et al.* 2000). This species was removed from the BBRC list after 2005.

Key (1997) concluded that a minimum of 15 birds occurred in Derbyshire during the period, and that as many as 25 may have been involved. The records are shown in the table. Since then, the only other occurrence was of one at Flash Lane on 24th February 2007.

Year	Location and date
1995	Ramsley Reservoir, an adult female trapped and ringed on 10th December
1995	Williamthorpe Nature Reserve, one, probably an adult female, on 14th December; a probable first-winter on 20th–21st December
1995	Barbrook Plantation, one on 17th December. Two, probably an adult male and a first-year male, on 19th December. Two, probably an adult male and female, on 24th December. A first-winter on 25th December
1995	Foremark Reservoir, three, a first-winter, a probable adult male and another, on 31st December
1996	Foremark Reservoir, a first-winter male trapped and ringed on 13th January
1996	Williamthorpe Nature Reserve, two females, probably adult and first-winter, on 15th January
1996	Carver's Rocks Nature Reserve, an adult male on 29th January
1996	Unstone Green, one on 13th February
1996	Hurst Clough, a male on 30th March
1996	Ladybower Reservoir, five on 30th March
1996	Derwentdale, a male on 3rd April and one on 7th April

Two-barred Crossbill
Loxia leucoptera
A very rare vagrant.

Two-barred Crossbills inhabit larch and cedar forests from Finland eastwards across northern Russia, and into Siberia and northern China. They are extremely rare in the British Isles, though during eruption years one or two are sometimes found among flocks of Common Crossbills. There had been 253 records in Britain by the end of 2011, of which 73 were before 1950 (Hudson *et al.* 2012).

There have been three Derbyshire records, the last of which was part of one of a highest ever totals (23) in the UK, between July and December 1990. The same period saw massive numbers of Common Crossbills and at least 200 Parrot Crossbills arrive in Britain from Fennoscandia.

Year	Location and date
1845	A female was shot in a Mickleover garden, where it had arrived with a flock of Fieldfares, on 21st November (Whitlock)
1983	A male was present with a small flock of Common Crossbills in the Howden Reservoir area from 9th January to 27th February
1990	A male was at Slippery Stones in Upper Derwentdale on 11th November

Common Crossbill
Loxia curvirostra
A scarce resident. An uncommon and erratic migrant, mainly in late summer.

Common Crossbills are rarely encountered away from coniferous trees since they are specialist feeders on the seeds, especially of spruce and larch, though pine is also commonly eaten. They are noisy in flight but feeding birds can be quiet and easily overlooked.

Former writers stressed the erratic pattern of their occurrences and, as recently as 1978, Frost said that they were less than annual. Breeding was recorded in 1916, 1958 and 1977, and a 1917 record has since come to light (Jourdain additions). There have now been records every year since 1975, especially in the Win Hill–Ladybower–Derwentdale area. Breeding was proved in this area in 1981, when several nests were found, 1996 (at least three pairs), 1997, 2001, 2007, 2008 (at least five pairs), 2010 (at least two pairs) and 2011, and has been strongly suspected in other years. In view of the difficulties in obtaining proof of breeding for this species, it seems reasonable to assume that the Derwent area now has a resident population, albeit in varying numbers. In the Matlock Forest complex, Crossbills were proved to breed in the late 1990s, in 2006–08 and 2010, and it seems likely that there is also a regular breeding population here. Since 1978, breeding has also been proved at Arnfield Reservoir, Chatsworth, Longshaw and Bunker's Hill Wood. Rather surprisingly, the only lowland breeding record

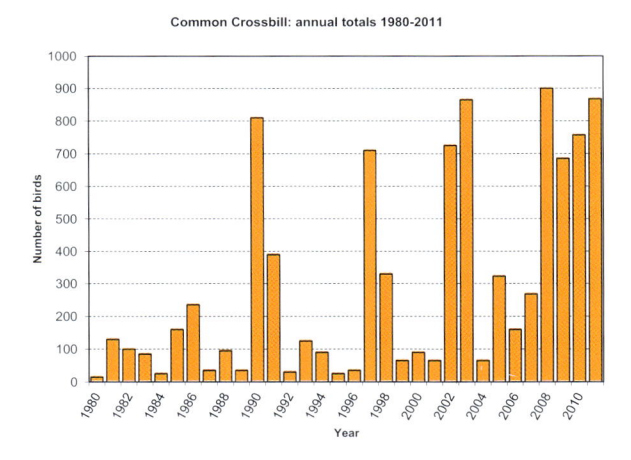

Large influxes of birds, presumed to be of mainly Continental origin, are often recorded. The chart shows the approximate number of birds seen annually in the period 1980–2011, showing the variation in numbers, and the major influxes.

Typically, the first arrivals are in June and July, with migrant parties often seen flying over open countryside at this time. Further flocks may continue to arrive until the late autumn. Many then overwinter and early in the following year much courtship activity is observed, though the proportion of birds which subsequently attempt to breed is unknown. All of the recorded Derbyshire nests with eggs have been found between February and April. Finding nests in conifer woodland, often on steep slopes with snow on the ground, is challenging, and breeding will have taken place on many more occasions than published records suggest.

In irruption years, Common Crossbills may be seen in any local conifer wood, though typically the northern half of the county will attract most birds. The largest site counts are shown in the table.

Location	Date	Birds
Derwentdale	24th February 2003	350
Bottom Moor	1st June 2008	170
Flash Lane	7th October 1990	100
Upper Derwentdale	24th June 2008	100
Derwent Reservoir	20th June 2008	85
South Wood	15th July 1997	74
Longshaw	5th July 1986	70
Osmaston	3rd December 1997	70
Ouzelden Clough	20th June 2008	70
Bottom Moor	5th July 2011	70
Chatsworth	29th June 1988	60

The only ringing recovery concerned a first-year male, trapped on 7th July 1991 at Theddlethorpe Dunes on the Lincolnshire coast, which died when it hit a conservatory window at Highoredish, Ashover, 117km west-south-west, five weeks later.

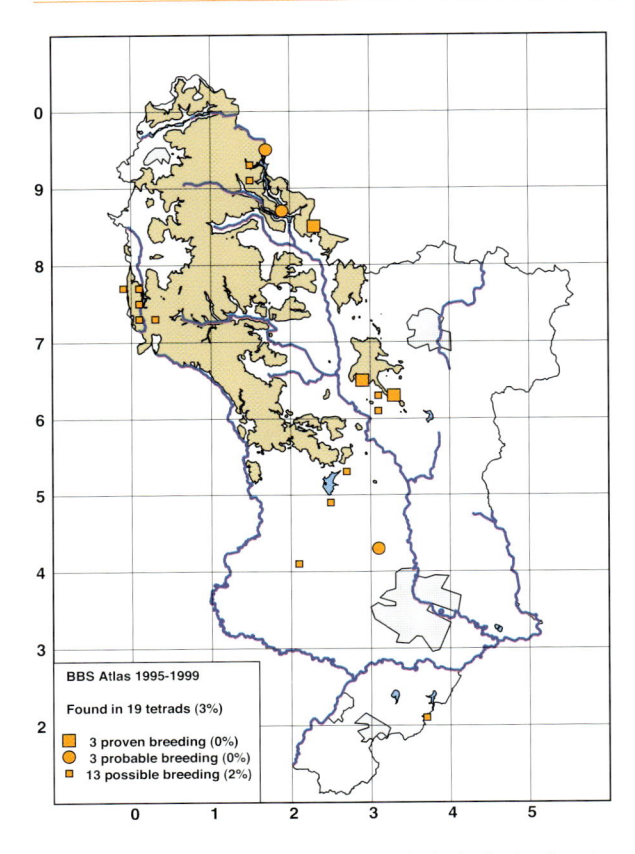

came from Scarcliffe in 2006. There can be little doubt that the increased regularity of Common Crossbills in Derbyshire results from the maturation of a greater area of coniferous woodland than before.

Breeding was confirmed in three 10km squares during the Derbyshire BBS (1995–99). There was one confirmed record in the 1988–91 Atlas and none in the 1968–72 Atlas.

Parrot Crossbill
Loxia pytyopsittacus
A very rare vagrant.

The Parrot Crossbill is a rare vagrant to Britain that breeds in mature pine forests in Norway, Sweden, Finland and Russia. Recently, a few pairs have been found breeding in the Scottish Highlands. They are subject to eruptive movements when their food supply is short and there were notable influxes into Britain in 1982/83 and 1990/91.

In Derbyshire there have been two records involving 28 birds. Up to 25 (ten males, 11 females and four immatures) were in the Howden Reservoir area of Upper Derwentdale from 30th October 1982 to 13th February 1983. The initial flock of seven birds increased to 25 from 15th November 1982 to 10th January 1983. Thereafter, there were 20 until 3rd February followed by a rapid dispersal, with the last, a male, seen on 13th February.

These birds were part of the major invasion of Parrot Crossbills into Britain in the autumn of 1982, during which an estimated 104 birds were seen. The invasion started with arrivals on the east coast and in the Northern Isles in the late autumn of 1982, followed by sporadic wintering of small flocks inland. It is thought that the invasion, which also reached southern Sweden, Denmark and the Netherlands, may have been due to an almost total failure of the pine seed crop in Norway in 1982 and that migrating birds possibly passed south without stopping (Catley & Hursthouse 1985).

The second county record was of three juveniles in the Longshaw–Padley area on 27th June and 3rd–13th July 1985.

Common Rosefinch
Carpodacus erythrinus
A very rare vagrant.

Common Rosefinches breed in the Palearctic from western Europe to the Pacific and have considerably expanded their range to the west and north in recent decades. Though breeding has occasionally taken place in the UK since 1982, they are mainly regular spring and autumn migrants in the UK. They are most frequently found on the east coast or on the Northern Isles of Scotland, and inland records are very rare.

There are two Derbyshire records. The first concerned a first-summer male, which was found singing in a hawthorn bush at Carr Vale at 1600hrs on 3rd June 1998. It flew into a field of oil-seed rape, where it was later seen feeding, before returning to the hawthorn. It was last seen singing in willows near the River Doe Lea from 1930hrs to 2005hrs. This bird constituted the first Midlands area record of this species since 1885, when one was at Adderbury, Oxfordshire. Beevers (1999b) supplied an account of the event.

The second county record was of a female or first-summer male, with a brood-patch, trapped and ringed in an area of mixed woodland and rhododendrons at Uppertown on 21st June 2003. It was not seen again after its release.

Bullfinch
Pyrrhula pyrrhula
A fairly common resident.

The Bullfinch is a fairly common, rather unobtrusive, bird, which frequents woods and spinneys, thickets, dense hedgerows, parks and large gardens. It has one of the quieter and least known songs of any British finch, but the piping call is distinctive and is often the first indication of the bird's presence. They occur in pairs for much of the year and might be found in small parties outside the breeding season but, unlike most other seed-eaters, they do not form large, mixed flocks with other species.

Bullfinches are found throughout much of the county, but are most numerous in well-wooded, lowland areas and scarcest in upland moorland areas and on the limestone plateau of the White Peak, where the pastures are bounded by drystone walls rather than hedges. The recent planting with woodland of many of the county's former colliery spoil-heap sites has provided this species with a large amount of new habitat, which it is one of the earliest woodland birds to colonize.

The tetrad map from the Derbyshire BBS (1995–99) shows their widespread distribution. They were present in all of the complete 10km squares, as they were in the 1968–72 and 1988–91 Atlases, with 22 or 23 confirmed breeding records in the 10km core squares in all three periods. Only high ground in the north-western Peak District was apparently devoid of Bullfinches, as was much of urban Derby. They were present in 426 tetrads overall, with breeding proved in 165 (23% of the total) despite nests often being well hidden in thick vegetation and adults with young foraging at some distance from their breeding sites.

Despite there being no apparent reduction in breeding distribution, Derbyshire Bullfinches are believed to be in serious decline. Whitlock considered the bird fairly common, while Frost was able to report an increase around 1943–44 and a more notable one from 1957. Legal protection from bird-catchers in the cage-bird industry and the demise of the Sparrowhawk were thought to be the main reasons for this growth in numbers. However, a national decline began during the 1970s and has continued ever since with Eaton *et al.* (2010) revealing a population crash of 49% in the period 1970–2008. The reasons for this are not fully understood but may include the intensification of farming, including hedgerow loss and the removal of weedy field corners, and the recovery of the Sparrowhawk population.

As with many common species, there is rather little precise information on local breeding numbers. At the woodland CBC plots surveyed during the 1990s, there was an average of four pairs a year (equating to some 28 pairs per km^2) at the Shirebrook site, which contains large areas of scrub, but only one pair was found at Shire Hill Wood and none at Shiningcliff Wood. None were found at Farfield Farm (Hope), while Culland and Broadhay Farm averaged 1.6 and 0.5 territories a year. At Scarcliffe Woods, Frost (2008a) recorded a population averaging 12 pairs a year, with a maximum of 21 pairs in 1974, and an overall decrease of 31% between the mid-1970s and the mid-2000s. Results from the Carsington Water combined census of 2003–07 suggested an impressive 26 pairs.

Outside the breeding season, Bullfinches may wander from their nesting areas and can sometimes be seen in habitats where they do not breed, including heather moorland. They occur only in small numbers, and records of more than 20 are unusual. The largest recorded counts at individual sites are of 44 at Scarcliffe Woods in December 1975 with 35 or more there on other occasions; 35 at Hardwick Park, also in December 1975, and 35 at Ogston Reservoir in October 1999, at a time when some numbers were seen on the east coast. A notable record was of 30 feeding on heather at Little Hayfield in December 1971. There is some evidence of a small movement at migration watch-points in autumn, with 14 flying south-west in 75 minutes at Highoredish Hill on 7th October 1997 perhaps the most interesting record.

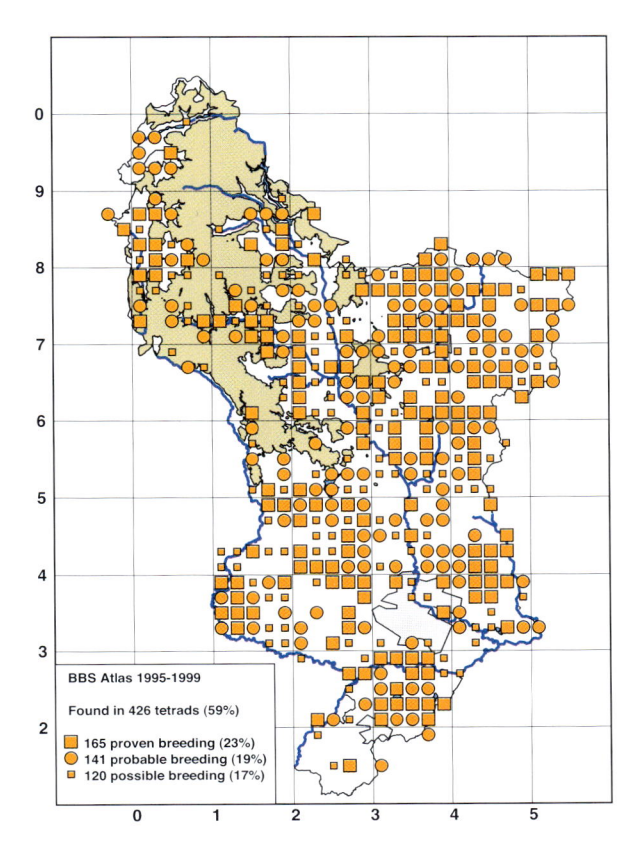

However, ringing records suggest that British Bullfinches are very sedentary, with most recovered within 10km of their ringing site. Of the 58 records for Derbyshire, 38 were within 2km. Two birds that travelled much further were a male, ringed at Ailsworth, Cambridgeshire in October 1962 that was shot 139km to the north-west, at Whaley Bridge in June 1963, and one ringed at Aston-on-Trent in September 1987 that travelled 56km west-south-west to Coven, Staffordshire, only to be killed by a cat. The same fate befell one that travelled 23km south-south-east from Eckington to Pinxton between January and June 1977. A total of 72% of the county records were recovered within a year of ringing, with the oldest well into its fourth year.

BBS Atlas 1995-1999

Found in 426 tetrads (59%)

- 165 proven breeding (23%)
- 141 probable breeding (19%)
- 120 possible breeding (17%)

Hawfinch
Coccothraustes coccothraustes
A scarce or uncommon resident.

At the start of the nineteenth century these engaging finches were regarded as winter visitors to the county, but a century later they were known to breed in all parts except the High Peak. In his classic monograph on the species, Mountfort (1957) described its Derbyshire status as 'well distributed in small numbers throughout the county. The Ashbourne, Ilkeston, Shipley and Derby districts are the best established breeding areas, but I have seen fair numbers in the breeding season around Matlock, Buxton and Radbourne; Hawfinches are seen regularly throughout the year between Wirksworth and Belper. Winter flocks are not uncommon.'

Frost reported that they bred almost throughout the county, but stated that numbers were in decline, a situation, which is still ongoing, leading to concern for the bird's future as a Derbyshire breeding bird.

The table shows the approximate number of sites and birds recorded annually in the period 1980–2011. Despite small fluctuations, the bird totals show a large overall decline during the period.

Hawfinches are notoriously difficult to locate on account of their arboreal habitats and shyness. Most are found by their hard 'tzik' call, but the song is quiet and easily overlooked. Nests are usually high in the canopy and hard to see. In the 1968–72 Atlas, breeding was confirmed in two western 10km squares, but was not proved anywhere in the 1988–91 Atlas. Lack of observer effort or competence is not thought to account for the decrease in records.

Since 1980, breeding has also been proved at Cromford, Rose End Meadows, Chatsworth, Great Longstone, Bakewell, Somercotes, Pleasley, Shirebrook, Barlborough and Scarcliffe. At the latter site there was a population of up to 50 pairs in the early 1960s, but this then collapsed, believed to be as a consequence of reforestation (Frost 1971b). Since 1970, up to five pairs have been present in the breeding season here, though with only one by the late 1990s and none since. At the Shirebrook CBC site, one to three pairs nested in 1978–84, but with no definite territories subsequently.

The tetrad map generated by the Derbyshire BBS (1995–99) demonstrates clearly the scarcity of this bird in Derbyshire. During the 1995–99 survey, breeding was proved in only one tetrad, SK33P (Darley Park, Derby), with probable breeding and presence in a further nine and 13 tetrads respectively. Subsequent to publication of the 1995–99 survey data, additional records came to light for the same survey period of one proven breeding record (a nest in SK26S, Rowsley), a probable breeding location (SK57A, Scarcliffe Park) and three other tetrads (SK17R, SK27F, SK37G) in which presence or possible breeding had been recorded but not submitted to the survey. Since 1999 there have been only two proven breeding records: at Chatsworth in 2002 and Cromford in 2005, with a possible third record from July 2003 when a juvenile was killed in collision with a window at Rose End Meadows near Cromford.

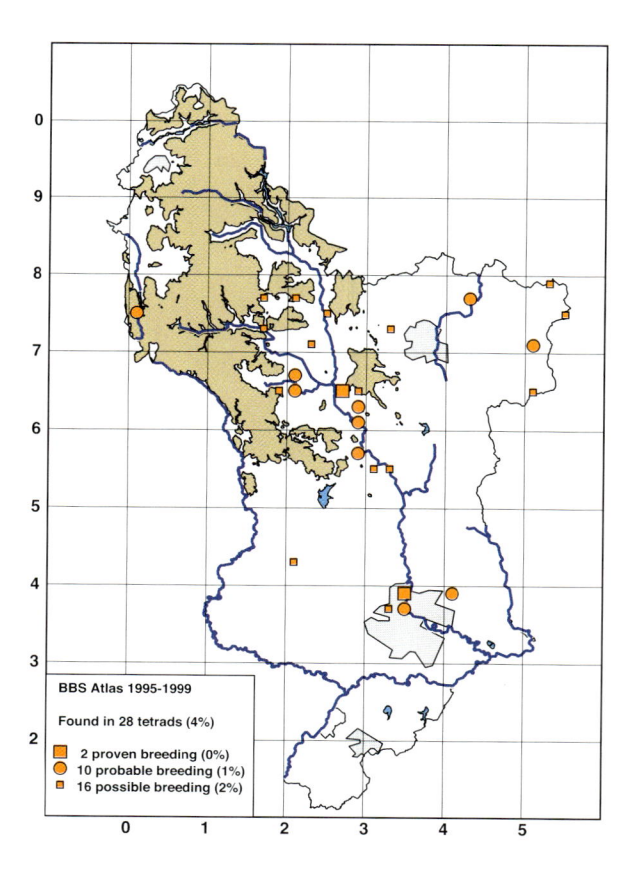

Year	Locations	Birds
1980	13	67
1981	13	67
1982	16	48
1983	11	54
1984	16	38
1985	11	32
1986	13	52
1987	13	48
1988	10	39
1989	14	44
1990	16	33
1991	13	34
1992	9	39
1993	11	39
1994	12	29
1995	14	36
1996	9	22
1997	14	37
1998	9	26
1999	7	14
2000	9	30
2001	8	11
2002	7	26
2003	6	16
2004	3	11
2005	11	37
2006	11	38
2007	3	10
2008	10	36
2009	5	23
2010	5	22
2011	2	12

BBS Atlas 1995-1999

Found in 28 tetrads (4%)

- 2 proven breeding (0%)
- 10 probable breeding (1%)
- 16 possible breeding (2%)

The reasons for the decline are unclear. Hawfinches feed mainly on seeds in winter, and in spring eat buds and also the tips of plants, while in summer invertebrates such as caterpillars are taken. Locally, they are seen most often in areas of beech, lime, hornbeam, sycamore, yew and cedar, with hawthorn often favoured in winter. At most of their favoured sites there has been little or no obvious change to their food resources. Brown and Grice (2005) thought that higher rates of nest predation by grey squirrels might be a factor.

Winter feeding areas are often the same as breeding sites, or close to them, suggesting that most of our Hawfinches are sedentary. The Derwent Valley is now the main area for finding these birds in winter and this is the only location to have produced double-figure winter flocks in the past 20 years. Chatsworth has hosted the largest numbers, with up to 50 roosting in ornamental woodland in the 1979/80 winter, and up to 14 during the 1990s. The birds seen in the Cromford Wharf–Rose End Meadows–Willersley Castle area are thought to be of one population, which reached a maximum of 19 on 30th January 2002, while Allestree Park held 11 in March 1997. Other recent groups include eight at Shiningcliff Wood on 22nd January 2005, ten at Two Dales on 15th November 2006, and eight at Cromford Moor on 23rd February 2008.

Very occasionally Hawfinches are seen at some of the county's regular autumn migration watch-points, suggesting arrivals from elsewhere. Since 1985 there have been such records at Ramsley, Strines Top and Ashover Fabric. Very unusually, one was in stubble at Hardwick on 19th October 2005 in an autumn when Hawfinches were unusually widespread, both in Derbyshire and elsewhere.

More curiously, a male was trapped and ringed at Ramsley Moor, well away from known breeding sites, on 6th July 1991 and two flew high to the south-west over the moorland watershed near Derwent Reservoir on 17th June 1989. Fortunate observers have seen Hawfinches in their gardens at Curbar in July and August 2004, Littleover in November 2005 and Wessington in October 2009.

Snow Bunting
Plectrophenax nivalis
A scarce winter visitor and passage migrant.

For most birdwatchers a typical image of Snow Buntings would be of a winter flock, feeding restlessly on a shingle beach or in sand dunes, on the east coast. However, Snow Buntings regularly occur inland. In Derbyshire, in the 54 years from 1958 to 2011, there were only six years without any records, the most recent being 2009. Many are merely seen as fly-overs but grounded birds occur mainly on moorland, especially stony or burnt stretches, and to a lesser degree on other areas of sparse and short vegetation, such as colliery spoil heaps, opencast sites, gravel pit margins and bare hilltops. Although the great majority of sightings have been in the Peak District, there are records from sites scattered throughout the county, in all of the Natural Areas.

Whitlock and Jourdain quoted may sightings, including small groups, in both upland and lowland regions. The earliest was one shot by Francis Gisborne at Staveley in December 1767 and referred to as a 'Greater Brambling.' They were said to sometimes occur in considerable numbers on the Sheffield side of the Peak District. Frost said that considerable numbers occurred in the early 1930s, when John Armitage recorded flocks of 50 at Cown Edge, Axe Edge and Raven's Low. These gatherings were associated with an infestation of the purple moor-grass by the larvae of the gall-midge *Oligotrophus* (now *Pemphiocesis*) *ventricola*. The largest flock after that was of 36 on Totley Moss on 27th December 1965.

Since 1978, there have been about 100 records of Snow Buntings involving about 201 birds. The largest flocks during this period were of 25 over Howden Reservoir on 29th December 1988 and 13 over Abbey Clough on 18th November 2002. Most records involve brief stays but notable exceptions were a flock of up to nine that stayed on upland pasture at Middleton Moor from 10th November 1996 to 2nd February 1997, and a group of five that remained from 16th January to 8th March 1999 at a newly reseeded area on the summit of Mam Tor.

The numbers of birds recorded in the period 1978–2011 are as illustrated in the chart.

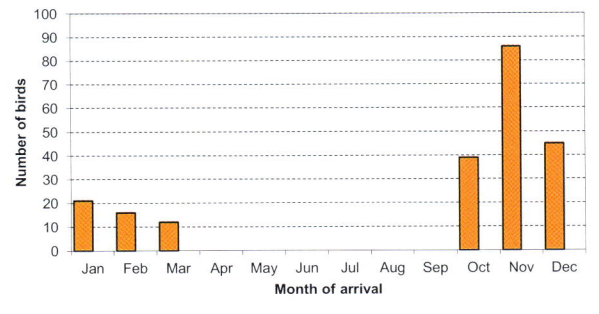

Snow Bunting: distribution by month 1978-2011

Extreme dates are 2nd October 1957, when one was at Whaley Bridge, and 10th April 1977, with one at Ogston Reservoir. However, there is a surprising, but well-authenticated, record of a male that took up territory on a drystone wall at Dove Holes during thick hill fog on 18th–19th June 1958.

Lapland Bunting
Calcarius lapponicus
A rare passage migrant and very rare winter visitor.

In the UK, Lapland Buntings are usually found wintering along the east coast of England, often associating with Skylarks, finches or bunting flocks in coastal stubble fields.

The first Derbyshire record (and the following six) was of one over Big Moor on 26th October 1966. There have now been 45 records, involving 49 birds, up to the end of 2011. The table shows the temporal spread of the birds.

Period	Birds
1960s	1
1970s	2
1980s	16
1990s	13
2000–11	17

The great majority of records were of birds flying over, identified by their distinctive call. Observer awareness probably accounts for the fact that over half have been seen at just two sites, namely Barbrook Reservoir (Pools)/Big Moor (13) and Williamthorpe (eight). Almost all occurred singly, the exceptions being three flying south at Ashover Fabric on 18th October 1986, two at Pleasley Colliery on 23rd September 2000 and two at Barbrook Pools on 25th November 2005. Apart from sites already mentioned, Lapland Buntings have also occurred at Strines Top (three), Stanedge (two), Totley Moss, Ramsley, Sawley, Killamarsh, Owler Bar, Willington Gravel Pits, Carr Vale, Upper Loads, Screetham Lane, Shirebrook Colliery, Beeley 'Triangle', and Carsington Water.

October and November are the prime months to see this species in the county, with 40 (88%) recorded then, as shown in the chart.

The latest date was at Pleasley Colliery in 2000, with one on 25th April and the earliest was 22nd September 2010 at Carsington Water.

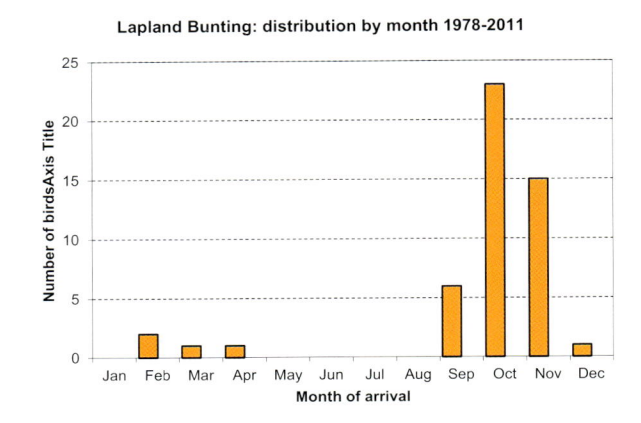

Yellowhammer
Emberiza citrinella
A common resident.

Yellowhammers are characteristic birds of farmland throughout much of Derbyshire. They also breed in areas of scrub, bushy wasteland, young plantations and along woodland edges. Whitlock described them as abundant, and breeding up to the moorland edge. Frost said they were common but had undergone a decline in the previous two decades.

The Derbyshire BBS (1995–99) showed the population to be well distributed throughout the lowlands of the county, although there was also a notable absence from the Derby urban area. There are few records of confirmed breeding from upland areas of the north-west with only eight squares showing proven breeding in the White Peak. Those records from higher ground are mainly from moorland fringe sites close to farms and farming activity. By way of illustrating their scarcity in upland regions, a record of a male on 14th December 1998 at Combs Reservoir was described as the first record in the Chapel-en-le-Frith area since 1983.

The tetrad map reveals the bird was found in 444 tetrads of which 189 had proven breeding (42% of those found and 26% of the county as a whole), while probable and possible breeding made for another 255 tetrads. The confirmed breeding records came from 20 of the 23 10km squares, the same number as in the 1968–72 Atlas; the 1988–91 Atlas confirmed breeding in 21 of these squares.

The maps show the breeding status by 10km squares in 1995–99 and 2007–11 and strongly suggest that the decline in western Derbyshire is continuing.

The BTO CBC has indicated that, overall, Yellowhammer numbers declined by about 43% during the period 1970–98. However, the 1984–88 Winter Atlas states that the breeding population has remained constant for the 20 years to 1984 and, therefore, the decline has probably accelerated since the mid-1980s.

Further, CBC results also show that the population of farmland Yellowhammers has been fairly stable since 1980, whereas there has been a decline in Yellowhammers in woodland habitats. Eaton *et al*. (2010) recorded an overall UK decline of 55% between 1970 and 2008. At Scarcliffe Woods there were up to 46 territories during the mid-1970s when much of the area was newly restocked with conifer plantations; by the mid-2000s there was an average of three territories a year. The overall decrease between the two periods was 91%, the largest of any species (Frost 2008a). More generally, since 1960 there has been a switch away from spring to autumn sowing of cereals, which must have impacted on the ecology of a bird characteristic of winter stubbles. Frost also considered the loss of hedgerows and a general tidying up of farmland to have been detrimental to this species.

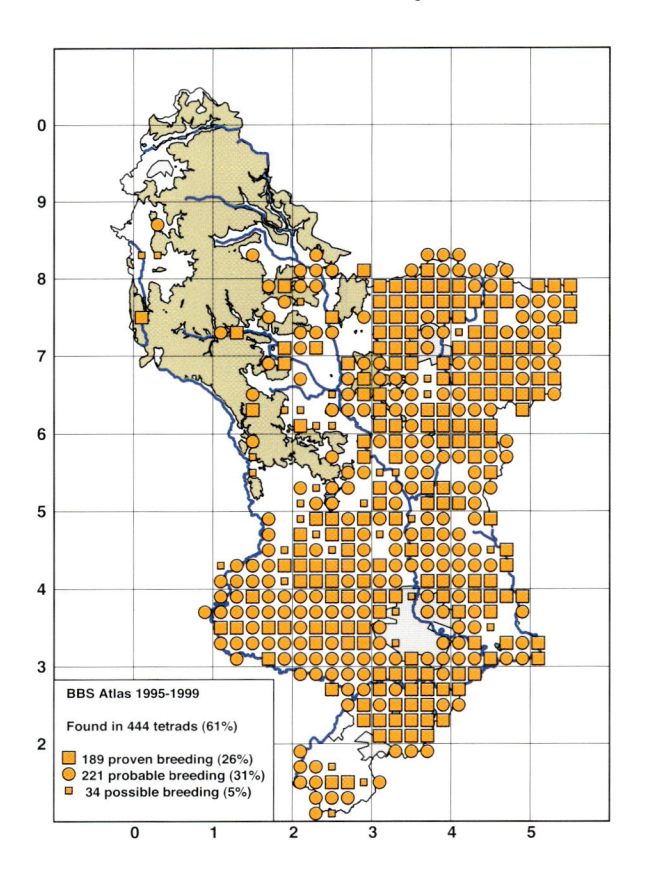

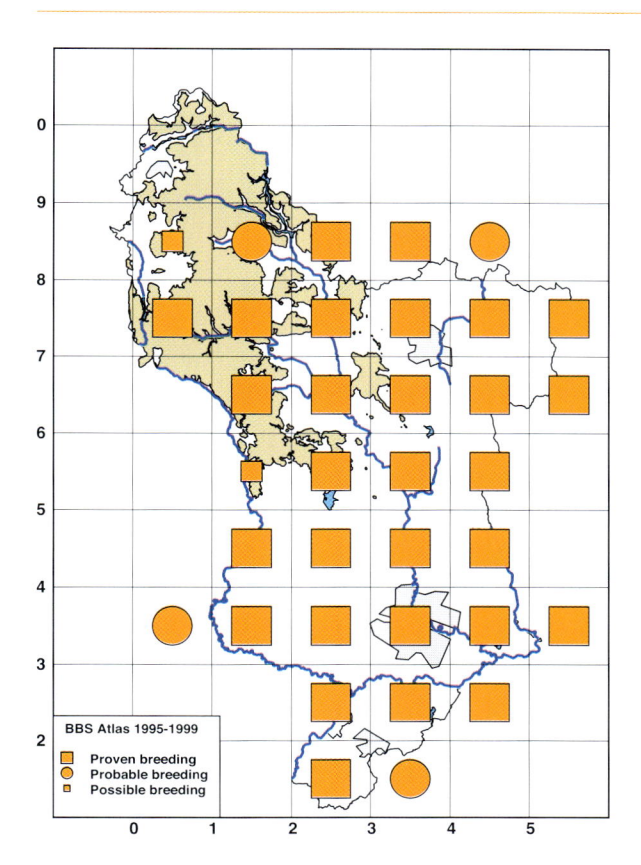

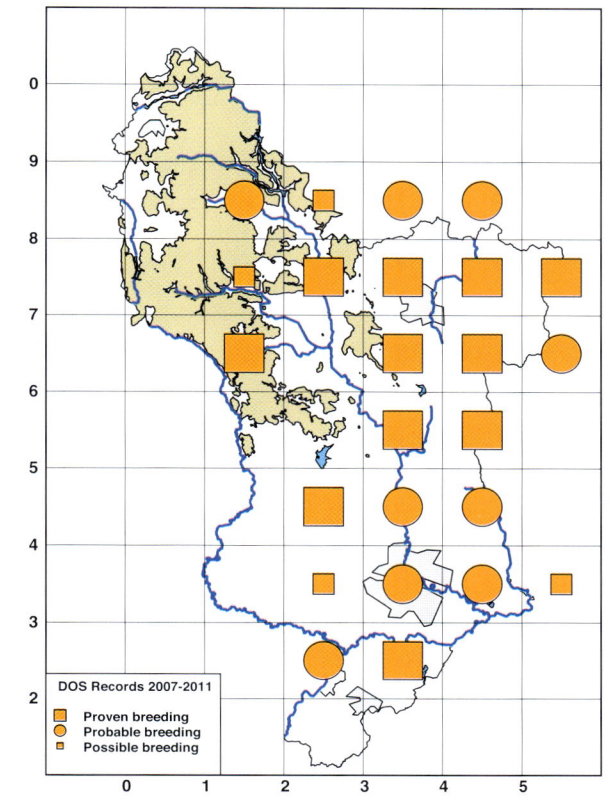

In more recent years, there have been numerous records of five or more singing birds or territorial pairs at numerous sites. The largest such counts have been at Oxcroft Estate, Bolsover, 12 on 27th June 1995; Breck Farm, 15 on 3rd July 1997; Williamthorpe, 15 in 2003; Clowne Common, 13 on 26th May 2007; Whitwell Quarry, 14 on 26th March 2008; Shirebrook Colliery, 12 in June 2008 and 13 on 25th May 2011; Pleasley Colliery, 14 on 18th March and 15 on 1st June 2010; Carr Vale, 17 on 25th June 2010 and 13 on 25th May 2011. Nine singing males at Baslow Edge on 23rd April 2008 was a high number for a Peak District locality.

Counts on a BBS plot at Ticknall between 1994 and 2009 showed that the number of singing males varied between seven in 1997 and 2003, and one in 2005 and 2008. The number of territories on another farmland BBS plot at North Wingfield over the same period of time varied between two in 1994 and 2004, and nine in 2006. At Weston Fields, five males were singing in a linear 1.2km on 12th May 2002, and at Stonebroom, six pairs were present in 1.5km on 16th May 2004.

In winter, Yellowhammers are typically flocking birds, feeding on a diet of cereal grains and other seeds, all of which are obtained almost exclusively from the ground. Their only distributional change between summer and winter is a tendency towards withdrawal from more upland areas during the winter months. Caution has to be exercised when reviewing the number of records of winter flocks and their size, as it is clear that the quality and number of records submitted to and published in the *Derbyshire Bird Report* since 1978 has increased significantly, which is as much a product of the growth in popularity of bird-recording in the county, and should not be mistaken for changes in the fortunes of the species. However, it is worth noting that during the 1980s there were 19 flocks of 100–200 birds recorded and three flocks of 200–230 birds. The highest counts were of 400 birds on recently abandoned arable land at Shirebrook on 14th December 1984, and 450 birds at Pebley on 20th January 1988.

During the 1990s there were very many more records of flocks of up to 100 birds, most containing 40–70 birds. There were 20 records of flocks of 100–199 birds and six of 200–250, with the highest counts during that decade being of 350 birds at Sinfin Moor on 27th November 1990 and 300 at Manor Floods on 23rd January 1992. In 2000–11 there were 19 flocks of 100 birds. Exceptional flocks during this period were of 250 at Creswell on 6th March 2004 and 500 there on 31st January 2007, 300 at Church Wilne on 15th March 2005, and 250 at Elmton on 27th December 2009.

Yellowhammers roost communally in winter, favouring areas of dense scrub and marshy vegetation. Counts made in most winters at a bed of *Phragmites* at Doe Lea show a reduction, with up to 160 roosting in the early 1980s, reducing to maxima of 40 in the 1990s and 22 in the 2000s.

Although, as previously mentioned, the Yellowhammer is described as rarely visiting gardens, there are a few records of this occurring. Three birds visited a garden in Matlock on 18th December 1981, increasing to seven there on 25th December. In 1996 there were up to 15 birds visiting a Bolsover garden in January and up to 12 birds during March. In 1998, again in Bolsover, there were ten birds in the observer's garden on 27th January.

The Yellowhammer is a very sedentary farmland species, and both national and county ringing data show that birds are very likely to remain in their natal area. Of 24 local records, nine birds were controlled or found dead at their ringing sites. Birds that travelled more than most were one ringed near Market Bosworth, Leicestershire, on 24th March 1977, which was shot near Swadlincote on 9th June 1978, a distance of 26km; one ringed at Doe Lea on 22nd January 1978 that was controlled 13km away at Thieves Wood, Nottinghamshire, on 24th April 1983; and one ringed at Barrow Hill on 13th February 1991 that was taken by a cat 12km away at Nether Langwith, Nottinghamshire, on 10th June 1996. One ringed at Staveley in February 1971 was killed by traffic at Derby in September of the same year.

The oldest Derbyshire record concerned a first-year male ringed at Barrow Hill on 30th July 1975 that was taken by a cat at the same location over eight years later on 20th January 1984.

Cirl Bunting
Emberiza cirlus
A very rare vagrant.

There have been about eight permissible Derbyshire records. One was seen at Bladon Wood, near Repton around 1881, and it had been seen once or twice in the Chellaston area (Whitlock). Jourdain quoted E.A. Brown as recording one near Burton upon Trent, but it seems likely that this was a Staffordshire record. A male was at Ashopton on 20th April 1926.

A singing male was seen at Hackenthorpe (now in Sheffield) in 1950, but it did not stay, while in Peter Dale, near Tideswell, a pair, of which the male was singing, was present on 11th March 1956. More recently, a male was at Snelston on 23rd March 1960 and a pair was at Osmaston from 27th November to 27th December 1965.

The closest breeding to Derbyshire in recent times took place in Worcestershire. However, this small relict population last bred there in 1977 (Harrison & Harrison 2005). This sedentary species is now restricted to Devon and the possibility of Cirl Buntings occurring again in Derbyshire in the near future seems very remote.

Ortolan Bunting
Emberiza hortulana
A very rare vagrant.

This species breeds across much of Europe, from Iberia and Scandinavia eastwards to Mongolia, wintering in sub-Saharan Africa. In the UK it is a scarce migrant, mainly in autumn.

The only Derbyshire record is of a male that was found feeding among long grass and weeds on an embankment at Aston-on-Trent Gravel Pits on 6th May 2000 in the mid-afternoon. It showed well, down to 10m at times, but also sometimes disappeared into the vegetation. It was present until at least 1930hrs but could not be relocated on the following day: see Key (2001c). This bird was one of only two inland spring records of Ortolan Bunting in Britain in 2000, in what was a below-average year for the species (Fraser & Rogers 2002).

Little Bunting
Emberiza pusilla
A very rare vagrant.

Little Buntings breed across much of the northern Palearctic and winter from Turkestan to south-east Asia. They are scarce migrants in the UK, though there are also a few records of overwintering.

The only Derbyshire record is of one found at Drakelow Nature Reserve on 11th March 1994, which remained until 27th March, by which time over 300 observers had seen it. Throughout its stay it was to be seen around the reserve's winter feeding station, close to the main hide. Though many Reed Buntings were attracted to this, the Little Bunting tended to feed alone and did not associate closely with other birds. Cockburn (1995) wrote an account of the event.

Reed Bunting
Emberiza schoeniclus
A fairly common resident and passage migrant.

Reed Buntings, as the name implies, are quite commonly found in a variety of wetland habitats such as marshes, reed-beds, sewage works and the margins of lakes, reservoirs and gravel pits. Whitlock described them as abundant in all low-lying parts of Derbyshire. Frost documented a more recent spread into drier habitats, such as cereal fields and forestry plantations, and said they bred on moorland up to 490m amsl. In the latter areas, bracken beds are particularly favoured.

Outside the breeding season they are not confined to wetland habitats and may also be found on farmland, moorland and waste ground. They are largely granivorous in winter, taking many seeds from the ground and can therefore be found associating with other buntings and finches at this time.

Overall, Reed Buntings are more numerous in lowland areas and their winter distribution shows a partial withdrawal from upland areas. The population is susceptible to very cold weather, showing marked declines following severe weather and peaks following series of milder winters. Overall, Eaton *et al.* (2010) stated that there had been a UK decline of 30% between 1970 and 2008. It is the winter shortage of naturally occurring weed seeds which may have led to the increasing use of gardens by Reed Buntings recorded since the late 1970s.

As shown on the tetrad map, Reed Buntings occur most frequently in the lower regions of the north-east, east and south of the county. But countywide they were found in 271 tetrads in the Derbyshire BBS (1995–99), and breeding was proved in 92 of these, which represents just 13% of the area. Breeding was proved in 19 of the 23 10km core squares, compared with 18 in the 1988–91 Atlas and 17 in the 1968–72 Atlas. Breeding Reed Buntings are not difficult to find, the males singing on prominent song-posts such as hedgerows, bushes and bracken. The number of confirmed cases is slightly lower, perhaps because of the rather inaccessible nature of sites within its aquatic habitat.

The comparative maps for 1995–99 and 2007–11 suggest some local losses.

In recent years there have been many site counts of up to 19 singing birds or territorial pairs. Greater numbers have been at Williamthorpe, where there were 34 territories in May 1990, 20 in 1997, 1998 and 2000, and 34 in May 2002. Similarly, in the Doe Lea Valley, there were 49 singing males in 1995, 44 in 1996, 50 in 1998 and 23 in 2005; on the Eastern Moors (Beeley to Strines), 62 territories in a survey in 1998; and at Willington Gravel Pits, 51 singing males on 19th March 2005 and 32 on 17th May 2007. A total of 65 territories was found on the EMP moors in a 2010 survey (Frost & Taylor 2011). Though most were in wetter areas (especially where *juncus* was present), with 19 on Big Moor and 18 on Leash Fen, many were found in drier areas such as beds of bracken. Frost (2008a) recorded up to 20 pairs in young forestry plantations at Scarcliffe during the 1970s, all of which disappeared as the trees matured.

The use of alternative habitats is illustrated by a count carried out in 1988 on the River Trent between Newton Solney and King's Mill, where eight singing males were all in cereal fields, with none in the marshes. Similarly, records of birds singing from fields of oil-seed rape, began with one in May 1991 at Scarcliffe, two in June 1992 at Sinfin, three in June 1993 at Stenson and three in June 1997 at Killamarsh Meadows. This had increased by 1998 and 1999 when there were many reports of birds singing in oil-seed rape. No fewer than 16 were singing in this crop at Egginton Sewage Farm on 29th June 2008.

Outside the breeding season there has been a continuing trend for birds to use artificial feeding stations. In 1978 and

1979 there were several records of birds feeding in gardens or at bird tables and records in most subsequent years to 1992. The number of records, and the numbers of birds involved have steadily increased. In 1981 there were six records, one of which was of eight birds in Walton (Chesterfield), in February. In 1984 there was a most unusual record of Reed Buntings visiting orange plastic nut-bags at Willington on 29th January. In 1986 there were several records, with one of 27 birds in a Melbourne garden in February being exceptional. In 1992 about 40 Reed Buntings were recorded visiting a feeding station at Drakelow Nature Reserve.

Small numbers are seen on autumn migration watches. There are several such records for Ramsley, with 73 birds moving west-south-west on 17th October 1987, and 12 birds moving south-west in two hours on 27th October 1999. At Strines Top, larger counts have included 20 to the north on 12th October 1992, 20 to the north-west on 14th October 1993 and 28 moving south-west on 30th September 1994. Autumn totals for Strines Top were 120 in 1993, and 170 in both 1994 and 1995. At Barbrook Pools, 23 moved west in 90 minutes on 30th October 2010 and 55 west, also in 90 minutes, on 6th November 2010.

Records of winter gatherings of Reed Buntings since 1978 usually refer to flocks of 10–40 birds. Roost counts of 90 at Doe Lea on 28th January 1981 and 150 at Williamthorpe on 25th October 1988 were noteworthy, but Frost referred to roosts of 250–300 in reed-beds at Killamarsh and Bolsover. There are quite numerous records of flocks of over 80 birds, including 90 at Etwall Gravel Pits on 29th December 1990, 100 at Elvaston Castle on 14th February 1991, 150 on 1st January 1995 at Drakelow Nature Reserve, an exceptional record of 250 at Manor Floods on 25th December 1996, 83 at Ramsley Moor on 8th January 2003 and 200 at Barbrook Pools on 29th December 2005. The two latter counts were made in snowy conditions.

British Reed Buntings are fairly sedentary and males in particular show strong site fidelity. They perform partial migratory movements under the influence of weather conditions but this is generally within Britain. There are 81 recovery records for the county, of which about 10% moved more than 100km from their ringing site.

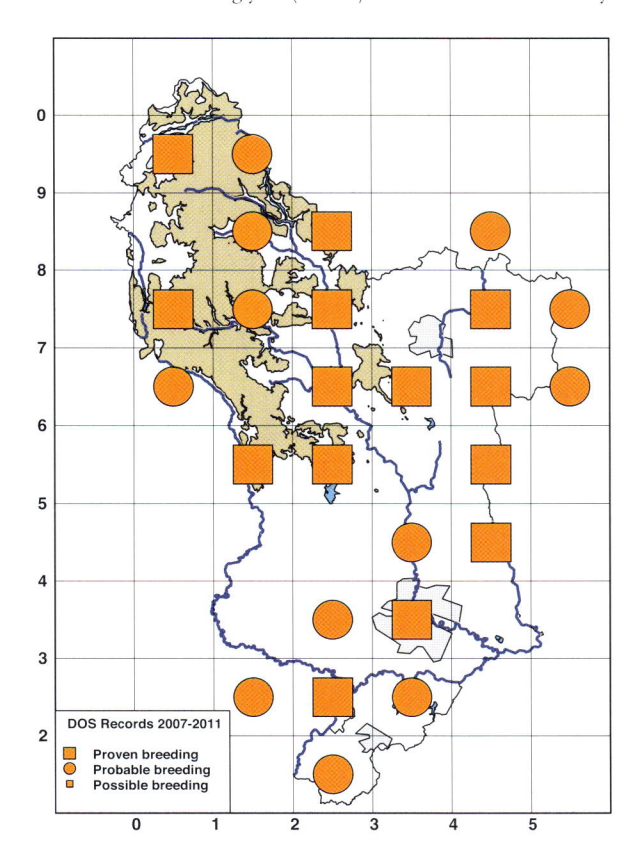

There are few national data of birds moving abroad, but there is one such county record of a bird ringed at Brabant, Belgium, in October 1989 which was controlled at Elvaston Castle Country Park in February 1992. It is possible that this bird's origin was Scandinavia and it had wintered in different regions. Other long-distance recoveries include an adult female ringed at Drakelow Nature Reserve in May 1988 that was controlled near Chislehurst, Dorset five months later (230km), a first-year female ringed in Dorset in October 1988 that was controlled at Palterton in March the following year (287km) and a female road casualty in Cumbria in June 1995 that had been ringed at Elvaston Castle Country Park in January the previous year (239km).

The Derbyshire recoveries are made up of 49 males, 22 females and ten birds not sexed. Most birds are ringed at nests and these figures reflect the bias towards males seen in the figures for birds ringed at roosts across central and southern England (Prŷs-Jones 1977). The suggestion is that females do not gather into roosts and/or disperse over greater distances in the winter months. Of the birds ringed or recovered in the county during September to April, 33% of males and 21% of females stayed within 10km of their ringing site, while 10% of males and 26% of females moved over 100km.

Corn Bunting
Emberiza calandra
A scarce resident, mainly in the south and north-east.

The status of the Corn Bunting in Derbyshire has undergone various fluctuations over the last 100 years or so, but never before has it been so close to extinction as a breeding bird as it now is. In 1893, Whitlock stated that Corn Buntings were common in the valleys of the Trent, lower Dove and Derwent but scarce and local elsewhere in the county. In contrast, Jourdain stated in 1905 that the limestone wall country around Tideswell and Brough was the stronghold of the species, with smaller numbers in the south, central and north-eastern areas of the county. By 1934, the species was stated to be very local in the county, and three years later had disappeared from the Trent Valley and the Winster areas, but still bred in 'one locality in the north'. From the 1940s onwards there were further reports of declining numbers and the species disappeared from some areas altogether.

In 1973, Miss K.M. Hollick correlated an increase in the number of Corn Buntings in the Pike Hall–Minninglow area, at the southern end of the Carboniferous Limestone region, with a change from permanent grassland to barley cultivation. Despite this and a few other small increases, Frost considered that, overall, the species had probably declined in the twentieth century.

Since 1978, Corn Buntings have undergone further serious declines and have suffered a marked contraction in range. This decline is widespread and Eaton *et al.* (2010) recorded a staggering loss of 89% of the national population between 1970 and 2008.

The song is distinctive and usually delivered from a prominent place, such as a bush top, but breeding is rather difficult to prove in the often inaccessible farmland habitat.

The Derbyshire BBS (1995–99) revealed 11 possible, 45 probable and 16 confirmed breeding tetrads, in two separate areas in the north-east and south, having been found in 72 tetrads in total. This represents a substantial decrease from the 1968–72 Atlas, highlighting some contraction in range, and in particular a withdrawal from the north-west. Since 2000, territorial birds have been confined to the north-east and south of the county, except for two surprising records from Mayfield and Wolfscote Dale. The last confirmed breeding away from lowland areas was on the upland fringe at Butterley in 1983.

Corn Buntings inhabit various kinds of farmland, favouring tilled land rather than grassland; cereals are the most favoured crops, although other crops are occasionally used. Less frequently they breed in grassland, usually preferring temporary rather than permanent pasture.

This preference for farmland habitats has led to a tendency for Corn Buntings to be underrecorded in the county, as these areas tend to be rather neglected by birdwatchers. This was clearly demonstrated by a detailed survey carried out in the area south of the Trent during 1976, when T. Cockburn located 30 singing birds, bringing the overall county total to 48 for that year, compared with just six reported the previous year. Similarly a survey of the north-eastern stronghold in 1992 and 1993 by M.A. Beevers revealed possible totals there of 55 (1992) and 76 pairs (1993). These figures boosted the county totals to a minimum of 75 and 105 singing bird or territories respectively for those years, compared with an average of around 26 reported pairs

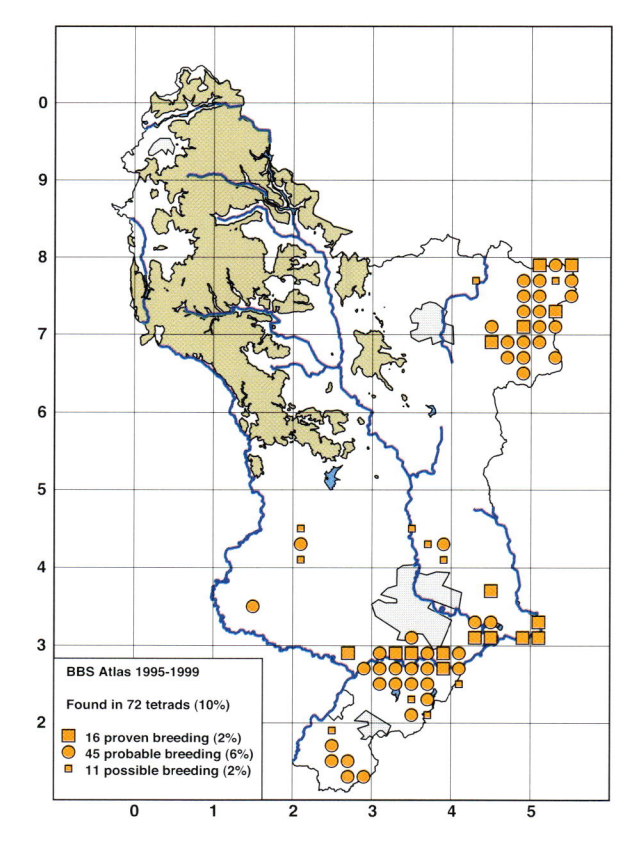

BBS Atlas 1995-1999
Found in 72 tetrads (10%)
- 16 proven breeding (2%)
- 45 probable breeding (6%)
- 11 possible breeding (2%)

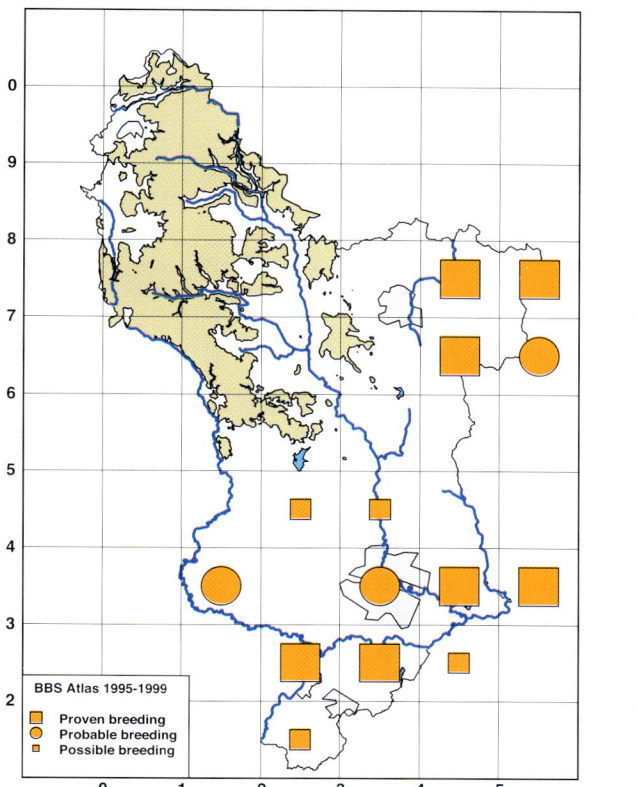

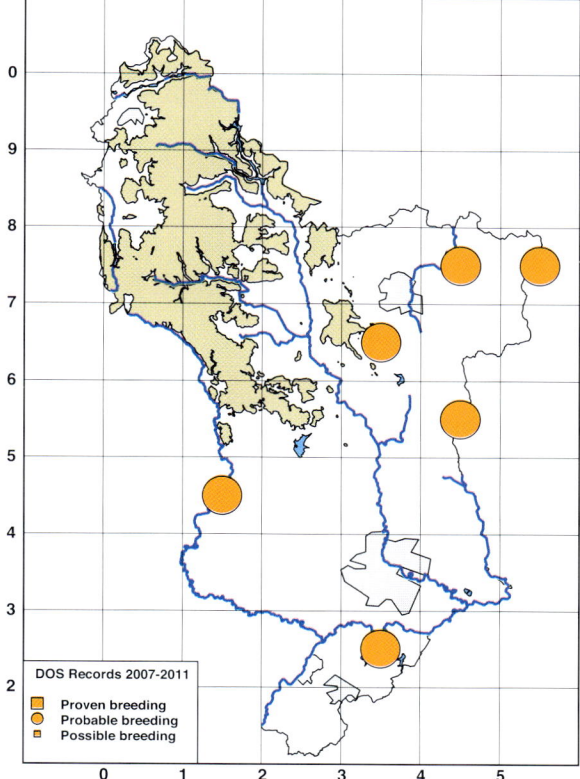

in the five years prior to this survey. Beevers (1994) concluded that the population appeared to be stable in the south and the north-east of the county at that time and that underrecording was responsible for the apparent decline. However, other observers disagreed with Beevers' conclusions, saying that the species was still declining; they have, unfortunately, been proved correct and since then numbers have declined further in both of the county strongholds. Although more observers are aware of the decline and are reporting all singing birds, figures suggested a total county population of not many more than 50 singing males during the breeding season in 1998 and 41 in 1999. There were 39 singing males in 2000, followed by a devastating collapse to just eight in 2001. There was a small increase to 15 singing males in 2003 but only between five and seven in 2004–06, one in 2008, two in 2010 and three in 2011, with none at all in 2007 and 2009. The maps for 1995–99 and 2007–11 illustrate the severity of the decline.

In Derbyshire, as in the rest of Britain, the Corn Bunting has, or rather had, a rather patchy distribution with small areas of high density, surrounded by larger areas of lower density. It has been suggested that this appears to fit a 'source-sink' distribution pattern, where a small area of extinction-resistant population (the source) is surrounded by a larger area consisting of a series of pockets with less viable populations (sinks). These sinks rely on immigration of birds dispersing from the source area, either because production is too low, or mortality too high, to support themselves. Consequently this has implications for survey work in that a decline in a certain area may not necessarily be due to any changes or problems within that area. Also, as a large proportion of an area's population may be present within the sinks, high numbers of breeding territories in a particular habitat may not necessarily mean that this is the prime habitat.

Although the reasons for the decline of Corn Buntings are still unclear, recent studies have suggested the most likely causes to be reduced winter stubbles resulting from the loss of spring tillage, increased pesticide use and improved harvesting and storage techniques. In grassland areas, the change from traditional hay meadows to earlier and more frequently harvested silage, has probably had an effect on breeding success, as the Corn Bunting nests rather late in the season. This is thought less likely to be a major problem in cereal areas, as in practice winter wheat tends to be harvested at about the same time as spring sown cereals, though winter sown barley can often be harvested on average around two weeks earlier. Between the 1968–72 and 1988–91 Atlases, they tended to be lost from squares which were higher in altitude and had a greater proportion of grassland to arable land than those squares which retained Corn Buntings.

One glimmer of hope for Derbyshire Corn Buntings is that they are still occasionally seen in flocks in winter. In 2004–06 there were counts of 18–55 at Creswell, and in December 2007 and January 2008, 17 were at Pebley Pond. The same site hosted a flock of 18 in December 2008, 40 in January 2009, 28 in January 2010 and 24 (possibly 31) in January 2011. Prior to that, flocks of up to 140 (at Church Wilne in February 1995) had been recorded.

Very few instances of visible migration have been recorded, though four flew north-west over Barbrook Reservoir on 5th November 1983 (the first record for this moorland site), and birds are occasionally reported from unusual locations such as Ogston Reservoir, suggesting at least some dispersal.

Larger numbers were formerly recorded at communal roosts in reed-beds, with up to 300 at Bolsover and 200 at Williamthorpe, but by the 1990s the only three-figure roost was at Markham, where the highest count was of 127. Since 1996, no roost has reached even double figures.

At Williamthorpe, a melanistic bird was seen on 24th February 1981 and a partial albino, described as all white except for a few flight feathers, was at Etwall Brook on 27th and 28th February 1984.

This is a difficult species to catch for the purposes of ringing, because of its open-country habitat, and almost all captures have been at winter roosts. The most interesting records concerned singles ringed at Wath-on-Dearne, South Yorkshire and near Gainsborough, Lincolnshire, which were found at Ilkeston and Palterton respectively; while birds ringed at Barrow Hill travelled to West Burton Power Station (Nottinghamshire) and Rotherham (South Yorkshire).

Important Records for 2012

This list for 2012 includes species recorded fewer than ten times in the county; largest flocks; earliest and latest ever dates for migrants; interesting extensions of breeding range and other important records.

Red-crested Pochard
Netta rufina

There was a record count of 22 at Long Eaton Gravel Pits on 12th February.

Velvet Scoter
Melanitta fusca

One remained at Steetley Quarry from 2nd December to 7th April 2013, by far the longest stay by this species.

Goosander
Mergus merganser

Present on the River Rother in the Staveley area during the breeding season and may well be breeding in the area.

Cormorant
Phalacrocorax carbo

A new breeding colony was found at British Celanese Lakes Nature Reserve, where ten pairs nested.

Great White Egret
Egretta alba

On 16th September, two, together with a Little Egret, were seen in flight at Ogston Reservoir, Leash Fen and Miller's Dale. Previous records have been of single birds.

Red Kite
Milvus milvus

Sightings continued to increase with reports from 29 localities in March and 34 in May. Four were seen together at Mickleover Meadows on 7th April.

Hobby
Falco subbuteo

Intensive fieldwork in parts of south Derbyshire suggested that the average population in 2010–12 was over twice that of 1999–2001. In 2012, breeding was recorded within the Derby City boundary for the first time and, in north-east Derbyshire and the Peak District, 16 breeding pairs were located, far more than previously. It is possible that the current county population is over 100 pairs.

Peregrine
Falco peregrinus

Pairs nested unsuccessfully on the East Mill in Belper and on an electricity pylon in north-east Derbyshire.

Temminck's Stint
Calidris temminckii

One at Middleton Moor on 19th–20th May constituted a first record for the Derbyshire Peak District.

Whiskered Tern
Chlidonias hybridus

One was at Long Eaton Gravel Pits on 25th April. The only previous records were in 1883 and 2009.

Sand Martin
Riparia riparia

The latest ever record was of one at Long Eaton Gravel Pits on 27th October.

Red-rumped Swallow
Cecropis daurica

One seen at Staunton Harold Reservoir and then later at Swarkestone Lake on 8th May was the eighth record for the county.

Cetti's Warbler
Cettia cettia

Breeding was proved at two sites in the Trent Valley. In the north-east, nest-building was recorded at one site and breeding was suspected at a second.

Chiffchaff
Phylloscopus collybita

Eight were seen at Pools Brook Country Park on 10th December. This was the largest wintering flock ever recorded in Derbyshire.

Garden Warbler
Sylvia borin

One at West Handley from 24th to 26th November was easily the latest ever record.

Waxwing
Bombycilla garrulus

The 2012/13 winter saw another large invasion, with records from most parts of Derbyshire. Flocks of up to 110 were seen in November and 150 in December.

Escaped or Released Species

The *Derbyshire Bird Report* of 1971 was the first issue to contain records of species under this heading, but it was not until 1980 that it became an established feature. An 'Introduction' was included from 1996 which stated that all records of escaped or released species would be welcomed, in order to monitor any population growth and to help establish any pattern of occurrence of potential vagrants.

Up to that time the collection and submission of records for the *Derbyshire Bird Report* was somewhat erratic, and moreover, the strict adjudication which was habitually applied to species in the main Systematic List was not generally applied to those in this category. This meant that some species listed may have been wrongly identified, while misunderstanding about, or changes of, nomenclature has confused recording. The latter problem was partly addressed by the introduction of scientific names, starting in 1991. Where species were not definitely identified, this is indicated in the text.

Considering the large number of potential escapees which must now be in captivity in private collections, wildlife parks, pet shops, falconers' collections, and the like, it is surprising how relatively few have been recorded. A reluctance to report these species, perceived to be unworthy or of little interest, may well account for this.

It is noticeable that the number of species included in the *Derbyshire Bird Report* increased markedly in the 1990s, particularly those of the order Psittaciformes, with new and exotic species being added to the list. This phenomenon perhaps indicates increased interest in keeping caged birds as leisure time increased during this era, together with a greater interest in providing records.

The following list comprises 97 species recorded in this category in Derbyshire up to the end of 2011 and uses the Master IOC List v2.7.3 as utilized by the BOU (Gill & Wright 2006). Where alternative common names are given, this indicates that they have been used on some occasions in the *Derbyshire Bird Report*.

The very small and insignificant number of individual birds only identified at the time by genera (for example White-eye) have not been listed.

There are no known records of species, subsequently admitted to the British List, which were not submitted to the British Birds Rarities Committee because the observer considered that they were escapes.

Helmeted Guinea Fowl
Numida meleagris
Distribution – Africa, resident south of the Sahara with introductions elsewhere.

There have been records from 23 locations since 1973, with 17 birds at Locko Park in 2005, 13 at Stanton Woodhouse in 1987 and Osmaston Park in 2002, ten at Stubbing Court in 2011 and eight at Osmaston Park in 2001. Otherwise five or fewer at various other locations.

California Quail
Callipepla californica
Distribution – South-western United States with introductions elsewhere.

Single birds at Mackworth in 1985, at Church Wilne in 2006 and at Chaddesden in 2011.

Northern Bobwhite
Colinus virginianus
Distribution – Resident United States, Mexico and Cuba with introductions elsewhere.

Some were released in the Hardwick Park area during the 1960s but they are believed to have died out quickly.

Chukar
Alectoris chukar
Distribution – Resident Eurasia with introductions elsewhere.

Two very tame birds at Osmaston Park, and five or six at Combs Moss in 1995 (see also main species account under Red-legged Partridge *Alectoris rufa*).

Silver Pheasant
Lophura nycthemera
Distribution – Resident south-east Asia, south China and Hainan.

Three records, in 1982, 1983 and 1992, all from Osmaston Park.

Reeves's Pheasant
Symaticus reevesii
Distribution – Resident central and eastern China.

These beautiful pheasants were released at Osmaston Park during the 1970s. Most were subsequently shot and the rest 'caught up' for the summer. Records continued to be received from this site in most years until 1999, including a male Reeves's Pheasant x Pheasant in 1980. There are recent records in 2007 and 2008 from Kedleston Park.

Golden Pheasant
Chrysolophus pictus
Distribution – Resident central China.

The male Golden Pheasant is a highly decorative species which is kept in many collections and has been released on several private estates in Derbyshire. It is a difficult species to observe in the wild, its preferred habitat being conifer thickets or extensive rhododendron understorey in deciduous woods. Here it is most easily seen at dawn and dusk.

It has been recorded in 21 recent years at a number of sites but there have never been more than four records in any one year. The vast majority of these have been of single males and of a tameness suggesting recent domesticity. Only one general area around Osmaston has provided records on a regular enough basis to suggest that it is possible that breeding could have taken place. Here a male Golden Pheasant x Pheasant cross was recorded on 4th September 1988.

Other sites where this species has been recorded since 1978 are Bradley, Ednaston, Breaston Nature Reserve, Mickleover, Cubley, Duffield, Long Eaton, Quarndon, Spondon, Staunton Harold Reservoir, Matlock Golf Course, Hoo Moor, the Goyt Valley and Derbyshire Level, Glossop.

Lady Amherst's Pheasant
Chrysolophus amherstiae
Distribution – Resident south-west China and Myanmar with introductions elsewhere.

Like many species of pheasant, Lady Amherst's is commonly kept in private collections and some of these birds escape or are released from time to time. It has established itself as a breeding bird in one or two localities in England but there is no evidence that it has ever done so in Derbyshire. The only records are of a pair and three males at Ednaston on 2nd January 1997, and a male at the Bugsworth Basin on 20th September 1997, which was thought to have been there for one or two years.

It is noteworthy that Ednaston is in the same general area in which there have been a number of records of Golden Pheasant (see above).

Indian Peafowl (Common Peafowl, 'Peacock')
Pavo cristatus
Distribution – Bangladesh, Bhutan, India, Nepal, Pakistan, Sri Lanka.

Single records in most years since 1992, with two birds in 1992 at Holymoorside and in 1993 at Sinfin, with three at Arkwright Town in 2003. In 2006 a pair nested at Scarcliffe, hatching two young; a pair unsuccessfully nested there again in 2007 and in 2008, when one young was raised. There was one remaining bird in 2010.

Black-bellied Whistling Duck
Dendrocygna autumnalis
Distribution – Southernmost United States, Central and South America.

A single record from Carsington Water in 2009.

Swan Goose (Chinese Goose)
Anser cygnoides
Distribution – Inner Mongolia, northernmost China, and south-eastern Russian Federation. It is migratory and winters mainly in central and eastern China.

Birds bred at Osmaston Park between 1982 and 1987. They raised two young in 1982, but failed to raise any young from 23 eggs in 1983, while 17 eggs were laid (outcome unknown) in 1987. Up to 11 birds were present during the 1980s. Records of smaller numbers continued up to 1998, including a sighting of small goslings in 1992. At other sites (Staunton Harold Reservoir, Derby River Gardens, Carsington Water, Dove Valley Lake, Wingerworth Lido, Swarkestone Lake) up to four birds were recorded between 2002 and 2011.

Greylag Goose (Domestic Goose)
Anser anser
Distribution – Wide range through the Old World from Europe to China. It is the ancestor of domestic geese *A.a. domesticus* in Europe and North America. During the twentieth century, feral populations were established across much of England.

Four geese of the Embden type (a large white goose thought to originate in northern Germany) were at Drakelow Nature Reserve in 1990. Four geese of unspecified type were at Hardwick in 1995, and eight at Bakewell in 1996 were again seen in 1997. Records of singles at other sites included Queen's Park, Chatsworth Park, Markeaton Park and Walton Dam.

Bar-headed Goose
Anser indicus
Distribution – Widely distributed as a high-altitude breeder in Asia from Afghanistan to China, wintering mainly in India.

This is one of the more widely reported species (30 sites) with records in (possibly 1968–70), 1971, 1973, 1980–84, 1986, 1987 and 1991–2011. Breeding was noted at Queen's Park, Chesterfield in 1993 when a pair raised five young and they were successful here in most years to the end of the twentieth century.

Snow Goose
Chen caerulescens
Distribution – Breeds on North American Arctic tundra, wintering mainly in United States.

There have been 19 records involving 30 birds between 1967, when a blue-phase bird was seen at Drakelow Nature Reserve, and 2007. Most of the later records are of light-phase birds. Six were seen at Kedleston Park in 2004 when they joined the resident Greylag Geese. Three were at Foremark Reservoir in 1987, and two at Locko Park in 1991; otherwise records were of single birds. Also a further record of one flying over Whitwell with nine Canada Geese in 2011

Ross's Goose
Chen rossii
Distribution – Breeds on central Canadian Arctic tundra, wintering in United States.

Recorded at Drakelow Nature Reserve throughout December 1999 and January to April 2000, then from October 2000 to January 2001. The only other records are of one with Barnacle Geese at Carsington Water on several dates in April and May 2002, and seen at Long Eaton Gravel Pits in 2010 and 2011.

Emperor Goose
Chen canagica
Distribution – Breeds coastal Alaska and north-eastern Siberia, wintering mainly on coasts of Aleutian Islands chain and Gulf of Alaska.

A single record from Willington Gravel Pits in 1998.

Cackling Goose
Branta hutchinsii
Distribution – North America.

Up to three on ten dates in 2006 at Carsington Water and again in 2007, three at Dove Valley Lake in 2006 and up to four in 2007. This species was recorded at ten sites on several occasions in 2008 with up to four present, and at Scropton one was paired with a nominate Canadian Goose *Branta canadensis*. In 2010, two were at Swarkestone Lake and there were records later in the year from Willington Gravel Pits and Sudbury Lake where one was also seen in 2011.

Nene (Hawaiian Goose)
Branta sandvicensis
Distribution – Hawaiian Islands.

Single birds at Staunton Harold Reservoir in 2003 and Drakelow Nature Reserve in 2005.

Red-breasted Goose
Branta ruficollis
Distribution – Breeds in central Arctic Siberia, wintering mainly by the Black Sea.

An adult was noted with a flock of Canada Geese on the River Trent at Ingleby in June 2003 and remained locally until May 2005 when it was last observed at Barrow Gravel Pits.

Black Swan
Cygnus atratus
Distribution – Australia, with introductions elsewhere.

The earliest record was in 1975 and there is now a possible feral population, with records annually since 1995 including 13 sites in 2008. Several records of an adult bird on a nest as if incubating have been made in recent years, though no young have been reported.

Trumpeter Swan
Cygnus buccinator
Distribution – North America.

A single record in 2007 from Willington Gravel Pits.

Whistling Swan
Cygnus columbianus columbianus
Subspecies of Tundra Swan *Cygnus columbianus*
Distribution – Nearctic.

One recorded on three dates in July 2006 from Carsington Water.

Andean Goose
Chloephaga melanoptera
Distribution – High Andes.

Two records, from Poolsbrook Country Park in 2003 and Froggatt in 2004.

South African Shelduck (Cape Shelduck)
Tadorna cana
Distribution – Southern Africa.

The earliest record is from 1977 when a female was observed for ten minutes at Drakelow Nature Reserve in April, and another was seen at Egginton Sewage Farm in August of the same year. In 1995, nine were observed at Middleton Moor in July but only one male remained three days later. Three were present at Aston-on-Trent Gravel Pits in 2001, and a male and two females were at Wyver Lane in 2008 and were seen again at Carsington Water later that year. Two were present at Willington Gravel Pits in 2009. Almost annual records were received from 1996 to 2005 of a pinioned female, which was present initially at Derby River Gardens and later at Alvaston Lake. In 2011, records were received from five sites including two at Carsington Water on two occasions.

Australian Shelduck
Tadorna tadornoides
Distribution – Southern Australia and Tasmania.

A single record in 2002 from Combs Reservoir.

Paradise Shelduck
Tadorna variegata
Distribution – New Zealand.

Single birds were recorded in 1995 and 1996 from Willington Gravel Pits, in 1996 from Drakelow Nature Reserve, and in 1998 from Aston-on-Trent and Barrow Gravel Pits.

Muscovy Duck
Cairina moschata
Distribution – Mexico, Central and South America, with feral populations in North America and Europe.

The first record was from Sutton Scarsdale in 1973 and then there were records almost annually from 1980 from many Derbyshire localities, including ten sites in 2010. In 1982, a feral pair hatched 13 young at Ashbourne Hall Pond. In Bradford Dale in 1997, a female was seen with a brood of five, in 1998 a pair had nine young, and in June 2002, 26 were recorded, including a brood of 15, with broods of eight and seven in the following month. Counts of more than ten were made at Buxton in 2000 (12), 2001 (18), 2004 (10), 2006 (11), 2007 (27), 2008 (25), 2010 (16) and 2011 (19). Hybridization with Mallard was noted in 2005.

Wood Duck (Carolina Duck)
Aix sponsa
Distribution – North America.

This is the most commonly reported species in this category with records in the following years: 'mid-19th century', 1853, 1878, 1974, 1982, and almost annually from 1982 to 2008. In that time it has been reported from 23 sites (compared with 30 for Bar-headed Goose). Three reports in 2011 include two new sites with two at the confluence of the Rivers Trent and Dove. Breeding was reported from Osmaston Park in 1984, 85 and 86: Frost (1987) gave further details of the likely origin of the latter birds.

Maned Duck
Chenonetta jubata
Distribution – Australia.

A bird noted in April 1996 and occasionally to the end of the year, then again in January, May and October in 1997 at Combs Reservoir. The only other record is from Ladybower Reservoir in April 1996.

Ringed Teal
Callonetta leucophrys
Distribution – South America.

A single male was present at Mapperley Reservoir on several dates in 1997, 1998 and 1999.

Cape Teal
Anas capensis
Distribution – Central and southern Africa.

A bird was recorded at Ogston Reservoir on several dates in September and October 1983.

Chiloë Wigeon
Anas sibilatrix
Distribution – Southern South America, the southernmost populations migrating north in winter.

A male was seen at Cromford from October to December 1982 and again in January, March and April 1983. In 1991 a male was noted at Willington Gravel Pits and in 1996 a male and female, neither of which seemed to be fully winged, were seen on the River Derwent in Derby. Other records are from Markeaton Lake in 2008, Ogston Reservoir on six dates in 2009, and Carsington Water on 11 dates in 2009 and in January 2010.

Yellow-billed Duck (South African Yellow-bill)
Anas undulata
Distribution – Southern and eastern Africa.

A single record in 1985 from Drakelow Nature Reserve. In 1999, a bird was seen on several occasions at Willington Gravel Pits in August and September, and in August at Staunton Harold Reservoir.

Cinnamon Teal
Anas cyanoptera
Distribution – Several races in North and South America, with much movement south and north respectively, in winter.

A single record of an eclipse male in 1987 from Middleton Moor.

Chestnut Teal
Anas castanea
Distribution – Australia.

Two records, of a male at Staunton Harold Reservoir in 1993 and a female at Willington Gravel Pits in 1999.

White-cheeked Pintail (Bahama Pintail)
Anas bahamensis
Distribution – Caribbean, South America and Galapagos Islands.

Single birds recorded on ten occasions between 1978 and 2008 from eight sites. The 1997 record from Ogston Reservoir was of a pale-morph form. Two were seen at Willington Gravel Pits in August 1994 and a single bird was seen in 2011 at Trent Lock.

Speckled/Yellow-billed Teal
Anas flavirostris/oxyptera
Distribution – South America.

One was present at Chatsworth in April 1996 and in 1997, and another at Carsington Water in October 2009, with probably the same bird at Derby River Gardens in the following month. In early 2010, two were observed at Carsington Water

Canvasback
Aythya valisineria
Distribution – North America.

One recorded in Buxton Pavilion Gardens in January and April 2009.

Hooded Merganser
Lophodytes cucullatus
Distribution – North America.

A pair on a small pond at Chinley in 2008 reappeared in 2009.

Chilean Flamingo
Phoenicopterus chilensis
Distribution – South America.

A single record in 1991 from Willington Gravel Pits.

Lesser Flamingo
Phoeniconaias minor
Distribution – Africa (largely the Great Rift Valley), India and Pakistan.

A record of three in 1989 from Foremark Reservoir.

African Sacred Ibis (Sacred Ibis)
Threskiornis aethiopicus
Distribution – Africa, Iran and Iraq.

One that roosted at Ashford-in-the-Water in 1974 and fed by the river for several days, and one at Ogston Reservoir in 1999. These were the only records until 2011 when the species was recorded at three sites including two at Chatsworth Park in May.

Great White Pelican (Eastern White Pelican, European White Pelican)
Pelecanus onocrotalus
Distribution – South-eastern Europe, Asia and Africa.

One was seen flying, and later settled in a field, at an unspecified location in the Derwent Valley in 1905.

Harris's Hawk (Harris' Hawk)
Parabuteo unicinctus
Distribution – South-western USA, south to Chile and Argentina.

Records of this species have occurred in all years from 2000 to 2011, many of which are of birds with jesses. In 2000, one was recorded feeding on a Feral Pigeon, and another on ducklings. Long-staying birds were present at British Celanese Lakes Nature Reserve in 2001, Walton Dam in 2002, Carr Vale in 2005, and at Elvaston Castle in 2008 one was observed nest building. In 2009, a bird was seen on seven dates between February and October at Sutton Brook Lakes, and at Elvaston Castle a bird was seen on 16 dates between April 2010 and December 2011.

Red-tailed Hawk
Buteo jamaicensis
Distribution – North America (USA and Canada) to West Indies.

In November 1995, a large *Buteo* at Howden Reservoir was thought to have been of this species but Ferruginous Hawk *Buteo regalis* was not eliminated. Since 1999 there have been seven records, three of which referred to birds with jesses. In 2005, a jessed bird at Willington Gravel Pits was mobbed by three Buzzards, and in 2007 one circled with a Buzzard over Long Eaton Gravel Pits.

Ferruginous Hawk
Buteo regalis
Distribution – North America.

A single record over Ludworth Moor in 1994.

Lanner Falcon (Lanner)
Falco biarmicus
Distribution – Africa, south-eastern Europe and south westernmost Asia.

There have been five records, from Ladybower in 1990, one at Church Wilne with jesses in 1998, and one at Arleston in 2002. In 2007 an immature male, unringed and unapproachable, was present for four days at Barbrook Pools and later in the year probably the same individual was seen at Ogston Reservoir.

Lagger Falcon
Falco jugger
Distribution – Indian subcontinent and nearby countries.

Two records, four weeks apart, from Buxton in the spring of 1999.

Saker Falcon (Saker)
Falco cherrug
Distribution – Central and Eastern Europe, across Asia to Manchuria.

Four records of single birds in the south of the county in 1993, 1994 and 2002, one from Upper Derwentdale in 1989, and one from Ramsley Reservoir in 2001.

Crowned Crane sp. (Black Crowned Crane, Grey Crowned Crane)
Balearica regulorum/pavonina
Distribution – Africa, south of the Sahara.

A single record of two birds flying west over Swarkestone Lake in 1980.

Sarus Crane
Grus antigone
Distribution – Indian subcontinent, south-east Asia and Australia.

A record of a bird present from January to March 1968 (during the foot-and-mouth disease crisis) in the Coton Park–Lullington–Linton area.

Demoiselle Crane
Anthropoides virgo
Distribution – The Black Sea east to Central Asia, wintering in Africa and India.

Three records, including a long-staying bird in the Williamthorpe–North Wingfield area during September and October 1971, and one in the Great Hucklow–Little Hucklow area in September 2007.

Grey-hooded Gull (Grey-headed Gull)
Chroicocephalus cirrocephalus
Distribution – South America and Africa, south of the Sahara.

A single record of a moulting adult at Middleton Moor in July and August 1996.

Hartlaub's Gull
Chroicocephalus hartlaubii
Distribution – South Africa (Atlantic coast) and Namibia.

A single record from Willington Gravel Pits in May 2000.

Barbary Dove (African/Eurasian Collared Dove)
'Streptopelia risoria' (domestic hybrid)
Distribution – Domesticated form of African (*s. roseogrisea*) or Eurasian (*s. decaocto*) Collared Dove.

One at Barlborough in December 1980, one at Ogston Reservoir on several dates in September 1985, one at Sinfin Golf Course during July 1988, one present from December 1988 to May 1989 at Midway, and one in Chesterfield town centre in June 2011.

Diamond Dove
Geopelia cuneata
Distribution – Australia.

A single record from Alvaston in October 2007.

Sulphur-crested Cockatoo
Cacatua galerita
Distribution – Australia, New Guinea.

Two records, from Drakelow in 1985 and Botany Bay in 2002.

White Cockatoo
Cacatua alba
Distribution – Indonesia.

A single record of one flying east over Big Moor in January 1992.

Cockatiel (Australian Cockatiel, Grey Cockatiel)
Nymphicus hollandicus
Distribution – Australia.

Recorded five times between 1974 and 1978, this species was then recorded every year from 1986 to 2011, with six noted in 2003, one of which stayed for a few days at Borrowash. One of the records in 2010 concerned a white bird with orange ear-coverts, at Repton.

Crimson Rosella
Platycercus elegans
Distribution – Eastern and south-eastern Australia.

One present at Littleover during November and December 1981, and January 1982.

Yellow Rosella
Platycercus elegans flaveolus
Distribution – Murray and Murrumbidgee Rivers of Australia.

Two records. One at Arkwright in December 2000, and one, which had escaped from a local aviary, at Bakestone Moor in February 2001.

Eastern Rosella
Platycercus eximius
Distribution – Tasmania and south-eastern Australia.

Four records, from Lea Bridge in 2000, Willington Gravel Pits in 2001 and 2008, and Carr Vale in 2005.

Budgerigar
Melopsittacus undulatus
Distribution – Australia.

There were 47 records in the 34 years from 1978 to 2011, but it was not recorded in eight of these years.

Eclectus Parrot
Eclectus roratus
Distribution – Solomon Islands, Sumba, New Guinea, north-eastern Australia and Maluku Islands.

A single record of a male from Carr Vale in May 2005.

Rosy-faced Lovebird (Peach-faced Lovebird)
Agapornis roseicollis
Distribution – South-western Africa.

A single record from Midway in January 1992.

Grey Parrot (African Grey Parrot)
Psittacus erithacus
Distribution – West and central Africa.

Five records of this species from Wyver Lane in March 1984, Walton Dam in August 1990, Glossop in September 1994, Spondon in June 1996 and Beeley Moor in October 2001.

Senegal Parrot
Poicephalus senegulus
Distribution – West Africa

A single record in May 1991 from Rother Valley Country Park (now in South Yorkshire).

Scarlet Macaw (Red and Yellow Macaw)
Ara macao
Distribution – South-eastern Mexico, south to Amazonian Bolivia, Brazil and Peru.

A single record of a bird feeding on hawthorn berries and apples, and roosting in a local wood at Catton, from September to November 1974.

Blue-crowned Parakeet (Blue-crowned Conure)
Aratinga acuticaudata
Distribution – South America.

A bird seen at both Spondon and Raynesway, Derby in early 2009 was probably the same individual.

Nanday Parakeet
Nandayus nenday
Distribution – South America.

A single record from Willington Gravel Pits in July 2006.

Burrowing Parrot (Patagonian Conure)
Cyanoliseus patagonas
Distribution – Argentina, Chile.

Three birds at Overseal in early September 1998.

Monk Parakeet (Quaker Parakeet)
Myiopsitta monachus
Distribution – Argentina and surrounding countries.

There have been five records of this species, three of which indicated some degree of attempted breeding. In 1975, a pair built a Magpie-type nest high in an oak at Alfreton. At Ashgate in 1975, three were seen regularly at a winter bird table and in 1980 two were thought to be possibly breeding. In Chesterfield in 1988, a pair had their first nest destroyed, but relocated to a nearby Carrion Crow nest and reared two young, with three birds present until the end of the year. It was not recorded again until 2011 when a single bird was seen at Wingerworth.

Snowy Owl
Bubo scandiacus
Distribution – Arctic tundra of Canada, Alaska and Eurasia.

A single record from Newhall in November 2001 of one that had escaped from nearby Stapenhill. A photo of it appeared in the local press.

Eagle Owl (Eurasian Eagle Owl)
Bubo bubo
Distribution – Widespread in Eurasia and Palearctic North Africa.

One, recorded as a 'Great Horned Owl', was shot near Shardlow in 1828 (Whitlock).

From 1992 to 1994 a female held territory in Longdendale where an abandoned nest with four infertile eggs was found in May 1993. It was last sighted at Arnfield Reservoir in March 1994. In 1995 a dead bird was found in Longdendale, but this was not of the Eurasian race, and was a different bird from the previous record. In June 1977 a bird, which had been present feeding on rabbits in Coombs Dale for two weeks, was found dead under a TV mast at Calver Peak. In 2005 a bird was reported at Heanor surviving on squirrels and rabbits for over six weeks in May and June, and a bird was present at Elvaston Castle for four weeks in October and November. Other records of single birds came from Derby (with jesses) in September 1988, Bonsall in June 1992, Mossylea (seen several times) in February 2000, Pye Bridge (taken into care) in August 2005, Chaddesden Park in January 2007, and Ockbrook in May 2007.

Cape Eagle-owl
Bubo capensis
Mackinder's subspecies *B.c. mackinderi* is found in Zimbabwe, western Mozambique and west-central Kenya.

A bird photographed in January 1983 at Howden Reservoir was thought to be of the Mackinder's subspecies *B.c. mackinderi*.

Red-billed Blue Magpie (Red-billed Blue Pie)
Urocissa erythoryncha
Distribution – Western Himalayas, eastward to China and Vietnam.

A single record of a bird seen feeding on carrots (put out for domestic geese) at Overseal in January 1984.

Pied Crow
Corvus albus
Distribution – Africa.

Two records, one of a bird in late May 1999, that could have been present since April, in Bolsover, and one at Heath in May 2001.

Red-Whiskered Bulbul (Red-eared Bulbul)
Pycnonotus jocosus
Distribution – Asia, with introductions elsewhere.

A single record from Willington Gravel Pits in 1998.

Himalayan Bulbul (White-cheeked Bulbul)
Pycnonotus leucogenys
Distribution – Afghanistan, Bhutan, India, Nepal, Pakistan, Tajikistan.

A single bird recorded from Willington from April to August 2004.

White-eared Bulbul
Pycnonotus leucotis
Distribution – Kuwait, Iran, Iraq, Afghanistan, Pakistan, north-western India and the Arabian Peninsula.

A single record from Findern in April 2004.

Red-vented Bulbul
Pycnonotus cafer
Distribution – Southern Asia.

In 1974 one was present in Buxton throughout the year, remaining until May 1975, and was singing in December 1974 and January 1975. Another long-staying bird was at Willington from March to December 1999, with the same or another seen there in March 2001.

Vinous-throated Parrotbill
Sinosuthora webbiana
Distribution – China, Korea, Mongolia, Russia, Taiwan and Vietnam.

A single record from Lea Bridge in December 1999.

Common Myna (Common Mynah)
Acridotheres tristis
Distribution – Asia with widespread introductions elsewhere.

A single record from Brimington in March 2002.

Superb Starling
Lamprotornis superbus
Distribution – East Africa.

One was seen at Barlborough in April 2005. In 2006 a bird seen on the Stockley Trail in August was found dead on the following day in Bolsover.

Sudan Golden Sparrow
Passer luteus
Distribution – Sub-Saharan Africa from Mauritania and northern Senegal, east to Sudan, Ethiopia and the Arabian peninsula.

A single record from Lea Bridge in June 1993.

Village Weaver (Black-headed Weaver)
Ploceus cucullatus
Distribution – West, central and East Africa.

A single record from New Mills in January 1981.

Black-winged Red Bishop (Red-crowned Bishop)
Euplectes hordeaceus
Distribution – Tropical Africa.

A single record in August 2000 from Torside Reservoir.

Southern Red Bishop (Red Bishop)
Euplectes orix
Distribution – Africa, south of the equator.

A single record from Staveley in July 1981.

Orange-cheeked Waxbill
Estrilda melpoda
Distribution – Western and central Africa.

A single record from Drakelow Nature Reserve in July 1980.

Black-rumped Waxbill (Pink-cheeked Waxbill, Red-eared Waxbill)
Estrilda troglodytes
Distribution – Senegal to southwest Eritrea and west Kenya.

A record of two birds from Stockley Brook Sewage Farm (Palterton) in 1989.

Common Waxbill
Estrilda astrild
Distribution – sub-Saharan Africa with introductions elsewhere.

A single record from Carr Vale in June 2001.

Zebra Finch
Taeniopygia guttata
Distribution – Australia, Indonesia and Timor-Leste with introductions elsewhere.

A pair showing courtship behaviour was seen in a Hartshorne garden in March 1996, and another six records of single birds were received between 1985 and 2007.

White-rumped Munia
Lonchura striata
Distribution – At least six races, widely distributed in southern and eastern Asia.

A single record of one in Spondon in 2011

Chestnut Munia (Chestnut Manikin)
Lonchura atricapilla
Distribution – India through to mainland China, South East Asia, the Philippines and Indonesia.

Two records from Breaston Nature Reserve in July 1974 and Ilkeston in August 1994.

Atlantic Canary (Canary)
Serinus canaria
Distribution – Canary Islands, Azores and Madeira.

Only 13 records of this popular cage-bird were received between 1976 and 2010, two of which refer to singing birds in May 1993 at Willington Gravel Pits and in September 2008 at Darley Dale.

Yellow-fronted Canary (Green Singing Finch)
Crithagra mozambica
Distribution – Sub-Saharan Africa.

Two records, from Stonebroom in March 2001 and Codnor in November 2004, and a probable one from the upper Goyt Valley in August 1981.

Rufous-collared Sparrow
Zonotrichia capensis
Distribution – Central and South America.

A single bird noted at Newhall from April to June 2003.

Unacceptable Historic Records

The following species, records of which have been published in earlier literature and for which there are no subsequent records, are on the British List (except Passenger Pigeon *Ectopistes migratorius*), but are now considered unacceptable as Derbyshire records for the reasons stated.

King Eider
Somateria spectabilis

A female was said to have been shot by J.H. Towle on the River Derwent, Draycott in November 1887. It was recorded in the *Zoologist*, 1897, p. 131, but was not accepted by Witherby *et al.* (1938–41).

Griffon Vulture
Gyps fulvus

On 4th June 1927, Dr H.H. Hollick, Miss Kathleen Hollick and E.A. Sadler recorded the sighting of two Griffon Vultures over Ashbourne, while watching for the return of homing pigeons. At the time, this constituted the second British Record and none has occurred since. However, in its 1999 review, the BOU Records Committee stated that the details were considered insufficient to rule out other species of vulture or the possibility of escapes from captivity. The record was accordingly rejected.

Gyrfalcon
Falco rusticolus

What was probably an Iceland Falcon was shot in November 'pre-1789' at Spondon. This bird is described in Whitlock but the notes are inconclusive, as Whitlock rightly decreed.

Capercaillie
Tetrao urogallus

Glover (1829) included this bird in his list without any evidence to justify it.

Passenger Pigeon
Ectopistes migratorius

J.J. Briggs reported one near Melbourne in *The Field* for 10th September 1869. Jourdain placed the record in square brackets, while Whitlock did not mention it.

Tree Swallow
Tachycineta bicolor

One is thought to have been killed near Derby in the summer of 1850. It was recorded by Wolley (1853), who believed that the bird was indeed shot at Derby, while conceding the possibility of error. Accordingly, the national authorities have never been willing to accept this record. The first acceptable British record was of one in Scilly in 1990.

Chough
Pyrrhocorax pyrrhocorax

On the Derbyshire moors (possibly), Whitlock stated that Charles Doncaster recorded an example in his list of birds seen within ten miles of Sheffield.

White's Thrush
Zoothera dauma

The *DAJ* recorded one on 14th September 1935 at Priestcliffe, but there is no mention of it by Witherby *et al.* (1938–41) nor by BOU (1971), and thus it must be regarded as unacceptable.

Red-eyed Vireo
Vireo olivaceus

At Chellaston, two 'Red-eyed Flycatchers' were said to have been caught by a bird-catcher in May 1859 and the male was preserved. Whitlock was happy about the identification but doubted that the birds were genuine vagrants.

Pine Grosbeak
Pinicola enuncleator

Jourdain stated that two specimens in Derby Museum were said to have been obtained locally, but that no further details were available. An unsatisfactory sight record in the Buxton area was mentioned in *The Field* of 4th February 1860 (Jourdain).

Table of Breeding Species in Order of Frequency of Occurrence

Data obtained from the Derbyshire Breeding Bird Survey (1995–99) were used to create the following table, in which the species are arranged to express how widespread each one is in the county. The top of the list in particular would probably be very similar to an equivalent table generated for the overall UK species list, although Red Grouse would be a notable exception. Ten of the known 135 breeding species have been omitted on the grounds of their being very low numbers or likely escapes.

Rank	Species	Tetrads (n = 724)	% of county
1	Wren	697	96.27
2	Chaffinch	695	95.99
3	Blackbird	684	94.48
4	Woodpigeon	683	94.34
4	Blue Tit	683	94.34
6	Robin	675	93.23
7	Carrion Crow	667	92.13
8	Magpie	666	91.99
9	Great Tit	660	91.16
10	Swallow	654	90.33
11	Willow Warbler	641	88.54
12	Pied Wagtail	637	87.98
13	Dunnock	633	87.43
14	Starling	630	87.02
15	Kestrel	617	85.22
16	Skylark	613	84.67
17	Mistle Thrush	603	83.29
18	Goldfinch	586	80.94
19	Song Thrush	579	79.97
20	Greenfinch	572	79.01
21	House Sparrow	571	78.87
22	Linnet	562	77.62
23	Swift	553	76.38
23	House Martin	553	76.38
25	Jackdaw	532	73.48
26	Pheasant	531	73.34
27	Collared Dove	517	71.41
28	Long-tailed Tit	509	70.30
29	Lapwing	504	69.61
30	Mallard	503	69.48
31	Rook	493	68.09
32	Sparrowhawk	487	67.27
32	Blackcap	487	67.27
34	Chiffchaff	485	66.99
35	Moorhen	479	66.16
36	Meadow Pipit	466	64.36
37	Whitethroat	460	63.54
38	Yellowhammer	444	61.33
39	Great Spotted Woodpecker	443	61.19
40	Cuckoo	431	59.53
41	Bullfinch	426	58.84
42	Tawny Owl	423	58.43
43	Coal Tit	401	55.39
44	Stock Dove	400	55.25
45	Little Owl	394	54.42
46	Treecreeper	393	54.28
47	Curlew	356	49.17
48	Garden Warbler	355	49.03
49	Jay	348	48.07
50	Spotted Flycatcher	343	47.38
51	Grey Partridge	339	46.82
52	Grey Wagtail	336	46.41
53	Goldcrest	327	45.17
54	Green Woodpecker	326	45.03
55	Nuthatch	317	43.78
56	Grey Heron	314	43.37
57	Rock Dove	311	42.96
58	Coot	274	37.85
59	Redstart	272	37.57
60	Reed Bunting	271	37.43
61	Red-legged Partridge	252	34.81
62	Lesser Whitethroat	233	32.18
63	Canada Goose	226	31.22
64	Tufted Duck	212	29.28
65	Tree Sparrow	203	28.04
66	Willow Tit	202	27.90
67	Wheatear	196	27.07
68	Kingfisher	194	26.80
69	Little Grebe	192	26.52
70	Yellow Wagtail	185	25.55
71	Tree Pipit	174	24.03
72	Mute Swan	166	22.93
73	Dipper	155	21.41
74	Sand Martin	145	20.03
75	Black-headed Gull	138	19.06
76	Red Grouse	122	16.85
77	Lesser Redpoll	121	16.71
78	Whinchat	113	15.61
79	Buzzard	109	15.06
80	Great Crested Grebe	105	14.50
81	Sedge Warbler	98	13.54
82	Woodcock	84	11.60
83	Common Sandpiper	82	11.33
83	Raven	82	11.33

Rank	Species	Tetrads (n = 724)	% of county
85	Wood Warbler	81	11.19
86	Turtle Dove	78	10.77
87	Marsh Tit	77	10.64
88	Snipe	74	10.22
89	Corn Bunting	72	9.94
90	Ring Ouzel	69	9.53
91	Golden Plover	66	9.12
91	Little Ringed Plover	66	8.84
93	Peregrine	65	8.98
94	Pied Flycatcher	59	8.15
95	Grasshopper Warbler	57	7.87
96	Lesser Spotted Woodpecker	56	7.73
97	Reed Warbler	54	7.46
98	Hobby	50	6.91
99	Goosander	43	5.94
99	Common Tern	43	5.94
99	Siskin	43	5.94
102	Merlin	36	4.97
103	Ruddy Duck	35	4.83
104	Short-eared Owl	34	4.70
105	Barn Owl	33	4.56

Rank	Species	Tetrads (n = 724)	% of county
106	Redshank	31	4.28
107	Twite	30	4.14
108	Long-eared Owl	28	3.87
108	Hawfinch	28	3.87
110	Gadwall	27	3.73
110	Teal	27	3.73
112	Stonechat	26	3.59
113	Mandarin	22	3.04
113	Goshawk	22	3.04
115	Greylag Goose	21	2.90
116	Red-breasted Merganser	19	2.62
116	Crossbill	19	2.62
118	Shelduck	17	2.35
119	Oystercatcher	14	1.93
119	Ringed Plover	14	1.93
121	Cormorant	12	1.66
121	Water Rail	12	1.66
121	Dunlin	12	1.66
124	Nightjar	6	0.83
125	Black Redstart	1	0.14

Gazetteer

Four-figure grid references are given in accordance with the standard Ordnance Survey (OS) system. Almost all of the county falls within 100km square SK, except very small areas in the north and west which are in SE and SJ respectively; therefore all references are SK unless shown otherwise.

There has been a considerable number of boundary changes to the county over many years, but the text of the book is based on the administrative boundary as at 31st December 1999, when the Breeding Bird Survey ended. Some of the following locations are no longer in the county due to the revisions detailed in 'Changes to the County Boundary' above, but have been retained here as the text may refer to them.

The Trent Valley gravel pits referred to in the text (some of which have now been restored to farmland) and for which grid references are shown, were historically known as:

Gravel pit	Grid reference
Willington No. 1	SK291294
Willington No. 2	SK288289
Egginton No. 3	SK275282
Egginton No. 4	SK260294
Hilton No. 5	SK256304
Hilton No. 6	SK250312
Egginton No. 7	SK275274

The more modern gravel pit locations are given in the main list below.

Farms, granges, halls, houses, lodges and manors and minor features (such as bridges) have not been listed, except in some specific cases where they have been mentioned in the text in connection with survey or ringing work.

This is intended to be a comprehensive county gazetteer, but by no means all the locations listed are mentioned in the text.

Derbyshire is covered by the OS with the following maps:
- **Landranger** magenta-coloured cover series at 1:50,000 scale, largely by numbers 110, 119, 120 and 128, but small areas also lie on numbers 109, 118 and 129
- **Explorer** orange-coloured cover series at 1:25,000 scale, by numbers OL1 and OL24 (formerly **Outdoor Leisure** 1 and 24) 245, 259, 260, 269, 270 (formerly No. 8) and 278
- **Street Atlas for Derbyshire** at 1:18,103 (3.5 inches:1 mile) scale.

Location	Grid reference
Aaron Hole Plantation	2466
Abbey Bank	1791
Abbey Hill Floods	3639
Abbey Tip Plantation	1791
Abbot's Chair	0290
Abbotsholme School	1138
Abbott's Rough Plantation	3843
Abney	1980
Abney Clough	2079
Abney Low	2079
Abney Moor	1879
Accession Wood	1540
Acordis Lakes (aka British Celanese Lakes Nature Reserve and Courtaulds Lakes)	3934
Acrelane Bridge	4229
Acresford	3013
Adam's Well	1279
Agnesmeadow Bridge	2147
Ain Moor	3961
Alder Carr	2037/2343
Alder Carrs	1238
Alder Moor Pond	1535
Alder Moor Wood	1435

Location	Grid reference
Aldercar	4447
Alders Wood	3760
Alderwasley	3153
Alderwasley Park	3253
Aldery Cliff	0966
Aldwark	2257
Aleck Low	1759
Alfreton	4155
Alfreton Brook	4056
Alfreton Park	4055
Alicehead	3365
Alkmonton	1838
Alkmonton (medieval village)	1937
Alkmonton Bottoms	1938
All Hooks	4126
Allens Hill	2956
Allenton	3732
Allestree	3439
Allestree Lake	3540
Allstone Lee	0477
Alport	2264
Alport (River)	1292
Alport Castles	1491
Alport Dale	1391

Location	Grid reference
Alport Grain	1590
Alport Height	3051
Alport Low	0994
Alport Moor	1193
Alport Valley Plantation	1291
Alport Village	2264
Alsop-en-le-Dale	1655
Alsop Moor	1556
Alsop Moor Cottages	1656
Alsop Moor Plantation	1657
Alton	3664
Alton Brook	2850
Alvaston	3833
Alvaston Lake	3734
Ambaston	4232
Amber (River)	3462
Amber Hill	3262
Ambergate	3451
Ambervale Quarry	3362
Anchor Church	3327
Ancote Hill	SE0800
Andle Stone	2462
Anthony Hill	0470/2161
Apperknowle	3878

Location	Grid reference
Arbor Low	1663
Arbour Hill	4339
Arbourfield Covert	2533
Archer's Alders	3521
Arkwright Plantation	3068
Arkwright Town	4270
Arleston	3329
Armiston Cottages	4432
Arnfield Clough	0399
Arnfield Covert	0298
Arnfield Flats	SE0200
Arnfield Gutter	0299
Arnfield Low Moor	0198
Arnfield Moor	0299
Arnfield Reservoir	0197
Arrock Plantation	1869
Ash Cottages	2533
Ash Gorse	2633
Ash Plantation	2660/3130
Ashbourne	1746
Ashbourne Airfield	1945
Ashbourne Green	1847
Ashbourne Hall Pond	1846
Ashfield Plantation	4336
Ashford-in-the-Water	1969
Ashford Lake	2069
Ashgate	3671
Ashgate Plantation	3571
Ashop (River)	1489
Ashop Clough	0890
Ashop Head	0690
Ashop Moor	1388
Ashopton Viaduct	1986
Ashover	3463
Ashover Fabric(k)/Rocks	3563
Ashover Hay	3560
Ashover Quarries	3164
Ashton Clough	1689
Ashton Tor	1390
Ashwood Dale	0772
Askew Hill	3127
Aston	1631/1883
Aston Bridge	1631
Aston Hill	4030
Aston Lock	4229
Aston Moor	4230
Aston-on-Trent	4129
Aston-on-Trent Gravel Pits	4329
Astwith	4464
Astwith Dumbles	4464
Atlow	2348
Audernshaw Clough	SE1100
Ault Hucknall	4665
Avenue Coking Plant	3967
Avenue Washlands Nature Reserve	3967
Axe Edge	0369
Axe Edge End	0368
Axe Edge Moor	0270
Back Dale Mine	2372
Back Dale Wood	2373
Back Tor	1484/1990

Location	Grid reference
Back Wood	3269
Backside Wood	1588
Backtor Bridge	1385
Backtor Wood	1485
Bacon's Spring	3962
Badder Green	2133
Bagshaw	0781
Bagshaw Dale	1566
Baine's Wood	3373
Bakestone Delph Clough	0591
Bakestone Moor	5276
Bakewell	2168
Baldfield Covert	2533
Baldwin's Wood	3038
Baley Hill	1454
Balk Wood	3258
Ball Edge	2857
Ballidon	2054
Ballidon Quarry	2055
Ballidonmoor	2155
Baltic Wood	2265
Baltimore Bridge	3630
Bamford	2083
Bamford Edge	2084
Bamford Moor	2185
(The) Bank	2375
Bank Clough	1691
Bank Quarry	2961
Bank Top	1337/2381
Bank Top Hey	1593
Bank Top Plantation	1593
Bank Wood	2372/2566/3076
Bankend	0084
Banks Wood (Park)	0295
Bannell's Plantation	2834
Bar Brook	2672
Barber Booth	1184
Barbrook Bridge	2778
Barbrook Plantation	2774
Barbrook Reservoir (Barbrook Pools since 2003)	2777
Bareholme Moss	SE0601
Bargate	3646
Barker Bank	1484
Barlborough	4777
Barlborough Common	4776
Barley Hill	2850
Barlow	3474
Barlow Common	3375
Barlow Moor	3173
Barmoor	0879
Barmoor Clough	0779
Barren Clough	0281
Barrow Bridge	2528
Barrow Clough	1397
Barrow Gravel Pit	3527
Barrow Hill	4175
Barrow Stones	1396
Barrow upon Trent	3528
Barton Blount	2134
Barton Cottages	2034

Location	Grid reference
Barton Hill Quarries	2462
Bartonpark	1935
Baslow	2572
Baslow Bar	2673
Baslow Edge	2573
Bass's Recreation Ground	3536
Bateman's Tomb	1963
Batham Gate (Roman road)	0876
Beacon Rod	2273
Beaconhill Plantation	2824
Beans and Bacon Mine	2559
Bear Hole Plantation	2935
Beardsley's Plantation	2155
Bee Low	1964
Bee Low Quarry	0979
Bee Low Wood	1865
Bee Nest Mine	2354
Bee Wood	2475
Beech Square Plantation	2467
Beech Wood	2062
Beeley	2667
Beeley Brook	2767
Beeley Moor	2968
Beeley Plantation	2767
Beeley 'Triangle'	2967
Beet Wood	0373
Beggar's Bridge	0965
Beggerswell Wood	3351
Beighton Hill	2951
Beighton Houses	2464
Beightonfields Priory	4576
Belfit Hill	3766
Bellevue	1746
Bellhagg Wood	1589
Bellington Hill	4231
Bellington Wood	4231
Belmont Park	3470
Belper	3547
Belper Bridge	3448
Belper Lane End	3349
Belper River Gardens	3448
Belph	5475
Bendall's Clump	3325
Bennerley Marsh	4743
Bennetston Hall Pond	0879
Bennywall Brook	2649
Bennywall Wood	2649
Ben's Well	3645
(The) Bent	2133/3649
Bent Brook	2133
Bent Dumble	1852
Benthill Wood	3452
Bentley Bridge	3161
Bentley Brook	1646/1738/1850/3161
Bentley Brook Quarries	3161
Bentley's Plantation	4544
Beresford Dale	1259
Berry Clough	0272
Beryl's Gorse	1636
Bessalone Wood	3549
Betty's Pond	3622

Gazetteer

Location	Grid reference
Big Bumper Piece	2866
Big Covert	2552
Big Dungeon	2660
Big Moor	2776
Big Moor Plantation	2178
Big Plantation	2995
Big Rough	3123
Big Wood	3440
Biggin	1559/2648
Biggin Dale	1457
Bilberry Knoll	3057
Bilberry Wood	3452
Binkley Wood	4076
Binns	SE0902
Binns Moss	SE0902
Birch Hill Plantation	4967
Birch Low	2280
Birch Vale	0186
Birch Wood	3155/4038
Birchen Bank Moss	1098
Birchen Edge	2772
Birchen Orchard Clough	0793
Birches Brook	3756
Birchfield Park	1784
Birchill Bank Wood	2371
Birchin Clough	1191
Birchin Clough Bridge	1091
Birchin Hat	1491
Birchin Lee New Piece	1590
Birchin Wood	2382
Birchinlee Moor	1591
Birchinlee Pasture	1591
Birchinlee West Plantation	1691
Birchover	2362
Birchover Quarry	2462
Birchover Wood	2361
Birchwoodpark Quarries	1541
Birdholme	3869
Birdholme Brook	3668
Birdholme Wildfowl Reserve	3868
Birkinshaw Wood	3269
Birkinstyle	4050
Birley Brook	3172
Birley Wood	3272/4082
Birleyhay	3980
Black Ashop Moor	0890
Black Brook	0482/2744/ 3063/3248
Black Car Lumb	3376
Black Clough	1133/1393
Black Dale	0970
Black Edge	0676
Black Edge Plantation	0278
Black Edge Reservoir	0676
Black Hill	SE0704/2764
Black Hill End	SE0701
Black Knowle Plantation	2463
Black Moor	0691
Black Moss	1097
Black Nursery Plantation	2062
Black Piece	3676

Location	Grid reference
Black Plantation	1972/2154/ 4237
Black Pool	2744
Black Rock	2955
Black Rocks	2154
Black Tor	SE0600/2757
Black Wood	2935
Blackbrook	3347
Blackden Brook	1288
Blackden Edge	1288
Blackden Moor	1288
Blackden Rind	1188
Blackden View	1389
Blackleach Brook	2972
Blackley Clough	1588
Blacklow Court (ruins)	1493
Blackshaw Clough	0596
Blackstone Low	2055
Blackwall	2549
Blackwall Plantation	1386
Blackwell	4458
Blackwell Dale	1372
Bladon Castle	2625
Bladon Hill	2624
Bladon Paddocks	2624
Blake Low	2260
Blake Mere	2558
Blake Moor	0596/1563
Blakedon Hollow	2073
Blakedon Lagoon	2074
Blakelow Hill	2559/3360
Blakemoor Plantation	0595/1562
Bleak Knoll	1879
Bleakley Dike	2163
Bleakley Plantation	2162
Bleaklow	1096
Bleaklow Head	0995
Bleaklow Hill	1096
Bleaklow Meadows	1097
Bletch Brook	1853
Blue John Cavern	1383
Bluebank Wood/Pools	3272
Bluster Castle	3173
Boden's Sticks	2436
Bog Plantation	1939
Boggy Brook	3655
Bolderstone Plantation	1761
Bole Hill	0583/1075/ 1867/2177/ 2179/2284/ 2974/3170/ 3374/3665
Bole Hill Quarry	2479
Bolehill	2954/4170
Bolehill Wood	2283
Bolsover	4770
Bolsover Moor	4970
Bolsover Woodhouse	4672
Bolsovermoor Plantation	5071
Bolt Edge	0779
Bondhay Common	5178
Bondhay Dyke	5179
Bondhay Plantation	5078

Location	Grid reference
Bond's Main	4167
Bonds Quarries	2766
Bonsall	2758
Bonsall Dale	2758
Bonsall Hollow	2857
Bonsall Mine	2657
Bonsall Moor	2559
Bonsall Wood	2757
Booth	0587
Boothgate	3749
Booth's Edge	2480
Booth's Wood	3645
Border Bank	3948
Borough Hill	2117
Borough Holme	2016
Borrowash	4234
Bossemore Brook	3740
Bostock Plantation	0592
Botany Bay	2615
Bottle Brook	3644/3946
Bottlebrook Houses	3846
Bottom Covert	3240
Bottom Dumbles	4046
Bottom Moor	3162
(The) Bottoms	1534
Bottoms Reservoir	0296
Boulton	3832
Boulton Moor	3831
Boun's Corner	2246
Bow Wood	3156
Bowbridge Wood	3037
Bower Plantation	4271
Bowling Alley	1436
Bowling Green Wood	2171
Bowmer Rough	3452
Boylestone	1835
Boythorpe	3770
Brackendale Brook	2252
Brackenfield	3758
Bradbourne	2052
Bradbourne Brook	1951
Bradbourne Mill	2052
Bradbury Wood	3667
Bradfield Gate Head	1990
Bradford	2164
Bradford Dale	2063
Bradley	2245
Bradley Brook	2244
Bradley Dam	2245
Bradley Dumble	2151
Bradley Moor	2045
Bradley Wood	1946
Bradshaw Wood	5268
Bradwell	1781
Bradwell Brook	1781
Bradwell Dale	1780
Bradwell Edge	1880
Bradwell Hills	1780
Bradwell Moor	1480
Bradwell Sitch	0898
Brailsford	2541

Location	Grid reference
Brailsford Brook	2338
Brailsford Common	2642
Brailsford Gorse	2442
Bramah Edge	0597
Bramble Brook	3235
Bramley	4079
Bramley Moor	3978
Bramley Plantation	2373
Bramley Vale	4666
Bramley Wood	2373
Bramma Wood	3271
Brampton	3670
Brampton East Moor	2970
Brand End	0568
Brand Side	0468
Brand Top	0468
Brandy Bottle Mine	2074
Brassington	2354
Bray Clough	0591
Breach Gorse	1732
Breadsall	3739
Breadsall Hilltop	3638
Breadsall Moor	3742
Breadsall Priory	3841
Breaston	4535
Breaston Nature Reserve	4733
Breck Edge	0882
Breck Farm	4276
Bretby	2923
Bretby Castle	2923
Bretby Court	2822
Bretby Hall Hospital	3022
Bretby Mill	3023
Bretby Park Ponds	3022
Bretton Brook	1978
Bretton Clough	2078
Bretton Low	1778
Bretton Moor	2078
Bretton Mount	1977
Breward's Carr	3044
Briars Well	2757
Brick-kiln Covert	3041
Brickyard Plantation	4130
Brickyard Wood	3037
Bridge End	2572
Bridgefield	0293
Bridgehill	3348
Bridgeholm Green	0581
Bridle Road Wood	3780
Brier Low	0868
Brierley Wood	3675
Brierlow Bar	0869
Brierlow Dale	0970
Brightgate	2659
Brimington	4073
Brimington Common	4072
Brinsley Flashes	4450
British Celanese Lakes Nature Reserve (aka Acordis Lakes and Courtaulds Lakes)	3934
Britland Edge Hill	1002
Britton Wood	3764

Location	Grid reference
Broad Low	1778
Broadbottom	SE9993
Broadhey Hill	SJ9983
Broadholm	3449
Broadhurst Edge	SJ9987
Broadhurstedge Plantation	SJ9987
Broadlee-Bank Tor	1185
Broadmeadow Wood	3275
Broadoak Hill	4664
Brock Hill	4073
Brockhurst	3364
Brocksford Bridge	1233
Brocksford Brook	1233
Brocksford Cottages	1333
Brocksford Gorse	1332
Brockwell	3771
Bromehead Wood	4080
Brook Bottom	1477/SJ9886
Brook Wood	2279
Brookfield Manor	2382
Brookside	3470
Broom Park	3343
Broombank Plantation	3475
Broomfield Hall	3840
Broomfield Wood	3681
Broomfield's Plantation	4289
Broomhill Cottages	1333
Broomhill Plantation	2470
Broomridding Wood	4264
Broomy Wood	3763
Brough	1782
Broughton Brook	1532
Brow Wood	3657
Brown Cross Plantation	2934
Brown Edge	0575
Brown Edge Plantation	0574
Brown Knoll	0885
Brownhouse Wood	2950
Brown's Brook	1841
Brun Wood	3037
Brundcliffe	1661
Bruns Wood	2456
(The) Brushes	3775
Brushfield	1571
Bryan's Coppice	3619
Bubnell	2472
Bubnell Cliff	2471
Buck Stone	2384
Bucka Hill	2877
Buckford Bridge	3129
Buckland Hollow	3751
Buckwheat Plantation	2921
Bugsworth (latterly Buxworth)	0282
Bull Hill	2046
Bull Stones	1796
Bull Tor	1472/1773
Bullbridge	3552
Bullbridge Hill	3552
Bullhay Dale	1070
Bullhurst	2943
Bullock Storth	3881

Location	Grid reference
Bullock Wood	4053
Bumper Castle	2865
Bunker's Hill	3441
Bunker's Hill Wood	2769
Bunker's Wood	3133
Bunsal Cob	0175
Bunster Hill	1451
Bunting Wood	3154
Burbage Edge	0273
(The) Buries	2927
Burland-green Plantation	3043
Burley Brook	3440
Burley Hill	3541
Burley Wood	3341
Burnaston	2832
Burnaston Airfield	2930
Burnhill Wood	5176
Burnt Heath	2075
Burnt Hill	0490
Burnt Piece	2964
Burntheath	2431
Burntwood Quarry	2666
Burnwood	4239
Burrfields	0580
Burrs Wood Nature Reserve	3075
Burton Ashes Wood	2267
Burton Bole End	1980
Burton Moor	2067
Bushey Wood	1863
Busks Wood	3175
Buston Wood	2570
Butcherlawn	4878
Butcherlawn Pond	4878
Butcher's Wood	5275
Butterley	4051
Butterley Hill	3459
Butterley Moss	SE0801
Butterley Park	4151
Butterley Reservoir	4052
Butterley Top	3460
Buxton	0573
Buxton Bridge	0975
Buxton Quarry	0869
Buxworth (formerly Bugsworth)	0282
Cabin Clough	0793
Cackle Hill	1543
Cadborough Hill	2914
Cadley	2719
Cadley Hill	2719
Cadley Hill Colliery	2719
Calder Well	2742
Ca(u)ldwell	2517
Ca(u)ldwell Covert	2516
Ca(u)ldwell Hall Pond	2517
Cales Dale	1764
Calfhay Wood	0176/1589/1691
California	3335
Calke	3722
Calke Abbey	3622
Calke Park	3622
Calling Low	1764

Gazetteer

Location	Grid reference
Callow	2652
Callow Bank	2582
Callow Moor	2651
Callow Wood	2280
Calow	4070
Calow Brook	4069
Calow Green	4169
Calton Hill	1171
Calton Houses	2468
Calton Lees	2568
Calton Pastures	2468
Calton Plantations	2561
Calver	2474
Calver Low	2374
Calver Peak	2374
Calver Sough	2474
Cambridge Wood	2561
Camp Green	2381
Camp Hill	1878/5173
Cannon Hill	3340
Car Plantation	4764/4978
Car Wood	4766
Carder Low	1262
Carhead Rocks	2482
Carnfield Wood	4355
(The) Carr	2645
Carr Brook	3560/3659/3742/3925
Carr Hill	3957
Carr Plantation	3865
Carr Vale Nature Reserve	4669
Carr Wood	1940/2038/2640/3659/4051
Carrs Wood	2262
Carsington	2553
Carsington Pasture	2454
Carsington Water	2451
Carterhall Wood	3881
Cartledge	3277
Carver's Rocks Nature Reserve	3322
Caskin Low	1461
Castle Gresley	2718
Castle Hill	2268/3177/3854/4335/4279/5078
Castle Knob	2717
Castle Naze	0578
Castle Plantation	4350
Castle Wood	2725
Castlehill	4350
Castlehill Woods	0295
Castles Wood	1391
Castleton	1582
Cat Clough	SE1201
Cat Hole Hill	3268
Cathole	3267
Cathole Coppice	3368
Cathole Wood	2752
Cattis-side Moor	2483
Catton Hill	2015
Catton Park	2014
Catton Wood	2014
Caulkley Wood	3121
Cave Dale	1482
Cavendish Mill	2075
Cedarwood Houses	2813
Chaddesden	3737
Chaddesden Brook	3836
Chaddesden Cemetery	3736
Chaddesden Common	3839
Chaddesden Park	3836
Chaddesden Sidings Gravel Pits	3735
Chaddesden Wood	3839
Champion Carr	3143
Chanderhill	3370
Chaneyfield Wood	3172
Chapel-en-le-Frith	0680
Chapel Hill	3253/4461
Chapel Milton	0581
Chapel Plantation	1692/1958
Chapelwheel Dam	4479
Charlestown	0392
Charlesworth	0092
Chatsworth House	2670
Chatsworth Park	2570
Chee Dale	1172
Cheeks Hill	0269
Chellaston	3730
Chellaston Covert	3830
Chellaston East Junction	3828
Chellaston Hill	3829
Chellaston Junction	3729
Chelmorton	1169
Chelmorton Flat	1071
Chelmorton Low	1170
Cherry Holme	2015
Cherrytree Hill	3836
Chertpit Plantation	1872
Chester Green	3537
Chesterfield	3871
Chesterfield Canal start	3871
leaves county	4682
Chestnut Park	3924
Chevin	3445
Chevin Mount	3346
Chevinend	3445
Chevinside	3446
Chew	SJ9992
Chinley	0482
Chinley Churn	0383
Chinley Head	0484
Chisworth	SJ9992
Choughriddins	1951
Chrome Hill	0767
Chunal	0391
Chunal Moor	0490
Chunal Plantation	0390
Church Broughton	2033
Church Gresley	2918
Church Hill	4064/4458
Church Spinney	3226
Church Town	4680
Church Wilne	4431
Church Wilne Gravel Pits	4532
Church Wilne Reservoir	4632
Churchbalk	2436
Churchtown	2663
Churn Hole	1071
Cinderhill	3746
Cinderhill Coppice	4344
Cistern's Clough	0369
Clarke's Plantation	2963
Clattercotes Wood	3560
Clay Cross	3936
Clay Cross Lagoon	3964
Clay Mills Gravel Pits	2726
Claypit Hill	2132
Claypit Plantation	3523
Clayton Upper Wood	3568
Clemonseats Plantation	1265
(The) Cliff	2275
Cliff Hill Plantation	4026
Cliff Quarry	3455
Cliff Wood	2282
Cliffe Bank	3742
Clifton	1644
Clifton Row	2712
Clod Hall Lane	2972
Clough Edge	0697
Clough Head	0596
Clough Wood	2561
Cloves Wood	3942
Clowne	4976
Clowne Common	4775
Coal Aston	3679
Coalburn Hill	3753
Coalpit Hill	0190
Coalpit Wood	3568/3680
Coalpithole Mines	0981
Cobblersnook Plantation	1957
Cobnor Wood	3575
Cock Alley	4170
Cock Hill	0596
Cockhay	2926
Cockhill Plantation	3358
Cocking Tor	3461
Cockpit Hill	3536
Cock's Head Wood	2863
Cocks-hut-hill	3142
Cockshutt Wood	3077
Cockyard	0479
Coddington	3354
Codnor	4249
Codnor Breach	4147
Codnor Castle	4349
Codnor Gate	4150
Codnor Park Reservoir	4351
Colborne Moor	0983
Cold Eaton	1456
Cold Side	1284
Coldeaton Bridge	1456
Coldharbour Moor	0793
Coldspring Plantation	0474

Location	Grid reference
Coldwall Bridge	1449
Coldwell Clough	0585
Coldwell Plantation	4378
Colehill Quarry	2854
Combs	0478
Combs Edge	0578
Combs Moss	0576
Combs Reservoir	0379
(The) Common	3341
Common Plantation	3029/3122
Common Side	4346
Commonside	3375
Compton	2039
Coney Green	4063
Congreave	2465
Conies Dale	1280
Conksbury	2065
Conksbury Bridge	2165
Constitution Hill	4436
Conygree Wood	1932
Cook Wood	2367
Coombes	0191
Coombes Edge	0191
Coombes Tor	0191
Coombs Dale	2274
Cop Well	1279
Coplow Dale	1678
Coppershill Spinney	2217
(The) Coppice	3823
Coppice Plantation	2139
Coppice Wood	3449
Coppy Hill	3525
Copse Hill	1942
Copy Wood	2665/3172
Corbar Hill	0474
Corbar Wood	0574
Corbriggs	4168
Cordwell Valley	3176
Coronation Plantation	4032
Corporation Wood	3566
Cotespark	4254
Cotmanhay	4643
Cotmanhay Wood	4644
Coton-in-the-Elms	2415
Coton Park	2717
Coumbs Wood	3156
Countess Cliff	0570
Courtaulds Lakes (aka Acordis Lakes and British Celanese Lakes Nature Reserve)	3934
Cow Dale	0872
Cow Hey	1693
Cow Low	0678/0972
Cow-ways	3247
Cowberry Tor	1190
Cowburn Tunnel	0883
Cowdale	0872
Cowden Plantation	1969
Cowers Lane	3046
Cowhill	3546
Cowley	3377
Cowley Bar	3277

Location	Grid reference
Cowley Knoll	2561
Cowlishaw Wood	3865
Cowms Moor	1290
Cowms Rocks	1290
Cown Edge	0191
Cowper Stone	2583
Coxbench	3743
Crabtree Wood	4878
Cracken Edge	0383
Cracken Edge Quarry	0383
Cracknowl Wood	2070
Crake Low	1753
Cranfleet Cut	4931
Cratcliffe Tor	2262
Cressbrook	1772
Cressbrook Dale	1774
Creswell	5274
Creswell Colliery	5273
Creswell Crags	5374
Crewe's Pond	3027
Crewton	3733
Crich	3454
Crich Carr	3354
Crich Chase	3452
Crich Chase Woods	3452
Crich Common	3553
Cromford	2956
Cromford Canal	3155
Cromford Hill	2856
Cromford Mill Pond	2956
Cromford Moor	3055
Cronkston Low	1166
Crook Hill	1886
Crookdale Plantation	1663
Crooked Clough	0893
Crookstone Hill	1488
Crookstone Knoll	1488
Crookstone Out Moor	1488
Cropper	2335
Cross Carr	1534
Cross Hill	4148
Cross Lanes	3358
Cross o' the Hands	2846
Cross Wood	4665
Crossdale Head Mine	1873
Crossgreen	2761
Crow Chin	2285
Crow Wood	4138/4348
Crowdecote	1065
Crowden	0799
Crowden Brook	0799/1086
Crowden Great Brook	SE0601
Crowden Head	0988
Crowden Little Brook	SE0701
Crowden Little Moor	SE0701
Crowden Meadows	SE0702
Crowhole	3374
Crowhole Reservoir	3174
Cubley Brook	1637
Cubley Common	1639
Cubley Covert	1539

Location	Grid reference
Cuckoo Tors	0574
Cuckoostone Dale	3062
Cuckoostone Quarry	3162
Culland Wood	3654
Cunnery Pond	2836
Cunning Dale	0872
Cupola Ponds (aka Stanedge Ponds)	3366
Curbar	2574
Curbar Edge	2575
Cutler Brook	2941
Cutthorpe	3473
Cutthorpe Common	3475
Cutthorpe Common End	3573
Cutthroat Bridge	2187
Dalbury	2634
Dalbury Hollow	2634
Dale	4338
Dale Abbey	4338
Dale Bottom	2481
Dale Bridge	3856
Dale Brook	1732/2275/2624
Dale End	2161
Dale Hill	4338
Dale Moor	4438
Dale Side	2275
Dalebank	3661
Dalebrook	1732
Dalehead	0984
Dam Brook	3739
Dam Cliff	1278
Dam Dale	1178
Damstead Wood	4054
Dane (River)	0270
Dane Head	0270
Danesmoor	4063
Daniel Hayes farm	3518
Danish Barrow Cemetery	3325
Darfield Plantation	1851
Dark Plantation	3622
Darley Abbey	3438
Darley Abbey Park	3538
Darley Bridge	2661
Darley Dale	2663
Darley Hillside	2763
Darley Moor	1641
Darley Park	3538
Darlton Quarry	2175
Dayfield Brook	2247
Deadman's Clough	1879
Dean Hill	1389
Dean Hollow	2856
(The) Decoy	1532
Deep Clough	0172/0176
Deep Dale	0971
Deep Dale Bridge	3429
Deep Grain	1295
Deep Rake	2273
Deepdale	1669
Deer Holes	1596
Deer Knowl	0998

Gazetteer

Location	Grid reference
Deer's Cote Spinney	3622
(The) Delph	2276
Denby	3946
Denby Bottles	3846
Denby Common	4147
Dennis Knoll	2284
Derby	3536
Derby Canal start end	4835 3729
Derby Junction	3636
Derby Locomotive Works	3635
Derby Racecourse	3637
Derby River Gardens	3536
Derby Sewage Farm/ Incinerator	3834
Derbyshire Bridge	0171
Derbyshire Level	0493
Derbyshire Oaks Quarry	3360
Derventio (Roman fort)	3537
Derwent	1888
Derwent (River) source confluence with Trent confluence with Wye confluence with Noe	 1296 4530 2565 2082
Derwent Edge	1989
Derwent Moors	2088
Derwent Mouth	4530
Derwent Reservoir	1790
Derwentdale	1790 to 1696
Dethick	3258
Dethick Common	3359
Devil's Elbow	2434
Dewhill Naze	SE1101
Diamond Hill	0570
Didsbury Intake	0498
Dimminsdale	3721
Dimons Dale	2955
Dimple	2966
Dimpus Clough	0685
Dinas Sitch Tor	1190
Dingle Bank	4070
Dinting Vale	0194
(The) Dipping Stone	SJ9981
Dirtlow Plantation	1869
Dirtlow Rake	1481
Ditch Cliff	2167
Ditch Clough	1492
Ditch Clough Plantation	1592
Dixon's Lock	4274
Dizzybeard Plantation	2434
Dobb Edge	2671
Dobb's Hill Plantation	3842
Dobmeadow Wood	3275
Doctor's Gate (Roman road)	0893
Doe Hill	4159
Doe Hill Lake	4259
Doe Lea	4666
Doe Lea (River)	4569
Doe Lea Bridge	4569
Doehole	3558
Dog Kennel Pond	2835
Dog-kennel Wood	2272

Location	Grid reference
Dog Rock	0795
Doles Brook	3130
Donkhill Plantation	2114
Doswood	3065
Dove (River) source confluence with Trent	 0368 2726
Dove Bridge	1034/2328
Dove Cote Hill	3324
Dove Dale	1452
Dove Head	0468
Dove Holes	0778/1453
Dove Holes Quarry	0977
Dove Valley Lakes	2031
Dovebank	1631
Doveholes Dale	0877
Doveridge	1134
Doves Wood	2952
Dovestone Clough	1989
Dovestone Tor	1989
Dowel Cave	0767
Dowel Dale	0767
Dowlow Works	1067
Dowstone Clough	0795
Dowstone Rocks	0998
Drabber Tor	1357
Drakelow Nature Reserve (Drakelow Wildfowl Reserve until 2007)	2220
Drakelow Power Station	2319
Draycott	4433
Draycott Hospital	4634
Draycott Plantation	3043
Dronfield	3578
Dronfield Woodhouse	3378
Druids Stone	1387
Drum Hill	3742
Dry Clough	1494
Drysike Clough	SE0901
Duckmanton	4170/4472
Duckmanton Moor	4370
Duckpit Plantation	2733
Ducksick Wood	3472
Dud Wood	2261
Duffield	3443
Duffield Bank	3542
Duffield Meadows	3343
Duke's Quarries	3354
Dukesbank Plantation	2370
(The) Dumble	1848/3644
Dumble Wood	3272
(The) Dumps	2117
Dunge Brook	2180
Dunge Clough	1289
Dunge Wood	2180/3550
Dungeon Plantation	2362
Dunsa	2470
Dunshill	4238
Dunsley Springs	2656
Dunster's Plantation	2934
Dunston	3673
Dunston Brook	3375

Location	Grid reference
Durham Edge	1879
Duric Well	2078
Dutton's Quarry	3362
Eagle Stone	2673
Eagle Tor	2362
Eaglestone Flat	2674
Earl Sterndale	0967
East Deer Park	2143
East Moor	2970
Eaton Dale	1755
Eaton Dovedale Farm	1037
Eaton Wood	1136
Eatondale Wood	1655
Eatonpark Wood	3642
Eccles Pike	0381
Ecclesbourne	3145
Ecclesbourne Valley	3244
Eckington	4279
Eckington Marsh	4178
Eckington Park	4180
Edale	1285
Edale End	1686
Edale Head	0886
Edale Moor	0987
Eddlestow Lot	3263
Edensor	2569
(The) Edge	0889
Edge Moor	3555
Edge Plantation	0595
Edlaston Airfield	1742
Ednaston	2341
Egginton	2628
Egginton Airfield	2629
Egginton Bridge	2627
Egginton Brook	2727
Egginton Common	2729
Egginton Junction	2529
Egginton Sewage Farm (latterly known as Etwall Farm)	2824
Egstow	3963
Eldon Hill	1181
Eldon Hole	1180
Elliott's Spring	3647
Elmton	5073
Elton	2260
Elton Common	2159
Elvaston Avenue	4132
Elvaston Castle Country Park	4032
Elvaston Castle Lake	4033
Elvaston Quarry	4531
Emmett Carr	4577
Emmett Field Wood	3668
Emperor Lake	2670
Emperor Stream	2771
End Low	1560
End Moor	1365
Endcliff Wood	2168
Endcliffe Quarry	2563
Ends Bridge	2445
Erewash (River) enters county confluence with Trent	 4453 5133

Location	Grid reference
Erewash Canal start	4645
end	4931
Erewash Meadows Nature Reserve	4449
Errwood Reservoir	0175
Etherow (River)	1299
Etherow Valley	0095
Etwall	2631
Etwall Brook	2631
Etwall Common	2730
Etwall Farm (formerly Egginton Sewage Farm)	2824
Exhibition Plantation	4250
Eyam	2276
Eyam Dale	2175
Eyam Edge	2077
Eyam Moor	2278
Fagney Clough	1492
Fagney Plantation	1492
Fair Brook	1089
Fair Vage Clough	0898
Fairbrook Naze	0989
Fairfield Common	0774
Fairfield Low	0773
Fairholmes	1789
Fairvage Clough	0591
Fall Hill	3562
Fallange Edge	2867
Fallgate	3562
Fallinge Edge	2765
Fancy Dam	2863
Far Back Clough	1298
Far Broadslate	SE0503
Far Carr	2443
Far Cown Edge	0190
Far Deep Clough	1890
Far End	2672
Far Fork Grain	1095
Far Laund	3648
Far Moss	0996
Far Small Clough	1399
Farhill	3563
Farley	2962
Farley Moor	3063
Farlow Paddocks	2471
Farnah Green	3347
Fauld	1829
Fawnsdale Plantation	2266
Featherbed Moss	SE0400/0370/ 0792/0992
Featherbed Top	0992
Fenny Bentley	1750
Fern Dale	1565
Fernilee	0178
Fernilee Reservoir	0177
Ferny Bottom	1458
Ferny Hole	0795
Ferny Side	1291
Fernydale	0967
Ferriby Brook	3939
Fiddle Clough	1585
Fiddler's Folly	2542

Location	Grid reference
Fin Wood	1771
Findern	3030
Findern Lake (aka Willington Lake Trout Fishery)	3029
Finny Plantation	2139
Firbeck Common	5378
Firestone Hill	3346
Fishpond Pit	2036
Fishpond Plantation	1455/2552
Fishpond Wood	2061/3165
Five Wells	1271
Flag Dale	1173
Flagg	1368
Flagg Moor	1367
Flagshaw Brook	2938
Flamstead Plantation	4045
Flash Dam	3064
Flash Lane	2965
Flask Edge	2878
Flat Covert	1641
Flat Wood	3154
Flax Dale	1963
Flaxholme	3442
Fletcherhill	3761
Flint Clough	0575
(The) Flourish	4238
(The) Folly	1682
Folly Well	2952
Foolow	1976
Forbes Hole	4932
Ford	4080
Foremark Reservoir	3323
Forrest's Plantation	4976
Foston	1831
Foston Brook	1832
Foston Detention Centre	1831
Foufinside	1854
Four Acre Plantation	1341
Four Winds	2921
Fourlane Ends	3855
Fox Covert	2417/2829/ 3929/4767/ 4772
Fox Green	5273
Fox Hill	4969
Fox Hole	1833
Fox Hole Wood	3525
Fox Low	0671
Foxfield Plantation	2736
Foxhole Hollow	0172
Foxhole Plantation	4350
Foxlane Plantation	2975
Foxlow Edge	0075
Foxlowe Plantation	4375
Fox's Piece	1592
Foxstone Dam	4277
Foxstone Wood	4277
Franker Brook	3047
Freebirch	3073
Friar Gate Nature Reserve	3436
Friar's Ridge	2583
Friden	1760

Location	Grid reference
Friden Brickworks	1760
Fritchley	3552
(The) Frith	0569
Frith Hall Wood	3371
Frith Wood	3678/5172
Froggatt	2576
Froggatt Bridge	2475
Froggatt Edge	2576
Frost Covert	3041
Fulam's Wood	3037
Furnace Hillock	4069
Furness Quarry	2076
Furness Vale	0083
Gallow Inn	4740
Gamesley	0194
Gannow Hill	4681
Garden Plantation	4878
Gardom's Edge	2773
Gaskin's Carr	2344
Gateside Clough	1189
Gathering Hill	0894
Gentshill	4062
Giant's Hole	1182
Gib Hill	1563
Gibbet Moor	2870
Gibbet Wood	2771/2950
Gibhill Plantation	1563
(The) Gilkin	2953
Gillfield Wood	3078
Gilwiskaw Brook	3518
Gladwin's Mark	3066
Gladwin's Mark Wood	3066
Gladwin's Wood	3368
Glapwell	4766
Glasshouse Common	3976
Glead Hill	0791
Glethering Clough	1293
Glossop	0394
Glossop Low	0696
Glossop Lowe Quarries	0596
Glover Bank	2081
Glutton Bridge	0866
Gnat Hole	0392
Goatscliffe	2477
Goatscliffe Brook	2377
Goddard's Quarry	2275
Godfreyhole	2753
(The) Goit	4569
Golden Brook	4534
Golden Valley	3844/4251
Goodwin's Lumb	3346
Goodwin's Wood	3061
Goose Green	3959
Goosehill Bridge	1482
Gores Heights	1690
Gores Plantation	1690
(The) Gorse	2922
Gorse Covert	1533/1538/ 1642/3929
Gorseley Estate	3219
Gorsey Covert	3522
Gorsey Leys	3015/3525

Gazetteer

Location	Grid reference
Goseley Dale	3220
Gosforth Valley	3478
Gotham	1858
Gotham Plantation	1858
Gotherage Plantation	2178
Goyt (River)	0178
Goyt Forest	9977
Goyt Valley	0176
Goyt's Clough	0173
Goyt's Clough Quarry	0173
Goyt's Moss	0173
Grains in the Water	1094
Grains Moss	SE0603
Granby Wood	2579
Grange Hill	3173
Grange Mill Quarry	2457
Grange Wood	2714/3074
Grangemill	2457
Grangewood	2614
Grasscroft Wood	3476/3876
Grassmoor	4066
Gratton Dale	2060
Gratton Moor	1960
Grave Wood	5071
Gravelpit Covert	1643
Gravelpit Hill	3222
Gravelpit Plantation	2729
Graves Wood	3651
Great Brind Wood	3276
Great Cubley	1638
Great Hucklow	1777
Great Intake	SE1101
Great Longstone	2071
Great Low	1068
Great Pond (Hardwick)	4563
(The) Great Pond of Stubbing	3667
Great Rocks Dale	1073
Great Rocks Lees	1075
Great Shacklow Wood	1669
Great Top	2084
Great Wilne	4430
Great Wood	1688
Greatrake Mine	2453
Greave's Wood	2041
Greaves's Piece	2977
Green Clough	1592
Green Dale	1679
Green Fairfield	0873
Green Hill	SE0604
Green Low	2357
Green Plantation	2828
Greenhill Lane	4252
Greenhillocks	4049
Greenlowfield	1555
Greenrake Plantation	1557
Greenseats Plantation	1763
Greenside	3979
Greensides Farm	0668
Greenwich	4050
Greenwood	3567
Gregory Dam	3255

Location	Grid reference
Gresley Common	3018
Grey Tor	2360
Greystone Edge Quarries	SE1200
Greystone Slack	SE0702
Griff Wood	4665
Griffe Grange Valley	2556
Grimbocar Wood	1788
Grin Low	0571
Grin Plantation	0572
Grin Quarry	0472
Grinah Grain	1395
Grinah Stones	1396
Grindleford	2578
Grindlegrain Tor	1292
Grindlow	1877
Grindsbrook Clough	1187
Grinlow Tower	0571
Groaning Tor	2857
(The) Grove	3326
Grove Plantation	1633
Grove Wood	2319
Gun Hill	2544
Gun Hills	3144
Gunby Hill/Lea	2814
Gypsy Brook	3844
Haddon Fields	2265
Haddon Grove	1766
Haddon Hall	2366
Haddon Park	2366
Haddon Plantation	2265
Hadfield	0296
Hadfield Fold	0081
Hady	3970
Hady Wood	3971
Hag Wood	3175
Hagg Hill	4066/4163
Hagg Wood	3270
Haggside	1788
Haggtor Coppice	1688
Haggwater Bridge	1688
(The) Hague	0094
Hague Bar	SJ9885
Hague Bridge	SJ9885
Hales Green	1741
Halfmoon Plantation	4377/4878
Halfmoon Pond	4656
Hall Dale	2863
Hall Dale Quarry	2859
Hall Wood	2552/2818
Hallam Fields	4739
Hallcroft Pond	2331
Halldale Brook	2863
Halldale Wood	2864
Hallmoor Wood	2763
Hallowes	3677
Hall's Plantation	4056
(The) Halsteads	1882
Hammersmith	3951
Hammerton Hill	1573
Hamston Hill	1550
Hancock Plantation	1790

Location	Grid reference
Hancock Wood	1790
Hand Dale	1460
Handley	3761
Handley Bottom	2369
Handley Moor/Wood	3248
Hanger Wood	3777
Hanging Banks	3866
Hanging Bridge	1545
Hanging Rock	0276
Hangingbridge	1645
Hangman's Stone	3425
Harborough Rocks	2455
Hard Rake Plantation	1669
Harden Clough	1284
Hardstoft	4362
Hardstoft Common	4363
Hardwick	3364/4563
Hardwick Hall	4663
Hardwick Park	4664
Hardwick Wood	3766
Hare Edge	3072
Hare Park	2571
Harehill	1735
Harehill Plantation	3567
Harehill Wood	4463
Harepark	1232
Harepit Hill	3040
Harewood Moor	3067
Hargate Hill	0193
Hargatewall	1175
Harland Edge	2868
Harland Sick	2968
Harlesthorpe Dam	4976
Harp Edge	2957
Harper Hill	3567
Harper Lees	2380
Harpur Hill	0671
Harrington Bridge	4731
Harrop Moss	0796
Harry Hut	0490
Harry Moor	0686
Harthill Moor	2262
Hartington	1260
Hartington Dale	1360
Hartle Dale	1680
Hartshorn Bog	3222
Hartshorne	3220
Hartshorne Heath	3419
Hasland	3969
Hasland Green	3969
Hassop	2272
Hassop Common	2273
Hassop Park	2171
Hatch-a-way	0867
Hathersage	2381
Hathersage Booths	2380
Hathersage Sewage Farm	2380
Hatton	2129
Hatton Fields	2232
Havenhill Dale Brook	2152
Haverhill Dale	2153

Location	Grid reference
Hawke Brook	4773
Hawkenedge Well	2575
Hawkhurst Edge	SJ9981
Hawks Low	1756
Hawthorn Clough	SE1200
Hay Dale	1177
Hay Top	1772
Hay Wood	2577/3141
'Hayes' Conference Centre	4052
Hayes Wood	4041/3420
Hayfield	0386
Haytop	3353
Hazelbrow	3344
Hazelwood	3245
Heage	3750
Heage Firs	3550
Heanor	4346
Heanor Gate	4246
Hearnstone Lane Head	1278
Heath	4466
Heath Wood	2132/3425
Heathcote	1460
Heathcote Mere	1460
Heathend Plantation	3621
Heathfield Nook	0770
Heathtop	2032
Heathy Lea Brook	2722
Heights of Abraham	2958
Hell Bank Plantation	2868
Hell Brook	3232
Hell Meadow	3231
Hemming Green	3271
Henmoor	3747/3863
Henmore Brook	1645
Henson's Coppice	3421
Hepworth Lane	4065
Hermitage Pond	2271
Hern Clough	0994
Herod Clough	0292
Hewett's Bank	2976
Hey Edge	SE0800
Hey Moss	SE0701
Hey Ridge	1390
Heyden Brook/Head	SE0902
Hicken's Bridge	4229
Hickin Wood	5076
Hidebank	0085
Higgenholes	2169
High Bramley Wood	4178
High Bridge	2727
High Cross Bank	2817
High Dale	1571
High Edge	0668
High Field	1672
High Fields	2174
High Lee	SJ9986
High Lees	2481
High Low	1569/2280
High Low Bank	2180
High Moor	4680
High Neb	2285

Location	Grid reference
High Needham	1165
High Peak Junction	3155
High Plantation	0572
High Rake	2175
High Tor	2959
High Wheeldon	1066
High Wood	3646/4678
Higham	3959
Highcliffe	2177
Highclifflane	2947
Higher Ashen Clough	0484
Higher Bibbington	0876
Higher Buxton	0673
Higher Chisworth	SJ9991
Higher Crossings	0480
Higher Deep Clough	0497
Higher Dinting	0294
Higher Ridge	0893
Higher Shelf Stone	0894
Highfields	4265
Highlane	4082
Highlikely Quarry	3164
Highlow Brook	2380
Highlow Wood	2279
Highmoor Pits	0692
Highoredish	3559
Highshaw Clough	2187
Highstone Rocks	0699
Highwood Cottages	3646
Hilcote	4558
Hill Covert	2318
Hill Somersal	1434
Hill Top	3577
Hill Wood	2562
Hillbridge and Park Wood Reserve	0178
Hillcarr Wood	2563
Hillcrest	4358
Hillcross	3333
Hillhead Quarry	0669
(The) Hills	3726
Hillside	3249
Hillstown	4769
Hillyfields (latterly Pools Brook Country Park)	4373
Hilton	2430
Hilton Brook	2528
Hilton Common	2530
Hilton Depot	2430
Hilton Gorse	2331
Hilton Gravel Pits Nature Reserve	2431
Hinchley Wood	1648
Hindlow	0869
Hindlow Quarry	0967
Hipley Hill	2054
Hipper (River)	3368
Hipper Sick	3068
Hitter Hill	0866
Hob Hurst's House	2869
Hob Tor	0677
Hob Wood	2852/5577

Location	Grid reference
Hockerley	0082
Hockley Quarry	3562
Hodgelane Brook	3264
Hodthorpe	5476
Hognaston	2350
Hognaston Bridge	2349
Hognaston Winn	2250
Hogshaw Brook	0574
Holbrook	3645/4481
Holbrook Crossing	3643
Holbrook Moor	3645
Holden Clough	0792
Holderness Quarry	0878
Hole Wood	3560
Holehouse	0092
Holestone	3361
Hollin Clough	1790
Hollin Hill	5175
Hollin Wood	3175
Hollinclough Plantation	1790
Hollington	2239
Hollington Grove	2238
Hollingwood Estate	4173
Hollingworth Clough	0489
Hollingworth Head	0390
Hollingworth Wood	4665
Hollinhill Grips	5075
Hollins	3271
Hollins Cross	1384
Hollins Green	3763
Hollins Hill	0667
Hollinsmoor	0089
Hollow Brook	2376
Hollow Farm Pond	2163
Holloway	3256
Holly Wood	2564
Holm Brook	2849
Holme Brook	3672
Holme Moss	SE0804
Holme Nook	3539
Holmebrook Valley Park	3572
Holmesdale	3678
Holmesfield	3277
Holmesfield Common	3177
Holmesfield Park Wood	3178
Holmewood	4366
Holmgate	3863
Holmley Common	3579
Holt Wood	2862/3257
(The) Holts	1743
Holy Moor	3268
Holymoorside	3369
Home Wood	2725
Homestall Wood	2214
Hoo Moor	0077
Hooborough Brook	3014
Hood Brook	2382
Hoofies Wood	3022
Hookcar Sitch	2483
Hook's Car	2483
Hoon Mount	2331

Gazetteer

Location	Grid reference
Hoon Pond	2231
Hoon Well	2548
Hope	1883
Hope Brink	1785
Hope Cement Works	1682
Hope Wood	1342
Hopton	2553
Hopton Quarry	2656
Hopton Wood	2556
Hopwell Park	4435
Hordron Edge	2187
Horn Hill	3320
Horse Clough	0192
Horse Dale	2658
Horse Hay Coppice	2477
Horse Stead	1471
Horse Wood	3271/3569
Horsebottoms	1833
Horseclose Plantation	4336
Horsehill Tor	0984
Horseshoe Dale	0970
Horseshoe Hill Plantation	0971
Horseshoe Plantation	2158
Horsley	3744
Horsley Carr	3742
Horsley Castle	3743
Horsley Woodhouse	3944
Horsleygate	3176
Horwich End	0180
Houghton Basset	4966
Houghton Felley	4966
Houndsfield Bridge	4074
Housley	1975
Howden Reservoir	1692
Hucklow Moor	1578
Hucknall Wood	4665
Hufton's Coppice	4345
Hulland	2446
Hulland-hollow Brook	2445
Hulland Moss	2546
Hulland Ward	2547
Humblebees Hill	2644
Humphrey Gate	1470
Hundall	3877
Hunger Hill	1752/2843/3267
Hungerhill Brook	2843
Hungry Bentley (medieval village)	1738
Hunloke Estate	3966
Hurdlow	1166
Hurker Wood	3061
Hurkling Stone	2087
Hurling Stone	2677
Hurlow Town	1166
(The) Hurst	4561
Hurst Clough	1888/2183
Hurst Moor	0692
Hurst Reservoir	0593
Ible	2557
Ible Wood	2556
Idridgehay	2848

Location	Grid reference
Idridgehay Green	2849
Ilam Rock	1453
Ilkeston	4641
Ince Piece Wood	4278
Ingerholmes Wood	3625
Ingleby	3427
Ingleby Toft	3526
Inkersall	4272
Inkersall Green	4273
Intake Dale	1679
Intake Quarry	2755
Ireland Colliery	4373
Ireton Houses	3747
Ireton Rough	3142
Ireton Wood	2847
Iron Tors	1456
Ironbower Moss	1199
Ironbower Rocks	1199
Ironville	4351
Ivet Low	2554
Ivonbrook Quarry	2358
Ivy Brook	2263
Ivy House Plantation	1659
Ivyspring Wood	3666
Jack Bank	1682
Jack Flat	2673
Jacksdale	4452
Jackson's Dumble	3741
Jackson's Plantation	1179
Jacob's Cabin	0172
Jacob's Ladder	0886
Jagger's Clough	1487
James's Thorn	0794
Jarvis Clough	2186
Jeff's Wood	2823
Jenny Well	2846
Jep Clough	0176
Jessop's Monument	4351
John Field Howden	1990
John Port Woods	2631
John Roe's Covert	1541
John Track Well	0896
John Wood	4244
Johnnygate	3275
Johnson's Carr	3048
Johnson's Knoll	1557
Jordanthorpe Plantation	3681
Joseph Patch	0896
Jubilee Plantation	3522
Jubilee Rock	2671
Jughole Wood	2759
Jumber Brook	2177
Jumble Coppice	2672
Jumble Hole	3373
Kedleston	3041
Kedleston Hall/Lake/Park	3140
Kelstedge	3363
Kemp's Hill	1078
Kennel Wood	3253
Kenslow	1962
Kenslow Knoll	1861

Location	Grid reference
Kenslow Wood	1962
Kent Wood	4081
Kettle Wood	2380
Kid Tor	0871
Kidtor Dale	0872
Kilburn	3845
Kill Hill Bridge	1783
Killamarsh	4580
Killamarsh Meadows	4581
Killamarsh Pond	4780
Kiln Clough	SE1101
Kinder Bank	0486
Kinder Low	0787
Kinder Low End	0686
Kinder Reservoir	0588
Kinder Scout	0888
King Sterndale	0972
King's Chair	2553
King's Corner	4039
King's Covert	2215
King's Mills	4127
King's Newton	3826
King's Newton Fields	3826
King's Tree	1693
Kirk Dale	1869
Kirk Hallam	4540
Kirk Ireton	2650
Kirk Langley	2838
Kirkstead	4555
Kishfield Bridge	SJ9980
Kitchen Wood	3377
Kitchenflat Wood	3372
Kniveton	2050
Kniveton Brook	2148
(The) Knot	0489
Knot Low	1373
(The) Knowle	3245
Ladbitch Wood	9977
Ladder Hill	0279
Laddow Moss	SE0501
Laddow Rocks	SE0501
Ladmanlow	0471
Lads Grave	2315
Lad's Leap	0599
Lady Booth Brook	1486
Lady Clough	1091
Lady Coppice	1135
Lady Low	0678
Lady Wood	3371/4439
Ladyacre Wood	3525
Ladybank Wood	4280
Ladybower Brook	2086
Ladybower Reservoir	1986
Ladybower Tor	2086
Ladybower Wood	2086/4271
Ladybrook Pasture	1584
Ladyclough Moor	1092
Ladycroft Wood	5474
Ladycross Wood	3525
Ladyfield's Plantation	3321
Ladygrove	3652

Location	Grid reference
Lady's Pond	2245
Ladywall Well	2572
Lake Bank	1532
Lamb Pasture	3068
Lambhouse	3149
Lane End	2951/4461
Lane Ends	2334
Lane Head	1576
Langley	4446
Langley Common	2937
Langley Green	2738
Langley Mill	4447
Langley Mill Flash	4548
Langwith	5269
Langwith Junction	5268
Langwith Wood	5068
Lansdowne Hose	3131
Lantern Pike	0288
Lantlodge	3262
Larklands	4741
Lathkill (River) source confluence with Wye	1765 2465
Lathkill Dale	1865
Laughman Tor	1078
Lawm Bridge	3125
Lawrence Edge	0898
Lawrence Field	2579
Lea Bridge	3156
Lea Brook	3156
Lea Hurst Park	3255
Lea Wood	2795/3155/3256
Leabrooks	4253
Lead Hill	1988
Leadmill	2380
Leadmill Bridge	2380
Leak's Plantation	3978
Leam	2379
Lean Low	1462
Leap Edge	0469
Leash Fen	2973
Leashaw Wood	3355
Lee Brook	3937
Lee Head	0092
Lees	2637
Lees Bottom	1770
Lees Brook	4037
Lees Cross Quarries	2563
Lees Moor Wood	2567
Lees Plantation	3375
Lees Wood	2568/3021/3376
Leigh's Plantation	1241
Lemon's Holme	1931
Lendlow Wood	2551
Leygatehead Moor	0589
Lidgate	3077
(The) Liffs	1557
Light Wood	0574/4078
Lightside	0595
Lightwood	3781

Location	Grid reference
Lightwood Reservoir	0575
(The) Lillies	3045
Limbersitch Brook	2233
Limehouse Dam	3320
Limekiln Field	4771
Limetree Wood	2767
Lin Dale	1551
Linacre Brook	3472
Linacre Reservoirs	3272
Linch Clough	1594
Lindop Wood	2567
Lindup Low	2569
Lindup Plantation	2569
Lindway Springs	3557
Lindway Springs Brook	3657
Linen Dale	1976
Ling Hill	2843
Linndale	1551
Linton	2716
Linton Heath	2816
Little Barbrook Reservoir	2776
Little Bolderstone Plantation	1760
Little Bolehill	2954
Little Brind Wood	3276
Little Bumper Piece	2765
Little Carterhall Wood	3880
Little Chester	3537
Little Clough	SE0603/0794
Little Cubley	1637
Little Dungeon	2560
Little Eaton	3641
Little Foxstone Wood	4277
Little Hallam	4640
Little Hayfield	0388
Little Hucklow	1678
Little Intake	SE1101
Little John's Well	2679
Little Liverpool	2414
Little Longstone	1971
Little Matlock	5265
Little Moor	1491/1876
Little Rookery Plantation	1760
Little Rough	3124
Little Shacklow Wood	1869
Little Wisels Wood	2059
Little Wood	4041
Littlemoor	3663/4459
Littlemoor Wood	3158
Littleover	3233
Litton	1675
Litton Edge	1675
Litton Mill	1572
LLL Plantation	1342
Loads Head	3169
Lock Lane Tip	4831
Locker Brook	1698
Lockerbrook	1681
Lockerbrook North Plantation	1689
Lockerbrook South Plantation	1689
Locker's Knoll	1643
Locko Lake/Park	4038

Location	Grid reference
Lode Mill	1455
Lodge Plantation	4664
Loftend Quarry	0799
Lombardale Hall	1963
Lombard's Green	1855
Long Alders	3420
Long Cliff	1382
Long Clough	0391
Long Dale	1061/1361/1860
Long Duckmanton	4471
Long Eaton	4933
Long Eaton Gravel Pits	5033
Long Edge Plantation	0278
Long Plantation	4056
Long Rake Plantation	2171
Long Wood	2939/3154/3680/4454
Longcliffe	2255
Longdendale	0297 to 0999
Longford	2137
Longford Park	2138
Longfordlane	2236
Longhorse Bridge	4539
Longlands Plantation	3029
Longlane	2538
Longley Bank	1688
Longman Nook	4865
Longrybank Wood	4878
Longshaw Country Park	2679
Longside Edge	1399
Longside End	1399
Longside Moor	3168
Longside Moss	SE1300
Longside Plantation	SJ9982
Longstone Edge	1973
Longstone Moor	1973
Longway Bank	3255
Loose Hill	1178
Lord's Seat	1183
Lordship Hill	0693
Loscoe	4247
Loscoe Brook	4147
Loscoe Dam	4247
Lose Hill	1585
Losehill Hall	1583
Lost Lad Hillend	1991
Loundsley Green	3571
Lover's Leap	1451
Low Leighton	0085
Low Moor Plantation	1864
Low Wood	1765
Lower Ashen Clough	0484
Lower Bee Low	1079
Lower Birchwood	4353
Lower Brookfarm Dumble	1542
Lower Crossings	0480
Lower Dinting	0294
Lower Dumble	1643
Lower Hartshay	3851
Lower Kilburn	3745
Lower Midway	3120

Gazetteer

Location	Grid reference
Lower Misden Clough	1695
Lower Pilsley	4163
Lower Ridge	0793
Lower Shelf	0694
Lower Shelf Stone	0894
Lower Small Clough	1495
Lower Somercotes	4353
Lower Thurvaston	2236
Lower Vicarwood	3139
Lowgates	4475
Lowmoor Cottages	1956
Lowmoor Plantation	1856
Lud Well	1262
Ludworth Moor	SJ9990
Lullington	2412
(The) Lumb	3046
Lumb Brook	3347
Lumb Wood	3981
Lumsdale	3160
Lumsdale Quarry	3160
Lumshill Quarry	3161
Mackworth (estate)	3236
Mackworth (village)	3137
Mackworth Brook	3137
Mackworth Castle (remains)	3137
Madge Dale	1361
Madge Hill	2149
Madwoman's Stones	1388
Mag Clough	2377
Makeney	3544
Malcolmsley Plantation	1537
Mam Tor	1283
Manchester Plantation	1761
Manners Wood	2368
Mansell Park Sand Pit	2544
(The) Map Plantation	2266
Mapleton	1647
Mapperley	4343
Mapperley Brook	4342
Mapperley Park	4243
Mapperley Park Wood	4342
Mapperley Pond	4343
Mapperley Reservoir	4343
Mapperley Wood	4343
Marehay	3948
Mares Back	0191
Margey Bower (tumulus)	1644
Markeaton	3337
Markeaton Brook	3238
Markeaton Lake/Park	3337
Markeaton Stones	3135
Markham	4572
Markland Grips	5074
Markland Plantation	5074
Marks Hill	3843
Marks Rough	3251
Marlpit Plantation	2729/2831
Marlpit Spinney	2117
Marlpool	4345
Marplas Plantation	3042
(The) Marsh	2236

Location	Grid reference
Marsh Brook	3463
Marsh Lane	4079
Marston Brook	1236
Marston Crossing	2329
Marston Junction	2329
Marston Montgomery	1337
Marston-on-Dove	2328
Marston Park	1339
Martinside	0679
Marvel Stones	1077
Mason's Wood	2948
Massey's Bridge	3828
Masson Hill	2858
Masson Mills	2957
Mastin Moor	4575
Mathersgrave	3559
Matley Moor	0290
Matlock	2960
Matlock Bank	2960
Matlock Bath	2958
Matlock Bridge	2960
Matlock Dale	2958
Matlock Forest	3062
Matlock Green	3059
Matlock Moor	3062
Matlockmoor Quarry	3061
Maud's Plantation	2469
Mayfield	1545
Meadow	1173
Meadow Clough	SE0702
Meadow Place Wood	1965
Meadowgrain Clough	SE0603
Mease (River) enters county leaves county	2912 2311
Meekfield Wood	3075
Meekfields	3075
Melbourne	3825
Melbourne Common	3724
Melbourne Parks	3923
Melbourne Plantation	3823
Melbourne Pool	3824
Mercaston Brook	2742
Mercaston Green	2643
Mercaston Sand Pits	2644
Mere Brook	3154
Mere Pond	3622
Merefield Gorse	1433
Merlin's Cavern	2175
Mermaid's Pool	0788
Merrill Sick	4864
Meveril Brook	0379
Meynell Gorse	2939
Meynell Langley	3039
Michill Bank	1582
Micklemeadow	3132
Mickleover	3034
Mickley	3279
Mickley Estate	3960
Middle Black Clough	1198
Middle Handley	4077
Middle Hill	1077/1182
Middle Moor	0488/3163

Location	Grid reference
Middle Peak Quarry	2754
Middle Seal Clough	1089
Middle Wood	4128
Middlecroft	4274
Middleton	2755
Middleton-by-Wirksworth	2756
Middleton-by-Youlgreave	1963
Middleton Common	1763
Middleton Dale	2175
Middleton Moor	2074/2655
Middleton Wood	2756
Midland Terrace	4258
Midway	3020
Midway Ponds	3020
Mild Lane	2965
Milehill	4068
Milford	3545
Milk Hill	3018
Mill Brook	1889
Mill Clough	0078/1889
Mill Dale	1454
Mill Green	3553
Mill Hill	0690
Mill Plantation	3327/3739
Mill Pond Plantation	1751
Mill Wood	2179/3154
Millbank Wood	2851
Millbrook Plantation	1890
Miller's Dale	1473
Miller's Pond	4564
Millington Green	2647
Millstone Sick	3067
Millthorpe	3176
Millthorpe Brook	3176
Milltown	3561
Milltown Quarry	3562
Millwood Brook	5575
Milner Plantation	4377
Milton	3226
Milton Carr	3225
Milton Water Reclamation Works	3128
Minninglow Hill	2057
Miry Clough	1193
Misden Clough	1695
Mitchell Field	2481
Moat Low	1553
Moat Wood	4340
Moatless Plantation	2369
Mompesson's Well	2277
Moneystones	1561
Monk Wood	3576
Monk's Dale	1174
Monk's Meadows	0484
Monk's Pond	2342
Monsal Dale	1771
Monsal Head	1871
Monyash	1566
(The) Moor	3526
Moor Edge Plantations	2067
Moor Plantation	3631/3842
Moor Wood	3458

Location	Grid reference
Moorend	2145
Moorhall Wood	3075
Moorhay Plantation	3072
Moorlawn Coppice	3468
Moorseats Wood	2382
Moorspring Wood	3675
Moorway Lane Pond	3232
Moorwood Moor	3656
Moorwood Quarry	3660
Moravian Settlement	4235
Morley	3940
Morley Park	3748
Morley Smithy	3941
Morleyhayes Wood	4042
Morleymoor	3841
Morrell's Wood	3748
Morton	4060
Morton Brook	4158
Morton Hospital	4060
Moscar	2187
Moscar Field	2287
Moscar Moor	2285
Moscar Wood	2382
Mosey Low	1264
Moseyley	3044
Mosley Bank	1695
(The) Moss	3880
Moss Castle	0791
Moss Rake	1580
Moss Valley	4180
Mossey Yard Plantation	3836
Mossylea	0594
Mount Famine	0585
Mount Pleasant	1135/2233/ 2817/3126/ 3448/3649/ 3746/3825/ 3947/4358
(The) Mountain	2649
Mousley Bottom	SJ9985
Moxon's Hill	3021
Muggingtonlane End	2844
Mugginton	2842
Mulberry Wood	3865
Muster Brook	4268
Musterbrook Bridge	4267
Mycross Mine	1766
Mytham Bridge	2082
(The) Nab	1286
Nab Brow	0588
Nab Plantation	3368
Nab Quarry	3368
Nab Wood	1690
(The) Nabs	1453
Nabs Spring	1453
Nadin's, Newhall	2921
National Coal Board Central Engineering Establishment	2821
National Stone Centre	2855
National Tramway Museum	3454
Near Black Clough	1098
Near Bleaklow Stone	1096
Near Broadslate	SE0502

Location	Grid reference
Near Deep Clough	1890
Near Fork Grain	1095
Nelson's Monument	2772
Nether Biggin	2648
Nether Burrows	2639
Nether Chanderhill	3370
Nether End	2572
Nether Hall Wood	3121
Nether Handley	4077
Nether Heage	3650
Nether Hey	1893
Nether Loads	3269
Nether Low	1069
Nether Moor	1488/3866
Nether Padley	2578
Nether Pilsley	4262
Nether Reddale Clough	1193
Nether Reever Low	2287
Nether Seal Clough	1189
Nether Speighthill Wood	3768
Nether Sturston	1946
Nether Tor	1287
Nether Wood	2170
Nether Wood Plantation	1693
Nethergate Clough	0991
Nethergreen	4581
Netherhead Clough	SE1300
Nethermoor Plantation	3866
Netherseal	2813
Netherthorpe	4474/4580
New Barlborough	4876
New Birchwood	4354
New Bolsover	4670
New Bridge	2475/2972/ 3926
New Brimington	4073
New Gorse Fox Covert	2831
New Higham	3958
New Horwich	0181
New Houghton	4965
New Mills	0085
New Park Quarry	2462
New Pilhough Quarry	2564
New Plantation	1671/2512
New Sawley	4732
New Smithy	0582
New Stanton	4639
New Wessington	3757
New Whittington	3975
New Zealand	3336
Newbold	3772
Newbold Moor	3773
Newboundmill	4963
Newfield Spring Wood	3781
Newgate	3374
Newhall	2921
Newhall Wood	2720
Newhaven	1660
Newhaven Crossing	1859
Newkennel Plantation	3142
Newlands	4346
Newline Quarry	0977

Location	Grid reference
Newschool	3149
Newton	4459
Newton Green	4459
Newton Mount	2823
Newton Park	2725
Newton Solney	2725
Newtonlot Plantation	2764
Newton's Corner	4026
Newtown	SJ9984
Nickalum Mine	2353
Nine Acre Piece	2965
'Nine Ladies' Stone Circle	2463
Nine Miles Plantation	1958
Nithen End	0473
Nitticarhill	4878
Nitticarhill Wood	4878
Noah's Ark	3122
Noe (River) confluence with Derwent	1485 2082
(The) Nook	1957
Nor Wood	3680
Norbriggs flash	4475
Norbury	1242
Norcliff Wood	4864
Normanton (Derby)	3433
Normanton Brook	4357
Normanton Common	4355
North Britain	3065
North Cliff Plantation	2373
North Grain	SE0603
North Lees	2382
North Plantation	1689/4256
North Wingfield	4165
Northedge	3565
Northedge Quarry	3564
Northern Dale	2660
Northfield Plantation	3142
Northwood	2664
Northwood Carr	2664
Norwood	4681
Nun Brook	0675
Nungrain Brink	1190
Nunsclough Brook	2637
Nut Brook	4541
Nut Wood	2155/3539
Nutbrook Canal	4639
Nutseats Quarry	2365
Nuttal's Park	4050
Oak Covert	2243
Oak Rough	1634
Oaken Clough	SE0500/0685
Oaker Top	1585
Oakerthorpe	3955
Oaks Green	1533
Oaks Plantation	2036
Oaks Wood	3754
Oak's Wood	2179/2578
Oaksetts Clump	5475
Oakside Bridge	SE0900
Oakside Clough	SE0800
Oakwood	3838
Ockbrook	4235

Gazetteer

Location	Grid reference
Ockbrook Wood	4338
Odin Mine	1383
Offerton Edge	2080
Offerton Moor	2080
Office Coppice	4344
Ogden Clough	0496
Ogston Bridge	3859
Ogston Carr	3659
Ogston Reservoir	3760
Okeover Bridge	1648
Oker	2761
Old Brampton	3371
Old Clough	2081
Old Covert	2843
Old Dam	1179
Old Glossop	0494
Old Matlock	2959
Old Moor	1073/1380
Old Park Plantation	2668
(The) Old Rectory	1637
Old River Dove	2328
Old Spring Wood	3369
Old Trent Water	2927/3127
Old Tupton	3865
Old Whittington	3874
Oldfield Lane Bridge	2551
Oldfield Plantation	2370/2930
Oldpits Plantation	0487
Oleston	2437
Oleston (site of medieval village)	2537
Oller Brook	1286
Ollersett	0385
Open Hagg	1688
Openwoodgate	3647
Orangehill Bridge	3225
Orchard Plantation	2934
Ormes Moor	SE0200
Ormonde Fields	2449
Osbourne's Pond	4444
Osierbed Plantation	1141
Osierbed Wood	2934/3238
Osmaston	1943/3633
Osmaston Lake/Park/Wood	2042
Otter Brook	0482
Otwell Bank Quarry	0387
Outlane	2283
Ouzelden Clough	1590
Over Burrows	2639
Over Dale	1880
Over End	2572
Over Haddon	2066
Over Wood	3170
Over Wood Moss	1193
Over Woodhouse	4671
Overdale Brook	1881
Overend	3264
Overgreen	3273
Overseal	2915
Owler Bar	2978
Owler Car Wood	3780
Owler Tor	2580

Location	Grid reference
Ox Hey	1694
Ox Low	1280
Oxclose Plantation	4664
Oxclose Wood	2365
Oxcroft	4873
Oxcroft Estate	4872
Oxhay Wood	2479
Oxlow Rake	1279
Oxton Rakes	3273
Oyster Clough	1190
Paddock Pool Plantation	3923
Paddock's Plantation	2470
Padfield	0396
Padley Gorge/Wood	2579
Padley Wood	4061
Palace Cottage	3050
Palmerston Wood	1865
Palterton	4768
Parish Quarry	2764
(The) Park (Belper)	3547
Park Brook	3843/4479
Park Head	3654
Park Nook Wood	3241
Park Plantation	3352
Park Pond	3125
Park Wood	0079/2570/3054
Parker's Wood	4173
Parkhill Wood	2751
Parkhouse Hill	0760
Parkin Clough	1982
Parkside Brook	2249
Parkside Cottages	2039
Parkside Wood	2466
Parsley Hay	1463
Parsley Nature Reserve	1562
Parson's Hills	2926
Parson's Piece	2288
Parson's Wood	3881
Parwich	1954
Parwich Hill	1854
Parwich Lees	1754
Pasture Tor	1589
Pasture Wood	0798
Pavilion Gardens (Buxton)	0573
Peak Cavern	1482
Peak Dale	0976
Peak Forest	1179
Peak Forest Canal	0182
Peak Naze	0496
Peak Pasture	2373
Peak Tor	2565
Peakley Hill	3376
Peaknaze Moor	0597
Peakshole Water	1683
Pear Tree	3533
Pearson Wood	3756
Pearsons Wood	3879
Peasehill	4049
Peaslow Cross	0880
Peasunhurst	3166
Peatmoss Plantation	2440

Location	Grid reference
Peatpits Brook	3252
Pebley Pond	4879
Pedlicote	1079
Peewit Carr	4541
Pell's Dam	0774
Pendleton Brook	3253
Pennant Edge	SJ9980
Pennytown	4254
Pennywaste Wood	2031
Pentrich	3852
Pentrichlane-end	3751
Perry Dale	1080
Perryfoot	1081
Pessall Brook	2414
Peter Dale	1275
Peter's Stone	1775
Peveril Castle	1482
Peveril House	4471
Philosopher's Wood	3022
Pickering Tor	1453
Pickering Wood	2365
Picory Corner	2365
Pig Tor	0872
Piggin Wood	4237
(The) Pike	0793
Pike Pool	1258
Pikehall	1959
Pikenaze Hill	SE0900
Pikenaze Moor	SE1000
Pilhough	2565
Pilhough Quarry	2564
Pilldock Wood	2937
Pilsbury	1163
Pilsbury Castle Hills	1163
Pilsley	2471/4262
Pilsley Green	4261
Pin Dale	1582
Pinchom's Hill	3546
Pinder's Rock	2255
Pinelow Plantation	1555
Pingle Dyke	3175
Pingle Wood	2282
Pinxton	4555
Pinxtonwharf	4554
Pistern Hill	3420
Pistern Hill Plantation	3520
Pitholes Plantation	3351
Plague Stone	2376
Plaistow	3456
(The) Plantation	2565
Pleasley	5064
Pleasley Park	5165
Pleasley Vale	5165
Pleasure Ground Wood	3040
Poker's Leys	3522
Pomeroy	1167
Pond Plantation	4469
Poole's Cavern	0472
Pools Brook Country Park (formerly Hillyfields)	4373
Pools Head	2540
Pools Head Ponds	2540

Location	Grid reference
Smerrill Moor	1860
Smisby	3519
Smithcote Hill	3741
Smithfield	0580
Smith's Gorse	3322
Smith's Plantation	2940
Smith's Rough	3552
Smithy Brook	3861/4577
Smithy Clough	1099
Smithy Houses	3847
Snake Inn	1190
Snake Pass	1190
Snake Path	0790
Snake Plantation	1091
Snake Summit	0892
Snels Low	1181
Snelston	1543
Snelston Common	1541
Snelston Park	1643
Snitterton	2760
Soldiers Knoll	2652
Soldiers Lump	SE0704
Solomon's Temple	0571
Somercotes	4253
Somersal Herbert	1335
Somersall Park	3570
Sough Top	1370
South End	4066
South Head	0684
South Hill	3760
South Normanton	4456
South Wingfield	3755
South Wood	3620
Sow Brook	4539
Spa Well (disused)	2647
Span Clough	0692
Span Moor	0692
Spancarr	3465
Sparklow	1265
Sparrowpit	0980
Spath Covert	2234
Speedwell Mine	1382
Spink Wood	2752
Spinkhill	4578
(The) Spinney	4249
Spinneyford Brook	2444
Spital Green	4769
Spitalhill	1845
Spitewinter	3466
Spondon	3935
Spondon Power Station	4034
Spondon Wood	4137
(The) Spots	4437
(The) Spots Plantation	4337
Spout	3051
Spring Carr	3243
Spring Hill	3344
Spring Wood	2263/3722
Spur's Bottom	3224
Square Plantation	1751/3923
Square Pond	1632

Location	Grid reference
Squire's Nursery	2937
St Anne's Well	2926
St Augustines	3869
St Chads Water	4431
St Mary's Wood	2473
Stable Clough	1098
Staffordshire Way	1036
Stainsborough Quarry	2652
Stainsby	4465
Stainsby Common	4364
Stainsby Plantation	4464
Stainsby Pond	4464
Stainsbybrook	4465
Stake Clough	0072
Stake Side	0073
Stanage	2178
Stanage Edge	2385
Stand Wood	2670
Standcliffe Quarries	2663
Standen	0772
Standen Low	0772
Standlow	1553
Stanedge	1659
Stanedge Plantation	2483
Stanedge Pole	2484
Stanedge Ponds (aka Cupola Ponds)	3366
Stanfree	4773
Stanhope Bretby	2822
Stanley	4140
Stanley Brook	4040
Stanley Common	4142
Stanley Moor	0471/1776
Stanley Moor Reservoir	0471
Stanlow Dale	1679
Stanton	2719
Stanton & Staveley Ironworks	4638
Stanton Bridge	4639
Stanton-by-Bridge	3727
Stanton-by-Dale	4637
Stanton-by-Newhall	2719
Stanton Ford	2373
Stanton Gate	4838
Stanton Grove	4538
Stanton-in-Peak	2465
Stanton Lees	2563
Stanton Moor	2463
Stanton Moor Plantation	2463
Stanton Moor Quarries	2463
Stanton Park Quarry	2462
Stanton Pools	4272
Stanton Wood	3523
Stanton Woodhouse	2564
Starkholmes	3058
Stars Wood	3561
Starvehimvalley Bridge	3751
Staunton Harold Reservoir	3723
Staveley	4374
Staveley Sewage Farm	4476
Staveley Works	4274
Steetley	5478
Steetley Quarry	5478

Location	Grid reference
Steetley Wood	5479
Stenson	3230
Stenson Fields	3231
Stenson Junction	3129
Stenson Marina	3230
Sterndale Moor	1068
Stocker Flat	3932
Stockings Plantation	2721
Stockley	4667
Stockley Brook	4667
Stoke Brook	2375
Stoke Flat	2576
Stoke Wood	2476
Stokehall Quarry	2476
Stone Dene	2553
Stone Edge	3367
Stone Edge Plantation	3367
Stone Edge Pools	3366
Stonebrake Quarry	0297
Stonebroom	4059
Stonegravels	3872
Stoneheads	0081
Stoneley Wood	3882
Stonelow Bridge	2971
Stonepit Plantation	1554
Stoney Clouds	4743
Stoney Houghton	4966
Stoney Ley Wood	2363
Stoney Low	1456
Stoney Middleton	2375
Stoneyford	4449
Straw's Bridge	4541
Street's Rough	3350
Stretton	3961
Stretton Hillside	3960
Strickle Brook	4665
Strines Edge	2189
Strines Top	2288
Stubbing Court	3567
Stubbing Wood	3977
Stubley Hollow	3479
Sturgess Fields	3337
Sturston Mill	2046
Sud Brook	3374
Sudbury Coppice	1535
Sudbury House	1532
Sudbury Lake	1532
Sudbury Park	1633
Sudbury Prison	1533
Sulphur Spring	3140
Summer Cross	1475
Summer Wood	4079
Summerley	3778
Summerwood Top	3478
Sunny Dale Park	3333
Sunny Hill	3332
Sunnybank Wood	2751
Sutcliffe Wood	3866
Sutton Brook Lakes	2332
Sutton Heath	2233
Sutton-on-the-Hill	2333

Gazetteer

Location	Grid reference
Sutton Scarsdale Flash	4468
Sutton Scarsdale Hall	4468
Sutton Springs Wood	4268
Swadlincote	2919
Swain's Greave	1197
Swain's Head	1398
Swainspark Wood	2917
Swallow Brook	0667
Swallow Tor	0667
(The) Swamp	1094
Swan Clough	1299
Swanwick	4053
Swarkestone	3628
Swarkestone Bridge	3627
Swarkestone Lake (Swarkestone Gravel Pits until 2005)	3627
Swarkestone Lows	3629
Swathwick	3667
Swine Sty	2775
Swinepark Wood	3257
Swine's Back	0786
Swineshaw Reservoir	0495
Swint Clough	1291
Swiss Lake	2770
Sydnope Brook	2963
Sydnope Hall	2964
Sydnope Stand	2963
Sykes Moor	0797
Taddington	1471
Taddington Dale	1671
Taddington Moor	1370
Taddington Wood	1670
Tags Naze	0984
Tansley	3259
Tansley Dale	1774
Tansley Knoll	3260
Tansley Moor	3261
Tansley Moor Quarries	3459
Tanyard	4251
Tapton	3972
Tapton Grove	4072
Tapton House	3972
Tarasiyka	3927
Taxal	0079
Taxal Edge	9978
Taxal Moor	9979
Temple Moor	0672
Temple Normanton	4167
Terrace Wood	4766
(The) Terret	0371
Terret Plantation	0371
Thacker Barn Cottages	4441
Thacker Wood	4538
Thacker's Wood	3551
Thirteen Bends	2371
Thomason's Hollow	0992
Thornbridge Hall	1970
Thornhill	1983
Thornhill Carrs	1984
Thornsett	0187
Thornsett Brows	0187

Location	Grid reference
Thornton Park Wood	4153
Thorpe	1550
Thorpe Cloud	1551
Thorpe Pasture	1551
Three Knolls	0787
Three Men	2772
Three Ships	2772
Three Shire Heads	0068
Throstle Nest	2380
Throstledale	0181
Thulston	4031
Thurvaston	1338/2437
Tibshelf	4360
Ticknall	3523
Ticknall Hill	3846
Ticknall Limeyards SSSI	3523
Tideslow Rake	1577
Tideswell	1575
Tideswell Dale	1573
Tideswell Moor	1378
Timlodge Plantation	0872
Tin Wood	3469
Tinkers Pit	0270
Tinkersley	2665
(The) Tinklers	4341
Tintwistle	0297
Tintwistle Knarr	0399
Tintwistle Low Moor	2098
Tissington	1752
Tissington Gates	1751
Tissington Spires	1452
Toadhole Footbridge	1443
Toadhole Furnace	3856
Toad's Mouth	2680
Todd Brook	SJ9981
Toddbrook Reservoir	0080
Toll's Wood	2364
Tom Wood	SJ9993
Tomlinson Carr	2246
Tomlinson Wood	2162
Tomthorn	0775
Tooleyshaw Moor	SE0802
Toost Bank Wood	2371
Toost Wood	2372
Toot Hill	0883
Toot Hills	4336
Topley Pike	1072
Topley Pike Quarry	1072
Topshill Brook	2751
Tor Rock	0667
Tor Wood	2279
(The) Tors	3453
Torside Bridge	0698
Torside Castle	0796
Torside Clough	0797
Torside Grain	0797
Torside Naze	0797
Torside Reservoir	0698
Totley Brook	3179
Totley Moss	2779
Tournament Field	3418

Location	Grid reference
Town Head	1269/2758
Townend	0681/2375
Townend Wood	2473
Townhead	2276
Townhead Bridge	1684
Treak Cliff	1383
Trent (River) enters county leaves county confluence with Derwent confluence with Dove confluence with Erewash	2014 5133 4530 2726 5133
Trent and Mersey Canal enters county end	2626 4530
Trent College	4833
Trent Lock	4931
Trent Meadows	5032
Trent Station (site of)	4932
Tricket Brook	3766
Trough Brook	4172
Troway	3879
Trusley	2535
Trusley Brook	2535
Trusley Coppice	2435
Tumbling Hill	2578
Tunstead	1176
Tunstead Milton	0308
Tunstead Quarry	0974
Tupton	3965
Turlow Fields	2449
Turnclife Common	0470
Turnditch	2946
Turner Lodge Reservoir	0675
Tutbury Bridge	2129
Twelve Acre Wood	4180
Twin Dales	1966
(The) Twitchlings	0491
Two Dales	2864
Two Meres	2558
Twyford	2228
Twyford Brook	3229
Typeclose Plantation	3252
Umber Mine	1861
Umberley Brook	2870
Umberley Sick	2969
Umberley Well	2869
Unstone	3777
Unstone Green	3776
Unthank	3076
Upper Biggin	2548
Upper Birchwood	4354
Upper Booth	1085
Upper Brookfarm Dumble	1542
Upper Dogkennel Plantation	2966
Upper Dumble	1643
Upper Edge	0668
Upper End	0876
Upper Gate Clough	0991
Upper Hackney	2861
Upper Hartshay	3850
Upper Heyden	SE0903
Upper Hurst Brook	2183

Location	Grid reference
Upper Langwith	5169
Upper Loads	3169
Upper Misden Clough	1695
Upper Moor	0687/1388/3064
Upper Newbold	3573
Upper North Grain	1093
Upper Padley	2478
Upper Pilsley	4262
Upper Pleasley	4964
Upper Reddale Clough	1193
Upper Reever Low	2287
Upper Seal Clough	1089
Upper Small Clough	1496
Upper Speighthill Wood	3767
Upper Taylor's Wood	1453
Upper Town	2461/2758
Upper Wood	1693
Upperdale	1772
Upperthorpe	4580
Uppertown	3265
Upperwood	2957
Urchin Clough	0893/1090
Valehouse Reservoir	0397
Valehouse Wood	0397
(The) Verge	2420
Vernon's Oak Plantation	1436
Via Gellia	2656
Vicar Wood	3139
Victory Plantation	2724
Victory Quarry	0776
View Quarry	2564
Virginsalley	1542
Wadshelf	3170
Wadshelf Brook	2971
Waggon Low	1164
Waingroves	4149
Wakebridge	3355
Waldley	1236
Wall Cliff	1477
Wall Hill	3326
Walling Brook	5576
Wallingbrook Wood	5576
Wallis's Gorse	4250
Walton	3669
Walton Bridge	2118
Walton Dam	3670
Walton Plantation	3669
Walton-upon-Trent	2118
Walton Wood	2116/3668
Wardlow	1874
Wardlow Hay Cop	1773
Wardlow Mires	1875
Ward's Cottages	4537
Ward's End	3058
Ward's Piece	1585
Warm Brook	0579
Warney Brook	2762
(The) Warren	3743
Warrencarr	2562
Wash Brook	1650
Wash Brow	0694
Wash Green	2954
Water-cum-jolly-Dale	1673
Waterlagg Brook	2745
Waterloo	4163
Waterswallows Quarry	0874
Waterworks Plantation	4336
Watford Bridge	0086
Watford Lodge Pond	0086
Watford Moor	0374
Watford Wood	0374
Wayne Corner Plantation	2864
Wayne Piece	2865
Wellclose Wood	3568
Wellhole Wood	3146
Wellington's Monument	2673
Wenley Hill Plantation	2063
Wensley	2661
Wensley Dale	2660
Wessington	3757
West Brook	2412
West Broughton	1433
West Cable Tip Plantation	1692
West Hallam	4341
West Hallam Common	4241
West Handley	3977
West Park (Long Eaton)	4833
West Withens Clough	SE1202
West Wood	4172
Westend	1493
Westend (River)	1494
Westend Head	1195
Westend Moor	1393
Westend Moss	SE0801
Wester Head Mine	2354
Westhorpe	4579
Westhouses	4257
Weston Cliff	4027
Weston Fields	3929
Weston-on-Trent	4028
Weston Underwood	2942
Westwood	4172
Whaley	5171
Whaley Bridge	0181
Whaley Moor	5272
Whaley Quarry	5071
Whaley Thorns	5270
Whatstandwell	3354
Wheatcroft	3557
Wheel Stone	2088
Wheeldon Trees	1066
Wheston	1376
Whibbersley Cross	2972
Whim Plantation	2480
Whinacre Wood	3780
Whinnybank Wood	4277
Whinstone Lee Tor	1988
White Brow	0588
White Clough	0894
White Edge	2154/2676
White Edge Moor	2678
White Hall Centre	0376
White Hollow	3122
White Hollows	3422
White Low	SE0802
White Moor	3648
White Path Moss	2483
White Tor	1988
Whitebrick Moor	4977
Whitefield Pits	1490
Whitehough	0382
Whiteley	4049
Whiteley Nab	0292
Whiteley's Plantation	2641/4244
Whitelow Mines	2558
Whitelow Slack	SE0802
Whitesprings Plantation	2865
Whitestones	1197
Whitethorn Clough	0491
Whitle	SJ9986
Whittington Moor	3873
Whittington Sewage Farm	3874
Whitwell	5276
Whitwell Common	5177
Whitwell Quarry	5375
Whitwell Wood	5278
Wibben Hill	1852
(The) Wicken	1289
Widdowson Spring Wood	3668
Widdowson's Plantation	4044
Wigan Clough	0795
Wigber Low	2051
Wiggens Clough	SE0702
Wigger Dale	2266
(The) Wiggs	4026
Wigley	3171
Wike Head	SE1300
Wild Moor	0274
Wild Park	2741
Wild Park Brook	2741
Wilday Green	3274
Wildboar Clough	0897
Wildboar Grain	0896
Wilder Brook	3249
(The) Wilderness	2420
Wildmoorstone Brook	0274
Wilkin Hill	3474
Willersley Castle	2957
Williams Clough	0689
Williamthorpe Nature Reserve	4366
Willington	2928
Willington Bridge	2927
Willington Gravel Pits	2827
Willington Lake Trout Fishery (aka Findern Lake)	3029
Willington Power Station	3028
Willington Sewage Farm	3029
Willowbed Plantation	4378
Wilmorton	3634
Wilne Cross	4532
Wilsthorpe	4733
Wimble Holme Hill	2879
Win Hill	1885
Win Hill Pike	1885

Gazetteer

Location	Grid reference
Windgate Edge	SE0300
Windgather Rocks	9978
Windley	3045
Windley Meadows	3244
Windmill	1677
Windmill Hill	3326
Windmill Spinney	2821
Windy Arbour	2740
Windy Harbour	0396
Windyharbour	0396
Wingerworth	3767
Wingerworth Lido	3767
Wingfield Manor House	3754
Wingfield Park	3653/3752
Winn Brook	2251
Winnats Pass	1382
Winny Brook	3758
Winsick	4068
Winster	2460
Wire Stone	3263
Wirestone Quarry	3263
Wirksworth	2853
Wirksworth Moor	3053
Withens Brook	SE1000
Withens Edge	SE1202
Withens Moor	SE1201
Withered Low	1076
Within Clough	0791
Withing's Clough	0791

Location	Grid reference
Withinleach Moor	9975
Wolfie Pond	4166
Wolfscote Dale	1357
Wolfscote Hill	1358
Woo Dale	0973
Wood Moor	1189
Woodbrook Quarry	2865
Woodcock Dumble	1849
Woodend Bridge	SJ9885
Woodhead	0999
Woodhead Reservoir	0899
Woodlands Valley	1588
Woodlinkin	4348
Woodseats	SJ9992
Woodside	1950
Woodstock Plantation	3054
Woodthorpe	4574
Woodville	3119
Wool Packs	0986
Wooler Knoll	1786
Woollens Plantation	2412
Woolley	3760
Woolley Bridge	0195
Woolley Moor	3661
Worm Stones	0491
Worm Wood	2169
Wormhill	1274
Wormhill Moor	1076
Wormhill Springs	1274

Location	Grid reference
Wragg's Quarry	2866
Wraglands Plantation	2724
Wren Wood	4056
Wrenhey Coppice	1690
Wyaston	1842
Wyaston Brook	1942
Wye (River) source confluence with Derwent confluence with Lathkill	0374 2565 2465
Wye Dale	1071
Wynds Point	3962
Wythen Lache	0377
Wyver Lane	3449
Wyver Wood	3349
Wyvern Centre	3835
Yarncliff Wood	2579
Yeaveley	1840
Yeaveley (Stydd) Preceptory (remains of)	1739
Yeld Wood	2672
Yeldersley	2144
Yeldersley Hollies	2243
Yeldersley Pond	2044
Yellowslacks	0695
Yellowslacks Brook	0694
Yeman's Bridge	0695
Yoke Cliffe	2853
Yorkcliffe Rake	2753
Yorkshire Bridge	1984
Youlgr(e)ave	2064

Bibliography

Primary sources

Derbyshire Ornithological Society. *Derbyshire Bird Report*, 1955–2011.

Derbyshire Ornithological Society. *Bulletin*, 1 (1954) to 631 (January 2013).

Frost, R.A. 1978. *Birds of Derbyshire*. Moorland, Hartington.

Jourdain, F.C.R. 1905. 'Birds' section of *The Victoria County History of Derbyshire*. Vol. 1, pp. 119–145. Addenda and corrigenda, XXIX. Institute of Historical Research, London.

Journal of the Derbyshire Archaeological and Natural History Society, 1893–1954.

South Peak Raptor Study Group. *Annual Report*, 1998–2009.

Whitlock, F.B. 1893. *The Birds of Derbyshire*. Bemrose, London and Derby.

Secondary sources

Adams, A. and Frost, R.A. 1983. Probable breeding of Garganey. *Derbyshire Bird Report*, 1982: 55.

Adams, A. and Thornhill, J.S. 1986. Marsh Warblers at Etwall Brook and Poolsbrook. *Derbyshire Bird Report*, 1985: 63.

Adams, M.C. 1966. Firecrests breeding in Hampshire. *British Birds*, 59: 240–246.

Alsop, D. 1975. The Ring Ouzel *Turdus torquatus* in Derbyshire. *Derbyshire Bird Report*, 1974: 10–14.

——. 1987. Rook populations in north-west Derbyshire. *Derbyshire Bird Report*, 1986: 68–70.

Alström, P. and Mild, K. 2003. *Pipits and Wagtails of Europe, Asia and North America*. Helm, London.

Anderson, P. and Radford, E. 1994. Changes in vegetation following reduction in grazing pressure on the National Trust's Kinder Estate, Peak District, Derbyshire, England. *Biological Conservation*, 69: 155–163.

Anderson, P. and Tallis, J. 1981. The nature and extent of soil and peat erosion in the Peak District – Field Survey. In Phillips, J., Yalden, D.W. and Tallis, J. *Moorland Erosion Study, Phase 1, Report*. Peak Park Joint Planning Board, Bakewell: 52–68.

Anderson, P. and Yalden, D.W. 1981. Increased sheep numbers and the loss of heather moorland in the Peak District, England. *Biological Conservation*, 20: 195–213.

Anderson, P., Tallis, J.H. and Yalden, D.W. 1997. *Restoring Moorland. Peak District Moorland Management Project Phase III Report*. Peak Park and English Nature, Bakewell.

Appleyard, I. 1994. *Ring Ouzels of the Yorkshire Dales*. Maney and Son, Leeds.

Archer, M.G. 2005. Eurasian Nuthatch flycatching. *British Birds*, 98: 380.

——. 2008. The effects of winter temperatures on the survival of Winter Wrens *Troglodytes troglodytes*. *Sorby Record*, 44: 47–50.

Atkin, J. and Falshaw, C. 2004. A survey of Ring Ouzels *Turdus torquatus* at Stanage. *Birds in the Sheffield area*, 2002: 155–160.

Baillie, S.R., Marchant, J.H., Crick, H.P.Q., Noble, D.G., Balmer, D.E., Barimore, C., Coombes, R.H., Dowina, I.S., Freeman, S.N., Joys, A.C., Leech, D.I., Raven, M.J., Robinson, R.A. and Thewlis, R.M. 2007. *Breeding Birds in the Wider Countryside: their conservation status 2007*. BTO Research Report 487. BTO, Thetford.

Ballance, D.K. and Smith, A.J. 2008. Recording Areas of Great Britain. *British Birds*, 101: 364–375.

Batten, L., Flegg, J., Sorenson, J., Wareing, M.J., Watson, D. and Wright, M. 1973. *Birdwatchers' Year*. Poyser, Berkhamsted.

Beevers, M.A. 1994. The Corn Bunting in Derbyshire. *Derbyshire Bird Report*, 1993: 100–107.

——. 1998a. Black Kite at Carr Vale. *Sheffield Bird Report*, 1997: 100.

——. 1998b. Chiffchaff of the race *tristis* at Carr Vale. *Derbyshire Bird Report*, 1997: 125–126.

——. 1999a. Lesser Yellowlegs *Tringa flavipes* at Carr Vale: a new species for Derbyshire. *Derbyshire Bird Report*, 1998: 128–129.

——. 1999b. Common Rosefinch *Carpodacus erythrinus* at Carr Vale: a new species for Derbyshire. *Derbyshire Bird Report*, 1998: 126–127.

Bevan, J.M.S., Robinson, D.P., Spencer, J.W. and Whitbread, A.S. 1992. *Derbyshire Inventory of Ancient Woodland (Provisional)*. Nature Conservancy Council, Peterborough.

Boisseau, S. and Yalden, D.W. 1998. The former status of the Crane *Grus grus* in Britain. *Ibis*, 140: 482–500.

Bolton, M., Tomsom, C. and Skelhorn, K. 2007. *Monitoring of Lapwing Recovery in the Peak District 2003–2006*. RSPB North West Regional Office, Denby Dale.

Bramwell, D. 1976. The vertebrate fauna of Wetton Mill Rock Shelter. In Kelly, J.H. *The excavation of Wetton Mill Rock Shelter, Manifold Valley*. City Museum and Art Gallery, Stoke-on-Trent.

——. 1978. The fossil birds of Derbyshire. In Frost, R.A. *Birds of Derbyshire*. Moorland, Hartington: Appendix 3, 160–163.

Bramwell, D. and Yalden, D.W. 1988. Birds from the Mesolithic of Demen's Dale, Derbyshire. *Naturalist*, 113: 141–148.

Bramwell, D., Yalden, D.W. and Yalden, P.E. 1990. Ossom's Eyrie Cave: an archaeological contribution to the recent history of vertebrates in Britain. *Zoological Journal of the Linnean Society*, 98: 1–25.

British Ornithologists' Union (BOU). 1971. *The status of birds in Britain and Ireland*. Blackwell, London and Edinburgh.

——. 2013. The British List: a checklist of birds of Britain. 8th ed. *Ibis*, 155: 635–676.

Broome, A. 1986. Black Kite at Chisworth. *Derbyshire Bird Report*, 1985: 65.

Brown, A. and Grice, P. 2005. *Birds in England*. Poyser, London.

Brown, A.F. 1993. The status of Golden Plover *Pluvialis apricaria* in the south Pennines. *Bird Study*, 40: 196–202.

Brown, A.F. and Shepherd, K. 1991. *Breeding Birds of the South Pennine Moors*. JNCC Report No. 7. JNCC, Peterborough.

Brown, N. 2007. Derby Cathedral's Peregrines; their lives exposed and their prey identified. *Derbyshire Bird Report*, 2006: 142–144.

Cain-Black, A.P.E. 1975. The General Breeding Ecology and Behaviours of the House Martin in Derbyshire. DOS *Bulletin*, 220: 6.

Calladine, J.R. 1989. Bonaparte's Gull at Ogston Reservoir. *Derbyshire Bird Report*, 1987: 79.

Cameron, K. 1959. *Place-names of Derbyshire*. English Placename Society, vols. 27–29. Cambridge University press, Cambridge.

Campbell, L.H. 1982. *Peak District 1981: Report of the survey for the RSPB Conservation Planning Department*. Unpublished report. RSPB, Sandy.

Carr, G. and Middleton, P. 2004. *Breeding Bird Survey of the Peak District Moorlands 2004*. Moors for the Future Report No. 1. Moors for the Future Partnership, Castleton.

Carrington, R. 2000. *Slinter Wood Birds 1999*. Arkwright Society, Cromford.

——. 2001. *Slinter Wood Birds 2000*. Arkwright Society, Cromford.

——. 2002. Red-spotted Bluethroat *Luscinia svecica svecica* at Beeley Moor. *Derbyshire Bird Report*, 2001: 129–130.

——. 2008. Summary of Breeding Bird Surveys 2002 to 2007. *Carsington Bird Club Annual Bird Report*, 16 (2007): 29–33.

Carrington, R. and Bradley, J. 2009. Common Gull *Larus canus* at Carsington Water: the first attempted breeding in Derbyshire. *Derbyshire Bird Report*, 2008: 164.

Carsington Bird Club. 2004. *Carsington Bird Club Annual Bird Report*, 12 (2003).

Catley, G.P. and Hursthouse, D. 1985. Parrot Crossbills in Britain. *British Birds*, 78: 482–505.

Clarke, R. and Watson, D. 1990. The Hen Harrier *Circus cyaneus* winter roost survey in Britain and Ireland. *Bird Study*, 37: 84–100.

Cockburn, T. 1976. 1975 Rookery survey. DOS *Bulletin*, 226: 5–6.

——. 1995. Little Bunting *Emberiza pusilla* at Drakelow Wildfowl Reserve: a new bird for Derbyshire. *Derbyshire Bird Report*, 1994: 96–98.

——. 1996a. Gull-billed Tern *Gelochelidon nilotica* at Drakelow Wildfowl Reserve: a new bird for Derbyshire. *Derbyshire Bird Report*, 1995: 116–117.

——. 1996b. Chiffchaff *Phylloscopus collybita* at Drakelow Wildfowl Reserve singing the song of Iberian Chiffchaff *P.c.brehmii*. *Derbyshire Bird Report*, 1995: 122–123.

——. 2004. Great White Egret *Ardea alba* at Drakelow Wildfowl Reserve 12th August to 12th October 2003. *Derbyshire Bird Report*, 2003: 141–142.

——. 2006. Cormorants apparently rearing two broods. *Derbyshire Bird Report*, 2005: 142.

Cole, A.C. and Trobe, W.M. 2000. *The egg collectors of Great Britain and Ireland*. Peregrine Books, Leeds.

Cole, S.R. 1989. Savi's Warbler at Drakelow Wildfowl Reserve. *Derbyshire Bird Report*, 1987: 80.

Coulson, J.C., Monaghan, P., Butterfield, J.E.L., Duncan, N., Ensor, K., Shedden, C. and Thomas, C. 1984. Scandinavian Herring Gulls wintering in Britain. *Ornis Scandinavica*, 15: 79–88.

Cramp, S., Simmons, K.E.L. and Perrins, C.M. (eds). (1977–94) *Handbook of the Birds of Europe, the Middle East and North Africa: the Birds of the Western Palearctic*. 9 vols. Oxford University Press, Oxford.

Crick, H.P.Q., Dudley, C., Glue, D.E. and Thomson, D.L. 1997. UK birds are laying eggs earlier. *Nature*, 388: 526.

Cross, L.R. 1989. Yellow-browed Warbler at Breadsall Cutting. *Derbyshire Bird Report*, 1988: 72–73.

Davies, C. 1986. Cave- and cliff-nesting Swallows in Derbyshire and the Peak. *Derbyshire Bird Report*, 1986: 62–67.

Davies, N.B. 1992. *Dunnock behaviour and social evolution*. Oxford University Press, Oxford.

Dymond, J.N, Fraser, P.A. and Gantlett, S.J.M. 1989. *Rare Birds in Britain and Ireland*. Poyser, Calton.

Eaton, M.A., Balmer, D., Burton, N., Grice, P.V., Musgrove, A.J., Hearn, R., Hilton, G., Leech, D., Noble, D.G., Ratcliffe, N., Rehfisch, M.M., Whitehead, S. and Wotton, S. 2008. *The state of the UK's birds 2007*. RSPB, BTO, Wildfowl & Wetlands Trust, Countryside Council for Wales, Natural England and Scottish Natural Heritage, Sandy.

Eaton, M.A., Appleton, G.F., Ausden, M.A., Balmer, D.E., Grantham, M.J., Grice, P.V., Hearn, R.D., Holt, C.A., Musgrove, A.J., Noble, D.G., Parsons, M., Risely, K., Stroud, D.A. and Wotton, S. 2010. *The state of the UK's birds 2010*. RSPB, BTO, Wildfowl & Wetlands Trust, Countryside Council for Wales, JNCC, Natural England, Northern Ireland Environment Agency and Scottish Natural Heritage, Sandy.

Elkington, T.T. 1986. *The Nature of Derbyshire*. Barracuda Books, Buckingham.

Evans, L.G.R. 1994. *Rare Birds in Britain 1800–1990*. LGRE Productions, Little Chalfont.

——. 1996. *The Ultimate Site Guide To Scarcer British Birds*. LGRE Productions, Little Chalfont.

Evans, L.G.R. and Proctor, B. 1997. The Subspecific Identification of Lesser Black-Backed Gulls and their status in Britain. *Rare Birds*, 3, no. 5: 216–218.

Falshaw, C. 2005. Waterways Bird Survey 2003. *Birds in the Sheffield Area*, 2003: 137–138.

Falshaw, C., Hornbuckle, J. and Wilson, A. 1999. The Waterways Bird Survey on the Rivers Derwent and Noe, Derbyshire: 1973 to 1996. *The Magpie*, 5 (1999): 29–40.

Fell, D.W. 2000. Pallas's Warbler *Phylloscopus proregulus* at Bondhay; a new species for Derbyshire. *Derbyshire Bird Report*, 1999: 121–122.

Finnegan, S.K, Pearce-Higgins, J.W. and Yalden, D.W. 2005. The effect of recreational disturbance on an upland breeding bird, the Golden Plover *Pluvialis apricaria*. *Biological Conservation*, 121: 53–63.

Fisher, E.A. 1997. Blue-winged Teal at Middleton Moor. *Sheffield Bird Report*, 1996: 99–100.

Foster, B.T. 1994. A survey of breeding Dippers *Cinclus cinclus* in Derbyshire in 1993. *Derbyshire Bird Report*, 1993: 92–98.

Fraser, P.A. and Rogers, M.J. 2002. Report on scarce migrants in Britain in 2000. *British Birds*, 95: 606–630.

——. 2005. Report on scarce migrants in Britain in 2002 – Part 2: American Wigeon to Ring-billed Gull. *British Birds*, 98: 73–88.

Fraser, P.A. and the Rarities Committee. 2007. Report on rare birds in Great Britain in 2006. *British Birds*, 100: 694–754.

Frith, M. and Gedge, D. 2000. The Black Redstart in Britain – a conservation conundrum? *British Wildlife*, 11: 381–388.

Frost, R.A. 1971a. A history of Westhouses 'Flashes'. *Derbyshire Bird Report*, 1969: 11–12.

——. 1971b. The Hawfinch at Scarcliffe. *Derbyshire Bird Report*, 1969: 9–10.

——. 1980. The first breeding occurrences of the Ringed Plover in Derbyshire. *Derbyshire Bird Report*, 1979: 10.

——. 1982. Firecrests breeding in Derbyshire. *Derbyshire Bird Report*, 1981: 53–54.

——. 1983. Insect food of Hobby. *British Birds*, 76: 449–450.

——. 1985. The 1984 Little Ringed Plover survey. *Derbyshire Bird Report*, 1984: 61–64.

——. 1986. Decline of certain winter visitors. *British Birds*, 79: 508–509.

——. 1987. Mandarins and Wood Ducks breeding In Derbyshire. *Derbyshire Bird Report*, 1986: 60–61.

——. 1993. The breeding birds of a North-east Derbyshire Wood. *Derbyshire Bird Report*, 1992: 104–108.

——. 1996. A second breeding record of Firecrests in Derbyshire. *Derbyshire Bird Report*, 1995: 122.

——. 2003. In Memoriam: Barbrook Reservoir. *Derbyshire Bird Report*, 2002: 138–141.

———. 2008a. A long-term study of bird populations at Scarcliffe Woods. *Derbyshire Bird Report*, 2007: 144–153.

———. 2008b. Cliff-nesting Twites in the Peak District. *British Birds*, 101: 263.

Frost, R.A. and Gould, K.R. 1989. Least Sandpiper at Middleton Moor. *Derbyshire Bird Report*, 1983: 71.

Frost, R.A. and Shooter, P. 1983. Fieldfares breeding in the Peak District. *British Birds*, 76: 62–65.

Frost, R.A. and Taylor, M.E. 2011. Breeding birds on the Eastern Moors in 2010. *Derbyshire Bird Report*, 2010: 171–175.

Gantlett, S.J.M. 2007. The Leach's Petrels in December 2006. *Birding World*, 19: 497–498.

Gantlett, S.J.M. and Millington, R.G. 2000. Honey Buzzards in September 2000. *Birding World*, 13: 363–365.

Garner, R. 1844. *Natural History of the County of Stafford*. Van Voorst, London (also supplement, 1860).

Garton, A. 2005–07. New habitats in South Derbyshire. DOS *Bulletin*, 543–566.

Gauton, S. 2012. Squacco Heron *Ardeola ralloides* adjacent to Attenborough Gravel Pits: a new species for the Society. *Derbyshire Bird Report*, 2011: 159.

Gibbons, D.W., Reid, J.B. and Chapman, R.A. 1993. *The New Atlas of Breeding Birds in Britain and Ireland 1988–1991*. Poyser, London.

Gill, F. and Wright, M. 2006. *Birds of the World: Recommended English Names*. Princeton University Press, Princeton. Version 2.7.3 generated on 2010–12–29, http://www.world-birdnames.org/names.html.

Glover, S. 1829. *History and Gazetteer of the County of Derby*. Henry Mozley and Son, London.

Gould, K.R. 1985. Sutton Scarsdale flash. *Derbyshire Bird Report*, 1985: 54–55.

———. 1997a. American Golden Plover *Pluvialis dominica* at Middleton Moor: second record for Derbyshire. *Derbyshire Bird Report*, 1996: 140.

———. 1997b. Red-throated Pipit *Anthus cervinus* at Hillyfields; a second record for Derbyshire. *Derbyshire Bird Report*, 1996: 138–139.

Greenall, P. 2012. Western Bonelli's Warbler *Phylloscopus bonelli* at Arnfield Reservoir: a new species for Derbyshire. *Derbyshire Bird Report*, 2011: 163–165.

Grimshaw, T. 1991. The status of the Peregrine in Derbyshire and the Peak District. *Derbyshire Bird Report*, 1990: 81–83.

Hallam, N. and Lewington, I. 2007. The Dix Pit gull. *Birding World*, 20: 503–505.

Harris, M.P. 1968. Manx Shearwater in Derbyshire with apparent puffinosis. *British Birds*, 61: 226–227.

Harrison, G. and Harrison, J. 2005. *The new birds of the West Midlands*. West Midland Bird Club, Studley.

Harrison, G.R., Dean, A.R., Richards, A.J. and Smallshire, D. 1982. *The Birds of the West Midlands*. West Midlands Bird Club, Studley.

Hatfield, D. 1989. Crane at Middleton Moor. *Derbyshire Bird Report*, 1987: 78.

Hattersley, A.P. 1990. Wintering Blackcaps in Derbyshire. *Derbyshire Bird Report*, 1989: 75–79.

———. 2002. Puffin *Fratercula arctica* found near Chesterfield. *Derbyshire Bird Report*, 2001: 132.

Hawker, D.M. 1970. Common Scoters inland. *British Birds*, 63: 382–384.

Heath, A. and Armstrong, H. 2008. Artificial feeding of Hen Harriers in the Peak District. *British Birds*, 101: 152–154.

Herremans, M. 1993. Clustering of territories in the Wood Warbler. *Bird Study*, 40: 12–23.

Hickling, R.A.O. 1978. *Birds in Leicestershire and Rutland*. Leicestershire and Rutland Ornithological Society, Leicester.

Holland, P.K. and Yalden, D.W. 1991. Population dynamics of the Common Sandpipers *Actitis hypoleucos* breeding along an upland river system. *Bird Study*, 38: 151–159.

Holland, P.K., Robson, J.E. and Yalden, D.W. 1982. The status and distribution of the Common Sandpiper *Actitis hypoleucos* in the Peak District. *Naturalist*, 107: 77–86.

Hollick, K.M. 1982. The Little Owl in the Ashbourne area. *Derbyshire Bird Report*, 1981: 52.

Holling, M. and the Rare Breeding Birds Panel. 2010. Rare Breeding Birds in the United Kingdom in 2008. *British Birds*, 103: 482–538.

———. 2011. Rare Breeding Birds in the United Kingdom in 2009. *British Birds*, 104: 476–537.

———. 2012. Rare breeding birds in the United Kingdom in 2010. *British Birds*, 105: 352–416.

Holloway, S. 1996. *The Historical Atlas of Breeding Birds in Britain and Ireland 1875–1900*. Poyser, London.

Hoodless, A. 1995. Studies of west palearctic birds 195. Eurasian Woodcock *Scolopax rusticola*. *British Birds*, 88: 578–592.

Hornbuckle, J. 1980. Roosting Hen Harriers – Winter 1979/80. *Derbyshire Bird Report*, 1979: 9.

———. 1984. Summering male Brambling attempting to mate with female Chaffinch. *Derbyshire Bird Report*, 1983: 62–63.

———. 1985. The Return of the Peregrine. *Derbyshire Bird Report*, 1984: 50.

———. 1989. Crane at Ringinglow Bog. *Derbyshire Bird Report*, 1987: 78.

Hornbuckle, J. and Herringshaw, D. 1985. *Birds of the Sheffield Area*. Sheffield City Libraries, Sheffield.

Hudson, G.W. 1998. Breeding Hen Harriers in the Goyt Valley. *Derbyshire Bird Report*, 1997: 122–124.

Hudson, N. and the Rarities Committee. 2010. Report on rare birds in Great Britain in 2009. *British Birds*, 103: 562–638.

———. 2011. Report on rare birds in Great Britain in 2010. *British Birds*, 104: 557–629.

———. 2012. Report on rare birds in Great Britain in 2011. *British Birds*, 105: 556–625.

Hudson, P. 1992. *Grouse in Space and Time*. Game Conservancy Trust, Fordingbridge.

Hudson, R. 1974. Feral Parakeets near London. *British Birds*, 67: 33, 174.

Hume, R.A. 1976. Inland records of Kittiwakes. *British Birds*, 69: 62–63.

Hunt, A.E. 1977. Lead Poisoning in Swans, *BTO News*, 90: 1–2.

Hutchinson, R.O. 1999. Pallid Swift *Apus pallidus* at Willington GP: a new species for Derbyshire. *Derbyshire Bird Report*, 1998: 130–131.

Irons, A. 1991. First breeding of Garganey in Derbyshire. *Derbyshire Bird Report*, 1990: 84–90.

Jackson, S. 2000. Green Sandpiper *Tringa ochropus* apparently holding territory in Derbyshire, summer 1999. *Derbyshire Bird Report*, 1999: 123–124.

James, R.M.R. 2007. Glossy Ibis *Plegadis falcinellus* at Nadin's, Newhall; a new species for the Society. *Derbyshire Bird Report*, 2006: 146–147.

James, R.M.R. and Key, R.W. 1999. Cormorant *Phalacrocorax carbo* at Willington GP; first breeding record in Derbyshire. *Derbyshire Bird Report*, 1998: 136.

James, R.M.R. and Roome, M. 2009. Mediterranean Gulls *Larus melanocephalus* at Willington Gravel Pits: the first breeding in Derbyshire. *Derbyshire Bird Report*, 2009: 151–152.

Jenkinson, R.D.S. 1984. *Creswell Crags. Late Pleistocene Sites in the East Midlands*. British Series No. 122. British Archaeological Reports, Oxford.

Kelsey, M.G., Green, G.H., Garnett, M.C. and Hayman, P.V. 1989. Marsh Warblers in Britain. *British Birds*, 82: 239–256.

Key, R.W. 1982. Kittiwakes in Derbyshire. *Derbyshire Bird Report*, 1981: 51–52.

———. 1983. Common Scoters in Derbyshire. *Derbyshire Bird Report*, 1982: 60–61.

—— 1993. Occurrence of a possible *taimyrensis* race Herring Gull at Church Wilne Reservoir. *Derbyshire Bird Report*, 1992: 91–93.

—— 1997. Arctic Redpoll *Carduelis hornemanni* in Derbyshire during the winter of 1995/96: a new species for the county. *Derbyshire Bird Report*, 1996: 136–139.

—— 1998a. Black-throated Thrush *Turdus ruficollis* at Hollingwood: a new species for Derbyshire. *Derbyshire Bird Report*, 1997: 128.

—— 1998b. Serin *Serinus serinus* at Combs Reservoir: a new species for Derbyshire. *Derbyshire Bird Report*, 1997: 127.

—— 2000a. Spotted Sandpiper *Actitis macularia* at Willington GP: a new species for Derbyshire. *Derbyshire Bird Report*, 1999: 118–119.

—— 2000b. Cetti's Warbler *Cettia cetti* at Drakelow WR: a new species for Derbyshire. *Derbyshire Bird Report*, 1999: 120.

—— 2001a. Honey Buzzards *Pernis apivorus* in Derbyshire during September 2000. *Derbyshire Bird Report*, 2000: 129–130.

—— 2001b. A partially albinistic Water Pipit *Anthus spinoletta* at Willington GP. *Derbyshire Bird Report*, 2000: 128.

—— 2001c. Ortolan Bunting *Emberiza hortulana* at Aston-on-Trent GP: a new species for Derbyshire. *Derbyshire Bird Report*, 2000: 126–127.

—— 2002. Rose-coloured Starling *Sturnus roseus* at Hilton, first modern-day record for Derbyshire. *Derbyshire Bird Report*, 2001: 131.

—— 2003a. American Wigeon in the Erewash valley – the first county record. *Derbyshire Bird Report*, 2002: 133–134.

—— 2003b. White Storks *Ciconia ciconia* in Derbyshire. *Derbyshire Bird Report*, 2002: 135.

—— 2003c. Two Rose-coloured Starlings *Sturnus roseus* in Derbyshire. *Derbyshire Bird Report*, 2002: 136–137.

—— 2004. Tawny Pipit *Anthus campestris* at Aston-on-Trent Gravel Pits: a new species for Derbyshire. *Derbyshire Bird Report*, 2003: 143–144.

—— 2005. Lesser Grey Shrike *Lanius minor* at Egginton Sewage Farm: a new species for Derbyshire. *Derbyshire Bird Report*, 2004: 148–149.

—— 2006a. Surf Scoter *Melanitta perspicillata* at Foremark Reservoir: a new species for Derbyshire. *Derbyshire Bird Report*, 2005: 138–139.

—— 2006b. Dartford Warbler *Sylvia undata* at The Sanctuary, Derby: a new species for the Society. *Derbyshire Bird Report*, 2005: 141–142.

—— 2010a. Glossy Ibis *Plegadis falcinellus* in Derbyshire in 2009: second and third Society records. *Derbyshire Bird Report*, 2009: 158–160.

—— 2010b. Whiskered Terns *Chlidonias hybrida* in Derbyshire: a new species for the Society. *Derbyshire Bird Report*, 2009: 153–156.

—— 2011. Great Reed Warbler *Acrocephalus arundinaceus* at Straw's Bridge Pond, Ilkeston; a new species for Derbyshire. *Derbyshire Bird Report*, 2010: 166–167.

Key, R.W. and James, R.M.R. 2005a. Bufflehead *Bucephala albeola* at Barrow GP: a new species for Derbyshire. *Derbyshire Bird Report*, 2004: 144.

——. 2005b. Broad-billed Sandpiper *Limicola falcinellus* at Aston-on-Trent GP; a new species for Derbyshire. *Derbyshire Bird Report*, 2004: 146–147.

Kitchen, A. 1978. Notes on the decline of the Black Grouse population of the Goyt Valley. *Derbyshire Bird Report*, 1977: 6–7.

Knox, A.G. 2001. The Bufflehead in Britain. *British Birds*, 94: 61–73.

Kramer, D. 1995. Inland spring passage of Arctic Terns in southern Britain. *British Birds*, 88: 211–217.

Lacey, M. 2000. The Status of the Raven *Corvus corax* in Derbyshire. *Derbyshire Bird Report*, 1999: 125–126.

Lacey, M. and Frost, R.A. 1988. Richard's Pipit at Staveley. *Derbyshire Bird Report*, 1987: 79–80.

Lacey, M. and Messenger, A.P. 2002. The return of the Buzzard *Buteo buteo*. *Derbyshire Bird Report*, 2001: 124–128.

Lack, P.C. 1986. *The Atlas of Wintering Birds in Britain and Ireland*. Poyser, London.

Lees, A.C. and Gilroy, J.J. 2004. Pectoral Sandpipers in Europe. *British Birds*, 97: 638–646.

Lichfield, J. 1977a. Notes on the decline of the Black Grouse population of Matlock Forest. *Derbyshire Bird Report*, 1976: 15–16.

——. 1977b. Notes on the decline of the Black Grouse population of Longshaw Estate and Big Moor area. *Derbyshire Bird Report*, 1976: 16.

Lock, L. and Cook, K. 1998. The Little Egret in Britain: a successful colonist. *British Birds*, 91: 273–280.

Lomas, P.D.R. 1968. The decline of the Rook population in Derbyshire. *Bird Study*, 15: 198–205.

Lovegrove, R. 2007. *Silent Fields. The long decline of a nation's wildlife*. Oxford University Press, Oxford.

Lovenbury, G.A., Waterhouse, M. and Yalden, D.W. 1978. The status of Black Grouse in the Peak District. *Naturalist*, 103: 3–14.

Lundberg, A. and Alatalo, R.V. 1992. *The Pied Flycatcher*. Poyser, London.

Macdonald, J.D. 1953. Black-browed Albatross in Derbyshire. *British Birds*, 46: 110–111, 307–310.

Mann, S. 1987. Red-rumped Swallow at Williamthorpe. *Derbyshire Bird Report*, 1986: 67.

——. 1990. Ring-billed Gull at Ogston Reservoir. *Derbyshire Bird Report*, 1989: 80–81.

——. 2011. Citrine Wagtail *Motacilla citreola* at Ogston Reservoir; a new species for Derbyshire. *Derbyshire Bird Report*, 2010: 168–170.

Marchant, J.H. and Gregory, R.D. 1999. Numbers of nesting Rooks *Corvus frugilegus* in the United Kingdom in 1996. *Bird Study*, 46: 258–273.

Marchant, J.H., Hudson, R., Carter, S.P. and Whittingham, P. 1990. *Population Trends in British Breeding Birds*. BTO/JNCC, Thetford.

Mather, J.R. 1986. *The Birds of Yorkshire*. Helm, London.

Mawson, G.P. 1979. House Martin Breeding Population in the Dronfield District. *Derbyshire Bird Report*, 1978: 10–13.

——. 1981. The Rookery census of 1980. *Derbyshire Bird Report*, 1980: 67–70.

——. 2006. A Ringing Study of Siskins in a Dronfield Garden. *Birds in the Sheffield Area*, 2004: 173–181.

——. 2009. Lesser Redpoll *Carduelis cabaret* migration through Ramsley Moor during autumn 2008. *Derbyshire Bird Report*, 2008: 152–154.

——. 2010. Apparent nesting association of Goshawks and Firecrests. *Derbyshire Bird Report*, 2009: 157.

Mearns, B. and Mearns, R. 1998. *The Bird Collectors*. Academic Press, San Diego.

Meek, E.R. and Little, B. 1977. The spread of the Goosander in Britain and Ireland. *British Birds*, 70: 229–237.

Messenger, A.P. and Taylor, M.E. 2007. Breeding Hen Harriers in the Upper Derwent Valley in 2006. *Derbyshire Bird Report*, 2006: 139–141.

Morris, A.J., Burgess, D., Fuller, R.J., Evans, A.D. and Smith, K.W. 1994. The Status and Distribution of Nightjars *Caprimulgus europaeus* in Britain in 1992. A report to the British Trust for Ornithology. *Bird Study*, 41: 181–191.

Mosley, O. and Brown, E. 1863. *Natural History of Tutbury and Neighbourhood*. Van Voorst, London.

Moulden, N. 2012. Black Stork *Ciconia nigra* at Beeley Moor: a new species for Derbyshire. *Derbyshire Bird Report*, 2011: 160–161.

Mountfort, G. 1957. *The Hawfinch*. New Naturalist Monograph No. 15. Collins, London.

Nightingale, B. and Allsopp, K. 1997. The ornithological year 1996. *British Birds*, 90: 538–548.

Nightingale, B. and Sharrock, J.T.R. 1982. Seabirds inland in Britain in late April 1981. *British Birds*, 75: 558–566.

Norman, D. 2008. *Birds in Cheshire and Wirral. A Breeding and Wintering Atlas*. Liverpool University Press, Liverpool.

Ogilvie, M.A. and the Rare Breeding Birds Panel. 2001. Rare breeding birds in the United Kingdom in 1999. *British Birds*, 94: 344–381.

———. 2004. Rare breeding birds in the United Kingdom in 2002. *British Birds*, 97: 492–536.

Ormerod, S. 1990. Time of passage, habitat use and mass change of *Acrocephalus* warblers in a South Wales reed swamp. *Ringing and Migration*, 11: 1–11.

Oulsnam, D. 2011. Franklin's Gull *Larus pipixcan* at Willington Gravel Pits: a new species for Derbyshire. *Derbyshire Bird Report*, 2010: 165.

Owen, M., Atkinson-Willes, G.L. and Salmon, D.G. 1986. *Wildfowl in Great Britain*. Second edition. Cambridge University Press, Cambridge.

Parrinder, E.A. 1989. Little Ringed Plover distribution in Britain in 1984. *Bird Study*, 36: 147–153.

PDNPA (Peak District National Park Authority). 2002. *Stanage Forum/North Lees Estate Management Plan*. Peak District National Park Authority, Bakewell.

Pearce, D.M. 2009a. *Status of Lapwing Vanellus vanellus in the Peak District*. Peak District National Park Authority, Bakewell.

———. 2009b. *Populations of breeding Curlew, Common Snipe and Twite in the Peak District*. Peak District National Park Authority, Bakewell.

Pilkington, J. 1789. *A View of the Present State of Derbyshire*. Drewry, Derby.

Pollitt, M.S., Cranswick, P.A., Musgrove, A.J., Hall, C., Hearn, R.D., Robinson, J.A. and Holloway, S.J. 2000. *The Wetland Bird Survey 1998–99; Wildfowl and Wader Counts*. BTO, Wildfowl & Wetlands Trust, RSPB and JNCC, Slimbridge.

Poyser, T. and Yalden, D.W. 2009. The loss of the native Black Grouse population from the Peak District. *West Midland Bird Club Annual Report*, 74 (for 2007): 210–218.

Prater, A.J. 1989. Ringed Plover *Charadrius hiaticula* breeding population of the United Kingdom in 1984. *Bird Study*, 36: 154–159.

Prŷs-Jones, R.P. 1977. Aspects of Reed Bunting ecology with comparisons with the Yellowhammer. DPhil thesis, University of Oxford.

Ratcliffe, D. 1972. The Peregrine population of Great Britain in 1971. *Bird Study*, 19: 117–156.

———. 1980. *The Peregrine Falcon*. Poyser, Calton.

———. 1984. The Peregrine breeding population of the UK in 1981. *Bird Study*, 31: 1–18.

———. 1993. *The Peregrine Falcon*. Second edition. Poyser, London.

———. 1997. *The Raven*. Poyser, London.

Rayner, M. 1963. The Lesser Black-backed Gull in Derbyshire. *Bird Study*, 10: 211–218.

Redpath, S.M. and Thirgood, S.J. 1997. *Birds of Prey and Red Grouse*. HMSO, London.

Richardson, D.A. 2001. Computerisation of Records. *Derbyshire Bird Report*, 2000: 131–140.

Riddington, R., Votier, S.C. and Steele, J. 2000. The influx of redpolls into Western Europe, 1995/96. *British Birds*, 93: 59–67.

Roddis, S.J. 1996. Firecrests breeding in the Sheffield area, 1995. *Birds in the Sheffield Area*, 1995: 95.

Rodgers, H.C. 1975. The extension of the breeding range of the Nuthatch in Derbyshire. *Derbyshire Bird Report*, 1974: 7–9.

Roebuck, A. 1933. A Survey of Rooks in the Midlands. *British Birds*, 27: 4–23.

Rogers, M.J. and the Rarities Committee. 2003. Report on rare birds in Great Britain in 2002. *British Birds*, 96: 542–609.

———. 2004. Report on rare birds in Great Britain in 2003. *British Birds*, 97: 558–625.

———. 2005. Report on rare birds in Great Britain in 2004. *British Birds*, 98: 628–694.

Roome, M. 1992. The Long-eared Owl in Derbyshire. *Derbyshire Bird Report*, 1991: 90–95.

Roome, M. and James, R.M.R. 1995. A dark rumped Whimbrel at Willington Gravel Pits. *Derbyshire Bird Report*, 1994: 98–100.

Roworth, P.C. 1981. The Little Owl in Derbyshire. *Derbyshire Bird Report*, 1980: 62–65.

Scott, D. 1997. *The Long-eared Owl*. Hawk and Owl Trust, London.

Scott, G.W., Jardine, D.C., Hills, G. and Sweeney, B. 1998. Changes in Nightjar populations in upland forests in Yorkshire. *Bird Study*, 45: 219–225.

Sharrock, J.T.R. 1976. *The Atlas of Breeding Birds in Britain and Ireland*. Poyser, Calton.

Shaw, A. 1978. BTO Golden Plover survey, winters 1976/77 and 1977/78. *Derbyshire Bird Report*, 1977: 16–23.

Shaw, J. and Shooter, P. 1985. Goosanders breeding in north Derbyshire. *Derbyshire Bird Report*, 1984: 56.

Shooter, P. 1970. The Dipper population of Derbyshire, 1958–68. *British Birds*, 63: 158–163.

Siriwardena, G. 2001. Why are 'brown tits' declining? *BTO News*, 235: 23–24.

Smith, A.H.V. and Vilkaitis, H. 2000. House Martin nests at selected and other sites in the Sorby recording area 1999–2000. *Sorby Record*, 36: 3–15.

Smith, K. 2012. Black Stork *Ciconia nigra* at Two Dales: a second record for Derbyshire. *Derbyshire Bird Report*, 2011: 162.

Smith, S. 1950. *The Yellow Wagtail*. New Naturalist Monograph No. 4. Collins, London.

Smith, T. 1938. *The Birds of Staffordshire*. Issued as Appendices 1–9 of the *Transactions and Annual Report of the North Staffordshire Field Club*, 64 (1930) to 72 (1938).

Snow, D. 2003. Song and territories of Song Thrushes in a Buckinghamshire village: a ten-year study. *British Birds*, 96: 119–131.

Snow, D.W. and Perrins, C.M. 1998. *The Birds of the Western Palearctic Concise Edition*. 2 vols. Oxford University Press, Oxford.

Spencer, K.G. 1969. Overland Migration of Common Scoter. *British Birds*, 62: 332–333.

Staley, B.A. 2009. Wintering Chiffchaffs in Derbyshire. *Derbyshire Bird Report*, 2008: 158–163.

Sugrue, A. 2002. *Lapwing and wader survey 2002: Peak District and surrounding area*. RSPB North West Regional Office, Denby Dale.

Summers-Smith, D. 1963. *The House Sparrow*. New Naturalist Monograph No. 19. Collins, London.

Taylor, M., Allard, P., Seago, M. and Dorling, D. 1999. *The Birds of Norfolk*. Pica Press, Mountfield.

Taylor, M.E. 2006. White-tailed Eagle *Haliaeetus albicilla* at Beeley Moor and Harland Edge: a new species for the Society. *Derbyshire Bird Report*, 2005: 140.

Thornhill, J.S. 1994. Sociable Plover at Egginton Sewage Farm. A new bird for Derbyshire. *Derbyshire Bird Report*, 1993: 98–100.

Thorpe, S. 1996. White-throated Needletail *Hirundapus caudacutus* near Belper; a new bird for Derbyshire. *Derbyshire Bird Report*, 1995: 119–121.

Tomlinson, K. 1999. Alpine Swift *Apus melba* at Bennerley Marsh: a new species for Derbyshire. *Derbyshire Bird Report*, 1998: 132.

Topliss, N. 1996. Blue-winged Teal *Anas discors* at Willington Gravel Pits; a new bird for Derbyshire. *Derbyshire Bird Report*, 1995: 118–119.

Tyler, S. and Ormerod, S. 1994. *The Dippers*. Poyser, London.

Vinicombe, K.E. 2000. Identification of Ferruginous Duck and its status in Britain and Ireland. *British Birds*, 93: 4–21.

Vinicombe, K.E. and Harrop, A.H.J. 1999. Ruddy Shelducks In Britain And Ireland 1986–94. *British Birds*, 92: 225–255.

Voous, K.H. 1977. *List of Recent Holarctic Bird Species*. BOU/Academic Press, London.

Wernham, C.V., Toms, M., Marchant, J., Clark, J., Siriwardena, G. and Baillie, S. 2002. *The Migration Atlas. Movements of the Birds of Britain and Ireland*. Poyser, London.

Whitaker, A. 1929. Notes on the Birds of the Sheffield District. *Proceedings Sorby Scientific Society*, 1: 15–33.

Wilson, A. and Slack, R. 1996. *Rare and Scarce Birds in Yorkshire*. Published privately.

Wilson, A.M., Vickery, J.A. and Browne, S.J. 2001. Numbers and distribution of Lapwings *Vanellus vanellus* breeding in England & Wales in 1998. *Bird Study*, 48: 2–17.

Witherby, H.F., Jourdain, F.C.R., Ticehurst, N.F. and Tucker, B.W. 1938–41. *The Handbook of British Birds*. 5 vols. Witherby, London.

Wolley, J. 1853. Supposed occurrence of the Severn Swallow (*Hirundo bicolour*, Viell), at Derby in 1850. *Zoologist*, 1853: 3806–07.

Yalden, D.W. 1972. The Red Grouse (*Lagopus lagopus scoticus* Lath.) in the Peak District. *Naturalist*, 930: 89–102.

———. 1974. The status of Golden Plover (*Pluvialis apricaria*) and Dunlin (*Calidris alpina*) in the Peak District. *Naturalist*, 930: 81–91.

———. 1986a. The further decline of Black Grouse in the Peak District 1975–1985. *Naturalist*, 976: 3–8.

———. 1986b. The status of Golden Plovers in the Peak Park, England, in relation to access and recreational disturbance. *Wader Study Group Bulletin*, 46: 34–35.

———. 1992. The influence of recreational disturbance on Common Sandpipers *Actitis hypoleucos* breeding by an upland reservoir. *Biological Conservation*, 61: 41–50.

———. 1994. The changing status of Red Grouse *Lagopus lagopus* on peripheral moorlands in the Peak District. *Naturalist*, 119: 61–65.

———. 1999. Canada Geese in the Dark Peak. *Derbyshire Bird Report*, 1998: 133–135.

Yalden, D.W. and Pearce-Higgins, J.W. 1997. Density-dependence and winter weather as factors affecting the size of a population of Golden Plovers *Pluvialis apricaria*. *Bird Study*, 44: 227–234.

Yalden, D.W. and Yalden, P.E. 1989. The starvation of Curlew *Numenius arquata* chicks. *Wader Study Group Bulletin*, 56: 15.

Yalden, P.E. and Yalden, D.W. 1990. Recreational disturbance of breeding Golden Plovers *Pluvialis apricaria*. *Biological Conservation*, 51: 243–262.

Index

Page numbers in **bold** type refer to the relevant species account, and the scientific names refer only to these accounts. This index excludes the 'Table of Breeding Species in Order of Frequency of Occurrence' (p. 343).

Accipiter gentilis   143
Accipiter nisus   144
Acrocephalus arundinaceus   281
Acrocephalus paludicola   277
Acrocephalus palustris   279
Acrocephalus schoenobaenus   278
Acrocephalus scirpaceus   279
Actitis hypoleucos   188
Actitis macularius   189
Aegithalos caudatus   263
Aix galericulata   91
Alauda arvensis   257
Albatross, Black-browed   42, 73, **122**
Alca torda   202
Alcedo atthis   233
Alectoris rufa   115
Alle alle   202
Alopochen aegyptiaca   89
Anas acuta   98
Anas americana   93
Anas carolinensis   96
Anas clypeata   99
Anas crecca   95
Anas discors   99
Anas penelope   92
Anas platyrhynchos   97
Anas querquedula   98
Anas strepera   93
Anser albifrons   84
Anser anser   85
Anser brachyrhynchus   83
Anser erythropus   85
Anser fabilis   83
Anthus campestris   309
Anthus cervinus   312
Anthus petrosus   312
Anthus pratensis   311
Anthus richardi   309
Anthus spinoletta   312
Anthus trivialis   309
Apus apus   232
Apus melba   233
Apus pallidus   233
Aquila chrysaetos   147
Ardea cinerea   131
Ardea purpurea   132
Ardeola ralloides   129
Arenaria interpres   176
Asio flammeus   230
Asio otus   229
Athene noctua   227
Auk, Little   32, 38, 39, 41, **202**
Avocet   41, **159**
Aythya collaris   102

Aythya ferina   101
Aythya fuligula   102
Aythya marila   104
Aythya nyroca   102

Bee-eater   42, **234**
Bishop, Black-winged Red   341
Bishop, Red   341
Bishop, Red-crowned   341
Bishop, Southern Red   341
Bittern   41, 46, **128**
Bittern, Little   42, **128**
Blackbird   12, 13, 27, 28, 36, 44, 145, 225, 227, 228, 271, **288**, 290, 291, 294
Blackcap   29, **270**, 272, 273
Blueback, Michigan   119
Bluethroat   38, 42, **295**
Bobwhite, Northern   335
Bombycilla garrulus   281
Botaurus stellaris   128
Brambling   13, 36, 281, 313, **314**
Branta bernicla   89
Branta canadensis   87
Branta leucopsis   88
Bubulcus ibis   129
Bucephala albeola   108
Bucephala clangula   108
Budgerigar   153, 339
Bufflehead   38, 42, **108**
Bulbul, Himalayan   340
Bulbul, Red-eared   340
Bulbul, Red-vented   340
Bulbul, Red-Whiskered   340
Bulbul, White-cheeked   340
Bulbul, White-eared   340
Bullfinch   43, 44, **325**
Bunting, Cirl   42, **330**
Bunting, Corn   vii, 14, 29, 33, 34, 38, 39, 56, 58, 78, **332**
Bunting, Lapland   42, **327**
Bunting, Little   38, 42, **330**
Bunting, Ortolan   38, 42, **330**
Bunting, Reed   26, 33, 34, 40, 225, **330**
Bunting, Snow   26, 41, **327**
Burhinus oedicnemus   159
Bustard, Little   41, **158**
Buteo buteo   145
Buteo lagopus   147
Buzzard   vii, 27, 29, 34, 36, 39, 78, 139, 140, 144, **145**, 236, 249, 338
Buzzard, Honey   41, **139**
Buzzard, Rough-legged   1, 26, 41, **147**

Calcarius lapponicus   327
Calidris alba   182
Calidris alpina   183
Calidris bairdii   185
Calidris canutus   177
Calidris falcinellus   180
Calidris ferruginea   180
Calidris maritima   184
Calidris melanotos   186
Calidris minuta   185
Calidris minutilla   186
Calidris pugnax   179
Calidris temminckii   181
Canary   341
Canary, Atlantic   341
Canary, Yellow-fronted   341
Canvasback   338
Capercaillie   43, 44, 78, 342
Caprimulgus europaeus   231
Carduelis cabaret   320
Carduelis cannabina   318
Carduelis carduelis   316
Carduelis flammea   322
Carduelis flavirostris   319
Carduelis hornemanni   323
Carduelis spinus   317
Carpodacus erythrinus   324
Cecropis daurica   263
Certhia familiaris   283
Cettia cetti   263
Chaffinch   14, 27, 28, 29, 30, 35, 36, 44, 145, **313**, 314
Charadrius alexandrinus   169
Charadrius dubius   167
Charadrius hiaticula   168
Charadrius morinellus   170
Charadrius vociferus   170
Chiffchaff   44, **267**, 269, 270, 334
Chiffchaff, Iberian   269
Chlidonias hybrida   204
Chlidonias leucopterus   205
Chlidonias niger   204
Chloris chloris   315
Chough   342
Chroicocephalus philadelphia   210
Chroicocephalus ridibundus   210
Chukar   115, 335
Ciconia ciconia   133
Ciconia nigra   132
Cinclus cinclus   286
Circus aeruginosus   141
Circus cyaneus   141
Circus pygargus   143
Clangula hyemalis   105

Index

Coccothraustes coccothraustes 326
Cockatiel 339
Cockatiel, Australian 339
Cockatiel, Grey 339
Cockatoo, Sulphur-crested 339
Cockatoo, White 339
Columba livia 220
Columba oenas 220
Columba palumbus 221
Conure, Blue-crowned 340
Conure, Patagonian 340
Coot 28, 29, 31, 33, 37, 43, 156, **157**, 161, 201, 207, 214
Coracias garrulus 234
Cormorant vii, 27, 31, 33, 38, 40, **126**, 132, 334
Corncrake vii, 31, 32, 36, 41, 153, **155**
Corvus corax 248
Corvus cornix 247
Corvus corone 246
Corvus frugilegus 244
Corvus monedula 243
Coturnix coturnix 114
Crake, Baillon's 41, 43, 44, **155**
Crake, Little 43, 44
Crake, Spotted 41, 154, **155**
Crane 23, 31, 42, **158**
Crane, Black Crowned 339
Crane, Demoiselle 339
Crane, Grey Crowned 339
Crane, Sarus 339
Crex crex 155
Crossbill 27, 36, 41, 61
Crossbill, Common 323
Crossbill, Parrot 42, 323, **324**
Crossbill, Two-barred 41, **323**
Crow, Carrion 152, 165, 202, 228, 242, 243, 244, **246**, 247, 340
Crow, Hooded 41, **247**
Crow, Pied 340
Cuckoo 26, 67, 145, 153, **224**
Cuculus canorus 224
Curlew 26, 27, 28, 29, 30, 31, 36, 66, 171, **172**, 231
Curlew, Stone 30, 42, **159**
Cyanistes caeruleus 251
Cygnus columbianus 81
Cygnus cygnus 82
Cygnus olor 80

Delichon urbicum 261
Dendrocopos major 237
Dendrocopos minor 238
Dipper 27, 28, 29, 31, 34, 35, 64, 188, **286**
Diver, Black-throated 31, 40, 42, **120**, 121
Diver, Great Northern 31, 41, **121**
Diver, Red-throated 37, 41, **120**
Dotterel 26, 41, 69, **170**
Dove, African Collared 339
Dove, Australian Crested 3
Dove, Barbary 339
Dove, Collared vii, 28, 42, **222**
Dove, Diamond 339
Dove, Eurasian Collared 339
Dove, Rock **220**
Dove, Stock 29, 34, 36, 52, **220**
Dove, Turtle 33, 34, 56, 58, 78, **223**
Duck, Black-bellied Whistling 336
Duck, Carolina 337

Duck, Ferruginous 31, 33, 35, 38, 42, 72, **102**
Duck, Long-tailed 30, 31, 41, 46, **105**
Duck, Mandarin 27, 30, 78
Duck, Maned 337
Duck, Muscovy 337
Duck, Ring-necked 31, 32, 35, 38, 39, 42, **102**
Duck, Ruddy 36, 38, 42, **112**
Duck, Tufted 29, 32, 33, 36, 37, 38, 39, 94, 101, **102**, 107
Duck, White-headed 113
Duck, Wood 36, 91, 337
Duck, Yellow-billed 338
Dunlin 26, 28, 44, 65, 153, 180, **183**
Dunnock 13, 27, 36, 44, 224, 225, **301**

Eagle, Golden 23, 41, 44, **147**
Eagle-owl, Cape 340
Eagle, White-tailed 23, 41, **141**
Egret, Cattle 31, 32, 38, 42, **129**
Egret, Great White 31, 32, 36, 38, 42, 130, 334
Egret, Little vii, 36, 38, 42, 46, **129**, 334
Egretta alba 130
Egretta garzetta 129
Eider 32, 34, 42, **104**
Eider, King 342
Emberiza calandra 332
Emberiza cirlus 330
Emberiza citrinella 328
Emberiza hortulana 330
Emberiza pusilla 330
Emberiza schoeniclus 330
Eremophila alpestris 258
Erithacus rubecula 294

Falco columbarius 150
Falcon, Gyr 1
Falcon, Iceland 342
Falcon, Lagger 339
Falcon, Lanner 338
Falcon, Red-footed 38, 42, 71, **149**
Falcon, Saker 339
Falco peregrinus 152
Falco subbuteo 151
Falco tinnunculus 148
Falco vespertinus 149
Ficedula hypoleuca 295
Fieldfare 27, 29, 43, 44, 288, **289**, 291, 323
Finch, Green Singing 341
Finch, Zebra 341
Firecrest 27, 28, 34, 36, 41, 61, **250**
Flamingo, Chilean 338
Flamingo, Lesser 338
Flycatcher, Pied 26, 27, 28, 29, 30, 60, **295**, 297
Flycatcher, Red-eyed 342
Flycatcher, Spotted 29, 33, 40, 225, **292**
Fratercula arctica 202
Fringilla coelebs 313
Fringilla montifringilla 314
Fulica atra 157
Fulmar 31, 34, 41, **122**
Fulmarus glacialis 122

Gadwall 32, 33, 35, 42, 44, **93**
Gallinago gallinago 198
Gallinago media 199

Gallinula chloropus 156
Gannet 40, 42, **125**
Garganey 32, 35, 37, 44, 49, **98**
Garrulus glandarius 242
Gavia arctica 120
Gavia immer 121
Gavia stellata 120
Gelochelidon nilotica 203
Godwit, Bar-tailed 41, 153, **175**
Godwit, Black-tailed 42, 153, **173**
Goldcrest 27, 28, 29, 44, **249**, 250, 283
Goldeneye 27, 37, 43, 44, 106, **108**, 144
Goldfinch 29, 33, **316**
Goosander vii, 27, 29, 30, 31, 33, 34, 36, 37, 39, 40, 44, 45, 110, **111**, 334
Goose, Andean 337
Goose, Bar-headed 33, 336, 337
Goose, Barnacle 41, 43, 85, **88**, 336
Goose, Bean 41, **83**, 84
Goose, Brent 37, 41, **89**
Goose, Cackling 88, 337
Goose, Canada 12, 27, 28, 33, 36, 40, 80, 84, 85, **87**, 88, 89, 336, 337
Goose, Canadian 337
Goose, Chinese 336
Goose, Domestic 336
Goose, Egyptian 37, 41, **89**
Goose, Emperor 337
Goose, Greylag 33, 36, 38, 40, 41, 43, **85**, 88, 89, 336
Goose, Hawaiian 337
Goose, Lesser Canada 88
Goose, Lesser White-fronted 41, 42, **85**
Goose, Pink-foot 43
Goose, Pink-footed **83**, 84, 85
Goose, Red-breasted 337
Goose, Ross's 336
Goose, Snow 41, 336
Goose, Swan 336
Goose, Tundra Bean 83
Goose, White-fronted 37, 41, **84**
Goshawk vii, 27, 29, 31, 39, 41, 43, 44, 61, 122, **143**, 251
Grebe, Black-necked 35, 36, 41, **138**
Grebe, Great Crested 28, 33, 35, 36, 37, 39, 40, 52, **135**, 141
Grebe, Little 29, 31, 36, 37, 39, **134**, 138, 216
Grebe, Red-necked 35, 37, 41, **136**
Grebe, Slavonian 35, 36, 41, **137**
Greenfinch 28, 33, 36, 38, 44, 168, 225, 313, **315**
Greenshank **192**
Grosbeak, Pine 342
Grouse, Black vii, 27, 28, 41, 43, 44, **117**, 119
Grouse, Red 18, 26, 27, 28, 29, 43, 70, 78, **116**, 119, 145
Grouse, Willow 43
Grus grus 158
Guinea Fowl, Helmeted 335
Gull, Baltic 214
Gull, Black-headed 4, 27, 30, 32, 37, 38, 39, 40, 127, 141, 203, 209, **210**, 213, 214, 219, 236
Gull, Bonaparte's 31, 38, 42, **210**
Gull, Caspian 42, **217**
Gull, Common 38, **214**
Gull, Franklin's 38, 39, 42, 72, **213**
Gull, Glaucous 42, **218**

Gull, Great Black-backed **219**
Gull, Grey-headed 339
Gull, Grey-hooded 339
Gull, Hartlaub's 339
Gull, Herring **215**, 216, 219
Gull, Heuglin's 216
Gull, Iceland 42, 215, **217**, 219
Gull, Kumlien's 217, 218
Gull, Laughing 31, 42, **212**
Gull, Lesser Black-backed 30, 31, 39, 201, **214**, 215, 216, 217
Gull, Little 38, 41, **212**
Gull, Mediterranean vii, 36, 38, 42, **213**
Gull, Ring-billed 42, **214**
Gull, Sabine's vii, 30, 31, 32, 42, 205, **208**
Gull, Siberian 216
Gull, Thayer's 217, 218
Gull, Yellow-legged 42, 135, **216**
Gyrfalcon 342

Haematopus ostralegus 160
Haliaeetus albicilla 141
Harrier, Hen vii, 26, 28, 66, 116, 117, **141**, 150, 222, 231
Harrier, Marsh 41, **141**
Harrier, Montagu's 42, **143**
Hawfinch 29, 31, 33, 34, 40, 41, 43, 44, 50, 51, 294, **326**
Hawk, Ferruginous 338
Hawk, Harris's 119, 338
Hawk, Red-tailed 338
Heathwren, Shy 3
Heron, Grey vii, 33, 36, 37, 38, **131**
Heron, Night 32, 40, 41, **129**
Heron, Purple 31, 32, 41, **132**, 241
Heron, Squacco 42, 71, **129**
Hirundapus caudacutus 232
Hirundo rustica 260
Hobby vii, 12, 13, 29, 34, 36, 38, 41, 149, **151**, 204, 231, 334
Honeyeater, Grey 3
Hoopoe 41, **235**
Hydrobates pelagicus 124
Hydrocoloeus minutus 212
Hydroprogne caspia 204

Ibis, African Sacred 338
Ibis, Glossy 31, 38, 39, 41, **133**
Ibis, Sacred 338
Ixobrychus minutus 128

Jackdaw 28, 29, 39, 43, 44, 239, 242, **243**, 246, 247, 285
Jay 43, 44, 241, **242**
Jynx torquilla 235

Kestrel vii, 29, 39, 43, 44, **148**, 153, 228, 231, 290
Killdeer 38, 42, **169**
Kingfisher 31, 34, 37, 46, **233**
Kite, Black 32, 42, **140**
Kite, Red vii, 41, **140**, 334
Kittiwake 40, 41, 206, **209**
Knot 37, 43, 44, 153, **177**

Lagopus lagopus 116
Lanius collurio 240
Lanius excubitor 240
Lanius minor 240
Lanius senator 241

Lanner 338
Lapwing vii, 27, 29, 30, 31, 33, 34, 35, 36, 40, 43, 75, 153, 163, **165**, 172, 184, 227
Lark, Shore 31, 32, 35, **258**
Larus argentatus 215
Larus atricilla 212
Larus cachinnans 217
Larus canus 214
Larus delawarensis 214
Larus fuscus 214
Larus glaucoides 217
Larus hyperboreus 218
Larus marinus 219
Larus melanocephalus 213
Larus michahellis 216
Larus pipixcan 213
Limosa lapponica 175
Limosa limosa 173
Linnet vii, 33, 38, 44, 225, 315, **318**, 319
Locustella luscinioides 277
Locustella naevia 276
Lovebird, Peach-faced 339
Lovebird, Rosy-faced 339
Loxia curvirostra 323
Loxia leucoptera 323
Loxia pytyopsittacus 324
Lullula arborea 257
Luscinia megarhynchos 295
Luscinia svecica 295
Lymnocryptes minimus 195

Macaw, Red and Yellow 340
Macaw, Scarlet 340
Magpie 43, 44, 228, 231, **241**, 243, 246, 247, 340
Magpie, Red-billed Blue 340
Mallard 27, 29, 33, 36, 37, 43, 44, 91, **97**, 98, 144, 153, 156, 157, 180, 201, 337
Mandarin 29, 30, 34, 36, 39, 40, 42, 52, **91**
Manikin, Chestnut 341
Martin, House 28, 30, 44, 54, 145, 251, 259, 260, 261, 294
Martin, Sand 27, 30, 33, 37, 40, **258**, 285, 334
Melanitta fusca 107
Melanitta nigra 106
Melanitta perspicillata 107
Merganser, Hooded 338
Merganser, Red-breasted vii, 27, 34, 37, 40, 42, 106, **110**, 111
Mergus albellus 109
Mergus merganser 111
Mergus serrator 110
Merlin vii, 26, 28, 41, 66, 149, **150**
Merops apiaster 234
Milvus migrans 140
Milvus milvus 140
Moorhen 29, 33, 37, 43, 138, **156**, 157
Morus bassanus 125
Motacilla alba 308
Motacilla cinerea 307
Motacilla citreola 306
Motacilla flava 304
Munia, Chestnut 341
Munia, White-rumped 341
Muscicapa striata 292
Myna, Common 341

Mynah, Common 341

Needletail, White-throated 42
Nene 337
Netta rufina 100
Nightingale 38, 41, **295**
Nightjar 27, 28, 31, 41, 61, 62, **231**
Numenius arquata 172
Numenius phaeopus 170
Nuthatch 29, 36, 40, 44, 228, **282**
Nycticorax nycticorax 129

Oceanodroma leucorhoa 124
Oenanthe oenanthe 300
Onychoprion fuscata 203
Oriole, Golden 38, 41, **239**
Oriolus oriolus 239
Osprey 41, 49, **148**
Ouzel, Ring 26, 28, 43, 68, **287**, 288
Owl, Barn 13, 31, 39, 44, 57, **226**, 228, 237
Owl, Eagle 41, 43, 44, 340
Owl, Eurasian Eagle 340
Owl, Little 29, 31, 36, 39, 63, 226, **227**, 228
Owl, Long-eared 27, 29, 32, 34, 36, 41, 44, 61, 62, 226, 228, **229**
Owl, Moor 230
Owl, Short-eared 26, 28, 39, 43, 67, 117, 229, **230**
Owl, Snowy 41, 340
Owl, Tawny 28, 44, 226, **228**, 229, 285
Owl, Wood 228
Oxyura jamaicensis 112
Oystercatcher 27, 30, 31, 36, 37, 41, **160**

Pandion haliaetus 148
Panurus biarmicus 256
Parakeet, Blue-crowned 340
Parakeet, Monk 340
Parakeet, Nanday 340
Parakeet, Quaker 340
Parakeet, Ring-necked 41, **224**
Parakeet, Rose-ringed 224
Parrot, African Grey 339
Parrot, Burrowing 340
Parrot, Eclectus 339
Parrot, Grey 339
Parrot, Night 3
Parrot, Senegal 340
Parrotbill, Vinous-throated 340
Partridge, Grey vii, 34, 36, 44, 57, 115, **118**, 151
Partridge, Red-legged 34, 36, 41, **115**, 118, 119, 335
Parus major 252
Passer domesticus 302
Passer montanus 303
Peacock 336
Peafowl, Common 336
Peafowl, Indian 336
Pelican, Eastern White 338
Pelican, European White 338
Pelican, Great White 338
Perdix perdix 118
Peregrine vii, 16, 26, 29, 30, 31, 33, 40, 41, 53, 54, 78, 79, 84, 114, 116, 145, **152**, 164, 171, 174, 176, 177, 196, 197, 204, 205, 209, 220, 222, 231, 334
Periparus ater 253
Pernis apivorus 139

Petrel, Leach's   31, 41, **124**
Petrel, Storm   31, 36, 41, **124**
Phalacrocorax aristotelis   127
Phalacrocorax carbo   126
Phalarope, Grey   27, 30, 31, 38, 41, **188**
Phalarope, Red-necked   30, 31, 38, 42, **187**
Phalarope, Wilson's   vii, 31, 42, **187**
Phalaropus fulicarius   188
Phalaropus lobatus   187
Phalaropus tricolor   187
Phasianus colchicus   119
Pheasant   117, **119**, 253, 335, 336
Pheasant, Bohemian   119
Pheasant, Golden   36, 41, 336
Pheasant, Lady Amherst's   41, 336
Pheasant, Reeves's   36, 335
Pheasant, Silver   36, 335
Phoenicurus ochruros   296
Phoenicurus phoenicurus   297
Phylloscopus bonelli   265
Phylloscopus collybita   267
Phylloscopus inornatus   265
Phylloscopus proregulus   264
Phylloscopus sibilatrix   265
Phylloscopus trochilus   269
Pica pica   241
Picus viridis   236
Pie, Red-billed Blue   340
Pigeon, Feral   220, 338
Pigeon, Passenger   342
Pintail   **98**
Pintail, Bahama   338
Pintail, White-cheeked   338
Pipit, Meadow   13, 26, 29, 33, 34, 35, 39, 44, 67, 150, 224, 258, 309, 310, **311**
Pipit, Red-throated   42, **312**
Pipit, Richard's   42, 309
Pipit, Rock   27, 35, 42, **312**, 313
Pipit, Tawny   38, 42, **309**
Pipit, Tree   26, 27, 28, 29, 33, 225, **309**, 320
Pipit, Water   40, 42, **312**
Platalea leucorodia   134
Plectrophenax nivalis   327
Plegadis falcinellus   133
Plover, American Golden   30, 42, **162**
Plover, Golden   13, 18, 26, 27, 28, 30, 32, 34, 38, 58, 65, 78, 153, **162**, 164, 183, 184, 219
Plover, Grey   42, 44, 153, **164**, 175
Plover, Kentish   vii, 31, 38, 42, **170**
Plover, Little Ringed   vii, 27, 28, 30, 32, 33, 35, 37, 40, 42, 54, 145, **167**
Plover, Ringed   33, 35, 37, 40, 54, 55, 78, **168**
Plover, Sociable   38, 42, **165**
Pluvialis apricaria   162
Pluvialis dominica   162
Pluvialis squatarola   164
Pochard   31, 40, **101**, 102, 113
Pochard, Red-crested   42, **100**, 334
Podiceps auritus   137
Podiceps cristatus   135
Podiceps grisegena   136
Podiceps nigricollis   138
Poecile montanus   254
Poecile palustris   255
Porzana porzana   155
Porzana pusilla   155

Prunella modularis   301
Psittacula krameri   224
Ptarmigan   43, 44
Puffin   41, **202**
Puffinus puffinus   123
Pyrrhula pyrrhula   325

Quail   34, 36, 39, 41, 57, **114**, 153
Quail, California   335

Rail, Water   32, 33, 38, 41, 153, **154**
Rallus aquaticus   154
Raven   vii, 23, 26, 29, 30, 31, 36, 41, 44, 54, 70, 153, 231, **248**
Razorbill   39, 42, **202**
Recurvirostra avosetta   159
Redpoll, Arctic   39, 42, **323**
Redpoll, Common   322, 323
Redpoll, Lesser   26, 33, 34, 39, 317, 319, **320**, 322
Redpoll, Mealy   **322**
Redshank   vii, 26, 35, 153, **194**
Redshank, Spotted   41, **191**
Redstart   26, 27, 28, 29, 30, 60, **297**
Redstart, Black   33, 40, 41, **296**
Redwing   27, 29, 44, 289, 290, **291**
Regulus ignicapilla   250
Regulus regulus   249
Riparia riparia   258
Rissa tridactyla   209
Robin   12, 27, 29, 30, 36, 44, 145, 153, 288, **294**
Roller   41, 234
Rook   28, 29, 75, 79, 200, 242, 243, **244**, 246, 247
Rosefinch, Common   32, 42, 72, **324**
Rosella, Crimson   339
Rosella, Eastern   339
Rosella, Yellow   339
Ruff   36, 37, 44, **179**

Saker   339
Sanderling   37, 40, 42, **182**
Sandgrouse, Pallas's   41, **219**
Sandpiper, Baird's   27, 31, 38, 42, **185**
Sandpiper, Broad-billed   38, 42, **180**
Sandpiper, Common   13, 27, 28, 29, 37, 78, 79, **188**, 286
Sandpiper, Curlew   35, 40, 42, **180**
Sandpiper, Green   37, 41, **190**
Sandpiper, Least   30, 42, **186**
Sandpiper, Pectoral   30, 31, 32, 38, 39, 42, **186**
Sandpiper, Purple   27, 30, 31, 38, 39, 42, **184**
Sandpiper, Spotted   31, 38, 42, **189**
Sandpiper, Wood   42, **192**
Saxicola rubetra   298
Saxicola torquatus   299
Scaup   37, **104**
Scolopax rusticola   196
Scoter, Common   30, **106**
Scoter, Surf   39, 42, **107**
Scoter, Velvet   35, 36, 37, 38, 40, 41, **107**, 334
Serin   42, **315**
Serinus serinus   315
Shag   42, **127**
Shearwater, Manx   31, 40, 42, **123**
Shelduck   30, 36, 37, **90**
Shelduck, Australian   337
Shelduck, Cape   337

Shelduck, Paradise   337
Shelduck, Ruddy   42, **90**
Shelduck, South African   337
Shorelark   42
Shoveler   33, 35, 40, 44, **99**
Shrike, Great Grey   26, 39, 41, 67, **240**
Shrike, Lesser Grey   38, 42, **240**
Shrike, Red-backed   vii, 4, 41, 44, **240**
Shrike, Woodchat   38, 41, 72, **241**
Siskin   26, 27, 28, 29, 31, 34, 144, **317**
Sitta europaea   282
Skua, Arctic   42, 200, 201
Skua, Great   42, 124, **201**
Skua, Long-tailed   31, 38, 42, **201**
Skua, Pomarine   31, 38, 39, 42, **200**
Skylark   26, 27, 29, 33, 34, 35, 36, 39, 44, 240, 257, 305, 327
Smew   37, 38, **109**
Snipe   vii, 26, 27, 29, 32, 33, 36, 43, 44, 50, 145, 153, 187, **198**, 228
Snipe, Great   38, 42, **199**
Snipe, Jack   1, 32, 33, 35, 50, 153, **195**
Somateria mollissima   104
Sparrowhawk   vii, 12, 27, 28, 29, 39, **144**, 148, 236, 290, 325
Sparrow, House   28, 262, **302**, 303, 304, 315
Sparrow, Rufous-collared   341
Sparrow, Sudan Golden   341
Sparrow, Tree   33, 36, 38, 39, 44, **303**
Spoonbill   41, **134**
Starling   29, 33, 44, 237, **285**, 315
Starling, Rose-coloured   41, 73, **286**
Starling, Superb   341
Stercorarius longicaudus   201
Stercorarius parasiticus   200
Stercorarius pomarinus   200
Stercorarius skua   201
Sterna dougallii   207
Sterna hirundo   206
Sterna paradisaea   208
Sterna sandvicensis   205
Sternula albifrons   203
Stint, Little   35, 42, 180, **185**
Stint, Temminck's   35, 42, **181**, 334
Stonechat   26, 68, 69, 275, **299**
Stork, Black   42, **132**
Stork, White   41, **133**
Streptopelia decaocto   222
Streptopelia turtur   223
Strix aluco   228
Sturnus roseus   286
Sturnus vulgaris   285
Swallow   12, 13, 14, 28, 35, 39, 44, 227, 228, 259, **260**, 261, 262, 284, 294, 297
Swallow, Red-rumped   31, 32, 42, **263**, 334
Swallow, Tree   342
Swan, Bewick's   37, **81**, 82
Swan, Black   337
Swan, Mute   33, 37, **80**, 82, 88, 125
Swan, Trumpeter   337
Swan, Tundra   337
Swan, Whistling   337
Swan, Whooper   30, 34, 37, 49, 81, **82**
Swift   13, 28, 75, 153, 232, 233
Swift, Alpine   31, 32, 42, **233**
Swift, Needle-tailed   **232**
Swift, Pallid   38, 42, **233**
Sylvia atricapilla   270

Sylvia borin 272
Sylvia communis 274
Sylvia curruca 273
Sylvia undata 275
Syrrhaptes paradoxus 219

Tachybaptus ruficollis 134
Tadorna ferruginea 90
Tadorna tadorna 90
Teal 27, 30, 32, 33, 35, 40, 43, 44, 94, **95**, 96
Teal, Blue-winged 30, 38, 42, 73, 98, **99**
Teal, Cape 338
Teal, Chestnut 338
Teal, Cinnamon 338
Teal, Green-winged 31, 38, 42, **96**
Teal, Ringed 337
Teal, Speckled 338
Teal, Yellow-billed 338
Tern, Arctic 41, 153, 206, **208**
Tern, Black 39, 40, 41, **204**, 212
Tern, Caspian 31, 38, 42, **204**
Tern, Common 32, 33, 36, 37, 38, 180, **206**, 207, 208
Tern, Gull-billed 38, 42, **203**
Tern, Little 41, **203**
Tern, Roseate 31, 38, 39, 42, **207**
Tern, Sandwich 42, **205**
Tern, Sooty 41, 79, **203**
Tern, Whiskered 31, 38, 42, 72, **204**, 334
Tern, White-winged Black 31, 38, 39, 42, 73, **205**, 208
Tetrao tetrix 117
Tetrax tetrax 158
Thalassarche melanophris 122
Thrush, Black-throated 42, 73, **289**
Thrush, Mistle 44, 75, 288, 290, **292**
Thrush, Song 28, 44, 225, 271, 288, **290**, 292, 294
Thrush, White's 342
Tit, Bearded 31, 36, 42, **256**
Tit, Blue 14, 27, 28, 29, 30, 44, 145, 221, **251**, 252, 255
Tit, Coal 27, 28, 29, **253**, 255
Tit, Great 27, 28, 30, 44, 251, **252**, 253, 255
Tit, Long-tailed 28, **263**, 264
Tit, Marsh 29, 33, 39, 253, 254, **255**

Tit, Willow 29, 33, 36, 39, 253, **254**, 255
Treecreeper 29, **283**
Tringa erythropus 191
Tringa flavipes 192
Tringa glareola 192
Tringa nebularia 192
Tringa ochropus 190
Tringa totanus 194
Troglodytes troglodytes 284
Turdus atrogularis 289
Turdus iliacus 291
Turdus merula 288
Turdus philomelos 290
Turdus pilaris 289
Turdus torquatus 287
Turdus viscivorus 292
Turnstone 42, 153, **176**
Twite 26, 28, 29, 30, 54, 318, **319**
Tyto alba 226

Upupa epops 235

Vanellus gregaria 165
Vanellus vanellus 165
Vireo, Red-eyed 342
Vulture, Griffon 342

Wagtail, Ashy-headed 306
Wagtail, Blue-headed 306
Wagtail, Channel 306
Wagtail, Citrine 31, 42, **306**
Wagtail, Grey 27, 28, 29, 31, 34, 35, 36, 64, **307**, 308
Wagtail, Grey-headed 306
Wagtail, Pied 27, 33, 44, 145, 225, 307, **308**
Wagtail, Sykes's 306
Wagtail, White 309
Wagtail, Yellow 12, 29, 33, 34, 35, 36, 39, 240, 261, **304**
Warbler, Aquatic 38, 42, **277**
Warbler, Cetti's 14, 32, 33, 37, 38, 40, 42, **263**, 334
Warbler, Dartford 40, 41, **275**
Warbler, Garden 29, 270, 271, **272**, 334
Warbler, Grasshopper 26, 39, 225, **276**
Warbler, Great Reed 33, 42, **281**
Warbler, Marsh 33, 42, 239, **279**
Warbler, Pallas's 42, **264**
Warbler, Reed 12, 33, 35, 36, 38, 39, 225, 271, 278, **279**

Warbler, Savi's 38, 42, **277**
Warbler, Sedge 33, 39, 225, 271, **278**
Warbler, Western Bonelli's 42, **265**
Warbler, Willow 12, 26, 27, 29, 30, 36, 267, 268, **269**
Warbler, Wood 27, 29, 40, 60, **265**, 297
Warbler, Yellow-browed 32, 42, **265**
Waxbill, Black-rumped 341
Waxbill, Common 341
Waxbill, Orange-cheeked 341
Waxbill, Pink-cheeked 341
Waxbill, Red-eared 341
Waxwing 1, 28, 41, 153, **281**, 334
Weaver, Black-headed 341
Weaver, Village 341
Wheatear 26, 29, 30, 31, 40, 44, 63, **300**
Wheatear, Greenland 301
Whimbrel 153, **170**
Whinchat 26, 27, 29, 68, 117, 225, **298**, 300, 320
Whitethroat 14, 29, 240, 260, 273, **274**
Whitethroat, Lesser 225, **273**, 274, 275
Wigeon 32, 33, 36, 37, 38, 44, 89, **92**, 93
Wigeon, American 32, 38, 42, **93**
Wigeon, Chiloë 338
Wigeon, Eurasian 93
Woodcock 31, 33, 34, 59, 145, 153, **196**, 228
Woodlark 32, 35, 41, **257**
Woodpecker, Great Spotted 27, 30, 33, 36, 39, 40, 43, 236, **237**, 238, 239, 255
Woodpecker, Green 30, 33, 36, 39, 40, 144, 145, **236**, 237
Woodpecker, Lesser Spotted 30, 33, 36, 39, 40, 237, **238**
Woodpigeon 28, 34, 144, 153, **221**, 228, 251
Wren 27, 29, 30, 31, 35, 43, 44, 78, 225, **284**, 308, 313
Wryneck 35, 41, **235**

Xema sabini 208

Yellow-bill, South African 338
Yellowhammer vii, 31, 34, 39, 151, 225, 241, 315, **328**
Yellowlegs, Lesser 32, 42, **192**